WILEY

Practitioner's Guide to GAAS 2004

Covering all SASs, SSAEs, SSARSs, and Interpretations

Subscriber Update Service

BECOME A SUBSCRIBER!

Did you purchase this product from a bookstore?

If you did, it's important for you to become a subscriber. John Wiley & Sons, Inc. may publish, on a periodic basis, supplements and new editions to reflect the latest changes in the subject matter that you ***need to know*** in order stay competitive in this ever-changing industry. By contacting the Wiley office nearest you, you'll receive any current update at no additional charge. In addition, you'll receive future updates and revised or related volumes on a thirty-day examination review.

If you purchased this product directly from John Wiley & Sons, Inc., we have already recorded your subscription for this update service.

To become a subscriber, please call **1-877-762-2974** or send your name, company name (if applicable), address, and the title of the product to:

mailing address: **Supplement Department**
John Wiley & Sons, Inc.
One Wiley Drive
Somerset, NJ 08875

e-mail: **subscriber@wiley.com**
fax: **1-732-302-2300**
online: **www.wiley.com**

For customers outside the United States, please contact the Wiley office nearest you:

Professional & Reference Division
John Wiley & Sons Canada, Ltd.
22 Worcester Road
Etobicoke, Ontario M9W 1L1
CANADA
416-236-4433
Phone: 1-800-567-4797
Fax: 416-236-4447
Email: canada@jwiley.com

John Wiley & Sons Australia, Ltd.
33 Park Road
P.O. Box 1226
Milton, Queensland 4064
AUSTRALIA
Phone: 61-7-3859-9755
Fax: 61-7-3859-9715
Email: brisbane@johnwiley.com.au

John Wiley & Sons, Ltd.
The Atrium
Southern Gate, Chichester
West Sussex, PO19 8SQ
ENGLAND
Phone: 44-1243-779777
Fax: 44-1243-775878
Email: customer@wiley.co.uk

John Wiley & Sons (Asia) Pte. Ltd.
2 Clementi Loop #02-01
SINGAPORE 129809
Phone: 65-64632400
Fax: 65-64634604/5/6
Customer Service: 65-64604280
Email: enquiry@wiley.com.sg

WILEY

Practitioner's Guide to GAAS 2004

Covering all SASs, SSAEs, SSARSs, and Interpretations

Dan M. Guy, CPA, PhD
D. R. Carmichael, CPA, CFE, PhD
Linda A. Lach, CPA

JOHN WILEY & SONS, INC.

Published simultaneously in Canada.

For general information on our other products and services please contact our Customer Care Department within the US at 800-762-2974, outside the US at 317-572-3993, or fax 317-572-4002.

Wiley also publishes its books in a variety of electronic formats. Some content that appears in print may not be available in electronic books.

ISBN 0-471-35250-0

Printed in the United States of America
10 9 8 7 6 5 4 3 2 1

CONTENTS

	Preface	**vii**
	About the Authors	**ix**
	Update on the PCAOB and the Sarbanes-Oxley Act/New Exposure Drafts	**xi**
100-230	The Auditor's Responsibilities and Functions, Introduction to GAAS and the General Standards	1
310	Appointment of the Independent Auditor	12
311	Planning and Supervision	18
312	Audit Risk and Materiality in Conducting an Audit	31
313	Substantive Tests prior to the Balance Sheet Date	48
315	Communications between Predecessor and Successor Auditors	54
316	Consideration of Fraud in a Financial Statement Audit	63
316A	Consideration of Fraud in a Financial Statement Audit	88
317	Illegal Acts by Clients	102
319	Consideration of Internal Control in a Financial Statement Audit	107
322	The Auditor's Consideration of the Internal Audit Function in an Audit of Financial Statements	121
324	Service Organizations	132
325	Communication of Internal Control Related Matters Noted in an Audit	145
326	Evidential Matter	153
328	Auditing Fair Value Measurements and Disclosures	169
329	Analytical Procedures	177
330	The Confirmation Process	193
331	Inventories	207
332	Auditing Derivative Instruments, Hedging Activities, and Investments in Securities	219
333	Management Representations	235
334	Related Parties	248
336	Using the Work of a Specialist	261
337	Inquiry of Client's Lawyer Concerning Litigation, Claims, and Assessments	272
339	Audit Documentation	286
341	The Auditor's Consideration of an Entity's Ability to Continue as a Going Concern	297
342	Auditing Accounting Estimates	310
350	Audit Sampling	317
380	Communication with Audit Committees	338
390	Consideration of Omitted Procedures After the Report Date	351
410/411	Adherence to GAAP (410) and the Meaning of "Present Fairly in Conformity with GAAP" (411)	357
420	Consistency of Application of Generally Accepted Accounting Principles	366
431	Adequacy of Disclosure in Financial Statements	372
504	Association with Financial Statements	374

508	Reports on Audited Financial Statements	381
530	Dating of the Independent Auditor's Report	407
532	Restricting the Use of an Auditor's Report	411
534	Reporting on Financial Statements Prepared for Use in Other Countries	414
543	Part of Audit Performed by Other Independent Auditors	419
544	Lack of Conformity with Generally Accepted Accounting Principles	430
550	Other Information in Documents Containing Audited Financial Statements	432
551	Reporting on Information Accompanying the Basic Financial Statements in Auditor-Submitted Documents	440
552	Reporting on Condensed Financial Statements and Selected Financial Data	449
558	Required Supplementary Information	456
560	Subsequent Events	462
561	Subsequent Discovery of Facts Existing at the Date of the Auditor's Report	471
623	Special Reports	476
625	Reports on the Application of Accounting Principles	500
634	Letters for Underwriters and Certain Other Requesting Parties	506
711	Filings under Federal Securities Statutes	547
722	Interim Financial Information	554
722A	Interim Financial Information	577
801	Compliance Auditing Considerations in Audits of Governmental Entities and Recipients of Governmental Financial Assistance	598
901	Public Warehouses: Controls and Auditing Procedures for Goods Held	605
2101	Attestation Standards	611
2201	Agreed-upon Procedures Engagements	631
2301	Financial Forecasts and Projections	642
2401	Reporting on Pro Forma Financial Information	667
2501	Reporting on an Entity's Internal Control over Financial Reporting	677
2601	Compliance Attestation	693
2701	Management's Discussion and Analysis (MD&A)	706
3100	Compilation and Review of Financial Statements	712
3200	Reporting on Comparative Financial Statements	741
3300	Compilation Reports on Financial Statements Included in Certain Prescribed Forms	748
3400	Communications between Predecessor and Successor Accountants	750
3600	Reporting on Personal Financial Statements Included in Written Personal Financial Plans	755

Appendix A: Cross-References to SASs, SSAEs, and SSARSs **757**

Appendix B: List of AICPA Audit and Accounting Guides and Statements of Position **761**

Appendix C: Other Auditing Publications in the GAAS Hierarchy **763**

Index **765**

PREFACE

This book reduces the official language of Statements on Auditing Standards (SAS), Statements on Standards for Attestation Engagements (SSAE), Statements on Standards for Accounting and Review Services (SSARS), and the interpretations of those standards to easy-to-read and understandable advice. It is designed to help CPAs in the application of, and compliance with, authoritative standards. One of its key features is the separation of those things specifically required from advice, observations, and other subordinate information. Thus, a user may quickly identify the minimum requirements of an SAS, an SSAE, or an SSARS.

This book follows the sequence of sections of the AICPA *Codification of Statements on Auditing Standards*, the *Codification of Statements on Standards for Attestation Engagements*, and the *Codification of Statements on Standards for Accounting and Review Services*. Sections are divided into the following easy-to-understand parts:

Effective Date and Applicability
Definitions of Terms
Objectives of Section
Fundamental Requirements
Interpretations
Techniques for Application
Illustrations

Effective Date and Applicability. A handy, brief identification of the original standard for the section, its effective date, and the circumstances that require the application of the section.

Definitions of Terms. A glossary of official definitions that gathers in one place explanations of terms that are ordinarily scattered throughout a standard.

Objectives of Section. A behind-the-scenes explanation of the reasons for the pronouncement and a capsule explanation of the most basic ideas of the section.

Fundamental Requirements. Concise listing and descriptions of those things specifically mandated by the section.

Interpretations. A brief summary of each interpretation.

Techniques for Application. Helpful techniques for complying with the fundamental requirements of the section.

Illustrations. Examples of the application of the fundamental requirements of the section.

Selected AICPA Practice Alerts and Audit Issues Task Force Advisories have also been summarized in certain sections.

This book is designed for practitioners to use as a trusted reference.

We bring to this book over 60 years of experience in accounting and audit practice and education. In fact, Dan Guy and Doug Carmichael have cumulatively been responsible, as former Vice Presidents at the AICPA, for over 90% of the authoritative standards covered herein. We have borrowed freely from our experience with clients and international, national, regional, and local accounting firms to provide what we consider the best advice on applying the standards.

As with all accounting and auditing publications, this book is merely a guide. It is not a substitute for professional judgment. It can, however, be a valuable reference tool.

To improve this book, we welcome comments, suggestions, and questions on the application of audit, attest, review and compilation standards in practice. Comments and suggestions will be incorporated in the annual update of the book. Please direct all correspondence to:

Dan M. Guy, PhD, CPA	Linda A. Lach, CPA
314 Paseo de Peralta	21 Papurah Rd
Santa Fe, NM 87501	Fairfield, CT 06432
dmguy@worldnet.att.net	LindaLach@aol.com

The 2004 edition of this book is current through SAS 101, *Auditing Fair Value Measurements and Disclosures,* SSAE 12, *Amendment to SSAE 10, "Attestation Standards: Revision and Recodification,"* and SSARS 9, *Omnibus Statement on Standards for Accounting and Review Services—2002.* We have also noted sections of the book impacted by Sarbanes-Oxley requirements and sections affected by outstanding Exposure Drafts. This book will be updated continuously at the John Wiley & Sons, Inc. website at www.wiley.com/gaas and updated annually in paperback.

Dan M. Guy
Douglas R. Carmichael
Linda A. Lach

September 2003

ABOUT THE AUTHORS

Dan M. Guy, PhD, CPA, lives in Santa Fe, New Mexico, where he has a litigation consulting practice. He completed an eighteen-year career with the AICPA in New York City in January 1998, where he had overall responsibility for, among other things, the Auditing Standards Board and the Accounting and Review Services Committee. Dr. Guy was Vice President, Auditing, at the AICPA from 1983 until 1996, when he became Vice President, Professional Standards and Services. Dr. Guy has written numerous books on auditing, sampling, and compilation and review. He has represented the profession on numerous occasions before Congress, various regulatory agencies, and at the international level. Prior to joining the AICPA, Dr. Guy was a professor of accounting at Texas Tech University and a visiting professor at the University of Texas at Austin. He was in public practice with KPMG Peat Marwick. In 1998, he received the John J. McCloy Award for outstanding contributions to audit quality in the US. The award was presented by the Public Oversight Board of the SEC Practice Section of the AICPA's Division for CPA Firms.

D. R. Carmichael, PhD, CPA, CFE, is the Chief Auditor and Director of Professional Standards of the Public Company Accounting Oversight Board (PCAOB). He has not participated in the current edition of this book. The views of Dr. Carmichael expressed herein are solely his and not necessarily those of the PCAOB or any other member of its staff. Formerly, he was Director of the Center for Financial Integrity and the Wollman Distinguished Professor of Accountancy at Baruch College, City University of New York. Until 1983, he was the Vice President, Auditing, at the AICPA, where he directly participated in the development of accounting and auditing standards. Dr. Carmichael has written numerous books and articles on accounting and auditing. He has acted as a consultant on accounting, auditing, and control matters to CPA firms, public corporations, attorneys, government agencies, and financial institutions. Dr. Carmichael has served as a consultant to the AICPA, the Securities and Exchange Commission (SEC), the General Accounting Office (GAO), the Federal Deposit Insurance Corporation (FDIC), the Federal Trade Commission (FTC), and other federal and state government agencies. He has also investigated numerous cases involving allegations of fraudulent financial reporting and provided expert witness testimony on those matters.

Linda Lach, CPA, lives in Fairfield, Connecticut. She is the former Associate Director for the Center for Financial Integrity at Baruch College and the former Director of Professional Development for the American Institute of Certified Public Accountants. At the AICPA, Linda was responsible for conferences, seminars, and self-study courses developed for the accounting profession. She has made numerous presentations and written articles on continuing education issues. Before joining the AICPA, she held various financial management positions and worked as an auditor for Touche Ross (currently Deloitte & Touche).

UPDATE ON THE PCAOB AND THE SARBANES-OXLEY ACT

Under the provisions of the Sarbanes-Oxley Act of 2002, the Public Company Accounting Oversight Board (PCAOB) has replaced the AICPA's Auditing Standards Board as the standards-setting authority for public company audits. The PCAOB has adopted the existing AICPA auditing standards as transitional standards, pending further deliberations by the PCAOB. However, the AICPA's outstanding Exposure Drafts will not be issued as final standards. The drafts will be considered by the PCAOB in developing future standards or amendments to the existing transitional standards.

The outstanding Exposure Drafts would create two new SASs that would not supersede or amend any other SASs.

- *Review of SEC Engagements by a Reviewing Partner.* This proposed SAS, which would be created under the *Sarbanes-Oxley Omnibus SAS,* would require that a reviewing partner perform reviews of audits and interim reviews for SEC engagements. This new statement would be effective for audits or reviews of SEC engagements for periods ending on or after September 15, 2003.
- *Auditing an Entity's Internal Control over Financial Reporting in Conjunction with the Financial Statement Audit.* This proposed SAS establishes standards and guidance for audits required under the Sarbanes-Oxley Act to have an audit of the entity's internal control over financial reporting. (Non-SEC entities could also use this guidance.).

The authors will provide updates on the PCAOB's activities and the Sarbanes-Oxley Exposure Drafts at www.wiley.com/gaas. Practitioners may also wish to monitor the PCAOB's website at www.pcaobus.org.

NEW EXPOSURE DRAFTS ISSUED BY THE AUDITING STANDARDS BOARD RELATED TO THE AUDITOR'S RISK ASSESSMENT PROCESS

The Auditing Standards Board (ASB) has issued Exposure Drafts of seven proposed SASs that relate to the risk assessment process. The Auditing Standards Board notes, in an explanatory memorandum to the audit risk Exposure Drafts, that the proposed SASs "represent a significant strengthening of auditing standards that will improve the quality and effectiveness of audits."

The Exposure Drafts, issued in response to the recommendations of the Public Oversight Board's Panel on Audit Effectiveness, were jointly developed by the ASB and International Auditing and Assurance Standards Board of the International Federation of Accountants. The proposed SASs are thus also representative of the effort among standard setters to promote convergence between US and international standards.

The Exposure Drafts are designed to make the following key changes in audit practice:

- Enhance the quality and depth of the required understanding of the entity and its environment, including its internal control.
- Require that the auditor assess the risks of material misstatement at the financial statement level and at the assertion level on all audits based on the understanding obtained.
- Encourage testing of controls.
- Emphasize the entity's risk assessment process.
- Link assessed risks and audit procedures to respond to those risks.
- Emphasize testing of disclosures.
- Expand documentation requirements.

Although the standards will not be issued as final standards by the AICPA, the authors have noted which sections may be impacted by the issuance of these Exposure Drafts. In addition, a new SAS, *Understanding the Entity and Its Environment and Assessing the Risks of Material Misstatement,* would be created. The PCAOB may consider these Exposure Drafts in developing new standards or amendments to the transitional standards. Therefore, practitioners may want to be aware of the changes proposed by the Exposure Draft. Please check for updates on the John Wiley & Sons, Inc. website at www.wiley.com/gaas.

100-230 THE AUDITOR'S RESPONSIBILITIES AND FUNCTIONS, INTRODUCTION TO GAAS, AND THE GENERAL STANDARDS (INCLUDING THE QUALITY CONTROL STANDARDS)[1]

EFFECTIVE DATE AND APPLICABILITY

Original Pronouncements	Statement of Auditing Standards (SAS) 1, November 1972; SAS 5, July 1975; SAS 25, November 1979; SAS 41, April 1982; SAS 43, August 1982; SAS 78, December 1995; SAS 82, February 1997; SAS 95, December 2001; SAS 98, September 2002; and SAS 99, October 2002.
Effective Date	When issued, November 1972, except for amendments on quality control (November 1979), services other than audits of financial statements (August 31, 1982), and consideration of fraud (February 1997). SAS 95 is effective for audits of financial statements for periods beginning on or after December 15, 2001. The amendments for SAS 98 are effective upon issuance, and the amendment for SAS 99 is effective for audits of financial statements for periods beginning on or after December 15, 2002, with earlier application permitted.

---

[1] *The Auditing Standards Board (ASB) has issued Exposure Drafts of seven proposed SASs that relate to the risk assessment process. A summary of key changes is provided immediately before Section 100-230. This section would be amended to expand the understanding required under the second standard of fieldwork to "the entity and its environment, including its internal control." The purpose of this understanding would also be amended to "assessing the risk of material misstatement of the financial statements whether due to error or fraud." The Public Company Accounting Oversight Board (PCAOB) has replaced the ASB as the standards-setting authority for public company audits. Therefore, the ASB's Exposure Draft will not be issued as a final standard by the AICPA. The document will, however, be considered by the PCAOB in developing a standard or amendments to an existing standard. Please check for updates to this section on the John Wiley & Sons, Inc. website at www.wiley.com/gaas.*

Applicability

All audits in accordance with generally accepted auditing standards and other services covered by SASs.

NOTE: All sections apply whether the financial statements are presented in conformity with GAAP or OCBOA unless otherwise noted.

DEFINITIONS OF TERMS

Auditing standards. Measures of audit quality and the objectives to be achieved in an audit.

Auditing procedures. Acts to be performed by the auditor during the course of an audit to comply with auditing standards.

Professional skepticism. An attitude that includes a questioning mind and a critical assessment of audit evidence.

OBJECTIVES OF SECTION

Most of the discussion in Sections 100-230 can be traced to the combination of generally accepted auditing standards with statements on auditing procedure in 1963. It was issued as Statement on Auditing Procedure (SAP) 33. Some of the material dates all the way back to the original tentative statement of auditing standards in 1947 and is primarily philosophical.

In December 2001, the Auditing Standards Board issued SAS 95, *Generally Accepted Auditing Standards.* This SAS superseded Section 150, "Generally Accepted Auditing Standards" of SAS 1, *Codification of Auditing Standards and Procedures.* It established a GAAS hierarchy, identified the auditing publications that auditors should follow in performing the audit, and clarified the authority of such publications. In September 2002, SAS 98 amended SAS 95 to clarify that appendixes to SASs are interpretive publications.

In October 2002, SAS 99 amended Section 230, "Due Professional Care in the Performance of Work," to add a discussion about the characteristics of fraud and collusion.

FUNDAMENTAL REQUIREMENTS

OBJECTIVE OF ORDINARY AUDIT

To express an opinion on the fairness, in all material respects, with which the financial statements present financial position, results of operations, and cash flows in conformity with generally accepted accounting principles or another comprehensive basis of accounting.

AUDITOR RESPONSIBILITIES

In every audit, the auditor has to obtain reasonable assurance about whether the financial statements are free of material misstatement. Material misstatement includes

1. Material error. (See Section 312)
2. Material fraud. (See Section 316)
3. Certain illegal acts. (See Section 317)

MANAGEMENT RESPONSIBILITIES

The fairness of the representations made through financial statements is an implicit and integral part of management's responsibility. Management is responsible for

1. Adopting sound accounting policies.
2. Establishing and maintaining internal control that will, among other things, record, process, summarize, and report financial data that are consistent with management's assertions embodied in the financial statements.

The auditor's participation in preparing financial statements does not change the character of the statements as representations of management. In brief, management is responsible for the financial statements; the auditor is responsible for expressing an opinion on those financial statements.

GENERALLY ACCEPTED AUDITING STANDARDS (GAAS) AND THE GAAS HIERARCHY

The auditor is responsible for planning, conducting, and reporting the results of an audit according to generally accepted auditing standards (GAAS). The hierarchy of GAAS consists of the following three tiers:

Tier 1: Auditing Standards (which include the Statements on Auditing Standards)
Tier 2: Interpretive publications
Tier 3: Other auditing publications

Tier 1: Auditing Standards

Tier 1 consists of (1) the ten general, fieldwork, and reporting standards, and (2) the Statements on Auditing Standards (SASs). As stated in AU 150.02 the generally accepted auditing standards (GAAS) approved by the American Institute of Certified Public Accountants (AICPA) membership are

A. General Standards

1. **Training and proficiency.** The audit is to be performed by a person or persons having adequate technical training and proficiency as an auditor.
2. **Independence.** In all matters relating to the assignment, an independence in mental attitude is to be maintained by the auditor or auditors.
3. **Due care.** Due professional care is to be exercised in the planning and performance of the audit and the preparation of the report.

B. Fieldwork Standards

4. **Planning and supervising.** The work is to be adequately planned, and assistants, if any, are to be properly supervised.
5. **Internal control.** A sufficient understanding of internal control is to be obtained to plan the audit and to determine the nature, timing, and extent of tests to be performed.
6. **Evidential matter.** Sufficient competent evidential matter is to be obtained through inspection, observation, inquiries, and confirmations to afford a reasonable basis for an opinion regarding the financial statements under audit.

C. Reporting Standards

7. **GAAP.** The report shall state whether the financial statements are presented in accordance with generally accepted accounting principles.
8. **Consistency.** The report shall identify those circumstances in which such principles have not been consistently observed in the current period in relation to the preceding period.
9. **Disclosure.** Informative disclosures in the financial statements are to be regarded as reasonably adequate unless otherwise stated in the report.
10. **Reporting obligation.** The report shall contain either an expression of opinion regarding the financial statements taken as a whole or an assertion to the effect that an opinion cannot be expressed. When an overall opinion cannot be expressed, the reasons should be stated. In all cases where an auditor's name is associated with financial statements, the report should contain

    a. A clear-cut indication of the character of the auditor's work, if any.
    b. The degree of responsibility the auditor is taking.

NOTE: Materiality and audit risk underlie the application of the ten standards and the SASs (see Section 312).

The preceding ten formal standards apply to all other services covered by SASs unless they are clearly not relevant or the SAS specifies that they do not apply.

These ten general, fieldwork, and reporting standards provide the framework for the SASs promulgated by the Auditing Standards Board (ASB). Auditors are required under Rule 202, *Compliance with Standards,* of the AICPA Code of Professional Conduct to comply with these standards. Auditors should have sufficient knowledge of the SASs to determine when they apply and should be prepared to justify departures from the SASs.

Tier 2: Interpretive Publications

Interpretive publications are recommendations, issued under the authority of the ASB, on how to apply the SASs in specific circumstances, including engagements for entities in specialized industries. Interpretive publications are not auditing standards. They consist of the following:

- Auditing Interpretations of SASs
- Auditing guidance in AICPA Audit and Accounting Guides
- Auditing Statements of Positions
- Appendixes to the SASs

NOTE: SAS 95 notes that certain "previously issued appendices to original pronouncements" that modified other SASs are Tier 1 publications, not interpretative publications.

Auditors should be aware of and consider interpretive publications that apply to their audits. Auditors who do not follow the guidance in an applicable interpretive publication should be prepared to explain how they complied with the relevant SAS requirements addressed by such guidance.

NOTE: Any "should" statements in audit guides now have a formal level of authority in the GAAS hierarchy. Auditing Interpretations are presented in this book in the related sections. A list of AICPA Audit and Accounting Guides and auditing Statements of Position are presented in Appendix B.

Tier 3: Other Auditing Publications

Other auditing publications are not authoritative but may help auditors to understand and apply SASs. Such publications include all AICPA auditing publications not included under Tier 1 or Tier 2 and other auditing publications, including

- Auditing articles in the *Journal of Accountancy* and other professional journals
- Auditing articles in AICPA *CPA Letter*
- Continuing professional education programs and other instructional materials
- Textbooks
- Guide books
- Audit programs
- Checklists
- Other auditing publications from state CPA societies, other organizations, and individuals

An auditor should evaluate such guidance to determine whether it is both (1) **relevant** for a particular engagement and (2) **appropriate** for the particular situation. When evaluating whether the guidance is appropriate, the auditor should consider whether the publication is recognized as helpful in understanding and applying SASs, and whether the author is recognized as an auditing authority. (AICPA auditing publications that have been reviewed by the AICPA Audit and Attest Standards staff are presumed to be appropriate.)

NOTE: The auditor is not required to be aware of the full body of other auditing publications. However, the authors believe that some of the most important Tier 3 publications are AICPA PITF Practice Alerts. All auditors of public companies should be familiar with these. A list of all Practice Alerts is included in Appendix C.

Quality Control Standards

An audit firm should establish a quality control system to provide it with reasonable assurance that its staff meet the requirements of GAAS in its audit engagements.

Training and Proficiency

The auditor holds out himself or herself as being proficient in accounting and auditing. Attaining proficiency begins with formal education and continues through later experience. The auditor must be aware of and understand new authoritative pronouncements on accounting and auditing.

Independence[2]

According to AU 230.03, to **be** independent, the auditor must be intellectually honest; to be **recognized** as independent, he or she must be free from any obligation to or interest in the client, its management, or its owners. For specific guidance, the auditor should look to

---

[2] *Section 201 of Sarbanes-Oxley Act of 2002 and the related SEC implementing rules created significant new independence requirements for auditors of public companies. For example, the SEC prohibits certain nonaudit services such as bookkeeping, internal audit outsourcing, and valuation services. All audit and nonaudit services performed by the auditor, including tax services, must be preapproved by the company's audit committee. In March 2003, the SEC issued final rules implementing Section 201 of the Act. The rules,* ***Strengthening the Commission's Requirements Regarding Auditor Independence****, can be found at http://www.sec.gov/rules/final/33-8183.htm.*

AICPA and the state society rules of conduct and, if relevant, the requirements of the Securities and Exchange Commission (SEC) and the Independence Standards Board (ISB).[3]

Due Care

The auditor should observe the standards of fieldwork and reporting, possess the degree of skill commonly possessed by other auditors, and should exercise that skill with reasonable care and diligence. The auditor should also exercise professional skepticism, that is, an attitude that includes a questioning mind and a critical assessment of audit evidence. However, the auditor is not an insurer and the audit report does not constitute a guarantee because it is based on reasonable assurance. The auditor should be alert to the possibility of collusion when performing the audit and how management may override controls in a way that would make the fraud particularly difficult to detect.

INTERPRETATIONS

There are no interpretations for this section.

TECHNIQUES FOR APPLICATION

Management's Responsibilities

Many times, clients do not understand their responsibilities for the audited financial statements. These financial statements are **management's**. They contain management's representations. The form and content of the financial statements are management's responsibility even though the auditor may have prepared them or participated in their preparation. The SEC has stated

> *The fundamental and primary responsibility for the accuracy of information filed with the Commission and disseminated among the investors rests upon management.* ***Management does not discharge its obligations in this respect by the employment of independent accountants, however reputable*** *(Accounting Series Release No. 62, June 27, 1947; emphasis added).*

Management Representation Letter

Generally accepted auditing standards require the auditor to obtain a management representation letter (see Section 333). In the letter, management acknowledges its responsibility for the financial statements and states its belief that the financial statements are fairly presented in conformity with generally accepted accounting principles. Sometimes, the client objects to this acknowledgment because of the auditor's role in the preparation of the financial statements. To avoid this misunderstanding, the auditor's engagement letter may include a paragraph such as the following:

> Generally accepted auditing standards require that we obtain from you a representation letter about the financial statements and the underlying accounting records and an acknowledgment that

---

[3] *The ISB went out of existence in July 2001, because the SEC, in issuing its new independence requirements in November 2000, basically obviated the need for the ISB. During its existence, the ISB issued guidance including Independence Standard 1,* ***Independence Discussions with Audit Committees.*** *This standard requires the external auditor to communicate and discuss independence issues with the audit committee, and continues to be effective. See the summary of Professional Issues Task Force Practice Alert 99-1 in Section 380 for more information on this standard.*

the financial statements are management's responsibility, and that they are presented in accordance with generally accepted accounting principles.

The annual reports of many public companies contain statements acknowledging management's responsibility for the financial statements and the underlying accounting records (see *Illustrations*).

AUDITOR'S RESPONSIBILITIES

The auditor's responsibility for the financial statements he or she audits is confined to the expression of an opinion on those statements. In performing the audit, the auditor is responsible for compliance with generally accepted auditing standards, including the statements on auditing standards.

Under the GAAS hierarchy, the auditor has a responsibility to consider SASs and interpretive publications in all audits. If such guidance is not followed, an auditor must be prepared to

- For Tier 1 SASs, justify a departure from SASs.
- For Tier 2 interpretive publications, explain that an alternative approach achieved the objectives of GAAS.

In other words, the first two categories of GAAS are "must know." When applying the Tier 3 level of GAAS, other auditing publications, the auditor should determine whether such guidance is relevant and appropriate.

To provide reasonable assurance that it is conforming with generally accepted auditing standards in its audit engagements, an accounting firm should establish quality control policies and procedures. These policies and procedures should apply not only to audit engagements but also to attest, and accounting and review services for which professional standards have been established.

ESTABLISHMENT OF QUALITY CONTROL POLICIES AND PROCEDURES

The nature and extent of a firm's quality control policies and procedures depend on the following:

1. Firm size and the number of its offices.
2. The degree of autonomy of personnel and practice offices.
3. The knowledge and experience of its personnel.
4. The nature and complexity of the firm's practice.
5. The cost of developing and implementing quality control policies and procedures in relation to the benefits provided.

When a firm establishes quality control policies and procedures, it also should do the following:

1. Assign responsibilities to qualified personnel to implement quality control policies and procedures.
2. Communicate quality control policies and procedures to personnel (see below).
3. Monitor the effectiveness of the quality control system. The purpose is to determine that policies and procedures and the methods of implementing and communicating them are still appropriate.

NOTE: Flaws in, or a violation of, a firm's quality control do not necessarily indicate that an audit was not performed in accordance with GAAS.

Communicating Quality Control Policies and Procedures

Quality control policies and procedures do not have to be in writing. They may be communicated orally when personnel are employed and repeated once a year at a firm meeting.

It is strongly recommended that firms, no matter what their size, document their quality control policies and procedures. The nature and extent of the documentation depend primarily on firm size and the nature of the practice.

Elements of Quality Control

When a firm establishes its quality control policies and procedures, it should follow the five elements of quality control (see Statement on Quality Control Standard 2, *System of Quality Control for a CPA Firm's Accounting and Auditing Practice,* as amended by SQCS 4, *Amendment to System of Quality Control for a CPA Firm's Accounting and Auditing Practice).*

NOTE: CPA firms or individuals that are enrolled in an AICPA approved practice-monitoring program are obligated to adhere to quality controls standards. In addition, the Principles of Professional Conduct indicate that members should practice in firms that have in place quality control procedures to provide reasonable assurance that services are competently delivered and adequately supervised. The Statements on Quality Control apply to a CPA firm's accounting, auditing, and attest practice.

Personnel Management

Policies and procedures should provide reasonable assurance that personnel

1. Have the characteristics to enable competent performance.
2. Have the technical training and proficiency needed.
3. Participate in continuing education to enable them to fulfill responsibilities and satisfy appropriate educational requirements of the AICPA and regulatory agencies.
4. Selected for advancement have the necessary qualifications.

Statement on Quality Control Standards 5, *The Personnel Management Element of a Firm's System of Quality Control—Competencies Required by a Practitioner-in-Charge of an Attest Engagement*, clarifies that a partner-in-charge of accounting, auditing, and attestation engagements should ordinarily possess the following competencies:

1. An understanding of the role of a system of quality control and the Code of Professional Conduct.
2. An understanding of the service to be performed.
3. Technical proficiency.
4. Familiarity with the industry.
5. Professional judgment.
6. An understanding of the organization's information technology systems.

Firm policies and procedures should address other competencies necessary in the circumstances.

NOTE: A practitioner-in-charge is defined as an individual responsible for supervising the engagement or signing the report on such engagement.

Acceptance and Continuance of Clients and Engagements

Policies and procedures should provide reasonable assurance that the firm will not be associated with clients whose management lacks integrity. A firm should

1. Undertake only engagements that can be completed with professional competence.
2. Consider the risks associated with the engagement.

Moreover, a firm should obtain an understanding with the client regarding the engagement.

Additional guidance on this subject is provided in the summary of Professional Issues Task Force Practice Alert 94-3, *Acceptance and Continuance of Audit Clients*, which can be found in Section 315.

Engagement Performance

Policies and procedures should provide reasonable assurance that personnel meet

1. Professional standards.
2. Regulatory requirements.
3. The firm's standards.
4. Concurring partner review requirements applicable to SEC engagements.

Policies and procedures should also provide reasonable assurance that personnel refer to authoritative literature and consult, on a timely basis, with appropriate individuals when dealing with complex, unusual, or unfamiliar issues.

Monitoring

Policies and procedures should provide reasonable assurance that the above elements of quality control are suitably designed and effectively applied. Monitoring involves

1. Relevant and adequate polices and procedures that are complied with by members of the firm.
2. Appropriate guidance and practice aids.
3. Effective professional development activities.

NOTE: A firm's monitoring procedures may include inspection procedures and preissuance or postissuance review of selected engagements by a qualified person not directly associated with performance of the engagement (may be a partner with final responsibility for the engagement in a small firm) (see Statement on Quality Control Standard 3, ***Monitoring a CPA Firm's Accounting and Auditing Practice****).*

Independence, Integrity, and Objectivity

Policies and procedures should provide reasonable assurance that personnel maintain independence when required and perform all responsibilities with integrity and objectivity.

1. Independence is an impartiality that recognizes an obligation for fairness.
2. Integrity pertains to being honest and candid, and requires that service and public trust not be subordinated to personal gain.
3. Objectivity is a state of mind that imposes an obligation to be impartial, intellectually honest, and free of conflicts of interest.

Administration of a Quality Control System

A partner or partners, depending on the size of the firm, should be responsible for monitoring the effectiveness of the firm's quality control system. The objective is to determine on a timely basis that the firm's quality control policies and procedures, assignment of responsibilities, and communication of policies and procedures continue to be appropriate.

ILLUSTRATIONS

The following are (1) a chart illustrating the GAAS hierarchy, and (2) an example of a management report of the American Institute of Certified Public Accountants acknowledging responsibility for the financial statements and the internal control system.

Illustration 1. GAAS Hierarchy

Level	*Elements*	*Authority*
Tier 1 Auditing Standards	• 10 Formal Standards listed in *Fundamental Requirements* • Statements on Auditing Standards (SASs)	Auditors must be familiar with all guidance in this category. Any departures must be justified.
Tier 2 Interpretive Publications	• Auditing Interpretations of SASs • Auditing guidance in AICPA Audit and Accounting Guides • Auditing Statements of Position • Appendices to SASs	Auditors must be familiar with all guidance in this category. Any departures must be justified.
Tier 3 Other Auditing Publications	• AICPA auditing publications not referred to under Tier 1 or Tier 2, such as PITF Practice Alerts • Auditing articles in the *Journal of Accountancy* and other professional journals • Auditing articles in *The CPA Letter* published by the AICPA • Continuing professional education programs and other instructional materials • Textbooks • Guide books • Audit programs • Checklists • Other auditing publications from state CPA societies, other organizations and individuals	Guidance in this category is not authoritative. Auditors must determine whether guidance is appropriate and relevant in particular circumstances.

Illustration 2. Report of Management on Financial Statements and Internal Control

Management's Responsibilities for Financial Statements and Internal Control

Financial Statements

The financial statements of the American Institute of Certified Public Accountants and related organizations (the "Institute") were prepared by management, which is responsible for their reliability and objectivity. The statements have been prepared in conformity with accounting principles generally accepted in the United States of America and, as such, include amounts based on informed estimates and judgments of management. Financial information elsewhere in this annual report is consistent with that in the financial statements.

The Board of Directors, operating through its Audit Committee, which is composed entirely of directors who are not officers or employees of the Institute, provides oversight of the financial reporting process and safeguarding of assets against unauthorized acquisition, use, or disposition. The Audit Committee annually recommends the appointment of independent public accountants and submits its recommendation to the Board of Directors, and then to the Council, for approval.

The Audit Committee meets with management, the independent public accountants, and the internal auditor; approves the overall scope of audit work and related fee arrangements; and reviews audit reports and findings. In addition, the independent public accountants and the internal auditor meet separately with the Audit Committee, without management representatives present, to discuss the results of their audits, the adequacy of the Institute's internal control system, the quality of its financial reporting, and the safeguarding of assets against unauthorized acquisition, use, or disposition.

The financial statements have been audited by an independent public accounting firm, J.H. Cohn LLP, which was given unrestricted access to all financial records and related data, including minutes of all meetings of the Council, the Board of Directors, and committees of the Board. The Institute believes that all representations made to the independent public accountants during their audits were valid and appropriate.

The report of the independent public accountants follows this statement.

Internal Control

The Institute maintains internal control over financial reporting and over safeguarding of assets against unauthorized acquisition, use, or disposition which is designed to provide reasonable assurance to the Institute's management and Board of Directors regarding the preparation of reliable financial statements and the safeguarding of assets. Internal control includes a documented organizational structure, a division of responsibility, and established policies and procedures, including a code of conduct, to foster a strong ethical climate.

Established policies are communicated throughout the Institute and enhanced through the careful selection, training, and development of its staff. Internal auditors monitor the operation of the internal control system and report findings and recommendations to management and the Board of Directors. Corrective actions are taken, as required, to address control deficiencies and implement improvements.

There are inherent limitations in the effectiveness of any system of internal control, including the possibility of human error and the circumvention or overriding of controls. Accordingly, even the most effective internal control system can provide only reasonable assurance with respect to financial statement preparation and the safeguarding of assets. Furthermore, the effectiveness of internal control can change with circumstances.

The Institute has assessed its internal control over financial reporting in relation to criteria described in *Internal Control—Integrated Framework* issued by the Committee of Sponsoring Organizations of the Treadway Commission. Based on this assessment, the Institute believes that, as of July 31, 2002, its internal control over financial reporting and over safeguarding of assets against unauthorized acquisition, use, or disposition met those criteria.

J.H. Cohn LLP also was engaged to report separately on the Institute's assessment of its internal control over financial reporting and over safeguarding of assets against unauthorized acquisition, use, or disposition.

The report of the independent public accountants follows this statement.

Barry C. Melancon

Barry C. Melancon
President & CEO

Clarence A. Davis

Clarence A. Davis
Chief Financial Officer

310 APPOINTMENT OF THE INDEPENDENT AUDITOR[1]

EFFECTIVE DATE AND APPLICABILITY

Original Pronouncements	SAS 1, November 1972; SAS 45, August 1983; SAS 83, October 1997; and SAS 89, December 1999.
Effective Date	When issued; November 1972, as amended by SAS 83 and SAS 89, effective for audits of financial statements periods beginning on or after December 15, 1999.
Applicability	Audits of financial statements in accordance with generally accepted auditing standards, reviews of interim financial information of public companies, and application of agreed-upon procedures to elements, accounts, or items of a financial statement.

DEFINITIONS OF TERMS

This section contains no definitions of terms. However, see the other sections related to planning and supervision listed in *Objectives of Section* for relevant terms.

---

[1] *The Auditing Standards Board (ASB) has issued an Exposure Draft of a proposed SAS that would affect this section,* ***Sarbanes-Oxley Omnibus SAS.*** *The Exposure Draft is designed to address certain provisions of the Sarbanes-Oxley Act of 2002. Among other things, the proposed amendment to this section would clarify that the audit committee normally engages the auditor on behalf of the entity, expand matters to be included in the required understanding between the auditor and the client, require documentation of the understanding, and state that the auditor should establish an understanding between the auditor and the client about an audit of internal control.*

The ASB has also issued Exposure Drafts of seven proposed SASs that relate to the risk assessment process. A summary of key changes is provided immediately before Section 100-230. Under the Exposure Draft, the guidance in Sections 310 and 311 would be combined. The proposed new SAS would cover, among other things, organizing the engagement, documenting the audit program, determining the extent that specialists are involved, and supervising assistants.

The Public Company Accounting Oversight Board (PCAOB) has replaced the ASB as the standards-setting authority for public company audits. Therefore, the ASB's Exposure Drafts will not be issued as final standards by the AICPA. The documents will, however, be considered by the PCAOB in developing standards or amendments to existing transitional standards.

Please check for updates to this section on the John Wiley & Sons, Inc. website at www.wiley.com/gaas.

OBJECTIVES OF SECTION

SAS 1, Section 310, discusses two matters—early appointment of the auditor and the need to establish an understanding with the client about the engagement. The first discussion about early appointment has been a long-standing good practice. The second item is a requirement that was added by SAS 83, *Establishing an Understanding with the Client*, in January 1998. The addition was made because of Statement on Quality Control Standard 2, *System of Quality Control for a CPA Firm's Accounting and Auditing Practice*. That standard requires a CPA firm to establish policies and procedures for obtaining an understanding with the client about the services to be performed. The Auditing Standards Board considered requiring a written engagement letter, but, because of restraint of trade concerns, SAS 83 expresses a preference, not a requirement, for an engagement letter.

FUNDAMENTAL REQUIREMENTS

BEFORE ACCEPTANCE

Before accepting an engagement near or after the close of the fiscal year, the auditor should

1. Determine whether circumstances of the engagement are likely to allow for an adequate audit and expression of an unqualified opinion.
2. If they will not, discuss with the client the possible need for a qualified opinion or disclaimer of opinion.

   NOTE: This requirement applies specifically to appointment near or after year end. However, any time the possible necessity of a qualified opinion or disclaimer of opinion becomes apparent, it is prudent for the auditor to discuss the matter with the client.

ESTABLISHING AN UNDERSTANDING WITH THE CLIENT

The auditor should establish an understanding with the client about the services to be performed for each audit, review of a public company's financial statements, or agreed-upon procedures engagement. According to AU 310.05, the understanding should include

1. Objectives of the engagement.
2. Management's responsibilities.
3. Auditor's responsibilities.
4. Limitations of the engagement.

The auditor should document the understanding, preferably through a written communication with the client. If the auditor fails to establish an understanding, the auditor should decline the engagement.

NOTE: This does not require an engagement letter, but the best way to meet the requirement is to always use an engagement letter.

According to AU 310.06, the understanding with the client generally includes the following matters:

1. The objective of the audit is the expression of an opinion.
2. Management is responsible for
   a. The financial statements.
   b. Effective internal control over financial reporting.
   c. Compliance with laws and regulations.
   d. Providing all financial records and related information to the auditor.

e. Providing a written representation letter to the auditor at the end of the engagement.
f. Adjusting the financial statements to correct material misstatements.
g. Affirming in the management representation letter that any uncorrected misstatements are immaterial.

3. The auditor is responsible for

a. Conducting the audit in accordance with generally accepted auditing standards (including a summary of the limitations of an audit).
b. Obtaining an understanding of internal control sufficient to plan the audit.

NOTE: All these matters are generally included, but the auditor is not required to include them.

Other matters may be included in the understanding, such as arrangements about

- The conduct of the engagement (for example, timing, client assistance).
- Specialists or internal auditors.
- A predecessor auditor.
- Fees and billing.
- Indemnification arrangements if the client knowingly provides false information to the auditor.

NOTE: The AICPA's Code of Professional Conduct permits indemnification arrangements limited to knowing misrepresentations made by the client, but regulators, such as the SEC, may prohibit or restrict these agreements.

- Conditions for access to the auditor's audit documentation.
- Additional services.

INTERPRETATIONS

There are no interpretations for this section.

TECHNIQUES FOR APPLICATION

APPOINTMENT OF THE AUDITOR

A significant factor in planning fieldwork and timing auditing procedures is the timing of the auditor's appointment.

Early Appointment

Early appointment of the auditor is ideal. It allows him or her to plan the work so that it may be done effectively. An early appointment is helpful in planning the following:

1. Observation of the taking of the physical inventories.
2. Confirmation of cash, receivables, and other balances.
3. Count of cash and securities.

Early appointment also is helpful because it allows the auditor to perform some procedures before the end of the period (interim work) such as obtaining and documenting knowledge of internal control and testing of details of transactions. Also, as explained in Section 313, some substantive tests of the details of balances may be applied at an interim date.

By doing interim work, the auditor can complete the audit at an early date after year-end. Early appointment also allows early consideration of difficult accounting and reporting problems and reduction of pressures to meet filing deadlines, such as those of the SEC.

Appointment Near or After Year-End

Appointment near or after the client's year-end date presents planning and timing problems for the auditor; however, these problems may be resolved. Ordinarily, the problems concern inventory observation, cash and securities counts, and confirmation requests.

Because of the late appointment, the auditor may not be able to observe the physical count of the inventory and the cash and securities at year-end. In this circumstance, the auditor should consider the client's accounting records. If the client maintains perpetual inventory records, the auditor can observe the physical count on a date after the client's year-end date and adjust that count back to year-end by using information in the perpetual inventory records. If the client maintains adequate and up-to-date securities records, the auditor can observe the count on a date after the client's year-end and adjust that count back to year-end by using information in the securities subsidiary ledger. Whenever the auditor observes a count on a date after the client's year-end date and adjusts that count back to year-end, he or she should examine, on a test basis, relevant transactions that occurred between year-end and the date of the count.

If the appointment is not too late after year-end, the auditor may be able to obtain necessary year-end confirmations, such as cash, receivables, prepayments, deposits, payables, and so on. If, however, the appointment is a month or two after year-end, the auditor may have to confirm account balances as of a date other than year-end and adjust the confirmed balances back to year-end. This procedure requires the examination on a test basis of relevant transactions that occurred between year-end and the confirmation date.

MATTERS COVERED IN ENGAGEMENT LETTER

The understanding with the client is specifically required to include

1. Objectives of the engagement,
2. Responsibilities of management,
3. Responsibilities of the auditor, and
4. Limitations of the engagement.

These four subject areas must be covered in the understanding. The manner and precise wording of that coverage is flexible.

Matters that are generally included in the understanding with the client are covered in *Fundamental Requirements*, under the section "Establishing an Understanding with the Client." For example, some auditors, in explaining responsibilities, describe responsibilities for detection of error, fraud, and reportable conditions of internal control, including a statement that matters of that nature that come to the auditor's attention will be communicated to management and the audit committee. These promises to communicate have sometimes been held to be separate undertakings in litigation that expand the auditor's legal duty. The auditor may wish to omit them or seek advice of legal counsel before including them.

ILLUSTRATION

The following is an illustration of an engagement letter.

ILLUSTRATION 1. ILLUSTRATIVE ENGAGEMENT LETTER

Auditor's Letterhead Guy and Carmichael
Certified Public Accountants
October 7, 2003

Addressed to Client	Brock Warner Plainsmen, Inc. 2320 Tiger Blvd. Lancaster, Pennsylvania 19701 To the Audit Committee[2]: This letter will confirm our understanding of the arrangements covering our audit of the financial statements of Plainsmen, Inc. for the period ending December 31, 2003.
Scope of Engagement	We will audit the company's balance sheet as of December 31, 2003, and the related statements of income, retained earnings, and cash flows for the year then ended. Our audit will be made in accordance with auditing standards generally accepted in the United States of America and will include obtaining an understanding of your internal controls over financial reporting sufficient to plan the audit and making such tests of the accounting records and such other auditing procedures as we consider necessary in the circumstances. Our audit is not designed to provide any assurance on internal control.
Objective of Engagement and Form of Report	The objective of our audit is to express an unqualified opinion on the financial statements, although it is possible that facts or circumstances encountered may require us to express a less than unqualified opinion. If for any reason, we are not able to complete the audit, we will not issue a report.
Client's Representations	Our procedures will include tests of documentary evidence supporting the transactions recorded in the accounts, tests of the physical existence of inventories, and direct confirmation of receivables and certain other assets and liabilities by correspondence with selected customers, creditors, legal counsel, and banks. At the conclusion of our audit, we will require a letter from management that confirms certain representations made about the financial statements and related matters during the audit.
Client's Responsibilities	The fair presentation of financial position and results of operations in conformity with accounting principles generally accepted in the United States of America is management's responsibility. Management is responsible for the development, implementation, and maintenance of an adequate internal control system, compliance with laws and regulations, and for the accuracy of the financial statements. Management is also responsible for making all financial records and related information available to us. Although we may advise you about appropriate accounting principles and their application, the selection and method of application are responsibilities solely of management.
Audit Adjustments	Management is responsible for adjusting the financial statements to correct material misstatements and for confirming to us in the representation letter that the effects of any uncorrected misstatements are immaterial, both individually and in the aggregate, to the financial statements.
Limitations of the Audit	We plan and perform our audit to obtain reasonable assurance about whether the financial statements are free of material misstatements. Because of the concept of reasonable assurance and because we do not perform a detailed examination of all transactions, there is a risk that material errors, fraud, or other illegal acts may exist and not be detected by us. However, we will inform you of any material errors that come to our attention and any fraud that comes to our attention. We will also inform you of any other illegal acts that come to our attention, unless clearly inconsequential.
Communications about Internal Control	During the course of our audit we may observe opportunities for economy in, or improved controls over, your operations. We will bring such matters to the attention of the appropriate level of management either orally or in writing. However, our audit is not designed and cannot be relied on to detect significant deficiencies in the design or operation of internal controls.

---

[2] *For a public entity that is listed on a stock exchange, the Sarbanes-Oxley Act requires the audit committee to be directly responsible for the appointment, compensation, and oversight of the external auditor.*

Fees	Fees for our services are based on our regular per diem rates plus travel and other out-of-pocket expenses. Invoices will be rendered every two weeks and are payable upon presentation. We estimate that our fee for this audit will be between $25,000 and $30,000. Should any situation arise that would materially increase this estimate we will, of course, advise you.
Use of Client Personnel	Whenever possible, we will attempt to use your company's personnel. This effort could substantially reduce our time requirements and help you hold down audit fees.
Other Work	We will also prepare federal and state tax returns for the year ended December 31, 2003. The fee for tax return preparation should be approximately $2,000.
Acknowledgement	Please indicate your agreement to these arrangements by signing the attached copy of this letter and returning it to us.
	We appreciate your confidence in retaining us as your certified public accountants and look forward to working with you and your staff.
	Sincerely,
	Guy and Carmichael
Signed by CPA	Guy and Carmichael
Signed by Client and Returned to CPA	Approved
	By *Brock Warner*
	Title *President*
	Plainsmen, Inc.
	Date *10/7/03*

311 PLANNING AND SUPERVISION[1]

EFFECTIVE DATE AND APPLICABILITY

Original Pronouncements	SAS 22, March 1978; SAS 47, December 1983; SAS 48, July 1984; SAS 77, November 1995.
Effective Date	Audits of financial statements for periods ending after September 30, 1978, unless amended by subsequent statements.
Applicability	Audits of financial statements in accordance with generally accepted auditing standards (also relevant for engagements involving special reports on specified elements, accounts, and items of financial statements).

DEFINITIONS OF TERMS

Auditor. Either the auditor with final responsibility for the audit or the auditor's assistants.

Assistants. Firm personnel other than the auditor with final responsibility for the audit.

Audit program. A reasonably detailed listing of audit procedures the auditor believes are necessary to accomplish the objectives of the audit. (It aids in instructing assistants in the work to be done.)

Audit planning. Developing an overall strategy for the expected conduct and scope of the audit.

Supervision. Directing the efforts of assistants who are involved in accomplishing the objectives of the audit and determining whether those objectives were accomplished. It includes

1. Instructing assistants.
2. Keeping informed of significant problems in conducting audits.
3. Reviewing assistants' work.
4. Dealing with differences of opinion among firm personnel.

---

[1] *The Auditing Standards Board (ASB) has issued Exposure Drafts of seven proposed SASs that relate to the risk assessment process. A summary of key changes is provided immediately before Section 100-230. Under the Exposure Draft, the guidance in Sections 310 and 311 would be combined. The proposed new SAS would cover, among other things, organizing the engagement, documenting the audit program, determining the extent that specialists are involved, and supervising assistants. The Public Company Accounting Oversight Board (PCAOB) has replaced the ASB as the standards-setting authority for public company audits. Therefore, the ASB's Exposure Drafts will not be issued as final standards by the AICPA. The documents will, however, be considered by the PCAOB in developing standards or amendments to existing transitional standards. Please check for updates to this section on the John Wiley & Sons, Inc. website at www.wiley.com/gaas.*

OBJECTIVES OF SECTION

The first standard of fieldwork requires adequate planning and proper supervision, but until SAS 22 was issued, the only observations on planning in the authoritative literature related to the advantages of early appointment of the auditor.

The need for more guidance on planning and supervision was identified when the general area of quality control received extensive attention in the early 1970s. It was recognized that quality control involved policies and procedures of CPA firms in the administration of a practice (see page 3) and policies and procedures of an individual auditor in planning and supervising an audit.

In the development of the SAS the need for answers to the following questions was identified:

1. What documentation of planning is required in every engagement? (A written audit program or programs.)
2. What knowledge of the client is required? (Enough to understand the events, transactions, and practices that significantly affect the financial statements.)
3. How should assistants' disagreements with significant conclusions be handled? (Assistants should be able to document disagreement if they want to disassociate themselves from the resolution.)

These matters are covered in more detail in *Fundamental Requirements*.

FUNDAMENTAL REQUIREMENTS

PLANNING

Planning Documentation

In planning the audit, the auditor should

1. Consider the nature, extent, and timing of work to be performed.
2. Prepare a written audit program (or a set of written audit programs).

   NOTE: Preparation of a memorandum on the preliminary audit plan is desirable, particularly for large and complex entities, but is not required.

Planning Considerations

These matters, among others, should be considered in planning the audit.

1. **Client.** The nature of the entity's business and industry.
2. **Accounting.** The entity's accounting policies and procedures.
3. **Processing methods.** The processing methods used by the entity for significant accounting applications.
4. **Control risk.** Planned assessed level of control risk (see Section 319).
5. **Materiality.** Preliminary estimate of what amount or amounts will be considered material in the audit (see Section 312).
6. **Other risks.** Audit areas likely to cause problems or require unusual attention (see Section 312).
   a. Financial statement items likely to require adjustment.
   b. Conditions likely to require modification of audit tests, such as related-party transactions or possible fraud. (See Sections 334 and 316.)
7. **Reports.** The kind of reports to be issued, such as filings with regulatory agencies or special reports on compliance with contractual provisions.

Knowledge of Business and Industry

The auditor should obtain enough knowledge about the client's business, organization, and operations to understand the events, transactions, and practices that may have an effect on financial statements. According to AU 311.07, the auditor should obtain knowledge of matters such as

1. Type of business.
2. Types of products and services.
3. Capital structure.
4. Related parties.
5. Business locations.
6. Production and distribution methods.
7. Compensation methods.

Industry matters the auditor should consider include

1. Economic conditions.
2. Government regulations.
3. Technological changes.
4. Accounting practices common in the industry.
5. Competitive conditions.
6. Available financial trends and ratios.

NOTE: The auditor's consideration of these matters, particularly industry matters, is directed at aspects that relate to the audit. General or extensive background research on the industry is not required.

Use of Computer Processing

In considering the effect of computer processing on internal control and audit procedures, the auditor should consider the

1. Extent of computer processing in each significant accounting application.
2. Complexity of that processing, including use of outside service organizations.
3. Organizational structure of computer processing.
4. Availability of data, since some data may exist only for a short period.
5. Use of computer-assisted audit techniques.
6. Need for specialized computer skills from the auditor's staff or outside consultants. If used, the auditor should
   a. Have sufficient computer knowledge to **communicate** the audit objectives.
   b. Evaluate whether the objectives will be achieved.
   c. Evaluate the results.

Specific Planning Procedures

The auditor's procedures for planning purposes usually involve

1. Review of his or her own records on the entity.
2. Discussions with others in the firm.
3. Discussions with the client's personnel.

Examples of these procedures are

1. Reviewing correspondence files, prior year's audit documentation, permanent files, prior years' financial statements, and auditor's reports.
2. Discussions with firm personnel responsible for nonaudit services to the client.

3. Asking about current business developments affecting the entity.
4. Reading current interim financial statements.
5. Discussions with management and the board of directors, or its audit committee, about the type, scope, and timing of the audit.
6. Considering implications of relevant accounting and auditing pronouncements, particularly recent pronouncements.
7. Coordinating the assistance of client personnel in preparing data and schedules.
8. Determining the involvement of consultants, specialists, and internal auditors.
9. Establishing the timing of audit work.
10. Establishing and coordinating staffing requirements.
11. Reviewing various sources of industry information, such as AICPA guides, industry publications, and annual reports of other entities in the industry.

SUPERVISION

Instructing Assistants

The auditor with final responsibility for the audit should inform assistants about

1. Their responsibilities.
2. The objectives of the procedures they are to perform.
3. Matters that may affect the scope of the procedures they are to perform, such as
   a. Aspects of the entity's business relevant to their assignment.
   b. Possible accounting and auditing problems.
4. The need to bring to his or her attention significant accounting and auditing questions raised during the audit,

Extent

The extent of supervision necessary depends on such factors as

1. Complexity of the subject matter.
2. Qualifications of the assistants.

Reviewing Work

The auditor should review the work of each assistant to

1. Determine whether it was adequately performed.
2. Evaluate whether the results support the conclusions to be expressed in the auditor's report.

Disagreements

If differences of opinion arise among firm personnel about accounting or auditing issues in an audit, there should be

1. Consultation to attempt resolution.
2. Documentation of an assistant's disagreement, if he or she wants to be disassociated from the final resolution.
3. Documentation of the basis for the final resolution.

INTERPRETATIONS

Communications between the Auditor and Firm Personnel Responsible for Nonaudit Services (February 1980)

The auditor should

1. Consider the nature of nonaudit services that have been performed.
2. Assess whether the services affect the financial statements or performance of the audit.
3. Discuss the nonaudit services with personnel who performed such services, if they have implications for the audit.

Responsibility of Assistants for the Resolution of Accounting and Auditing Issues (February 1986)

Each assistant has a responsibility to

1. Bring to the attention of the appropriate auditor significant disagreements about accounting and auditing issues.
2. Document his or her disagreement and disassociate himself or herself from the resolution of the matter, if the issue is not satisfactorily resolved.

TECHNIQUES FOR APPLICATION

The extent of the auditor's planning depends on the nature of the client and the experience of the auditor with that client. For example, planning for the audit of a new client is more extensive than planning for the audit of an existing client. When planning an audit, the auditor should consider the following:

1. The economy.
2. The client's industry.
3. The client's business.
4. Firm requirements.

These factors are discussed below. All factors are not appropriate for every audit. The size and complexity of the client determine which factors are relevant.

The Economy

There are certain economic conditions that significantly influence the industry and the business of the client. The auditor should be aware of these conditions and should consider them when planning the audit. Some economic factors that might affect client operations and, therefore, should be considered in planning an audit follow:

1. Interest rates.
2. Unemployment rates.
3. Money supply.
4. Foreign currency exchange rates.
5. International trade agreements.
6. Government regulations and legislation.
7. Overall business conditions—depression, recession, inflation.

CLIENT'S INDUSTRY

When planning the audit, the auditor should be aware of conditions in the client's industry. Factors to consider include the following:

1. Growth and financial results of the industry. Possible sources of this information are the following:
   a. Industry trade association literature.
   b. Publications issued by agencies such as Moody's, Standard & Poor's, and Robert Morris Associates (see Section 329).
   c. Government publications issued by the Government Printing Office, Washington, D.C.
2. Cyclical and seasonal nature of the industry.
3. Is the industry labor intensive or capital intensive?
4. Industry labor conditions.
   a. Is the industry unionized?
   b. Has the industry recently experienced a strike?
5. Industry accounting practices. This information may be obtained from firm members with clients in the same industry and AICPA Industry Audit and Accounting Guides.
6. Industry price patterns and consumer reactions to price changes.
7. State of industry technology.
8. Competitiveness of industry.
   a. Number of bankruptcies during the past year.
   b. Number of new companies organized during the current year.

In addition to the information the auditor obtains about the client's industry from industry-related publications, he or she may obtain industry information from bankers, client management, auditors with clients in the same industry, and general business publications, such as the *Wall Street Journal, Business Week, Forbes,* and *Fortune*.

CLIENT'S BUSINESS: NEW CLIENT

When planning the audit, the auditor should have a knowledge of the client's operations. For a new client, the primary sources of information are discussions with the predecessor auditor and inquiries of client management.

For a new client, the auditor should learn about the client and plan the audit by doing the following:

1. Communicate with predecessor auditor (see Section 315).
2. Visit client's administrative office and major facilities.
3. Review year-end financial statements of prior year and interim financial statements of current and prior year.
4. Review auditor's report on prior year's financial statements.
   a. Was there a scope limitation?
   b. Were certain matters emphasized?
   c. Did the auditor disclaim an opinion or issue an adverse opinion?
   d. Were there other modifications of the auditor's standard report?
5. Review prior year's income tax returns.
6. Obtain the results of the most recent income tax examination.

7. Review reports issued to agencies, such as the following:
   a. Securities and Exchange Commission.
   b. Federal Housing Administration, Small Business Administration, and Department of Labor.
   c. Credit agencies and banks.

Visit to Administrative Office

During his or her visit to the client's administrative office, the auditor should do the following:

1. Meet with financial and administrative officers and obtain or determine the following:
   a. The functions of each executive.
   b. The executive responsible for the audit.
   c. Organization charts.
   d. Locations and relative importance of all offices, showrooms, warehouses and factories.
   e. Obtain corporate manuals or memoranda that provide information about the following:
      (1) Nature and description of the entity's products.
      (2) Production and distribution methods.
      (3) Internal control (see Section 319).
      (4) General ledger chart of accounts.
   f. Methods of financing the entity's operations.
   g. Schedule of long-term debt.
   h. Names of banks and account executive at each bank. For each bank, determine the following:
      (1) Outstanding indebtedness and terms of payment.
      (2) Lines of credit.
      (3) Other banking services.
   i. For nonpublic companies, a schedule of stockholders with the following information:
      (1) Names.
      (2) Addresses.
      (3) Certificate numbers.
      (4) Number of shares held.
      (5) Shareholder function in the business.
   j. Purchase terms.
      (1) Terms of payment.
      (2) Are letters of credit used for foreign purchases?
   k. Sales terms.
      (1) Terms of payment.
      (2) Are letters of credit used for foreign sales?
   l. The existence of related-party transactions such as the following:
      (1) Purchases and sales.

(2) Loans.
(3) Receiving or providing services, such as management, legal, and administrative.

m. Schedule of all affiliates and nonconsolidated subsidiaries.
n. Customers and suppliers on whom the entity is economically dependent.
o. Most recent trial balance.
p. General ledger and books of original entry.

(1) Are accounting records up-to-date?
(2) What is the quality of accounting records?

q. Extent of client responsibility for preparation of the following:

(1) Trial balance.
(2) Schedules.
(3) Adjustments and accruals.
(4) Confirmations.
(5) Inventory instructions.
(6) Financial statements.
(7) Income tax returns.

r. Tentative audit schedule. Agree to dates for the following:

(1) Physical inventory.
(2) Cash and securities count.
(3) Mailing and confirmations.
(4) Start of fieldwork.

2. Obtain the entity's forms and documents, such as the following:

a. Purchase requisitions.
b. Purchase orders.
c. Sales authorizations.
d. Sales orders.
e. Sales invoices.
f. Production orders.
g. Production requisitions.
h. Receipts.
i. Checks.
j. Payroll cards.
k. Sales returns and credits.
l. Purchase returns and credits.

3. Examine work area that will be allocated to the auditor.
4. Walk through the accounting area.

a. Observe work conditions.
b. Meet employees.
c. Determine employee functions.

Visit to Facility

During the visit to the client's facility, the auditor should do the following:

1. Meet with management.
2. Walk through a production cycle and note the following:

   a. Initiation of order.
   b. Requisition of materials.
   c. Movement of production.
   d. Completion of production.
   e. Storage of completed product.
   f. Shipment to customer.

3. Document flow of production.
4. Note conditions of facility and equipment.
5. Visit materials stockroom, observe condition of the inventory, and review the following:

   a. Inventory records.
   b. Receiving reports.
   c. Inventory reports.

CLIENT'S BUSINESS: CONTINUING CLIENT

For a continuing client, information about the business is obtained from the following:

1. Client permanent file.
2. Prior year's audit documentation.
3. Prior year's audit team.
4. Client's current year budgets.
5. Client's current year interim financial statements.
6. Members who had professional assignments with the client during the year. These assignments include the following:

   a. Review of interim financial statements.
   b. Income tax planning.
   c. Systems and other consulting services.

7. Discussions with client management.

Discussions with Client Management

The in-charge auditor and the staff member who will supervise the audit should visit the client before beginning the audit to determine the following:

1. Change in product line.
2. Addition or deletion of factories, offices, warehouses, or showrooms.
3. Addition of new administrative departments.
4. Acquisition of subsidiaries.
5. Existence of new or continuing related parties.
6. Changes in production or distribution methods.
7. Changes in sources of financing.
8. Changes in internal control.
9. Acquisition of new office equipment such as a computer.
10. Changes in key personnel.
11. New long-term commitments, such as

    a. Leases.
    b. Employment contracts.

12. Adoption of employee compensation and benefit plans.

During the discussion with management, items that are discussed with a new client also should be discussed with a continuing client. These include

1. Timing of audit.
2. Auditor working conditions.
3. Client participation.

FIRM REQUIREMENTS

After he or she has obtained knowledge of the client and agreed with the client about the timing of, and client participation in, the audit, the auditor should do the following:

1. Obtain an engagement letter or prepare a memo about the understanding with the client.
2. Estimate staff requirements.
3. Prepare audit plan (if considered appropriate) and audit programs.
4. Prepare time budgets.

Staff Requirements

Staff requirements include the following:

1. Number of staff members required for the audit.
2. The levels of staff required—supervisor, manager, senior, semisenior staff.
3. Timing of need for staff.
    a. Year-end work, such as inventory observation, cash and securities counts, mailing of confirmations.
    b. Beginning of fieldwork.
    c. During fieldwork.
4. Number of staff members with previous audit experience with client.
5. Expertise required of staff.
    a. Taxes.
    b. Statistics.
    c. Computer applications.
    d. Familiarity with industry.

Preparation of Audit Plan

The audit plan provides the framework for the design of detailed audit procedures to be performed during the audit. The decision to use an audit planning memorandum and the content of the memorandum are matters of firm policy and there is substantial variation in practice.

Time Budgets

A time budget indicates time allocated to each aspect of the audit and what staff level will perform the specific audit task. Factors to be considered in the preparation of time budgets are the following:

1. Preliminary assessment of control risk.
2. Audit materiality levels.
3. Prior year's time budget and its relationship to actual time.
4. Key audit areas.

ILLUSTRATION

The following questionnaire will help the auditor assess risk. The existence of a condition covered by the questionnaire does not mean errors or fraud have occurred; it is a warning sign indicating increased risk in the audit areas affected. The questionnaire should be modified in accordance with the size and complexity of the entity.

ILLUSTRATION 1. RISK ASSESSMENT QUESTIONNAIRE

____
(Client)

____
(Audit Date)

________________________ (Prepared by / Date) ________________________ (Reviewed by / Date)

Instructions

This questionnaire should be completed before the start of fieldwork. Its purpose is to document and assess audit risk.

The information required to complete this questionnaire comes from the following sources:

1. Client responses to our inquiries.
2. Our knowledge of general and industry economic conditions.
3. Our knowledge of the client.

This questionnaire is divided into two major sections: external and internal factors. It is designed so that every "Yes" answer adversely affects risk exposure.

For every "Yes" answer, the item should be referenced to the appropriate audit documentation. The audit documentation should state our assessment of the effect of the condition on the risk of material errors or fraud.

EXTERNAL FACTORS

	Yes	*No*	*Working paper reference*
General Economic and Financial Conditions			
1. Are there trade or other barriers to the client's international business?			
2. Have the client's domestic markets suffered from high unemployment?			
3. Have the client's domestic markets suffered from high inflation?			
4. Has legislation passed that adversely affects client?			
5. Are interest rates high in relation to the client's capital needs?			
6. Has the client's business been adversely affected by changes in the following:			
a. Interest rates?			
b. Unemployment rates?			
c. Money supply?			
d. Foreign currency exchange rates?			
e. Overall business conditions (depression, recession, inflation)?			
Industry Economic and Financial Conditions			
1. Are the products of this industry subject to rapid obsolescence?			
2. Is the industry highly competitive?			
3. Have there been an unusual number of bankruptcies in this industry?			
4. Does the estimated income for the year deviate significantly from the industry?			
5. Did the industry experience a strike or other labor unrest?			
Uses and Users of Financial Statements			
1. Will the financial statements be filed with the Securities and Exchange Commission?			
2. Will the financial statements be submitted to the client's bank?			

	Yes	*No*	*Working paper reference*
3. Will the financial statements be submitted to credit agencies?			
4. Will the financial statements be submitted to stockholders?			
5. Will the financial statements be submitted to employees with reference to			
a. Profit-sharing plans?			
b. Pension plans?			
c. Bonus arrangements?			
d. Other compensation arrangements?			
6. Will the financial statements be used in connection with negotiations relating to an acquisition or a disposal of a business or a segment of a business?			
7. Will the financial statements be used in connection with negotiations for			
a. A loan?			
b. Performance bond?			
c. Private sale of stock?			
8. Are there other uses or users of these financial statements which may affect our risk? If so, list.			

INTERNAL FACTORS

	Yes	*No*	*Working paper reference*
Management's Integrity			
1. Are there any indications that management may lack integrity?			
2. Does management desire favorable earnings because of the following:			
a. Need to meet forecasts?			
b. Need to support price of the entity's stock?			
c. Existence of management profit-sharing agreements?			
3. Does management desire low earnings to reduce income taxes?			
4. Is management dominated by one or a few individuals?			
5. Does management have a poor reputation in the industry?			
6. Does management have a reputation for taking unusual or unnecessary risks?			
7. Has there been considerable turnover in senior management positions?			
8. Are there other characteristics of management personnel that may affect our risk? If so, list.			
Entity Organization			
1. Does the entity lack an audit committee?			
2. Does the entity fail to document its accounting system?			
3. Does the entity fail to use internal auditors?			
4. Do internal auditors, if any, not report to the audit committee or some other high organizational level of the entity?			
5. Is the organization owner- or manager-dominated?			
6. Does the entity fail to document job requirements?			
7. Does management lack an understanding of accounting and administrative controls?			
8. Does management fail to implement accounting and administrative controls?			
9. Has management failed to correct material weaknesses in internal accounting control that can be corrected?			
10. Are the entity's records generated to a significant degree by an EDP system?			
11. Does the entity fail to maintain perpetual records of			
a. Inventories?			
b. Long-lived assets?			
c. Investments?			
12. If the entity maintains perpetual records, does it periodically compare them with physical counts?			

	Yes	No	Working paper reference
13. Does management fail to communicate to other personnel a commitment to control?			
14. Does the entity fail to maintain policy and procedures manuals?			
15. Is there a high turnover of accounting and finance personnel?			
16. Has the client recently changed auditors or attorneys?			
17. Does a hostile relationship exist between our staff and management?			
18. Has the client recently organized or acquired a subsidiary?			
Financial Condition of Entity			
1. Does the entity have insufficient working capital?			
2. Does the entity have sufficient lines of credit?			
3. Does the entity depend on relatively few customers?			
4. Does the entity depend on relatively few suppliers?			
5. Are there violations of debt covenants?			
6. Has the entity recently experienced a significant period of losses?			
7. Is the entity using short-term obligations to finance long-term projects?			
8. Does the entity have excess productive capacity?			
9. Does the entity have high fixed costs?			
10. Has the entity experienced rapid expansion?			
11. Does the entity have a significantly long operating cycle?			
12. Does the entity have significant contingent liabilities?			
13. Is the entity the defendant in any significant litigation?			
14. Do major valuation problems exist, such as			
a. Allowance for doubtful accounts?			
b. Inventories?			
c. Investment?			
d. Long-term construction contracts?			
15. Has the client experienced severe losses from investments or joint ventures?			
Nature of Transactions			
1. Does the entity engage in a significant number of consignment purchases or sales?			
2. Does the entity engage in significant cash transactions?			
3. Does the entity engage in significant related-party transactions?			
4. Has the entity engaged in significant unusual transactions during the year or near the end of the year?			
5. Are there any questions on the timing of revenue recognition?			

312 AUDIT RISK AND MATERIALITY IN CONDUCTING AN AUDIT[1]

EFFECTIVE DATE AND APPLICABILITY

Original Pronouncement	SAS 47, December 1983; as amended by SAS 82, February 1997; SAS 96, January 2002; and SAS 98, September 2002.
Effective Date	Audits of financial statements for periods beginning after June 30, 1984, unless amended by subsequent statements. (SAS 96 is effective for audits of financial statements for periods beginning on or after May 15, 2002, with earlier application permitted. The amendments for SAS 98 are effective upon issuance.)
Applicability	Audits of financial statements in accordance with generally accepted auditing standards. (Specific requirements apply to **planning** audit tests and **evaluating** the results of audit tests.)

DEFINITIONS OF TERMS

Audit risk. The risk that the auditor may unknowingly fail to appropriately modify his or her opinion on financial statements that are materially misstated. At the account balance or class of transactions level, it consists of inherent risk, control risk, and detection risk. (It does not include business risk, inappropriate audit reporting decisions unrelated to detection and evaluation of misstatements, or erroneously concluding that the statements are materially misstated.)

Business risk. The risk of loss or injury to an auditor's professional practice from litigation, adverse publicity, or other event arising in connection with financial statements examined or reported on. (Not included in audit risk. Low business risk does not permit performance of less extensive procedures than would otherwise be appropriate under generally accepted auditing standards.)

---

[1] *The Auditing Standards Board (ASB) has issued Exposure Drafts of seven proposed SASs that relate to the risk assessment process. A summary of key changes is provided immediately before Section 100-230. Among other things, the Exposure Draft would amend this section to clarify risk assessment, clarify guidance on performing a combined assessment of inherent and control risk, and eliminate guidance on assessing risk at the maximum. The Public Company Accounting Oversight Board (PCAOB) has replaced the ASB as the standards-setting authority for public company audits. Therefore, the ASB's Exposure Draft will not be issued as a final standard by the AICPA. The document will, however, be considered by the PCAOB in developing new standards or amendments to existing standards. Please check for updates to this section on the John Wiley & Sons, Inc. website at www.wiley.com/gaas.*

*NOTE: **Business risk** is not a component of audit risk, but the concept is defined in a footnote to SAS 47.*

Misstatement. All errors and fraud, including certain illegal acts.

Inherent risk. The susceptibility of an assertion to a material misstatement, assuming that there are no internal controls. (Consists of the relative risk of misstatements of some assertions [for example, cash is more likely to be stolen than an inventory of coal] and to external factors such as technological developments or a declining industry characterized by many business failures.)

Control risk. The risk that a material misstatement that could occur in an assertion will not be prevented or detected on a timely basis by the entity's internal controls.

Detection risk. The risk that the auditor will not detect a material misstatement that exists in an assertion. (Inherent risk and control risk exist independently of the audit of financial statements. Detection risk relates to the auditor's procedures and can be changed at the auditor's discretion. Detection risk should be varied by the auditor inversely in relation to the assessment of inherent risk and control risk.)

Likely misstatement. The auditor's best estimate of the total misstatements in the account balances or classes of transactions examined.

Known misstatement. The amount of misstatements specifically identified by the auditor.

Materiality. This key term is not explicitly defined in the section, but, as explained in the next section, the FASB's definition is quoted. Also, the following observations are made about materiality:

1. Financial statements are materially misstated when they contain misstatements whose effect, individually or in the aggregate, is important enough to cause them not to be presented fairly in accordance with generally accepted accounting principles.
2. When reaching a conclusion as to whether the effect of misstatements, individually or in the aggregate, is material, an auditor ordinarily should consider their nature and amount in relation to the nature and amount of other items in the financial statements under audit.

These observations may be combined to specify that an item is material when its nature and amount in relation to the nature and amount of other items in the financial statements are important enough to affect the fair presentation of the financial statements in conformity with GAAP or an OCBOA.

*NOTE: The practitioner may want to consider the guidance provided in Staff Accounting Bulletin (SAB) 99, **Materiality.** This SAB addresses the application of materiality thresholds to the preparation and audit of financial statements filed with the SEC and provides guidance on qualitative factors to consider when evaluating materiality. The full text of the SAB can be viewed at www.sec.gov.*

OBJECTIVES OF SECTION

SAS 47 provides a framework for considering audit risk and materiality in planning audit procedures and evaluating the results of those procedures. It establishes how consideration of materiality and audit risk should affect planning audit procedures and evaluating audit findings.

SAS 47 was amended by SAS 82, *Consideration of Fraud in a Financial Statement Audit*, to provide for explicit consideration of the risk of fraud within the audit risk model and to incorporate guidance on errors that was formerly included in superseded SAS 53 on fraud and errors. The SAS 82 amendments to SAS 47 also (1) added factors auditors should consider for entities with multiple locations or components, (2) conformed the internal control terminology to SAS 78, *Consideration of Internal Control in a Financial Statement Audit: An Amendment to Statement on Auditing Standard No. 55,* and (3) included specific documentation requirements for consideration of fraud risk factors.

In January 2002, SAS 96, *Audit Documentation,* amended SAS 47 to add a requirement that an auditor document the nature and effect of aggregated misstatements, as well as his or her conclusion as to whether the aggregated misstatements cause the financial statements to be materially misstated.

Background

In 1975 the FASB published a discussion memorandum on materiality, and as the FASB project neared completion, there was some anticipation that the FASB would establish quantitative guidelines for materiality judgments. An auditing standards project was started in 1979 to consider how guidelines that might be established as accounting standards would affect the auditor's judgments in audit planning and evaluation of the presentation of financial statements. Ultimately, the FASB concluded that no general quantitative standards could be established. In 1980 the FASB issued Statement of Financial Accounting Concepts 2 on the qualitative characteristics of accounting data. The statement contained the following definition of materiality:

> *The magnitude of an omission or misstatement of accounting information that, in the light of surrounding circumstances, makes it probable that the judgment of a reasonable person relying on the information would have been changed or influenced by the omission or misstatement.*

Both SAS 47 and Statement of Financial Accounting Concepts 2 recognize that materiality judgments involve both quantitative and qualitative considerations, and the FASB definition encompasses both categories. In other words, the FASB's definition is **conceptual** and encompasses both quantitative and qualitative considerations.

Audit Concept of Materiality

When the FASB failed to establish general quantitative guidelines, the Auditing Standards Board decided to continue with its own project and to resolve several issues that had been identified. One of these issues was whether there was a separate concept of materiality in auditing distinguishable from accounting materiality as typified by the FASB definition.

SAS 47 does not tackle the issue directly. However, the description of the consideration of materiality in audit judgments supports the view that materiality in auditing is related to accounting materiality but can be distinguished particularly as it is used in planning. The SAS makes the point that the auditor's consideration of materiality is **influenced** by his or her perception of the needs of a reasonable person who will rely on the financial statements. In contrast, the FASB defines materiality as **dependent** on the needs of such a person.

SAS 47 states that "the auditor plans the audit to obtain reasonable assurance of detecting misstatements that he [or she] believes could be large enough, individually or in the aggregate, to be **quantitatively** material to the financial statements" [emphasis added]. This is a concept of materiality as an allowance or "cushion" for misstatement in the financial statements. Materiality in planning is a gauge on the effectiveness of audit procedures; the auditor uses it as a quantitative measure of how effective audit procedures should be to detect misstatements that, individually or in the aggregate, would exceed the dollar amount considered material to the financial statements.

The use of materiality in the evaluation stage of the audit employs essentially the same concept described in the FASB definition. SAS 47 observes that "as a result of the interaction of quantitative and qualitative considerations in materiality judgments, misstatements of relatively small amounts detected by the auditor could have a material effect on the financial statements.

ISSUES ON MATERIALITY IN AUDITING

There are several other issues that SAS 47 was intended to resolve.

Does the auditor need to estimate a single amount material to the financial statements at the start of the audit and explicitly relate that amount to individual account balances in planning procedures? The short answer is no. However, an auditor ordinarily would estimate a single amount material to the financial statements taken as a whole because most misstatements affect both the balance sheet and the income statement, and using the smallest amount that would be material to one of the statements is the only practical approach. This amount does not necessarily have to be quantified and documented, and it does not have to be explicitly related to individual account balances. However, some auditors believe those steps are necessary to implement use of a preliminary judgment about materiality.

Does business risk (potential loss or injury to the auditor's professional practice) affect the scope of the auditor's procedures? Things that make a client risky because of increased likelihood of litigation or adverse publicity may, as a practical matter, increase audit scope either because they also affect inherent risk or because the auditor elects to reduce business risk. If, however, the auditor assesses business risk as low, it is not appropriate to perform less extensive procedures than would otherwise be appropriate under generally accepted auditing standards

How does the reasonableness of accounting estimates affect the auditor's evaluation of whether financial statements are materially misstated? Before SAS 47, some auditors believed that evaluation of accounting estimates should be considered separately from known misstatements because of the inherent subjectivity of estimates. Also, there was disagreement about whether a difference between the client's estimate and the auditor's **best** estimate should be considered a misstatement. The SAS takes the position that the amount of misstatement in an estimate should be measured by the difference between the client's estimate and the closest end of the auditor's **range** of reasonableness, and that this misstatement should be combined with other known and likely misstatements in evaluating whether financial statements are materially misstated. For example, if the client's estimate of uncollectible accounts receivable is $10,000, and the auditor believes a reasonable estimate would be between $12,000 and $15,000, then $2,000 is the misstatement to be aggregated with other uncorrected likely misstatements. The auditor does not need to use the midpoint of the range. However, if a client's estimates consistently are all different in the same direction from the auditor's best estimates, the auditor should consider the possibility of management bias.

How does the auditor's knowledge of uncorrected immaterial misstatements in financial statements of prior periods influence the auditor's consideration of materiality in planning and evaluation in the current audit? The SAS does not take an unequivocal position on how prior periods' misstatements are to be considered in the current audit. It is clear that such misstatements should not be ignored, but their accounting treatment if they are to be corrected is not dealt with explicitly in accounting pronouncements. The auditor is reminded that an accumulation of uncorrected immaterial misstatements in the balance sheet could become material. Also, the auditor is advised to consider the nature (cause) and amount of such misstatements in planning procedures. If the misstatements of prior periods **affect the current period's financial statements,** the auditor should aggregate the prior periods' misstatements with uncorrected likely misstatements in considering whether the financial statements are materially misstated. However, the criteria for deciding when such misstatements affect the current statements are not specified.

Does the judgment about materiality used in planning audit tests have to be used in evaluating the financial statements? No. The evaluation of whether the financial statements taken as a whole are materially misstated may be affected by qualitative considerations and other information obtained during the audit. (See *Techniques for Application* "Evaluation of Financial Statements," for further discussion.)

FUNDAMENTAL REQUIREMENTS

GENERAL

According to AU 312.12, the auditor should consider audit risk and materiality both in (1) planning the audit and designing auditing procedures and (2) evaluating whether the financial statements taken as a whole are presented fairly in conformity with GAAP.

PLANNING—FINANCIAL STATEMENT LEVEL

According to AU 312.13, the auditor should plan the audit so that audit risk will be limited to a low level that is appropriate for issuing an opinion on the financial statements.

In planning the audit, the auditor should make a preliminary judgment about materiality levels. Ordinarily, the auditor plans the audit by considering the **smallest aggregate level of misstatements** that could be considered material to any one of the financial statements.

1. Ordinarily, it is not practical to design procedures to detect **qualitatively** material misstatements. However, when performing planned procedures, the auditor should be alert for such misstatements.
2. If a preliminary judgment about materiality is made before the financial statements to be audited are prepared, or if significant accounting adjustments can reasonably be expected, the preliminary judgment may be based on
   a. Annualized interim financial statements.
   b. Financial statements of one or more prior annual periods, after considering major changes in the entity's circumstances, its industry, or the economy.

The auditor should assess the risk of misstatement during planning, including a specific assessment about the risk of misstatement due to fraud. This should affect the overall audit strategy and the conduct and scope of the audit.

If the auditor concludes that there is a significant risk of material misstatement, this should affect

1. The nature, timing, and extent of procedures.
2. The assignment of staff and level of supervision.

The auditor should consider the extent of procedures to be performed at selected locations. According to AU 312.7, factors that could influence selection include the

1. Nature and amounts of assets and transactions executed.
2. Degree of centralization of records.
3. Effectiveness of control.
4. Frequency, timing, and scope of management's monitoring activities.
5. Judgments about materiality.

In planning auditing procedures, the auditor should consider the nature, cause (if known), and amount of misstatements the auditor is aware of from the audit of the prior period's financial statements.

Planning—Account Balance or Class of Transactions Level

According to AU 312.25, the auditor should design auditing procedures to detect misstatements (whether caused by error or fraud) that the auditor believes, based on the preliminary judgment about materiality, could be material when aggregated with misstatements in other balances or classes to the financial statements taken as a whole.

NOTE: The section observes that some auditors explicitly estimate for planning purposes the maximum amount of misstatement in a balance or class that, combined with misstatements in other balances or classes, could exist without causing the financial statements to be materially misstated, and that other auditors do not explicitly estimate such misstatement. In SAS 39 on audit sampling (Section 350), this maximum amount of misstatement is called ***tolerable misstatement****.*

The auditor should attempt to restrict audit risk at the individual balance or class level in a way that will enable the auditor at the completion of the audit to express an opinion on the financial statements taken as a whole at an appropriate low level of audit risk.

1. At the account balance or class of transactions level, audit risk consists of
   a. The risk (consisting of inherent risk and control risk) that the balance or class contains a misstatement that could be material when aggregated with misstatements in other balances or classes to the financial statements, and
   b The risk (detection risk) that the auditor will not detect such misstatement.
2. The auditor should vary detection risk in response to the assessment of inherent risk and control risk.
   a. The less inherent and control risk thc auditor believes exists, the greater the detection risk that can be accepted.
   b. The greater inherent and control risk the auditor believes exists, the less detection risk that can be accepted.

   NOTE: The section observes that audit risk at the account balance or class of transactions level may be assessed in quantitative terms, such as percentages, or in qualitative terms that range, for example, from a minimum to a maximum.
3. Assessment of inherent and control risk may be separate or combined. The assessment may be based on questionnaires, checklists, instructions, or similar generalized materials, and, in the case of control risk, the auditor's understanding of internal control and the results of the performance of suitable tests of controls.

   NOTE: Any assessment at less than maximum risk needs to be supported.
4. The auditor should not rely completely on the assessment of inherent and control risk and decide not to perform substantive tests of account balances or classes of transactions where material misstatements could exist.

Evaluating Audit Findings

The auditor should consider the effects, both individually and in the aggregate, of uncorrected misstatements.

1. The aggregation should include likely misstatement as well as known misstatement. The aggregation consists of
   a. Projected misstatement from substantive audit samples and known misstatement in nonsampling applications.
   b. Differences between any estimated amounts in the financial statements that the auditor considers unreasonable and the **closest reasonable** estimates.

c. Uncorrected prior period misstatements that affect the current period's financial statements.

2. Qualitative as well as quantitative considerations should be included in evaluating materiality.
3. It is ordinarily not feasible when planning an audit to anticipate all of the circumstances that may ultimately influence judgment about materiality levels in evaluating audit findings at the completion of the audit. Thus, the preliminary judgment about materiality levels will ordinarily differ from the judgment about materiality levels used in evaluating audit findings.

If the auditor determines that the effect of likely misstatements, individually or aggregated, causes the financial statements to be materially misstated, the auditor ordinarily should ask management to eliminate the misstatement. If the material misstatement is not eliminated, the auditor should issue a qualified or adverse opinion.

If the auditor concludes that the effects of likely misstatement, individually or aggregated, do not cause the financial statements to be materially misstated, the auditor should recognize that they could still be materially misstated due to further undetected misstatement.

1. The risk that the financial statements may be materially misstated increases as aggregated likely misstatement increases.
2. If the auditor believes that the risk of further misstatement is unacceptably high, the auditor should perform additional auditing procedures or obtain satisfaction that the entity has adjusted the financial statements to reduce the risk of material misstatement to an acceptable level.

Modification of Planned Procedures

The auditor may need to reevaluate planned auditing procedures as the audit progresses because of revised consideration of audit risk and materiality for all or certain account balances or classes of transactions, or the auditor may need to reevaluate the sufficiency of procedures already performed.

1. The extent of misstatements the auditor detects may alter the assessment of inherent and control risks, and other information about the financial statements may alter the preliminary judgment about materiality.
2. If significantly lower materiality levels are determined to be appropriate in evaluating audit findings, the auditor should reevaluate the sufficiency of auditing procedures performed.

Documentation Requirements

According to AU 312.40, the auditor should document both the nature and effect of aggregated misstatements, as well as his or her conclusion as to whether the financial statements are materially misstated.

INTERPRETATIONS

The Meaning of the Term *Misstatement* (December 2000)

This interpretation states that a misstatement may consist of

- A difference between the amount, classification, or presentation in the financial statements and the amount, classification, or presentation under GAAP.
- An omission of a financial statement element, account, or item, or information required to be disclosed under GAAP.

- Financial statement disclosures that are not in accordance with GAAP.

Misstatements may be known or likely, as discussed in the section on evaluation of financial statements in *Techniques for Application*.

Evaluating Differences in Estimates (December 2000)

When determining the amount of the likely misstatements to be aggregated, the auditor should consider the "closest reasonable estimate," which may be either a range of acceptable amounts or a point estimate. If the auditor uses a range, the amount of the likely misstatement would be the difference between the recorded amount and the amount at the closest end of the range. If the auditor uses a point estimate, the likely misstatement would be the difference between the point estimate and the amount recorded by the client.

The auditor should be alert to the possibility that a cluster of management's recorded estimates at either end of the auditor's range of acceptable amounts may indicate a bias on the part of management. In this case, the auditor should reconsider whether other estimates reflect a similar bias and perform additional audit procedures as necessary. The auditor should also be alert to the possibility that recorded estimates may be clustered at one end of the acceptable range in a preceding year, and the other end of the range in the current year. This may indicate that management is using swings in accounting estimates to manage earnings, in which case the auditor should consider whether this needs to be communicated to the audit committee as required by SAS 61.

Quantitative Measures of Materiality in Evaluating Audit Findings (December 2000)

The auditor should use professional judgment when evaluating quantitative aspects of identified misstatements. Materiality should be based on the financial statement elements most likely considered important by financial statement users. For publicly traded entities, this is generally recognized as after-tax income from continuing operations. However, this measure may not be appropriate if the after-tax income or loss from continuing operations fluctuates widely from year to year due to unusual or infrequent items. Depending on an entity's circumstances, other useful elements may be current assets, net working capital, total assets, total revenues, gross profit, total equity, and cash flows from operations.

Considering the Qualitative Characteristics of Misstatements (December 2000)

The auditor should also consider qualitative factors when evaluating misstatements, since misstatements of relatively small amounts may have a material effect on the financial statement. This interpretation lists a number of qualitative factors that the auditor may want to consider including

- The potential effect of the misstatement on profitability or other trends, or compliance with loan covenants, other contractual agreements, and regulatory provisions.
- Whether the misstatement changes a loss into income (or vice versa) or increases management's compensation.
- The effect of the misstatement on segment information or the effect of a misclassification (e.g., a misclassification between operating and nonoperating income).
- Statutory or regulatory requirements that affect materiality thresholds.
- The sensitivity of the circumstances of the misstatements (e.g., a misstatement that involves a fraud or illegal act).

- The significance of the financial statement element impacted by the misstatement (e.g., a misstatement that affects recurring earnings versus a nonrecurring charge or credit) or the significance of the misstatement or disclosures as they relate to the needs of users (e.g., the effect of misstatements on earnings contrasted with expectations).
- The character of the misstatement (e.g., an error in an objectively determinable amount versus an error in an estimate, which by its nature involves a degree of subjectivity).
- Management's motivation.
- Whether individually significant but different misstatements have offsetting effects.
- The likelihood that a currently immaterial misstatement may become material.
- The cost of correcting the misstatement.
- The risk that there are possible additional undetected misstatements that might impact the auditor's evaluation.

PROFESSIONAL ISSUES TASK FORCE PRACTICE ALERTS

94-1 Dealing with Audit Differences

This practice alert advises auditors to consider the following issues when evaluating audit differences and deciding whether to communicate them to audit committees:

- Are audit differences material when evaluated in light of factors such as debt covenants?
- Will an agreement with management to waive "hard" audit differences and errors because "soft" credit differences offset them be appropriate if these "soft" differences never materialize?
- Do many of the audit differences trend in the same direction, indicating the possibility of management trying to achieve an earnings forecast, or even the possibility of fraud?
- Are accumulated unrecorded audit differences that are not material now likely to become more significant if the entity's leadership changes or other conditions change?

The auditor should remember that audit committees and outsiders who find out about waived audit differences may ask why those differences were not recorded. The practice alert advises auditors to encourage management to record material and immaterial audit differences because it sends a clear message about management's responsibilities. If the client still does not record audit differences, the auditor should try to agree on a plan for recording differences in the following year.

The full text of this Practice Alert can be obtained from the AICPA website at www.aicpa.org/members/div/secps/lit/practice.htm.

TECHNIQUES FOR APPLICATION

In applying SAS 47, the auditor is faced with the following questions:

1. How to make a preliminary judgment about materiality for the financial statements taken as a whole.
2. How to relate the preliminary judgment about materiality to individual account balances and classes of transactions in planning auditing procedures.
3. How to consider audit risk at the financial statement level and account balance or class of transactions level and to relate the assessment of inherent risk and control risk to planning auditing procedures.
4. How to relate the required assessment of the risk of material misstatement due to fraud to inherent and control risk.

5. How to evaluate whether the financial statements are materially misstated based on audit findings.

MAKING A PRELIMINARY JUDGMENT ABOUT MATERIALITY

To make a preliminary judgment about the amount to be considered material to the financial statements, the auditor should first recognize the nature of this amount. It is an allowance or "cushion" for undetected or uncorrected misstatement remaining in the financial statements after all audit procedures have been applied. The auditor's goal is to plan audit procedures so that if misstatements exceed this amount, there is a relatively low risk of failing to detect them.

SAS 47 does not require quantification of the preliminary judgment about materiality. However, it is usually more efficient and effective to estimate a single dollar amount to be used in planning the audit. Since the amount is to be used as an aid in planning the scope of auditing procedures, use of a general rule of thumb is both practical and acceptable. For example, many auditors use 5 to 10% of before-tax income or .5 to 1% of the larger of total assets or total revenue. Adoption of a rule of thumb requires consideration of the appropriate base and the percentage of that base to be used to make the calculation.

Determining the Base

If the current financial statements are available, amounts from these statements may be used, or interim financial statements may be annualized. However, if significant audit adjustments are expected, an average from prior financial statements may be used. When historical data is used, the auditor should adjust the data for unusual items that affected prior years and for any known changes that can be expected to affect the current period.

Usually a single base is necessary because the auditor expresses an opinion on the financial statements taken as a whole rather than on individual financial statements. Also, many misstatements affect both the income statement and the balance sheet. This means that, as SAS 47 states, "the auditor ordinarily considers materiality for planning purposes in terms of the smallest aggregate level of misstatements that could be considered material to any one of the financial statements." However, this does not dictate the financial statement to use as the base. For example, the balance sheet (total assets) may be used as the base providing the percentage chosen for the base results in a suitably small amount.

The most common bases for materiality judgments are

1. Income before tax.
2. Total revenue.
3. Total assets.

Some common approaches to using these bases include, but are not limited to the following:

1. Select from among the bases recognizing differences in client and industry circumstances. For example
   a. If income fluctuates significantly or approaches breakeven, use total revenue.
   b. If the entity is in an industry that is asset intensive, such as a financial institution, use total assets; if the entity is a nonprofit organization, use total revenue.
   c. Otherwise, use income before taxes.
2. Use a single base that is likely to be valid across most client circumstances or industries. For example, always use the larger of total assets or total revenue.
3. Consider using appropriate percentages applied to different bases as the outside limits on a range, and select an amount within the range based on judgment. For ex-

ample, select an amount between X% of income before taxes and Y% of total revenue.

The choice of approach is influenced by judgments about the importance of stability of the base versus flexibility in using judgment in the circumstances.

Determining a Percentage

The percentage should be suitably small in relation to the base. Common approaches for determining percentages are

1. Select a single percentage for particular bases. For example, 5% of before-tax income or 1% of total revenue.
2. Select a range of percentages for particular bases to be adjusted for judgments about client circumstances or size. For example, use .5 to 1% of total revenue or 5 to 10% of before-tax income depending on
   a. Risk assessment—lower percentage as risk increases.
   b. Client size—lower percentage as size of entity increases.

Illustration of an Approach

One large CPA firm at one point used the following percentage scale applied to the larger of total assets or total revenue:

If the base is		*Planning materiality is the base*	
Over	*But not over*	*Times*	*Plus*
$ 0	$ 30 thousand	.54	$ 0
30 thousand	100 thousand	.029	750
100 thousand	300 thousand	.018	1,850
300 thousand	1 million	.0125	3,500
1 million	3 million	.0083	7,700
3 million	10 million	.006	14,600
10 million	30 million	.004	34,600
30 million	100 million	.00272	73,000
100 million	300 million	.0019	155,000
300 million	1 billion	.00125	350,000
1 billion	3 billion	.00087	730,000
3 billion	10 billion	.00058	1,600,000
10 billion	30 billion	.0004	3,400,000
30 billion	--	.00027	7,300,000

For example, if an entity has estimated revenues for the year of $9 million and estimated total assets of $11 million, the preliminary judgment about materiality would be $78,600 ($11,000,000 x .004 + $34,600). As is explained in the next section, this amount is not intended for evaluation of individual detected misstatements. In other words, the auditor would not decide that one of several detected misstatements was not material because the misstatement did not exceed this amount.

Nature of a Materiality Rule of Thumb

Several matters should be recognized in using a rule of thumb to estimate an amount to be used for planning materiality. First, the amount expresses the auditor's judgment about the total acceptable amount of undetected misstatement and detected but uncorrected misstatement. Thus, this amount in some circumstances may be larger than some auditors have considered to be material.

Second, because the amount includes an allowance for **undetected** misstatements and includes the **combined** effect of misstatements, it is not suitable as a threshold for evaluating the materiality of individual misstatements. Also, in evaluation the auditor should consider qualitative matters and additional information obtained during the audit.

Finally, although this approach is called a rule of thumb, it is in no sense a rule. It is simply a guide to making a planning decision. If the rule of thumb produces an amount that an auditor believes is unreasonable, the auditor's considered judgment should prevail over arbitrary adherence to the rule of thumb.

USING THE PRELIMINARY JUDGMENT IN PLANNING PROCEDURES

The auditor needs to plan audit procedures for a specific account balance or class of transactions so that misstatements in that balance or class when combined with misstatement in other balances or classes will not exceed the preliminary judgment about materiality. This may be done explicitly or judgmentally. A quantitative allocation of the preliminary judgment is not required.

Necessary Reduction of Preliminary Judgment

The first step in relating the preliminary judgment to individual balances and classes is to reduce the preliminary judgment for the amount of misstatement that is expected to be uncorrected when the audit report is issued. Naturally, known uncorrected misstatement reduces the allowance or cushion for undetected misstatement. In the following discussion, for convenience, uncorrected misstatements are assumed to be negligible, and the amount estimated in making the preliminary judgment is used in planning procedures.

Nonsampling Applications

In the application of audit procedures that do not involve audit sampling (see Section 350), the relation of the preliminary judgment to balances or classes depends on the approach to examining the account.

Some accounts are examined 100% because the account is affected by very few transactions and all of them are expected to be material. For example, stockholders' equity and long-term debt usually fall in this category, and property and equipment may be in this category. For these accounts, no relation to the preliminary judgment is relevant. The preliminary judgment is an allowance for undetected misstatement, and the normal audit approach would detect all misstatements.

For some accounts no substantive tests are applied. The total of these accounts should be clearly immaterial. A common rule of thumb is that the total amount of these accounts should not exceed 1/3 of the preliminary judgment.

Some accounts are examined by selecting all items above a specified "material" amount. A common rule of thumb is that this amount should be between 1/6 and 1/3 of the preliminary judgment. All items larger than 1/3 of the preliminary judgment would be examined if little or no misstatement was expected or if the procedure applied to the items was one of several directed toward the same audit objective. All items larger than 1/6 of the preliminary judgment would be examined if many misstatements were expected or if the procedure applied to the items was extremely important to the auditor's conclusion. An amount between 1/3 and 1/6 could be used for circumstances between these extremes.

Sampling Applications

The relation of the preliminary judgment to tolerable misstatement (see Section 350) depends on the type of sampling plan used.

If a classical statistical sampling method is used (mean-per-unit estimation, difference estimation, and ratio estimation), the allocation is based on the classical statistics measurement of variance. It is

$$\text{Tolerable misstatement} = \text{Preliminary judgment} \times \sqrt{\frac{\text{Account balance}}{\text{Total of all sampled balances}}}$$

Many auditors have been confused about this method of allocation. It does not apply universally; it is used only for classical statistical sampling.

If a probability-proportional-to-size (PPS) statistical plan is used, no allocation of the preliminary judgment is necessary. If little or no misstatement is expected, tolerable misstatement may be equal to the preliminary judgment. However, if some misstatement is expected, the preliminary judgment may need to be reduced so that sample sizes will not be too small. Some auditors reduce the preliminary judgment by the anticipated effect of expected misstatement plus an extra cushion to allow for the unexpected. Other auditors use the preliminary judgment for tolerable misstatement and then adjust sample size for expected misstatement.

Nonstatistical sampling plans that approximate PPS plans generally use tolerable misstatement equal to the preliminary judgment and adjust sample size for expected misstatement.

Other nonstatistical plans take a variety of forms, and it is not possible to generalize about the relation of the preliminary judgment to tolerable misstatement.

CONSIDERATION OF AUDIT RISK (INCLUDING FRAUD RISK)

The auditor's goal is to plan the audit to restrict audit risk to a relatively low level. Audit risk cannot be objectively measured for the financial statements taken as a whole, and the requirements of SAS 47 are easier to understand and apply if one focuses on relationships at the account balance and class of transactions level. At that level, audit risk has the following three components:

1. Inherent risk.
2. Control risk.
3. Detection risk.

The basic idea is that the auditor assesses the existing inherent risk and existing control risk and then plans audit procedures with a suitably low detection risk to reduce the overall risk (audit risk) to an acceptably low level. Inherent risk and control risk exist independently, and all the auditor can do is assess them. Detection risk is a function of the effectiveness of audit procedures; the more effective the audit procedures, the lower the detection risk. At the balance or class level, audit risk is the risk that the auditor will fail to detect an amount of misstatement that would be material when combined with misstatement in other balances or classes.

Risk of Material Misstatement Due to Fraud

The auditor is obligated to assess the risk of misstatement due to fraud even if inherent or control risk is assessed at the maximum. Furthermore, as discussed in Section 316, as long as the auditor assesses the two types of fraud risk (misstatements arising from fraudulent financial reporting and misstatements arising from misappropriation of assets) and the various categories of risk factors under each, he or she may combine the fraud risk, inherent risk, and control risk assessments. SAS 82, *Consideration of Fraud in a Financial Statement*

Audit, recognizes that the fraud risk factors encompass both inherent and control risk attributes.

Inherent Risk

This risk is the susceptibility of an account balance or class of transactions to misstatement that could be material. Inherent risk is influenced by the nature of the account balance or class of transactions and by other factors that may affect several or all of the balances or classes.

Assessment of inherent risk is usually based on the auditor's knowledge of the nature of the client's business, its organization, and its operating characteristics. The need for the auditor to obtain knowledge of such matters and the factors that affect them are explained in Section 311. Some auditors have formalized the approach to obtaining this knowledge through the use of questionnaires or checklists. (See Section 311 for an illustration of such a questionnaire.) Other auditors gather this information less formally but nevertheless explicitly consider it in planning procedures for specific balances or classes. SAS 47 does not require documentation of the assessment of inherent risk unless the auditor considers inherent risk to be less than the maximum.

SAS 47 gives the following examples of how the nature of an account balance could influence inherent risk:

- Complex calculations are more likely to be misstated than simple calculations.
- Cash is more susceptible to theft than an inventory of coal.
- Accounts consisting of amounts derived from accounting estimates pose greater risks than do accounts consisting of relatively routine factual data.

This aspect of inherent risk has been recognized in the auditing literature for several decades under the term **relative risk**.

SAS 47 gives the following examples of other factors that influence inherent risk:

- Technological developments might make a particular product obsolete, thereby causing inventory to be more susceptible to overstatement.
- A declining industry characterized by a large number of business failures or a lack of sufficient working capital to continue operations might predispose management to misstate financial statements.

The relation of inherent risk assessment to planning is considered further in the following discussions of control risk and detection risk.

Control Risk

This is the risk that material misstatement may occur in an assertion and not be prevented or detected on a timely basis by the entity's internal controls. SAS 47 states that the auditor may make a separate assessment of control risk or a combined assessment of inherent and control risk. However, some auditors believe that at the balance or class level, the assessment is necessarily combined from either a theoretical or practical perspective.

These auditors point out that superseded Section 320 states that a conceptually logical approach to evaluation of accounting control is the direct focus on the purpose of preventing or detecting **material** errors or fraud in financial statements by applying the following steps:

1. Consider the types of errors and fraud that could occur. (This is basically an assessment of inherent risk.)[2]

---

[2] *Parenthetical comments are added to relate evaluation of accounting control to assessment of risk.*

2. Determine the controls that should prevent or detect such errors and fraud.
3. Determine whether the necessary procedures are prescribed and are being followed satisfactorily. (This is the assessment of control risk.)
4. Determine the effect of control weaknesses (control risk) on the nature, timing, or extent of auditing procedures. (This is the consideration of acceptable detection risk based on the assessment of inherent risk and control risk.)

Although Section 320 has been replaced by SAS 55 (AU 319), this remains a valid description of the conceptual approach.

The first two steps are usually performed through the development of generalized materials such as checklists and questionnaires. The third step is accomplished by analysis of the information obtained through the use of generalized materials and tests of controls.

Other auditors believe that a separate assessment of inherent risk may be made by considering factors such as the relative complexity of transaction processing, the susceptibility of the item to misstatement without regard to controls, the relative size of individual items, and the relative stability of operations. The important aspect of the assessment is that it must be made independently of control procedures. For example, the likelihood of understatement errors in payroll may be considered low no matter what control procedures exist, but overstatement caused by errors or fraud may be influenced significantly by controls.

Detection Risk—Nonsampling Considerations

The assessment of inherent risk created by factors that affect several or all balances or classes is often responded to in a general way rather than by specific modification of auditing procedures. For example, the auditor may assign more experienced personnel to the engagement, increase the level and extent of supervision, and generally conduct the audit with a heightened degree of professional skepticism. In this area, the auditor's focus is really on whether the risk level is above the ordinary for the entire audit.

At the account balance or class of transactions level, some of the factors that affect all balances or classes may influence the planned auditing procedures for a specific balance or class. Substantive tests may be applied at year-end rather than at interim dates, and unusual rather than normal procedures may be selected. Some auditors have formalized the assessment of inherent risk at the balance or class level by requiring documentation of an explicit qualitative judgment of whether the risk of material misstatement is high, moderate, or low when the audit program is prepared. Although SAS 47 states that the auditor must have an "appropriate basis" whenever inherent risk is assessed at less that the maximum, SAS 47 stops short of requiring this degree of formalization in audit program planning.

Detection Risk—Sampling Considerations

The assessment of inherent risk and control risk and the resultant effect on detection risk can have a dramatic effect on the sample sizes necessary to hold audit risk to an acceptably low level. The way the detection risk is considered is determined by whether the planned audit sample is statistical or nonstatistical and whether the nonstatistical plan is a formal plan (usually a PPS approximation) or an informal one.

If the sampling plan is an informal, nonstatistical one, there is no point in quantifying the assessment of inherent or control risk. As inherent and control risk increase, sample sizes should increase because the auditor must achieve a low detection risk to reduce audit risk to an acceptable level. However, about the only generalization that can be made is this relationship between risk level and sample size.

In a formal nonstatistical plan, the auditor usually has to identify one of three or four qualitative levels of assessment of inherent and control risk, and one of three or four levels of reliance on audit procedures other than the one applied using sampling (an assessment of detection risk for all relevant nonsampling procedures). For example, the auditor will select from among **maximum, moderate,** and **low** assessment of control risk and inherent risk, and this selection will have a predetermined effect on the sample size required. The following relationships may be used:

Control risk	*Effect on sample size*	*Implicit detection risk in sample*
Low	1	20%
Moderate	1.33	10%
Maximum	2	5%

This means that assuming that the only audit procedure applied to achieve a particular audit objective uses sampling, a qualitative assessment of control risk of "low" results in a sample size that is one half the sample size required with an assessment at the maximum level.

If a statistical plan is used, it is necessary to assess inherent risk, control risk, and detection risk applicable to nonsampling procedures, such as analytical procedures, as specific percentages and to use these percentages in a formula to determine the acceptable detection risk for the sample. The formula is explained in the appendix to SAS 39 (see Section 350). The only time it is necessary to reduce the risk assessment to specific percentages is when a statistical sampling plan is used. In all other cases, use of specific percentages and the SAS 39 formula are unnecessary. The SAS 39 formula assumes that inherent risk is at the maximum and no separate assessment is made. Some CPA firms use statistical or nonstatistical plans that incorporate a separate assessment.

Evaluation of Financial Statements

Usually the only practical way to consider whether financial statements are materially misstated at the conclusion of the audit is to use a worksheet that determines the combined effect of uncorrected misstatement on important totals or subtotals in the financial statements, for example, current assets, current liabilities, income before taxes, income taxes, net income, total assets, total liabilities, and stockholders' equity. Use of such worksheets is fairly common in auditing practice. However, it is important to recognize that the auditor may use a different amount in evaluating whether the financial statements are materially misstated than was used in planning the audit. Qualitative considerations may cause the auditor to consider smaller detected misstatements to be material. Also, for misstatements that have an effect only on the balance sheet or that affect only classification within a financial statement, an amount may have to be larger to be considered material.

In explaining the misstatements that should be combined to consider whether the financial statements are materially misstated, SAS 47 refers to **known** misstatement and **likely** misstatement. Known misstatement is the amount of misstatement actually detected in applying audit procedures. Likely misstatement is essentially the same as projected misstatement in sampling applications. (See Section 350 and, in particular, "Substantive Tests" under *Techniques for Application.*) In addition to considering the combined effect of uncorrected known and likely misstatement, the auditor should consider the risk of further misstatement remaining undetected. For example, the amount estimated for planning materiality usually includes an allowance for undetected misstatement.

Prior Period Misstatements

SAS 47 requires that prior period misstatements be considered, but permits either the "rollover" or "iron curtain" approach. Under the "iron curtain" approach, the effects of all cumulative uncorrected misstatements are deemed to affect the current period's income statement as well as the balance sheet. Under the "rollover" approach, the cumulative uncorrected misstatements, net of the uncorrected misstatements carried over from the prior year, are deemed to affect the current period's income statement. If, for example, warranties payable were understated by $150 in the prior period and $200 in the current period, the rollover approach would compare only $50 to the current income to evaluate quantitative materiality while the iron curtain approach would compare the full $200. The auditor should be alert to the fact that neither the iron curtain nor the rollover approach can be applied mechanically. While the SEC has taken the position that the iron curtain approach is preferable, because the rollover effect postpones adjustments to another period and may facilitate earnings management and abuse, the two approaches are clear alternatives only in complex situations in which a misstatement accumulates in the balance sheet. In fact, the authors have noted that the mechanical application of the iron curtain approach in a more complex situation may have the opposite of the intended effects. For example, if warranties payable were **overstated** in the prior period by $300, and **understated** in the current period by $200, the aggregate effect on the current period income statement would be a $500 overstatement of income before tax. The uncorrected prior period misstatement would have a $300 carryover effect in the current period income statement. Therefore, careful consideration of the impact of prior period adjustments is needed, and individual facts and circumstances must be considered.

313 SUBSTANTIVE TESTS PRIOR TO THE BALANCE SHEET DATE[1]

EFFECTIVE DATE AND APPLICABILITY

Original Pronouncement	SAS 45, August 1983.
Effective Date	Audits of financial statements for periods ended after September 30, 1983.
Applicability	Audits of financial statements in accordance with generally accepted auditing standards. (Because of some complexities in applicability, additional explanation is provided below.)

APPLICABILITY

As a practical matter, this section applies when procedures such as receivables confirmation and inventory observation (principal substantive tests of details) are applied to an account balance as of a date before the balance sheet date (at an interim date). This means that the requirements of the section do not apply to the following types of audit tests.

CONVENIENCE-TIMED TESTS

Some audit tests can be applied at any convenient selected date before the balance sheet date and completed as part of year-end procedures. Examples are

1. Tests of details of the additions to, and reduction of, accounts such as property, investments, debt, and equity.
2. Tests of details of transactions affecting income and expense accounts.
3. Tests of accounts that are not generally audited by testing the details of items composing the balance, such as warranty reserves and certain deferred charges.
4. Analytical procedures applied to income or expense accounts.

The common denominator in these tests is that the nature and extent of procedures applied are not necessarily influenced by doing a portion of the testing before the balance

---

1 *The Auditing Standards Board (ASB) has issued Exposure Drafts of seven proposed SASs that relate to the risk assessment process. A summary of key changes is provided immediately before Section 100-230. This section would be superseded by a new SAS,* ***Performing Audit Procedures in Response to Assessed Risks and Evaluating the Audit Evidence Obtained.*** *The Public Company Accounting Oversight Board (PCAOB) has replaced the ASB as the standards-setting authority for public company audits. Therefore, the ASB's Exposure Drafts will not be issued as final standards by the AICPA. The documents will, however, be considered by the PCAOB in developing standards or amendments to existing transitional standards. Please check for updates to this section on the John Wiley & Sons, Inc. website at www.wiley.com/gaas.*

sheet date. For example, the auditor may decide to vouch all property additions and retirements over a specified dollar amount. The nature and extent of the test are not influenced by whether the testing is done all at year-end, or a portion at an interim date and the remainder at year-end.

Tests of Controls

Considerations that influence the timing of tests of controls are explained in Section 319 as part of assessing control risk at below the maximum level.

Alternative Procedures

In some cases, the auditor may apply principal substantive tests **after** the balance sheet date as an alternative procedure. For example, the auditor may make inventory test counts after the balance sheet date or review subsequent collections of receivables. This section does not apply to such tests.

Coordinating the Timing of Procedures

SAS 45 does cover the coordination of the timing of auditing procedures. However, no specific requirements are imposed, and it is important to recognize that the discussion of coordination is independent of the requirements that apply to principal substantive tests at an interim date.

DEFINITIONS OF TERMS

Incremental audit risk. The increase in the risk that the auditor will not detect misstatements that may exist at the balance sheet date caused by applying principal substantive tests to the details of asset and liability accounts at an interim date.

Principal substantive tests. Tests of details of asset or liability accounts that provide the principal, or primary, assurance that a particular audit objective for an account is achieved. For example, confirmation with customers provides the principal assurance for audit objectives related to the existence of trade accounts receivable.

Balance sheet date. The date of the balance sheet being audited.

Interim date. A date before the balance sheet date as of which principal substantive tests are applied to asset and liability accounts. (Technically, the date is the "as of" date of the balance to which the procedures are applied and not the date the procedures are applied.)

Remaining period. The period between the interim date and the balance sheet date.

OBJECTIVES OF SECTION

The considerations that influence the desirability of applying principal substantive tests at an interim date are related to **efficiency**. The auditor may want to apply such tests at an interim date to meet a deadline for audited financial statements or to spread audit work out over the year.

SAS 45 establishes requirements to ensure that the **effectiveness** of audit tests is not impaired to achieve the efficiency of interim testing. Assurance that audit objectives have been achieved for a particular asset or liability account at the balance sheet date may be provided by a combination of the following:

- Substantive tests of the details of the balance at an interim date.
- Assessed level of control risk. (As the following discussion explains, an assessed level below maximum is not required.)
- Substantive tests that cover the remaining period.

The total assurance from the combination has to be equivalent to what would be obtained from applying principal substantive tests at the balance sheet date.

Before SAS 45 was issued, the common wisdom was that interim substantive testing was possible only when internal control was assessed below the maximum. SAS 45 changed that. It makes clear that assessing control risk at below the maximum level is not required to have a reasonable basis for extending audit conclusions from an interim date to the balance sheet date.

The relationship between internal control and interim principal substantive tests of details, as explained in SAS 45, is that if effective internal controls over completeness or asset safeguarding are lacking, the effectiveness of substantive tests related to assertions on completeness or existence for the remaining period may be impaired. This means that the auditor will ordinarily conclude that it is necessary to reperform principal substantive tests at year-end or otherwise significantly increase the scope of substantive tests for the remaining period. In that case, applying principal substantive tests at an interim date is not cost effective.

FUNDAMENTAL REQUIREMENTS

ASSESS INCREMENTAL AUDIT RISK AND COST

Before applying principal substantive tests to the details of asset or liability accounts at an interim date, the auditor should assess

1. The difficulty in controlling incremental audit risk.
2. The cost of substantive tests necessary to cover the remaining period to provide appropriate audit assurance at the balance sheet date.

   NOTE: SAS 45 observes that interim tests may not be cost effective without effective internal control, but assessing control risk at below the maximum is not a requirement for interim tests of details.

FACTORS THAT INCREASE INCREMENTAL AUDIT RISK

The auditor might conclude that substantive tests to cover the remaining period would not be effective in controlling incremental audit risk and thus apply principal substantive tests at year-end if the following conditions or circumstances exist:

1. Rapidly changing business conditions.
2. Circumstances that might predispose management to misstate financial statements (see Section 316).

FACTORS THAT INFLUENCE CONTROLLING AUDIT RISK

If the auditor concludes that evidential matter related to any of the following is not sufficient for controlling audit risk, principal substantive tests should be applied at year-end.

1. **Predictability.** Whether year-end balances of asset or liability accounts being considered for interim testing are reasonably predictable as to amount, composition, and relative significance.
2. **Procedures.** Whether the client's proposed procedures for analyzing and adjusting such accounts at interim dates and for establishing proper accounting cutoffs are appropriate.
3. **Information provided by accounting system.** Whether the accounting system will provide sufficient information on balances at year-end and transactions in the remaining period to allow investigation of

   a. Significant unusual transactions or entries, including those at or near year-end.

b. Other causes of significant fluctuations or expected fluctuations that did not occur.
c. Changes in the composition of balances.

REQUIRED SUBSTANTIVE TESTS FOR REMAINING PERIOD

Substantive tests to cover the remaining period ordinarily should include

1. Comparing information on the year-end balance with comparable information at the interim date to identify amounts that appear unusual.
2. Investigating any amounts that appear unusual.
3. Other analytical procedures or substantive tests of details, or a combination of both.

NOTE: This means that the minimum tests for the remaining period are comparison to identify unusual amounts and other analytical procedures applied to the balances at year-end. Whether analytical procedures need to be augmented by tests of details is discussed in the following requirement.

NATURE AND EXTENT OF TESTS OF DETAILS FOR REMAINING PERIOD

The relative mix of tests of details and analytical procedures to provide a reasonable basis for extending to the balance sheet date the audit conclusions about assertions tested at an interim date is influenced by

1. The nature of the transactions and balances relating to the assertion involved.
2. The availability of records necessary for effective tests of details and the nature of the tests to which they are susceptible.
3. The availability of historical data or other criteria for use in analytical procedures.

MISSTATEMENTS DETECTED AT INTERIM DATES

The auditor should evaluate the results of principal substantive tests at an interim date to assess the possibility of misstatement at the balance sheet date. According to AU 313.09, this evaluation is influenced by

1. The possible implications of the nature and cause of the misstatements detected at the interim date.
2. The possible relationship to other phases of the audit.

   NOTE: For example, do the misstatements detected indicate a need to reconsider planned assessment of control risk? Does the extent of misstatement indicate audit sampling is not efficient?

3. The corrections subsequently recorded by the entity.

   NOTE: For example, uncorrected misstatements might reduce the auditor's preliminary judgment about tolerable misstatement.

4. The results of auditing procedures covering the remaining period.

This assessment may cause the auditor to reperform principal substantive tests at year-end or to otherwise expand the scope of substantive tests at year-end.

NOTE: Even if the misstatement detected at an interim date is corrected prior to year-end, there may be implications for evaluation of misstatements at year-end. Unless the auditor has applied procedures sufficient to provide reasonable assurance that similar misstatements have not occurred, the auditor may need to project a misstatement from interim to year-end.

Assessing Control Risk

If the auditor assesses control risk at the maximum during the remaining period, the auditor should consider whether the effectiveness of substantive tests to cover the remaining period will be impaired. For example

1. If effective internal controls are lacking over internal documents that indicate transactions have been executed, substantive tests applied to such documents related to the completeness assertion could not be extended to the balance sheet date.
2. If effective internal controls are lacking over custody and physical movement of assets, substantive tests related to the existence assertion could not be extended to the balance sheet date.

NOTE: In both examples, the auditor would ordinarily need to reperform principal substantive tests at the balance sheet date, and interim testing would not be efficient.

Coordinating Timing of Procedures

According to AU 313.10, the timing of auditing procedures also includes

1. Coordinating procedures applied to related-party transactions and balances.
2. Coordinating testing of interrelated accounts and cutoffs.
3. Maintaining temporary audit control over negotiable assets, such as securities, and simultaneously testing related items such as cash on hand and in banks, and bank loans.

NOTE: Timing considerations that apply to these procedures are relevant whether principal substantive tests are applied at an interim date or at year-end.

INTERPRETATIONS

There are no interpretations for this section.

TECHNIQUES FOR APPLICATION

Assessment of Incremental Audit Risk

The factors that influence incremental audit risk are essentially the same as those factors that influence the inherent risk that applies to several or all account balances (see Section 312).

The auditor usually obtains information about these factors as part of obtaining knowledge of the client entity, its business, and its operations (see Section 311). When these risks are assessed as relatively high, principal substantive tests ordinarily should be applied at year-end.

Assessing Control Risk at below the Maximum

The primary focus on internal control for purposes of interim principal substantive tests is on asset safeguarding and completeness controls. If such policies and procedures are not effective enough to assess control risk at below the maximum, substantive tests to achieve audit objectives related to existence and completeness should be applied at year-end. However, this advice applies only to substantive tests designed to achieve those particular audit objectives. For example, the auditor usually does not rely on confirmation of accounts receivable to achieve audit objectives related to completeness. This means that receivables could be confirmed at an interim date even if completeness controls over receivables were lacking. However, the auditor would still need to consider the nature, timing, and extent of other procedures relevant to achieving audit objectives related to completeness of receivables.

Length of Remaining Period

How long can the remaining period be? SAS 45 does not offer any specific advice; it only observes that "the potential for increased audit risk tends to become greater as the remaining period is lengthened."

In practice, some rules of thumb are commonly used. Many auditors believe the remaining period should not exceed three months. For example, for a calendar-year entity, the earliest that principal substantive tests of details would be applied would be the asset or liability balance as of September 30. This timing can be conveniently coordinated with tests of controls for which a common rule of thumb is to cover the first nine months' transactions.

Another rule of thumb is to consider a remaining period of one month as creating a relatively low increase in audit risk. Ordinarily, if the remaining period is one month, substantive tests to cover the remaining period can be restricted to the minimum of

1. Comparison of the account balance at year-end with the balance at the interim date to identify unusual amounts.
2. Investigation of unusual amounts.
3. Application of other analytical procedures to the year-end balance. (This is usually a predictive test of what the balance should be based on existing relationships.)

Naturally, as with any rule of thumb, the auditor cannot ignore the circumstances. The auditor should be aware that in specific circumstances, factors may increase incremental audit risk or preclude adequately controlling audit risk, and the principal substantive test will have to be applied at year-end.

315 COMMUNICATIONS BETWEEN PREDECESSOR AND SUCCESSOR AUDITORS[1]

EFFECTIVE DATE AND APPLICABILITY

Original Pronouncement	SAS 84, October 1997; and SAS 93, October 2000.
Effective Date	For acceptance of engagements after March 31, 1998.
Applicability	Because of some complexities in applicability, additional explanation is provided below.

APPLICABILITY

This section applies when a change of auditors has occurred or is in process for an audit of financial statements in accordance with generally accepted auditing standards. This section applies to both predecessor and successor auditors. SAS 84 also provides guidance when a successor becomes aware of possible misstatements in financial statements reported on by a predecessor auditor.

The section applies whenever an auditor is considering accepting an engagement to audit or reaudit financial statements, and after such auditor has been appointed to perform such an engagement. The provisions are not required if the most recent audited financial statements are more than two years prior to the beginning of the earliest period to be audited by the successor auditor.

The section also applies to engagements when a successor auditor is replaced before completing an audit engagement and issuing a report. In such situations, there are two predecessor auditors: the auditor who reported on the most recent audited financial statements and the auditor who was engaged to perform but did not complete the engagement.

---

[1] *The Auditing Standards Board has issued an Exposure Draft of a proposed SAS that would affect this section,* ***Sarbanes-Oxley Omnibus SAS.*** *The Exposure Draft is designed to address certain provisions of the Sarbanes-Oxley Act of 2002. The proposed amendment to this section notes that if the successor auditor becomes aware of information that leads him or her to believe that financial statements reported on by a predecessor auditor may require revision, the successor should not report on revised audited financial statements prior to communicating information described in Section 315 to the predecessor. The Public Company Accounting Oversight Board (PCAOB) has replaced the ASB as the standards-setting authority for public company audits. Therefore, the ASB's Exposure Draft will not be issued as a final standard by the AICPA. The document will, however, be considered by the PCAOB in developing a standard or amendments to an existing standard to comply with the Sarbanes-Oxley Act and the related SEC implementing rules. Please check for updates to this section on the John Wiley & Sons, Inc. website at www.wiley.com/gaas.*

This section does not discuss quality control policies pertaining to client acceptance. One of the procedures for client acceptance required by Statement of Quality Control Standards 2, however, is communication with the predecessor auditor.

DEFINITIONS OF TERMS

Predecessor auditor. An auditor who (1) has reported on the most recent audited financial statements or was engaged to perform, but did not complete, an audit of the financial statements, and (2) has resigned, declined to stand for reappointment, or been notified that his or her services have been, or may be, terminated.

Successor auditor. An auditor who is considering accepting an engagement to audit financial statements but has not yet communicated with the predecessor auditor, and an auditor who has accepted such an engagement.

OBJECTIVES OF SECTION

SAS 84 superseded SAS 7 (same title) and its related interpretations. SAS 7, issued in October 1975, was a response to a few cases that resulted in litigation that showed that some predecessor auditors were not candid and forthright in their responses to successor inquiries. This continues to be a practice problem.

SAS 84 modernizes SAS 7 to reflect good practices in the existing environment. In summary it

- Revises the definitions of predecessor and successor auditors to reflect the existing proposal environment.
- Expands the required communications with the predecessor auditor before the successor auditor accepts an engagement to include inquiries about communications made by the predecessor auditor to audit committees or others with equivalent authority and responsibility as described in SAS 82, *Consideration of Fraud in a Financial Statement Audit* (Section 316), SAS 54, *Illegal Acts by Clients* (Section 317), and SAS 60, *Communication of Internal Control Related Matters Noted in an Audit* (Section 325).
- Clarifies the successor auditor's responsibility for obtaining evidence used in analyzing opening balances for the current year financial statements and consistency of accounting principles.
- Expands the audit documentation ordinarily made available to the successor auditor by the predecessor auditor to include documentation of planning, internal control, audit results, and other matters of continuing audit significance.
- Introduces an illustrative client consent and acknowledgment letter and an illustrative successor auditor acknowledgment letter (see *Illustrations*). A predecessor auditor may conclude that obtaining written communications from both the former client and the successor auditor will allow greater communication between both parties and greater access to the audit documentation than would be the case in the absence of such communications. The Auditing Standards Board believes that it is in the public interest for successor auditors to have greater access to the audit documentation and, accordingly, for all auditors to have access to these letters and to use them in their practice. However, these letters are presented for illustrative purposes only and not required.

SAS 93, *Omnibus Statement on Auditing Standards—2000*, was issued in October 2000. It clarifies that any auditor who is engaged to perform an audit, but does not complete the audit, is considered a predecessor auditor for the purposes of SAS 84.

FUNDAMENTAL REQUIREMENTS

Change of Auditors

According to AU 315.03, an auditor should not accept an engagement until the communications described in "Communications Before Acceptance" below have been evaluated. However, an auditor may make a proposal for an audit engagement before communicating with the predecessor auditor.

Other communications, described in "Other Communications" below, are advisable to assist in the planning of the engagement. However, the decision whether to make these other communications and the timing of them is more flexible (i.e., they may be initiated prior to engagement acceptance or subsequent thereto).

When more than one auditor is considering accepting an engagement, the predecessor auditor should not be expected to be available to respond to inquiries until a successor auditor has accepted the engagement subject to the evaluation of the "Communications Before Acceptance."

Initiative for Communicating

The successor auditor should initiate the communication. The communication may be either written or oral. Both the predecessor and successor auditors should hold in confidence information obtained from each other.

Communications before Acceptance

Inquiry of the predecessor auditor is required because the predecessor may provide information that will assist the successor auditor in determining whether to accept the engagement.

The successor auditor should request permission from the prospective client to make an inquiry of the predecessor *prior to final acceptance of the engagement.* The successor auditor should ask the prospective client to authorize the predecessor to respond fully to the successor auditor's inquiries. If a prospective client refuses to permit the predecessor auditor to respond or limits the response, the successor auditor should inquire as to the reasons and consider the implications of that refusal in deciding whether to accept the engagement.

The successor auditor should make specific and reasonable inquiries of the predecessor about

1. Information about the integrity of management.
2. Disagreements with management as to accounting principles, auditing procedures, or other similarly significant matters.
3. Communications to audit committees or others with equivalent authority and responsibility regarding fraud (SAS 82, see Section 316), illegal acts by clients (SAS 54, see Section 317), and internal control related matters (SAS 60, see Section 325).
4. The predecessor auditor's understanding as to the reasons for the change of auditors.

The predecessor auditor should respond promptly, fully, and factually. However, should the predecessor decide, due to unusual circumstances such as impending, threatened, or potential litigation; disciplinary proceedings; or other unusual circumstances, not to respond fully, he or she should indicate that the response is limited.

If the successor auditor receives a limited response, its implications should be considered in deciding whether to accept the engagement.

Other Communications

The successor auditor should request that the client authorize the predecessor to allow a review of the predecessor auditor's audit documentation. (*Illustrations* contains a client consent and acknowledgment letter that may be used by the predecessor auditor.) Before permitting access to the audit documentation, the predecessor auditor may obtain a written communication from the successor auditor about the use of the audit documentation. (*Illustrations* contains a successor auditor acknowledgment letter.)

The predecessor auditor should determine the audit documentation that will be made available for review and whether the documentation may be copied. The predecessor auditor should ordinarily permit the successor auditor to review audit documentation, including documentation of planning, internal control, audit results, and other matters of continuing accounting and auditing significance, such as the documented analysis of balance sheet accounts, and those relating to contingencies. Also, the predecessor auditor should reach an understanding with the successor auditor about the use of the audit documentation. The extent, if any, to which a predecessor auditor permits access to the audit documentation is a matter of judgment.

SUCCESSOR AUDITOR'S USE OF COMMUNICATIONS

The successor auditor should obtain sufficient competent evidence to afford a basis for expressing an opinion. The audit evidence used in analyzing the impact of the opening balances on the current year financial statements and consistency of accounting principles is a matter of professional judgment. Audit evidence may include

1. The most recent audited financial statements.
2. The predecessor auditor's report.
3. The results of inquiry of the predecessor auditor.
4. The results of the successor auditor's review of the predecessor's audit documentation relating to the most recently completed audit.
5. Audit procedures performed on the current period's transactions.

The successor auditor may wish to make inquiries about the professional reputation and standing of the predecessor auditor. (See SAS 1, Section 543, "Part of Audit Performed by Other Independent Auditors.")

In reporting on the audit, the successor auditor should not make reference to the report or work of the predecessor auditor in his or her audit report to support the successors auditor's opinion.

AUDITS OF FINANCIAL STATEMENTS THAT HAVE BEEN PREVIOUSLY AUDITED

If an auditor is asked to audit financial statements that have been previously audited (i.e., a reaudit), the auditor considering acceptance of the reaudit engagement is also a successor auditor, and the auditor who previously reported is also a predecessor auditor.

In addition to the communications described in "Communications before Acceptance" above, the auditor should state that the purpose of the inquiries is to obtain information about whether to accept an engagement to perform a reaudit. If the successor auditor accepts the reaudit engagement, he or she may consider the information obtained from inquiries of the predecessor auditor and review of the predecessor auditor's report and audit documentation in planning the reaudit. However, the information obtained from those inquiries and any review of the predecessor auditor's report and audit documentation is not sufficient to afford a basis for expressing an opinion.

The successor auditor should plan and perform the reaudit in accordance with GAAS. The successor auditor should not assume responsibility for the predecessor auditor's work or issue a report that reflects divided responsibility. Furthermore, the predecessor auditor is not a specialist (Section 336) or an internal auditor (Section 322).

If, in a reaudit engagement, the successor auditor is unable to obtain sufficient competent evidential matter to express an opinion on the financial statements, the successor auditor should qualify or disclaim an opinion because of the inability to perform procedures.

The successor auditor should request audit documentation for the period or periods under reaudit and the period prior to the reaudit period. However, the extent, if any, to which the predecessor auditor permits access to the audit documentation is a matter of judgment.

The successor auditor performing the reaudit should, if material, observe or perform some physical counts of inventory at a date subsequent to the period of the reaudit, in connection with a current audit or otherwise, and apply appropriate tests of intervening transactions.

Discovery of Possible Misstatements in Financial Statements Reported on by a Predecessor

If, during the audit or reaudit, the successor auditor becomes aware of information that leads him or her to believe that financial statements reported on by the predecessor auditor may require revision, the successor auditor should request that the client inform the predecessor auditor of the situation and arrange for the three parties to discuss this information and attempt to resolve the matter.

The successor auditor should communicate to the predecessor auditor any information that the predecessor auditor may need to consider in accordance with Section 561, "Subsequent Discovery of Facts Existing at the Date of the Auditor's Report."

If the client refuses to inform the predecessor auditor or if the successor auditor is not satisfied with the resolution of the matter, the successor auditor should evaluate (1) possible implications on the current engagement, and (2) whether to resign from the engagement. Furthermore, the successor auditor may wish to consult with his or her legal counsel in determining an appropriate course of further action.

INTERPRETATIONS

There are no interpretations for this section.

PROFESSIONAL ISSUES TASK FORCE PRACTICE ALERTS

94-3 Acceptance and Continuance of Audit Clients

The practice alert highlights matters that a firm may consider when establishing firm policies and procedures for client acceptance and continuance. It provides the following list of procedures that a firm may perform when deciding whether to accept or continue with a client:

- Understand the client's business and operations.
- Ask about the reputation of high-ranking employees, influential directors and shareholders, and the entity.
- Consider how management responds to observations about, or suggestions for, improvements in internal controls made by the predecessor auditor or internal auditor.
- Evaluate the composition, including the number of independent outside directors, and autonomy of the Board of Directors and the Audit Committee.
- Communicate with the predecessor auditor as required by this section.

- Read both the Form 8-K reporting the termination of the predecessor auditor, and the predecessor's response, to identify disagreements with management or reportable events.
- Consider whether any financial interests or relationships exist that would impair the appearance of the firm's independence from the client and preclude its expression of an opinion. The auditor should consider the requirements of Rule 101 of the AICPA's *Code of Conduct* and the requirements of the SEC.
- Consider whether the services to be provided are compatible with the firm's policies and whether qualified personnel are available.
- Consider any potential conflicts of interest that could result from acceptance of the client.
- Consider the willingness and ability of the prospective client to pay an acceptable fee.
- Consider the significance of specific risk factors identified as a result of the above procedures.

The alert also states that these same matters should be actively considered in the decision of whether to continue to serve a client.

Finally, the alert provides a list of factors related to an entity's business risk, the auditor's business risk, and the auditor's audit risk that should be considered and addressed when assessing whether to accept or continue a client relationship.

The full text of this Practice Alert can be obtained from the AICPA website at www.aicpa.org/members/div/secps/lit/practice.htm.

97-3 Changes in Auditors and Related Topics

This Practice Alert provides guidance on the pertinent issues that a practitioner must face when there is a change of auditors and summarizes guidance in SAS 82, *Consideration of Fraud in a Financial Statement Audit* (Section 316), SAS 84, *Communications between Predecessor and Successor Auditors* (Section 315), and SAS 85, *Management Representations* (Section 333). The alert clarifies the successor auditor's responsibility for

- Initiating contact with a predecessor auditor after obtaining the client's permission and for making specific and reasonable inquiries of the predecessor.
- Requesting that the client authorize a review of the predecessor auditor's audit documentation.
- Analyzing the impact of the opening balances on the current year financial statements and for consistency of accounting principles.

If the successor auditor is not allowed access to the predecessor auditor's audit documentation, the successor auditor should use professional judgment in determining the nature, timing, and extent of procedures to be performed on opening balances, including determining the need to audit the previous financial statements.

The practice alert also gives guidance on requests to reissue reports, which is summarized in Section 508.

The full text of this Practice Alert can be obtained from the AICPA website at www.aicpa.org/members/div/secps/lit/practice.htm.

TECHNIQUES FOR APPLICATION

REVISIONS OF FINANCIAL STATEMENTS REPORTED ON BY THE PREDECESSOR AUDITOR

It is possible that during the audit the successor auditor will become aware of information that leads him or her to believe that financial statements reported on by the predecessor may require revision. The successor should prepare a worksheet with appropriate supporting documentation and should request the client to arrange a meeting between the predecessor, the successor, and the client.

NOTE: If the client refuses, or if the successor is not satisfied with the results of the conference, the successor should consult his or her attorney.

At the meeting, the predecessor auditor is advised to do the following:

1. Review the worksheet and supporting documentation of the successor auditor.
2. Determine if the report should be revised.

If the predecessor auditor determines that the report should be revised, the guidance provided in Section 561, "Subsequent Discovery of Facts Existing at the Date of the Auditor's Report," may be pertinent.

REISSUANCE OF PREDECESSOR'S REPORT

Generally, business enterprises present their financial statements for the current and preceding years. For example, the SEC requires presentation of the two most recent annual balance sheets and the three most recent statements of income and cash flows. In these situations, the successor auditor may do the following:

1. Refer to the predecessor's previously issued report in his or her report, but only as it relates to the financial statements of the prior year on which the predecessor reported.
2. Request that the client ask the predecessor auditor to reissue the previously issued report.

Guidance and illustrations on reference to, and reissuance of, the predecessor's previously issued report are provided in Section 508.

ILLUSTRATIONS

Following are illustrations of (1) client consent and acknowledgment, and (2) a successor auditor acknowledgment letter. Both letters are adapted from SAS 84.

ILLUSTRATION 1. ILLUSTRATIVE CLIENT CONSENT AND ACKNOWLEDGMENT LETTER

The predecessor auditor may request a consent and acknowledgment letter from the client to reduce misunderstandings about the scope of the communications being authorized. The following letter is presented for illustrative purposes only and is not required by professional standards.

June 30, 20X2

Widget Enterprises
Anytown, NY

You have given your consent to allow [*name of successor CPA firm*], as successor independent auditors for Widget Enterprises (Widget), access to our audit documentation for our audit of the December 31, 20X1 financial statements of Widget. You also have given your consent to us to respond fully to [*name of successor CPA firm*] inquiries. You understand and agree that the review of our audit documentation is undertaken solely for the purpose of obtaining an understanding about Widget and certain information about our audit to assist [*name of successor CPA firm*] in planning the audit of the December 31, 20X2 financial statements of Widget.

Please confirm your agreement with the foregoing by signing and dating a copy of this letter and returning it to us.

Attached is the form of the letter we will furnish [*name of successor CPA firm*] regarding the use of the audit documentation.

Very truly yours,

[*Predecessor Auditor*]
By: ______________________

Accepted:

Widget Enterprises

By: ______________________ Date: ______________________

ILLUSTRATION 2. ILLUSTRATIVE SUCCESSOR AUDITOR ACKNOWLEDGMENT LETTER

The following letter is presented for illustrative purposes only and is not required by professional standards.

August 30, 20X2

[*Successor Auditor*]
Anytown, NY

We have previously audited, in accordance with auditing standards generally accepted in the United States of America, the December 31, 20X1 financial statements of Widget Enterprises (Widget). We rendered a report on those financial statements and have not performed any audit procedures subsequent to the audit report date. In connection with your audit of Widget's 20X2 financial statements, you have requested access to our audit documentation prepared in connection with that audit. Widget has authorized our firm to allow you to review that audit documentation.

Our audit, and the audit documentation prepared in connection therewith, of Widget's financial statements were not planned or conducted in contemplation of your review. Therefore, items of possible interest to you may not have been specifically addressed. Our use of professional judgment and the assessment of audit risk and materiality for the purpose of our audit means that matters may have existed that would have been assessed differently by you. We make no representation as to the sufficiency or appropriateness of the information in our audit documentation for your purposes.

We understand that the purpose of your review is to obtain information about Widget and our 20X1 audit results to assist you in planning your 20X2 audit of Widget. For that purpose only, we will provide you access to our audit documentation that relate to that objective.

Upon request, we will provide copies of that audit documentation that provide factual information about Widget. You agree to subject any such copies or information otherwise derived from our audit documentation to your normal policy for retention of audit documentation and protection of confidential client information. Furthermore, in the event of a third-party request for access to our audit documentation prepared in connection with your audits of Widget, you agree to obtain our permission before voluntarily allowing any such access to our audit documentation or information otherwise derived from our audit documentation, and to obtain on our behalf any releases that you obtain from such third party. You agree to advise us promptly and provide us a copy of any subpoena, summons, or other court order for access to your audit documentation that include copies of our audit documentation or information otherwise derived therefrom.

Please confirm your agreement with the foregoing by signing and dating a copy of this letter and returning it to us.

Very truly yours,

[*Predecessor Auditor*]
By: ______________________

Accepted:

[*Successor Auditor*]
By: ______________________ Date: ______________________

NOTE: Even with the client's consent, access to the predecessor auditor's audit documentation may still be limited. Experience has shown that the predecessor auditor may be willing to grant broader access if given additional assurance concerning the use of the audit documentation. Accordingly, the successor auditor might consider agreeing to the following limitations on the review of the predecessor auditor's audit documentation to obtain broader access:

- *The successor auditor will not comment, orally or in writing, to anyone as a result of the review as to whether the predecessor auditor's engagement was performed in accordance with GAAS.*

- *The successor auditor will not provide expert testimony or litigation services or otherwise accept an engagement to comment on issues relating to the quality of the predecessor auditor's audit.*
- *The successor auditor will not use the audit procedures or results thereof documented in the predecessor auditor's audit documentation as evidential matter in rendering an opinion on the 20X2 financial statements of Widget Enterprises, except as contemplated in SAS 84.*

The following paragraph in SAS 84 (AU 315) illustrates the above:

Because your review of our audit documentation is undertaken solely for the purpose described above and may not entail a review of all our audit documentation, you agree that (1) the information obtained from the review will not be used by you for any other purpose, (2) you will not comment, orally or in writing, to anyone as a result of that review as to whether our audit was performed in accordance with auditing standards generally accepted in the United States of America, (3) you will not provide expert testimony or litigation services or otherwise accept an engagement to comment on issues relating to the quality of our audits, and (4) you will not use the audit procedures or results thereof documented in our audit documentation as evidential matter in rendering your opinion on the 20X2 financial statements of Widget, except as contemplated in Statement on Auditing Standards 84.

316 CONSIDERATION OF FRAUD IN A FINANCIAL STATEMENT AUDIT[1,2]

EFFECTIVE DATE AND APPLICABILITY

Original Pronouncement	SAS 99, October 2002.
Effective Date	Audits of financial statements for periods beginning on or after December 15, 2002, with earlier application permitted.
Applicability	Audits of financial statements in accordance with generally accepted auditing standards.

DEFINITIONS OF TERMS

Fraud. An intentional act that results in a material misstatement in financial statements that are the subject of an audit. The primary distinction between fraud and error is whether the underlying action that causes the misstatement of the financial statements is intentional or unintentional.

Misstatements arising from fraudulent financial reporting. Intentional misstatements or omissions of amounts or disclosures in financial statements designed to deceive financial statement users when the effect causes the financial statements not to be presented, in all material respects, in conformity with GAAP.

Misstatements arising from misappropriation of assets. The theft of an entity's assets where the effect of the theft causes the financial statements not to be presented in conformity with generally accepted accounting principles (sometimes referred to as defalcation).

---

1 *SAS 82 remains in effect for audits of financial statements for periods ending before December 15, 2002, although earlier application of SAS 99 is permitted. The guidance in SAS 82 can be found in Section 316A.*

2 *The Auditing Standards Board has issued an Exposure Draft of a proposed SAS that would affect this section,* ***Sarbanes-Oxley Omnibus SAS.*** *The Exposure Draft is designed to address certain provisions of the Sarbanes-Oxley Act of 2002. The proposed amendment to this section requires that auditors of SEC clients ask the audit committee about procedures to handle complaints about accounting, internal accounting controls, or auditing matters and concerns submitted regarding questionable accounting or auditing matters. The Public Company Accounting Oversight Board (PCAOB) has replaced the ASB as the standards-setting authority for public company audits. Therefore, the ASB's Exposure Draft will not be issued as a final standard by the AICPA. The document will, however, be considered by the PCAOB in developing a standard or amendments to an existing transitional standard to comply with the Sarbanes-Oxley Act and the related SEC implementing rules. Please check for updates to this section on the John Wiley & Sons, Inc. website at www.wiley.com/gaas.*

Fraud risk factors. Events or conditions that indicate incentives/pressures to perpetrate fraud, opportunities to carry out the fraud, or attitudes/rationalizations to justify a fraudulent action. These conditions that may alert the auditor to a possibility that fraud may exist.

OBJECTIVES OF SECTION

The accounting profession has always had trouble explaining to critics why an audit conducted in accordance with professional standards might fail to detect a material misstatement of financial statements caused by fraud.

Over the years, there have been several pronouncements issued to attempt to explain the auditor's responsibility for fraud detection. This section is the latest attempt.

In 1992, the AICPA convened a conference of educators and practitioners, known as the Expectation Gap Roundtable, to present papers and discuss several auditing standards that had been issued in 1988 (the expectation gap standards). The deliberations at the conference raised questions concerning whether SAS 53, *The Auditor's Responsibility to Detect and Report Errors and Irregularities*, had been successful in narrowing the expectation gap relating to the detection of material financial statement fraud.

In its March 1993 report, titled *In the Public Interest*, the Public Oversight Board (POB) of the AICPA SEC Practice Section noted: "Attacks on the accounting profession from a variety of sources suggested a significant public concern over the profession's performance. Of particular moment is the widespread belief that auditors have a responsibility for detecting management fraud which they are not now meeting." The POB, in its report, made two recommendations addressing fraud. They were

1. Accounting firms should ensure that auditors more consistently implement, and be more sensitive to the need to exercise, the professional skepticism required by SAS 53.
2. The ASB, the SEC Practice Section, or some other appropriate body should develop guidelines to assist auditors in assessing the likelihood that fraud which may affect financial information may be occurring, and to specify additional auditing procedures when there is a heightened likelihood of management fraud.

In 1993, the AICPA's Board of Directors also issued a report, *Meeting the Financial Reporting Needs of the Future: A Public Commitment from the Public Accounting Profession*. In this report, the AICPA's Board of Directors supported recommendations and initiatives of others to assist auditors in the detection of material misstatements in financial statements resulting from fraud, and encouraged every participant in the financial reporting process—management, their advisors, regulators, and independent auditors—to share in this responsibility.

The Auditing Standards Board (ASB) decided to undertake a project on fraud in large measure because of the Expectation Gap Roundtable findings and the reports of the POB and the AICPA's Board of Directors. In keeping with its commitment to serve the public interest by improving the detection of material fraud in financial statements, the ASB issued SAS 82, *Consideration of Fraud in a Financial Statement Audit*, in February 1997. SAS 82 provided expanded operational guidance on the consideration of fraud in conducting a financial statement audit. It also strengthened the auditor's ability to fulfill his or her responsibility to plan and perform the audit to obtain reasonable assurance about whether financial statements are free of material misstatements, whether caused by error or fraud.

After SAS 82 was issued, several developments occurred.

- The ASB formed the Fraud Research Steering Task Force, which sponsored five academic research projects to reexamine fraud.

- The Public Oversight Board's Panel on Audit Effectiveness, in its "Report and Recommendations" on August 31, 2000, included a number of recommendations concerning earnings management and fraud.
- The International Auditing Practices Committee of the International Federation of Accountants issued International Standard on Auditing (ISA) 240, *The Auditor's Responsibility to Consider Fraud and Error in an Audit of Financial Statements.* The ISA incorporated many of the concepts in SAS 82, but also provided guidance beyond that included in SAS 82.

In response to these developments, the ASB formed a new Fraud Task Force in September 2000 to revise SAS 82. In October 2002, the Auditing Standards Boards issued SAS 99, *Consideration of Fraud in a Financial Statement Audit.* The new SAS does not change the auditor's responsibility to plan and perform the audit to obtain reasonable assurance about whether the financial statements are free of material misstatement, whether caused by error or fraud. However, SAS 99 does establish specific new performance requirements and provides guidance to auditors in fulfilling that responsibility, as it relates to fraud.

FUNDAMENTAL REQUIREMENTS

BASIC REQUIREMENT

In every audit, the auditor is obligated to plan and perform the audit to obtain reasonable assurance about whether the financial statements are free of material misstatement, whether caused by error or fraud.

NOTE: SAS 99 states that the guidance in the statement is meant to be integrated into an overall audit process that is consistent with the requirements in other sections, including

Section 311, ***Planning and Supervision***
Section 312, ***Audit Risk and Materiality in Conducting an Audit***
Section 319, ***Consideration of Internal Control in a Financial Statement Audit***

Also, since auditing involves a continuous, rather than a sequential process, the sequence of the requirements of this statement may be implemented differently in various audit engagements.

PROFESSIONAL SKEPTICISM

As defined in Section 100-230, professional skepticism is an attitude that includes a questioning mind and critical assessment of audit evidence. The auditor should conduct the entire engagement with an attitude of professional skepticism, recognizing that fraud could be present, regardless of past experience with the entity or beliefs about management's integrity. The auditor should not let his or her beliefs about management's integrity allow the auditor to be satisfied with any audit evidence that is less than persuasive. Finally, the auditor should continuously question whether information and evidence obtained suggest that material misstatement caused by fraud has occurred.

ENGAGEMENT TEAM DISCUSSION ABOUT FRAUD

When planning the audit, members of the audit team should discuss where and how the financial statements may be susceptible to material misstatement caused by fraud. This discussion should include

- Exchanging ideas and brainstorming about where the financial statements are susceptible to fraud, how assets could be stolen, and how management might engage in fraudulent financial reporting.

- Emphasizing the need to maintain the proper mindset throughout the audit regarding the potential for fraud. As previously discussed, the auditor should continually exercise professional skepticism and have a questioning mind when performing the audit and evaluating audit evidence. Engagement team members should thoroughly probe issues, acquire additional evidence when necessary, and consult with other team members and firm experts as needed.
- Considering known external and internal factors affecting the entity that might create incentives and opportunities to commit fraud, and indicate an environment that enables rationalizations for committing fraud.
- Considering the risk that management might override controls.
- Considering how to respond to the susceptibility of the financial statements to material misstatement caused by fraud.
- For the purposes of this discussion, setting aside any of the audit team's prior beliefs about management's honesty and integrity.

The discussion would normally include key audit team members. Other factors that should be considered when planning the discussion include

- Whether to have multiple discussions if the audit involves more than one location.
- Whether to include specialists assigned to the audit.

NOTE: The SAS specifically notes that the auditor with final responsibility for the audit should be present for the exchange of ideas and brainstorming about fraud. The auditor should document this discussion, including how and when the discussion occurred, the audit team members involved, and the subject discussed.

Audit team members should continue to communicate throughout the audit about the risks of material misstatement due to fraud.

OBTAINING INFORMATION NEEDED TO IDENTIFY FRAUD RISKS

In addition to performing procedures required under Section 311, *Planning and Supervision*, the auditor should obtain information needed to identify the risks of material misstatement due to fraud by

a. Asking management and others within the entity about their views on the risk of fraud and how such risks are addressed.
b. Considering unusual or unexpected relationships identified by analytical procedures performed while planning the audit.
c. Considering whether any fraud risk factors exist.
d. Considering other information that may be helpful in identifying fraud risk.

NOTE: The auditor should document the procedures performed to obtain information to identify and assess fraud risks.

Inquiries of Management

The auditor should make the following inquiries of management:

- Does management know about actual or suspected fraud?
- Have there been any allegations of actual or suspected fraud from employees, former employees, analysts, regulators, short sellers, and others?
- Does management understand the entity's fraud risk, including any identified risk factors or account balances or classes of transactions for which a fraud risk is likely to exist?

- What programs and controls does the entity have to help prevent, deter, and detect fraud? How does management monitor such programs?
- When there are multiple locations, how are operating locations or business segments monitored? Is fraud more likely to exist at any one of the locations or business segments?
- Does management communicate its views on business practices and ethical behavior to employees, and if so, how?
- Has management reported to the audit committee or equivalent body how the entity's internal control prevents, deters, and detects fraud?

When evaluating management's responses to these inquiries, auditors should remember that management is often in the best position to commit fraud. Therefore, the auditor should determine when it is necessary to corroborate those responses with other information. When responses are inconsistent, the auditor should obtain additional audit evidence.

Inquiries of the Audit Committee

The auditor should make the following inquiries of the audit committee:

- What are the audit committee's (or at least the chair's) views of the risk of fraud?
- Does the audit committee know about actual or suspected fraud in the entity?

The auditor should also understand how the audit committee oversees the entity's assessment of fraud risks and the mitigating programs and controls.

Inquiries of Internal Auditors

The auditor should make the following inquiries of internal auditors.

- What are the internal auditors' views on the risk of fraud?
- Have the internal auditors performed procedures to identify or detect fraud during the year?
- Has management satisfactorily responded to any finding from procedures performed to identify or detect fraud?
- Are the internal auditors aware of any actual or suspected fraud?

Inquiries of Others within the Organization

The auditor should also ask others within the entity about whether they are aware of actual or suspected fraud. According to AU 316.25, the following are examples of people that the auditor may wish to consider directing inquiries to:

a. Anyone at varying levels of authority that the auditor deals with during the audit, such as when the auditor is obtaining an understanding of the entity's internal controls, observing inventory, performing cutoff procedures, or getting explanations for fluctuations noted during analytical procedures.
b. Operating personnel not directly involved in financial reporting.
c. Employees involved in initiating, recording, or processing complex or unusual transactions.
d. In-house legal counsel.

Considering the Results of Analytical Procedures

When performing the required analytical procedures in planning the audit as discussed in Section 329, "Analytical Procedures," the auditor may find unusual or unexpected relationships as a result of comparing the auditor's expectations with recorded amounts or ratios developed from such amounts. The auditor should consider those results in identifying the risk of material misstatement due to fraud.

The auditor should also perform analytical procedures **relating to revenue** with the objective of identifying unusual or unexpected relationships involving revenue accounts that may indicate a material misstatement due to fraudulent financial reporting. Examples of such procedures include

- Comparing sales volume with production capacity. (Sales volume greater than production capacity might indicate fraudulent sales.)
- Trend analysis of revenues by month and sales return by month shortly before and after the reporting period. (The analysis may point to undisclosed side agreements with customers to return goods.)

Although analytical procedures performed during audit planning may be helpful in identifying the risk of material misstatement due to fraud, they may only provide a broad indication since such procedures use data aggregated at a high level, Therefore, the results of such procedures should be considered along with other information obtained by the auditor in identifying fraud risk.

Considering Fraud Risk Factors

Using professional judgment, the auditor should consider whether information obtained about the entity and its environment indicates that fraud risk factors are present, and, if so, whether it should be considered when identifying and assessing the risk of material misstatement due to fraud.

Examples of fraud risk factors are presented in Illustrations 1 and 2. These risk factors are classified based on the three conditions usually present when fraud exists.

1. Incentive/pressure
2. Opportunity
3. Attitude/rationalization

Considering Other Information

The auditor should evaluate other information that may be helpful in identifying fraud risk. The auditor should consider

- Any information from procedures performed when deciding to accept or continue with a client.
- Results of review of interim financial statements.
- Identified inherent risks.
- Information from the discussion among engagement team members.

IDENTIFYING FRAUD RISKS

Attributes

The auditor should use professional judgment and information obtained when identifying the risks of material misstatement due to fraud. The auditor should consider the following attributes of the risk when identifying risks:

- Type. (Does the risk involve fraudulent financial reporting or misappropriation of assets?)
- Significance. (Could the risk lead to a material misstatement of the financial statements?)

- Likelihood. (How likely is it that the risk would lead to a material misstatement of the financial statements?)
- Pervasiveness. (Does the risk impact the financial statements as a whole or does it relate to an assertion, account, or class of transactions?)

The auditor should evaluate whether identified fraud risks can be related to certain account balances or classes of transactions and related assertions, or whether they relate to the financial statements as a whole. Examples of accounts or classes of transactions that might be more susceptible to fraud risk include

- Liabilities from a restructuring because of the subjectivity in estimating them.
- Revenues for a software developer, because of their complexity.

NOTE: The auditor should document the identified fraud risks.

Presumption about Improper Revenue Recognition as a Fraud Risk

Since fraudulent financial reporting often involves improper revenue recognition, the auditor should ordinarily presume that there is a risk of material misstatement due to fraudulent revenue recognition.

NOTE: The auditor should document the reasons supporting his or her conclusion when improper revenue recognition is not identified as a fraud risk.

Consideration of the Risk of Management Override of Controls

The auditor should also recognize that, even when other specific risks of material misstatement are not identified, there is a risk that management can override controls. The auditor should address this risk as discussed in the section below on "Addressing the Risk of Management Override."

ASSESSING IDENTIFIED RISKS

As part of the understanding of internal control required by Section 319, the auditor should

1. Evaluate whether the entity's programs and controls that address identified risks have been appropriately designed and placed in operation. Programs and controls may involve specific controls, such as those designed to prevent theft, or broad programs, such as one which promotes ethical behavior.
2. Consider whether programs and controls mitigate identified risks of material misstatement due to fraud or whether control deficiencies exacerbate risks.
3. Assess identified risks, taking into account the evaluation of programs and controls.
4. Consider this assessment when responding to the identified risks of material misstatement due to fraud.

RESPONDING TO THE RESULTS OF THE ASSESSMENT

The auditor responds to assessment of risk of material misstatement due to fraud by

- Exercising professional skepticism.
- Evaluating audit evidence.
- Considering programs and controls to address those risks.

Examples of the use of professional skepticism would include

- Designing additional or different audit procedures to obtain more reliable evidence.
- Obtaining additional corroboration of management's responses or representations.

The auditor should respond to the risk of material misstatement in the following ways:

1. Evaluate the overall conduct of the audit.
2. Adjust the nature, timing, and extent of audit procedures performed in response to identified risks.
3. Perform certain procedures to address the risk that management will override controls.

NOTE: The auditor should document a description of the auditor's response to identified fraud risks.

If the auditor concludes that it is not practical to design audit procedures to sufficiently address the risks of material misstatement due to fraud, the auditor should consider withdrawing from the engagement and communicating the reason to the audit committee.

Overall Response to Risk

Judgments about the risk of material misstatements due to fraud may affect the audit in the following ways:

1. **Assignment of personnel and supervision.** The personnel assigned to the engagement should have the knowledge, skill, and experience necessary to address the auditor's assessment of the level of risk of the engagement. The extent of supervision should also reflect the level of risk.
2. **Accounting principles.** The auditor should evaluate management's selection and application of significant accounting principles, particularly those relating to subjective measurements and complex transactions. The auditor should also consider whether the collective application of the principles indicates a bias that may create a material misstatement.
3. **Predictability of audit procedures.** The auditor should vary procedures from year to year to create an element of unpredictability. For example, the auditor may perform unannounced procedures or use a different sampling method.

Adjusting Audit Procedures

The auditor may respond to identified risks by adjusting the nature, timing, and extent of audit procedures performed. Specifically

- The **nature** of procedures may need to be modified to provide more reliable and persuasive evidence, or to corroborate management's representations. For example, the auditor may need to rely more on independent sources, physical observation of assets, or computer-assisted audit techniques.
- The **timing** of procedures may need to be changed. For example, the auditor may decide to perform more procedures at year-end, rather than relying on tests from an interim date.
- The **extent** of procedures applied should reflect the assessment of fraud risk and may need to be adjusted. For example, the auditor may increase sample sizes, perform more detailed analytical procedures, or perform more computer-assisted audit techniques.

Additional examples of ways to modify the nature, timing, and extent of tests to respond to the fraud risk assessment, examples of responses to identified risks arising from fraudulent financial reporting, and examples of responses to risks from misstatements arising from the misappropriation of assets can be found in *Techniques for Application.*

NOTE: Audit procedures may involve both substantive tests and tests of controls. However, since management may be able to override controls, it is unlikely that audit risk can be reduced to an appropriate level by performing only tests of controls.

Addressing the Risk of Management Override

The auditor should perform the following procedures to specifically address the risk for management's override of controls.

Examine journal entries and other adjustments for evidence of possible material misstatement due to fraud, and test the appropriateness and authorization of such entries. The following procedures should help the auditor in addressing possible recording of inappropriate or unauthorized journal entries or making financial statement adjustments, such as consolidating adjustments, report combinations, or reclassifications not reflected in formal journal entries. According to AU 316.58, the auditor should specifically:

a. Understand the financial reporting process, understand the design of controls over journal entries and other adjustments, and determine that such controls are suitably designed and placed in operation.
b. Identify and select journal entries and other adjustments for testing, while considering the following factors identified in AU 316.61:
    - The auditor's assessment of the risk of material misstatement due to fraud. (The auditor may identify a specific class of journal entries to examine after considering a specific fraud risk factor.)
    - The effectiveness of controls that have been implemented over journal entries and other adjustments. (Even if controls are implemented and operating effectively, the auditor should identify and test specific items.)
    - The entity's financial reporting process and the nature of evidence that can be examined. (Regardless of whether journal entries are automated or processed manually, the auditor should select journal entries to be tested from the general ledger, and examine support for those items. In addition, if journal entries and adjustments are in electronic form only, the auditor may require that an information technology [IT] specialist extract the data. Similarly, in an IT environment, the auditor may need computer-assisted audit techniques to identify and select journal entries and adjustments for testing.)
    - The characteristics of fraudulent entries or adjustments, or the nature and complexity of accounts. Illustration 3 provides a worksheet to use in identifying characteristics of fraudulent journal entries or adjustments, or accounts that may be more likely to contain inappropriate journal entries or adjustments. (When audits involve multiple locations, the auditor should consider whether to select journal entries from various locations.)
    - Journal entries or other adjustments processed outside the normal course of business, (i.e., nonstandard or nonrecurring entries). The auditor should consider placing additional emphasis in identifying and testing items processed outside the normal course of business, because such items may not be subject to the same level of internal control as other entries.
c. Determine the timing of testing. Fraud may occur throughout a period, and so the auditor should consider the need to test journal entries throughout the period under audit. However, the auditor should also consider that fraudulent journal entries are often made at the end of the reporting period, and should focus on entries made during that time.

d. Ask individuals in the financial reporting process about inappropriate or unusual activity relating to journal entries and adjustments.

NOTE: The auditor should document the results of procedures performed to address the possibility that management might override controls.

Reviewing accounting estimates for biases that could result in fraud. The auditor should consider whether differences between amounts supported by audit evidence and the estimates included in the financial statements, even if individually reasonable, indicate a possible bias on the part of entity's management. If so, the auditor should reconsider the estimates taken as a whole.

The auditor should retrospectively review significant accounting estimates in prior year's financial statements to determine whether there is a possible bias on the part of management. (Significant accounting estimates are those based on highly sensitive assumptions or significantly affected by management's judgment.) The review should provide information to the auditor about a possible management bias that can be helpful in evaluating the current year's estimates. If a management bias is identified, the auditor should evaluate whether the bias represents a risk for material misstatement due to fraud.

Evaluating whether the rationale for significant unusual transactions is appropriate. Personnel at the entity engaged in trying to hide a theft or commit fraudulent financial reporting might use unusual or nonstandard transactions to conceal the fraud. The auditor should understand the business rationale for such transactions and whether the rationale suggests that the transactions are fraudulent. When evaluating the transactions, the auditor should consider

- Is the transaction overly complex?
- Has management discussed the nature and accounting for the transaction with the audit committee or board of directors?
- Is management focusing more on achieving a particular accounting treatment than the underlying economics?
- Have any transactions involving special-purpose entities or other unconsolidated related parties been approved by the audit committee or board of directors?
- Do transactions involve previously unidentified related parties?
- Do transactions involve parties that cannot support the transaction without the help of the audited entity?

EVALUATING AUDIT EVIDENCE

The auditor should

1. Assess the risk of material misstatement due to fraud throughout the audit.
2. Evaluate whether analytical procedures performed as substantive tests or in the overall review indicate a previously unidentified fraud risk.
3. Evaluate the risk of material misstatement due to fraud at or near the completion of fieldwork.
4. Respond to misstatements that may result from fraud.
5. Consider whether identified misstatements may be indicative of fraud, and if so, evaluate their implications.

Assessing the Risk of Material Misstatements Due to Fraud

The auditor should continuously assess the risk of material misstatement due to fraud throughout the audit. The auditor should be alert for conditions that may change or support a judgment regarding the risk assessment. These conditions are listed in Illustration 4.

Evaluating Analytical Procedures

The auditor should consider whether analytical procedures performed as substantive tests or in the overall review stage of the audit indicate a risk of material misstatement due to fraud. The auditor should perform analytical procedures relating to revenue through the end of the reporting period, either as part of the overall review of the audit or separately. If not included during the overall review stage of the audit, the auditor should perform analytical procedures specifically related to potentially fraudulent revenue recognition.

The auditor should be alert to responses to inquiries about analytical relationships that are

- Vague or implausible
- Inconsistent with other audit evidence

NOTE: The auditor should document other conditions or analytical relationships that result in additional procedures, and any other responses the auditor feels are necessary.

Evaluating Fraud Risk at or near the Completion of Fieldwork

The auditor should, at or near the end of fieldwork, evaluate whether the results of auditing procedures and observations affect the earlier assessment of the risk of material misstatement due to fraud. When making this evaluation, the auditor with final responsibility for the audit should confirm that all audit team members have been communicating information about fraud risks to each other throughout the audit.

Responding to misstatements that may result from fraud. When misstatements are identified, the auditor should consider whether they are indicative of fraud. The auditor may need to consider the impact on materiality and other related responses.

If the auditor believes that the misstatements are or may result from fraud, but the effect is not material to the financial statements, the auditor should evaluate the implications for the rest of the audit. If the auditor determines that there are implications, such as implications about management's integrity, the auditor would reevaluate the assessment of the risk of material misstatement due to fraud and its impact on the nature, timing, and extent of substantive tests and the assessment of control risk if control risk was assessed below the maximum.

If the auditor believes that the misstatements are fraudulent, or may result from fraud, and the effect is material (or if the auditor cannot evaluate the materiality of the effect) the auditor should

1. Try to obtain additional evidence to determine whether fraud occurred and what its effect would be.
2. Consider how it affects the rest of the audit.
3. Discuss the matter and a plan for further investigation with a level of management at least one level above those involved, as well as senior management and the audit committee. If senior management is involved, it may be appropriate for the auditor to hold the discussion with the audit committee.
4. Consider suggesting that the client consult legal counsel.

After evaluating the risk of material misstatement, the auditor may determine that he or she should withdraw from the engagement and communicate the reason to the audit committee. The auditor may wish to consult legal counsel when considering withdrawing from the engagement.

NOTE: Because of the wide variety of circumstances involved, the SAS points out that it is not possible to definitively point out when the auditor should withdraw. However, the auditor may want to consider the implications of the fraud for management's integrity and the cooperation and effectiveness of management and/or board of directors when considering whether to withdraw.

Communication about Possible Fraud to Management, the Audit Committee, and Others

The auditor should communicate any evidence that fraud may exist, even if such fraud is inconsequential, to the appropriate level of management.

The auditor should directly inform the audit committee about

- Fraud involving senior management.
- Fraud that causes a material misstatement of the financial statements.

The auditor should reach an understanding with the audit committee about the nature and extent of communications that need to be made to the committee about misappropriations committed by lower-level employees.

The auditor should consider whether the following are reportable conditions that should be communicated to senior management and the audit committee:

- Identified risks of material misstatement due to fraud that have continuing control implications (whether or not transactions or adjustments that could result from fraud have been detected).
- A lack of, or deficiencies in, programs and controls to mitigate the risk of fraud.

The auditor may also want to communicate other identified risks of fraud to the audit committee, either in the overall communication of business and financial statement risks affecting the entity or in the communication about the quality of the entity's accounting principles (see Section 380).

Ordinarily, the auditor is not required to disclose possible fraud to anyone other than the client's senior management and audit committee, and in fact, would be prevented by the duty of confidentiality from doing so. However, a duty to disclose to others outside the entity may exist when

1. Complying with certain legal and regulatory requirements.
2. Responding to a successor auditor's inquiries.
3. Responding to a subpoena.
4. Complying with requirements of a funding agency or other specified agency for audits that receive governmental financial assistance.

The auditor may wish to consult legal counsel before discussing these matters outside the client to evaluate the auditor's ethical and legal obligations for client confidentiality.

NOTE: The auditor should document these communications to management, the audit committee, and others.

Documentation

According to AU 316.83, the auditor should document

- The engagement team's discussion, when planning the audit, about the entity's susceptibility to fraud. The documentation should include how and when the discussion occurred, audit team members participating, and the subject matter covered.
- Procedures performed to obtain the information for identifying and assessing the risks of material misstatements due to fraud.
- Specific risks of material misstatement due to fraud identified, and a description of the auditor's response to those risks.
- If improper revenue recognition has not been identified as a risk factor, the reasons supporting such conclusion.
- The results of procedures performed that addressed the risk that management would override controls.
- Other conditions and analytical relationships that caused the auditor to believe that additional procedures or responses were required, and any other further responses to address risks or other conditions.
- The nature of communications about fraud to management, the audit committee, and others.

INTERPRETATIONS

There are no interpretations for this section.

PROFESSIONAL ISSUES TASK FORCE PRACTICE ALERTS

98-2 Professional Skepticism and Related Topics

This Practice Alert was written after SAS 82 was issued and highlights two areas that warrant professional skepticism and attention to audit evidence.

1. A review of nonstandard journal entries. SAS 99, issued after SAS 82, also highlights the importance of attention to nonstandard entries.
2. Review of original and final source documents. SAS 82, which preceded SAS 99, highlighted the need for skepticism when only photocopies, and not originals, exist. The Practice Alert reemphasized the need to consider obtaining original documents. The alert also emphasized the importance of certain precautions with facsimile responses, such as confirming information with sender via telephone and asking the sender to send an original directly to the auditor.

The full text of this Practice Alert can be obtained from the AICPA website at www.aicpa.org/members/div/secps/lit/practice.htm.

98-3 Revenue Recognition Issues

This Practice Alert notes that a substantial portion of litigation against accounting firms reported to the AICPA SEC Practice Section Quality Control Inquiry Committee and a number of SEC Accounting and Auditing Enforcement Releases involve revenue recognition issues. This Practice Alert

1. Reminds auditors of certain factors or conditions that can indicate improper, aggressive, or unusual revenue recognition practices.
2. Suggests ways that auditors may reduce the risk of failing to detect such practices, including the use of professional skepticism and having an understanding of the client's industry and business, its products, its marketing and sales policies and strategies, its internal control, and its accounting policies and procedures related to revenue recognition.

An understanding of the revenue cycle is particularly important when

- The entity has new product or service introductions or begins new sales arrangements.
- The auditor is reviewing sales to distributors. The auditor should consider asking whether the client has offered to assist the distributor in placing the product with end users and whether concessions have been made with the distributor in the form of return product rights or other arrangements.

3. Provides guidance on confirmations and management representations related to revenue transactions. The auditor may need to consider performing additional audit procedures such as

   - Discussions with representatives of the client's sales, marketing, customer service and returns department.
   - Confirmations of sales terms.
   - Review of sales contracts.
   - Use of a specialist to interpret contractual agreements.

   Standard confirmation requests that confirm only the outstanding balance may not always provide sufficient audit evidence to determine whether revenue transactions have been recorded properly. Confirmations can be designed to provide information about

   - Payment terms.
   - Right-of-return privileges.
   - Continuing obligations on the part of the client.
   - Significant risks retained by the client.
   - Oral modifications or "side agreements" for unusual transactions.
   - Terms of individually significant revenue transactions.

   Auditors may also wish to obtain written representations from management about revenue recognition issues, such as the terms and conditions of unusual or complex sales agreements, confirmation that there are no contingencies that affect the obligation of customers to pay for merchandise purchased, or the existence of any side agreements.

4. Refers to professional guidance which addresses the accounting considerations for revenue recognition, such as

   - FASB Concept Statement 5, *Recognition and Measurement in Financial Statements of Business Enterprises.*
   - Accounting Research Bulletin 45, *Long-Term Construction-Type Contracts.*
   - Statement of Financial Accounting Standards 48, *Revenue Recognition When Right of Return Exists.*
   - AICPA Statement of Position (SOP) 81-1, *Accounting for Performance of Construction-Type and Certain Production-Type Contracts.*
   - AICPA SOP 97-2, *Software Revenue Recognition.*
   - SEC Accounting and Auditing Enforcement Release 108 (states that recognition of revenue on "bill and hold" transactions, prior to shipment or exchange with the customer, is a departure from the "general rule of revenue recognition," and is appropriate only if certain conditions described in Release 108 are met)
   - Various other Emerging Issues Task Force abstracts which provide guidance on specific revenue recognition issues.

5. Reminds auditors of their responsibilities to communicate with the board of directors and audit committees.

   The Alert notes that the auditor should have a discussion with the board of directors/audit committee related to revenue recognition practices of the company, including topics such as a change in the company's revenue recognition policy, a lack of involvement by the accounting/finance department in sales transactions or in the monitoring of arrangements with distributors, significant sales or volume of sales that are recorded at or near the end of the reporting period, sales terms that do not comply with the company's normal policies, etc. The SEC Practice Section has developed best practices guidance on communications with board of directors/audit committees, which includes recommendations regarding the following:

   - The establishment of firm policies and procedures for communications with board of directors/audit committees.
   - The establishment of a relationship with board of directors/audit committees which fosters candid and open discussions.
   - The nature of communication by the auditor regarding the qualitative assessment of the company's accounting principles and the clarity of the company's financial statement disclosures.
   - The timing of when such communication should occur.

The SEC Practice Section best practices guidance can be obtained from the AICPA website at www.aicpa.org/members/div/secps/lit/best/index.htm. The full text of this Practice Alert can be obtained from the AICPA website at www.aicpa.org/members/div/secps/lit/practice.htm.

03-02 Journal Entries and Other Adjustments

This Practice Alert assists auditors in designing and performing audit procedures to fulfill the requirements of SAS 99 regarding journal entries and other adjustments. Highlights of the alert include guidance on

- How to obtain an understanding of the entity's financial reporting process and its controls over journal entries and other adjustments.
- Assessing the risk of material misstatement resulting from journal entries and other adjustments, including when such entries exist only in electronic form. The alert also suggest that auditors discuss, in their brainstorming session, the ways in which management could originate and post inappropriate entries or adjustments, the kinds of unusual combinations of debits and credits to watch for, and the types of entries and adjustments that could result in a material misstatement that might not be detected by standard audit procedures.
- Making inquiries about fraud of those involved in the financial reporting process. The alert recommends that where practical and regardless of the fraud risk assessment, the auditor should ask (1) accounting and data entry personnel about whether those individual were asked to make unusual entries, and (2) selected programmers and IT staff about any unusual and/or unsupported entries.
- Assessing the completeness of journal entry and other sources of adjustments. Since journal entries and other adjustment may be made outside the general ledger, the auditor should completely understand how the various general ledgers are combined and the accounts grouped to create the consolidated financial statements.
- Identifying and selecting entries and adjustments for testing. The alert points out that the auditor may need to employ computer-assisted audit techniques to identify entries and adjustments to test. These techniques are often designed to detect entries made at

unusual times of day, by unusual users, or electronic entries not documented in the general ledger.

- Testing other adjustments, including comparing the adjustments to underlying supporting information, and considering the rationale underlying the adjustment and the reason it was not in a formal journal entry.
- Documenting the results of procedures related to journal entries and other adjustments.

The full text of this Practice Alert can be obtained from the AICPA website at www.aicpa.org/members/div/secps/lit/practice.htm.

TECHNIQUES FOR APPLICATION

MANAGEMENT'S RESPONSIBILITIES

Management is responsible for designing and implementing programs to prevent, deter, and detect fraud. When management and others, such as the audit committee and board of directors, set the proper tone of proper ethical conduct, the opportunities for fraud are significantly reduced.

DESCRIPTION AND CHARACTERISTICS OF FRAUD

Although fraud is a broad legal concept, the auditor's interest specifically relates to fraudulent acts that cause a material misstatement of financial statements. Two types of misstatements are relevant to the auditor's consideration in a financial statement audit.

1. Misstatements arising from fraudulent financial reporting.

   NOTE: SAS 99 points out that fraudulent financial reporting does not need to involve a grand plan or conspiracy. Management may rationalize that a misstatement is appropriate because it is an aggressive interpretation of accounting rules, or that it is a temporary misstatement that will be corrected later.

2. Misstatements arising from misappropriation of assets.

   NOTE: The scope of SAS 99 applies only to misappropriation of assets that cause the financial statements not to be fairly presented, in all material respects, in conformity with GAAP.

Fraudulent financial reporting and misappropriation of assets differ in that fraudulent financial reporting is committed, usually by management, to deceive financial statement users while misappropriation of assets is committed against an entity, most often by employees.

Fraud generally involves the following:

1. A pressure or an incentive to commit fraud.
2. A perceived opportunity to do so.
3. Rationalization of the fraud by the individual(s) committing it.

However, not all three conditions must be observed to conclude that there is an identified risk. It is particularly difficult to observe that the correct environment for rationalizing fraud is present.

The auditor should be aware that the presence of each of the three conditions may vary, and is influenced by factors such as the size, complexity, and ownership of the entity. These three conditions usually are present for both types of fraud.

The auditor should also be alert to the fact that fraudulent financial reporting often involves the override of controls, and that management's override of controls can occur in unpredictable ways. Also, fraud may be concealed through collusion, making it particularly difficult to detect.

Although fraud usually is concealed, the presence of risk factors or other conditions may alert the auditor to its possible existence.

FRAUD RISK FACTORS

Fraud risk factors may come to the auditor's attention while performing procedures relating to acceptance or continuance of clients, during engagement planning or obtaining an understanding of an entity's internal control, or while conducting fieldwork. Accordingly, the assessment of the risk of material misstatement due to fraud is a cumulative process that includes a consideration of risk factors individually and in combination. As noted earlier, assessment of fraud risk factors is not a simple matter of counting the factors present and converting to a level of fraud risk. A few or even a single risk factor may heighten significantly the risk of fraud.

Identifying Fraud Risks

When identifying fraud risks, the auditor may find it helpful to consider information obtained along with the three conditions—incentives/pressures, opportunities, and attitudes/rationalizations—usually present when fraud exists. However, as stated above, the auditor should not assume that all three conditions must be present or observed. In addition, the extent to which any condition is present may vary.

The size, complexity, and ownership of the entity may also affect the identification of fraud risks.

Modifying the Nature, Timing and Extent of Audit Procedures to Address Risk

According to AU 316.53, the following are examples of ways to modify the nature, timing and extent of tests in response to identified risks of material misstatement due to fraud:

- Perform unannounced or surprise procedures at locations.
- Ask that inventories be counted as close as possible to the end of the reporting period.
- Orally confirm with major customers and suppliers in addition to sending written confirmations.
- Send confirm requests to a specific party in an organization.
- Perform substantive analytical procedures using disaggregated data, such as comparing gross profit or operating margins by location, line of business, or month to auditor-developed expectations.
- Interview personnel involved in areas where a fraud risk has been identified to get their views about the risk and how controls address the risk.
- Discuss with other independent auditors auditing other subsidiaries, divisions, or branches the extent of work that should be performed to address the risk of fraud resulting from transactions and activities among those components.

Examples of Responses to Identified Risks of Misstatements from Fraudulent Financial Reporting

The following examples are from AU 316.54:

Revenue recognition. The auditor may consider

- Performing substantive analytical procedures relating to revenue using disaggregated data, such as comparing revenue reported by month or by product line or business segment during the current reporting period with comparable prior periods.

- Confirming with customers certain relevant contract terms and the absence of side agreements because the appropriate accounting often is influenced by such terms or agreements. For example, acceptance criteria, delivery and payment terms, the absence of future or continuing vendor obligations, the right to return the product, guaranteed resale amounts, and cancellation or refund provisions often are relevant in such circumstances.
- Inquiring of the entity's sales and marketing personnel or in-house legal counsel regarding sales or shipments near the end of the period and their knowledge of any unusual terms or conditions associated with these transactions.
- Being physically present at one or more locations at period-end to observe goods being shipped or being readied for shipment (or returns processing) and performing other appropriate cutoff procedures.
- For those situations for which revenue transactions are electronically initiated, processed, and recorded, testing controls to determine whether they provide assurance that recorded revenue transactions occurred and are properly recorded.

Inventory quantities. The auditor may consider

- Examining the entity's inventory records to identify locations or items that require specific attention during or after the physical inventory count.
- Performing additional procedures during the count, such as rigorously examining the contents of boxes, checking the manner in which goods are stacked for hollow squares, or examining the quality of liquid substances for purity, grade, or concentration.
- Performing additional testing of count sheets, tags, or other records to reduce the possibility of subsequent alteration or inappropriate compilation.
- Performing additional procedures to test the reasonableness of quantities counted, such as comparing quantities for the current period with prior periods by class or category of inventory or location.
- Using computer-assisted audit techniques.

Management estimates. The auditor may want to supplement the audit evidence obtained. The auditor may

- Engage a specialist.
- Develop an independent estimate for comparison.
- Evaluate information gathered about the entity and its environment.
- Retrospectively review similar management judgments and assumptions from prior periods.

Examples of Responses to Identified Risks of Misstatements Arising from Misappropriation of Assets

The auditor will usually direct a response to identified risks of misstatements arising from misappropriation of assets to certain account balances. The scope of the work should be linked to the specific information about the identified misappropriation risk. The auditor may consider some of the procedures listed in "Examples of Responses to Identified Risks of Misstatements Arising from Fraudulent Financial Reporting." However, in some cases, the auditor may

- Obtain an understanding of the controls related to preventing or detecting the misappropriation and testing of such controls.
- Physically inspect assets near the end of the period.

- Apply substantive analytical procedures, such as the development by the auditor of an expected dollar amount at a high level of precision to be compared with a recorded amount.

Evaluating Analytical Procedures as Part of Audit Evidence

As part of the auditor's evaluation of analytical procedures performed as substantive tests or in the overall review stage of the audit, and those analytical procedures that relate to revenue through the end of the reporting period, the auditor may find it helpful to consider

1. Are there any unusual relationships involving revenues and income at year-end, such as an unexpectedly large amount of revenue reported at the very end of the reporting period from nonstandard transactions, or income that is not consistent with cash flow trends from operations?
2. Are there other unusual or unexpected analytical relationships that should be evaluated? AU 316.72 provides the following examples:
   - An unusual relationship between net income and cash flows from operations may occur if management recorded fictitious revenues and receivables but was unable to manipulate cash.
   - Inconsistent changes in inventory, accounts payable, sales or cost of sales between the prior period and the current period may indicate a possible employee theft of inventory, because the employee was unable to manipulate all of the related accounts.
   - Comparing the entity's profitability to industry trends, which management cannot manipulate, may indicate trends or differences for further consideration.
   - Unexplained relationships between bad debt write-offs and comparable industry data, which employees cannot manipulate, may indicate a possible theft of cash receipts.
   - Unusual relationships between sales volume taken from the accounting records and production statistics maintained by operating personnel—which may be more difficult for management to manipulate—may indicate a possible misstatement of sales.

In planning the audit, the auditor will most likely use a list of fraud risk factors to serve as a "memory jogger." This list may be taken from the examples listed in the next section (*Illustrations*), or the examples provided may be tailored to the client. The documentation of this list of fraud risk factors considered is **not** required, but represents good practice.

During the planning and performance of the audit, the auditor may identify some of the fraud risk factors from the list as being present at the client. Of those risk factors present, some will be addressed sufficiently by the planned audit procedures; others may require the auditor to extend audit procedures.

Required Actions/Communication Required for Discovered Fraud

When the auditor discovers or suspects fraud, the actions and communications required by SAS 99 are somewhat complex, especially when an SEC client is involved. The actions/communications required by Title III of the Private Securities Litigation Reform Act of 1995, by the SEC Practice Section (SECPS) for its members, and by the SEC in Form 8-K add to the complexity.

To operationalize SAS 99, and to also give appropriate consideration to the SEC and SECPS requirements, the best approach is to decide which of the following three situations governs and follow the guidance presented below for the applicable situation.

Situation 1.

SAS 99 Actions/Communications Requirements for Material Fraud + Any Fraud Involving Senior Management for Non-SEC Clients

Auditor should

1. Consider implications for other aspects of audit.
2. Reevaluate the assessment of the risk of fraud.
3. Discuss matter and the approach to further investigation with appropriate level of management.[3]
4. Obtain additional evidential matter, including suggesting that client consult with legal counsel.
5. Consider whether any risk factors identified represent reportable conditions (Section 325).
6. Consider withdrawing from the engagement and communicating reasons to the audit committee (or board of directors, etc.).
7. Report the fraud to the audit committee or, in a small business, to the owner-manager.

   NOTE: If perpetrator controls audit committee or board of directors, go directly to client's legal counsel. If perpetrator is a general partner acting against interest of limited partners, obtain legal advice and consider communicating to limited partners. If perpetrator is owner-manager of a small business, auditor has little choice but to communicate with perpetrator and has no obvious course of action but to withdraw. However, first the auditor should consult with his or her legal counsel.

8. Insist that the financial statements be revised and, if they are not, express a qualified or adverse opinion. If precluded from obtaining needed evidence, disclaim an opinion or withdraw.

Situation 2.

Actions/Communications Requirements for Material Fraud + Any Fraud Involving Senior Management for SEC Clients

Auditor should

1. Follow steps in Situation 1. checklist (SAS 99 requirements) + additional items 2. - 4. below.
2. Consider Section 10A(b) of the Securities Exchange Act of 1934 (Title III, Private Securities Litigation Reform Act of 1995).
   a. Matter is reported to board of directors and it does not take appropriate action.
   b. Auditor concludes that failure to take remedial action is expected to cause departure from standard audit report or cause withdrawal.
   c. Auditor should report conclusion in b. above to board of directors (e.g., on Monday).
   d. Client is required to notify SEC (within one business day) of auditor's conclusion described in b. above (e.g., by Tuesday).
   e. Client is required to furnish report to SEC in d. above to auditor within one business day (e.g., by Tuesday).
   f. If auditor doesn't receive report in e. above, auditor notifies SEC within one business day following failure to receive (e.g., on Wednesday).

---

[3] *Fraud that involves senior management or fraud that causes a material misstatement of the financial statements should be reported directly to the audit committee.*

3. For SEC Practice Section members, if auditor withdraws or resigns from engagement, auditor must send copy of resignation to the SEC within five business days.
4. Follow SEC requirements for reporting on Form 8-K.

   a. Upon auditor's withdrawal, client must disclose within five business days[4] the following information on a Form 8-K, filed with the SEC, with a copy to the auditor on the same day

      - Auditor's resignation.
      - Auditor's conclusion that the information coming to his/her attention **has a material impact** on the fairness or reliability of the client's financial statements or audit report and that this matter was not resolved to the auditor's satisfaction before resignation.

   b. Auditor must prepare a letter stating agreement or disagreement with client's statements after reading Form 8-K. If auditor disagrees, he/she must disclose differences of opinion in a letter to client as promptly as possible. Client must then file the letter with the SEC within ten business days after filing the Form 8-K. Notwithstanding the ten-business-day requirement, client has two business days from the date of receipt to file the letter with the SEC.

Situation 3.

SAS 99 Actions/Communication Requirements for Immaterial Fraud + Not Involving Senior Management for All Clients (Public and Nonpublic)

Auditor should

1. Evaluate implications for other aspects of audit, especially organizational position of persons involved.
2. Bring to attention of, and discuss with, appropriate level of management (even if inconsequential).
3. Communicate matter to audit committee unless matter is clearly below communication threshold previously agreed to by auditor and the audit committee.
4. Consider whether any risk factors identified represent reportable conditions (Section 325).

MANAGEMENT ANTIFRAUD PROGRAMS AND CONTROLS

In an exhibit to SAS 99 titled *Management Antifraud Programs and Controls*, the AICPA provides guidance to help prevent, deter, and detect fraud. The SAS states that the exhibit is printed for the reader's convenience but is not an integral part of the SAS. The document identifies the key participants in this effort, including boards of directors, management, internal and independent auditors, and certified fraud examiners. Auditors may wish to review the guidance provided in this exhibit, which can be found at www.aicpa.org/antifraud/management/20.htm.

---

[4] *Practitioners with publicly-traded clients should be aware that the SEC is proposing modifications to the Form 8-K requirements. The proposals would shorten the filing deadline for Form 8-K to two business days after an event triggering the form's disclosure requirements. (The proposals will also expand the list of significant events requiring disclosure in Form 8-K.) Practitioners should monitor the status of the proposed rules at www.sec.gov.*

ILLUSTRATIONS

ILLUSTRATION 1. RISK FACTORS—FRAUDULENT FINANCIAL REPORTING

The following are examples of risk factors, reproduced with permission from SAS 99, relating to misstatements arising from fraudulent financial reporting:

Incentives/Pressures

a. Financial stability or profitability is threatened by economic, industry, or entity operating conditions, such as (or indicated by)
   - High degree of competition or market saturation, accompanied by declining margins.
   - High vulnerability to rapid changes, such as changes in technology, product obsolescence, or interest rates.
   - Significant declines in customer demand and increasing business failures in either the industry or overall economy.
   - Operating losses making the threat of bankruptcy, foreclosure, or hostile takeover imminent.
   - Recurring negative cash flows from operations or an inability to generate cash flows from operations while reporting earnings and earnings growth.
   - Rapid growth or unusual profitability, especially compared to that of other companies in the same industry.
   - New accounting, statutory, or regulatory requirements.

b. Excessive pressure exists for management to meet the requirements or expectations of third parties due to the following:
   - Profitability or trend level expectations of investment analysts, institutional investors, significant creditors, or other external parties (particularly expectations that are unduly aggressive or unrealistic), including expectations created by management in, for example, overly optimistic press releases or annual report messages.
   - Need to obtain additional debt or equity financing to stay competitive—including financing of major research and development or capital expenditures.
   - Marginal ability to meet exchange listing requirements or debt repayment or other debt covenant requirements.
   - Perceived or real adverse effects of reporting poor financial results on significant pending transactions, such as business combinations or contract awards.

c. Information available indicates that management or the board of directors' personal financial situation is threatened by the entity's financial performance arising from the following:
   - Significant financial interests in the entity.
   - Significant portions of their compensation (for example, bonuses, stock options, and earn-out arrangements) being contingent upon achieving aggressive targets for stock price, operating results, financial position, or cash flow[5]
   - Personal guarantees of debts of the entity

d. There is excessive pressure on management or operating personnel to meet financial targets set up by the board of directors or management, including sales or profitability incentive goals.

Opportunities

a. The nature of the industry or the entity's operations provides opportunities to engage in fraudulent financial reporting that can arise from the following:
   - Significant related-party transactions not in the ordinary course of business or with related entities not audited or audited by another firm.
   - A strong financial presence or ability to dominate a certain industry sector that allows the entity to dictate terms or conditions to suppliers or customers that may result in inappropriate or non-arm's-length transactions.
   - Assets, liabilities, revenues, or expenses based on significant estimates that involve subjective judgments or uncertainties that are difficult to corroborate.
   - Significant, unusual, or highly complex transactions, especially those close to period end that post difficult "substance over form" questions.

---

[5] *Management incentive plans may be contingent upon achieving targets relating only to certain accounts or selected activities of the entity, even though the related accounts or activities may not be material to the entity as a whole.*

- Significant operations located or conducted across international borders in jurisdictions where differing business environments and cultures exist.
- Significant bank accounts or subsidiary or branch operations in tax-haven jurisdictions for which there appears to be no clear business justification.

b. There is ineffective monitoring of management as a result of the following:
- Domination of management by a single person or small group (in a nonowner-managed business) without compensating controls.
- Ineffective board of directors or audit committee oversight over the financial reporting process and internal control.

c. There is a complex or unstable organizational structure, as evidenced by the following:
- Difficulty in determining the organization or individuals that have controlling interest in the entity.
- Overly complex organizational structure involving unusual legal entities or managerial lines of authority.
- High turnover of senior management, counsel, or board members.

d. Internal control components are deficient as a result of the following:
- Inadequate monitoring of controls, including automated controls and controls over interim financial reporting (where external reporting is required).
- High turnover rates or employment of ineffective accounting, internal audit, or information technology staff.
- Ineffective accounting and information systems, including situations involving reportable conditions.

Attitudes/Rationalizations

Risk factors reflective of attitudes/rationalizations by board members, management, or employees, that allow them to engage in and/or justify fraudulent financial reporting, may not be susceptible to observation by the auditor. Nevertheless, the auditor who becomes aware of the existence of such information should consider it in identifying the risks of material misstatement arising from fraudulent financial reporting. For example, auditors may become aware of the following information that may indicate a risk factor:

- Ineffective communication, implementation, support, or enforcement of the entity's values or ethical standards by management or the communication of inappropriate values or ethical standards.
- Nonfinancial management's excessive participation in or preoccupation with the selection of accounting principles or the determination of significant estimates.
- Known history of violations of securities laws or other laws and regulations, or claims against the entity, its senior management, or board members alleging fraud or violations of laws and regulations.
- Excessive interest by management in maintaining or increasing the entity's stock price or earnings trend.
- A practice by management of committing analysts, creditors, and other third parties to achieve aggressive or unrealistic forecasts
- Management failing to correct known reportable conditions on a timely basis.
- An interest by management in employing inappropriate means to minimize reported earnings for tax-motivated reasons.
- Recurring attempts by management to justify marginal or inappropriate accounting on the basis of materiality.
- The relationship between management and the current or predecessor auditor is strained, as exhibited by the following:
  - Frequent disputes with the current or predecessor auditor on accounting, auditing, or reporting matters.
  - Unreasonable demands on the auditor, such as unreasonable time constraints regarding the completion of the audit or the issuance of the auditor's report.
  - Formal or informal restrictions on the auditor that inappropriately limit access to people or information or the ability to communicate effectively with the board of directors or audit committee.
  - Domineering management behavior in dealing with the auditor involving attempts to influence the scope of the auditor's work or the selection or continuance of personnel assigned to or consulted on the audit engagement.

ILLUSTRATION 2. RISK FACTORS—MISAPPROPRIATION OF ASSETS

The following are examples of risk factors, reproduced with permission from SAS 99, relating to misstatements arising from misappropriation of assets:

Incentives/Pressures

a. Personal financial obligations may create pressure on management or employees with access to cash or other assets susceptible to theft to misappropriate those assets.

b. Adverse relationships between the entity and employees with access to cash or other assets susceptible to theft may motivate those employees to misappropriate those assets. For example, adverse relationships may be created by the following:

- Known or anticipated future employee layoffs.
- Recent or anticipated changes to employee compensation or benefit plans.
- Promotions, compensation, or other rewards inconsistent with expectations.

Opportunities

a. Certain characteristics or circumstances may increase the susceptibility of assets to misappropriation. For example, opportunities to misappropriate assets increase when there are the following:

- Large amounts of cash on hand or processed.
- Inventory items that are small in size, of high value, or in high demand.
- Easily convertible assets, such as bearer bonds, diamonds, or computer chips.
- Fixed assets that are small in size, marketable, or lacking observable identification of ownership.

b. Inadequate internal control over assets may increase the susceptibility of misappropriation of those assets. For example, the misappropriation of assets may occur because there is the following:

- Inadequate segregation of duties or independent checks
- Inadequate management oversight of employees responsible for assets, for example, inadequate supervision or monitoring of remote locations.
- Inadequate job applicant screening of employees with access to assets.
- Inadequate recordkeeping with respect to assets.
- Inadequate system of authorization and approval of transactions (for example, in purchasing)
- Inadequate physical safeguards over cash, investments, inventory, or fixed assets.
- Lack of complete and timely reconciliations of assets.
- Lack of timely and appropriate documentation of transactions, for example, credits for merchandise returns.
- Lack of mandatory vacations for employees performing key control functions.
- Inadequate management understanding of information technology, which enables information technology employees to perpetrate a misappropriation.
- Inadequate access controls over automated records, including controls over and review of computer systems events logs.

Attitudes/Rationalizations

Risk factors reflective of employee attitudes/rationalizations that allow them to justify misappropriation of assets, are generally not susceptible to observation by the auditor. Nevertheless, the auditor who becomes aware of the existence of such information should consider it in identifying the risks of material misstatement arising from misappropriation of assets. For example, auditors may become aware of the following attitudes or behavior of employees who have access to assets susceptible to misappropriation:

- Disregard for the need for monitoring or reducing risks related to misappropriation of assets.
- Disregard for internal control over misappropriation of assets by overriding existing controls or by failing to correct known internal control deficiencies.
- Behavior indicating displeasure or dissatisfaction with the company or its treatment of the employee.
- Changes in behavior or lifestyle that may indicate assets have been misappropriated.

ILLUSTRATION 3. WORKSHEET TO IDENTIFY FRAUDULENT ENTRIES OR ADJUSTMENTS (ADAPTED FROM AU 316.61)

Inappropriate journal entries and other adjustments often have certain unique characteristics. The auditor should use the following questions to help identify characteristics of inappropriate journal entries and other adjustments:

- Is the entry made to an unrelated, unusual, or seldom-used account?
- Is the entry made by an individual who typically does not make journal entries?
- Is the entry made at closing of the period or postclosing with little or no explanation or description?
- Do entries made during the preparation of financial statements lack account numbers?

- Does the entry contain round numbers or a consistent ending number?

The auditor should use the following questions to identify journal entries and adjustments made to accounts that have the following characteristics:

- Does the account consist of transactions that are complex or unusual in nature?
- Does the account contain significant estimates and period-end adjustments?
- Has the account been prone to errors in the past?
- Has the account not been regularly reconciled on a timely basis?
- Does the account contain unreconciled differences?
- Does the account contain intercompany transactions?
- Is the account otherwise associated with an identified risk of material misstatement due to fraud?

ILLUSTRATION 4. LIST OF CONDITIONS THAT MAY CHANGE OR SUPPORT THE FRAUD RISK ASSESSMENT (FROM AU 316.68)

Conditions may be identified during fieldwork that change or support a judgment regarding the assessment of the risks, such as the following:

- Discrepancies in the accounting records, including
  - Transactions that are not recorded in a complete or timely manner or are improperly recorded as to amount, accounting period, classification, or entity policy.
  - Unsupported or unauthorized balances or transactions.
  - Last-minute adjustments that significantly affect financial results.
  - Evidence of employees' access to systems and records inconsistent with that necessary to perform their authorized duties.
  - Tips or complaints to the auditor about alleged fraud.
- Conflicting or missing evidential matter, including
  - Missing documents.
  - Documents that appear to have been altered.
  - Unavailability of other than photocopies or electronically transmitted documents when documents in original form are expected to exist.
  - Significant unexplained items on reconciliations.
  - Inconsistent, vague, or implausible responses from management or employees arising from inquiries procedures.
  - Unusual discrepancies between the entity's records and confirmation replies.
  - Missing inventory or physical assets of significant magnitude.
  - Unavailable or missing electronic evidence, inconsistent with the entity's record retention practices or policies.
  - Inability to produce evidence of key systems development and program change testing and implementation activities for current year system changes and deployments.
- Problematic or unusual relationships between the auditor and management, including
  - Denial of access to records, facilities, certain employees, customers, vendors, or others from whom audit evidence might be sought.
  - Undue time pressures imposed by management to resolve complex or contentious issues.
  - Complaints by management about the conduct of the audit or management intimidation of audit team members, particularly in connection with the auditor's critical assessment of audit evidence or in the resolution of potential disagreements with management.
  - Unusual delays by the entity in providing requested information.
  - Unwillingness to facilitate auditor access to key electronic files for testing through the use of computer-assisted audit techniques.
  - Denial of access to key IT operations staff and facilities, including security, operations, and systems development personnel.
  - An unwillingness to add or revise disclosures in the financial statements to make them more complete and transparent.

316A CONSIDERATION OF FRAUD IN A FINANCIAL STATEMENT AUDIT[1]

EFFECTIVE DATE AND APPLICABILITY

Original Pronouncement	SAS 82, February 1997.
Effective Date	Audits of financial statements for periods ending on or after December 15, 1997.
Applicability	Audits of financial statements in accordance with generally accepted auditing standards.

DEFINITIONS OF TERMS

Fraudulent financial reporting. Intentional material misstatement of financial statements.

Misstatements arising from fraudulent financial reporting. Intentional misstatements or omissions of amounts or disclosures in financial statements to deceive financial statement users.

Misstatements arising from misappropriation of assets. The theft of an entity's assets where the effect of the theft causes the financial statements not to be presented in conformity with generally accepted accounting principles (sometimes referred to as defalcation).

Fraud risk factors. Conditions that may alert the auditor to a possibility that fraud may exist.

OBJECTIVES OF SECTION

The accounting profession has always had trouble explaining to critics why an audit conducted in accordance with professional standards might fail to detect a material misstatement of financial statements caused by fraud.

Over the years, there have been several pronouncements issued to attempt to explain the auditor's responsibility for fraud detection. This section is the latest attempt.

In 1992, the AICPA convened a conference of educators and practitioners, known as the Expectation Gap Roundtable, to present papers and discuss several auditing standards that had been issued in 1988 (the expectation gap standards). The deliberations at the conference raised questions concerning whether SAS 53, *The Auditor's Responsibility to Detect and Report Errors and Irregularities*, had been successful in narrowing the expectation gap relating to the detection of material financial statement fraud.

---

[1] *SAS 82 remains in effect for audits of financial statements for periods ending before December 15, 2002. SAS 82 is superseded by SAS 99,* ***Consideration of Fraud in a Financial Statement Audit,*** *for audits of financial statements beginning on or after December 15, 2002, with earlier application permitted. Guidance on SAS 99 can be found in Section 316.*

In its March 1993 report, titled *In the Public Interest*, the Public Oversight Board (POB) of the AICPA SEC Practice Section noted: "Attacks on the accounting profession from a variety of sources suggested a significant public concern over the profession's performance. Of particular moment is the widespread belief that auditors have a responsibility for detecting management fraud which they are not now meeting." The POB, in its report, made two recommendations addressing fraud. They were

1. Accounting firms should ensure that auditors more consistently implement, and be more sensitive to the need to exercise, the professional skepticism required by SAS 53.
2. The ASB, the SEC Practice Section, or some other appropriate body should develop guidelines to assist auditors in assessing the likelihood that fraud which may affect financial information may be occurring, and to specify additional auditing procedures when there is a heightened likelihood of management fraud.

In 1993, the AICPA's Board of Directors also issued a report, *Meeting the Financial Reporting Needs of the Future: A Public Commitment from the Public Accounting Profession*. In this report, the AICPA's Board of Directors supported recommendations and initiatives of others to assist auditors in the detection of material misstatements in financial statements resulting from fraud, and encouraged every participant in the financial reporting process—management, their advisors, regulators, and independent auditors—to share in this responsibility.

The Auditing Standards Board (ASB) decided to undertake a project on fraud in large measure because of the Expectation Gap Roundtable findings and the reports of the POB and the AICPA's Board of Directors. In keeping with its commitment to serve the public interest by improving the detection of material fraud in financial statements, the ASB issued SAS 82, *Consideration of Fraud in a Financial Statement Audit*, in February 1997. SAS 82 provides expanded operational guidance on the consideration of fraud in conducting a financial statement audit. It also strengthens the auditor's ability to fulfill his or her responsibility to plan and perform the audit to obtain reasonable assurance about whether financial statements are free of material misstatements, whether caused by error or fraud.

FUNDAMENTAL REQUIREMENTS

Basic Requirement

According to AU 110.02, the auditor should plan and perform the audit to obtain reasonable assurance about whether the financial statements are free of material misstatement, whether caused by error or fraud.

Assessment of the Risk of Material Misstatement Due to Fraud

According to AU 316.12, the auditor should specifically assess the risk of material misstatement of the financial statements due to fraud and should consider that assessment in designing the audit procedures to be performed.

In making this assessment, the auditor should consider fraud risk factors that relate to fraudulent financial reporting and misappropriation of assets in each of the following categories.

According to AU 316.16, risk factors that relate to fraudulent financial reporting

1. **Management's characteristics and influence over the control environment.** These pertain to management's abilities, pressures, style, and attitude relating to in-

ternal control and the financial reporting process. An example is a strained relationship between management and the current or predecessor auditor.
2. **Industry conditions.** These involve the economic and regulatory environment in which the entity operates. An example is a declining industry with increasing business failures.
3. **Operating characteristics and financial stability.** These pertain to the nature and complexity of the entity and its transactions, the entity's financial condition, and its profitability. An example is a significant related-party transaction not in the ordinary course of business or with related entities not audited or audited by another firm.

According to AU 316.18, risk factors that relate to misappropriation of assets

1. **Susceptibility of assets to misappropriation.** These pertain to the nature of an entity's assets and the degree to which they are subject to theft. Examples are easily convertible assets, such as bearer bonds, diamonds, or computer chips.
2. **Controls.** These involve the lack of controls designed to prevent or detect misappropriation of assets. An example is an accounting system in disarray.

The auditor also should inquire of management to obtain management's understanding regarding the risk of fraud in the entity, and to determine if management has knowledge of fraud that has been perpetrated on or within the entity.

The auditor should use professional judgment when assessing the significance and relevance of fraud risk factors and determining the appropriate audit response.

Although the auditor is not required to plan the audit to discover information that is indicative of financial stress of employees or adverse relationships between the entity and its employees, the auditor may become aware of such information. An example is an anticipated future employee layoff that is known to the work force. If the auditor becomes aware of such information, he or she should consider it in assessing the risk of material misstatement arising from misappropriation of assets.

The auditor should exercise professional judgment when considering risk factors individually or in combination and whether there are specific controls that mitigate the risk.

The auditor may consider the effectiveness of any programs established by the entity that include steps to prevent, deter, and detect fraud. The auditor also should ask those persons overseeing such programs whether the program has identified any fraud risk factors.

Other conditions may be identified during fieldwork that change or support a judgment regarding the assessment. Examples include availability of only photocopied documents when documents in original form are expected to exist, or auditors being denied access to records, facilities, certain employees, customers, vendors, or others from whom audit evidence might be sought. Accordingly, the assessment is an ongoing process as work is performed.

NOTE: There is no formula for converting identified risk factors into an assessment of the level of fraud risk. The evaluation does not depend on a simple count of the number of risk factors identified. Although the presence of a large number of risk factors may indicate increased risk of fraud, one or a few factors may have a significant effect on the evaluation.

The Auditor's Response to the Results of the Assessment

The auditor should consider whether the assessment of the risk of material misstatement due to fraud indicates a need for an overall response; one that is specific to a particular account balance, class of transactions or assertions; or both.

EVALUATION OF AUDIT TESTS RESULTS

Prior to the completion of the audit, the auditor should consider whether the accumulated results of audit procedures and other observations affect the assessment of the risk of material misstatement due to fraud made when planning the audit.

When audit test results identify misstatements in the financial statements, the auditor should consider whether such misstatements may be indicative of fraud. When the auditor has determined that a misstatement is or may be the result of fraud, but the effect of the misstatement is not material to the financial statements, the auditor should evaluate the implications, especially those dealing with the organizational position of the employee(s) involved.

When the matter involves higher level management, even though the amount itself is not material to the financial statements, it may be indicative of a more pervasive problem. In such circumstances, the auditor should reevaluate the assessment of the risk of material misstatement due to fraud and its resulting impact on the audit.

According to AU 316.35, if the auditor has determined that the misstatement is, or may be, the result of fraud, and either has determined that the effect could be material to the financial statements or has been unable to evaluate whether the effect is material, the auditor should

1. Consider the implications for other aspects of the audit.
2. Discuss the matter and the approach to further investigation with an appropriate level of management that is at least one level above those involved and with senior management.
3. Attempt to obtain sufficient competent evidential matter to determine whether, in fact, material fraud exists, and, if so, its effect.
4. If appropriate, suggest that the client consult with legal counsel.

According to AU 316.16, the auditor's consideration of the risk of material misstatement due to fraud and the results of audit tests may indicate such a significant risk of fraud that the auditor should consider withdrawing from the engagement and communicating the reasons for withdrawal to the audit committee or others with equivalent authority and responsibility.

DOCUMENTATION OF THE AUDITOR'S RISK ASSESSMENT AND RESPONSE

According to AU 316.37, in planning the audit, the auditor should document evidence of the performance of the assessment of the risk of material misstatement due to fraud, including how fraud risk factors were considered. Where risk factors are identified, the documentation should include

1. Risk factors identified.
2. The auditor's response to those risk factors, individually or in combination.

If, during the performance of the audit, fraud risk factors or other conditions are identified that cause the auditor to believe that an additional response is required, such risk factors or other conditions, and any further response that the auditor concluded was appropriate, also should be documented.

COMMUNICATIONS ABOUT FRAUD TO MANAGEMENT, THE AUDIT COMMITTEE AND OTHERS

Whenever the auditor has determined that there is evidence that a fraud may exist, this should be brought to the attention of an appropriate level of management. Fraud involving senior management and fraud that causes a material misstatement of the financial statements should be reported directly to the audit committee or, in the case of a small business, to the owner-manager. In addition, the auditor should establish an understanding with the audit committee regarding the expected nature and extent of communications about misappropriations perpetrated by lower-level employees.

When the auditor has identified risk factors that have continuing control implications, the auditor should consider whether those factors are reportable conditions, and if they are, the auditor should report these factors to senior management and the audit committee.

The auditor is not ordinarily responsible for the disclosure of fraud to parties other than the client's senior management and its audit committee and ordinarily would be precluded by the auditor's ethical or legal obligations of confidentiality. The auditor should recognize, however, that in the following circumstances a duty to disclose outside the entity may exist.

1. To comply with certain legal and regulatory requirements. (For example, an intentional material misstatement of a financial statement may be a violation of securities laws and may be regarded as a material illegal act that requires disclosure to the SEC under Section 10A of the 1934 Act.)
2. To a successor auditor when the successor make inquiries in accordance with SAS 84, *Communications between Predecessor and Successor Auditors*, (Section 315).
3. In response to a subpoena.
4. To a funding agency or other specified agency in accordance with requirements for the audits of entities that receive governmental financial assistance.

INTERPRETATIONS

There are no interpretations for this section.

PROFESSIONAL ISSUES TASK FORCE PRACTICE ALERTS

98-2 Professional Skepticism and Related Topics

This Practice Alert provides guidance to practitioners in two areas that may warrant a relatively high level of professional skepticism and attention to audit evidence.

Review of nonstandard journal entries. Nonstandard journal entries are ones that are made outside the normal course of business, such as the provision for loan losses, provision for inventory obsolescence, and cut-off or period-end adjustments. Nonstandard journal entries may pose increased risk to the auditor in that they might conceal attempts by management to manipulate earnings and can be recorded in practically any account. (Because most accounting systems are computerized, nonstandard journal entries may be backdated and posted to months throughout the period in numerous transactions of relatively small amounts.)

To identify nonstandard journal entries, the auditor should consider whether the client has an established routine, or set of procedures, for processing transactions on a recurring basis. Since most processing involves a combination of manual and automated steps and procedures, the auditor may need to use computer-assisted audit techniques, such as report writers, software, or data-extraction tools and should follow the guidance in SAS 31, *Evidential Matter*, as amended by SAS 80.

Account balances which might be subject to misstatement may be identified by the auditor in assessing whether each significant account balance

- Contains journal entries processed outside the normal course of business.
- Contains transactions that are complex or unusual in nature.
- Contains estimates and period-end adjustments.
- Contains journal entries indicative of potential problems with the accounting systems.
- Has been prone to client error in the past.

- Has not been reconciled on a timely basis or contains old reconciling items.
- Represents a particular risk specific to the client's industry.
- Represents account balances affecting the client's value and liquidity.

Review of original and final versions of source documents rather than photocopies or draft versions in these two areas. SAS 82, *Consideration of Fraud in a Financial Statement Audit*, states that the unavailability of other than photocopied documents when original documents are expected to exist may pose a risk of material misstatement due to fraud. When presented with photocopied documents, the auditor should exercise professional skepticism and consider the need to obtain the original source documents to ensure conformity to the photocopied documents.

Similarly, a facsimile response may create risk for the auditor because it may be difficult to ascertain the source of the response. Section 330, "The Confirmation Process," states that to restrict the risk associated with facsimile responses and treat the confirmations as valid audit evidence, the auditor should consider taking certain precautions, such as

- Verifying the source and contents of the facsimile response in a telephone call to the purported sender.
- Requesting the purported sender to mail the original confirmation directly to the auditor.

The full text of this Practice Alert can be obtained from the AICPA website at www.aicpa.org/members/div/secps/lit/practice.htm.

98-3 Revenue Recognition Issues

A substantial portion of litigation against accounting firms reported to the AICPA SEC Practice Section Quality Control Inquiry Committee and a number of SEC Accounting and Auditing Enforcement Releases continue to involve revenue recognition issues. This Practice Alert

1. Reminds auditors of certain factors or conditions that are listed in the practice aids that can be indicative of increased audit risk of improper, aggressive or unusual revenue recognition practices.
2. Suggests ways that auditors may reduce the risk of failing to detect such practices. The alert suggests that to reduce such risk, the audit should be planned and executed with an appropriate degree of professional skepticism. In planning the audit, the auditor should obtain a sufficient understanding of the client's industry and business, its products, its marketing and sales policies and strategies, its internal control, and its accounting policies and procedures related to revenue recognition.

   An understanding of the revenue cycle is particularly important when

   - The entity has new product or service introductions or begins new sales arrangements.
   - The auditor is reviewing sales to distributors. The auditor should consider inquiring as to whether the client has offered to assist the distributor in placing the product with end users and whether concessions have been made with the distributor in the form of return product rights or other arrangements.

   This understanding is critical for determining the nature, timing, and extent of audit procedures to be applied and for assessing the extent of experience or supervision required of the personnel assigned to audit revenue transactions.

The alert also notes that well-planned analytical procedures performed during the planning process and the audit itself may be helpful in identifying situations that warrant additional consideration.

3. Provides guidance on confirmations and management representations related to revenue transactions. Since unusual or complex revenue transactions increase inherent risk, the auditor may need to consider performing additional audit procedures such as

   - Discussions with representatives of the client's sales, marketing, customer service and returns department.
   - Confirmations of sales terms.
   - Review of sales contracts.
   - Use of a specialist to interpret contractual agreements.

   Standard confirmation requests that confirm only the outstanding balance may not always provide sufficient audit evidence to determine whether revenue transactions have been recorded properly. Confirmations can be designed to solicit information from customers about

   - Payment terms.
   - Right-of return-privileges.
   - Continuing obligations on the part of the client.
   - Significant risks retained by the client.
   - Oral modifications or "side agreements" for unusual transactions.
   - Terms of individually significant revenue transactions.

   Auditors may also wish to obtain written representations from management concerning specific revenue recognition issues, such as the terms and conditions of unusual or complex sales agreements, confirmation that there are no contingencies that affect the obligation of customers to pay for merchandise purchased, or the existence of any side agreements.

4. Refers to professional guidance which addresses the accounting considerations for revenue recognition, such as

   - FASB Concept Statement 5, *Recognition and Measurement in Financial Statements of Business Enterprises.*
   - Accounting Research Bulletin 45, *Long-Term Construction-Type Contracts.*
   - Statement of Financial Accounting Standards 48, *Revenue Recognition When Right of Return Exists.*
   - AICPA Statement of Position (SOP) 81-1, *Accounting for Performance of Construction-Type and Certain Production-Type Contracts.*
   - AICPA SOP 97-2, *Software Revenue Recognition.*
   - SEC Accounting and Auditing Enforcement Release 108 (states that recognition of revenue on "bill and hold" transactions, prior to shipment or exchange with the customer, is a departure from the "general rule of revenue recognition," and is appropriate only if certain conditions described in Release 108 are met)
   - Various other Emerging Issues Task Force abstracts which provide guidance on specific revenue recognition issues.

5. Reminds auditors of their responsibilities to communicate with the board of directors and audit committees.

   The communication by the auditor to the board of directors/audit committee should include a discussion related to revenue recognition practices of the company, including matters such as a change in the company's revenue recognition policy, a lack of involvement by the accounting/finance department in sales transactions or in the monitoring of arrangements with distributors, significant sales or volume of sales that are recorded at or near the end of the reporting period, sales terms that do not comply with the company's normal policies, etc. The SEC Practice Section has developed best practices guidance on communications with board of directors/audit committees, which includes recommendations regarding the following:

- The establishment of firm policies and procedures for communications with board of directors/audit committees.
- The establishment of a relationship with board of directors/audit committees which fosters candid and open discussions.
- The nature of communication by the auditor regarding the qualitative assessment of the company's accounting principles and the clarity of the company's financial statement disclosures.
- The timing of when such communication should occur.

The SEC Practice Section best practices guidance can be obtained from the AICPA website at www.aicpa.org/members/div/secps/lit/best/index.htm. The full text of this Practice Alert can be obtained from the AICPA website at www.aicpa.org/members/div/secps/lit/practice.htm.

TECHNIQUES FOR APPLICATION

Description and Characteristics of Fraud

Although fraud is a broad legal concept, the auditor's interest specifically relates to fraudulent acts that cause a material misstatement of financial statements. Two types of misstatements are relevant to the auditor's consideration in a financial statement audit.

1. Misstatements arising from fraudulent financial reporting.
2. Misstatements arising from misappropriation of assets.

Fraudulent financial reporting and misappropriation of assets differ in that fraudulent financial reporting is committed, usually by management, to deceive financial statement users while misappropriation of assets is committed against an entity, most often by employees.

Fraud frequently involves the following:

1. A pressure or an incentive to commit fraud.
2. A perceived opportunity to do so.

These two conditions usually are present for both types of fraud.

Although fraud usually is concealed, the presence of risk factors or other conditions may alert the auditor to its possible existence.

Fraud Risk Factors

Fraud risk factors may come to the auditor's attention while performing procedures relating to acceptance or continuance of clients, during engagement planning or obtaining an understanding of an entity's internal control, or while conducting fieldwork. Accordingly, the assessment of the risk of material misstatement due to fraud is a cumulative process that includes a consideration of risk factors individually and in combination. As noted earlier, assessment of fraud risk factors is not a simple matter of counting the factors present and converting to a level of fraud risk. A few or even a single risk factor may heighten significantly the risk of fraud.

RESPONDING TO THE FRAUD RISK ASSESSMENT

In some cases, even though some of the fraud risk factors are identified as being present, the auditor's judgment may be that audit procedures otherwise planned are sufficient to respond to the risk factors, individually or in combination. In other circumstances, the auditor may conclude that the conditions indicate a need to modify procedures. The auditor also may conclude that it is not practicable to modify the procedures sufficiently to address the risk, in which case withdrawal and communication to the appropriate parties may be appropriate.

Judgments about the risk of material misstatement due to fraud may affect the audit in the following ways:

1. **Professional skepticism.** Due professional care requires the auditor to exercise professional skepticism, that is, an attitude that includes a questioning mind and critical assessment of audit evidence.
2. **Assignment of personnel.** The knowledge, skill, and ability of personnel assigned significant engagement responsibilities should be commensurate with the assessment of the level of risk of the engagement. In addition, the extent of supervision should recognize the risk of material misstatement due to fraud and the qualifications of persons performing the work.
3. **Accounting principles and policies.** The auditor may conclude that there is a risk of fraudulent financial reporting that requires the auditor to consider further management's selection and application of significant accounting policies, particularly those related to revenue recognition, asset valuation, or capitalizing vs. expensing.
4. **Controls.** When a risk of material misstatement due to fraud relates to risk factors that may have control implications, the auditor's ability to assess control risk below the maximum may be reduced.

The nature, timing, and extent of procedures may need to be modified in the following ways:

1. The **nature** of audit procedures may need to be changed to obtain evidence that is more reliable or obtain additional corroborative information.
2. The **timing** of substantive tests may need to be altered to be closer to, or at, year-end.
3. The **extent** of the procedures applied should reflect the assessment of the risk of material misstatement due to fraud.

DOCUMENTATION REQUIREMENTS

SAS 82 requires the auditor to document **evidence of the performance** of the assessment of the risk of material misstatement due to fraud. The auditor is **not** required to quantify the assessment (for example, as "high" or "low"), or to describe how he or she made the assessment.

To document evidence of performance of this fraud risk assessment, the workpapers should clearly indicate

1. The risk factors identified as present.
2. The auditor's response to those risk factors.
3. If, during the performance of the audit, additional fraud risk factors or other conditions come to the auditor's attention and these cause the auditor to believe that an additional audit response is required, those risk factors and other conditions, and

any further response that the auditor concluded was appropriate, also should be documented.

Although not required, it is good practice to document the inquiries (and responses) made by the auditor of management

1. Regarding the risk of fraud in the entity.
2. Whether management has knowledge of fraud that has been perpetrated.
3. If the entity has a program that includes steps to prevent, deter and detect fraud, whether the program has identified any fraud risk factors.

In planning the audit, the auditor will most likely use a list of fraud risk factors to serve as a "memory jogger." This list may be taken from the examples listed in the next section (*Illustrations*), or the examples provided may be tailored to the client. The documentation of this list of fraud risk factors considered is **not** required, but represents good practice.

NOTE: The AICPA's implementation aid, ***Considering Fraud in a Financial Statement Audit: Practical Guidance for Applying SAS No. 82,*** *presents industry-specific fraud risk factors and guidance for (1) banks, savings institutions, and credit unions, (2) brokers and dealers in securities, (3) employee benefit plans, (4) governmental entities, (5) health care organizations, (6) insurance companies, (7) investment companies, (8) not-for-profit organizations, (9) public utilities, (10) real estate entities, and (11) small privately owned businesses.*

During the planning and performance of the audit, the auditor may identify some of the fraud risk factors from the list as being present at the client. Of those risk factors present, some will be addressed sufficiently by the planned audit procedures; others may require the auditor to extend audit procedures. SAS 82 requires the auditor to document **all risk factors identified as present** (and the response) regardless of whether the presence of those risk factors requires modification in the planned audit approach.

REQUIRED ACTIONS/COMMUNICATION REQUIRED FOR DISCOVERED FRAUD

When the auditor discovers or suspects fraud, the actions and communications required by SAS 82 are somewhat complex, especially when an SEC client is involved. The actions/communications required by Title III of the Private Securities Litigation Reform Act of 1995, by the SEC Practice Section (SECPS) for its members, and by the SEC in Form 8-K add to the complexity.

To operationalize SAS 82, and to also give appropriate consideration to the SEC and SECPS requirements, the best approach is to decide which of the following three situations governs and follow the guidance presented below for the applicable situation.

Situation 1.

SAS 82 Actions/Communications Requirements for Material Fraud + Any Fraud Involving Senior Management for Non-SEC Clients

Auditor should

1. Consider implications for other aspects of audit.
2. Reevaluate the assessment of the risk of fraud.
3. Discuss matter and the approach to further investigation with appropriate level of management.
4. Obtain additional evidential matter, including suggesting that client consult with legal counsel.
5. Consider whether any risk factors identified represent reportable conditions (Section 325).

6. Consider withdrawing from the engagement and communicating reasons to the audit committee (or board of directors, etc.).
7. Report the fraud to the audit committee or, in a small business, to the owner-manager.

   NOTE: If perpetrator controls audit committee or board of directors, go directly to client's legal counsel. If perpetrator is a general partner acting against interest of limited partners, obtain legal advice and consider communicating to limited partners. If perpetrator is owner-manager of a small business, auditor has little choice but to communicate with perpetrator and has no obvious course of action but to withdraw. However, first the auditor should consult with his or her legal counsel.

8. Insist that the financial statements be revised and, if they are not, express a qualified or adverse opinion. If precluded from obtaining needed evidence, disclaim an opinion or withdraw.

Situation 2.

Actions/Communications Requirements for Material Fraud + Any Fraud Involving Senior Management for SEC Clients

Auditor should

1. Follow steps in Situation 1. checklist (SAS 82 requirements) + additional items 2. - 4. below.
2. Consider Section 10A(b) of the Securities Exchange Act of 1934 (Title III, Private Securities Litigation Reform Act of 1995).
   a. Matter is reported to board of directors and it does not take appropriate action.
   b. Auditor concludes that failure to take remedial action is expected to cause departure from standard audit report or cause withdrawal.
   c. Auditor should report conclusion in b. above to board of directors (e.g., on Monday).
   d. Client is required to notify SEC (within one business day) of auditor's conclusion described in b. above (e.g., by Tuesday).
   e. Client is required to furnish report to SEC in d. above to auditor within one business day (e.g., by Tuesday).
   f. If auditor doesn't receive report in e. above, auditor notifies SEC within one business day following failure to receive (e.g., on Wednesday).
3. For SEC Practice Section members, if auditor withdraws or resigns from engagement, auditor must send copy of resignation to the SEC within five business days.
4. Follow SEC requirements for reporting on Form 8-K.
   a. Upon auditor's withdrawal, client must disclose within five business days[2] the following information on a Form 8-K, filed with the SEC, with a copy to the auditor on the same day
      - Auditor's resignation.
      - Auditor's conclusion that the information coming to his/her attention **has a material impact** on the fairness or reliability of the client's financial state-

---

[2] *Practitioners with publicly-traded clients should be aware that the SEC is proposing modifications to the Form 8-K requirements. The proposals would shorten the filing deadline for Form 8-K to two business days after an event triggering the form's disclosure requirements. (The proposals will also expand the list of significant events requiring disclosure in Form 8-K.) Practitioners should monitor the status of the proposed rules at www.sec.gov.*

ments or audit report and that this matter was not resolved to the auditor's satisfaction before resignation.

b. Auditor must prepare a letter stating agreement or disagreement with client's statements after reading Form 8-K. If auditor disagrees, he/she must disclose differences of opinion in a letter to client as promptly as possible. Client must then file the letter with the SEC within ten business days after filing the Form 8-K. Notwithstanding the ten-business-day requirement, client has two business days from the date of receipt to file the letter with the SEC.

Situation 3.

SAS 82 Actions/Communication Requirements for Immaterial Fraud + Not Involving Senior Management for All Clients (Public and Nonpublic)

Auditor should

1. Evaluate implications for other aspects of audit, especially organizational position of persons involved.
2. Bring to attention of, and discuss with, appropriate level of management (even if inconsequential).
3. Communicate matter to audit committee unless matter is clearly below communication threshold previously agreed to by auditor and the audit committee.
4. Consider whether any risk factors identified represent reportable conditions (Section 325).

ILLUSTRATIONS

ILLUSTRATION 1. RISK FACTORS—FRAUDULENT FINANCIAL REPORTING

The following are examples of risk factors from SAS 82 relating to misstatements arising from fraudulent financial reporting:

1. Risk factors relating to management's characteristics and influence over the control environment. Examples include
   - A motivation for management to engage in fraudulent financial reporting. Specific indicators might include
     - A significant portion of management's compensation represented by bonuses, stock options, or other incentives, the value of which is contingent upon the entity achieving unduly aggressive targets for operating results, financial position, or cash flow.
     - An excessive interest by management in maintaining or increasing the entity's stock price or earnings trend through the use of unusually aggressive accounting practices.
     - A practice by management of committing to analysts, creditors, and other third parties to achieve what appear to be unduly aggressive or clearly unrealistic forecasts.
     - An interest by management in pursuing inappropriate means to minimize reported earnings for tax-motivated reasons.
   - A failure by management to display and communicate an appropriate attitude regarding internal control and the financial reporting process. Specific indicators might include
     - An ineffective means of communicating and supporting the entity's values or ethics, or communication of inappropriate values or ethics.
     - Domination of management by a single person or small group without compensating controls such as effective oversight by the board of directors or audit committee.
     - Inadequate monitoring of significant controls.
     - Management failing to correct known reportable conditions on a timely basis.
     - Management setting unduly aggressive financial targets and expectations for operating personnel.
     - Management displaying a significant disregard for regulatory authorities.
     - Management continuing to employ an ineffective accounting, information technology, or internal auditing staff.

- Nonfinancial management's excessive participation in, or preoccupation with, the selection of accounting principles or the determination of significant estimates.
- High turnover of senior management, counsel, or board members.
- Strained relationship between management and the current or predecessor auditor. Specific indicators might include
  - Frequent disputes with the current or predecessor auditor on accounting, auditing, or reporting matters.
  - Unreasonable demands on the auditor including unreasonable time constraints regarding the completion of the audit or the issuance of the auditor's reports.
  - Formal or informal restrictions on the auditor that inappropriately limit his or her access to people or information, or his or her ability to communicate effectively with the board of directors or the audit committee.
  - Domineering management behavior in dealing with the auditor, especially involving attempts to influence the scope of the auditor's work.
- Known history of securities law violations or claims against the entity or its senior management alleging fraud or violations of securities laws.

2. Risk factors relating to industry conditions. Examples include
   - New accounting, statutory, or regulatory requirements that could impair the financial stability or profitability of the entity.
   - High degree of competition or market saturation, accompanied by declining margins.
   - Declining industry with increasing business failures and significant declines in customer demand.
   - Rapid changes in the industry, such as high vulnerability to rapidly changing technology or rapid product obsolescence.
3. Risk factors relating to operating characteristics and financial stability. Examples include
   - Inability to generate cash flows from operations while reporting earnings and earnings growth.
   - Significant pressure to obtain additional capital necessary to stay competitive considering the financial position of the entity—including need for funds to finance major research and development or capital expenditures.
   - Assets, liabilities, revenues, or expenses based on significant estimates that involve unusually subjective judgments or uncertainties, or that are subject to potential significant change in the near term in a manner that may have a financially disruptive effect on the entity, such as ultimate collectibility of receivables, timing of revenue recognition, realizability of financial instruments based on the highly subjective valuation or collateral of difficult-to-assess repayment sources, or significant deferral of costs.
   - Significant related-party transactions not in the ordinary course of business or with related entities not audited or audited by another firm.
   - Significant, unusual, or highly complex transactions, especially those close to year-end, that pose difficult "substance over form" questions.
   - Significant bank accounts or subsidiary or branch operations in tax-haven jurisdictions for which there appears to be no clear business justification.
   - Overly complex organizational structure involving numerous or unusual legal entities, managerial lines of authority, or contractual arrangements without apparent business purpose.
   - Difficulty in determining the organization or individual(s) that control(s) the entity.
   - Unusually rapid growth or profitability, especially compared with that of other entities in the same industry.
   - Especially high vulnerability to changes in interest rates.
   - Unusually high dependence on debt or marginal ability to meet debt repayment requirements; debt covenants that are difficult to maintain.
   - Unrealistically aggressive sales or profitability incentive programs.
   - Threat of imminent bankruptcy or foreclosure, or hostile takeover.
   - Adverse consequences on significant pending transactions, such as a business combination or contract award, if poor financial results are reported.
   - Poor or deteriorating financial position when management has personally guaranteed significant debts of the entity.

Illustration 2. Risk Factors—Misappropriation of Assets

The following are examples of risk factors from SAS 82 relating to misstatements arising from misappropriation of assets:

1. Risk factors relating to susceptibility of assets to misappropriation
   - Large amounts of cash on hand or processed.
   - Inventory characteristics, such as small size, high value, or high demand.
   - Easily convertible assets, such as bearer bonds, diamonds, or computer chips.
   - Fixed asset characteristics, such as small size, marketability, or lack of ownership identification.
2. Risk factors relating to controls
   - Lack of appropriate management oversight (for example, inadequate supervision or monitoring of remote locations).
   - Lack of job applicant screening procedures relating to employees with access to assets susceptible to misappropriation.
   - Inadequate recordkeeping with respect to assets susceptible to misappropriation.
   - Lack of appropriate segregation of duties or independent checks.
   - Lack of appropriate system of authorization and approval of transactions (for example, in purchasing).
   - Poor physical safeguards over cash, investments, inventory, or fixed assets.
   - Lack of timely and appropriate documentation for transactions (for example, credits for merchandise returns).
   - Lack of mandatory vacations for employees performing key control functions.

As noted earlier, fraud risk factors are not readily susceptible to a quantitative analysis. The auditor has to qualitatively translate the factors present into an assessed level of fraud risk and consider the appropriate audit response. A few or a single factor may be important in a particular situation.

317 ILLEGAL ACTS BY CLIENTS

EFFECTIVE DATE AND APPLICABILITY

Original Pronouncement	SAS 54, April 1988.
Effective Date	Audits of financial statements for periods beginning on or after January 1, 1989.
Applicability	Audits of financial statements in accordance with generally accepted auditing standards.

DEFINITIONS OF TERMS

Illegal acts. Violations of laws or governmental regulations. For purposes of this section, a distinction is made between the following types of illegal acts:

- Illegal acts with a direct and material effect on determination of financial statement amounts.
- Other illegal acts.

OBJECTIVES OF SECTION

Illegal acts are so diverse that articulating the auditor's responsibility for their detection and reporting has proven to be very complex. Some laws and regulations such as the Internal Revenue Code regulations concerning income tax expense clearly fall within the auditor's expertise, and the audit of financial statements normally includes testing compliance with such laws and regulations. Other laws and regulations such as those on occupational safety and health or food and drug administration are clearly outside the auditor's expertise and are not susceptible to testing by customary auditing procedures. Some laws and regulations fall in between these extremes.

Simple criteria for distinguishing those laws and regulations that should be of greater concern to the auditor have not been found. The materiality of the consequences of violation is not suitable. Many laws and regulations outside the auditor's expertise and not susceptible to audit testing could have consequences very material to the financial statements if violated. Even the relation to financial matters is not conclusive. For example, laws concerning securities trading are financially related, but involve complex legal concepts.

This section takes the approach of dividing illegal acts into two broad categories or types. The auditor's responsibility for detection of illegal acts differs depending on the type of illegal act. The auditor's responsibility to detect misstatements resulting from illegal acts having a direct and material effect on the determination of financial statement amounts (except disclosure of contingencies) is the same as that for errors (see Section 312) and fraud (see Section 316). For other illegal acts, the auditor should be aware of the possibility that such illegal acts may have occurred. If specific information comes to the auditor's attention that such acts may have occurred, the auditor should apply audit procedures specifically directed to ascertaining whether an illegal act has occurred. However, an audit in accordance with generally accepted auditing standards provides no assurance that illegal acts will be detected or that any contingent liabilities that may result will be disclosed.

In other respects, this section is essentially the same as the one it replaced (superceded SAS 17). The requirements are directed primarily to what the auditor should do when a possible illegal act comes to his or her attention and there is no general obligation to apply any audit procedures specifically designed to detect illegal acts.

FUNDAMENTAL REQUIREMENTS[1]

AUDIT PROCEDURES ABSENT EVIDENCE OF POSSIBLE ILLEGAL ACTS

An audit does not normally include audit procedures specifically designed to detect illegal acts. However, audit procedures may bring possible illegal acts to the auditor's attention. The auditor should be aware of the possibility that illegal acts may have occurred. If information indicates that illegal acts may have occurred, the auditor should apply audit procedures to address the matter.

The auditor should ask management about the client's compliance with laws and regulations. Where applicable, the auditor should also ask management about

1. Policies relating to prevention of illegal acts.
2. Use of directives issued by the client.
3. Periodic representations obtained by the client from management at appropriate levels of authority concerning compliance with laws and regulations.

The auditor also ordinarily obtains written representations from management concerning the absence of violations or possible violations of laws or regulations whose effects should be considered for disclosure in the financial statements or as a basis for recording a loss contingency (see Section 333). The auditor does not need to perform any further procedures in this area absent specific information concerning possible illegal acts.

EVIDENCE OF POSSIBLE ILLEGAL ACTS

According to AU 317.09, the auditor should be aware that specific information such as the following may raise a question concerning possible illegal acts:

1. Violations of laws or regulations cited in reports of examinations by regulatory agencies that have been made available to the auditor.
2. Large payments for unspecified services to consultants, affiliates, or employees.
3. Failure to file tax returns or pay government duties or similar fees that are common to the entity's industry or the nature of its business.

RESPONSE TO POSSIBLE ILLEGAL ACTS

According to AU 317.10, when the auditor becomes aware of information concerning a possible illegal act, the auditor should obtain an understanding of the nature of the act, the circumstances in which it occurred, and sufficient other information to evaluate the effect on the financial statements.

The auditor should inquire of management at a level above those involved, if possible. If management does not provide satisfactory information that there has been no illegal act, the auditor should

---

[1] *The requirements apply to those illegal acts with an indirect and contingent effect. Those illegal acts with a direct and material effect are treated the same as errors (see Section 312) or fraud (see Section 316).*

1. Consult with the client's legal counsel (with the client's permission) or other specialists about the application of relevant laws and regulations to the circumstances and the possible effects on the financial statements.
2. Apply additional procedures, if necessary, to obtain further understanding of the nature of the acts. The additional procedures might include
   a. Examining supporting documents, such as invoices.
   b. Confirming significant information with other parties to the transaction.
   c. Determining if the transaction was properly authorized.
   d. Considering whether other similar transactions may have occurred.
   e. Applying procedures to identify other similar transactions.

Evaluation of Detected or Expected Illegal Acts

The auditor should consider the quantitative and qualitative aspects of the illegal act. Loss contingencies resulting from illegal acts that may be required to be disclosed should be evaluated similar to other loss contingencies.

The auditor should consider the implications of an illegal act for the rest of the audit, particularly whether the auditor can rely on client representations. Factors to consider include the relationship of the perpetration and concealment, if any, of the illegal act to specific control procedures and the level of management or employees involved.

Effect on the Audit Report

According to AU 313.18, if the auditor concludes that an illegal act has a material effect on the financial statements and the act has not been properly accounted for or disclosed, the auditor should express a qualified or an adverse opinion.

According to AU 313.19, if the auditor is precluded by the client from obtaining sufficient competent evidential matter to evaluate whether an illegal act that could be material to the financial statements has occurred, or is likely to have occurred, the auditor generally should disclaim an opinion.

Consideration of Withdrawal

If the client refuses to accept the auditor's report as modified because of an illegal act, the auditor should withdraw from the engagement and indicate the reasons for withdrawal in writing to the audit committee or to the board of directors.

Even when the illegal act is not material to the financial statements, the auditor may decide to withdraw from the engagement when the client does not take the remedial action the auditor considers necessary in the circumstances.

Internal Communications

The auditor should be sure that the audit committee or others with equivalent authority and responsibility are adequately informed about illegal acts that come to the auditor's attention. The communication should describe the act, the circumstances of its occurrence, and the effect on the financial statements.

The auditor need not communicate matters that are clearly inconsequential and may reach agreement in advance with the audit committee on the nature of such matters to be communicated. The communication may be oral or written, but if oral, it should be documented in audit workpapers.

If senior management is involved in an illegal act, the auditor should communicate directly with the audit committee.

EXTERNAL COMMUNICATIONS

The auditor is not ordinarily responsible for disclosing an illegal act outside the client's organization and such disclosure would be precluded by the auditor's ethical or legal obligation of confidentiality, unless the matter affects his opinion on the financial statements. The auditor should recognize, however, that in the following circumstances, a duty to notify parties outside the client may exist:

1. To the SEC when the client reports an auditor change on Form 8-K (or to comply with other legal and regulatory requirements, such as the Private Securities Litigation Reform Act of 1995, i.e., Section 10A of the 1934 Act).
2. To a successor auditor under Section 315.
3. To a court in response to a subpoena.
4. To a funding agency or other specified agency in audits of entities that receive financial assistance from a government agency.

INTERPRETATIONS

CONSIDERATION OF INTERNAL CONTROL IN A FINANCIAL STATEMENT AUDIT AND THE FOREIGN CORRUPT PRACTICES ACT (OCTOBER 1978)

An auditor of an entity subject to the Securities Exchange Act of 1934 is not required to expand the consideration of internal control because of the Foreign Corrupt Practices Act of 1977.

MATERIAL WEAKNESSES IN INTERNAL CONTROL AND THE FOREIGN CORRUPT PRACTICES ACT (OCTOBER 1978)

A specific material weakness in internal control may be a violation of the Foreign Corrupt Practices Act and also an illegal act. In this situation, the auditor should consult with the client's legal counsel to determine if the material weakness is a violation. After consulting with management and legal counsel

a. If management has concluded that corrective action is not cost-beneficial, the auditor should consider the underlying reasons.
b. If a determination is made that there has been a violation of the Act and appropriate consideration is not given to the violation, the auditor should consider withdrawing from the engagement or dissociating from any future relation with the client.

A violation of the internal control provisions of the Act would not have a direct effect on the financial statements, but the contingent monetary fine could be material to the financial statements.

TECHNIQUES FOR APPLICATION

DISTINCTION BETWEEN RESPONSIBILITY FOR DETECTION OF ILLEGAL ACTS AND FRAUD

The auditor should plan and perform the audit to provide reasonable assurance that material fraud will be detected. The same responsibility applies to material, direct-effect illegal acts. An intentional material misstatement or omission in financial information filed with the SEC is a violation of federal securities laws and should be regarded as a material illegal act. However, the appropriate guidance for the audit approach to these matters is SAS 82 (Section 316). For indirect-effect illegal acts, the auditor should be aware of the possibility that such illegal acts may have occurred. If a possible indirect-effect illegal act having a material effect on the financial statements is detected, the auditor should apply specific procedures to determine if an illegal act has occurred. Examples of customary audit procedures that might bring possible illegal acts to the auditor's attention include

1. Reading minutes.
2. Making inquiries of management and legal counsel concerning litigation, claims, and assessments.
3. Performing substantive tests of sensitive transactions.
4. Making inquiries of management concerning compliance with laws and regulations.
5. Obtaining a representation letter that includes comments concerning the absence of violations of laws and regulations.

Required Procedures

In spite of the fact that this section states that the auditor does not apply procedures specifically directed to the detection of illegal acts, there are some required procedures. The required procedures are

1. Inquire of management concerning the client's compliance with laws and regulations.
2. If applicable, inquire of management concerning
   a. Policies on prevention of illegal acts and
   b. Use of directives and periodic representations obtained from management at appropriate levels of authority concerning compliance with laws and regulations.

AU 317.08 also mentions that written representations concerning the absence of illegal acts are usually included in the management representation letter.

A question that often arises in practice is whether obtaining a management representation letter meets the separately stated requirement to inquire of management concerning the client's compliance with laws and regulations. Practice differs on this point. Some auditors obtain the typical written representations from management and make no separate oral inquiries on illegal acts.

Other auditors believe it is prudent to make separate inquiries near the conclusion of the audit. As part of the closing conference with the client, they obtain additional oral assurances from the client on the absence of violations of laws and regulations. This oral communication is intended to evoke candor and stress the importance the auditor attaches to being fully informed on such matters. Because SAS 82 does require the auditor to inquire about fraud, in practice the inquiries about fraud and illegal acts are typically combined. These inquiries are a separate audit step and are normally documented in the audit program or other working papers.

The inquiries concerning policies on illegal acts and use of directives and obtaining written representations from management personnel are required only when applicable. For example, if management personnel are required to complete a questionnaire on compliance with a code of conduct, it would be prudent for the auditor to become familiar with the process and review returned questionnaires. However, if an entity does not have a code of conduct or does not require management personnel to make representations on compliance, the entity's policies and procedures are not necessarily deficient.

319 CONSIDERATION OF INTERNAL CONTROL IN A FINANCIAL STATEMENT AUDIT[1, 2]

EFFECTIVE DATE AND APPLICABILITY

Original Pronouncement	SAS 55, April 1988; as amended by SAS 78, December 1995; and SAS 94, May 2001.
Effective Date	Originally effective for audits of financial statements for periods beginning on or after January 1, 1990; revised to reflect SAS 78, effective for audits on or after January 1, 1997; and SAS 94, effective for audits of financial statements for periods beginning on or after June 1, 2001, with early application permitted.
Applicability	Audits of financial statements in accordance with generally accepted auditing standards.

---

[1] *Section 404, "Management Assessment of Internal Controls" of the Sarbanes-Oxley Act of 2002, and the related SEC implementing rules require that all public company annual reports on Form 10-K include a report containing a statement of management's responsibility to establish and maintain internal control over financial reporting, and an assessment, as of the end of the company's most recent fiscal year, of the effectiveness of those controls. The company's auditors must attest to and report on management's assessment of the effectiveness of internal control. The Act states that these attestations will not be separate engagements. A company that is an "accelerated filer" (Exchange Act Rule 12b-2) must comply with Section 404 at the end of its first fiscal year ending on or after June 15, 2004. Other companies, including foreign private issuers, must comply on or after April 15, 2005.*

[2] *The Auditing Standards Board has issued Exposure Drafts of seven proposed SASs that relate to the risk assessment process that would supercede the guidance in this section. A summary of key changes is provided immediately before Section 100-230. The Public Company Accounting Oversight Board (PCAOB) has replaced the ASB as the standards-setting authority for public company audits. Therefore, the ASB's Exposure Drafts will not be issued as final standards by the AICPA. The documents will, however, be considered by the PCAOB in developing new standards or amendments to existing standards. Please check for updates to this section on the John Wiley & Sons, Inc. website at www.wiley.com/gaas.*

DEFINITIONS OF TERMS

Internal control. A process effected by an entity's board of directors, management, and other personnel that is designed to provide reasonable assurance about the achievement of the entity's objectives in the following categories:

1. Reliability of financial reporting.
2. Effectiveness and efficiency of operations.
3. Compliance with applicable laws and regulations.

Components of internal control. The five interrelated components of internal control are

1. Control environment.
2. Risk assessment.
3. Control activities.
4. Information and communication systems support.
5. Monitoring.

Control environment. The tone of an entity that influences the control consciousness of its people. It is the foundation for all other components of internal control, providing discipline and structure.

Risk assessment. From a financial reporting perspective, an entity's risk assessment is its identification, analysis, and management of risks relevant to the preparation of financial statements.

Control activities. The policies and procedures that help ensure that management directives are carried out.

Information and communication. The information system which includes the accounting system that consists of the methods and records that the entity has to record, process, summarize, and report entity transactions, events, and conditions, and to maintain accountability for the related assets, liabilities, and equity.

Monitoring. A process to assess whether controls are operating as intended and whether they are modified as appropriate for changes in conditions.

Risk of material misstatement in financial statement assertions. The product of inherent risk and control risk.

Inherent risk. The susceptibility of an assertion to a material misstatement assuming there are no related internal controls.

Control risk. The risk that a material misstatement that could occur in an assertion will not be prevented or detected on a timely basis by the entity's internal control.

Detection risk. The risk that the auditor will not detect a material misstatement that exists in an assertion.

Tests of controls. Procedures directed toward either the (1) effectiveness of the design or (2) operation of an internal control procedure.

Placed in operation. An internal control procedure that is actually being used by the entity.

Tests of controls directed toward effectiveness of design. Procedures concerned with whether an internal control procedure is suitably designed to prevent or detect material misstatements in specific financial statement assertions. Tests of controls used for generating evidence about effectiveness of design include inquiries of appropriate entity personnel, inspection of documents and reports, and observation of the application of specific controls.

Tests of controls directed toward operating effectiveness. Procedures concerned with how an internal control procedure was applied, the consistency with which it was applied during the audit period, and by whom it was applied. Tests of controls used for generating evidence about operating effectiveness include inquiries, inspection, observation, and reperformance of the application of the control.

Assessed level of control risk. The conclusion reached as a result of assessing control risk. Control risk may be assessed at the maximum level or at some level below the maximum if supported by appropriate tests of controls.

Maximum level of assessed control risk. The greatest probability that a material misstatement that could occur in a financial statement assertion will not be prevented or detected on a timely basis by an entity's internal control.

Information technology (IT). IT encompasses automated means of originating, processing, storing, and communicating information, and includes recording devices, communication systems, computer systems (including hardware and software components and data), and other electronic devices. (The auditor is primarily interested in the entity's use of IT to initiate, record, process, and report transactions or other financial data.)

Application controls. Control activities that apply to the processing of individual applications (e.g., edit checks of input data, sequence checks, manual follow-up of exception reports).

General controls. Control activities that relate to many applications and that support application controls (e.g., controls over data center and network operations, access security, and systems and software acquisitions and maintenance).

OBJECTIVES OF SECTION

This section originally superseded Section 320, "The Auditor's Study and Evaluation of Internal Control." It was issued and then amended in 1995 by SAS 78, *Consideration of Internal Control in a Financial Statement Audit: An Amendment to Statement on Auditing Standards No. 55,* (1) to broaden and clarify the auditor's responsibility to understand and assess internal control in an audit; and (2) to incorporate the definition and description of internal control contained in *Internal Control-Integrated Framework*, published by the Committee of Sponsoring Organizations of the Treadway Commission (COSO Report). The primary new concepts articulated after issuance of Section 320 are control risk, financial statement assertions, and COSO terminology. Their incorporation into the literature results in a complete change in the terminology related to the auditor's responsibility to gather information about and evaluate the client's controls.

The key changes subsequent to Section 320 are as follows:

- The concept of internal control is replaced with a broader concept of internal control that consists of the control environment, risk assessment, control activities, information and communication, and monitoring.
- The auditor is required to obtain an understanding of the five components of internal control (listed above) to the extent necessary to plan the audit.
- The auditor's responsibility for internal control is discussed in terms of control risk as defined in SAS 47 (312) and financial statement assertions as defined in SAS 31 (326).

The changes made subsequent to Section 320 resulted in a revision of the second standard of fieldwork of the ten generally accepted auditing standards. The revised standard is worded as follows:

> *A sufficient understanding of internal control is to be obtained to plan the audit and to determine the nature, timing, and extent of the tests to be performed.*

The second standard of fieldwork implicitly relates the extent of the understanding that is necessary to the need to plan the audit effectively.

The objectives behind the change were diverse, but involved primarily the following matters:

- Shifting to a focus on risk assessment makes clear that the auditor does not make a yes or no decision to rely or not rely on controls. The risk level can be assessed anywhere along a continuum from maximum (100%) to a relatively low level.
- Requiring an understanding of all five components of internal control in all audits will help ensure that the auditor has a sufficient understanding of the potential misstatements that can occur to design effective substantive tests.

The auditor should obtain a sufficient understanding of internal control to recognize the potential material misstatements and design substantive tests effective in detecting those misstatements.

In May 2001, SAS 94, *The Effect of Information Technology on the Auditor's Consideration of Internal Control in a Financial Statement Audit,* was issued to amend SAS 55. The SAS provides guidance to auditors about the effect of information technology (IT) on internal control, and on the auditor's understanding of internal control and assessment of control risk. Among other things, SAS 94

1. States that it may not be practical or possible to restrict detection risk to an acceptable level by performing only substantive tests for a given assertion, especially when evidence exists only in electronic form.
2. Requires the auditor to obtain evidence about the accuracy and completeness of information in circumstances where the auditor is performing only substantive tests in restricting detection risk to an acceptable level and where the information used by the auditor to perform such substantive tests is produced by the entity's information system.
3. Requires the auditor to consider whether information technology specialized skills are needed for the audit.
4. Requires that the auditor gain an understanding of the automated and manual procedures an entity uses to prepare financial statements and related disclosures, and how misstatements may occur. This understanding should include
   a. The procedures for entering transaction totals into the general ledger,
   b. The procedures for initiating, recording, and processing journal entries in the general ledger, including standard journal entries required on a recurring basis and nonstandard journal entries to record nonrecurring or unusual transactions or adjustments, and
   c. The procedures for recording recurring and nonrecurring adjustments to the financial statements that are not reflected in formal journal entries, such as consolidating adjustments, report combinations, and reclassifications.

FUNDAMENTAL REQUIREMENTS

BASIC REQUIREMENT

In all audits, the auditor should obtain a sufficient understanding of each of the five components of internal control (control environment, risk assessment, control activities, information systems support, communication, and monitoring) to plan the audit by performing procedures to

1. Understand the design of controls relevant to audit planning.
2. Determine whether they have been placed in operation.

NOTE: Controls that are relevant to an audit usually pertain to the reliability of the entity's external financial statements.

APPLICATION OF THE FIVE COMPONENTS TO A FINANCIAL STATEMENT AUDIT

The five components should be considered in the context of the entity's

1. Size.
2. Organization and ownership characteristics.
3. Business.
4. Diversity and complexity of operations.
5. Applicable legal and regulatory requirements.
6. The nature and complexity of the systems that are part of the entity's internal control, including the use of service organizations (see Section 324).

NOTE: The auditor's primary focus is on whether a control affects financial statement assertions, not its classification into one of the five components of control.

LIMITATIONS OF INTERNAL CONTROL

The auditor should recognize that internal control, no matter how well designed and operated, provides only reasonable assurance about achievement of an entity's objectives. Limitations of internal control include

1. Human judgments/decisions can be faulty.
2. Breakdown in controls can occur because of error or mistake (e.g., errors may occur in designing, maintaining, or monitoring automated controls).
3. Controls can be circumvented by collusion or management override (e.g., edit routines in a software program that are designed to identify and report transactions that exceed specified credit limits may be overridden or disabled).

NEED FOR INFORMATION TECHNOLOGY SKILLS

The auditor should consider whether a professional possessing IT skills is needed on the audit team to consider the effect of IT on the audit, to understand IT controls, or to design and perform tests of IT controls or substantive tests.

According to AU 319.31, in doing so, the auditor should consider

1. The complexity of the entity's systems, and IT controls and the manner in which they are used in conducting the entity's business.
2. The significance of changes made to existing systems, or the implementation.
3. The extent to which data is shared among systems.
4. The extent of the entity's participation in electronic commerce.

5. The entity's use of emerging technologies.
6. The significance of audit evidence that is available only in electronic form.

Obtaining an Understanding of Internal Control

The auditor's understanding of internal control should be used to

1. Identify types of potential misstatements.
2. Consider factors that affect the risk of material misstatements.
3. Design tests of controls, when applicable.
4. Design substantive tests.

Control Environment

The auditor should obtain a sufficient knowledge of the control environment to understand management's and the board of directors' attitude, awareness, and actions concerning the environment. According to AU 319.34, control environment factors include

1. Integrity and ethical values.
2. Commitment to competence.
3. Board of directors or audit committee participation.
4. Management's philosophy and operating style.
5. Organizational structure.
6. Assignment of authority and responsibility.
7. Human resource policies and practices.

NOTE: The auditor should concentrate on the substance of controls (established and acted upon), not their form.

Risk Assessment

The auditor should obtain sufficient knowledge of the entity's risk assessment process to understand how management considers and addresses risks relevant to financial reporting. According to AU 319.38, risks can occur because of the following:

1. Changes in operating environment.
2. New personnel.
3. New or revamped information systems.
4. Rapid growth.
5. New technology.
6. New business models, products, or activities.
7. Corporate restructurings.
8. Expanded foreign operations.
9. New accounting pronouncements.

NOTE: The auditor's assessment of inherent and control risks is a separate consideration and not part of the entity's risk assessment.

Control Activities

The auditor should obtain an understanding of those control activities, whether automated or manual, needed to plan the audit. Control activities that may be relevant to audit planning include

1. Performance reviews (e.g., actual vs. budget comparisons).

2. Information processing (e.g., general and application controls in a data center operation).
3. Physical controls (e.g., access to computer programs and data files).
4. Segregation of duties (e.g., assigning different people the responsibility for authorizing transactions, recording transactions, and maintaining custody of assets).

The auditor should also obtain an understanding of how IT affects control activities that are relevant to planning the audit.

Information and Communication

According to AU 319.49, the auditor should obtain sufficient knowledge of the accounting information system to understand

1. The classes of transactions that are significant to the financial statements.
2. The procedures, both automated and manual, by which those transactions are initiated, recorded, processed, and reported from their occurrence to inclusion in the financial statements.
3. The related accounting records, whether electronic or manual, supporting information, and specific accounts involved in initiating, recording, processing and reporting transactions.
4. How the information system captures other events and conditions that are significant to the financial statements.
5. The financial reporting process.

The auditor should understand the automated and manual procedures used to prepare financial statements and related disclosures, and how misstatements may occur. Such procedures include

1. The procedures used to enter transaction totals into the general ledger.

   NOTE: The auditor should be aware that when IT is used to automatically transfer information from transaction processing systems to general ledger or financial reporting systems, there may be little or no visible evidence of intervention in the information systems (e.g., an individual may inappropriately override automated processes by changing the amounts being automatically passed to the general ledger or financial reporting system).

2. The procedures used to initiate, record and process standard (e.g., monthly sales and purchase transactions) and nonstandard (e.g., business combinations or disposals, or a nonrecurring accounting estimate) journal entries in the general ledger.

   NOTE: The Panel on Audit Effectiveness points out that "nonstandard entries" is a term that is not precisely defined, although it is commonly used among accountants and auditors. Such entries sometimes are referred to as "top-side entries," "postclosing entries," "manual adjustments," "management entries," or "unusual adjustments." In general, they are financial statement changes or entries made in books and records (including computer records) of an entity that usually are initiated by management-level personnel and are not routine or associated with the normal processing of transactions. Auditors should be aware that

   a. When IT is used to maintain the general ledger and prepare financial statements, such nonstandard entries may exist only in electronic form and may be more difficult to identify through physical inspection of printed documents.

   b. Financial statement misstatements are often perpetrated by using nonstandard entries to record fictitious transactions or other events and circumstances, particularly near the end of the reporting period.

3. Other procedures used to record recurring and nonrecurring adjustments (e.g., consolidating adjustments and reclassifications that are not made by formal journal entries).

The auditor should also obtain sufficient knowledge of the means the entity uses to communicate financial reporting roles and responsibilities and significant matters about financial reporting.

Monitoring

The auditor should obtain sufficient knowledge of the major types of activities that the entity uses to monitor internal control over financial reporting, including internal auditors (Section 322).

DOCUMENTING THE UNDERSTANDING

The auditor should document the understanding of the components of the entity's internal controls over financial reporting. Documentation formats may include

1. Memoranda.
2. Flowcharts.
3. Questionnaires.
4. Decision tables.

NOTE: The more complex the internal control system and the more extensive the procedures performed, the more extensive the documentation should be.

ASSESSMENT OF CONTROL RISK

After obtaining this understanding, the auditor should assess control risk for the assertions embodied in the account balance, transaction class, and disclosure components of the financial statements.

1. According to AU 319.67, in assessing control risk for specific assertions, the auditor should consider
   a. The nature of the assertion.
   b. The volume of transactions or data related to the assertion.
   c. The nature and complexity of the systems, including the use of IT, by which the entity processes and controls information supporting the assertion.
   d. The nature of the available evidential matter, including audit evidence that is available only in electronic form.
2. The auditor may assess control risk at the maximum level for some assertions because
   a. Controls are unlikely to pertain to an assertion.
   b. Controls are unlikely to be effective.
   c. Evaluating the effectiveness of controls would be inefficient.
3. The auditor needs to be satisfied that the performance of substantive tests only would effectively restrict detection risk to an acceptable level. When the auditor performs only substantive tests to restrict detection risk to an acceptable level and when the information used by the auditor to perform such substantive tests is produced by the entity's information system, the auditor should obtain evidence about the accuracy and completeness of the information.

4. If the auditor determines that
   a. Assessing control risk below the maximum level for certain assertions would be effective and more efficient than performing only substantive tests, or
   b. It is not practical or possible to restrict detection risk to an acceptable level by performing only substantive tests for one or more financial statement assertions,

   the auditor should obtain evidential matter about the effectiveness of both the design and operation of controls to reduce the assessed level of control risk.
5. When assessing control risk at less than the maximum, the auditor should do the following:
   a. Identify specific controls relevant to specific assertions.
   b. Perform tests of controls (inquiry, inspection, observation, and reperformance of the control).
   c. Recognize that results of procedures performed to obtain an understanding of control may be considered tests of controls if they provide sufficient evidential matter about the effectiveness of design and operation.
   d. Conclude on the assessed level of control risk.
6. When a significant amount of information supporting one or more financial statement assertions is electronically initiated, recorded, processed, or reported, the auditor may determine that it is not possible to design effective substantive tests that by themselves would provide sufficient evidence that the assertions are not materially misstated. In this case, the auditor should perform tests of controls to gather evidential matter to use in assessing control risk.

   NOTE: For example, an entity uses IT to initiate orders for goods based on predetermined decision rules and to pay the related payables based on system-generated information regarding receipt of goods. No other documentation of orders or goods received is produced or maintained. In this situation, the auditor may find it impossible to design effective substantive tests that by themselves would provide sufficient evidence that certain assertions are not materially misstated.

FURTHER REDUCTION IN ASSESSED LEVEL OF CONTROL RISK

After obtaining the understanding and assessing control risk, the auditor may want to further reduce the assessed level of control risk for some assertions.

1. The auditor considers whether evidential matter sufficient to support a further reduction is likely to be available and whether performing additional tests of controls to obtain such evidential matter would be efficient.
   a. Is a further reduction in the assessed level of control risk desired for some assertions?
   b. Is it likely that additional evidential matter could be obtained to support a lower assessed level of control risk for these assertions?
2. The auditor may then perform additional tests of controls to obtain evidential matter for these assertions and assess control risk for these assertions based on such evidential matter.

3. The auditor then uses the knowledge provided by the understanding of internal control and the assessed level of control risk in determining the nature, timing, and extent of substantive tests for financial statements assertions.

DOCUMENTING THE ASSESSED LEVEL OF CONTROL RISK

In addition to the documentation of the understanding of internal control, the auditor should document his or her conclusions about the assessed level of control risk for financial statement assertions.

1. If the assessed level of control risk is less than the maximum, the basis for that conclusion should be documented.
2. If the assessed level of control risk is the maximum, only that conclusion need be documented.

When the auditor assesses control risk below the maximum, sufficient evidence should support the lower assessment.

NOTE: Inquiry alone generally will not support a conclusion about the effectiveness of design or operation of a control.

Other factors that the auditor should consider in evaluating tests of controls evidence are

1. A control might not be performed in the same manner when the auditor is not present.
2. Observation tests of controls pertain only to the point in time at which the auditing procedure was applied.
3. Tests of controls evidence from prior audits may be used by the auditor in the current audit provided the auditor considers
    a. The significance of the assertion.
    b. The specific controls that were previously evaluated.
    c. The degree to which those controls were evaluated.
    d. The results of the prior audit tests of controls.
    e. The substantive tests results from the current audit.
    f. The time elapsed since the performance of the tests of controls.
4. When considering tests of controls evidence from prior audits, the auditor should obtain current evidence about changes in internal control, including policies, procedures, and personnel.
5. When tests of controls evidence is generated during an interim period, the auditor should determine what additional evidence is needed for the remaining period. In making that determination, the auditor should consider the matters listed at 3. and 4. above.
6. The auditor should consider the combined effect of various types of evidence related to the same assertion in evaluating the assurance provided.
7. Regardless of the assessed level of control risk, the auditor should perform substantive tests for significant account balances and transaction classes.
8. When the auditor performs a combined substantive test of details and a test of controls (i.e., a dual-purpose test), he or she should ensure that both tests' objectives are accomplished.

INTERPRETATIONS

There are no interpretations for this section.

TECHNIQUES FOR APPLICATION

ASSESSING CONTROL RISK

After obtaining an understanding of all five components of internal control, the auditor makes assessments of control risk based on the information obtained for assertions related to significant account balances or transaction classes.

Although assessments of control risk are required, the auditor would always be permitted to base those assessments solely on the understanding of internal control obtained to plan the audit. For many assertions, this may mean that the auditor may assess the level of control risk as maximum because the information obtained about control from the required understanding may not support lower assessments.

Extended assessments of control risk are not required. Typically, the auditor elects to make an extended control risk assessment when it improves audit efficiency. When the auditor extends the control risk assessment, support may be obtained for a lower level of control risk for some assertions. As discussed in Section 326, in some circumstances where significant information is transmitted, processed, maintained, or accessed electronically, the auditor may have to perform tests of controls to reduce detection risk to an acceptable level.

The auditor uses the assessed level of control risk in determining the detection risk to accept for a financial statement assertion and, accordingly, in determining the nature, extent, and timing of substantive tests. This level may vary along a range from maximum to minimum as long as the auditor has obtained evidential matter to support that assessed level. When the auditor assesses control risk below the maximum level, he or she should obtain evidential matter sufficient to support that assessed level. The evidential matter necessary to support a specific level of control risk is strictly a matter of audit judgment. Evidential matter varies substantially in the assurance it provides the auditor. The type of evidential matter, its source, its timeliness, and the existence of other evidential matter related to the conclusions to which it leads, all bear on the degree of assurance evidential matter provides.

An important step in assessing control risk is identifying the control activities that pertain to a specific audit objective for a specific financial statement assertion. Financial statement assertions relate to existence, completeness, rights and obligations, valuation, and presentation and disclosure. For example, a specific audit objective for accounts receivable related to the completeness assertion would be that accounts receivable at the balance sheet date include all amounts owed by customers. Relevant control procedures that pertain to this objective might be use of prenumbered shipping documents with sequence accounted for, or periodic client reconciliation of goods shipped with goods billed. The auditor then evaluates the effectiveness of those policies and procedures in achieving, or contributing to the achievement of, the audit objective. For example, do the client's controls provide reasonable assurance that all goods shipped are billed? Is there more than a relatively low risk of material misstatement arising from unrecorded sales?

After considering the level to which the auditor seeks to restrict the risk of material misstatement and the assessed level of inherent risk and control risk, the auditor plans substantive tests to restrict detection risk to an acceptable level. As the assessed level of control risk decreases, the acceptable level of detection risk increases. Accordingly, the auditor may alter the nature, extent, and timing of the substantive tests performed. The inverse relationship between control risk and detection risk may permit the auditor to change the nature or the timing of substantive tests or limit their extent, but ordinarily the assessed level of control risk cannot be sufficiently low to eliminate the need to perform any substantive tests to restrict detection risk for all of the assertions relevant to significant account balances or transaction classes. Thus, regardless of the assessed level of control risk, the auditor should perform some substantive tests for significant account balances and transaction classes.

The auditor may determine that assessing control risk below the maximum level for certain assertions would be effective and more efficient than performing only substantive tests. In addition, the auditor may determine that it is not practical or possible to restrict detection risk to an acceptable level by performing only substantive tests for one or more financial statement assertions. In such circumstances, the auditor should obtain evidential matter about the effectiveness of both the design and operation of controls to reduce the assessed level of control risk. If the auditor wishes to further reduce the assessed level of control risk for certain assertions, the auditor should consider whether evidential matter sufficient to support a further reduction is likely to be available and whether performing additional tests on controls to obtain such evidential matter would be efficient.

Effect of Information Technology on Internal Control

IT affects the way in which transactions are initiated, recorded, processed, and reported. IT controls consist of automated controls (e.g., controls embedded in computer programs) and manual controls. Manual controls may be independent of IT, may use information produced by IT, or may be limited to monitoring the effective function of IT and of automated controls, and to handling exceptions. An entity's mix of controls varies with the nature and complexity of its use of IT. IT enables an entity to

1. Consistently apply predefined business rules and perform complex calculations in processing large volumes of transactions or data.
2. Enhance the timeliness, availability, and accuracy of information.
3. Facilitate the additional analysis of information.
4. Enhance the ability to monitor the performance of activities and its policies and procedures.
5. Reduce the risk that controls will be circumvented.
6. Enhance the ability to achieve effective segregation of duties by implementing security controls.

IT also poses specific risks to an entity's internal control, including

1. Reliance on systems or programs that are inaccurately processing data, processing inaccurate data, or both.
2. Unauthorized access to data that may result in destruction of data or improper changes to data, including the recording of unauthorized or nonexistent transactions or inaccurate recording of transactions.
3. Unauthorized changes to data in master files.
4. Unauthorized changes to systems or programs.
5. Failure to make necessary changes to systems or programs.
6. Inappropriate manual intervention.
7. Potential loss of data.

ILLUSTRATION

This section contains a flowchart that illustrates the consideration of internal control in a financial statement audit.

ILLUSTRATION 1. CONSIDERATION OF INTERNAL CONTROL IN A FINANCIAL STATEMENT AUDIT

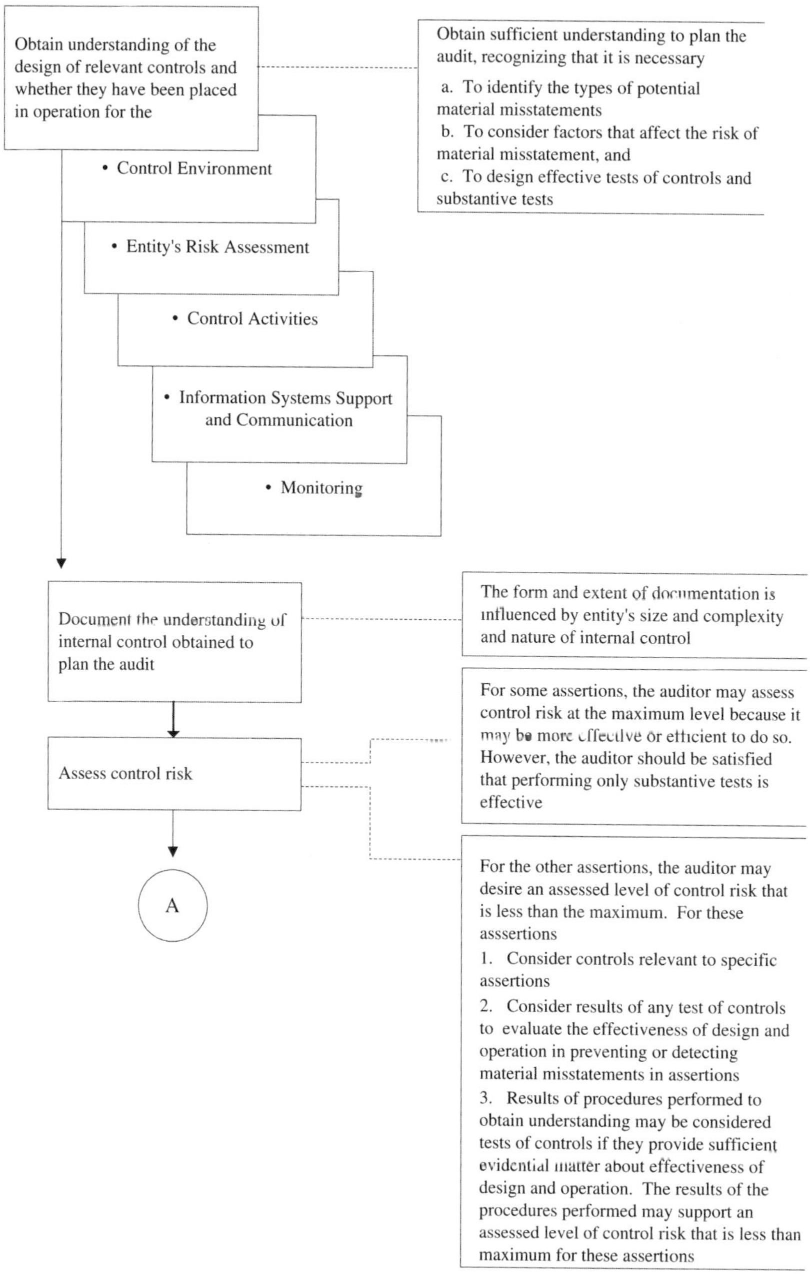

CONSIDERATION OF INTERNAL CONTROL IN A FINANCIAL STATEMENT AUDIT (CONTINUED)

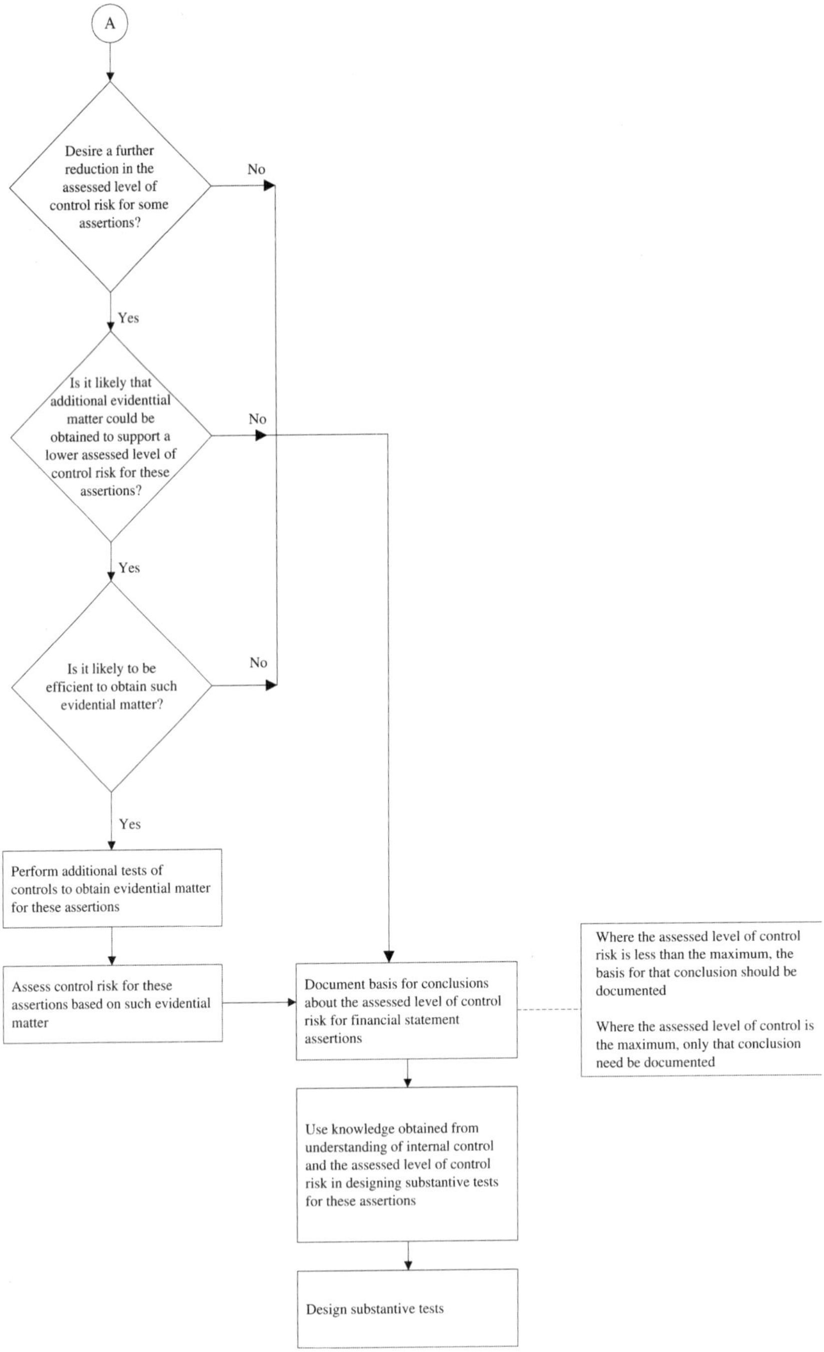

322 THE AUDITOR'S CONSIDERATION OF THE INTERNAL AUDIT FUNCTION IN AN AUDIT OF FINANCIAL STATEMENTS

EFFECTIVE DATE AND APPLICABILITY

Original Pronouncement	SAS 65, April 1991.
Effective Date	Audits of financial statements for periods ending after December 15, 1991.
Applicability	Audits of financial statements in accordance with generally accepted auditing standards.

DEFINITIONS OF TERMS

Internal auditors. Client personnel responsible for providing (1) analyses, (2) evaluations, (3) assurances, (4) recommendations, and (5) other information to management and the board of directors or to others with equivalent authority and responsibility.

Internal audit function. Consists of one or more individuals who perform internal auditing activities. It is an independent appraisal function and part of the control environment that requires internal auditors to be independent of the activity they audit. An important responsibility of the internal audit function is to monitor the performance of an entity's controls.

OBJECTIVES OF SECTION

SAS 65 supersedes SAS 9, *The Effect of an Internal Audit Function on the Scope of the Independent Auditor's Examination.* It expands the guidance to independent auditors concerning the use of internal auditors' work.

The SAS does not require the independent auditor to use the work of internal auditors. However, SAS 55 (Section 319), *Consideration of Internal Control in a Financial Statement Audit*, requires the auditor to obtain a sufficient understanding of internal control to plan the audit. The internal audit function is part of internal control; it is part of the control environment. SAS 65 provides sources of information and appropriate inquiries for the auditor to make to obtain the required understanding.

The major points of SAS 65 are as follows:

1. If the entity has an internal audit function that acts as a higher level of control over the operation of control procedures, it will usually influence the independent auditor's assessment of control risk and, as a result, may influence the scope of the audit procedures. The independent auditor should determine what work of the internal

auditors is relevant to a financial statement audit and whether it is efficient to use that work.

2. Internal auditors may be used to provide direct assistance to the independent auditor by performing substantive tests or tests of controls.
3. For either use (1. or 2.), the independent auditor should review the competence and objectivity of internal auditors and evaluate their work.
4. The only limitation on the use of internal auditors for either purpose, assuming that the independent auditor is satisfied with competence, objectivity, and work performance, is that significant audit judgments should be made by the independent auditor.
5. The work of internal auditors may affect the independent auditor's procedures; however, the independent auditor should perform enough of his or her own procedures to obtain sufficient, competent evidential matter to support the auditor's report. In making judgments about the extent of the effect of the internal auditors' work on the independent auditor's procedures, the independent auditor considers the following about the financial statement amounts worked on by internal auditors:
   a. The materiality of financial statement amounts; that is, account balances or classes of transactions.
   b. The risk, inherent risk and control risk, of material misstatement of the assertions (see Section 326, "Evidential Matter") related to these financial statement amounts.
   c. The degree of subjectivity involved in the evaluation of the audit evidence gathered in support of the assertions.

As the materiality of the financial statement amounts increases and either the risk of material misstatement or the degree of subjectivity increases, the need for the auditor to perform his or her own tests of the assertions increases. As these factors decrease, the need for the independent auditor to perform his or her own tests of the assertions decreases.

As a practical matter, the SAS permits the independent auditor to use the work of internal auditors to reduce audit costs. In effect, the SAS officially sanctions the use of internal auditors—it is permissible—but the SAS does not provide a mandate on minimum use.

Another important point to recognize is that the SAS is concerned with the internal audit **function** and not client personnel that simply have the title of internal auditor. For example, personnel who reconcile bank accounts or recompute the amount of invoices might be called auditors, but the independent auditor would not view their work any differently than that of other personnel who perform those specific procedures. The SAS is concerned with internal auditors who act as a higher level of control—an additional layer of control to ensure that routine control procedures are operating.

FUNDAMENTAL REQUIREMENTS

BASIC REQUIREMENT

When the independent auditor obtains an understanding of internal control, he or she should obtain an understanding of the internal audit function sufficient to identify those internal audit activities that are relevant to planning the audit.

To obtain an understanding of the internal audit function, the independent auditor ordinarily should make inquiries, listed in AU 322.04, of appropriate management and internal audit personnel about the internal auditors'

- Organizational status within the entity.
- Audit plan, including the nature, timing, and extent of audit work.

- Access to records and whether there are limitations on the scope of their activities.
- Application of professional internal audit standards.

NOTE: Standards for the professional practice of internal auditing have been developed by the Institute of Internal Auditors and the General Accounting Office.

Competence and Objectivity

If the independent auditor decides to consider how the internal auditors' work might affect the scope of the audit, he or she should assess the competence and objectivity of the internal auditors.

NOTE: After obtaining the required understanding of internal auditing, the auditor may decide that the internal auditors' work is not relevant to the audit or that it is not efficient to use their work.

Assessing Competence

According to AU 322.09, when the independent auditor assesses the internal auditors' competence, he or she should obtain or update information from prior years about factors such as the following:

- Educational level and professional experience of internal auditors.
- Professional certification and continuing education.
- Audit policies, programs, and procedures.
- Practices regarding assignment of internal auditors.
- Supervision and review of internal auditors' activities.
- Quality of audit documentation, reports, and recommendations.
- Evaluation of internal auditors' performance.

Assessing Objectivity

When the independent auditor assesses the internal auditors' objectivity, he or she should obtain or update information from prior years about factors such as (1) the organizational status of the person responsible for the internal audit function, and (2) policies to maintain the internal auditors' objectivity about the areas audited.

Procedures

When the internal auditors' work is expected to affect the audit, the independent auditor should (1) consider the extent of the effect, (2) coordinate work with internal auditors, and (3) evaluate and test the effectiveness of the internal auditors' work.

Evaluating the Effectiveness of Internal Auditors' Work

The independent auditor should perform procedures to evaluate the quality and effectiveness of the internal auditors' work that significantly affects the nature, timing, and extent of the auditors' procedures. According to AU 322.25, in developing evaluation procedures, the auditor should consider whether the internal auditors'

- Scope of work is appropriate to meet the objectives.
- Audit programs are adequate.
- Work performed, including evidence of supervision and review, is adequately documented.
- Conclusions are appropriate in the circumstances.
- Reports are consistent with the results of the work performed.

Testing the Effectiveness of Internal Auditors' Work

The independent auditor should test some of the internal auditors' work related to significant financial statement assertions. These tests may be made by (1) reperforming some of the work done by internal auditors or by (2) examining similar controls, transactions, or balances. Afterwards, the auditor should compare the results of his or her work to the results of the internal auditors' work.

SUFFICIENCY OF EVIDENCE

Even though the internal auditors' work may impact the auditor's procedures, the auditor is responsible for gathering sufficient competent evidential matter to support his or her audit report.

DIRECT ASSISTANCE TO THE INDEPENDENT AUDITOR

When internal auditors provide direct assistance to the independent auditor, the independent auditor should

- Assess the internal auditors' competence and objectivity.
- Supervise, review, evaluate, and test the work performed by the internal auditors.
- Inform the internal auditors of their responsibilities, the objectives of the procedures they are to perform, and matters that may affect the scope of the audit procedures.
- Inform the internal auditors that all significant accounting and auditing issues identified during the audit should be brought to the independent auditors' attention.

INTERPRETATIONS

There are no interpretations for this section.

TECHNIQUES FOR APPLICATION

EFFECT OF USE OF INTERNAL AUDITORS' WORK ON THE AUDIT

The use of the internal auditors' work affects the scope of the audit, especially when the independent auditor performs

1. Procedures to obtain an understanding of the entity's internal control.
2. Procedures to assess risk.
3. Substantive procedures.

Obtaining an Understanding of Internal Control

The independent auditor's understanding of the entity's internal control should include knowledge about the design of relevant policies, procedures, and records and whether they have been placed in operation (see Section 319). The independent auditor, when obtaining an understanding of the internal audit function (see below), may review flowcharts prepared by the internal auditors to obtain information about the design of policies and procedures.

To obtain information about whether the controls have been placed in operation, the independent auditor may consider the results of procedures performed by the internal auditors on the controls.

Risk Assessment

If the independent auditor plans to assess control risk below the maximum, he or she should test controls (see Section 319). The results of the internal auditors' tests of controls may provide information about the effectiveness of the entity's internal control and change the nature, timing, and extent of testing the auditor would otherwise need to perform.

Substantive Procedures

Internal auditors may perform substantive tests, such as the confirmation of receivables and the observation of inventories. The independent auditor, therefore, may be able to change the timing of the confirmation procedures, the number of receivables to be confirmed, or the number of locations of inventories to be observed.

OBTAINING AN UNDERSTANDING OF THE INTERNAL AUDIT FUNCTION

As part of the independent auditor's obtaining an understanding of internal control, he or she should obtain an understanding of the internal audit function.

To obtain an understanding of the internal audit function, the independent auditor might do the following:

1. Read the entity's manuals.
2. Review the entity's policies and management directives concerning the internal audit function.
3. Make inquiries of management and internal audit personnel about the internal audit function, as described in *Fundamental Requirements.*
4. Review internal auditors' audit documentation.
5. Consider the entity's organization chart and organization chart of the internal audit department.

Inquiries

As described in *Fundamental Requirements*, the independent auditor should make inquiries of appropriate management and internal audit personnel about the internal auditors' work. The inquiries should answer the following questions:

1. What are the primary responsibilities of internal auditors?
2. What do internal auditors do when
   a. They believe misstatements have occurred?
   b. They believe the entity's policies are not being properly executed?
   c. They believe weaknesses exist in internal control?
3. What importance does management attach to the internal audit function?
4. What does management do with recommendations and reports of internal auditors?

To determine how the internal audit department functions, the independent auditor should seek answers to the following questions:

1. How are scopes of examinations determined?
2. How are audit procedures determined?
3. How are reports prepared?
4. Who receives the reports?
5. What are the follow-up procedures?

Review of Audit Documentation

SAS 55 (Section 319) requires the independent auditor to obtain an understanding of internal control and to determine whether relevant policies, procedures, and records have been placed in operation. A review of the internal auditors' audit documentation, schedules, flowcharts, questionnaires, checklists, etc. will help the independent auditor determine if the relevant policies, procedures, and records have been placed in operation. It also will help the independent auditor obtain an understanding of the internal audit function.

Organization Charts

To determine the position of the internal audit department in the organization, the independent auditor might obtain an organization chart of the entity. The independent auditor would then determine the following:

1. To whom do internal auditors report?
2. To what extent do internal auditors have access to top management and to the audit committee or the full board of directors?

Ready access to top management and to the audit committee indicates that the internal audit department could act independently.

To determine the size of the internal audit department and the responsibilities of each member, the independent auditor might obtain an organization chart of the department. The responsibilities of the members indicate whether the department performs an internal audit function or an accounting control function.

Assessing Relevance and Efficiency

Relevance

When the independent auditor reviews the internal auditors' audit documentation (see above, "Obtaining an Understanding of the Internal Audit Function"), he or she can determine which of the internal auditors' work is relevant to a financial statement audit. According to AU 322.07, other procedures that may be used by the independent auditor to determine the relevancy of the internal auditors' work include the following:

1. Consider knowledge from prior year audits.
2. Review how the internal auditors allocate their audit resources to financial or operating areas.
3. Read internal audit reports to obtain detailed information about the scope of internal audit activities.

Efficiency

Determining whether it is efficient to use the internal auditors' work requires the professional judgment of the independent auditor. The independent auditor should answer the question: Is it less time-consuming and cheaper, and as effective, to use the internal auditors' work than to do original work himself or herself?

Assessing Competence and Objectivity of Internal Auditors

In assessing competence and objectivity, the auditor will consider information obtained from the following sources:

1. Previous experience with internal auditors.
2. Discussions with management.
3. Results of any recent external quality review of the internal audit function.

When assessing competence and objectivity, the independent auditor should consider using the guidance provided in professional internal auditing standards, such as those promulgated by the Institute of Internal Auditors and the General Accounting Office.

Competence

Information that the independent auditor should obtain about the competence of internal auditors is specified in *Fundamental Requirements.* The independent auditor should apply the following procedures to obtain that information:

1. Determine personnel policies relative to hiring, training, job assignment, promotion, supervision, and review.
2. Review personnel files.
3. Determine entity policy on training programs.
4. Scan audit documentation of internal auditors.
5. Consider adequacy of audit documentation review by supervisors in internal audit department.

Objectivity

The independent auditor should obtain or update information from prior years about the organizational status of the internal auditor responsible for the internal audit function and policies to maintain internal auditors' objectivity about the areas audited.

According to AU 322.10, the information about the organizational status of the internal auditor responsible for the internal audit function should include the following:

1. Whether the internal auditor reports to an officer of sufficient status to ensure broad audit coverage and adequate consideration of, and action on, the findings and recommendations of the internal auditors.
2. Whether the internal auditor has direct access and reports regularly to the board of directors, the audit committee, or the owner-manager.
3. Whether the board of directors, the audit committee, or the owner-manager oversees employment decisions related to the internal auditor.

Policies to maintain auditors' objectivity about the areas audited should include the following:

1. Policies prohibiting internal auditors from auditing areas where relatives are employed in important or audit-sensitive positions.
2. Policies prohibiting internal auditors from auditing areas where they were recently assigned or are scheduled to be assigned on completion of responsibilities in the internal audit function.

The independent auditor also should determine the scopes of examinations of the internal auditors. He or she should ascertain that the scopes were not restricted and that they were established solely by the internal audit department.

Extent of the Effect of the Internal Auditors' Work

Factors affecting the extent of the effect of the internal auditors' work on the scope of the audit were described in *Objectives of Section.* These factors are (1) materiality, (2) risk, and (3) subjectivity.

The independent auditor may decide to use the internal auditors' work for assertions related to material financial statement amounts where the risk of material misstatement or the degree of subjectivity involved is high. In these circumstances, the internal auditors' work cannot alone reduce audit risk to a level that would eliminate the need for the independent auditor to apply any procedures to those assertions. Examples of those assertions are (1) valuation of assets and liabilities involving significant accounting estimates (for example, accounts receivable; property, plant, and equipment; product warranties), (2) existence and disclosure of related-party transactions, (3) contingencies, (4) uncertainties, and (5) subsequent events. The independent auditor should apply some audit procedures to these assertions, in addition to considering the internal auditors' work.

The independent auditor may decide to use the internal auditors' work for assertions related to less material financial statement amounts where the risk of material misstatement or the degree of subjectivity involved is low. In these circumstances, the internal auditors' work may reduce audit risk to an acceptable level so that the independent auditor does not have to apply any further procedures to those assertions. Examples of those assertions are the existence of cash, prepaid assets, and fixed-asset additions.

Coordination of Work

According to AU 322.23, if the internal auditors' work will have an effect on the independent auditor's procedures, it would be efficient for them to coordinate their work by doing the following:

1. Holding periodic meetings.
2. Scheduling audit work.
3. Providing access to internal auditors' audit documentation.
4. Reviewing audit reports.
5. Discussing possible accounting and auditing issues.

Evaluating and Testing Effectiveness of Internal Auditors' Work

Evaluating

Procedures to evaluate the work of internal auditors include a review of the following:

1. Scope of work.
2. Instructions to internal audit staff.
3. Audit documentation.

Scope of work. The independent auditor should review the scope of the internal auditors' work to determine that it was established by them and was in no way restricted.

Instructions to staff. To determine that the internal auditors were properly instructed, the independent auditor should read all written instructions. The independent auditor also should review audit programs to determine that they were adequate.

Review of audit documentation. To determine the quality of internal auditors' work, the independent auditor should review their audit documentation to determine that

1. Audit documentation adequately records work performed, including evidence of supervision and review.
2. There is evidence of follow-up and disposition of questions and errors.
3. Conclusions are appropriate in the circumstances.
4. Reports are consistent with the results of work performed.

Testing

To determine the effectiveness of the internal auditors' work, the independent auditor should test their work by examining documentary evidence of work performed. He or she should either (1) examine some of the controls, transactions, or balances examined by the internal auditors or (2) examine similar controls, transactions, or balances not actually examined by the internal auditors. In either case, the independent auditor should compare the results of his or her tests with the results of the internal auditors' work.

Using Internal Auditors to Provide Direct Assistance to the Independent Auditor

When the independent auditor uses internal auditors to provide him or her with direct assistance, he or she should apply the procedures described above (see *Fundamental Requirements*). In addition, the independent auditor should review and evaluate the internal auditors' audit documentation to the same extent he or she would review and evaluate the audit documentation of the independent auditors' staff.

ILLUSTRATIONS

This section contains (1) a checklist that may be used by the independent auditor when he or she uses the work of internal auditors and (2) a copy of the flowchart from SAS 65 (AU 322) that describes its requirements.

Illustration 1. Checklist for Using Work of Internal Auditors

____
[*Client*]

____
[*Audit date*]

This checklist should be used on all engagements where the firm intends to use the work of internal auditors. The work of internal auditors should be evaluated in two situations as follows:

1. Internal audit as a separate, higher level of control.
2. Use of internal auditors to assist firm in testing controls, gaining an understanding of controls, and substantive testing.

	Performed by	*Date*
Acquire an Understanding of Internal Audit Function		
1. Review internal audit department and note the following:		
a. Hiring policies.		
b. Total number of employees.		
c. Number of employees by title; for example, supervisor, senior, and so on.		
d. Department's place in organization structure.		
e. To whom department reports.		
2. Review current year's reports and note the following:		
a. Number and nature of audits.		
b. Scope of audits.		
c. Recommendations.		
d. To whom issued.		
e. Action on recommendations.		
Relevancy and Efficiency		
1. Determine what work of the internal auditors is relevant to a financial statement audit.		
2. Determine whether it is efficient to use the internal auditors' work as part of our audit.		
Competence of Internal Auditors		
1. Determine if entity conducts training programs for internal auditors.		
2. If entity does not conduct training programs, determine if internal auditors attend outside seminars.		
3. Review personnel files and compare with hiring policies		
4. Review department library.		
5. Review, on a test basis, current year's audit documentation and note the following:		
a. Quality of work.		

	Performed by	Date
b. Adequacy of documentation.		
c. Adequacy of supervision.		
Objectivity of Internal Audits		
1. Review, on a test basis, scope of audits.		
2. Determine how scope was established.		
3. Determine work performed by internal auditors and ascertain that work was independent of accounting functions.		
4. Review, on a test basis, reports of internal audit department		
a. Recommendations.		
b. To whom issued.		
c. Action on recommendations.		
Evaluating Work of Internal Auditors		
1. Select, on a test basis, audits performed by the department during the year and do the following:		
a. Determine if scope is appropriate for job.		
b. Review audit programs.		
c. Review preaudit instructions.		
d. Review audit documentation for		
(1) Completeness of documentation.		
(2) Follow-up and disposition of questions and errors.		
2. Determine if audit reports and conclusions are consistent with findings noted in audit documentation.		
3. Test work of internal auditors		
a. Examine the same transactions and account balances.		
b. Examine similar transactions and account balances.		
c. Compare results to findings of internal auditors.		
Direct Assistance of Internal Auditors		
1. Meet with internal auditors		
a. Discuss areas of work.		
b. Review program.		
c. Review procedures.		
2. Review completed audit documentation of internal auditors.		
3. Consider the need to test the work performed by internal auditors.		

ILLUSTRATION 2. THE AUDITOR'S CONSIDERATION OF THE INTERNAL AUDIT FUNCTION IN AN AUDIT OF FINANCIAL STATEMENTS

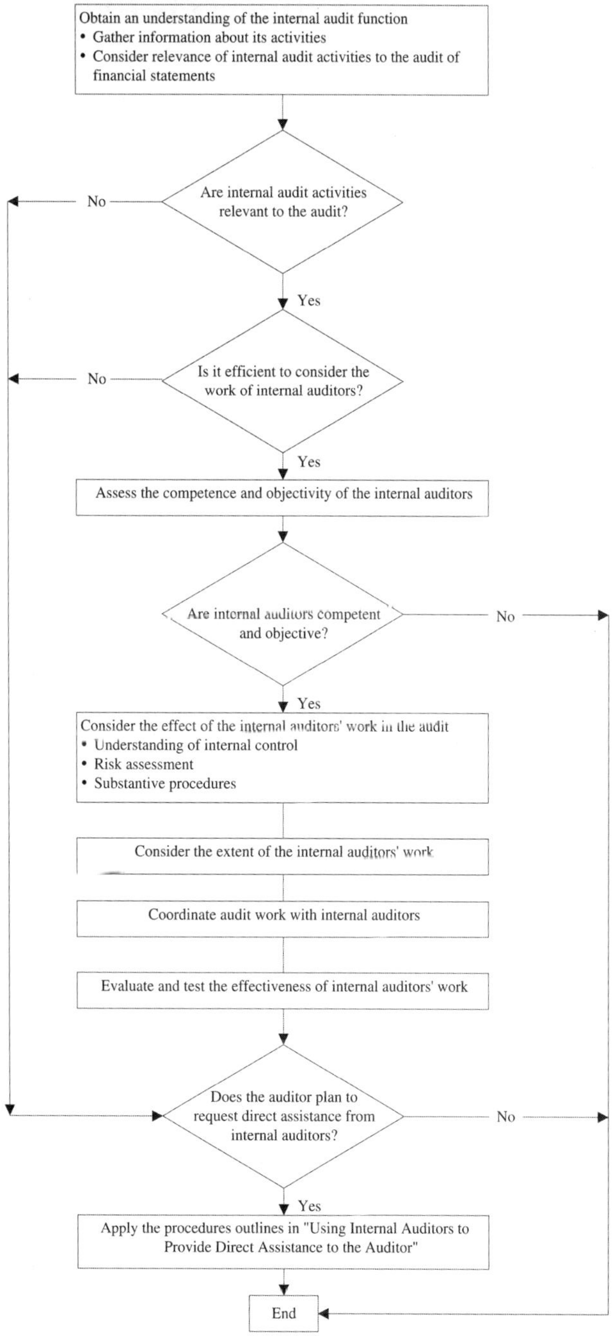

324 SERVICE ORGANIZATIONS

EFFECTIVE DATE AND APPLICABILITY

Original Pronouncement	SAS 70, April 1992; as amended by SAS 78, December 1995; SAS 88, December 1999; and SAS 98, September 2002.
Effective Date	Originally effective for service auditor's reports dated as of or after March 31, 1993; revised to reflect SAS 78, effective for service auditor's reports covering descriptions as of or after January 1, 1997; and SAS 88, effective upon issuance, and SAS 98, effective for reports issued on or after January 1, 2003, with earlier application permitted.
Applicability	Practitioners auditing financial statements of an entity that uses a service organization, such as a data processing service center, a bank trust department, or a mortgage banker servicing mortgages for others. Practitioners issuing service auditor reports.

DEFINITIONS OF TERMS

User organization. The entity that has engaged a service organization and whose financial statements are being audited.

User auditor. The auditor who reports on the financial statements of the user organization.

Service organization. The entity (or segment of an entity) that provides services to the user organization.

Service auditor. The auditor who reports on the processing of transactions by the service organization.

Reports on controls placed in operation. A service auditor's report on a service organization's description of controls addressing (1) whether controls were suitably designed to achieve specified control objectives, and (2) whether controls had been placed in operation at a specific date.

Reports on controls placed in operation and tests of operating effectiveness. A service auditor's report on a service organization's description of controls that covers (1) suitability of control design, (2) controls placed in operation, and (3) whether controls tested were sufficiently effective to provide reasonable assurance that control objectives were achieved during the period specified.

Subsequent events. Changes in a service organization's controls that could affect user organizations' information systems that occur subsequent to the period covered by the service auditor's report but before the date of the service auditor's report.

OBJECTIVES OF SECTION

The Statement provides guidance to auditors of financial statements of an entity that uses a service organization to process transactions. The Statement applies when an entity obtains services from another entity that are part of its information system. A service organization's services are part of an entity's information system if they affect any of the following:

1. Transaction initiation.
2. Accounting records and supplemental detail.
3. Processing of accounting information.
4. Financial reporting process.

Bank trust departments are service organizations because they invest and service assets for others. An example of a user organization for a bank trust department is an employee benefit plan. Data processing service centers are service organizations because they process transactions and related data for others. Similarly, mortgage bankers that service mortgages for other entities are service organizations.

A bank that processes checking account transactions or a broker who executes securities transactions is not included under the Statement definition of **service organizations**. When services are limited to executing transactions specifically authorized by the client, the Statement is not applicable. The Statement also is not applicable to the audit of transactions arising from financial interest in partnerships, corporations, and joint ventures (see Section 332 for guidance on financial instruments).

More and more entities are outsourcing activities to service organizations. There is often a belief by the user organization that the service organization can be totally relied upon and that the user organization needs only to have limited, if any, controls. SAS 88 was issued to clarify the use of Section 324. The statement is intended to help auditors determine what additional information they might need when auditing an entity that uses a service organization. SAS 88 makes it clear that the guidance in this section applies if an entity obtains services from another organization that are part of the entity's information system. Also, SAS 88 clarifies the factors that an auditor should use in determining the significance of service organization's controls to the user organization's control. In other words, the audit procedures that are appropriate when a service organization's procedures are significant to the audited entity are not optional. The auditor has to evaluate the interaction between the audited entity and all service organizations used by that entity.

In November 2002, SAS 98 amended this section to require that an auditor ask management about whether management is aware of subsequent events that would have a significant effect on user organizations, rather than merely suggesting that the auditor make such an inquiry. SAS 98 also incorporated the guidance from Interpretation 6, *Responsibilities of Service Organizations and Service Auditors with Respect to Subsequent Events in a Service Auditor's Engagement.*

FUNDAMENTAL REQUIREMENTS: USER AUDITORS

When an entity uses a service organization, part of the processing that the auditor usually finds in the client's internal control is physically and operationally separate from that entity (the user organization). In some circumstances, the user organization may be able to implement effective internal controls. This occurs when the user organization authorizes all transactions and maintains accountability that would detect unauthorized transactions or activity.

In other circumstances, the service organization's procedures relevant to the user organization need to be included when the user auditor is obtaining an understanding of internal control. One source of additional information to obtain this understanding is a service auditor's report.

The key factors for a user auditor to consider in deciding whether additional information such as a service auditor's report is needed are

1. Degree of interaction between the activity at the service organization and that of the user organization.
2. Nature of the transactions processed.
3. Materiality of the transaction processed.

According to SAS 55, the auditor's understanding of internal control should be sufficient to "plan the audit." Additional information from the service center or a service auditor's report may not be needed if the auditor obtains at the user organization a sufficient understanding of the controls placed in operation by the service organizations whose services are part of the entity's information system to identify types of potential misstatements, to consider factors that affect the risk of material misstatement, and to design substantive tests.

Information about a service organization's controls may be obtained from a wide variety of sources, including

1. User manuals.
2. System overviews.
3. Technical manuals.
4. The contract between the user organization and the service organization.
5. Reports by service auditors, internal auditors, or regulatory authorities on the service organization's controls.
6. The user auditor's prior experience with the service organization (if the services and the service organization's controls are highly standardized).

If the user auditor cannot obtain sufficient evidence to achieve the audit objectives, the user auditor should issue a qualified opinion or disclaim an opinion because of a scope limitation.

AU 324.17 defines two types of service auditor's reports.

1. Report on controls placed in operation.

   NOTE: This type of report can help in obtaining an understanding of internal control to plan the audit, but it is not usually an adequate basis for reducing the assessed level of control risk below maximum.

2. Report on controls placed in operation and tests of operating effectiveness.

Both types of service auditor's reports provide an opinion on whether

1. The accompanying description presents fairly, in all material respects, the aspects of the service organization's controls that may be relevant to a user organization's internal control, and
2. The controls have been placed in operation as of a date, and
3. The controls are suitably designed to provide reasonable assurance that the specified control objectives would be achieved.

The second type of service auditor's report adds a list of tests of controls performed by the service auditor, and an opinion on whether the controls tested were operating with sufficient effectiveness to provide reasonable, but not absolute, assurance that the related control objectives were achieved during the period specified.

Before using a service auditor's report, the user auditor should make inquiries about the service auditor's professional reputation (see Section 543). Also, the user auditor should consider

1. Discussing the audit procedures and their results with the service auditor.
2. Reviewing the service auditor's audit program.
3. Reviewing the service auditor's audit documentation.

FUNDAMENTAL REQUIREMENTS: SERVICE AUDITORS

According to AU 324.22, the service auditor is responsible for the representations in his or her report and for exercising due care in the application of procedures that support those representations.

The service auditor should perform the engagement in accordance with the general standards and the relevant fieldwork and reporting standards. The service auditor should be independent from the service organization, but need not be independent from each user organization.

If the service auditor becomes aware of illegal acts, fraud, or uncorrected errors attributable to the service organization, the service auditor should discuss the matter with an appropriate level of management of the service organization to determine whether this information has been communicated to the affected user organizations. If management is unwilling to make the communication, the service auditor should inform the service organization's audit committee or its equivalent, and if the audit committee fails to respond appropriately, consult with an attorney and consider resigning from the engagement.

The service auditor should obtain written representations from the service organization's management. See *Illustrations* for an example of such a representation letter.

If the service auditor is asked to apply substantive procedures to user transactions or assets at the service organization, the auditor may make specific reference in his or her report to having carried out the designated procedures and include a sufficient description of the procedures to allow user auditors to decide whether to use the results as evidence to support their opinions.

RESPONSIBILITY FOR SUBSEQUENT EVENTS

A service auditor should consider the following types of subsequent events that come to his or her attention:

1. *Events that provide additional information about conditions that existed during the period covered by the service auditor's report.* The service auditor should use this information to determine whether controls at the service organization that could affect user organizations' information systems were placed in operation, suitably designed, and operating effectively during the engagement period.
2. *Events that provide information about conditions that arose subsequent to the period covered by the service auditor's report that require disclosure to prevent users from being misled.* This type of information usually will not affect the service auditor's report if the information is appropriately disclosed by the service organization's management. The service auditor should determine whether management has disclosed such information in the section of the service auditor's report titled "Other Information Provided by the Service Organization." If the information is not disclosed, the service auditor should consider disclosing it in the section of the service auditor's report titled "Other Information Provided by the Service Auditor" and/or in the service auditor's report.

A service auditor is not responsible for detecting subsequent events. However, a service auditor should ask management whether it is aware of any subsequent events through the date of the service auditor's report that would have a significant effect on user organizations and should obtain a representation from management regarding subsequent events.

INTERPRETATIONS

Describing Tests of Operating Effectiveness and the Results of Such Tests (April 1995)

Paragraph .44f of SAS 70 requires that a service auditor's report that includes tests of operating effectiveness describe "tests applied" and the "results of the tests."

In describing "tests applied," the service auditor should indicate whether sampling was used or all of the items in a population were tested.

In describing the "results of the tests," the service auditor should include exceptions and other information (whether or not control objective has been achieved) that in his or her judgment could be relevant to user auditors. The following should be included:

1. Sample size.
2. Number of exceptions.
3. Nature of exceptions.

If no exceptions are noted, that should be indicated.

Service Organizations That Use the Services of Other Service Organizations (Subservice Organizations) (Issued April 1995, Revised February 1997)

When a service organization uses a subservice organization, the user auditor should determine whether the subserver's processing significantly affects assertions in the user organization's financial statements. To obtain the required understanding of control, the user auditor may need to consider control at both the service and subservice organizations.

A service auditor also may need to consider functions performed at both organizations and the effect of controls at the subserver on the service organization.

The service organization's description of control should include a description of the processing performed by the subservice organization (identity of subserver is not required).

There are two alternative methods of presenting the description of controls by the subserver and reporting on those controls by the service auditor.

1. Carve-out method (control objectives and controls of subserver are excluded).
2. Inclusive method (control objectives and controls of subserver are included).

Both methods require the description of processing discussed above. If that description is omitted or the service organization does not disclose the existence of a subserver, the auditor may need to issue a qualified or adverse opinion as to the fairness of the presentation.

The interpretation provides illustrative service auditor reports using the carve-out and the inclusive methods.

Responsibilities of Service Organizations and Service Auditors with Respect to Forward-Looking Information in a Service Organization's Description of Controls (February 2002)

This interpretation clarifies that Section 324 does not apply to design deficiencies that potentially could affect processing of user organizations' transactions in **future periods.** A service auditor would **not** be required to identify, in his or her report, design deficiencies that do not affect processing during the period covered by the service auditor's examination but that may represent potential problems in future periods, such as a lack of contingency planning or provisions for disaster recovery. However, if a service auditor becomes aware of such design deficiencies, the service auditor may choose to communicate this information to the service organization's management and advise management to disclose this information and its plans for correcting the design deficiencies in a section of the service auditor's document titled "Other Information Provided by the Service Organization." In this case, the service auditor should read the information, consider applying by analogy the guidance in Section 550, and include a paragraph in his or her report such as the following that disclaims an opinion on the information provided by the service organization:

> The information in Section 4 describing ABC Service Organization's plans to modify its disaster recovery plan is presented by the Service Organization to provide additional information and is not a part of the Service Organization's description of controls that may be relevant to a user organization's internal control. Such information has not been subjected to the procedures applied in the examination of the description of the controls applicable to the processing of transactions for user organizations and, accordingly, we express no opinion on it.

A service auditor also may decide to communicate information about the design deficiencies in the section of the service auditor's document titled "Other Information Provided by the Service Auditor."

STATEMENTS ABOUT THE RISK OF PROJECTING EVALUATIONS OF THE EFFECTIVENESS OF CONTROLS TO FUTURE PERIODS (FEBRUARY 2002)

This interpretation clarifies that sample service auditor's reports in Section 324 may be expanded to describe the risk of projecting to the future conclusions about the effectiveness of controls. The sentence in the sample report in Illustrations 1 and 4 could be expanded, as illustrated below, to describe the risk of projecting an evaluation of the controls to future periods because of changes to the system or controls, or the failure to make needed changes to the system or controls (new language is in italics).

> Furthermore, the projection of any conclusions, based on our findings, to future periods is subject to the risk that changes *made to the system or controls, or the failure to make needed changes to the system or controls,* may alter the validity of such conclusions.

PROFESSIONAL ISSUES TASK FORCE PRACTICE ALERT

99-2 HOW THE USE OF A SERVICE ORGANIZATION AFFECTS INTERNAL CONTROL CONSIDERATIONS

More and more entities are outsourcing activities to service organizations. This alert states that in these situations, it is critical for the user auditor to consider the guidance in Section 324 (SAS 70) and the implications the service organization may have to the audit. Therefore, the alert clarifies and highlights factors that an auditor should consider in those audits. Some of the key points covered in the alert are

- A user auditor should consider the guidance in Section 324 (SAS 70) whenever a service organization's services are part of the user organization's information system. The alert notes that a service organization's services meet that criterion if they affect
  - —How the user organization's transactions are initiated.
  - —The accounting records, supporting information, and specific accounts in the financial statements involved in the processing and reporting of the user organization's transactions.

—The accounting processing for transactions from initiation to inclusion in financial statements.
—The financial reporting process used to prepare the user organization's financial statements, including significant accounting estimates and disclosures.

- The nature and materiality of the transactions processed for the user organization and the effectiveness of the user organization's internal controls over the activities of the service organization determine the significance of the service organization's controls.
- After obtaining a service auditor's report, the user auditor should consider whether the service auditor's report is satisfactory for his or her purposes. This may include making inquiries concerning the service auditor's professional reputation (see Section 543), reading the report to determine whether the service auditor demonstrates an understanding of the subject matter, and if necessary, contacting the service organization to perform additional testing.
- If a service auditor's report on controls placed in operation is dated before the beginning of the period under audit, the user auditor should consider updating the information to determine whether there have been any relevant changes in the service organization's controls, and if so, what the effect of those changes are on his/her audit.

The full text of this Practice Alert can be obtained from the AICPA website at www.aicpa.org/members/div/secps/lit/practice.htm.

TECHNIQUES FOR APPLICATION: USER AUDITORS

REPORTS ON CONTROLS PLACED IN OPERATION

This report has two elements.

1. The service auditor's report on whether the service organization's description of its controls presents fairly the controls placed in operation as of a specific date, and
2. The service auditor's opinion that the controls have been suitably designed to provide reasonable assurance that the stated control objectives would be achieved if the controls were complied with satisfactorily.

This type of report generally helps in obtaining an understanding of the entity's internal control sufficient to plan the audit. It does not allow the user auditor to reduce the assessed level of control risk below the maximum.

REPORT ON CONTROLS PLACED IN OPERATION AND TESTS OF OPERATING EFFECTIVENESS

This report includes both elements of a "placed in operation" report and adds a third; it refers to a list of tests performed by the service auditor of specific controls. The test period covered is described and is a minimum of six months. The user auditor decides what evidential matter is needed to reduce the assessed level of control risk. In some cases, the tests of operating effectiveness performed by the service auditor may provide such evidence. (Other potential sources of this evidence are tests of the user organization's controls over the activities of the service organization, or tests of controls performed by the user auditor at the service organization.)

The user auditor selects the audit approach.

1. Is it more efficient to obtain evidential matter about the operating effectiveness to permit assessing control risk below the maximum, or
2. Is the more efficient approach to assess control risk at the maximum and plan other audit procedures suitable for that level of risk of material misstatement?

Considerations in Using a Service Auditor's Report

A service auditor's report with a "clean opinion" does not mean the service organization controls are effective for the user organization. It means that the control objectives listed and their related controls are described accurately. For example

1. The report may not address all of the control objectives that the user auditor would find helpful. Key control objectives relating to transactions processed by service organizations are often defined in the description as responsibilities of the user organization, not of the service organization.
2. The description may state that the system was designed with the assumption that certain internal controls would be implemented by the user organization. In this case, the service auditor's report includes "and user organizations applied the internal controls contemplated in the design of the service organization's controls" in the scope and opinion paragraphs.
3. One criterion used by service auditors to determine whether a **significant deficiency** exists is whether user organizations would "generally be expected to have controls in place to mitigate such design deficiencies." The user auditor needs to consider whether his or her client has these expected controls in place.

Obtaining a service auditor's report is the starting point for careful reading of the description to obtain an understanding of internal control and how it is integrated between the service organization and the user organization.

The user auditor should make inquiries concerning the service auditor's professional reputation. (See Section 543.)

The user auditor should consider the scope and results of the service auditor's work to decide whether the report provides the needed information and evidential matter that the user auditor needs to achieve the audit objectives. In some cases, the user auditor may clarify his or her understanding of the service auditor's procedures and conclusions by discussing the scope and results of the work with the service auditor and reviewing the service auditor's audit program and workpapers.

The user auditor's audit report on the financial statements should **not** make reference to the report of the service auditor. The service auditor is not responsible for examining any portion of the financial statements.

When the user auditor wishes to reduce the assessed level of control risk and is using a service auditor's report that reports the results of tests of controls over a specified time period, the user auditor should consider the appropriateness of the time period covered in evaluating the tests performed and results to assess the level of control risk for the user organization.

TECHNIQUES FOR APPLICATION: SERVICE AUDITORS

Reports on Controls Placed in Operation

To evaluate the description of the service organization's controls, the service auditor

1. Obtains information on the controls through
   a. Discussions with service organization personnel.
   b. Reference to documentation, such as system flowcharts and narratives.
2. Considers whether the information needed by the user auditors is included.
   a. Controls that affect user organization's internal control are included. The linkage of the controls to the stated control objectives should be considered.

   b. Sufficient information is presented for user auditors to obtain an understanding of those controls.
   c. Specific control objectives of the service organization relevant to user organizations are presented. The control objectives should be "reasonable in the circumstances" and consistent with the service organization's contractual obligations.
3. Obtains evidence of whether controls have been placed in operation by
   a. Previous experience with the service organization.
   b. Inquiry of service organization personnel.
   c. Inspection of service organization documents and records.
   d. Observation of service organization activities and operations.
4. Evaluates whether significant deficiencies exist that either
   a. Preclude reasonable assurance that specified control objectives would be achieved, or
   b. Could adversely affect the ability to record, process, summarize, or report financial data to user organizations without error when user organizations would not generally be expected to have controls to mitigate such design deficiencies. (Such deficiencies should be included in the report even if they do not relate to the specified control objectives.)
5. Considers whether changes in controls made within twelve months before the date being reported on would be considered significant to user organizations and their auditors. If so, the description should communicate the changes. If management does not include the changes that the service auditor considers significant, the changes should be described in the service auditor's report.
6. Considers whether the system was designed with the assumption that certain controls would be implemented by the user organization. If so, such presumed user organization controls should be included in the description. The service auditor's report will then have an added phrase referring to the user organization controls. (See *Illustrations*.)

REPORTS ON CONTROLS PLACED IN OPERATION AND TESTS OF OPERATING EFFECTIVENESS

The service auditor performs the procedures described above under "Reports on Controls Placed in Operation." In addition, the service auditor performs tests of controls to determine whether specified controls are operating with sufficient effectiveness to achieve specified control objectives.

NOTE: Section 350, "Audit Sampling," provides guidance on the application and evaluation of audit sampling in performing tests of controls.

Management of the service organizations specifies whether all or selected applications and control objectives will be addressed by the tests. The service auditor determines, in his or her judgment

1. Which controls are necessary to achieve the control objectives to be addressed.
2. The nature, timing, and extent of tests of controls needed to evaluate operating effectiveness.

The tests should be applied to controls throughout the period covered by the report.

MODIFICATION OF THE SERVICE AUDITOR'S REPORT

Incomplete or Inaccurate Description

If the service auditor concludes that the service organization's description is inaccurate or incomplete, the service auditor's report should be modified to state the conclusion and provide a description sufficient to provide user auditors with an understanding. For this situation, the service auditor adds an explanatory paragraph before the opinion paragraph, and the first sentence of the opinion includes the phrase "except for the matter . . ." (see *Illustrations*).

Significant Deficiencies

If the service auditor concludes that significant deficiencies in the design or operation exist, the deficiencies are included in an explanatory paragraph before the opinion paragraph, and the **second** sentence of the opinion includes the phrase "except for the deficiency . . ." (see *Illustrations*).

The Statement provides an example of a significant deficiency in the **design** of the policies and procedures. However, it does not specifically illustrate the situation wherein the results of the service auditor's tests of controls indicate a deficiency in the operation that precludes the service auditor from expressing the opinion that the controls tested were operating with sufficient effectiveness to provide reasonable assurance that the control objectives were achieved during the period.

ILLUSTRATIONS

Following are illustrative service auditor reports adapted from SAS 70 (Section 324) on

1. Controls placed in operation—no exceptions.
2. Controls placed in operation—inaccurate or incomplete description.
3. Controls placed in operation—significant deficiencies in the design or operation.
4. Controls placed in operation and tests of operating effectiveness—no exceptions.

All service auditor reports should be accompanied by a description of the service organization's controls. Illustration 5 presents a service organization management representation letter, which is required.

ILLUSTRATION 1. SERVICE AUDITOR'S REPORT ON CONTROLS PLACED IN OPERATION—NO EXCEPTIONS NOTED

To Basic Service Organization:

We have examined the accompanying description of controls related to the ______ application of Basic Service Organization. Our examination included procedures to obtain reasonable assurance about whether (1) the accompanying description presents fairly, in all material respects, the aspects of Basic Service Organization's controls that may be relevant to a user organization's internal control as it relates to an audit of financial statements, (2) the controls included in the description were suitably designed to achieve the control objectives specified in the description, if those controls were complied with satisfactorily [and user organizations applied the controls contemplated in the design of Basic Service Organization's controls], and (3) such controls had been placed in operation as of [*date*]. The control objectives were specified by [*the service organization, regulatory authorities, a user group or others*]. Our examination was performed in accordance with standards established by the American Institute of Certified Public Accountants and included those procedures we considered necessary in the circumstances to obtain a reasonable basis for rendering our opinion.

We did not perform procedures to determine the operating effectiveness of controls for any period. Accordingly, we express no opinion on the operating effectiveness of any aspects of Basic Service Organization's controls, individually or in the aggregate.

In our opinion, the accompanying description of the aforementioned application presents fairly, in all material respects, the relevant aspects of Basic Service Organization's controls that had been placed in operation as of [*date*]. Also, in our opinion, the controls, as described above, are suitably designed to provide reasonable assurance that the specified control objectives would be achieved if the described controls were complied with satisfactorily (and user organizations applied the internal controls contemplated in the design of Basic Service Organization's controls).

The description of controls at Basic Service Organization is as of [*date*] and any projection of such information to the future is subject to the risk that, because of change, the description may no longer portray the controls in existence. The potential effectiveness of specific controls at the Service Organization is subject to inherent limitations and, accordingly, errors or fraud may occur and not be detected. Furthermore, the projection of any conclusions, based on our findings, to future periods is subject to the risk that changes may alter the validity of such conclusions.

This report is intended solely for use by the management of Basic Service Organization, its customers, and the independent auditors of its customers.

Illustration 2. Service Auditor's Report on Controls Placed in Operation—Inaccurate or Incomplete Description

To Basic Service Organization:

We have examined the accompanying description of controls related to the ______ application of Basic Service Organization. Our examination included procedures to obtain reasonable assurance about whether (1) the accompanying description presents fairly, in all material respects, the aspects of Basic Service Organization's controls that may be relevant to a user organization's internal control as it relates to an audit of financial statements, (2) the controls included in the description were suitably designed to achieve the control objectives specified in the description, if those controls were complied with satisfactorily [and user organizations applied the controls contemplated in the design of Basic Service Organization's controls], and (3) such controls had been placed in operation as of [*date*]. The control objectives were specified by [*the service organization, regulatory authorities, a user group or others*]. Our examination was performed in accordance with standards established by the American Institute of Certified Public Accountants and included those procedures we considered necessary in the circumstances to obtain a reasonable basis for rendering our opinion.

We did not perform procedures to determine the operating effectiveness of controls for any period. Accordingly, we express no opinion on the operating effectiveness of any aspects of Basic Service Organization's controls, individually or in the aggregate.

The accompanying description states that Basic Service Organization uses operator identification numbers and passwords to prevent unauthorized access to the system. Based on inquiries of staff personnel and inspection of activities, we determined that such procedures are employed in Applications A and B, but are not required to access the system in Applications C and D.

In our opinion, except for the matter referred to in the preceding paragraph, the accompanying description of the aforementioned applications presents fairly, in all material respects, the relevant aspects of Basic Service Organizations controls that had been placed in operation as of [*date*]. Also, in our opinion, the controls as described are suitably designed to provide reasonable assurance that the specified control objectives would be achieved if the described controls were complied with satisfactorily (and user organizations applied the controls contemplated in the design of Basic Service Organization's controls).

The description of controls at Basic Service Organization is as of [*date*] and any projection of such information to the future is subject to the risk that, because of change, the description may no longer portray the controls in existence. The potential effectiveness of specific controls at the Service Organization is subject to inherent limitations and, accordingly, errors or fraud may occur and not be detected. Furthermore, the projection of any conclusions, based on our findings, to future periods is subject to the risk that changes may alter the validity of such conclusions.

This report is intended solely for use by the management of Basic Service Organization, its customers, and the independent auditors of its customers.

Illustration 3. Service Auditor's Report on Controls Placed in Operation—Significant Deficiencies in the Design or Operation

To Basic Service Organization:

We have examined the accompanying description of controls related to the ______ application of Basic Service Organization. Our examination included procedures to obtain reasonable assurance about whether (1) the accompanying description presents fairly, in all material respects, the aspects of Basic Service Organization's controls that may be relevant to a user organization's internal control as it relates to an audit of financial statements, (2) the controls included in the description were suitably designed to achieve the control objectives specified in the description, if those controls were complied with satisfactorily (and user organizations applied the controls contemplated in the design of Basic Service Organization's controls), and (3) such controls had been placed in operation as of [*date*]. The control objectives were specified by [*the service organization, regulatory authorities, a user group or others*]. Our examination was performed in accordance with standards established by the American Institute of Certified Public Accountants and included those procedures we considered necessary in the circumstances to obtain a reasonable basis for rendering our opinion.

We did not perform procedures to determine the operating effectiveness of controls for any period. Accordingly, we express no opinion on the operating effectiveness of any aspects of Basic Service Organization's controls, individually or in the aggregate.

As discussed in the accompanying description, from time to time the Service Organization makes changes in application programs to correct deficiencies or to enhance capabilities. The procedures followed in determining whether to make changes, in designing the changes, and in implementing them do not include review and approval by authorized individuals who are independent from those involved in making the changes. There are also no specified requirements to test such changes or provide test results to an authorized reviewer prior to implementing the changes.

In our opinion, the accompanying description of the aforementioned application presents fairly, in all material respects, the relevant aspects of Basic Service Organization's controls that had been placed in operation as of [*date*]. Also, in our opinion, except for the deficiency referred to in the preceding paragraph, the controls as described are suitably designed to provide reasonable assurance that the specified control objectives would be achieved if the described controls were complied with satisfactorily (and user organizations applied the controls contemplated in the design of Basic Service Organization's controls).

The description of controls at Basic Service Organization is as of [*date*] and any projection of such information to the future is subject to the risk that, because of change, the description may no longer portray the controls in existence. The potential effectiveness of specific controls at the Service Organization is subject to inherent limitations and, accordingly, errors or fraud may occur and not be detected. Furthermore, the projection of any conclusions, based on our findings, to future periods is subject to the risk that changes may alter the validity of such conclusions.

This report is intended solely for use by the management of Basic Service Organization, its customers, and the independent auditors of its customers.

Illustration 4. Service Auditor's Report on Controls Placed in Operation and Tests of Operating Effectiveness—No Exceptions Noted

To Basic Service Organization.

We have examined the accompanying description of controls related to the ______ application of Basic Service Organization. Our examination included procedures to obtain reasonable assurance about whether (1) the accompanying description presents fairly, in all material respects, the aspects of Basic Service Organization's controls that may be relevant to a user organization's internal control as it relates to an audit of financial statements, (2) the controls included in the description were suitably designed to achieve the control objectives specified in the description, if those controls were complied with satisfactorily [and user organizations applied the controls contemplated in the design of Basic Service Organization's controls], and (3) such controls had been placed in operation as of [*date*]. The control objectives were specified by [*the service organization, regulatory authorities, a user group or others*]. Our examination was performed in accordance with standards established by the American Institute of Certified Public Accountants and included those procedures we considered necessary in the circumstances to obtain a reasonable basis for rendering our opinion.

In our opinion, the accompanying description of the aforementioned applications presents fairly, in all material respects the relevant aspects of Basic Service Organization's controls that had been placed in operation as of [*date*]. Also, in our opinion, the controls as described are suitably designed to provide reasonable assurance that the specified control objectives would be achieved if the described controls were complied with satisfactorily [and user organizations applied the controls contemplated in the design of Basic Service Organization's controls].

In addition to the procedures we considered necessary to render our opinion as expressed in the previous paragraph, we applied tests to specific controls, listed in Schedule X, to obtain evidence about their effectiveness in meeting control objectives, described in Schedule X, during the period from [*date*] to [*date*]. The specific controls and the nature, timing, and extent, and results of the tests are listed in Schedule X. This information has been provided to user organizations of Basic Service Organization and to their auditors to be taken into consideration, along with information about control at user organizations, when making assessments of control risk for user organizations. In our opinion the controls that were tested, as described in Schedule X, were operating with sufficient effectiveness to provide reasonable, but not absolute, assurance that the control objectives specified in Schedule X were achieved during the period from [*date*] to [*date*]. [However, the scope of our engagement did not include tests to determine whether control objectives not listed in Schedule X were achieved; accordingly we express no opinion on the achievement of control objectives not included in Schedule X.]

The relative effectiveness and significance of specific controls at Basic Service Organization and their effect on assessments of control risk at user organizations are dependent on their interaction with the controls and other factors present at individual user organizations. We have performed no procedures to evaluate the effectiveness of controls at individual user organizations.

The description of controls at Basic Service Organization is as of [*date*] and information about tests of the operating effectiveness of specific controls covers the period from [*date*] to [*date*]. Any projection of such information to the future is subject to the risk that, because of change, the description may no longer portray the system in existence. The potential effectiveness of specific controls at the Service Organization is subject to inherent limitations and, accordingly, errors or fraud may occur and not be detected. Furthermore, the projection of any conclusions, based on our findings, to future periods is subject to the risk that changes may alter the validity of such conclusions.

This report is intended solely for use by the management of Basic Service Organization, its customers, and the independent auditors of its customers.

Illustration 5. Service Organization Management Representation Letter (Applies to Both Types of Reports)

[*Client Letterhead*]

[*Date of service auditor's report*]

[*Name of service auditor*]
[*Address*]
[*City, State*]

We have engaged you to examine the description of controls related to the _______ application of Basic Service Organization as of [*date*] for the purpose of expressing an opinion as to whether the description presents fairly, in all material respects, the relevant aspects of Basic Service Organization's controls that had been placed in operation as of [*date*], and as to whether the controls, as described, are suitably designed to provide reasonable assurance that the specified control objective would be achieved if the described controls were complied with satisfactorily. In connection with this examination, we confirm, to the best of our knowledge and belief, the following representations made to you during your examination.

1. We are responsible for establishing and maintaining appropriate controls relating to the processing of transactions for user organizations.
2. We believe the control objectives we have specified in the description are appropriate. They are both reasonable in the circumstances and consistent with our contractual obligations.
3. The description of controls presents fairly, in all material respects, the aspects of Basic Service Organization's controls that may be relevant to a user organization's internal control.
4. The controls, as described, had been placed in operation as of [*date*].
5. We believe the controls were suitably designed to achieve the specified control objectives.
6. We have disclosed to you all significant changes in controls that have occurred since Basic Service Organization's last examination.
7. There are no (We have disclosed to you all) illegal acts, fraud, or uncorrected errors attributable to Basic Service Organization's management or employees that may affect one or more user organizations.
8. There are no (We have disclosed to you all) design deficiencies in controls of which we are aware, including those for which we believe the cost of corrective action may exceed the benefits.
9. There are no (We have disclosed to you all) subsequent events that would have a significant effect on user organizations.
10. We have disclosed to you all instances, of which we are aware, when controls have not operated with sufficient effectiveness to achieve the specified control objective during the period [*date*] to [*date*].

Very truly yours,

NOTE: SAS 70 requires that representation 10. above be included in the report when the scope of work includes tests of operating effectiveness. The authors believe that it is also beneficial to include in the report on controls placed in operation.

325 COMMUNICATION OF INTERNAL CONTROL RELATED MATTERS NOTED IN AN AUDIT[1]

EFFECTIVE DATE AND APPLICABILITY

Original Pronouncements	SAS 60, April 1988; as revised to reflect the conforming changes necessary due to the issuance of SAS 78, December 1995; and SAS 87, September 1998.
Effective Date	Audits of financial statements for periods beginning on or after January 1, 1989; revised to reflect SAS 78, effective for audits on or after January 1, 1997; and SAS 87, effective for reports issued after December 31, 1998.
Applicability	Audits of financial statements in accordance with generally accepted auditing standards. SAS 60 supersedes SAS 20 (Section 323), *Required Communication of Material Weaknesses in Internal Accounting Control*, and paragraphs 47 through 53 of SAS 30 (Section 642), *Reporting on Internal Accounting Control*. (Section 642 was subsequently superseded by SSAE 2.)

[1] *The Auditing Standards Board (ASB) has issued an Exposure Draft of a proposed SAS,* ***Communication of Internal Control Related Matters Noted in an Audit.*** *The proposed SAS would supersede SAS 60 and would, among other things, redefine a reportable condition as a "significant deficiency," require that significant deficiencies and material weaknesses be reported to the audit committee, enhance reporting and documentation guidance, and establish that a material misstatement detected by the auditor but not by the entity ordinarily indicates a material weakness in internal control. This proposed SAS does not apply to SEC audits, other than registered investment companies, in which the auditor of the financial statements is also required to audit the entity's internal control over financial reporting. The proposed SAS,* ***Auditing an Entity's Internal Control over Financial Reporting in Conjunction with the Financial Statement Audit,*** *would apply to audits of these entities. The Public Company Accounting Oversight Board (PCAOB) has replaced the ASB as the standards-setting authority for public company audits. Therefore, the ASB's Exposure Draft will not be issued as a final standard by the AICPA. The document will, however, be considered by the PCAOB in developing a standard or amendments to existing transitional standard to comply with the Sarbanes-Oxley Act and the related SEC implementing rules. Please check for updates to this section on the John Wiley & Sons, Inc. website at www.wiley.com/gaas.*

DEFINITIONS OF TERMS

Reportable conditions. Matters coming to the auditor's attention that, in his or her judgment, should be communicated to the audit committee or individuals with equivalent authority and responsibility because they represent significant deficiencies in the design or operation of internal control (see Section 319), which could adversely affect the organization's ability to record, process, summarize, and report financial data consistent with the assertions of management in the financial statements. (At the end of this section, under *Illustrations*, are examples of reportable conditions.)

Material weakness. A reportable condition in which the design or operation of one or more of the specific internal control components does not reduce to a relatively low level the risk that misstatements caused by error or fraud in amounts that would be material in relation to the financial statements being audited may occur and not be detected within a timely period by employees in the normal course of performing their assigned functions.

NOTE: This Statement has no further definitions; however, it uses terms defined in SAS 55, ***Consideration of Internal Control in a Financial Statement Audit*** *(Section 319).*

OBJECTIVES OF SECTION

This section provides guidance in identifying and reporting conditions observed during an audit that relate to an entity's internal control. The communication of these conditions would generally be to the audit committee, or to persons with authority and responsibility equivalent to an audit committee in entities that do not have one, such as the board of directors, board of trustees, owner in an owner-managed company, or others who may have engaged the auditor. (For the remainder of this section, the term audit committee will be used for convenience whether referring to an audit committee or its equivalent.)

SAS 60 clarified and simplified the language of the auditor's report on internal control previously prescribed by SAS 20. However, it also substituted for the requirement to report **material weaknesses in internal accounting control,** described in SAS 20, a requirement to report a **reportable condition**.

The section provides guidance in identifying and reporting conditions that relate to an entity's internal control observed during an audit of financial statements. It does not apply to the reporting of material weaknesses noted in an attest engagement to report on entity's internal control.

The section also provides for establishing, between the auditor and client, agreed-upon criteria for identifying and reporting on matters in addition to those required to be reported on by this section.

FUNDAMENTAL REQUIREMENTS

General

Reportable conditions or conditions considered reportable because of agreement between the auditor and the client should be reported, preferably in writing.

The auditor should document the communication in the audit documentation if the reportable condition is communicated orally.

The auditor may communicate matters that he or she considers to be not reportable conditions but which nonetheless may be of benefit to the entity.

AUDITOR'S OBLIGATION

The auditor is not obligated to search for reportable conditions. However, the auditor is obligated to communicate reportable conditions to the audit committee (or to individuals with equivalent authority and responsibility such as a board of directors, board of trustees, or an owner in an owner-managed entity).

The auditor should consider various factors relating to the entity, such as its size, complexity and diversity of activities, organizational structure, and ownership characteristics when making the decision concerning which matters are reportable conditions.

Management may be aware of a reportable condition and decide not to correct it because of costs or other considerations. The auditor may decide the condition does not have to be reported **if the audit committee has acknowledged its understanding and consideration of the condition and the related risk**. Periodically, however, the auditor should consider whether it is appropriate and timely to report such a condition because of changes in management, the audit committee, or because of the passage of time.

CONTENT OF REPORT

1. The report should state that the communication is intended solely for the information and use of the audit committee, management, and others within the organization. Specific reference may be made to a regulatory authority if the regulatory authority has established requirements to furnish such reports.
2. All reports on reportable conditions should include
   a. An indication that the purpose of the audit was to report on the financial statements and not to provide assurance on internal control.
   b. The definition of reportable conditions.
   c. The restriction on distribution described in 1. above.
3. The auditor may include additional statements in the report regarding the inherent limitations of internal control in general, the specific extent and nature of the consideration of internal control during the audit, or other matters regarding the basis for the comments made.
4. In a communication that contains both reportable conditions and other comments, it may be appropriate to identify those in each category.
5. If a reportable condition is considered to be a material weakness in internal control, the auditor may, but is not required to, separately identify and communicate that material weakness.

NO REPORTABLE CONDITIONS

The auditor should **not** issue a report stating that no reportable conditions were noted during the audit.

NOTE: If no reportable conditions are noted, the auditor should not issue an SAS 60 letter but may, as discussed below, issue a management letter.

TIMING OF COMMUNICATION AND OTHER MATTERS

The auditor may communicate reportable conditions after the audit has been completed or may choose to communicate significant matters during the course of the audit.

The auditor may communicate to the client observations and suggestions about matters relating to internal control that are not deemed to be reportable conditions or information that goes beyond internal control.

INTERPRETATIONS

Reporting on the Existence of Material Weaknesses (February 1989, Revised February 1999)

1. An auditor may issue a report on material weaknesses separate from the report on reportable conditions (see example at the end of this section under *Illustrations*).
2. In issuing such a report, the auditor should not imply that no reportable conditions were noted.
3. In some cases reports on material weakness may include comments on specific aspects of internal control or additional matters. A regulatory agency may require such reports. In this situation the report in *Illustrations* should be modified to
   a. Clearly identify the additional matters covered.
   b. Distinguish a. from internal control.
   c. Describe the scope of the review and tests of the additional matters.
   d. Express conclusions in language comparable to language in other reports in *Illustrations*.

TECHNIQUES FOR APPLICATION

Identification of Reportable Conditions

The auditor is not required to search for reportable conditions. However, during the course of the audit, the auditor may become aware of reportable conditions as a result of obtaining an understanding of internal control, assessing control risk, or performing substantive tests. Identifying whether a weakness in controls is a reportable condition requires judgment about both the likelihood and magnitude of the misstatement permitted by the weakness. A significant deficiency in the design or operation of controls is less significant than a material weakness and, thus, both the risk and materiality of misstatement have lower thresholds.

Documentation of Reportable Conditions

During the audit, as the auditor becomes aware of reportable conditions, he or she should document them in a workpaper specifically prepared to list reportable conditions, describe their nature, and may indicate possible corrective measures.

Agreed-Upon Criteria

The auditor and the client may agree that the auditor will report conditions that go beyond those described in the Statement. The auditor and the client also may agree that the auditor will report on matters of less significance than reportable conditions. These agreements may require the auditor to perform procedures not required by generally accepted auditing standards. In these circumstances, the auditor would be wise to document these agreements, preferably in the engagement letter.

Communications of Reportable Conditions

Written Communication

It is preferable that reportable conditions and other matters, if applicable, be communicated in writing. Examples of written communications are presented in the following section, *Illustrations*.

Oral Communication

Reportable conditions may be reported orally. If the communication is oral, the auditor should note the following in the audit documentation:

1. Date of communication.
2. Person or persons informed of the reportable condition.
3. Nature of the reportable condition.
4. Response of the person or persons informed of the reportable condition.

Communication of Reportable Conditions and Other Matters

For communications that contain both reportable conditions and other matters, it would be appropriate for the auditor to indicate which comments apply to each category.

Timing of Communication

Usually, the auditor will communicate reportable conditions after the audit has been completed. However, if a reportable condition exposes the client to significant immediate risk, the auditor should communicate it when discovered. Reportable conditions that would normally warrant prompt communication are the following:

1. Possible loss of records. For example, a client may decide to implement a new computer program without simultaneous processing using the old program.
2. Possible loss of assets, such as stock held for investment purposes made out to bearer.
3. Possible fraud permitted by a change in procedures. For example, the person doing the bank reconciliation is given responsibility to handle cash.

Requirements of Governmental Authorities

If a governmental authority requires a report on reportable conditions, it would be advisable for the auditor to make specific reference to the governmental authority in the last paragraph of the report (see *Illustrations*).

Recommended Corrective Action

Although the auditor is not required to recommend corrective action for a reportable condition, he or she may do so as a matter of client service.

Material Weakness

The Statement does not require the auditor to separately identify and communicate as material weaknesses those reportable conditions that the auditor believes are material weakness. The auditor may, however, communicate as follows:

1. Identify those reportable conditions that he or she considers to be material weaknesses. (For example, lack of segregation of certain functions.) This may be done in the report on reportable conditions or in a separate report (see *Illustrations*).
2. State that none of the reportable conditions are material weaknesses.

Known Reportable Condition

Management may be aware of a reportable condition and decide not to correct it because of costs or other considerations. The auditor is not required to report the condition if the audit committee has acknowledged (the authors recommend that this acknowledgment be in writing) its understanding of the condition and the risk of not correcting it.

When the auditor communicates a previously noted reportable condition that has not been corrected, he or she should indicate that this condition was previously reported. For example, the communication might contain a paragraph similar to the following:

> It should be noted that some of the items discussed here have been commented on before and are repeated since they are still applicable. Such comments are indicated by an asterisk (*).

ILLUSTRATIONS

The following illustrations are adapted from SAS 60:

1. Examples of possible reportable conditions.
2. Report on reportable conditions observed.
3. Report indicating that the reportable conditions are not deemed to be material weaknesses.
4. Report on material weaknesses separate from report on reportable conditions (from interpretation of SAS 60).

ILLUSTRATION 1. EXAMPLES OF POSSIBLE REPORTABLE CONDITIONS (FROM AU 325)

Deficiencies in Internal Control Design

- Inadequate overall internal control design.
- Absence of appropriate segregation of duties consistent with appropriate control objectives.
- Absence of appropriate reviews and approvals of transactions, accounting entries, or systems output.
- Inadequate procedures for appropriately assessing and applying accounting principles.
- Inadequate provisions for the safeguarding of assets.
- Absence of other control techniques considered appropriate for the type and level of transaction activity.
- Evidence that a system fails to provide complete and accurate output that is consistent with objectives and current needs because of design flaws.

Failures in the Operation of Internal Control

- Evidence of failure of identified controls in preventing or detecting misstatements of accounting information.
- Evidence that a system fails to provide complete and accurate output consistent with the entity's control objectives because of the misapplication of controls.
- Evidence of failure to safeguard assets from loss, damage, or misappropriation.
- Evidence of intentional override of internal control by those in authority to the detriment of the overall objectives of the system.
- Evidence of failure to perform tasks that are part of internal control, such as reconciliations not prepared or not timely prepared.
- Evidence of willful wrongdoing by employees or management.
- Evidence of manipulation, falsification, or alteration of accounting records or supporting documents.
- Evidence of intentional misapplication of accounting principles.
- Evidence of misrepresentation by client personnel to the auditor.
- Evidence that employees or management lack the qualifications and training to fulfill their assigned functions.

Others

- Absence of a sufficient level of control consciousness within the organization.
- Failure to follow up and correct previously identified internal control deficiencies.
- Evidence of significant or extensive undisclosed related-party transactions.
- Evidence of undue bias or lack of objectivity by those responsible for accounting decisions.

ILLUSTRATION 2. REPORT ON REPORTABLE CONDITIONS OBSERVED (ADAPTED FROM AU 325)

To the Audit Committee of ABC Corporation:

In planning and performing our audit of the financial statements of the ABC Corporation for the year ended December 31, 20X1, we considered its internal control in order to determine our auditing procedures for the purpose of expressing our opinion on the financial statements and not to provide assurance on internal control. However, we noted certain matters involving internal control and its operation that we consider to be reportable conditions under standards established by the American Institute of Certified Public Accountants.

Reportable conditions involve matters coming to our attention relating to significant deficiencies in the design or operation of internal control that, in our judgment, could adversely affect the organization's ability to record, process, summarize, and report financial data consistent with the assertions of management in the financial statements.

General

A standard accounting manual should be prepared that describes in detail all accounting policies and procedures of the Company. This manual would be useful in controlling operations of the various reporting units and would be a significant help in training new employees. This manual would include the following:

1. A description and a chart of the accounting organization.
2. A description of duties and responsibilities.
3. A description and an explanation of methods and procedures to be followed.
4. A chart of accounts.
5. Reporting deadlines.
6. Other documents, forms, or instructions for which uniformity is desired.

Sales

We noted that several bills of lading were not dated by the carrier. To provide adequate proof of delivery and to safeguard the Company's assets, all bills of lading should be dated by the carrier.

A number of credit memos were not approved and were not supported with adequate documentation. To reduce the possibility of unauthorized credits, all credit memos should be reviewed for proper authorization and documentation before being processed.

[*Include additional paragraphs to describe other reportable conditions noted.*]

This report is intended solely for the information and use of the audit committee [*board of directors, board of trustees, or owners in owner-managed enterprises*], management, and others within the organization [*or specified regulatory agency*] and is not intended to be and should not be used by anyone other than these specified parties.

Illustration 3. Report Indicating That the Reportable Conditions Are Not Deemed to Be Material Weaknesses (Adapted from AU 325)

To the Audit Committee of ABC Corporation:

[*Include the same first paragraph as Illustration 2.*]

[*Include paragraphs to describe the reportable conditions noted.*]

A material weakness is a reportable condition in which the design or operation of one or more of the internal control components does not reduce to a relatively low level the risk that errors or fraud in amounts that would be material in relation to the financial statements being audited may occur and not be detected within a timely period by employees in the normal course of performing their assigned functions.

Our consideration of internal control would not necessarily disclose all matters in internal control that might be reportable conditions and, accordingly, would not necessarily disclose all reportable conditions that are also considered to be material weaknesses as defined above. However, none of the reportable conditions described above is believed to be a material weakness.

[*Include the same final paragraph as Illustration 2.*]

Illustration 4. Report on Material Weaknesses Separate from Report on Reportable Conditions (Adapted from an Interpretation of AU 325)

To the Audit Committee of ABC Corporation:

In planning and performing our audit of the financial statements of ABC Corporation for the year ended December 31, 20X1, we considered its internal control to determine our auditing procedures for the purpose of expressing our opinion on the financial statements and not to provide assurance on internal control. Our consideration of internal control would not necessarily disclose all matters in internal control that might be material weaknesses under standards established by the American Institute of Certified Public Accountants. A material weakness is a condition in which the design or operation of the specific internal control component does not reduce to a relatively low level the risk that misstatements caused by error or fraud in amounts that would be material in relation to the financial statements being audited may occur and not be detected within a timely period by employees in the normal course of performing their assigned functions. However, we noted no matters involving internal control and its operation that we consider to be material weaknesses as defined above. [*Or*: However, we noted the following matters involving internal control and its operation that we consider to be material weaknesses as defined above: *Insert paragraphs describing the material weaknesses.*]

Some practitioners add the following paragraph for clarity and to avoid misunderstandings:

[Our consideration of internal control was for the limited purpose described in the preceding paragraph and would not necessarily disclose all matters that might be material weaknesses. In addition, because of inherent limitations in any internal control, errors or fraud may occur and not be detected by internal control.]

This report is intended solely for the information and use of the audit committee [*or board of directors, board of trustees, or owners in owner-managed enterprises*], management, and others within the organization [*or specified regulatory agency*] and is not intended to be and should not be used by anyone other than these specified parties.

326 EVIDENTIAL MATTER[1]

EFFECTIVE DATE AND APPLICABILITY

Original Pronouncements	SAS 31, August 1980; as amended by SAS 48, July 1984 and SAS 80, December 1996.
Effective Date	When issued, August 1980, except SAS 80 amendment is effective for engagements beginning on or after January 1, 1997.
Applicability	Audits of financial statements in accordance with generally accepted auditing standards (also applies to special reports on financial statements prepared in conformity with a comprehensive basis of accounting other than GAAP and on specified elements, accounts, or items expressing an opinion).

DEFINITIONS OF TERMS

Assertions. Representations by management that are embodied in financial statement components. They are classified in these broad categories.

- Existence or occurrence.
- Completeness.
- Rights and obligations.
- Valuation or allocation.
- Presentation and disclosure.

Existence or occurrence. Whether assets or liabilities included in the financial statements exist at the balance sheet date and whether recorded transactions occurred during the period covered by the income statement.

Completeness. Whether all transactions and accounts that should be in the financial statements are included.

Rights and obligations. Whether assets are rights of the entity and liabilities are its obligations at a given date.

---

[1] *The Auditing Standards Board (ASB) has issued Exposure Drafts of seven proposed SASs that relate to the risk assessment process. A summary of key changes is provided immediately before Section 100-230. This section would be superseded by a new SAS,* ***Audit Evidence****. The proposed new SAS would, among other things, provide additional guidance on the third standard of fieldwork, including a new definition of audit evidence and provide guidance on risk assessment procedures. The Public Company Accounting Oversight Board (PCAOB) has replaced the ASB as the standards-setting authority for public company audits. Therefore, the ASB's Exposure Drafts will not be issued as final standards by the AICPA. The documents will, however, be considered by the PCAOB in developing standards or amendments to existing transitional standards. Please check for updates to this section on the John Wiley & Sons, Inc. website at www.wiley.com/gaas.*

Valuation or allocation. Whether asset, liability, revenue, and expense components are included in the financial statements at appropriate amounts.

Presentation and disclosure. Whether components of financial statements are properly classified, described, and disclosed.

Audit objectives. Specific objectives to be achieved by applying audit procedures, developed from assertions, to enable the auditor to obtain evidential matter sufficient to form conclusions on the validity of the assertions.

Evidential matter. Underlying accounting data and corroborating information.

Underlying accounting data. Books of original entry, general and subsidiary ledgers, related accounting manuals, as well as informal and memorandum records (such as worksheets, computations, and reconciliations) supporting the financial statements.

Corroborating information. Documentary material (such as checks, invoices, contracts, and minutes of meetings), confirmations and other written representations, as well as any other information obtained by the auditor from inquiry, observation, inspection, physical examination, or valid reasoning.

Competence. A quality of evidential matter that relates to its **validity** and **relevance**.

Sufficiency. A quality of evidential matter that relates to the **amount** necessary to support an informed opinion on the financial statements.

NOTE: Competence indicates the kind of evidential matter, and sufficiency indicates the amount of evidence.

OBJECTIVES OF SECTION

SAS 31 combines an explanation of evidential matter that was developed in 1963 with the more current notion of financial statement assertions and audit objectives. More than most SASs, this one is a diverse mixture of the following:

Broad generalizations. The nature, timing, and extent of the procedures to be applied on a particular engagement are a matter of professional judgment to be determined by the auditor, based on specific circumstances.

Protective observations. An auditor typically works within economic limits; his or her opinion, to be economically useful, must be formed within a reasonable length of time and at reasonable cost.

Specific advice. In designing substantive tests to achieve an objective related to the assertion of existence or occurrence, the auditor selects from items contained in a financial statement amount and searches for relevant evidential matter. (This example, then, points out that the direction of testing is the opposite for completeness—from evidence of what should be included to the accounting record.)

General requirements. The procedures should be adequate to achieve the audit objectives developed by the auditor, and the evidential matter obtained should be sufficient for the auditor to form conclusions concerning the validity of the individual assertions embodied in the component of financial statements.

The SAS retains basic relationships from the earlier material, such as

Evidential matter = Underlying accounting data + Corroborating information

To this basic material is added the concepts of financial statement assertions and audit objectives. For example

Financial statement component	Inventories
Assertion	Existence or occurrence
Audit objective	Inventories included in the balance sheet physically exist
Procedure	Observe physical inventory counts

For each financial statement component, the auditor develops specific audit objectives using the broad categories of assertions as a guide. Then the auditor selects procedures designed to achieve those specific objectives. Several procedures may be needed to achieve some objectives, and some procedures contribute information on more than one objective.

This is a conceptually logical approach to the selection of the nature of procedures in planning an audit. In practical application, even though the practice is not explicitly recognized in the SAS, the auditor may use generalized material such as checklists, questionnaires, or standardized audit programs to accomplish the same thing. These generalized materials should be adapted to the circumstances of a particular engagement but remain a valid approach.

SAS 80 amended SAS 31 to recognize that in some situations in entities where significant information is transmitted, processed, maintained, or accessed electronically, the auditor may have to perform tests of controls. In other words, the auditor may determine that it is not practical or possible to reduce detection risk to an acceptable level by performing only substantive tests in certain circumstances.

FUNDAMENTAL REQUIREMENTS

DEVELOPING AUDIT OBJECTIVES

In developing audit objectives the auditor should consider

1. The nature of the entity's economic activity.
2. Accounting practices unique to its industry.
3. Assertions, both explicit and implicit, embodied in its financial statements.

SELECTING SUBSTANTIVE TESTS

The auditor selects substantive tests to achieve the audit objectives he or she has developed by considering

1. The nature of the audit objective to be achieved.
2. The nature and materiality of the items being tested.
3. The risk of material misstatement of the financial statements.
4. The assessed level of control and inherent risks.
5. The kinds and competence of available evidential matter.
6. The expected efficiency and effectiveness of possible substantive tests.

TESTS OF UNDERLYING ACCOUNTING DATA

The auditor tests the internal consistency of the accounting records by

1. Analysis and review.
2. Retracing procedural steps in the accounting process.
3. Recalculating.
4. Reconciling related information.

NOTE: By itself, underlying accounting data cannot be considered sufficient support for financial statements. However, unless adequate attention is paid to the underlying accounting data, the audit cannot be sufficient. For example, a trial balance of the general ledger is part of the underlying accounting data, but must be tested by comparison to the general ledger itself.

TESTS TO DEVELOP CORROBORATING INFORMATION

The auditor develops corroborating evidential matter by

1. Inspection of documents such as checks, invoices, contracts, and minutes of meetings.
2. Obtaining confirmation and other written representation from knowledgeable people within and outside the entity.
3. Physical examination of assets with a physical existence.
4. Observation of entity personnel and conditions within the entity.
5. Obtaining other information from inquiry, observation, inspection, physical examination, or valid reasoning.

General Guides to Competence of Evidence

Validity of evidence depends on the circumstances, so there are important exceptions to the following presumptions. They are, however, useful general guides.

1. Evidential matter from independent sources outside an entity is more reliable than that secured solely within the entity.
2. Accounting data developed under satisfactory internal control are more reliable than data developed under unsatisfactory conditions.
3. Direct personal knowledge obtained from the auditor's own physical examination, inspection, observation, or computation is more reliable than information obtained indirectly.

General Guides to Sufficiency of Evidence

The amount of competent evidential matter necessary to provide a reasonable basis for an opinion depends largely on the exercise of professional judgment.

1. Usually the auditor must rely on evidence that is persuasive rather than convincing; an auditor is seldom convinced beyond all doubt about all aspects of the statements being audited.
2. There should be a rational relationship between the cost and usefulness of evidence, but the difficulty and expense of a test is not a valid reason for omitting it.

Evaluation of Evidential Matter

The auditor should be **thorough** in searching for evidence and **unbiased** in evaluating it; he or she should consider relevant evidential matter whether it corroborates or contradicts assertions in the financial statements and recognize the possibility that the statements may not warrant an unqualified opinion.

If the auditor remains in doubt about any material assertion, he or she should refrain from forming an opinion until enough evidence has been obtained to remove the doubt, or the auditor should express a qualified opinion, or disclaim an opinion.

Basic Requirements

Professional judgment determines the specific procedures to be applied, but the auditor should meet these requirements.

1. The procedures adopted should be adequate to achieve the objectives developed by the auditor.
2. The procedures should reduce detection risk to an acceptable level.
3. The evidential matter obtained should be sufficient for the auditor to form conclusions on the validity of the individual assertions embodied in the components of the financial statements.

4. In some circumstances, the auditor should perform tests of control because it is not practical or possible to reduce detection risk to an acceptable level by performing only substantive tests.

   NOTE: These circumstances may be encountered in entities where significant information is transmitted, processed, maintained, or accessed electronically. In this situation, the potential for improper initiation or alteration of information to occur and not be detected may be greater.

5. Because certain electronic evidence may exist at a point in time, the auditor should consider the time during which information exists or is available for substantive or test of controls testing.

INTERPRETATIONS

EVIDENTIAL MATTER FOR AN AUDIT OF INTERIM FINANCIAL STATEMENTS (ISSUED FEBRUARY 1974; MODIFIED OCTOBER 1980)

1. The third standard of fieldwork on evidential matter also applies to an audit of interim financial information.
2. Because additional estimates are used in measuring certain times for interim financial information, the evidence that is needed to test those estimates may differ from evidence required for the audit of annual financial information.

THE EFFECT OF AN INABILITY TO OBTAIN EVIDENTIAL MATTER RELATING TO INCOME TAX ACCRUALS (ISSUED MARCH 1981; REVISED APRIL 2003)

1. Occasionally, the client may not (a) prepare or maintain appropriate documentation of the calculation or contents of the income tax accrual, or (b) permit the auditor access to the documentation or necessary information, or to entity personnel with information about the income tax accrual.
2. In these circumstances, the client has imposed a scope limitation on the audit, and the auditor should determine the effect of the limitation on his or her ability to express an opinion on the financial statements. The auditor may express an unqualified opinion, a qualified opinion, or disclaim an opinion (see Section 508).
3. The auditor should document all relevant information that he or she obtains about the income tax accrual. The documentation should include results of auditing procedures and should include significant elements of the client's analysis of the tax contingencies or reserves.
4. The opinion of the client's legal counsel about the appropriateness of the income tax accrual is **not** sufficient competent evidential matter for the accrual.
5. Similarly, an auditor cannot rely solely on the conclusions of a third-party tax adviser without careful consideration by the auditor. The auditor should have access to the tax adviser's opinions and supporting evidence. If the auditor cannot obtain sufficient competent evidence, the auditor has a scope limitation.

THE AUDITOR'S CONSIDERATION OF THE COMPLETENESS ASSERTION (APRIL 1986)

1. Management's written representations about the completeness assertions and the auditor's assessment of control risk, by themselves, do not constitute sufficient competent evidential matter as to the completeness assertion.

2. The auditor should obtain other evidence by performing substantive tests, such as analytical procedures and tests of details of accounts related to the account that may not include all transactions.
3. The auditor should consider that for some transactions (e.g., revenues in cash at a casino or a charitable organization) it may be necessary to perform tests of controls and assess control risk below the maximum.

Applying Auditing Procedures to Segment Disclosures in Financial Statements (August 1998)

Statement of Financial Accounting Standards (SFAS) 131, *Disclosures About Segments of an Enterprise and Related Information*, established standards for the way that public business enterprises disclose information about segments in annual financial statements and in interim reports. (See the following for a summary of SFAS 131.) An auditor should consider segment disclosures in relation to the financial statements taken as a whole and is not required to apply procedures as extensive as would be necessary to express an opinion on the segment information taken by itself.

In planning the audit, the auditor should understand

- Who performs the function of the chief operating decision maker.
- How management organized the entity into operating segments for internal reporting.
- The nature of, and differences between, information systems used to generate data for allocation to segments versus those used for external reporting.

The auditor should perform procedures designed to

- Evaluate whether the entity appropriately identified its reportable operating segments according to SFAS 131.
- Evaluate the adequacy and completeness of management's disclosures.

The auditor's standard report on financial statements prepared in conformity with generally accepted accounting principles implicitly applies to segment information in the same manner as other informative disclosures. The auditor's report does not refer to segment information unless

- The audit revealed a material misstatement or omission of the segment information.
- The auditor was unable to apply the necessary auditing procedures.

In these situations, the auditor should consider the reporting guidance in Section 508. Furthermore, the auditor is not obligated to refer to changes required by SFAS 131 or to subsequent changes in segments if

1. The prior financial statements have been restated and the restatement is disclosed, or
2. The financial statements disclose why the earlier period has not been restated.

Summary of SFAS 131

NOTE: The following summary of SFAS 131 is not part of this Interpretation, but has been included for the practitioner's information.

SFAS 131 establishes standards for the way that public business enterprises report information about operating segments in annual financial statements and requires that those enterprises report selected information about operating segments in interim financial reports issued to shareholders. It also establishes standards for related disclosures about products and services, geographic areas, and major customers. The Statement supersedes SFAS 14, *Financial Reporting for Segments of a Business Enterprise*, but retains the requirement to report information about major customers. It amends SFAS 94, *Consolidation of All Majority-Owned Subsidiaries*, to remove the special disclosure requirements for previously unconsolidated subsidiaries. The Statement does not apply to nonpublic business enterprises or to not-for-profit organizations.

SFAS 131 requires that a public business enterprise report financial and descriptive information about its reportable operating segments. Operating segments are components of an enterprise about which separate financial information is available that is evaluated regularly by the chief operating decision maker in deciding how to allocate resources and in assessing performance. Generally, financial information is required to be reported on the basis that it is used internally for evaluating segment performance and deciding how to allocate resources to segments.

The Statement requires that a public business enterprise report a measure of segment profit or loss, certain specific revenue and expense items, and segment assets. It requires reconciliations of total segment revenues, total segment profit or loss, total segment assets, and other amounts disclosed for segments to corresponding amounts in the enterprise's general-purpose financial statements. It requires that all public business enterprises report information about the revenues derived from the enterprise's products or services (or groups of similar products or services), about the countries in which the enterprise earns revenues and holds assets, and about major customers regardless of whether that information is used in making operating decisions. However, the Statement does not require an enterprise to report information that is not prepared for internal use if reporting it would be impracticable.

The Statement also requires that a public business enterprise report descriptive information about the way that the operating segments were determined, the products and services provided by the operating segments, differences between the measurements used in reporting segment information and those used in the enterprise's general-purpose financial statements, and changes in the measurement of segment amounts from period to period.

TECHNIQUES FOR APPLICATION

There is an almost infinite variety of approaches that an auditor can use in practice to comply with Section 326. One approach is to go through all the steps in SAS 31 in each engagement for each financial statement component. The following illustration, included in the appendix to SAS 31 (AU 326) and reprinted here with the permission of the AICPA, shows what this approach might look like for the financial statement component of inventories.

Illustrative audit objectives	*Examples of substantive tests*
	Existence or Occurrence
Inventories included in the balance sheet physically exist.	Observing physical inventory counts. Obtaining confirmation of inventories at locations outside the entity. Testing of inventory transactions between a preliminary physical inventory date and the balance sheet date.
Inventories represent items held for sale or use in the normal course of business.	Reviewing perpetual inventory records, production records, and purchasing records for indication of current activity. Comparing inventories with a current sales catalog and subsequent sales and delivery reports. Using the work of specialists to corroborate the nature of specialized products.

Illustrative audit objectives	*Examples of substantive tests*
Completeness	
Inventory quantities include all products, materials, and supplies on hand.	Observing physical inventory counts. Analytically comparing the relationship of inventory balances to recent purchasing, production, and sales activities. Testing shipping and receiving cutoff procedures.
Inventory quantities include all products, materials, and supplies owned by the entity that are in transit or stored at outside locations.	Obtaining confirmation of inventories at locations outside the entity. Analytically comparing the relationship of inventory balances to recent purchasing, production, and sales activities. Testing shipping and receiving cutoff procedures.
Inventory listings are accurately compiled and the totals are properly included in the inventory accounts.	Tracing test counts recorded during the physical inventory observation to the inventory listing. Accounting for all inventory tags and count sheets used in recording the physical inventory counts. Testing the clerical accuracy of inventory listing. Reconciling physical counts with perpetual records and general ledger balances and investigating significant fluctuations.
Rights and Obligations	
The entity has legal title or similar rights of ownership to the inventories.	Observing physical inventory counts. Obtaining confirmation of inventories at locations outside the entity. Examining paid vendors' invoices, consignment agreements, and contracts.
Inventories exclude items billed to customers or owned by others.	Examining paid vendor's invoices, consignment agreements, and contracts. Testing shipping and receiving cutoff procedures.
Valuation or Allocation	
Inventories are properly stated at cost (except when market is lower).	Examining paid vendors' invoices. Reviewing direct labor rates. Testing the computation of standard overhead rates. Examining analyses of purchasing and manufacturing standard cost variances.
Slow-moving, excess, defective, and obsolete items included in inventories are properly identified.	Examining an analysis of inventory turnover. Reviewing industry experience and trends. Analytically comparing the relationship of inventory balances to anticipated sales volume. Touring the plant. Inquiring of production and sales personnel concerning possible excess of obsolete inventory items.
Inventories are reduced, when appropriate, to replacement cost or net realizable value.	Obtaining current market value quotations. Reviewing current production costs. Examining sales after year-end and open purchase order commitments.
Presentation and Disclosure	
Inventories are properly classified in the balance sheet as current assets.	Reviewing drafts of the financial statements.
The major categories of inventories and their bases of valuation are adequately disclosed in the financial statements.	Reviewing the drafts of the financial statements. Comparing the disclosures made in the financial statements to the requirements of generally accepted accounting principles.
The pledge or assignment of any inventories is appropriately disclosed.	Obtaining confirmation of inventories pledged under loan agreements.

This approach can be time-consuming and result in a substantial amount of repetition. For example, developing specific audit objectives for the existence of each asset normally results in the repetitive statement that the particular asset does, in fact, exist and is available for its intended use. There is more variation for specific audit objectives related to presentation and disclosure, but disclosure checklists are available for that assertion and related specific objectives.

EXAMPLES OF EVIDENTIAL MATTER THAT MAY SUPPORT THE SPECIFIC ASSERTIONS EMBODIED IN FINANCIAL STATEMENTS

Another approach is a source list of procedures or evidential matter to be used as a resource in developing audit programs. The following chart indicates what this approach might look like for some common financial statement components. Usually such source lists present either evidential matter or procedures, but to avoid repetition, not both. For example, if the evidential matter is minutes of board meetings, the procedure is to read the minutes. Or if the procedure is to inspect a broker's advice, the evidential matter is the broker's advice.

Another approach is to use standardized audit programs developed for common components of financial statements. This approach is not illustrated here. Many auditors prefer source lists to packaged programs because of a concern that standardized programs promote routine application and do not encourage exercise of judgment.

SOURCE LIST OF PROCEDURES OR EVIDENTIAL MATTER

Elements of financial statements	*Existence or occurrence*	*Completeness*	*Rights and obligations*	*Valuation or allocation*	*Presentation and disclosure*
Cash	Bank confirmations	Bank reconciliations	Bank confirmations	Foreign currency exchange rates from newspapers, and so on	Confirmation of restrictions on bank balances
	Cash counts	Interbank transfer schedules			Contractual agreements relating to escrow funds, compensating balances, sinking funds, and so on
	Certificates of deposit and savings account books	Subsequent "cutoff" bank statements			
		Review of controls over cash receipts and disbursements			
Marketable securities	Security counts	Analyses of general ledger account activity	Certificate of ownership	Broker's advices and documents supporting purchases of securities	Representation and other information regarding management's intention to retain securities
	Security confirmations	Confirmations of security positions with brokers and dealers	Security confirmations	Market value quotations	Minutes of board or committee meetings
	Custodian's reports	Custodian's reports		Appraised values of infrequently traded securities	Contractual terms of debt securities and preferred stocks
		Review of subsequent transactions		Foreign currency exchange rates from newspapers, and so on	Confirmation of securities pledged under loan agreements, and so on
		Review of controls over security of investments and transactions			
Receivables	Confirmation of account balances	Tests of year-end sales and shipping cutoff procedures	Confirmation of account balances	Aging of open balances	Confirmation of terms with debtors

Receivables (continued)	Underlying customer orders and agreements, invoices, and shipping documents	Reconciliation of trial balances and general control accounts	Subsequent collections	Credit experience and terms	Sales agreement and contract terms
	Subsequent collections	Analytical relationship of balances to recent sales volume	Sales records	Credit reports on customers	Terms of notes receivable and collateral held
	Customer correspondence	Analyses of general ledger account activity	Customer correspondence	Correspondence on collection follow-up	Confirmation of receivables sold with recourse, discounted, pledged, and so on
	Sales records	Review of controls over billings and cash receipts	Promissory notes	History of sales returns and allowances Industry experience and trends Subsequent collections, credits, and write-offs Discussion with credit and collection personnel Review of controls over credit extension and collection Foreign currency exchange rate from newspapers, and so on	
Inventory	Physical counts	Tests of year-end shipping and receiving cutoff procedures	Physical counts and confirmations	Purchasing and manufacturing cost records	Confirmation of inventories pledged under loan agreements, and so on
	Confirmation of inventories not on hand	Reconciliations of physical counts with perpetual records and general ledger balances	Paid vendors' invoices	Vendors' invoices	
	Perpetual inventory records	Analytical relationship of balances to recent purchasing, production, and sales activity	Consignment agreements	Review of labor rates	

Elements of financial statements	*Existence or occurrence*	*Completeness*	*Rights and obligations*	*Valuation or allocation*	*Presentation and disclosure*
Inventory (continued)	Underlying purchasing records, including purchase orders, vendors' invoices, and receiving reports	Analyses of general ledger account activity	Purchase agreements and contracts	Analyses of purchasing and manufacturing standard cost variances	
	Underlying production records	Review of controls over accounting for receiving, production, and shipping activities	Physical observations and confirmations	Open purchase commitments	
	Subsequent sales and delivery reports	Review of controls over inventory records		Current market value quotations and replacement cost information	
				Plant tour for possible excess and obsolescence	
				Discussion with production and sales personnel	
				Inventory turnover schedules	
				Industry experience and trends	
				Analytical relationship of balances to anticipated sales volume	
Prepaid assets and deferred charges	Invoices, contracts, agreements, and other documents supporting additions to balances	Analyses of general ledger account activity	Documents supporting additions to balances	Documents supporting additions to balances	Terms of insurance policies, tax bills, and so on (current vs. noncurrent)
		Review of controls over accounts payable and cash disbursements		Recalculation of amortization	
		Review of subsequent transactions		Recomputation of ending account balances	
				Analytical relationship of balances to estimated future utilization of assets	

Prepaid assets and deferred charges (continued)				Discussion of realizability of deferred charges with appropriate personnel	
				Industry experience and trends	
Fixed assets	Physical observations	Plant tour	Documents supporting confirmations	Documents supporting acquisitions	Minutes, representations, and other information regarding management's intention to abandon or dispose of fixed assets
	Documents supporting acquisitions, including authorizations in minutes, construction contracts, purchase orders, invoices, work orders, and so on	Analyses of general ledger activity	Lease agreements	Lease agreement terms	Confirmation of fixed assets pledged under loan agreements, and so on
	Confirmation of equipment maintained at outside locations	Reconciliation of account activity to subsidiary property records		Appraisal reports, replacement cost quotations, and so on	Terms of lease agreements
		Analytical relationship of fixed asset dispositions to replacements		Recalculation of depreciation and amortization	
		Confirmation of construction contracts payable		Analytical relationship of current year's depreciation and amortization to fixed asset costs	
		Vouching of repair and maintenance expense accounts		Industry experience and trends	

Elements of financial statements	*Existence or occurrence*	*Completeness*	*Rights and obligations*	*Valuation or allocation*	*Presentation and disclosure*
Fixed assets (continued)		Review of controls over accounts payable and cash disbursements Review of controls over construction work in progress			
Intangible assets	Documents supporting acquisitions, including authorizations in minutes, purchase agreements, contracts, and so on	Review of controls over accounts payable and cash disbursements	Documents supporting acquisition	Documents supporting acquisitions	Terms of contracts and purchase agreement
				Appraisal reports	Minutes of board or committee meetings
				Recalculation of amortization Representations and other information regarding use and realizability of assets Industry experience and trends Verification of foreign currency exchange rates	
Accounts payable	Confirmation of selected accounts	Circularization of vendors	Confirmations of selected balances	Foreign currency exchange rate from newspapers, and so on	Confirmation of terms with creditors
	Supporting documents including purchase orders, invoices, receiving reports, check requests, and so on	Tests of year-end purchasing and receiving cutoff procedures	Purchase contracts and vendor statements		Purchase agreement and contract terms

Accounts payable (continued)	Vendor statements	Reconciliation of trial balances and general ledger control accounts Review of subsequent payments Review of unmatched vendor invoices and receiving reports Review of controls over purchasing, receiving, and cash disbursements			
Accrued taxes and other expenses	Tax bills, invoices, and other documents supporting charges for services	Analysis of general ledger account activity	Tax bills, invoices, and other documents supporting charges for services	Documents relating to items accrued	Terms of tax bills, and so on
	Subsequent payments	Comparison of account balances between years	Subsequent payments	Recalculation of amortization	Internal Revenue Service agents' reports
	Industry experience	Review of controls over recording of cash disbursements		Recomputation of ending account balance Discussion of estimated future costs with entity personnel	
Debt	Confirmation with lenders	Bank confirmations	Notes and loan agreements	Current interest rate quotations	Confirmation of terms with lenders
	Note and loan agreements	Representations from management	Lease agreements	Foreign currency exchange rate from newspapers, and so on	Terms of note and loan agreements
	Lease agreements	Reference in minutes to commitments, obligations, acquisitions, and so on			Terms of lease
	Authorization in minutes of board meetings	Correspondence from legal counsel			Current bank prime rate schedules
Revenue	Documents in support of selected revenue transactions including customer orders, contracts, shipping documents, and sales invoices	Tests of year-end sales and shipping cutoff procedures	Not applicable	Discussions with engineers regarding percentage of completion of long-term projects	Terms of documents supporting revenue transactions, including long-term contracts

Elements of financial statements	*Existence or occurrence*	*Completeness*	*Rights and obligations*	*Valuation or allocation*	*Presentation and disclosure*
Revenue (continued)	Review of controls over shipping and billing activities	Review of subsequent transactions		Recalculations of percentage of completion computations	
	Documents in support of selected expense transactions including purchase orders, contracts, check requests, and so on	Review of controls over shipping and billing activities		History of sales returns and allowances	
	Review of controls over recording long-term contract activity		Industry experience and trends	Subsequent credit memos	

NOTE: Revenue recognition continues to pose significant audit risk to auditors. Therefore, auditors should be aware that the AICPA recently issued an Audit and Accounting Guide, ***Auditing Revenue in Certain Industries,*** *that summarizes key accounting guidance regarding whether and when revenue should be recognized in accordance with GAAP, identifies circumstances and transactions that may signal improper revenue recognition, and provides guidance on auditing revenue transactions in selected industries not covered by existing AICPA Audit and Accounting Guides. In addition, the SEC has issued Staff Accounting Bulletin 101,* ***Revenue Recognition in Financial Statements,*** *which summarized certain of the SEC staff's views in applying GAAP to revenue recognition in financial statements. These two publications may be useful to auditors in evaluating revenue recognition issues.*

Expense	Documents in support of selected expense transactions including purchase order contracts, check requests, and so on	Test of year-end purchasing cutoff procedures	Not applicable	Recomputation of depreciation and amortization	Terms of documents supporting selected expense transactions, including large and unusual purchases
	Confirmation of large and unusual purchases with suppliers	Review of subsequent transactions		Recomputation of amortization of prepaid and accrued expense and deferred charges	
	Review of controls over accounts payable and cash disbursements	Comparison of account balances between years		Analytical relationship of balances to total revenue	
		Review of control over accounts payable and cash disbursements			

328 AUDITING FAIR VALUE MEASUREMENTS AND DISCLOSURES[1]

EFFECTIVE DATE AND APPLICABILITY

Original Pronouncement	SAS 101, January 2003.
Effective Date	Audits of financial statements for periods beginning on or after June 15, 2003, with earlier application permitted.
Applicability	Audits of financial statements in accordance with generally accepted auditing standards.
	NOTE: The SAS does not address specific types of assets, liabilities, components of equity, transactions, or industry-specific practices. Such guidance can be found in other SASs, such as Section 332, "Auditing Derivative Instruments, Hedging Activities, and Investments in Securities."

DEFINITIONS OF TERMS

Fair value. According to FASB Statement of Financial Accounting Concepts 7, *Using Cash Flow Information and Present Value in Accounting Measurements,* the fair value of an asset or liability is the amount at which that asset (liability) could be bought (incurred) or sold (settled) in a current transaction between willing parties, that is, other than in a forced or liquidation sale.

Significant assumptions. Generally, significant assumptions cover matters that materially affect the fair value measurement and may include those that are

a. Sensitive to variation or uncertainty in amount or nature of the item. For example, assumptions about short-term interest rates may be less susceptible to variation compared to assumptions about long-term interest rates.
b. Susceptible to misapplication or bias.

OBJECTIVES OF SECTION

More and more GAAP pronouncements require the use of fair value measurements when presenting and disclosing certain assets, liabilities, and components of equity in the

---

[1] *In 2002, the AICPA developed* ***Auditing Fair Value Measurements and Disclosures: A Toolkit for Auditors.*** *This publication assists auditors by presenting recommendations on applying GAAS to audits of financial statements that recognize fair value measurements under SFAS 141,* ***Business Combinations,*** *SFAS 142,* ***Goodwill and Other Intangible Assts,*** *and SFAS 144,* ***Accounting for the Impairment or Disposal of Long-Lived Assets.*** *The full test of the toolkit can be obtained for free from the AICPA website at http://www.aicpa.org/memebers/div/auditstd/fasb123002.asp.*

financial statements. Such measurements have become both increasingly complex and yet important for financial statement users. The ASB decided that practitioners needed overall guidance when auditing fair value measurements and disclosures.

Since assumptions used in measuring fair value are similar to those used in developing other accounting estimates, this section addresses issues similar to those in Section 342, "Auditing Accounting Estimates," along with guidance that is specific to fair value estimates.

SAS 101 provides the standards and guidance for auditing fair value measurements in financial statements and the related disclosures.

FUNDAMENTAL REQUIREMENTS

According to AU 328.03, the auditor should obtain sufficient competent audit evidence to provide reasonable assurance that fair value measurements and disclosures conform with GAAP.

UNDERSTANDING HOW FAIR VALUE IS DETERMINED AND ASSESSING RISK

The auditor should understand the entity's process for determining fair value measurements and disclosures and the relevant controls sufficient to develop an effective audit approach. The auditor uses this understanding when assessing the risk of material misstatement and then determining the nature, timing and extent of audit procedures to perform. The auditor should be aware that, as the accounting and financial reporting requirements for fair value measurements become more complex, the risk of material misstatement may increase.

NOTE: The SAS notes that since fair value measurements often involve subjective judgments, this may affect the nature of controls, the possibility of management override of controls, and the inherent limitations of internal control.

EVALUATING CONFORMITY OF FAIR VALUE MEASUREMENTS AND DISCLOSURES WITH GAAP

According to AU 328.15, the auditor should evaluate whether the fair value measurements and disclosures in the financial statements are in conformity with GAAP. The auditor uses the understanding of GAAP requirements, knowledge of the entity's business and industry, and the results of audit procedures to evaluate the accounting for and disclosure of fair values. The auditor's understanding of the business is particularly important in certain cases, such as the following:

1. When the asset or liability or the valuation method is highly complex, such as when valuing complex derivatives.
2. When valuing items that may be affected by the entity's circumstances and operations, such as the valuation of intangible assets acquired in a business combination.
3. When assessing the need to recognize an impairment loss under GAAP. The results of audit procedures should also be considered when making this assessment.

The auditor should also evaluate the intent and ability of management to carry out specific courses of action where intent is relevant to the use of fair value measurements, the related presentation and disclosure requirements, and how changes in fair value are reported in the financial statements. The auditor's procedures ordinarily include reviewing budgets, minutes, written plans and other documentation and making inquires of management, corroborating management's responses as necessary, to

1. Evaluate management's history of carrying out its stated intentions regarding assets or liabilities.

2. Evaluate management's reasons for choosing a particular course of action and its ability to carry out the action in light of economic circumstances and contractual commitments.

When the entity uses a valuation method, the auditor should evaluate whether the entity's measurement method is appropriate in the circumstances. The evaluation requires the use of professional judgment along with an understanding of management's rationale for selecting a particular method, obtained by discussing the reasons for selecting the valuation method with management. The auditor also considers the following:

1. Has management sufficiently evaluated and applied required GAAP criteria, if any, to support the selected method?
2. Is the valuation method appropriate in light of the nature of the item valued and the entity's business, industry, and operating environment?
3. If different valuation methods result in significantly different fair value measurements, how has the entity investigated the reasons for these differences in establishing its fair value measurements?

The auditor should evaluate whether the entity's method for determining fair value measurements is applied consistently, and if so, whether such consistency is appropriate in light of any changes in the entity's circumstances, environment, or changes in accounting principles.

If management changes the method for determining fair value, the auditor considers whether management can adequately demonstrate that the new method is more appropriate.

NOTE: SAS 101 notes that an example of an appropriate change might be discontinuing an old valuation method when an active market for an equity security is created.

Engaging a Specialist

The auditor should consider whether to engage and use the work of a specialist as evidential matter in performing substantive tests of material financial statement assertions. If the auditor decides to use a specialist, he or she considers whether the specialist's understanding of fair value and the method to be used by the specialist are consistent with those of management and with GAAP. The auditor may discuss such matters with the specialist or read the specialist's report. The auditor should also apply the guidance in Section 336, "Using the Work of a Specialist."

Testing the Entity's Fair Value Measurements and Disclosures

Based on the auditor's assessment of the risk of material misstatement, the auditor should test the entity's fair value measurements and disclosures. The nature, timing, and extent of audit procedures may vary widely because of differences in the complexity of fair value measurements and levels of the risk of material misstatement. Such substantive tests may involve

1. Testing management's significant assumptions, the valuation model, and the underlying data,
2. Developing corroborating independent fair value estimates, or
3. Reviewing subsequent events and transactions.

Testing Significant Assumptions, the Valuation Model, and the Underlying Data

The auditor evaluates the following when testing the entity's fair value measurements and disclosures:

1. Are management's assumptions reasonable and consistent with market information?
2. Was the fair value determined using an appropriate model?
3. Did management use relevant and reasonably available information?

The auditor should evaluate whether management's significant assumptions taken individually and as a whole, provide a reasonable basis for the entity's fair value measurements and disclosures. The auditor pays particular attention to significant assumptions that support complex valuation methods and consider whether they are reasonable and consistent with market information. The auditor should keep in mind, however, that he or she is not required to obtain evidence to provide an opinion on the assumptions, but rather evaluate whether such assumptions provide a reasonable basis for the fair value measurements in the context of the audit.

The auditor should test the data used in preparing the fair value measurements and disclosures and evaluate whether the fair value measurements have been properly determined from the data and assumptions. The auditor evaluates whether the data is accurate, complete, and relevant. The auditor also evaluates whether the data and management's assumptions support the measurements. Such tests of data may include

- Verification of the data's source.
- Mathematical recomputation of inputs.
- Review of the consistency of information, including consistency with management's intent and ability to carry out planned actions.

Developing Corroborating Independent Fair Value Estimates

If the auditor decides to develop an independent fair value estimate to corroborate management's estimate, the auditor evaluates management's assumptions. The auditor may decide to develop his or her own assumptions to make a comparison with management's fair value measurements. However, the auditor should still understand and evaluate management's assumptions. This understanding will help to ensure that the auditor's independent estimate considers all significant variables, and will help in evaluating significant differences in the auditor's estimate and management's estimate. The auditor should also test the data that management uses to develop the fair values, as discussed previously.

Reviewing Subsequent Events and Transactions

Subsequent events and transactions that reflect circumstances existing at the balance sheet date may substantiate fair value measurements and reduce the need to apply other audit procedures to substantiate the measurements. However, if subsequent events or transactions reflect changes in circumstances occurring after the balance sheet date, then such events are not competent evidence of the fair value measurement at the balance sheet date.

NOTE: For example, a change in the price of an equity security with an active market change reflects a change in circumstances and would not provide competent evidence of the fair value measurement of the security at the balance-sheet date. The SAS notes that this consideration of subsequent events is a substantive test and differs from the review of subsequent events in Section 560, "Subsequent Events."

FAIR VALUE DISCLOSURES

The auditor should evaluate whether the entity's fair value disclosures are adequate and are in conformity with GAAP. The auditor would use essentially the same procedures to audit the fair value disclosures as used in auditing fair value measurements in the financial statements. The auditor obtains sufficient competent audit evidence that the valuation principles are appropriate and consistently applied, and that the valuation method and significant assumptions used are properly disclosed as required by GAAP.

When evaluating the adequacy of disclosure, the auditor considers whether disclosures of items with a high degree of measurement uncertainty sufficiently inform users of this uncertainty.

When fair value information required under GAAP is not included because it is not practicable to reliably determine fair value, the auditor evaluates whether the disclosures in these circumstances are adequate or whether the lack of disclosure causes the financial statements to be materially misstated.

Evaluating the Results of Audit Procedures

The auditor should evaluate the sufficiency and competence of audit evidence obtained for fair value measurements and disclosures and whether the evidence is consistent with other audit evidence. The auditor's evaluation of whether the fair value measurements and disclosures are in conformity with GAAP is done in the context of the financial statements as a whole. (See Section 312.)

Written Management Representations

The auditor should obtain written management representations about whether significant assumptions are reasonable and whether they appropriately reflect management's intent and ability to carry out specific courses of action relevant to the use of fair value measurements and disclosures.

The auditor may also obtain written representations concerning whether

- The measurement methods and related assumptions are appropriate and whether the methods are consistently applied.
- Fair value disclosures are complete and adequate.
- Subsequent events would require that fair value measurements and disclosures be adjusted.

Communication with Audit Committees

Section 380, "Communication with Audit Committees," requires that certain significant accounting estimates be communicated to audit committees. The auditor should determine that the audit committee is informed about management's process for formulating sensitive accounting estimates including fair value estimates, and the basis for the auditor's conclusions about those estimates. The auditor may consider communicating

- The nature of significant assumptions underlying fair value measurements.
- The subjectivity of the assumptions.
- The materiality of the measurements to the financial statements as a whole.

NOTE: In determining the nature and form of communication, the auditor should follow the guidance in Section 380, "Communication with Audit Committees."

TECHNIQUES FOR APPLICATION

General

Fair value of an asset, liability, or component of equity may be measured when the item is initially recorded or at a later date when the value of the item changes. GAAP requires that certain items be recorded at fair value, but may provide for different treatments of changes in fair value that occur over time. For example, certain changes in fair value are reflected in net income, while others may be shown as an element of other comprehensive income.

The Nature of Fair Value Measurements

Fair value measurements, other than those with observable market prices, are inherently imprecise because such measurements involve uncertainty and are based on assumptions that may change over time. The auditor is responsible for considering information available to the auditor at the time of the audit and is not responsible for predicting future conditions, transactions, or events that, had they been known at the time of the audit, might affect actions and assumptions underlying fair value measurements and disclosures.

Measuring fair value may be relatively simple for certain assets or liabilities, such as actively traded securities. For other items, fair value measurement may be much more complex and require the use of a valuation method.

Relation to Other Audit Procedures

Other audit procedures may also provide evidence about fair value measurements and disclosures. For example, examining an asset to verify its existence may also provide evidence about the physical condition that would affect its valuation.

MANAGEMENT'S RESPONSIBILITIES

Management is responsible for determining the fair value measurements and disclosures in the financial statements, including

1. Establishing the process for determining fair values and disclosures.
2. Selecting appropriate valuation methods.
3. Identifying and supporting significant assumptions.
4. Performing the valuation.
5. Determining that the presentation and disclosure of the fair value measurements are in conformity with GAAP.

UNDERSTANDING HOW FAIR VALUE IS DETERMINED AND ASSESSING RISK

The auditor should consider the following when obtaining an understanding of the entity's process for determining fair values and disclosures:

1. General considerations, including
   a. The role of information technology in the fair value process.
   b. The types of accounts or transactions requiring fair value (e.g., do the accounts consist of routine recurring transactions or unusual transactions?)
   c. Whether the entity uses a service organization.
2. Information about management's assumptions, including
   a. Significant assumptions used to determine fair value,
   b. The process for developing and applying assumptions and monitoring changes in them, and
   c. The documentation supporting the assumptions.

   NOTE: The auditor should consider whether management used available market information in developing assumptions.

3. Information about controls over
   a. The process for determining fair values, including data controls and whether duties are segregated between personnel responsible for committing the entity to the underlying transactions and those responsible for making the valuation.
   b. The ability to change controls and security procedures for valuation models and the associated information systems.
   c. Consistency, timeliness, and reliability of the data for valuation models.
4. Information about the personnel involved, including
   a. The expertise and experience of the personnel making the fair value measurements.
   b. Whether a specialist is used.

TESTING THE ENTITY'S FAIR VALUE MEASUREMENTS AND DISCLOSURES

Complex fair value measurements normally tend to be more uncertain, resulting from

- A longer forecast period.
- More significant and complex assumptions.
- Greater subjectivity in the assumptions and factors used in the process.
- Greater uncertainty as to future events underlying the assumptions used.
- Less or no objective data when highly subjective factors are used.

Examples of considerations when developing auditing procedures include

- Fair value measurements may be made at a date other than the required financial statement reporting date. When this happens, the auditor obtains evidence that management has accounted for any changes affecting the measurements that occur between the measurement and reporting dates.
- If collateral is a factor when measuring fair value, the auditor obtains sufficient competent audit evidence regarding the existence, value, rights, and access to or transferability of the collateral. The auditor should consider whether all appropriate liens have been filed and whether the collateral has been appropriately disclosed.
- The auditor considers whether additional procedures are needed to obtain sufficient competent audit evidence about the appropriateness of a fair value measurement, such as physically inspecting an asset to verify the current physical condition and the effect on fair value.

Tests of Significant Assumptions

When evaluating significant assumptions used by management, the auditor considers the following:

- Assumptions will vary depending upon the characteristics of the item valued and the valuation method used.
- Assumptions will be supported by different types of internal and external evidence, and the auditor evaluates the source and reliability of such evidence.
- Because assumptions are often interdependent, assumptions should be evaluated individually and as a whole. Auditors should be alert to the fact that an assumption can appear reasonable when considered individually but not when considered along with other assumptions.
- The valuation may be sensitive to changes in significant assumptions, such as market conditions. If necessary, the auditor encourages management to use sensitivity analy-

sis or other techniques to identify sensitive assumptions. If management does not do so, the auditor should consider whether to employ such techniques.
- If assumptions are based on historical information, whether that basis is justified.

Assumptions should be realistic and consistent with

- The overall economic climate, the economic climate of the industry, the entity's own economic circumstances, and market information.
- The entity's plans.
- Prior period assumptions if still appropriate, and any applicable past experience.
- Risk related to cash flows, including possible variations in the amount and timing of cash flows and the effect on the discount rate, if applicable.
- The extent to which management relies on historical financial information and whether such reliance is appropriate.
- Any other financial statement matters, such as assumptions used for other types of accounting estimates.

The auditor may also compare fair value measurements from prior periods to help evaluate the reliability of the entity's process for making such measurements. If variances from prior period measurements exist, the auditor considers whether they result from changes in market or economic circumstances.

Testing the Valuation Model

The auditor does not function as an appraiser and does not substitute his or her judgment for management's when evaluating valuation models. Instead, the auditor should review the model and determine whether

- The assumptions are reasonable.
- The model is appropriate for that entity.

NOTE: SAS 101 notes that an example of where a method might not be appropriate is the use of discounted cash flows by a start-up entity for valuing an equity investment if there is no current revenue stream on which to base future forecasts of earnings or cash flows.

329 ANALYTICAL PROCEDURES

EFFECTIVE DATE AND APPLICABILITY

Original Pronouncement	SAS 56, April 1988; and SAS 96, January 2002.
Effective Date	Audits of financial statements for periods beginning on or after January 1, 1989.
Applicability	Audits of financial statements in accordance with generally accepted auditing standards. (SAS 96 is effective for audits of financial statements for periods beginning on or after May 15, 2002. *NOTE: Some of the guidance provided in this Statement might be useful in other engagements in which analytical procedures are normally applied, such as reviews of interim information or examinations of prospective financial information, even though it is not required to be applied in those engagements.*

DEFINITIONS OF TERMS

Analytical procedures. Analytical procedures consist of evaluations of financial information made by an auditor of **plausible and expected** relationships among both financial and nonfinancial data. They range from simple comparisons (the current year with the preceding year) to the use of complex models involving many relationships and elements of data (regression analysis).

A basic premise underlying the application of analytical procedures is that plausible relationships among data may reasonably be expected to exist and continue except as particular conditions (specific unusual transactions or events, accounting changes, business changes, random fluctuations, or misstatements) cause changes.

OBJECTIVES OF SECTION

INTRODUCTION

The term "analytical review procedures" was introduced in the official auditing literature in 1972 when SAP 54 on the auditor's study and evaluation of internal control was issued. Such procedures were used in practice well before then and were commonly referred to as ratio and trend analysis and comparisons. SAP 54 was the first official recognition, however, that such procedures could provide the auditor with evidential matter that satisfies the third standard of fieldwork on sufficient competent evidential matter. SAS 23, *Analytical Review Procedures*, issued in 1978, stated that the auditor's reliance on substantive tests might be derived from

1. Tests of details of transactions and balances.
2. Analytical review procedures.
3. Any combination of those two types of substantive tests.

SAS 23 did not require that analytical review procedures be applied. Nor did it specify what proportion of reliance on substantive tests might be derived from analytical procedures. The proportion of reliance to be placed on analytical procedures was left entirely to the auditor's judgment based on his or her evaluation of the expected efficiency and effectiveness of audit tests. SAS 23 did, however, require that the auditor investigate significant fluctuations identified when analytical review procedures were applied.

This SAS supersedes SAS 23 and shortens the term for this type of procedure by dropping the word "review." The major change is that analytical procedures are **required** in the planning and final review stages of an audit. The primary motivation for the requirement is that analytical procedures are effective in identifying misstatements and alerting the auditor to the possibility of certain types of material fraud.

Planning the Audit

The objective of using analytical procedures in planning the audit is to increase the auditor's understanding of the client and identify specific audit risks by considering unusual or unexpected balances or relationships in aggregate data. Specifically, the objective is to identify the existence of unusual transactions and events, and amounts, ratios, and trends that might identify matters that have audit planning ramifications.

Overall Review

The objective of using analytical procedures in the overall review of the audited financial statements near the completion of the audit is to help the auditor in assessing the validity of the conclusions reached during the audit, including the opinion on the financial statements.

Substantive Tests

The Statement does not require the auditor to use analytical procedures as a substantive test (see *Fundamental Requirements*). The auditor may, however, use these procedures as a substantive test. When used as a substantive test, the objective of analytical procedures is to accumulate evidence supporting the validity of a specific account balance assertion. For example, the results of applying an average interest rate to average debt outstanding would provide evidence supporting the amount of interest expense.

Updates

In January 2002, SAS 96, *Audit Documentation*, amended SAS 56 to add documentation requirements when an analytical procedure is used as the principal substantive test of a significant financial statement assertion.

FUNDAMENTAL REQUIREMENTS

Planning the Audit

The auditor is **required** to use analytical procedures in planning the audit. The purpose of analytical procedures at this stage of the audit is to assist the auditor in planning the nature, timing, and extent of the auditing procedures that will be used to obtain evidence in support of specific account balances or classes of transactions.

Overall Review

The auditor is **required** to use analytical procedures in the overall review of the audited financial statements. The results of this review may indicate that additional audit evidence may be needed.

Substantive Tests

The auditor **may** use analytical procedures to obtain evidential matter about particular assertions related to account balances or classes of transactions. When used for this purpose, analytical procedures are substantive tests.

1. According to AU 329.16, when using analytical procedures for substantive testing, the auditor should assess the reliability of the data by considering whether
   - The data was obtained from independent sources outside the entity.
   - Data sources within the entity were independent of those who are responsible for the data being audited.
   - The data was developed under a reliable system with adequate controls.
   - The data was subject to audit testing in the current or prior year.
   - The expectations were developed from data using a variety of sources.
2. The auditor should consider the amount of difference from his or her expectation that can be accepted without additional investigation.
3. The auditor should evaluate significant unexpected differences.
4. Management explanations should ordinarily be corroborated with other evidence.
5. If an explanation for a difference cannot be obtained, the auditor should perform other audit procedures if a likely misstatement has occurred.
6. The auditor should consider that an unexplained difference might increase the risk of material misstatement.

NOTE: To be used as a substantive test, an analytical procedure has to provide persuasive evidence. Audit objectives cannot be achieved by the application of analytical procedures that only provide overall comfort—the evidence has to be persuasive.

According to AU 329.22, the auditor should document all of the following when an analytical procedure is used as the principal substantive test for an assertion:

- The expectation and factors considered in its development, when the expectation is not readily determinable from the existing documentation.
- Results of the comparison between the expectation and the recorded amounts or ratios developed from the recorded amounts.
- Any additional auditing procedures performed in response to significant unexpected differences arising from the analytical procedure and the results of such procedures.

NOTE: These documentation requirements were established by SAS 96, which is effective for audits of financial statements for periods beginning on or after May 15, 2002, with earlier application permitted.

INTERPRETATIONS

There are no interpretations for this section.

PROFESSIONAL ISSUES TASK FORCE PRACTICE ALERTS

98-1 The Auditor's Use of Analytical Procedures

This Practice Alert provides guidance to practitioners on

1. **Applying substantive analytical procedures.** Analytical procedures are based on expectations, which are the auditor's prediction of what a recorded account balance

or ratio should be. In forming an expectation, the auditor should determine that a relationship is plausible. Plausible relations are relationships expected to exist based on the auditor's understanding of the client and the client's industry.

The auditor might consider the following items included in the Practice Alert:

- Forces external to the client's industry.
- The client's position within the industry.
- The client's processes for achieving its objectives.
- The prior years' audits and results.
- The client's budgeted and actual amounts.
- Discussions held with client personnel responsible for preparing recorded account balances or ratios and financial and nonfinancial results of comparable entities operating in the industry.

An expectation is typically developed using one or more of the following:

- Prior year data adjusted for expected change.
- Current period data.
- Budgets or forecasts.
- Nonfinancial data from within the entity.

These types of data are considered independent and reliable if they are

- Consistent with current business conditions.
- Not subject to influence or manipulation by persons involved in the accounting functions.

The account balance being tested can be estimated using data external to the entity, sources of which include

- Government agencies.
- Industry regulators.
- Trade associations.
- Industry surveys.
- Published financial information.

The auditor should consider whether the following limit or preclude the use of external information:

- Industry statistics may be biased by the results of one or two major players within the industry.
- The client activities may not match those that are covered by the information.
- Industry statistics may only reflect prior year history.
- The quality of industry statistics depends upon the degree of care taken by the industry participants in completing periodic returns.

In assessing the relationship between data used and the account balance being tested, the auditor should give consideration to the following factors:

- Data may exist for only part of the account balance being tested.
- The relationship may be circular or deterministic.
- The effects of changes in relationships, seasonality, and lags.

The reliability of the data is influenced by whether the data is

- Audited.
- From independent sources outside the entity.

- From sources within the entity that are independent from those responsible for the amount being tested.
- Subject to a reliable system of internal controls.

2. **Identifying difficulties[1] noted in the performance of analytical procedures and ways to avoid them.** The Practice Alert highlights difficulties such as
    - Using unaudited balances as a starting point. Auditors should not use management's unaudited balance as a starting point in determining what a recorded balance should be, without first looking to other predicative factors.
    - Unusual fluctuations might reflect a pattern. Examining each account without noting combinations of financial discrepancies may result in problematic situations being overlooked.
    - Placing reliance on management's explanations. Auditors should use discretion in using management as a first resource in explaining unexpected fluctuations, since the client's explanation might limit the auditor's consideration of other likely causes.
    - Developing expectations at the appropriate level of disaggregation. The auditors should be careful while performing substantive analytical procedures to use data at an appropriate level of disaggregation. Generally, the higher the level of disaggregation of the data, the more precise the expectation will be.
3. **How analytical procedures can assist the auditor in evaluating the risk of fraud.** The Alert provides guidance on how analytical procedures can assist the auditor in evaluating the risk of fraud. The results of analytical procedures do not provide the auditor with evidence to determine if fraud has resulted in a material misstatement to the financial statements, but they do help the auditor to determine if account balances have an increased chance of being subjected to fraud.

Finally, the Practice Alert also covers various bases for developing expectations, such as trend analysis, ratio analysis, reasonableness testing, and regression analysis, as well as consideration of the precision of the expectation. These topics are covered in the *Techniques for Application* section.

The full text of this Practice Alert can be obtained from the AICPA website at www.aicpa.org/members/div/secps/lit/practice.htm.

TECHNIQUES FOR APPLICATION

INTRODUCTION

Analytical procedures include (1) comparisons, (2) ratio analysis, (3) trend analysis, (4) variance analysis, (5) preparation of common-size financial statements, and (6) regression analysis. The specific procedures used are determined by the nature of the client's business and its industry, availability of data, degree of precision required, and auditor judgment.

When applying analytical procedures, the auditor may use data from outside the accounting system or financial statements, such as

1. Units produced or sold.
2. Number of employees.

---

[1] *The Practice Alert notes that some of the difficulties posed and ways to address them are discussed in the November 1997 article in the Journal of Accountancy, "When Judgment Counts." Members of the AICPA may obtain reprints of this article from the AICPA library at (888) 777-7077.*

3. Hours worked by nonsalaried employees.
4. Square feet of selling space.
5. Budget information. If, however, the budget is primarily a motivational tool—goals instead of expectations—its usefulness for analytical procedures is limited.

The remainder of this section, *Techniques for Application*, contains a general discussion of various techniques for the application of analytical procedures, followed by an explanation of how these procedures could be applied to the specific phases of the audit—planning, accumulation of audit evidence (substantive tests), and overall review.

ANALYTICAL PROCEDURES: GENERAL

When the auditor applies analytical procedures, he or she usually **computes**, **compares**, and **analyzes ratios**, **trends**, and **variances**. Generally, ratio analysis, trend analysis, and variance analysis are used together. In addition to these analyses, some auditors use regression analysis in applying analytical procedures.

Ratio analysis involves the following:

1. The computation of significant financial relationships, such as current assets to current liabilities.
2. The comparison of current period ratios with one or more of the following:
   a. Similar ratios of a prior period or periods.
   b. Similar ratios of the industry.
   c. Similar ratios generally viewed as acceptable by bankers or other credit grantors.
3. The analysis of unexpected deviations between current period ratios and those with which they are compared.

Trend analysis involves the following:

1. The selection of a base period.
2. The computation of subsequent periods' financial data, such as sales as a percentage of base period data.
3. The comparison of current period's percentages with those of prior periods.
4. The analysis of unexpected changes in percentages between the current period and prior periods.

Variance analysis involves the following:

1. The determination of acceptable levels for the financial data being analyzed.
2. The comparison of current period financial data with the acceptable levels.
3. The analysis of unexpected deviations between current period financial data and the acceptable level for such data.

COMPARISONS WITH INDUSTRY

In applying analytical procedures, the auditor may wish to compare the financial data of the client with those of the client's industry. For a diversified entity, however, comparisons may not be effective unless the auditor compares client segment data with appropriate industry data.

OBTAINING INDUSTRY DATA

Industry data may be obtained from publications issued by the following:

1. Dun & Bradstreet
   One Diamond Hill Road
   Murray Hill, NJ 07974
2. Robert Morris Associates
   1650 Market St. #2300
   1 Liberty Place
   Philadelphia, PA 19103
3. Standard & Poor's Corporation
   1221 Avenue of the Americas
   New York, NY 10020
4. Industry trade associations such as
   a. National Retail Merchants Association.
   b. American Association of Advertising Agencies.
   c. National Association of Tobacco Distributors.
5. Industry trade journals such as
   a. *Advertising Age.*
   b. *Chemical Week.*
   c. *Progressive Grocer.*

In addition, business publications such as *Business Week, Forbes,* and *Fortune* annually present financial data on the top 500 or 1000 companies. The auditor should use his or her ingenuity to locate the industry trade association or the industry trade publication if the client cannot provide the information. The auditor may do the following:

1. Consult the library of the American Institute of Certified Public Accountants.
2. Request help from business publications such as *Business Week, Forbes,* and *Fortune.*
3. Check the New York and Chicago telephone books, because *many* trade associations and trade journals are located in these cities.

Comparisons with National Economic Data

The auditor may wish to compare the client's financial data with national economic data such as the following:

1. Economic indicators—leading, lagging, coincident.
2. Gross domestic product.
3. Disposable income.
4. Consumer price index.
5. Wholesale price index.
6. Unemployment rate.

The data are issued monthly, the first five by the US Department of Commerce, the sixth by the US Department of Labor. All of the data and other national economic data are reported in the *Wall Street Journal.*

Ratio Analysis

The most common analytical procedure is ratio analysis. Ratios may be classified based on their sources as follows:

1. Balance sheet ratios.
2. Income statement ratios.
3. Mixed ratios. These ratios contain numbers from more than one financial statement.

Some of the more common ratios, their classification, method of computation, and the attribute measured are shown in the following list:

Ratios	*Formula*	*Purpose*
Liquidity ratios—Measure the entity's ability to meet its short-term obligations, and provide an indication of the entity's solvency.		
Current ratio	$= \dfrac{\text{Current assets}}{\text{Current liabilities}}$	Indicates whether claims of short-term creditors can be met with current assets.
Quick ratio or acid test	$= \dfrac{\text{Current assets} - \text{Inventory}}{\text{Current liabilities}}$	Measures the entity's ability to pay off short-term creditors without relying on the sale of inventories.
Leverage ratios—Measure the extent to which the entity is financed by debt and provide a measure of the risk of the entity borne by the creditors.		
Debt ratio	$= \dfrac{\text{Total debt}}{\text{Total assets}}$	Indicates percentage of total funds provided by creditors; high ratios when economy is in downturn indicate more risk for creditors.
Times interest earned	$= \dfrac{\text{Earnings before interest and taxes}}{\text{Interest charges}}$	Measures extent to which earnings can decline and still provide entity with ability to meet annual interest costs; failure to meet this obligation may result in legal action by creditors, possibly resulting in bankruptcy.
Long-term debt to equity	$= \dfrac{\text{Long-term debt}}{\text{Stockholder's equity}}$	Indicates the proportion of the entity financed through long-term debt vs. owners' equity.
Activity ratios—Measure how effectively an entity employs its resources.		
Inventory turnover	$= \dfrac{\text{Cost of goods sold}}{\text{Average inventory}}$	Estimates how many times a year inventory is sold.
Age of inventory	$= \dfrac{\text{360 days}}{\text{Inventory turnover}}$	Indicates number of days of inventory on hand at year-end.
Accounts receivable turnover	$= \dfrac{\text{Net credit sales}}{\text{Average accounts receivable}}$	Estimates how many times a year accounts receivable are collected.
Age of accounts receivable	$= \dfrac{\text{360 days}}{\text{Accounts receivable turnover}}$	Indicates the age of accounts receivable or number of days sales not collected.
Total asset turnover	$= \dfrac{\text{Net sales}}{\text{Total assets}}$	Estimates volume of sales based on total assets
Profitability ratios—Measure how effectively the entity is being managed.		
Sales to total assets	$= \dfrac{\text{Net sales}}{\text{Total assets}}$	Indicates the ability of an entity to use its assets to generate sales.
Gross margin	$= \dfrac{\text{Gross margin}}{\text{Net sales}}$	Provide a percentage relationship based on sales.
Profit margin on sales	$= \dfrac{\text{Net income}}{\text{Net sales}}$	Indicates the return an entity receives on sales.
Net operating margin	$= \dfrac{\text{Operating income}}{\text{Net sales}}$	Indicates management's effectiveness at using entity's assets to generate operating income.

Ratios		*Formula*	*Purpose*
Return on total assets	=	$\frac{\text{Net income} + \text{Interest expense}}{\text{Total assets}}$	Indicates the return an entity receives for its assets.
Return on common stockholders' equity	=	$\frac{\text{Net income} - \text{Preferred dividends}}{\text{Average stockholder's equity}}$	Indicates return on investment to common stockholders.

These ratios are some, but not all, of the ratios that may be used in applying analytical procedures. The auditor should use his or her knowledge of the client and its industry to develop relevant and meaningful ratios.

Ratio analysis has limitations in that it concentrates on the past and deals in aggregates. Ratios serve as warning signs and indicators, however, that are helpful in discovering existing or potential trouble spots when applied in trend analysis and variance analysis.

TREND ANALYSIS

Trend analysis indicates the relevant changes in data from period to period. For example, assume the following sales in successive income statements:

Year	20X1	20X2	20X3	20X4	20X5
Sales	$200	$300	$350	$450	$500

If 20X1 is selected as the base year, sales for that year are 100% and sales for 20X2 are 150% (300 ÷ 200). Sales in a trend statement are as follows:

Year	20X1	20X2	20X3	20X4	20X5
Sales	100%	150%	175%	225%	250%

Any year may be the base year, and the auditor may select a moving base year. At the end of 20X6, he or she may decide to develop a new five-year trend statement by eliminating 20X1 and making 20X2 the base year or 100%.

Trend statements may be developed from any data. For example, assume the following gross profit percentages:

Year	20X1	20X2	20X3	20X4	20X5
Profit	42%	43%	45%	45%	40%

If 20X1 is selected as the base year, its gross profit percentage would be 100.0%, and 20X2 would be 102.4% (43% ÷ 42%). Gross profit percentages in a trend statement are as follows:

Year	20X1	20X2	20X3	20X4	20X5
Profit	100.0%	102.4%	107.1%	107.1%	95.2%

The unusual decline in the trend from 20X4 to 20X5 alerts the auditor to an area (sales and cost of goods sold) requiring special attention and, perhaps, additional audit procedures.

Maintaining trend statements for significant numbers, sales, cost of goods sold, repairs and maintenance, selling expenses, and so on, and for significant ratios aids the auditor in detecting unusual deviations from prior periods.

VARIANCE ANALYSIS

An auditor may wish to compare current data with predetermined acceptable levels (the norms). Deviations from these levels require investigation. This process is known as variance analysis.

When applying variance analysis, the auditor may use data for his or her norms from the following sources:

1. Entity budgets.
2. Entity forecasts.
3. Industry data.
4. Prior period data.

When using industry data in analytical procedures, the auditor may convert the client's financial statements to common-size financial statements.

COMMON-SIZE FINANCIAL STATEMENTS

A common-size financial statement is one in which the numbers are converted to percentages. The dollars of cash, receivables, inventory, and other assets in the balance sheet are converted to percentages based on the relationship of each asset to total assets.

Common-size financial statements aid the auditor in comparing financial data of businesses of different sizes because not numbers but proportions are being compared. Further, most industry data such as those issued by Robert Morris Associates and Dun & Bradstreet are common size.

The following balance sheet is presented in amounts and in common size.

	Amount	*Common size*
Cash	$ 200	6.7%
Accounts receivable	500	16.7
Inventories	700	23.3
Property, plant and equipment, net	1,500	50.0
Other assets	100	3.3
Total	$3,000	100.0%
Accounts payable	$ 300	10.0%
Other current liabilities	100	3.3
Long-term debt	900	30.0
Stockholders' equity	1,700	56.7
Total	$3,000	100.0%

Common-size income statements also may be prepared based on sales as the 100% figure.

REGRESSION ANALYSIS

Regression analysis is the means by which cause-and-effect relationships are used to make inferences. The relationships are expressed in terms of a dependent variable and one or more independent variables.

Regression is used in auditing to make inferences as to what account balances **should be** for comparison with what account balances **are**. Ordinarily, a linear regression model is used when the auditor applies regression analysis.

Linear Regression

The linear regression model defines the relationship between the dependent variable and the independent variable or variables in terms of a straight line. To determine meaningful relationships, the auditor should identify those independent variables that affect the dependent variable. Although these relationships will never be exact and will differ at various times, useful inferences are possible as long as the relationships indicate that a relatively stable pattern exists between the dependent variable and the independent variable or variables.

Defining the Variables

To develop the regression model, the auditor should define the variables. In defining the variables, the auditor will use his or her knowledge of the client and previously audited historical data. In developing regression models, the auditor also may use external independent variables, such as gross national product, disposable net income, unemployment rate, and so on.

The Linear Regression Formula

The linear regression formula is as follows:

$$Y = a + bX$$

In this formula, *a* is the value of *Y* when *X* is equal to 0. The slope of the regression line is *b*, which indicates the change in *Y* for each unit of change in *X*. For example, assume the auditor wishes to make inferences about the amount of recorded selling expenses. Based on his or her knowledge of the client, the auditor determines the following:

1. Fixed selling expenses amount to $10,000. In the regression formula, this amount is *a*.
2. Selling expenses (*Y*) increase as sales (*X*) increase.
3. From prior data, the auditor determines that for each dollar of sales, selling expenses increase by $.05. In the regression formula, this amount is *b*.

In the regression formula, the preceding information is expressed as follows:

$$\text{Selling expense } (Y) = \$10{,}000\ (a) + [.05\ (b) \times \text{Sales } (X)]$$

Therefore, if sales were $10 million, the auditor would expect selling expenses to be $510,000, determined as follows:

$$Y = \$10{,}000 + .05 \times \$10{,}000{,}000$$
$$Y = \$510{,}000$$

Applying Regression Analysis

After defining the variables and determining the values for *a* and *b*, the auditor should perform other steps before making inferences. These steps are as follows:

1. Calculate the correlation coefficient.
2. Calculate point estimates.
3. Determine the standard deviation.
4. Determine the standard error.
5. Calculate the precision interval.
6. Calculate the confidence interval.

PERMANENT FILE FOR ANALYTICAL PROCEDURES

Because analytical procedures are based in part on industry data and client prior period data, this data may be maintained in the client permanent file for subsequent use. The data to be maintained depend on the nature of the analytical procedures.

When the auditor compares current period results with prior periods, the comparisons may include the following:

1. Quarter to quarter during the current year.
2. Month to month during the current year.
3. Season to season during the current year.
4. Current year's quarter, month, or season with the similar period of prior years.

The auditor may maintain in the client permanent file all periodic data used in the analysis.

The auditor also may include in the permanent file, when applicable, the following:

1. The percentages used in trend analysis.
2. The percentages used in common-size financial statements.
3. The ratios used in ratio analysis.
4. The industry data used and the source of the data.

There is no specified period of time for which permanent file data should be retained; however, it is advisable to retain these data for at least five years.

PLANNING THE AUDIT

Analytical procedures used in planning the audit are directed to (1) improving the auditor's understanding of the client's business and the transactions and events that have occurred since the last audit, and (2) identifying areas that may represent risks relevant to the current audit. For example, a lower than usual accounts receivable turnover ratio indicates possible collectibility problems. The auditor, therefore, should prepare an audit program for accounts receivable that emphasizes testing for the adequacy of the allowance for doubtful accounts.

Recommended Procedures

The Statement does not require the auditor to apply specific procedures. The sophistication, extent, and timing of the procedures are based on the auditor's judgment and may vary widely, depending on the size and complexity of the client.

Analytical procedures used in planning the audit might include the following:

1. **Account balance comparison.** Compare unadjusted trial balance amounts of the current period to adjusted trial balance amounts of the prior period.
2. **Computation of significant ratios.** Compute ratios, such as gross margin, inventory turnover, receivables turnover, and compare them to prior year ratios or industry ratios.
3. **Other ratios.** Compute ratios using nonfinancial and financial data; for example, sales per square foot of sales space.

For a large, complex entity, analytical procedures might include regression analysis to estimate the amount of certain account balances and extensive analysis of quarterly financial information.

The results of analytical procedures used in planning the audit combined with the auditor's knowledge of the client's business and industry serve as a basis for inquiries and the effective planning of substantive tests.

OVERALL REVIEW

The application of analytical procedures in the overall review stage of the audit is one of the last tests of the audit. Analytical procedures at this stage of the audit assist the auditor in assessing the conclusions reached concerning certain account balances and in evaluating the overall financial statement presentation.

Recommended Procedures

The overall review generally includes reading the financial statements and accompanying notes and considering the following:

1. The adequacy of evidence accumulated for account balances considered unusual or unexpected in the planning stage or during the audit.
2. Unusual or unexpected balances or relationships that were not previously identified.
3. The overall reasonableness of the financial statements and the adequacy of the financial statement disclosures.

In addition to reading the financial statements and accompanying notes, the auditor may consider using other analytical procedures, such as the following:

1. Comparison to similar financial data for the prior year or the client's industry.
2. Ratio analysis.
3. Trend analysis.
4. Development of common-size financial statements.

Results of Overall Review

The results of the overall review may indicate that additional audit evidence is needed. Because of this possibility, the auditor should try to complete the overall review before the end of fieldwork.

SUBSTANTIVE TESTS

The extent to which the auditor uses analytical procedures as a substantive test depends on the level of assurance he or she wants in achieving a particular audit objective. The higher the level of assurance desired, the more predictable the relationship should be. As a general rule, relationships involving income statement accounts are more predictable than relationships involving only balance sheet accounts.

It may be difficult or impossible to achieve certain substantive audit objectives without relying to some extent on analytical procedures (e.g., this is often the case in testing for unrecorded transactions).

Some audit objectives may be difficult or impossible to achieve by relying solely on analytical procedures (e.g., testing an account balance that is not expected to show a predictable relationship with other operating or financial data).

Analytical procedures may be more effective and efficient than tests of details for assertions in which potential misstatements would not be apparent from an examination of the detailed evidence or in which detailed evidence is not readily available (e.g., comparison of aggregate purchases with quantities received may indicate duplication payments that may not be apparent from testing individual transactions).

Differences from expected relationships would often be good indicators of potential omissions, whereas evidence that an individual transaction should have been recorded may not be readily available.

The expected effectiveness and efficiency of an analytical procedure in detecting errors or fraud depends on, among other things

- The nature of the assertion.
- The plausibility of the relationship.
- The reliability of the data used to develop the expectation.
- The precision of the expectation.

Availability and Reliability of Data

The auditor obtains assurance from analytical procedures based upon the consistency of the recorded amounts with the expectations developed from data derived from other sources. Other sources for data include industry trade associations; data service organizations, such as Dun & Bradstreet, Robert Morris Associates, and Standard & Poor's Corp., industry trade journals; and the client's prior year's audited financial statements. In circumstances where the auditor specializes in a specific industry, the auditor may use clients' data to develop plausible expectations (for example, gross margin percentage, other income statement ratios, and receivable and inventory turnover ratios).

The reliability of the data used to develop the expectations should be appropriate for the desired level of assurance from the analytical procedures.

Precision of the Expectation

The expectation of the relationship that exists should be precise enough to provide the desired level of assurance that differences that may be potential material misstatements would be identified for the auditor to investigate. Expectations developed at a detailed level ordinarily have a greater chance of detecting misstatements of a given amount than do broad comparisons. For example, expectations developed at a division level will have a greater chance of detecting misstatement than expectations developed at an entity level.

DOCUMENTATION

As with any other auditing procedure, the auditor should document the application of analytical procedures. SAS 96 requires certain documentation when an analytical procedure is used as the principal substantive test for an assertion. In addition, the following are recommended:

1. Procedures to be applied should be listed in the audit program.
2. Audit documentation should record the results of the procedures applied.
3. Auditor conclusions should appear in the audit documentation.
    a. What effect did the results have in planning the audit?
    b. If procedures applied in the overall review indicated that additional procedures were required, reference should be made in the audit documentation to those sections that document the additional procedures.
    c. If procedures applied as substantive tests indicated unexpected fluctuations, an explanation of these fluctuations should appear in the audit documentation. The auditor's explanation should include audit evidence supporting that explanation.

ILLUSTRATIONS

The following illustrations give examples of the application of analytical procedures and suggested follow-up audit procedures.

ILLUSTRATION 1

Facts

A company had sales (all credit) for the year of $120,000. Its accounts receivable at year-end amounted to $20,000. Its day's sales in accounts receivable is computed as follows:

1. Sales	$120,000
2. Accounts receivable	$ 20,000
3. Average daily sales (Sales $120,000 ÷ 360 days	$ 333
4. Day's sales in accounts receivable [Accounts receivable ÷ Average daily sales ($20,000 ÷ $333)]	60

In the previous year, the day's sales in accounts receivable was forty-five.

Analysis

The company is not collecting its receivables as rapidly as it did in the previous year. This increase in the day's sales in accounts receivable indicates a possible problem in the collectibility of the receivables.

Auditing Procedures

The auditor may consider doing some or all of the following:

1. Review cash receipts and remittance advices for the subsequent period.
2. Obtain credit reports on significant past due accounts.
3. Analyze year-end sales to determine any unusually large sales. Determine the nature of these sales and ascertain that they were recorded in the proper accounting period.

ILLUSTRATION 2

Facts

A company has cost of sales for the year of $108,000. Its inventory amounted to $20,000 at the beginning of the year and $16,000 at the end of the year. Its inventory turnover is determined as follows:

1. Average inventory		
Beginning balance	$20,000	
Ending balance	16,000	
Total	$36,000	
Total divided by 2		$18,000

NOTE: A better indication of the average inventory may be obtained by using month-end inventories, if available.

2. Cost of goods sold		$108,000
3. Cost of goods sold ÷ Average inventory = Inventory turnover		6

In the previous year, the inventory turnover was four.

Analysis

An increase in the inventory turnover ratio may occur because of improved purchasing, production, and pricing policies. It may also be caused by one of the following:

1. Poor credit rating of client. If the client has a poor credit rating, it may not be getting all of the inventory it requires. This will cause inventory levels to decline, and if sales do not decline as rapidly, the inventory turnover ratio will increase.
2. Unrecorded purchases.
3. Unusual inventory shrinkage.
4. Overly conservative inventory valuation.
5. Error in computing the inventory.

Auditing Procedures

There are no specific auditing procedures when the high turnover is caused by insufficient inventory because of a poor credit rating. In that situation, however, the auditor might want to obtain a credit report on the client and should approach the audit with more skepticism than usual.

If the auditor believes the high turnover is caused by other than a poor credit rating, he or she may do the following:

1. Review debit balances in the accounts payable schedule. A debit balance might indicate a payment without the accompanying entry for a purchase.
2. Review inventory controls to determine the possibility of theft. Also, if the company is a manufacturer, review production records to determine spoilage and waste.
3. Compare inventory costs with inventory values.
4. Review inventory computations.

ILLUSTRATION 3

Facts

Following is a trend statement of selected income and expense items:

Year	20X1	20X2	20X3	20X4	20X5
Sales	100	116	133	151	168
Selling expenses	100	115	132	150	175

Analysis

Sales have increased at a steady rate over the five-year period, and selling expenses matched this increase for the first four years. In the fifth year, however, the increase in selling expenses was disproportionate to previous years' increases and to the current year's increase in sales. The increase may have been caused by one of the following:

1. Misclassification of expenses.
2. Classification of prepayments as expenses.
3. Recording of nonbusiness expenses.

Auditing Procedures

If a trend statement indicates a disproportionate increase in an expense, the auditor should apply additional substantive tests to this expense. To determine the reason for the disproportionate increase in selling expenses in the preceding example, the auditor may review invoices for major expense items in order to answer the following:

1. Were administrative or nonselling expenses classified as selling expenses?
2. At year-end, did the entity make advance payments for the subsequent year's selling program and classify these payments as an expense rather than as a prepayment?
3. Are expenses of executives that are personal in nature being charged to the entity?

330 THE CONFIRMATION PROCESS

EFFECTIVE DATE AND APPLICABILITY

Original Pronouncement	SAS 67, November 1991.
Effective Date	Audits of fiscal periods ending after June 15, 1992.
Applicability	Audits of financial statements or other financial information made in accordance with generally accepted auditing standards.

DEFINITIONS OF TERMS

The confirmation process. The process of obtaining and evaluating a direct communication from a third party in response to a request for information about a particular item affecting financial statement assertions. The process includes

1. Selecting items for confirmation.
2. Designing the confirmation request.
3. Communicating the confirmation request to the appropriate third party.
4. Obtaining the response from the third party.
5. Evaluating the information, or lack thereof, provided by the third party about the audit objectives, including the reliability of that information.

Accounts receivable. An entity's claims against customers that have arisen from the sale of goods or services in the normal course of business, and a financial institution's loans.

Positive form of confirmation request. Recipient is asked to respond whether he or she agrees or disagrees with the information stated on the request. Positive forms provide audit evidence only when responses are received from the recipients.

Blank form of confirmation request. A blank form—a type of positive confirmation request—does not state amounts or other information on the confirmation request. The recipient is asked to provide the amount or furnish other information.

Negative form of confirmation request. Recipient is asked to respond only if he or she disagrees with the information given. Negative requests may be used to reduce audit risk to an acceptable level when **all** of the following exist:

1. The combined assessed level of inherent risk and control risk is low.
2. A large number of small balances is involved.
3. The auditor has no reason to believe that the recipients of the requests are unlikely to give them consideration.

OBJECTIVES OF SECTION

The auditor uses the confirmation process to obtain sufficient competent evidential matter. Confirmation is performed to obtain evidence from third parties about financial statement assertions made by management.

Section 326 (SAS 31), "Evidential Matter," states that, in general, it is presumed that "evidential matter...obtained from independent sources outside an entity...provide greater assurance of reliability for the purposes of an independent audit than that secured solely within the entity." Confirmation requests do not, however, address all assertions equally well. For example, accounts receivable confirmations are likely to be more effective for the existence and the rights-and-obligations assertions (see Section 326 for the five categories of assertions) than for the valuation assertion.

Since 1939, confirmation of receivables has been a generally accepted auditing procedure. The independent auditor who issued an opinion on financial statements and did not confirm receivables had the burden of justifying the opinion expressed on those financial statements (Section 331, formerly "Receivables and Inventory"). However, because of problems uncovered in peer reviews and mentioned in SEC Enforcement Releases, the Auditing Standards Board issued SAS 67.

SAS 67 addresses **all** types of confirmations including, but not limited to, accounts receivable confirmations. It relates the confirmation process to inherent and control risk. The greater the combined assessed level of inherent and control risk, the greater the assurance that the auditor needs from substantive tests. As this combined level of risk increases, the auditor designs substantive tests to obtain more or different evidence about a financial statement assertion. In those circumstances, the auditor should consider using confirmation procedures instead of, or in conjunction with, tests directed toward documents or parties within the entity. In circumstances where the combined assessed level of inherent and control risk is low, it may be appropriate for the auditor to consider not using confirmations. For example, if the combined assessed level of inherent and control risk over the existence of cash is low, the auditor might limit substantive procedures to inspecting client-provided bank statements rather than confirming cash balances.

Another factor that influences the use of confirmations is the nature of transactions. Confirmation of the terms of a transaction would be appropriate if that transaction was unusual or complex and the combined assessed level of inherent and control risk was high.

FUNDAMENTAL REQUIREMENTS

GENERAL

The auditor should consider the use of confirmations for situations where the combined assessed level of inherent risk and control risk is high.

The auditor should consider confirming the terms of unusual or complex transactions when the combined assessed level of inherent risk and control risk is high.

The auditor should consider the materiality of an account balance and his or her assessment of inherent risk and control risk when deciding whether the evidence provided by confirmations reduces audit risk for the related assertions to an acceptably low level.

The auditor should perform additional procedures when he or she concludes that evidence provided by confirmations alone is not sufficient to reduce audit risk to an acceptably low level. For example, the auditor may perform sales cutoff tests in addition to confirming accounts receivable to obtain sufficient evidence concerning the completeness and existence assertions for accounts receivable.

The auditor should exercise an appropriate level of professional skepticism throughout the confirmation process.

DESIGNING THE CONFIRMATION REQUEST

The auditor should design the confirmation request to satisfy the specific audit objective. Factors the auditor should consider include the following:

1. Assertions addressed (see Section 326, "Evidential Matter").
2. Conditions likely to affect the reliability of the confirmations.
3. Form of the confirmation request.
4. Prior experience on the audit or similar engagements.
5. Nature of information being confirmed.
6. Intended respondent.

When using negative confirmations, the auditor should

1. Perform other substantive procedures to supplement the use of the negative confirmations.
2. Investigate relevant information provided on returned negative confirmations.
3. Reconsider the combined assessed level of inherent and control risk and consider the effect on planned audit procedures when his or her investigation of responses indicates a pattern of misstatements.
4. Be aware that unreturned negative confirmation requests rarely provide significant evidence concerning financial statement assertions.
5. Be aware that negative confirmation requests are more likely to generate responses indicating misstatements if a larger number of requests are sent.

The auditor should consider the type of information respondents will be readily able to confirm when designing confirmation requests. For example, respondents, because of the nature of their accounting system, may not be able to confirm account balances but may be able to confirm transactions, terms of loans, and other information.

The auditor should obtain an understanding of the substance of the client's arrangements and transactions with third parties to determine the appropriate information to include on the confirmation request. For example

1. The auditor should consider confirming the **terms** of unusual transactions or sales, such as bill and hold sales, in addition to amounts.
2. If the auditor believes there is at least a moderate degree of risk that there may be significant oral modifications to agreements (for example, unusual payment terms or liberal rights of return), he or she should inquire about those modifications. A method of doing this is to confirm both the terms of the agreement and whether oral modifications exist.

THE RESPONDENT

The confirmation request should be addressed to a person who the auditor believes is knowledgeable about the information to be confirmed.

If a question arises about the respondent's competence, knowledge, motivation, ability, objectivity, or willingness to respond, the auditor should consider the effect in designing the confirmation request and evaluating the response. In those circumstances, the auditor should also determine whether other procedures are necessary.

If there are unusual circumstances where the auditor should exercise a heightened degree of professional skepticism concerning the respondent's competence, knowledge, motivation, ability, objectivity, or willingness to respond, the auditor should consider whether there is sufficient basis for concluding that the confirmation request is being sent to a respondent who the auditor believes will provide meaningful and competent evidence. Examples of such circumstances are significant unusual year-end transactions that have a material effect on the financial statements and when the respondent is the custodian of a material amount of the audited entity's assets.

CONTROL OF CONFIRMATIONS

The auditor should maintain control of the confirmation requests and responses. There should be no client intervention from the mailing of the requests to the receipt of the responses.

Because of the risks associated with facsimile responses (difficulty of ascertaining the sources of the responses), the auditor should consider performing the following in order to treat the confirmation as valid audit evidence:

1. Verifying the source and contents of the response through a telephone call to the purported sender.
2. Asking the purported sender to mail the original confirmation directly to the auditor.

Oral confirmations should be documented in the workpapers. If the information is significant, the auditor should ask the parties involved to submit written confirmation of that information directly to the auditor.

NONRESPONSES

If the recipients do not respond to the confirmation request, other than a negative confirmation request, the auditor should generally follow up with a second and sometimes a third request to those who did not respond.

If the auditor does not receive replies to positive confirmation requests, he or she should apply alternative procedures to the nonresponse to obtain the necessary evidence (see *Techniques for Application*). The auditor does not have to apply alternative procedures if

1. He or she has not identified unusual qualitative factors or systematic characteristics related to the nonresponses (for example, all nonresponses pertain to year-end transactions).
2. He or she is testing for overstatement and the nonresponses in the aggregate, when projected as 100% misstatements to the population and added to the total of all other unadjusted differences, would not affect the auditor's decision about whether the financial statements are materially misstated.

EVALUATING THE RESULTS

According to AU 330.33, the auditor should evaluate the combined evidence provided by the confirmations and the alternative procedures to determine whether sufficient evidence has been obtained. In performing the evaluation, the auditor should consider the following:

1. The reliability of the evidence.
2. The nature of any exceptions, including quantitative and qualitative implications of those exceptions.
3. The evidence provided by other procedures.
4. Whether additional evidence is needed.

If additional evidence is needed, the auditor should request additional confirmations or extend other tests, such as tests of details or analytical procedures.

CONFIRMATION OF ACCOUNTS RECEIVABLE

Confirmation of accounts receivable, including a financial institution's loans, is a generally accepted auditing procedure. It is therefore presumed that the auditor will request the confirmation of accounts receivable during an audit.

The presumption that the auditor will confirm accounts receivable may be overcome if one of the following exists:

1. Accounts receivable are not material to the financial statements.
2. The use of confirmations would be ineffective (for example, based on experience, the auditor concludes that response rates will be inadequate or that responses will be unreliable).
3. In some circumstances, the auditor's combined assessed level of inherent and control risk may be low, and that level, in conjunction with evidence expected to be provided by substantive tests, is sufficient to reduce audit risk to an acceptably low level for the applicable financial statement assertions.

NOTE: If confirmations are not used because experience with the entity indicates the procedure would not be effective, the auditor needs to design suitable alternative procedures to achieve audit objectives.

If the auditor does not confirm accounts receivable, he or she should document the reasons for not doing so.

INTERPRETATIONS

There are no interpretations for this section.

PROFESSIONAL ISSUES TASK FORCE PRACTICE ALERTS

03-01 AUDIT CONFIRMATIONS

This Practice Alert provides additional guidance to auditors on using confirmations. To improve the confirmation response rate, the alert suggests that auditors request information that the recipient is likely and able to confirm. Confirmations should also include relevant information required for the recipient's response.

The alert suggests the following techniques to improve the confirmation response rate:

- Use clear wording.
- Send the confirmation to a specified individual.
- Identify the organization being audited.
- Consider asking the client to hand-sign the request.
- Set response deadlines.
- Send second, and possibly third, requests.
- Call the respondent to obtain oral confirmation and request that the written confirmation be returned.

The alert also provides guidance on negative versus positive confirmation requests, nonresponses to positive confirmations, verifying fax confirmations, the use of alternative procedures, and using client personnel. Among other things, the alert notes that

- The auditor should thoroughly investigate all exceptions to positive confirmation requests.
- The auditor should carefully consider any requests by management not to confirm certain balances or other information. The auditor should challenge those reasons, and seek corroborating evidence.

Finally, the Alert provides guidance on the confirmation of specific areas, including accounts receivable, related-party transactions, accounts payable, and the terms of unusual or complex agreements or transactions.

The full test of this Practice Alert can be obtained from the AICPA website at www.aicpa.org/members/div/secps/lit/practice.htm.

TECHNIQUES FOR APPLICATION: CONFIRMATION OF RECEIVABLES

TIMING OF CONFIRMATION REQUEST

For both positive and negative confirmation requests, the debtor is provided with the balance as of a specified date. The date may be as follows:

1. Year-end date.
2. Date prior to year-end. This date generally is one or two months prior to year-end.

It is recommended that confirmation requests be sent to debtors approximately a week before the date specified in the request. If the debtor is in a foreign country, the request should be mailed earlier.

Confirming Prior to Year-End

The auditor may decide to request that the debtor confirm the balance as of a date before year-end. If the auditor follows this procedure, however, he or she should perform the following procedures during the year-end procedures:

1. Perform selective other substantive tests of transactions from the confirmation date to the balance sheet date. These tests would include the following:
   a. Review subsequent sales invoices and related bills of lading.
   b. Review subsequent customer cash receipts and related remittance advices.
2. If balances change significantly from confirmation date to year-end, it is recommended that the auditor reconfirm. In making this decision the auditor should follow the guidance in Section 313.

USE OF NEGATIVE FORM OF CONFIRMATION REQUEST

If the negative form of confirmation request is used, the auditor should normally do one of the following:

1. Send out more requests than if the positive form is used.
2. Apply other auditing procedures to a greater extent than if the positive form is used. Other auditing procedures include examination of the following:
   a. Subsequent cash receipts.
   b. Subsequent cash remittance advices.
   c. Sales and shipping documents.

STEPS IN CONFIRMATION PROCESS

The steps in the process of confirming receivables follow:

1. Obtain aged schedule of accounts receivable.
2. Select accounts for confirmation.
3. Prepare and mail confirmation requests.
4. Process responses to confirmation requests.
5. Summarize confirmation results.

Obtain Aged Schedule of Accounts Receivable

The auditor should obtain an aged schedule of accounts receivable as of the confirmation date. He or she should apply the following procedures to this schedule:

1. Determine that totals are correct.
2. Compare all or a selected sample of account balances with the account balances in the accounts receivable subsidiary ledger.
3. Investigate credit balances.

Select Accounts for Confirmation

Auditors have used, and some continue to use, judgment in selecting accounts for confirmation. Statistical sampling methods, however, are ideal for the selection process. Whatever method of selection is used, the auditor generally considers the following accounts:

1. All accounts with a balance over a predetermined amount. The predetermined amount is based on the auditor's assessment of materiality.
2. Some or all accounts with zero balances.
3. Accounts with old unpaid items, especially when subsequent sales have been paid.
4. Accounts written off during the year under review.
5. Accounts with entities related to the client but not audited by the auditor.
6. Certain accounts that appeared on the prior year's accounts receivable schedule but not on the current year's.
7. Accounts with credit balances.

   a. Occasionally, the client will not want confirmation requests sent to these accounts. If the amounts are material, it might result in a scope limitation; however, this is generally not the case.
   b. If accounts with credit balances are not confirmed, alternative auditing procedures should be applied.

8. Of the remaining accounts, a representative portion both in dollar amount and number of accounts should be selected.

Prepare and Mail Confirmation Requests

The auditor should observe the following procedures in preparing and mailing confirmation requests:

1. Prepare schedule of accounts to be confirmed (see *Illustrations*).

   a. Alphabetically.
   b. Address.
   c. Amount.
   d. Assign each account a number. This number also should be placed on the confirmation request.
   e. Total the dollar amount of receivables selected for confirmation and compute as a percentage of the total dollar amount of the receivables.
   f. Determine the number of confirmation requests and compute as a percentage of the total number of accounts.
   g. Leave sufficient blank columns after the customer's name to insert the following information when the confirmation reply is received:

      (1) Date reply received.
      (2) Amount confirmed.

   (3) Explanation of difference between amount customer confirmed and client amount.

   h. Leave a blank column for insertion of the date the second request was mailed.
   i. Indicate at bottom the date the first requests were mailed.

2. Request that client address confirmation forms and prepare customer statements.
   a. If auditor desires that client not know which accounts are to be confirmed, he or she should have his or her staff address confirmations.
   b. If auditor desires that client not know which accounts are to be confirmed but wants client to address confirmations, he or she should request client to address confirmation to all accounts and then eliminate the accounts not selected for confirmation.
3. When the auditor receives the addressed confirmation with the account balance and the customer statement, he or she should compare that balance with the balance on the schedule.
4. Independently, some customer addresses should be checked. These tests can be made by comparing the address on confirmation with the address in the telephone book.
5. After confirmations have been reviewed and numbered, the auditor should insert them and the customer statement in his or her firm's envelopes, that is, envelopes with the firm's return address.
6. In addition to inserting the confirmation request in the envelope, insert a postage-paid return envelope bearing the auditor's address.
7. When the requests have been stamped, the auditor should mail them.

From the time the auditor receives the addressed confirmation requests containing the account balances, he or she should never lose control. The confirmation requests always should remain in the auditor's custody or under his or her supervision until mailed.

Process Responses to Confirmation Requests

When confirmation replies are received, the auditor should do the following:

1. Enter for each account the following:
   a. Date received.
   b. Amount confirmed.
2. If the amount confirmed differs from the account balance, the following should be done:
   a. Photocopy confirmation reply.
   b. Give photocopy to client and request that the difference be reconciled and provide documentation for reconciling items.
   c. Review documentation for reconciling items.
   d. If documentation is satisfactory, enter reasons for difference in receivable confirmation schedule.
3. If the amount confirmed differs from the account balance and the client cannot satisfactorily reconcile the difference, the auditor should do the following:
   a. If the difference is small, the auditor may ignore it. If there are a significant number of small differences, however, the auditor should analyze them. If the analysis of the significant number of small differences indicates a deficiency in

the receivable controls, the auditor may have to apply additional auditing procedures to satisfy himself or herself of the accounts receivable balance.

b. If the difference is significant, request the client to correspond with the debtor. Make certain the correspondence states that the debtor response should be sent directly to the auditor.

A CPA firm needs to establish a mechanism for ensuring that responses mailed to the CPA firm are obtained and considered by the audit team in the field on a timely basis. Also, a firm needs to ensure that responses that relate to transaction terms and other complex matters (such as compliance with laws and regulations for a governmental entity) are considered by appropriately experienced audit team members.

Summarize Confirmation Results

Near the conclusion of the engagement, the auditor should prepare a worksheet summarizing confirmation results. The worksheet should contain the following:

1. Number and dollar amount of confirmations sent and the percentage of these to the total receivables.
2. Number and dollar amount of confirmations received with no exceptions indicated and the percentage of these to the total confirmations requests.
3. Number and dollar amount of confirmations received with exceptions that were satisfactorily reconciled by the client. Compute the percentage of these to the total confirmations requested.
4. Number and dollar amount of confirmations received with exceptions that were not satisfactorily reconciled by the client.
   a. Determine total dollar amount of differences between client records and confirmation responses.
   b. Determine reasons for differences and materiality of differences.
   c. Compute the percentage of these to the total confirmations requested.
5. Review statistics and determine if the results of the confirmation procedures provided sufficient competent evidential matter as to the existence of the receivables. If the auditor is not satisfied with the results of the confirmation procedures, he or she should perform other procedures such as the following:
   a. Review subsequent cash receipts and accompanying remittance advices.
   b. Review individual sales invoices and related shipping documents.

A confirmation worksheet is presented below in *Illustrations*.

NONRESPONSE TO CONFIRMATION REQUESTS

If a response to a confirmation request is not received within a reasonable period of time—two to three weeks—a second request should be sent. The auditor should note in the receivable confirmation worksheet the date the second request was mailed.

Telephone Call to Debtor

If the nonresponse pertains to an account with a significant balance, the auditor should consider making a telephone call to the customer. If the auditor confirms by telephone, he or she should do the following:

1. Obtain the name and title of the person providing the information.
2. Request that the information provided be confirmed in writing.

Other Auditing Procedures

If the nonresponse pertains to an account with a significant balance, the auditor should consider reviewing the customer file to determine the following:

1. Cash receipts subsequent to year-end.
2. Items paid for subsequent to year-end. This is done by reviewing customer remittance advices.

NONDELIVERY OF CONFIRMATION REQUEST

If a confirmation request is returned to the auditor because it was not delivered, the auditor should do the following:

1. Determine customer's new address and mail confirmation request.
2. If customer went out of business, ascertain that client has established appropriate allowance.

CONFIRMATION RESPONSES NOT EXPECTED

Sometimes the auditor does not expect a response to a confirmation request based on past experience with the entity or with customers similar to those of the entity.

When the auditor does not expect a response to a traditional confirmation request, he or she should do the following:

1. Request confirmation of specific items included in the account balance.
2. Review subsequent customer remittances. Where these amounts are significant, it is recommended that for a period of time subsequent to the balance sheet date, the auditor be present whenever the client receives mail. The auditor should open all mail from customers unable to confirm balances and compare remittance advices to ledger balances.
3. Undertake other procedures to validate the existence of the customer and sales to the customer. (For example, the customer could be looked up in a phone directory and called.)

When fraud risk factors are present and confirmation of receivables is not possible, the auditor should employ unusual procedures if necessary to validate the existence of the customer and the sales to that customer.

CONFIRMATION CHECKLIST

To make certain all procedures have been applied in the confirmation of receivables, the auditor should design a confirmation checklist. One is presented in *Illustrations*.

ILLUSTRATIONS

This section contains illustrations of the following for accounts receivable:

1. Confirmation checklist.
2. Positive confirmation with statement.
3. Positive confirmation without statement.
4. Negative confirmation.
5. Subsequent payments confirmation.
6. Confirmation of selected transactions.
7. Description of confirmation worksheet.

Illustration 1. Accounts Receivable Confirmation Checklist

____

[Client]

____

[Audit date]

Instructions. This checklist is divided into two sections, as follows:

1. General information.
2. Procedures.

If a procedure listed is not applicable, insert "N/A" in the column "Performed by" and explain why in the "Explanation" column.

General Information

1. Date confirmation sent.

	Positive confirmation	*Negative confirmation*
First request		
Second request		N/A
Third request		N/A

2. For positive confirmation, list the following:

	Number of receivables	*Amount of receivables*
a. Accounts receivable		
b. Confirmations sent		
c. Percentage		
d. Responses		
e. Percentage of confirmations sent		
f. Percentage of total receivables		

3. For negative confirmation, list the following:

	Number of receivables	*Amount of receivables*
a. Accounts receivable		
b. Confirmations sent		
c. Percentage		
d. Responses		
e. Percentage of confirmations sent		
f. Percentage of total receivables		

Procedure	*Performed by*	*Date*	*Explanation*
1. Obtain from client aged schedule of accounts receivable.			
2. Determine that all accounts listed in the accounts receivable schedule are customer accounts.			
3. Check that total in accounts receivable is correct and compare total with balance for accounts receivable in general ledger.			
4. Compare all or a selected sample of account balances in the schedule with account balances in the accounts receivable subsidiary ledger.			
5. Select accounts for positive confirmations.			
6. Select accounts for negative confirmations.			
7. Prepare schedule of accounts to be confirmed, listing the following:			
a. Confirmation number.			
b. Name of account.			
c. Address of account.			
d. Receivable balance.			
c. Balance confirmed.			
f. Difference.			
g. Explanation of difference.			

Procedure	Performed by	Date	Explanation
8. On a test basis, check account addresses to source independent of accounts receivable department, such as a. Customer file. b. Telephone book. 9. Mail confirmation requests in envelope with firm return address. Include the following: a. Customer statement. b. Letter requesting confirmation. c. Firm postage-paid envelope. 10. For confirmation responses, do the following: a. Enter balance confirmed. b. Require client to reconcile any differences. c. Review documentation for reconciling items. 11. Send second requests. 12. Send third requests. 13. For nonresponses of significant balances, do the following: a. Review subsequent cash receipts. b. Review customer remittance advices. 14. If customer indicates it cannot confirm balance owed, request confirmation of a. Specified invoices. b. Specified cash receipts. 15. Nondelivery of request. Mail to new address. 16. Facsimile response. a. Photocopy response. b. Verify source and contents of response by telephone call to sender. c. Request sender to mail original confirmation request.			

ILLUSTRATION 2. ACCOUNTS RECEIVABLE: POSITIVE CONFIRMATION WITH STATEMENT

[*Control number*]

[*Client letterhead*]

[*Date*]

[*Name and address of customer*]

Gentlemen:

Our auditors, [*name and address*], are conducting an audit of our financial statements. Please examine the accompanying statement and either confirm its correctness or report any differences to our auditors.

Your prompt attention to this request will be appreciated. An envelope is enclosed for your reply.

Very truly yours,

____

[*Client signature and title*]

Confirmation

The balance receivable from us of [*amount*] as of [*date*] is correct except as noted below:

____

[*Debtor name*]

Date ____________________ By ____________________

NOTE: This confirmation also may be used as a second request by stamping or printing in a prominent location "SECOND REQUEST" and mailing with a copy of the statement.

ILLUSTRATION 3. ACCOUNTS RECEIVABLE: POSITIVE CONFIRMATION WITHOUT STATEMENT

[*Control number*]

[*Client letterhead*]

[*Date*]

[*Name and address of customer*]

Gentlemen:

Our auditors, [*name and address*], are conducting an audit of our financial statements. Please confirm to them our receivable from you of [*amount*] as of [*date*].

Your prompt attention to this request will be appreciated. An envelope is enclosed for your reply.

Very truly yours,

____

[*Client signature and title*]

Confirmation

The balance receivable from us of [*amount*] as of [*date*] is correct except as noted below:

____

[*Debtor name*]

Date ____________________ By ____________________

NOTE: This confirmation also may be used as a second request by stamping or printing in a prominent location "SECOND REQUEST."

ILLUSTRATION 4. ACCOUNTS RECEIVABLE: NEGATIVE CONFIRMATION WITH STATEMENT, GUMMED STICKER, OR RUBBER STAMP

Auditor's Confirmation Request

Please examine this statement. If it does not agree with your records, please report any exceptions directly to our auditors

[*Auditor's name*]
[*Auditor's address*]

who are conducting an audit of our financial statements. An envelope is enclosed for your reply.

NOTE: This format may be used as a gummed sticker attached to a statement or as a rubber stamp imprinted on a statement.

ILLUSTRATION 5. ACCOUNTS RECEIVABLE: SUBSEQUENT PAYMENTS CONFIRMATION

[*Control number*]

[*Client letterhead*]

[*Date*]

[*Name and address of customer*]

Gentlemen:

Our records indicate that between [*date*] and [*date*], you made payments to us of [*amount*].

In connection with an audit of our financial statements, please confirm the payments and their allocation listed below or report any differences to our auditors, [*name and address*].

Check or voucher				Applicable to invoices dated	
Date	Number	Amount	Deductions	Before	After

Your prompt attention to this request will be appreciated. An envelope is enclosed for your reply.

Very truly yours,

____

[*Client signature and title*]

Confirmation

The payments and their allocation listed above agree with our records except as noted below:

____

[Debtor name]

Date _________________________ By ________________

ILLUSTRATION 6. ACCOUNTS RECEIVABLE: CONFIRMATION OF SELECTED TRANSACTIONS, OPEN INVOICE SYSTEM

[Control number]

[Client letterhead]

[Date]

[Name and address of customer]

Gentlemen:

We understand that you do not maintain an accounts payable ledger showing balances due each vendor. However, we would appreciate your assistance in providing limited confirmation of specific transactions to permit the completion of our annual audit.

Please confirm to our auditors, [name and address], that the invoices listed below were proper and were unpaid as of [date].

Invoice		Customer		
No.	Date	P.O. No.	Location	Amount

Your prompt response will be appreciated. An envelope is enclosed for your reply.

Very truly yours,

____

[Client signature and title]

Confirmation

The invoices listed above were properly charged to our account and were unpaid as of [date] except as noted below.

____

[Debtor name]

Date _________________________ By ____________

ILLUSTRATION 7. ACCOUNTS RECEIVABLE: DESCRIPTION OF CONFIRMATION WORKSHEET

Description. An accounts receivable confirmation worksheet ordinarily should include the following columns:

1. Customer name.
2. Control number.
3. Indication of second request.
4. Balance per client.
5. Amount confirmed.
6. Differences.
7. Explanation of differences.
   a. Receipts in transit.
      (1) Date deposited.
      (2) Amount.
   b. Credits issued.
      (1) Date.
      (2) Amount.
   c. Shipments in transit.
      (1) Date shipped.
      (2) Amount.
   d. Other.

331 INVENTORIES

EFFECTIVE DATE AND APPLICABILITY

Original Pronouncements	SAP 43, September 1970 (codified in SAS 1, November 1972); SAS 43, August 1982; and SAS 67, November 1991.
Effective Date	When issued, September 1970.
Applicability	Audits of financial statements in accordance with generally accepted auditing standards and special reports involving inventories.

DEFINITIONS OF TERMS

Observing Inventories. Being present when the inventory is counted and, by observation, tests, and inquiries, becoming satisfied about the following:

1. The effectiveness of the methods of counting the inventory.
2. The extent of reliance that may be placed on the client's representations about the quantities and physical condition of the inventories.

OBJECTIVES OF SECTION

Observation of inventories has been a "generally accepted auditing procedure" since 1939. The first auditing statement, SAP 1, was issued as a result of a study of the McKesson & Robbins fraud. The statement dealt with the procedures of confirming receivables and observing inventories. It was revised or amended three times before this section was originally issued in September 1970 as SAP 43. The significant changes made in SAP 43 follow:

1. No modification of the audit report is required if it is impractical or impossible to observe inventories. The auditor should satisfy himself or herself, however, by alternative procedures.
2. There are no alternative procedures for **ending** inventories. The auditor **always** should make or observe some physical counts.

FUNDAMENTAL REQUIREMENTS: OBSERVATION

Quantities Determined Solely by Physical Count

When quantities are determined solely by physical count and all counts are made as of the balance sheet date or within a reasonable time before or after the balance sheet date, the auditor should ordinarily be present when inventory is counted.

Perpetual Inventory Records

If these records are well kept and checked by the client periodically by comparisons with physical counts, the auditor may observe inventory either during or after the end of the period under audit.

Client Use of Statistical Sampling Methods

When used in determining inventory quantities, an annual physical count of each item of inventory may not be necessary. In these circumstances the auditor should

1. Be satisfied that the sampling plan is statistically valid, that it has been properly applied, and that the results are reasonable.
2. Be present to observe some physical counts to satisfy himself or herself of the effectiveness of the counting procedures used.

NOTE: Sampling to determine financial statement amount generally must be more rigorous and precise than might be appropriate for audit sampling.

Necessity to Observe Physical Count

The auditor should make, or observe, some physical counts of the ending inventory. Tests of the accounting records alone are not sufficient for the auditor to become satisfied about inventory quantities at the balance sheet date.

Beginning Inventories

Sometimes the auditor may not have observed the beginning inventory of a period he or she is being asked to report on. Ordinarily, this occurs in new engagements. **If the auditor is satisfied about the current year-end inventory,** he or she may be able to satisfy himself or herself of prior period inventories by the following procedures:

1. Tests of prior transactions.
2. Reviews of records of prior counts.
3. Tests of gross profit.

Inventories Held in Public Warehouses

Ordinarily the auditor should obtain direct confirmation, in writing, from the custodian. If these inventories represent a significant proportion of current or total assets, however, the auditor should also apply one or more of the following procedures:

1. Review and test client's procedures for investigating the warehouseman and evaluating his or her performance.
2. Observe physical counts of goods, if practicable.
3. If warehouse receipts have been pledged as collateral, confirm with lenders details of pledged receipts.
4. Do one of the following:
   a. Obtain an independent auditor's report on the warehouseman's control procedures affecting the custody of goods and pledging of receipts.
   b. Apply alternative procedures at the warehouse to gain reasonable assurance that information obtained from the warehouseman is reliable.

FUNDAMENTAL REQUIREMENTS: REPORTING

SCOPE LIMITATION IMPOSED BY CLIENT

Section 508, "Reports on Audited Financial Statements," deals with scope limitations. Generally, if the client restricts the scope of the audit as to observation of inventories, the auditor should disclaim an opinion on the financial statements.

SCOPE LIMITATION IMPOSED BY CIRCUMSTANCES

Circumstances may make it impracticable or impossible for the auditor to observe inventories. If the auditor is able to satisfy himself or herself of these assets by applying alternative procedures, there is no significant scope limitation. In these circumstances, the auditor's report should not refer to the omission of procedures or the use of alternative procedures.

NOTE: There are no alternative procedures for inventory observation. The auditor should make or observe some inventory counts for ending inventory.

INTERPRETATIONS

There are no interpretations for this section. (However, see Section 508 on a report of an outside inventory-taking firm as an alternative procedure and the discussion on the same topic in *Techniques for Application*, "Outside Inventory-Taking Firm" in this section.)

PROFESSIONAL ISSUES TASK FORCE PRACTICE ALERT

PRACTICE ALERT 94-2 AUDITING INVENTORIES—PHYSICAL OBSERVATIONS

This practice alert, which focuses on the physical existence of inventories, discusses some ways in which inventory frauds have been perpetrated and presents information that might help prevent such frauds from going undetected. The main message of the alert is that the following may help to reduce inadvertent and intentional misstatements:

- An understanding of the client's business, its count procedures and controls, and a resulting assessment of where quantity errors might occur.
- Appropriate planning for physical inventory observation together with healthy audit skepticism.

The alert also provides guidance on taking inventories at multiple locations. To help discourage the shifting of inventory from one location to another, the auditor should consider taking physical inventory at all significant locations at the same time. When the physical count at each significant location will not be observed, the auditor should consider informing management that observations will be performed at some locations without advance notice. The auditor may perform alternative procedures for locations not visited.

Other topics covered in this alert include

- Inventories held for or by others. The auditor should make sure that consigned goods are properly identified and excluded from inventory. The auditor should also follow the guidance in *Fundamental Requirements* of this section.
- Use of a specialist. The auditor may need to use a specialist to determine quantities or value special-purpose inventory and would therefore follow the guidance in Section 336.
- Postobservation matters. The auditor should consider the guidance in Section 313 if observing inventory at other than the balance sheet date. The auditor should also consider testing significant items in the reconciliation of physical inventory to the general

ledger, examining significant reconciling items for those locations not observed, and testing goods-in-transit and inventory transfers.

The full text of this Practice Alert can be obtained from the AICPA website at www.aicpa.org/members/div/secps/lit/practice.htm.

TECHNIQUES FOR APPLICATION

TIMING AND EXTENT OF INVENTORY OBSERVATION

The timing and extent of inventory observation are determined by the client's inventory system and the effectiveness of its inventory controls. If the client maintains perpetual inventory records and the inventory controls are effective, the auditor may limit the extent of his or her observation and may observe the physical count at various times during the year.

For inventory observation prior to year-end, the auditor should follow the guidance of Section 313, "Substantive Tests Prior to the Balance Sheet Date."

Periodic Inventory System

If the client has a periodic inventory system, a physical inventory should be taken at least once during the year. No matter how many times during the year the client takes a physical inventory, the auditor should observe the count that occurs at or near year-end.

For purposes of this section, it is assumed that the client has a periodic inventory system. However, the same procedures, with minor modifications, may be used when observing inventory accounted for under a perpetual system.

INVENTORY IN A PUBLIC WAREHOUSE

A client may have a significant amount of inventory in a public warehouse. Auditing procedures in these circumstances are described in *Fundamental Requirements*.

INVENTORY HELD BY CUSTODIAN OTHER THAN A PUBLIC WAREHOUSE

Occasionally, the client's inventory is held by a consignee or a subcontractor.

Procedures

When the amount held by the custodian is significant, the auditor should observe the count of the inventory, if it is practicable. If observation is not practicable, the auditor should do the following:

1. Review all documents underlying the transaction.
2. Determine the reliability of the custodian by doing the following:
   a. Obtain credit report, if available.
   b. If custodian is a public company, obtain last annual and most recent quarterly reports.
   c. Make inquiries of client, bankers, and industry.
3. Confirm with custodian as to quantities of inventory held.

STEPS IN THE OBSERVATION OF INVENTORY

The two major steps in the observation of a physical inventory are as follows:

1. Planning the physical inventory.
2. Taking the physical inventory.

Planning the Physical Inventory

Planning the physical inventory is essential. The auditor should review or prepare the client instructions and should work closely with the client in the planning stage. The inventory should be taken at a time when operations are suspended or minimal.

The client has primary responsibility for planning and conducting the physical inventory. Because of the auditor's important role in the taking of the inventory, however, he or she should participate in the planning stage.

Before taking the inventory, the client should submit a plan containing the following:

1. Date and time inventory is to be taken.
2. Locations of inventory.
3. Method of counting and recording.
4. Instructions to employees.
5. Provisions for the following:
   a. Receipts and shipments of inventory during the counts.
   b. Segregation of inventory not owned by client.
   c. Physical arrangement of inventory.

Date and time of inventory. If the client has a periodic inventory system, the physical inventory should be taken at or near year-end. The inventory should be taken at a time when operations have ceased or are at a reduced level. Ideally, the physical inventory should be taken when the client is not operating, such as weekends or after hours.

Locations of inventory. The client's plan should indicate the location of all inventory. Inventory usually is located at the following:

1. Client's premises. Client should indicate where on its premises inventory is located.
2. Plants at locations other than the client's major premises.
3. In transit.
4. On consignment.
5. In a public warehouse.
6. At nonrelated factories for processing.

The client's plan should indicate how inventory will be taken at the various locations.

Method of counting and recording. When a physical inventory is taken, it ordinarily requires two people; one to call the count and the other to record it, or one to count the inventory and the other to check the count. Ordinarily, it is recorded in duplicate on one of the following:

1. Prenumbered inventory sheets.
2. Prenumbered inventory tags.

When the count is completed, the auditor keeps one copy of the sheets or tags.

Instructions to employees. Before the client counts the inventory, the auditor should review the instructions to the employees. Instructions should include the following:

1. Method of counting and recording.
   a. Will one person count and record and then have another check?
   b. Will one person call the count to a second person, who will record it?
2. Method of arranging inventory before physical count.
   a. Will inventory be segregated by style number, serial number, or in some other way?
   b. Will inventory be moved to a specific area?

3. Method of description. How will inventory be described when recorded?
   a. Style number.
   b. Serial number.
   c. Part number.
   d. Other.
4. Method of controlling inventory tags or inventory sheets.
   a. Who will have custody?
   b. How will they be distributed to employees taking the physical inventory?
5. How and when should inventory tags or sheets be gathered?
6. Custody of inventory tags or sheets when the count is completed.

If the client is a manufacturer, the instructions to the employees also should indicate how the stage of completion is determined for work in process.

Other considerations. The plan for the physical inventory also should provide for the following:

1. Receipts and shipments of inventory during the count.
   a. Whenever possible, no merchandise should be shipped until after the physical count. If this is not feasible, merchandise that will be shipped should be segregated.
   b. A designated area on the client's premises should be used for merchandise received during the count.
2. Segregation of inventory not owned by the client such as the following:
   a. Inventory on consignment.
   b. Bill-and-hold merchandise. This is merchandise invoiced to a customer but not yet shipped.
   c. Customer merchandise being repaired by the client.
3. The physical arrangement of the inventory.

Preplanning for Inventory Observation

Before the client counts the inventory, the auditor should prepare his or her program for the observation. Before preparing this program, the auditor should do the following:

1. Review last year's inventory observation audit documentation to ascertain the following:
   a. Nature of inventory.
   b. Materiality of specific items.
   c. Components of inventory.
   d. Nature of any problems.
2. Review and discuss with client its physical inventory plan.
3. Visit all locations where significant amounts of inventory are held. Determine if the location is conducive to the physical count.
4. Consider the need for using the services of an outside specialist to assist in identification and valuation problems of certain inventory items.
5. Prepare personnel assignments for inventory observation.

TAKING THE PHYSICAL INVENTORY

Audit Program for Inventory Observation

After preliminary reviews, the auditor should prepare his or her observation program (see *Illustrations*). The program should include the following:

1. Obtain cutoff numbers (i.e., last receiving number and last shipping number prior to physical count).
2. Inform staff of client inventory procedures.
3. Assign sufficient staff to observe that client procedures are properly executed.
4. Determine the extent to which client counts will be test counted.
5. Randomly select cartons of inventory and have them opened to ascertain that inventory does, in fact, exist.
6. Randomly select inventory items and, as appropriate, do the following:
   a. Have client measure them.
   b. Have client weigh them.
7. When client counts are test counted, compare count with what appears on inventory tag, sheet, or card. Also, compare inventory serial number, style number, and description with what appears on the inventory tag, sheet, or card. List numbers where these procedures were applied.
8. Obtain the range of numbers for the inventory tags, sheets, or cards used to record the inventory.
   a. At conclusion of count, ascertain that all numbers distributed for the count are accounted for.
   b. Be sure to specifically identify for later reference the numbers of all unused inventory tags, sheets, or cards.
9. Make a note of all tags, sheets, or cards that represent obsolete, defective, excess, or slow-moving inventory.
10. For work in process, review with knowledgeable employees the following:
    a. Estimated cost to complete per production records.
    b. Estimated costs to date. Review, on a test basis, documentation such as
       (1) Material invoices.
       (2) Labor costs.
11. After the inventory has been completed, tour area with supervisor and ascertain that all items have been tagged.
12. Account for all numbers distributed.
13. Supervise the collection of all tags, sheets, or cards, being careful to note that none of the inventory is moved.
14. Make certain that inventory not owned by the client is not included in the count.
15. If specialists are used, observe their procedures.
16. For finished goods inventory, do, on a test basis, the following:
    a. Inspect them to ascertain that they are complete.
    b. If feasible, have some units disassembled to ascertain that all components have been included.
17. After all tags, sheets, or cards have been collected, review numbers to ascertain that all numbers are accounted for. (See 8. a. and b.)

18. Separate the original and the copy of the tags, sheets, or cards, leaving the original with the client and taking the copy for audit files.

At completion of the physical inventory, the auditor should prepare an inventory observation memorandum that includes the following:

1. Receiving and shipping cutoff numbers.
2. Entity personnel who supervised the count.
3. Number range for inventory tags, sheets, or cards.

OUTSIDE INVENTORY-TAKING FIRM

Clients may retain outside firms of nonaccountants to take their physical inventories. This does not relieve the auditor, however, of the responsibility to observe physical inventories.

Auditor's Procedures

If a client retains an outside inventory firm to count its inventories, the auditor's primary concern is the effectiveness of the outside firm's procedures. To evaluate the procedures of the outside firm, the auditor should do the following:

1. Examine the firm's inventory observation program.
2. Observe the firm's procedures and controls.
3. Observe some physical counts of inventory.
4. Recompute calculations of the submitted inventory on a test basis.

If the auditor is satisfied with the procedures of the outside firm, he or she may reduce, **not eliminate,** his or her work on the physical count of the inventory.

Restrictions on Auditor

Any restrictions on the auditor's judgment concerning the extent of his or her contact with the inventory counted by an outside firm is a scope limitation.

INVENTORY OBSERVATION CHECKLIST

To make certain all procedures have been applied in the observation of inventories, the auditor should design an inventory observation checklist. One is presented below in *Illustrations.*

ILLUSTRATIONS

This section contains illustrations of the following:

1. Inventory observation checklist.
2. Confirmation of inventories on consignment.
3. Confirmation of inventories in public warehouses.

ILLUSTRATION 1. INVENTORY OBSERVATION CHECKLIST

____
(Client)

____
(Audit Date)

____
(Date of Physical Inventory)

Instructions

This checklist is divided into four sections.

1. General information.
2. Procedures performed prior to date of physical inventory.
3. Procedures performed at date of physical inventory.
4. Procedures performed after date of physical inventory.

If a procedure is not applicable, insert N/A in the column "Performed by" and explain why in the "Explanation" column.

GENERAL

1. List inventory locations.
   a. ____________________
   b. ____________________
   c. ____________________
   d. ____________________
2. List staff members assigned to observe the inventory count.
   a. ____________________
   b. ____________________
   c. ____________________
   d. ____________________
   e. ____________________
   f. ____________________
3. List client personnel supervising the inventory count.
   a. ____________________
   b. ____________________
   c. ____________________
   d. ____________________
4. If inventory was ticketed—inventory tags, etc.—indicate range of ticket numbers.
   a. From____________________
   b. To____________________
5. If inventory was not ticketed, explain briefly how inventory was counted.
6. Nature of inventory.
   a. Finished goods____________________
   b. Work in process____________________
   c. Raw materials____________________
7. Describe client's physical inventory procedures. Instead of this description, attach copy of client's instructions.
8. Indicate the following:
   a. Last receiving number prior to physical count ____
   b. Last sales number prior to physical count.
      (1) Bill of lading number _____
      (2) Sales invoice number _____
9. Indicate the following:
   a. Inventory tickets.
      (1) Number used _____
      (2) Number checked _____
   b. Inventory value.
      (1) Total $_____
      (2) Amount checked $_____

Procedure	*Performed by*	*Date*	*Explanation*
Prior to Date of Physical Inventory			
1. Visit inventory locations. Note critical areas.			
a. Receiving.			
b. Shipping.			
c. Production.			
d. Stock.			
e. ________________.			
2. Review inventory instructions.			
a. Date and time.			
b. Locations.			
c. Method of counting and recording.			
d. Segregation of inventory.			
(1) By style number.			
(2) By serial number.			
(3) By part number.			
(4) ______________			
3. Discuss with client the following:			
a. Physical arrangement of inventory.			
b. Segregation of inventory not owned.			
c. Receipts and shipments of inventory during count.			
d. Production during count.			
4. Ascertain other locations of inventory.			
a. In transit.			
b. On consignment.			
c. In public warehouse.			
d. At contractor.			
e. Bill and hold.			
f. Merchandise for repair.			
5. Review prior year's observation audit documentation for			
a. Nature of inventory.			
b. Materiality of specific items.			
c. Components of inventory.			
d. Nature of any problems.			
6. Consider need for using the services of outside specialist.			
7. Discuss inventory observation with staff.			
At Date of Physical Inventory			
1. Obtain cutoff numbers for shipments and receipts.			
2. Obtain first and last inventory ticket numbers.			
3. Ascertain that inventory was arranged and segregated as required by inventory instructions.			
4. Ascertain that operations were halted during the count.			
a. Receiving.			
b. Shipping.			
c. Production.			
5. If operations were not halted during the counts, prepare memo indicating how control was maintained.			
6. Ascertain when counting and tagging was completed.			
a. Before your arrival.			
b. After your arrival.			
7. If inventory is counted and tagged after your arrival, observe if method of counting and tagging conforms with instructions.			
8. Determine that all inventory was tagged.			
9. Count the inventory on a test basis and compare with quantity entered on inventory tag.			

Procedure	*Performed by*	*Date*	*Explanation*
10. Prepare schedule indicating your count and client's count for tags checked.			
11. If test count indicates significant difference, increase number of tags tested.			
12. Have client correct tags with errors.			
13. Where inventory is in sealed containers, have client open them on a test basis and count inventory.			
a. Compare count with that indicated on tag.			
14. For finished goods, ascertain on a test basis that they are in fact completed.			
a. Lift some of them.			
b. Have some of them disassembled, if feasible.			
15. For work in process, note on a test basis, the following:			
a. Amount of material.			
b. Amount of labor.			
16. Review inventory for old and obsolete items.			
a. Discuss with client.			
b. Amount of labor.			
17. Tour inventory area and ascertain that all inventory has been tagged or otherwise counted.			
18. Observe the pulling of the inventory tickets and obtain your copies immediately. Make certain that none of the tickets are altered.			
19. Account for all inventory ticket numbers.			
After Date of Physical Inventory			
1. Compare client's inventory sheets with your copies of inventory tickets for the following:			
a. All ticket numbers have been accounted for.			
b. Description and quantity on tickets agrees with inventory sheets.			
2. If client maintains perpetual inventory records, test check inventory tickets against those records.			

ILLUSTRATION 2. INVENTORIES: CONFIRMATION OF INVENTORIES ON CONSIGNMENT

[*Control number*]

[*Client letterhead*]

[*Date*]

[*Name and address*
of consignee]

Gentlemen:

Our auditors, [*name and address*], are conducting an audit of our financial statements. Please confirm to them our merchandise consigned to you as of [*date*], as described below:

Description	Quantity

Your prompt attention to this request will be appreciated. An envelope is enclosed for your reply.

Very truly yours,

____
[*Client signature and title*]

Confirmation:

The consigned merchandise listed above is all that is held by us as of [*date*] except as noted below:

____
[*Consignee name*]

Date ____________________ By____________________

ILLUSTRATION 3. INVENTORIES: CONFIRMATION OF INVENTORIES IN PUBLIC WAREHOUSES

[*Control number*]

[*Client letterhead*]

[*Date*]

[*Name and address
of warehouse*]

Gentlemen:

Our auditors, [*name and address*], are conducting an audit of our financial statements. Please furnish them with a list of our inventory at your warehouse as of [*date*] and a statement that this merchandise was stored on your premises for our account at that date.

Your prompt attention to this request will be appreciated. An envelope is enclosed for your reply.

Very truly yours,

____

[*Client signature and title*]

Confirmation:

The attached list, prepared by us, represents all merchandise stored on our premises as of [*date*] for the account of [*Client name*].

____

[*Warehouse name*]

Date ____________________ By__________________

332 AUDITING DERIVATIVE INSTRUMENTS, HEDGING ACTIVITIES, AND INVESTMENTS IN SECURITIES[1]

EFFECTIVE DATE AND APPLICABILITY

Original Pronouncement	SAS 92, August 2000. (Supersedes SAS 81.)
Effective Date	Audits of financial statements for fiscal years ending on or after June 30, 2001. (Early application is permitted.)
Applicability	Derivative instruments, including certain derivative instruments embedded in contracts; debt and equity securities; and hedging activities in which the entity designates a derivative or a nonderivative financial instrument as a hedge for which GAAP permits hedge accounting.

DEFINITIONS OF TERMS

DERIVATIVE INSTRUMENTS AND HEDGING ACTIVITIES

This section uses the definitions of derivatives and hedging activities in SFAS 133, *Accounting for Derivative Instruments and Hedging Activities*, as amended (AC section D50), hereinafter referred to as SFAS 133. SFAS 133 addresses the accounting for derivatives that are either freestanding or embedded in contracts or agreements. For purposes of applying the guidance in this SAS, a derivative is a financial instrument or other contract with all three of the characteristics listed in SFAS 133; that is

---

[1] *The Auditing Standards Board has issued Statement of Position (SOP) 01-3,* ***Performing Agreed-upon Procedures Engagements That Address Internal Control over Derivative Transactions as Required by the New York State Insurance Law,*** *which is effective upon issuance. (See August 2001, Journal of Accountancy, pages 97-103.) The SOP provides guidance to practitioners on performing an agreed-upon procedures engagement that enables insurance companies to meet the requirements of the New York Derivative Law (the Law) that amends Article 14 of the New York Insurance Law. The Law requires insurers who enter into derivative transactions to file with the State of New York Insurance Department (Department) a statement describing an independent CPA's assessment of the insurance company's internal control over derivative transactions. This assessment is considered part of the evaluation of internal control prescribed by Section 307(b) of the New York State Insurance Law. An assessment is required regardless of whether the derivative transactions are material to the insurer's financial statements.*

1. It has
   a. One or more underlyings (a specified interest rate, security price, commodity price, foreign exchange rate, or other variable) and
   b. One or more notional amounts or payment provisions or both.

   Those terms determine the amount of the settlement or settlements, and, in some cases, whether settlement is required.
2. It requires no initial net investment or an initial net investment that is smaller than would be required for other types of contracts that would be expected to have a similar response to changes in market factors.
3. Its terms require or permit net settlement, it can readily be settled net by a means outside the contract, or it provides for delivery of an asset that puts the recipient in a position not substantially different from net settlement.

An entity may enter into a derivative for investment purposes or to designate it as a hedge of exposure to changes in fair value (referred to as a fair value hedge), exposure to variability in cash flows (referred to as a cash flow hedge), or foreign currency exposure. The guidance in this section applies to hedging activities in which the entity designates a derivative or a nonderivative financial instrument as a hedge of exposure for which SFAS 133 permits hedge accounting.

OBJECTIVES OF SECTION

As the accounting standards for investing and related activities have become more complex and detailed, the related auditing guidance has followed suit.

The original auditing pronouncement on investments was issued primarily to deal with the auditing procedures that should be applied to investments of Small Business Investment Corporations (SBICs). The difficult audit issue for an SBIC's investments was that the investments were, by definition, in small and new companies that could not obtain financing from traditional sources. The guidance focused on the fact that only audited financial statements of these investees provided sufficient competent evidential matter.

The first revision of that pronouncement was necessitated by the issuance of APB Opinion 18, *The Equity Method of Accounting for Investments in Common Stock,* and the next revision was necessitated by a FASB statement on accounting for certain marketable securities. SAS 92 is the most comprehensive pronouncement yet issued on auditing investing and hedging activities. It applies to investments in all securities as well as to derivative instruments and hedging activities.

There are two types of securities—debt securities and equity securities. SAS 92 uses the definitions of debt security and equity security that are in SFAS 115, *Accounting for Certain Investments in Debt and Equity Securities.* However, SAS 92 applies to debt and equity securities without regard to whether they are covered by SFAS 115. For example, it applies to assertions about securities accounted for under the equity method following the requirements of APB Opinion 18.

SAS 92 retains the basic notion that an investee's unaudited financial statements generally do not provide sufficient evidential matter. However, it adds a cautionary note that even audited financial statements might not be sufficient because of factors such as significant differences in fiscal year-ends or accounting principles between the investor and investee or changes in ownership or conditions.

SAS 92 adds substantial guidance on the effect on audit approach and procedures of complexities and risks related to derivatives, involvement of service organizations, and accounting requirements applicable to hedging activities.

The AICPA issued an Audit Guide concurrent with SAS 92 entitled *Auditing Derivative Instruments, Hedging Activities, and Investments in Securities* (Guide). The Committee of Sponsoring Organizations of the Treadway Commission (COSO) issued *Internal Control Issues in Derivatives Usage: An Information Tool for Considering the COSO "Internal Control—Integrated Framework" in Derivatives Applications* in 1996. Although the COSO document precedes SFAS 133, its guidance may be useful to entities in developing controls over derivatives transactions and to auditors in assessing control risk for assertions about those transactions.

The Independence Standards Board[2] issued Interpretation 99-1 on assisting clients in implementing SFAS 133. It includes guidance on the effect of assistance on accounting application of SFAS 133 and derivative valuation consulting on the auditor's independence.

Although the focus of SFAS 92 is on more complex financial instruments, its guidance is generally still applicable to more simple investment interests such as partnerships and loans, and advances in the nature of investments such as those made by certain investment companies.

FUNDAMENTAL REQUIREMENTS

Required Risk Assessment in Planning

The auditor should consider the inherent risk and control risk for assertions about derivatives and securities when designing audit procedures.

Control Risk Assessment

The auditor should assess control risk for the related assertions after obtaining an understanding of internal control over derivatives and securities transactions.

For assertions for which the auditor plans to assess control risk below the maximum, the auditor should

- Identify specific controls relevant to the assertions that are likely to prevent or detect material misstatements that have been placed in operation by either the entity or a service organization.
- Gather evidential matter about whether controls are operating effectively.

NOTE: Gathering evidential matter about controls is often referred to simply as testing controls.

Confirmations of balances or transactions from a service organization do not provide evidence about its controls.

Designing Auditing Procedures

In designing auditing procedures for assertions about derivatives and securities, the auditor should consider the following about the entity:

- Its size.

---

[2] *The ISB was dissolved on July 31, 2001.*

- Its organizational structure.
- The nature of its operations.
- The types, frequency, and complexity of its derivatives and securities transactions.
- Its controls over those transactions.

Importance of Identifying and Testing Controls

In some circumstances, the auditor will need to identify controls placed in operation by the entity or service organization and gather evidence about the operating effectiveness of the controls to reduce audit risk to an acceptable level.

For example, the auditor likely would be unable to reduce audit risk to an acceptable level without identifying and testing controls for assertions about the occurrence of earnings if the entity has a large number of derivatives or securities transactions. Relevant controls include those over the authorization, recording, custody, and segregation of duties.

Designing Substantive Procedures Based on Risk Assessment

According to AU 332.19, the auditor should use the assessed levels of inherent risk and control risk for assertions about derivatives and securities to determine the nature, timing, and extent of substantive procedures to be performed to detect material misstatements of the financial statement assertions.

The auditor should consider whether the results of other audit procedures conflict with management's assertions about derivatives and securities, and, if so, the impact on the sufficiency of evidential matter.

Completeness Assertion for Derivatives

In designing tests of the completeness assertion for derivatives, the auditor should not focus exclusively on evidence relating to cash receipts and disbursements. Derivatives may involve only a commitment to perform under a contract and not an initial exchange of tangible considerations.

The auditor should consider the following procedures:

1. Make inquiries, including inquiries about operating activities that might present risks hedged by derivatives.
2. Inspect agreements.
3. Read minutes of meetings of the board of directors or the finance, investment, or other committees.
4. Read any other relevant information.

Tests of Valuation Assertions

The auditor should design tests of valuation assertions according to the valuation method used for measurement or disclosure in accordance with GAAP.

GAAP may

1 Require that a derivative or security be valued based on cost, the investee's financial results, or fair value.
2. Require disclosures about the value of a derivative or security and specify that impairment losses should be recognized in earnings prior to realization.

3. Vary depending on the type of security, the nature of the transaction, management's objectives related to the security, and the type of entity.

VALUATION BASED ON COST

If GAAP requires that the derivative or security be valued based on cost, the auditor should evaluate management's conclusion about recognizing an impairment loss for an other-than-temporary decline in a security's fair value below its cost.

VALUATION BASED ON AN INVESTEE'S FINANCIAL RESULTS

If GAAP required that the derivative or security be valued based on the investee's financial results, the auditor should obtain sufficient evidence to support those financial results, including but not limited to the equity method of accounting (see APB Opinion 18). The investor's auditor should

- Read financial statements and the audited report of the investee, if available. Audited financial statements of the investee and an audit report satisfactory for the investor auditor's purpose may constitute sufficient evidential matter.
- Ask that the investor arrange with the investee to have another auditor apply appropriate auditing procedures if the investee's financial statements are not audited or the investee's audit report is not satisfactory.
- Obtain sufficient evidence to support the carrying amount of the security if this amount reflects factors not recognized in the investee's financial statements or if the asset's fair values are materially different from the carrying amounts.
- Add an explanatory paragraph to the auditor's report because of the change in reporting period if a change in time lag occurs that materially affects the investor's financial statements.

  NOTE: A time lag in reporting between the date of the financial statements of the investor and the investee should be consistent from period to period. The effect may be material when, for example, the time lag is not consistent with the prior period in comparative statements or if a significant transaction occurred during the time lag. In this case, the auditor should determine if management has properly considered the lack of comparability.

- Evaluate management's conclusion about recognizing an impairment loss for an other-than-temporary decline in a security's fair value below its cost.
- Obtain evidence about (1) whether unrealized profits and losses on transactions between the entity and the investee are properly eliminated when the equity method of accounting is used to account for an investment under GAAP and (2) the disclosures of material related-party transactions are adequate.
- Read the investee's interim financial statements and make inquiries of the investor to identify subsequent events (those occurring after the date of the investee's financial statements but before the date of the investor auditor's report) that are material to the investor's financial statements. Subsequent events discussed in Section 560, "Subsequent Events," should be disclosed in the notes to the investor's financial statements and labeled "unaudited."

  NOTE: The events or transactions discussed in Section 560 should be recognized when recording the investor's share of the investee's results of operations.

VALUATION BASED ON FAIR VALUE

If GAAP requires that the derivative or security be valued based on fair value, the auditor should obtain evidence supporting management's assertions about the fair value of derivatives and securities measured or disclosed at fair value. The auditor should

- Determine whether GAAP specifies the method to be used for calculating the fair value of the derivatives and securities, and evaluate whether the fair value calculations are consistent with that valuation method.
- Consider the guidance in Section 342, "Auditing Accounting Estimates," if appropriate, and the guidance in Section 312, "Audit Risk and Materiality in Conducting an Audit," guidance on considering a difference between an estimated amount best supported by the audit evidence and the estimated amount in the financial statements.

SOURCES OF FAIR VALUE INFORMATION

If derivatives or securities are listed on national exchanges or over-the-counter markets, quoted market prices are available in financial publications, the exchange, the National Association of Securities Dealers Automated Quotations Systems (NASDAQ), pricing services and other sources.

Quoted market prices for certain other derivatives and securities can be obtained from broker-dealers who are market makers or through the National Quotation Bureau. However, special knowledge may be necessary for understanding the way in which the quote was developed. For example, National Quotation Bureau quotes may not be based on recent trades and may only indicate interest and not an actual price for the underlying derivative or security.

If quoted market prices for derivatives or securities are not available, broker-dealers or other third-party sources can often develop fair value estimates using internally or externally developed valuation models. The auditor should understand the method used in developing the estimate. The auditor may also decide to obtain estimates from more than one pricing source. AU 332.39 points out that this may be appropriate if either

- The pricing source has a relationship with an entity that might impair its objectivity, such as an affiliate or a counterparty involved in selling or structuring the product.
- The valuation is based on assumptions that are highly subjective or particularly sensitive to changes in the underlying circumstances.

NOTE: When fair value estimates are obtained from broker-dealers and other third-party sources, the auditor should consider whether guidance in Section 336 "Using the Work of a Specialist," applies. The guidance in Section 350 may be applicable if the third-party source derives the fair value of the derivative or security by using modeling or similar techniques. If the entity uses a pricing service to obtain prices of securities and derivatives, the guidance in Section 324, "Service Organizations," may be appropriate.

FAIR VALUE DETERMINED USING A MODEL

The entity may use a valuation model, such as the present value of expected future cash flows, option-pricing models, matrix pricing, option-adjusted spread models, and fundamental analysis, to value a derivative or security.

NOTE: SAS 92 notes that when the entity uses a valuation model, the auditor should not assume the role of an appraiser and is not expected to substitute his or her judgment for that of management.

When GAAP requires that quoted market prices be used to determine fair value, a valuation model should ***not*** *be used.*

The auditor should perform the following procedures to obtain evidence about management's assertions about fair value as determined by the model:

- Assess whether the model is reasonable and appropriate. (For example, estimates of future cash flows should be based on reasonable and supportable assumptions.) Since evaluating appropriateness may require knowledge of valuation techniques and other factors, the auditor may need to involve a specialist to assess the model.
- Calculate the value using the auditor's model or a model developed by the auditor's specialist to corroborate the reasonableness of the entity's value.
- Compare the fair value with subsequent or recent transactions.

USE OF COLLATERAL IN EVALUATING FAIR VALUE

If collateral is important in evaluating the security, the auditor should obtain evidence regarding the

- Existence.
- Fair value.
- Transferability.
- Investor's rights to the collateral.

NOTE: Negotiable securities, real estate, chattels, or other property is often assigned as collateral for debt securities.

IMPAIRMENT LOSSES

The auditor should evaluate management's conclusion about the need to recognize in earnings an impairment loss for a decline in fair value that is other than temporary. In doing so, the auditor should evaluate (1) whether management has considered relevant information about whether a decline is other than temporary and (2) management's conclusions about recognizing an impairment loss. The auditor is required to obtain evidence about such factors that tend to corroborate or conflict with management's conclusions. When an impairment loss is recognized, the auditor should obtain evidence supporting the recorded amount of the impairment adjustment and determine whether the entity has appropriately followed GAAP.

UNREALIZED APPRECIATION OR DEPRECIATION IN FAIR VALUE OF A DERIVATIVE

The auditor should obtain evidence to support the amount of unrealized appreciation or depreciation in the fair value of a derivative that is recognized in earnings or other comprehensive income or that is disclosed because of the ineffectiveness of a hedge.

NOTE: GAAP may specify how to account for unrealized appreciation and depreciation of the fair value of the entity's derivatives and securities. AU 332.45 provides the following examples of when GAAP requires the entity to report a change in the unrealized appreciation or depreciation in the fair value of

- *A derivative that is designated as a fair value hedge in earnings, with disclosure of the ineffective portion of the hedge.*

- *A derivative that is designated as a cash flow hedge in two components, with the ineffective portion reported in earnings and the effective portion reported in other comprehensive income.*
- *A derivative that was previously designated as a hedge but is no longer highly effective, or a derivative that is not designated as hedge, in earnings.*
- *An available-for-sale security in other comprehensive income.*

GAAP may also require reclassification of amounts from accumulated other comprehensive income to earnings. For example, such reclassifications may be required because a hedged transaction is determined to no longer be probable of occurring.

ASSERTIONS ABOUT PRESENTATION AND DISCLOSURE

The auditor should evaluate whether the presentation and disclosures of derivatives and securities are in conformity with GAAP.

ADDITIONAL CONSIDERATIONS RELATED TO GATHERING EVIDENTIAL MATTER ABOUT HEDGING ACTIVITIES

The auditor should gather evidential matter to

- Determine whether management complied with hedge accounting requirements, including designation and documentation requirements.
- Support management's expectation at the inception of the hedge that the relationship will be highly effective and periodically assess ongoing effectiveness.
- Support the recorded change in the hedged item's fair value attributable to the hedged risk.
- Determine whether management has properly applied GAAP to the hedged item.
- Evaluate whether a forecasted transaction that is hedged is probable of occurring.

NOTE: The likelihood that a forecasted transaction will take place cannot be based solely on management intent.

ASSERTIONS RELATED TO MANAGEMENT'S ABILITY AND INTENT

According to AU 332.56, if GAAP requires that management's intent and ability be considered in valuing securities, in evaluating management's intent and ability the auditor should

- Obtain an understanding of the process used by management to classify securities as trading, available-for-sale, or held-to-maturity.
- For an investment accounted for using the equity method, inquire of management as to whether the entity has the ability to exercise significant influence over the operating and financial policies of the investee and evaluate the attendant circumstances that serve as a basis for management's conclusions.
- If the entity accounts for the investment contrary to the presumption established by GAAP for use of the equity method, obtain sufficient competent evidential matter about whether that presumption has been overcome and whether appropriate disclosure is made regarding the reasons for not accounting for the investment in keeping with that presumption.
- Consider whether management's activities corroborate or conflict with its stated intent. For example, the auditor should evaluate an assertion that management intends to hold debt securities to their maturity by examining evidence such as documentation

of management's strategies and sales and other historical activities with respect to those securities and similar securities.

- Determine whether GAAP requires management to document its intentions and specify the content and timeliness of that documentation. The auditor should inspect the documentation and obtain evidential matter about its timeliness. Unlike the formal documentation required for hedging activities, evidential matter supporting the classification of debt and equity securities may be more informal.
- Determine whether management's activities, contractual agreements, or the entity's financial condition provide evidence of its ability. For example
  - The entity's financial position, working capital needs, operating results, debt agreements, guarantees, alternate sources of liquidity, and other relevant contractual obligations, as well as laws and regulations, may provide evidence about an entity's ability to hold debt securities to their maturity.
  - Management's cash flow projections may suggest that it does not have the ability to hold debt securities to their maturity.
  - Management's inability to obtain information from an investee may suggest that it does not have the ability to significantly influence the investee.
  - If the entity asserts that it maintains effective control over securities transferred under a repurchase agreement, the contractual agreement may be such that the entity actually surrendered control over the securities and therefore should account for the transfer as a sale instead of a secured borrowing.

Management Representations

The auditor ordinarily should obtain written management representations confirming management's intent and ability concerning assertions about derivatives and securities, and consider obtaining representations about other aspects of derivatives and securities transactions that affect assertions about them.

NOTE: Examples of such representations might include management's intent and ability to hold a debt security to maturity or to enter into a forecasted transaction to which hedge accounting is applied

TECHNIQUES FOR APPLICATION

Special Skill or Knowledge Might Be Needed to Plan or Perform Auditing Procedures Related to Derivatives or Securities

According to AU 332.05, examples of situations that might require special skill or knowledge to plan or perform auditing procedures related to derivatives or securities are as follows:

- Obtaining an understanding of an entity's information system for derivatives and securities, including services provided by a service organization, may require that the auditor have special skill or knowledge with respect to computer applications when significant information about derivatives and securities is transmitted, processed, maintained, or accessed electronically.
- Identifying controls placed in operation by a service organization that provides services to an entity that are part of the entity's information system for derivatives and

securities may require that the auditor have an understanding of the operating characteristics of entities in a certain industry.

- Understanding the application of GAAP for assertions about derivatives might require that the auditor have special knowledge because of the complexity of those principles. In addition, a derivative may have complex features that require the auditor to have special knowledge to evaluate the measurement and disclosure of the derivative in conformity with generally accepted accounting principles. For example, features embedded in contracts or agreements may require separate accounting as a derivative, and complex pricing structures may increase the complexity of the assumptions used in estimating the fair value of a derivative.
- Understanding the determination of the fair values of derivatives and securities, including the appropriateness of various types of valuation models and the reasonableness of key factors and assumptions, may require knowledge of valuation concepts.
- Assessing inherent risk and control risk for assertions about derivatives used in hedging activities may require an understanding of general risk management concepts and typical asset/liability management strategies.

If the auditor seeks assistance from employees of the auditor's firm, or others outside the firm, with the necessary skill or knowledge, the auditor should consider the guidance in Section 311, "Planning and Supervision." If the auditor plans to use the work of a specialist, the auditor should consider the guidance in Section 336, "Using the Work of a Specialist."

Assessing Inherent Risk for an Assertion about a Derivative or Security

The primary inherent risk is the susceptibility of an assertion about a derivative or security to a material misstatement, assuming there are no related controls. According to AU 332.08, examples of considerations that might affect the auditor's assessment of inherent risk are as follows:

- **Management's objectives.** The complexity of accounting requirements based on management's objectives may increase the inherent risk for certain assertions.
- **The complexity of the features of the derivative or security.** The complexity of the features of the derivative or security may increase the complexity of measurement and disclosure considerations required by GAAP.
- **Whether the transaction that gave rise to the derivative or security involved the exchange of cash.** Derivatives that do not involve an initial exchange of cash are subject to an increased risk that they will not be identified for valuation and disclosure considerations.
- **The entity's experience with the derivative or security.** An entity's inexperience with a derivative or security increases the inherent risk for assertions about it.
- **Whether a derivative is freestanding or an embedded feature of an agreement.** Embedded derivatives are less likely to be identified by management, which increases the inherent risk for certain assertions.
- **Whether external factors affect the assertion.** Assertions about derivatives and securities may be affected by a variety of risks related to external factors, such as
  - **Credit risk,** which exposes the entity to the risk of loss as a result of the issuer of a debt security or the counterparty to a derivative failing to meet its obligation.

- **Market risk,** which exposes the entity to the risk of loss from adverse changes in market factors that affect the fair value of a derivative or security, such as interest rates, foreign exchange rates, and market indexes for equity securities.
- **Basis risk,** which exposes the entity to the risk of loss from ineffective hedging activities. Basis risk is the difference between the fair value (or cash flows) of the hedged item and the fair value (or cash flows) of the hedging derivative. The entity is subject to the risk that fair values (or cash flows) will change so that the hedge will no longer be effective.
- **Legal risk,** which exposes the entity to the risk of loss from a legal or regulatory action that invalidates or otherwise precludes performance by one or both parties to the derivative or security.

Changes in external factors can also affect assertions about derivatives and securities. The following are examples:

- The increase in credit risk associated with amounts due under debt securities issued by entities that operate in declining industries increases the inherent risk for valuation assertions about those securities.
- Significant changes in, and the volatility of, general interest rates increase the inherent risk for the valuation of derivatives whose value is significantly affected by interest rates.
- Significant changes in default rates and prepayments increase the inherent risk for the valuation of retained interests in a securitization.
- The fair value of a foreign currency forward contract will be affected by changes in the exchange rate, and the fair value of a put option for an available-for-sale security will be affected by changes in the fair value of the underlying security.

- **The evolving nature of derivatives and the applicable GAAP.** As new forms of derivatives are developed, interpretive accounting guidance for them may not be issued until after the derivatives are broadly used in the marketplace. In addition, GAAP for derivatives may be subject to frequent interpretation by various standard-setting bodies. Evolving interpretative guidance and its applicability increase the inherent risk for valuation and other assertions about existing forms of derivatives.
- **Significant reliance on outside parties.** An entity that relies on external expertise may be unable to appropriately challenge the specialist's methodology or assumptions. This may occur, for example, when a valuation specialist values a derivative.
- **GAAP may require developing assumptions about future conditions.** As the number and subjectivity of those assumptions increase, the inherent risk of material misstatement increases for certain assertions. For example, inherent risk for valuation assertions based on assumptions about debt securities whose value fluctuates with changes in prepayments (for example, interest-only strips) increases as the expected holding period lengthens. Similarly, the inherent risk for assertions about cash flow hedges fluctuates with the subjectivity of the assumptions and probability, timing, and amounts of future cash flows.

Assessing Control Risk for Assertions about Derivatives or Securities

According to AU 332.10, to achieve its objectives, management of an entity with extensive derivatives transactions may implement controls that call for

- Monitoring by a control staff that is fully independent of derivatives activities.
- Derivatives personnel to obtain at least oral approval from senior management independent of derivatives activities prior to exceeding limits.
- Senior management to properly address limit excesses and divergences from approved derivatives strategies.
- Derivatives positions to be accurately transmitted to the risk measurement systems.
- Performing appropriate reconciliations to ensure data integrity across the full range of derivatives, including any new or existing derivatives that may be monitored apart from the main processing networks.
- Derivatives traders, risk managers, and senior management to define constraints on derivatives activities and justify identified excesses.
- Senior management, an independent group, or an individual that management designates to perform a regular review of the identified controls and financial results of the derivatives activities to determine whether controls are being effectively implemented and the entity's business objectives and strategies are being achieved.
- A review of limits in the context of changes in strategy, risk tolerance of the entity, and market conditions.

The required extent of the auditor's understanding of internal control over derivatives and securities depends on how much information the auditor needs to identify the types of potential misstatements, consider factors that affect the risk of material misstatement, design tests of controls where appropriate, and design substantive tests. The understanding could include controls over derivatives and securities transactions from initiation to inclusion in the financial statements and might encompass controls placed in operation by the entity and by service organizations whose services are part of the entity's information system.

The Effect of a Service Organization on Audit Approach and Procedures

AU 332 provides guidance on how service organizations apply to audits of derivatives and securities.

1. **Determining applicability of Section 324.** According to AU 322.11, a service organization's services are part of an entity's information system for derivatives and securities if they affect any of the following:
   - How the entity's derivatives and securities transactions are initiated.
   - The accounting records, supporting information, and specific accounts in the financial statements involved in the processing and reporting of the entity's derivatives and securities transactions.
   - The accounting processing involved from the initiation of those transactions to their inclusion in the financial statements, including electronic means (such as computers and electronic data interchange) used to transmit, process, maintain, and access information.

- The process the entity uses to report information about derivatives and securities transactions in its financial statements, including significant accounting estimates and disclosures.

2. **Examples where Section 324 applies.** According to AU 322.12, a service organization's services that would be part of an entity's information system include, for example

   - The initiation of the purchase or sale of equity securities by a service organization acting as investment advisor or manager.
   - Services that are ancillary to holding an entity's securities, such as
     - Collecting dividend and interest income and distributing that income to the entity.
     - Receiving notification of corporate actions.
     - Receiving notification of security purchase and sale transactions.
     - Receiving payments from purchasers and disbursing proceeds to sellers for security purchase and sale transactions.
     - Maintaining records of securities transactions for the entity.

     Maintaining custody of securities, either in physical or electronic form, is referred to as **holding** securities, and performing ancillary services is referred to as **servicing** securities.
   - A pricing service providing fair values of derivatives and securities through paper documents or electronic downloads that the entity uses to value its derivatives and securities for financial statement reporting.

According to AU 322.13 a service organization's services that would not be part of an entity's information system include, for example

- The execution by a securities broker of trades that are initiated by either the entity or its investment advisor.
- The holding of an entity's securities.

3. **Obtaining information.** An auditor who needs information about the nature of a service organization's services that are part of an entity's information system for derivative and securities transactions, or its controls over those services, to plan the audit may be able to gather the information from a variety of sources, such as

   - User manuals.
   - System overviews.
   - Technical manuals.
   - The contract between the entity and the service organization.
   - Reports by auditors, internal auditors, or regulatory authorities on the information system and other controls placed in operation by a service organization.
   - Inquiry or observation of personnel at the entity or at the service organization.
   - Prior experience with the service organization if the services and the service organization's controls over those services are highly standardized.

4. **Effect on audit procedures.** According to AU 322.20, the provision by a service organization of services that are part of an entity's information system may affect

the nature, timing, and extent of the auditor's substantive procedures for assertions about derivatives and securities in a variety of ways. The following are examples:

- Supporting documentation, such as derivative contracts and securities purchases and sales advices, may be located at the service organization's facilities. As a result, either the auditor of the entity's financial statements, an auditor working under the direction of that auditor, or an auditor engaged by the service organization may need to visit the facilities to inspect the documentation.
- Data processors, investment advisors, holders of securities, recordkeepers, and other service organizations may electronically transmit, process, maintain, or access significant information about an entity's securities. In such situations, it may not be practicable or possible for the auditor to reduce audit risk to an acceptable level without identifying controls placed in operation by the service organization or the entity and gathering evidential matter about the operating effectiveness of those controls.
- Service organizations may initiate securities transactions for an entity and hold and service the securities. In determining the level of detection risk for substantive tests, the auditor should consider whether there is a segregation of duties and other controls for the services provided. For example
    - When one service organization initiates transactions as an investment advisor and another service organization holds and services those securities, the auditor may corroborate the information provided by the two organizations. For example, the auditor may confirm holdings with the holder of the securities and apply other substantive tests to transactions reported by the entity based on information provided by the investment advisor. Depending on the facts and circumstances, the auditor also may confirm transaction or holdings with the investment advisor and review the reconciliation of differences.
    - If one service organization initiates transactions as an investment advisor and also holds and services the securities, all of the information available to the auditor is based on the service organization's information. The auditor may be unable to sufficiently limit audit risk without obtaining evidential matter about the operating effectiveness of one or more of the service organization's controls. An example of such controls is establishing independent departments that provide the investment advisory services and the holding and servicing of securities, then reconciling the information about the securities that is provided by each department.

ILLUSTRATIONS

ILLUSTRATION 1. EXAMPLES OF SUBSTANTIVE PROCEDURES FOR EXISTENCE OR OCCURRENCE ASSERTIONS[3] (FROM AU 332)

Examples of substantive procedures for existence or occurrence assertions about derivatives and securities are

- Confirmation with the issuer of the security.
- Confirmation with the holder of the security, including securities in electronic form, or with the counterparty to the derivative.
- Confirmation of settled transactions with the broker-dealer or counterparty.
- Confirmation of unsettled transactions with the broker-dealer or counterparty.
- Physical inspection of the security or derivative contract.
- Reading executed partnership or similar agreements.
- Inspecting underlying agreements and other forms of supporting documentation, in paper or electronic form, for
  - Amounts reported.
  - Evidence that would preclude the sales treatment of a transfer.
  - Unrecorded repurchase agreements.
- Inspecting supporting documentation for subsequent realization or settlement after the end of the reporting period.
- Performing analytical procedures. For example, the absence of a material difference from an expectation that interest income will be a fixed percentage of a debt security based on the effective interest rate determined when the entity purchased the security provides evidence about existence of the security.

ILLUSTRATION 2. EXAMPLES OF SUBSTANTIVE PROCEDURES FOR COMPLETENESS ASSERTIONS[4] (FROM AU 332)

Examples of substantive procedures for completeness assertions about derivatives and securities are

- Requesting the counterparty to a derivative or the holder of a security to provide information about it, such as whether there are any side agreements or agreements to repurchase securities sold.
- Requesting counterparties or holders who are frequently used, but with whom the accounting records indicate there are presently no derivatives or securities, to state whether they are counterparties to derivatives with the entity or holders of its securities.

---

[3] *Existence assertions relate to whether the derivatives and securities reported in the financial statements through recognition or disclosure exist at the date of the statement of financial position. Occurrence assertions relate to whether derivatives and securities transactions reported in the financial statements, as a part of earnings, other comprehensive income, or cash flows or through disclosure, occurred.*

[4] *Completeness assertions relate to whether all the entity's derivatives and securities are reported in the financial statements through recognition or disclosure. They also relate to whether all derivatives and securities transactions are reported in the financial statements as a part of earnings, other comprehensive income, or cash flows or through disclosure. The extent of substantive procedures for completeness may vary in relation to the assessed level of control risk. The auditor should consider that derivatives may not involve an initial exchange of tangible consideration, and, thus, it may be difficult to limit audit risk for assertions about the completeness of derivatives to an acceptable level with an assessed level of control risk at the maximum.*

- Inspecting financial instruments and other agreements to identify embedded derivatives.
- Inspecting documentation in paper or electronic form for activity subsequent to the end of the reporting period.
- Performing analytical procedures. For example, a difference from an expectation that interest expense is a fixed percentage of a note based on the interest provisions of the underlying agreement may indicate the existence of an interest rate swap agreement.
- Comparing previous and current account detail to identify assets that have been removed from the accounts and testing those items further to determine that the criteria for sales treatment have been met.
- Reading other information, such as minutes of meetings of the board of directors or finance, asset/liability, investment, or other committees.

Derivatives may involve only a commitment to perform under a contract and not an initial exchange of tangible consideration. Thus, auditors designing tests related to the completeness assertion should not focus exclusively on evidence relating to cash receipts and disbursements. When testing for completeness, auditors should consider making inquiries, inspecting agreements, and reading other information, such as minutes of meetings of the board of directors or finance, asset/liability, investment, or other committees. Auditors should also consider making inquiries about aspects of operating activities that might present risks hedged using derivatives. For example, if the entity conducts business with foreign entities, the auditor should inquire about any arrangements the entity has made for purchasing foreign currency. Or, if an entity is in an industry in which commodity contracts are common, the auditor should inquire about any commodity contracts with fixed prices that run for unusual durations or involve unusually large quantities. The auditor also should consider inquiring as to whether the entity has converted interest-bearing debt from fixed to variable, or vice versa, using derivatives.

If one or more service organizations provide services that are part of the entity's information system for derivatives, the auditor may be unable to sufficiently limit audit risk for assertions about the completeness of derivatives without obtaining evidential matter about the operating effectiveness of controls at one or more of the service organizations. Testing reconciliations of information provided by two or more of the service organizations may not sufficiently limit audit risk for assertions about the completeness of derivatives.

Illustration 3. Examples of Substantive Procedures for Rights and Obligations Assertions[5] (From AU 332)

Examples of substantive procedures for assertions about rights and obligations associated with derivatives and securities are

- Confirming significant terms with the counterparty to a derivative or the holder of a security, including the absence of any side agreements.
- Inspecting underlying agreements and other forms of supporting documentation, in paper or electronic form.
- Considering whether the findings or other auditing procedures, such as reviewing minutes of meetings of the board of directors and reading contracts and other agreements, provide evidence about rights and obligations, such as pledging of securities as collateral or selling securities with a commitment to repurchase them.

---

[5] *Assertions about rights and obligations relate to whether the entity has the rights and obligations associated with derivatives and securities, including pledging arrangements, reported in the financial statements.*

333 MANAGEMENT REPRESENTATIONS[1]

EFFECTIVE DATE AND APPLICABILITY

Original Pronouncement	SAS 85, November 1997; SAS 89, December 1999, and SAS 99, October 2002.
Effective Date	Audits of financial statements for period ending on or after June 30, 1998; revised to reflect SAS 89, effective for audits of financial statements for periods beginning on or after December 15, 1999, and SAS 99, effective for audits of financial statements for periods beginning on or after December 15, 2002, with early application permitted.
Applicability	Audits of financial statements in accordance with generally accepted auditing standards.

DEFINITIONS OF TERMS

Representation letter. Written representations obtained from management to confirm oral representations explicitly or implicitly given to the auditor, to indicate and document the continuing appropriateness of such representations, and to reduce the possibility of misunderstanding concerning the matters that are the subject of the representations. It has the following characteristics:

1. Presented in writing and covers all periods addressed in audit report.
2. Addressed to the auditor.
3. Dated no earlier than the date of the auditor's report.
4. Signed by management on client letterhead.
5. Acknowledges management's responsibility for the financial statements and management's belief that the financial statements are presented in accordance with GAAP.

---

[1] *In May 2002, the Auditing Standards Board (ASB) issued an Exposure Draft of a proposed SAS that would affect this section,* ***Sarbanes-Oxley Omnibus SAS****. The Exposure Draft is designed to address certain provisions of the Sarbanes-Oxley Act of 2002. The proposed amendment to this section would require representations concerning disclosure of all significant deficiencies, including material weaknesses in internal controls. Also, if the auditor of a public company chooses to get a combined representation letter covering the financial statement audit and the audit of internal control, the auditor should also obtain additional management representations covering the audit of internal control required under the Sarbanes-Oxley Act. The Public Company Accounting Oversight Board (PCAOB) has replaced the ASB as the standards-setting authority for public company audits. Therefore, the ASB's Exposure Draft will not be issued as a final standard by the AICPA. The document will, however, be considered by the PCAOB in developing a standard or amendments to an existing standard to comply with the Sarbanes-Oxley Act and the related SEC implementing rules. Please check for updates to this section on the John Wiley & Sons, Inc. website at www.wiley.com/gaas.*

6. Confirms management's oral and written representations to the auditor during the course of the audit.
7. Tailored to the entity's circumstances.

OBJECTIVES OF SECTION

SAS 19, *Client Representations*, was issued in June 1977 and needed updating to reflect changes in accounting standards and auditing practice. As a result, SAS 85, *Management Representations*, superseded SAS 19. SAS 85 accomplishes a number of objectives. The significant changes are as follows:

1. Clarifies the requirement for an auditor to obtain written representations for all periods covered by the audit report. (This was required by an interpretation of SAS 19 that was sometimes overlooked. The interpretation was incorporated in SAS 85.)
2. Adds a required representation in which management states its belief that the financial statements are fairly presented in accordance with generally accepted accounting principles or other comprehensive basis of accounting (footnote 3 of SAS 85 requires that a representation letter be obtained for OCBOA financial statements).
3. Expands the list of specific representations to be obtained that are consistent with practice and that reflect new standards (e.g., SAS 82, *Consideration of Fraud in a Financial Statement Audit* [Section 316], and SOP 94-6, *Disclosure of Certain Significant Risks and Uncertainties*).
4. States that the representation letter should be tailored to cover representations unique to entity's business and industry (see *Illustrations* for additional representations that may be needed).
5. Requires that auditor investigate and consider the reliability of representations that are contradicted by other evidence.
6. Includes guidance about explicit materiality levels that may be included in the representation letter (see the illustrative representation letter in *Illustrations* that includes a materiality discussion).
7. Amends SAS 58, *Reports on Audited Financial Statements* (Section 508), to require that a predecessor auditor obtain an updated representation letter from the client when requested by a former client to reissue the audit report on prior period financial statements (see *Illustrations* for an illustrative updating management representation letter). SAS 19 required only a representation letter from the successor auditor. SAS 85 retains that requirement.

SAS 89, *Audit Adjustments*, was issued in December 1999 to require management to acknowledge its responsibility for any uncorrected misstatements that management deems to be immaterial.

The representation letter is valid corroborative evidence. It is competent evidence; however, it is **not** sufficient evidence. It complements other auditing procedures, but it is **not** a substitute for these procedures.

In October 2002, SAS 99, *Consideration of Fraud in a Financial Statement Audit*, amended this section to require that the auditor obtain management representations concerning fraud and the risk of fraud.

FUNDAMENTAL REQUIREMENTS

RELIANCE ON MANAGEMENT REPRESENTATIONS

Management representation letters represent evidential matter and they serve to

1. Establish and remind management that they are primarily responsible for the financial statements.

2. Document representations explicitly or implicitly given to the auditor.
3. Reduce the possibility of misunderstanding.

Representation letters complement other auditing procedures and are not a substitute for those auditing procedures needed to support an opinion on the financial statements.

According to AU 333.04, if a representation made by management is contradicted by other audit evidence, the auditor should investigate the circumstances and consider the reliability of the representations made. In this situation, the auditor should consider whether reliance on other representations made by management is appropriate and justified.

Obtaining Written Representations

The auditor should obtain written representations from management should be obtained for all financial statements and periods covered by his or her report. If comparative financial statements are reported on, the representation letter should address all periods reported on.

NOTE: If the auditor is reporting on consolidated financial statements, the representation letter should relate to those statements. If the auditor is reporting on the separate financial statements of a component of a consolidated group, including the parent company, the representation letter should also relate to the separate statements.

According to AU 333.06, specific representations in a representation letter for financial statements presented in accordance with generally accepted accounting principles should cover the following (see *Illustrations* for an illustrative management representation letter):

Financial Statements

1. Management's acknowledgement of its responsibility for the fair presentation in the financial statements of financial position, results of operations, and cash flows in conformity with GAAP.
2. Management's belief that the financial statements are fairly presented in conformity with GAAP.

Completeness of Information

3. Availability of all financial records and related data.
4. Completeness and availability of all minutes of meetings of stockholders, directors, and committees of directors.
5. Communications from regulatory agencies concerning noncompliance with, or deficiencies in, financial reporting practices.
6. Absence of unrecorded transactions.

Recognition, Measurement, and Disclosure

7. Management's belief that any uncorrected misstatements (a summary of which is included in or attached to the letter) are immaterial, both individually and in the aggregate.
8. Management's acknowledgement of its responsibility for designing and implementing programs and controls to prevent and detect fraud.
9. Knowledge of actual or suspected fraud involving (1) management, (2) employees who have significant roles in internal control, or (3) others where the fraud could have a material effect on the financial statements.
10. Knowledge of any allegations of actual or suspected fraud made by current or former employees, analysts, regulators, short sellers, or others.
11. Plans or intentions that may affect the carrying value or classification of assets or liabilities.
12. Information concerning related-party transactions and amounts receivable from, or payable to, related parties.

13. Guarantees, whether written or oral, under which the entity is contingently liable.
14. Significant estimates and material concentrations known to management that are required to be disclosed in accordance with the AICPA's Statement of Position 94-6, *Disclosure of Certain Significant Risks and Uncertainties*.
15. Violations or possible violations of laws and regulations whose effects should be considered for disclosure in the financial statements or as a basis for recording a loss contingency.
16. Unasserted claims or assessments that the entity's lawyer has advised are probable of assertion and must be disclosed in accordance with the Financial Accounting Standards Board (FASB) Statement 5, *Accounting for Contingencies*.
17. Other liabilities or loss contingencies that are required to be accrued or disclosed by FASB Statement 5.
18. Satisfactory title to assets, liens or encumbrances on assets, and assets pledged as collateral.
19. Compliance with aspects of contractual agreements that may affect the financial statements.

Subsequent Events

18. Information concerning subsequent events.

Tailoring the Representation Letter

The representation letter ordinarily should also be modified to include additional representations from management covering matters specific to the entity's business or industry.

NOTE: Consult relevant AICPA industry audit and accounting guides for additional representations that are unique to a particular industry.

Materiality Considerations

Management's representations may be limited to material matters, provided management and the auditor have reached an understanding on materiality. Materiality may be different for different representations. Materiality may be addressed explicitly in the representation letter, in either qualitative or quantitative terms. Materiality considerations do not apply to items that are not directly related to amounts included in the financial statements, for example, items 1., 3., 4., and 5. under "Obtaining Written Representations." Likewise, materiality does not apply to item 9. for management and employees who have significant roles in internal control.

Addressing and Dating the Letter

The representation letter should be addressed to the auditor and should be dated no earlier than the date of the auditor's report. If the report is dual dated, the auditor should consider whether to obtain additional representations for subsequent events.

Signing the Letter

The management representation letter should be signed by those in management with overall financial and operating responsibility who the auditor believes are responsible for, and knowledgeable about, directly or through others in the organization, the matters covered by the representations. Normally this includes the chief executive officer and chief financial officer or others with equivalent positions in the entity.

The auditor should obtain a representation letter from current management for all periods covered by the auditor's report, even if current management was not present during all such periods.

The auditor may also want to have other individuals provide written representations. For example, the auditor could obtain from the person responsible for keeping minutes of stockholders, directors, and committees of directors, a written representation stating that such minutes are complete.

Updating Letters

As discussed in Section 508, a predecessor auditor in certain circumstances is required to obtain an updating representation letter. Also, auditors should obtain updated written representations from management when performing subsequent events procedures in connection with Securities Act of 1933 filings. The updated letter should state whether previous representations should be modified or whether subsequent events necessitate adjustment or disclosures in the financial statements.

Scope Limitations

If management refuses to furnish a representation letter, the auditor should ordinarily issue a disclaimer of opinion because of the limitation on audit scope or withdraw from the engagement. If the auditor concludes that a qualified opinion is appropriate, he or she should consider the effects of the refusal in relying on other management representations.

If the auditor is precluded from performing necessary procedures on a matter that is material to the financial statements, even though management has given representations on the matter, the auditor should qualify the opinion or disclaim an opinion because of the scope limitation.

INTERPRETATIONS

Management Representations on Violations and Possible Violations of Laws and Regulations (March 1979)

One of the required representations in a management letter is "violations or possible violations of laws or regulations whose effects should be considered for disclosure in the financial statements or as a basis for recording a loss contingency." The reference to "possible violations" does not change or go beyond the guidance in FASB Statement 5, *Accounting for Contingencies*, or SAS 54, *Illegal Acts by Clients* (Section 317).

TECHNIQUES FOR APPLICATION

Auditor's Relationship with a Small Nonpublic Client

The **independent** auditor's relationship with a small or nonpublic client usually is closer than the relationship with a large or publicly held client. In these circumstances, the independent auditor may significantly influence **client** decisions, such as the following:

1. Depreciation methods.
2. Accounting for start-up and similar costs.
3. Accounting for revenues.
4. Accounting for leases.
5. Inventory valuation methods.

Even though the auditor's influence may be significant, it is management's responsibility to decide whether to accept the auditor's recommendations. The client representation letter is management's acknowledgment of this responsibility.

To avoid problems at the date of completion of fieldwork, when the auditor asks management to sign the client representation letter, he or she should consider some or all of the following approaches:

1. Describe management's responsibilities in the engagement letter.
2. Discuss accounting policies and choices with management during the year and at the end of the year.
3. Define technical terms that appear in the representation letter.

Engagement Letter

The engagement letter is a written agreement signed by both the client and the auditor. It establishes the nature and terms of the engagement.

Because the engagement letter formalizes the terms of retention, it is suggested that a paragraph such as the following be added to the letter:

> We may prepare or help prepare the financial statements of XYZ Corp., but these financial statements are solely the representations of management. We may advise as to which accounting principles should be applied to the financial statements and the method of application, but the selection and the method of application are determinations made solely by management.

When the engagement letter is signed, it is advisable to tell the client what the paragraph means and that at the end of the fieldwork management must sign a representation letter in which it acknowledges its responsibility.

Although it is important to agree about management responsibility at the beginning of the engagement, it is equally important to remind management of its responsibility during the year.

Procedures during the Year

For the audit of a nonpublic client, the auditor usually is involved throughout the year. Decisions about accounting principles and methods are made during the year. For example, depreciation methods are determined, decisions are made to capitalize start-up costs and similar expenditures, and the method of accounting for various revenue streams may be established. In these circumstances, it is recommended that the auditor do the following:

1. Review the decision with management.
2. Explain financial statements effect of the decision to management.
3. Document the decision.

   NOTE: Include name of person who made the decision.

Procedures at End of Year

At the end of the year, the auditor should review with management the accounting principles applied during the year. The auditor should prepare a list of the accounting principles and explain their financial statement effect.

Before asking management to sign the representation letter, the auditor should review with them the draft of the financial statements, including the notes and the auditor's report. If the auditor has not prepared the notes and the report, he or she should tell management about their content.

Date of Representation Letter

The auditor is concerned with material events and transactions that occur to the date of completion of fieldwork. This is the date of the auditor's report and the date to which he or she wants information from client lawyers and management. For this reason, the subsequent events review extends to this date. **Also, the management representation letter should be signed as of the date the fieldwork is completed.** (For more information about dating representation letters and reports, see Section 560.)

EXPLICITLY ADDRESSING MATERIALITY IN THE REPRESENTATION LETTER

The auditor is permitted to reach an understanding with management on materiality and then management representations may be limited to material matters, except for certain items. Materiality may be addressed in quantitative or qualitative terms. An example of a quantitative expression would be 3% of before-tax income. A qualitative expression would be, for example, a significant change in the trend of earnings or revenue. The FASB's definition of materiality from Concepts Statement 2 is applicable to both quantitative and qualitative aspects of materiality. The conceptual description used alone, if read literally, would permit management to omit items larger than would be quantitatively material based on qualitative considerations. The authors do not recommend using it for that reason. The authors recommend that a quantitative expression of materiality, well below the planning materiality amount, be used, in conjunction with the FASB's conceptual definition. A common rule of thumb is one-sixth of planning materiality for the quantitative expression.

ILLUSTRATIONS

The following items presented in this section are from SAS 85 (AU 333).

1. Illustrative Management Representation Letter for GAAP Financial Statements.
2. Additional Illustrative Representations.
3. Illustrative Updating Management Representation Letter.

ILLUSTRATION 1. ILLUSTRATIVE MANAGEMENT REPRESENTATION LETTER FOR GAAP FINANCIAL STATEMENTS (FROM SAS 86 [AU 333])

The following representation letter, which is based on GAAP financial statements, is presented for illustrative purposes only.

If matters exist that should be disclosed to the auditor, they should be indicated by modifying the related representation. For example, if an event subsequent to the date of the balance sheet has been disclosed in the financial statements, the final paragraph could be modified as follows: "To the best of our knowledge and belief, except as discussed in Note X to the financial statements, no events have occurred. . ." In appropriate circumstances, item 9 could be modified as follows: "The company has no plans or intentions that may materially affect the carrying value or classification of assets and liabilities, except for its plans to dispose of segment A, as disclosed in Note X to the financial statements, which are discussed in the minutes of the December 7, 20X1, meetings of the board of directors." Similarly, if management has received a communication regarding an allegation of fraud or suspected fraud, item 8 could be modified as follows: "Except for the allegation discussed in the minutes of the December 7, 20X1, meeting of the board of directors (or disclosed to you at our meeting on October 15, 20X1), we have no knowledge of any allegations of fraud or suspected fraud affecting the company received in communications from employees, former employees, analysts, regulators, short sellers, or others."

Certain terms are used in the illustrative letter that are described elsewhere in authoritative literature. Examples are fraud (SAS 82, *Consideration of Fraud in a Financial Statement Audit),* and related parties, (SAS 45, *Omnibus Statement on Auditing Standards).* The auditor may wish to furnish those definitions to management or request that the definitions be included in the written representations.

[*Client Letterhead*]

[*Date*]

To [*Independent Auditor*]

We are providing this letter in connection with your audit(s) of the [*identification of financial statements*] of [*name of entity*] as of [*dates*] and for the [*periods*] for the purpose of expressing an opinion as to whether the [*consolidated*] financial statements present fairly, in all material respects, the financial position, results of operations, and cash flows of [*name of entity*] in conformity with accounting principles generally accepted in the United States of America. We confirm that we are responsible for the fair presentation in the [*consolidated*] financial statements of financial position, results of operations, and cash flows in conformity with accounting principles generally accepted in the United States of America.

Certain representations in this letter are described as being limited to matters that are material. Items are considered material if they exceed [*insert dollar amount*] or if they, regardless of size, involve an omission or misstatement of accounting information that, in the light of surrounding circumstance, makes it probable that the judgment of a reasonable person relying on the information would be changed or influenced by the omission or misstatements.

We confirm, to the best of our knowledge and belief [*as of (date of auditor's report)*], the following representations made to you during your audit(s).

1. The financial statements referred to above are fairly presented in conformity with accounting principles generally accepted in the United States of America.
2. We have made available to you all
   a. Financial records and related data.
   b. Minutes of the meetings of stockholders, directors, and committees of directors, or summaries of actions of recent meetings for which minutes have not yet been prepared.
3. There have been no communications from regulatory agencies concerning noncompliance with, or deficiencies in, financial reporting practices.
4. There are no material transactions that have not been properly recorded in the accounting records underlying the financial statements.
5. We believe that the uncorrected financial statement misstatements summarized in the accompanying schedule[2] are immaterial, both individually and in the aggregate.
6. We acknowledge our responsibility for the design and implementation of programs and controls to prevent and detect fraud.
7. We have no knowledge of any fraud or suspected fraud affecting the entity involving
   a. Management, or
   b. Employees who have significant roles in internal control, or
   c. Others where the fraud could have a material effect on the financial statements.
8. We have no knowledge of any allegations of fraud or suspected fraud affecting the entity received in communications from employees, former employees, analysts, regulators, short sellers, or others.
9. The entity has no plans or intentions that may materially affect the carrying value or classification of assets and liabilities.
10. The following have been properly recorded or disclosed in the financial statements:
    a. Related-party transactions, including sales, purchases, loans, transfers, leasing arrangements, and guarantees, and amounts receivable from or payable to related parties.
    b. Guarantees, whether written or oral, under which the entity is contingently liable.
    c. Significant estimates and material concentrations known to management that are required to be disclosed in accordance with the AICPA's Statement of Position 94-6, *Disclosures of Certain Significant Risks and Uncertainties.* (Significant estimates are estimates at the balance sheet date that could change materially within the next year. Concentrations refer to volumes of business, revenues, available sources of supply, or markets or geographic areas for which events could occur that would significantly disrupt normal finances within the next year.)
11. There are no
    a. Violations or possible violations of laws or regulations whose effects should be considered for disclosure in the financial statements or as a basis for recording a loss contingency.
    b. Unasserted claims or assessments that our lawyer has advised us are probable of assertion and must be disclosed in accordance with Financial Accounting Standards Board (FASB) Statement 5, *Accounting for Contingencies.*
12. The entity has satisfactory title to all owned assets, and there are no liens or encumbrances on such assets nor has any asset been pledged as collateral.
13. The entity has compiled with all aspects of contractual agreements that would have a material effect on the financial statements in the event of noncompliance.

[*Add additional representations that are unique to the entity's business or industry. See Illustration 2.*]

---

[2] *Schedule not included in this illustration.*

To the best of our knowledge and belief, no events have occurred subsequent to the balance sheet date and through the date of this letter that would require adjustment to or disclosure in the aforementioned financial statements.

____

[*Name of Chief Executive Officer and Title*]

____

[*Name of Chief Financial Officer and Title*]

ILLUSTRATION 2. ADDITIONAL ILLUSTRATIVE REPRESENTATIONS (FROM SAS 85 [AU 333])

Representation letters ordinarily should be tailored to include additional appropriate representations from management relating to matters specific to the entity's business or industry. The auditor also should be aware that certain AICPA Audit Guides recommend that the auditor obtain written representations concerning matters that are unique to a particular industry. The following is a list of additional representations that may be appropriate in certain situations. This list is not intended to be all-inclusive.

General

Condition	*Illustrative Example*
Unaudited interim information accompanies the financial statements.	The unaudited interim financial information accompanying [*presented in Note X to*] the financial statements for the [*identify all related periods*] has been prepared and presented in conformity with generally accepted accounting principles applicable to interim financial information [*and with Item 302(a) of Regulation S-K*]. The accounting principles used to prepare the unaudited interim financial information are consistent with those used to prepare the audited financial statements.
The impact of a new accounting principle is not known.	We have not completed the process of evaluating the impact that will result from adopting Financial Accounting Standards Board (FASB) Statement [*XXX, Name*], as discussed in Note [*X*]. The company is therefore unable to disclose the impact that adopting FASB Statement [*XXX*] will have on its financial position and the results of operations when such Statement is adopted.
There is justification for a change in accounting principles.	We believe that [*describe the newly adopted accounting principle*] is preferable to [*describe the former accounting principle*] because [*describe management's justification for the change in accounting principles*].
Financial circumstances are strained, with disclosure of management's intentions and the entity's ability to continue as a going concern.	Note [*X*] to the financial statements discloses all of the matters of which we are aware that are relevant to the company's ability to continue as a going concern, including significant conditions and events, and management's plans.
The possibility exists that the value of specific significant long-lived assets or certain identifiable intangibles may be impaired.	We have reviewed long-lived assets and certain identifiable intangibles to be held and used for impairment whenever events or changes in circumstances have indicated that the carrying amount of its assets might not be recoverable and have appropriately recorded the adjustment.

General

Condition	*Illustrative Example*
The entity engages in transactions with special-purpose entities	We have evaluated all transactions involving special-purpose entities to determine that the accounting for such transactions is in accordance with generally accepted accounting principles. Specifically [*indicate appropriate accounting principles*] • Conditions pursuant to paragraph 35 of FASB Statement 140, *Accounting for Transfers and Servicing of Financial Assets and Extinguishment of Liabilities.* • EITF Issue No. 96-16, *Investor's Accounting for an Investee When the Investor Has a Majority of the Voting Interest but the Minority Shareholder or Shareholders Have Certain Approval or Veto Rights.* • EITF Issue 90-15, *Impact of Nonsubstantive Lessors, Residual Value Guarantees, and Other Provisions in Leasing Transactions.* • EITF Issue 96-21, *Implementation in Accounting for Leasing Transactions Involving Special-Purpose Entities.* • EITF 97-1, *Implementation Issues in Accounting for Lease Transactions, Including Those Involving Special-Purpose Entities.* • EITF Issue No. 97-2, *Application of FASB Statement No. 94 and APB Opinion No. 16 to Physician Practice Management [PPM] Entities and Certain Other Entities with Contractual Management Arrangements.* • EITF Issue No. 00-04, *Majority Owner's Accounting for a Transaction in the Shares of a Consolidated Subsidiary and a Derivative Indexed to the Minority Interest in That Subsidiary,*
The work of a specialist has been used by the entity.	We agree with the finding of specialists in evaluating the [*describe assertion*] and have adequately considered the qualifications of the specialist in determining the amounts and disclosures used in the financial statements and underlying accounting records. We did not give or cause any instructions to be given to specialists with respect to the values or amounts derived in an attempt to bias their work, and we are not otherwise aware of any matters that have had an impact on the independence or objectivity of the specialists.

Assets

Condition	*Illustrative Example*
Cash	
Disclosure is required of compensating balances or other arrangements involving restrictions on cash balances, line of credit, or similar arrangements.	Arrangements with financial institutions involving compensating balances or other arrangements involving restrictions on cash balances, line of credit, or similar arrangements have been properly disclosed.
Financial Instruments	
Management intends to, and has the ability to, hold to maturity debt securities classified as held-to-maturity.	Debt securities that have been classified as held-to-maturity have been so classified due to the company's intent to hold such securities to maturity and the company's ability to do so. All other debt securities have been classified as available-for-sale or trading.

Assets

Condition	*Illustrative Example*
Management considers the decline in value of debt or equity securities to be temporary.	We consider the decline in value of debt or equity securities classified as either available-for-sale or held-to-maturity to be temporary.
Management has determined the fair value of significant financial instruments that do not have readily determinable market values.	The methods and significant assumptions used to determine fair values of financial instruments are as follows: [*describe methods and significant assumptions used to determine fair values of financial instruments*]. The methods and significant assumptions used result in a measure of fair value appropriate for financial statement measurement and disclosure purposes.
There are financial instruments with off-balance-sheet risk and financial instruments with concentrations of credit risk.	The following information about financial instruments with off-balance-sheet risk and financial instruments with concentrations of credit risk has been properly disclosed in the financial statements: 1. The extent, nature, and terms of financial instruments with off-balance-sheet risk. 2. The amount of credit risk of financial instruments with off-balance-sheet risk and information about the collateral supporting such financial instruments. 3. Significant concentrations of credit risk arising from all financial instruments and information about the collateral supporting such financial instruments.
Receivables	
Receivables have been recorded in the financial statements.	Receivables recorded in the financial statements represent valid claims against debtors for sales or other charges arising on or before the balance sheet date and have been appropriately reduced to their estimated net realizable value.
Inventories	
Excess or obsolete inventories exist.	Provision has been made to reduce excess or obsolete inventories to their estimated net realizable value.
Investments	
There are unusual considerations involved in determining the application of equity accounting.	[*For investments in common stock that are either nonmarketable or of which the entity has a 20% or greater ownership interest, select the appropriate representation from the following:*] • The equity method is used to account for the company's investment in the common stock of [*investee*] because the company has the ability to exercise significant influence over the investee's operating and financial policies. • The cost method is used to account for the company's investment in the common stock of [*investee*] because the company does not have the ability to exercise significant influence over the investee's operating and financial policies.
Deferred Charges	
Material expenditures have been deferred.	We believe that all material expenditures that have been deferred to future periods will be recoverable.

Assets

Condition	Illustrative Example
Deferred Tax Assets	
A deferred tax asset exists at the balance sheet date.	The valuation allowance has been determined pursuant to the provisions of FASB Statement 109, *Accounting for Income Taxes*, including the company's estimation of future taxable income, if necessary, and is adequate to reduce the total deferred tax asset to an amount that will more likely than not be realized. [*Complete with appropriate wording detailing how the entity determined the valuation allowance against the deferred tax asset.*] or A valuation allowance against deferred tax assets at the balance sheet date is not considered necessary because it is more likely than not the deferred tax asset will be fully realized.

Liabilities

Condition	Illustrative Example
Debt	
Short-term debt could be refinanced on a long-term basis and management intends to do so.	The company has excluded short-term obligations totaling $[*amount*] from current liabilities because it intends to refinance the obligations on a long-term basis. [*Complete with appropriate wording detailing how amounts will be refinanced as follows:*] • The company has issued a long-term obligation [*debt security*] after the date of the balance sheet but prior to the issuance of the financial statements for the purpose of refinancing the short-term obligations on a long-term basis. • The company has the ability to consummate the refinancing, by using the financing agreement referred to in Note [*X*] to the financial statements.
Tax-exempt bonds have been issued.	Tax-exempt bonds issued have retained their tax-exempt status.
Taxes	
Management intends to reinvest undistributed earnings of a foreign subsidiary.	We intend to reinvest the undistributed earnings of [*name of foreign subsidiary*].
Contingencies	
Estimates and disclosures have been made of environmental remediation liabilities and related loss contingencies.	Provision has been made for any material loss that is probable from environmental remediation liabilities associated with [*name of site*]. We believe that such estimate is reasonable based on available information and that the liabilities and related loss contingencies and the expected outcome of uncertainties have been adequately described in the company's financial statements.
Agreements may exist to repurchase assets previously sold.	Agreements to repurchase assets previously sold have been properly disclosed.
Pension and Postretirement Benefits	
An actuary has been used to measure pension liabilities and costs.	We believe that the actuarial assumptions and methods used to measure pension liabilities and cost for financial accounting purposes are appropriate in the circumstances.
There is involvement with a multiemployer plan.	We are unable to determine the possibility of a withdrawal liability in a multiemployer benefit plan. or We have determined that there is the possibility of a withdrawal liability in a multiemployer plan in the amount of $[*XX*].

Liabilities

Condition	*Illustrative Example*
Postretirement benefits have been eliminated.	We do not intend to compensate for the elimination of postretirement benefits by granting an increase in pension benefits. or We plan to compensate for the elimination of postretirement benefits by granting an increase in pension benefits in the amount of $[*XX*].
Employee layoffs that would otherwise lead to a curtailment of a benefit plan are intended to be temporary.	Current employee layoffs are intended to be temporary.
Management intends to either continue to make or not make frequent amendments to its pension or other postretirement benefit plans, which may affect the amortization period of prior service cost, or has expressed a substantive commitment to increase benefit obligations.	We plan to continue to make frequent amendments to its pension or other postretirement benefit plans, which may affect the amortization period of prior service cost. or We do not plan to make frequent amendments to its pension or other postretirement benefit plans.

Equity

Condition	*Illustrative Example*
There are capital stock repurchase options or agreements or capital stock reserved for options, warrants, conversions, or other requirements.	Capital stock repurchase options or agreements or capital stock reserved for options, warrants, conversions, or other requirements have been properly disclosed.

Income Statement

Condition	*Illustrative Example*
There may be a loss from sales commitments.	Provisions have been made for losses to be sustained in the fulfillment of, or from inability to fulfill, any sales commitments.
There may be losses from purchase commitments.	Provisions have been made for losses to be sustained as a result of purchase commitment for inventory quantities in excess of normal requirements or at prices in excess of prevailing market prices.
Nature of the product or industry indicates the possibility of undisclosed sales terms.	We have fully disclosed to you all sales terms, including all rights of return or price adjustments and all warranty provisions.

Illustration 3. Illustrative Updating Management Representation Letter (From SAS 85 [AU 333])

[*Client Letterhead*]

[*Date*]

To [*Auditor*]

In connection with your audit(s) of the [*identification of financial statements*] of [*name of entity*] as of [*dates*] and for the [*periods*] for the purpose of expressing an opinion as to whether the [*consolidated*] financial statements present fairly, in all material respects, the financial position, results of operations, and cash flows of [*name of entity*] in conformity with accounting principles generally accepted in the United States of America, you were previously provided with a representation letter under the date of [*date of previous representation letter*]. No information has come to our attention that would cause us to believe that any of those previous representations should be modified.

To the best of our knowledge and belief, no events have occurred subsequent to [*date of latest balance sheet reported on by auditor*] and through the date of this letter that would require adjustment to or disclosure in the aforementioned financial statements.

____

[*Name of Chief Executive Officer and Title*]

____

[*Name of Chief Financial Officer and Title*]

334 RELATED PARTIES[1]

EFFECTIVE DATE AND APPLICABILITY

Original Pronouncement	SAS 45, August 1983.
Effective Date	Effective for periods ended after September 30, 1983, unless subsequently amended.
Applicability	Audits of financial statements in conformity with generally accepted auditing standards.

DEFINITIONS OF TERMS

The section itself has no general definitions, but it uses terms defined in paragraph 1 and the glossary of SFAS 57, *Related-Party Disclosures* (March 1982).

Related parties.

- Affiliates of the enterprise.
- Entities for which investments are accounted for by the equity method.
- Trusts for the benefit of employees, such as pension and profit-sharing trusts that are managed by or under the trusteeship of management.
- Principal owners.
- Management.
- Members of the immediate families of principal owners and management.
- Other parties if one party controls or can significantly influence the management or operating policies of the other to an extent that one of the parties might be prevented from pursuing its own separate interest.
- Another party that can significantly influence the management or operating policies of the transacting parties or that has an ownership interest in one of the transacting parties and can significantly influence the other to an extent that one or more of the transacting parties might be prevented from pursuing its own separate interests.

Affiliate. A party that, directly or indirectly though one or more intermediaries, controls, is controlled by, or is under common control with an enterprise.

---

[1] *The Auditing Standards Board (ASB) has issued an Exposure Draft of a proposed SAS that would affect this section,* ***Sarbanes-Oxley Omnibus SAS****. The Exposure Draft is designed to address certain provisions of the Sarbanes-Oxley Act of 2002. The proposed amendment to this section states that related-party transactions may represent illegal acts. For example, certain loans to a director or an executive officer of a public company may be prohibited. The Public Company Accounting Oversight Board (PCAOB) has replaced the ASB as the standards-setting authority for public company audits. Therefore, the ASB's Exposure Draft will not be issued as a final standard by the AICPA. The document will, however, be considered by the PCAOB in developing a standard or amendment to an existing transitional standard to comply with the Sarbanes-Oxley Act and the related SEC implementing rules. Please check for updates to this section on the John Wiley & Sons, Inc. website at www.wiley.com/gaas.*

Control. The possession, direct or indirect, of the power to direct or cause the direction of the management and policies of an enterprise through ownership, by contract, or otherwise.

Immediate family. Family members whom a principal owner or a member of management might control or influence, or by whom they might be controlled or influenced because of the family relationship.

Management. Persons who are responsible for achieving the objectives of the enterprise and who have the authority to establish policies and make decisions by which those objectives are to be pursued. Management normally includes members of the board of directors, the chief executive officer, chief operating officer, vice presidents in charge of principal business functions (such as sales, administration, or finance), and other persons who perform similar policymaking functions. Persons without formal titles also may be members of management.

Principal owners. Owners of record or known beneficial owners of more than 10% of the voting interests of the enterprise.

OBJECTIVES OF SECTION

Special attention to related parties has a long history in auditing. The first publication on generally accepted auditing standards in the United States contained the following illustration of relative risk in auditing:

> *Arm's-length transactions with outside parties are usually subjected to less detailed scrutiny than intercompany transactions or transactions with officers and employees, where the same degree of disinterested dealing cannot be assumed.*

From the auditor's perspective, related-party transactions have two distinct, but not mutually exclusive, aspects: adequate disclosure and fraud detection.

The disclosure aspect is emphasized in SFAS 57. Some related-party transactions may be the direct result of the relationship. Without that relationship, the transaction might not have occurred at all or might have had substantially different terms. Thus, disclosure of the nature and amount of transactions with related parties is necessary for a proper understanding of the financial statements.

Inadequate disclosure of related-party transactions may result in misleading financial statements, and so the auditor should be concerned with identifying such transactions in the audit and evaluating the adequacy of disclosure of them. The auditor should also be concerned, however, with the possibility that an undisclosed relationship with a party to a material transaction has been used to fabricate transactions. That is, the transactions may be fraudulent or without substance. SAS 45 clearly acknowledges the possibility that a related-party relationship may be a tool for fraud by management.

SAS 6 was issued in 1975 primarily in response to some spectacular fraud cases in which management's involvement in material transactions was obscured either by inadequate disclosure or outright concealment. The SAS was more disclosure-oriented than fraud-oriented, however, because fraud is the exception rather than the norm. Nevertheless, the auditor should be aware of the possibility of fraud. The SAS observed

> *In the absence of evidence to the contrary, transactions with related parties should not be assumed to be outside the ordinary course of business.*
>
> *The auditor should view related-party transactions within the framework of existing pronouncements, placing primary emphasis on the adequacy of disclosure. In addition, the auditor should be aware that the substance of a particular transaction could be significantly different from its form.*

When issued, SAS 6 provided guidance on disclosure of related-party transactions because accounting literature did not contain such guidance. SFAS 57 essentially transferred that guidance to the authoritative accounting literature. It was, therefore, no longer necessary or appropriate for an auditing standard to contain accounting standards. SAS 45 eliminated references to accounting considerations and disclosure requirements that were in SAS 6, but coverage of SFAS 57 is included here for the reader's convenience.

FUNDAMENTAL REQUIREMENTS

ACCOUNTING CONSIDERATIONS

SFAS 57, *Related-Party Disclosures*, provides that

1. Material related-party transactions, other than compensation arrangements, expense allowances, and other similar items in the ordinary course of business should be disclosed. (Disclosure of transactions eliminated in consolidated or combined statements is not required in those statements.)
2. The disclosures shall include
   a. The nature of the relationship(s).
   b. A description of the transactions for each of the periods for which income statements are presented and such other information necessary to understand the effects of the transactions on the financial statements (including transactions to which no amounts or nominal amounts were ascribed).
   c. The dollar amounts of transactions for each period for which an income statement is presented. (The effects of any change in the method of establishing the terms from the prior period should also be disclosed.)
   d. Amounts due from or to related parties as of each balance sheet date presented and the terms and manner of settlement.

AUDIT PROCEDURES

An audit cannot be expected to provide assurance that all related-party transactions will be discovered. Nevertheless, the auditor should be aware of

1. The possibility that material related-party transactions exist that could affect the financial statements.
2. Common ownership or management control relationships that are required by SFAS 57 to be disclosed even though there are no transactions.

In determining the scope of work to be performed, the auditor should obtain an understanding of management responsibilities and the relationship of each of the entity's component to the total entity. The auditor should consider controls over management activities and the business purpose served by the various components.

NOTE: Business structure and operating style are occasionally deliberately designed to obscure related-party transactions.

The auditor should recognize that the following transactions may indicate related parties:

1. Borrowing or lending at no interest or at rates significantly different from market rates.
2. Selling real estate at a price significantly different from its appraised value.
3. A nonmonetary exchange of property for similar property.
4. Making loans with no scheduled terms for the time or method of repayment.

AU 334.07 also enumerates the following factors that the auditor should be aware of that may motivate transactions with related parties:

1. Lack of sufficient working capital or credit to continue the business.
2. An urgent desire for a continued favorable earnings record to support the price of the entity's stock.
3. An overly optimistic earnings forecast.
4. Dependence on one or a few products, customers, or transactions for continued success.
5. A declining industry with many business failures.
6. Excess capacity.
7. Significant litigation, especially between stockholders and management.
8. Significant dangers of obsolescence because the entity is in a high-technology industry.

NOTE: These are fraud "warning signs" or risk factors. The presence of one or more factors is not proof of fraud, but the auditor should increase his or her awareness of the possibility of fraud. If the risk is high, the auditor might increase the scope of substantive tests designed to identify undisclosed relationships or use some of the expanded procedures enumerated in SAS 45. (See also Section 316.)

Basic Approach

To identify material related-party transactions the auditor should

1. Identify related parties (through inquiry and review of relevant information to determine the identity of related parties so that material transactions with these parties known to be related can be examined).

   NOTE: According to SAS 45, the auditor should place emphasis on testing identified material related-party transactions.

2. Identify material transactions (consider whether there are indications of previously undisclosed relationships for material transactions).
3. Examine identified material related-party transactions.

NOTE: In SAS 45, the procedures are grouped essentially in the preceding categories. In the following discussion, a different grouping is used to emphasize distinctions between specific procedures for related parties and general procedures.

Specific Procedures

SAS 45 includes some procedures performed solely for the purpose of identifying related parties or related-party transactions.

1. Inquire of management
   a. Names of all related parties.
   b. Whether there were any transactions with these parties during the period.
   c. Whether the entity has procedures for identifying and properly accounting for related-party transactions. If so, evaluate these procedures.

      NOTE: This is covered in the management representation letter. It is helpful to give management the technical definition of related parties at the time of initial inquiry and in the letter.

2. Obtain the names of all pension and other trusts established for the benefit of employees and the names of officers and trustees of the trusts.

3. Review stockholder listings of closely held entities to identify principal stockholders.
4. Provide audit staff with the names of known related parties so that they can identify transactions with such parties.
5. For indications of undisclosed relationships, review the nature and extent of business transacted with major
   a. Customers.
   b. Suppliers.
   c. Borrowers.
   d. Lenders.
6. Consider whether transactions are occurring but not being given accounting recognition, such as the client receiving or providing accounting, management, or other services at no charge, or a major stockholder absorbing corporate expenses.

General Procedures

The procedures in SAS 45 for identifying related parties and for identifying transactions with related parties include several procedures that are usually performed in an audit. These are normal procedures performed for several purposes that may also identify related parties.

General procedure	*Relevance to related parties*
Review prior years' audit documentation.	Identify names of known related parties.
Review minutes of meetings of board of directors and executive or operating committees.	Obtain information on material transactions authorized or discussed.
Review confirmations of compensating balance arrangements.	Identify whether balances are or were maintained for or by related parties.
Review invoices from law firms for regular or special services.	Identify indications of related parties or related-party transactions.
Review confirmations of loans receivable and payable.	Identify whether there are guarantees and the nature of relationship to guarantor.
Review material investment transactions.	Determine whether investment created related party.
Review accounting records for large, unusual, or nonrecurring transactions or balances, particularly at or near end of reporting period.	Consider whether transactions are with related parties.
Inquire of predecessor, principal, or other auditors of related entities (this inquiry should be made at an early stage of the audit).	Obtain their knowledge of related parties or related-party transactions.

Procedures: Public Companies

Some procedures in SAS 45 are relevant only for public companies.

1. Review filings with the SEC and other regulatory agencies for the names of related parties and for other businesses in which officers and directors occupy directorships or other management positions.
2. Review proxy and other material filed with the SEC and comparable data filed with other regulatory agencies for information on material transactions with related parties.
3. Review "conflict-of-interest" statements obtained by the entity from its management.

Procedures for Identified Transactions

After a related-party transaction is identified, the auditor should apply substantive tests to that transaction. Inquiry of management is not sufficient. According to AU 334.09, procedures that should be considered are

1. Obtain an understanding of the business purpose of the transaction.

   NOTE: Until the auditor understands the business sense of the transaction, he or she cannot complete the audit.

2. Examine invoices, executed copies of agreements, contracts, and other pertinent documents, such as receiving reports and shipping documents.
3. Determine whether the transaction has been approved by the board of directors or other appropriate officials.
4. Test for reasonableness the compilation of amounts to be disclosed or considered for disclosure.
5. Inspect or confirm and obtain satisfaction as to the transferability and value of collateral.
6. For intercompany account balances

   a. Arrange for examination at concurrent dates, even if fiscal years differ.
   b. Arrange for examination of specified, important, and representative related-party transactions by auditors for each of the parties with an exchange of relevant information.

   NOTE: A principal auditor-other auditor relationship may exist and the component not audited by the principal auditor may have conducted related-party transactions that are complex or unusual. In these circumstances, the principal auditor should request access to the other auditor's audit documentation concerning this matter.

Expanded Procedures

If the auditor concludes that it is necessary to fully understand a related-party transaction, he or she should consider the following procedures that might otherwise be unnecessary:

1. Confirm the amount and terms of the transaction, including guarantees and other significant data, with the other party.
2. Inspect evidence in the other party's possession.
3. Confirm or discuss significant information with intermediaries (banks, guarantors, agents, or attorneys).
4. If there is reason to believe that material transactions with unfamiliar customers, suppliers, or others may lack substance, refer to financial publications, trade journals, credit agencies, and other information sources.
5. Obtain information on the financial capability of the other party for material uncollected balances, guarantees, or other obligations.

Equivalence Representations

No representations need be made in the financial statements that related-party transactions were consummated on terms equivalent to those that prevail in arm's-length transactions. If representations are made that state or imply that, SFAS 57 requires that the entity be able to substantiate them. Thus, the auditor should consider whether there is sufficient support for such a representation, if made, and appropriately qualify his or her opinion if there is not such support.

NOTE: Lack of substantiation of representations made on equivalence of material related-party transactions should result in a qualified or adverse opinion because of a departure from GAAP.

INTERPRETATIONS

Exchange of Information between the Principal and Other Auditor on Related Parties (April 1979)

The principal auditor and the other auditor should, at an early stage in the audit, obtain from each other the names of known related parties.

Examination of Identified Related-Party Transactions with a Component (April 1979)

Audit procedures may have to be applied to a component audited by another auditor. When unusual or complex related-party transactions exist, the principal auditor may need access to the relevant portions of the other auditor's workpapers. Access ordinarily should be provided.

The Nature and Extent of Auditing Procedures for Examining Related-Party Transactions (May 1986)

The higher the auditor's assessment of risk regarding related-party transactions, the more extensive or effective the audit tests should be. To understand the business purpose or to obtain sufficient evidence about the transaction, the auditor may

1. Refer to audited or unaudited financial statements of the related party.
2. Apply procedures at the related party.
3. Audit the financial statements of the related party.

The auditor should consider obtaining representations from senior management and its board of directors about whether they or other related parties engaged in any transactions with the entity during the period.

Management's and Auditor's Responsibilities for Related-Party Disclosures Prefaced by Terminology Such as "Management Believes That" (May 2000)

As discussed above under "Equivalence Representations," if management makes an assertion in financial statements about equivalency that is prefaced by "management believes that" or "it is the company's belief that," the auditor's responsibility is not changed. That is, the auditor must obtain evidence relating to the equivalency assertion, and management must still substantiate the asserted equivalence. If the auditor believes that the representation is unsubstantiated, depending on the materiality of the related-party transaction, the auditor should express either a qualified or adverse opinion because of a GAAP departure.

PROFESSIONAL ISSUES TASK FORCE PRACTICE ALERT

95-3 Auditing Related Parties and Related-Party Transactions

This practice alert lists examples of events that may indicate that transactions with undisclosed related parties are occurring and offers suggestions on how to respond to those events. The alert states that the number one rule for potentially identifying related parties and related-party transactions that management does not disclose is simply to be alert to that possibility. When assessing risk, the auditor should also consider whether the following factors exist:

- Complex corporate structures
- Entities that have material intercompany transactions with one another with audit responsibilities divided among two or more auditing firms, or in which one of the entities is not audited
- Highly complex business practices that help management to mask their economic substance
- Unique, highly complex, and material transactions close to year-end that raise difficult "substance over form" concerns.

The alert also offers suggestions on how to respond to related parties and related-party transactions not voluntarily disclosed by management. If the auditor thinks that a related-party transaction exists, he or she should consider the performance of additional audit procedures to determine whether it exists. If an undisclosed related party is identified, the audit team should assess whether management's failure to disclose was an oversight or a deliberate attempt to mask the relationship. If it is a deliberate attempt to mask the relationship, the auditor should reassess the overall audit scope and ability to rely on other management representations. The auditor should consider withdrawing from the engagement (and consulting legal counsel) if he or she can no longer trust management.

The full text of this Practice Alert can be obtained from the AICPA website at www.aicpa.org/members/div/secps/lit/practice.htm.

ACCOUNTING AND AUDITING FOR RELATED PARTIES AND RELATED-PARTY TRANSACTIONS: A TOOLKIT FOR ACCOUNTANTS AND AUDITORS

In 2001, the AICPA developed a nonauthoritative toolkit to assist accountants and auditors in better understanding some of the current issues pertaining to related parties and related-party transactions. The toolkit points out that related parties and related-party transactions are difficult to audit for several reasons.

- Transactions with related parties are not always easily identifiable.
- Although other procedures are ordinarily performed, the auditor relies primarily upon management and principal owners to identify all related parties and related-party transactions.
- Such transactions may not be easily tracked by a company's internal control.

The toolkit summarizes the accounting and auditing literature. In addition, the toolkit points out that some business entities make use of off-balance-sheet arrangements to conduct financing or other business activities. These arrangements may involve unconsolidated, nonindependent, limited-purpose entities called structured finance or special-purpose entities (SPEs). These entities may be corporations, partnerships, limited liability companies, trusts, structured finance entities, or other types of agreements, relationships, or understandings. Such entities may be used to provide financing, liquidity, market risk or credit support, or involve leasing, hedging, and/or research and development services.

Auditors should

- Be alert to the existence or creation of SPEs.
- Understand the ownership structure of, and transactions with, the SPE.
- Evaluate management's conclusions regarding nonconsolidation and off-balance-sheet treatment.

- Consider whether transactions with the SPE represent related-party transactions.

The full text of this toolkit can be obtained from the AICPA website at www.aicpa.org/news/relpty1.htm.

TECHNIQUES FOR APPLICATION

PRELIMINARY EVALUATION OF RISK

A preliminary evaluation concerning the likelihood of related-party transactions is usually made during the planning of the audit when the risk assessment questionnaire is completed (see Section 311). This evaluation includes

1. Obtaining an understanding of the structure of the entity and management responsibilities.
2. Considering the business purpose of the various components of the entity.
3. Considering the control consciousness within the entity and controls over management activities.

PURPOSE OF AUDITING PROCEDURES DESIGNED SPECIFICALLY FOR RELATED-PARTY TRANSACTIONS

The purpose of auditing procedures designed specifically for related-party transactions is to determine the **existence** of related parties and to **identify** significant related-party transactions, including those not recognized in the accounting records.

If the auditor identifies significant related-party transactions, he or she should **examine** these transactions and **evaluate the adequacy** of their disclosure.

The auditor also is concerned with the adequacy of disclosure of economic dependence (see below).

DETERMINING THE EXISTENCE OF RELATED PARTIES

The existence of some related parties, such as parent-subsidiary, investor-investee and affiliates, is obvious. To determine the existence of other related parties, specific audit procedures are necessary. These procedures were described in *Fundamental Requirements* and are listed in the related-party checklist in *Illustrations*.

IDENTIFYING RELATED-PARTY TRANSACTIONS

Related-party transactions and similar transactions that require disclosure may be classified as follows:

1. Those recognized in the accounting records.
2. No-charge transactions.
3. Those that create economic dependence.

Related-Party Transactions Recognized in the Accounting Records

To identify these transactions, specific audit procedures are necessary. These procedures were described in Fundamental Requirements and are listed in the related-party checklist in Illustrations.

No-Charge Transactions

Sometimes a related party provides services that are not given accounting recognition. Examples of these services are the following:

1. Accounting and managerial.
2. Credit and collection.
3. Professional.

To identify no-charge transactions, the auditor should compare expenses with sales and

1. Investigate deviations from industry standards.
2. Investigate deviations from prior year.

These are essentially analytical procedures (see Section 329).

Transactions That Create Economic Dependence

SFAS 57 does not address the issue of economic dependence. Related parties do not exist solely because one party is economically dependent on another. If one party exercises significant influence over the other, however, a related-party situation does exist and should be disclosed. In situations where economic dependence does not create related parties, disclosure may still be necessary to keep the financial statements from being misleading.

EXAMINING RELATED-PARTY TRANSACTIONS

When the auditor identifies related-party transactions, he or she should analyze them to determine the following:

1. The purpose of the transactions.
2. The nature of the transactions.
3. The extent of the transactions.
4. The effect of the transactions on the financial statements.

To determine the preceding, the auditor applies normal auditing procedures and also may have to apply extended auditing procedures.

MANAGEMENT REPRESENTATION LETTER

Much of the information about related parties is obtained through inquiry of management. The responses to these inquiries should be formalized in the management representation letter (see Section 333).

If no related-party transactions occurred, a statement to that effect should appear in the management representation letter. If related party transactions occurred, the following should be noted:

1. Identification of the related parties.
2. Identification of the transactions.
3. The nature of the transactions.
4. The amount of the transactions.

The auditor should also consider obtaining written representations from the client's senior management and its board of directors about whether they or other related parties engaged in any transactions with the entity.

ILLUSTRATIONS

This section contains the following illustrations:

1. Paragraph in auditor's report calling attention to the existence of related parties.
2. Notes to financial statements disclosing the existence of related parties.
3. Related-party checklist.

Illustration 1. Auditor's Report Paragraph Calling Attention to the Existence of Related Parties

This section does not require the auditor to note the existence of related-party transactions in the report. If the auditor decides to call the user's attention to related-party transactions, however, he or she may include a separate explanatory paragraph in the report. Following is a separate paragraph from an auditor's report on the audit of the combined financial statements of the leasing and financing subsidiaries of Pullman Incorporated:

> The leasing and financing subsidiaries engage in significant transactions with Pullman Incorporated as described in Note 2 of the notes to combined financial statements.

Illustration 2. Disclosure in Notes to Financial Statements

Following are illustrations of the disclosure of related-party transactions in the notes to financial statements.

> Related-Party Transactions
>
> A Director of the Company is a principal in two companies that are distributors of the Company's products. Total sales to these related companies aggregated $86,000 in 20X2 and $91,000 in 20X1. At August 31, 20X2, these companies owed the company $35,983, of which $25,525 was owed beyond the Company's normal credit terms.
>
> Related-Party Transactions
>
> The Company occupies premises leased from two officer-shareholders for which $74,000 was paid in 20X2 and $27,000 was paid in 20X1. The lease agreement calls for minimum future payments of $86,000 in 20X3, $94,000 in 20X4, $101,000 in 20X5 and $114,000 in 20X6. The Company loaned $102,000 to these officer-shareholders to provide the down payment for their purchase of the property in 20X0. This loan was repaid during 20X1.

Illustration 3. Related-Party Checklist

Checklist

____

Related Parties

____

____

(Client)

__________	__________	__________	______
(Audit date)	(Date completed)	(Reviewed by)	(Date)

Instructions. This checklist is designed to assist the auditor in complying with the requirement that material related-party transactions be identified and evaluated for disclosure. If this checklist is not used, the audit program should include appropriate procedures for related-party transactions. This checklist does not apply to transactions that are eliminated in consolidation.

Many procedures performed for related-party transactions are normal auditing procedures executed during other phases of the audit. These procedures are indicated in this checklist by an asterisk (*).

Procedures for auditing related-party transactions involve the following:

1. Gaining an understanding of management's responsibilities, internal accounting controls related to management's activities, and the relationship of each component of the entity to the total business.
2. Obtaining knowledge of related parties and planning and executing the audit so that material transactions—individually or in the aggregate—with related parties are identified and evaluated for disclosure.

Part 1 of this checklist is concerned with the existence and identification of related parties and related-party transactions. Part 2 is concerned with the examination and evaluation of identified related-party transactions and the adequacy of disclosure of these transactions in the client's financial statements. Part 2 should **not** be done if Part 1 has been completed and it is concluded that no related-party transactions exist.

The "Inquiry of, W/P reference" column should provide the name and position of the client personnel queried and, where applicable, reference to the supporting audit documentation, including client permanent files. If a procedure is not applicable "N/A" should be placed in the "Inquiry of, W/P reference" column.

PART 1: EXISTENCE AND IDENTIFICATION

	Procedure	*Performed by*	*Inquiry of, W/P reference*
*1.	Review prior year's audit documentation for names of known related parties and related-party transactions.		
2.	Evaluate client procedures for identifying, accounting for, and disclosing related-party transactions, including procedures established to monitor or avoid conflicts of interest in purchasing, contracting, or similar business activities.		
3.	Review conflict-of-interest statements obtained by the entity from its management.		
4.	For nonpublic entities, review stock certificate book or schedule of stockholders to identify principal stockholders.		
*5.	Review material filed with the SEC, taxing authorities, and other regulatory bodies.		
6.	Inquire about the names of related parties and whether there were transactions with them.		
7.	Inquire about whether the client is under common ownership or management control with another entity.		
8.	Obtain the names of all pension and profit-sharing trusts established for the benefit of employees, and the names of the officers and trustees and their trusts. (If the trusts are managed by or under the trusteeship of management, they are related parties.)		
*9.	Inquire of predecessor auditor and principal auditor or other auditors of related entities about their knowledge of existing related parties and the extent of management involvement in material transactions.		
*10.	Review the extent and nature of business transacted with major customers, suppliers, borrowers, and lenders for indications of previously undisclosed relationships.		
11.	Inquire about transactions occurring but not being given accounting recognition, such as receiving or providing accounting, management, or other services at no charge, or a major stockholder absorbing corporate expenses.		
*12.	Review confirmations of compensating balance arrangements for indications that balances are maintained for or by related parties.		
*13.	Review confirmations of loans receivable and payable for indications of guarantees. If guarantees are indicated, determine their nature and the relationship of the guarantors to the client.		
*14.	Review material investment transactions to determine if the nature and extent of the investments created related parties.		
*15.	Review minutes of meetings of board of directors and executive committees or operations for discussions or authorization of material or unusual transactions.		
*16.	Review large, unusual, or nonrecurring transactions, especially those recognized at or near the end of the period under audit. If appropriate, inquire whether the transactions involved a related party.		
*17.	Review invoices from law firms and other specialists for indications of related parties or related-party transactions.		
18.	Prepare or update a carryforward schedule of related parties and information on known continuing related-party transactions. Provide copy of schedule to audit personnel and other auditors of related entities.		

PART 2: EXAMINATION AND EVALUATION

(To be filled out only if Part 1 indicates the existence of related-party transactions.)

Procedure	*Performed by*	*Inquiry of, W/P reference*
1. Obtain an understanding of the business purpose of the transactions. If necessary, consult with attorney or other specialist.		
2. Examine invoices, agreements, contracts, and other relevant documents, such as receiving reports and shipping documents.		
3. Determine that the transactions have been authorized by the appropriate party.		
4. Arrange for audits of intercompany account balances at the same date.		
5. Arrange for the examination of specific related-party transactions by auditors for each of the parties and for the exchange of relevant information.		
6. Inspect or confirm collateral received in connection with related-party transactions and obtain satisfaction regarding the value and transferability of the collateral.		
7. To understand fully a specific related-party transaction, consider doing the following:		
a. Confirm transaction amounts and terms, including guarantees and other significant data, with other parties to the transaction.		
b. Inspect evidence in the possession of other parties to the transaction.		
c. Confirm or discuss significant information with intermediaries, such as banks, guarantors, agents, or lawyers.		
d. Refer to financial publications, trade journals, credit agencies, and other sources if there is reason to believe that unfamiliar customers, suppliers, or other business enterprises with which material amounts of business have been transacted may lack substance.		
e. For material uncollected balances, guarantees, and other obligations, obtain information about the financial capability of other parties to the transaction.		
8. Recompute the compilation of amounts to be disclosed.		
9. Determine that the financial statements adequately disclose related-party transactions.		

336 USING THE WORK OF A SPECIALIST

EFFECTIVE DATE AND APPLICABILITY

Original Pronouncement SAS 73, July 1994.

Effective Date Audits of financial statements for periods ending on or after December 15, 1994.

Applicability Audits of financial statements in accordance with generally accepted auditing standards.

NOTE: Clarifying applicability was the main reason SAS 73 was issued to replace SAS 11. Applicability is further explained in several components of this section.

Applies to all audit engagements and to engagements performed under SAS 62 (Section 623), *Special Reports*.

Guidance in this section is applicable when

1. Management engages or employs a specialist and the auditor uses that specialist's work as evidential matter in performing substantive tests to evaluate material financial statement assertions.
2. Management engages a specialist employed by the auditor's firm to provide advisory services, and the auditor uses that specialist's work as evidential matter in performing substantive tests to evaluate material financial statement assertions.
3. The auditor engages a specialist, and uses that specialist's work as evidential matter in performing substantive tests to evaluate material financial statement assertions.

NOTE: If a specialist employed by the auditor's firm participates in the audit, the specialist should be properly supervised in the same manner as others on the audit team. In this situation SAS 22 (Section 311), ***Planning and Supervision,*** *applies.*

DEFINITIONS OF TERMS

Specialist. A person (or firm) possessing special skill or knowledge in a particular field other than accounting or auditing. Specialists include, but are not limited to actuaries, appraisers, engineers, environmental consultants, and geologists.

OBJECTIVES OF SECTION

SAS 11 was issued in December 1975 to serve as an umbrella SAS to provide a basis for more detailed guidance to be provided in industry audit guides on the use of particular types of specialists in various specialized industries. For example, audit guides related to insurance companies provide guidance on the use of the work of actuaries who determine loss reserves. Before SAS 11, the views of auditors were not necessarily uniform concerning matters such as how aggressively the auditor should challenge the work of a specialist. Some believed the auditor should be able to accept a qualified specialist's work at face value. Others believed the auditor had to be familiar enough with a specialist's methods to challenge the validity of the result. There was also disagreement about the appropriateness of making reference to the specialist's work in the audit report in much the same manner that an auditor would divide responsibility for the audit of financial statements with another auditor.

SAS 11 took the position that the auditor should obtain an understanding of the specialist's methods and assumptions but would ordinarily be able to use the work of the specialist unless the auditor believed the specialist's findings were unreasonable. In other words, the auditor would not have to substantiate the reasonableness of the specialist's findings but would be expected to have done enough to recognize clearly unreasonable findings. SAS 11 also prohibited reference to the specialist in the auditor's report unless the auditor was qualifying the opinion based at least in part on the specialist's findings.

SAS 73 does not change these basic positions. The primary changes made by SAS 73 are as follows:

1. Clarifies the applicability of the guidance.
2. Relaxes the need to document the understanding among the client, auditor, and specialist.
3. Provides additional guidance for situations in which the specialist is related to the client or employed by the audit firm.

SAS 73 also updates the examples of using the work of a specialist. For example, use of an environmental consultant's findings related to an environmental cleanup obligation is mentioned.

The primary reason that SAS 11 was revised was to clarify when the SAS had to be applied. What circumstances dictate use of a specialist's work? Or is use of a specialist always an option? The intent of SAS 11 was that the guidance applied in two broad types of circumstances. In the most common circumstance, the client would have engaged a specialist who determined an amount or developed information for disclosure that was material to the financial statements. For example, an insurance company normally uses an actuary to determine loss reserves. In that circumstance, the auditor's use of the work of a specialist could not be an option; the guidance in SAS 11 would have to be applied.

In other circumstances, an auditor might engage a specialist to assist in applying audit procedures. For example, an auditor might engage an engineer to assist in determining the quantity of material stored in stockpiles. This type of use of a specialist would most likely be discretionary.

Some auditors misinterpreted SAS 11 as always permitting, but never requiring, the use of the work of a specialist. They believed that use of a specialist was an auditor's option to be used to provide assistance in applying audit procedures. Clearly this was not the intent of SAS 11. The example of use of a specialist that was discussed most extensively during the development of SAS 11 was use of the work of an actuary who had determined insurance loss reserves. The primary motivation for issuing SAS 11 was disagreement concerning the proper guidance to provide in the property and casualty insurance audit guide on use of the work of an actuary. The loss reserves of an insurance company are usually critical to its financial statements. The auditor cannot fail to evaluate the work of the actuary who determined the loss reserves.

SAS 73 was intended to clarify the circumstances when the guidance concerning use of the work of a specialist would have to be applied. Essentially, the guidance applies when an auditor uses a specialist's work as evidential matter in performing substantive tests to evaluate material financial statement assertions. The applicability of the guidance is not influenced by who engaged the specialist. SAS 73 notes that an auditor may encounter complex or subjective matters potentially material to the financial statements that may require special skill or knowledge, and that in the auditor's judgment require using the work of a specialist to obtain competent evidential matter. In those cases, such as insurance loss reserves, in which a material financial statement amount or disclosure is developed by a specialist, use of the work of a specialist would be essential unless the audit team includes an auditor with the knowledge, training, and experience of such a specialist.

FUNDAMENTAL REQUIREMENTS

QUALIFICATIONS OF A SPECIALIST

The auditor should consider the following to evaluate whether the specialist has the necessary qualifications:

1. Professional certification, license, or other recognition of competence.
2. Reputation and standing in the view of peers and other knowledgeable parties.
3. Experience in the kind of work under consideration.

NOTE: For example, an actuary determining property and casualty loss reserves should have experience in the property and casualty insurance field.

WORK OF A SPECIALIST

The auditor should obtain an understanding of the nature of the specialist's work that covers the following:

1. Objectives and scope.
2. Relationship to client.
3. Methods or assumptions used.
4. Comparison of 3. with methods or assumptions used in preceding period.
5. Appropriateness for intended purpose.
6. Form and content of specialist's findings.

NOTE: Sometimes it may be necessary to contact the specialist to ensure the specialist is aware of the auditor's intended use of the work.

RELATIONSHIP TO CLIENT

The auditor should evaluate whether the specialist's relationship to the client, if any, might impair the specialist's objectivity and, if so, perform additional procedures to determine whether the specialist's assumptions, methods, or findings are not unreasonable, or engage another specialist for that purpose.

USING FINDINGS

The auditor should perform procedures to

1. Obtain an understanding of the methods and assumptions used.

2. Test data (accounting and other data) provided to the specialist and, in considering the extent of testing, assess the control risk relevant to the data.
3. Evaluate whether the findings support the related financial statement assertions.
4. In the circumstance in which the auditor believes the findings are unreasonable, apply additional procedures.

NOTE: Additional procedures might include obtaining the opinion of another specialist.

EFFECT ON AUDIT REPORT

If there is a material difference between the specialist's findings and the assertions in the financial statements, the auditor should do the following:

1. If the matter cannot be resolved by applying additional audit procedures, obtain the opinion of another specialist, unless it appears that the matter cannot be resolved.
2. If the matter has not been resolved, qualify the opinion or disclaim an opinion because of the inability to obtain sufficient competent evidence.
3. If the auditor concludes the difference indicates the assertions are not in conformity with GAAP, qualify the opinion or express an adverse opinion.

REPORT REFERENCE TO SPECIALIST

The auditor should not refer to the work or findings of, or identify the specialist in the audit report, unless the findings of the specialist cause the auditor to depart from an unqualified opinion or add explanatory language to the standard report.

NOTE: If the auditor concludes there is a scope limitation or GAAP departure, the auditor would qualify the audit opinion. An explanatory paragraph should not be added for an uncertainty that is adequately presented and disclosed in accordance with GAAP.

INTERPRETATIONS

THE USE OF LEGAL INTERPRETATIONS AS EVIDENTIAL MATTER TO SUPPORT MANAGEMENT'S ASSERTION THAT A TRANSFER OF FINANCIAL ASSETS HAS MET THE ISOLATION CRITERION IN PARAGRAPH 9(a) OF FINANCIAL ACCOUNTING STANDARDS BOARD STATEMENT 140 (DECEMBER 2001)

SFAS 140, *Accounting for Transfers and Servicing of Financial Assets and Extinguishment of Liabilities* (AC Section F38), requires that a transferor of financial assets must surrender control over the financial assets to account for the transfer as a sale. Paragraph 9(a) states several conditions that must be met to provide evidence of surrender of control. One of these conditions is that the transferred assets must have been isolated from the transferor and its creditors. The determination of whether this isolation criterion has been met depends on facts and circumstances and should be assessed primarily from a legal perspective.

Decision to Use a Specialist

The auditor should first consider whether to use the work of a legal specialist to support management's assertion that the isolation criterion has been met. The specialist can be the client's internal or external attorney who is knowledgeable about applicable law. While the use of a legal specialist will not be necessary for routine transfers of assets, a legal specialist is necessary for transfers involving complex legal structures, continuing involvement by the transferor, or other legal issues.

If the auditor uses a legal opinion to support the accounting conclusion, the auditor may need, in certain circumstances, to obtain updates of the opinion to confirm that there have been no subsequent changes in relevant law or applicable regulations or in the pertinent facts of the transaction that would change the previous opinion. Updates may be necessary when

- The legal opinion relates to multiple transfers under a single structure, and such transfers occur over an extended period of time under that structure.
- Management asserts that a new transaction has a structure that is the same as a prior structure for which a legal opinion that complies with this interpretation was used as evidence to support an assertion that the transfer of assets met the isolation criterion.

The auditor should also consider whether management needs to obtain period updates to confirm that there have been no subsequent changes in relevant law or applicable regulations that may affect the conclusions in the previous opinion in the case of other transfers.

Assessing the Adequacy of the Legal Opinion

In assessing the adequacy of the legal opinion, the auditor should

- Consider whether the legal specialist has experience with relevant matters, including knowledge of the US Bankruptcy Code and other federal, state, and foreign law.
- Consider whether the legal specialist has knowledge of the transaction on which management's assertion is based.
- For transactions that may be affected by provisions of the Federal Deposit Insurance Act, consider whether the legal specialist has experience with the rights and powers of receivers, conservators, and liquidating agents under that Act.
- Obtain an understanding of the assumptions used by the legal specialist and make appropriate tests of information.
- Consider the form and content of the document provided by the legal specialist.
- Evaluate whether the legal specialist's findings support management's assertions about the isolation criterion.

A legal opinion that includes any of the following would not be persuasive evidence that a transfer of assets has met the isolation criterion:

- An inadequate opinion, inappropriate opinion, or a disclaimer of opinion.
- A limit on the scope of the opinion to facts and circumstances that are not applicable to the transaction.
- Language that does not provide persuasive evidence, such as the following examples provided in the interpretation:
  - "We are unable to express an opinion. . ."
  - "It is our opinion, based upon limited facts. . ."
  - "We are of the view. . ." or "it appears. . ."
  - "There is a reasonable basis to conclude that. . ."
  - "In our opinion, the transfer would be *either* a sale *or* a grant of a perfected security interest. . ."
  - "In our opinion, there is a reasonable possibility. . ."
  - "In our opinion, the transfer *should* be considered a sale. . ."
  - "It is our opinion that the entity will be able to assert meritorious arguments. . ."
  - "In our opinion, it is more likely than not. . ."
  - "In our opinion, the transfer would *presumptively* be. . ."
  - "In our opinion, it is probable that. . ."
- Conclusions about hypothetical transactions if they are not relevant to management's assertions or do not contemplate all the facts and circumstances of the transaction.

If a legal specialist's response does not provide persuasive evidence that a transfer of assets has met the isolation criterion, and no other relevant evidential matter exists, derecognition of the transferred assets is not in conformity with GAAP, and the auditor should consider expressing a qualified or adverse opinion (see Section 508).

Restricted Use Legal Opinions

Legal opinions that restrict the use of the opinion to the client, or to third parties other than the auditor, would **not** be acceptable audit evidence. In this case, the auditor should ask the client to obtain the legal specialist's written permission for the auditor to use the opinion for the purpose of evaluating management's assertion that the isolation criterion has been met.

If the legal specialist does not grant permission for the auditor to use a legal opinion that is restricted to the client or to third parties other than the auditor, a scope limitation exists, and the auditor should consider qualifying or disclaiming an opinion (see Section 508).

The following example from the interpretation illustrates a letter from a legal specialist to a client that adequately communicates permission for the auditor to use the legal specialist's opinion for the purpose of evaluating management's assertion that a transfer of financial assets meets the isolation criterion of SFAS 140:

> Notwithstanding any language to the contrary in our opinions of even date with respect to certain bankruptcy issues relating to the above-referenced transaction, you are authorized to make available to your auditors such opinions solely as evidential matter in support of their evaluation of management's assertion that the transfer of the receivables meets the isolation criterion of SFAS 140, provided a copy of this letter is furnished to them in connection therewith. In authorizing you to make copies of such opinions available to your auditors for such purpose, we are not undertaking or assuming any duty or obligation to your auditors or establishing any lawyer-client relationship with them. Further, we do not undertake or assume any responsibility with respect to financial statements of you or your affiliates.

The following would **not** adequately communicate permission for the auditor to use:

- "Use but not rely on" language in which a letter from a legal specialist authorizes the client to make copies available to the auditor but states that the auditor is not authorized to rely thereon.
- Other language that similarly restricts the auditor's use of the legal specialist's opinion.

The auditor may wish to consult with his or her legal counsel in circumstances where it is not clear that the auditor may use the legal specialist's opinion.

Finally, the interpretation provides

- Two examples of the conclusions in a legal opinion for an entity that is subject to receivership or conservatorship under provisions of the Federal Deposit Insurance Act. The conclusions in the examples provide persuasive evidence, in the absence of contradictory evidence, to support management's assertion that the transferred financial assets have been put presumptively beyond the reach of the entity and its creditors, even in conservatorship or receivership.
- Examples of additional paragraphs addressing substantive consolidation that applies when the entity to which the assets are sold or transferred is an affiliate of the selling entity. These paragraphs may also apply in other situations as noted by the legal specialist.

Effective Date and Applicability

This interpretation is effective for auditing procedures related to transfers of financial assets that are required to be accounted for under SFAS 140 as amended by FASB Technical Bulletin 01-1, *Effective Date for Certain Financial Institutions of Certain Provisions of Statement 140 Related to the Isolation of Transferred Financial Assets*.

TECHNIQUES FOR APPLICATION

EXAMPLES OF USE OF A SPECIALIST

The following are examples of common uses of specialists:

1. Determination of postemployment and postretirement benefit-related amounts by an actuary.
2. Determination of environmental cleanup obligations by an environmental consultant.
3. Determination of oil and gas reserves by a petroleum engineer.
4. Determination of the valuation of a financial institution's real estate investments or real estate collateral by an appraiser.
5. Determination of loss reserves of an insurance company by an actuary.

The auditor is not required to use a specialist automatically whenever the client has engaged a specialist. The distinction between the circumstances that require use and other circumstances involving use of real estate appraisers discussed by the Auditing Standards Board provides an instructive example. The key is the relation of the specialist's work to the financial statement assertions. A financial institution normally obtains a real estate appraisal for loans collateralized by real estate as part of the loan origination process. In testing controls over the loan origination process, the auditor normally would inspect the appraisal to see that it conformed with the institution's policies and procedures. This is not use of a specialist's work that requires application of the guidance in SAS 73. This is a test of controls, not a substantive test, and the specialist's work is not being used to evaluate a material financial statement assertion.

In contrast, in the evaluation of the need for a reserve on a problem loan, the auditor might inspect an appraisal to consider whether the collateral value is below the loan amount. This is a substantive test involving the valuation assertion, and loss reserves are usually material to a financial institution's financial statements. Application of the guidance in SAS 73 is required.

USE OF A LAWYER AS A SPECIALIST

SAS 73 applies to attorneys engaged as specialists in situations other than to provide services to a client concerning litigation, claims, or assessments. SAS 12 (Section 337) applies to an attorney's response to audit inquiries concerning litigation, claims, and assessments. SAS 73 applies to other use of an attorney's work, such as interpreting the provisions of a contractual agreement.

An auditor, however, cannot use an attorney's work to evaluate material assertions related to income tax matters. Generally, the auditor's education, training, and experience enable him or her to be competent to assess the presentation of income tax matters in financial statements.

Documentation of the Understanding of the Work to Be Performed by the Specialist

SAS 73 relaxes the documentation required concerning the understanding of the nature and purpose of the work to be performed by the specialist. SAS 11 had indicated that, preferably, this understanding should be documented. SAS 73 indicates only that in **some** cases the auditor may decide it is necessary to contact the specialist to determine that the specialist is aware that his or her work will be used for evaluating the assertions in the financial statements.

While SAS 11 stated a preference for documenting the understanding with the specialist, there was considerable diversity in practice. Frequently, the nature and purpose of the specialist's work is clearly understood within the industry, such as the use of a petroleum engineer to determine oil and gas reserves by an oil and gas producer. In some cases, such as for a real estate appraiser, the specialist's report routinely documents the specialist's qualifications and purpose of the engagement.

Thus, under SAS 73, the auditor has considerable discretion in deciding whether it is necessary to contact the specialist and in documenting the understanding with the specialist.

For those circumstances in which documentation is appropriate, the *Illustrations* section provides an engagement letter form.

Specialist Related to Client

SAS 11 indicated that use of an "unrelated" specialist was preferable. The term **unrelated** was used rather than **independent** because it was not considered feasible to impose the ethics rules of the accounting profession on other disciplines.

SAS 73 more clearly indicates that the purpose of considering the specialist's relationship is to evaluate whether there are circumstances that might impair the specialist's objectivity. If the client has the ability to directly or indirectly control or significantly influence the specialist, objectivity might be impaired. The influence might arise from employment, ownership, contractual right, family relationship, or otherwise.

A specialist without a relationship to the client is more likely to be objective, and that specialist's work will provide the auditor with greater assurance of reliability.

If the specialist has a relationship with the client, the auditor should assess the risk that the specialist's objectivity might be impaired. If the auditor believes the relationship might impair the specialist's objectivity, the auditor should perform additional procedures.

The additional procedures involve heightened scrutiny of the specialist's assumptions, methods, or findings to determine that the findings are not unreasonable. The auditor might decide another specialist should be engaged for this purpose.

The *Illustrations* section contains a form that can be used to document information concerning the relationship of the specialist to the client.

Specialist Employed by CPA Firm

Some CPA firms have employed specialists to provide consulting services to clients. For example, some CPA firms employ actuaries, real estate appraisers, or environmental specialists.

If the client has engaged a specialist employed by the CPA firm to determine an amount or disclosure that is material to the financial statements, the guidance in SAS 73 applies to the auditor's use of that specialist's work. This means the auditor has to apply the same procedures that SAS 73 would require to be applied to the work of a specialist unrelated to the CPA firm. For example, the auditor would have to obtain an understanding of the methods and assumptions used by the specialist and evaluate whether the specialist's findings support the related assertions in the financial statements.

In some cases, the auditor might decide to engage a specialist. For example, a specialist might be engaged by the auditor to apply additional procedures when the client uses a related specialist. In these circumstances, a specialist employed by the CPA firm might be used. In this case, the specialist is functioning as a member of the audit team. The auditor would need to provide proper supervision of that specialist in the same manner as any other member of the audit team. On the other hand, if the auditor engages a specialist not employed by the CPA firm, then the guidance in SAS 73 applies. When the CPA firm uses a firm specialist as a member of the audit team, the specialist is an assistant on the audit with all that such status implies. The specialist has to adhere to GAAS and be properly supervised. Extra supervision is required when the specialist is not knowledgeable about GAAP, GAAS, and the Code of Professional Conduct.

TESTS OF DATA USED BY THE SPECIALIST

In many cases, the client has to provide data to the specialist. For example, the management of an insurance company would provide data on insurance in force to an actuary engaged to determine loss reserves, and a financial institution might provide a real estate appraiser with income statements of a project that collateralizes a loan.

SAS 11 indicated that the auditor should test accounting data the client provided to the specialist. SAS 73 indicates that the auditor should make appropriate tests of data provided to the specialist. In other words, the data to be tested is not limited to accounting data.

In deciding the extent of testing of data that is necessary, the auditor should consider the control risk associated with production of the data. SAS 73 does not mention inherent risk. Thus, the implication is that the auditor would need to substantiate data provided to the specialist unless the data is produced by a system with a relatively low control risk. Also, the extent of testing considered necessary would depend on the nature and materiality of the related financial statement assertion.

NEED TO REFER TO AUDIT GUIDES OR SOPS

SAS 73 is still an umbrella SAS. If there is more specific guidance on the use of a specialist in an audit guide or SOP, the auditor should refer to the more detailed guidance. An audit guide or SOP cannot reduce the procedures needed when a specialist's work is used. However, the guidance might specify additional procedures or limit the auditor's discretion in determining the scope of procedures. For example, SOP 92-4, *Auditing Insurance Entities' Loss Reserves*, provides that an outside loss reserve specialist, that is, one who is not an officer or employee of the insurance company, should be used. When the auditor has the necessary knowledge and experience, the auditor may serve as the loss reserve specialist.

An AICPA audit guide or SOP might also provide informative guidance on the methods and assumptions of a specialist that is useful in evaluating whether a specialist's findings support financial statement assertions. For example, there is an AICPA guide on real estate appraisals that describes the various methods used by an appraiser. Some methods might produce a value that is not suitable for supporting financial statement assertions in certain circumstances. For example, the market value determined by an appraiser based on stabilized net operating income might not be appropriate when the real estate's fair value is the appropriate measure.

AUDITOR WITH RELEVANT TRAINING AND EXPERIENCE

SAS 11 indicated that the auditor's knowledge, training, and experience in a specialized field should not influence the extent of procedures considered necessary. The intent of

SAS 11 was that an auditor with relevant training and experience in the specialized field would not necessarily be expected to do more than an auditor without that knowledge.

SAS 73 is silent on this point. Naturally an auditor with the necessary training and experience can apply additional procedures to the work of a specialist related to the client without the aid of another specialist. Also, SOP 92-4 indicates that an auditor with the proper background may serve as a loss reserve specialist.

Would an auditor with training and experience in a field be expected to more readily recognize inappropriate methods or unreasonable assumptions or findings? Officially, the answer under SAS 11 was **no**. SAS 73 provides no guidance on the matter. Presumably an auditor with relevant training and experience would, in the exercise of due care, reasonably be expected to bring that knowledge to bear in evaluating the specialist's methods, assumptions, or findings. Such an auditor would not be expected to do more work, but would be better equipped to recognize inappropriate methods or unreasonable assumptions and findings and would need to act accordingly.

ILLUSTRATIONS

The following are illustrations of

1. An engagement letter from a client to a specialist.
2. An independence letter for a specialist.

Illustration 1. Engagement Letter from Client to Specialist

[*Client's letterhead*]

[*Addressed to specialist's firm*]

This letter confirms our understanding for the services you provide as an independent specialist in connection with the audit of the financial statements of [*name of client*] for the year ended [*date*]. If you agree to this understanding, please sign one copy of this letter and return it to us.

Our understanding is as follows:

1. You understand that the results of your work will be used by our auditors, [*name of auditors*], as corroborating evidence in connection with their audit of the aforementioned financial statements for the purpose of expressing an opinion on whether the statements are presented fairly in all material respects in conformity with accounting principles generally accepted in the United States of America.
2. The objectives of your work are as follows:

   [*List objectives, such as determining fair market value of inventory, fair value of stock in a closely held corporation, pension expense, and pension liability, etc.*]
3. The scope of your work is as follows:

   [*List procedures that it is anticipated the specialist will apply. In this list, indicate that scope is in no way restricted.*]
4. The methods and assumptions you will use will cover the following areas:

   [*List methods and assumptions such as the following: estimated rate of return and estimated life expectancy of employees for pension expense and pension liability, estimated rate of return and estimated cash flows for valuation of stock in a closely held corporation, etc.*]
5. Your report will be submitted directly to us with a copy to our auditors no later than [*date*]. Your report will include the following:

   a. Scope of work.
   b. Methods used and statement of consistency of the methods used with those used in the prior year.
   c. Assumptions used.
   d. Results, in detail, of your work.
   e. Your opinion on the information that will appear in our financial statements and accompanying notes.

6. You are independent with respect to us and our management. Principals, officers, owners of your firm and members of their immediate families, and members of your staff in the office working on this engagement are not in any way—nor have you been in any way—associated with us and our management except in your capacity as an outside specialist. [*This paragraph would be modified if there is a relationship between the specialist and the client.*]
7. Fees for your services will be at your usual per diem rate of [*amount*].

Very truly yours,

____
[*Client's name*]

____
[*Signature and title*]

Agreed to:

____
[*Name and title of specialist*] [*Date*]

ILLUSTRATION 2. STATEMENT OF SPECIALIST'S INDEPENDENCE

[*Client's letterhead*]

[*Addressed to specialist firm*]

In connection with their audit of our financial statements for the year ended [*date*], please describe directly to our auditors, [*name of firm*], the nature and extent of any relationship noted below that you have with the Entity, exclusive of your engagement as [*type of work, i.e., actuary, appraiser, etc.*]. A stamped, self-addressed envelope is enclosed for your convenience.

Very truly yours,

____
[*Client's name*]

By ______________________________

____
[*Title*]

Specialist Representation:

Except as noted below, the principals, officers, owners of our firm and members of their immediate families, and members of our staff in the office doing the work described above are not associated with [*name of client*], as follows:

1. By direct or indirect financial interest.
2. As an officer, employee, or member of the board of directors.
3. In any capacity, other than our normal business relationship, where we have a vested interest in the success of the Entity.

Exceptions:____
____
____
____
____
____

[*Date*] [*Firm*] [*Signature*] [*Title*]

337 INQUIRY OF A CLIENT'S LAWYER CONCERNING LITIGATION, CLAIMS, AND ASSESSMENTS

EFFECTIVE DATE AND APPLICABILITY

Original Pronouncement	SAS 12, January 1976.
Effective Date	When issued, January 1976.
Applicability	Audits of financial statements in accordance with generally accepted auditing standards.

DEFINITIONS OF TERMS

The section itself has no general definitions, but it uses terms that have been defined by the FASB and the American Bar Association (ABA). SFAS 5, *Accounting for Contingencies*, paragraphs 1 and 3 define the following terms used in the section.

Loss contingency. An existing condition, situation, or set of circumstances involving uncertainty as to possible loss to an enterprise that will ultimately be resolved when one or more future events occur or fail to occur. (The likelihood that the future event will confirm the loss or impairment of an asset or the incurrence of a liability can range from probable to remote.)

Probable. The future event is **likely** to occur.

Reasonably possible. The chance of the future event occurring is more than remote but less than likely.

Remote. The chance of the future event occurring is slight.

The ABA has defined the following terms used in the section:

Threatened litigation. A potential claimant has manifested to the client an awareness of, and present intention to assert, a possible claim or assessment.

Unasserted claim or assessment. No claimant has manifested an awareness or intention to assert a claim or assessment, but it is probable a claim will be asserted, and there is a reasonable possibility the outcome will be unfavorable.

Probable. An unfavorable outcome is probable if the prospects of the claimant not succeeding are judged to be extremely doubtful and the prospects for success by the client in its defense are judged to be slight.

Remote. The prospects for the client not succeeding in its defense are judged to be extremely doubtful, and the prospects of success by the claimant are judged to be slight.

OBJECTIVES OF SECTION

Before SAS 12 was issued, auditors generally viewed lawyers as the primary source of evidence on litigation, claims, and assessments. For many years, auditors thought they were able to obtain all the information they needed. About two years before SAS 12 was issued (January 1976), however, there was a growing movement among lawyers that threatened to halt the flow of information from lawyers to auditors. Also, preliminary discussions between the ABA and the AICPA indicated that lawyers' responses to inquiries from auditors were far more limited than they appeared on the surface.

SAS 12 and the ABA Statement of Policy provide for an exchange of information within a framework that should be understandable and acceptable to lawyers and auditors. Nevertheless, care is necessary in phrasing audit inquiry letters and evaluating responses to ensure that sufficient information is obtained. Suggestions for achieving that are made in *Techniques for Application.*

SAS 12 is the result of a cooperative effort between the AICPA and the ABA to prescribe procedures to be followed by auditors and lawyers in discharging their separate professional responsibilities. The procedures developed for pending or threatened litigation differ from those applicable to unasserted claims. A lawyer will, with the client's consent, confirm the completeness of a list of pending or threatened litigation and furnish information on that litigation.

For unasserted claims, the procedures are more complex and less conclusive. Essentially, a lawyer will confirm that he or she has advised the client of unasserted claims that have come to his or her attention that the client should consider disclosing. The auditor then informs the lawyer of unasserted claims the client has brought to the auditor's attention. Presumably, if this exchange makes the lawyer aware that the client is concealing information from the auditor, the lawyer will persuade the client to furnish the information and, failing that, resign from the engagement. The lawyer will not explicitly confirm the completeness of the list of unasserted claims, however, or furnish information on them directly to the auditor. This complex process was agreed to by the AICPA and the ABA to preserve the attorney-client privilege and yet make it possible for the auditor to assess the adequacy of disclosure in financial statements.

Lawyers also agreed to evaluate the chance of an unfavorable outcome and to provide an estimate, if one can be made, of the amount or range of potential loss. The ABA Statement of Policy imposes significant constraints, however, on the circumstances when an evaluation or estimate is appropriate.

FUNDAMENTAL REQUIREMENTS

This section establishes requirements in four areas.

1. Accounting considerations.
2. Audit procedures other than inquiry of lawyers.
3. Inquiry of the client's lawyer and related considerations.
4. Evaluation of the lawyer's response.

ACCOUNTING CONSIDERATIONS

The relevant accounting standards are found in SFAS 5.

1. Accrual of a loss is required if
   a. The amount can be reasonably estimated, and

   b. At the date of the financial statements, it is **probable** that an asset has been impaired or a liability incurred. (That is, it is probable that a future event will occur confirming the loss.)

2. Disclosure of a loss contingency is required if
   a. No accrual is made because either the amount cannot be estimated or it was not probable that an asset was impaired or a liability incurred at the financial statement date or there is exposure to loss in excess of an accrual.
   b. There is at least a reasonable possibility that a loss or an additional loss may have been incurred.
3. Disclosure should be made of
   a. The nature of the contingency.
   b. The possible loss or range of loss or a statement that an estimate cannot be made.
4. Disclosure of the nature of an accrual, and sometimes the amount accrued, should be made if it is necessary for the financial statements not to be misleading.
5. Disclosure of an unasserted claim or assessment is required if
   a. It is probable that a claim will be asserted.
   b. There is at least a reasonable possibility that the outcome will be unfavorable.
6. In evaluating whether accrual or disclosure is required of pending or threatened litigation or possible claims or assessments, the following factors must be considered:
   a. The period in which the cause for legal action occurred. (The date of the underlying cause of action rather than the date of a lawsuit or claim affects whether accrual is appropriate.)
   b. The likelihood of an unfavorable outcome.
   c. The ability to estimate the loss.

   NOTE: These same factors are the focus of the auditor's procedures.
7. In evaluating the likelihood of an unfavorable outcome, the following factors must be considered:
   a. The nature of the litigation, claim, or assessment.
   b. The progress of the case up to the date the financial statements are issued.
   c. The opinions of legal counsel and other advisers.
   d. The experience of the entity or other entities in similar cases.
   e. Any decision of management on how the entity intends to respond.

   NOTE: The same factors are the focus of the auditor's inquiry of the client's lawyer.

AUDIT PROCEDURES OTHER THAN INQUIRY OF LAWYERS

Several customary audit procedures other than inquiry of the client's lawyer are required.

1. Inquire of, and discuss with, the client's management its procedures for identifying, evaluating, and accounting for litigation, claims, and assessments.
2. Examine documents held by the client, such as correspondence and invoices from lawyers.

   NOTE: This does not include documents subject to the lawyer-client privilege.
3. Read minutes of meetings of stockholders, board of directors, and related client committees.

4. Read contracts, loan agreements, leases, and correspondence from taxing or other government agencies.
5. Obtain information from banks concerning loan agreements.
6. Inspect other documents for possible guarantees made by the client.

INQUIRY OF CLIENT'S LAWYER

The primary audit procedures for litigation, claims, and assessments are a combination of inquiries of the client's management and lawyers. The auditor should

1. Ask the client's management to send letters of inquiry to those lawyers consulted on litigation, claims, and assessments.
2. Obtain written assurances from management that
    a. It has disclosed all matters required to be disclosed by SFAS 5.
    b. It has disclosed all unasserted claims that the lawyer has advised are probable of assertion and must be disclosed under SFAS 5.

    NOTE: These two assurances obviously overlap, but the separate assurance is required for unasserted claims because of the different treatment accorded them to preserve the lawyer-client privilege. These assurances may be included in the management representation letter (see Section 333).
3. Inform the lawyer, with the client's permission, that the client has given the assurance concerning unasserted claims.

    NOTE: Usually this is covered in the inquiry letter.

Content of Inquiry to Lawyer

According to AU 337.08, the inquiry letter to the lawyer should cover the following matters:

1. Identification of the client, the financial statements under audit, and the date of the audit.
2. A list that describes and evaluates pending or threatened litigation, claims, and assessments. For each matter on the list, the lawyer should be asked to furnish
    a. A description of the nature of the matter.
    b. The progress of the case to date.
    c. The action the entity intends to take.
    d. An evaluation of the likelihood of an unfavorable outcome and an estimate, if possible, of the amount or range of possible loss.
    e. An identification of any omissions or a statement that the list of matters is complete.

    NOTE: The list may be prepared by management or by the lawyer. Under either approach, management normally consults with the lawyer on the response to the auditor.
3. A list that describes and evaluates unasserted claims (that are probable of assertion and reasonably possible of having an unfavorable outcome) prepared by management.
4. A statement on the client's understanding of the lawyer's professional responsibility concerning unasserted claims.
5. A request that the lawyer confirm the understanding stated in 4.
6. A request that the lawyer specifically identify the nature of and reasons for any limitation on his or her response.
7. The date by which the lawyer's response should be sent to the auditor.

8. A request that the lawyer specify the latest date covered by his or her review (the effective date).

Oral Response

In special circumstances, representations may be made orally by the lawyer. For example, evaluation of the effect of legal advice on unsettled points of law might be covered in a conference among auditor, client, and lawyer. The auditor should document significant conclusions reached on accounting matters in such a conference in the audit workpapers.

Client Changes Lawyer or Lawyer Resigns

Because the special treatment accorded unasserted claims rests on the lawyer's professional responsibility, the auditor should consider the need to make inquiries concerning why the lawyer is no longer associated with the client.

Evaluation of Lawyer's Response

In evaluating the lawyer's response, the auditor needs to be aware that some limitations on responses may affect his or her opinion. Others have no effect.

Limitations with No Effect

A lawyer may appropriately limit his or her response in the following ways:

1. To matters to which he or she has given substantive attention in the form of legal consultation or representation.

   NOTE: This means essentially that the lawyer does not do a legal audit. He or she does not undertake to evaluate all legal exposures or reconsider earlier conclusions.

2. To matters that are considered individually or collectively material, provided the lawyer and auditor have agreed on the amounts to be used.

Limitations with Effect

A limitation such as the following may preclude an unqualified opinion:

1. **Scope.** If a lawyer refuses to furnish information requested in the ordinary inquiry letter, it is a limitation on the scope of the audit that results in a qualified or disclaimed opinion.
2. **Uncertainty.** If a lawyer is unable to evaluate the likelihood of an unfavorable outcome or estimate the amount or range of potential loss, it is an uncertainty. The guidance in Section 508, "Reports on Audited Financial Statements," should be followed, which may result in the auditor qualifying or disclaiming an opinion because of the scope limitation.

INTERPRETATIONS

Specifying Relevant Date in an Audit Inquiry Letter (March 1977)

The audit inquiry letter should specify the effective date of the lawyer's response and the latest date that the response should be mailed. Ordinarily, a two-week period should be allowed between the effective date and the mail date. If the lawyer's response does not specify an effective date, the auditor can assume that the date of the response is the effective date.

Relationship between Date of Lawyer's Response and Auditor's Report (March 1977)

The effective date of the lawyer's response should be specified to reasonably approximate the expected date of completion of fieldwork.

Form of Audit Inquiry Letter When Client Represents That No Unasserted Claims and Assessments Exist (March 1977)

When clients have stated that no unasserted claims exist that portion of the inquiry letter may be worded as follows:

> Unasserted Claims and Assessments—we have represented to our auditors that there are no unasserted possible claims that you have advised us are probable of assertion and must be disclosed, in accordance with Statement of Financial Accounting Standards 5.

Documents Subject to Lawyer-Client Privilege (March 1977)

An inability to review documents or correspondence that is subject to lawyer-client privilege is not a scope limitation. The auditor may want to confirm with the lawyer that such information is subject to privilege and was considered by the lawyer in his or her response to the inquiry letter.

Alternative Wording of the Illustrative Audit Inquiry Letter to a Client's Lawyer (June 1983)

This interpretation recognizes the acceptability of the alternative inquiry letter that is presented in *Illustrations*. The letter presented in *Illustrations* has been adapted from the interpretation.

Client Has Not Consulted a Lawyer (June 1983)

If the client has not consulted a lawyer, the auditor normally relies on a review of internally available evidence and management representations regarding litigation, claims, and assessments. *Illustrations* contains a suitable management representation in this situation.

Assessment of a Lawyer's Evaluation of the Outcome of Litigation (Issued June 1983; Revised February 1997)

Written responses from lawyers may contain wording that is vague or ambiguous and may be of limited use to auditors. Lawyers are not required to use terms such as "probable" or "remote" in their evaluations. Other wording may be acceptable if the response can be classified according to the three probability classifications in SFAS 5 (probable, reasonably possible, and remote).

Some examples of acceptable language, even through "remote" is not used, are as follows:

- "We are of the opinion that this action will not result in any liability to the company."
- "It is our opinion that the possible liability to the company in this proceeding is nominal in amount."
- "We believe the company will be able to defend this action successfully."
- "We believe that the plaintiff's case against the company is without merit."
- "Based on the facts known to us, after a full investigation, it is our opinion that no liability will be established against the company in these suits."

The following are examples of unacceptable lawyers' evaluations since they are unclear as to the likelihood of an unfavorable outcome.

- "This action involves unique characteristics wherein authoritative legal precedents do not seem to exist. We believe that the plaintiff will have serious problems establishing the company's liability under the act; nevertheless, if the plaintiff is successful, the award may be substantial."
- "It is our opinion that the company will be able to assert meritorious defenses to this action." (The term "meritorious defenses" indicates that the company's defenses will not be summarily dismissed by the court; it does not necessarily indicate counsel's opinion that the company will prevail.)
- "We believe the action can be settled for less than the damages claimed."
- "We are unable to express an opinion as to the merits of the litigation at this time. The company believes there is absolutely no merit to the litigation." (If client's counsel, with the benefit of all relevant information, is unable to conclude that the likelihood of an unfavorable outcome is "remote," it is unlikely that management would be able to form a judgment to that effect.)
- "In our opinion, the company has a substantial chance of prevailing in this action." (A "substantial chance," a "reasonable opportunity," and similar terms indicate more uncertainty than an opinion that the company will prevail.)

If the auditor is uncertain about the lawyer's evaluation, he or she should clarify the communication via a follow-up letter or conference.

USE OF THE CLIENT'S INSIDE COUNSEL IN THE EVALUATION OF LITIGATION, CLAIMS, AND ASSESSMENTS (JUNE 1983)

Audit inquiry letters should be sent to those lawyers who have the primary responsibility for, and knowledge about, particular litigation, claims, and assessments. Such lawyers may be inside counsel or outside lawyers. If inside counsel has the primary responsibility, their response ordinarily would be considered adequate. However, there may be circumstances when outside lawyers have significant involvement in the matter. In these situations, the opinion of inside counsel should be confirmed by the outside lawyers. If differences exist, the auditor should discuss the matter with the parties involved to resolve the conflict in views. Failure to reach agreement between the lawyers may require the auditor to consider appropriate modification of the audit report. (See "Reliance on House or Inside Counsel" in *Techniques for Application*.)

USE OF EXPLANATORY LANGUAGE ABOUT THE ATTORNEY-CLIENT PRIVILEGE OR THE ATTORNEY WORK-PRODUCT PRIVILEGE (FEBRUARY 1990)

In some cases, to emphasize the attorney-client privilege or the attorney work-product privilege, some clients and attorneys in the audit inquiry letter and in the attorney's response letter include explanatory language indicating that the privileges are not waived. This explanatory language does not result in a limitation of the scope of the audit. Such explanatory language simply makes explicit what has been implicit; therefore, inclusion or noninclusion of the language does not change the attorney-client or work-product privileges.

Use of Explanatory Language Concerning Unasserted Possible Claims or Assessments in Lawyer's Responses to Audit Inquiry Letters (January 1997)

To emphasize the preservation of attorney-client privilege for unasserted claims, some lawyers include additional comments in their response letters stating that it would be inappropriate to respond to a general inquiry about unasserted claims. The explanation continues to state that they cannot comment on the adequacy of the entity's listing of unasserted claims, if any. The inclusion of this kind of explanatory information is not a limitation on the scope of the audit.

TECHNIQUES FOR APPLICATION

Until litigation, claims, and assessments are finally settled, they might not enter the flow of data to the client's accounting records. Therefore, they might be difficult to identify.

This section provides the auditor with guidance on procedures he or she should consider for identifying litigation, claims, and assessments when performing an audit in accordance with generally accepted auditing standards. In practice, questions often arise about applying this section in the following areas:

1. Ensuring adequate description of case.
2. Client without a lawyer.
3. Effective date of lawyer's response.
4. Evaluating lawyer's opinion.
5. Lawyers on board of directors.
6. Litigation not investigated by lawyers.
7. Litigation with insurance companies.
8. Reliance on house or inside counsel.
9. Refusal of attorney to respond.
10. Resignation of attorney.
11. Review of interim financial information.
12. Alternative form letter of inquiry.

Ensuring Adequate Description of Case

There are two types of lawyer's letters, either of which the client may send.

1. The form illustrated in SAS 12 in which the client lists the pending and threatened litigation.
2. An alternative or short form in which the client requests the lawyer to list the pending and threatened litigation.

Both types of letters are included in *Illustrations*.

When the client sends the short-form letter to its lawyer, the lawyer may not provide a sufficiently detailed description of the pending or threatened litigation in his or her response. To avoid this type of inadequate response, the client should request the lawyer to list for each pending or threatened litigation the following:

1. The nature of the litigation.
2. Identification of the proceedings.
3. Description of the asserted claim.
4. The amount of monetary or other damages sought.
5. Statement as to whether the potential damages are covered by insurance and to what extent they are covered.

6. The progress of the case.
7. Entity's response or intended response to the litigation.

CLIENT WITHOUT A LAWYER

As discussed in *Interpretations*, a client not having a lawyer should not present unusual audit problems. Inquiry of a client's lawyer is a procedure applied by the auditor to identify pending or threatened litigation. Other procedures described in this section are the following:

1. Inquires of management.
2. Discussions with management.
3. Examination of relevant documents.

These procedures are described earlier in *Fundamental Requirements*. The auditor may conclude that the client has no litigation, claims, or assessments that require disclosure or these procedures may identify such matters.

Client Assertions

When the client does not retain an attorney, it ordinarily will state that there are no asserted or unasserted litigation, claims, and assessments. In these circumstances, the client should include these assertions on absence of litigation and lack of an attorney in the client representation letter (see *Illustrations*).

Auditor Discovery of Claims

In the application of other procedures, the auditor may discover the following:

1. A material asserted claim.
2. A situation in which a material unasserted claim exists.

In these circumstances, the auditor should recommend that the client seek legal advice. If the client does not accept this recommendation, the auditor should consider it a scope limitation and may need to modify his or her report.

EFFECTIVE DATE OF LAWYER'S RESPONSE

If the effective date of the lawyer's response is the balance sheet date or a date not close enough to the date the fieldwork is completed, the auditor will have to initiate a second inquiry to the lawyer. This second inquiry may be either another letter to the lawyer or a telephone call from the auditor to the lawyer. Responses to a telephone call should be documented.

EVALUATING LAWYER'S OPINION

The auditor does not have the expertise of a lawyer. Therefore, he or she requires the opinion of a lawyer on legal matters relating to the client. It is the lawyer's opinion on litigation, claims, and assessments that helps the auditor reach a conclusion on the appropriateness of accounting for, and disclosure of, litigation and other contingent liabilities. However, the lawyer's opinion on a legal matter might not be clear and, thus, not acceptable for the auditor's purposes. Examples of such responses are presented in *Interpretations*.

Unacceptable Attorney Response

If the auditor receives a response from a client attorney that is not helpful in evaluating the litigation for accounting purposes, he or she should review the matter with the attorney and the client. The purpose of this review is to obtain a more complete and acceptable response from the attorney.

The auditor may not be able to obtain a satisfactory response from the client's attorney and may not be able to obtain sufficient other corroborating evidence to support management's evaluation of the litigation. In these circumstances, the auditor has a scope limitation that may require a qualified or disclaimed opinion.

Avoidance of Unacceptable Attorney Response

To avoid unacceptable attorney responses, the letter of inquiry should specifically request that the evaluation of the litigation reflect the attorney's opinion. Also, the attorney should be requested to specify litigation for which he or she can express no opinion on a probable outcome or a range of potential loss. The attorney should be requested to state reasons for this type of response.

LAWYERS ON BOARD OF DIRECTORS

In response to the client's letter of inquiry, the lawyer is not required to include information he or she received as a director or officer of the client unless he or she also received the information in the capacity of attorney for the client.

A reply that excludes information the attorney obtained solely as a member of the board of directors or as an officer of the client is acceptable. The letter of inquiry should request that the attorney indicate if he or she is excluding such information. If the attorney indicates that he or she is excluding this information, the auditor may wish to obtain specific written representations from the attorney concerning the information.

LITIGATION NOT INVESTIGATED BY THE LAWYER

A lawyer's response is limited to those matters to which he or she has given substantive attention. If a lawyer is not able to investigate adequately a matter and render a satisfactory opinion regarding material litigation, the auditor generally should attempt to arrange a meeting with the client's management and the lawyer. The purpose of this meeting is to determine what can be done to enable the lawyer to respond satisfactorily.

Delay Issuance of Financial Statements

If a lawyer cannot render a satisfactory opinion concerning material litigation because he or she has not given the matter substantive attention, the problem may be resolved if the client is able to and agrees to delay the issuance of its financial statements. The delay will give the lawyer time to study the matter and formulate a satisfactory opinion.

Audit Scope Limitation

A lawyer's **inability** to evaluate material litigation is not a limitation on the scope of an audit. If the lawyer cannot evaluate the litigation, and if the auditor cannot obtain sufficient other evidence to corroborate the information about the matter, however, the matter is a limitation on the scope of the audit.

LITIGATION WITH INSURANCE COMPANY

In some cases, litigation, claims, and assessments are defended by the client's insurance company. In these circumstances, the client's attorney may decline to provide an opinion. The attorney may be knowledgeable, however, about the litigation and its probable outcome, especially those matters in which there is a reasonable prospect that the liability will exceed the insurance coverage. In these circumstances, the client should request that the lawyer provide the auditor with an opinion on the probable outcome of the litigation.

If the client's lawyer cannot render an opinion on litigation handled by the client's insurance company, the auditor should ask the client to send a letter of inquiry to the insurance company or the insurance company's counsel.

RELIANCE ON HOUSE OR INSIDE COUNSEL

The letter to the client's lawyer is the auditor's primary means of obtaining corroboration of the information furnished by management concerning litigation, claims, and assessments. As discussed in Interpretation 8 of SAS 12, in certain circumstances the corroboration may come from evidential matter provided by the client's legal department or inside general counsel.

Many entities employ inside counsel or house counsel. Some entities maintain legal departments. Attorneys employed by the client are bound by the American Bar Association's Code of Professional Ethics. Therefore, the auditor may accept as corroborative evidence responses from house counsel. In these circumstances, the usual distinction between internal evidence and external independent evidence does not apply.

A response from house counsel is generally acceptable; however, it cannot be substituted for a response from outside counsel when outside counsel refuses to respond to a valid inquiry or when outside counsel is clearly more knowledgeable about litigation.

House counsel and outside counsel may have devoted substantive attention to a matter, and their opinions may differ on the possible outcome. In this situation, the auditor should attempt to resolve the difference by discussion with the parties involved.

Although inside counsel and outside counsel are both subject to the same ethical responsibilities, the auditor has to be aware that house counsel is a member of management and operates within the client's control environment. Thus, the auditor has to consider the presence of fraud risk indicators and the nature of the representations in evaluating a response from house counsel.

REFUSAL OF ATTORNEY TO RESPOND

An auditor may encounter a situation in which the attorney refuses to respond to the client's letter of inquiry. In these situations, the auditor is faced with a scope limitation sufficient to preclude an unqualified opinion.

If the attorney refuses to respond, the auditor should attempt to have a meeting with the attorney and the client to resolve the problem. If the attorney continues to refuse to respond to the letter of inquiry, the auditor should decide whether to issue an "except for" opinion or to disclaim an opinion (see Section 508).

RESIGNATION OF ATTORNEY

The auditor always should be concerned when a client's attorney is replaced or has resigned. If the auditor has reason to believe an attorney has been replaced or has resigned, he or she should ask management about the reasons for the resignation or replacement. If an attorney has resigned, the auditor, with the client's consent, should discuss the matter with the attorney.

REVIEW OF INTERIM FINANCIAL INFORMATION

When an accountant reviews interim financial information under SAS 71, *Interim Financial Information* (Section 722), it is not necessary to send an inquiry letter to the client's lawyer concerning litigation, claims, and assessments. The accountant would be prudent, however, to communicate, at least orally, with the attorney regarding updated information on the previous audit inquiry responses concerning litigation, claims, and assessments.

Securities Act of 1933

When an accountant's report on audited financial statements is included in a filing under the Securities Act of 1933, regardless of whether unaudited interim information is included, he or she should inquire of the client's legal counsel concerning litigation, claims, and assessments. In this situation, the lawyer should be requested to update his or her previous audit inquiry response to the estimated effective date of the registration statement.

Ordinarily, a request to the lawyer to update a previous audit inquiry response is limited to the following:

1. Changes from the lawyer's previous evaluation of litigation, claims, and assessments.
2. Any new matters arising since the previous response.

ALTERNATIVE FORM LETTER OF INQUIRY

SAS 12 provides an example of a letter of inquiry in which the client lists all pending and threatened litigation, claims, and assessments. This illustration assumes either that the client had house counsel prepare the list or that the client management consulted with the attorney.

SAS 12 indicates that the client may request that the attorney prepare the list of pending and threatened litigation, claims, and assessments. A letter of inquiry of this nature is referred to as the alternative form letter and is permitted by an interpretation of SAS 12.

ILLUSTRATIONS

The following are illustrated below.

1. Standard form letter of inquiry (from SAS 12 [AU 337]).
2. Alternative form letter of inquiry (from an interpretation of SAS 12 [AU 337]).
3. Management representation when entity has no attorney.

ILLUSTRATION 1. INQUIRY OF A CLIENT'S LAWYER CONCERNING LITIGATION, CLAIMS, AND ASSESSMENTS: STANDARD FORM LETTER OF INQUIRY

[*Client letterhead*]

[*Date*]

[*Name and address*
of lawyer and salutation]

In connection with an audit of our financial statements at [*balance sheet date*] and for the [*period*] then ended, management of the Company has prepared and furnished to our auditors, [*name and address of auditors*], a description and evaluation of certain contingencies, including those set forth below [*or attached*] involving matters with respect to which you have devoted substantive attention on behalf of the Company in the form of legal consultation or representation. These contingencies are regarded by management of the Company as material for this purpose [*or for the purpose of your response to this letter, we believe that as to each contingency an amount in excess of $_____ would be material, and in total, $_____*]. Your response should include matters that existed at [*balance sheet date*] and during the period from that date to the date of completion of their audit, which is anticipated to be on or about [*date*].

Pending or Threatened Litigation, Claims, and Assessments (Excluding Unasserted Claims and Assessments)

[*Ordinarily, management of the Company would provide for each matter the following information: (1) the name of the case, (2) the nature of the litigation, (3) description of the asserted claim, (4) the amount of monetary or other damages sought, (5) how management is responding or intends to respond to the litigation, (6) statement of whether potential damages are covered by insurance and, if covered, to what extent, and (7) management's evaluation of the likelihood of an unfavorable outcome and an estimate, if one can be made, of the amount or range or potential loss. After all matters have been listed, the following paragraph appears.*]

Please furnish to our auditors such explanation, if any, that you consider necessary to supplement the foregoing information, including an explanation of those matters on which your views may differ from those stated and an identification of the omission of any pending or threatened litigation, claims, and assessments or a statement that the list of these matters is complete.

Unasserted Claims and Assessments Considered by Management to Be Probable of Assertion and That, If Asserted, Would Have at Least a Reasonable Possibility of an Unfavorable Outcome

[*Ordinarily, management of the company would state that it had represented to the auditor that there were no unasserted claims that required accrual or disclosure or, if such matters had been identified, provide for each matter the following information: (1) the nature of the matter, (2) how management intends to respond if the claim is asserted, and (3) management's evaluation of the likelihood of an unfavorable outcome and an estimate, if one can be made, of the amount or range of potential loss. After all matters have been listed, the following paragraph appears.*]

Please furnish to our auditors such explanation, if any, that you consider necessary to supplement the foregoing information, including an explanation of those matters on which your views may differ from those stated.

We understand that in the course of performing legal service for us with respect to a matter recognized to involve an unasserted possible claim or assessment that may call for financial statement disclosure, if you have formed a professional conclusion that we should disclose or consider disclosure concerning such possible claim or assessment, as a matter of professional responsibility to us, you will so advise us and will consult with us concerning the question of such disclosure and the applicable requirements of Statement of Financial Accounting Standards 5. Please specifically confirm to our auditors that our understanding is correct.

Other Matters

Please specifically identify the nature of and reasons for any limitations on your response.

Please indicate the amount owed to you for services and expenses, billed and unbilled, at [*balance sheet date*].

Very truly yours,

____

[*Client signature and title*]

ILLUSTRATION 2. INQUIRY OF A CLIENT'S LAWYER CONCERNING LITIGATION, CLAIMS, AND ASSESSMENTS: ALTERNATIVE FORM LETTER OF INQUIRY

[*Client letterhead*]

[*Date*]

[*Name and address*
of lawyer and salutation]

In connection with an audit of our financial statements at [*balance sheet date*] and for the [*period*] then ended, please furnish our auditors, [*name and address of auditors*], with the information requested below concerning certain contingencies involving matters with respect to which you have devoted substantive attention on behalf of the Company in the form of legal consultation or representation. [*If a materiality limit has been agreed to by management and the auditor, the following sentence should be added.*] For the purpose of your response to this letter, we believe that for each contingency an amount in excess of $_____ would be material, and in total, $______. Your response should include matters that existed at [*balance sheet date*] and during the period from that date to the date of completion of their audit, which is anticipated to be on or about [*date*].

Pending or Threatened Litigation, Claims and Assessments (Excluding Unasserted Claims and Assessments)

Please prepare a description of all litigation, claims, and assessments. The description of each case should include, but not be limited to, the following:

1. The nature of the litigation, including the following:
   a. Identification of the proceedings.
   b. The claims asserted.
   c. The amount of monetary or other damages sought.
   d. Whether potential damages are covered by insurance and if so, to what extent.
   e. Objectives of plaintiff other than monetary or other damages.
2. The progress of the case to date.
3. How management is responding, or intends to respond, to the litigation.
4. Your evaluation of the likelihood of an unfavorable outcome.
5. An estimate of the amount or range of potential loss.

Unasserted Claims and Assessments

We understand that in the course of performing legal service for us with respect to a matter recognized to involve an unasserted possible claim or assessment that may call for financial statement disclosure, if you have formed a professional conclusion that we should disclose or consider disclosure concerning such possible claim or assessment, you will so advise us and will consult with us concerning the question of such disclosure and the applicable requirements of Statement of Financial Accounting Standards 5, as a matter of professional responsibility to us. Please specifically confirm to our auditors that our understanding is correct.

We have represented to our auditors that you have not advised us of any unasserted claims or assessments that are probable of assertion and must be disclosed in accordance with Statement of Financial Accounting Standards 5.

Other Matters

Please specifically identify the nature of, and reasons for, any limitation on your response.

Please indicate the amount owed to you for services and expenses [*billed and unbilled*] at [*balance sheet date*].

Very truly yours,

____

[*Client signature and title*]

ILLUSTRATION 3. MANAGEMENT REPRESENTATION WHEN ENTITY HAS NO ATTORNEY

[*Client letterhead*]

[*Date*]

[*Name and address*
of CPA firm and salutation]

We are not aware of any pending or threatened litigation, claims, or assessments or unasserted claims or assessments that are required to be accrued or disclosed in the financial statements in accordance with Statement of Financial Accounting Standards 5, and we have not consulted a lawyer concerning litigation, claims, or assessments.

Very truly yours,

____

[*Client signature and title*]

339 AUDIT DOCUMENTATION[1]

EFFECTIVE DATE AND APPLICABILITY

Original Pronouncement	SAS 96, December 2001.
Effective Date	Audits of financial statements for periods beginning on or after May 15, 2002, with earlier application permitted.
Applicability	Audits of financial statements in accordance with generally accepted auditing standards.

DEFINITIONS OF TERMS

Audit documentation. Records prepared by the auditor of the following:

1. Procedures applied.
2. Tests performed.
3. Information obtained.
4. Pertinent conclusions reached.

The following are examples of audit documentation:

1. Audit program.
2. Analyses.
3. Memoranda.
4. Letters of confirmation.
5. Representation letters.
6. Abstracts or photocopies of documents.
7. Schedules or commentaries.

Audit documentation may be in paper form, electronic form, or other media.

Audit documentation serves the following functions:

1. Provides principal support for the auditor's report.

---

[1] *The Auditing Standards Board has issued an Exposure Draft of a proposed SAS that would affect this section,* ***Sarbanes-Oxley Omnibus SAS.*** *The Exposure Draft is designed to address certain provisions of the Sarbanes-Oxley Act of 2002. The proposed amendment to this section would require that the auditor retain audit documentation and certain other records for at least seven years after the auditor concludes the audit. The Public Company Accounting Oversight Board (PCAOB) has replaced the ASB as the standards-setting authority for public company audits. Therefore, the ASB's Exposure Draft will not be issued as a final standard by the AICPA. The document will, however, be considered by the PCAOB in developing a standard or amendments to an existing standard to comply with the Sarbanes-Oxley Act and the related SEC implementing rules. Please check for updates to this section on the John Wiley & Sons, Inc. website at www.wiley.com/gaas.*

2. Provides principal support for the auditor's representation that the audit was made in accordance with generally accepted auditing standards, especially the standard of fieldwork.
3. Aids the auditor in conducting and supervising the audit.

OBJECTIVES OF SECTION

The information contained in audit documentation is the principal record of the work the auditor has done. Audit documentation also contains the conclusions of the auditor on significant matters and the evidence supporting these conclusions.

SAS 41 was issued in 1982 to remove apparent confusion about whether working papers are required to conform with professional standards. SAS 41 made it clear that the auditor should prepare working papers, but did not require specific working papers. It also did not change the provisions of other SASs that specify particular documentation requirements. For example, in every audit, the working papers should contain audit programs (Section 311) and management representation letters (Section 333) because they are required by other SASs.

In January 2002, the Auditing Standards Board issued SAS 96, *Audit Documentation.* SAS 96 replaced SAS 41, *Working Papers.* The standard

- Uses the term **audit documentation** in place of **working papers**.
- Replaces the SAS 41 list of factors affecting the auditor's judgment about the quantity, type, and content of the working papers for a particular engagement with a new list of factors that the auditor should consider in determining the nature and extent of the documentation for a particular audit area or auditing procedure.
- Specifies that audit documentation now must include (1) abstracts or copies of significant contracts or agreements that were examined in evaluating the accounting for significant transactions, and (2) an identification of the items tested in tests of the operating effectiveness of controls and substantive tests of details that involve inspection of documents or confirmation.
- Expands the "sufficiency" guidance to require that audit documentation be sufficient to (1) enable members of the engagement team with supervision and review responsibilities to understand the nature, timing, extent, and results of the auditing procedures performed, and the evidence obtained; and (2) indicate the engagement team member(s) who performed and reviewed the work.
- Requires documentation of audit findings or issues where judgment is significant, actions taken to address them (including any additional evidence obtained), and the basis for the final conclusions reached.
- Requires that record-retention procedures enable the auditor to access electronic audit documentation throughout the retention period.
- Requires that the auditor adopt reasonable procedures to maintain the confidentiality of confidential client information contained in audit documentation and prevent unauthorized access to the audit documentation.
- Amends Section 312, *Audit Risk and Materiality,* Section 329, *Analytical Procedures,* and Section 341, *Consideration of an Entity's Ability to Continue as a Going Concern.*

The precise form and content of working papers are matters the auditor decides based on several factors listed in the SAS (see *Fundamental Requirements*).

FUNDAMENTAL REQUIREMENTS

REQUIREMENT FOR AUDIT DOCUMENTATION

The auditor should prepare and maintain audit documentation. The form and content of the audit documentation should be designed for the specific engagement.

CONTENT OF AUDIT DOCUMENTATION

The quantity, type, and content of the audit documentation are based on the auditor's professional judgment and vary with the engagement. Factors to consider in determining the content of audit documentation are discussed in the following paragraphs. Additional factors to consider in designing audit documentation are explained in *Techniques for Application.*

Standards of Fieldwork

According to AU 339.04, audit documentation ordinarily should be sufficient to show that the three standards of fieldwork have been observed.

1. The work has been adequately planned and supervised.
2. A sufficient understanding of internal control has been obtained to plan the audit and determine the nature, timing, and extent of tests to be performed.
3. The evidence obtained, procedures applied, and testing done have provided sufficient competent evidential matter to afford a reasonable basis for an opinion.

Sufficiency of Audit Documentation

Audit documentation should be sufficient to

- Enable those supervising and reviewing the engagement to understand the nature, timing, extent, and results of auditing procedures performed and the evidence obtained.
- Indicate who performed and reviewed the work.
- Show the agreement or reconciliation of accounting records with financial statements or other information being reported on.

Factors to Consider in Determining the Nature and Extent of Audit Documentation

According to AU 339.07, the auditor should consider the following factors in determining the nature and extent of the documentation for an audit area or auditing procedure:

- Risk of material misstatement associated with the assertion, or account or class of transactions.
- Extent of judgment involved in performing the work and evaluating results.
- Nature of the auditing procedure.
- Significance of evidence obtained to the tested assertion.
- Nature and extent of identified exceptions.
- Need to document a conclusion or basis for a conclusion not readily determinable from the documentation of the work performed.

Required Audit Documentation

Audit documentation should also include

- Abstracts or copies of significant contracts or agreements examined by the auditor in evaluating the accounting for significant transactions.
- An identification of the items tested in tests of operating effectiveness of controls and substantive tests of details that involve document inspection or confirmation. This can be accomplished by indicating the source of the items selected and the specific selection criteria.

NOTE: The following indicate ways in which the identification of selected items can be accomplished.

- *Identifying characteristics, such as specific invoice numbers of the items included in the sample, when a haphazard or random sample is selected.*
- *When all items over a specified dollar amount are selected, describe the scope and identification of the listing, (for example, all payables over $10,000 from the December accounts payable journal).*
- *When a systematic sample is selected from a population of documents, identify the source of the documents and indicate the starting point and the sampling interval.*

Auditors can determine whether the identification is accomplished by asking themselves whether another auditor on the engagement would be able to identify the particular items selected for testing by reviewing the audit program and related documentation.

- Documentation of significant audit findings or issues, actions taken to address them (including additional evidence obtained) and the basis of the conclusions reached. According to AU 339.09, significant audit findings or issues include
  - Matters that are both significant and involve the appropriate selection, application, and consistency of accounting principles with regard to the financial statements, including related disclosures. Such matters often relate to (1) accounting for complex or unusual transactions or (2) estimates and uncertainties, and the related management assumptions, if applicable.
  - Results of auditing procedures that indicate that the financial statements or disclosures could be materially misstated or that the auditing procedures need to be significantly modified.
  - Circumstances that cause significant difficulty in applying necessary auditing procedures.
  - Other findings that could result in a modified auditor's report.

OWNERSHIP AND CONFIDENTIALITY

The auditor owns the audit documentation, but his or her ownership rights are limited by ethical and legal rules on confidential relationships with clients. The auditor should adopt reasonable procedures to protect the confidentiality of client information. The auditor should also adopt reasonable procedures to prevent unauthorized access to the audit documentation. The auditor should retain the audit documentation for a period sufficient to meet the needs of the auditor's practice and to satisfy pertinent legal requirements of records retention. Record-retention procedures should allow the auditor to access electronic audit documentation throughout the retention period.

NOTE: Rules of the Securities and Exchange Commission and other federal and local governmental agencies may be pertinent.

Sometimes audit documentation may serve as a source of reference for the client, but it should not be considered as a part of, or a substitute for, the client's accounting records.

DOCUMENTATION REQUIREMENTS IN OTHER SASS

Certain other SASs require documentation of specific matters. These requirements are presented in Illustration 1. In addition, other standards, such as government auditing standards, laws, or regulations may also contain specific documentation requirements.

INTERPRETATIONS

PROVIDING ACCESS TO, OR PHOTOCOPIES OF, AUDIT DOCUMENTATION TO A REGULATOR (ISSUED JULY 1994; REVISED JUNE 1996; REVISED OCTOBER 2000; REVISED JANUARY 2002)

A regulator may request access to an auditor's audit documentation to fulfill a quality review requirement or to assist in establishing the scope of a regulatory examination. In making the request, the regulator may ask to make photocopies and may also make such copies available to others. When regulators make a request for access, the auditor should

1. Consider advising the client about the request and indicating that he or she intends to comply. In some cases the auditor may wish or be required to confirm in writing the requirements to provide access (see Illustration 1).
2. Make arrangement with the regulator for the review.
3. Maintain control over the original audit documentation.
4. Consider submitting a letter to the regulator (see Illustration 2).
5. Obtain the client's consent to provide access when not required to provide access (see Illustration 3).

TECHNIQUES FOR APPLICATION

STANDARDIZATION OF AUDIT DOCUMENTATION

Audit documentation should be designed for the specific engagement; however, audit documentation supporting certain accounting records may be standardized.

The auditor should analyze the nature of his or her clients and the complexity of their accounting systems. This analysis will indicate accounts for which audit documentation may be standardized. An auditor ordinarily may be able to standardize audit documentation for a small business client as follows:

1. Cash, including cash on hand.
2. Short-term investments.
3. Trade accounts receivable.
4. Notes receivable.
5. Other receivables.
6. Prepaid expenses.
7. Property, plant, and equipment.
8. Long-term investments.
9. Intangible assets.
10. Deposits.
11. Accrued expenses.
12. Taxes payable.
13. Long-term debt.
14. Stockholders' equity accounts.

PREPARATION OF AUDIT DOCUMENTATION

All audit documentation should have certain basic information, such as the following:

1. Heading
    a. Name of client.
    b. Description of audit documentation, such as

(1) Proof of cash—Fishkill Bank & Trust Company.
(2) Accounts receivable—confirmation statistics.

c. Period covered by engagement.

(1) For the year ended. . .

2. An index number

a. All audit documentation should be numbered for easy reference. Audit documentation is identified using various systems, such as the following:

(1) Alphabetic.
(2) Numbers.
(3) Roman numerals.
(4) General ledger account numbers.
(5) A combination of the preceding.

3. Preparer and reviewer identification

a. Identification of person who prepared audit documentation and date of preparation.

(1) If client prepared the audit documentation, this should be noted. Person who checked papers also should be identified.

b. Identification of person who reviewed the audit documentation and date of review.

4. Explanation of symbols

a. Symbols used in the audit documentation should be explained. Symbols indicate matters such as the following:

(1) Columns were footed.
(2) Columns were cross-footed.
(3) Data were traced to original sources.

5. Source of information

a. The audit documentation should indicate source of information.

(1) Client records.
(2) Client personnel.

Related Accounts

One page of audit documentation may provide documentation for more than one account. Many balance sheet accounts are related to income statement accounts. In these circumstances, the audit work on the accounts should be documented in one page of audit documentation. Examples of related accounts are the following:

1. Notes receivable and interest income.
2. Depreciable assets, depreciation expense, and accumulated depreciation.
3. Prepaid expenses and the related income statement expenses, such as insurance, interest, and supplies.
4. Long-term debt and interest expense.
5. Deferred income taxes and income tax expense.

Client Preparation of Audit Documentation

It is advisable to have the client's employees prepare as much as possible of the auditor's audit documentation. This increases the efficiency of the audit. The auditor should identify the audit documentation as "Prepared by the Client" (PBC) and note the auditor who reviewed the client-prepared audit documentation. The preparation of audit documentation by the client does not impair the auditor's independence. However, the auditor should test the information in client-prepared audit documentation.

QUALITY OF AUDIT DOCUMENTATION

Audit documentation aids the execution and supervision of the current year's engagement. Also, such documentation helps the auditor in planning and executing the following year's audit. Audit documentation also serves as the auditor's reference for answering questions from the client. For example, a bank or a credit agency may want information that the auditor can provide to the client for submission to the third party from the audit documentation.

In case of litigation against the client, the auditor's audit documentation may be subpoenaed. In litigation against the auditor, the audit documentation will be used as evidence. Therefore audit documentation should be accurate, complete, and understandable. After audit documentation is reviewed, additional work, if any, is done, and modifications are made to the audit documentation, all review notes and all to-do points should be discarded because the issues they addressed have been appropriately responded to in the audit documentation.

Likewise, miscellaneous notes, memoranda, e-mails, and other communications among members of the audit engagement team created during the audit should be included or summarized in the audit documentation when needed to identify issues or support audit conclusions; otherwise, they should be discarded. Any information added after completion of fieldwork should be dated at the date added.

AUDIT DOCUMENTATION DEFICIENCIES

Some of the more common audit documentation deficiencies are failure to

1. Express a conclusion on the account being analyzed.
2. Explain exceptions noted.
3. Obtain sufficient information for note disclosure.
4. Reference information.
5. Update and revise permanent file.
6. Post adjusting and reclassification journal entries to appropriate audit documentation.
7. Indicate source of information.
8. Promptly review audit documentation prepared by assistants.
9. Sign or date audit documentation.
10. Foot client-prepared schedules.
11. Explain tick marks.

ILLUSTRATIONS

Illustrations 1, 2, and 3 are adapted from AICPA Interpretations of AU 339.

1. An auditor's written communication to client when not required to provide access.
2. An auditor's letter to a regulator.
3. A confirmation that the auditor may be required to provide access when required by law or regulation.

Illustration 4, which lists audit documentation requirements in other SASs, is adapted from the appendix to AU 339.

ILLUSTRATION 1. AUDITOR'S WRITTEN COMMUNICATION TO CLIENT WHEN NOT REQUIRED TO PROVIDE ACCESS (ADAPTED FROM AN INTERPRETATION OF AU 339)

The audit documentation for this engagement is the property of Guy & Co. and constitutes confidential information. However, we have been requested to make certain audit documentation available to [*name of regulator*] for [*describe the regulator's basis for its request*]. Access to such audit documentation will be provided under the supervision of Guy & Co. personnel. Furthermore, upon request, we may provide photocopies of selected audit documentation to [*name of regulator*].

You have authorized Guy & Co. to allow [*name of regulator*] access to the audit documentation in the manner discussed above. Please confirm your agreement to the above by signing below and returning it [*name of auditor, address*].

Firm signature

____

Agreed and acknowledged:

____

[Name and title]

____

[Date]

ILLUSTRATION 2. AUDITOR'S LETTER TO REGULATOR (FROM AN INTERPRETATION OF AU 339)

[*Date*]

[*Name and Address of Regulatory Agency*]

Your representatives have requested access to our audit documentation in connection with our audit of December 31, 20X1 financial statements of Widget Company. It is our understanding that the purpose of your request is [*state purpose: for example, "to facilitate your regulatory examination"*].

Our audit of Widget Company December 31, 20X1 financial statements was conducted in accordance with auditing standards generally accepted in the United States of America, the objective of which is to form an opinion as to whether the financial statements, which are the responsibility and representations of management, present fairly, in all material respects, the financial position, results of operations and cash flows in conformity with generally accepted accounting principles. Under generally accepted auditing standards, we have the responsibility, within the inherent limitations of the auditing process, to design our audit to provide reasonable assurance that errors and fraud that have a material effect on the financial statements will be detected, and to exercise due care in the conduct of our audit. The concept of selective testing of the data being audited, which involves judgment both as to the number of transactions to be audited and as to the areas to be tested, has been generally accepted as a valid and sufficient basis for any auditor to express an opinion on financial statements. Thus, our audit, based on the concept of selective testing, is subject to the inherent risk that material errors or fraud, if they exist, would not be detected. In addition, an audit does not address the possibility that material errors or fraud may occur in the future. Also, our use of professional judgment and the assessment of materiality for the purpose of our audit means that matters may have existed that would have been assessed differently by you.

The audit documentation was prepared for the purpose of providing principal support for our report on Widget Company December 31, 20X1 financial statements and to aid in the conduct and supervision of our audit. The audit documentation is the principal record of the auditing procedures performed, the evidence obtained, and the conclusions reached in the engagement. The auditing procedures that we performed were limited to those we considered necessary under generally accepted auditing standards to enable us to formulate and express an opinion on the financial statements taken as a whole. Accordingly, we make no representation as to the sufficiency or appropriateness, for your purposes, of either the information continued in our audit documentation or our audit procedures. In addition, any notations, comments, and individual conclusions appearing on any of the audit documentation do not stand alone, and should not be read as an opinion on any individual amounts, accounts, balances, or transactions.

Our audit of Widget Company December 31, 20X1 financial statements was performed for the purpose stated above and has not been planned or conducted in contemplation of your [*state purpose: for ex-*

ample, "regulatory examination"] or for the purpose of assessing Widget Company compliance with laws and regulations. Therefore, items of possible interest to you may not have been specifically addressed. Accordingly, our audit and the audit documentation prepared in connection therewith, should not supplant other inquiries and procedures that should be undertaken by the [*name of regulatory agency*] for the purpose of monitoring and regulating statements of Widget Company. In addition, we have not audited any financial statements of Widget Company since [*date of audited balance sheet referred to in the first paragraph above*] nor have we performed any audit procedures since [*date*], the date of our auditor's report, and significant events or circumstances may have occurred since that date.

The audit documentation constitutes and reflects work performed or evidence obtained by [*name of auditor*] in its capacity as independent auditor for Widget Company. The documents contain trade secrets and confidential commercial and financial information of our firms and Widget Company that is privileged and confidential, and we expressly reserve all rights with respect to disclosures to third parties. Accordingly, we request confidential treatment under the Freedom of Information Act or similar laws and regulations when requests are made for the audit documentation or information contained therein or any documents created by the [*name of regulatory agency*] containing information derived therefrom. We further request that written notice be given to our firm before distribution of the information in the audit documentation [or photocopies thereof] to others, including other governmental agencies, except when such distribution is required by law or regulation.

[*If it is expected that photocopies will be requested, add:*

Any photocopies of our audit documentation we agree to provide you will be identified as "Confidential Treatment Requested by (*name of auditor, address, telephone number*)."]

Firm signature

ILLUSTRATION 3. CONFIRMATION THAT AUDITOR MAY BE REQUIRED TO PROVIDE ACCESS WHEN REQUIRED BY LAW OR REGULATION (FROM AN INTERPRETATION OF AU 339)

The audit documentation for this engagement is the property of [*name of auditor*] and constitute confidential information. However, we may be requested to make certain audit documentation available to [*name of regulator*] for [*describe the regulator's basis for its request*]. Access to such audit documentation will be provided under the supervision of [*name of auditor*] personnel. Furthermore, upon request, we may provide photocopies of selected audit documentation to [*name of regulator*].

You have authorized [*name of auditor*] to allow [*name of regulator*] access to the audit documentation in the manner discussed above. Please confirm your agreement to the above by signing below and returning to [*name of auditor, address*].

Firm signature

____

Agreed and acknowledged:

____

[Name and title]

____

[Date]

ILLUSTRATION 4. AUDIT DOCUMENTATION REQUIREMENTS IN OTHER STATEMENTS ON AUDITING STANDARDS (ADAPTED FROM AU 339)

Reference	Documentation requirement(s)
Section 310: *Establishing an Understanding with the Client*	Understanding with the client.
Section 311: *Planning and Supervision*	A written audit program (or set of programs) for every audit.
Section 312: *Audit Risk and Materiality in Conducting an Audit*	The nature and effect of aggregated misstatements and the auditor's conclusion as to whether the aggregated misstatements cause the financial statements to be materially misstated.

Reference	Documentation requirement(s)
Section 316A: *Consideration of Fraud in a Financial Statement Audit* [2]	1. Evidence of the performance of the assessment of the risk of material misstatement due to fraud and the auditor's response to risk factors identified. 2. Any fraud risk factors or other conditions identified during the audit and any further response that the auditor concluded was appropriate.
Section 317: *Illegal Acts by Clients*	Oral communications to the audit committee or others with equivalent authority and responsibility regarding illegal acts that come to the auditor's attention.
Section 319: *Consideration of Internal Control in a Financial Statement Audit*	1. Understanding of the entity's internal control components obtained to plan the audit. 2. Auditor's conclusions about the assessed level of control risk.
Section 325: *Communication of Internal Control Related Matters Noted in an Audit*	Oral communications with the audit committee or others with equivalent authority and responsibility of conditions noted by the auditor that are considered reportable or that are the result of agreement with client.
Section 329: *Analytical Procedures*	When an analytical procedure is used as the principal substantive test of an assertion, 1. The expectation and factors considered in its development (where that expectation is not otherwise readily determinable from the documentation of the work performed). 2. Results of the comparison of the expectation to the recorded amounts or ratios developed from recorded amounts. 3. Any additional auditing procedures performed in response to significant unexpected differences arising from the analytical procedure and the results of such additional procedures.
Section 330: *The Confirmation Process*	Oral confirmations. Also, when the auditor has not requested confirmations in the examination of accounts receivable, document how the auditor overcame this presumption.
Section 333: *Management Representations*	Written representations from management.
Section 337: *Inquiry of a Client's Lawyer Concerning Litigation, Claims, and Assessments*	1. That the client has assured the auditor that it has disclosed **all** unasserted claims that the lawyer has advised the client are probable of assertion and must be disclosed in accordance with SFAS 5, *Accounting for Contingencies*. 2. The conclusions reached as a result of responses obtained in any conference relating to matters covered by the audit inquiry letter.
Section 341: *The Auditor's Consideration of an Entity's Ability to Continue as a Going Concern*	1. The conditions or events that led the auditor to believe that there is substantial doubt about the entity's ability to continue as a going concern, 2. The work performed in connection with the auditor's evaluation of management's plans, 3. The auditor's conclusion as to whether substantial doubt about the entity's ability to continue as a going concern for a reasonable period of time remains or is alleviated, and 4. The consideration and effect of that conclusion on the financial statements, disclosures, and the audit report.
Section 380: *Communications with Audit Committees*	Any oral communications with the audit committee regarding the scope and results of the audit.
Section 508: *Reports on Audited Financial Statements*	Predecessor auditor: representation letters from management of the former client and from the successor auditor before reissuing (or consenting to the reissue of) a report previously issued on the financial statements of a prior period.

---

[2] *See Section 316 for requirements under SAS 99, **Consideration of Fraud in a Financial Statements Audit**, which is effective for periods beginning on or after December 15, 2002.*

Reference	Documentation requirement(s)
Section 534: *Reporting on Financial Statements Prepared for Use in Other Countries*	Written representations from management regarding the purpose and uses of financial statements prepared in conformity with the accounting principles of another country.
Section 801: *Compliance Auditing Considerations in Audits of Governmental Entities and Recipients of Governmental Financial Assistance*	Oral communications to management and the audit committee or others with equivalent authority and responsibility when the auditor becomes aware during a GAAS audit that the entity is subject to an audit requirement that may not be encompassed in the terms of the engagement.

341 THE AUDITOR'S CONSIDERATION OF AN ENTITY'S ABILITY TO CONTINUE AS A GOING CONCERN

EFFECTIVE DATE AND APPLICABILITY

Original Pronouncements

SAS 59, April 1988; SAS 64, December 1990; SAS 77, November 1995, and SAS 96, January 2002.

Effective Date

Audits of financial statements for periods beginning on or after January 1, 1989 (SAS 59); auditors' reports issued after December 31, 1990 (SAS 64). (SAS 96 is effective for audits of financial statements for periods beginning on or after May 15, 2002, with earlier application permitted.)

Applicability

Audits of financial statements in accordance with generally accepted auditing standards.

NOTE: The Statement applies in the audit of any type of entity. It is applicable to both profit-making and not-for-profit organizations. Thus, it would apply, for example, in the audit of a municipality. Also, the Statement applies to both GAAP basis financial statements and OCBOA (Other Comprehensive Bases of Accounting) basis financial statements, (e.g., cash or modified cash basis, tax basis, or regulatory basis). However, it does not apply to liquidation basis financial statements.

DEFINITIONS OF TERMS

The section itself has no general definitions. The section is based on the "going concern" concept (see below, *Objectives of Section*).

OBJECTIVES OF SECTION

The "going concern" concept has long been a tenet of financial accounting. It has been called an assumption, a concept, a basic fixture, and a postulate and has usually been stated somewhat as follows:

Continuation of entity operations is usually assumed in financial accounting in the absence of evidence to the contrary.

There has been little guidance in the accounting literature, however, on when an entity may not be a going concern and what to do in that case. Until SAS 34 was issued in 1980, there was also little guidance in the auditing literature. The Auditing Standards Board decided it was necessary to replace SAS 34 because of complaints that an audit should provide an adequate warning of impending failure. Unfortunately, SAS 34 read as if an auditor must stumble over a going concern problem before recognizing its existence.

A new affirmative obligation was imposed by SAS 59, codified in this section, to make an assessment of ability to continue as a going concern. Some believe this is not too different from the auditor's prior responsibility. The big change is that the auditor's responsibility is stated in affirmative, nondefensive language.

Note that the section still does not mandate any procedures especially and solely directed to searching for conditions or events that would indicate a going concern problem. The obligation is to assess the information obtained from procedures used for other purposes.

Another change made by the section is that report modification may result solely from substantial doubt about continued existence regardless of whether there is any uncertainty associated with the recoverability and classification of recorded amounts. SAS 34 made the decision to modify the audit report hinge on uncertainty about recoverability and classification. Under this section, continued existence has a separate status. There could be substantial doubt about continued existence even when there is no question about recoverability and classification.

Also, the section makes a significant change in the way the audit report is modified for a material uncertainty. No longer is there a "subject to" qualification. The opinion is unqualified, but disclosure of the going concern uncertainty is made in an explanatory paragraph that follows the opinion paragraph. This type of uncertainty is now the only one that requires a report modification.

The section states that "a reasonable period of time" is a period not to exceed one year beyond the balance sheet date.

In January 2002, SAS 96, *Audit Documentation*, amended SAS 59 to add a requirement to document certain specific aspects of the work performed and conclusions reached about the auditor's going concern considerations. (See *Fundamental Requirements* for the specific documentation requirements.)

FUNDAMENTAL REQUIREMENTS

AUDITOR'S RESPONSIBILITY

The auditor should evaluate whether there is substantial doubt about the entity's ability to continue as a going concern for a reasonable period of time, not to exceed one year beyond the date of the financial statements being audited (i.e., the balance sheet date). However, the auditor is **not** required to design audit procedures specifically to identify conditions and events that indicate a "going concern" problem.

PROCEDURES REQUIRED

The auditor should consider whether the results of his or her usual audit procedures indicate that there could be substantial doubt.

ADDITIONAL PROCEDURES

If the auditor has substantial doubt about the entity's ability to continue as a going concern for a reasonable period of time, he or she should

1. Obtain information about management's plans to mitigate the problem.
2. Assess the likelihood of effective implementation of the plans.
3. Identify those elements that are especially significant to mitigating the going concern problem and should plan and perform auditing procedures to obtain evidential matter about those elements.

Prospective Financial Information

If prospective financial information is significant to management's plans, the auditor should obtain that information and should consider the adequacy of support for the significant assumptions. According to AU 341.09, the auditor should give special attention to those assumptions that are

1. Material to the prospective financial information.
2. Especially sensitive or susceptible to change.
3. Inconsistent with historical trends.

Auditor Conclusions—Substantial Doubt Exists

If the auditor concludes that there is substantial doubt about the entity's ability to continue as a going concern for a reasonable period of time, he or she should (1) consider the adequacy of disclosure of the condition and (2) modify the auditor's standard report by including an explanatory paragraph (following the opinion paragraph) or disclaim an opinion. The auditor's conclusion should be expressed in the report using the terms "substantial doubt" and "going concern."

Auditor Conclusions—Substantial Doubt Does Not Exist

If the auditor concludes that substantial doubt does not exist about the entity's ability to continue as a going concern for a reasonable period of time, he or she should consider the need for the disclosure of the matter.

NOTE: The absence of reference to substantial doubt in the auditor's report does not mean that the auditor is providing assurance about an entity's ability to continue as a going concern.

Inadequate Disclosure

If the auditor concludes that the entity's disclosures about its ability to continue as a going concern for a reasonable period of time are inadequate, the auditor's report should be qualified or adverse because of a departure from generally accepted accounting principles.

NOTE: The need to consider the adequacy of disclosure of going concern problems is independent of the auditor's decision to modify the audit report, that is, disclosure may be necessary even when the report is not modified.

Documentation Requirements

If, after considering the aggregate of events and conditions identified during the audit, the auditor believes that there is substantial doubt about the ability of the entity to continue as a going concern for a reasonable period of time, the auditor should document all of the following:

1. The conditions or events that led to the auditor's belief that there is substantial doubt about the entity's ability to continue as a going concern.
2. Those parts of management's plans that are particularly significant to overcoming the adverse effects of conditions or events.
3. The auditing procedures performed and evidence obtained to evaluate management's plans.
4. The auditor's conclusions about whether substantial doubt about the going concern issue remains.
    - If substantial doubt exists, document the possible effects of the conditions or events on the financial statements and the adequacy of the related disclosures.

- If substantial doubt is alleviated, document the conclusion about whether disclosure of the principal conditions and events that led the auditor to believe there was substantial doubt is needed.

5. The auditor's conclusion about whether to include an explanatory paragraph in the audit report to reflect the conclusion that substantial doubt remains. If going concern disclosures are inadequate, the auditor should document the conclusion about whether to express a qualified or adverse opinion to reflect the GAAP departure.

INTERPRETATIONS

ELIMINATING A GOING CONCERN EXPLANATORY PARAGRAPH FROM A REISSUED REPORT (AUGUST 1995)

An auditor may be asked by the client to reissue the audit report and eliminate the going concern paragraph. Such requests usually occur after the going concern matter has been resolved. The auditor has no obligation to reissue the audit report. However, if the auditor decides to reissue the report, he or she should

1. Audit the event or transaction that prompted the request to reissue.
2. Perform the procedures in Section 560.
3. Consider at the date of reissue the conditions and events that related to negative trends, internal matters, external matters, and other indications of financial difficulty. Also consider at the date of reissue management plans, including prospective financial information, the financial statement effects, and the effects on the audit report.
4. Perform any audit procedures considered necessary.
5. Reassess the going concern status of the entity.

TECHNIQUES FOR APPLICATION

PROCEDURES

The auditor's evaluation of whether there is a substantial doubt about the entity's ability to continue as a going concern for a reasonable period of time (not to exceed one year beyond the balance sheet date) is based on his or her knowledge of relevant **conditions** and **events** that exist at, or occurred before, completion of fieldwork. It is not necessary for the auditor to design audit procedures specifically to identify conditions and events that indicate a going concern problem. **Regular auditing procedures are sufficient.**

Regular auditing procedures that may identify conditions and events that indicate a going concern problem include the following:

1. **Analytical procedures.** Analytical procedures used as a substantive test or used in the planning and overall review stages of the audit may indicate

   a. Negative trends.
   b. Slow-moving inventory.
   c. Receivable collectibility problems.
   d. Liquidity and solvency problems.

2. **Review of subsequent events.** Subsequent events, such as the bankruptcy of a major customer, confirm adverse conditions that existed at the balance sheet date. Other subsequent events that indicate a possible going concern problem include

a. Collapse of the market price of the entity's inventory.
b. Withdrawal of line of credit by bank.
c. Expropriation of entity's assets.

3. **Review of compliance with the terms of debt and loan agreements.** Violation of debt covenants results in debt default.
4. **Reading of minutes.** Minutes of meetings of stockholders, board of directors, and board committees may indicate

   a. Potentially expensive litigation.
   b. Loss of lines of credit.
   c. Loss of a major supplier.
   d. Changes in the operation of the business that could result in significant losses.

5. **Inquiry of legal counsel.** Responses to inquiries of the entity's legal counsel about litigation, claims, and assessments could indicate possible significant losses because of product liability claims, copyright or patent infringement, contract violations, and illegal acts.
6. **Confirmations concerning financial support.** Confirmation with related parties and third parties of the details of arrangements to provide or maintain financial support may indicate loss of bank lines of credit or loss of third-party guarantees of entity indebtedness.

INDICATIONS OF GOING CONCERN PROBLEMS

Regular audit procedures such as those described above may reveal conditions and events that indicate there could be substantial doubt about the entity's ability to continue as a going concern for a reasonable period of time. Examples of these conditions and events (going concern warning signs or red flags) are as follows:

1. Negative trends.

   a. Declining sales.
   b. Increasing costs.
   c. Recurring operating losses.
   d. Working capital deficiencies.
   e. Negative cash flows from operations.
   f. Adverse key financial ratios.

2. Internal matters.

   a. Chaotic and inefficient accounting system.
   b. Loss of key management or operations personnel.
   c. Work stoppages or other labor difficulties.
   d. Substantial dependence on the success of a particular project.
   e. Uneconomic long-term commitments.
   f. Need to significantly revise operations.

3. External events that have occurred.

   a. Legal proceedings.
   b. Legislation or similar matters that might jeopardize operating ability.
   c. Loss of a key franchise, license, or patent.
   d. Loss of a principal customer or supplier.
   e. Uninsured catastrophes such as drought, earthquake, or flood.

4. Other indications of possible financial difficulties.
    a. Default on loan or similar agreements.
    b. Arrearages in dividends.
    c. Denial of usual trade credit from suppliers.
    d. Noncompliance with statutory capital requirements.
    e. Seeking new sources or methods of financing.

Consideration of Management's Plans

If, after considering the conditions and events described above, the auditor believes there is substantial doubt about the entity's ability to continue as a going concern for a reasonable period of time, he or she should consider management's plans for addressing these conditions and events.

Management's plans may be classified as follows:

1. Plans to dispose of assets.
2. Plans to borrow money or restructure debt.
3. Plans to reduce or delay expenditures.
4. Plans to increase ownership equity.

Plans to Dispose of Assets

If management plans to dispose of assets, the auditor should consider the following:

1. Marketability of assets that management plans to sell.
2. Restrictions on the disposal of assets.
3. Effects of disposal.

Marketability of Assets

The auditor should do the following:

1. If the assets are securities, review market quotations to determine price and volume.
    a. If the securities are unlisted, review management documentation and correspondence with prospective buyer.
2. If the assets are intangible assets—patents, franchises, copyrights—review the following:
    a. Cash generated by the asset over the previous years.
    b. Management's documentation of estimated sales price.
    c. Correspondence with prospective buyer.
3. If the assets are long-lived assets—property, plant, and equipment—review the following:
    a. Current market for the assets and current market value.
    b. Management's documentation of estimated sales price.
    c. Correspondence with prospective buyer.
4. If management contemplates sales of receivables to a financial institution, review the following:
    a. Allowances for doubtful accounts, and sales returns and allowances.
    b. Management's documentation of estimated sales price.
    c. Correspondence with financial institution.

5. If the assets are a complete segment of the entity, review the following:
   a. Segment operations over the previous years.
   b. Management's documentation of estimated sales price.
   c. Correspondence with prospective buyer.

Restrictions on Disposal of Assets

Under certain circumstances, the entity may be prohibited from disposing of assets. If management contemplates disposal, the auditor should do the following:

1. Review all loan agreements.
2. Review mortgages, financing arrangements, and other asset encumbrances.

Effects of Disposal

The auditor should consider possible adverse effects of the proposed disposal of assets. He or she should do the following:

1. Discuss with management the estimated effect of the disposal on the continuing operations of the entity.
2. Prepare pro forma financial statements of the entity, after excluding the assets that will be disposed.
3. Analyze the pro forma financial statements to determine the effect of the disposal on operations and cash flows.

PLANS TO BORROW MONEY OR RESTRUCTURE DEBT

If management plans to borrow money or restructure debt, the auditor should consider the following:

1. Availability of debt financing.
2. Availability and sufficiency of collateral.
3. Restrictions on additional borrowing.
4. Existing or committed arrangements to restructure or subordinate debt or to obtain guarantees of loans to the entity.

Availability of Debt Financing

The auditor should do the following:

1. Review management's plan.
2. Determine if there are existing or committed arrangements, such as lines of credit.
3. Determine feasibility of factoring receivables. Consider the impact on operations of factor's fees and interest charges.
4. Ascertain the availability of assets for sale-leaseback arrangements.

Availability and Sufficiency of Collateral

If there is a question about an entity's continued existence, it is probable that it will not be able to borrow funds without collateral. The auditor should consider the availability and sufficiency of assets as collateral. Assets to be considered are the following:

1. Marketable securities.
2. Receivables.
3. Inventories.
4. Property, plant, and equipment.

Restrictions on Additional Borrowing

Existing loan agreements may prohibit the entity from borrowing additional funds. To determine this, the auditor should do the following:

1. Review mortgage agreements.
2. Review bond indentures.
3. Review bank loan agreements.

Existing or Committed Arrangements

If there are existing plans or commitments to modify existing loans or to guarantee existing or new loans, the auditor should do the following:

1. Review management's plans for
   a. Debt restructuring.
   b. Subordination of existing debt.
   c. Obtaining loan guarantees.
2. Review correspondence and documents pertaining to the arrangements.
3. Confirm the arrangement with the other party, for example, the bank.

PLANS TO REDUCE OR DELAY EXPENDITURES

When a question arises about the continued existence of an entity, it is not uncommon for the entity to reduce or delay expenditures, such as the following:

1. Repairs and maintenance.
2. Advertising.
3. Research and development.
4. Additions to property, plant, and equipment.

If management plans to reduce or delay these expenditures, the auditor should do the following:

1. Review management's plans.
2. Discuss with management the plan's effects on operations.

PLANS TO INCREASE OWNERSHIP EQUITY

When a question arises about the continued existence, it is not uncommon for the entity to offer equity capital to an investor. Also, it is not uncommon for investors to search for entities in need of additional capital.

Ordinarily, in these circumstances, the entity will sell its stock to the investor at a discount from market value. In certain circumstances, the investor may have plans to bring profitable businesses into the troubled entity to use the troubled entity's net operating loss carryforward. In these situations, the auditor should do the following:

1. Review the plan.
2. Determine the tax consequences of the plan.
3. Determine the plan's impact on existing shareholders.
4. Discuss with management the adequacy of the investment.

The auditor's concern is that the funds will be sufficient to ease the liquidity problem and to provide sufficient working capital.

Consideration of Management Forecasts

The auditor is not required to examine management forecasts; however, he or she should read these forecasts and apply his or her knowledge of the client. The auditor should pay special attention to cash flows and the implementation of management plans. The auditor is interested in whether the forecasts provide a reasonable basis for the belief that the entity will be in business a year from the current balance sheet date.

Obtain Management Assumptions

The auditor should ask management for its assumptions, especially assumptions about the following:

1. General economic conditions.
2. Industry economic conditions.
3. Sales.
4. Cost of sales.
5. Cost of labor.
6. Expenditures for plant and equipment.
7. Selling, general, and administrative expenses.
8. Borrowings, interest expense, and extension of lines of credit.
9. Income taxes, if any.

Sources of Management Assumptions

The auditor should ask management for sources for its assumptions in developing the prospective data, especially the following:

1. Assumptions material to the forecasts or projections.
2. Assumptions that are unusually uncertain or sensitive to variation.
3. Assumptions that deviate from historical trends.

Possible sources for assumptions are the following:

1. Government publications.
2. Industry publications.
3. Economic forecasts.
4. Entity budgets.
5. Labor agreements.
6. Sales backlog.
7. Debt agreements.

When the auditor reads management's assumptions, he or she may want to consider the following:

1. Historical trends of the entity.
2. Historical trends of the industry.
3. Comparison of prior year's forecasts with actual results.

Internal Consistency of Assumptions

Management assumptions should be internally consistent. Examples of this internal consistency are the following:

1. There should be a logical relationship between net cash flow and the following:
   a. Sales.
   b. Expenses.

   c. Expenditures.
   d. Receivables.
   e. Payables.

2. There should be a logical relationship between sales and the following:
   a. Cost of sales.
   b. Labor.
   c. Rent.
   d. Advertising.

3. There should be a logical relationship between income statement items and balance sheet items such as the following:
   a. Sales to receivables.
   b. Cost of sales to inventories.
   c. Sales to working capital.

FINANCIAL STATEMENT EFFECTS

Substantial Doubt Exists

If the auditor concludes after considering management's plans, that there is substantial doubt about the entity's ability to continue as a going concern for a reasonable period of time, he or she should consider possible effects on the financial statements and the adequacy of the related disclosure. Disclosure might include the following:

1. Conditions and events creating the doubt, such as recurring operating losses, negative cash flows, working capital deficiency, and violation of debt covenants.
2. Possible effect of conditions and events, such as a cutback in operations, a layoff of employees, or a bankruptcy filing.
3. Management's evaluation of the significance of the conditions and events and any mitigating factors.
4. Possible discontinuance of operations.
5. Management's plans, including relevant prospective financial information.

   NOTE: It is not intended that the prospective financial information should meet the minimum presentation guidelines of Statement on Standards for Accountants' Services on Prospective Financial Information, ***Financial Forecasts and Projections****. Also, the inclusion of prospective financial information does not require procedures beyond those required by generally accepted auditing standards (see above, "Consideration of Management Forecasts").*

6. Information about recoverability or classification of recorded asset amounts or the amounts or classification of liabilities.

Substantial Doubt Does Not Exist

After considering management's plans, the auditor may conclude that substantial doubt about the entity's ability to continue as a going concern for a reasonable period of time does not exist. In these circumstances, the auditor should nonetheless consider the need to disclose the conditions and events responsible for the initial doubt and any mitigating factors, including management's plans.

EFFECTS ON THE AUDITOR'S REPORT

If the auditor concludes that substantial doubt exists about the entity's ability to continue as a going concern for a reasonable period of time, the auditor's standard report should include an explanatory paragraph, **following the opinion paragraph**, to reflect that conclusion. In these circumstances, the auditor ordinarily expresses an unqualified opinion (see below "Disclaimer of Opinion"). The auditor may no longer express a "subject to" opinion for any uncertainty (see SAS 58, *Reports on Audited Financial Statements*, Section 508). The auditor's conclusion should be expressed using a phrase such as "substantial doubt about its (the entity's) ability to continue as a going concern." The report wording must include the terms "substantial doubt" and "going concern" and should be stated unconditionally.

The following (from SAS 59 [AU 341]) is an example of an explanatory paragraph:

> The accompanying financial statements have been prepared assuming that the Company will continue as a going concern. As discussed in Note X to the financial statements, the Company has suffered recurring losses from operations and has a net capital deficiency that raise substantial doubt about its ability to continue as a going concern. Management's plans in regard to these matters are also described in Note X. The financial statements do not include any adjustments that might result from the outcome of this uncertainty.

Disclaimer of Opinion

Instead of issuing an unqualified opinion with an explanatory paragraph following the opinion paragraph, the auditor may disclaim an opinion if he or she concludes that there is substantial doubt about the entity's ability to continue as a going concern for a reasonable period of time. A disclaimer of opinion is permitted at the auditor's discretion, but never required.

Inadequate Disclosure

If the auditor concludes that the entity's disclosures about its ability to continue as a going concern for a reasonable period of time are inadequate, the auditor's report should be modified for a departure from generally accepted accounting principles. This may result in either a qualified (except for) or adverse opinion (see Section 508).

Prior Period Audit Report

The fact that the auditor is issuing a "going concern" report on the current period financial statements does not imply that a going concern problem existed in the prior period. Therefore, the auditor's report on prior period financial statements presented for comparative purposes with the current period financial statements need not be changed.

Subsequent Period Audit Report

The auditor may have issued a "going concern" report on the prior period financial statements that are presented for comparative purposes with the current period financial statements. If the going concern problem has been resolved during the current period, the explanatory paragraph included in the auditor's report on those prior period financial statements should **not** be repeated.

ILLUSTRATION

The following checklist may be used by the auditor to assess his or her doubt about a client's ability to continue as a going concern and to evaluate management's plans for addressing the issue.

ILLUSTRATION 1. GOING CONCERN CHECKLIST

____
[Client]

____
[Audit Date]

Instructions

This checklist should be used in every audit of financial statements to assess whether there is significant doubt about the "going concern" assumption. It is divided into two parts. Part I should always be completed. Part II should be completed only when as a result of completing Part I the auditor concludes that significant doubt may exist.

If an item is not applicable, insert "N/A" in the Yes/No column.

Part I

	Yes/No	*Date*	*Comment*
1. Have audit procedures identified any of the following conditions or events that may raise a question about the client's continued existence?			
a. Recurring operating losses.			
b. Working capital deficiencies.			
c. Negative cash flows from operations.			
d. Adverse key financial ratios, such as the current ratio and the quick asset ratio.			
e. Default on loan or similar agreements.			
f. Dividend arrearages.			
g. Denial of usual trade credit from suppliers.			
h. Noncompliance with statutory capital requirements.			
i. Necessity of seeking new sources or methods of financing.			
j. Loss of key management or operations personnel.			
k. Work stoppages or other labor difficulties.			
l. Substantial dependence on the success of a particular project.			
m. Uneconomic long-term commitments.			
n. Legal proceedings, legislation, or similar matters that might jeopardize entity's ability to operate.			
o. Loss of key franchise, license, or patent.			
p. Loss of a principal customer or supplier.			
q. Uninsured catastrophe.			
r. Other factors that create an uncertainty about going-concern status.			
2. Analyze the conditions or events identified in 1. above and conclude whether they raise a question about ability to continue as a going concern. (If the conclusion is "Yes," complete the procedures described in Part II.)			

Part II

	Performed by	*Date*	*Explanation or conclusion*
Consideration of Management Plans			
1. Discuss situation with management and determine plans for correcting conditions. Is management planning to			
a. Dispose of assets?			
b. Borrow money or restructure debt?			
c. Reduce or delay expenditures?			
d. Increase ownership equity?			
2. Fill out appropriate section or sections below.			
Liquidate assets			
3. Inquire about marketability of assets.			
4. Inquire about restrictions on the disposal of assets.			
5. Inquire about effects on operations of disposal.			

	Performed by	*Date*	*Explanation or conclusion*
Borrow money or restructure debt			
6. Inquire about the availability of new debt.			
7. Inquire about the availability of collateral to support new debt.			
8. Inquire about restrictions on additional debt.			
9. Read management's plans for			
a. Debt restructuring.			
b. Subordination of existing debt.			
c. Obtaining loan guarantees.			
Reduce or delay expenditures			
10. Read management's plans for reducing or delaying expenditures for the following:			
a. Repairs and maintenance.			
b. Advertising.			
c. Research and development.			
d. Property, plant, and equipment.			
e. Other.			
11. Discuss with management the effect on operations of the reduction or delay.			
12. Read management's plan to sell equity securities.			
13. Discuss tax consequences of plan with our tax department.			
14. Inquire about plan's impact on existing shareholders.			
15. Discuss with management the adequacy of the investment.			
Management Forecasts			
1. Read management's assumptions about the following:			
a. General economic conditions.			
b. Industry economic conditions.			
c. Sales.			
d. Cost of sales.			
e. Cost of labor.			
f. Capital expenditures.			
g. Selling, general, and administrative expenses.			
h. Interest expenses.			
i. New borrowings.			
j. Income taxes.			
2. Recompute mathematical calculations.			
3. Consider the internal consistency of the forecasts.			
Adequacy of Disclosure and Auditor's Report			
1. Consider the need to disclose the following:			
a. Conditions and events that created the doubt about continued existence.			
b. Possible effects of significant conditions and events.			
c. Management's evaluation of conditions and events.			
d. Possible disposal of a component of an entity.			
e. Management's plans, including relevant prospective financial information.			
f. Information about recoverability or classification of recorded asset amounts or the amounts or classification of liabilities.			
2. Consider need to modify report.			
a. Add explanatory paragraph.			
b. Disclaim an opinion (discretionary).			

342 AUDITING ACCOUNTING ESTIMATES[1]

EFFECTIVE DATE AND APPLICABILITY

Original Pronouncement	SAS 57, April 1988.
Effective Date	Audits of financial statements for periods beginning on or after January 1, 1989.
Applicability	Audits of financial statements in accordance with generally accepted auditing standards.

DEFINITIONS OF TERMS

Accounting estimate. An accounting estimate is an approximation of a financial statement element, item, or account. Accounting estimates are included in historical financial statements because (1) the measurement of some amounts or the valuation of some accounts is uncertain, pending the outcome of future events, or (2) relevant data concerning events that have already occurred cannot be accumulated on a timely cost-effective basis.

Accounting estimates in historical financial statements measure the effects of past business transactions or events, or the present status of an asset or liability. Examples of accounting estimates include (1) net realizable values of inventory and accounts receivable, (2) property and casualty insurance loss reserves, (3) revenue from contracts accounted for by the percentage-of-completion method, and (4) pension and warranty expenses. (*Illustrations* contain a list of typical accounting estimates. The examples are taken from SAS 57.)

Key factors. The Statement does not define this term; however, it states that the auditor normally concentrates on key factors in evaluating the reasonableness of accounting estimates. The term is defined in Section 2301, "Financial Forecasts and Projections," as follows:

> *Significant matters on which an entity's future results are expected to depend. Key factors encompass matters that affect items such as sales, production, service, and financing activities. They are the foundation for prospective financial statements and are the bases for assumptions.*

---

[1] *Practitioners with publicly traded clients should be aware that the SEC is proposing disclosure requirements on accounting estimates. A company would have to identify the accounting estimates reflected in its financial statements that required it to make assumptions about matters that were highly uncertain at the time of estimation. Disclosure about those estimates would then be required if different estimates that the company reasonably could have used in the current period, or changes in the accounting estimate that are reasonably likely to occur from period to period would have a material impact on the presentation of the company's financial condition, changes in financial condition, or results of operations. A company's disclosure about these critical accounting estimates would include discussion of the method and assumptions underlying them, the effect the accounting estimates have on the company's financial presentation, and the effect of changes in the estimates. Practitioners should monitor the status of the proposed rule, "Disclosure in Management's Discussion and Analysis about the Application of Critical Accounting Policies," Rule No. 33-8098, at www.sec.gov.*

OBJECTIVES OF SECTION

Estimation is essential in the preparation of financial statements. Exact measurement of some amounts or the valuation of some accounts is uncertain until (1) the outcome of future events is known, or (2) all relevant data concerning events that have already occurred are accumulated.

Because they involve uncertainty and subjectivity, and because controls over them are more difficult to establish than controls over factual information, accounting estimates ordinarily are more susceptible to material misstatements than factual data. It is, therefore, necessary for the auditor to devote adequate audit resources to accounting estimates in light of the degree of uncertainty and subjectivity, quality of controls, and other relevant circumstances.

SAS 57 provides guidance to auditors (1) on identifying circumstances that require accounting estimates, and (2) on obtaining and evaluating sufficient competent evidential matter to support accounting estimates in an audit of financial statements in accordance with generally accepted auditing standards.

FUNDAMENTAL REQUIREMENTS

AUDITOR'S RESPONSIBILITY

The auditor is responsible for evaluating the reasonableness of accounting estimates made by management. The auditor should consider, with an attitude of professional skepticism, both the subjective and objective factors on which accounting estimates are based in planning and performing procedures to evaluate those estimates.

AUDITOR'S OBJECTIVE

The auditor should evaluate accounting estimates to obtain reasonable assurance that

1. All accounting estimates that could be material have been developed by management.
2. Those estimates are reasonable.
3. The estimates are presented and disclosed in conformity with generally accepted accounting principles.

IDENTIFYING CIRCUMSTANCES THAT REQUIRE MATERIAL ACCOUNTING ESTIMATES

According to AU 342.08, in evaluating whether management has identified all accounting estimates that could be material to the financial statements, the auditor should consider performing the following procedures:

1. Consider assertions embodied in the financial statements to determine the need for accounting estimates (see *Illustrations* for examples of accounting estimates included in financial statements).
2. Evaluate information obtained in performing other auditing procedures (see *Techniques for Application*).
3. Inquire of management about the existence of circumstances that may indicate the need to make an accounting estimate.

NOTE: In evaluating whether all material estimates have been identified, the auditor considers the circumstances of the industry, the entity's method of conducting business, new accounting pronouncements, and other relevant internal or external factors.

EVALUATING REASONABLENESS

According to AU 342.09-.10, in evaluating reasonableness of accounting estimates, the auditor should do the following:

1. As a general rule, consider the historical experience of the entity in making past estimates and the auditor's experience in the industry.
2. Obtain an understanding of how management developed the estimate.
3. Based on the understanding obtained in 2., the auditor should do one or a combination of the following:
   a. Review and test the process used by management to develop the estimate.
   b. Develop an independent expectation of the estimate to corroborate the reasonableness of management's estimate.
   c. Review subsequent events or transactions occurring before the completion of fieldwork.

NOTE: In evaluating reasonableness, the auditor should concentrate on key factors and assumptions that are

1. *Significant.*
2. *Sensitive to variations.*
3. *Deviations from historical patterns.*
4. *Subjective and susceptible to misstatement and bias.*

INTERPRETATIONS

PERFORMANCE AND REPORTING GUIDANCE RELATED TO FAIR VALUE DISCLOSURES (FEBRUARY 1993; REVISED OCTOBER 2000)

The auditor should determine if the fair value disclosures presented represent only those required by FASB Statement 107, *Disclosures About Fair Value of Financial Instruments*, or whether additional voluntary disclosures are also presented.

For both required and voluntary disclosures, the auditor should reasonably assure that

1. The valuation of principles are acceptable, consistently applied, and supported by underlying documentation.
2. The methods of estimation and significant assumptions used are properly disclosed.

Only Required Information Presented

If no other report modifications are needed, the auditor may issue a standard audit report. The auditor may elect to add an emphasis-of-matter paragraph calling attention to the nature and possible range of fair values. If required information is not presented, the auditor should consider whether a qualified or adverse opinion is required because of the departure from GAAP.

Both Required and Voluntary Information Presented

The auditor may audit the voluntary information only if

1. The measurement and disclosure criteria used are reasonable.
2. Competent persons using the measurement and disclosure criteria would ordinarily obtain similar results.

Voluntary fair values may be presented as a complete balance sheet presentation or a less than complete balance sheet. When a complete balance sheet is presented, the following paragraph should be added to the audit report:

> We have also audited in accordance with auditing standards generally accepted in the United States of America the supplemental fair value balance sheet of ABC Company as of December 31, 20X1. As described in Note X, the supplemental fair value balance sheet has been prepared by management to present relevant financial information that is not provided by the historical-cost balance sheets and is not intended to be a presentation in conformity with generally accepted accounting principles. In addition, the supplemental fair value balance sheet does not purport to present the net realizable, liquidation, or market value of ABC Company as a whole. Furthermore, amounts ultimately realized by ABC Company from the disposal of assets may vary significantly from the fair values presented. In our opinion, the supplemental fair value balance sheet referred to above presents fairly, in all material respects, the information set forth therein as described in Note X.

When the required and voluntary fair values do not constitute a complete balance sheet and are located on the face of the financial statements or in footnotes, the standard audit report may be presented. However, if the partial disclosures are included in a separate schedule or exhibit in an auditor-submitted document, the auditor should add an additional paragraph to the audit report (see Section 551) indicating that the fair value information is presented for additional analysis purposes and is not a required part of the basic financial statements. In situations when the auditor is not engaged to audit the voluntary fair value information or is unable to audit it and the information is presented in an auditor-submitted document (on the face of the financial statements or in notes thereto or in a supplemental format), the voluntary information should be labeled "unaudited" and the auditor should disclaim an opinion on it (see Section 551). Finally, when the audited disclosures are presented on the face of the financial statements, in footnotes, or as supplements in a client-prepared document, the information should simply be labeled "unaudited."

TECHNIQUES FOR APPLICATION

CLIENT'S RESPONSIBILITIES

In applying procedures to identify circumstances that require accounting estimates and evaluate the reasonableness of the estimates, the auditor should be aware of the entity's responsibilities in the development of accounting estimates.

Developing Accounting Estimates

Management is responsible for establishing the process for preparing accounting estimates. The process, presented in AU 342.05, may not be documented or formally applied; however, it usually consists of

1. Identifying when accounting estimates are required.
2. Identifying the factors that affect the accounting estimate.
3. Accumulating data on which to base the estimate.
4. Developing appropriate assumptions.
5. Estimating the amount.
6. Determining that the estimate is presented in the financial statements in conformity with appropriate accounting principles and that disclosure is adequate.

If management's process for developing accounting estimates is documented, generally the auditor should review the documentation. If the process is not documented, the auditor should make inquiries of management to determine how management developed its accounting estimates.

Internal Control

An entity's internal control may reduce the likelihood of material misstatements of accounting estimates. Aspects of control related to accounting estimates include the following:

1. Does management communicate the need for proper accounting estimates?
2. Are appropriate data on which to base the estimate accumulated?
3. Are estimates prepared by qualified personnel?
4. Are accounting estimates and supporting data adequately reviewed and approved?
5. Are past accounting estimates compared with actual results?
6. Has management considered whether the accounting estimate is consistent with its plans?

When the auditor documents his or her understanding of the entity's internal control (see Section 319), he or she should document those aspects related to accounting estimates.

IDENTIFYING CIRCUMSTANCES THAT REQUIRE ACCOUNTING ESTIMATES

1. **Read the financial statements.** The auditor should read the financial statements, including the notes, to determine if any elements, accounts, or items require an accounting estimate. The auditor's knowledge of the client's operations and industry help the auditor determine those components of the financial statements that require accounting estimates.
2. **Obtain information by performing other procedures.** By performing customary auditing procedures—reading minutes, inquiries, substantive tests of account balances—the auditor may obtain information that might indicate the need for an accounting estimate. The auditor should evaluate this information which includes the following:
    a. Information about changes made or to be made in the entity's business that may indicate the need to make an account estimate (see Section 311). For example, estimates must be made if the entity has disposed of, or plans to dispose of, a segment of the business.
    b. Changes in methods of accumulating financial information. Documenting the auditor's understanding of the entity's internal control would provide this information.
    c. Information concerning identified litigation, claims, and assessments, and other contingencies. Inquiring of client's lawyer and analysis of client's legal expenses would provide this information (see Section 337).
    d. Information from reading available minutes of meetings of stockholders, directors, and appropriate committees.
    e. Information included in regulatory or examination reports, supervisory correspondence, and similar materials from regulatory agencies.

In addition, other auditing procedures, such as confirmation of receivables and observation of inventories might provide information about the need to reconsider the estimate for allowance for doubtful accounts or provide an estimate for inventory obsolescence.

3. **Make inquiries of management.** Throughout the audit the auditor makes inquiries of management. An inquiry should be made concerning the need for an accounting estimate.

EVALUATING THE REASONABLENESS OF ACCOUNTING ESTIMATES

Review and Test Management's Process

In evaluating the reasonableness of accounting estimates, the auditor may consider performing the following procedures:

1. Consider the understanding that has been obtained of the process established by management to develop accounting estimates and whether the process is appropriate in the circumstances.
2. Identify controls over the process and the supporting data.
3. Identify the sources of information that management used in forming the assumptions and consider whether the information is reliable and sufficient for the purpose based on information gathered in other audit tests.
4. Consider whether there are additional key factors or alternative assumptions about the factors.
5. Evaluate whether the assumptions are consistent with one another, the supporting data, and relevant historical data.
6. Analyze historical data used in developing the assumptions to assess its comparability and consistency with data of the period under audit, and determine whether it is sufficiently reliable for the purpose.
7. Consider whether changes in the business or industry may cause other factors to become significant to the assumptions.
8. Review available documentation of the assumptions used in developing the accounting estimates and inquire about any other plans, goals, and objectives of the entity, as well as considering their relationship to the assumptions.
9. Test the calculations used to translate the assumptions and key factors into the accounting estimate.
10. Consider whether there are more appropriate ways to translate assumptions into estimates.
11. Consider obtaining the opinion of a specialist regarding certain assumptions (see Section 336).

Develop an Expectation

Based on his or her understanding of the facts and circumstances and knowledge of the client and its industry, the auditor may develop an independent expectation of the estimate by using factors and assumptions not used by the entity and compare that to the client's estimate. Analytical procedures are a common method used in this approach (see Section 329).

Review Subsequent Events

In evaluating the reasonableness of an accounting estimate, the auditor may review subsequent events to confirm the estimate or the appropriateness of the factors and assumptions used to develop the estimate or to obtain additional relevant information. For example, a loan that was sixty days past due at year-end might be 180 days past due near the completion of the audit.

UNREASONABLE ESTIMATE

The audit evidence might indicate that an accounting estimate is not reasonable. In these circumstances, the auditor should refer to paragraph 29 of SAS 47, *Audit Risk and*

Materiality in Conducting an Audit (see Section 312), which states that "If the auditor believes the estimated amount is unreasonable, he should treat the difference between that estimate and the closest reasonable estimate as a likely misstatement and aggregate it with other likely misstatements." In addition, SAS 47 indicates, "The auditor should also consider whether the differences between estimates best supported by the audit evidence and the estimates included in the financial statements, which are individually reasonable, indicate a possible bias on the part of the entity's management." In these circumstances, the auditor should reconsider significant estimates and similar matters influenced by management's judgment.

ILLUSTRATIONS

The following list is taken from SAS 57 (AU 342). It is not all-inclusive.

ILLUSTRATION 1. EXAMPLES OF ACCOUNTING ESTIMATES

Receivables:
- Uncollectible receivables
- Allowance for loan losses
- Uncollectible pledges

Inventories:
- Obsolete inventory
- Net realizable value of inventories where future selling prices and future costs are involved
- Losses on purchase commitments

Financial instruments:
- Valuation of securities
- Trading vs. investment security classification
- Probability of high correlation of a hedge
- Sales of securities with puts and calls

Productive facilities, natural resources and intangibles:
- Useful lives and residual values
- Depreciation and amortization methods
- Recoverability of costs
- Recoverable reserves

Accruals:
- Property and casualty insurance company loss reserves
- Compensation in stock option plans and deferred plans
- Warranty claims
- Taxes on real and personal property
- Renegotiation refunds
- Actuarial assumptions in pension costs

Revenues:
- Airline passenger revenue
- Subscription income
- Freight and cargo revenue
- Dues income
- Losses on sales contracts

Contracts:
- Revenue to be earned
- Costs to be incurred
- Percent of completion

Leases:
- Initial direct costs
- Executory costs
- Residual values

Litigation:
- Probability of loss
- Amount of loss

Rates:
- Annual effective tax rate in interim reporting
- Imputed interest rates on receivables and payables
- Gross profit rates under program method of accounting

Other:
- Losses and net realizable value on disposal of segment or restructuring of a business
- Fair values in nonmonetary exchanges
- Interim period costs in interim reporting
- Current values in personal financial statements

350 AUDIT SAMPLING[1]

EFFECTIVE DATE AND APPLICABILITY

Original Pronouncements	SAS 39, June 1981; SAS 43, August 1982; SAS 45, August 1983.
Effective Date	June 25, 1983 (as amended by SAS 43); effective date relates to audits of financial statements for periods ended on that date.
Applicability	Audits of financial statements in accordance with generally accepted auditing standards. The SAS applies to **audit sampling** whether the sampling is statistical or nonstatistical (see *Definitions* and *Objectives of Section*).

DEFINITIONS OF TERMS

Audit sampling. The application of an audit procedure to less than 100% of the items within an account balance or class of transactions for the purpose of evaluating some characteristics of the balance or class.

Audit risk. A combination of the risk that material misstatements will occur in the accounting process used to develop the financial statements and the risk that any material misstatements that occur will not be detected by the auditor. (Audit risk is the product of these two individual risks.)

Sampling risk. The risk that the auditor's conclusions may be different from the conclusions he or she would reach if the (audit) test were applied in the same way to all items in the account balance or class of transactions (varies inversely with sample size).

Nonsampling risk. All aspects of audit risk that are not due to sampling (for example, selecting auditing procedures that do not achieve a specific objective, or failing to recognize misstatements).

Risk of incorrect acceptance. The risk that the sample supports the conclusion that the recorded account balance is not materially misstated when it is materially misstated (aspect of sampling risk for substantive test).

---

[1] *The Auditing Standards Board (ASB) has issued Exposure Drafts of seven proposed SASs that relate to the risk assessment process. A summary of key changes is provided immediately before Section 100-230. This section would be amended to move guidance from an appendix in SAS 39 to the proposed SAS on audit risk and materiality, to incorporate guidance on fraud and performing procedures from other SASs, and to provide guidance on tolerable misstatement for audit procedures and how to apply sampling to tests of controls. The Public Company Accounting Oversight Board (PCAOB) has replaced the ASB as the standards-setting authority for public company audits. Therefore, the ASB's Exposure Drafts will not be issued as final standards by the AICPA. The documents will, however, be considered by the PCAOB in developing standards or amendments to existing transitional standards. Please check for updates to this section on the John Wiley & Sons, Inc. website at www.wiley.com/gaas.*

Risk of incorrect rejection. The risk that the sample supports the conclusion that the recorded account balance is materially misstated when it is not materially misstated (aspect of sampling risk for substantive test).

Risk of assessing control risk too low. The risk that the assessed level of control risk based on the sample is less than true operating effectiveness of the control (aspect of sampling risk for tests of controls).

Risk of assessing control risk too high. The risk that the assessed level of control risk based on the sample is greater than the true operating effectiveness of the control (aspect of sampling risk for tests of controls).

Tolerable misstatement. The maximum monetary misstatement for an account balance or class of transactions that may exist without causing the financial statements to be materially misstated. (A planning concept—tolerable misstatement combined for the entire audit plan should not exceed preliminary estimates of materiality levels.)

Tolerable rate. The maximum rate of deviations from a prescribed internal control that the auditor would be willing to accept without altering his or her assessment of the level of control risk.

Dual-purpose sample. A sample designed (1) to assess control risk, and (2) to test whether the recorded monetary amount of transactions is correct.

Population. The items comprising the account balance or class of transactions.

Unexamined items. Selected sample items that cannot be examined because they are missing (for example, supporting documentation for a selected sample item cannot be located).

OBJECTIVES OF SECTION

SAS 39 is not just for statistical samplers. It applies equally to nonstatistical and statistical sampling. The SAS makes clear that either approach to audit sampling, **when properly applied,** can provide sufficient evidential matter. And it establishes specific requirements essential for proper application.

Because the SAS establishes requirements that apply whenever audit sampling is used, the definition of audit sampling becomes very important. Audit sampling is defined as "the application of an audit procedure to less than 100% of the items within an account balance or class of transactions for the purpose of evaluating some characteristic of the balance or class." Thus, whenever the auditor intends to reach a conclusion about whether an account balance or class of transactions is misstated based on an examination of less than all the items in the balance or class, he or she should adhere to the requirements of SAS 39.

One effect of SAS 39 on practice should be to place a premium on the auditor's decision to sample. If the auditor is sampling, he or she should adhere to the SAS. If the auditor has some other audit objective, the SAS does not apply. Thus, the auditor can no longer simply decide that a procedure will be applied on a test basis. Careful consideration should go into a decision that the best approach to an audit test involves use of audit sampling (see *Techniques for Application*).

SAS 39 marks an important milestone in the development of statistical sampling in the auditing literature.

1. In 1963, SAP 33 acknowledged that the use of statistical sampling in an audit was in accordance with generally accepted auditing standards. This meant that statistical sampling was permissible under professional standards.
2. In 1972, SAP 54 was issued with an appendix on the use of statistical sampling in audit tests. The appendix explained the relationship of statistical terms to established auditing concepts, such as materiality and risk, and provided guidance on the incorporation of statistical sampling in planning and applying audit procedures.

3. In 1981, SAS 39 moved statistical sampling from the subordinate status of an appendix to the body of the statement and equated statistical and nonstatistical sampling in a common approach. Basically, the SAS says that there is an underlying rationale for sampling in auditing that is applicable whether the sampling is statistical or nonstatistical. Whether that parity is a boon or a burden for nonstatistical audit sampling will depend on distinguishing the specific requirements of the SAS from its other aspects (see *Techniques for Application*).

If the auditor is sampling, the selection of sample items should not be judgmental. It must be expected to be representative. SAS 39 effectively eliminated "judgmental" sampling as a permissible audit approach. All audit sampling has to be either statistical or nonstatisitical.

FUNDAMENTAL REQUIREMENTS

In planning a particular sample, the auditor should

1. Determine the specific audit objective to be achieved.
2. Determine that the audit procedure, or combination of procedures, to be applied will achieve that objective.
3. Determine that the population from which he or she draws the sample is appropriate for the specific audit objective.

NOTE: The following requirements apply equally to nonstatistical and statistical audit samples.

EXAMINED 100 PERCENT

Some items exist for which, in the auditor's judgment, acceptance of some sampling risk is not justified. All of these items should be examined. (Items examined 100% are not part of the items subject to sampling.)

NOTE: Some items may individually be so significant or may have such a high likelihood of being misstated that they should not be sampled.

SAMPLE SELECTION

According to AU 350.24, sample items should be selected in such a way that the sample can be expected to be representative of the population. That is, the auditor should select a sample he or she believes is representative of the items comprising the pertinent account balance or class of transactions.

STRATIFICATION

According to AU 350.22, the auditor may be able to reduce required sample size by separating items subject to sampling into relatively homogeneous groups on the basis of some characteristic related to the specific audit objective.

UNEXAMINED SAMPLE ITEMS

The treatment of unexamined selected sample items depends on their effect on the auditor's evaluation of the sample. In a substantive test, if considering the unexamined items to be misstated would not alter the auditor's evaluation of sample results, the items may be ignored. If the evaluation would be changed, the auditor should apply alternative procedures for those items and consider the implications of the reasons for his or her inability to examine the items. In a test of controls, selected items that cannot be examined should be treated as deviations.

NOTE: Before ignoring or simply considering unexamined or missing items as misstated or deviations, the auditor should consider whether the unexamined items might be indicative of fraud.

Sample Size: Substantive Test

To determine the number of items to be selected in a sample for a particular substantive test of details, the auditor should consider

1. Tolerable misstatement.
2. Allowable risk of incorrect acceptance.
3. Characteristics of the population.

NOTE: For a statistical audit sample, these factors should be reduced to specific amounts for use in a formula or table to calculate sample size. For a nonstatistical sample, specific amounts are often neither required nor possible, and the auditor considers qualitative relationships. For example, as tolerable misstatement increases, sample size decreases.

Sample Size: Test of Controls

To determine the number of items to be selected for a particular sample for a test of controls, the auditor should consider

1. Tolerable rate of deviation from controls being tested, based on the planned assessed level of control risk.
2. Expected or likely rate of deviation.
3. Allowable risk of assessing control risk too low.

Projection of Misstatements

The auditor should project the misstatement results of the sample to the account balance or class of transactions from which the sample was selected.

Aggregation of Misstatements

The auditor should aggregate projected misstatements for all audit sampling applications and all known misstatements from nonsampling applications when he or she evaluates whether the financial statements taken as a whole may be materially misstated.

Qualitative Aspects

In addition to evaluating quantitative sample results (frequency of deviations or frequency and amount of monetary misstatements), the auditor should consider the qualitative aspects of sample results, such as the nature and cause of deviations or monetary misstatements.

NOTE: The qualitative evaluation includes consideration of whether sample results might be indicative of fraud.

INTERPRETATIONS

Applicability (January 1985)

The auditor's examination of less than 100% of the items comprising an account balance or class of transactions is not an audit sampling application under SAS 39 in the following circumstances:

1. It is not the auditor's intent to extend the conclusions reached from the sample to the remaining items in the account balance or class of transactions.
2. The auditor examines 100% of the items in a given population (or breaks an account balance or class of transactions down into two populations and examines 100% of the subpopulation while considering the second subpopulation immaterial).

3. The auditor is testing controls that do not leave a documentary trail (for example, the auditor's observation of a client's physical inventory).
4. The auditor is not performing a test of details for a given substantive test.

TECHNIQUES FOR APPLICATION: NONSAMPLING

DISTINGUISHING SAMPLING FROM OTHER AUDIT TESTS

Because SAS 39 applies equally to nonstatistical sampling (often called judgment sampling) and statistical sampling, whether a procedure involves audit sampling becomes a critical decision. Some audit procedures obviously do not involve sampling, such as

- Analytical procedures.
- Inquiries and observation used in tests of controls that do not result in documentary evidence of performance and in audit planning.
- Examination of 100% of the items in an account balance or class of transactions.

In general, an audit procedure involves sampling whenever evidence relating to individual items is used as a basis for a conclusion about the population from which the items were selected. However, there are two types of audit tests that do not involve audit sampling that should be carefully distinguished because they are commonly thought of as being done on a test basis.

- Key-item tests.
- Flow-of-transaction tests (walk-throughs).

Key-Item Tests

These tests are substantive tests of details of all the items in a population that individually or in total could contain monetary misstatements that approximate tolerable misstatement. This approach does not test those items that in total are not material. The results of this kind of test cannot be projected to the balance or class as a whole. The evidence obtained only supports evaluation of the items tested.

This kind of test can be used primarily when most of the dollar amount of an account balance is concentrated in a comparatively few key items such that the remainder of the items in the balance could be entirely misstated without having a material effect on the financial statements.

Flow-of-Transactions Tests

If the auditor's objective is to obtain a better understanding of the flow of a particular class of transactions through the accounting system, sampling is not involved. In this kind of test the auditor traces one or a few of the different types of transactions through the related documents and records. It is often called a walk-through. This test does not involve sampling if the auditor is trying to confirm his or her understanding of how the accounting system works.

TECHNIQUES FOR APPLICATION: NONSTATISTICAL AUDIT SAMPLING

INTRODUCTION

The auditor performs two separate groups of procedures in audit sampling.

1. Sample selection and evaluation of the sample results.
2. Audit procedures in examining the sample items.

The audit procedures performed on the sample items do not depend on the method of sample selection. **Items selected by either nonstatistical or statistical sampling methods are subject to the same audit procedures.**

A properly designed nonstatistical sampling plan can provide results that are as effective as results from a properly designed statistical sampling plan. The significant difference between nonstatistical and statistical sampling is that statistical sampling measures the sampling risk associated with sampling procedures. Sampling risk arises from the possibility that when a test of controls or substantive test is applied to a sample, the auditor's conclusions might be different from those that would have been made if the tests were applied in the same way to all items in the population. That is, the sample selected from the population might not be representative of that population. For tests of controls, sampling risk is the risk of assessing control risk too low or too high. For substantive testing, sampling risk is the risk of incorrect acceptance or incorrect rejection of the amount tested.

METHODS OF SAMPLE SELECTION

Sample items should be selected in a way so that the sample can be expected to be representative of the population; therefore, all items in the population should have a chance of being selected. Common methods of selecting samples are

- Block sampling.
- Haphazard sampling.
- Random number sampling.
- Systematic sampling.

Block sampling does not meet the requirements for a representative sample. The other three do. Ordinarily, only the last two methods are used in statistical sampling.

Block Sampling

A block sample is obtained by selecting several items in sequence. Once the first item in the block is selected, the remainder of the block is chosen automatically. For example, the sample may consist of all vouchers processed during a two-week period or all vouchers processed on specific days. Block samples could theoretically be representative samples but are rarely used because they are inefficient. The time and expense to select sufficient blocks so that the sample could be considered representative of the total population is prohibitive.

Haphazard Sampling

A haphazard sample is obtained by selecting, without any conscious bias, items regardless of their size, source, or other distinguishing characteristics. It is not the selection of sample units in a careless manner; the units are selected in a manner so that the sample can be expected to be representative of the population. For example, the sample may consist of vouchers pulled from all vouchers processed for the year. Excluding items from the sample on the basis of judgment invalidates the requirement for a representative sample.

Random Number Sampling

A random sample is obtained by selecting numbers from a random number table or by generating numbers randomly by computer and matching them with document numbers, such as check numbers and invoice numbers.

Systematic Sampling

A systematic sample is obtained by selecting items at uniform intervals. The interval is determined by dividing the number of physical units in the population by the sample size. A starting point is selected at random in the first interval, and one item is selected from the population at each of the uniform intervals from the random starting point. For example, in a population of 20,000 units and a desired sample of 100 units, every two hundredth item will be selected from the starting point. Neither the size nor the unusualness of an item should be allowed to influence selection. The auditor can select large and unusual items in addition to items sampled, however.

TESTS OF CONTROLS

After the auditor obtains and documents his or her understanding of internal control, he or she may wish to assess control risk at below the maximum for certain assertions. For these assertions, the auditor should perform tests of controls (see Section 319). When testing controls, the auditor may use attribute sampling.

Attribute Sampling

An attribute is a characteristic of interest. For example, some attributes of a sale that are of interest to the auditor may be the following:

1. Authorization by the sales order department.
2. Approval by the credit department.
3. Comparison of merchandise shipped and merchandise listed on the sales invoice for agreement.

In testing for attributes, the auditor is concerned with how many times a prescribed internal control failed to operate. Based on the occurrence rate in the sample, the auditor decides if he or she can assess control risk at below the maximum.

For nonstatistical attribute sampling, the auditor does the following:

1. Judgmentally determines sample size.
2. Selects the sample.
3. Applies audit procedures to the sample units.
4. Evaluates the results of the application of audit procedures to the sample.

Determination of sample size. The auditor determines sample size and evaluates sample results using subjective judgment to apply the criteria specified in SAS 39 and his or her own experience with the client. The auditor may, but is not required to, use statistical tables to determine sample size for nonstatistical compliance tests. (See *References* at the end of this section.) Sample sizes, according to SAS 39, should be based on the tolerable rate of deviation from the control procedures being tested, the expected rate of deviations, and the allowable risk of assessing control risk too low.

The auditor is not required to select a number of items comparable to a statistical sample size. If his or her past experience with a continuing client has been good, the auditor might continue to use sample sizes that have proven effective.

Selection of sample units. The auditor may use one of the methods described earlier for selecting the sample. In selecting the sample, the auditor may encounter the following:

1. Voided documents.
2. Unused or inapplicable documents.
3. Inability to examine selected items.

Voided documents. If the auditor selects a voided document—for example, a voided sales invoice—he or she should replace it with another. The auditor should obtain reasonable assurance, however, that the document was properly voided and was not a deviation from prescribed internal control.

Unused or inapplicable documents. If the auditor selects an unused or inapplicable document, he or she should treat it the same as a voided document.

Inability to examine selected items. If for any reason—for example, the document cannot be located—he or she cannot examine a selected item, the auditor should consider this a deviation from prescribed policies or procedures. Also, the auditor should consider reasons for this deviation and the effect it has on his or her understanding and assessed level of control risk of particular control procedures.

Evaluating sample results. After he or she has completed the examination of the sample units and noted the deviation from prescribed policies or procedures, the auditor

1. Calculates the deviation rate.
2. Considers sampling risk.
3. Considers qualitative aspects of deviations.
4. Reaches a conclusion.

Calculation of deviation rate. The deviation rate is the number of observed deviations divided by the sample size. This is the auditor's best estimate of the deviation rate for the population from which the sample was selected. In statistics, it is called a point estimate.

Consideration of sampling risk. When he or she evaluates a sample for a test of controls, the auditor should consider sampling risk (see *Definitions*). For a nonstatistical sample, sampling risk cannot be quantified. Generally, however, sample results do not support assessed risk below the maximum if the actual deviation rate exceeds or is close to the expected population deviation rate used in designing the sample.

Qualitative aspects of deviations. The qualitative aspects of the observed deviations should be considered by the auditor. Each deviation from a prescribed policy procedure should be analyzed to determine its nature and cause. Deviations that occurred when the person responsible for performing the task was on vacation are not as serious as intentional failure to perform prescribed policies or procedures or misunderstood instructions of prescribed policies or procedures. The nature and cause of deviations may influence the auditor's decision to assess control risk below the maximum or perform additional audit procedures.

Reaching a conclusion. Based on the sample results and on his or her experience and judgment, the auditor reaches a conclusion about the level of control risk. If the auditor concludes that he or she cannot assess control risk below the maximum, he or she may

- Test additional items with the hope of reducing sampling risk.
- Modify planned substantive tests.

Documentation of Sampling Procedures

This section does not require specific documentation of audit sampling applications; however, the auditor might consider including the following in the audit documentation:

1. A description of the control tested.
2. Objectives of the sampling application, including its relationship to planned substantive testing.
3. Definitions of the population and the sampling unit.
4. Definition of a deviation.
5. Assessments of
    a. Risk of assessing control risk too low.
    b. Tolerable deviation rate.
    c. Expected population deviation rate.
6. Method of determining sample size.
7. Method of selecting sample.
8. Description of how sampling procedure was performed and a list of sample deviations.

9. Evaluation of sample and summary of conclusions, including
   a. Number of sample deviations.
   b. Explanation of how sampling risk was considered.
   c. Determination of whether sample results supported planned assessed level of control risk.
   d. Qualitative aspects of deviations.
   e. Effects of evaluation of results on planned substantive tests.

SUBSTANTIVE TESTS

In using nonstatistical sampling for substantive tests, the auditor should do the following:

1. Identify individually significant items.
2. Define the population.
3. Define the sample unit.
4. Determine the sample size.
5. Select the sample.
6. Evaluate the sample results (quantitatively and qualitatively).
7. Consider sampling risk.
8. Document the sampling procedures.

Identify Individually Significant Items

In using sampling for substantive tests, the auditor may decide that for certain items, accepting some sampling risk is not justified. For example, the auditor may decide to examine **all** items over a specified dollar amount. Items tested 100% are not part of the sample. Dividing a population into relatively homogeneous units is known as stratification. Excluding individually significant items provides an initial stratification. The auditor may further subdivide the remaining population, however, into subgroups of items with similar values.

Define the Population

The population consists of the class of transactions or the account balance to be tested. Because the auditor will project the results of the sample to the population, he or she must specify the population so that the sample units come from that population. For example, accounts receivable has four different populations.

1. All accounts.
2. Accounts with zero balances.
3. Accounts with debit balances.
4. Accounts with credit balances.

The audit objective determines which population is appropriate.

Define the Sample Unit

A sampling unit is any item in the population. For example, a sampling unit may be a customer account or an individual transaction.

Determine Sample Size

For nonstatistical sampling, sample size can be subjectively determined. Factors 1 to 4 should be considered and 5 might be considered.

1. Amounts of the individual items in the population.

2. Variability and size of the population.
3. Risk of incorrect acceptance.
4. Tolerable misstatement and expected misstatement.
5. Statistical table or formula.

Amounts of individual items. Accounting populations usually include a few very large amounts, a number of moderately large amounts, and a large number of small amounts. In these circumstances, if the population is not stratified, much larger sample sizes are necessary.

Variability and size of the population. Populations are characterized by some variability; that is, not every item in the population is the same amount. Statistically, this variation is measured by the standard deviation. The larger the variability of the population, the larger the standard deviation is. For nonstatistical sampling, the standard deviation is not quantified; it is estimated in qualitative terms, such as small variability or large variability. **The larger the estimated variability of the population, the larger the sample size required is.** To estimate variability, the auditor may use

- His or her judgment.
- Prior year results.
- A pilot sample.

The number of items in the population generally has little effect on the sample size for substantive tests; therefore, it is generally not efficient to determine sample size as a fixed percentage of the population.

Risk of incorrect acceptance. In determining sample size, the auditor should consider the risk of incorrect acceptance (an aspect of sampling risk). As the level of risk of incorrect acceptance increases, the sample size for the substantive test decreases. For example, a 10% level of risk of incorrect acceptance requires a smaller sample to achieve the same results than does a 5% level of risk. If he or she assessed control risk at lower than the maximum for a given assertion, the auditor can accept a larger risk of incorrect acceptance for the substantive test related to the assertion.

Tolerable misstatement and expected misstatement. For an account balance or a class of transactions, the sample size, given the risk of incorrect acceptance, increases as the tolerable misstatement for that balance or class of transactions decreases. As the size or frequency of expected misstatements decreases, the sample size also decreases.

Statistical table or formula. After he or she determines sample size for nonstatistical sampling, the auditor may wish to, but is not required to, compare it with the sample size from a statistical table or formula. The auditor may also use a statistical table or formula to determine sample size for a nonstatistical sample. The distinguishing feature of statistical sampling is mathematical evaluation of sample results using the laws of probability. Use of statistical methods for sample size determination and selection of sample items do not by themselves make the audit sample a statistical sample.

Select the Sample

The auditor should select the sample units by using any method that can be expected to result in a representative sample. For substantive tests of account balances, the auditor ordinarily stratifies the population before selecting the sample.

Evaluate Sample Results

The section requires the auditor to project the misstatement results of the sample to the population from which the sample was selected.

One method of projecting the misstatement is to divide the dollar amount of the misstatement in the sample by the percentage of the sample dollars to the total dollars in the population. For example, if the sample amounted to 5% of the population (in dollars), and if $1,000 of misstatement was observed in the sample, the misstatement projected to the population is $20,000 ($1,000 ÷ 5%). This is the best estimate of the misstatement in the population.

Another method of projecting the misstatement is to multiply the average unit misstatement in the sample by the number of units in the population. For example, if there were 200 units in the sample and $600 in misstatements was observed, the average misstatement in the sample is $3 ($600 ÷ 200). If there are 30,000 units in the population, the misstatement projected to the population is $90,000 (30,000 x $3).

Projected misstatement is the best estimate of the misstatement in the population. In statistics, it is called the point estimate.

Consider Sampling Risk

For nonstatistical sampling, the auditor uses his or her experience with the client and professional judgment when considering sampling risk. If the projected misstatement does not exceed expected misstatement, the auditor may reasonably conclude that there is an acceptably low risk that the true misstatement exceeds the tolerable misstatement. However, if the projected misstatement exceeds or approximates expected misstatement, the auditor may reasonably conclude that there is an unacceptably high risk that the true misstatement exceeds the tolerable misstatement.

If he or she believes the recorded amount may be misstated, the auditor ordinarily suggests that the entity investigate the misstatements and, if appropriate, adjust the recorded amount.

Document Sampling Procedures

This section does not require specific documentation of audit sampling applications; however, the auditor might consider including the following in the audit documentation:

1. Objectives of the test and a description of other procedures, if any, directed to these same objectives.
2. Definitions of the population and the sampling unit.
3. Definition of a misstatement.
4. Assessment of
    a. Risk of incorrect acceptance.
    b. Risk of incorrect rejection (solely a matter of **efficiency**).
    c. Tolerable misstatement.
    d. Expected population misstatement.
5. Sampling technique used.
6. Method of selecting sample.
7. Description of how sampling procedure was performed and a list of sample errors.
8. Evaluation of sample and summary of conclusions, including
    a. Projection of misstatements.
    b. Consideration of sampling risk.
    c. Qualitative aspects of the misstatements.

TECHNIQUES FOR APPLICATION: STATISTICAL AUDIT SAMPLING

INTRODUCTION

The following discussion was prepared by Neal Hitzig, CPA. Mr. Hitzig was a partner with Ernst & Young and is currently a professor of accounting at Fordham University. We are indebted to him for this contribution.

There are many valid ways of applying statistical sampling. The method described in this section is a highly efficient application.

Statistical samples can be designed to satisfy either or both of the following objectives:

1. **The detection objective.** The detection of a misstatement or deviation if it exists in the population at a specified rate or amount.
2. **The estimation objective.** The estimation of the extent of detected misstatements or deviations.

Random sampling enables the auditor to project sample results mathematically and to state, with measurable precision and confidence, the estimated rate of deviation in the population under audit (attribute sampling), or the estimated dollar amount of misstatement in the population (dollar value,[2] or variables, sampling).

CALCULATING SAMPLE SIZE

Given that the auditor is willing to accept some sampling risk, the most important risk to consider in the planning of a test procedure is the risk of incorrect acceptance (or risk of assessing control risk too low). In the simplified approach to be presented below, this risk, whether for substantive tests or tests of control, will be referred to as the detection risk. Detection risk is the chance that an audit sample will fail to disclose misstatement if the misstatement in the population exceeds the tolerable misstatement (or tolerable rate of deviation). The complement of the detection risk is the detection confidence. The sample size approach that controls the detection risk is known as a discovery sample size.

Discovery Sampling

A discovery sample is the smallest sample size that is capable of providing a specified chance (confidence) of detecting misstatement when the misstatement in the population exceeds tolerable misstatement. If a discovery sample is selected and discloses no misstatement, then the auditor can assert, with specified confidence, that the population misstatement does not exceed tolerable misstatement.

Discovery sampling is an efficient, yet powerful, approach in determining the extent of testing required to satisfy an audit test objective and is especially useful for testing populations that are nearly free of misstatement. If misstatements exist, they are likely to be detected. If misstatements are detected, the sample results can then be used to project the detected misstatements to the population from which the sample was selected.

Discovery sample sizes are easily calculated. For tests of controls, the sample size (n) is obtained by dividing the confidence factors (CF) by the tolerable deviation rate (TDR) or

$$n = \text{CF/TDR}$$

Confidence factors for discovery sample size follow.

Confidence level (%)	80.0	90.0	95.0	97.5	99.0	99.5
RISK (%) (1 – confidence level)	20.0	10.0	5.0	2.5	1.0	.5
Confidence factor (CF)	1.61	2.31	3.00	3.69	4.61	5.30

---

[2] *Dollar value sampling is also referred to as probability-proportional-to-size sampling.*

For substantive tests, the confidence factor is multiplied by the population book value (B) and divided by the tolerable misstatement amount (TMA), or

$$n = (\text{B x CF})/\text{TMA}$$

For example, assume that a population has a book value of $3,530,000. The auditor wishes to have an 80% chance of detecting misstatement in the sample if the amount of misstatement in the population exceeds $70,000. The discovery sample size is

$$\begin{aligned} n &= (3{,}530{,}000 \text{ x } 1.61)/70{,}000 \\ &= 82 \text{ items (rounded up)} \end{aligned}$$

Note that when the foregoing method is applied to samples selected with equal chance, it is assumed that misstatements tend to be randomly distributed throughout the population. If this is not likely to be the case, the auditor should consider stratifying the population so as to segregate those portions of the population that, in his or her judgment, are more likely to be prone to misstatement.

Sample Sizes When Deviations or Misstatements Are Expected

If a population is not expected to be nearly free of deviation or misstatement, a discovery sample size will often be too small to enable the auditor to conclude that the population deviation or misstatement is less than tolerable deviation or misstatement. In addition to the aforementioned factors, the auditor considers the expected deviation rate (EDR) when planning a test of controls or the expected misstatement amount (EMA) when planning a substantive test. For a test of controls, the sample size formula is

$$n = \left(\frac{\text{CF}}{\text{TDR} - \text{EDR}}\right)\left[1 + \left(\frac{\text{EDR}}{\text{TDR} - \text{EDR}}\right)\right]$$

For a substantive test using dollar unit sampling, or when sampling with equal chance for randomly distributed errors or overstatement

$$n = \left[\frac{(\text{B})(\text{CF})}{(\text{TMA} - \text{EMA})}\right]\left[1 + \left(\frac{\text{EMA}}{\text{TMA} - \text{EMA}}\right)\right]$$

The confidence factor is determined from the list of confidence factors given earlier. There is a tendency to understate somewhat the sample size for confidence levels of 97.5% or higher. This can be corrected by using the following factors:

Confidence level	Confidence factor
97.5	3.84
99.0	5.43
99.5	6.63

Suppose, in the previous example, the auditor expects as much as $20,000 of misstatement in the population, based on his or her previous experience. The sample size is

$$\begin{aligned} n &= \left[\frac{(3{,}530{,}000)(1.61)}{70{,}000 - 20{,}000}\right]\left[1 + \left(\frac{20{,}000}{70{,}000 - 20{,}000}\right)\right] \\ &= 160 \text{ items (rounded up)} \end{aligned}$$

Note that the foregoing formula applies only when EDR is less than TDR (or EMA is less than TMA). As a practical matter, the auditor should consider applying this formula only if EDR or EMA is no more than TDR/2 or TMA/2, respectively.

As the expected deviation or misstatement approaches or exceeds one-half the tolerable deviation or misstatement, it becomes increasingly difficult to establish, with a reasonable sample size, that the population deviation or misstatement does not exceed the specified tolerable level. Tests of controls may not be appropriate when numerous deviations are expected—the auditor may choose not to assess control risk lower than the maximum. Accordingly, the auditor may modify his or her substantive testing objective to obtaining an estimate of the dollar amount of misstatement in the population.

In this case, the auditor specifies the desired precision (P) for the estimate to be obtained. This is usually an amount between TMA/2 and TMA. The sample size formula is

$$n = \left(\frac{(B)(CF)}{P}\right)\left(1 + \frac{EMA}{P}\right)$$

For example, the expected misstatement in a $9,450,000 population may be as high as $600,000. The auditor wishes to obtain an estimate of the maximum amount of overstatement that could exist. The auditor's desired precision is $400,000. The confidence level is 97.5%. The sample size is

$$n = \left[\frac{(9{,}450{,}000)(3.84)}{400{,}000}\right]\left(1 + \frac{600{,}000}{400{,}000}\right)$$

$$= 227 \text{ items (rounded up)}$$

Other Methods for Calculating Sample Size

The preceding parts of this section describe the simplest methods for calculating sample sizes. The methods are well suited to testing controls and substantive tests for overstatement (such as tests of existence, collectibility, or lower of cost or market). Numerous other methods exist, particularly for substantive tests. (See *References* at end of this section.)

Risk and Confidence in Substantive Tests of Details

The **detection risk** (SAS 39 refers to it as the risk of incorrect acceptance) is the chance that the statistical sampling results will lead the auditor incorrectly to conclude that the misstatement in the population does not exceed the tolerable misstatement.

The complement of the detection risk is a one-sided confidence level that may be expressed in either of two ways: (1) the confidence that the magnitude of misstatement in the population is greater than zero; or (2) the confidence that the magnitude of misstatement in the population is less than the tolerable misstatement.

The audit test risk is associated with the detection objective. When planning a test it is specified by the auditor.

The **estimation risk** (SAS 39 refers to it as the risk of incorrect rejection) is the chance that the calculated confidence interval does not include the true value of the population. This confidence interval is two-sided because it makes simultaneous use of two confidence limits, an upper misstatement limit and a lower misstatement limit.

The simultaneous use of two confidence limits is associated with the estimation objective. When planning to achieve the estimation objective, the auditor specifies a two-sided confidence level that will achieve the auditor-specified precision. When evaluating the results of a sample, the auditor calculates the precision (and confidence limits) associated with the specified confidence level.

The following list gives the relationship between a one-sided confidence level and a two-sided confidence level:

One-sided confidence level (%)	*Two-sided confidence level (%)*
99.5	99.0
99.0	98.0
97.5	95.0
95.0	90.0
90.0	80.0
80.0	60.0
75.0	50.0

STATISTICAL EVALUATION OF A SAMPLE IN SUBSTANTIVE TESTS OF DETAILS

The auditor can evaluate a statistical sample by calculating a **point estimate** and a **confidence interval** around the point estimate at the specified **confidence level**. The point estimate is the projection of the detected misstatements to the population from which the sample was selected. The confidence interval and the confidence level are related measurements. The confidence level is the chance that a confidence interval that is calculated as a result of a random sample will include the actual misstatement within its limits. The width of this interval indicates the amount of precision that the auditor has achieved with the estimate. The two end points of the confidence interval are called the upper and lower confidence limits (UCL and LCL, respectively).

The confidence interval for a specified confidence level can be expressed in three ways.

1. The population misstatement is not more than the UCL (a one-sided confidence limit).
2. The population misstatement is not less than the LCL (a one-sided confidence limit).
3. The population misstatement is included between the LCL and the UCL (two-sided confidence limits).

For example, suppose the evaluation is as follows:

Two-sided confidence: 90%

$LCL	=	$ 5,000 of overstatement error
$UCL	=	$15,000 of overstatement error

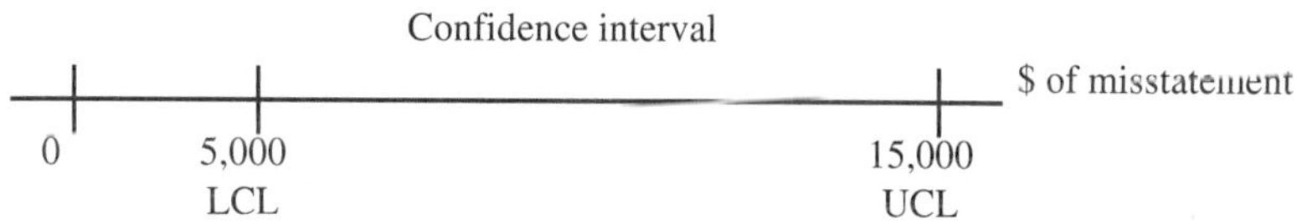

The auditor could conclude, with 90% confidence (two-sided), that the misstatement in the population is $5,000 – $15,000 of overstatement. The auditor could, alternatively, conclude, with 95% confidence, that the misstatement was no less than $5,000 of overstatement, or that the misstatement was no more than $15,000 of overstatement. If the tolerable misstatement is $10,000, the auditor concludes that the population is overstated (because the lower confidence limit is greater than $0) and that the misstatement may exceed the tolerable misstatement (because the upper confidence limit is greater than the tolerable misstatement). Only if the upper confidence limit were less than $10,000 would the auditor be able to conclude that any existing misstatement was not likely to exceed the tolerable misstatement.

The complement of confidence is risk. In statistical sampling there are two aspects of risk: detection risk, which is associated with the detection objective; and estimation risk, which is associated with the estimation objective. Both aspects and their related confidence levels are discussed in the following sections.

CALCULATING CONFIDENCE LIMITS

The calculations for a point estimate and confidence limits depend on the method by which the sample was selected and on certain data assumptions—for example, the assumption that an item cannot be overstated by more than its recorded value. A variety of evaluation methods are given in Arkin's *Handbook*.

Three basic methods for evaluating statistical samples are presented. The methods presented do not cover all situations, but they provide the auditor with the means to evaluate samples on an attributes basis for tests of controls and on a dollar-value basis for substantive tests for overstatement.

Equal-Probability Sampling: Attributes Evaluation

Point Estimate

The point estimate of the rate of deviation in the population (D) is obtained by dividing the number of deviations (m) that occurred in the sample by the sample size (n). The formula is

$$D\% = (100)\,(m/n)$$

For example, if 3 deviations are disclosed in a sample of 150 items, the point estimate is

$$\begin{aligned} D\% &= (100)\,(3/150) \\ &= 2.0\% \end{aligned}$$

Confidence Limits

The upper confidence limit (UCL%) of the rate of deviation in the population is obtained by dividing the upper confidence limit factor (ULF) in Table 1 by the sample size (n). The formula is

$$\text{UCL\%} = (100)\,(\text{ULF}/n)$$

The appropriate row in Table 1 is determined by the number of deviations in the sample. The appropriate column is determined by the auditor's specified confidence level, which, in Table 1, is given as a one-sided confidence level.

A lower confidence limit is obtained in the same manner, except that Table 2 is used to obtain the lower limit factor (LLF). The formula is

$$\text{LCL\%} = (100)\,(\text{LLF}/n)$$

For example, to obtain an upper 95% confidence limit for a sample of 150 that disclosed three deviations, first obtain the upper limit factor from Table 1 (ULF = 7.76). The upper limit is

$$\begin{aligned} \text{UCL\%} &= (100)\,(7.76/150) \\ &= 5.17\% \end{aligned}$$

Thus, the auditor can be 95% confident that the population deviation rate does not exceed 5.17%.

To obtain a lower 95% confidence limit for the same sample outcome, obtain the lower limit factor from Table 2 (LLF = 0.81). The lower limit is

$$\begin{aligned} \text{LCL\%} &= (100)\,(.81/150) \\ &= .54\% \end{aligned}$$

Thus, the auditor can also be 95% confident that the population deviation rate is at least .54%.

If the auditor wishes to express the sample results on a two-sided basis, he or she would be 90% confident that the population deviation rate is between .54% and 5.17%. (See the list given earlier for the relationship between one-sided and two-sided confidence levels.)

Dollar Value Evaluation

The following procedures are applicable to the most common type of substantive tests of details—the test for overstatement in an account balance or class of transactions. They may be used (1) for tests of the existence assertion, such as in the confirmation of receivables, (2) for tests of the valuation assertion, such as collectibility, lower of cost or market, or obsolescence, or (3) for tests of the classification assertion. The following conditions should apply to the population:

1. The population does not consist of commingled debit-balance, or credit-balance, and zero-balance items. For example, if the auditor is testing an asset account, the population should consist only of debit-balance items.
2. The maximum amount by which an item may be overstated is its recorded value.

It should be noted that these data conditions are not unduly restrictive and are appropriate for testing the aforementioned financial statement assertions.

EQUAL-PROBABILITY SAMPLING: VARIABLES EVALUATION

Point Estimate

The point estimate of the amount of misstatement in the population ($M_\$$) is determined by (1) calculating the ratio (R) of the total overstatement misstatement in the sample (Σm) to the total book value of the sample (Σb), and (2) multiplying the ratio by the total book value (B) of the population from which the sample was selected. The formula is

$$\begin{aligned} M_\$ &= (B)(R) \\ &= (B)(\Sigma m/\Sigma b) \end{aligned}$$

For example, 3 misstatements are disclosed in a sample of 150 items.
The total misstatement in the 3 items is $225.
The total book value of the 150 items is $15,300.
The total book value of the population is $1,492,000.
The misstatement ratio R is

$$\begin{aligned} R &= 225/15{,}300 \\ &= .0147 \end{aligned}$$

The point estimate of the total misstatement in the population is

$$\begin{aligned} M_\$ &= 1{,}492{,}000 \times .0147 \\ &= \$21{,}932 \end{aligned}$$

Confidence Limits

The upper confidence limit ($UCL_\$$) of the amount of overstatement misstatement in the population is obtained by dividing the upper confidence limit factor (ULF) in Table 1 by the sample size (n) and multiplying the result by the population book value (B). The formula is

$$UCL_\$ = (B)(ULF/n)$$

The appropriate row in Table 1 depends on the sample total equivalent misstatement (m'), which is obtained by multiplying the misstatement ratio (R) by the sample size (n). The formula is

$$m' = (n)(R)$$

In the example the total equivalent misstatement is

$$\begin{aligned} m' &= (150)(.0147) \\ &= 2.21 \end{aligned}$$

Locate the upper limit factor in the column of Table 1 that is headed by the desired one-sided confidence level. Note that it may be necessary to interpolate between two successive values of TEM. In the example, the 95% confidence ULF is 6.30 for m equal to 2. The ULF is 7.76 for m equal to 3. Thus, the appropriate ULF, obtained by linear interpolation, is 6.61. The calculation is

$$\begin{aligned} ULF &= 6.30 + (.21)(7.76 - 6.30) \\ &= 6.61 \text{ (rounded off)} \end{aligned}$$

The upper 95% confidence limit of the amount of misstatement in the population is

$$\begin{aligned} UCL_\$ &= (1{,}492{,}000)(6.61/150) \\ &= \$65{,}700 \text{ (rounded off)} \end{aligned}$$

The lower confidence limit is calculated using the sample procedure, except that the lower confidence limit factor is obtained from Table 2. The formula is

$$LCL_{\$} = (B)\,(LLF/n)$$

Table 1. Upper Limit Factors, *m* Deviations or Misstatements in Sample (*m´* Equivalent Deviations of Misstatements)

Deviations or Misstatements in Sample (*m*)	Confidence (One-sided)						
	99.5	99.0	97.5	95.0	90.0	80.0	75.0
0	5.30	4.61	3.69	3.00	2.31	1.61	1.39
1	7.43	6.64	5.58	4.75	3.89	3.00	2.70
2	9.28	8.41	7.23	6.30	5.33	4.28	3.93
3	10.98	10.05	8.77	7.76	6.69	5.52	5.11
4	12.60	11.61	10.25	9.16	8.00	6.73	6.28
5	14.15	13.11	11.67	10.52	9.28	7.91	7.43
6	15.66	14.58	13.06	11.85	10.54	9.08	8.56
7	17.14	16.00	14.43	13.15	11.78	10.24	9.69
8	18.58	17.41	15.77	14.44	13.00	11.38	10.81
9	20.00	18.79	17.09	15.71	14.21	12.52	11.92
10	21.40	20.15	18.40	16.97	15.41	13.66	13.02
11	22.78	21.50	19.69	18.21	16.60	14.78	14.13
12	24.15	22.83	20.97	19.45	17.79	15.90	15.22
13	25.50	24.14	22.24	20.67	18.96	17.02	16.32
14	26.84	25.45	23.49	21.89	20.13	18.13	17.40
15	28.17	26.75	24.75	23.10	21.30	19.24	18.49
16	29.49	28.04	25.99	24.31	22.46	20.34	19.58
17	30.80	29.31	27.22	25.50	23.61	21.44	20.66
18	32.10	30.59	28.45	26.70	24.76	22.54	21.74
19	33.39	31.85	29.68	27.88	25.91	23.64	22.81
20	34.67	33.11	30.89	29.07	27.05	24.73	23.89
21	35.95	34.36	32.11	30.25	28.19	25.82	24.96
22	37.22	35.61	33.31	31.42	29.33	26.91	26.03
23	38.49	36.85	34.52	32.59	30.46	28.00	27.10
24	39.75	38.08	35.72	33.76	31.59	29.09	28.17
25	41.01	39.31	36.91	34.92	32.72	30.17	29.24
26	42.26	40.54	38.10	36.08	33.84	31.25	30.31
27	43.50	41.76	39.29	37.24	34.96	32.33	31.37
28	44.74	42.98	40.47	38.39	36.08	33.41	32.43
29	45.98	44.19	41.65	39.55	37.20	34.49	33.50
30	47.21	45.41	42.83	40.70	38.32	35.57	34.56
31	48.44	46.61	44.01	41.84	39.43	36.64	35.62
32	49.67	47.82	45.18	42.99	40.55	37.72	36.68
33	50.89	49.02	46.35	44.13	41.66	38.79	37.74
34	52.11	50.22	47.52	45.27	42.77	39.86	38.79
35	53.33	51.41	48.68	46.41	43.88	40.93	39.85
36	54.54	52.61	49.84	47.55	44.98	42.00	40.91
37	55.75	53.80	51.00	48.68	46.09	43.07	41.96
38	56.96	54.98	52.16	49.81	47.19	44.14	43.02
39	58.17	56.17	53.32	50.94	48.29	45.21	44.07
40	59.37	57.35	54.47	52.07	49.39	46.27	45.12
41	60.57	58.53	55.63	53.20	50.49	47.34	46.18
42	61.77	59.71	56.78	54.33	51.59	48.40	47.23
43	62.96	60.89	57.93	55.45	52.69	49.47	48.28
44	64.15	62.06	59.07	56.58	53.79	50.53	49.33
45	65.35	63.24	60.22	57.70	54.88	51.59	50.38
46	66.53	64.41	61.36	58.82	55.98	52.66	51.43
47	67.72	65.58	62.51	59.94	57.07	53.72	52.48
48	68.91	66.74	63.65	61.08	58.16	54.78	53.53
49	70.09	67.91	64.79	62.18	59.25	55.84	54.58
50	71.27	69.07	65.92	63.29	60.34	56.90	55.62

Table 2. Lower Limit Factors, *m* Deviations or Misstatements in Sample (*m´* Equivalent Deviations of Misstatements)

Deviations or Misstatements in Sample (m)	Confidence (One-sided)						
	99.5	99.0	97.5	95.0	90.0	80.0	75.0
0	0.	0.	0.	0.	0.	0.	0.
1	.01	.01	.03	.05	.11	.22	.29
2	.10	.14	.24	.35	.53	.82	.96
3	.33	.43	.61	.81	1.10	1.53	1.72
4	.67	.82	1.08	1.36	1.74	2.29	2.53
5	1.07	1.27	1.62	1.97	2.43	3.08	3.36
6	1.53	1.78	2.20	2.61	3.15	3.90	4.21
7	2.03	2.33	2.81	3.28	3.89	4.73	5.08
8	2.57	2.90	3.45	3.98	4.65	5.57	5.95
9	3.13	3.50	4.11	4.69	5.43	6.42	6.83
10	3.71	4.13	4.79	5.42	6.22	7.28	7.72
11	4.32	4.77	5.49	6.16	7.02	8.15	8.61
12	4.94	5.42	6.20	6.92	7.82	9.03	9.51
13	5.58	6.09	6.92	7.68	8.64	9.91	10.42
14	6.23	6.78	7.65	8.46	9.46	10.79	11.32
15	6.89	7.47	8.39	9.24	10.29	11.68	12.23
16	7.56	8.18	9.14	10.03	11.13	12.57	13.15
17	8.25	8.89	9.90	10.83	11.97	13.46	14.06
18	8.94	9.61	10.66	11.63	12.82	14.36	14.98
19	9.64	10.34	11.43	12.44	13.67	15.26	15.90
20	10.35	11.08	12.21	13.25	14.52	16.17	16.83
21	11.06	11.82	12.99	14.07	15.38	17.07	17.75
22	11.79	12.57	13.78	14.89	16.24	17.98	18.68
23	12.52	13.32	14.58	15.71	17.10	18.89	19.60
24	13.25	14.08	15.37	16.54	17.97	19.81	20.53
25	13.99	14.85	16.17	17.38	18.84	20.72	21.47
26	14.74	15.62	16.98	18.21	19.71	21.64	22.40
27	15.49	16.39	17.79	19.05	20.59	22.55	23.33
28	16.24	17.17	18.60	19.90	21.46	23.47	24.27
29	17.00	17.95	19.42	20.74	22.34	24.39	25.20
30	17.76	18.74	20.24	21.59	23.22	25.32	26.14
31	18.53	19.53	21.06	22.44	24.11	26.24	27.08
32	19.30	20.32	21.88	23.29	24.99	27.16	28.02
33	20.07	21.12	22.71	24.15	25.88	28.09	28.96
34	20.85	21.91	23.54	25.01	26.77	29.02	29.90
35	21.63	22.72	24.37	25.86	27.66	29.94	30.84
36	22.42	23.52	25.21	26.73	28.55	30.87	31.79
37	23.20	24.33	26.05	27.59	29.44	31.80	32.73
38	23.99	25.14	26.89	28.45	30.34	32.73	33.68
39	24.79	25.95	27.73	29.32	31.24	33.67	34.62
40	25.58	26.77	28.57	30.19	32.13	34.60	35.57
41	26.38	27.58	29.42	31.06	33.03	35.53	36.51
42	27.18	28.40	30.26	31.93	33.93	36.47	37.46
43	27.98	29.22	31.11	32.81	34.83	37.40	38.41
44	28.79	30.05	31.97	33.68	35.74	38.34	39.36
45	29.59	30.87	32.82	34.56	36.64	39.27	40.31
46	30.40	31.70	33.87	35.44	37.55	40.21	41.28
47	31.21	32.53	34.53	36.31	38.45	41.15	42.21
48	32.03	33.38	35.39	37.20	39.36	42.09	43.16
49	32.84	34.19	36.25	38.08	40.27	43.03	44.11
50	33.86	35.03	37.11	38.96	41.17	43.97	45.06

In the example, the 95% confidence LLF, obtained by interpolation, is .45. Thus, the lower confidence limit is

$$LCL_{\$} = (1{,}492{,}000)\,(.45/150)$$
$$\$4{,}500 \text{ (rounded off)}$$

Thus, the auditor can be 95% confident that the total misstatement in the population is no more than $65,700. The auditor can also be 95% confident that the total misstatement is at least \$4,500. Furthermore, the auditor can be 90% confident that the total misstatement is between \$4,500 and \$65,700. (See the earlier list for the relationship between one-sided and two-sided confidence levels.)

It should be noted that to apply the foregoing procedure, the total book value of the population (B) must be known to be accurately footed, because both the estimate and the confidence limits are obtained directly from this number.

Other procedures for calculating confidence limits for dollar value estimates, including those that handle understated items, are given in Arkin's *Handbook*.

Point Estimate

The point estimate of the amount ($M_\$$) of overstatement misstatement in the population is obtained by multiplying the population book value (B) by the average item misstatement ratio ($\bar{r}$). The misstatement ratio (r) for a sample item is obtained by dividing the amount of misstatement (m) in the item by the item's book value (b). Thus,

$$r = m/b$$

for each item in the sample. Note that r will be zero for most of the sample items in a typical audit application. This greatly simplifies the calculation of the average ratio $\bar{r}$. The formula for the average misstatement ratio is

$$\bar{r} = (\Sigma r)/n$$

or the total equivalent misstatement (m'), which is the sum of the item ratios divided by the sample size. The formula for the point estimate of the population misstatement amount is

$$M_\$ = (B)(\bar{r})$$

Suppose the data of the previous example were obtained for a sample that was selected with probability proportional to size (that is, dollar unit sampling), instead of equal-probability sampling. The sample data follow:

Population book value (B): \$1,492,000
Sample size: 150 items

	Item	Book value (b)	Misstatement amount (m)	Misstatement ratio (r)	
	1	183	37	.20	
	2	452	185	.41	
	3	3	3	1.00	
	4	95	0	.00	
	--	--	--	--	
	--	--	--	--	
	--	--	--	--	
n =	150	214	0	0.00	
		\$15,300	\$225	1.61	= m'

The average misstatement ratio is

$$\bar{r} = 1.61/150$$
$$= .011$$

The point estimate of population misstatement is

$$M_\$ = 1{,}492{,}000 \times .011$$
$$= \$16{,}412$$

Confidence Limits

The upper confidence limit ($UCL_\$$) of the amount of overstatement misstatement in the population is obtained by dividing the upper confidence limit factor (ULF) in Table 1 by the sample size (n), and multiplying the result by the population book value (B). The formula is

$$UCL_\$ = (B)(ULF/n)$$

For any specified confidence level the ULF is determined by the total equivalent misstatement (m'), which, in dollar unit sampling, is the sum of the sample item misstatement ratios ($\sum r$). The formula is

$$m' = \sum r$$

If the calculated m' is between two successive values of m in Table 1, the auditor can determine the ULF by interpolation. In the example, m' is calculated to be 1.61 equivalent misstatements. The 95% confidence factors for 1 and 2 misstatements are 4.75 and 6.30, respectively. Thus, the interpolated confidence factor for $m' = 1.61$ is

$$\begin{aligned} \text{ULF} &= 4.75 + (.61)(6.30 - 4.75) \\ &= 5.70 \text{ (rounded off)} \end{aligned}$$

Thus, the upper 95% confidence limit is

$$\begin{aligned} \text{UCL}_{\$} &= (1{,}492{,}000)(5.70/150) \\ &= \$56{,}700 \text{ (rounded off)} \end{aligned}$$

The lower confidence limit is calculated in the same manner, except that the lower limit factor is obtained by interpolating between successive values of LLF in Table 2. Thus,

$$\text{LCL}_{\$} = (B)(\text{LLF}/n)$$

In the example, the lower 95% confidence factor is

$$\begin{aligned} \text{LLF} &= .05 + (.61)(.35 - .05) \\ &= .23 \text{ (rounded off)} \end{aligned}$$

The lower confidence limit is

$$\begin{aligned} \text{LCL}_{\$} &= (1{,}492{,}000)(.23/150) \\ &= \$2{,}300 \text{ (rounded off)} \end{aligned}$$

The auditor can state, with 95% confidence, that the population overstatement does not exceed \$56,700. The auditor can also state, with 95% confidence, that the misstatement is at least \$2,300. Moreover, the auditor can be 90% confident that the actual population overstatement misstatement is between \$2,300 and \$56,700. (See the earlier list for the relationship between one-sided and two-sided confidence levels.)

REFERENCES

An auditor who uses statistical sampling is well-advised to refer to the *Practitioner's Guide to Audit Sampling*, (New York: John Wiley & Sons, 1998) by Dan M. Guy, D. R. Carmichael, and R. Whittington.

The following books may also be helpful. They are no longer in print, but may be available at a college or university business library.

1. Herbert Arkin, *Handbook of Sampling for Auditing and Accounting* (New York: McGraw-Hill, 1974).
2. Herbert Arkin, *Sampling Methods for the Auditor* (New York: McGraw-Hill, 1982).
3. Donald H. Roberts, *Statistical Auditing* (New York: AICPA, 1978).

380 COMMUNICATION WITH AUDIT COMMITTEES[1]

EFFECTIVE DATE AND APPLICABILITY

Original Pronouncement	SAS 61, April 1988; SAS 89, December 1999; and SAS 90, December 1999.[2]
Effective Date	Audits of financial statements for periods beginning on or after January 1, 1989; revised to reflect SAS 89, effective for audits of financial statements for periods beginning on or after December 15, 1999; and SAS 90, effective for audits of financial statement for periods ending on or after December 15, 2000.

---

[1] *The Auditing Standards Board (ASB) has issued an Exposure Draft of a proposed SAS that would affect this section,* ***Sarbanes-Oxley Omnibus SAS****. The proposed amendment to this section would, among other things, require that the auditor report to the audit committee information about all of the entity's critical accounting policies and practices and all alternative treatments within GAAP for accounting policies and practices related to material items. The Public Company Accounting Oversight Board (PCAOB) has replaced the ASB as the standards-setting authority for public company audits. Therefore, the ASB's Exposure Draft will not be issued as a final standard by the AICPA. The document will, however, be considered by the PCAOB in developing a standard or amendments to an existing standard to comply with the Sarbanes-Oxley Act of 2002 and the related SEC implementing rules.*

Section 204, "Auditor Reports to Audit Committees" and the related SEC implementing rule 33-8138, "Strengthening the Commission's Requirements Regarding Auditor Independence," requires that the auditor communicate:

1. *All critical accounting policies and practices.*
2. *All alternative accounting and disclosure treatments of material financial information that has been discussed with management, including the ramifications of the use of such alternative treatments and disclosures and the treatment preferred by the auditor.*

The SEC's Financial Reporting Release 60, "Cautionary Advice Regarding Disclosure about Critical Accounting Policies," defines "critical accounting policies" as those policies that are both most important to the company in portraying the company's financial position and results, and that require management's most difficult, subjective, or complex judgments, often as a result of the need to make estimates about highly uncertain matters.

Please check for updates to this section on the John Wiley & Sons, Inc. website at www.wiley.com/gaas.

[2] *See also the requirement at Section 328, "Auditing Fair Value Measurements and Disclosures", to determine that certain information about fair values is communicated to audit committees.*

Applicability

Audits of financial statements in accordance with generally accepted auditing standards of entities who have an audit committee (or other committee formally designated with oversight for financial reporting) and all public entities (i.e., SEC engagements—see *Definitions of Terms*).

DEFINITIONS OF TERMS

Audit adjustment. An audit adjustment, **whether or not recorded by the entity,** is a proposed correction of the financial statements that, in the auditor's judgment, may not have been detected except through auditing procedures performed.

NOTE: The auditor cannot redefine an amount that is not supported sufficiently by audit evidence as something other than an audit adjustment by failing to propose corrections of the financial statements.

Securities and Exchange Commission (SEC) engagements. An SEC engagement, for purposes of this Statement, is defined as one that involves the audit of the financial statements of

1. An issuer making an initial filing, including amendments, under the Securities Act of 1933 and the Securities Exchange Act of 1934.
2. A registrant that files periodic reports with the SEC under the Investment Company Act of 1940 or the Securities Exchange Act of 1934, except a broker or dealer registered only because of Section 15(a) of the 1934 Act.
3. A bank or other lending institution that files periodic reports with the Comptroller of Currency, the Federal Reserve System, the Federal Deposit Insurance Corporation, or the Federal Home Loan Bank Board.

   NOTE: The following companies are excluded: (1) those with less than $5 million in total assets on the last day of each of the company's three most recent fiscal years and fewer than 500 shareholders and (2) those with fewer than 300 shareholders.
4. A company whose financial statements appear in the annual report or proxy statements of any investment fund because it is a sponsor or manager of such a fund, but which is not by itself a registrant required to file periodic reports under the Investment Company Act of 1940 or Section 13 or 15(d) of the Securities Exchange Act of 1934.

OBJECTIVES OF SECTION

During audits of financial statements, auditors obtain information that may be useful for audit committees. In the past, while some of the information may have been passed on to appropriate parties, communication of all information was not required and ordinarily was informal. Communication of information is currently required by the following pronouncements:

1. SAS 71 (Section 722)—*Interim Financial Information.*
2. SAS 82 (Section 316A)—*Consideration of Fraud in a Financial Statement Audit.*
3. SAS 54 (Section 317)—*Illegal Acts by Clients.*
4. SAS 70 (Section 324)—*Service Organizations.*
5. SAS 60 (Section 325)—*Communication of Internal Control Related Matters Noted in an Audit.*
6. SAS 74 (Section 801)—*Compliance Auditing Considerations in Audits of Governmental Entities and Recipients of Governmental Financial Assistance.*
7. SAS 99 (Section 316)—*Consideration of Fraud in a Financial Statement Audit.*
8. SAS 101 (Section 328)—*Auditing Fair Value Measurements and Disclosures.*

In addition to the above requirements, Section 311, "Planning and Supervision," indicates that the auditor may consider discussing the type, scope, and timing of the audit with the audit committee.

This section does not modify the requirements of the standards listed above.

NOTE: The Independence Standards Board (ISB) issued Independence Standard 1, ***Independence Discussions with Audit Committee,*** *in January 1999, effective for audits of companies (governed by the Securities Acts administered by the SEC) with fiscal years ending after July 15, 1999.*[3] *ISB 1 requires the auditor to*

1. *Disclose in writing to the audit committee (or board of directors) all relationships between the auditor (and related entities) and the company (and related entities) that* ***in the auditor's judgment*** *may reasonably bear on independence.*
2. *Confirm in the letter in 1. above that he or she is independent of the company within the meaning of the Securities Acts.*
3. *Discuss independence with the audit committee.*

The objective of this section is to increase the flow of useful information from auditors to those who have responsibility for oversight of the financial reporting process. The communications are required in the following types of engagements:

1. Entities that either have an audit committee or that have otherwise formally designated oversight of the financial reporting process to a group equivalent to an audit committee, such as a finance committee or a budget committee. (For purposes of this section the recipient of the required communications is referred to as the **audit committee**.)
2. All Securities and Exchange Commission (SEC) engagements—see *Definitions of Terms.*

SAS 89, *Audit Adjustments*, amended SAS 61 to require the auditor to communicate uncorrected misstatements to the audit committee even if not believed to be material by management or the auditor. SAS 90, *Audit Committee Communications,* amended SAS 61 to require an auditor of an SEC client to discuss the quality of accounting principles with the audit committee. The Blue Ribbon Committee on Improving the Effectiveness of Corporate Audit Committees (formed by the New York Stock Exchange and the National Association of Securities Dealers) suggested that the discussion about the quality of accounting principles be required.

The section establishes a requirement for the auditor to **determine** that certain matters related to the conduct of an audit are communicated to the audit committee. Some of these matters should be communicated by the auditor; others may be communicated by management.

FUNDAMENTAL REQUIREMENTS

GENERAL RESPONSIBILITY

The auditor **should ensure** that the audit committee receives information regarding the scope and results of the audit. Some of this information should be communicated by the auditor; some may be communicated by management. The auditor is not required to repeat information that management has communicated; however, he or she is not precluded from communicating the information to management or others within the entity.

---

[3] *The ISB was dissolved on July 31, 2001. However, ISB 1 continues in effect.*

METHOD OF COMMUNICATION

The communication may be either oral or written.

1. If it is oral, the auditor should document the communication (see *Techniques for Application*).
2. If it is written, the communication should indicate that it is intended solely for the use of the audit committee or the board of directors and, if appropriate, management.

TIMING OF COMMUNICATION

The communications are not required to be made before issuance of the auditor's report on the entity's financial statements. Some information may, however, need to be communicated to and discussed with the audit committee before the auditor's report is issued.[4]

AUDITOR'S LEVEL OF RESPONSIBILITY

The auditor **should communicate** to the audit committee the level of responsibility assumed under generally accepted auditing standards for internal control and the financial statements. The auditor should explain to the audit committee the concepts of materiality, audit tests and reasonable, as opposed to absolute, assurance.

SIGNIFICANT ACCOUNTING POLICIES

The auditor **should determine** that the audit committee is informed about the initial selection of, and changes in, significant accounting policies or their application. (AU 380.07)

SIGNIFICANT UNUSUAL TRANSACTIONS

The auditor **should determine** that the audit committee is informed about the methods used to account for significant unusual transactions. The audit committee also should be informed of the effect and implications of existing accounting policies in controversial or emerging accounting areas, such as revenue recognition, off-balance-sheet financing, and accounting for equity investments.

ACCOUNTING ESTIMATES

The auditor **should determine** that the audit committee is informed about (1) the process used by management in formulating particularly sensitive accounting estimates, and (2) the basis for the auditor's conclusions about the reasonableness of those estimates.

AUDIT ADJUSTMENTS

The auditor **should inform** the audit committee about audit adjustments—both those recorded by the entity and those not recorded by the entity—arising from the audit that could, in his or her judgment, either individually or in the aggregate, have a significant effect on the financial reporting process.

---

[4] *Section 204, "Auditor Reports to Audit Committees," of the Sarbanes-Oxley Act, and the related SEC implementing rule which apply beginning on or after May 6, 2003, require that certain communications occur prior to the filing of the issuer's annual report. In addition, the communications are required to occur prior to filing registration statements and other current filings when audit reports are included in those filings.*

The auditor also **should inform** the audit committee about uncorrected misstatements aggregated by the auditor that pertain to the latest period presented and were determined by management to be immaterial.

NOTE: The auditor's summary of uncorrected misstatements is usually included in or attached to the management representation letter (see Section 333). The summary presented to the audit committee should be the same as, or similar to, the summary presented to management.

OTHER INFORMATION

The auditor **should discuss** with the audit committee his or her responsibility for other information, including "Management's Discussions and Analysis of Financial Condition and Results of Operations," in documents containing audited financial statements, any procedures performed, and the results.

AUDITOR'S JUDGMENTS ABOUT THE QUALITY OF THE ENTITY'S ACCOUNTING PRINCIPLES

The auditor **should discuss** his or her judgments about the quality, not just the acceptability, of the company's accounting principles with the audit committees of SEC clients. Such discussion should include management as a participant and should include

- Matters such as the consistency of application of the entity's accounting policies and the clarity and completeness of the entity's financial statements and related disclosures
- Certain items that have a significant impact on the representational faithfulness,[5] verifiability,[6] neutrality,[7] and consistency of the accounting information included in the financial statements, such as
  - New or changed accounting policies
  - Estimates, judgments, and uncertainties
  - Unusual transactions
  - Accounting policies for significant financial statement items, including the timing of transactions and the period recorded

NOTE: The auditor may wish to review the audit committee's minutes to determine if the minutes are consistent with what he or she communicated.

DISAGREEMENTS WITH MANAGEMENT

The auditor **should discuss** with the audit committee any disagreements with management (as management is defined in Statement of Financial Accounting Standards 57, see Section 334) whether or not resolved, about matters that individually or in the aggregate could be significant to the entity's financial statements or the auditor's report. (AU 380.13) Disagreements may arise over (1) the application of accounting principles, (2) scope of audit, (3) financial statements disclosures, and (4) wording of the auditor's report.

NOTE: Disagreements do not include differences of opinion based on incomplete or preliminary information that is resolved.

---

[5] *Representational faithfulness means that the amounts and disclosures in the company's financial statements represent what really happened. It includes the concept of substance over form.*

[6] *Verifiability means that accountants using the same measurement method would obtain similar results.*

[7] *Neutrality means that information in financial statements cannot be selected to favor one set of financial statement users over another.*

CONSULTATION WITH OTHER ACCOUNTANTS (SECOND OPINIONS)

If management consults with other accountants about auditing and accounting matters, the auditor **should discuss** with the audit committee his or her views about significant matters that were the subject of the consultations (see also Section 625).

ISSUES DISCUSSED PRIOR TO RETENTION

The auditor **should discuss** with the audit committee any major issues that were discussed with management in connection with the initial or recurring retention of the auditor. Issues include, among other matters, any discussions regarding the application of accounting principles and auditing standards.

DIFFICULTIES ENCOUNTERED DURING AUDIT

The auditor **should inform** the audit committee of any significant difficulties encountered in dealing with management related to the performance of the audit. (AU 380.16) Difficulties include, among others (1) unreasonable delays by management in permitting the commencement of the audit or in providing needed information, (2) whether the timetable set by management was unreasonable under the circumstances, (3) unavailability of client personnel, and (4) failure of client personnel to complete client-prepared schedules on a timely basis.

RECURRING MATTERS

Generally, it is not necessary to repeat the communication of recurring matters each year. Periodically, however, the auditors **should consider,** because of the passage of time or changes in the members of the audit committee, the appropriateness of communicating these matters.

INTERPRETATIONS

APPLICABILITY OF SECTION 380 (AUGUST 1993)

If a non-SEC client has no designated group equivalent to an audit committee with formal responsibility for the financial reporting process, the auditor is not required to communicate the matters required by this section, but may elect to make the communications.

PROFESSIONAL ISSUES TASK FORCE PRACTICE ALERTS

99-1 GUIDANCE FOR INDEPENDENCE DISCUSSIONS WITH AUDIT COMMITTEES

Independence Standard 1, *Independence Discussions with Audit Committees* (the Standard),[8] requires annual written and oral communications between the auditor and the audit committee (or board of directors if there is no audit committee) of a public company client regarding relationships that, in the auditor's professional judgment, may reasonably be thought to bear on the independence. The standard also requires written confirmation that the auditor is independent of the company within the meaning of the Securities Acts administered by the SEC.

The Report and Recommendations of the Blue Ribbon Committee on Improving Effectiveness of Corporate Audit Committees (the Blue Ribbon Committee Report), issued in Feb-

---

[8] *The Independence Standards Board, which adopted this statement, was dissolved on July 31, 2001. However, ISB1 will continue in effect.*

ruary 1999, included a recommendation that the listing rules for both the New York Stock Exchange and the National Association of Securities Dealers require audit committee charters to specify that the audit committee is responsible for ensuring receipt of the communication required by this standard, and that the audit committee is responsible for discussing with the auditors any relationships or services that may impact the objectivity and independence of the auditor and should take appropriate action, if necessary, to ensure the continued independence of the auditor. (The New York Stock Exchange, American Stock Exchange, and National Association of Securities Dealers subsequently amended their listing rules to implement these requirements).

This practice alert is designed to address implementation issues relative to the Standard and is designed to assist firms in

- Evaluating and enhancing policies and procedures for identifying and communicating with audit committees those matters that may bear on the auditor's independence, which should in turn assist audit committees/board of directors in fulfilling certain of their responsibilities relative to corporate governance.
- Assisting auditors in fulfilling their responsibilities to serve the public interest and strengthen the public's confidence in audited financial information.

Although the guidance in the alert focuses on communications between the auditor and the audit committee/board of directors, the auditor is also encouraged to have similar communications with senior management.

The alert provides the following guidance:

- Firms should establish policies and procedures for independence communications with audit committees. The alert provides examples of relationships that may impact the auditor's independence, along with relevant safeguards. The alert also suggests that the auditor not conclude that a relationship need not be disclosed because independence is not impaired, especially when information about the relationship may help the audit committee understand auditor independence for this entity's specific circumstances.
- The auditor should consider engaging the audit committee chair in discussions concerning the chair's views on relationships that may reasonably be thought to bear on independence and what should be disclosed. The alert provides a sample letter to the audit committee chair that could be used to initiate these discussions.
- To assist audit committees in expanding their knowledge of independence issues, auditors should periodically discuss new or revised independence standards, emerging independence issues, and common threats to auditor objectivity. The alert provides a summary of common threats to auditor objectivity and related safeguards that mitigate these threats.
- The ISB Standard requires written communications that summarize relationships that may reasonably be thought to bear on independence and confirm that, in the auditor's professional judgment, the auditor is independent of the company within the meaning of the Securities Acts.

Without reducing the importance of the independence discussion, the alert recognizes that communications with audit committees, whether written or oral, are broader than independence and therefore the auditor may choose a more comprehensive form of communication to cover some or all of these matters.

The alert also emphasizes that disclosure of relationships that may reasonably be thought to bear on independence should not be construed to imply that the auditor's independence has been impaired, but rather as a tool to foster discussion between the auditor and the audit committee regarding the nature of the relationship.

The auditor should meet with the audit committee to discuss all applicable relationships (actual and ideally, proposed) between the company and the auditor. The ISB intentionally left timing flexible as long as the communication is done annually.

The alert provides a sample letter relating to annual independence discussions with audit committees and confirmation that the auditor is independent of the company within the meaning of the Securities Acts.

Finally, the alert also provides guidance on initial public offerings, the initial year of application, prospective clients, and failure to comply with the standard. The alert was updated in 2000 to provide guidance on ISB Interpretation 00-1 that relates to the applicability of ISB Statement 1 to secondary auditors.

The full text of the practice alert can be obtained from the AICPA website at www.aicpa.org/members/div/secps/lit/practice.htm. The ISB's Standard can be obtained from the ISB website at www.cpaindependence.org.

Quality of Accounting Principles—Guidance for Discussions with Audit Committees

In December 1999, the Auditing Standards Board issued SAS 90, which requires that the independent auditor of an SEC client discuss with a client's audit committee the quality, not just acceptability, of the entity's accounting principles. (See "Auditor's Judgments About the Quality of the Entity's Accounting Principles" under *Fundamental Requirements*.)

This Practice Alert is intended to assist auditors in identifying relevant matters to the discussion with an entity's audit committee of the quality of accounting principles used in the preparation of entity's financial statements. To meet the objectives of SAS 90, the Alert recommends that

- Communications should be understandable to all members of the audit committee.
- Discussions with the audit committee should be sufficiently frequent to ensure that audit committee members are advised of issues on a timely basis.
- Periodic communications with the audit committee need not encompass all accounting principles, estimates, and judgments, but should build on prior communications and address accounting principles and unusual transactions that are more significant in any particular period's financial statements.

Topics that management and the auditor should consider discussing with the audit committee would include, but not be limited to

1. The accounting principles applied by the entity for which acceptable alternative principles are available.
2. Judgments and estimates that affect the financial statements.
3. Consideration of factors affecting asset and liability carrying values.
4. Use of special structures and timing of actions that affect financial statements.
5. Evolving issues and choices that affect financial reporting.
6. The frequency and significance of transactions with related parties, particularly those that are not in the ordinary course of business.
7. Unusual arrangements (e.g., bill-and-hold transactions, self-insurance, multielement arrangements contemporaneously negotiated, and sales of assets or licensing arrangements with continuing involvement by the enterprise).
8. Clarity and transparency of financial statements and disclosures.
9. Audit adjustments identified in the audit.
10. Materiality thresholds and cost/benefit judgments.

The practice alert also provides guidance if the auditor or the audit committee wants to address the degree of aggressiveness or conservatism of the accounting principles applied in the financial statements.

The full text of the practice alert can be obtained from the AICPA website at www.aicpa.org/members/div/secps/lit/practice.htm.

TECHNIQUES FOR APPLICATION

GENERAL

To make certain that all communications required by this section have been made, the authors recommend that a questionnaire similar to the one at the end of this section (see *Illustrations*) be used.

TIMING OF COMMUNICATION[9]

If the matters that should be communicated to the audit committee have no impact on the conduct of the audit, these matters may be communicated before or after the audit has been completed, whichever is more convenient.

If the matters that should be communicated to the audit committee have some impact on the audit (for example, unavailability of client personnel, unresolved disagreements with management over the application of accounting principles), it is recommended that these matters be communicated immediately.

WHO SHOULD COMMUNICATE?

The authors recommend that the partner in charge of the audit should personally communicate with the audit committee. The partner should sign all communications to the audit committee, meet with the audit committee, and complete the questionnaire illustrated at the end of the section.

ORAL COMMUNICATION

The authors recommend that communications to the audit committee be in writing. However, if the communications are oral, the auditor should note the following in the working papers:

1. Date of communication.
2. Matters communicated.
3. Person or persons who received the communication.
4. Resolution of matters covered by the communication.

COMMUNICATION IN ENGAGEMENT LETTER

The auditor should communicate to the audit committee the level of responsibility assumed by the auditor under generally accepted auditing standards and the concepts of materiality, audit tests, and reasonable assurance. Furthermore, the auditor's responsibility for other information, such as supplemental information, and management's discussion and analysis has to be communicated. All of these matters may be communicated in the engagement letter (see Section 310 for an illustrative engagement letter).

---

[9] *See footnote 4.*

WRITTEN COMMUNICATION

The authors recommend that communications to the audit committee be in writing unless they involve sensitive personnel matters. A suggested format for written communications is provided under *Illustrations.*

ORAL COMMUNICATION SUPPLEMENTED BY WRITTEN COMMUNICATION

The best way to communicate with the audit committee is for the partner in charge of the audit to meet with the committee after the audit has been completed. Before the meeting, the partner should submit a proposed agenda of the matters he or she intends to discuss. Naturally, members of the committee may have matters other than those outlined by the auditor that they would like to discuss. The partner would be wise to have the manager in charge of the audit attend the meeting.

Immediately after the meeting with the audit committee, the partner should prepare a written communication to the audit committee summarizing all matters discussed and conclusions reached.

ILLUSTRATIONS

The following illustrations are presented:

1. A questionnaire concerning communications to the audit committee.
2. Written communication to the audit committee.

ILLUSTRATION 1. QUESTIONNAIRE: COMMUNICATIONS TO AUDIT COMMITTEE

____
(Client)

____
(Audit Date)

____________	______	____________	______
(Prepared by)	(Date)	(Reviewed by)	(Date)

Instructions. This questionnaire should be used on all audits of entities who have an audit committee (or other committee formally designated with oversight for financial reporting) and all public entities governed by the Securities Acts (as defined). However, the addendum, "Communication About Independence" only applies to audits when SEC Regulation S-X governs. For all questions, "No" and "N/A" answers should be explained.

Communications may be written or oral and may be made by the auditor or by client management. This and the substance of the matters communicated should be documented and the audit documentation reference should be entered in the appropriate column of the questionnaire.

The questionnaire is divided into four sections, as follows:

A. General.
B. Communications that may be made by management and the auditor.
C. Communications that should be made by the auditor.
D. Communications about independence.

Question	*Yes*	*No*	*N/A*	*Explanation*	*W/P ref.*
A. General					
1. Has there been oral communication of required matters with the audit committee?					
2. If the answer to 1. is "yes," has the following been documented:					
a. Date of communication?					
b. Matters communicated?					
c. Person or persons who received the communication?					
d. Resolution of matters covered by the communication?					

Question	Yes	No	N/A	Explanation	W/P ref.
3. If the communication with the audit committee was written, did it indicate that it was solely for use of the audit committee or the board of directors and, where appropriate, management?					
B. Communications about the Quality of Accounting Principles That May Be Made by Management and the Auditor					
4. Were accounting policies relating to significant financial statement items, including the timing of transactions and the period in which they were recorded, discussed with the audit committee?					
5. Was the audit committee informed about the initial selection of and changes in significant accounting policies and their application?					
6. Was the entity involved in significant unusual transactions?					
7. If the answer to 6. is "yes," was the audit committee informed of the following:					
a. Methods used to account for them?					
b. Effects and implications of methods used?					
8. Did the entity make sensitive accounting estimates material to the financial statements?					
9. If the answer to 8. is "yes," was the audit committee informed about the following:					
a. The process used to develop the estimates?					
b. The basis for our conclusions that the estimated amounts are reasonable?					
NOTE: Section 204, "Auditor's Reports to Audit Committees" of the Sarbanes-Oxley Act and the SEC implementing rule require the auditor to communicate to the audit committee					
1. All critical accounting policies and practices.					
2. All alternative accounting and disclosure treatments that have been discussed with management, including the ramifications of the use of such alternative treatments/disclosures and the treatments performed by the auditor.					
C. Communications That Should Be Made by Auditor					
10. For audit adjustments, have we					
a. Informed the audit committee of the recorded adjustments?					
b. Explained the implications of the adjustments?					
c. Informed the audit committee of any uncorrected misstatements that management determined were immaterial?					
d. Presented a summary of uncorrected misstatements to the audit committee?					
11. Does information prepared by management accompany the audited financial statements?					
12. If the answer to 11. is "yes," did we					
a. Discuss with the audit committee the procedures we performed and the results of these procedures?					
b. Explain our responsibility for the information prepared by management?					

Question	*Yes*	*No*	*N/A*	*Explanation*	*W/P ref.*
13. With reference to generally accepted auditing standards, did we explain (or does the engagement letter include) the following to the audit committee:					
a. Our level of responsibility?					
b. The concept of materiality (both planning and evaluation)?					
c. The concept of audit tests?					
d. The concept of reasonable, as opposed to absolute, assurance?					
14. Did we have disagreements with management over significant matters, such as the application of accounting principles, scope of audit, financial statement disclosures, and wording of our report?					
15. If the answer to 14. is "yes," did we discuss with the audit committee those disagreements, whether or not resolved, about matters that could be significant to the financial statements or the auditor's report?					
16. Did management consult with other accountants about the auditing and accounting matters?					
17. If the answer to 16. is "yes," did we discuss these matters with the audit committee?					
18. Were we selected this year by management to audit the entity's financial statements?					
19. If the answer to 18. is "yes," did we discuss with the audit committee major issues that were discussed with management, such as the application of accounting principles and auditing standards?					
20. Did we encounter serious difficulties with entity personnel, including management, during the audit?					
21. If the answer to 20. is "yes," did we inform the audit committee of these difficulties?					
22. Did we consider communicating recurring matters that have not been communicated within the past three years?					
23. Is the client an SEC client?					
24. If the answer to 22. is "yes," did we discuss the quality of the company's accounting principles with the audit committee?					
D. Addendum—Communications about Independence					
25. If the answer to 23. is "yes," have we disclosed in writing before issuance of the audit report all relationships between us/related entities and the client/related entities that may reasonably bear on independence (include relationships where we have concluded that we are independent)?					
26. Did we confirm in the letter in 25. above that we are independent of the entity within the meaning of the Securities Act?					
27. If the answer to 23. is "yes," did we discuss audit independence with the audit committee (or Board of Directors)?					

Illustration 2. Written Communication to Audit Committee

To the Audit Committee
XYZ Corporation

The purpose of this report is to communicate our understanding of the matters discussed at the meeting of [*date*] between the Audit Committee of the XYZ Corporation and representatives of our firm. The meeting was attended by all members of the Committee and [*identify firm representatives*] of our firm. The purpose of the meeting was to discuss matters related to the audit of the consolidated financial statements of XYZ Corporation and subsidiaries for the year ended December 31, 20X1.

The purpose of our engagement was to audit the consolidated financial statements of the Company and its subsidiaries and evaluate the fairness of presentation of these statements in conformity with accounting principles generally accepted in the United States of America.

Our audit was performed in accordance with auditing standards generally accepted in the United States of America. Those standards require that an audit be designed to evaluate whether the financial statements are materially misstated. To make this evaluation, evidence supporting the amounts included in the financial statements was examined on a test basis, accounting principles used and significant estimates made by management were evaluated to determine their appropriateness, and the overall financial statement presentation and disclosures were examined to determine their propriety. Since evidence was examined on a test basis only, the audit provided us with reasonable, not absolute, assurance as to the fair presentation, in all material respects, of the Company's financial statements in conformity with generally accepted accounting principles.

To determine the nature, timing, and extent of our tests, we obtained a sufficient understanding of the Company's internal control. The Company's internal control consists of five interrelated components, which are: (1) the control environment, (2) risk assessment, (3) control activities, (4) information and communication, and (5) monitoring. Our understanding of the Company's internal control was obtained by inquiry, tests of controls, observation, review of Company manuals, and experience gained in prior year audits. We communicated to you in a separate report certain matters pertaining to internal control that came to our attention during the audit.

We direct your attention to the fact that management has responsibility for developing an internal control system that will assure the proper recording of transactions in the books of account, the safeguarding of assets, and the substantial accuracy of the Company's financial statements. These statements are the representation of management.

The matters noted below were discussed by us with members of the audit committee at our meeting on [*date*].

Significant Accounting Policies

You told us that management informed you about the initial selection of significant accounting policies and the application of these policies.

Significant Unusual Transactions

You told us that management informed you about the method used to account for the sale of real estate that occurred during the year. You were also informed about how the profit on this sale will be recognized.

(Other matters discussed—refer to Illustration 1)

Independence Matters

We informed you that we are not aware of any relationships between our firm and XYZ Corporation audits subsidiaries that, in our professional judgment, may reasonably be thought to bear on our independence which have occurred during 20X1 through [*date of this meeting*]. We also hereby confirm that as of [*date of meeting*] we are independent accountants within the meaning of the Securities Acts administered by the Securities and Exchange Commission and the requirements of the Independence Standards Board.

This report is intended solely for the information and use of the audit committee and is not intended to be, and should not be, used by anyone other than the Audit Committee, the Board of Directors, management, and others within XYZ Corporation. We will be happy to respond to any questions you may have concerning this report.

Firm's signature

City, State
Date

390 CONSIDERATION OF OMITTED PROCEDURES AFTER THE REPORT DATE

EFFECTIVE DATE AND APPLICABILITY

Original Pronouncement	SAS 46, September 1983.
Effective Date	October 31, 1983.
Applicability	Circumstances when

- Subsequent to the date of the auditor's report on audited financial statements, the auditor concludes that one or more auditing procedures **considered necessary at the time of the audit in the circumstances then existing** were omitted from the audit, but
- There is no indication that the financial statements are not fairly presented in conformity with generally accepted accounting principles or, if applicable, another comprehensive basis of accounting.

NOTE: This section does not apply in the following circumstances:

1. *An engagement in which an auditor's work is at issue in a threatened or pending legal proceeding (see* ***Definitions of Terms****) or regulatory investigation.*
2. *An engagement in which an auditor subsequent to the date of his or her report on audited financial statements becomes aware that facts regarding those financial statements may have existed at that date and might have affected the financial statements or the audit report had he or she then been aware of them (see Section 561).*

DEFINITIONS OF TERMS

Threatened legal proceeding. Circumstances in which a potential claimant has indicated to the auditor an awareness of, and present intention to assert, a possible claim.

Omitted procedure. An auditing procedure that was not applied in the audit of financial statements and that subsequent to the date of the auditor's report on those financial statements was considered to be necessary at the time of the audit in the circumstances then existing.

Present ability to support previously expressed opinion. The professional judgment of the auditor that (1) based on auditing procedures applied in a previous audit of financial statements and the facts and circumstances existing at the time of that audit, or (2) based on additional information or analysis since that audit, the auditor's report on those financial statements still is appropriate.

OBJECTIVES OF SECTION

GENERAL

The issuance of SAS 46 (Section 390) is an indirect result of the development of peer review and quality control standards (see Statement on Quality Control Standards 2, *System of Quality Control for a CPA Firm's Accounting and Auditing Practice*). An auditor is not required to carry out retrospective review of his or her work once a report has been issued on audited financial statements. Audit documentation is reviewed, however, in connection with peer reviews and in-house inspections. These reviews may reveal the omission of necessary auditing procedures. This section provides guidance to the auditor on considerations and procedures to be applied when omitted auditing procedures are discovered after the audit report has been issued.

BACKGROUND

The initial stimulus for the section resulted from peer reviews of members of the AICPA Division for Firms and the oversight program on peer reviews of the Public Oversight Board (POB). In October 1980, the POB informed the AICPA of its concern when reviewers concluded that an audit had not been conducted in accordance with generally accepted auditing standards (GAAS). At the time, auditors had no guidance on appropriate procedures in these circumstances. The POB recommended that the proper standard-setting body issue guidance on procedures a firm should apply when it becomes aware of an audit that may not have been made in accordance with GAAS. This section is the response to the POB recommendation.

PROFESSIONAL DISAGREEMENTS

This section does not apply to professional disagreements about whether an auditing procedure is necessary in a specific engagement under circumstances existing at the time of the audit. For example, a peer reviewer may suggest that an auditing procedure was necessary (e.g., confirming additional receivables), and the auditor may disagree.

The alleged omitted auditing procedure might be one that professionals could reasonably disagree about (e.g., judgments about materiality). In these circumstances, every effort should be made to convince the reviewer that the auditor's judgment was appropriate.

NO SUBSTITUTE FOR OMITTED PROCEDURES

The omitted procedure may be one for which there is no alternative (e.g., making or observing some inventory counts), or the omission may be the failure to apply any auditing procedures to obtain evidential matter for a significant audit objective (e.g., accepting management representations and not testing percentage of completion on a material construction contract). In these circumstances, the auditor cannot maintain that these are matters about which reasonable professionals might disagree.

DISTINCTION FROM SECTION 561

Section 561 provides guidance when the auditor becomes aware, subsequent to the date of the report on the audited financial statements, that facts may have existed at that date which might have affected the financial statements or the audit report had the auditor been aware of those facts. The "facts" usually relate to the financial statements and whether those financial statements are presented fairly in all material respects in conformity with generally accepted accounting principles.

Section 561 applies to facts that indicate possible misstatement of financial statements. On the other hand, Section 390 applies to the possible omission of auditing procedures. The application of Section 561 is initiated by a possible GAAP failure; the application of Section 390 is initiated by a possible GAAS failure. However, when omitted auditing procedures are applied, the auditor may become aware that facts may have existed at the date of the auditor's report and might have affected the report had the auditor been aware of those facts (see *Fundamental Requirements*). In that situation, Section 561 is applicable.

FUNDAMENTAL REQUIREMENTS

Importance of Omitted Procedures

If the auditor decides that a situation involving an omitted procedure exists, he or she should determine if the omitted procedure currently affects his or her ability to support the previously expressed opinion (see *Techniques for Application*).

NOTE: In these circumstances, the auditor would be well advised to consult with his or her attorney.

Applying Omitted Procedures

The auditor should promptly attempt to apply the omitted procedure or alternative procedures that would provide a satisfactory basis for the original opinion on the financial statements if he or she

1. Decides that the omitted procedure impairs his or her present ability to support the previously expressed opinion, and
2. Believes that there are persons currently relying, or likely to rely, on the financial statements and the related auditor's report.

Inability to Apply Omitted Procedures

If the auditor is not able to apply the omitted procedure or appropriate alternative procedures, the auditor should consult his or her attorney to determine the proper action concerning the auditor's responsibilities to

1. The client.
2. Regulatory authorities having jurisdiction over the client.
3. Persons relying, or likely to rely, on the auditor's report.

NOTE: This section does not require the auditor to notify the client of the omitted auditing procedures.

Subsequent Discovery of Facts Existing at Date of Auditor's Report

When the auditor subsequently applies the omitted procedure or alternative procedures, he or she may become aware of facts regarding the financial statements that existed at the date of the auditor's report and would have affected the report had the auditor been aware of them. In these circumstances, the auditor should

1. Advise the client to disclose the newly discovered facts and their impact on the financial statements to persons known to be currently relying, or who are likely to rely, on the financial statements and the related auditor's report.
2. Take whatever steps he or she believes necessary to be satisfied that the client has made the specified disclosures.

The auditor also would be well advised to consult with his or her attorney.

If the client refuses to make the disclosures requested, the auditor should follow the guidance in Section 561 under *Fundamental Requirements*.

INTERPRETATIONS

There are no interpretations for this section.

TECHNIQUES FOR APPLICATION

GENERAL

The objective of the auditor's assessment of the importance of the omitted procedure is to determine if it is

1. Necessary to apply the omitted procedure.
2. Necessary to apply alternative procedures.
3. Appropriate not to apply either the omitted procedure or alternative procedures.

URGENCY OF RESOLUTION

Whenever the auditor becomes aware of an omitted procedure, he or she should act promptly. In these circumstances, a client has issued what it represented to be audited financial statements that may not have been audited properly. The client may be able to wait a short period of time (to be determined by the client, the auditor, and their lawyers) for the matter to be resolved; however, it cannot wait too long before notifying interested parties. The urgency of resolution may differ for public versus nonpublic companies.

Public Companies

Public companies file audited financial statements with the Securities and Exchange Commission. If the auditor becomes aware of an omitted procedure concerning these financial statements, he or she should consider the client's possible obligation for timely disclosure of significant events. Form 8-K must be filed within fifteen calendar days after occurrence of most significant events.

Nonpublic Companies

Nonpublic companies may submit audited financial statements to banks, bonding companies, credit agencies, and others. If these financial statements were not audited properly **and** are misleading, the client should notify immediately anyone relying on them. Although there is no specified time period within which to notify interested parties, the client probably will consider its reputation and its exposure to lawsuits in determining when to notify them. It would therefore be prudent for the auditor to complete all procedures before a significant period of time has elapsed.

DETERMINING IMPORTANCE OF OMITTED PROCEDURES

To determine the importance of the omitted procedure to the auditor's present ability to support the previously expressed opinion, he or she should

1. Review documentation of the audit.
2. Discuss circumstances with audit personnel and others.
3. Review documentation of the subsequent audit.

Review Audit Documentation

The auditor should review relevant audit documentation to determine if

1. Other procedures were applied that compensated for the one omitted or made the one omitted less important. For example, the review of subsequent cash collected and the related customer remittance advices might compensate for inadequate confirmation of receivables or make the failure to obtain enough receivable confirmations less important than usual.
2. A lower level of control risk was justified so that the omitted procedure was not necessary. The auditor should review audit documentations on
   a. The documentation of the understanding of internal control.
   b. Tests of controls.

Discussions with Audit Personnel

The auditor should discuss the audit with audit personnel to determine if

1. The omitted procedure or a related procedure was discussed.
2. The omitted procedure was performed but not documented.
3. The omitted procedure affected an item considered not material.

The auditor should determine if the alleged omitted procedure was performed, and if not, why not.

Review Subsequent Period Audit Documentation

The auditor should review audit documentation for the subsequent period to determine if procedures applied provide audit evidence to support the previously expressed opinion. For example

1. Costing of subsequent period sales may provide audit evidence about existence of prior period inventory.
2. A review of subsequent period changes in receivables may provide audit evidence about existence of prior period receivables.
3. A review of subsequent period liabilities may provide evidence that a contingency did not exist at the end of the prior period.

ILLUSTRATION

ILLUSTRATION 1. APPLYING THE OMITTED PROCEDURE

If the auditor concludes that the omitted procedure should be performed, he or she should apply it promptly. In these circumstances, the auditor would have to discuss the matter with the client. Below are possible omitted procedures and suggested methods of correcting the omission.

	Possible Omitted Procedure	*Remedy*
1.	Failure to obtain management representation letter.	Obtain letter retroactive to date of auditor's report.
2.	Failure to obtain a sufficient number of confirmations of receivables.	Confirm retroactive to balance sheet date. If control risk is assessed at less than the maximum, confirm currently, and work back to balance sheet date.
3.	Failure to observe a sufficient quantity of inventory.	If control risk is assessed at less than the maximum, observe count of specific styles or components, and work back to year-end. If control risk is assessed at the maximum, the entire inventory may have to be taken currently before the auditor can work back to year end.
4.	Failure to make inquiry of client's lawyer.	Make inquiry retroactive to date of auditor's report.

	Possible Omitted Procedure	*Remedy*
5.	Failure to obtain sufficient evidence about the value of investments in nonpublic investees.	Review recent audited financial statements, if available. If recent audited financial statements are not available, review recent unaudited financial statements, and apply selected audit procedures. Consult with investee's accountant.
6.	Failure to apply procedures for identifying related-party transactions.	Apply procedures for current and prior period (see Section 334).

410 AND 411 ADHERENCE TO GAAP (410) AND THE MEANING OF "PRESENT FAIRLY IN CONFORMITY WITH GAAP" (411)

EFFECTIVE DATE AND APPLICABILITY

Original Pronouncements	Section 410: SAS 1, November 1972 (adapted from SAP 33); SAS 62, April 1989.
	Section 411: SAS 69, January 1992 (superseded the Section 411 in effect at that date); SAS 91, April 2000; and SAS 93, January 2001.
Effective Date	Section 410: November 1972.
	Section 411: Audits of financial statements ending after March 15, 1992. (See *Fundamental Requirements* for transition requirements.) Revised to reflect SAS 91, which is effective upon issuance.
Applicability	Audits of GAAP financial statements in accordance with generally accepted auditing standards.

DEFINITIONS OF TERMS

Generally accepted accounting principles (GAAP). A technical accounting term that encompasses all the conventions, rules, and procedures necessary to define accepted accounting practice at a particular time. (As used in the reporting standards, GAAP includes accounting principles and practices as well as the methods of applying them.)

Generally accepted accounting principles recognize the importance of reporting transactions and events in accordance with their substance.

OBJECTIVES OF SECTION

To express an opinion on the "fairness" of financial statements, the independent auditor requires a standard to determine if those financial statements are, in fact, presented fairly. That standard or framework is generally accepted accounting principles. Without that framework, the auditor would have no uniform standard for judging the presentation of financial position, results of operations, and cash flows in financial statements. SAS 69 provides a hierarchy of generally accepted accounting principles. The SASs that were sources of the original section were SASs 5, 43, and 52.

In 1989, the Financial Accounting Foundation, which has oversight responsibilities for the Financial Accounting Standards Board and the Governmental Accounting Standards Board, stated that "an entity subject to the jurisdiction of one board should not be required to change its reporting principles as a result of a standard issued by the other board." Because of this policy, the GAAP hierarchy had to be revised to establish two separate hierarchies—one for nongovernmental entities and the other for state and local governments. SAS 69 established two separate but parallel hierarchies.

SAS 69 also increased the categories in the hierarchies from four to five and added new types of pronouncements that had come into existence after the most recent prior revision.

In 2000, SAS 91 amended this section to add a GAAP hierarchy for federal government entities and in 2001, SAS 93 amended this section to reflect the requirement to include in the auditor's report an identification of the USA as the country of origin of GAAP. SAS 93 also changed the title of this section from *The Meaning of Present Fairly in Conformity with Generally Accepted Accounting Principles in the Independent Auditor's Report* to its current title.

FUNDAMENTAL REQUIREMENTS

FRAMEWORK FOR OPINION

The independent auditor's judgment concerning the fairness of presentation of the overall financial statements should be applied within the framework of generally accepted accounting principles. The auditor should consider whether the substance of transactions or events differs materially from their form.

REPORTING STANDARD

The first standard of reporting is: "The report shall state whether the financial statements are presented in accordance with generally accepted accounting principles." AU 410.02 states that this standard is construed not to require a statement of fact by the auditor but an opinion.

BASIS FOR AUDITOR'S OPINION

According to AU 411.04, the auditor's opinion that financial statements are presented fairly in conformity with accounting principles generally accepted in the United States of America should be based on his or her judgment about whether

1. The accounting principles selected and applied have **general acceptance**.
2. The accounting principles are appropriate in the circumstances.
3. The financial statements and related notes are informative of matters that may affect their use, understanding, and interpretation (see Section 431).
4. The information presented in the financial statements is classified and summarized in a reasonable manner (see Section 431).
5. The financial statements reflect the underlying transactions and events in a manner that presents financial position, results of operations, and cash flows within a range of acceptable limits (the concept of materiality).

GAAP HIERARCHY—NONGOVERNMENTAL ENTITIES[1]

The categories of GAAP, in rank order, are as follows:

1. Accounting principles promulgated by bodies designated by the AICPA Council to establish such principles, pursuant to Rule 203 of the AICPA Code of Professional Conduct. Those principles are
   - Financial Accounting Standards Board (FASB) Statements of Financial Accounting Standards and Interpretations.
   - Accounting Principles Board (APB) Opinions.
   - AICPA Accounting Research Bulletins.
2. FASB Technical Bulletins and, if cleared by the FASB, AICPA Industry Audit and Accounting Guides and AICPA Statements of Position.
3. AICPA Accounting Standards Executive Committee (AcSEC) Practice Bulletins that have been cleared by the FASB and consensus positions of the FASB Emerging Issues Task Force (EITF).
4. AICPA Accounting Interpretations, Implementation Guides (Qs and As) published by the FASB staff, and practices that are widely recognized and prevalent either generally or in the industry.
5. Other accounting literature (nonauthoritative). This category includes, but is not limited to
   - FASB Statements of Financial Accounting Concepts.
   - AICPA Issues Papers.
   - International Accounting Standards of the International Accounting Standards Committee.
   - Governmental Accounting Standards Board (GASB) Statements, Interpretations, and Technical Bulletins.
   - FASAB Statements, Interpretations, and Technical Bulletins.
   - Pronouncements of other professional associations or regulatory agencies.
   - Technical Information Service Inquiries and Replies included in AICPA Technical Practice Aids.
   - Accounting textbooks, handbooks, and articles.

GAAP HIERARCHY—STATE AND LOCAL GOVERNMENT ENTITIES[2]

The categories of GAAP, in rank order, are as follows:

---

[1] ***Transition Requirements***

Most of the pronouncements or practices in categories 2., 3., and 4. of hierarchies had equal authoritative standing before the issuance of SAS 69. Therefore

1. *An entity following an accounting treatment in category 3. or 4. as of March 15, 1992, is not required to change to an accounting treatment in a category 2. or 3. pronouncement whose effective date is **before** March 15, 1992.*
2. *For pronouncements whose effective date is **after** March 15, 1992, and for entities initially applying an accounting principle **after** March 15, 1992 (see FASB EITF on p. 362), the auditor should follow the applicable hierarchy established by SAS 69 in determining whether an entity's financial statements are fairly presented in conformity with GAAP.*

FASB EITF. *Consensus positions of the EITF issued **before** March 16, 1992, become effective in the GAAP hierarchy for initial application of an accounting principle **after** March 15, 1993.*

[2] *See footnote on page 340.*

1. GASB Statements and Interpretations, as well as AICPA and FASB pronouncements specifically made applicable to state and local governmental entities by GASB Statements or Interpretations.
2. GASB Technical Bulletins and, if specifically made applicable to state and local governmental entities by the AICPA and cleared by the GASB, AICPA Industry Audit and Accounting Guides and AICPA Statements of Position.
3. AICPA AcSEC Practice Bulletins, if specifically made applicable to state and local governmental entities and cleared by the GASB, and consensus positions on accounting issues applicable to state and local governmental entities of a group of accountants organized by the GASB.
4. Implementation Guides (Qs and As) published by the GASB staff and practices that are widely recognized and prevalent in state and local government.
5. Other accounting literature (nonauthoritative). This category includes but is not limited to

   - GASB Concepts Statements.
   - Pronouncements referred to in categories 1. through 4. of the GAAP Hierarchy—Nongovernmental entities above, when not specifically made applicable to state and local governmental entities by either the GASB or the organization issuing them.
   - FASB Concepts Statements.
   - FASAB Statements, Interpretations, and Technical Bulletins.
   - AICPA Issues Papers.
   - International Accounting Standards of the International Accounting Standards Committee.
   - Pronouncements of other professional associations or regulatory agencies.
   - Technical Information Service Inquiries and Replies included in AICPA Technical Practice Aids.
   - Accounting textbooks, handbooks, and articles.

GAAP Hierarchy—Federal Governmental Entities

The categories of GAAP, in rank order, are as follows:

1. Federal Accounting Standards Advisory Board (FASAB) Statements and Interpretations, as well as AICPA and FASB pronouncements specifically made applicable to federal governmental entities by FASAB Statements or Interpretations. FASAB Statements and Interpretations will be periodically incorporated in a publication by the FASAB.
2. FASAB Technical Bulletins and, if specifically made applicable to federal governmental entities by the AICPA and cleared by the FASAB, AICPA Industry Audit and Accounting Guides and AICPA Statements of Position.
3. AICPA AcSEC Practice Bulletins, if specifically made applicable to federal governmental entities and cleared by the FASAB, as well as Technical Releases of the Accounting and Auditing Policy Committee of the FASAB.
4. Implementation Guides published by the FASAB staff as well as practices that are widely recognized and prevalent in federal government.
5. Other accounting literature (nonauthoritative). This category includes but is not limited to

   - FASAB Concepts Statements.

- Pronouncements referred to in categories 1. through 4. of the GAAP Hierarchy—Nongovernmental Entities, when not specifically made applicable to federal governmental entities by the FASAB.
- FASB Concepts Statements.
- GASB Statements, Interpretations, Technical Bulletins, and Concept Statements.
- AICPA Issues Papers.
- International Accounting Standards of the International Accounting Standards Committee.
- Pronouncements of other professional associations or regulatory agencies.
- AICPA Technical Practice Aids.
- Accounting textbooks, handbooks, and articles.

RULE 203 PRONOUNCEMENTS

An auditor should **not** express an unqualified opinion on financial statements that contain a material departure from a pronouncement covered by Rule 203 of the AICPA Code of Professional Conduct (category 1. under both the nongovernmental and the governmental hierarchies).

Rule 203 pronouncements: Exception. An auditor should express an unqualified opinion on financial statements that contain a material departure from a pronouncement covered by Rule 203 of the AICPA Code of Professional Conduct in those unusual circumstances where literal application of that pronouncement might result in misleading financial statements. In those unusual circumstances, the auditor should

1. Add a separate paragraph to the report that describes the departure, its approximate effects, if practicable, and the reasons why the departure is necessary to prevent the financial statements from being misleading.
2. Express an unqualified opinion on conformity with GAAP.

NOTE: Circumstances that would cause adherence to a Rule 203 pronouncement to result in misleading financial statements are likely to be exceedingly rare in practice. Only a handful of such reports have ever been issued. (See ***Illustrations****. Also see Section 508.)*

No applicable Rule 203 pronouncement. If the accounting treatment of a transaction or event is not specified by a pronouncement covered by Rule 203, the auditor should consider whether the accounting treatment is specified by another source of established accounting principles (categories 2., 3., and 4. of the nongovernmental or the governmental hierarchies).

FAILURE TO APPLY ANOTHER SOURCE OF ESTABLISHED ACCOUNTING PRINCIPLES

If an established accounting principle from category 2., 3., or 4. is relevant to the circumstances, the auditor should be able to justify a conclusion that another treatment is generally accepted.

CONFLICT BETWEEN ACCOUNTING PRINCIPLES

If there is a conflict between relevant accounting principles from one or more sources in category 2., 3., or 4., the auditor should follow the guidance specified by the source in the higher category; for example, follow category 2. guidance over category 3. If the auditor concludes that the guidance specified by a source in the lower category better presents the substance of the transaction, the auditor must be able to justify that conclusion.

SECURITIES AND EXCHANGE COMMISSION (SEC)

Rules and interpretive releases of the SEC have a level of authority equal to that of category 1. pronouncements for SEC registrants. The SEC also expects registrants to follow the positions agreed to under a consensus of the FASB Emerging Issues Task Force.

INTERPRETATIONS

THE IMPACT ON THE AUDITOR'S REPORT OF A FASB STATEMENT PRIOR TO THE STATEMENT'S EFFECTIVE DATE (ISSUED OCTOBER 1979, REVISED DECEMBER 1992, JUNE 1993, AND FEBRUARY 1997)

The auditor should not qualify his or her opinion if an entity does not adopt a FASB statement prior to its effective date as long as the accounting principles being followed are currently acceptable.

For financial statements that are prepared on the basis of accounting principles that are acceptable at the financial statement date but that will not be acceptable in the future, the auditor should consider whether disclosure of the impending change in principle and resulting restatement are essential. In cases where the estimated impact of the impending changes is unusually material, disclosure is best made by supplementing the historical financial statements with pro forma financial data that give effect to the future adjustment as if it had occurred on the date of the balance sheet. The auditor may also decide to include an explanatory paragraph that highlights the changes. If essential information is not disclosed, the auditor should express a qualified or adverse opinion.

THE AUDITOR'S CONSIDERATION OF MANAGEMENT'S ADOPTION OF ACCOUNTING PRINCIPLES FOR NEW TRANSACTIONS OR EVENTS (MARCH 1995; REVISED OCTOBER 2000)

When an entity adopts an accounting principle for which there are no established sources of accounting principles, the auditor should understand the basis used by the entity to select the new principle. In assessing the appropriateness of the new principle, the auditor may consider whether there are analogous transactions or events for which there are established accounting principles. Furthermore, when SAS 61, *Communication with Audit Committees* (Section 380) applies, the auditor should determine that the audit committee is informed about the new accounting principle.

TECHNIQUES FOR APPLICATION

AUDITOR AWARENESS

The auditor should be aware of the content of the pronouncements listed in categories 1. through 4. of the GAAP hierarchies. The auditor may obtain this awareness by subscribing to the various services published by the FASB, GASB, and AICPA.

EVALUATION APPROACH

When the auditor evaluates the accounting treatment of a transaction or event, he or she should consider the content of the pronouncements listed in the GAAP hierarchies, starting with the highest level of authority (category 1.) and working down toward the lowest level (category 4.).

The auditor should rely on the first category that contains a pronouncement that specifies the accounting treatment applicable to the transaction or event.

If the transaction or event is not covered in categories 1. through 4., the auditor should then consider other accounting literature (category 5.).

NO ESTABLISHED ACCOUNTING PRINCIPLES

The auditor should reason by analogy from existing GAAP in developing an accounting treatment for a new type of business transaction or a new development that is not covered by established accounting principles.

METHODS OF APPLICATION

The auditor should also be aware of the different methods of applying accounting principles. For example, inventory cost may be computed under the FIFO, LIFO, or average cost method.

OTHER SOURCES OF ACCOUNTING GUIDANCE

Sources available, other than those noted in *Fundamental Requirements,* include the following:

1. *Accounting Trends and Techniques.* This publication contains data on accounting practices followed in 600 reports of public companies to stockholders.
2. *Financial Report Surveys.* These provide illustrations of financial statement disclosure of specific items, such as income taxes, significant accounting policies, and related-party transactions.
3. *AICPA Technical Information Service.* The AICPA has a staff available to respond to technical inquiries. The toll-free telephone number is 1-888-777-7077.
4. *PPC/AICPA Practitioner's Library—Accounting and Auditing.* This CD-ROM contains all of Practitioners Publishing Company's accounting and auditing guides along with all AICPA, FASB, and GASB authoritative pronouncements.

ILLUSTRATIONS

The following are illustrated:

1. Table of GAAP hierarchy from SAS 69 (AU 411).
2. Auditor's report and explanatory note to the financial statements when adherence to an authoritative pronouncement would, in a very rare circumstance, make the financial statements misleading.

ILLUSTRATION 1. GAAP HIERARCHY SUMMARY FROM SAS 69 (AU 411)*

		Nongovernmental Entities		*State and Local Governments*		*Federal Government*
Established Accounting Principles	10a	FASB Statements and Interpretations, APB Opinions, and AICPA Accounting Research Bulletins	12a	GASB Statements and Interpretations, plus AICPA and FASB Pronouncements if made applicable to state and local governments by a GASB Statement or Interpretation	14a	Federal Accounting Standards Advisory Board (FASAB) Statements and Interpretations, as well as AICPA and FASB pronouncements specifically made applicable to federal governmental entities by FASAB Statements or Interpretations
	10b	FASB Technical Bulletins, AICPA Industry Audit and Accounting Guides, and AICPA Statements of Position	12b	GASB Technical Bulletins, and the following pronouncements if specifically made applicable to state and local governments by the AICPA: AICPA Industry Audit and Accounting Guides and AICPA Statements of Position	14b	FASAB Technical Bulletins and, if specifically made applicable to federal governmental entities by the AICPA and cleared by the FASAB, AICPA Industry Audit and Accounting Guides and AICPA Statements of Position
	10c	Consensus positions of the FASB Emerging Issues Task Force and AICPA Practice Bulletins	12c	Consensus positions of the GASB Emerging Issues Task Force*** and AICPA Practice Bulletins if specifically made applicable to state and local governments by the AICPA	14c	AICPA AcSEC Practice Bulletins if specifically made applicable to federal governmental entities and cleared by the FASAB, as well as Technical Releases of the Accounting and Auditing Policy Committee of the FASAB
	10d	AICPA accounting interpretations, "Qs and As," published by the FASB staff, as well as industry practices widely recognized and prevalent	12d	"Qs and As" published by the GASB staff, as well as industry practices widely recognized and prevalent	14d	Implementation guides published by the FASAB staff, as well as practices that are widely recognized and prevalent in the federal government
Other Accounting Literature **	11	Other accounting literature, including FASB Concepts Statements, AICPA Issues Papers; International Accounting Standards Committee Statements; GASB Statements, Interpretations, and Technical Bulletins; FASAB Statements, Interpretations, and Technical Bulletins; pronouncements of other professional associations or regulatory agencies; AICPA *Technical Practice Aids*; and accounting textbooks, handbooks, and articles	13	Other accounting literature, including GASB Concepts Statements; pronouncements in categories (1) through (4) of the hierarchy for nongovernmental entities when not specifically made applicable to state and local governments; FASB Concepts Statements; FASAB Statements, Interpretations, and Technical Bulletins; AICPA Issues Papers; International Accounting Standards Committee Statements; pronouncements of other professional associations or regulatory agencies; AICPA *Technical Practice Aids*; and accounting textbooks, handbooks, and articles	15	Other accounting literature, including FASAB Concepts Statements; pronouncements in categories (a) through (d) of the hierarchy for federal governmental entities when not specifically made applicable to federal governmental entities; FASB Concepts Statements; GASB Statements, Interpretations, Technical Bulletins, and Concept Statements; AICPA Issues Papers; International Accounting Standards of the International Accounting Standards Committee; pronouncements of other professional associations or regulatory agencies; AICPA *Technical Practice Aids*; and accounting textbooks, handbooks, and articles

* *Paragraph references correspond to the paragraphs of SAS 69 that describe the categories of the GAAP hierarchy*
** *In the absence of established accounting principles, the auditor may consider other accounting literature, depending on its relevance in the circumstances.*
*** *As of the date of this Statement, the GASB had not organized such a group*

ILLUSTRATION 2. AUDITOR'S REPORT AND NOTE TO FINANCIAL STATEMENTS FOR RULE 203 DEPARTURE[3]

To the Stockholders and Board of Directors of US Industries, Inc.

We have examined the consolidated balance sheets of US Industries, Inc. and consolidated subsidiaries as of December 31, 1975 and 1974, and the related consolidated statements of income, additional capital and changes in financial position for the years then ended. Our examinations were made in accordance with generally accepted auditing standards and, accordingly, included such tests of the accounting records and such other auditing procedures as we considered necessary in the circumstances. We did not examine the financial statements of the Corporation's health spa subsidiaries for the years ended December 31, 1975 and 1974, which statements reflect total assets and revenues constituting 7% and 4% in 1975 and 6% and 3% in 1974, respectively, of the related consolidated totals. These statements were examined by other independent accountants whose reports thereon have been furnished to us and our opinion expressed herein, insofar as it relates to the amounts included for such subsidiaries, is based solely upon the reports of the other independent accountants.

As explained in Note A (9), the Corporation's health spa subsidiaries have changed their method of recording revenues from the recognition of revenue at the time of sale to the recognition of revenue over the membership term and have applied this change retroactively in their financial statements. The other independent accountants' reports, referred to above, stated, "Accounting Principles Board (APB) Opinion Number 20, 'Accounting Changes,' provides that such a change be made by including, as an element of net earnings during the year of change, the cumulative effect of the change on prior years. Had APB Opinion Number 20 been followed literally, the cumulative effect of the accounting change would have been included as a charge in the 1975 statement of operations. Because of the magnitude and pervasiveness of this change, we believe a literal application of APB Opinion Number 20 would result in a misleading presentation, and that this change should therefore be made on a retroactive basis." Accordingly, the accompanying consolidated financial statements for 1974 have been restated.

In our opinion, based upon our examination and the aforementioned reports of the other independent accountants, the financial statements referred to above present fairly the consolidated financial position of US Industries, Inc. and consolidated subsidiaries at December 31, 1975 and 1974, and the consolidated results of their operations and changes in financial position for the years then ended, in conformity with generally accepted accounting principles applied on a consistent basis, after restatement for the change, with which the other independent accountants and we concur, in the method of revenue recognition by the health spa subsidiaries referred to in the preceding paragraph.

Ernst & Ernst

New York, NY
February 27, 1976
(March 6, 1976, as to the reports of other independent accountants)

(9) Change in Accounting for Membership Revenues

The corporation has two subsidiaries, one of which is 80% owned, which operate health spas. These **companies** sell health club memberships that have specific terms, which presently range up to thirty months. In prior years, revenue from sale of memberships, less a deferred portion, was taken into income at time of sale. The deferred portion was taken into revenue on a straight-line basis over the membership terms and was equivalent to the estimated future costs of providing facilities and services. These costs consisted of a pro rata share of estimated future operating expenses. In December 1974, Touche Ross & Co., independent accountants for the Corporation's health spa subsidiaries, informed the Corporation that they had taken a position as a firm, which they suggested should be effective for fiscal years ended after December 31, 1974, to recognize membership fee revenue and associated costs over the period of membership.

The subsidiaries have concluded that, even though the change has not been required by an authoritative accounting body, there is sufficient authoritative support within similar industries and they have accepted the change suggested by their independent accountants.

Accounting Principles Board (APB) Opinion Number 20, "Accounting Changes," provides that such a change be made by including, as an element of net earnings during the year of change, the cumulative effect of the change on prior years. Had APB Opinion Number 20 been followed literally, the cumulative effect of the accounting change would have been included as a charge, net of tax benefits, in the 1975 consolidated statement of income and would have resulted in reporting a consolidated net loss of $3,398,000 ($.24 per common share) in 1975 and a consolidated net income of $18,171,000 ($.44 per common share) in 1974. Because of the magnitude and pervasiveness of this change, the Corporation believes a literal application of APB Opinion Number 20 would result in a misleading presentation, and that this change should, therefore, be made on a retroactive basis. The Corporation's and the subsidiaries' independent accountants concur in this treatment.

As a result of retroactive treatment of the change in the method of accounting for membership revenues, the consolidated financial statements for prior years have been restated. The effect of the change was to reduce consolidated net income for 1975 by $90,000 and to increase consolidated net income previously reported for 1974 by $5,160,000 ($.16 per share). The increase in deferred revenue at January 1, 1974, net of related tax benefits, resulted in an adjustment to opening retained earnings of $19,037,000.

---

[3] *This report example does not reflect the new report form required by SAS 58 (see Section 508). The authors are not aware of any Rule 203 exception reports that have been issued under the SAS 58 report format.*

420 CONSISTENCY OF APPLICATION OF GENERALLY ACCEPTED ACCOUNTING PRINCIPLES

EFFECTIVE DATE AND APPLICABILITY

Original Pronouncements	SAP 53, November 1972 (codified in SAS 1, November 1972); SAS 43, and SAS 88, December 1999.
Effective Date	When issued, November 1972. Revised to reflect SAS 88, which is effective upon issuance.
Applicability	Audit of financial statements in accordance with generally accepted auditing standards.

NOTE: The consistency standard does not apply in the audit of the financial statements of a new entity. It applies either to financial statements prepared in accordance with GAAP or another comprehensive basis of accounting.

DEFINITIONS OF TERMS

Comparability. Comparison of financial statements between years may be affected by

1. Accounting changes.
2. An error in financial statements of prior years.
3. Changes in classification.
4. Events or transactions that are substantially different from those of prior periods.

NOTE: All these things affect comparability, but only certain accounting changes affect consistency.

Accounting change. A change in

1. An accounting principle.
2. An accounting estimate.
3. The reporting entity (a special type of change in accounting principle).

NOTE: Only a change in accounting principle (1. or 3., above) affects consistency.

Accounting principle. Accounting principles, practices, and the methods of applying them.

NOTE: Other definitions are presented in ***Fundamental Requirements*** *because the definition is the substance of the requirement.*

OBJECTIVES OF SECTION

Before APB Opinion 20, *Accounting Changes*, was issued, most of the accounting guidance as well as audit reporting guidance on accounting changes was covered in the auditing literature. An important feature of the auditing guidance was a distinction between changes in circumstances that caused accounting changes and other, presumably discretionary, changes. Only a discretionary change affected consistency reporting.

Opinion 20 established several new accounting requirements and codified some existing practices. Opinion 20

1. Created a presumption that an accounting principle once adopted should not be changed in accounting for similar transactions or events. The presumption can be overcome only if the new accounting principle is justified as being **preferable**.
2. Specified the accounting treatment of the effect of accounting changes on the financial statements. This is essentially a cumulative-effect adjustment except for certain specified changes made by retroactive restatement.
3. Specified the disclosure requirements for various types of accounting changes.

Opinion 20 does not apply to changes made to conform to new authoritative pronouncements, but such pronouncements specify the applicable accounting treatment and disclosure.

The auditing literature was modified to mesh with Opinion 20. The old distinction between changes in circumstances and other changes disappeared. The auditing literature adopted the classification of accounting changes of Opinion 20 and specified those that affect consistency and those that do not. Once a change is put in the slot specified in Opinion 20, reference to lists of changes affecting and not affecting consistency reporting in this section determines the appropriate reporting on consistency.

Although these refinements have been made in consistency reporting, the basic objective of consistency reporting by the auditor has remained the same. It is

1. To give assurance that the comparability of financial statements between periods has not been materially affected by changes in accounting principle.
2. If comparability has been materially affected by changes in accounting principle, to require appropriate reporting by the independent auditor on the changes.

FUNDAMENTAL REQUIREMENTS

REPORTING STANDARD

The second standard of reporting is: "The report shall identify those circumstances in which such principles have not been consistently observed in the current period in relation to the preceding period."

CONSISTENCY IMPLICATION OF AUDITOR'S STANDARD REPORT

According to AU 411.02, the auditor's standard report implies that the auditor is satisfied that the comparability of financial statements between periods has not been materially affected by changes in accounting principles and that such principles have been consistently applied between or among periods because either (1) no change in accounting principles has occurred, or (2) there has been a change in accounting principles or in the method of their application, but the effect of the change on the comparability of the financial statements is not material. In these cases, the auditor would not refer to consistency in his or her report.

A change in accounting principle that has a material effect on the comparability of financial statements requires an explanatory paragraph after the opinion paragraph in the auditor's report.

PERIODS TO WHICH CONSISTENCY STANDARD RELATES

The financial statements included in the consistency implication depend on what financial statements are covered by the auditor's report.

1. Current period only—the consistency of application of accounting principles in relation to the preceding period only (even if financial statements for one or more preceding periods are presented).
2. Two or more years (no other statements presented)—the consistency of application of accounting principles between such years.
3. Two or more years (prior year presented but not included in auditor's report)—consistency between years included in report and also the consistency of such years with the prior year.

CHANGES AFFECTING CONSISTENCY

The following changes, if they have a material effect, require the addition of an explanatory paragraph after the opinion paragraph that describes the inconsistency.

1. Change in Accounting Principle

Adoption of a generally accepted accounting principle different from the one used in the prior period. An example is a change from the straight-line method to the declining balance method of depreciation for all newly acquired assets in a class. An investee accounted for by the equity method may change an accounting principle. If this change causes a material lack of comparability in the financial statements of the investor, the auditor should add an explanatory paragraph to the auditor's report following the opinion paragraph.

2. Change in Reporting Entity

This is a special type of change in accounting principle and is limited mainly to

a. Presenting consolidated or combined statements instead of statements of individual entities.
b. Changing specific subsidiaries included in the group of entities in the consolidation.

   NOTE: This means a change in consolidation policy and not the creation, cessation, purchase, or disposition of a subsidiary.

c. Changing entities included in combined financial statements.

A change in reporting entity also results from a business combination under the pooling-of-interests method. However, a change in the reporting entity that results from a transaction or event, such as a pooling of interests, or the creation, cessation, or complete or partial purchase or disposition of a subsidiary or business unit, does **not** require the addition of an explanatory paragraph that describes the inconsistency.

If a pooling of interests occurs and is not accounted for retroactively in the financial statements, the auditor should express a qualified or adverse opinion because of a GAAP departure.

NOTE: SFAS 141, ***Business Combinations,*** *prohibits the pooling-of-interests method for all business combinations within its scope initiated after June 30, 2001. (Combinations of nonprofit organizations, acquisitions of for-profit business entities by nonprofit organizations, and combinations of mutual enterprises are not included within the scope of SFAS 141.)*

3. Correction of an Error in Principle

A change from an accounting principle that is not generally accepted to one that is, including correcting a mistake in applying a principle.

NOTE: APB Opinion 20 specifies that the accounting treatment of the change is the correction of an error, but the method of accounting for the change does not affect its classification as a change in accounting principle for audit reporting purposes.

4. Change in Principle Inseparable from Change in Estimate

A change in estimate that is achieved by changing an accounting principle. An example is changing from deferring and amortizing a cost to expensing it when incurred because future benefits of the cost have become doubtful.

NOTE: Again, although the accounting treatment is that for a change in estimate, the change in principle affects audit reporting.

5. Changes in Presentation of Cash Flows

A change in an entity's policy for determining which items are treated as cash equivalents. SFAS 95, *Statement of Cash Flows*, requires this type of change to be effected by restating financial statements for earlier years presented for comparative purposes. This change in the presentation of cash flows requires the addition of an explanatory paragraph after the opinion paragraph.

CHANGES NOT AFFECTING CONSISTENCY

The following changes, if they have a material effect on comparability, require disclosure in the financial statements but have no effect on the auditor's report and its implications for consistency.

1. Change in Accounting Estimate

Examples of items for which estimates are made include uncollectible receivables, inventory obsolescence, warranty costs, and service lives and salvage values of depreciable assets. As new events occur or additional information is obtained, a change in such accounting estimates may be necessary.

2. Error Correction Not Involving Principle

Correction of an error not involving an accounting principle includes mathematical mistakes, oversight, or misuse of facts that existed when the financial statements were originally prepared.

3. Changes in Classification or Reclassification

Use of classifications within the financial statements different from classifications in prior years may be made. For example, "cash on hand" might be combined with "cash in bank" in a new classification "cash."

NOTE: A change in classification that significantly affects measurement of financial position or operating results requires a consistency modification—for example, a change in types of items reported as extraordinary.

4. Substantially Different Transactions or Events

Accounting principles are adopted when events or transactions first become material. Initial adoption or modification of an accounting principle necessitated by transactions or events clearly different in substance from past transactions or events does not affect consistency.

5. **Changes Expected to Have a Material Future Effect**

   If an accounting change has no material effect on the current financial statements but is reasonably certain to have a substantial future effect, disclosure of the change should be made whenever the statements of the period of the change are presented but **need not** cause modification of the audit report.

   NOTE: This means that the auditor does not have to modify the audit report for the inconsistency, but modification is permissible if the auditor wishes.

First Year Audits

If the independent auditor has not audited an entity's financial statements for the preceding year, he or she should apply reasonable and practicable procedures, such as reviewing underlying financial records and predecessor auditor's audit documentation, to obtain assurance as to the consistency of accounting principles employed in the current and the preceding year.

The independent auditor may not be able to obtain sufficient, competent evidential matter about the consistent application of accounting principles and the amounts of assets and liabilities at the beginning of the current year. In these circumstances, if these amounts could materially affect current operating results, in addition to modifying the auditor's report for a scope limitation as to consistency, the independent auditor would also be unable to express an opinion on the current year's results of operations and cash flows.

INTERPRETATIONS

The Effect of APB Opinion 28 on Consistency (February 1974)

Auditors may be engaged to report on financial information for an annual period and a subsequent interim period. APB Opinion 28 may appear to produce changes in the methods of applying accounting principles. For example, the entity, as permitted under APB Opinion 28, may use the gross profit method to estimate the interim inventory; whereas, for the annual financial statements, a physical inventory may be taken. The modifications permitted by APB Opinion 28 constitute a difference in circumstances, not a change in accounting principle. Therefore, the auditor should not add an explanatory paragraph to the audit report because of an inconsistency.

Impact on the Auditor's Report of FIFO to LIFO Change in Comparative Financial Statements (January 1975, Amended April 1989)

For a FIFO to LIFO change made in the earlier year presented and reported on (20X2 and 20X1 comparative financial statements presented—change made in 20X1), there is no inconsistency in the application of accounting principles. Comparability between the earliest year and subsequent year(s) is not affected since no cumulative effect is reported in the year of change. (There is no cumulative effect since the ending inventory for 20X0 is the beginning inventory for 20X1 for LIFO purposes.) The auditor should not refer to the change from FIFO to LIFO in his or her report.

THE EFFECT OF ACCOUNTING CHANGES BY AN INVESTEE ON CONSISTENCY (ISSUED JULY 1980, REVISED JUNE 1993)

As discussed in *Fundamental Requirements*, a change in accounting principles by an investee accounted for by the equity method requires the auditor to add an explanatory paragraph because of an inconsistency.

CHANGE IN PRESENTATION OF ACCUMULATED BENEFIT INFORMATION IN THE FINANCIAL STATEMENTS OF A DEFINED BENEFIT PENSION PLAN (DECEMBER 1980)

A change in the format of presentation of accumulated benefit information (e.g., on the face of a financial statement or in a separate statement) or a change in the date as of which such information is presented, is a reclassification, not an inconsistency.

THE EFFECT ON THE AUDITOR'S REPORT OF AN ENTITY'S ADOPTION OF A NEW ACCOUNTING STANDARD THAT DOES NOT REQUIRE THE ENTITY TO DISCLOSE THE EFFECT OF THE CHANGE IN THE YEAR OF ADOPTION (APRIL 2002)

If an entity adopts an accounting standard (for example, SFAS 133, *Accounting for Derivative Instruments and Hedging Activities*) and the standard does not require the entity to disclose the effect of the change in the year of adoption, Section 420 does not require the auditor to independently determine the effect of that change. However, this section requires that the auditor add an explanatory paragraph to his or her report for **material** changes in accounting principles. In determining whether such a paragraph is necessary, the auditor should consider

- The materiality of the change's cumulative effect
- The entity's voluntary disclosure about the effect of the change in accounting principle.

431 ADEQUACY OF DISCLOSURE IN FINANCIAL STATEMENTS

EFFECTIVE DATE AND APPLICABILITY

Original Pronouncement	SAS 32, October 1980.
Effective Date	When issued, October 1980.
Applicability	Audits of financial statements in accordance with generally accepted auditing standards.

DEFINITIONS OF TERMS

Adequate disclosure. Material matters include the (1) form, (2) arrangement, and (3) content of the financial statements and the appended notes, including

- Terminology used.
- Amount of detail given.
- Classification of items.
- Bases of amounts.

OBJECTIVES OF SECTION

This section is a carryover from the explanation of the reporting standard on adequate disclosure issued when generally accepted auditing standards were originally proposed in 1947. Thus, it is more philosophical than operational.

The section was modified in 1980, but the primary changes deleted some archaic advice on the possibility of not disclosing sensitive information that appeared contrary to current GAAP.

FUNDAMENTAL REQUIREMENTS

REPORTING STANDARD

The third standard of reporting is "Informative disclosures in the financial statements are to be regarded as reasonably adequate unless otherwise stated in the report."

BASIC REQUIREMENT

If management fails to disclose information required by GAAP, the auditor should

1. Express a qualified or adverse opinion.
2. Provide the information in the report (see below for exceptions to this requirement).

EXCEPTIONS TO NEED TO INCLUDE INFORMATION

The auditor may omit the information from the audit report if

1. The omission is recognized as appropriate by an SAS.
2. The information is **not** reasonably obtainable from management's accounts and records.
3. Providing the information would require the auditor to assume the position of a preparer of financial information. For example, an auditor would not be expected to provide
   a. A basic financial statement, such as a statement of cash flows.
   b. Segment information.

ACCOUNTING SERVICES PERMISSIBLE

An independent auditor may participate in preparing financial statements, including accompanying notes. This participation does not change the character of the statements as management's representations.

NOTE: This means that providing accounting services in conjunction with an audit is permissible and the fact that the auditor rather than management has prepared disclosure information does not create any reporting requirement. (However, for an SEC reporting company, the auditor would lose his or her independence by performing accounting services such as bookkeeping.)

INTERPRETATIONS

There are no interpretations for this section.

TECHNIQUES FOR APPLICATION

To aid the auditor in determining that all material matters have been adequately disclosed, a disclosure checklist may be completed at the end of the audit. The auditor may prepare his or her own disclosure checklists; however, checklists may be obtained from many sources, such as the AICPA.

504 ASSOCIATION WITH FINANCIAL STATEMENTS

EFFECTIVE DATE AND APPLICABILITY

Original Pronouncements	SAS 26, November 1979; SAS 35, April 1981; SAS 72, February 1993.
Effective Date	When issued, November 1979, unless subsequently amended.
Applicability	Accountants' reports on 1. Unaudited financial statements of public entities. 2. Comparative financial statements of public or nonpublic entities when the financial statements of one period are audited. 3. Financial statements of public entities when the accountant is not independent.

DEFINITIONS OF TERMS

Association. An accountant is associated with financial statements when he or she has consented to the use of his or her name in a report, document, or written communication containing the statements, or when he or she submits to the client or others financial statements that he or she has prepared or assisted in preparing.

NOTE: The accountant would be associated with the financial statements even though his or her name did not appear.

Public entity. Any entity (1) whose securities trade in a public market either on a domestic or foreign stock exchange or in the over-the-counter market, including securities quoted only locally or regionally, (2) that makes a filing with a regulatory agency in preparation for the sale of any class of its securities in a public market, or (3) a subsidiary, corporate joint venture, or other entity controlled by an entity described in (1) or (2).

OBJECTIVES OF SECTION

In December 1978, the Accounting and Review Services Committee of the AICPA issued Statement on Standards for Accounting and Review Services (SSARS) 1, *Compilation and Review of Financial Statements*. SSARS 1 applies to unaudited financial statements of nonpublic entities.

The basic purpose of this section was to replace existing sections that covered all unaudited financial statements. It updated the SASs for SSARSs by removing guidance for unaudited financial statements of nonpublic entities.

This section provides guidance to the accountant when he or she is associated with a **public entity's** unaudited financial statements

1. Prepared in conformity with generally accepted accounting principles (GAAP).
2. Prepared in accordance with a comprehensive basis of accounting (OCBOA) other than GAAP (see Section 623).
3. Not in conformity with GAAP or OCBOA.
4. On which the accountant provides negative assurance.

The section also provides guidance to the accountant when he or she is associated with

1. A public entity's financial statements that are unaudited because the accountant is not independent.
2. A **public or a nonpublic** entity's unaudited and audited financial statements presented in comparative form.

FUNDAMENTAL REQUIREMENTS

UNAUDITED FINANCIAL STATEMENTS

The basic requirements are

1. When an accountant is associated with financial statements of a public entity, but has not audited or reviewed them, the accountant should disclaim an opinion. His or her report should only identify the financial statements and state that they were not audited and that no opinion is expressed.
2. Each page of the financial statements should be marked "UNAUDITED."
3. The accountant should read the financial statements. He or she has no responsibility to apply any other procedures.
4. Procedures applied should not be described in the accountant's report.
5. For public entities that do not have annual audits, the accountant should refer to SSARSs for guidance.

Report on GAAP Financial Statements

An accountant associated with a **public** entity's unaudited GAAP financial statements should follow the preceding guidance and issue the following report illustrated in AU 504.05:

> The accompanying balance sheet of Widget Company as of December 31, 20X1, and the related statements of income and retained earnings, and cash flows for the year then ended, were not audited by us and, accordingly, we do not express an opinion on them.
>
> [*Signature*]
>
> [*Date*]

Report on OCBOA Financial Statements

An accountant associated with a **public** entity's unaudited OCBOA financial statements should basically follow the guidance in "Unaudited Financial Statements," earlier, but the report language should be modified to recognize the basis of accounting. An example of such a report is illustrated in AU 504.07.

> The accompanying statement of assets and liabilities resulting from cash transactions of Widget Corporation as of December 31, 20X1, and the related statement of revenues collected and expenses paid during the year then ended were not audited by us and, accordingly, we do not express an opinion on them.
>
> [*Signature*]
>
> [*Date*]

A note to the financial statements should describe the basis of accounting and how it differs from generally accepted accounting principles; however, the monetary effect of the difference does not have to be presented.

Report Modified for Lack of Independence

An accountant who is not independent with respect to a **public** entity's financial statements should basically follow the guidance in "Unaudited Financial Statements," explained earlier in this section, but the report language should be modified to recognize the lack of independence. The accountant should disclaim an opinion on the financial statements and state that he or she is not independent. The reason the accountant is not independent, however, should not be described in the report. An example of such a report is illustrated in AU 504.10.

> We are not independent with respect to Widget Company, and the accompanying balance sheet as of December 31, 20X1, and the related statements of income and retained earnings and cash flows for the year then ended were not audited by us and, accordingly, we do not express an opinion on them.
>
> [*Signature*]
>
> [*Date*]

If he or she is not independent with respect to the financial statements of a nonpublic entity, the accountant should follow the guidance in Statements on Standards for Accounting and Review Services (SSARSs).

Financial Statements Not in Conformity with GAAP

An accountant associated with a public entity's unaudited financial statements that are not in conformity with GAAP (for inadequate disclosure, see below) should suggest that they be revised. If the statements are not revised, the accountant should describe the departure in his or her report. The description should refer to the nature of the departure and, if practicable, state the effects on the financial statements. If the effects are not reasonably determinable, the report should state this fact. (Accountants' reports on unaudited financial statements not in conformity with GAAP are presented in *Illustrations*.) If management does not revise the financial statements or does not accept the accountant's report with the description of the departure, the accountant should refuse to be associated with the financial statements and, if necessary, withdraw from the engagement.

Inadequate Disclosure in Financial Statements

An accountant associated with a public entity's unaudited financial statements that do not contain adequate disclosure should describe this departure from GAAP in his or her report and, if practicable, include the necessary information for adequate disclosure. When it is not practicable to include omitted disclosures in the report, the accountant should state this fact. For example, when all, or substantially all, disclosures have been omitted, the accountant should indicate this in the report; however, he or she is not expected to include the omitted disclosures. (An accountant's report on unaudited financial statements that do not include adequate disclosure is presented in *Illustrations*.) If the client does not revise the financial statements or does not accept the accountant's report with the description of the inadequate disclosure, the accountant should refuse to be associated with the financial statements and, if necessary, withdraw from the engagement.

NOTE: If a nonpublic entity omits all, or substantially all, disclosures from its unaudited financial statements, the accountant should follow the guidance of SSARSs in reporting on these financial state-

ments. SSARSs prescribe specific wording for this situation. That wording may be used in a similar report on a public entity, but this section does not require use of that specific language.

AUDITED AND UNAUDITED FINANCIAL STATEMENTS IN COMPARATIVE FORM

For documents filed with the SEC, unaudited financial statements presented in comparative form with audited financial statements should be marked "UNAUDITED." The unaudited financial statements should **not** be referred to in the auditor's report.

NOTE: The reason for this different treatment is the legal significance of including a "report" in an SEC filing.

For all other documents, the unaudited financial statements should be marked "UNAUDITED," **and** the report on the prior period should be reissued or the report on the current period should include a separate paragraph describing the responsibility assumed for the prior period's financial statements.

NOTE: For information on the reissuance of auditors' reports, see Section 530; for information on the reissuance of compilation or review reports, see SSARS 2 (Section 3200).

Prior Period Audited—Current Period Unaudited

According to AU 504.16, when the financial statements of the prior period were audited and the report on the current period is to contain a separate paragraph about those financial statements, the separate paragraph should indicate the following:

1. The financial statements of the prior period were audited previously.
2. The date of the previous period's report.
3. The type of opinion expressed previously.
4. If the opinion of the previous period was other than unqualified, the reason.
5. No auditing procedures were performed after the date of the previous period's report.

An example of an appropriate separate paragraph is as follows:

> The financial statements for the year ended December 31, 20X1, were audited by us, and we expressed an unqualified opinion on them in our report dated March 1, 20X2, but we have not performed any auditing procedures since that date.

Prior Period Unaudited—Current Period Audited

According to AU 504.17, when the financial statements of the prior period were not audited and the report on the current period is to contain a separate paragraph about those financial statements, the separate paragraph should indicate the following:

1. A statement of the service performed in the prior period.
2. The date of the previous period's report.
3. A description of material modifications, if any, noted in the report of the previous period.
4. A statement that the service was less in scope than an audit and that the service does not provide a basis for the expression of an opinion on the financial statements taken as a whole.

Public Entity Financial Statements

If the financial statements are those of a public entity, the separate paragraph should include an "unaudited" disclaimer of opinion or a description of a review, whichever is appropriate.

Nonpublic Entity Financial Statements

If the financial statements are those of a nonpublic entity and they were compiled or reviewed, the separate paragraph should describe the service performed. The separate paragraph describing a review, illustrated in AU 504.17, might be as follows:

> The 20X1 financial statements were reviewed by us, and our report thereon, dated March 1, 20X2, stated we were not aware of any material modifications that should be made to those statements for them to be in conformity with generally accepted accounting principles. However, a review is substantially less in scope than an audit and does not provide a basis for the expression of an opinion on the financial statements taken as a whole.

The separate paragraph describing a compilation, also illustrated in AU 504.17, might be as follows:

> The 20X1 financial statements were compiled by us, and our report thereon, dated March 1, 20X2, stated we did not audit or review those financial statements and, accordingly, express no opinion or other form of assurance on them.

NEGATIVE ASSURANCE

Ordinarily, when a disclaimer of opinion is issued, it should not be modified by the accountant's expression of assurance that he or she has no knowledge of departures from generally accepted accounting principles. Exceptions to this general rule follow:

1. Review reports as described in SSARS 1.
2. Letters for underwriters in which the auditor reports on his or her limited procedures with respect to unaudited financial statements or other financial data necessary for a securities offering (see Section 634, "Letters for Underwriters and Certain Other Requesting Parties").
3. Review reports on interim financial information (see Section 722, "Interim Financial Information").

CLIENT-PREPARED COMMUNICATION

A public entity may prepare a written communication containing financial statements that have not been audited or reviewed and name the accountant in the document. In these circumstances, the accountant should request that (1) his or her name not be included or (2) that the financial statements be marked "unaudited" and a notation made that he or she does not express an opinion on them. If the client does not comply, the accountant should advise the client that the accountant has not consented to the use of his or her name and should consider other actions, such as consulting his or her lawyer.

INTERPRETATIONS

ANNUAL REPORT DISCLOSURE OF UNAUDITED FOURTH QUARTER INTERIM DATA (ISSUED NOVEMBER 1979; REVISED NOVEMBER 2002)

Unless specifically engaged to do so, the auditor does not have an obligation to audit interim data—such as disclosure of fourth quarter adjustments—presented in a note to annual audited financial statements. Disclosure of fourth quarter adjustments is a requirement, in certain circumstances, of APB Opinion 28 on interim financial information, and is not essential for fair presentation of annual financial statements in conformity with GAAP. The note would ordinarily be marked to indicate it has not been audited. Omission of the note disclosure when required should be mentioned in the audit report, but would not result in a qualified opinion because the annual financial statements reported on would conform with GAAP.

AUDITOR'S IDENTIFICATION WITH CONDENSED FINANCIAL DATA (NOVEMBER 1979)

Financial reporting services, such as Dun & Bradstreet, furnish subscribers with information that frequently includes identification of the entity's auditor, condensed financial information, and other data. The auditor and the entity do not have the ability to restrain a financial reporting service from publishing this information. In this context, the accountant has not consented to the use of his or her name, there is no "association" in the sense of Section 504, and there is no reporting obligation.

APPLICABILITY OF GUIDANCE ON REPORTING WHEN NOT INDEPENDENT (NOVEMBER 1979)

In determining whether he or she is independent and whether the reporting requirements of Section 504 therefore apply, the accountant should consider the ethical requirements of the AICPA and the relevant state society of CPAs or state board of accountancy. These ethics requirements should be considered in evaluating independence whether the financial statements are audited or unaudited.

TECHNIQUES FOR APPLICATION

REPORTING ON TAX RETURNS

SAS and SSARS requirements do not apply to **any** tax returns or other forms (such as Form 990) filed solely with taxing authorities. This means: **If it is a tax form, the accountant may sign it and not issue a report.** Financial statements that correlate with the data in the return may be attached as a supplement to the return without triggering a reporting obligation. If the client wants it or if the CPA firm adopts a policy requiring it, however, an accountant's report in conformity with the applicable SAS or SSARS is permissible.

UNAUDITED FINANCIAL STATEMENTS IN SEC FILINGS

The Securities Act of 1933 imposes a heavy legal burden on the auditor and other professionals. Section 11 of the Act allows any person who purchased securities described in the registration statement to sue the auditor. Under this section, all the purchaser must do is prove that the financial statements were misleading or materially misstated. The auditor has the burden of demonstrating as a defense that, among other things, an adequate audit was conducted in the circumstances.

Because of the burden placed on the auditor by Section 11 of the 1933 Act, he or she should not explicitly report on unaudited statements in a registration statement filed with the SEC under the 1933 Act.

ILLUSTRATIONS

When an accountant reads a public company's unaudited financial statements, he or she may become aware of departures from GAAP including inadequate disclosures. Following are reports describing these departures in the following situations:

1. Inventories stated below cost—effects of departure not determined.
2. Land recorded at appraised values—effects of departure determined.
3. Omission of disclosure—restrictions on retained earnings.

If the effects of a GAAP departure have been determined, the effects should be disclosed, but the accountant need not undertake to determine the effects.

ILLUSTRATION 1. INVENTORIES STATED BELOW COST—EFFECTS OF DEPARTURE NOT DETERMINED

The accompanying balance sheet of the XYZ Company as of December 31, 20X1, and the related statements of income and retained earnings and cash flows for the year then ended were not audited by us, and accordingly, we do not express an opinion on them.

Under generally accepted accounting principles, the components of inventory cost are material, labor, and overhead. Management has informed us that the inventory of finished goods is stated in the accompanying financial statements at material cost only. The effects of this departure from generally accepted accounting principles on the accompanying financial statements have not been determined.

ILLUSTRATION 2. LAND RECORDED AT APPRAISED VALUES—EFFECTS OF DEPARTURE DETERMINED

The accompanying balance sheet of the XYZ Company as of December 31, 20X1, and the related statements of income and retained earnings and cash flows for the year then ended were not audited by us, and accordingly, we do not express an opinion on them.

Under generally accepted accounting principles, land is ordinarily stated at cost. Management has informed us that the Company has recorded its land at appraised value and that if generally accepted accounting principles had been followed, the land account would have been decreased by $______.

ILLUSTRATION 3. OMISSION OF DISCLOSURE—RESTRICTIONS ON RETAINED EARNINGS

The accompanying balance sheet of the XYZ Company as of December 31, 20X1, and the related statements of income and retained earnings and cash flows for the year then ended were not audited by us, and accordingly, we do not express an opinion on them.

The financial statements do not disclose that the debentures issued on July 31, 20X1, limit the payment of cash dividends to 50% of earnings for 20X1 and thereafter. Generally accepted accounting principles require disclosure of matters of this nature.

508 REPORTS ON AUDITED FINANCIAL STATEMENTS

EFFECTIVE DATE AND APPLICABILITY

Original Pronouncements

SAS 58, April 1988; SAS 64, December 1990; SAS 79, December 1995; SAS 85, November 1997; SAS 93, October 2000; and SAS 98, September 2002.

Effective Date

Auditor's reports issued or **reissued** on or after January 1, 1989, unless subsequently amended. The amendments for SAS 93 are effective for reports issued or reissued on or after June 30, 2001, with earlier application permitted. The amendment for SAS 98 is effective upon issuance.

Applicability

Auditor's reports issued in connection with audits of historical financial statements that are intended to present financial position, results of operations, and cash flows in conformity with generally accepted accounting principles (GAAP).

The Statement does not apply to unaudited financial statements as described in Section 504, "Association with Financial Statements." It also does not apply to reports on incomplete financial information or other special presentations as described in Section 623, "Special Reports."

DEFINITIONS OF TERMS

Auditor's standard report. The auditor's standard report states that the financial statements present fairly, in all material respects, an entity's financial position, results of operations, and cash flows in conformity with generally accepted accounting principles. It has a title that includes the word **independent,** and **three paragraphs**—an **introductory paragraph** that identifies the financial statements audited and the division of responsibility between the auditor and management, a **scope paragraph** that describes the nature of an audit, and an **opinion paragraph** that expresses the auditor's opinion on the financial statements audited.

Audit. An audit, as referred to in the standard report, is an audit of historical financial statements performed in accordance with generally accepted auditing standards in effect at the time the audit is performed. Generally accepted auditing standards include the ten standards as well as Statements on Auditing Standards that interpret those standards and, when relevant, AICPA Audit and Accounting Guides.

Unqualified opinion. An unqualified opinion states that the financial statements present fairly, in all material respects, the financial position, results of operations, and cash flows of the entity in conformity with generally accepted accounting principles. This is the opinion expressed in the auditor's standard report.

Explanatory language added to the auditor's standard report. Certain circumstances, while not affecting the auditor's unqualified opinion on the financial statements, may require that the auditor add an explanatory paragraph (or other explanatory language) to the report.

Qualified opinion. A qualified opinion states that, except for the effects of the matter(s) to which the qualification relates, the financial statements present fairly, in all material respects, the financial position, results of operations, and cash flows of the entity in conformity with generally accepted accounting principles.

Adverse opinion. An adverse opinion states that the financial statements do not present fairly the financial position, results of operations, and cash flows of the entity in conformity with generally accepted accounting principles. An adverse opinion is an opinion, even though negative, and cannot be expressed unless an audit in accordance with GAAS has been performed.

Disclaimer of opinion. A disclaimer of opinion means that the auditor is unable to and does not express an opinion on the financial statements.

Continuing auditor. An auditor who has audited the financial statements of the current period and of one or more consecutive periods immediately prior to the current period.

Updated report. A report issued in conjunction with the report on current period financial statements by a continuing auditor that takes into consideration information that the auditor has become aware of during the audit of the current period financial statements.

OBJECTIVES OF SECTION

The primary objective of this section is to help assure the public's understanding of the auditor's role by requiring the auditor's report to more explicitly address in nontechnical language the following matters: (1) responsibility assumed, (2) procedures performed, and (3) degree of assurance provided.

SAS 58 prescribed a new form of standard report for auditors and deleted all reference to "consistency," eliminated "subject to" qualifications, and substituted "audited" for "examined." It required all auditors' reports to have a title that includes the word **independent** (for example, Independent Auditor's Report).

SAS 58 superseded previous guidance in SAS 2 (Section 509), *Reports on Audited Financial Statements*, and revised reporting guidance in other SASs and related interpretations.

In conjunction with deleting the routine reference to "consistency" in the auditor's standard report, SAS 58 revised the second standard of reporting in the ten generally accepted auditing standards as follows:

> *The report shall identify those circumstances in which such principles (GAAP) have not been consistently observed in the current period in relation to the preceding period.*

Thus, the auditor does not include an explicit opinion on consistency in normal circumstances, but adds an explanatory paragraph to highlight an inconsistency.

SAS 79 eliminated the reporting requirement to add an explanatory paragraph for all uncertainties, except substantial doubt about ability to continue as a going concern (see Section 341).

The removal of the uncertainties reporting requirement culminated a long debate about the relevance of this form of reporting that was set in motion by FASB Statement 5 on loss contingencies. Under GAAP, when an uncertainty is properly disclosed, the financial statements are not deficient and no audit report modification is warranted.

SAS 93, *Omnibus Statement on Auditing Standards—2000,* issued in January 2001, amends SAS 58 to include a reference to the United States of America as the country of origin of the accounting principles used to prepare the financial statements and the auditing standards that the auditor follows in performing the audit. This change was made because financial statements in conformity with US GAAP and audited according to US GAAS are increasingly available beyond US borders.

FUNDAMENTAL REQUIREMENTS: AUDITOR'S STANDARD REPORT

COMPONENTS OF AUDITOR'S STANDARD REPORT

The auditor's standard report should include the following:

1. A title that includes the word **independent** (for example, Independent Auditor's Report). A title is not required for an auditor's report if the auditor is not independent. (Section 504, "Association with Financial Statements," provides guidance on reporting when an auditor is not independent.)
2. An introductory paragraph with statements that
   a. The financial statements explicitly identified in the report as to title and date were audited.
   b. The financial statements are the responsibility of the entity's management.
   c. The auditor's responsibility is to express an opinion on the financial statements based on the audit.
3. A scope paragraph with statements that
   a. The audit was conducted in accordance with generally accepted auditing standards and an identification of the United States of America as the country of origin of those standards (e.g., auditing standards generally accepted in the United States of America or US generally accepted auditing standards).
   b. Those standards require that the auditor plan and perform the audit to obtain reasonable assurance about whether the financial statements are free of material misstatement.
   c. An audit includes
      (1) Examining, on a test basis, evidence supporting the amounts and disclosures in the financial statements.
      (2) Assessing the accounting principles used and significant estimates made by management.
      (3) Evaluating the overall financial statement presentation.
   d. The auditor believes that the audit provides a reasonable basis for the opinion.
4. An opinion paragraph that presents the auditor's opinion as to whether the financial statements present fairly, in all material respects, the financial position of the entity as of the balance sheet date and the result of its operations and its cash flows for the period then ended in conformity with generally accepted accounting principles. The opinion should include an identification of the United States of America as the country of origin of those accounting principles (e.g., accounting principles gener-

ally accepted in the United States of America or US generally accepted accounting principles).[1]

5. The manual or printed signature of the auditing firm and the date of the audit report, which is normally the date of completion of fieldwork.

The illustrations at the end of this section contain examples of the auditor's standard report on financial statements covering a single year (Illustration 1) and on comparative financial statements (Illustration 2). The illustrations also contain examples of audit reports on comparative financial statements when the opinions differ between years (Illustrations 14 and 15).

Addressee

The auditor's report may be addressed to the entity whose financial statements are being audited, its board of directors, or its shareholders. For an unincorporated entity, the report should be addressed as circumstances dictate. For example

- **Unincorporated entity.** The report should be addressed to the partners, or to the general partner of a limited partnership, to joint venturers, or to the proprietor of a sole proprietorship.
- **Audit of entity not the client of the auditor.** When an auditor is retained to audit the financial statements of an entity that is not the auditor's client, the report should be addressed to the one who retained the auditor and not to the directors or shareholders of the entity whose financial statements were audited.

NOTE: Under Section 301, "Public Company Audit Committees," and the SEC's related implementing Rule No. 33-8138, "Strengthening the Commission's Requirements Regarding Auditor Independence," the audit committee is "directly responsible for the appointment, compensation, and oversight of the work of any registered public accounting firm employed by that issuer. . . for the purpose of preparing or issuing an audit report or related work, and each such registered public accounting firm shall report directly to the audit committee." Therefore, the authors recommend that audit reports of listed companies be addressed to the audit committee. The authors believe that it is acceptable to also address the report to the stockholders and boards of directors.

FUNDAMENTAL REQUIREMENTS: EXPLANATORY LANGUAGE ADDED TO THE AUDITOR'S STANDARD REPORT

General

Circumstances may require the auditor to add an explanatory paragraph or explanatory language to the standard report, even though the circumstances do not affect the auditor's unqualified opinion. Unless specifically stated otherwise, the explanatory paragraph may either precede or follow the opinion paragraph. AU 508.11 lists the following circumstances that may require explanatory language:

1. The auditor's opinion is based in part on the report of another auditor (see *Illustrations* and Section 543).
2. The financial statements contain a departure from a promulgated accounting principle to prevent them from being misleading. (These situations are covered by Rule 203 of the AICPA Code of Professional Ethics. Also, see Section 410/411.)

---

[1] *A US auditor may also be engaged to report on a US entity's financial statements that have been prepared in conformity with accounting principles generally accepted in another country, in which case the auditor should refer to Section 534.*

3. There is substantial doubt about the entity's ability to continue as a going concern (see Section 341, "The Auditor's Consideration of an Entity's Ability to Continue as a Going Concern").
4. There has been a material change between periods in accounting principles or in the method of their application.
5. Certain circumstances relating to reports on comparative financial statements exist (e.g., prior year audited by another accountant whose report is not presented).
6. Selected quarterly financial data required by SEC Regulation S-K has been omitted or has not been reviewed (see Section 722, "Review of Interim Financial Information").
7. The following circumstances pertaining to supplementary information required by the Financial Accounting Standards Board (FASB), the Governmental Accounting Standards Board (GASB), or the Federal Accounting Standards Advisory Board (FASAB) exist:
   a. The information has been omitted.
   b. The information presented departs materially from FASB, GASB, or FASAB guidelines.
   c. The auditor is unable to complete prescribed procedures on the information.
   d. The auditor has doubts about whether the information conforms to FASB, GASB, or FASAB guidelines.
8. Other information in a document containing audited financial statements is materially inconsistent with information appearing in the financial statements (see Section 550, "Other Information in Documents Containing Audited Financial Statements").
9. The auditor may, but is not required to, add an explanatory paragraph when he or she wishes to emphasize a matter concerning the financial statements.

Opinion Based in Part on Report of Another Auditor

When the auditor decides to make reference to the report of another auditor as a basis, in part, for the opinion on the financial statements, he or she should disclose this fact in the introductory paragraph of the report and should refer to the report of the other auditor in the opinion paragraph (see Illustration 4 and Section 543).

Departure from a Promulgated Principle

Rule 203 of the AICPA Code of Professional Conduct states that the auditor should not express an unqualified opinion if the financial statements contain a material departure from an accounting principle promulgated by the bodies designated by Council of the AICPA to establish such principles. Rule 203, however, provides for the possibility that literal application of a principle may, in unusual circumstances, result in misleading financial statements. In those unusual circumstances, the auditor's report should include a separate paragraph or paragraphs containing the following:

1. A description of the departure.
2. The approximate effects of the departure, if practicable.
3. Reasons why compliance with the principle would result in misleading financial statements.

The explanatory paragraph(s) may either precede or follow the opinion paragraph. In these circumstances, the auditor may express an unqualified opinion with respect to the conformity of the financial statements with GAAP. Illustration 10 presents an example of an auditor's report in these circumstances.

NOTE: The financial statements conform with GAAP because the departure from a promulgated principle (pronouncement) is necessary to keep the financial statements from being misleading.

LACK OF CONSISTENCY

If there has been a change in accounting principles or in the method of their application that has a material effect on the comparability of financial statements, the auditor should add an explanatory paragraph **following** the opinion paragraph which (1) notes the change, (2) identifies the nature of the change, and (3) refers to the note in the financial statements that discusses the change.

The auditor does not indicate concurrence with the change. If he or she does not concur, the opinion should be qualified because of the GAAP departure or be an adverse opinion (see *Fundamental Requirements: Departures from Unqualified Opinions*).

Explanatory Paragraph

The following is an example of an appropriate explanatory paragraph (following the opinion paragraph) for a change in accounting principle or the method of application:

> As discussed in Note X to the financial statements, the Company changed its method of computing depreciation in 20X2.

Reports on Financial Statements of Subsequent Years

The explanatory paragraph described above is required in the auditor's report of financial statements of subsequent years as long as the year of change is presented and reported on. An exception to this requirement occurs when a change in accounting principle that does not require a cumulative effect adjustment is made at the beginning of the earliest year presented and reported on (for example, a change from FIFO to LIFO).

If the accounting change is accounted for by retroactive restatement of the financial statements affected, the explanatory paragraph is required only in the year of change.

EMPHASIS OF A MATTER

The auditor may add an explanatory paragraph, either preceding or following the opinion paragraph, to emphasize a matter regarding the financial statements, but nonetheless express an unqualified opinion on these statements. The auditor should not refer to this type of explanatory paragraph in the opinion paragraph.

FUNDAMENTAL REQUIREMENTS: DEPARTURES FROM UNQUALIFIED OPINIONS

GENERAL

Circumstances may require that the auditor not express an unqualified opinion on the financial statements. Depending on the circumstances, the auditor should express a qualified opinion ("except for") or an adverse opinion or disclaim an opinion.

QUALIFIED OPINIONS

When the auditor expresses a qualified opinion, he or she should

1. Add one or more separate explanatory paragraph(s) **preceding** the opinion paragraph of the report that discloses all of the substantive reasons for the qualified opinion.
2. Add appropriate qualifying language to the opinion paragraph, including the word **except** or **exception** in a phrase such as **except for** or **with the exception of**.
3. Add a reference in the opinion paragraph to the explanatory paragraph(s).

Qualified opinions are expressed when there is a scope limitation or a departure from generally accepted accounting principles, and the auditor has decided not to disclaim an opinion or express an adverse opinion, respectively.

The illustrations contain examples of auditors' reports qualified because of a scope limitation (Illustration 5) and qualified because of a departure from generally accepted accounting principles (Illustrations 7 and 8).

NOTE: Disclosing all the substantive reasons for an opinion means that all GAAP departures and scope limitations that are material and known to the auditor should be disclosed. For example, the auditor should disclose a known misapplication of the lower of cost or market method in inventory evaluation even though the opinion has been qualified for a scope limitation related to inventory.

Scope Limitation

Restrictions on the audit's scope, whether imposed by the client or by circumstances, may require the auditor to qualify the opinion or to disclaim an opinion. **Ordinarily,** the auditor should disclaim an opinion on the financial statements when restrictions that significantly limit the scope of the audit are imposed by the client.

Uncertainties and scope limitations. If the auditor has not obtained sufficient evidential matter concerning an uncertainty, he or she should consider the need to express a qualified opinion ("except for") or to disclaim an opinion. Qualifying or disclaiming an opinion because of a scope limitation is appropriate when sufficient evidential matter does or did exist but was not available to the auditor (for example, management did not retain certain records or management imposed a scope restriction). If it is expected that evidence concerning the resolution of the uncertainty will become available in the future, an unqualified opinion with an explanatory paragraph is appropriate.

Notes to financial statements. Notes to financial statements may contain unaudited information that should be subjected to auditing procedures. If the auditor is not able to apply necessary auditing procedures to these disclosures, he or she should qualify the opinion or disclaim an opinion because of the scope limitation. However, some disclosures, such as the pro forma effects of a business combination or a subsequent event, are not necessary to fairly present the financial statements in accordance with generally accepted accounting principles and, therefore, may be identified as **unaudited** or as **not covered by the auditor's report**.

Reporting on one basic financial statement. The auditor may audit and express an unqualified opinion on one of the basic financial statements if the scope of the audit is not restricted. Illustration 3 contains an example of an auditor's report on the audit of a balance sheet.

Departure from a Generally Accepted Accounting Principle

When financial statements are materially affected by a departure from GAAP, the auditor should express a qualified opinion or an adverse opinion.

When the auditor expresses a qualified opinion, he or she should include a separate explanatory paragraph or paragraphs **preceding** the opinion paragraph disclosing (1) all substantive reasons that led to the conclusion that there was a departure from GAAP and (2) the principal effects of the departure on the financial statements, if practicable (see Section 431,

"Adequacy of Disclosure in the Financial Statements"). If the effects of the departure are not reasonably determinable, the auditor's report should state that fact.

The opinion paragraph of a report qualified because of a departure from GAAP should include appropriate qualifying language and a reference to the explanatory paragraph(s).

Illustrations 7 and 8 contain an example of an auditor's report qualified because of a departure from GAAP.

NOTE: Disclosing all substantive reasons for a GAAP departure means that all known instances of violation of GAAP involved should be mentioned. For example, the auditor should not disclose that a building is stated at appraised value and fail to mention that the increase to appraised value was made to capitalize a realized loss on the sale of another asset.

Inadequate disclosure. If the financial statements, including the notes to the financial statements, do not disclose information required by GAAP, the auditor should express a qualified or adverse opinion because of this departure from GAAP and should provide the information in the auditor's report, if practicable (see Section 431, "Adequacy of Disclosure in the Financial Statements"). Illustration 13 contains an example of an auditor's report qualified because of inadequate disclosure.

NOTE: At times, current year financial statements are prepared on the basis of accounting principles acceptable at the financial statement date but that will have to be restated in the following year because of the issuance of a statement of financial accounting standards whose effective date is after the date of the current year's financial statements. In those circumstances, if the auditor decides that the matter should be disclosed in the current year's financial statements and it is not, the auditor should express a qualified or adverse opinion as to conformity with GAAP.

Omission of statement of cash flows. If an entity issues a balance sheet and an income statement but fails to present a statement of cash flows, the auditor normally should qualify the opinion. The auditor is not required to prepare a basic financial statement and include it in the auditor's report if the entity's management does not present the statement.

Illustration 11 contains an example of an auditor's report qualified because of the omission of the statement of cash flows.

Uncertainties and departures from GAAP. Matters involving risks or uncertainties may cause a departure from generally accepted accounting principles because of the following:

1. Inadequate disclosure.
2. Inappropriate accounting principles.
3. Unreasonable accounting estimates.

The auditor should qualify the opinion or express an adverse opinion if he or she concludes that a matter involving a risk or an uncertainty is not adequately disclosed in the financial statements (see Statement of Financial Accounting Standards [SFAS] 5, *Accounting for Contingencies*, for the required disclosures of some uncertainties).

The auditor should qualify the opinion or express an adverse opinion if he or she concludes that the accounting principle used to report a transaction involving an uncertainty causes the financial statements to be materially misstated. An example is a sale on account where collection is uncertain that is reported under the accrual method instead of under the installment or cost recovery method as required by GAAP.

The auditor should qualify the opinion or express an adverse opinion if he or she concludes that management has made an unreasonable estimate of the future outcome of an uncertainty and that its effect is to cause the financial statements to be materially misstated (see Section 312, "Audit Risk and Materiality in Conducting an Audit" and Section 342, "Auditing Accounting Estimates").

Accounting changes—general. The auditor should express a qualified opinion if (1) a newly adopted accounting principle is not a generally accepted accounting principle, (2) the method of accounting for the effect of the change is not in conformity with generally accepted accounting principles, or (3) management has not provided reasonable justification for the change in accounting principle. If the effects of the change are sufficiently material, the auditor should express an adverse opinion on the financial statements.

If management has not provided reasonable justification for a change in accounting principle, the auditor should, in subsequent years, continue to qualify the opinion on the financial statements of the year of change as long as those financial statements are presented and reported on. The auditor's opinion on financial statements of subsequent years need not be qualified.

Illustration 12 contains an example of an auditor's report qualified because management did not provide reasonable justification for a change in accounting principle.

Accounting changes—subsequent years. Whenever the auditor expresses a qualified or an adverse opinion on the conformity of financial statements with GAAP for the year of change, the auditor should do the following when reporting on subsequent year's financial statements:

1. Disclose the reservations with respect to the financial statements for the year of change if those financial statements are presented and reported on with the subsequent year's financial statements.
2. If an entity has adopted an accounting principle that is not generally accepted, the auditor should express a qualified or an adverse opinion on the subsequent year's financial statements, depending on the materiality of the departure of those financial statements.
3. If an entity accounts for the effects of a change in accounting principle prospectively when it should have reported the cumulative effects of the change in the year of change, the auditor should express a qualified or an adverse opinion on the subsequent year's financial statements, depending on the materiality of the effect of the departure from generally accepted accounting principles on those financial statements.

ADVERSE OPINIONS

An adverse opinion is expressed when the auditor believes the financial statements taken as a whole are not presented fairly in conformity with GAAP.

When the auditor expresses an adverse opinion, he or she should do the following:

1. Disclose in a separate explanatory paragraph **preceding** the opinion paragraph of the report all substantive reasons for the opinion.
2. State the principal effects of the subject matter that caused the adverse opinion on financial position, results of operations, and cash flows, if practicable (see SAS 32, Section 431, "Adequacy of Disclosure in the Financial Statements"). If the effects are not reasonably determinable, the auditor's report should state this fact.
3. Include in the opinion paragraph a direct reference to the separate explanatory paragraph.

Illustration 9 contains an example for an auditor's report expressing an adverse opinion.

NOTE: Because an adverse opinion is an opinion, it should not be expressed unless the auditor has performed an audit of sufficient scope to be able to express an opinion.

DISCLAIMER OF OPINION

The auditor disclaims an opinion when he or she has not performed an audit sufficient in scope to enable him or her to form an opinion on the financial statements. Ordinarily, the auditor should disclaim an opinion on the financial statements when significant scope restrictions are imposed by the client.

The auditor should **not** disclaim an opinion because he or she believes there are material departures from generally accepted accounting principles.

The auditor should do the following when disclaiming an opinion because of a scope limitation:

1. Indicate in a separate explanatory paragraph the reasons why the audit did not comply with generally accepted auditing standards.
2. State in the disclaimer of opinion paragraph that the scope of the audit was not sufficient to warrant the expression of opinion.
3. The auditor's report should not include a scope paragraph.

Illustration 6 contains an example of an auditor's report disclaiming an opinion because of a scope limitation.

NOTE: Even though the auditor disclaims an opinion, the auditor should disclose any known GAAP departures.

FUNDAMENTAL REQUIREMENTS: REPORTS ON COMPARATIVE FINANCIAL STATEMENTS

GENERAL

A continuing auditor should update his or her report on the prior period financial statements presented on a comparative basis with those of the current period. When updating his or her report, the auditor should consider the effects of circumstances or events coming to his or her attention during the audit of the current period financial statements that may affect the prior period financial statements (see below, "Change of Opinion").

The auditor's report on comparative financial statements should be dated as of the date of completion of fieldwork for the most recent audit.

CHANGE OF OPINION

In an updated report, if the auditor expresses an opinion different from the one previously expressed on prior period financial statements, he or she should do the following:

1. Disclose all substantive reasons for the different opinion in a separate explanatory paragraph **preceding** the opinion paragraph of the report.
2. The explanatory paragraph should disclose the following:
   a. The date of the auditor's previous report.
   b. The type of opinion previously expressed.
   c. The circumstances or events that caused the auditor to express a different opinion.
   d. The updated opinion on the prior period financial statements is different from the opinion previously expressed on those financial statements.

Illustration 16 contains an example of an auditor's report with an opinion different from the one previously expressed on prior period financial statements.

Reissuance of Predecessor Auditor's Report

Predecessor's Procedures

Before reissuing or consenting to the reuse of a report previously issued on financial statements of a prior period, when those financial statements are to be presented on a comparative basis with audited financial statements of a subsequent period, a predecessor auditor should consider whether the previous report on those statements is still appropriate. The predecessor should do the following:

1. Read the financial statements of the current period.
2. Compare the prior period financial statements that the predecessor reported on with the financial statements to be presented for comparative purposes.
3. Obtain letters of representation from
   a. The successor auditor stating whether the successor's audit revealed matters that might have a material effect on, or require disclosure in, the financial statements reported on by the predecessor auditor, and
   b. Management of the former client stating
      (1) Whether any information has come to management's attention that would cause them to believe that any previous representations should be modified, and
      (2) Whether any events have occurred subsequent to the balance sheet date of the latest prior period financial statements reported on by the predecessor auditor that would require adjustment to, or disclosure in, those financial statements. (Illustration 17D contains an example of a letter of representation from a successor auditor and from management.)

Based on the above procedures, if the predecessor auditor believes the previously issued report must be revised, he or she should make inquiries about the matter and perform other procedures considered necessary.

Revision of Previously Issued Report

If the predecessor auditor concludes that the previously issued report should be revised, the updated report should disclose all substantive reasons for the different opinion in a separate explanatory paragraph **preceding** the opinion paragraph of the report. The explanatory paragraph should disclose the following:

1. The auditor's previous report date.
2. The type of opinion previously expressed.
3. The circumstances or events that caused the auditor to express a different opinion.
4. The updated opinion on the prior period financial statements is different from the opinion previously expressed on those financial statements.

Dating of Reissued Report

When reissuing the auditor's report on prior period financial statements, the predecessor auditor should use the date of the previous report.

If the predecessor revises the report or the previously reported-on financial statements are restated, the predecessor auditor should dual date the report.

PREDECESSOR AUDITOR'S REPORT NOT PRESENTED

GENERAL

When the predecessor auditor's report on prior period financial statements is not presented, the successor auditor should disclose in the introductory paragraph of his or her report the following:

1. The prior period financial statements were audited by another auditor.
2. The predecessor auditor's report date.
3. The type of report issued by the predecessor auditor.
4. The substantive reasons for a report other than the standard report.

Illustration 17 contains examples of successor auditor reports when the predecessor auditor's report is not presented.

Prior Period Financial Statements Restated

When the prior period financial statements have been restated, the introductory paragraph of the successor auditor's report should indicate that a predecessor auditor reported on the financial statements of the prior period before restatement. If the successor auditor is able to satisfy himself or herself as to the appropriateness of the restatement, he or she may also include the following paragraph from AU 508.74 in the report:

> We also audited the adjustments described in Note X that were applied to restate the 20X1 financial statements. In our opinion, such adjustments are appropriate and have been properly applied.

INTERPRETATIONS

REPORT OF AN OUTSIDE INVENTORY-TAKING FIRM AS AN ALTERNATIVE PROCEDURE FOR OBSERVING INVENTORIES (ISSUED JULY 1975; REVISED OCTOBER 2000)

Some companies, such as retail stores or automobile dealers, use outside specialists in the taking of physical inventories to count, list, price, and subsequently compute the dollar amount of inventory on hand. The fact that inventory is counted by outside specialists is not by itself a satisfactory substitute for the auditor's own observation or taking of some physical counts.

The auditor would ordinarily apply the following procedures:

1. Examine the outside specialist's work program.
2. Observe its counting procedures.
3. Make or observe some physical counts.
4. Recompute calculations of submitted inventory on a test basis.
5. If appropriate, apply tests to intervening transactions.

The independent auditor might, as a matter of professional judgment, decide to reduce the extent of work because of the work of outside specialists, but any restrictions imposed by management or others would be a scope limitation.

REPORTING ON FINANCIAL STATEMENTS PREPARED ON A LIQUIDATION BASIS OF ACCOUNTING (ISSUED DECEMBER 1984; REVISED JUNE 1993 AND FEBRUARY 1997; REVISED OCTOBER 2000)

An entity is not viewed as a going concern if liquidation is imminent. In these circumstances, the liquidation basis of accounting is GAAP. If the liquidation basis has been properly applied and adequate disclosures are made, the auditor should issue an unqualified opinion.

If financial statements on the liquidation basis are presented in comparative form with a prior period's going-concern basis financial statements, the auditor's report should include an explanatory paragraph that describes the change in basis of accounting. (Illustrations 19 and 20 present examples of auditor's reports on financial statements on the liquidation basis of accounting.)

REFERENCE IN AUDITOR'S STANDARD REPORT TO MANAGEMENT'S REPORT (JANUARY 1989)

The auditor's standard report on financial statements should not refer to a separate report by management, if management chooses to present one, that describes management's financial reporting responsibilities. The standard auditor's report should still state that management is responsible for the financial statements, but a cross-reference to a report by management might be misinterpreted by users.

REPORTING ON AUDITS CONDUCTED IN ACCORDANCE WITH AUDITING STANDARDS GENERALLY ACCEPTED IN THE UNITED STATES OF AMERICA AND IN ACCORDANCE WITH INTERNATIONAL STANDARDS ON AUDITING (MARCH 2002)

As discussed in this section, the auditor is required to (1) indicate in his or her report that the audit was conducted in accordance with generally accepted auditing standards and (2) identify the United State of America as the country of origin of those standards. However, nothing in this section prohibits an auditor from stating that the audit was conducted in accordance with another set of auditing standards. If the audit was also conducted in accordance with International Standards on Auditing in their entirety, the auditor may indicate this in his or her report.

When reporting on an audit performed in accordance with US GAAS and International Standards on Auditing, the auditor should comply with US reporting standards.

The following is an example from the interpretation (AU 9508.59) of a paragraph in a report for an audit performed in accordance with US GAAS and International Standards on Auditing:

> We conducted our audit in accordance with auditing standards generally accepted in the United States of America and in accordance with International Standards on Auditing. Those standards require that we plan and perform the audit to obtain reasonable assurance about whether the financial statements are free of material misstatement. An audit includes examining, on a test basis, evidence supporting the amounts and disclosures in the financial statements. An audit also includes assessing the accounting principles used and significant estimates made by management, as well as evaluating the overall financial statement presentation. We believe that our audit provides a reasonable basis for our opinion.

Reporting as Successor Auditor When Prior-Period Audited Financial Statements Were Audited by a Predecessor Auditor Who Has Ceased Operations (November 2002)

If prior period financial statements were audited by a predecessor auditor who has ceased operations, and such statements are presented for comparative purposes with the current financial statements, the successor auditor should indicate in the introductory paragraph of his or her report that the financial statements of the prior period were audited by another auditor and should indicate the date and type of report. (If the report was not unqualified, the auditor should also indicate the substantive reasons for the report qualifications.) The successor auditor also should state that the other auditor has ceased operations, but should not name the other auditor.

The interpretation presents the following example of such a report (AU 9508.61):

> The financial statements of ABC Company as of December 31, 20X1, and for the year then ended were audited by other auditors who have ceased operations. Those auditors expressed an unqualified opinion on those financial statements in their report dated March 31, 20X2.

For SEC engagements (particularly involving Arthur Andersen LLP), the SEC staff has stated that in annual reports, the predecessor's latest prior period report should be reprinted with a legend indicating that the report is a copy of the previously issued report and that the report has not been reissued.

If the prior period financial statements are subsequently restated, the successor auditor cannot report on the restated adjustments until the audit of the current period financial statements is complete. If the successor auditor is asked to report on the restated financial statements without also reporting on the current period audited financial statements, the successor auditor would need to reaudit the prior period statements.

Effect on Auditor's Report of Omission of Schedule of Investments by Investment Partnerships That Are Exempt from Securities and Exchange Commission Registration under the Investment Company Act of 1940 (April 2003)

When an auditor is reporting on financial statements of an investment partnership that is exempt from SEC registration and that does not include required Schedule of Investments information, the auditor is required to include the missing information in a qualified or an adverse report, if practicable. The auditor should not describe "the nature of the omitted disclosures" in the qualified or adverse report.

PROFESSIONAL ISSUES TASK FORCE PRACTICE ALERTS

97-3 Changes in Auditors and Related Topics

Predecessor auditors need to consider relevant issues when asked by a former client to reissue reports, since the predecessor auditor is essentially being asked to reestablish a client relationship. This practice alert states that before consenting to the inclusion of his or her report on previously audited financial statements, a predecessor auditor should perform procedures similar to its client acceptance and continuation procedures as required by Statement on Quality Control Standards 2, *System of Quality Control for a CPA Firm's Accounting and Auditing Practice*, and may wish to consider the recommendations of the AICPA Joint Task Force on Quality Control Standards in its *Guide for Establishing and Maintaining a System of Quality Control for a CPA Firm's Accounting and Auditing Practice*.

The auditor typically would evaluate whether specific events have occurred, such as a major change in

- Management
- Directors
- Ownership
- Legal counsel
- Financial condition
- Litigation status
- Nature of the entity's business
- Scope of the engagement

Consideration of

- Whether the client has selected an underwriter that has been the subject of adverse publicity.
- The professional reputation and experience of both the successor auditor and legal counsel associated with subsequent years' financial statements.

After consideration of these factors, the predecessor auditor should then consider whether his or her report is still appropriate under the circumstances, using guidance provided in this section under *Fundamental Requirements: Reports on Comparative Financial Statements.* If after performing the appropriate procedures, a predecessor becomes aware of subsequent events or transactions that require adjustment, additional disclosure or reclassification, the predecessor auditor should make inquiries and perform any other necessary procedures.

An auditor may decide not to consent to the use of his or her previously issued report, and is not required to subsequently sign a consent for inclusion of that report in a registration statement or for any other reason. The auditor does not need to disclose or communicate the reasons for not issuing the report to either the entity or its audit committee. If the predecessor does not reissue his or her report, the successor may be engaged to audit the financial statements previously reported on and should follow the guidance in *Fundamental Requirements* of Section 315, "Communications between Predecessor and Successor Auditors."

Finally, the alert discusses the use of indemnification clauses when reissuing reports. SEC independence rules prohibit indemnification agreements between auditors and current publicly held clients. However, the SEC staff has agreed not to question a predecessor auditor's independence with respect to a former client for indemnification agreements provided that

1. Such indemnification letter would be void and any advanced funds would be returned to a client if a court finds the former auditor liable for malpractice, and
2. The indemnification provision is entered into after a successor auditor has issued an audit report on the former client's most recent financial statements included in the client's registration statement.

The full text of this Practice Alert can be obtained from the AICPA website at www.aicpa.org/members/div/secps/lit/practice.htm.

TECHNIQUES FOR APPLICATION

The following table lists the circumstances requiring modification of the auditor's standard report and the effect of the modification on the auditor's standard report.

Circumstances	Types of Opinion: Unqualified	Qualified	Adverse	Disclaimer
1. Opinion based in part on report of another auditor.	x			
2. Rule 203 opinion.	x			
3. Lack of consistency.	x			
4. Required quarterly data omitted or not reviewed.	x			
5. Required supplementary information omitted or not reviewed.	x			
6. Other information in a document containing audited financial statements is materially inconsistent with financial statement information.	x			
7. Emphasis of matter.	x			
8. Scope limitation.		x		x
9. Report on one financial statement only.	x			
10. Departure from GAAP.		x	x	
11. Inadequate disclosure.		x	x	
12. Change in accounting principle.				
a. Newly adopted principle not generally accepted.		x	x	
b. Incorrect method of accounting for the effect of the change.		x	x	
c. Reasonable justification for change not provided.		x	x	

SCOPE LIMITATION

GENERAL

The decision to qualify the opinion or to disclaim an opinion depends on the auditor's assessment of the importance of the omitted procedure to his or her ability to form an opinion on the financial statements being audited. The auditor's assessment is affected by the following:

1. Nature and magnitude of the potential effects.
2. Significance to financial statements of item to scope limitation.
3. Pervasiveness of the item.

Pervasiveness generally relates to the number of items in the financial statement; that is, is the matter isolated to a few items or does it affect many? For example, ending inventory affects many items—current assets, current ratio, gross profit, income taxes, and net income—whereas an investment accounted for by the equity method affects few line items in the financial statements.

Common Restrictions on Scope

Common restrictions on the scope of the audit involve (1) observation of physical inventories, (2) confirmation of accounts receivable, and (3) long-term investments accounted for by the equity method when the auditor is unable to obtain audited financial statements of the investee.

If the auditor did not observe the ending inventory because of circumstances such as appointment after year-end, he or she should apply alternative procedures. Alternative procedures may include observing all or part of the physical inventory after year-end and rolling it back to year-end by adjusting for additions and sales between year-end and the date the physical inventory was observed. Whatever alternative procedures are used, the auditor should always make, or observe, some physical counts of the inventory and apply appropriate tests to the transactions between year-end and the date of the observation. (See Section 331.)

If the auditor did not confirm accounts receivable at year-end because of circumstances such as appointment after year-end, he or she might do either of the following at the time of appointment:

1. Try to confirm year-end balances or individual sales and cash receipts.
2. Confirm balances at a date subsequent to year-end and apply appropriate tests to transactions between year-end and the confirmation date.

Some debtors are unable to confirm balances at any time. In these circumstances, the auditor should consider examining subsequent cash receipts or specific sales invoices. In all instances in which accounts receivable are not substantiated by confirmation, the auditor has to document how the presumption that receivables will be confirmed was overcome (see Section 330).

If the auditor is unable to obtain audited financial statements of the investee for investments accounted for by the equity method, he or she should examine other types of financial statements (compiled, reviewed, internal) and, depending on the materiality of the investment, apply appropriate auditing procedures to these statements.

If there is a scope limitation and the auditor satisfies himself or herself as to the account balance by applying alternate procedures, the auditor's report should not make reference to these circumstances.

Restrictions Imposed by Client

As noted under *Fundamental Requirements*, when scope limitations are imposed by the client, the auditor should ordinarily disclaim an opinion on the financial statements. The rationale for a disclaimer in these circumstances is that the client is in a position to avoid the limitation and the auditor cannot know what would be found by release of the restriction.

DEPARTURE FROM GAAP

The decision to express a qualified or an adverse opinion because of a departure from GAAP depends on the degree of materiality of the departure. Criteria for determining the degree of materiality of a departure from GAAP are

1. Dollar magnitude of the effects.
2. Significance of the item to the entity (for example, inventories to a manufacturing company).
3. Pervasiveness of the misstatements.
4. Impact of the misstatement on the financial statements taken as a whole.

In practice, auditors also consider the likely purpose of management in departing from GAAP. A judgment that management intended to mislead users would ordinarily cause the auditor to express an adverse opinion.

LITIGATION SERVICES

A practioner engaged to provide expert consulting or witness services is not subject to the requirements of GAAS, including the reporting standards. However, an expert engaged by plaintiffs or defendants in an auditor malpractice matter may testify about the application of GAAS to the circumstances.

ILLUSTRATIONS

The following are illustrations of auditors' reports, explanatory paragraphs, a letter from successor auditor to predecessor auditor, and a letter from management to the predecessor auditor.

Illustration 1. Auditor's Standard Report: Financial Statements Covering a Single Year (Adapted from SAS 58)

Independent Auditor's Report

We have audited the accompanying balance sheet of Widget Company as of December 31, 20X1, and the related statements of income, retained earnings, and cash flows for the year then ended. These financial statements are the responsibility of the Company's management. Our responsibility is to express an opinion on these financial statements based on our audit.

We conducted our audit in accordance with auditing standards generally accepted in the United States of America. Those standards require that we plan and perform the audit to obtain reasonable assurance about whether the financial statements are free of material misstatement. An audit includes examining, on a test basis, evidence supporting the amounts and disclosures in the financial statements. An audit also includes assessing the accounting principles used and significant estimates made by management, as well as evaluating the overall financial statement presentation. We believe that our audit provides a reasonable basis for our opinion.

In our opinion, the financial statements referred to above present fairly, in all material respects, the financial position of Widget Company as of [*at*] December 31, 20X1, and the results of its operations and its cash flows for the year then ended in conformity with accounting principles generally accepted in the United States of America.

Guy and Carmichael
February 15, 20X2

Illustration 2. Auditor's Standard Report on Comparative Financial Statements (Adapted from SAS 58)

Independent Auditor's Report

We have audited the accompanying balance sheet of Widget Company as of December 31, 20X2 and 20X1, and the related statements of income, retained earnings, and cash flows for the years then ended. These financial statements are the responsibility of the Company's management. Our responsibility is to express an opinion on these financial statements based on our audit.

We conducted our audits in accordance with auditing standards generally accepted in the United States of America. Those standards require that we plan and perform the audit to obtain reasonable assurance about whether the financial statements are free of material misstatement. An audit includes examining, on a test basis, evidence supporting the amounts and disclosures in the financial statements. An audit also includes assessing the accounting principles used and significant estimates made by management, as well as evaluating the overall financial statement presentation. We believe that our audits provide a reasonable basis for our opinion.

In our opinion, the financial statements referred to above present fairly, in all material respects, the financial position of Widget Company as of [at] December 31, 20X2 and 20X1, and the results of its operations and its cash flows for the years then ended in conformity with accounting principles generally accepted in the United States of America.

Guy and Carmichael
February 15, 20X3

Illustration 3. Auditor's Report on One Basic Financial Statement (Adapted from SAS 58)

Independent Auditor's Report

We have audited the accompanying balance sheet of Widget Company as of December 31, 20X1. This financial statement is the responsibility of the Company's management. Our responsibility is to express an opinion on this financial statement based on our audit.

We conducted our audit in accordance with auditing standards generally accepted in the United States of America. Those standards require that we plan and perform the audit to obtain reasonable assurance about whether the financial statements are free of material misstatement.

An audit includes examining, on a test basis, evidence supporting the amounts and disclosures in the financial statements. An audit also includes assessing the accounting principles used and significant estimates made by management, as well as evaluating the overall financial statement presentation. We believe that our audit provides a reasonable basis for our opinion.

In our opinion, the balance sheet referred to above presents fairly, in all material respects, the financial position of Widget Company as of December 31, 20X1, in conformity with accounting principles generally accepted in the United States of America.

Guy and Carmichael
February 15, 20X2

ILLUSTRATION 4. AUDITOR'S REPORT: OPINION BASED IN PART ON REPORT OF ANOTHER AUDITOR (ADAPTED FROM SAS 58)

Independent Auditor's Report

We have audited the consolidated balance sheets of Widget Company and subsidiaries as of December 31, 20X2 and 20X1, and the related consolidated statements of income, retained earnings, and cash flows for the years then ended. These financial statements are the responsibility of the Company's management. Our responsibility is to express an opinion on these financial statements based on our audits. We did not audit the financial statements of B Company, a wholly owned subsidiary, which statements reflect total assets of $_____ and $_____ as of December 31, 20X2 and 20X1, respectively, and total revenues of $_____ and $_____ for the years then ended. Those statements were audited by other auditors whose report has been furnished to us, and our opinion, insofar as it relates to the amounts included for B Company, is based solely on the report of the other auditors.

We conducted our audits in accordance with auditing standards generally accepted in the United States of America. Those standards require that we plan and perform the audit to obtain reasonable assurance about whether the financial statements are free of material misstatement. An audit includes examining, on a test basis, evidence supporting the amounts and disclosures in the financial statements. An audit also includes assessing the accounting principles used and significant estimates made by management, as well as evaluating the overall financial statement presentation. We believe that our audits and the report of other auditors provide a reasonable basis for our opinion.

In our opinion, based on our audits and the report of other auditors, the consolidated financial statements referred to above present fairly, in all material respects, the financial position of Widget Company as of December 31, 20X2 and 20X1, and the results of its operations and its cash flows for the years then ended in conformity with accounting principles generally accepted in the United States of America.

Guy and Carmichael
February 15, 20X3

ILLUSTRATION 5. AUDITOR'S REPORT: QUALIFIED OPINION—SCOPE LIMITATION (ADAPTED FROM SAS 58)

Independent Auditor's Report

[*Same first paragraph as the standard report*]

Except as discussed in the following paragraph, we conducted our audits in accordance with auditing standards generally accepted in the United States of America. Those standards require that we plan and perform the audit to obtain reasonable assurance about whether the financial statements are free of material misstatement. An audit includes examining, on a test basis, evidence supporting the amounts and disclosures in the financial statements. An audit also includes assessing the accounting principles used and significant estimates made by management, as well as evaluating the overall financial statement presentation. We believe that our audits provide a reasonable basis for our opinion.

We were unable to obtain audited financial statements supporting the Company's investment in a foreign affiliate stated at $_____ and $_____ at December 31, 20X2 and 20X1, respectively, or its equity in earnings of the affiliate of $_____ and $_____, which is included in net income for the years then ended as described in Note X to the financial statements; nor were we able to satisfy ourselves as to the carrying value of the investment in the foreign affiliate or the equity in its earnings by other auditing procedures.

In our opinion, except for the effects of such adjustment, if any, as might have been determined to be necessary had we been able to examine evidence regarding the foreign affiliate investment and earnings, the financial statements referred to in the first paragraph above present fairly, in all material respects, the financial position of Widget Company as of December 31, 20X2 and 20X1, and the results of its operations and its cash flows for the years then ended in conformity with accounting principles generally accepted in the United States of America.

Guy and Carmichael
February 15, 20X3

Illustration 6. Auditor's Report: Disclaimer of Opinion—Scope Limitation (Adapted from SAS 58)

Independent Auditor's Report

We were engaged to audit the accompanying balance sheets of Widget Company as of December 31, 20X2 and 20X1, and the related statements of income, retained earnings, and cash flows for the years then ended. These financial statements are the responsibility of the Company's management.

[*Second paragraph of standard report should be omitted*]

The Company did not make a count of its physical inventory in 20X2 or 20X1, stated in the accompanying financial statements at $_____ as of December 31, 20X2, and at $_____ as of December 31, 20X1. Further, evidence supporting the cost of property and equipment acquired prior to December 31, 20X1, is no longer available. The Company's records and circumstances do not permit the application of other auditing procedures to inventories or property and equipment.

Since the Company did not take physical inventories and we were not able to apply other auditing procedures to satisfy ourselves as to inventory quantities and the cost of property and equipment, the scope of our work was not sufficient to enable us to express, and we do not express, an opinion on these financial statements.

Guy and Carmichael
February 15, 20X3

Illustration 7. Auditor's Report: Qualified Opinion—Departure from GAAP Explained in Report (Adapted from SAS 58)

Independent Auditor's Report

[*Same first and second paragraphs as the standard report*]

The Company has excluded, from property and debt in the accompanying balance sheets, certain lease obligations that, in our opinion, should be capitalized in order to conform with accounting principles generally accepted in the United States of America. If these lease obligations were capitalized, property would be increased by $_____ and $_____, long-term debt by $_____ and $_____, and retained earnings by $_____ and $_____ as of December 31, 20X2 and 20X1, respectively. Additionally, net income would be increased (decreased) by $_____ and $_____ and earnings per share would be increased (decreased) by $_____ and $_____, respectively, for the years then ended.

In our opinion, except for the effects of not capitalizing certain lease obligations as discussed in the preceding paragraph, the financial statements referred to above present fairly, in all material respects, the financial position of Widget Company as of December 31, 20X2 and 20X1, and the results of its operations and its cash flows for the years then ended in conformity with accounting principles generally accepted in the United States of America.

Guy and Carmichael
February 15, 20X3

Illustration 8. Auditor's Report: Qualified Opinion—Departure from GAAP Explained in a Note (Adapted from SAS 58)

Independent Auditor's Report

[*Same first and second paragraphs as the standard report*]

As more fully described in Note X to the financial statements, the Company has excluded certain lease obligations from property and debt in the accompanying balance sheets. In our opinion, accounting principles generally accepted in the United States of America require that such obligations be included in the balance sheets.

In our opinion, except for the effects of not capitalizing certain lease obligations as discussed in the preceding paragraph, the financial statements referred to above present fairly, in all material respects, the financial position of Widget Company as of December 31, 20X2 and 20X1, and the results of its operations and its cash flows for the years then ended in conformity with accounting principles generally accepted in the United States of America.

Guy and Carmichael
February 15, 20X3

ILLUSTRATION 9. AUDITOR'S REPORT: ADVERSE OPINION—DEPARTURE FROM GAAP (ADAPTED FROM SAS 58)

Independent Auditor's Report

[*Same first and second paragraphs as the standard report*]

As discussed in Note X to the financial statements, the Company carries its property, plant, and equipment accounts at appraisal values, and provides depreciation on the basis of such values. Further, the Company does not provide for income taxes for differences between financial income and taxable income arising because of the use, for income tax purposes, of the installment method of reporting gross profit from certain types of sales. Accounting principles generally accepted in the United States of America require that property, plant, and equipment be stated at an amount not in excess of cost, reduced by depreciation based on such amount, and that deferred income taxes be provided.

Because of the departures from accounting principles generally accepted in the United States of America identified above, as of December 31, 20X2 and 20X1, inventories have been increased $_____ and $_____ by inclusion in manufacturing overhead of depreciation in excess of that based on cost; property, plant, and equipment, less accumulated depreciation, is carried at $_____ and $_____ in excess of an amount based on the cost to the Company; deferred income taxes of $_____ and $_____ have not been recorded; resulting in an increase of $_____ and $_____ in retained earnings and in appraisal surplus of $_____ and $_____, respectively. For the years ended December 31, 20X2 and 20X1, cost of goods sold has been increased $_____ and $_____, respectively, because of the effects of the depreciation accounting referred to above and deferred income taxes of $_____ and $_____ have not been provided, resulting in an increase in net income of $_____ and $_____, respectively.

In our opinion, because of the effects of the matters discussed in the preceding paragraphs, the financial statements referred to above do not present fairly, in conformity with accounting principles generally accepted in the United States of America, the financial position of Widget Company as of December 31, 20X2 and 20X1, or the results of its operations or its cash flows for the years then ended.

Guy and Carmichael
February 15, 20X3

ILLUSTRATION 10. AUDITOR'S REPORT: RULE 203 OPINION

Independent Auditor's Report

[*Same first and second paragraphs as the standard report*]

As explained in Note X to the financial statements, the Company has changed its method of recording revenues from the recognition of revenue at the time of sale to the recognition of revenue over the membership term and has applied this change retroactively in its financial statements. Accounting Principles Board [APB] Opinion 20, *Accounting Changes*, provides that such a change be made by including, as an element of net earnings during the year of change, the cumulative effect of the change on prior years. Had APB Opinion 20 been followed literally, the cumulative effect of the accounting change would have been included as a change in the 20X2 income statement. Because of the magnitude and pervasiveness of this change, we believe a literal application of APB Opinion 20 would result in a misleading presentation, and that the change should therefore be made on a retroactive basis. Accordingly, the accompanying consolidated financial statements for 20X1 have been restated.

In our opinion, the financial statements referred to above present fairly, in all material respects, the consolidated financial position of Widget Corporation and consolidated subsidiaries as of December 31, 20X2 and 20X1, and the consolidated results of their operations and their cash flows for the years then ended in conformity with accounting principles generally accepted in the United States of America.

Guy and Carmichael
February 15, 20X3

Illustration 11. Auditor's Report: Omission of Statement of Cash Flows (Adapted from SAS 58)

Independent Auditor's Report

We have audited the accompanying balance sheets of Widget Company as of December 31, 20X2 and 20X1, and the related statements of income and retained earnings for the years then ended. These financial statements are the responsibility of the Company's management. Our responsibility is to express an opinion on these financial statements based on our audit.

[*Same second paragraph as the standard report*]

The Company declined to present a statement of cash flows for the years ended December 31, 20X2 and 20X1. Presentation of such statement summarizing the Company's operating, investing, and financing activities is required by accounting principles generally accepted in the United States of America.

In our opinion, except that the omission of a statement of cash flows results in an incomplete presentation as explained in the preceding paragraph, the financial statements referred to above present fairly, in all material respects, the financial position of Widget Company as of December 31, 20X2 and 20X1, and the results of its operations for the years then ended in conformity with accounting principles generally accepted in the United States of America.

Guy and Carmichael
February 15, 20X3

Illustration 12. Auditor's Report: Management Has Not Provided Reasonable Justification for Change in Accounting Principle (Adapted from SAS 58)

Independent Auditor's Report

[*Same first and second paragraphs as the standard report*]

As disclosed in Note X to the financial statements, the Company adopted, in 20X2, the first-in, first-out method of accounting for its inventories, whereas it previously used the last-in, first-out method. Although use of the first-in, first-out method is in conformity with accounting principles generally accepted in the United States of America, in our opinion the Company has not provided reasonable justification for making this change as required by those principles.

In our opinion, except for the change in accounting principle discussed in the preceding paragraph, the financial statements referred to above present fairly, in all material respects, the financial position of Widget Company as of December 31, 20X2 and 20X1, and the results of its operations and its cash flows for the years then ended in conformity with accounting principles generally accepted in the United States of America.

Guy and Carmichael
February 15, 20X3

Illustration 13. Auditor's Report: Inadequate Disclosure (Adapted from SAS 58)

Independent Auditor's Report

[*Same first and second paragraphs as the standard report*]

The Company's financial statements do not disclose [*describe the nature of the omitted disclosures*]. In our opinion, disclosure of this information is required by accounting principles generally accepted in the United States of America.

In our opinion, except for the omission of the information discussed in the preceding paragraph, the financial statements referred to above present fairly, in all material respects, the financial position of Widget Company as of December 31, 20X2 and 20X1, and the results of its operations and its cash flows for the years then ended in conformity with accounting principles generally accepted in the United States of America.

Guy and Carmichael
February 15, 20X3

ILLUSTRATION 14. AUDITOR'S STANDARD REPORT ON THE PRIOR YEAR FINANCIAL STATEMENTS AND A QUALIFIED OPINION ON THE CURRENT YEAR FINANCIAL STATEMENTS (ADAPTED FROM SAS 58)

Independent Auditor's Report

[*Same first and second paragraphs as the standard report*]

The Company has excluded, from property and debt in the accompanying 20X2 balance sheet, certain lease obligations that were entered into in 20X2 which, in our opinion, should be capitalized in order to conform with accounting principles generally accepted in the United States of America. If these lease obligations were capitalized, property would be increased by $_____, long-term debt by $_____, and retained earnings by $_____, as of December 31, 20X2, and net income and earnings per share would be increased (decreased) by $_____ and $_____, for the year then ended.

In our opinion, except for the effects on the 20X2 financial statements of not capitalizing certain lease obligations as described in the preceding paragraph, the financial statements referred to above present fairly, in all material respects, the financial position of Widget Company as of December 31, 20X2 and 20X1, and the results of its operations and its cash flows for the years then ended in conformity with accounting principles generally accepted in the United States of America.

Guy and Carmichael
February 15, 20X3

ILLUSTRATION 15. AUDITOR'S STANDARD REPORT ON THE CURRENT YEAR FINANCIAL STATEMENTS WITH A DISCLAIMER OF OPINION ON THE PRIOR YEAR STATEMENTS OF INCOME, RETAINED EARNINGS, AND CASH FLOWS (ADAPTED FROM SAS 58)

Independent Auditor's Report

[*Same first paragraph as the standard report*]

Except as explained in the following paragraph, we conducted our audits in accordance with auditing standards generally accepted in the United States of America. Those standards require that we plan and perform our audit to obtain reasonable assurance about whether the financial statements are free of material misstatement. An audit includes examining, on a test basis, evidence supporting the amounts and disclosures in the financial statements. An audit also includes assessing the accounting principles used and significant estimates made by management, as well as evaluating the overall financial statements presentation. We believe that our audits provide a reasonable basis for our opinion.

We did not observe the taking of physical inventory as of December 31, 20X1, because that date was prior to our appointment as auditors for the Company, and we were unable to satisfy ourselves regarding inventory quantities by means of other auditing procedures. Inventory amounts as of December 31, 20X1, enter into the determination of net income and cash flows for the year ended December 31, 20X2.

Because of the matter discussed in the preceding paragraph, the scope of our work was not sufficient to enable us to express, and we do not express, an opinion on the results of operations and cash flows for the year ended December 31, 20X2.

In our opinion, the balance sheets of Widget Company as of December 31, 20X3 and 20X2, and the related statements of income, retained earnings, and cash flows for the year ended December 31, 20X3, present fairly, in all material respects, the financial position of Widget Company as of December 31, 20X3 and 20X2, and the results of its operations and its cash flows for the year ended December 31, 20X3, in conformity with accounting principles generally accepted in the United States of America.

Guy and Carmichael
February 15, 20X4

ILLUSTRATION 16. AUDITOR'S REPORT: OPINION DIFFERENT FROM OPINION PREVIOUSLY EXPRESSED (ADAPTED FROM SAS 58)

Independent Auditor's Report

[*Same first and second paragraphs as the standard report*]

In our report dated March 1, 20X2, we expressed an opinion that the 20X1 financial statements did not fairly present financial position, results of operations, and cash flows in conformity with accounting principles generally accepted in the United States of America because of two departures from such principles: (1) the Company carried its property, plant, and equipment at appraisal values, and provided for depreciation on the basis of such values and (2) the Company did not provide for deferred income taxes with respect to differences between income for financial reporting purposes and taxable income. As described in Note X, the Company has changed its method of accounting for these items and restated its 20X1 financial statements to conform with accounting principles generally accepted in the United States of America. Accordingly, our present opinion on the 20X1 financial statements, as presented herein, is different from that expressed in our previous reports.

In our opinion, the financial statements referred to above present fairly, in all material respects, the financial position of Widget Company as of December 31, 20X2 and 20X1, and the results of its operations and its cash flows for the years then ended in conformity with accounting principles generally accepted in the United States of America.

Guy and Carmichael
February 15, 20X3

Illustration 17. Auditor's Report: Predecessor Auditor's Report Not Presented (Adapted from SAS 58)

A. Independent Auditor's Report—Financial Statements Not Restated

We have audited the balance sheet of Widget Company as of December 31, 20X2, and the related statements of income, retained earnings, and cash flows for the year then ended. These financial statements are the responsibility of the Company's management. Our responsibility is to express an opinion on these financial statements based on our audit. The financial statements of Widget Company as of December 31, 20X1, were audited by other auditors whose report dated March 31, 20X2, expressed an unqualified opinion on those statements.

[*Same second paragraph as the standard report*]

In our opinion, the 20X2 financial statements referred to above present fairly, in all material respects, the financial position of Widget Company as of December 31, 20X2, and the results of its operations and its cash flows for the year then ended in conformity with accounting principles generally accepted in the United States of America.

Guy and Carmichael
February 15, 20X3

B. Modification of First Paragraph

[*If the predecessor auditor's report was other than the standard report, the wording that may be included in the successor's report would be as follows:*]

. . .were audited by other auditors whose report dated March 1, 20X2, on those statements included an explanatory paragraph that described the change in accounting principle discussed in Note X to the financial statements.

C. Independent Auditor's Report—Predecessor Auditor's Report Not Presented—Financial Statements Restated

We have audited the balance sheet of Widget Company as of December 31, 20X2, and the related statements of income, retained earnings, and cash flows for the year then ended. These financial statements are the responsibility of the Company's management. Our responsibility is to express an opinion on these financial statements based on our audit. The financial statements of Widget Company as of December 31, 20X1, were audited by other auditors whose report dated March 31, 20X2, expressed an unqualified opinion on those statements before restatement. We also audited the adjustments described in Note X that were applied to restate the 20X1 financial statements. In our opinion, such adjustments are appropriate and have been properly applied.

[*Same second paragraph as the standard report*]

In our opinion, the 20X2 financial statements referred to above present fairly, in all material respects, the financial position of Widget Company as of December 31, 20X2, and the results of its operations and its cash flows for the year ended in conformity with accounting principles generally accepted in the United States of America.

Guy and Carmichael
February 15, 20X3

NOTE: This illustration assumes that the successor auditor was engaged to audit and applied sufficient procedures to be satisfied as to the appropriateness of the restatement adjustments.

D. Letter of Representation from Successor Auditor to Predecessor Auditor

[*Date*]

Name of Predecessor Auditor
Address

Dear Sir:

In connection with the reissuance of your report on the consolidated financial statements of Widget Inc. and subsidiaries for the years ended December 31, 20X2 and 20X1, we wish to advise you that we have audited the consolidated financial statements of Widget Inc. and subsidiaries as of December 31, 20X3. As set forth in our report dated March 10, 20X4, our audit was made in accordance with auditing standards generally accepted in the United States of America.

Our audit of the consolidated financial statements of Widget Inc. and subsidiaries as of December 31, 20X3, disclosed no events or transactions to March 10, 20X4, that, in our opinion, would require modification of the financial statements of Widget Inc. and subsidiaries for the years ended December 31, 20X2, and 20X1.

This letter is solely for your information in connection with your previously mentioned reports.

Very truly yours,

ILLUSTRATION 18. ILLUSTRATIVE UPDATING MANAGEMENT REPRESENTATION LETTER (ADAPTED FROM SAS 85)

[*Date*]

To [*Auditor*]

In connection with your audit(s) of the [*identification of financial statements*] of [*name of entity*] as of [*dates*] and for the [*periods*] for the purpose of expressing an opinion as to whether the [*consolidated*] financial statements present fairly, in all material respects, the financial position, results of operations, and cash flows of [*name of entity*] in conformity with accounting principles generally accepted in the United States of America, you were previously provided with a representation letter under the date of [*date of previous representation letter*]. No information has come to our attention that would cause us to believe that any of those previous representations should be modified.

To the best of our knowledge and belief, no events have occurred subsequent to [*date of latest balance sheet reported on by the auditor*] and through the date of this letter that would require adjustment to or disclosure in the aforementioned financial statements.

____
[*Name of Chief Executive Officer and Title*]

____
[*Name of Chief Financial Officer and Title*]

NOTE: If matters exist that should be disclosed to the auditor, they should be indicated by listing them. For example, if an event subsequent to the date of the balance sheet has been disclosed in the financial statements, the final paragraph could be modified as follows: "To the best of our knowledge and belief, except as discussed in Note X to the financial statements, no events have occurred. . . ."

ILLUSTRATION 19. AUDITOR'S REPORT ON SINGLE-YEAR FINANCIAL STATEMENTS IN YEAR OF ADOPTION OF LIQUIDATION BASIS (ADAPTED FROM INTERPRETATION OF SAS 58)

Independent Auditor's Report

We have audited the statement of net assets in liquidation of Widget Company as of December 31, 20X2, and the related statement of changes in net assets in liquidation for the period from April 26, 20X2, to December 31, 20X2. In addition, we have audited the statements of income, retained earnings, and cash flows for the period from January 1, 20X2, to April 25, 20X2.

These financial statements are the responsibility of the Company's management. Our responsibility is to express an opinion on these financial statements based on our audit.

We conducted our audit in accordance with auditing standards generally accepted in the United States of America. These standards require that we plan and perform the audit to obtain reasonable assurance about whether the financial statements are free of material misstatement. An audit includes examining, on a test basis, evidence supporting the amounts and disclosures in the financial statements. An audit also includes assessing the accounting principles used and significant estimated made by management, as well as evaluating the overall financial statement presentation. We believe that our audit provides a reasonable basis for our opinion.

As described in Note X to the financial statements, the stockholders of Widget Company approved a plan of liquidation on April 25, 20X2, and the company commenced liquidation shortly thereafter. As a result, the company has changed its basis of accounting for periods subsequent to April 25, 20X2, from the going-concern basis to a liquidation basis.

In our opinion, the financial statements referred to above present fairly, in all material respects, the net assets in liquidation of Widget Company as of December 31, 20X2, the changes in its net assets in liquidation for the period from April 26, 20X2 to December 31, 20X2, and the results of its operations and its cash flows for the period from January 1, 20X2, to April 25, 20X2, in conformity with accounting principles generally accepted in the United States of America applied on the bases described in the preceding paragraph.

Guy and Carmichael
February 15, 20X3

ILLUSTRATION 20. AUDITOR'S REPORT ON COMPARATIVE FINANCIAL STATEMENTS IN YEAR OF ADOPTION OF LIQUIDATION BASIS (ADAPTED FROM INTERPRETATION OF SAS 58)

Independent Auditor's Report

We have audited the balance sheet of Widget Company as of December 31, 20X1, and the related statements of income, retained earnings, and cash flows for the year then ended, and the statements of income, retained earnings, and cash flows for the period from January 1, 20X2, to April 25, 20X2. In addition, we have audited the statement of net assets in liquidation as of December 31, 20X2, and the related statement of changes in net assets in liquidation for the period from April 25, 20X2, to December 31, 20X2. These financial statements are the responsibility of the Company's management. Our responsibility is to express an opinion on these financial statements based on our audits.

We conducted our audits in accordance with auditing standards generally accepted in the United States of America. Those standards require that we plan and perform the audit to obtain reasonable assurance about whether the financial statements are free of material misstatements. An audit includes examining, on a test basis, evidence supporting the amounts and disclosures in the financial statements. An audit also includes assessing the accounting principles used and significant estimates made by management, as well as evaluating the overall financial statement presentation. We believe that our audits provide a reasonable basis for our opinion.

As described in Note X to the financial statements, the stockholders of Widget Company approved a plan of liquidation on April 25, 20X2, and the company commenced liquidation shortly thereafter. As a result, the company has changed its basis of accounting for periods subsequent to April 25, 20X2, from the going-concern basis to a liquidation basis.

In our opinion, the financial statements referred to above present fairly, in all material respects, the financial position of Widget Company as of December 31, 20X1, the results of its operations and its cash flows for the year then ended and for the period from January 1, 20X2, to April 25, 20X2, its net assets in liquidation as of December 31, 20X2, and the changes in its net assets in liquidation for the period from April 26, 20X2, to December 31, 20X2, in conformity with accounting principles generally accepted in the United States of America applied on the bases described in the preceding paragraph.

Guy and Carmichael
May 20, 20X2

530 DATING OF THE INDEPENDENT AUDITOR'S REPORT

EFFECTIVE DATE AND APPLICABILITY

Original Pronouncements	SAP 47, September 1971 (codified in SAS 1, November 1972); SAS 29, July 1980; and SAS 98, September 2002.
Effective Date	When issued, September 1971, unless subsequently amended. (The amendments for SAS 98 are effective upon issuance of the SAS.)
Applicability	Audits of financial statements in accordance with generally accepted auditing standards.

DEFINITIONS OF TERMS

Date of auditor's report. Date of completion of auditor's fieldwork.

NOTE: Ordinarily, this is the date that the auditor and the client agree on the form and content of the financial statements. Sometimes, the date is a matter of judgment (see ***Techniques for Application****). It is the date up to which the auditor is responsible for keeping informed about events affecting the financial statements being reported on.*

Date of issuance. Date the auditor's report is delivered to the client.

Reissued report. Auditor's report issued subsequent to the date the original report was issued.

NOTE: "Reissued report" is used to refer broadly to subsequent reprinting by the auditor of a prior audit report with release to the client as well as reuse by the client in conjunction with issuance of a new document of a prior report. Reuse by the client requires that certain procedures be performed before the auditor can consent (see Section 508).

Dual-dated report. Auditor's report with different dates: (1) the date of completion of fieldwork, and (2) the date a specific event occurred after completion of the fieldwork but before issuance of the auditor's report.

NOTE: An auditor also may dual date a reissued audit report because of an event that occurs after issuance of the original audit report.

Subsequent events. For purposes of this section, events occurring after the date of the auditor's report but before issuance of the related financial statements that require adjustment of or disclosure in the financial statements (see Section 560).

OBJECTIVES OF SECTION

SAP 47, *Subsequent Events*, covered the subject matter of this section and Section 560. This section codifies those parts of the SAP that told the auditor how to date the report in the following circumstances:

1. Under ordinary conditions.
2. Subsequent events.
3. Reissuance of report.

SAS 29, effective December 31, 1980 (see Section 551), created a difference in responsibilities for types of reissued reports. If the client is furnished with additional copies of a previously issued report, the auditor has no responsibility to perform any procedures prior to reprinting the report unless the auditor has become aware of the need to adjust or make disclosure in the financial statements. In the case of a predecessor auditor consenting to reuse a previous report, additional procedures are always required (see Section 508).

FUNDAMENTAL REQUIREMENTS

ORDINARY CONDITIONS

Under ordinary conditions, the auditor should date his or her report as of the date of completion of fieldwork. The auditor does not have to make inquiries or apply other auditing procedures after the date of his or her report under ordinary conditions. However, additional procedures might be required (see "Reissuance of Report" and "Unusual Conditions").

Subsequent Events Requiring Adjustment of Financial Statements

Some events that require adjustment might be made without disclosure, but some events require additional disclosure to be understood.

1. **Financial statements adjusted, no disclosure.** When the adjustment is made but disclosure of the event is not necessary, the auditor's report should be dated as of the date of completion of fieldwork.
2. **Financial statements adjusted, disclosure.** When the adjustment is made with disclosure of the event, the auditor should dual date the report or date it as of the date of the event (see "Subsequent Events Review").
3. **Financial statements not adjusted.** If the financial statements are not adjusted, the auditor should qualify his or her opinion or, if appropriate, express an adverse opinion.

Subsequent Events Requiring Disclosure

Some subsequent events only require disclosure of information in the notes to the financial statements.

1. **Disclosure made.** Disclosure would be made in a note to the financial statements, but might also be referred to in the auditor's report. In either circumstance, the auditor should dual date his or her report or date it as of the event (see "Subsequent Events Review").
2. **No disclosure.** If the subsequent event is not disclosed, the auditor should qualify the opinion, or if appropriate, express an adverse opinion. In these circumstances, the auditor should either dual date the report or date it as of the date of the event (see "Subsequent Events Review").

SUBSEQUENT EVENTS REVIEW

A subsequent events review is the auditor's review of transactions and events occurring after the date of the balance sheet and up to the date of the auditor's report. Its purpose is to determine whether the financial statements being reported on require adjustment or additional disclosures (see Section 560).

If the auditor dates the report as of the date of the subsequent event rather than dual dating the report he or she should extend the subsequent events review to that date (see Section 560).

REISSUANCE OF REPORT

When the auditor reissues the report and uses the original report date, he or she does not have to investigate or inquire about events affecting the financial statements reported on that may have occurred between the original date and the reissuance date.

NOTE: However, see Section 508 for additional requirements that apply when there are comparative financial statements. If the auditor is a continuing auditor, the report has to be updated. If the auditor is a predecessor auditor and the client is reusing the report, additional procedures are required, including a requirement to obtain an updating representation letter from management and a representation letter from the successor auditor.

Events Requiring Adjustment or Disclosure

The auditor may be aware of an event that occurred between the original report date and the reissuance date that affects the financial statements reported on. This event may require disclosure to prevent the financial statements from being misleading. Events occurring between the original report date and the reissuance date do not require adjustment of the financial statements unless the adjustment results in the correction of an error (see Section 560).

When the auditor reissues the report and the financial statements have been adjusted or events have been disclosed in the notes, he or she should dual date the report or date it as of the date of the event responsible for the adjustment or the disclosure.

NOTE: The effect of the event may cause the auditor to express an opinion different from the one he or she originally expressed.

UNAUDITED NOTE

An event that requires disclosure only may be disclosed in a note to the financial statements marked "unaudited." In these circumstances, the auditor's report would have the original date. An example of the heading to use for this type of note follows:

Event (Unaudited) Subsequent to the Date of the Report of the Independent Auditor.

UNUSUAL CONDITIONS

Under ordinary conditions, the auditor has no responsibility to make any inquiry or carry out any procedures for the period after the date of his or her report. An exception might arise if the audit report is reissued as explained previously. An exception might also arise in either of the following circumstances.

Subsequent Discovery of Facts

If, subsequent to the date of the report, the auditor becomes aware of facts that may have existed at that date which might have affected the report, additional procedures are required (see Section 561).

Filing under the 1933 Act

If the financial statements subsequently are incorporated in a filing under the Securities Act of 1933, additional procedures are required (see Section 711).

INTERPRETATIONS

There are no interpretations for this section.

TECHNIQUES FOR APPLICATION

DETERMINING THE DATE OF COMPLETION OF FIELDWORK

There is no authoritative pronouncement that provides guidance on how to determine the date of completion of fieldwork. The date is usually the **same** as the date of the management representation letter (see Section 333) and the date up to which lawyers are asked to respond (see Section 337) concerning litigation, claims, and assessments.

Ordinarily, the date of completion of the fieldwork is the date on which the auditor in charge of the engagement and the client's chief financial officer agree on the form and content of the financial statements. The auditor and the client may arrange for a formal closing conference to review the financial statements. The conclusion of this conference may be considered the date of completion of the fieldwork. If there is no formal closing conference, the date of completion of the fieldwork may be considered to be the date the audit staff finally leaves the client's premises, provided no significant adjustments are expected after that date.

If any procedures that are necessary to the expression of an opinion are performed after the audit staff leaves the client's premises, the substantial completion of those procedures is the completion of fieldwork. Additional advice on issues concerning dating of the audit report is presented in the *Techniques for Application* section of Section 560.

PERIOD BETWEEN COMPLETION OF FIELDWORK AND ISSUANCE OF AUDITOR'S REPORT

Ordinarily, there is a lapse of two to three weeks between the date of the auditor's report (the date of completion of the fieldwork) and its issuance. During this period, the auditor might review the audit documentation a final time to make certain there are no open items, put the audit documentation in a form suitable to be filed, and prepare the final audit report and financial statements. During this period, the auditor is not required to apply any procedures unless information about subsequent events comes to the attention of the auditor (see Section 530).

If the period between the date of the auditor's report and the issuance of the financial statements exceeds approximately three weeks, it would be prudent for the auditor to call the client and inquire about subsequent events. If the delay is unusually long, it may be advisable to extend the subsequent events review and redate the report.

DUAL DATING REPORT

When an event that requires disclosure or adjustment of financial statements occurs between the date of the auditor's report and the issuance of the financial statements, or between the date of issuance and the date of reissuance, the auditor may dual date the report or extend the date of the report and the subsequent events review to the date of the event. Because extending the date of the report extends the auditor's responsibility, the auditor is acting prudently in always dual dating reports requiring disclosure of subsequent events.

An example of the dual dating of an auditor's report is as follows:

> February 16, 20X1, except for Note X as to which the date is February 25, 20X1.

532 RESTRICTING THE USE OF AN AUDITOR'S REPORT

EFFECTIVE DATE AND APPLICABILITY

Original Pronouncement

SAS 87, September, 1998. Revised October 2000 to reflect conforming changes necessary due to the issuance of SAS 93.

Effective Date

Audit reports issued after December 31, 1998.

Applicability

Engagements involving the issuance of reports based on

1. Subject matter or presentations on measurement or disclosure criteria contained in contractual agreements or regulatory provisions.
2. A by-product of a financial statement audit.

*NOTE: SAS 87 does not apply to SAS 70, **Reports on the Processing of Transactions by Service Organizations** (see Section 324) or reports issued under SAS 72, **Letters for Underwriters and Certain Other Requesting Parties** (see Section 634).*

DEFINITIONS OF TERMS

General-use reports. Reports that are not restricted to specified parties such as reports on financial statements prepared in conformity with generally accepted accounting principles or certain comprehensive bases of accounting (OCBOA).

Restricted-use reports. Reports intended for specified parties. Restriction may result from the following:

- Purpose of report.
- Nature of procedures applied.
- Basis of assumptions used.
- Extent of knowledge of procedures.
- Potential for report to be misunderstood.

OBJECTIVES OF SECTION

SAS 87 was issued to identify when an auditor's (or an accountant's) report should be restricted and to specify the language in the restricted-use report paragraph. The standard serves as a conceptual document in that other SASs presenting restricted-use reports were amended or conformed to the requirements herein. SAS 87 replaces the terms **restricted distribution** and **general distribution** with **restricted use** and **general use** and defines the last two terms.

The standard reminds auditors that they may restrict the use of any general-use report and requires auditors to restrict combined reports that contain general-use and restricted-use reports on different subject matter. SAS 87 amended SAS 60 on reportable conditions (see Section 325) to unify the fundamental requirements with guidance herein.

FUNDAMENTAL REQUIREMENTS

REPORTS REQUIRED TO BE RESTRICTED

The auditor should restrict the use of a report when

1. The subject matter or the presentation being reported on is based on measurement or disclosure criteria contained in contractual agreements or regulatory provisions that are not in conformity with GAAP or OCBOA.
2. The auditor's report is a by-product of a financial statement audit and the procedures applied were designed for the audit, not to provide assurance on the subject matter of the report.

IDENTIFICATION OF RESTRICTED PARTIES

The auditor should restrict reports based on contractual agreements or regulatory provisions to parties to the agreement or to the responsible regulatory agency.

The auditor should restrict by-product reports to an entity's audit committee, board of directors, management, or others within the organization, specified regulatory agencies, and parties to the contract for compliance with contractual agreements.

COMBINED REPORTS COVERING BOTH RESTRICTED-USE AND GENERAL-USE SUBJECT MATTER OR PRESENTATIONS

The auditor should restrict the use of a single combined restricted-use and general-use report to specified parties.

INCLUSION OF A SEPARATE RESTRICTED-USE REPORT AND A SEPARATE GENERAL-USE REPORT IN THE SAME DOCUMENT

A separate restricted-use report may be included in a document that contains a separate general-use report, provided the combined report is restricted.

ADDING NEW SPECIFIED PARTIES

After the engagement is completed or in the course of such an engagement, the client may ask the auditor to add other specified parties. An auditor should not agree to add other specified parties to a by-product report.

For a subject matter or presentation type report, the auditor may agree to add other specified parties after considering such factors as identity of the other parties and intended use of the report. If the auditor adds other specified parties, he or she should obtain affirmative acknowledgment, ordinarily in writing, from the other parties about their understanding of the engagement, measurement or disclosure criteria, and the report.

If other parties are added after issuance of the auditor's report, the auditor may reissue the report or provide other acknowledgment that new parties have been added. If the report is reissued, the report date should not be changed. If the auditor provides written acknowledgment of the addition, the acknowledgment should state that no subsequent or new procedures have been performed.

LIMITING REPORT DISTRIBUTION

The auditor should consider informing the client that restricted-use reports are not intended for distribution to nonspecified parties. However, an auditor is not responsible for controlling the client's restricted-use report distribution.

REQUIRED RESTRICTED-USE REPORT LANGUAGE

The auditor should add a separate paragraph at the end of the report that contains

1. A statement that the report is intended solely for the information and use of the specified parties.
2. An identification of the parties.
3. A statement indicating that the report is not intended to be, and should not be, used by nonspecified parties.

Illustrations contains an example of a restricted-use paragraph.

INTERPRETATIONS

There are no interpretations for this section.

TECHNIQUES FOR APPLICATION

The following SASs present by-product reports:

1. SAS 60, *Communication of Internal Control Related Matters Noted in an Audit* (see Section 325).
2. SAS 61, *Communication with Audit Committees* (see Section 380).
3. SAS 62, *Special Reports*, for reports on compliance with contractual agreements or regulatory requirements (see Section 623).

The auditor should refer to the aforementioned sections for guidance that conforms to SAS 87.

Note that auditors will rarely have to apply SAS 87 because the amendments and conforming changes have been made in the relevant sections throughout this book.

ILLUSTRATION

The following example of a restricted-use paragraph is from SAS 87.

> This report is intended solely for the information and use of [*the specified parties*] and is not intended to be, and should not be, used by anyone other than these specified parties.

534 REPORTING ON FINANCIAL STATEMENTS PREPARED FOR USE IN OTHER COUNTRIES

EFFECTIVE DATE AND APPLICABILITY

Original Pronouncement	SAS 51, July 1986.
Effective Date	Audits of financial statements for periods beginning after July 31, 1986.
Applicability	Engagements to report on the financial statements of a US entity that have been prepared in conformity with accounting principles generally accepted in another country for use outside the US.

DEFINITIONS OF TERMS

US entity. An entity that is either organized or domiciled in the United States.

US-style report modified. The auditor's standard report as described in SAS 58 (see Section 508) modified for use outside the US.

Limited distribution in US. Distribution of financial statements to parties (such as banks, institutional investors, and similar knowledgeable parties) that deal with the entity directly in a manner that permits such parties to discuss differences from US GAAP and their significance.

Dual statements. Two sets of financial statements for the same entity—one prepared in conformity with US GAAP and another prepared in conformity with accounting principles generally accepted in another country.

OBJECTIVES OF SECTION

A US entity may need to prepare financial statements for use outside the US that are prepared in conformity with accounting principles that are generally accepted in another country, but not in conformity with US GAAP. For example, this situation may arise in the following circumstances:

1. The financial statements are to be included in the consolidated financial statements of a non-US parent.
2. The financial statements are to be used by a significant group of foreign investors.
3. The financial statements are to be used to raise capital in another country.

SAS 51 was developed to provide guidance on appropriate reporting in these circumstances. An SAS was necessary because of a provision of the AICPA ethics code that was in effect at the time. ET Section 92.02 of the Code indicated that in circumstances that would entitle a reader to assume US practices were followed, the auditor must adhere to Rule 202 (GAAS) and Rule 203 (GAAP).

Practice varied considerably because of uncertainty about the conditions that would entitle a reader to assume that US practices were followed. Some auditors believed that it was appropriate to follow foreign standards—both accounting and auditing. Others believed that it was necessary to adhere to US standards. The new Code of Professional Conduct adopted in January 1988 is applicable to **all** AICPA members including those who practice outside the US.

SAS 51 takes the position that in all circumstances it is necessary for a US auditor (whether practicing within the US or outside the US) to adhere to the general and fieldwork standards of US GAAS. However, it relaxes the reporting standards for financial statements prepared for foreign use with no, or limited, US distribution. In those circumstances, the auditor may issue a specially worded US-style report that expresses an unqualified opinion on conformity with foreign accounting principles or the standard report of another country.

FUNDAMENTAL REQUIREMENTS

Purpose and Use of Financial Statements

Before reporting on financial statements prepared in conformity with accounting principles of another country, the auditor should

1. Have a clear understanding of their purpose and use.
2. Obtain **written** representation from management on such purpose and use.

General and Fieldwork Standards

In auditing financial statements prepared in conformity with accounting principles of another country, the auditor should

1. Perform the procedures that are necessary to comply with the general and fieldwork standards of US GAAS.
2. Modify such procedures as necessary for differences in financial statement assertions caused by the accounting principles of the other country.

   NOTE: For example, procedures for testing deferred tax balances would not be needed if the other country's principles do not require or permit recognition of deferred taxes.

3. Obtain an understanding of accounting principles generally accepted in the other country by reading statutes or professional literature and, if necessary, by consulting with persons with appropriate expertise.

Compliance with Foreign Auditing Standards

If the auditor is asked to apply the auditing standards of another country in auditing financial statements prepared for use in the other country, the auditor should

1. Read the statutes or professional literature that describes auditing standards generally accepted in that country.
2. Consider consulting persons having expertise in the auditing standards of the other country.
3. Comply with the general and fieldwork standards of both the other country and US GAAS.

Reporting Standards

If financial statements are prepared for use only outside the US or have only limited distribution within the US, the auditor may report using either

1. A US-style report modified to report on the accounting principles of another country; or
2. The report form of the other country.

Modified US-Style Report

A US-style report modified to report on financial statements prepared in conformity with the accounting principles of another country should include the following:

1. A title that includes the word independent (for example, Independent Auditor's Report).
2. An introductory paragraph with statements that
   a. The financial statements identified in the report were audited.
   b. Refers to the note to the financial statements that describes the basis of presentation of the financial statements on which the auditor is reporting, including identification of the nationality of the accounting principles.
   c. The financial statements are the responsibility of the entity's management and that the auditor's responsibility is to express an opinion based on the audit.
3. A scope paragraph with statements that
   a. The audit was conducted in accordance with auditing standards generally accepted in the United States of America and, if appropriate, with the auditing standards of the other country.
   b. US standards require that the auditor plan and perform the audit to obtain reasonable assurance about whether the financial statements are free of material misstatement.
   c. An audit includes
      (1) Examining, on a test basis, evidence supporting the amounts and disclosures in the financial statements.
      (2) Assessing the accounting principles used and significant estimates made by management.
      (3) Evaluating the overall financial statement presentation.
   d. The auditor believes that the audit provides a reasonable basis for the opinion.
4. An opinion paragraph that presents the auditor's opinion as to whether the financial statements are presented fairly, in all material respects, in conformity with the basis of accounting described. If the auditor concludes that the financial statements are not fairly presented on the basis of accounting described, he or she should add an explanatory paragraph, preceding the opinion paragraph, to the auditor's report that discloses all substantive reasons for that conclusion. The opinion paragraph of the auditor's report should be appropriately modified, and reference should be made to the explanatory paragraph.
5. An explanatory paragraph following the opinion paragraph if the auditor is auditing comparative financial statements and the described basis of accounting has not been applied in a manner consistent with that of the preceding period. The explanatory paragraph should describe the change in accounting principle and refer to the note to the financial statements that discusses the change and its effect on the financial statements.
6. The manual or printed signature of the auditing firm and the date of the report.

Foreign Report Form

The auditor may use the standard report of another country if

1. Such a report would be used by auditors in the other country in similar circumstances.
2. The auditor understands and is in a position to make the attestations contained in such a report.
3. The other country is identified in the report when the auditor believes the report or the financial statements may otherwise be misunderstood because they resemble those prepared in conformity with US standards.

If the auditor uses the standard report of another country, the auditor should comply with the reporting standards of that country and should recognize the following points:

1. Even if the report appears similar to a US-style report, it may convey a different meaning and entail different responsibilities due to custom or culture.
2. The report may also require the auditor to provide explicit or implicit assurance of statutory compliance or otherwise require understanding of local law.
3. In addition to foreign professional standards, the auditor needs to understand applicable legal responsibilities.
4. The auditor should consider consulting with persons with expertise in the audit reporting practices of the other country.

Dual Statements

If financial statements are needed for use both in another country and within the US, the auditor may report on two sets of financial statements.

1. One set prepared in conformity with foreign accounting standards for use outside the US; and
2. Another set prepared in conformity with US GAAP.

If dual statements are prepared, the auditor may wish to include, in one or both of the reports, a statement that another report has been issued on the entity's statements prepared in conformity with accounting principles of another country. (See *Illustrations*.)

US Distribution

If financial statements prepared in conformity with accounting principles of another country will have more than limited US distribution, the auditor should use the US standard report modified (qualified or adverse) for departures from US GAAP. The auditor may also, in a separate paragraph to the report, express an opinion on whether the financial statements are presented in conformity with accounting principles generally accepted in another country.

INTERPRETATIONS

Financial Statements for General Use Only Outside of the US in Accordance with International Accounting Standards and International Standards on Auditing (May 1996)

An independent auditor practicing in the US may report on the financial statements of a US entity presented in conformity with International Accounting Standards for general use only outside of the US. The auditor may perform the audit of these statements in accordance with International Standards on Auditing, but should also comply with the general and fieldwork standards of US GAAS. The form of the audit report may be either a US-style modified for reference to International Standards or the form in International Standards on Auditing.

TECHNIQUES FOR APPLICATION

The most difficult aspect of applying SAS 51 in practice is the time and effort required to obtain an adequate understanding of the following:

1. Accounting principles generally accepted in the other country.
2. General and fieldwork auditing standards of the other country.
3. Audit reporting practices of the other country.

In all these areas, the SAS suggests that the auditor should consider consulting with persons with expertise in the area. The need for consultation is a matter of professional judgment and depends, in part, on the formality and extensiveness of promulgated standards in the particular country.

In some countries, accounting principles may not be well-developed. A broad range of practices may be acceptable and professional literature may not have sufficient authority or general acceptance. In these circumstances, the auditor should establish that the client's principles and practices are appropriate in the circumstances and are disclosed in a clear and comprehensive manner. For guidance on the appropriateness of the accounting principles used, the auditor may refer to International Accounting Standards established by the International Accounting Standards Committee.

ILLUSTRATIONS

The following examples of reporting are adapted from SAS 51 (AU 534).

1. A US-style report modified for use outside the US.
2. An additional paragraph for a report on dual statements.

ILLUSTRATION 1. US-STYLE REPORT MODIFIED FOR USE OUTSIDE US

Independent Auditor's Report

We have audited the accompanying balance sheet of Worldwide Company as of December 31, 20X1, and the related statements of income, retained earnings, and cash flows for the year then ended which, as described in Note X, have been prepared on the basis of accounting principles generally accepted in [*name of country*]. These financial statements are the responsibility of the Company's management. Our responsibility is to express an opinion on these financial statements based on our audit.

We conducted our audit in accordance with auditing standards generally accepted in the United States of America (and in [*name of country*]). US Standards require that we plan and perform the audit to obtain reasonable assurance about whether the financial statements are free of material misstatement. An audit includes examining, on a test basis, evidence supporting the amounts and disclosures in the financial statements. An audit also includes assessing the accounting principles used and significant estimates made by management, as well as evaluating the overall financial statement presentation. We believe that our audit provides a reasonable basis for our opinion.

In our opinion, the financial statements referred to above present fairly, in all material respects, the financial position of Worldwide Company as of [*at*] December 31, 20X1, and the results of its operations and its cash flows for the year then ended in conformity with accounting principles generally accepted in [*name of country*].

ILLUSTRATION 2. ADDITIONAL PARAGRAPH FOR REPORT ON DUAL STATEMENTS

We also have reported separately on the financial statements of Worldwide Company for the same period presented in accordance with accounting principles generally accepted in [*name of country*]. (The significant differences between the accounting principles accepted in [*name of country*] and those generally accepted in the United States of America are summarized in Note X.)

543 PART OF AUDIT PERFORMED BY OTHER INDEPENDENT AUDITORS

EFFECTIVE DATE AND APPLICABILITY

Original Pronouncements	SAP 45, July 1971 (codified in SAS 1, November 1972); SAS 64, December 1990.
Effective Date	When issued, July 1971, except for form of auditor's report which is for reports issued after December 31, 1990 (SAS 64).
Applicability	Audits of financial statements in accordance with generally accepted auditing standards when the auditor uses the work and reports of other independent auditors.

DEFINITIONS OF TERMS

Principal auditor. The auditor who expresses an opinion on the financial statements of the reporting entity. (The financial statements may be consolidated or combined, or the reporting entity may have significant investments accounted for by the equity method.) The principal auditor performs a significant portion of the work and has sufficient knowledge of the operations of the reporting entity. There is no strict quantitative measure for determining the principal auditor (see *Techniques for Application*).

Other independent auditor. The auditor who expresses an opinion on the financial statements of a subsidiary, division, branch, or investee that are incorporated in the financial statements of the reporting entity.

OBJECTIVES OF SECTION

The financial statements of a part of a reporting entity may be audited by auditors other than the principal auditor. The parts audited by other auditors may be subsidiaries, divisions, branches, or investments accounted for by the equity method.

This section provides guidance on the professional judgments the auditor makes in deciding

1. Whether he or she may serve as principal auditor and use the work and reports of other auditors.
2. The form and content of the principal auditor's report when he or she uses the work and reports of other auditors.

NOTE: A principal auditor may refer to the work of other auditors in the report (see below) to indicate the divided responsibility of the auditors. ***This reference is not a qualification of the principal auditor's opinion. A report that makes reference to other auditors is not inferior to a report without such reference.***

The basic notion of a report that makes reference to the report of the other auditor is **divided responsibility**. The principal auditor divides responsibility with the other auditor. For this reason the report should clearly describe the portion of the financial statements audited by the other auditor.

FUNDAMENTAL REQUIREMENTS

THE PRINCIPAL AUDITOR DECISION

When more than one auditor is involved in auditing the financial statements of the reporting entity, a decision must be made on which one is the principal auditor. In making the decision, the auditor should consider

1. Proportions of assets, revenue, and income audited.
2. Materiality and significance of the components audited.
3. Overall knowledge and understanding of the reporting entity.

RESPONSIBILITY FOR THE WORK OF OTHER AUDITORS

The principal auditor should decide whether to assume responsibility for the work of other auditors insofar as that work relates to his or her expression of an opinion on the financial statements taken as a whole.

Decision to Assume Responsibility

If the principal auditor decides to assume responsibility for the work of other auditors, he or she should **not** make reference in the report to the work of the other auditors.

Decision Not to Assume Responsibility

If the principal auditor decides not to assume responsibility for the work of other auditors, he or she should make reference in the report to the work of the other auditors (see Illustrations 1 and 2).

NOTE: The decision to assume or not assume responsibility has significant legal as well as professional consequences. In a report that makes reference, the principal auditor does not intend to assume any legal responsibility for the work of the other auditor.

Principal Auditor's Report with Reference

In the introductory paragraph of the report, the principal auditor should indicate the division of responsibility for the audited financial statements by disclosing the magnitude of the portion of those statements audited by other auditors. This is done by stating either the dollar amounts or the percentages that these amounts are to total assets, total revenues, net income or other criteria. The criteria selected depend on what most clearly indicates the portion of the financial statements audited by other auditors. The scope paragraph should also refer to the other auditors. The opinion paragraph should indicate that the opinion is based in part on the report of the other auditors.

NOTE: The other auditor may be named only if he or she gives permission and if the report is presented with that of the principal auditor.

REQUIRED PROCEDURES

Whether the principal auditor decides to make reference to the work of other auditors or makes no reference, he or she should

1. Make inquiries concerning the professional reputation and independence of the other auditors.
2. Coordinate his or her activities with those of the other auditors.

(See *Techniques for Application.*)

ADDITIONAL PROCEDURES UNDER DECISION TO ASSUME RESPONSIBILITY

The extent of additional procedures is determined by the principal auditor. These procedures might include the following:

1. Visit the other auditor and discuss his or her audit procedures.
2. Review the other auditor's audit program.

NOTE: The principal auditor should consider directing the other auditor as to the scope of his or her work.

3. Review the other auditor's audit documentation.
4. Participate in discussions with management of the component whose financial statements are being audited by the other auditor.
5. Perform supplemental tests of the accounting records of the component whose financial statements are being audited by the other auditor.

MODIFICATION OF OPINION

If he or she decides neither to assume responsibility for the other auditor's work nor to accept a division of responsibility with him or her, the principal auditor should qualify his or her opinion or disclaim an opinion. The reasons should be stated, and the magnitude of the portion of the financial statements responsible for the qualification or disclaimer should be disclosed.

POOLING OF INTERESTS

After the consummation of a business combination accounted for as a pooling of interests, an auditor may be asked to report on restated combined financial statements for prior years when other auditors audited the financial statements of some of the entities included in the combination. In this situation, the auditor should decide if he or she can serve as principal auditor. Sometimes it is not possible or necessary for the auditor to be satisfied with the restated financial statements. In these circumstances, if the auditor has audited the financial statements of one of the entities included in the restatement, he or she may express an opinion solely on the combining of the financial statements (see *Illustrations*).

Before the auditor expresses an opinion on the combining of the financial statements, he or she should apply certain procedures, such as testing the combination for clerical accuracy and conformity with generally accepted accounting principles. Also, the auditor should make inquiries and apply procedures about the following:

1. Elimination of intercompany transactions and accounts.
2. Combining adjustments and reclassifications.
3. Adjustments to treat like items in a comparable manner, if appropriate.
4. Disclosures in the restated financial statements and notes.

The auditor should also consider applying the additional procedures in "Additional Procedures under Decision to Assume Responsibility."

*NOTE: SFAS 141, **Business Combinations,** prohibits the pooling-of-interests method for all business combinations within its scope initiated after June 30, 2001. (Combinations of nonprofit organizations, acquisitions of for-profit business entities by nonprofit organizations, and combinations of mutual enterprises are not included within the scope of SFAS 141.)*

Modifications in Other Auditor's Report

If the other auditor's opinion is other than a standard report, the principal auditor should decide whether to recognize the modification in his or her own report. The decision is based on the nature and significance of the modification and its materiality in relation to the financial statements of the reporting entity taken as a whole.

NOTE: If the subject of the modification is not material and the other auditor's report is not presented, the principal auditor is not required to make reference to the matter in the report. If the other auditor's report is presented, however, the principal auditor may decide to refer to the modification even if the matter is not material to the financial statements of the reporting entity. For example, he or she may state that the matter is not material.

INTERPRETATIONS

Specific Procedures Performed by the Other Auditor at the Principal Auditor's Request (Issued April 1979; Revised November 1996)

When the principal auditor requests that the other auditor perform procedures, the principal auditor should provide specific instructions on procedures to be performed, materiality considerations for that purpose, and other information that may be necessary in the circumstances. The other auditor should perform the requested procedures in accordance with the instructions and report the findings solely for the use of the principal auditor. These auditor-to-auditor communications do not have to meet the requirements of an agreed-upon procedures engagement.

Inquiries of the Principal Auditor by the Other Auditor (April 1979)

The other auditor should inquire of the principal auditor regarding related-party transactions. The other auditor should consider whether to make additional inquiries based on whether there are unusual or complex transactions or relationships between the component he or she is auditing and the components audited by the principal auditor. Also, the other auditor should consider whether in the past, matters relevant to his or her own audit were known by the principal auditor.

The other auditor might provide the principal auditor with a draft of the financial statements and audit report expected to be issued to facilitate the principal auditor's response.

Form of Inquiries of the Principal Auditor Made by the Other Auditor (April 1979)

See *Illustrations* for an example of the form of inquiry letter the other auditor might send the principal auditor.

If the principal auditor's response is limited because his or her audit has not progressed to a point that enables a meaningful response, the other auditor should consider whether acceptable alternative procedures can be applied, whether to delay report issuance, or whether to qualify or disclaim an opinion because of the scope limitation.

Form of Principal Auditor's Response to Inquiries from Other Auditors (April 1979)

The principal auditor's response may be written or oral depending on what the other auditor has requested.

See *Illustrations* for an example of a principal auditor's written response. Information that may have a significant effect on the other auditor's audit should be in writing.

PROCEDURES OF THE PRINCIPAL AUDITOR (APRIL 1979)

The principal auditor's response should ordinarily be made by the auditor with final responsibility for the engagement. This auditor should take reasonable steps to be informed of matters pertinent to the other auditor's inquiry, such as inquiring of principal assistants and directing them to keep him or her informed of significant matters. Procedures directed solely toward responding to the other auditor that would not affect his or her own audit are not required. However, the principal auditor should update the response for significant matters that come to his or her attention after the original response, but before completion of the audit.

APPLICATION OF ADDITIONAL PROCEDURES CONCERNING THE AUDIT PERFORMED BY THE OTHER AUDITOR (DECEMBER 1981)

The principal auditor's judgment about the extent of additional procedures to be applied, if any, to obtain information about the adequacy of the other auditor's audit may be affected by knowledge of the other auditor's quality control policies and procedures.

Other factors that might affect the extent of additional procedures are previous experience with the other auditor, the materiality of the portion of the financial statements audited by the other auditor, the extent of control of the principal auditor over the other auditor's work, and results of the principal auditor's other procedures.

TECHNIQUES FOR APPLICATION

DETERMINATION OF PRINCIPAL AUDITOR

There are no simple rules or precise formulas for determining who is the principal auditor. The decision is based on professional judgment; however, consideration should be given to the following:

1. Proportions of assets, revenue, and income audited.
2. Materiality and significance of the components audited.
3. Overall knowledge and understanding of the reporting entity.

Presumption of Securities and Exchange Commission

There is no rule that the principal auditor should audit a specific proportion of the financial statement amounts; however, the SEC staff informally has taken the position that a majority coverage of total assets, revenue, or net income, whichever is appropriate, is presumed necessary.

Many auditors use the same guidelines that the SEC follows. Before serving as principal auditor, they would ordinarily need to audit at least a majority of total assets or total revenue. This guideline is used as a goal, however, rather than as an arbitrary cutoff. Some of the factors that may cause auditors not to adhere to percentages of total assets or total revenue are

1. **Unusual years.** The financial position or operating results in a particular year may have been affected by unusual circumstances that cause the normal relationships among components to be temporarily out of line.
2. **Centralization of control.** The parent or controlling entity may exert such control over the operations and accounting of other components that the auditor of that entity has sufficient knowledge of the other components without auditing them.

3. **Unusual components.** The nature of the business of components may be such that asset size is out of proportion to the importance of such components. For example, a financial institution may be large in size but not proportionately important to a consolidated group.
4. **Equal components.** The components may be nearly equal in size so that no single component has a majority of assets or revenue, and each component may historically have had different auditors. In this case, someone has to act as principal auditor, and the principal auditor will ordinarily gain sufficient knowledge of the other components by applying some of the procedures suggested in the section for circumstances when there is a decision not to make reference.
5. **Past experience.** The auditor may have audited the financial statements of some components in prior years and, thus, have sufficient knowledge of them to act as principal auditor.
6. **Change of auditors planned.** A change in auditors may be planned so that an auditor who will audit a majority of assets or revenue in future years considers it efficient to obtain sufficient knowledge of those components in the current year.

Decision to Assume Responsibility

Ordinarily the principal auditor is able to assume responsibility for the work of other auditors when

1. The other auditor is an associated or correspondent firm.
2. The other auditor was retained by the principal auditor, **and** the work was supervised by the principal auditor.
3. The principal auditor applies procedures he or she considers necessary to be satisfied about the quality of the other auditor's audit.
4. The portion of the financial statements audited by other auditors is not material to the financial statements reported on by the principal auditor.

Other factors the principal auditor should consider are

1. The quality control policies and procedures of the other auditor and the results of past peer reviews (see discussion following in "Reputation and Independence of Other Auditors").
2. Previous experience with the other auditor.
3. Control that he or she will exercise over the conduct of the other auditor's audit.

Decision Not to Assume Responsibility

The principal auditor may decide not to assume responsibility for the work of other auditors because

1. It is impracticable to review their work or perform other procedures.
2. The financial statements of the components audited by other auditors may be extremely material in relation to the total, regardless of any other considerations.

Reputation and Independence of Other Auditors

To determine the reputation and independence of the other auditors, the principal auditor might apply such procedures as

1. Communicate with the AICPA, the applicable state societies of CPAs, or, in the case of a foreign auditor, the corresponding professional organization.

a. The Professional Ethics Division will respond to inquiries about whether individuals are members of the Institute and whether complaints against members have been adjudicated.
b. The Division for CPA Firms will
   (1) Respond to inquiries about whether specific firms are members of either the AICPA Alliance for CPA Firms (formerly the Private Companies Practice Section) or the SEC Practice Section.
   (2) Indicate whether a firm has undergone peer review. (For a fee, copies of peer review reports will be supplied.)
   (3) Indicate whether any sanctions against a firm have been announced.
c. The AICPA Practice Monitoring Staff or the appropriate state society can respond as to whether firms are members and indicate whether the firm had a quality review.

2. Make inquiries of bankers, credit agencies, other credit grantors, attorneys, and other professionals about the reputation of the other auditors.
3. Obtain a representation (see *Illustrations*) from the other auditors that they are independent as required by the AICPA and, if appropriate, the SEC.

COORDINATION OF ACTIVITIES

The principal auditor may wish to have the other auditor perform certain procedures. In these circumstances, he or she should provide specific instructions on procedures to be performed, materiality considerations for this purpose, and other necessary information.

NOTE: The other auditor should perform the requested procedures in accordance with the principal auditor's instructions.

The principal auditor should communicate with the other auditor to determine that

1. The auditor is aware that the financial statements he or she will audit will be included in the financial statements on which the principal auditor will report.
2. The auditor is aware that his or her report will be relied on or, if applicable, referred to by the principal auditor.
3. The auditor has knowledge of financial reporting requirements of regulatory agencies, such as the SEC, if appropriate.
4. The auditor is aware that a review will be made to determine uniformity of accounting practices and elimination of intercompany transactions and accounts.

NOTE: For foreign auditors, the principal auditor should determine that they are familiar with US GAAP and GAAS and that they will conduct their audits and report in accordance with these principles and standards.

LONG-TERM INVESTMENTS

Equity Method

For investments accounted for under the equity method, the investor's auditor is similar to a principal auditor. In these circumstances, it is prudent for the investor's auditor to refer to the work of the investee's auditor.

Cost Method

For investments accounted for under the cost method, the work and reports of other auditors may be a significant part of the evidence for these investments. In these circumstances, depending on the materiality of the investments in relation to the financial statements taken as a whole, the investor's auditor may be similar to a principal auditor.

ILLUSTRATIONS

The following principal auditor reports are illustrated below.

1. Reference to subsidiary's auditor.
2. Reference to investee's auditor.

The following also are illustrated:

3. Auditor's report following a pooling of interests when the auditor is unable to serve as the principal auditor for the restated financial statements.
4. Representation letter from the other auditor.
5. Letter of inquiry from other auditor to principal auditor.
6. Principal auditor's response to letter of inquiry from other auditor.

ILLUSTRATION 1. REFERENCE TO SUBSIDIARY'S AUDITOR (ADAPTED FROM SECTION 543)

Independent Auditor's Report

We have audited the accompanying balance sheet of Widget Company and subsidiaries as of December 31, 20X1, and the related consolidated statements of income and retained earnings and cash flows for the year then ended. These financial statements are the responsibility of the Company's management. Our responsibility is to express an opinion on these financial statements based on our audits. We did not audit the financial statements of Basic Company, a wholly owned subsidiary, which statements reflect total assets and revenues constituting 20% and 22%, respectively, of the related consolidated totals. Those statements were audited by other auditors whose report has been furnished to us, and our opinion, insofar as it relates to the amounts included for Basic Company, is based solely on the report of the other auditors.

We conducted our audit in accordance with auditing standards generally accepted in the United States of America. Those standards require that we plan and perform the audit to obtain reasonable assurance about whether the financial statements are free of material misstatement. An audit includes examining, on a test basis, evidence supporting the amounts and disclosures in the financial statements. An audit also includes assessing the accounting principles used and significant estimates made by management, as well as evaluating the overall financial statement presentation. We believe that our audit and the report of the other auditors provides a reasonable basis for our opinion.

In our opinion, based on our audit and the report of the other auditors, the consolidated financial statements referred to above present fairly, in all material respects, the financial position of Widget Company as of [*at*] December 31, 20X1, and the results of its operations and its cash flows for the year then ended in conformity with accounting principles generally accepted in the United States of America.

ILLUSTRATION 2. REFERENCE TO INVESTEE'S AUDITOR

Independent Auditor's Report

We have audited the consolidated balance sheet of Widget Company and subsidiaries as of December 31, 20X1, and the related consolidated statements of income and retained earnings and cash flows for the year then ended. These financial statements are the responsibility of the Company's management. Our responsibility is to express an opinion on these financial statements based on our audit. We did not audit the financial statements of Basic Company, an affiliated company, owned 25% in 20X1, which is accounted for in the accompanying financial statements by the equity method of accounting. The equity in net income of this affiliated company constitutes 15% of net income for the year ended December 31, 20X1. The financial statements of the affiliated company were audited by other auditors, whose report has been furnished to us, and our opinion, insofar as it relates to the amounts included for Basic Company, is based solely on the report of the other auditors.

We conducted our audit in accordance with auditing standards generally accepted in the United States of America. Those standards require that we plan and perform the audit to obtain reasonable assurance about whether the financial statements are free of material misstatement. An audit includes examining, on a test basis, evidence supporting the amounts and disclosures in the financial statements. An audit also includes assessing the accounting principles used and significant estimates made by management, as well as evaluating the overall financial statement presentation. We believe that our audit and the report of the other auditors provides a reasonable basis for our opinion.

In our opinion, based on our audit and the report of the other auditors, the consolidated financial statements referred to above present fairly, in all material respects, the financial position of Widget Company as of [*at*] December 31, 20X1, and the results of its operations and its cash flows for the year then ended in conformity with accounting principles generally accepted in the United States of America.

Illustration 3. Report Following a Pooling of Interests (Adapted from Section 543)

Independent Auditor's Report

We have audited the consolidated balance sheet of Widget Company as of December 31, 20X2, and the related statements of income, retained earnings, and cash flows for the year then ended. These financial statements are the responsibility of the Company's management. Our responsibility is to express an opinion on these financial statements based on our audit.

We conducted our audit in accordance with auditing standards generally accepted in the United States of America. Those standards require that we plan and perform the audit to obtain reasonable assurance about whether the financial statements are free of material misstatement. An audit includes examining, on a test basis, evidence supporting the amounts and disclosures in the financial statements. An audit also includes assessing the accounting principles used and significant estimates made by management, as well as evaluating the overall financial statement presentation. We believe that our audit provides a reasonable basis for our opinion.

In our opinion, the financial statements referred to above present fairly, in all material respects, the financial position of Widget Company as of December 31, 20X2, and the results of its operations and its cash flows for the year then ended in conformity with accounting principles generally accepted in the United States of America.

We previously audited and reported on the consolidated statements of income and cash flows of Widget Company and subsidiaries for the year ended December 31, 20X1, prior to their restatement for the 20X2 pooling of interests. The contribution of Widget Company and subsidiaries to revenues and net income represented __ percent and __ percent of the respective restated totals. Separate financial statements of the other companies included in the 20X1 restated consolidated statements of income and cash flows were audited and reported on separately by other auditors. We also have audited the combination of the accompanying consolidated statements of income and cash flows for the year ended December 31, 20X1, after restatement for the 20X2 pooling of interests; in our opinion, such consolidated statements have been properly combined on the basis described in Note A of notes to consolidated financial statements.

Illustration 4. Representation Letter from Other Auditor

[*Other auditor's letterhead*]

[*Date*]

Principal Auditor
[*Address*]

Gentlemen:

We have audited the financial statements of ABC, Inc., for the year ended December 31, 20X1. Because you will report on the consolidated financial statements of Widget Company for the year ended December 31, 20X1, which will include the financial statements of ABC, Inc., we have been requested to furnish you with the following information for the period covered by our report.

1. Our firm is independent with respect to the parent company, any subsidiary, or affiliated companies following the provisions of the AICPA Code of Professional Conduct and the independence rulings of the Securities and Exchange Commission; for example

    a. None of the partners of our firm, nor any of the staff members employed by any office doing the work on this audit, has any direct or material indirect financial interest in or indebtedness owing from the parent company, any subsidiary, or affiliated companies.

b. None of the partners of our firm, nor any of the staff members employed by any office doing the work on this audit, is connected with the parent company, any subsidiary, or affiliated companies as a promoter, underwriter, voting trustee, director, officer, or employee.

c. To the best of our knowledge there are no other relationships or circumstances that would impair our independence with respect to the parent company or any subsidiary or affiliate companies.

2. In connection with our audit of ABC, Inc., nothing has come to our attention that in our judgment would have a material effect on, or require mention in, the financial statements of Widget Company.
3. The financial statements as reported on by us are suitable for consolidation with Widget Company, with adjustment only for normal consolidation and elimination entries, as follows:

[*Itemization*]

____

____

4. We understand that in reporting on XYZ Company, you will cite your reliance on our report covering our audit of ABC, Inc.

Yours very truly,

[*Other auditor's firm signature*]

Illustration 5. Letter of Inquiry from Other Auditor to Principal Auditor (from Section 543 Interpretation)

We are auditing the financial statements of [*name of client*] as of [*date*] and for the [*financial statement period*] for the purpose of expressing an opinion on whether the financial statements present fairly, in all material respects, the financial position, results of operations, and cash flows of [*name of client*] in conformity with accounting principles generally accepted in the United States of America.

A draft of the financial statements referred to above and a draft of our report are enclosed solely to aid you in responding to this inquiry. Please provide us [*in writing, orally*] with the following information in connection with your current audit of the consolidated financial statements of [*name of parent company*]:

1. Transactions or other matters [*including adjustments made during consolidation or contemplated at the date of your reply*] that have come to your attention that you believe require adjustment to or disclosure in the financial statements of [*name of client*] being audited by us.
2. Any limitation on the scope of your audit that is related to the financial statements of [*name of client*] being audited by us, or that limits your ability to provide us with the information requested in this inquiry.

Please make your response as of a date near [*expected date of the auditor's report*].

NOTE: The letter should be addressed to the principal auditor and signed by the other auditor.

Illustration 6. Principal Auditor's Response to Letter of Inquiry from Other Auditor (from Section 543 Interpretation)

This letter is furnished to you in response to your request that we provide you with certain information in connection with your audit of the financial statements of [*name of components*], and [*subsidiary, division, branch, or investment*] of Parent Company for the year ended [*date*].

We are in the process of performing an audit of the consolidated financial statements of Parent Company for the year ended [*date*] (but have not completed our work as of this date). The objective of our audit is to enable us to express an opinion on the consolidated financial statements of Parent Company and, accordingly, we have performed no procedures directed toward identifying matters that would not affect our audit or our report. However, solely for the purpose of responding to your inquiry, we have read the draft of the financial statements of [*name of component*] as of [*date*] and for the [*period of audit*] and the draft of your report on them, included with your inquiry dated [*date of inquiry*].

Based solely on the work we have performed [*to date*] in connection with our audit of the consolidated cash flows, which would not necessarily reveal all or any of the matters covered in your inquiry, we advise you that

1. No transactions or other matters (including adjustments made during consolidation or contemplated at this date) have come to our attention that we believe require adjustment to, or disclosure in, the financial statements of [*name of component*] being audited by you.
2. No limitation has been placed by Parent Company on the scope of our audit that, to our knowledge, is related to the financial statements [*of name of component*] being audited by you that has limited our ability to provide you with the information requested in your inquiry.

NOTE: The letter should be addressed to the other auditor and signed by the principal auditor.

544 LACK OF CONFORMITY WITH GENERALLY ACCEPTED ACCOUNTING PRINCIPLES

EFFECTIVE DATE AND APPLICABILITY

Original Pronouncements	SAP 33, December 1963 (codified in SAS 1, November 1972); SAS 2, October 1974; SAS 62, April 1989; SAS 77, November 1995.
Effective Date	When issued, December 1963, unless subsequently amended.
Applicability	Audits of financial statements of regulated companies in accordance with generally accepted auditing standards when the financial statements are presented for purposes other than regulatory filings.

DEFINITION OF TERM

Regulated companies. Companies, such as public utilities and insurance companies, whose accounting practices are prescribed by governmental regulatory authorities or commissions.

OBJECTIVES OF SECTION

Governmental regulatory authorities or commissions may prescribe accounting practices for regulated companies. Examples of these companies include public utilities, common carriers, insurance companies, and financial institutions. Sometimes the prescribed accounting practices are not in conformity with GAAP. This section tells the auditor the kind of report he or she should issue when a regulated company presents financial statements for purposes other than regulatory filings that follow accounting practices prescribed by regulatory authorities or commissions that are not in conformity with GAAP.

Differences between prescribed accounting practices and accounting practices applicable to nonregulated businesses that are caused by the rate-making process can be in conformity with GAAP. Guidance on accounting for regulated enterprises is contained in several FASB Statements of Financial Accounting Standards, particularly SFAS 71, *Accounting for the Effects of Certain Types of Regulation,* SFAS 90, *Regulated Enterprises—Accounting for Abandonments and Disallowances of Plant Costs,* SFAS 92, *Regulated Enterprises—Accounting for Phase-in Plans,* and SFAS 101, *Regulated Enterprises—Accounting for the Discontinuation of Application of FASB Statement 71.*

FUNDAMENTAL REQUIREMENTS

DEPARTURES FROM GAAP

The auditor should express a qualified opinion or an adverse opinion when a regulated company issues financial statements to anyone other than its regulatory agency that are prepared in conformity with accounting practices prescribed by regulatory authorities or commissions that do not conform with GAAP.

FINANCIAL STATEMENTS SOLELY FOR FILING WITH REGULATORY AGENCY

The auditor may report on a regulated company's financial statements as being prepared in accordance with a comprehensive basis of accounting other than generally accepted accounting principles (see Section 623) **only** if the statements are **solely** for filing with the regulatory agency.

FINANCIAL STATEMENTS FOR OTHER THAN FILING WITH REGULATORY AGENCY

The auditor may be asked to report on the fair presentation of financial statements in conformity with a regulatory prescribed basis of accounting in presentations other than filings with the regulatory agency. In these circumstances, the auditor's standard report should be modified because of the departure from GAAP, and, in an additional paragraph, an opinion may be expressed on the conformity of the financial statements with the prescribed method.

NOTE: The additional paragraph is added at the auditor's discretion; it is never required.

INTERPRETATIONS

There are no interpretations for this section.

550 OTHER INFORMATION IN DOCUMENTS CONTAINING AUDITED FINANCIAL STATEMENTS

EFFECTIVE DATE AND APPLICABILITY

Original Pronouncement	SAS 8, December 1975; and SAS 98, September 2002.
Effective Date	When issued, December 1975.
Applicability	Audits of financial statements in accordance with generally accepted auditing standards, but only if the audited financial statements are in certain documents. The amendment for SAS 98 is effective upon issuance. *NOTE: Because applicability is unusually complex, it is explained below.*

APPLICABILITY

Basically, the applicability of the SAS depends on the type of document that includes audited financial statements. The SAS is applicable to several types of annual reports and only to other documents at the client's request.

ANNUAL REPORTS

Three kinds of annual reports that involve a responsibility to read and evaluate other information are specifically enumerated.

1. Annual reports to holders of securities or beneficial interests.

   NOTE: Essentially, this means the glossy annual report to shareholders issued by public corporations or similar formal financial reports of other entities issued to those with ownership interests.

2. Annual reports of organizations for charitable or philanthropic purposes.

   NOTE: This means that some nonprofit organizations are covered but others are not covered. Also, the annual reports of state and local governmental entities are not covered.

3. Annual reports filed with regulatory authorities under the Securities Exchange Act of 1934.

   NOTE: A registration statement filed under the 1933 act is specifically excluded because the responsibilities are covered in other sections.

CLIENT'S REQUEST

If the client informs the auditor that the audited financial statements and the audit report are to be included in some document prepared by the client, then the section applies.

NOTE: This circumstance is described as "other documents to which the auditor, at the client's request, devotes attention" to avoid any implication that the auditor needs to keep informed of what the client does with the auditor's report once it has been issued. If the client brings the subsequent use of the audit report to the auditor's attention before release of the document, then he or she has the responsibilities imposed by this section.

AUDITED OTHER INFORMATION

This section does not apply if the auditor has been engaged to express an opinion on other information. For example, the auditor may be requested by the client to express an opinion on consolidating schedules (Section 551).

The auditor is cautioned in a footnote that the limited procedures required by this section (reading and comparing) are not a sufficient basis to express an opinion on other information.

DEFINITIONS OF TERMS

Other information. Any information, other than audited financial statements and the auditor's report thereon, contained in a document published by an entity that contains audited financial statements.

NOTE: The document would always be client-prepared, that is, a financial report prepared by the client, such as an annual report. SAS 29 (Section 551) applies to auditor-submitted documents.

Material inconsistency. A material difference between information in the audited financial statements and the same information appearing elsewhere in the document, or a material difference in the manner of presentation.

Material misstatement of fact. A statement that appears to the auditor to be untrue and significant that is not a material inconsistency.

NOTE: The section is vague on the precise meaning of this term. It includes virtually anything that the auditor believes is materially misleading that is outside the financial statements.

OBJECTIVES OF SECTION

Generally, before SAS 8 was issued, auditors considered it a prudent practice to read the entire document that contained audited financial statements. The practice was considered prudent because an auditor has a natural concern with the way that his or her audit report is to be used and there is always at least a possibility that something outside the financial statements might be alleged to be misleading. Even if misleading information appears outside audited financial statements, the auditor might be involved in any resulting litigation and, at the very least, might be exposed to unfavorable publicity.

The SAS made this prudent practice a part of professional responsibility. The responsibility is carefully worded, however, to avoid the implication that the auditor assumes anything remotely resembling audit responsibility for the information. For the same reason, no reference is made to responsibility for other information in the standard audit report.

The SAS states that the auditor's reason for reading the entire document is that "other information in a document may be relevant to an audit performed by an independent auditor or to the continuing propriety of his report." Also, the SAS limits responsibility by noting that "the auditor has no obligation to perform any procedures to corroborate other information contained in a document." The auditor may have a responsibility, however, to reach out to information outside the financial statements if there is a material inconsistency or misstatement.

In September 2002, SAS 98 amended this section to clarify that an auditor may issue a report providing an opinion, in relation to the basic financial statements taken as a whole, or supplementary information and other information that has been subjected to auditing procedures applied to the audit of those basic financial statements.

FUNDAMENTAL REQUIREMENTS

The auditor should

1. Read the other information.

   NOTE: This is the knowledgeable study of information by an auditor who has an understanding of the client's business, organization, and operating characteristics as well as its financial statements.

2. Consider whether the other information is materially inconsistent with information in the audited financial statements. This consideration includes the manner of presentation of both the other information and comparable information in the financial statements.
3. If there is a material inconsistency
   a. Determine whether the financial statements, the report, or both require revision.

      NOTE: This means the auditor should decide if the difference is caused by a misstatement in the financial statements.

   b. Request that the client revise the other information if it, rather than the financial statements, is misstated.
   c. If the other information is not revised, consider other actions such as
      (1) Revising the report to include an explanatory paragraph describing the material inconsistency.
      (2) Withholding the use of the report in the document.
      (3) Withdrawing from the engagement.
4. If the auditor's reading makes him or her aware of a material misstatement of fact, he or she should
   a. Discuss the matter with the client.
   b. Consider that
      (1) He or she may not have the expertise to assess the validity of the statement.
      (2) There may be no standards by which to assess its presentation.
      (3) There may be valid differences of judgment or opinion.

      NOTE: This means that concluding there is a material misstatement is a lot more subjective than concluding there is a material inconsistency.

   c. Request that the client seek the advice of legal counsel on the matter.
   d. If the auditor concludes after discussion with the client that there is, in fact, a material misstatement of fact, he or she should consider steps such as
      (1) Notifying the client in writing of his or her views.
      (2) Consulting his or her own legal counsel on what other action is appropriate.
   e. If the supplementary or other information has been subjected to audit procedures, the auditor can report on supplementary and other information, indicating that such information is fairly stated in all material respects in relation to the financial statements. The auditor may report using the guidance in AU 551.

INTERPRETATIONS

REPORT BY MANAGEMENT ON INTERNAL CONTROL OVER FINANCIAL REPORTING (ISSUED MAY 1994; REVISED JANUARY 2001)

If management includes an assertion on internal control in a document containing audited financial statements, the auditor's responsibility depends on the nature of the engagement.

If the auditor has been engaged to examine and report on management's assertion on internal control effectiveness, the auditor should follow the guidance in Section 2501 for an attestation engagement to report on internal control over financial reporting.

If the auditor has not been engaged to examine and report on management's assertion, then the assertion is **other information** and should be read and evaluated for the existence of a material misstatement of fact.

The auditor may, but is not required to, add the following paragraph to the standard auditor's report:

> We were not engaged to examine management's assertion about the effectiveness of [*name of entity*]'s internal control over financial reporting as of [*date*] included in the accompanying [*title of management's report*] and, accordingly, we do not express an opinion thereon.

OTHER REFERENCES BY MANAGEMENT TO INTERNAL CONTROL OVER FINANCIAL REPORTING, INCLUDING REFERENCES TO THE INDEPENDENT AUDITOR (ISSUED MAY 1994; REVISED JANUARY 2001)

If management's assertion on internal control includes references to the independent auditor or to the audit, the auditor should consider whether the references would lead a reader to assume the auditor had performed more work than required under GAAS, or to believe that the auditor was providing assurance on internal control, or whether the reference otherwise implies the auditor's involvement was greater than supported by the facts. If management misstates the auditor's involvement or responsibility, the auditor should treat the misstatement as a material misstatement of fact.

If management's assertion refers to the auditor's communication that there are no material weaknesses in internal control, the auditor should advise management to delete the reference because it might be misunderstood by users. If management does not revise its report, the auditor should notify management that the auditor has not consented to this reference and consider what other actions might be appropriate. The auditor may wish to consult legal counsel.

OTHER INFORMATION IN ELECTRONIC SITES CONTAINING AUDITED FINANCIAL STATEMENTS (ISSUED MARCH 1997; REVISED JANUARY 2001)

Electronic sites, such as the World Wide Web area of the Internet or the SEC's EDGAR system, are a means of distributing information and are not documents under Section 550. The auditor is not required to read information contained in electronic sites that also contain financial statements the auditor has audited, or consider whether there are material inconsistencies.

PROFESSIONAL ISSUES TASK FORCE PRACTICE ALERTS

97-1 Financial Statements on the Internet

This Practice Alert restates the advice provided by the interpretation entitled, "Other Information in Electronic Sites Containing Audited Financial Statements." (See *Interpretations.*) In addition, it states that

- The auditor may wish to discuss concerns about the security and integrity of information published on the Internet with the client, so that the client may review safeguards used to protect the data.
- A client who distributes audited financial statements and the auditor's report on the Internet can set it up so that a user knows when they are hyperlinking to matters outside of that document. Also, entities may wish to allow easy access to an entire document or the ability to download or print an entire document on their sites to make sure that users can easily locate complete documents.

The full text of this Practice Alert can be obtained from the AICPA website at www.aicpa.org/members/div/secps/lit/practice.htm.

TECHNIQUES FOR APPLICATION

Location of Other Information

Other information that is more likely to contain material inconsistencies or material misstatements of fact might be found in the following places:

1. Letter from the chairman of the board or the chief executive officer.
2. Management statement on its responsibilities for financial reports and internal control.
3. Financial highlights.
4. Financial review.
5. Management's discussion and analysis (MD&A).
6. Schedules.
7. Graphic presentations and charts of financial data accompanied by explanations.

Who Should Read the Document?

The document containing the other information and the audited financial statements should be read by the auditor with final responsibility for the engagement or the responsibility should be delegated to a knowledgeable and experienced assistant. Generally, a partner or manager should assume this responsibility. The auditor reading the document should have overall knowledge of the client's operations and financial condition. Also, he or she should be aware of the problems encountered during the audit.

Reading the Document and Additional Procedures

The auditor is not required to perform any procedures to corroborate the other information contained in the document. As matters of prudence and professionalism, however, many auditors do the following in addition to comparing the other information with audited financial statements:

1. Recompute numerical data.
2. Trace numerical data to audit documentation.

Comparisons with Information in the Audited Financial Statements

The other information should be read, and, if it contains data included in the financial statements, that data should be compared with similar data in the audited financial statements. For example, the letter from the chairman of the board may refer to current year's sales, net income, or capital expenditures. The data in the chairman's letter should be compared with the data in the audited financial statements.

Recomputations

Occasionally, other information may contain disaggregated financial statement data. For example, the financial review may indicate sales by product line or salaries by function—sales, administrative, production. Also, operating ratios such as gross margin and net income, and balance sheet ratios such as the current ratio, may be presented.

Any information that is disaggregated is generally footed to determine that its total agrees with the total in the audited financial statements.

All ratios presented in other information are generally recomputed based on data in the audited financial statements. The recomputed ratios should be compared with the ratios presented in the other information.

Tracing to Audit Documentation

Occasionally, other information may contain schedules supporting information that appears in the audited financial statements. For example, other information may contain schedules of cost of goods sold and selling, general, and administrative expenses. The components of these schedules are generally traced to the extended trial balance in the auditor's audit documentation.

MATERIAL INCONSISTENCIES

Examples

The following are examples of material inconsistencies in information outside the audited financial statements:

1. Referring to an item as net income when it is income before extraordinary loss.
2. Referring to cash flow from operations as net income.
3. Including in working capital cash that was classified as a noncurrent asset.

Auditor Procedures

When the auditor finds a material inconsistency between data in the audited financial statements and data in the other information, he or she should generally bring the inconsistency to the attention of the chief financial officer. The auditor and the chief financial officer should analyze the inconsistency to determine the following:

1. The nature of the inconsistency.
2. Actions required to eliminate the inconsistency.

Refusal of Client to Revise Other Information

If a client refuses to revise other information to eliminate a material inconsistency, the auditor should consider actions such as the following:

1. Revise the report by including an explanatory paragraph describing the inconsistency.
2. Withhold the use of the report in the document containing the other information.
3. Withdraw from the engagement.

Revision of Auditor's Report

If the auditor decides to explain the material inconsistency in the report, he or she should add an explanatory paragraph, such as the following:

> A letter from the chairman of the board of directors appears on page ___ of this document. In this letter, the chairman refers to net income of $____. However, this amount is the net income before an extraordinary loss. Net income for the period as reported in the income statement on page ___ amounted to $____.

The introductory, scope, and opinion paragraphs would not be modified.

Withholding Use of Auditor's Report

If the auditor decides to withhold the use of the report in the document containing the other information, he or she should notify the board of directors and management of this decision. If the client ignores the auditor's decision and uses the report, the auditor should consider doing the following:

1. Consult with his or her lawyer.
2. Notify the agency, if any, to whom the document has been submitted.
3. Notify all those known to have received the document.

Withdrawal from Engagement

Withdrawal from the engagement is an exceptionally strong and serious reaction to a material inconsistency. The material inconsistency generally has to be very serious and significant for the auditor to take this action. If the auditor decides to withdraw from the engagement, he or she should consider doing the following:

1. Consult with his or her lawyer.
2. Notify board of directors and management.
3. If the client's document, with the auditor's report, has been released
   a. Notify the agency, if any, to whom the document has been submitted.
   b. Notify all those known to have received the document.

Material Misstatement of Fact

General

It might be exceptionally difficult for the auditor to identify a material misstatement of fact in other information in documents containing audited financial statements. Most of the other information usually is nonaccounting in nature and beyond the expertise of the auditor.

Examples

Material misstatements of fact are virtually anything other than material inconsistencies that cause the auditor concern. They can range from outright lies to mere exaggeration of the facts, but generally the auditor is concerned only with serious distortions of the facts. Some obvious examples of material misstatements of fact in information outside the financial statements are the following:

1. Using a photograph of a factory that the entity does not own and describing the factory as company property.
2. Statement that the entity has settled litigation, for example, with the IRS when it has not.
3. Statement that the entity has obtained valuable franchises or patents when it has not.
4. Statement that the entity has fully integrated the operations of a major newly acquired subsidiary when it has not.

Auditor Procedures

When the auditor finds a material misstatement of fact in the other information, he or she should generally bring the misstatement to the attention of the chief financial officer. The auditor and the chief financial officer should analyze the misstatement to determine the following:

1. The nature of the misstatement. Is it a misstatement, or is it an exaggeration? It may be necessary for the officer and the auditor to consult with an expert, such as the client's lawyer.
2. Actions required to eliminate the misstatement.

Refusal of Client to Revise Other Information

If a client refuses to revise other information to eliminate a material misstatement of fact, the auditor should consider actions such as the following:

1. Write to the management and the board of directors and express his or her views about the misstatement.
2. Consult with his or her lawyer.

PROVISION IN ENGAGEMENT LETTER

To have the opportunity to review documents containing audited financial statements, the auditor might wish to include in the engagement letter (see Section 310) a provision that the client must submit these documents to the auditor before they are issued. An example of such a provision follows:

> It is our firm's policy that if you reproduce or publish our report, or any portion of it, in a document containing other information, copies of printer's proofs of the **entire document** must be submitted to us in sufficient time for our review. It is necessary that we specifically give permission for the use of our name on our report in any such document. Also, it will be necessary for you to furnish us with [*number*] copies of the printed document.

COMMUNICATION WITH AUDIT COMMITTEES

SAS 61 (see Section 380), when applicable, requires the auditor to discuss

1. Responsibility for other information.
2. Any procedure performed on the information.
3. Results of those procedures.

551 REPORTING ON INFORMATION ACCOMPANYING THE BASIC FINANCIAL STATEMENTS IN AUDITOR-SUBMITTED DOCUMENTS

EFFECTIVE DATE AND APPLICABILITY

Original Pronouncements SAS 29, July 1980; SAS 52, April 1988; and SAS 98, September 2002.

Effective Date Effective for auditors' reports dated on or after December 31, 1980, and (for SAS 52) when issued, April 1988. The amendment for SAS 98 is effective upon issuance.

Applicability Audits of financial statements in accordance with generally accepted auditing standards if the statements and the auditor's report on them are included in a document that the auditor submits to the client or others.

NOTE: The form of reporting specified is not required but may be used in a client-prepared document, such as an annual report to shareholders.

DEFINITIONS OF TERMS

Basic financial statements. A balance sheet, statement of income, statement of retained earnings or changes in stockholders' equity, statement of cash flows, and

- Description of accounting policies.
- Notes to financial statements.
- Schedules and explanatory material that **are identified** as part of the basic financial statements.

NOTE: Schedules and explanatory material may be either part of the basic statements or accompanying information, depending on whether the information is incorporated in the statements by a cross-reference in the statements.

Accompanying information. Information presented outside the basic financial statements that is not required for presentation of financial position, results of operations, or cash flows in conformity with generally accepted accounting principles. Examples are

- Additional details of items in, or related to, the basic financial statements (e.g., a schedule of investments).

- Consolidating information (e.g., schedules presenting separate financial statements of components of a consolidated group).
- Historical summaries of items extracted from the basic financial statements (e.g., a five- or ten-year presentation of sales, gross profit, and net income).
- Statistical data.
- Other material, some of which may be from outside the accounting system or outside the entity (e.g., sales or production data by unit, number of employees, or industry statistics).

Coexisting financial statements. Financial statements for an entity covering the same time period presented in different types of documents.

Auditor-submitted document. A document containing audited financial statements and the auditor's report on them that the auditor submits to the client or others.

NOTE: The usual form is a bound report prepared by the auditor with an identifying cover containing the auditor's logo or letterhead.

Client-prepared document. A document prepared by the client that contains audited financial statements and the auditor's report on them, including financial reports prepared by the client but reproduced by the auditor on the client's behalf.

NOTE: The usual form is the glossy annual report of an entity, but the distinguishing feature is that the identifying characteristics, particularly the cover, are those of the entity and not the auditor.

OBJECTIVES OF SECTION

This section is potentially confusing. The key to understanding it is recognizing that the auditor's reporting responsibility is determined by the type of document containing audited financial statements rather than the nature of the information that might be included in the document in addition to the statements. The auditor's obligation to report on information other than audited statements depends on whether the document is client-prepared or auditor-submitted.

In a client-prepared document, the presumption is that the auditor has audit responsibility only for the information explicitly identified in the introductory paragraph of the standard audit report. For example, the usual type of client-prepared document is the glossy annual report of a public company. The presumption is that any information within the glossy covers is the responsibility of the entity's management. The auditor reports on the financial statements audited and explicitly describes the degree of responsibility assumed for them.

The presumption changes for auditor-submitted documents. An auditor-submitted document usually is a bound document prepared by the auditor with a distinctive typeface, paper, and format that usually carries the logo or identifying letterhead of the auditor. Because this type of document obviously comes from the auditor, there is a presumption of responsibility for all the information included. To clarify the degree of responsibility, it is necessary for the auditor explicitly to report on all the information.

The nature of the information included in addition to the financial statements typically has no influence on the auditor's obligation to report. Customarily there are some differences, however, in the nature of the information. For example, a glossy annual report usually has a president's letter to shareholders and an auditor-submitted document usually does not. An auditor-submitted document is more likely to contain schedules of the items included in an account balance, such as a schedule of investments; an annual report is more likely to contain a management's discussion and analysis (MD&A).

Information outside the financial statements in a client-prepared document is normally not reported on explicitly unless the auditor has been specifically engaged to provide audit or attest services on the information. The auditor has a very limited responsibility for it, as described in Section 550, "Other Information in Documents Containing Audited Financial Statements." One of the confusing aspects is that in a client-prepared document, information outside the financial statements is called **other information,** but the same type of information may appear in an auditor-submitted document and would then be called **accompanying information**. Generally the nature of the information has no bearing on reporting responsibility; the type of document is the sole determinant.

Another potential source of confusion is that the type of document usually determines whether the auditor should report on information, but the auditor may at the client's request report on information in a client-prepared document using the same form of reporting as for an auditor-submitted document. For certain types of information, namely, condensed financial statements or selected financial data (Section 552) and supplementary information required by GAAP (Section 558), however, there are separate reporting requirements, and the form of reporting differs, depending on whether the document including the information is client-prepared or auditor-submitted.

At one time auditor-submitted documents with information accompanying the basic financial statements were called long-form reports. An auditor-submitted document with only the basic financial statements and an auditor's report on them was called a short-form report. The audit report itself, however, was also generally referred to as a short-form report. In 1972, the term **short-form** report was replaced with **standard** report in the authoritative literature, and the once-common distinction between short-form and long-form reports was obscured. This section resolved the matter by linking reporting responsibility to the type of document rather than to the length of report or the nature of the information covered.

FUNDAMENTAL REQUIREMENTS

Reporting Responsibility

According to AU 551.04, when an auditor submits a document containing audited financial statements to the client or to others, he or she has a responsibility to report on all the information included in the document.

Form of Report

In an auditor-submitted document, the report on information accompanying the basic financial statements should

1. State that the audit has been made for the purpose of forming an opinion on the basic financial statements taken as a whole.
2. Identify the accompanying information by descriptive title or page of the document.
3. State that the accompanying information is presented for purposes of additional analysis and is not a required part of the basic financial statements.
4. Either express an opinion on whether the accompanying information is fairly stated in all material respects in relation to the basic financial statements taken as a whole, or disclaim an opinion.
    a. Whether an opinion can be expressed depends on whether the information has been subjected to the auditing procedures applied in the audit of the basic financial statements.
    b. The auditor may express an opinion on a **portion** of the accompanying information and disclaim an opinion on the remainder.

LOCATION OF REPORT

The report on accompanying information may be added to the standard report on the basic statements or may appear separately in the auditor-submitted document.

MATERIALITY

In reporting on accompanying information, the measurement of materiality is the same as that used in forming an opinion on the basic financial statements.

NOTE: This means that in applying auditing procedures and in deciding about report modifications, the basis is what would be material to the basic financial statements and not what would be material to a separate presentation of accompanying information.

REPORT MODIFICATIONS

The auditor should consider the effect of any modifications in the standard report on the report on the accompanying information.

1. If the auditor expresses a qualified opinion on the basic financial statements, he or she should make clear the effects of that matter on the accompanying information.
2. If the auditor expresses an adverse opinion or disclaims an opinion on the basic financial statements, he or she should not express an unqualified opinion on the accompanying information.

   NOTE: Presumably the auditor should give the same kind of report on accompanying information as on the basic financial statements—adverse opinion or disclaimer.

3. If the auditor concludes that accompanying information is materially misstated in relation to the basic financial statements, he or she should

   a. Propose a revision of the information to the client.
   b. If the client refuses, modify the report on accompanying information, or
   c. Refuse to include the information in the document.

   NOTE: This guidance assumes that there could be a material misstatement in the accompanying information that did not result in a qualified opinion on the basic financial statements that would still preclude an unqualified opinion on the accompanying information. Although the section does not explicitly say so, the only basis for this reporting decision is a matter that is material to the accompanying information but not the basic financial statements.

SUPPLEMENTARY INFORMATION REQUIRED BY GAAP

If supplementary information required by GAAP is presented outside the basic financial statements in an auditor-submitted document, the auditor should

1. Opine on the information if the auditor has been engaged to examine the information,
2. Report on the information if the information has been subjected to audit procedures, or
3. Disclaim an opinion on it.

CONDENSED STATEMENTS OR SELECTED DATA

In an auditor-submitted document, the auditor reports on condensed statements or selected data (see Section 552) in the same manner as on other accompanying information. In a client-prepared document, the auditor is not required to report on this type of information, but if the auditor does report, the form of the report differs from that used for an auditor-submitted document (see Section 552).

Consolidating Information

If the auditor is associated with consolidated financial statements that include consolidating information or schedules presenting the separate financial statements of components to the consolidated group, there are two equally acceptable approaches to reporting.

1. The auditor may issue the standard report on the consolidated statements and report on the consolidating information or schedules in the same manner as reporting on other accompanying information outside the basic financial statements.

   NOTE: In this case, it is important to identify the consolidating information to distinguish it from the consolidated statements. The easiest way is to present it in separate schedules.

2. The auditor may issue a standard report that covers both the consolidated statements and the consolidating information.

   NOTE: In this case, the scope of the audit has to be extensive enough to express an opinion on the individual financial statements of the components, and the disclosure has to be adequate for each of the individual components.

The same guidance applies to combined statements and combining information or schedules.

NOTE: For the same reason as explained in the note on Report Modifications, if a misstatement known to the auditor is material to the consolidating information, but not the consolidated financial statements, the auditors should modify the opinion on the consolidating information.

Additional Comments on Audit Procedures

An auditor-submitted document may contain a more detailed description of the audit procedures applied than does the standard report. If audit procedures are described

1. The description should not contradict or detract from the standard report.

   NOTE: This means the description should not imply a scope limitation that is not described in the standard report.

2. The description should be separate from the accompanying information rather than interspersed with it.

   NOTE: This means the auditor should not, for example, include a description of the procedures applied to investments as part of a schedule presenting investments. The description of audit procedures should be separate from the accounting information.

Coexisting Financial Statements

The auditor should be satisfied that information accompanying basic financial statements in an auditor-submitted document would not support a contention that the same basic financial statements in a client-prepared document are not in conformity with GAAP.

NOTE: For example, a schedule of accounts receivable may show a significant concentration with a few customers. If this information is material to the use or understanding of the basic financial statements, failure to include the information in a document that does not contain the accompanying information could support a contention that the basic financial statements are misleading.

INTERPRETATIONS

There are no interpretations for this section.

TECHNIQUES FOR APPLICATION

The following techniques for applying this section are explained:

- Content of accompanying information.

- Format of report document.
- Audit procedures applied to accompanying information. (Examples of reporting on accompanying information are presented in *Illustrations*.)

CONTENT OF ACCOMPANYING INFORMATION

There is no authoritative guidance on what information should accompany the basic financial statements in an auditor-submitted document. The content of accompanying information is entirely a matter of what is useful or desired in the circumstance. There is no required minimum or maximum.

Generally, in the preliminary stages of the engagement, the auditor should discuss with the client what information in addition to the basic financial statements might be useful in light of the intended use of the financial statements. Some auditors, however, for purposes of efficiency, adopt a standardized content for accompanying information. Some of the possible types of accompanying information are explained in the following discussion.

Schedules of Accounts

One of the most common forms of accompanying information is schedules of important components of the financial statements; for example, a schedule listing the investments held or the details of receivables or property, plant, and equipment, or the components of major expenses. Generally, this form of information is useful to management as well as to others, such as bankers, who extend credit to the entity.

Statistical Data

A table or schedule of significant financial ratios (current ratio, inventory and sales turnover, etc.) may be useful to both management and other users. (See Section 329 for a discussion of possible ratios.)

FORMAT OF REPORT DOCUMENT

There are several acceptable formats for auditor-submitted documents. For example, a format with a separate report on accompanying information might have the following table of contents:

- Auditor's standard report
- Basic financial statements including notes.
- Separate auditor's report on accompanying information.
- Accompanying information.

Generally auditors tend to prefer the preceding format. It has the advantage of making a clear separation of the basic financial statements and the accompanying information and the different degree of responsibility the auditor assumes for each.

If, however, the report on accompanying information is not separate, the format of the document might be as follows:

- Auditor's report.
  - Standard introductory paragraph.
  - Standard scope paragraph.
  - Standard opinion paragraph.
  - Separate paragraph on accompanying information.
- Basic financial statements including notes.
- Accompanying information.

AUDIT PROCEDURES APPLIED TO ACCOMPANYING INFORMATION

The auditor is not required to express an opinion on accompanying information. The requirement is to report on the information and describe the degree of responsibility assumed for it. If the scope of the audit of the basic financial statements includes sufficient procedures applied to accompanying information, then the auditor can express an opinion on whether the information is fairly stated in all material respects in relation to the basic financial statements taken as a whole. For example, if receivables and investments are material to the basic financial statements, then the procedures applied in the audit are normally adequate to say whether schedules of receivables and investments are fairly stated in all material respects in relation to the basic financial statements.

Sometimes the client may request the presentation of information that is not normally the subject of auditing procedures included in the audit of the basic financial statements. The auditor could simply disclaim an opinion on this accompanying information. It generally is advisable, however, to discuss with the client the cost of extending the scope of the audit to be able to express an opinion on the accompanying information.

ILLUSTRATIONS

The following are illustrative audit reports adapted from Section 551:

1. A separate report on information accompanying the basic financial statements in an auditor-submitted document.
2. A disclaimer on
   a. All accompanying information.
   b. Part of the accompanying information.
3. A qualification on part of the accompanying information when the auditor's report contains a qualification on the basic financial statements.
4. A disclaimer of opinion in an auditor-submitted document on supplementary information required by GAAP.
5. An example of an auditor's report when the consolidated financial statements include consolidating information that has not been separately audited.

ILLUSTRATION 1. SEPARATE REPORT ON INFORMATION ACCOMPANYING BASIC FINANCIAL STATEMENTS IN AUDITOR-SUBMITTED DOCUMENT

> Our audit was conducted for the purpose of forming an opinion on the basic financial statements taken as a whole. The [*identify accompanying information*] is presented for purposes of additional analysis and is not a required part of the basic financial statements. Such information has been subjected to the auditing procedures applied in the audit of the basic financial statements and, in our opinion, is fairly stated in all material respects in relation to the basic financial statements taken as a whole.

This report also may be included in the auditor's standard report as a fourth paragraph.

ILLUSTRATION 2. DISCLAIMER ON ACCOMPANYING INFORMATION

When the auditor disclaims an opinion on all or part of the accompanying information in a document that he or she submits to the client or to others, the information (on which a disclaimer is issued) should be marked "unaudited" and the report should disclaim an opinion on the information.

Disclaimer on All Accompanying Information

Following is an example from Section 551 of a separate disclaimer on all accompanying information. It should appear after the notes to the basic financial statements and just before the accompanying information.

> Our audit was conducted for the purpose of forming an opinion on the basic financial statements taken as a whole. The [*identify the accompanying information*] is presented for purposes of additional analysis and is not a required part of the basic financial statements. Such information has not been subjected to the auditing procedures applied in the audit of the basic financial statements, and accordingly, we express no opinion on it.

The report may also be included in the auditor's standard report as a fourth paragraph, as shown.

> We have audited the accompanying balance sheet of Widget Company as of December 31, 20X1, and the related statements of income, retained earnings, and cash flows for the year then ended. These financial statements are the responsibility of the Company's management. Our responsibility is to express an opinion on these financial statements based on our audit.
>
> We conducted our audit in accordance with auditing standards generally accepted in the United States of America. Those standards require that we plan and perform the audit to obtain reasonable assurance about whether the financial statements are free of material misstatement. An audit includes examining, on a test basis, evidence supporting the amounts and disclosures in the financial statements. An audit also includes assessing the accounting principles used and significant estimates made by management, as well as evaluating the overall financial statement presentation. We believe that our audit provides a reasonable basis for our opinion.
>
> In our opinion, the financial statements referred to above present fairly, in all material respects, the financial position of Widget Company as of December 31, 20X1, and the results of its operations and its cash flows for the year then ended in conformity with accounting principles generally accepted in the United States of America.
>
> Our audit was conducted for the purpose of forming an opinion on the basic financial statements taken as a whole. The [*identify the accompanying information*] is presented for purposes of additional analysis and is not a required part of the basic financial statements. Such information has not been subjected to the auditing procedures applied in the audit of the basic financial statements, and accordingly, we express no opinion on it.

Disclaimer on Part of Accompanying Information

Following is an example from Section 551 of a separate disclaimer on part of the accompanying information. It should appear after the notes to the basic financial statements and just before the accompanying information. The report also may be included in the auditor's standard report as a fourth paragraph.

> Our audit was conducted for the purpose of forming an opinion on the basic financial statements taken as a whole. The information on pages xx-xy is presented for purposes of additional analysis and is not a required part of the basic financial statements. Such information, except for the portion marked "unaudited," on which we express no opinion, has been subjected to the auditing procedures applied in the audit of the basic financial statements; and, in our opinion, the information is fairly stated in all material respects in relation to the basic financial statements taken as a whole.

Illustration 3. Qualification on Part of Accompanying Information When Auditor's Report Contains Qualification on Basic Financial Statements

Following is an example from Section 551 of a qualification on part of the accompanying information when the auditor expresses a qualification on the basic financial statements. It should appear after the notes to the basic financial statements and just before the accompanying information. The report also may be included in the auditor's standard report as the last paragraph.

> Our audit was conducted for the purpose of forming an opinion on the basic financial statements taken as a whole. The schedules of investments (page 7), property (page 8), and other assets (page 9) as of December 31, 20X1, are presented for purposes of additional analysis and are not a required part of the basic financial statements. The information in such schedules has been subjected to the auditing procedures applied in the audit of the basic financial statements; and, in our opinion, except for the effects on the schedule of investments of not accounting for the investments in certain companies by the equity method as explained in the second preceding paragraph (second paragraph of our report on page 1), such information is fairly stated in all material respects in relation to the basic financial statements taken as a whole.

Illustration 4. Supplementary Information Required by GAAP Pronouncements

Below is an example from Section 551 of the disclaimer of opinion in an auditor-submitted document on supplementary information required by GAAP.

The disclaimer of opinion should appear after the notes to the basic financial statements and just before the section containing supplementary information. This report also may be included in the auditor's report as the fourth paragraph.

> The [*identify the supplementary information*] on page xx is not a required part of the basic financial statements but is supplementary information required by accounting principles generally accepted in the United States of America. We have applied certain limited procedures, which consisted principally of inquiries of management regarding the methods of measurement and presentation of the supplementary information. However, we did not audit the information and express no opinion on it.

Illustration 5. Consolidating Information

Following is an example from Section 551 of an auditor's report when the consolidated financial statements include consolidating information that has not been separately audited. This report should appear just after the notes to the basic financial statements and just before the consolidating information. The report also may be included in the auditor's standard report as a fourth paragraph.

> Our audit was conducted for the purpose of forming an opinion on the consolidated financial statements taken as a whole. The consolidating information is presented for purposes of additional analysis of the consolidated financial statements rather than to present the financial position (results of operations and cash flows) of the individual companies. The consolidating information has been subjected to the auditing procedures applied in the audit of the consolidated financial statements and, in our opinion, is fairly stated in all material respects in relation to the consolidated financial statements taken as a whole.

This same form of report would be used for combining financial statements by substituting "combined" and "combining" for "consolidated" and "consolidating."

552 REPORTING ON CONDENSED FINANCIAL STATEMENTS AND SELECTED FINANCIAL DATA

EFFECTIVE DATE AND APPLICABILITY

Original Pronouncements SAS 42, September 1982; SAS 71, May 1992.

Effective Date Accountants' reports issued or reissued on or after January 1, 1989, unless subsequently amended.

Applicability Accountants' reports

1. On condensed financial statements in a client-prepared document for an annual or interim period, derived from audited financial statements of a public entity that is required to file, at least annually, complete audited financial statements with a regulatory agency; or
2. On selected financial data in a client-prepared document of a public or nonpublic entity, derived from audited financial statements that are presented in a document that includes audited financial statements, or that (if a public entity) incorporates such statements by reference. (See *Objectives of Section* for additional explanation of applicability.)

DEFINITIONS OF TERMS

Condensed financial statements. Financial statements presented in considerably less detail than complete financial statements that are intended to present financial position, results of operations, and cash flows in conformity with generally accepted accounting principles.

NOTE: The section has no informative explanation of the extent of condensation permissible. Because GAAP do not specify the extent of detail necessary in complete financial statements, this is understandable. Usually in condensed statements many financial statement components are combined and notes are omitted. The required form of reporting was intended to avoid forcing the accountant to evaluate the extent of condensation.

Selected financial data. Selected components of financial statements (usually of prior periods) that management has determined should be presented. Under SEC regulations, for example, management has to present the following selected data for each of the last five fiscal years:

1. Net sales or operating revenue.

2. Income or loss from continuing operations in total and per common share.
3. Total assets.
4. Long-term obligations and redeemable preferred stock.
5. Cash dividends declared per common share.

NOTE: In condensed financial statements all the components of financial statements are included, but many of them are combined. In selected financial data only specific components are presented.

Selected financial data includes specific components appearing in financial statements and data calculated from such components, such as working capital. It does not include nonfinancial information, such as number of employees.

OBJECTIVES OF SECTION

The goal at the inception of the project that led to issuance of this section was to provide some guidance on accountants' reports in SEC filings on some new kinds of required information so that there would be reasonable uniformity in practice. The more ambitious task of providing comprehensive guidance on reporting on condensed financial information was considered too complex and hence too time-consuming. By the time the section was in place, practice could be diverse, and less desirable practice might be entrenched. Protests during exposure about the narrow applicability of the proposed guidance forced a compromise of sorts. Through footnotes and cross-references to other literature, the section identifies the reporting guidance that applies to all forms of condensed financial statements.

AUDITOR-SUBMITTED DOCUMENTS

In an auditor-submitted document (see Section 551) condensed financial statements and selected financial data are treated no differently from any other information that might accompany the basic financial statements. Section 551 applies, and if the information has been subjected to sufficient auditing procedures, the auditor reports on whether it is fairly stated in all material respects in relation to the basic financial statements taken as a whole. Usually the auditor will have audited the basic financial statements from which the condensed financial statements and selected financial data are derived and will be able to give this assurance.

CLIENT-PREPARED DOCUMENTS: PUBLIC ENTITIES

Here the reporting guidance differs for condensed financial statements versus selected data.

Condensed Financial Statements

The form of reporting in this section for condensed financial statements can be used only in a client-prepared document containing annual or interim condensed financial statements, derived from audited financial statements of a public entity that is required to file, at least annually, complete audited financial statements with a regulatory agency. The justification for permitting the specified assurance on condensed financial statements is the discipline of an annual filing requirement and the guaranteed public availability of information on an entity that this discipline provides. Note that the audited financial statements from which the condensed financial statements are derived do not actually have to be filed. For example, complete audited financial statements for an interim period might never be filed.

The form of reporting in the section cannot be used in client-prepared documents of all public entities (only those subject to a regulatory agency's annual filing requirements). For public entities not subject to a filing requirement, there are two options. If the client-prepared document contains complete audited financial statements, the Section 551 form of report could be used. If the client-prepared document does not contain complete audited financial statements, an adverse opinion is required (see the discussion for nonpublic entities).

Selected Data

The section provides guidance on reporting on selected financial data in all client-prepared documents of public and nonpublic entities (see *Fundamental Requirements*).

CLIENT-PREPARED DOCUMENTS: NONPUBLIC ENTITIES

Selected financial data in a client-prepared document of a nonpublic entity are covered by the reporting guidance in this section. Condensed financial statements of such entities are not covered. This means the form of report described in this section cannot be issued on the condensed financial statements of a nonpublic entity. If the condensed financial statements are in a client-prepared document that contains audited financial statements, the Section 551 form of report could be used. If the condensed financial statements are in a client-prepared (or auditor-submitted) document that does not contain complete audited financial statements, there are two options.

1. An adverse opinion.
2. A compilation report for statements that omit substantially all disclosures.

Although the natural inclination may be to use a compilation report, the report illustrated in a footnote to the section (reproduced in *Illustrations*) has the following attractive features:

1. The first paragraph describes the fact that the complete financial statements from which the condensed financial statements are derived were audited.
2. The information omitted from the condensed financial statements does not need to be included in the report (an exemption from the usual requirements of an adverse opinion).
3. Although the opinion paragraph states that the condensed financial statements are not presented fairly in conformity with GAAP, this may be more acceptable to the client than the warning paragraph in a compilation report on the omission of substantially all disclosures.

FUNDAMENTAL REQUIREMENTS

CONDENSED FINANCIAL STATEMENTS

Form of Report

According to AU 552.04, the auditor's report on condensed financial statements that are derived from complete financial statements that he or she has audited should indicate

1. That the auditor has audited and expressed an opinion on the complete financial statements.
2. The date of the audit report on the complete financial statements.
3. The type of opinion expressed.
4. Whether, in the auditor's opinion, the information set forth in the condensed financial statements is fairly stated in all material respects in relation to the complete financial statements from which it has been derived.

NOTE: Several things should be noted about this requirement.

1. This form of report can be used only in a client-prepared document of a public entity subject to an annual filing requirement of a regulatory agency. Reporting is optional.

The auditor may report at the client's request, but see "Client Statements in Document" below.

2. *The report states that the information set forth in the condensed financial statements and not the condensed financial statements is fairly stated. This means that the report expresses no judgment on the extent of condensation.*
3. *An example of this form of report is given in* ***Illustrations****.*

Client Statements in Document

In a client-prepared document, a client might name the auditor and state that condensed financial statements are derived from audited financial statements. By itself, this kind of client statement does not trigger a reporting requirement for the auditor **if** the document contains audited statements or incorporates them by reference to information filed with a regulatory agency. If audited complete financial statements are not in the document or incorporated by reference and the company is public and subject to an annual filing requirement, the auditor should ask the client either to

1. Not include his or her name.
2. Include his or her report on the condensed financial statements.

   NOTE: Presumably, if the entity is not subject to an annual filing requirement, the only option is to ask not to be named or to express an adverse opinion on the condensed financial statements.

Comparative Presentation with Interim Information

Condensed financial statements might be presented in comparative form with interim information for a later period that has been reviewed. The auditor may append the report on the condensed financial statements to the review report. (An example combined report is presented in *Illustrations.*)

Marking Condensed Statements

It is desirable that the condensed financial statements be clearly marked as condensed.

NOTE: This is not a requirement.

Dating Report

A footnote in the section observes that reference to the date of the original audit report in the report on condensed financial statements removes any implication that records, events, or transactions after that date have been audited. Nothing else is mentioned about dating.

NOTE: Presumably, the report date for a separate report on condensed financial statements should be the date of the original audit report because that is when fieldwork was completed. A combined report on both a review of interim information and on condensed financial statements could be dated as of the completion of the review or might be dual-dated.

Selected Financial Data

Form of Report

According to AU 552.09, the auditor's report on selected financial data should specifically identify the data being reported on and indicate

1. That the auditor has audited and expressed an opinion on the complete financial statements.
2. The type of opinion expressed.

3. Whether, in the auditor's opinion, the information set forth in the selected financial data is fairly stated in all material respects in relation to the complete financial statements from which it has been derived.

NOTE: Several things should be noted about this requirement.

1. *This form of report may be used only in a client-prepared document (public or nonpublic entity) that contains audited financial statements or, for a public entity, that incorporates such statements by reference to information filed with a regulatory agency. Reporting on selected financial data is optional. The auditor may report at the client's request, but there is no requirement to report. However, see "Client Statements in Document" below.*
2. *The report states that the information set forth in the selected financial data and not the selected financial data is fairly stated. This means that the report expresses no judgment on the appropriateness of selection. However, if a regulatory agency has specified the selected financial data that have to be presented, the auditor should take exception to omission of the specified information.*
3. *Because the report on selected financial data is normally included as a paragraph in the standard report, dating is not an issue.*
4. *An example of this form of report is given in* ***Illustrations****.*

Client Statements in Document

A client might name the auditor and state that selected data are derived from financial statements he or she audited. If the client-prepared document contains audited financial statements or incorporates them by reference to information filed with a regulatory agency, the auditor is not required to report on the selected financial data. If the document does not contain audited financial statements or incorporate them by reference, the auditor should

1. Ask the client not to name or refer to him or her, or
2. Disclaim an opinion on the selected financial data and ask that the disclaimer be included.

NOTE: These requirements are more stringent than those for condensed financial statements. In effect, the auditor is not permitted to be associated, even if not named, with selected financial data unless audited financial statements are included in the document or incorporated by reference; a client may not even state that the selected financial data is derived from audited financial statements.

INTERPRETATIONS

There are no interpretations for this section.

ILLUSTRATIONS

The following reports adapted from Section 552 are illustrated:

1. A separate report on condensed financial statements.
2. A combined report on reviewed and condensed financial statements.
3. An adverse opinion on separately presented condensed financial statements.
4. A standard report with a report on selected financial data.

ILLUSTRATION 1. SEPARATE REPORT ON CONDENSED FINANCIAL STATEMENTS (FROM SECTION 552)

Independent Auditor's Report

We have audited, in accordance with auditing standards generally accepted in the United States of America, the consolidated balance sheet of Widget Company and subsidiaries as of December 31, 20X1, and the related consolidated statements of income, retained earnings, and cash flows for the year then ended (not presented herein); and in our report dated February 15, 20X2, we expressed an unqualified opinion on those consolidated financial statements.

In our opinion, the information set forth in the accompanying condensed consolidated financial statements is fairly stated, in all material respects, in relation to the consolidated financial statements from which it has been derived.

Guy and Carmichael
March 15, 20X2

Illustration 2. Combined Report on Reviewed and Condensed Financial Statements (from Section 552)

Independent Accountant's Report

We have reviewed the condensed consolidated balance sheet of Widget Company and subsidiaries as of March 31, 20X2, and the related condensed consolidated statements of income and cash flows for the three-month periods ended March 31, 20X2 and 20X1. These financial statements are the responsibility of the company's management.

We conducted our review in accordance with standards established by the American Institute of Certified Public Accountants. A review of interim financial information consists principally of applying analytical procedures to financial data, and making inquiries of persons responsible for financial and accounting matters. It is substantially less in scope than an audit in accordance with generally accepted auditing standards, the objective of which is the expression of an opinion regarding the financial statements taken as a whole. Accordingly, we do not express such an opinion.

Based on our review, we are not aware of any material modifications that should be made to the condensed consolidated financial statements referred to above for them to be in conformity with generally accepted accounting principles.

We have previously audited, in accordance with auditing standards generally accepted in the United States of America, the consolidated balance sheet as of December 31, 20X1, and the related consolidated statements of income, retained earnings, and cash flows for the year then ended (not presented herein); and in our report dated February 15, 20X2, we expressed an unqualified opinion on those consolidated financial statements. In our opinion, the information set forth in the accompanying condensed consolidated balance sheet as of December 31, 20X1, is fairly stated in all material respects in relation to the consolidated balance sheet from which it has been derived.

Guy and Carmichael
March 15, 20X2

Illustration 3. Adverse Opinion on Separately Presented Condensed Financial Statements (from Section 552)

Independent Auditor's Report

We have audited the consolidated balance sheet of Widget Company and subsidiaries as of December 31, 20X1, and the related earnings, and cash flows for the year then ended (not presented herein). These financial statements are the responsibility of the Company's management. Our responsibility is to express an opinion on these financial statements based on our audit.

We conducted our audit in accordance with auditing standards generally accepted in the United States of America. Those standards require that we plan and perform the audit to obtain reasonable assurance about whether the financial statements are free of material misstatement. An audit includes examining, on a test basis, evidence supporting the amounts and disclosures in the financial statements. An audit also includes assessing the accounting principles used and significant estimates made by management, as well as evaluating the overall financial statement presentation. We believe that our audit provides a reasonable basis for our opinion.

The condensed consolidated balance sheet as of December 31, 20X1, and the related condensed statements of income, retained earnings, and cash flows for the year then ended, presented on pages xx-xx, are presented as a summary and therefore do not include all of the disclosures required by accounting principles generally accepted in the United States of America.

In our opinion, because of the significance of the omission of the information referred to in the preceding paragraphs, the condensed consolidated financial statements referred to above do not present fairly, in conformity with accounting principles generally accepted in the United States of America, the financial position of Widget Company and subsidiaries as of December 31, 20X1, or the results of its operations or its cash flows for the year then ended.

Guy and Carmichael
March 15, 20X2

ILLUSTRATION 4. STANDARD REPORT WITH REPORT ON SELECTED FINANCIAL DATA (FROM SECTION 552)

Independent Auditor's Report

We have audited the consolidated balance sheets of Widget Company and subsidiaries as of December 31, 20X5 and 20X4, and the related consolidated statements of income, retained earnings, and cash flows for each of the three years in the period ended December 31, 20X5. These financial statements are the responsibility of the Company's management. Our responsibility is to express an opinion on these financial statements based on our audit.

We conducted our audits in accordance with auditing standards generally accepted in the United States of America. Those standards require that we plan and perform the audit to obtain reasonable assurance about whether the financial statements are free of material misstatement. An audit includes examining, on a test basis, evidence supporting the amounts and disclosures in the financial statements. An audit also includes assessing the accounting principles used and significant estimates made by management, as well as evaluating the overall financial statement presentation. We believe that our audits provided a reasonable basis for our opinion.

In our opinion, the consolidated financial statements referred to above present fairly, in all material respects, the financial position of the Widget Company and subsidiaries as of December 31, 20X5 and 20X4, and the results of their operations and their cash flows for each of the three years in the period ended December 31, 20X5, in conformity with accounting principles generally accepted in the United States of America.

We have also previously audited, in accordance with auditing standards generally accepted in the United States of America, the consolidated balance sheets as of December 31, 20X3, 20X2, and 20X1, and the related statements of income, retained earnings, and cash flows for the years ended December 31, 20X2 and 20X1 (none of which are presented herein); and we expressed unqualified opinions on those consolidated financial statements.

In our opinion, the information set forth in the selected financial data for each of the five years in the period ended December 31, 20X5, appearing on page xx, is fairly stated, in all material respects, in relation to the consolidated financial statements from which it has been derived.

Guy and Carmichael
March 15, 20X6

558 REQUIRED SUPPLEMENTARY INFORMATION

EFFECTIVE DATE AND APPLICABILITY

Original Pronouncement	SAS 52, April 1988, and SAS 98, September 2002.
Effective Date	When issued, April 1988. The amendments for SAS 98 are effective upon issuance.
Applicability	Audits of financial statements that are required to be accompanied by certain supplementary information (see below).

APPLICABILITY

GENERAL

This section applies to audits in accordance with generally accepted auditing standards of financial statements included in a document that should contain supplementary information required by GAAP. Individual GAAP statements specify the circumstances in which disclosure is necessary.

CLIENT-PREPARED DOCUMENTS: VOLUNTARY PRESENTATIONS

If the client voluntarily includes, in documents containing audited financial statements, supplementary information that GAAP requires of other entities, the provisions of this section apply, unless

1. The entity indicates that the auditor has not applied the procedures described in the section, or
2. The auditor disclaims an opinion on the supplementary information in the report on the audited financial statements.

If the auditor does not apply the procedures described in this section to supplementary information that is voluntarily included in client-prepared documents, the provisions of Section 550, "Other Information in Documents Containing Audited Financial Statements," apply.

AUDITOR-SUBMITTED DOCUMENTS

If supplementary information required by GAAP is presented outside the basic financial statements in documents that the auditor submits to the client or to others, the provisions of Section 551, "Reporting on Information Accompanying the Basic Financial Statements in Auditor-Submitted Documents," apply. Section 551 prescribes a special type of disclaimer for these circumstances.

AUDIT OF SUPPLEMENTARY INFORMATION

If an auditor is engaged to audit and express an opinion on supplementary information, Section 623, "Special Reports," applies. In that case, the information, though supplementary, is analogous to a specified element, account, or item of a financial statement.

DEFINITIONS OF TERMS

Basic financial statements. Balance sheet, statement of income, statement of retained earnings, and statement of cash flows, including accompanying notes (see Section 508).

Financial reporting. The basic financial statements and other means of communicating information that relates, directly or indirectly, to the information provided by the accounting system.

OBJECTIVES OF SECTION

Financial statements and the notes thereto have been the traditional means of communicating an entity's financial information to users. In recent years, however, the FASB, the GASB, the FASAB, and the SEC have expanded disclosure requirements to include supplementary information that is outside the basic financial statements and the related notes. Although this information is provided, in part, by the entity's accounting system, it is not as objective and, therefore, not as auditable as information provided in the basic financial statements. The Financial Accounting Standards Board, in Statement of Financial Accounting Concepts (SFAC) 1, *Objectives of Financial Reporting by Business Enterprises*, recognized the need for, and the usefulness of, this "soft" information by acknowledging that "some useful information is better provided by financial statements and some is better provided, or can only be provided, by means of financial reporting other than financial statements" (paragraph 5). The statement went on to indicate that "financial reporting includes not only financial statements but also other means of communicating information that relates, directly or indirectly, to the information provided by the accounting system—that is, information about an enterprise's resources, obligations, earnings, etc." (paragraph 7). Thus, the FASB expanded its scope from financial statements to financial reporting.

The GASB also recognized the need for, and usefulness of, "soft" information by acknowledging in GASB Concepts Statement 1 that "certain information is better provided by financial statements; other information is better provided, or can only be provided by financial reporting outside the financial statements" (paragraph 4).

Council of the AICPA has designated the FASB, the GASB, and the FASAB as having authority to establish accounting principles under Rule 203 for disclosure of financial information outside financial statements.

This section establishes the auditor's responsibility to apply certain limited procedures to all supplementary information required by the FASB, the GASB, or the FASAB and to report deficiencies in, or the omission of, the information. SAS 98, issued in November 2002, amended this section to apply to supplementary information required by all sources of GAAP, such as AICPA Industry Audit and Accounting Guides, and not just those of the FASB, GASB, and FASAB. SAS 98 also amended this section to indicate that an auditor may issue a report on supplementary and other information, indicating that such information is fairly stated in all material respects in relation to the financial statements, if the supplementary or other information has been subjected to audit procedures.

The section also describes the limited procedures to be applied to required supplementary information and the auditor's reporting under various circumstances.

FUNDAMENTAL REQUIREMENTS

AUDITOR RESPONSIBILITY

The auditor should apply certain limited procedures to supplementary information outside the basic financial statements required by GAAP.

LIMITED PROCEDURES

The auditor should consider whether the supplementary information is required by GAAP. If it is, he or she should apply the following procedures:

1. **Inquiries.** Ask management
   a. Whether the supplementary information is measured and presented in accordance with guidelines prescribed by GAAP.
   b. Whether methods of measurement or presentation have been changed from those of the prior period and if so, the reasons for the change.
   c. About any significant assumptions or interpretations underlying the measurement or presentation.
2. **Comparisons.** Compare the information for consistency with
   a. Management responses to inquiries.
   b. Audited financial statements.
   c. Other knowledge obtained during the audit.
3. **Management representation.** Consider whether representations about the information should be included in the management representation letter.

   NOTE: It is prudent for the auditor to obtain a written representation concerning required supplementary information.
4. **Other procedures.** Apply procedures that other statements, interpretations, guides, or SOPs prescribe for specific types of required supplementary information.
5. **Additional inquiries.** Make additional inquiries if the results of the preceding procedures cause the auditor to believe the information may not be measured or presented as required by GAAP.

NOTE: The preceding procedures also are appropriate when the auditor is involved with presentations of GAAP-required supplementary information by entities not required to present the information.

REPORTING ON SUPPLEMENTARY INFORMATION REQUIRED BY GAAP

Ordinarily, the auditor should not refer to the required supplementary information or to his or her limited procedures in the report on the basic financial statements.

Explanatory Paragraph on Supplementary Information

The auditor should refer to supplementary information in a separate explanatory paragraph added to the standard report on audited financial statements if the following conditions exist:

1. The information required to be presented by GAAP is omitted.
2. The measurement or presentation of the supplementary information departs materially from GAAP guidelines.
3. The auditor does not complete the prescribed procedures.
4. The auditor is not able to remove substantial doubts about whether the supplementary information conforms to prescribed guidelines.

Material departures from GAAP guidelines should be described in a separate paragraph of the audit report. The auditor should not modify his or her opinion on the financial statements if the preceding conditions exist. Also, the auditor should not present in his or her report supplementary information that is omitted by the entity. The information is not a required part of the basic financial statements.

Report or Disclaimer on Supplementary Information

When the client indicates that the auditor applied procedures to supplementary information without stating that the auditor does not express an opinion on it, the auditor should disclaim an opinion on the supplementary information or, if appropriate, report on such information. Also, unless the information is audited as part of the basic financial statements, the auditor should disclaim an opinion on the supplementary information whenever it is included as part of the basic financial statements (for example, in the notes to financial statements) and is not clearly marked "unaudited."

INTERPRETATIONS

SUPPLEMENTARY OIL AND GAS INFORMATION (FEBRUARY 1989)

SFAS 69, *Disclosures About Oil and Gas Producing Activities*, required publicly traded entities that have significant oil and gas producing activities to include, with complete sets of annual financial statements, disclosures of proved oil and gas reserve quantities, changes in reserve quantities, a standardized measure of discounted future net cash flows relating to reserve quantities, and changes in the standardized measure. The SEC requires that the disclosures related to annual periods be presented for each annual period for which an income statement is required and the disclosures as of the end of an annual period be presented as of the date of each audited balance sheet required. These disclosures are supplementary information and may be presented outside the basic financial statements. In these circumstances, the auditor should consider the provisions of this section.

When making the inquiries in this section, the auditor's inquiries should be directed to management's understanding of the specific requirements for disclosure of supplementary oil and gas reserve information, including the following:

1. The factors considered in determining the reserve quantity information to be reported, such as including in the information the following:
    a. Quantities of all domestic and foreign proved oil and gas reserves owned by the entity net of interests of others.
    b. Reserves attributable to consolidated subsidiaries.
    c. A proportionate share of reserves of investees that are proportionately consolidated.
    d. Reserves relating to royalty interests owned.
2. The separate disclosure of items such as the following:
    a. The entity's share of oil and gas produced from royalty interests for which reserve quantity information is unavailable.
    b. Reserves subject to long-term agreements with governments or authorities in which the entity participates in the operation or otherwise serves as producer.
    c. The entity's proportional interest in reserves of investees accounted for by the equity method.
    d. Subsequent events, important economic factors, or significant uncertainties affecting particular components of the reserve quantity information.

   e. Whether the entity's reserves are located entirely within its home country.
   f. Whether certain named governments restrict the disclosure of reserves or require that the reserve estimates include reserves other than proved.
3. The factors considered in determining the standardized measure of discounted future net cash flows to be reported.

The auditor should also do the following:

1. Inquire about whether the person who estimated the entity's reserve quantity information has appropriate qualifications (see Section 336).
2. Compare the entity's recent production with its reserve estimates for properties that have significant production or significant reserve quantities and inquire about disproportionate ratios.
3. Compare the entity's reserve quantity information with the corresponding information used for depletion and amortization, and make inquiries when differences exist.
4. Inquire about the calculation of the standardized measure of discounted future net cash flows. These inquiries might include matters such as the following:
   a. The prices used to develop future cash inflows from estimated production of the proved reserves are based on prices received at the end of the entity's fiscal year, and whether the calculation of future cash inflows appropriately reflects the terms of sales contracts and applicable governmental laws and regulations.
   b. The entity's estimate of the nature and timing of future development of the proved reserves and the future rates of production are consistent with available development plans.
   c. The entity's estimates of future development and production costs are based on year-end costs and assumed continuation of existing economic conditions.
   d. Future income tax expenses have been computed using the appropriate year-end statutory tax rates, with consideration of future tax rates already legislated, after giving effect to the tax basis of the properties involved, permanent differences, and tax credits and allowances.
   e. The future net cash flows have been appropriately discounted.
   f. With respect to full cost companies, the estimated future development costs are consistent with the corresponding amounts used for depletion and amortization purposes.
   g. With respect to the disclosure of changes in the standardized measure of discounted future net cash flows, the entity has computed and presented the sources of the changes in conformity with the requirements of SFAS 69.
5. Inquire about whether the methods and bases for estimating the entity's reserve information are documented and whether the information is current.

If the auditor believes that the information may not be presented within applicable guidelines, he or she should ordinarily make additional inquiries. However, the auditor may not be able to evaluate responses to the additional inquiries. In these circumstances, the auditor should report as follows:

> The oil and gas reserve information is not a required part of the basic financial statements, and we did not audit and do not express an opinion on such information. However, we have applied certain limited procedures prescribed by professional standards that raised doubts that we were unable to resolve regarding whether material modifications should be made to the information for it to conform with guidelines established by the Financial Accounting Standards Board. [The auditor should consider including in his report the reason(s) why he was unable to resolve his doubts. For example, the auditor may wish to state that the information was estimated by a person lacking appropriate qualifications.]

TECHNIQUES FOR APPLICATION

COORDINATION WITH OTHER AUDIT AREAS

The auditor should coordinate the application of procedures to supplementary information with procedures applied in other areas. For example, for an entity engaged in oil and gas producing activities, the entity might be required to pay state or federal taxes on oil and gas produced in particular geographical areas. In this circumstance, the auditor would want to coordinate work on tax expense and payables and segment disclosures with work on the required supplementary oil and gas information.

ILLUSTRATIONS

The following examples (adapted from SAS 52) illustrate the separate explanatory paragraphs that might be added to the standard report in the indicated circumstances.

ILLUSTRATION 1. OMISSION OF SUPPLEMENTARY INFORMATION REQUIRED BY GAAP

The [*Entity or Governmental Unit*] has not presented [*describe the supplementary information required by GAAP in the circumstances*] that accounting principles generally accepted in the United States has determined is necessary to supplement, although not required to be part of, the basic financial statements.

ILLUSTRATION 2. MATERIAL DEPARTURES FROM GUIDELINES

The [*specifically identify the supplementary information*] on page xx is not a required part of the basic financial statements, and we did not audit and do not express an opinion on such information. However, we have applied certain limited procedures, which consisted principally of inquiries of management regarding the methods of measurement and presentation of the supplementary information. As a result of such limited procedures, we believe that the [*specifically identify the supplementary information*] is not in conformity with accounting principles generally accepted in the United States because [*describe the material departure(s) from GAAP*].

ILLUSTRATION 3. PRESCRIBED PROCEDURES NOT COMPLETED

The [*specifically identify the supplementary information*] on page xx is not a required part of the basic financial statements, and we did not audit and do not express an opinion on such information. Further, we were unable to apply to the information certain procedures prescribed by professional standards because [*state the reasons*].

ILLUSTRATION 4. UNRESOLVED DOUBTS ABOUT ADHERENCE TO GUIDELINES

The [*specifically identify the supplementary information*] on page xx is not a required part of the basic financial statements, and we did not audit and do not express an opinion on such information. However, we have applied certain limited procedures prescribed by professional standards that raised doubts that we were unable to resolve regarding whether material modifications should be made to the information for it to conform with guidelines established by accounting principles generally accepted in the United States. [*The auditor should consider including in his or her report the reason(s) he or she was unable to resolve his or her substantial doubts.*]

NOTE: The auditor does not modify his or her opinion on the financial statements when conditions 1. through 4. above exist because they do not affect the presentation of the financial statements.

560 SUBSEQUENT EVENTS

EFFECTIVE DATE AND APPLICABILITY

Original Pronouncements	SAP 47, September 1971 (codified in SAS 1, November 1972); SAS 12, January 1976; and SAS 98, September 2002.
Effective Date	When issued, September 1971, unless subsequently amended. (The amendments for SAS 98 are effective upon issuance.)
Applicability	Audits of financial statements in accordance with generally accepted auditing standards. (The accounting considerations apply whenever the accountant is reporting on financial statements. Thus, the accounting guidance also applies in compilation or review engagements.)

DEFINITIONS OF TERMS

Subsequent events. Events or transactions that occur after the balance sheet date but before issuance of the financial statements that have a material effect on the financial statements and therefore require adjustment or disclosure in the statements.

Adjustment events. Events that provide additional evidence about conditions that existed at the date of the balance sheet and affect the estimates inherent in the process of preparing financial statements.

Disclosure events. Events that provide evidence about conditions that did not exist at the date of the balance sheet being reported on but arose after that date. These events should not result in adjustment of the financial statements, but disclosure of them may be required to keep the financial statements from being misleading.

Date of the independent auditor's report. The date of completion of fieldwork.

Subsequent period. The period from the date of the balance sheet to the date of the auditor's report.

OBJECTIVES OF SECTION

The date of the auditor's report is generally regarded as a cutoff point of significance for the auditor's responsibility for detection of important facts that arise after the date of the financial statements. Up through that date, the auditor should apply procedures specifically directed to keeping informed about events that have a material effect on the financial statements. After that date, the auditor cannot be expected to know of such events unless the information is brought to his or her attention.

This section deals with the procedures that should be applied specifically to search for material events in the subsequent period and explains how those events should be treated in the financial statements. The guidance on treatment of subsequent events in financial statements effectively establishes accounting standards (GAAP) in this area. When the standard was issued in 1971, the section made the following changes in authoritative literature:

1. **Adjustment versus disclosure.** The distinction between events that require adjustment versus those that need only to be disclosed is pinned entirely on whether there is a condition existing at the balance sheet date that leads to the event. This has been described as the **clean cutoff** approach. This means, for example, that whether a loss on receivables should be adjusted for or disclosed depends on the condition that caused the loss. If the loss resulted from a customer's major casualty that happened after the balance sheet date, then disclose (don't adjust). If the event was the culmination of a condition that existed at the balance sheet date, such as a customer's bankruptcy, then adjust.
2. **Nudge to adjust.** Because determining if a condition existed at the balance sheet date may not be easy, there is a nudge to adjust. Essentially, this means when in doubt, adjust.
3. **Extent of procedures.** The procedures specifically designed to search for subsequent events were expanded. Although the procedures, which were based on inquiry and review, were of the same nature as before 1971, the extent was increased.
4. **Disclosure events.** Before 1971, the literature contained a third category of events: those that did not require adjustment or disclosure. This category was removed because it was not possible to give examples of events that might not under some circumstances be necessary to disclose to keep the financial statements from being misleading.

A subtle point about the accounting guidance is that it establishes a duty for management to identify and disclose subsequent events through the issuance date of the financial statements. The auditor's duty to detect, in contrast, cuts off earlier at the audit report date.

FUNDAMENTAL REQUIREMENTS

ACCOUNTING CONSIDERATIONS

The auditor should evaluate whether management has

1. Adjusted the financial statements for any changes in estimates resulting from relevant events after the date of the statements but before issuance—adjustment events.

   NOTE: The SAS has a "nudge" toward adjustment. That is, there is encouragement to adjust for events that affect asset realization or settlement of estimated liabilities. The only exception is changes in quoted market price in securities, because the changes represent concurrent evaluation of new conditions rather than the culmination of existing conditions.

2. Disclosed events that occurred in the subsequent period that do not require adjustment but that require disclosure to keep the financial statements from being misleading—disclosure events.

   NOTE: A substantial amount of judgment is required in evaluating these events, but they usually involve significant changes in the composition or valuation of assets or liabilities presented in the financial statements being reported on, such as the issuance of bonds or stock, purchase of a business, or loss of plant or inventories from catastrophes.

AUDITING PROCEDURES

For the subsequent period, the auditor should apply the following procedures:

1. Compare latest interim financial statements with the financial statements being audited.

2. Ask officers and other executives responsible for financial and accounting matters whether
   a. Interim financial statements are prepared on the same basis as annual financial statements.
   b. During the subsequent period there were any
      (1) Unusual adjustments.
      (2) Significant changes in
         (a) Capital stock.
         (b) Long-term debt.
         (c) Working capital.
         (d) Status of items accounted for on the basis of tentative or inconclusive data.
         (e) Existence of substantial contingent liabilities or commitments.
3. Read minutes of meetings of stockholders, directors, and relevant committees. Inquire about matters dealt with at meetings for which minutes are not available.
4. Inquire of client's legal counsel about litigation, claims, and assessments (see Section 337).
5. Obtain a representation letter from management (see Section 333) that includes information concerning subsequent events.
6. Make additional inquiries or apply other procedures to dispose of any questions raised by the foregoing procedures.

INTERPRETATIONS

There are no interpretations for this section.

TECHNIQUES FOR APPLICATION

General

For subsequent events, the auditor is concerned about the following:

1. Types of events.
2. Procedures for becoming aware of them.
3. Their effect on the audit report.

Types of Subsequent Events

Subsequent events may be classified as follows:

1. Require adjustment.
2. Require disclosure.
3. Change in number of shares outstanding.

Require Adjustment

Ordinarily, the following subsequent events require adjustment of the current financial statements:

1. Customer bankruptcy arising from other than the customer's major casualty subsequent to the balance sheet date.
2. Investee bankruptcy arising from other than the investee's major casualty subsequent to the balance sheet date.
3. Resolution of an uncertainty concerning loss contingencies or asset realization.

Require Disclosure

Ordinarily, the following subsequent events require disclosure in the current financial statements:

1. Issuing bonds or capital stock.
2. Business combination.
3. Loss of assets or decline in value of assets because of the following events occurring in the subsequent period:
   a. Expropriation.
   b. Earthquake or similar event.
   c. Customer or investee experiences major casualty such as fire.

Events that require disclosure may be presented as follows:

1. Explanatory information in the notes to financial statements.
2. **Pro forma** (as if) financial information in the notes to financial statements.
3. **Pro forma** (as if) financial statements on the face of the historical statements.

Ordinarily, subsequent events that require disclosure are explained in the notes to financial statements. Sometimes the effect of this type of event is so significant, however, that disclosure should be made by using **pro forma** financial information or by presenting **pro forma** financial statements. In those circumstances, the **pro forma** presentation may be marked "unaudited."

Change in Number of Shares

Effect should be given to subsequent events that change the number of shares outstanding, such as stock dividends, stock splits, and reverse stock splits. Generally, the number of shares is adjusted even if the event occurred after the balance sheet date.

PROCEDURES

Specific procedures for becoming aware of subsequent events are in the checklist in *Illustration*. These procedures may be classified as inquiring, reviewing, and reading.

Inquiry

Management's responses to auditor inquiries about subsequent events should be included in the management representation letter (see Section 333).

In the letter to the client's lawyer (see Section 337), the auditor should make certain that he or she inquires about events that occurred up to the approximate date of the conclusion of the fieldwork. When the inquiry is sent, the auditor will estimate the date the fieldwork will end. If the response is received significantly before the audit report date, an updated response should be obtained.

Review

At the end of the fieldwork, the auditor should review the accounting records for unusual material transactions from the date of the balance sheet to the date of completion of the fieldwork. Records to be reviewed include the general ledger, the general journal, and other books of original entry.

The auditor should inquire about any subsequent unusual material transactions that come to his or her attention and determine their effect on the audited financial statements.

Read

The auditor should read subsequent client minutes and financial statements.

Minutes. The auditor should read minutes of meetings of stockholders, directors, and significant committees that occurred between the balance sheet date and the date of completion of the fieldwork. Items of concern include the following:

1. Issuance of debt or equity securities.
2. Declaration of stock dividends, stock splits, and reverse stock splits.
3. Debt modification.
4. Refinancing of short-term debt with long-term debt.
5. Business combinations.
6. Disposal or discontinuance of a segment.
7. Reduction in carrying value of assets.
8. Adoption of pension or profit-sharing plan.
9. Approval of long-term commitments.

Unavailability of minutes. Minutes for all meetings may not have been prepared by the completion of the fieldwork. In these circumstances, the auditor should do the following:

1. Meet with the secretary of the entity or whoever is responsible for preparing the minutes.
2. Review notes of the person who will prepare the minutes.
3. Obtain a letter from the person responsible for preparing the minutes, confirming matters discussed and decisions made.

Financial statements. The auditor should read the most recent interim financial statements of the entity. He or she should compare these statements with those of the corresponding prior period and the current audited statements. Explanations should be obtained for material fluctuations.

AUDITOR'S REPORT

When considering subsequent events and his or her report, the auditor is concerned with the following:

1. Dating the report.
2. Dual dating the report.
3. Reissuing the report.

Dating Auditor's Report

The report date signals the end of the auditor's responsibility for applying procedures specifically directed to obtaining knowledge of subsequent events. Section 530, "Dating of the Independent Auditor's Report," states: "Generally, the date of completion of the fieldwork should be used as the date of the independent auditor's report." Because completion of fieldwork is not defined, this is a flexible standard that can be adapted to meet the variety of circumstances that occur in audit engagements.

The ordinary meaning of **fieldwork** is work outside the auditor's office and usually on the client's premises. Because completion of all important audit procedures usually coincides with completion of work at the client's office, use of this ordinary meaning is usually acceptable.

The audit report, of course, should not be dated before the auditor has obtained all the information essential for an opinion on the financial statements. Therefore, there should be no significant potential for material adjustments to the financial statements after the report date.

For a small, noncomplex business, the auditor's report can usually be dated at the date the staff leaves the client's office.

For a larger, more complex business, more coordination and care are needed in fixing the report date. A common practice is to schedule the report date to coincide with the closing conference with the client at which agreement is reached on the financial statements. This practice requires coordination of the subsequent events review procedures with this expected date, including the dating of representation letters.

The auditor wants to issue the report as soon after its date as is reasonably possible; however, sometimes this is not feasible. When the report is not issued promptly, the auditor should decide what procedures, if any, to apply to events that occurred between the report date and the issuance date. Many firms establish an arbitrary period such as two or three weeks by which a report should be issued. If its report is not issued during this period, the auditor will extend the subsequent events review to a date closer to issuance of the report.

The section states that the subsequent events review procedures should be performed at or **near** completion of fieldwork. Near, in this case, refers to a period slightly **before** completion of fieldwork. Fieldwork does not end until the subsequent events review is completed.

Sometimes, an event requiring financial statement adjustment or disclosure occurs after the date of the auditor's report but before its issuance. In these circumstances, the auditor should decide whether to update or to dual date the report. Because updating the report makes the auditor liable for reviewing for events occurring up to the new date, he or she ordinarily will dual date the report.

Dual Dating the Auditor's Report

To limit his or her liability and avoid extending his or her procedures, the auditor dual dates the report for a subsequent event that occurred after the report date but before the issuance of the report. Ordinarily, the specific event is described in a separate note to the financial statements. The auditor should apply appropriate auditing procedures to this event. For example, if the subsequent event was the issuance of debt or stock, the auditor would examine documents pertaining to the issuance and accounting records recording the event. The auditor also would consider confirming the event directly with the other party to the transaction.

When the auditor's report is dual dated, the date of the report is presented in a manner such as the following:

> February 10, 20X1, except with respect to the matters discussed in Note___ as to which the date is March 31, 20X1.

Reissuing Auditor's Report

Sometimes, financial statements are reissued. The auditor generally has no responsibility to apply procedures to search for events that occur after issuance of the financial statements. However, sometimes events that are significant to the financial statements, but that occurred after the financial statements and audit report were originally issued, come to the auditor's attention. Events that occurred between the issuance date and the reissuance date do not require adjustment of the financial statements, unless the adjustment meets the criteria for the correction of an error or the subsequent discovery of facts existing at the date of the auditor's report (see Section 561).

To prevent financial statements from being misleading, subsequent events between issuance date and reissuance date might have to be disclosed. This disclosure may be labeled "unaudited" and does not require a change of date or a dual dating of the auditor's report.

ILLUSTRATION

The following pages illustrate a subsequent events checklist.

ILLUSTRATION 1. SUBSEQUENT EVENTS CHECKLIST

(Client)	(Prepared by)	(Date)
(Period ended)	(Reviewed by)	(Date)

Instructions

This checklist is designed to assist in complying with the requirement that a review be made of transactions and events occurring between the date of financial statements being audited and the date of the auditor's report. The purpose of the review is to determine whether transactions or events occurred that require adjustment of the financial statements or disclosure in the notes to the financial statements. If this checklist is not used, the audit program should include appropriate procedures concerning subsequent events. This checklist may be modified to fit the needs of a specific audit.

Subsequent events are classified as follows:

1. Events that provide additional evidence about conditions that existed at the balance sheet date and affect estimates in the financial statements. The financial statements should be adjusted for changes in estimates resulting from the use of this evidence.

   NOTE: Events affecting the realization of assets, such as receivables and inventories, or the settlement of estimated liabilities, ordinarily result in adjustment.

2. Events that provide evidence about conditions that did not exist at the balance sheet date but arose subsequent to that date. These events, except for stock dividends, stock splits, or reverse stock splits, do not result in adjustment of the financial statements. Some, however, may require disclosure to keep the financial statements from being misleading.

Ordinarily, the review of subsequent events is limited to transactions and events occurring between the date of the audited financial statements and the date of the issuance of financial statements. If there are circumstances where a significant time lag exists between the date of the auditor's report and the date of its issuance, however, the subsequent events review may have to be extended.

This checklist includes procedures to be performed before the release of the financial statements. These procedures should be coordinated with other auditing procedures, such as cutoff tests, confirmation follow-up, review of subsequent cash collections, and so on. In some circumstances, this checklist might be supplemented by supporting audit documentation.

For all procedures listed below, the "Completed by" and "Date" columns should be completed. The "Inquiry of" and "W/P reference" columns should include the name of the client personnel queried or reference to supporting audit documentation. If a procedure is not applicable, "N/A" should be entered in the "Inquiry of" and "W/P reference" columns.

Procedure	*Completed by*	*Date*	*Inquiry of*	*W/P reference*
1. Read minutes of meetings of stockholders, board of directors, and other appropriate committees up to the date of completion of the fieldwork.				
2. Read the most recent interim financial statements prepared after the balance sheet date and compare them with the financial statements being reported on, budgets and forecasts, if available, and interim financial statements for the same period of the prior year.				
3. Review accounting records—general ledger, general journal, other books of original entry—for unusual material transactions from the balance sheet date to the date of completion of the fieldwork.				
4. Review reports of internal auditors prepared after the balance sheet date. If reports have not been prepared, inquire about the findings of the internal auditors.				
5. Inquire of appropriate executives about matters and events such as the following:				
a. The most recent interim financial statements				

Procedure	*Completed by*	*Date*	*Inquiry of*	*W/P reference*
(1) Accounting practices that differ from those in the financial statements being reported on.				
(2) Components of operating results.				
(3) Significant changes in working capital.				
b. Property, plant, and equipment				
(1) Commitments for major additions or dispositions.				
(2) New or modified leases.				
(3) New or modified mortgages or other liens.				
(4) Fire or other casualty losses.				
c. Long-term debt and capital stock				
(1) New borrowings or modifications of existing debt.				
(2) Early extinguishment of debt.				
(3) Compliance with debt covenants.				
(4) Stock conversions or conversions of debt to stock.				
(5) Transactions involving equity securities, such as stock splits, stock options, and warrants.				
(6) Declaration of dividends.				
d. Personnel				
(1) Labor disputes.				
(2) Adoption of new or amended employee benefit plans.				
e. Contingencies				
(1) Status of contingencies existing at the balance sheet date.				
(2) New contingencies.				
(3) Notice of deficiencies from regulatory agencies.				
f. Other				
(1) Significant sales, purchases, or other commitments.				
(2) Unusual adjustments made subsequent to the balance sheet date.				
(3) Negotiations or agreements involving business combinations or dispositions of corporate assets.				
(4) Status of transactions with related parties entered into before or after the balance sheet date.				
(5) New information about items in the financial statements being reported on that were accounted for on the basis of tentative or inconclusive data.				
(6) Decisions that may affect carrying value or classification of assets or liabilities.				
(7) Changes in lines of credit or compensating balances.				
(8) Changes in financial policies.				

Procedure	*Completed by*	*Date*	*Inquiry of*	*W/P reference*
6. Review letters received from entity lawyers in response to inquiries on litigation, claims, and assessments. If these letters are not dated close to the report date, consider whether it is necessary to obtain an updated letter.				
7. Review documents and financial statements provided to regulatory agencies, credit agencies, financial institutions, potential investors, and others subsequent to the balance sheet date.				
8. For documents prepared by the client that include audited financial statements and other information, read the other information.				
9. Review the management representation letter to determine that it includes matters pertaining to subsequent events.				

561 SUBSEQUENT DISCOVERY OF FACTS EXISTING AT THE DATE OF THE AUDITOR'S REPORT

EFFECTIVE DATE AND APPLICABILITY

Original Pronouncement

SAP 41, October 1969 (codified in SAS 1, November 1972), and SAS 98, September 2002.

Effective Date

When issued, October 1969. The amendments for SAS 98 are effective upon issuance.

Applicability

The auditor's discovery of facts, after he or she has issued the report on the financial statements, that:

- Existed at the date of the report.
- Were not known by the auditor at the date of the report.
- Would have required the auditor to change the report had he or she been aware of them.

NOTE: The section does not apply to matters identified in a subsequent events review that covers the period after the financial statements but before the original issuance date of the auditor's report (see Section 560).

NOTE: The section applies only to audits; however, SSARSs refer to it in situations in which the accountant becomes aware of facts existing at the date of the report after he or she issued a compilation or review report. The accountant might wish to consider the section in an analogous situation in a compilation or review engagement.

DEFINITIONS OF TERMS

This section contains no authoritative definitions.

OBJECTIVES OF SECTION

Before the issuance of SAP 41, there was no authoritative guidance for the auditor if, after issuing the report on the financial statements, he or she became aware of facts that existed at the date of the report that would have required the auditor to change the report had he or she been aware of them. SAP 41 was a direct result of *Fischer v. Kletz*, commonly known as the *Yale Express* case.

In the case of *Yale Express*, a large CPA firm did not promptly disclose material errors in financial statements covered by its issued report that were subsequently discovered during a consulting services engagement. The court rejected the contention in the defendant's motion to dismiss the case that an auditor has no duty to those still relying on the report to disclose subsequently discovered errors in that report. The case was settled out of court, however, and the precise nature and extent of an auditor's duty to those relying on a previous report was unclear. SAP 41 was issued to delineate the nature and extent of the auditor's responsibility.

This section established the auditor's **continuing responsibility** for the validity of the report. It provides guidance on procedures the auditor should follow after the date of the report if he or she becomes aware of certain facts that may have existed when the report was issued.

This section is distinguishable from Section 560 on subsequent events. Under Section 560, the auditor has no responsibility to search for events subsequent to the date of the financial statements after the audit report has been issued. Under Section 561, an event subsequently comes to the auditor's attention that existed at the audit report date and the auditor is required to apply procedures to investigate whether the event would have affected the audit report if known at that earlier date.

FUNDAMENTAL REQUIREMENTS

CONSULTATION WITH ATTORNEY

Although it is not a requirement of the section, SAP 41 states that the **auditor is well-advised to consult with his or her attorney upon encountering circumstances to which this section applies.**

NOTE: The auditing standard setters have always avoided making the failure to consult legal counsel a departure from professional standards because consultation is undertaken to protect the auditor.

DETERMINATION OF RELIABILITY OF INFORMATION

Whenever he or she becomes aware of information covered by this section, the auditor should determine its reliability and whether it existed at the date of the report. The auditor should discuss the matter with whatever level of management is appropriate, including the board of directors, and request cooperation to whatever extent necessary.

NOTE: Information about facts existing at the date of the auditor's report may come from many sources, such as

1. *Tax engagements.*
2. *Consulting engagements.*
3. *Client executive or any other current or former employee of the client.*
4. *Audit staff performing interim work.*
5. *Unattributable rumors or an anonymous informant.*

AUDITOR ACTION

The auditor should advise the client to disclose the newly discovered facts and their effect on the financial statements to persons known to be currently relying, or who are likely to rely, on the financial statements and the related auditor's report if

1. The subsequently discovered information is reliable.
2. It existed at the date of the auditor's report.
3. The auditor's report would have been affected if all the information had been known to him or her at the date of the report and had not been reflected in the financial statements.

4. The auditor believes there are persons currently relying, or likely to rely, on the financial statements who would attach importance to the information.

The auditor should take whatever steps he or she believes necessary to satisfy himself or herself that the client has made the requested disclosures (see *Techniques for Application* for methods of disclosure).

Client Refusal to Make Disclosures

If the client refuses to make the disclosures requested, the auditor should notify each member of the board of directors of the refusal and of the auditor's intention to take steps to prevent future reliance on the report.

NOTE: In this situation, if the auditor has not already done so, it is prudent to consult his or her attorney.

Auditor Steps When Client Refuses to Make Disclosures

Unless his or her attorney recommends otherwise, the auditor should take the following steps when the client fails to make the requested disclosures:

1. Notify client that the audit report must no longer be associated with the financial statements.
2. Notify regulatory agencies with jurisdiction over the client that the report should no longer be relied on.
3. Notify each person known specifically by the auditor to be relying on the financial statements that the report should no longer be relied on (see *Techniques for Application*).

Content of Auditor Disclosure

If the auditor determines that the information is reliable and the client refuses to make appropriate disclosures, the auditor should disclose

1. The nature of the subsequently acquired information and its effect on the financial statements.
2. What effect the subsequently acquired information would have had on the auditor's report had it been known at the date of the report and not reflected in the financial statements.

NOTE: The disclosure should be precise and factual and should avoid comments concerning the conduct or motives of any person.

If the auditor takes the steps described in "Auditor Steps When Client Refuses to Make Disclosures," above, and has not been able to determine the reliability of the information because the client refused to cooperate, he or she should disclose that

1. Information has come to his or her attention that the client has not cooperated in attempting to substantiate.
2. If the information is true, the auditor believes the report must no longer be relied on or associated with the client's financial statements.

NOTE: These disclosures should be made only if the auditor believes that the financial statements may be misleading and that the report should not be relied on.

INTERPRETATIONS

Auditor Association with Subsequently Discovered Information When the Auditor Has Resigned or Been Discharged (February 1989)

The investigation of whether subsequently discovered information is reliable and whether facts existed at the date of the original audit report should be performed even when the auditor has resigned or been discharged prior to undertaking or completing the investigation. In other words, Section 561 is equally applicable to a predecessor auditor and a continuing auditor.

TECHNIQUES FOR APPLICATION

Parties to Be Notified

When the auditor has concluded that subsequently discovered information should be disclosed, some or all of the following might be notified:

1. Stockholders.
2. Banks.
3. Bond trustees.
4. Major note holders, such as insurance companies.
5. Major suppliers.
6. Credit agencies.
7. Securities and Exchange Commission.
8. Stock exchanges.
9. Regulatory agencies.
10. Other persons known to be currently relying or likely to rely on the financial statements and related auditor's report.

Notification of parties other than the client is a serious step and should be undertaken only under the guidance of legal counsel. The requirement to notify applies only for persons actually known by the auditor to be relying and not to persons that the auditor might infer could be relying. However, whether to notify and whom to notify should be considered with the advice of legal counsel.

Methods of Disclosure

The method of disclosing new information depends on the circumstances.

Revised Financial Statements and Auditor's Report

If the effect of the new information can be determined promptly, disclosure should consist of issuing, as soon as practicable, revised financial statements and auditor's report.

1. The reasons for the revision should be described in a note to financial statements and referred to in the auditor's report.
2. The opinion paragraph of the auditor's report accompanying revised financial statements would start as follows:

   > In our opinion, the aforementioned financial statements, revised as described in Note X, present fairly . . .

3. The auditor's report accompanying the revised financial statements should contain two dates: the date of the original report and the date of the revision described in a separate note to the financial statements (see Section 530).

Current Financial Statements and Auditor's Report

When audited comparative financial statements and the related auditor's report for a subsequent period are about to be issued, disclosure of the revisions can be made in these reissued statements.

1. In these circumstances, the prior financial statements will be revised and the revision disclosed, but the auditor's report need not refer to the revision.
2. This method may be used only if disclosure of the new information is not seriously delayed.

Effect Not Promptly Determinable

Occasionally, the effect of subsequently discovered facts cannot be determined without prolonged investigation. In these circumstances, the issuance of revised financial statements and auditor's report would be delayed. If it appears that the new information will require revision of the financial statements and the report, the auditor should request that the client do the following:

1. Notify persons known to be relying, or who are likely to rely on, the financial statements and the related auditor's report that they should not be relied on.
2. Inform these persons that revised financial statements and auditor's report will be issued when the current investigation is completed.
3. Communicate with SEC, stock exchanges, and regulatory agencies.

623 SPECIAL REPORTS

EFFECTIVE DATE AND APPLICABILITY

Original Pronouncements

SAS 62, April 1989; and SAS 77, November 1995; as revised to reflect the conforming changes necessary due to the issuance of SAS 87, September 1998.

Effective Date

Special reports dated on or after July 1, 1989. Revised to reflect SAS 87, effective for reports issued after December 31, 1998.

Applicability

Auditor's reports issued in connection with the following:

1. **Other Comprehensive Basis of Accounting (OCBOA).** Audited financial statements prepared in accordance with a comprehensive basis of accounting other than generally accepted accounting principles (see *Definitions of Terms*).
2. **Elements, accounts, or items.** Audited specified elements, accounts, or items of a financial statement.
3. **Compliance.** Compliance with aspects of contractual agreements or regulatory requirements related to audited financial statements.
4. **Special-purpose financial presentations.** Financial presentations prepared to comply with contractual agreements or regulatory provisions.
5. **Prescribed forms.** Financial information presented in prescribed forms or schedules that require a prescribed form of auditor's report.

Auditor's reports issued in connection with any of the above are special reports.

Not Applicable to

Reports issued in connection with the following:

1. Reviews of interim financial statements.
2. Financial forecasts, projections, or feasibility studies.
3. Compliance with aspects of contractual agreements or regulatory requirements unrelated to financial statements.

NOTE: When the auditor is engaged to perform an audit in accordance with ***Governmental Auditing Standards*** *(Yellow Book) issued by the Comptroller General of the United States or the Single Audit Act, he or she should follow guidance contained in SAS 74,* ***Compliance Auditing Considerations in Audits of Governmental Entities and Recipients of Gov-***

ernmental Financial Assistance. *(See Section 801.)*

A review of specified elements, accounts, or items in accordance with Statements on Standards for Accounting and Review Services is not appropriate. However, the auditor may be engaged to make a review in accordance with attestation standards (see Section 2101).

DEFINITIONS OF TERMS

Historical Financial Statements

Generally accepted auditing standards are applicable whenever an auditor is engaged to audit and report on any historical financial statement.

Characteristics. A financial statement has the following characteristics:

1. It is a presentation of financial data, including accompanying notes.
2. It is derived from accounting records.
3. It is intended to communicate an entity's economic resources or obligations at a point in time or the changes in the economic resources or obligations for a period of time in accordance with generally accepted accounting principles or a comprehensive basis of accounting.

Examples of financial statements. For reporting purposes, the following types of financial presentations are financial statements:

1. Balance sheet.
2. Statement of income or statement of operations.
3. Statement of retained earnings.
4. Statement of cash flows.
5. Statement of changes in owners' equity.
6. Statement of assets and liabilities that does not include owners' equity accounts.
7. Statement of revenue and expenses.
8. Summary of operations.
9. Statement of operations by product lines.
10. Statement of cash receipts and disbursements.

Entities. A financial statement may be presented for any of the following:

1. A corporation.
2. A consolidated group of corporations.
3. A combined group of affiliated entities.
4. A not-for-profit organization.
5. A governmental unit.
6. An estate or trust.
7. A partnership.
8. A proprietorship.
9. A segment of any of the preceding.
10. An individual.

Comprehensive Basis of Accounting other than Generally Accepted Accounting Principles

For purposes of this section, a comprehensive basis of accounting other than generally accepted accounting principles is a basis to which at least one of the following descriptions applies:

Regulatory. A basis of accounting used by the reporting entity in compliance with requirements or financial reporting provisions of a governmental regulatory agency with jurisdiction over the entity. Examples are the following:

1. Interstate Commerce Commission.
2. Department of Housing and Urban Development.
3. State insurance commissions.

NOTE: A special report cannot be used unless the statements are filed solely with the agency.

Tax. A basis of accounting that the reporting entity uses or expects to use in filing its income tax return for the period covered by the financial statements.

Cash. The cash receipts and disbursements basis of accounting and modifications of the basis that have substantial support. Modifications having substantial support include, for example

1. Recording depreciation on long-lived assets.
2. Accruing income taxes.

Other. A definite set of criteria having substantial support that is applied to all material items appearing in the financial statements. An example of this type is financial statements prepared on the price-level basis of accounting.

NOTE: Presentations in accordance with FASB Statement 89 of current-cost and constant-dollar data are not comprehensive bases of accounting because the prescribed data do not constitute financial statements.

Current-value financial statements that supplement historical-cost financial statements in a general-use presentation of real estate entities are not considered to be OCBOA financial statements. See ***Techniques for Application*** *and Illustration 16 for additional information.*

For this section to apply, the financial statements should conform to one of the four descriptions. Reporting on other kinds of financial statements is not necessarily prohibited; however, the guidance in this section is not applicable.

OBJECTIVES OF SECTION

Engagements That May Be Accepted

An independent auditor expresses an opinion about whether the audited financial statements are presented fairly, in all material respects, in conformity with generally accepted accounting principles (GAAP). GAAP requires financial statements to be prepared on the accrual basis. There are, however, organizations that believe that neither they nor the users of their financial statements need accrual-basis financial statements. Examples of these organizations are the following: (1) some not-for-profit entities, (2) certain nonpublic entities (e.g., service enterprises and small, closely held businesses), (3) regulated companies that must file financial statements based on accounting principles prescribed by a governmental regulatory agency, and (4) entities formed for special purposes, such as certain partnerships and joint ventures.

Sometimes an auditor is asked to express an opinion on parts (elements, accounts, or items) of a financial statement. Situations where this may occur include audits of sales for purposes of computing royalties or additional rent. Unions sometimes require a special audit of the allocation of their expenses between those chargeable and those not chargeable to nonunion workers whom they represent in collective bargaining arrangements.

The objectives of this section are (1) to identify those engagements that the auditor may accept to audit and report on financial statements that are not prepared in conformity with generally accepted accounting principles without expressing a qualified or adverse opinion and (2) to identify those engagements that the auditor may accept to audit and report on parts of financial statements.

GENERALLY ACCEPTED AUDITING STANDARDS

The section establishes that whenever the auditor is engaged to audit and report on financial statements prepared in accordance with a comprehensive basis of accounting other than generally accepted accounting principles, the audit should be performed in accordance with all of the generally accepted auditing standards.

For other audits described, the section indicates which of the generally accepted auditing standards apply.

AUDITOR'S REPORT

The section provides examples of reports that an auditor should issue under each type of engagement. It also provides guidance when the auditor's report contains wording prescribed by the regulatory body to whom the client's financial statements are submitted.

FUNDAMENTAL REQUIREMENTS: FINANCIAL STATEMENTS PREPARED IN CONFORMITY WITH AN OCBOA

COMPONENTS OF AUDITOR'S STANDARD REPORT

According to AU 623.05, when reporting on financial statements prepared in conformity with an other comprehensive basis of accounting (OCBOA), the independent auditor's report should include the following:

1. A title that includes the word **independent**.
2. A standard introductory paragraph.
3. A standard scope paragraph, including an identification of the United States of America as the country of origin of the auditing standards used.
4. A paragraph that
    a. Identifies the basis of presentation and refers to the note to the financial statements that describes that basis.
    b. Indicates that the basis of presentation is a comprehensive basis of accounting other than generally accepted accounting principles.
5. An opinion paragraph that presents the auditor's opinion as to whether the financial statements are presented fairly, in all material respects, in conformity with the basis of accounting described.
6. The manual or printed signature of the auditing firm.
7. The date.

NOTE: If the financial statements are prepared in conformity with the requirements or financial reporting provisions of a governmental regulatory agency, see the section on "Governmental Regulatory Agencies" below.

(See Illustrations 1 and 2.)

DEPARTURES FROM UNQUALIFIED OPINIONS

The auditor may conclude that he or she cannot express an unqualified opinion on the financial statements in the following circumstances:

1. The financial statements are not presented fairly on the basis of accounting described.
2. There is a limitation on the scope of the audit.

In these circumstances, the auditor should do the following:

1. Include an explanatory paragraph before the opinion paragraph that discloses all substantive reasons for the modified opinion.
2. Include in the opinion paragraph appropriate modifying language and a reference to the explanatory paragraph.

GOVERNMENTAL REGULATORY AGENCIES

Sometimes the auditor reports on financial statements prepared in conformity with the requirements on financial reporting of a governmental regulatory agency. (See Illustration 3.) In these circumstances, the auditor's report should include a paragraph after the opinion paragraph that restricts the use of the report solely to those within the entity and for filing with the regulatory agency. This paragraph is appropriate even though the auditor's report may be made a matter of public record by law or regulation.

FINANCIAL STATEMENTS NOT IN CONFORMITY WITH OCBOA

If the financial statements do not meet the conditions for presentation in conformity with a comprehensive basis of accounting other than generally accepted accounting principles (see *Definitions of Terms*), the auditor should issue the standard auditor's report modified because of a GAAP departure (see Section 508).

TITLE OF FINANCIAL STATEMENTS

Titles used for financial statements prepared in conformity with generally accepted accounting principles are not appropriate for financial statements prepared in conformity with a comprehensive basis of accounting other than generally accepted accounting principles. For example, cash-basis financial statements would be titled "Statement of Assets and Liabilities Arising from Cash Transactions" and "Statement of Revenue Collected and Expenses Paid."

If the auditor believes the financial statements are not titled appropriately, he or she should ask the client to change the titles and, failing that, disclose his or her reservations in an explanatory paragraph of the auditor's reports and qualify his or her opinion.

FINANCIAL STATEMENT DISCLOSURES

The notes to the financial statements prepared on an other comprehensive basis of accounting should include a summary of significant accounting policies that describes the basis of presentation and indicates how that basis differs from generally accepted accounting principles. The effects of the differences do not have to be quantified.

Items that are similar to those in GAAP financial statements (for example, depreciation in modified cash-basis financial statements) require the same informative disclosures.

FUNDAMENTAL REQUIREMENTS: SPECIFIED ELEMENTS, ACCOUNTS, OR ITEMS OF A FINANCIAL STATEMENT

EXAMPLES AND OTHER SERVICES

An auditor may accept an engagement to express an opinion on one or more specified elements, accounts, or items of a financial statement, either as a separate engagement or in conjunction with the audit of the financial statements. The specified elements, accounts, or items may be presented in the auditor's report or in a document accompanying the report.

Examples of specified elements, accounts, or items of a financial statement that an auditor may report on include accounts receivable, investments, rentals, royalties, provision for income taxes, total expenses. For specified elements, accounts, or items, the accountant may review the specified elements, accounts, or items in accordance with attestation standards (see Section 2201).

GENERALLY ACCEPTED AUDITING STANDARDS

Nine of the ten generally accepted auditing standards are applicable to any engagement to express an opinion on one or more elements, accounts, or items of a financial statement. The first standard of reporting (GAAP conformity) is not applicable unless the specified elements, accounts, or items are intended to be presented in conformity with generally accepted accounting principles.

SCOPE OF AUDIT AND LEVEL OF MATERIALITY

In these types of engagements, the auditor expresses an opinion on **each** of the specified elements, accounts, or items encompassed by the auditor's report. The measurement of materiality, therefore, should be related to each individual element, account, or item reported on, and not to the aggregate of them or to the financial statements taken as a whole.

Because the amount considered material is usually smaller in an audit of this nature, the audit of the specified element, account, or item usually is more extensive than it is when the same information is being considered in conjunction with an audit of the financial statements taken as a whole.

Many financial statement elements, such as sales and receivables, inventory and payables, long-lived assets and depreciation, are interrelated. The auditor may therefore also apply audit procedures to elements, accounts, or items that are interrelated with those on which he or she has been engaged to express an opinion.

ADVERSE OPINION OR DISCLAIMER ON THE BASIC FINANCIAL STATEMENTS

An auditor may have expressed an adverse opinion or disclaimed an opinion on the basic financial statements. In these circumstances, the auditor still may report on one or more specified elements, accounts, or items of the basic financial statements if the following conditions exist:

1. The matters to be reported on and the scope of the audit were not intended to and did not include so many elements, accounts, or items as to constitute a major portion of the basic financial statements.
2. The report on the elements, accounts, or items should be presented separately from the report on the financial statements of the entity.

Specified Element, Account, or Item Related to Net Income or Stockholders' Equity

The auditor should have audited the complete financial statements to express an opinion on a specified element, account, or item if that specified element, account, or item is, or is based upon, an entity's net income or stockholders' equity or their equivalent.

The Auditor's Report

According to AU 623.15, the auditor's report on one or more specified elements, accounts, or items of a financial statement should include the following:

1. A title that includes the word **independent**.
2. An introductory paragraph with statements that
   a. The specified elements, accounts, or items identified in the report were audited.
      (1) If the audit was made in conjunction with the audit of the entity's financial statements, this should be stated, and the date of auditor's report on those financial statements should be indicated.
      (2) Any departure from the auditor's standard report on the entity's financial statements should be noted if considered relevant to the presentation of the specified element, account, or item.
   b. The specified elements, accounts, or items are the responsibility of the entity's management and that the auditor's responsibility is to express an opinion on the specified elements, accounts, or items based on the audit.
3. A scope paragraph with statements that
   a. The audit was conducted in accordance with auditing standards generally accepted in the United States of America.
   b. Those standards require that the auditor plan and perform the audit to obtain reasonable assurance about whether the specified elements, accounts, or items are free of material misstatement.
   c. An audit includes
      (1) Examining on a test basis, evidence supporting the amounts and disclosures in the presentation of the specified elements, accounts, or items.
      (2) Assessing the accounting principles used and significant estimates made by management.
      (3) Evaluating the overall presentation of the specified elements, accounts, or items.
   d. The auditor believes that the audit provides a reasonable basis for the opinion.
4. A paragraph with statements that
   a. Describe the basis on which the specified elements, accounts, or items are presented and if applicable, any agreements specifying the basis if the basis is not in conformity with generally accepted accounting principles. (If the presentation is prepared in conformity with generally accepted accounting principles, the paragraph should include an identification of the United States of America as the country of origin of those accounting principles.)
   b. Describe significant interpretations, if any, made by the entity's management relating to the provisions of a relevant agreement.

5. A paragraph that expresses the auditor's opinion (or disclaims an opinion) on whether the specified elements, accounts, or items are fairly presented, in all material respects, in conformity with the basis of accounting described. If the auditor concludes that the specified elements, accounts, or items are not presented fairly on the basis of accounting described or if there has been a scope limitation, the auditor should
   a. Disclose all the substantive reasons for his or her conclusion in an explanatory paragraph preceding the opinion paragraph of the report.
   b. Modify the opinion and refer to the explanatory paragraph.
6. A paragraph that restricts the use of the auditor's report to those within the entity and parties to a contract or agreement if the specified element, account, or item is prepared to comply with the requirements of a contract or agreement that results in a presentation not in conformity with generally accepted accounting principles or an other comprehensive basis of accounting.
7. The manual or printed signature of the auditing firm and the date of the report.

(See Illustrations 4 to 8.)

FUNDAMENTAL REQUIREMENTS: COMPLIANCE WITH CONTRACTUAL OR REGULATORY REQUIREMENTS RELATED TO AUDITED FINANCIAL STATEMENT

AGREEMENTS REQUIRING COMPLIANCE REPORTS

Entities may be required by bond indentures, loan and other agreements, or regulatory agencies to give compliance reports by independent auditors. For example, loan agreements may contain covenants for borrowers, such as payments into sinking funds, payments of interest, maintenance of current ratios, restriction of dividend payments, and use of proceeds of sales of property. Also, these agreements may require that the borrower provide annual financial statements that have been audited by an independent auditor.

If the auditor is testing compliance with laws and regulations in an audit in accordance with *Government Auditing Standards* (Yellow Book) issued by the Comptroller General of the United States or a single audit act in accordance with an office of management budget circular, he or she should follow the guidance in SAS 74, *Compliance Auditing Considerations in Audits of Governmental Entities and Recipients of Governmental Financial Assistance*. (See Section 801.)

REQUEST FOR ASSURANCE

In certain circumstances, lenders request from the independent auditor assurance that the borrower has complied with the covenants of the agreements relating to accounting or auditing matters. (The lender's request is made to the client, not the auditor.) The independent auditor usually satisfies this request by giving negative assurance concerning the applicable covenants. Such assurance may **not** be given if the auditor has not audited the financial statements related to the contractual agreements or regulatory requirements, if the auditor has issued an adverse opinion or disclaimer of opinion on those statements, or if the assurance extends to covenants addressing matters not subjected to auditing procedures.

The negative assurance given by the auditor may be provided in a separate report or in one or more paragraphs of the auditor's report accompanying the financial statements.

ASSURANCE GIVEN IN AUDITOR'S REPORT ON THE FINANCIAL STATEMENTS

According to AU 623.21, when the auditor's report on compliance with contractual agreements or regulatory provisions is included in the auditor's report on the financial statements, the auditor should include a paragraph, after the opinion paragraph, that provides the negative assurance relative to compliance with the applicable covenants of the agreement, insofar as they relate to accounting matters. The paragraph also should state that (1) the negative assurance is being given in connection with the audit of the financial statements and (2) the audit was not directed primarily toward obtaining knowledge regarding compliance.

The auditor's report should also include a paragraph with the description and source of any significant interpretations made by the entity's management and a paragraph that restricts its use to those within the entity and the parties to the contract or agreement or for filing with the regulatory agency, if appropriate.

SEPARATE AUDITOR'S REPORT

According to AU 623.20, if an auditor's report on compliance with contractual agreements or regulatory provisions is a separate report, it should include the following:

1. A title that includes the word **independent**.
2. A paragraph that states that the financial statements were audited in accordance with auditing standards generally accepted in the United States of America and the date of the auditor's report on the financial statements. Any departure from the auditor's standard report on the financial statements should be disclosed.
3. A paragraph that
   a. Refers to the specific covenants or paragraphs of the agreement.
   b. Provides negative assurance relative to compliance with the applicable covenants of the agreement insofar as they relate to accounting matters.
   c. Specifies that the negative assurance is being given in connection with the audit of the financial statements.
   d. States that the audit was not directed primarily toward obtaining knowledge regarding compliance.
4. A paragraph that includes a description and the source of any significant interpretations made by the entity's management relating to provisions of the agreement.
5. A paragraph that restricts the use of the report to those within the entity and the parties to the contract or agreement or for filing with the regulatory agency, if appropriate.
6. The manual or printed signature of the auditing firm and the date of the report.

(See Illustrations 9 and 10.)

FUNDAMENTAL REQUIREMENTS: SPECIAL-PURPOSE FINANCIAL PRESENTATIONS TO COMPLY WITH CONTRACTUAL AGREEMENTS OR REGULATORY PROVISIONS

SPECIAL-PURPOSE FINANCIAL PRESENTATIONS

Sometimes an auditor is asked to report on special-purpose financial statements prepared to comply with a contractual agreement or regulatory provisions. In most circumstances, these types of financial presentations are intended for use of the parties to the agreement, regulatory bodies, or other specified parties. They include the following:

1. A financial presentation prepared in compliance with a contractual agreement or regulatory provision that is not a complete presentation of the entity's assets, liabilities, revenues, or expenses, but is otherwise prepared in conformity with generally accepted accounting principles or an other comprehensive basis of accounting (an incomplete presentation).
2. A financial presentation (a complete set of financial statements or a single financial statement) prepared on a basis of accounting prescribed in an agreement that is not a presentation in conformity with generally accepted accounting principles or an other comprehensive basis of accounting.

INCOMPLETE PRESENTATIONS

Situations That Would Involve Incomplete Presentations

The following situations involve incomplete presentations:

1. A governmental agency may require a schedule of gross income and certain expenses, exclusive of items such as interest, depreciation, and income taxes, of a entity's real estate operations.
2. A buy-sell agreement may specify a schedule of assets and liabilities measured in conformity with generally accepted accounting principles, but limited to certain designated assets and liabilities (for example, tangible assets and liabilities, exclusive of loans from stockholders).

These presentations should differ from complete financial statements only to the extent necessary to meet the special purposes for which they were prepared.

Disclosures

If these financial presentations contain items the same as, or similar to, those contained in a complete set of financial statements prepared in conformity with generally accepted accounting principles, similar informative disclosures should be made.

Title

The financial statements should be appropriately titled to avoid any implication that these incomplete presentations are intended to present financial position, results of operations, or cash flows.

Materiality

Although not complete financial statements, these financial presentations are considered to be financial statements for purposes of considering materiality. That is, the measurement of materiality for purposes of expressing an opinion should be related to the financial presentation taken as a whole.

Auditor's Report

According to AU 623.25, when the auditor reports on financial statements prepared on a basis of accounting prescribed in a contractual agreement or regulatory provision that results in an incomplete presentation, but one that is otherwise in conformity with generally accepted accounting principles or another comprehensive basis of accounting, the auditor's report should include the following:

1. A title that includes the word **independent**.
2. A standard introductory paragraph.

3. A standard scope paragraph, including an identification of the United States of America as the country of origin of the auditing standards used.
4. A paragraph that
   a. Explains what the presentation is intended to present and refers to the note to the financial statements that describes the basis of presentation.
   b. States that the presentation is not intended to be a complete presentation of the entity's assets, liabilities, revenues, and expenses if the basis of presentation is in conformity with generally accepted accounting principles or another comprehensive basis of accounting.
5. A paragraph that expresses the auditor's opinion related to the fair presentation, in all material respects, of the information the presentation is intended to present in conformity with generally accepted accounting principles or an other comprehensive basis of accounting. If the presentation is prepared in conformity with generally accepted accounting principles, the paragraph should include an identification of the United States of America as the country of origin of those accounting principles. If the auditor concludes that the information the presentation is intended to present is not presented fairly on the basis of accounting described or if there has been a scope limitation, the auditor should
   a. Disclose all the substantive reasons for his or her conclusion in an explanatory paragraph preceding the opinion paragraph of the report.
   b. Modify the opinion and refer to the explanatory paragraph.
6. A paragraph that restricts the use of the auditor's report to the parties to the contract or agreement, to those with whom the entity is negotiating directly, or for filing with a regulatory agency.

   NOTE: There should not be a restrictive paragraph when the report and related financial presentation are to be filed with a regulatory agency, such as the SEC, and are to be included in a document that is distributed to the general public, such as a prospectus.
7. The manual or printed signature of the auditing firm and the date of the report.

(See Illustrations 11 and 12.)

NON-GAAP OR NON-OCBOA PRESENTATIONS

Situations That Would Involve Non-GAAP or Non-OCBOA Presentations

The following situations in AU 623.27 involve special-purpose financial statements presented in conformity with a basis of accounting that departs from generally accepted accounting principles or an other comprehensive basis of accounting:

1. A loan agreement may require the borrower to prepare financial statements in which assets, such as inventory, are presented on a basis that is not in conformity with generally accepted accounting principles.
2. An acquisition agreement may require the financial statements of the entity being acquired to be prepared in conformity with generally accepted accounting principles, except for certain assets for which a valuation basis is stated in the agreement.

Another example would be when current-value financial statements supplement historical-cost financial statements in a general-use presentation of real estate entities.

Auditor's Report

According to AU 623.29, when the auditor reports on financial statements described above, the auditor's report should include

1. A title that includes the word **independent**.
2. A standard introductory paragraph.
3. A standard scope paragraph, including an identification of the United States of America as the country of origin of the auditing standards used.
4. A paragraph that
   a. Explains what the presentation is intended to present and refers to the note to the financial statements that describes the basis of presentation.
   b. States that the presentation is not intended to be a presentation in conformity with generally accepted accounting principles.
5. A paragraph that describes and provides the source of any significant interpretations made by the entity's management relating to provisions of a relevant agreement.
6. A paragraph that expresses the auditor's opinion related to the fair presentation, in all material respects, of the information the presentation is intended to present on the basis of accounting specified. If the auditor concludes that the information the presentation is intended to present is not presented fairly on the basis of accounting described or if there has been a limitation on the scope of the audit, the auditor should
   a. Disclose all the substantive reasons for his or her conclusion in an explanatory paragraph preceding the opinion paragraph of the report.
   b. Modify the opinion and refer to the explanatory paragraph.
7. A paragraph that restricts the use of the report to those in the entity, to parties to the contract or agreement, to those with whom the entity is negotiating directly, or for filing with a regulatory agency.

   NOTE: When current-value financial statements of a real estate entity supplement the historical-cost financial statements and are not presented as a stand-alone presentation, it is not necessary to restrict the distribution of the auditor's report.
8. The manual or printed signature of the auditing firm and the date of the report.

(See Illustration 13.)

FUNDAMENTAL REQUIREMENTS: CIRCUMSTANCES REQUIRING EXPLANATORY LANGUAGE IN AN AUDITOR'S SPECIAL REPORT

CIRCUMSTANCES REQUIRING EXPLANATORY LANGUAGE

Circumstances that do not affect the auditor's unqualified opinion may nonetheless require that the auditor add explanatory language to the special report. These circumstances include the following:

1. Lack of consistency in accounting principles.
2. Going concern uncertainties.
3. Other auditors.
4. Comparative financial presentations.

Lack of Consistency in Accounting Principles

A change in accounting principles or in the method of their application for the financial statements or specified elements, accounts, or items of financial statements may cause a material lack of comparability. In these circumstances, the auditor should add an explanatory paragraph to the auditor's report. The explanatory paragraph should

1. Follow the opinion paragraph.
2. Describe the change.
3. Refer to the note that discusses the change and the effect (see Section 508).

Change from GAAP to OCBOA. The auditor does not have to follow the above requirements if the financial statements or specified elements, accounts, or items were prepared in conformity with generally accepted accounting principles one year and an other comprehensive basis of accounting the following year. The auditor may, however, add an explanatory paragraph to the auditor's report to call attention to the difference in the bases of presentation.

GAAP and OCBOA financial statements. Sometimes, two sets of financial statements for the same year may be issued—one prepared in conformity with generally accepted accounting principles, the other in conformity with an other comprehensive basis of accounting. In these circumstances, the auditor may add an explanatory paragraph to each report stating that another set of financial statements prepared in conformity with another basis have been reported on and issued.

Change in the tax law. A change in the tax law is not considered to be a change in accounting principle for financial statements prepared in conformity with the tax basis of accounting. The auditor would not, therefore, need to add an explanatory paragraph to the auditor's report. However, disclosure of the tax law change may be necessary.

Going Concern Uncertainties

The auditor may have substantial doubt about the entity's ability to continue as a going concern for a period of time not to exceed one year beyond the date of the financial statements. In these circumstances, the auditor should add an explanatory paragraph after the opinion paragraph of the auditor's report if the going concern uncertainty is relevant to what the auditor is reporting on (see Section 341).

Other Auditors

If the auditor decides to make reference to the report of another auditor as a basis, in part, for his or her opinion, the auditor should disclose this in the introductory paragraph of the auditor's report and should refer to the other auditor's report in the opinion paragraph (see Section 508).

Comparative Financial Presentations

The auditor may express an opinion on prior period financial statements or specified elements, accounts, or items that is different from the opinion he or she previously expressed on the same information. In these circumstances, the auditor should disclose all substantive reasons for the different opinion in a separate explanatory paragraph preceding the opinion paragraph of the auditor's report.

FUNDAMENTAL REQUIREMENTS: FINANCIAL INFORMATION PRESENTED IN PRESCRIBED FORMS OR SCHEDULES

The Auditor's Report

Printed forms or schedules sometimes are designed or adopted by the agencies with which they are to be filed. These forms or schedules might prescribe wording of the auditor's report that is not acceptable to the auditor because it does not conform to the standards of reporting. When a printed auditor's report form contains an assertion that the independent auditor believes he or she is not justified in making, the auditor should either reword the form or attach a separate report.

INTERPRETATIONS

AUDITORS' SPECIAL REPORTS ON PROPERTY AND LIABILITY INSURANCE COMPANIES' LOSS RESERVES (MAY 1981; REVISED FEBRUARY 1999; REVISED OCTOBER 2000)

State regulatory agencies may require property and liability insurance companies to file the statement of a qualified loss reserve specialist setting forth his or her opinion on the loss and loss adjustment expense reserves.

An independent auditor who has the competence may be a qualified loss reserve specialist. In these circumstances, the auditor who expresses an opinion on the loss and loss expense reserves should be guided by the provisions of the section pertaining to auditors' reports expressing an opinion on one or more specified elements, accounts, or items of a financial statement.

A report issued under these circumstances and the schedule of liabilities for losses and loss adjustment expenses that would accompany the report are illustrated in the interpretation. (See Illustration 14.)

REPORTS ON THE FINANCIAL STATEMENTS INCLUDED IN INTERNAL REVENUE FORM 990, "RETURN OF ORGANIZATIONS EXEMPT FROM INCOME TAX" (ISSUED JULY 1982; REVISED FEBRUARY 1997; REVISED FEBRUARY 1999; REVISED OCTOBER 2000)

Form 990 may be used as a uniform annual report by charitable organizations in some states for reporting to both state and federal governments. Many states require an auditor's opinion on whether the financial statements included in Form 990 are presented fairly in conformity with generally accepted accounting principles. However, financial statements included in a Form 990 used by a charitable organization as a uniform annual report may contain certain material departures from the accounting principles in the AICPA Audit and Accounting Guides for *Health Care Organizations* and *Not-for-Profit Organizations.*

In most states, the report filed by the charitable organization is used to satisfy statutory requirements, but the regulators make the financial statements and the accompanying auditor's report a matter of public record. In some situations, there may be public distribution of the charitable organization's report.

Financial Statements in Conformity with GAAP

If the financial statements are in conformity with generally accepted accounting principles, the auditor can express an unqualified opinion.

Financial Statements Not in Conformity with GAAP

If the financial statements are not in conformity with generally accepted accounting principles, the auditor should consider the distribution of the report to determine whether it is appropriate to issue a special report on financial statements prepared on a basis prescribed by a regulatory agency solely for filing with that agency (see *Illustrations*). This type of reporting is appropriate if the report is intended solely for filing with regulatory agencies even though the regulatory agencies might make the auditor's report a matter of public record by law or regulation. (See Illustration 15.)

If there is public distribution of the report of the charitable organization and the financial statements included in it are not in conformity with generally accepted accounting principles, the auditor's report described in the preceding paragraph is not appropriate. In these circumstances, the auditor should express a qualified or adverse opinion. Public distribution occurs when the report is sent unsolicited to contributors or others by the charitable organization.

Reporting on Current-Value Financial Statements That Supplement Historical-Cost Financial Statements in a General-Use Presentation of Real Estate Entities (Issued July 1990; Revised February 1999; Revised October 2000)

The auditor may accept an engagement to report on current-value financial statements that supplement historical-cost financial statements in a general-use presentation of real estate entities only if the following two conditions are met:

1. The measurement and disclosure criteria used to prepare the current-value statements are reasonable.
2. Competent persons using the measurement and disclosure criteria would ordinarily obtain materially similar measurements or disclosures.

The auditor should consider the adequacy of disclosures relating to the current-value statements, including appropriate disclosure of the basis of presentation, nature of the reporting entity's properties, status of construction-in-process, valuation bases used for each classification of assets and liabilities, and sources of valuation. These disclosures should be made in the notes in a sufficiently clear and comprehensive manner that enables a knowledgeable reader to understand the current-value financial statements. A restriction on use of the auditor's report is not necessary because the presentation is only a supplement to historical financial statements rather than being a stand-alone presentation. (See Illustration 16.)

Evaluation of the Appropriateness of Informative Disclosures in Insurance Enterprises' Financial Statements Prepared on a Statutory Basis (Issued December 1991; Revised February 1997. Amended December 2001 by SOP 01-5, *Amendments to Specific AICPA Pronouncements for Changes Related to the NAIC Codification*)

When financial statements are presented on a statutory basis, the auditor should consider whether the financial statements and notes are informative of matters that may affect their use, understanding, and interpretation.

In the case of an insurance enterprise, most states are expected to adopt the updated *Accounting Practices and Procedures Manual,* revised by the National Association of Insurance Commissioners (NAIC). Since the revised Manual contains extensive disclosure requirements, the statutory basis of enterprises in states that have adopted the revised Manual will include informative disclosures appropriate for that basis of accounting. However, some states may not adopt the revised Manual or may adopt it with significant departures.

Disclosures in statutory-basis financial statements for items and transactions that are accounted for essentially the same or in a similar manner under a statutory basis as under GAAP should be the same as, or similar to, the disclosures required by GAAP unless the revised Manual specifically states the NAIC Codification rejected the GAAP disclosures. Disclosures should also include those required by the revised Manual. If the state's required accounting for an item or transaction differs from the accounting in the revised Manual, but is in accordance with GAAP or superseded GAAP, the statutory basis financial statement disclosures for that item or transaction should be the applicable GAAP or superseded GAAP disclosures. Finally, if the accounting required by the state for an item or transaction differs from the accounting in the revised Manual, GAAP, or superseded GAAP, sufficient relevant disclosures should be made.

If state requirements have not been revised to reflect new GAAP disclosure requirements, the statutory basis financial statements should include the new required GAAP disclosures that are relevant and significant to the statutory basis of accounting, pending inclusion in or exclusion from the revised Manual.

REPORTING ON A SPECIAL-PURPOSE FINANCIAL STATEMENT THAT RESULTS IN AN INCOMPLETE PRESENTATION BUT IS OTHERWISE IN CONFORMITY WITH GAAP (MAY 1995, REVISED FEBRUARY 1999)

An offering memorandum providing information as the basis for negotiating an offer to sell certain assets, or an entire business, or to simply raise funds does not constitute a contractual agreement. The auditor should follow the guidance for reporting GAAP departures in a standard audit report (Section 508) rather than the guidance for a special-purpose financial presentation as described in Section 623.

An agreement between a client and one or more third parties other than the auditor to prepare financial statements using a special-purpose presentation is a contractual agreement and Section 623 applies. The report's use should be restricted to the entity, parties to the agreement, or parties negotiating the agreement directly with the entity.

EVALUATING THE ADEQUACY OF DISCLOSURE IN FINANCIAL STATEMENTS PREPARED ON THE CASH, MODIFIED CASH, OR INCOME TAX BASIS OF ACCOUNTING (JANUARY 1998)

Note disclosures in these types of OCBOA financial statements should contain disclosures similar to GAAP for financial statement items that are the same as, or similar to, those prepared in conformity with GAAP. However, in applying that general guideline, the following modifications may be made:

1. Brief and less detailed is fine.
2. Quantification is not necessary.
3. Communication of substance of the disclosure is enough.
4. Disclosures not relevant to the measurement of the element, account, or item need not be considered.

Examples of these modifications are as follows:

- Disclosure of the basis of presentation may be limited to a brief identification of the basis and primary differences from GAAP. Quantification of the differences is not required.
- Disclosure of repayment terms of significant long-term borrowing communicates the substance of future principal reductions, and a schedule of payments for the next five years is not necessary.
- If the accounting basis does not adjust cost of securities to fair value, then fair value information is not relevant.
- Information on accounting changes, discontinued operations, and extraordinary items may be disclosed in a note without following the GAAP requirements for statement presentation and disclosing net-of-tax effects.
- Disclosure about use of estimates is not relevant in a presentation that has no estimates such as one based on cash receipts and disbursements.

ILLUSTRATIONS

Illustrations 1-16 illustrate auditor's reports adapted from AU Section 623 and its interpretations.

Illustration 1. Financial Statements Prepared on the Entity's Income Tax Basis

Independent Auditor's Report

We have audited the accompanying statements of assets, liabilities, and capital-income tax basis of Widget Partnership as of December 31, 20X2, and 20X1, and the related statements of revenue and expenses-income tax basis and of changes in partners' capital accounts-income tax basis for the years then ended. These financial statements are the responsibility of the Partnership's management. Our responsibility is to express an opinion on these financial statements based on our audits.

We conducted our audits in accordance with auditing standards generally accepted in the United States of America. Those standards require that we plan and perform the audit to obtain reasonable assurance about whether the financial statements are free of material misstatement. An audit includes examining, on a test basis, evidence supporting the amounts and disclosures in the financial statements. An audit also includes assessing the accounting principles used and significant estimates made by management, as well as evaluating the overall financial statement presentation. We believe that our audits provide a reasonable basis for our opinion.

As described in Note X, these financial statements were prepared on the basis of accounting the Partnership uses for income tax purposes, which is a comprehensive basis of accounting other than generally accepted accounting principles.

In our opinion, the financial statements referred to above present fairly, in all material respects, the assets, liabilities, and capital of Widget Partnership as of December 31, 20X2 and 20X1, and its revenue and expenses and changes in partners' capital accounts for the years then ended, on the basis of accounting described in Note X.

Illustration 2. Financial Statements Prepared on the Cash Basis

Independent Auditor's Report

We have audited the accompanying statements of assets and liabilities arising from cash transactions of Widget Company as of December 31, 20X2 and 20X1, and the related statements of revenue collected and expenses paid for the years then ended. These financial statements are the responsibility of the Company's management. Our responsibility is to express an opinion on these financial statements based on our audits.

We conducted our audits in accordance with auditing standards generally accepted in the United States of America. Those standards require that we plan and perform the audit to obtain reasonable assurance about whether the financial statements are free of material misstatement. An audit includes examining, on a test basis, evidence supporting the amounts and disclosures in the financial statements. An audit also includes assessing the accounting principles used and significant estimates made by management, as well as evaluating the overall financial statement presentations. We believe that our audits provide a reasonable basis for our opinion.

As described in Note X, these financial statements were prepared on the basis of cash receipts and disbursements, which is a comprehensive basis of accounting other than generally accepted accounting principles.

In our opinion, the financial statements referred to above present fairly, in all material respects, the assets and liabilities arising from cash transactions of Widget Company as of December 31, 20X2 and 20X1, and its revenues collected and expenses paid during the years then ended, on the basis of accounting described in Note X.

Illustration 3. Financial Statements Prepared on a Basis Prescribed by a Regulatory Agency Solely for Filing with That Agency[1]

Independent Auditor's Report

We have audited the accompanying statutory statements of admitted assets, liabilities, and surplus of Carmichael Insurance Company as of December 31, 20X2 and 20X1, and the related statutory statements of income and changes in surplus and cash flows for the years then ended. These financial statements are the responsibility of the Company's management. Our responsibility is to express an opinion on these financial statements based on our audits.

We conducted our audits in accordance with auditing standards generally accepted in the United States of America. Those standards require that we plan and perform the audit to obtain reasonable assurance about whether the financial statements are free of material misstatement. An audit includes examining, on a test basis, evidence supporting the amounts and disclosures in the financial statements. An audit also includes assessing the accounting principles used and significant estimates made by management, as well as evaluating the overall financial statement presentation. We believe that our audits provide a reasonable basis for our opinion.

As described more fully in Note X to the financial statements, these financial statements were prepared in conformity with the accounting practices prescribed or permitted by the Insurance Department of [*State*], which is a comprehensive basis of accounting other than generally accepted accounting principles.

In our opinion, the financial statements referred to above present fairly, in all material respects, the admitted assets, liabilities, and surplus of Carmichael Insurance Company as of [at] December 31, 20X2 and 20X1, and the results of its operations and its cash flows for the years then ended, on the basis of accounting described in Note X.

This report is intended solely for the information and use of the board of directors and the management of Carmichael Insurance Company and [*name of regulatory agency*] and is not intended to be, and should not be, used by anyone other than these specified parties.

Illustration 4. Report on Specified Elements, Accounts, or Items Relating to Accounts Receivable

Independent Auditor's Report

We have audited the accompanying schedule of accounts receivable of Widget Company as of December 31, 20X2. This schedule is the responsibility of the Company's management. Our responsibility is to express an opinion on this schedule based on our audit.

We conducted our audit in accordance with auditing standards generally accepted in the United States of America. Those standards require that we plan and perform the audit to obtain reasonable assurance about whether the schedule of accounts receivable is free of material misstatement. An audit includes examining, on a test basis, evidence supporting the amounts and disclosures in the schedule of accounts receivable. An audit also includes assessing the accounting principles used and significant estimates made by management, as well as evaluating the overall schedule presentation. We believe that our audit provides a reasonable basis for our opinion.

In our opinion, the schedule of accounts receivable referred to above presents fairly, in all material respects, the accounts receivable of Widget Company as of December 31, 20X2, in conformity with accounting principles generally accepted in the United States of America.

Illustration 5. Report on Specified Elements, Accounts, or Items Relating to Amount of Sales for the Purpose of Computing Rental

Independent Auditor's Report

We have audited the accompanying schedule of gross sales [*as defined in the lease agreement dated March 4, 20X0, between Widget Company, as lessor, and Carmichael Stores Corporation, as lessee*] of Carmichael Stores Corporation at its Main Street Store, [*City*], [*State*], for the year ended December 31, 20X2. This schedule is the responsibility of Carmichael Stores Corporation's management. Our responsibility is to express an opinion on this schedule based on our audit.

---

[1] *This report is presented in SOP 01-5,* ***Amendments to Specific AICPA Pronouncements for Changes Related to the NAIC Codification****. The amendments in SOP 01-5 are effective for audits of statutory financial statements for fiscal years ending on or after December 15, 2001. Retroactive application is not permitted.*

We conducted our audit in accordance with auditing standards generally accepted in the United States of America. Those standards require that we plan and perform the audit to obtain reasonable assurance about whether the schedule of gross sales is free of material misstatement. An audit also includes examining, on a test basis, evidence supporting the amounts and disclosures in the schedule of gross sales. An audit also includes assessing the accounting principles used and significant estimates made by management, as well as evaluating the overall schedule presentation. We believe that our audit provides a reasonable basis for our opinion.

In our opinion, the schedule of gross sales referred to above presents fairly, in all material respects, the gross sales of Carmichael Stores Corporation at its Main Street store, [*City*] [*State*], for the year ended December 31, 20X2, as defined in the lease agreement referred to in the first paragraph.

This report is intended solely for the information and use of the boards of directors and managements of Carmichael Stores Corporation and Widget Company and is not intended to be, and should not be, used by anyone other than these specified parties.

Illustration 6. Report on Specified Elements, Accounts, or Items Relating to Royalties with Disclosure of Management's Interpretation of Agreement

Independent Auditor's Report

We have audited the accompanying schedule of royalties applicable to engine production of the Q Division of Widget Corporation for the year ended December 31, 20X2, under the terms of a license agreement dated May 14, 20X0, between ABC Company and Widget Corporation. This schedule is the responsibility of Widget Corporation's management. Our responsibility is to express an opinion on this schedule based on our audit.

We conducted our audit in accordance with auditing standards generally accepted in the United States of America. Those standards require that we plan and perform the audit to obtain reasonable assurance about whether the schedule of royalties is free of material misstatement. An audit includes examining, on a test basis, evidence supporting the amounts and disclosures in the schedule. An audit also includes assessing the accounting principles used and significant estimates made by management, as well as evaluating the overall schedule presentation. We believe that our audit provides a reasonable basis for our opinion.

We have been informed that, under Widget Corporation's interpretation of the agreement referred to in the first paragraph, royalties were based on the number of engines produced after giving effect to a reduction for production retirements that were scrapped, but without a reduction for field returns that were scrapped, even though the field returns were replaced with new engines without charge to customers.

In our opinion, the schedule of royalties referred to above presents fairly, in all material respects, the number of engines produced by the Q Division of Widget Corporation during the year ended December 31, 20X2, and the amount of royalties applicable thereto, under the license agreement referred to above.

This report is intended solely for the information and use of the boards of directors and managements of Widget Corporation and ABC Company and is not intended to be, and should not be, used by anyone other than these specified parties.

Illustration 7. Report on Specified Elements, Accounts, or Items Relating to a Profit Participation with Identification of Relevant Agreements

Independent Auditor's Report

We have audited, in accordance with auditing standards generally accepted in the United States of America, the financial statements of Basic Company for the year ended December 31, 20X1, and have issued our report thereon dated March 10, 20X2. We have also audited Basic Company's schedule of Jane Doe's profit participation for the year ended December 31, 20X1. This schedule is the responsibility of the Company's management. Our responsibility is to express an opinion on this schedule based on our audit.

We conducted our audit of the schedule in accordance with auditing standards generally accepted in the United States of America. Those standards require that we plan and perform the audit to obtain reasonable assurance about whether the schedule of profit participation is free of material misstatement. An audit includes examining, on a test basis, evidence supporting the amounts and disclosures in the schedule. An audit also includes assessing the accounting principles used and significant estimates made by management, as well as evaluating the overall schedule presentation. We believe that our audit provides a reasonable basis for our opinion.

We have been informed that the documents that govern the determination of Jane Doe's profit participation are (a) the employment agreement between Jane Doe and Basic Company dated February 1, 20X0, (b) the production and distribution agreement between Basic Company and Television Network Incorporated dated March 1, 20X0, and (c) the studio facilities agreement between Basic Company and QRZ Studios dated April 1, 20X0, as amended November 1, 20X0.

In our opinion, the schedule of profit participation referred to above presents fairly, in all material respects, Jane Doe's participation in the profits of Basic Company for the year ended December 31, 20X1, in accordance with the provisions of the agreements referred to above.

This report is intended solely for the information and use of the boards of directors and management of Basic Company and Jane Doe and is not intended to be, and should not be, used by anyone other than these specified parties.

Illustration 8. Report on Specified Elements, Accounts, or Items Relating to Federal and State Income Taxes Included in Financial Statements with Reference to Audit Report on Related Financial Statements

Independent Auditor's Report

We have audited, in accordance with auditing standards generally accepted in the United States of America, the financial statements of Widget Company, Inc., for the year ended June 30, 20X1, and have issued our report thereon dated August 15, 20X1. We have also audited the current and deferred provision for the Company's federal and state income taxes for the year ended June 30, 20X1, included in those financial statements, and the related asset and liability tax accounts as of June 30, 20X1. This income tax information is the responsibility of the Company's management. Our responsibility is to express an opinion on it based on our audit.

We conducted our audit of the income tax information in accordance with auditing standards generally accepted in the United States of America. Those standards require that we plan and perform the audit to obtain reasonable assurance about whether the federal and state income tax accounts are free of material misstatement. An audit includes examining, on a test basis, evidence supporting the amounts and disclosures related to the federal and state income tax accounts. An audit also includes assessing the accounting principles used and significant estimates made by management, as well as evaluating the overall presentation of the federal and state income tax accounts. We believe that our audit provides a reasonable basis for our opinion.

In our opinion, the Company has paid or, in all material respects, made adequate provision in the financial statements referred to above for the payment of all federal and state income taxes and for related deferred income taxes that could be reasonably estimated at the time of our audit of the financial statements of Widget Company, Inc., for the year ended June 30, 20X1.

Illustration 9. Report on Compliance with Contractual Provisions Given in a Separate Report

Independent Auditor's Report

We have audited, in accordance with auditing standards generally accepted in the United States of America, the balance sheet of Widget Company as of December 31, 20X2, and the related statements of income, retained earnings, and cash flows for the year then ended, and have issued our report thereon dated February 16, 20X3.

In connection with our audit, nothing came to our attention that caused us to believe that the Company failed to comply with the terms, covenants, provisions, or conditions of Section XX to XX, inclusive, of the Indenture dated July 21, 20X0, with Basic Bank in so far as they relate to accounting matters. However, our audit was not directed primarily toward obtaining knowledge of such noncompliance.

This report is intended solely for the information and use of the boards of directors and management of Widget Company and Basic Bank and is not intended to be, and should not be, used by anyone other than these specified parties.

Illustration 10. Report on Compliance with Regulatory Requirements Given in a Separate Report When the Auditor's Report on the Financial Statements Included an Explanatory Paragraph Because of a Going Concern Uncertainty

Independent Auditor's Report

We have audited, in accordance with auditing standards generally accepted in the United States of America, the balance sheet of Widget Company as of December 31, 20X2, and the related statements of income, retained earnings, and cash flows for the year then ended, and have issued our report thereon dated March 5, 20X3, which included an explanatory paragraph that described the substantial doubt about Widget Company's ability to continue as a going concern discussed in Note X of those statements.

In connection with our audit, nothing came to our attention that caused us to believe that the Company failed to comply with the accounting provisions in sections (1), (2), and (3) of the [*name of state regulatory agency*]. However, our audit was not directed primarily toward obtaining knowledge of such noncompliance.

This report is intended solely for the information and use of the board of directors and management of Widget Company and the [*name of state regulatory agency*] and is not intended to be, and should not be, used by anyone other than these specified parties.

Illustration 11. Report on a Schedule of Gross Income and Certain Expenses to Meet a Regulatory Requirement and to Be Included in a Document Distributed to the General Public

Independent Auditor's Report

We have audited the accompanying Historical Summaries of Gross Income and Direct Operating Expenses of Basic Apartments, City, State (Historical Summaries), for each of the three years in the period ended December 31, 20X1. These Historical Summaries are the responsibility of the Apartments' management. Our responsibility is to express an opinion on the Historical Summaries based on our audits.

We conducted our audits in accordance with auditing standards generally accepted in the United States of America. Those standards require that we plan and perform the audit to obtain reasonable assurance about whether the Historical Summaries are free of material misstatement. An audit includes examining, on a test basis, evidence supporting the amounts and disclosures in the Historical Summaries. An audit also includes assessing the accounting principles used and significant estimates made by management, as well as evaluating the overall presentation of the Historical Summaries. We believe that our audits provide a reasonable basis for our opinion.

The accompanying Historical Summaries were prepared for the purpose of complying with the rules and regulations of the Securities and Exchange Commission (for inclusion in the registration statement on Form S-11 of DEF Corporation) as described in Note X and are not intended to be a complete presentation of the Apartments' revenues and expenses.

In our opinion, the Historical Summaries referred to above present fairly, in all material respects, the gross income and direct operating expenses described in Note X of Basic Apartments for each of the three years in the period ended December 31, 20X1, in conformity with accounting principles generally accepted in the United States of America.

Illustration 12. Report on Statement of Assets and Liabilities Transferred to Comply with a Contractual Agreement

Independent Auditor's Report

We have audited the accompanying statement of net assets sold of Widget Company as of June 8, 20X1. This statement of net assets sold is the responsibility of Widget Company's management. Our responsibility is to express an opinion on the statement of net assets sold based on our audit.

We conducted our audit in accordance with auditing standards generally accepted in the United States of America. Those standards require that we plan and perform the audit to obtain reasonable assurance about whether the statement of net assets sold is free of material misstatement. An audit includes examining, on a test basis, evidence supporting the amounts and disclosures in the statement. An audit also includes assessing the accounting principles used and significant estimates made by management, as well as evaluating the overall presentation of the statement of net assets sold. We believe that our audit provides a reasonable basis for our opinion.

The accompanying statement was prepared to present the net assets of Widget Company sold to Basic Corporation pursuant to the purchase agreement described in Note X, and is not intended to be a complete presentation of Widget Company's assets and liabilities.

In our opinion, the accompanying statement of net assets sold presents fairly, in all material respects, the net assets of Widget Company as of June 8, 20X1, sold pursuant to the purchase agreement referred to in Note X, in conformity with accounting principles generally accepted in the United States of America.

This report is intended solely for the information and use of the boards of directors and managements of Widget Company and Basic Corporation and is not intended to be, and should not be, used by anyone other than these specified parties.

ILLUSTRATION 13. REPORT ON FINANCIAL STATEMENTS PREPARED PURSUANT TO A LOAN AGREEMENT THAT RESULTS IN A PRESENTATION NOT IN CONFORMITY WITH GENERALLY ACCEPTED ACCOUNTING PRINCIPLES OR AN OTHER COMPREHENSIVE BASIS OF ACCOUNTING

Independent Auditor's Report

We have audited the special-purpose statement of assets and liabilities of Widget Company as of December 31, 20X2 and 20X1, and the related special-purpose statements of revenues and expenses and of cash flows for the years then ended. These financial statements are the responsibility of the Company's management. Our responsibility is to express an opinion on these financial statements based on our audits.

We conducted our audits in accordance with auditing standards generally accepted in the United States of America. Those standards require that we plan and perform the audit to obtain reasonable assurance about whether the financial statements are free of material misstatement. An audit includes examining, on a test basis, evidence supporting the amounts and disclosures in the financial statements. An audit also includes assessing the accounting principles used and significant estimates made by management, as well as evaluating the overall financial statement presentation. We believe that our audits provide a reasonable basis for our opinion.

The accompanying special-purpose financial statements were prepared for the purpose of complying with Section 4 of a loan agreement between Basic Bank and the Company as discussed in Note X, and are not intended to be a presentation in conformity with generally accepted accounting principles.

In our opinion, the special-purpose financial statements referred to above present fairly, in all material respects, the assets and liabilities of Widget Company as of December 31, 20X2 and 20X1, and the revenues, expenses and cash flows for the years then ended, on the basis of accounting described in Note X.

This report is intended solely for the information and use of the boards of directors and managements of Widget Company and Basic Bank and is not intended to be, and should not be, used by anyone other than these specified parties.

ILLUSTRATION 14. AUDITOR'S REPORT EXPRESSING AN OPINION ON AN INSURANCE COMPANY'S LOSS AND LOSS ADJUSTMENT EXPENSE RESERVES AND THE SCHEDULE THAT WOULD ACCOMPANY THE REPORT

Board of Directors

X Insurance Company

We are members of the American Institute of Certified Public Accountants (AICPA) and are the independent public accountants of Basic Insurance Company. We acknowledge our responsibility under the AICPA's Code of Professional Conduct to undertake only those engagements which we can complete with professional competence.

We have audited the financial statements prepared in conformity with accounting principles generally accepted in the United States of America [*or prepared in conformity with accounting practices prescribed or permitted by the Insurance Department of the State of . . . .*] of Basic Insurance Company as of December 31, 20X1, and have issued our report thereon dated March 1, 20X2. In the course of our audit, we have audited the estimated liabilities for unpaid losses and unpaid loss adjustment expenses of Basic Insurance Company as of December 31, 20X1, as set forth in the accompanying schedule including consideration of the assumptions and methods relating to the estimation of such liabilities.

In our opinion, the accompanying schedule presents fairly, in all material respects, the estimated unpaid losses and unpaid loss adjustment expenses of Basic Insurance Company that could be reasonably estimated at December 31, 20X1, in conformity with accounting practices prescribed or permitted by the Insurance Department of the State of. . . . . on a basis consistent with that of the preceding year.

This report is intended solely for the information and use of the board of directors and management of Basic Insurance Company and [*the state regulatory agencies to whose jurisdiction the entity is subject*] and is not intended to be, and should not be, used by anyone other than these specified parties.

[*Signature*]

[*Date*]

Basic Insurance Company
Schedule of Liabilities for Losses and Loss Adjustment Expenses
December 31, 20X1

Liability for losses	$xx,xxx,xxx
Liability for loss adjustment expenses	x,xxx,xxx
Total	$xx,xxx,xxx

Note 1—Basis of presentation

The above schedule has been prepared in conformity with accounting practices prescribed or permitted by the Insurance Department of the State of . . . . . . [*Significant differences between statutory practices and generally accepted accounting principles for the calculation of the above amounts should be described but the monetary effect of any such differences need not be stated.*]

Losses and loss adjustment expenses are provided for when incurred in accordance with the applicable requirements of the insurance laws [*and/or regulations*] of the State of . . . . . . Such provisions include (1) individual case estimates for reported losses, (2) estimates received from other insurers with respect to reinsurance assumed, (3) estimates for unreported losses based on past experience modified for current trends, and (4) estimates of expenses for investigating and settling claims.

Note 2—Reinsurance

The Company reinsures certain portions of its liability insurance coverages to limit the amount of loss on individual claims and purchases catastrophe insurance to protect against aggregate single occurrence losses. Certain portions of property insurance are reinsured on a quota share basis.

The liability for losses and the liability for loss adjustment expense were reduced by $xxx,xxx and $xxx,xxx, respectively, for reinsurance ceded to other companies.

Contingent liability exists with respect to reinsurance which would become an actual liability in the event the reinsuring companies, or any of them, might be unable to meet their obligations to the Company under existing reinsurance agreements.

ILLUSTRATION 15. AUDITOR'S REPORT ON THE FINANCIAL STATEMENTS INCLUDED IN INTERNAL REVENUE SERVICE FORM 990, "RETURN OF ORGANIZATIONS EXEMPT FROM INCOME TAX"

Independent Auditor's Report

We have audited the balance sheet, (Part IV) of Basic Charity as of December 31, 20X1, and the related statement of revenue, expenses, and changes in net assets (Part I) and statement of functional expenses (Part II) for the year then ended included in the accompanying Internal Revenue Service Form 990. These financial statements are the responsibility of Basic Charity's management. Our responsibility is to express an opinion on these financial statements based on our audit.

We conducted our audit in accordance with auditing standards generally accepted in the United States of America. Those standards require that we plan and perform the audit to obtain reasonable assurance about whether the financial statements are free of material misstatement. An audit includes examining, on a test basis, evidence supporting the amounts and disclosures in the financial statements. An audit also includes assessing the accounting principles used and significant estimates made by management, as well as evaluating the overall financial statement presentation. We believe that our audit provides a reasonable basis for our opinion.

As described in Note X, these financial statements were prepared in conformity with accounting practices prescribed by the Internal Revenue Service and the Office of the State of . . . . . ., which is a comprehensive basis of accounting other than generally accepted accounting principles.

In our opinion, the financial statements referred to above present fairly, in all material respects, the assets, liabilities and fund balances of Basic Charity as of December 31, 20X1, and its revenue, expenses, and changes in fund balances for the year then ended on the basis of accounting described in Note X.

Our audit was made for the purpose of forming an opinion on the above financial statements taken as a whole. The accompanying information on pages . . . to . . . is presented for purposes of additional analysis and is not a required part of the above financial statements. Such information, except for that portion marked "unaudited," on which we express no opinion, has been subjected to the auditing procedures applied in the audit of the above financial statements; and, in our opinion, the information is fairly stated in all material respects in relation to the financial statements taken as a whole.

This report is intended solely for the information and use of the board of directors and management of Basic Charity, the Internal Revenue Service, and the Office of the State of . . . . . . and is not intended to be, and should not be, used by anyone other than these specified parties.

[*Signature*]

[*Date*]

Illustration 16. Auditor's Report on Current-Value Financial Statements That Supplement Historical-Cost Financial Statements in a General-Use Presentation of a Real Estate Entity

Independent Auditor's Report

We have audited the accompanying historical-cost balance sheet of Basic Company as of December 31, 20X3 and 20X2, and the related historical-cost statements of income, shareholders' equity, and cash flows for each of the three years in the period ended December 31, 20X3. We have also audited the supplemental current-value balance sheets of Basic Company as of December 31, 20X3 and 20X2, and the related supplemental current value statements of income and shareholders' equity for each of the three years in the period ended December 31, 20X3. These financial statements are the responsibility of the Company's management. Our responsibility is to express an opinion on these financial statements based on our audits.

We conducted our audits in accordance with auditing standards generally accepted in the United States of America. Those standards require that we plan and perform the audit to obtain reasonable assurance about whether the financial statements are free of material misstatement. An audit includes examining, on a test basis, evidence supporting the amounts and disclosures in the financial statements. An audit also includes assessing the accounting principles used and significant estimates made by management, as well as evaluating the overall financial statement presentation. We believe that our audits provide a reasonable basis for our opinion.

In our opinion, the historical-cost financial statements referred to above present fairly, in all material respects, the financial position of Basic Company as of December 31, 20X3 and 20X2, and the results of its operations and its cash flows for each of the three years in the period ended December 31, 20X3, in conformity with accounting principles generally accepted in the United States of America.

As described in Note 1, the supplemental current-value financial statements have been prepared by management to present relevant financial information that is not provided by the historical-cost financial statements and are not intended to be a presentation in conformity with generally accepted accounting principles. In addition, the supplemental current-value financial statements do not purport to present the net realizable, liquidation, or market value of the Company as a whole. Furthermore, amounts ultimately realized by the Company from the disposal of properties may vary significantly from the current values presented.

In our opinion, the supplemental current-value financial statements referred to above present fairly, in all material respects, the information set forth in them on the basis of accounting described in Note 1.

[*Signature*]

[*Date*]

625 REPORTS ON THE APPLICATION OF ACCOUNTING PRINCIPLES

EFFECTIVE DATE AND APPLICABILITY

Original Pronouncement	SAS 50, July 1986; and SAS 97, June 2002.
Effective Date	SAS 50 was effective upon issuance in July 1986. SAS 97 is effective for written reports issued or oral advice provided on or after June 30, 2002, with earlier application of the provisions of SAS 97 permitted.
Applicability	Reports providing advice on the application of accounting principles to specific transactions or providing advice on the type of opinion that may by rendered made as a part of a proposal or otherwise by an accountant other than the entity's continuing accountant. (See below.)

APPLICABILITY

SAS 50 applies to providing **written** advice

1. On the application of accounting principles to specified transactions (completed or proposed) involving facts and circumstances of a specific entity.
2. On the type of opinion that may be rendered on a specific entity's financial statements.

The SAS applies to these situations whether the advice is provided as part of a proposal to obtain a new client or as a separate engagement.

SAS 50 applies to **oral** advice in the following circumstances:

1. The reporting accountant concludes the advice is intended to be used by a principal as an important factor in reaching a decision; and
2. The advice relates to the application of accounting principles to a specific transaction or the type of opinion that may be rendered on a specific entity's financial statements.

SAS 50 does not apply to

1. A **continuing** accountant engaged to report on the financial statements of a specific entity.
2. An engagement to either assist in litigation involving accounting matters or provide expert testimony in litigation (i.e., litigation service engagements).
3. Advice provided to another accountant in public practice.

4. Position papers on accounting principles or the type of opinion that may be rendered, including: newsletters, articles, speeches, lectures, or other public presentations; letters to standard-setting bodies.

However, if position papers are intended to provide guidance on specific transactions or the type of opinion on a **specific** entity's financial statements, the SAS applies.

When facing a hypothetical transaction, a reporting accountant cannot know whether a continuing accountant has reached a different conclusion on applying accounting principles to the same transaction or how the specific entity previously accounted for similar transactions. Therefore, written reports on hypothetical transactions are prohibited.

DEFINITIONS OF TERMS

Specific transactions. Completed or proposed specified transactions of a specific entity.

Hypothetical transactions. Transactions that do not involve facts and circumstances of a specific entity.

Reporting accountant. An accountant other than the continuing accountant, engaged in the practice of public accounting as defined by AICPA Rules of Conduct, who prepares a written report or provides oral advice on the application of accounting principles to specified transactions involving facts and circumstances of a specific entity, or the type of opinion that may be rendered on a specific entity's financial statements.

Continuing accountant. An accountant who has been engaged to report on the financial statements of a specific entity. An accountant engaged to perform services other than reporting on the entity's financial statements is not considered a continuing accountant.

Written report. For the purposes of applying this section, a written report includes any written communication that expresses a conclusion on the appropriate accounting principles to be applied or the type of opinion that may be rendered on an entity's financial statements.

OBJECTIVES OF SECTION

In today's complex financial reporting environment, there is an increasing tendency for entities to consult with CPA firms other than their own auditors on accounting or financial reporting issues. This practice is sometimes called "opinion shopping"—a term that implies that the client will shop around until it finds an auditor who will agree with its position and then hire that auditor. A less pejorative term for the practice is obtaining a "second opinion." The implication of the term "second opinion" is that the motivation of the client arises from lack of clear-cut answers to accounting problems created by the fluid and constantly evolving environment of business today.

The Auditing Standards Board (ASB) issued SAS 50 to address the concerns of financial statement users and regulators about opinion shopping. The ASB concluded that it would be inappropriate to prohibit second opinions because it would stifle the free exchange of ideas within the financial community and would restrict the ability of reporting entities and others to consider alternatives in determining appropriate financial reporting for new or emerging issues. Also, as a practical matter, the AICPA cannot afford to take action that might be viewed by the Federal Trade Commission as restricting competition.

Before providing advice to another CPA's client, a CPA should inform the entity of the need to consult with the other CPA and communicate with that CPA. The objective of this communication is primarily to determine whether the entity and its auditors have disagreed, and if so, whether the disagreement is about facts or about how relevant accounting principles should be applied.

SAS 50 permitted reports on hypothetical transactions, which were reports on the application of accounting principles not involving facts and circumstances of a particular principal. The SEC subsequently expressed concerns about the appropriate use of these reports, and whether such reports were in the best interest of the public. In response to the SEC's concerns, the Auditing Standards Board issued SAS 97, *Amendment to Statement on Auditing Standards No. 50,* ***Reports on the Application of Accounting Principles,*** in June 2002. SAS 97 revised SAS 50 to prohibit written reports on hypothetical transactions.

FUNDAMENTAL REQUIREMENTS

PERFORMANCE STANDARDS

1. According to AU 625.07-.09, the reporting accountant should
   a. Exercise due professional care.
   b. Have adequate technical training and proficiency.
   c. Plan the engagement adequately and supervise the work of assistants, if any.
   d. Accumulate sufficient information to provide a reasonable basis for the professional judgment described in the report.
2. The reporting accountant should consider
   a. The circumstances under which the written report or oral advice is requested.
   b. The purpose of the request.
   c. The intended use of the written report or oral advice.
3. The reporting accountant should perform the following procedures:
   a. Obtain an understanding of the form and substance of the transaction(s).
   b. Review applicable GAAP.
   c. If appropriate, consult with other professionals or experts.
   d. If appropriate, perform research or other procedures to identify credible precedents or analogies.
4. When evaluating accounting principles for a specific transaction or determining the type of opinion that may be rendered on a specific entity's financial statements, the reporting accountant should
   a. Consult with the continuing accountant of the entity to ascertain all the available facts relevant to forming a professional judgment.
   b. Obtain available facts that the continuing accountant may be able to provide that include
      (1) The form and substance of the transaction.
      (2) How management has applied accounting principles to similar transactions.
      (3) Whether management disputes the accounting method the continuing accountant recommends.
      (4) Whether the continuing accountant has reached a different conclusion than the reporting accountant.
   c. In communicating with the continuing accountant, follow the guidance on communications between predecessor and successor auditors (Section 315).

Reporting Standards

According to AU 625.10, a written report should be addressed to the requesting entity (for example, management or the board of directors of the entity) and should ordinarily include the following:

1. A brief description of the engagement.
2. A statement that the engagement was performed in accordance with applicable AICPA standards.
3. Identification of the specific entity and a description or statement concerning the following:
   a. The transactions.
   b. Relevant facts, circumstances, and assumptions.
   c. Sources of information.
4. A conclusion on the appropriate accounting principles (including an identification of the country of origin) to be applied or type of opinion that may be rendered.
5. If appropriate, a description of the reasons for the conclusion.
6. If appropriate, a statement that the responsibility for proper accounting treatment rests with preparers of financial statements who should consult their continuing accountants.
7. A statement that any differences in the facts, circumstances, or assumptions presented might change the report.
8. A separate paragraph at the end of the report that includes
   a. A statement that the report is intended solely for the information and use of the specified parties.
   b. An identification of the parties.
   c. A statement that the report is not intended to be, and should not be, used by nonspecified parties.

INTERPRETATIONS

There are no interpretations for this section.

TECHNIQUES FOR APPLICATION

The following practice problems that might arise are discussed:

1. Engagement acceptance.
2. Applicability to proposals.
3. Responding to intermediaries.
4. Documentation.

Engagement Acceptance

A CPA firm should adopt policies and procedures concerning the acceptance and approval of engagements to furnish an opinion letter on the application of accounting principles or the type of opinion to be rendered on financial statements.

It is important to understand the purpose of the request, the nature of the issue on which advice is requested, and whether there is a disagreement between the client and its continuing accountant. Before SAS 50 was issued, many CPAs would not accept such an engagement if the client would not permit contact with the continuing accountant. However, some firms made a distinction between completed and proposed transactions and did not insist on contact before providing advice on proposed transactions.

The rationale for not insisting on contact for proposed transactions was that future transactions could not affect current financial statements. Interpretation 201-3 of the Code of Professional Ethics, which was in effect at the time, referred to providing advice on matters in connection with the financial statements of another CPA's client. SAS 50 now clearly requires contact with the other CPA in these circumstances because it applies to specific transactions, both completed and proposed.

APPLICABILITY TO PROPOSALS

For many practitioners, the most common situation in which SAS 50 will apply is making a proposal for a new client. Not every proposal will be affected, but the requirements are applicable when a prospective client asks for the proposal to include the proposing firm's position on a specific accounting issue or the type of opinion that may be rendered on its financial statements in specific circumstances.

In all circumstances, before accepting an engagement, the successor auditor needs to communicate with the predecessor (Section 315). However, when SAS 50 applies, the communication should include more specific inquiries explicitly directed to disagreements about the subject on which a position is requested and should take place before the proposal is made rather than merely before acceptance of the audit engagement. In ordinary circumstances, communication does not take place until a predecessor has been terminated, and does not take place during the proposal process (see Section 315). A request to include an opinion on accounting principles or type of audit opinion in a proposal changes the requirements.

Note that SAS 50 focuses on accounting matters and the type of opinion that may be rendered. It does not broadly address auditing matters. This means that a proposal may discuss general matters of audit scope, such as overall approach, locations to be visited, and similar matters without creating a requirement to contact the continuing accountant before making the proposal.

DOCUMENTATION

SAS 50, as amended by SAS 97, does not impose any requirement to document the procedures used or information obtained to provide a basis for the professional judgment described in the report. However, the authors recommend the following documentation:

1. A description of the problem, including all relevant facts and circumstances. (Preferably this should be prepared by the client.)
2. If applicable, a summary of the discussions with the continuing accountant.
3. A description of the procedures followed to determine the accounting practices that would be appropriate in the circumstances, including citations to relevant authoritative literature.

If the engagement is terminated before a report is issued, documentation of the engagement to that point is generally desirable but not essential.

ILLUSTRATION

The following example of a report on the application of accounting principles to a specific transaction is adapted from SAS 97 (AU 625).

ILLUSTRATION 1. REPORT ON THE APPLICATION OF ACCOUNTING PRINCIPLES TO A SPECIFIC TRANSACTION

Introduction

We have been engaged to report on the appropriate application of accounting principles generally accepted in [*country of origin of such principles*] to the specific transaction described below. This report is being issued to Widget Company for assistance in evaluating accounting principles for the described specific transaction. Our engagement has been conducted in accordance with standards established by the American Institute of Certified Public Accountants.

Description of Transaction

The facts, circumstances, and assumptions relevant to the specific transaction as provided to us by the management of Widget Company are as follows:

[*Describe facts, circumstances, and assumptions or refer to attached description.*]

Appropriate Accounting Principles

[*Describe the advice on application of generally accepted accounting principles.*]

Concluding Comments

The ultimate responsibility for the decision on the appropriate application of accounting principles generally accepted in [*country of origin of such principles*] for an actual transaction rests with the preparers of financial statements, who should consult with their continuing accountants. Our judgment on the appropriate application of accounting principles generally accepted in [*country of origin of such principles*] for the described specific transaction is based solely on the facts provided to us as described above; should these facts and circumstances differ, our conclusion might change.

Restricted Use

This report is intended solely for the information and use of the board of directors and management of Widget Company and is not intended to be and should not be used by anyone other than these specified parties.

634 LETTERS FOR UNDERWRITERS AND CERTAIN OTHER REQUESTING PARTIES

EFFECTIVE DATE AND APPLICABILITY

Original Pronouncements	SAS 72, February 1993; SAS 76, September 1995; SAS 86, March 1998.
Effective Date	Comfort letters (see *Definitions of Terms*) issued on or after June 30, 1993, unless subsequently amended.
Applicability	Engagements to issue comfort letters for underwriters and certain other requesting parties in connection with financial statements and financial statement schedules contained in registration statements filed with the Securities and Exchange Commission (SEC) under the Securities Act of 1933 (the Act) and certain other securities offerings. (See *Applicability* section for additional discussion.)

APPLICABILITY

In addition to issuing a comfort letter to an underwriter, accountants may also issue a comfort letter to a broker-dealer or other financial intermediary, acting as principal or agent in an offering or a placement of securities in connection with the following types of securities offerings:

1. Foreign offerings, including Regulation S, Eurodollar, and other offshore offerings.
2. Transactions exempt from the registration requirements of Section 5 of the Act, including those pursuant to Regulation A, Regulation D, and Rule 144A.
3. Securities offerings issued or backed by governmental, municipal, banking, tax-exempt, or other entities that are exempt from registration under the Act.

In those offerings, the accountant may issue a comfort letter only if the party provides a representation letter that represents that the party's review process is substantially consistent with the review process under the 1933 Act.

An accountant may also issue a comfort letter in connection with acquisition transactions in which there is an exchange of stock and comfort letters that are requested by the buyer or seller, or both, as long as a representation letter is provided that represents that the party's review process is substantially consistent with the review process under the 1933 Act.

A comfort letter may also be addressed to parties with a statutory due diligence defense under Section 11 of the Act, other than a named underwriter, when a law firm or attorney for the requesting party issues a written opinion to the accountants that states that the party has a due diligence defense under Section 11 of the Act. If the requesting party cannot provide a law firm's or attorney's written opinion to the accountant, the requesting party should provide a representation letter.

When one of the parties identified in the preceding paragraphs (other than an underwriter or other party with due diligence responsibilities) requests a comfort letter, but does not provide a representation letter, a special type of letter is permissible. (See Illustration 17.)

DEFINITIONS OF TERMS

Comfort letter. A letter issued by accountants to underwriters, or to other parties with a statutory due diligence defense under Section 11 of the Act, in connection with financial statements and financial statement schedules included (incorporated by reference) in registration statements filed with the SEC under the Act. Comfort letters are not required under the Act, and copies are not filed with the SEC. It is, however, a common condition of an underwriting agreement in connection with the offering for sale of securities registered with the SEC under the Act that the accountants are to furnish a comfort letter. Subjects covered in a comfort letter usually are limited to those specified in the underwriting agreement. Subjects that may be addressed in a comfort letter include

1. The independence of the accountants.
2. Compliance in form, in all material respects, of the audited financial statements and financial statement schedules included (incorporated by reference) in the registration statement with applicable accounting requirements of the Act and the related rules and regulation adopted by the SEC.
3. Unaudited financial statements, condensed interim financial information, capsule financial information, pro forma financial information, financial forecasts, management's discussion and analysis (MD&A), and changes in selected financial statement items during a period subsequent to the date and period of the latest financial statements included (incorporated by reference) in the registration statement.
4. Tables, statistics, and other financial information included (incorporated by reference) in the registration statement.
5. Negative assurance about whether certain nonfinancial statement information included (incorporated by reference) in the registration statement complies as to form in all material respects with Regulation S-K.

Underwriter. Any person who has purchased from an issuer with a view to, or offers or sells for an issuer in connection with, the distribution of any security, or participates or has a direct or indirect participation in any such undertaking or participates or has a participation in the direct or indirect underwriting of any such undertaking. An underwriter does not include a person whose interest is limited to a commission from an underwriter or dealer not in excess of the usual and customary distributors' or sellers' commission (Section 2 of the Act).

Capsule financial information. Unaudited summarized interim information for periods subsequent to the periods covered by audited financial statements or unaudited condensed interim financial information. Capsule financial information (either in narrative or tabular form) often is provided for the most recent interim period and for the corresponding period of the prior year. It usually includes income statement items, often limited to sales and total and per share amounts for extraordinary items and net income.

Change period. The period that ends on the cutoff date (specified in the underwriting agreement) and which usually begins for balance sheet items immediately after the date of the latest balance sheet in the registration statement. For income statement items, the period usually begins immediately after the latest period for which those items are presented in the registration statement.

Closing date. The date on which the issuer or selling security holder delivers the securities to the underwriter in exchange for the proceeds of the offering.

Cutoff date. A date specified in the underwriting agreement to which certain procedures described in the comfort letter are to relate (for example, a date five days before the date of the letter).

Effective date. The date on which the registration statement becomes effective. It is the date when the issuer's or selling security holder's securities may first be sold to the public.

Filing date. The date on which the registration statement is first filed with the SEC.

Negative assurance. A statement by accountants that, as a result of performing specified procedures, nothing came to their attention that caused them to believe that specified matters do not meet a specified standard (for example, that nothing came to their attention that caused them to believe that any material modifications should be made to the unaudited financial statements or unaudited condensed financial statements for them to be in conformity with generally accepted accounting principles).

Shelf registration statement. A registration statement in which the issuer registers a designated amount of securities for continuous or delayed offerings during an extended period. Ordinarily, the issuer does not have to prepare and file a new prospectus and registration statement for each sale.

Underwriting agreement. An agreement between issuers of securities or selling stockholders and the underwriter specifying terms and conditions of the offering and sale of securities. It usually contains provisions that affect the accountant including the provision that the accountant is to furnish a comfort letter.

OBJECTIVES OF SECTION

SAS 72 superseded SAS 49, *Letters for Underwriters*. It provides guidance to accountants for performing and reporting on the results of engagements to issue comfort letters for underwriters and certain other requesting parties. Those engagements are in connection with financial statements and financial statement schedules contained in registration statements filed with the SEC under the Act and certain other securities offerings.

SAS 72 addresses various matters, such as the following:

1. Whether it is proper for independent accountants, acting in their professional capacity, to comment in a comfort letter on specific matters, and, if so, the form the comment should take.
2. Practical suggestions on which form of comfort letter is suitable in a given circumstance, procedural matters, the dating of letters, and what steps may be taken when information that may require special mention in a letter comes to the accountant's attention.
3. Suggestions of ways of reducing or avoiding the uncertainties regarding the nature and extent of accountants' responsibilities in connection with a comfort letter.

Providing comfort letters to underwriters is a service of accountants that developed after enactment of the Securities Act of 1933. Section 11 of the Act provides that underwriters, among others, could be liable if any part of a registration statement contains material omissions or misstatements. The Act also provides for an affirmative defense for underwriters if they can demonstrate that, after a reasonable investigation (called "due diligence"), the underwriter has reasonable grounds to believe that there were no material omissions or misstatements. In requesting a comfort letter, an underwriter is generally seeking assistance in performing a reasonable investigation of financial and accounting data in the registration statement that is not "expertized" (i.e., covered by a report of independent accountants, who consent to be named as experts, based on an audit in accordance with generally accepted auditing standards) as a defense against possible claims under Section 11 of the Act.

Ordinarily, underwriting agreements require comfort letters from the issuer's accountant to the underwriter. Comfort letters pertain primarily to financial data and information that have not been audited ("expertized"). What constitutes a reasonable investigation of unaudited data and information sufficient to satisfy the underwriter is not authoritatively established. Consequently, only the underwriter can determine what is sufficient for his or her purposes concerning procedures to be applied by the accountant.

The assistance the accountant can provide to the underwriter by way of the comfort letter is subject to limitations. Procedures short of an audit, such as those contemplated in a comfort letter, provide an accountant with a basis for expressing, at the most, negative assurance. Also, an accountant can properly comment only on matters to which the accountant's professional expertise is substantially relevant.

FUNDAMENTAL REQUIREMENTS: GENERAL

REPRESENTATION LETTER

According to AU 634.06, if the party requesting the comfort letter is a party other than a named underwriter with a due diligence defense under Section 11 of the Act, but is one of the types of parties described in the *Applicability* section, the accountant should obtain a representation letter that includes the following elements:

1. The letter should be addressed to the accountants.
2. The letter should contain the following:

   This review process, applied to the information relating to the issuer is (will be) substantially consistent with the due diligence review process that we would perform if this placement of securities (or issuance of securities in an acquisition transaction) were being registered pursuant to the Securities Act of 1933 (the Act). We are knowledgeable with respect to the due diligence review process that would be performed if this placement of securities were being registered pursuant to the Act.

3. The letter should be signed by the requesting party.

When the accountants receive the representation letter, they should refer in the comfort letter to the requesting party's representations (see Illustration 16 and Illustration 17 when requesting party has not provided the required representation letter).

REPORTS TO OTHER PARTIES

When a party other than those described in the *Applicability* section requests a report, the accountant should not provide a comfort letter or the letter in Illustration 17. Instead, the accountant should provide a report on agreed-upon procedures. (See Section 2201.)

COMMUNICATIONS WITH UNDERWRITER

The accountant should suggest to the underwriter that they meet with the client to discuss the procedures to be followed in connection with the comfort letter (procedures followed are described in the comfort letter; see Illustration 1). The underwriter should also provide the accountant with a draft of the underwriting agreement so that the accountant can indicate whether he or she will be able to furnish a letter in acceptable form.

DRAFT COMFORT LETTER

It is desirable for accountants to prepare a draft of the form of the comfort letter they expect to furnish as soon as they receive the draft of the underwriting agreement. The draft comfort letter should

1. Deal, as completely as possible, with all matters to be covered in the final comfort letter.
2. Use exactly the same terms as those to be used in the final comfort letter, with the understanding that the comments in the final letter cannot be determined until the underlying procedures have been performed.
3. Be identified as a draft.
4. Not contain statements or implications that the accountant is carrying out such procedures as he or she considers necessary.

The following (from AU 634.16) is a suggested form of the legend that may be placed on the draft comfort letter for identification and explanation of its purposes and limitations:

> This draft is furnished solely for the purpose of indicating the form of letter that we would expect to be able to furnish [*name of underwriter*] in response to their request, the matters to be covered in the letter, and the nature of the procedures that we would expect to carry out with respect to such matters. Based on our discussions with [*name of underwriter*], it is our understanding that the procedures outlined in this draft letter are those they wish us to follow.* Unless [*name of underwriter*] informs us otherwise, we shall assume that there are no additional procedures they wish us to follow The text of the letter itself will depend, of course, on the results of the procedures, which we would not expect to complete until shortly before the letter is given and in no event before the cutoff date indicated therein.

* If the accountant has not met with the underwriter, this sentence should be as follows:

> In the absence of any discussions with [*name of underwriter*] we have set out in this draft letter those procedures referred to in the draft underwriting agreement (of which we have been furnished a copy) that we are willing to follow.

PRINCIPAL ACCOUNTANT

If more than one accountant is involved in the audit of the financial statements and the reports of those accountants appear in the registration statement, the principal accountant (the accountant reporting on the consolidated financial statements) should read the comfort letters of the other accountants who are reporting on significant components of the consolidated group. According to AU 634.18, the principal accountant should state in his or her comfort letter that (see Illustration 10)

1. Reading comfort letters of the other accountants was one of the procedures followed.
2. The procedures performed by the principal accountant (other than reading the letters of the other accountants) related solely to companies audited by the principal accountant and to the consolidated financial statements.

SHELF REGISTRATION

If the registrant has not chosen an underwriter by the effective date of a shelf registration statement, the accountant should not agree to furnish a comfort letter addressed to the client, legal counsel designated to represent the underwriting group, or a nonspecific addressee. The accountant may, however, agree to provide the client or legal counsel for the underwriting group with a draft comfort letter that describes the procedures performed by the accountant and the comments the accountant is willing to express based on those procedures. The following (from AU 634.19) is a suggested form of the legend that should be placed on the draft comfort letter to describe the letter's purpose and limitations:

> This draft describes the procedures that we have performed and represents a letter we would be prepared to sign as of the effective date of the registration statement if the managing underwriter had been chosen at that date and requested such a letter. Based on our discussions with [*name of client or legal counsel*], the procedures set forth are similar to those that experience indicates underwriters often request in such circumstances. The text of the final letter will depend, of course, on whether the managing underwriter who is selected requests that other procedures be performed to meet his or her needs and whether the managing underwriter requests that any of the procedures be updated to the date of issuance of the signed letter.

A signed comfort letter may be issued to the underwriter selected for the portion of the issue then being offered when the underwriting agreement for an offering is signed and on each closing date.

Issuance of Letters or Reports under Other Standards

When issuing a comfort letter, the accountant may not issue any additional letters or reports under any other statements (SASs, SSAEs, or SSARSs) to the underwriter or other requesting parties in connection with the offering or placement of securities in which the accountant comments on items for which commenting is otherwise precluded by this section.

FUNDAMENTAL REQUIREMENTS: FORMAT AND CONTENTS OF COMFORT LETTERS

Dating of Comfort Letter

The following apply to the date of the comfort letter:

1. The letter normally is dated on or shortly before the effective date. (In rare instances, requests have been made to date letters on or shortly before the filing date.)
2. Cutoff date. The letter should state that the inquiries and other procedures described in the letter did not extend from the cutoff date (specified in the underwriting agreement) to the date of the letter.
3. Subsequent letters.
    a. A subsequent letter may be dated on or before the closing date.
    b. The specified procedures and inquiries noted in the comfort letter should be completed as of the cutoff date for each letter.
    c. Comments contained in an earlier letter may be incorporated by reference in a subsequent letter (see Illustration 3); but a subsequent letter should address only information in the most recently amended registration statement.

Addressee

The following apply to determining the addressee of the comfort letter:

1. The letter should be addressed to the client and the intermediary (usually the underwriter) who negotiated the agreement with the client and with whom the accountants discussed the scope and sufficiency of the letter. (An example of an appropriate form of address is, "X Corporation and John Doe and Company, as Representative of Several Underwriters.")
2. The letter should not be addressed or given to any parties other than the client and the named underwriters, broker-dealer, financial intermediary, or buyer or seller.

3. A comfort letter for other accountants should be addressed in accordance with 1. above, and copies should be given to the principal accountant and his or her client.

INTRODUCTORY PARAGRAPH

The following apply to the introductory paragraph of the comfort letter:

1. It is good practice to include an introductory paragraph similar to the following (from AU 634.26):

   > We have audited the [*identify the financial statements and financial statement schedules*] included (incorporated by reference) in the registration statement (No. 33-00000) on Form ____ filed by the company under the Securities Act of 1933 (the Act); our reports with respect thereto are also included (incorporated by reference) in that registration statement. The registration statement, as amended as of ____________, is herein referred to as the registration statement.

2. If the audit report on the financial statements included in the registration statement is not the standard report, for instance, if an explanatory paragraph has been added (see Illustration 9).
   a. Accountants should refer to that fact and discuss the content of the paragraph in the comfort letter.
   b. The accountants need not refer to or discuss explanatory paragraphs addressing the consistent application of accounting principles.
   c. If the SEC accepts a qualified opinion on historical financial statements, the accountants should refer to the qualification and discuss the subject matter in the comfort letter's opening paragraph.
3. The accountant should not repeat his or her opinion on the audited financial statements.
4. Negative assurance. Accountants should not give negative assurance concerning their audit report on the financial statements, nor should they give negative assurance concerning financial statements and financial statement schedules audited and reported on in the registration statement by other accountants.
5. Other reports issued by the accountants. The accountants may refer to their reports on
   a. Condensed financial statements that are derived from audited financial statements (see Section 552).
   b. Selected financial data (see Section 552).
   c. Interim financial information (see Section 722).
   d. Pro forma financial information (see Section 2401).
   e. A financial forecast (see Section 2301).
   f. Management's discussion and analysis (see Section 2701).

If the above reports are not included (incorporated by reference) in the registration statement, they may be attached to the comfort letter. According to AU 634.29, the accountant should not repeat the report in the comfort letter or otherwise imply that he or she is reporting as of the date of the comfort letter or that he or she assumes responsibility for the sufficiency of the procedures for the underwriter's purposes.

6. The accountant should not
   a. Attach to the comfort letter or refer to any restricted-use report except for a review report on MD&A.
   b. Mention reports on internal control related matters (Section 325).

c. Mention restricted use reports on internal control (Section 2501).
d. Comment on unaudited interim financial information required by item 302(a) of Regulation S-K to which Section 722 applies, or required supplementary information to which Section 558 applies unless the underwriter asks the accountant to perform procedures in addition to those required be Section 722 and 558. The accountant may then perform additional procedures and report the findings.

INDEPENDENCE

The following apply to statements on independence:

1. If, as is customary, the underwriting agreement in connection with a SEC filing requires a statement from the accountant concerning independence, the following wording from AU 634.31 is appropriate:

   We are independent certified public accountants with respect to the XYZ Company, within the meaning of the Act and the applicable rules and regulations thereunder adopted by the SEC.

2. For a non-SEC filing, the following wording from AU 634.31 is appropriate:

   We are independent certified public accountants with respect to XYZ Company, under Rule 101 of the AICPA's Code of Professional Conduct and its interpretations and rulings.

3. Accountants for previously nonaffiliated companies recently acquired by the registrant would make a statement similar to the following (from AU 634.32):

   As of [*date of the accountant's most recent report on the financial statements of his or her client*] and during the period covered by the financial statements on which we reported, we were independent certified public accountants with respect to [*name of client*] within the meaning of the Act and the applicable rules and regulations thereunder adopted by the SEC.

COMPLIANCE AS TO FORM WITH SEC REQUIREMENTS

The following apply to compliance with SEC requirements.

1. If the accountant is asked to express an opinion on whether the financial statements covered by his or her report comply as to form with pertinent accounting requirements adopted by the SEC, the following wording from AU 634.33 is appropriate:

   In our opinion [*include the phrase "except as disclosed in the registration statement," if applicable*], the [*identify the financial statements and financial statement schedules*] audited by us and included (incorporated by reference) in the registration statement comply as to form in all material respects with the applicable accounting requirements of the Act and the related rules and regulations adopted by the SEC.

2. Material departures from pertinent rules and regulations adopted by the SEC should be disclosed in the comfort letter (see Illustration 11).
3. The accountant may provide positive assurance on compliance as to form with requirements under rules and regulations adopted by the SEC only with respect to those rules and regulations applicable to the form and content of financial statements and financial statement schedules that they have audited. When the financial statements or financial statement schedules have not been audited, the accountant may only provide negative assurance on compliance as to form.

FUNDAMENTAL REQUIREMENTS: COMMENTING IN A COMFORT LETTER ON INFORMATION OTHER THAN AUDITED FINANCIAL STATEMENTS

General

The following apply to (1) unaudited condensed interim financial information, (2) capsule financial information, (3) pro forma financial information, (4) financial forecasts, and (5) changes in capital stock, increases in long-term debt, and decreases in other specified financial statement items.

1. Agreed-upon procedures performed by the accountant should be stated in the comfort letter. If, however, the accountants have been requested to provide negative assurance on interim financial information or capsule financial information, the procedures involved in a Section 722 review need not be specified. The accountant should not make any statements or imply that he or she has applied procedures determined to be necessary or sufficient for the underwriter's purposes.
2. If the underwriter requests that the accountant apply procedures in addition to those specified in Section 722, the accountant may perform those procedures and should describe them in the comfort letter. The criteria specified by the underwriter should be included in the descriptions of procedures in the comfort letter.
3. The accountant should not use terms such as **general review, limited review, reconcile, check,** or **test** to describe the work done unless the procedures required by those terms are described in the comfort letter.
4. The accountant should not make a general statement that, as a result of carrying out procedures specified in the underwriting agreement and draft comfort letter, nothing else came to his or her attention that would be of interest to the underwriter.

Knowledge of Internal Control

If the accountant has not obtained knowledge of a client's internal control over financial reporting as it relates to the preparation of both annual and interim financial information, he or she should not comment in the comfort letter on (1) unaudited condensed interim financial information, (2) capsule financial information, (3) a financial forecast when historical financial statements provide a basis for one or more significant assumptions for the forecast, or (4) changes in capital stock, increases in long-term debt, and decreases in selected financial statement items.

Unaudited Condensed Interim Financial Information

The following apply to unaudited condensed interim financial information:

1. Accountants may comment in the form of negative assurance on this type of financial information only when they have conducted a review of the interim financial information in accordance with Section 722.
2. The comfort letter may state that the accountants have conducted review procedures in accordance with Section 722. If the letter states that the accountants issued a review report, the report should be attached unless the review report is included in the registration statement.
3. If the accountants have not conducted a review in accordance with Section 722, they may not comment in the form of negative assurance. In those circumstances, the accountants are limited to reporting procedures performed and findings obtained (see Illustration 15). The comfort letter should identify any unaudited condensed

interim financial information and should state that the information has not been audited in accordance with generally accepted auditing standards and, therefore, no opinion is expressed concerning that information.

Capsule Financial Information

The following apply to capsule financial information:

1. Accountants may give negative assurance as to conformity with generally accepted accounting principles and may refer to whether the dollar amounts were determined on a basis substantially consistent with that of the corresponding amounts in the audited financial statements if (1) the capsule financial information meets the minimum disclosure requirements of Accounting Principles Board Opinion (APB) 28, *Interim Financial Reporting* (para 30), and (2) the accountants have reviewed the interim financial statements underlying the capsule financial information in accordance with Section 722.
2. If a review in accordance with Section 722 (SAS 71) was performed, the accountants may give negative assurance as to whether the dollar amounts were determined on a basis substantially consistent with that of the corresponding amounts in the audited financial statements, even if the capsule financial information is more limited than the minimum disclosure required by paragraph 30 of APB Opinion 28 (see Illustration 12).
3. If a review has not been performed, the accountants are limited to reporting procedures performed and findings obtained.

Pro Forma Financial Information

The following apply to pro forma financial information:

1. Accountants should not comment on this type of information unless they have appropriate knowledge of the accounting and reporting practices of the entity.
2. Accountants should not give negative assurance on the application of pro forma adjustments to historical amounts, the compilation of pro forma financial information, or whether the pro forma financial information complies as to form in all material respects with the applicable requirements of Rule 11-02 of Regulation S-X unless they have (1) obtained the required knowledge described in 1. and (2) performed an audit of the annual financial statements or a review of interim financial statements of the entity to which the adjustments were applied.
3. For a business combination, the historical financial statements of each part of the combined entity on which the pro forma financial information is based should be audited or reviewed (see Illustration 4).
4. If the accountants have the required knowledge of internal control described above in "Knowledge of Internal Control," but have not met the requirements for giving negative assurance, they are limited to reporting procedures performed and findings obtained (see Illustration 15). In those circumstances, the accountants should comply with the guidance on reporting the results of agreed-upon procedures (see Section 2201).

Financial Forecasts

The following apply to financial forecasts:

1. To perform agreed-upon procedures on a financial forecast and comment on it, accountants should obtain the knowledge described in "Knowledge of Internal Con-

trol" above and then perform the procedures prescribed in Section 2301 for reporting on the compilation of a forecast.

2. The accountant's report on the forecast should be attached to the comfort letter.
3. If the forecast is included in the registration statement, the forecast should be accompanied by an indication that the accountants have not examined the forecast and, therefore, do not express an opinion on it.
4. Accountants may perform additional procedures on the forecast and report their findings in the comfort letter (see Illustrations 5 and 15).
5. Accountants may not provide negative assurance on the results of procedures performed. They may also not provide negative assurance with respect to compliance of the forecast with Rule 11-03 of Regulation S-X unless they have performed an examination of the forecast in accordance with Section 2301.

SUBSEQUENT CHANGES

Comments on subsequent changes usually address

1. Whether there have been any change in capital stock, increase in long-term debt, or decreases in other specified financial statement items during the change period (see *Definitions of Terms*).
2. Issues such as subsequent changes in the amounts of net current assets or stockholders' equity, net sales, total and per share amounts of income before extraordinary items, and net income.

Accountants generally will be asked to read minutes and make inquiries of company officials concerning the change period. The accountants should, therefore, base their comments solely on those limited procedures, and clearly state this in the comfort letter. (see Illustration 1, paragraph 6).

The following apply to other aspects of subsequent changes:

1. Accountants may provide negative assurance on subsequent changes in specific financial statement items up to 135 days from the end of the most recent audit or review period (see Illustration 1, paragraphs 5b and 6, and Illustration 13).
2. For periods 135 days or greater, accountants may not provide negative assurance but may only report procedures performed and findings obtained (see Illustration 15).
3. Changes in an accounting principle during the change period should be stated in the comfort letter.
4. Comments on subsequent changes are limited to those increases or decreases not disclosed in the registration statement.
5. The date and the period used to determine if subsequent changes occurred should be specified in both the draft and final comfort letters.

TABLES, STATISTICS, AND OTHER FINANCIAL INFORMATION

The following apply to tables, statistics, and other financial information:

1. Accountants may comment only on the following:
   a. Information expressed in dollars, or percentages derived from those dollars, obtained from accounting records that are subject to the entity's internal control.
   b. Information derived directly from the accounting records by analysis or computation.

   c. Quantitative information obtained from an accounting record if the information is subject to the same controls as the dollar amounts.

2. Accountants should not comment on matters such as the following, unless they are subjected to internal control over financial reporting (which is not ordinarily the case):

   a. Square footage of facilities.
   b. Number of employees, except as related to a specific payroll period.
   c. Backlog information.

In addition to the above, accountants should not comment on

   d. Any matter or information subject to legal interpretation.
   e. Segment information or the appropriateness of allocations made to derive segment information included in financial statements.
   f. Tables, statistics, and other financial information relating to an unaudited period unless they have

      (1) Audited the client's financial statements for a period including or immediately prior to the unaudited period or have completed an audit for a later period.
      (2) Otherwise obtained knowledge of the client's internal control over financial reporting.

3. Procedures followed by the accountants with respect to this information should be described in both the draft and the final comfort letter. The letter should also contain a statement that the accountants are not furnishing any assurances with respect to the sufficiency of the procedures for the underwriter's intended purpose (see Illustration 7).
4. Regulation S-K requires the inclusion of certain financial information in registration statements. Accountants may comment and provide negative assurance about whether this information is in conformity with the disclosure requirements of Regulation S-K if the following conditions are met:

   a. The information is derived from the accounting records subject to the entity's internal control over financial reporting or has been derived directly from the accounting records by analysis or computation.
   b. The information is capable of evaluation against reasonable criteria established by the SEC.

   Regulation S-K disclosure requirements that meet those conditions are

   a. Item 301, "Selected Financial Data."
   b. Item 302, "Supplementary Financial Information."
   c. Item 402, "Executive Compensation."
   d. Item 503(d), "Ratio of Earnings to Fixed Charges."

   Accountants should not comment in a comfort letter on compliance as to form of MD&A with SEC rules and regulations, but may examine or review MD&A in an attestation engagement (see Illustration 18 and Section 2701).

5. Specific information commented on should be identified by referring to specific captions, tables, page numbers, paragraphs, or sentences. Descriptions of the procedures followed and the findings obtained may be stated individually for each item of specific information commented on.

6. Comments concerning tables, statistics, and other financial information included in the registration statement should include
   a. A description of the procedures followed.
   b. The findings, ordinarily expressed in terms of agreement between items compared.
   c. Statements with respect to the acceptability of methods of allocation used in deriving the figures commented on.
      (1) Whether comments on allocation may be made depends on the extent to which they are made in, or can be derived directly by analysis or computation from, the client's accounting records.
      (2) Comments, if made, should make clear that the allocations are to a substantial extent arbitrary, that the allocation method used is not the only acceptable one, and that other acceptable methods of allocation might produce significantly different results (see Illustrations 6, 7, and 8).

FUNDAMENTAL REQUIREMENTS: OTHER MATTERS

CONCLUDING PARAGRAPH

It is desirable that the comfort letter conclude with a paragraph such as the following wording from AU 634.31:

> This letter is solely for the information of the addressees and to assist the underwriters in conducting and documenting their investigation of the affairs of the company in connection with the offering of the securities covered by the registration statement, and it is not to be used, circulated, quoted, or otherwise referred to within or without the underwriting group for any other purpose, including, but not limited to, the registration, purchase, or sale of securities, nor is it to be filed with or referred to in whole or in part in the registration statement or any other document, except that reference may be made to it in the underwriting agreement or in any list of closing documents pertaining to the offering of the securities covered by the registration statement.

DISCLOSURE OF SUBSEQUENTLY DISCOVERED MATTERS

Accountants may discover matters that should be included in the final comfort letter but that were not mentioned in the draft comfort letter. If these matters are not to be disclosed in the registration statement, the accountant should let the client know that they will be mentioned in the final comfort letter. Also, the accountant should suggest that the underwriter be informed immediately. It is advisable for the accountant to be present when these matters are discussed between the client and the underwriter.

INTERPRETATIONS

LETTERS TO DIRECTORS RELATING TO ANNUAL REPORTS ON FORM 10-K (ISSUED APRIL 1981, MODIFIED MAY 1981, REVISED JUNE 1993)

Annual reports to the SEC on Form 10-K must be signed by at least a majority of the board of directors. The directors might seek assistance from the registrant's independent accountants. The accountant can report to the directors in accordance with the following guidelines:

- The auditor can express an opinion on whether the financial statements and schedules comply as to form with the accounting requirements of the 1934 Act.
- The auditor may affirm that GAAS require the auditor to read the information in addition to financial statements in the Form 10-K (see Section 550).

- The auditor may apply procedures requested by directors to tables, statistics, and other financial information. The guidance in Section 634 on comfort letters provides appropriate guidance in this area.
- The auditor may comment on whether information in Form 10-K is in conformity with disclosure requirements of Regulation S-K. The guidance in Section 634 provides appropriate general guidance in this area.
- The auditor may reaffirm independence in a manner similar to the guidance in Section 634.
- The auditor should clearly indicate to the directors that the auditor cannot make any representations as to whether any procedures performed at the request of the directors are sufficient for the directors' purposes.

COMMENTING IN A COMFORT LETTER ON QUANTITATIVE DISCLOSURES ABOUT MARKET RISK MADE IN ACCORDANCE WITH ITEM 305 OF REGULATION S-K (AUGUST 1998)

Regulation S-K, Item 305, *Quantitative and Qualitative Disclosures About Market Risk*, requires certain qualitative (descriptive) and quantitative disclosures with respect to the following, which are collectively referred to as "market-risk-sensitive instruments:"

1. Derivative financial instruments, generally as defined in SFAS 119, *Disclosure About Derivative Financial Instruments and Fair Value of Financial Instruments.*
2. Other financial instruments, generally as defined in SFAS 107.
3. Derivative commodity instruments, such as commodity futures, forwards, and swaps that are permitted by contract or custom to be settled in cash.

These required disclosures

- Generally include a combination of historical and fair value data and the hypothetical effects on such data of assumed changes in interest rates, foreign currency exchange rates, commodity prices, and other relevant market rates.
- Should be disclosed outside the financial statements and related notes thereto.

Assurance

An accountant may not provide either positive or negative assurance on conformity with Item 305 of Regulation S-K. Positive assurance is prohibited since Section 634 states that accountants may not give positive assurance on conformity of information with the disclosure requirements of Regulation S-K since this information is not in the form of financial statements and generally has not been audited by the accountants. Negative assurance is also not allowed since much of the information provided by the registrant is not derived from accounting records subject to the entity's controls over financial reporting.

Comments on Qualitative Disclosures

Accountants may not comment in a comfort letter on the registrant's Item 305 qualitative disclosures since such information is not

- Expressed in dollars or percentages obtained from dollar amounts.
- Obtained from accounting records subject to the entity's controls over financial reporting.
- Derived from such accounting records by analysis or computation.

Comments on Quantitative Disclosures

Item 305 requires quantitative disclosures that may be presented in the form of tabular presentation, sensitivity analysis, or value-at-risk disclosures. An accountant's ability to comment on such quantitative disclosures is largely dependent upon the degree to which the forward-looking information used to prepare these disclosures is linked to accounting records that are subject to the entity's controls over financial reporting. This link to the accounting records will vary with the three forms of presentation.

Tabular presentation. The tabular presentation includes the fair values of market-risk-sensitive instruments and contract terms to determine the future cash flows from these instruments that are categorized by expected maturity dates. This approach may require the use of yield curves and implied forward rates to determine expected maturity dates, as well as assumptions regarding prepayments and weighted-average interest rates.

The tabular presentation contains fewer assumptions and less complex mathematical calculations than the sensitivity analysis or value-at-risk disclosures. In addition, certain information, such as contractual terms in a tabular presentation, are derived from the accounting records. Therefore, the accountant may perform limited procedures related to tabular presentations to the extent that such information is derived from the accounting records.

When performing procedures related to tabular presentation disclosures, the accountant should

- Consider whether the entity's documentation of its contractual positions in derivatives, commodities, and other financial instruments is subject to the controls over financial reporting.
- Consider whether such documentation provides a complete record of the entity's market-risk-sensitive instruments.

The accountant also should disclaim as to the reasonableness of the assumptions underlying the disclosures.

Sensitivity analysis. This term describes a general class of models that are designed to assess the risk of loss in market-risk-sensitive instruments, based on hypothetical changes in market rates or prices. Sensitivity analysis does not refer to one specific model and may include duration analysis or other "sensitivity" mea-sures. The disclosures are dependent upon assumptions about theoretical future market conditions, and therefore, are not derived from the accounting records. Therefore, accountants should not agree to make any comments or perform any procedures related to these disclosures.

Value at risk. This term describes a general class of models that provide a probabilistic assessment of the risk of loss in market-risk-sensitive instruments over a selected period of time, with a selected likelihood of occurrences based upon selected confidence intervals. Value at risk disclosures are extremely aggregated and, in addition to the assumptions made for sensitivity analyses, may include additional assumptions regarding correlation between asset classes and future market volatilities.

As a result, these disclosures are not derived from the accounting records. Therefore, the accountant should not agree to make any comments or perform any procedures related to these disclosures.

Market Risk Category Disclosures

Item 305 requires registrants to stratify financial instruments according to market risk category (i.e., interest rate risk, foreign exchange risk, and equity price risk). If the instrument is at risk in more than one category, the instrument should be included in the disclosures for each applicable category. In reporting findings from agreed-upon procedures relating to market risk categories, the accountant should not provide any findings that the company's stratifications are complete or comply as to form with Item 305 requirements and should disclaim with respect to the company's determination of market risk categories.

Item 305 encourages registrants to provide quantitative and qualitative information about market risk in terms of, among other things, the magnitude of actual past market movements and estimates of possible near-term market movements. Accountants should not agree to perform any procedures related to such market data.

Understanding with the Underwriter/Need for Specialist

The accountant should establish a clear understanding with the underwriter as to the limitations of the procedures to be performed with respect to market risk disclosures. Accountants should also consider the need to utilize a specialist in performing procedures related to these disclosures.

TECHNIQUES FOR APPLICATION

Accountants, in comfort letters, describe procedures applied and findings obtained by applying those procedures. Negative assurances may be provided in certain circumstances. The procedures applied are described in the comfort letters. Examples of comfort letters are presented in the following section (*Illustrations*).

ILLUSTRATIONS

The following illustrations of comfort letters are reprinted from SAS 72, SAS 86, and SSAE 8.

1. Typical comfort letter.
2. Letter when a short-form registration statement is filed incorporating previously filed forms 10-K and 10-Q by reference.
3. Letter reaffirming comments in Illustration 1 (typical comfort letter) as of a later date.
4. Comments on pro forma financial information.
5. Comments on a financial forecast.
6. Comments on tables, statistics, and other financial information—complete description of procedures and findings.
7. Comments on tables, statistics, and other financial information—summarized description of procedures and findings regarding tables, statistics, and other financial information.
8. Comments on tables, statistics, and other financial information: description of procedures and findings, regarding tables, statistics, and other financial information—attached registration statement (or selected pages) identifies with designated symbols items to which procedures were applied.
9. Alternate wording when accountants' report on audited financial statements contains an explanatory paragraph.
10. Alternate wording when more than one accountant is involved.
11. Alternate wording when the SEC has agreed to a departure from its published accounting requirements.
12. Alternate wording when recent earnings data are presented in capsule form.
13. Alternate wording when accountants are aware of a decrease in a specified financial statement item.
14. Alternate wording of the letter for companies that are permitted to present interim earnings for a twelve-month period.

15. Alternate wording when the procedures that the underwriter has requested the accountant to perform on interim financial information are less than an SAS 71[1] review.
16. A typical comfort letter in a non-1933 Act offering, including the required underwriter representations.
17. Letter to a requesting party that has not provided the normally required representation letter.
18. Comfort letter that includes reference to examination of annual MD&A and review of interim MD&A.

Shelf registration statements may have several closing dates and different underwriters. Descriptions of procedures and findings regarding interim financial statements, tables, statistics, or other financial information that is incorporated by reference from previous 1934 Act filings may have to be repeated in several comfort letters. To avoid restating these descriptions in each comfort letter, accountants may initially issue the comments in a format (such as an appendix) that can be referred to in, and attached to, subsequently issued comfort letters.

Illustration 1. Typical Comfort Letter

A typical comfort letter includes

1. A statement regarding the independence of the accountants.
2. An opinion regarding whether the audited financial statements and financial statement schedules included (incorporated by reference) in the registration statement comply as to form in all material respects with the applicable accounting requirements of the Act and related rules and regulations adopted by the SEC.
3. Negative assurance on whether
    a. The unaudited condensed interim financial information included (incorporated by reference) in the registration statement complies as to form in all material respects with the applicable accounting requirements of the Act and the related rules and regulations adopted by the SEC.
    b. Any material modifications should be made to the unaudited condensed consolidated financial statements included (incorporated by reference) in the registration statement for them to be in conformity with generally accepted accounting principles.
4. Negative assurance on whether, during a specified period following the date of the latest financial statements in the registration statement and prospectus, there has been any change in capital stock, increase in long-term debt or any decrease in other specified financial statement items.

Illustration 1 is a letter covering all these items. Letters that cover some of the items may be developed by omitting inapplicable portions of Illustration 1.

Illustration 1 assumes the following circumstances.[2] The prospectus (part I of the registration statement) includes audited consolidated balance sheets as of December 31, 20X5 and 20X4, and audited consolidated statements of income, retained earnings (stockholders' equity), and cash flows for each of the three years in the period ended December 31, 20X5. Part I also includes an unaudited condensed balance sheet as of March 31, 20X6, and unaudited condensed consolidated statements of income, retained earnings (stockholders' equity) and cash flows for the three-month periods ended March 31, 20X6 and 20X5, reviewed in accordance with Section 722 but not previously reported on by the accountants. Part II of the registration statement includes audited consolidated financial statement

---

[1] *SAS 100,* ***Interim Financial Information,*** *supersedes SAS 71 for interim periods within fiscal years beginning after December 15, 2002.*

[2] *The example includes financial statements required by SEC regulations to be included in the filing. If additional financial information is covered by the comfort letter, appropriate modifications should be made.*

schedules for the three years ended December 31, 20X5. The cutoff date is June 23, 20X6, and the letter is dated June 28, 20X6. The effective date is June 28, 20X6.

Each of the comments in the letter is in response to a requirement of the underwriting agreement. For purposes of Illustration 1, the income statement items of the current interim period are to be compared with those of the corresponding period of the preceding year.

June 28, 20X6

[*Addressee*]

Dear Sirs:

We have audited the consolidated balance sheets of The Basic Company, Inc. (the company) and subsidiaries as of December 31, 20X5 and 20X4, and the consolidated statements of income, retained earnings (stockholders' equity), and cash flows for each of the three years in the period ended December 31, 20X5, and the related financial statements schedules all included in the registration statement (No. 33-00000) on Form S-1 filed by the company under the Securities Act of 1933 (the Act); our reports with respect thereto are also included in that registration statement. The registration statement, as amended on June 28, 20X6, is herein referred to as the registration statement.[3]

In connection with the registration statement

1. We are independent certified public accountants with respect to the company within the meaning of the Act and the applicable rules and regulations thereunder adopted by the SEC.
2. In our opinion [*include the phrase "except as disclosed in the registration statement," if applicable*], the consolidated financial statements and financial statement schedules audited by us and included in the registration statement comply as to form in all material respects with the applicable accounting requirements of the Act and the related rules and regulations adopted by the SEC.
3. We have not audited any financial statements of the company as of any date or for any period subsequent to December 31, 20X5; although we have conducted an audit for the year ended December 31, 20X5, the purpose (and therefore the scope) of the audit was to enable us to express our opinion on the consolidated financial statements as of December 31, 20X5, and for the year then ended, but not on the financial statements for any interim period within that year. Therefore, we are unable to and do not express any opinion on the unaudited condensed consolidated balance sheet as of March 31, 20X6, and the unaudited condensed consolidated statements of income, retained earnings (stockholders' equity), and cash flows for the three-month periods ended March 31, 20X6 and 20X5, included in the registration statement, or on the financial position, results of operations, or cash flows as of any date or for any period subsequent to December 31, 20X5.
4. For purposes of this letter we have read the 20X6 minutes of meetings of the stockholders, the board of directors, and [*include other appropriate committees, if any*] of the company and its subsidiaries as set forth in the minutes books at June 23, 20X6, officials of the company having advised us that the minutes of all such meetings[4] through the date were set forth herein; we have carried out other procedures from June 23, 20X6, as follows (our work did not extend to the period from June 24, 20X6, to June 28, 20X6, inclusive):
   a. With respect to the three-month periods ended March 31, 20X6 and 20X5, we have
      (1) Performed the procedures specified by the American Institute of Certified Public Accountants for a review of interim financial information as described in SAS 71[5], *Interim Financial Information*, on the unaudited condensed consolidated balance sheet

---

[3] *The example assumes that the accountants have not previously reported on the interim financial information. If the accountants have previously reported on the interim financial information, they may refer to that fact in the introductory paragraph of the comfort letter as follows:*

> *Also, we have reviewed the unaudited condensed consolidated financial statements as of March 31, 20X6 and 20X5, and for the three-month periods then ended, as indicated in our report dated May 15, 20X6, which is included (incorporated by reference) in the registration statement.*

The report may be attached to the comfort letter. The accountants may agree to comment in the comfort letter on whether the interim financial information complies as to form in all material respects with the applicable accounting requirements of the published rules and regulations of the SEC.

[4] *The accountants should discuss with the secretary those meetings for which minutes have not been approved. The letter should be modified to identify specifically the unapproved minutes of meetings that the accountants have discussed with the secretary.*

[5] *See footnote 1.*

as of March 31, 20X6, and unaudited condensed consolidated statements of income, retained earnings (stockholders' equity), and cash flows for the three-month periods ended March 31, 20X6 and 20X5, included in the registration statement.

(2) Inquired of certain officials of the company who have responsibility to financial and accounting matters whether the unaudited condensed consolidated financial statements referred to in a(1) comply as to form in all material respects with the applicable accounting requirements of the Act and the related rules and regulations adopted by the SEC.

b. With respect to the period from April 1, 20X6, to May 31, 20X6, we have

(1) Read the unaudited consolidated financial statements[6] of the company and subsidiaries for April and May of both 20X5 and 20X6 furnished us by the company, officials of the company having advised us that no such financial statements as of any date or for any period subsequent to May 31, 20X6, were available.

(2) Inquired of certain officials of the company who have responsibility for financial and accounting matters whether the unaudited consolidated financial statements referred to in b(1) are stated on a basis substantially consistent with that of the audited consolidated financial statements included in the registration statement.

The foregoing procedures do not constitute an audit conducted in accordance with generally accepted auditing standards. Also, they would not necessarily reveal matters of significance with respect to the comments in the following paragraph. Accordingly, we make no representations regarding the sufficiency of the foregoing procedures for your purposes.

5. Nothing came to our attention as a result of the foregoing procedures, however, that caused us[7] to believe that

a. (1) Any material modifications should be made to the unaudited condensed consolidated financial statements described in 4a(1), included in the registration statement, for them to be in conformity with generally accepted accounting principles.[8]

(2) The unaudited condensed and consolidated financial statements described in 4a(1) do not comply as to form in all material respects with the applicable accounting requirements of the Act and the related rules and regulations adopted by the SEC.

b. (1) At May 31, 20X6, there was any change in the capital stock, increase in long-term debt, or decrease in consolidated net current assets or stockholders' equity of the consolidated companies as compared with amounts shown in the March 31, 20X6 unaudited condensed consolidated balance sheet included in the registration statement, or (2) for the period from April 1, 20X6, to May 31, 20X6, there were any decreases, as compared to the corresponding period in the preceding year, in consolidated net sales or in the total or per share amounts of income before extraordinary items or of net income, except in all instances of changes, increases, or decreases that the registration statement discloses have occurred or may occur.

6. As mentioned in 4b, company officials have advised us that no consolidated financial statements as of any date or for any period subsequent to May 31, 20X6, are available; accordingly, the procedures carried out by us with respect to changes in financial statement items after May 31, 20X6, have, of necessity, been even more limited than those with respect to the periods referred to in 4. We have inquired of certain officials of the company who have responsibility for financial and accounting matters whether (1) at June 23, 20X6, there was any change in the capital stock, increase in long-term debt, or any decreases in consolidated net current assets or stockholders' equity of the consolidated companies as compared with amounts shown on the March 31, 20X6 unaudited condensed balance sheet included in the registration statement or (2) for the period from April 1, 20X6, to June 23, 20X6, there were any decreases, as compared with the corresponding period in the preceding year, in consolidated net sales or in the total or per share amounts of in-

---

[6] *If the interim financial information is incomplete, a sentence similar to the following should be added:*

"The financial information for April and May is incomplete in that it omits the statements of cash flows and other disclosures."

[7] *If there has been a change in accounting principle during the interim period, a reference to that change should be included herein.*

[8] *Section 722 does not require the accountants to modify the report on a review of interim financial information for a lack of consistency in the application of accounting principles provided that the interim financial information appropriately discloses such matters.*

come before extraordinary items or of net income. On the basis of these inquiries and our reading of the minutes as described in 4., nothing came to our attention that caused us to believe that there was any such change, increase, or decrease, except in all instances for changes, increases, or decreases that the registration statement discloses have occurred or may occur.

7. This letter is solely for the information of the addressees and to assist the underwriters in conducting and documenting their investigation of the affairs of the company in connection with the offering of the securities covered by the registration statements, and it is not to be used, circulated, quoted, or otherwise referred to within or without the underwriting group for any purpose, including but not limited to the registration, purchase, or sale of securities, nor is it to be filed with or referred to in whole or in part in the registration statement or any other document, except that reference may be made to it in the underwriting agreement or in any list of closing documents pertaining to the offering of the securities covered by the registration statement.

Illustration 2. Letter When a Short-Form Registration Statement Is Filed Incorporating Previously Filed Forms 10-K and 10-Q by Reference

Illustration 2. is applicable when a registrant uses a short-form registration statement (Form S-2 or S-3) which, by reference, incorporates previously filed Forms 10-K and 10-Q. It assumes that the short-form registration statement and prospectus include the Form 10-K for the year ended December 31, 20X5, and Form 10-Q for the quarter ended March 31, 20X6, which have been incorporated by reference. In addition to the information presented below, the letter would also contain paragraphs 6 and 7 of the typical letter in Illustration 1. A Form S-2 registration statement will often both incorporate and include the registrant's financial statements. In such situations, the language in the following illustration should be appropriately modified to refer to such information as being both incorporated and included.

June 28, 20X6

[*Addressee*]

Dear Sirs:

We have audited the consolidated balance sheets of The Basic Company, Inc. (the company) and subsidiaries as of December 31, 20X5 and 20X4, and the consolidated statements of income, retained earnings (stockholders' equity), and cash flows for each of the three years in the period ended December 31, 20X5, and the related financial statement schedules, all included (incorporated by reference) in the company's annual report on Form 10-K for the year ended December 31, 20X5, and incorporated by reference in the registration statement (No. 33-00000) on Form S-3 filed by the company under the Securities Act of 1933 (the Act); our report with respect thereto is also incorporated by reference in that registration statement. The registration statement as amended on June 28, 20X6, is herein referred to as the registration statement.

In connection with the registration statement

1. We are independent certified public accountants with respect to the company within the meaning of the Act and the applicable rules and regulations thereunder adopted by the SEC.
2. In our opinion, the consolidated financial statements and financial statement schedules audited by us and incorporated by reference in the registration statement comply as to form in all material respects with the applicable accounting requirements of the Act and the Securities Exchange Act of 1934 and the related rules and regulations adopted by the SEC.
3. We have not audited any financial statements of the company as of any date or for any period subsequent to December 31, 20X5; although we have conducted an audit for the year ended December 31, 20X5, the purpose (and therefore the scope) of the audit was to enable us to express our opinion on the consolidated financial statements as of December 31, 20X5, and for the year then ended, but not on the consolidated financial statements for any interim period within that year. Therefore, we are unable to and do not express any opinion on the unaudited condensed consolidated balance sheet as of March 31, 20X6, and the unaudited condensed consolidated statements of income, retained earnings (stockholders' equity), and cash flows for the three-month periods ended March 31, 20X6 and 20X5, included in the company's quarterly report on Form 10-Q for the quarter ended March 31, 20X6, incorporated by reference in the registration statement, or on the financial position, results of operations, or cash flows as of any date or for any period subsequent to December 31, 20X5.
4. For purposes of this letter, we have read the 20X6 minutes of meetings of the stockholders, the board of directors, and [*include other appropriate committees, if any*] of the company and its sub-

sidiaries as set forth in the minutes books at June 23, 20X6, officials of the company having advised us that the minutes of all such meetings[9] through the date were set forth herein; we have carried out other procedures from June 23, 20X6, as follows (our work did not extend to the period from June 24, 20X6, to June 28, 20X6, inclusive):

a. With respect to the three-month periods ended March 31, 20X6 and 20X5, we have

(1) Performed the procedures specified by the American Institute of Certified Public Accountants for a review of interim financial information as described in SAS 71,[10] *Interim Financial Information*, on the unaudited condensed consolidated financial statements for these periods, described in 3., included in the company's quarterly report on Form 10-Q for the quarter ended March 31, 20X6, incorporated by reference in the registration statement.

(2) Inquired of certain officials of the company who have responsibility for financial and accounting matters whether the unaudited condensed consolidated financial statements referred to in a(1) comply as to form in all material respects with the applicable accounting requirements of the Securities Exchange Act of 1934 as it applied to Form 10-Q and the related rules and regulations adopted by the SEC.

b. With respect to the period from April 1, 20X6, to May 31, 20X6, we have

(1) Read the unaudited consolidated financial statements[11] of the company and subsidiaries for April and May of both 20X5 and 20X6 furnished us by the company, officials of the company having advised us that no such financial statements as of any date or for any period subsequent to May 31, 20X6, were available.

(2) Inquired of certain officials of the company who have responsibility for financial and accounting matters whether the unaudited consolidated financial statements referred to in b(1) are stated on a basis substantially consistent with that of the audited consolidated financial statements incorporated by reference in the registration statement.

The foregoing procedures do not constitute an audit conducted in accordance with generally accepted auditing standards. Also, they would not necessarily reveal matters of significance with respect to the comments in the following paragraph. Accordingly, we make no representations about the sufficiency of the foregoing procedures for your purposes.

5. Nothing came to our attention as a result of the foregoing procedures, however, that caused us to believe that

a. (1) Any material modifications should be made to the unaudited condensed consolidated financial statements described in 3., incorporated by reference in the registration statement, for them to be in conformity with generally accepted accounting principles.

(2) The unaudited condensed and consolidated financial statements described in 3. do not comply as to form in all material respects with the applicable accounting requirements of the Securities Exchange Act of 1934 as it applies to Form 10-Q and the related rules and regulations adopted by the SEC.

b. (1) At May 31, 20X6, there was any change in the capital stock, increase in long-term debt, or decrease in consolidated net current assets or stockholders' equity of the consolidated companies as compared with amounts shown in the March 31, 20X6, unaudited condensed consolidated balance sheet incorporated by reference in the registration statement, or

(2) For the period from April 1, 20X6, to May 31, 20X6, there were any decreases, as compared with the corresponding period in the preceding year, in consolidated net sales or in the total or per share amounts of income before extraordinary items or of net income, except in all instances of changes, increases, or decreases that the registration statement discloses have occurred or may occur.

---

9 *See footnote 3.*

10 *See footnote 1.*

11 *See footnote 4.*

ILLUSTRATION 3. LETTER REAFFIRMING COMMENTS IN ILLUSTRATION 1 AS OF A LATER DATE

If more than one comfort letter is requested, the later letter may, in appropriate situations, refer to information appearing in the earlier letter without repeating such information. Illustration 3 reaffirms and updates the information in Illustration 1.

July 25, 20X6

[*Addressee*]

Dear Sirs:

We refer to our letter of June 28, 20X6, relating to the registration statement (No. 33-00000) of The Basic Company, Inc. (the company). We reaffirm as of the date hereof (and as though made on the date hereof) all statements made in that letter except that, for the purposes of this letter

1. The registration statement to which this letter relates is as amended on July 13, 20X6 [*effective date*].
2. The reading of minutes described in paragraph 4 of that letter has been carried out through July 20, 20X6 [*the new cutoff date*].
3. The procedures and inquiries covered in paragraph 4 of that letter were carried out to July 20, 20X6 [*the new cutoff date*] (our work did not extend to the period from July 21, 20X6 to July 25, 20X6 [*date of letter*], inclusive).
4. The period covered in paragraph 4b of that letter is changed to the period from April 1, 20X6, to June 30, 20X6, officials of the company having advised us that no such financial statements as of any date or for any period subsequent to June 30, 20X6, were available.
5. The references to May 31, 20X6, in paragraph 5b of that letter are changed to June 30, 20X6.
6. The references to May 31, 20X6, and June 23, 20X6, in paragraph 6 of that letter are changed to June 30, 20X6, and July 20, 20X6, respectively.

This letter is solely for the information of the addressees and to assist the underwriters in conducting and documenting their investigation of the affairs of the company in connection with the offering of the securities covered by the registration statement, and it is not to be used, circulated, quoted, or otherwise referred to within the underwriting group for any other purpose, including but not limited to the registration, purchase, or sale of securities, nor is it to be filed with or referred to in whole or in part in the registration statements or any other document, except that reference may be made to it in the underwriting agreement or any list of closing documents pertaining to the offering of the securities covered by the registration statement.

ILLUSTRATION 4. COMMENTS ON PRO FORMA FINANCIAL INFORMATION

Illustration 4 is applicable when the accountants are asked to comment on (1) whether the pro forma financial information included in a registration statement complies as to form in all material respects with the applicable accounting requirements of Rule 11-02 of Regulation S-X, and (2) the application of pro forma adjustments to historical amounts in the compilation of the pro forma financial information. The material in this illustration is intended to be inserted between paragraphs 6 and 7 in Illustration 1. The accountants have audited the December 31, 20X5 financial statements and have conducted an SAS 71[12] [Section 722] review of the March 31, 20X6 interim financial information of the acquiring company. Other accountants conducted a review of the March 31, 20X6 interim financial information of XYZ Company, the company being acquired. The illustration assumes that the accountants have not previously reported on the pro forma financial information. If the accountants did previously report on the pro forma financial information, they may refer in the introductory paragraph of the comfort letter to the fact that they have issued a report, and the report may be attached to the comfort letter. In that circumstance, therefore, the procedures in 7b(1) and 7c ordinarily would not be performed, and the accountants should not separately comment on the application of pro forma adjustments to historical financial information, since that assurance is encompassed in the accountants' report on pro forma financial information. The accountants may, however, agree to comment on compliance as to form with the applicable accounting requirements of Rule 11-02 of Regulation S-X.

---

[12] *See footnote 1.*

7. At your request we have
   a. Read the unaudited pro forma condensed consolidated balance sheet as of March 31, 20X6, and the unaudited pro forma condensed consolidated statements of income for the year ended December 31, 20X5, and the three-month period ended March 31, 20X6, included in the registration statement.
   b. Inquired of certain officials of the company and of XYZ Company (the company being acquired) who have responsibility for financial and accounting matters about
      (1) The basis for their determination of the pro forma adjustments, and
      (2) Whether the unaudited pro forma condensed consolidated financial statements referred to in 7a comply as to form in all material respects with the applicable accounting requirements of Rule 11-02 of Regulation S-X.
   c. Proved the arithmetic accuracy of the application of the pro forma adjustments to the historical amounts in the unaudited pro forma condensed consolidated financial statements.

   The foregoing procedures are substantially less in scope than an examination, the objective of which is the expression of an opinion on management's assumptions, the pro forma adjustments, and the application of those adjustments to historical financial information. Accordingly, we do not express such an opinion. The foregoing procedures would not necessarily reveal matters of significance with respect to the comments in the following paragraph. Accordingly, we make no representation about the sufficiency of such procedures for your purposes.
8. Nothing came to our attention as a result of the procedures specified in paragraph 7, however, that caused us to believe that the unaudited pro forma condensed consolidated financial statements referred to in 7a included in the registration statement do not comply as to form in all material respects with the applicable accounting requirement of Rule 11-02 of Regulation S-X and that the pro forma adjustments have not been properly applied to the historical amounts in the compilation of those statements. Had we performed additional procedures or had we made an examination of the pro forma condensed consolidated financial statements, other matters might have come to our attention that would have been reported to you.

Illustration 5. Comments on a Financial Forecast

Illustration 5 is applicable when accountants are asked to comment on a financial forecast. The material in this illustration is intended to be inserted between paragraphs 6 and 7 in Illustration 1. The illustration assumes that the accountants have previously reported on the compilation of the financial forecast and that the report is attached to the letter (see Illustration 15).

7. At your request, we performed the following procedure with respect to the forecasted consolidated balance sheet and consolidated statements of income and cash flows as of December 31, 20X6, and for the year then ending. With respect to forecasted rental income, we compared the occupancy statistics about expected demand for rental of the housing units to statistics for existing comparable properties and found them to be the same.
8. Because the procedure described above does not constitute an examination of prospective financial statements in accordance with standards established by the American Institute of Certified Public Accountants, we do not express an opinion on whether the prospective financial statements are presented in conformity with AICPA presentation guidelines or on whether the underlying assumptions provide a reasonable basis for the presentation. Had we performed additional procedures or had we made an examination of the forecast in accordance with standards established by the American Institute of Certified Public Accountants, matters might have come to our attention that would have been reported to you. Furthermore, there will usually be differences between the forecasted and actual results, because events and circumstances frequently do not occur as expected, and those differences may be material.

Illustration 6. Comments on Tables, Statistics, and Other Financial Information—Complete Description of Procedures and Findings

Illustration 6 is applicable when the accountants are asked to comment on tables, statistics, or other compilations of information appearing in a registration statement. Each of the comments is in response to a specific request. The paragraphs in Illustration 6 are intended to follow paragraph 6 in Illustration 1.

7. For purposes of this letter, we have also read the following, set forth in the registration statement on the indicated pages.[13]

Item	Page	Description
a	4	**Capitalization.** The amounts under the captions, "Amount Outstanding As of June 15, 20X6," and, "As Adjusted." The related notes, except the following in Note 2: "See 'Transactions With Interested Persons.' From the proceeds of this offering the company intends to prepay $900,000 on these notes, pro rata. See 'Use of Proceeds.'"
b	13	**History and Business—Sales and Marketing.** The table following the first paragraph.
c	22	**Executive Compensation—20X5 Compensation**.
d	33	**Selected Financial Data**.[14]

8. Our audit of the consolidated financial statements for the periods referred to in the introductory paragraph of this letter comprised audit tests and procedures deemed necessary for the purpose of expressing an opinion on such financial statements taken as a whole. For none of the periods referred to therein, or any other period, did we perform audit tests for the purpose of expressing an opinion on individual balances of accounts or summaries of selected transactions such as those enumerated above, and accordingly, we express no opinion thereon.
9. However, for purposes of this letter we have performed the following additional procedures, which were applied as indicated with respect to the items enumerated above.

Item in 7	Procedures and findings
a	We compared the amounts and numbers of shares listed under the caption "Amount Outstanding As of June 15, 20X6," with the balances in the appropriate accounts in the company's general ledger at May 31, 20X6 (the latest date for which postings had been made), and found them to be in agreement. We were informed by company officials who have responsibility for financial and accounting matters that there had been no changes in such amounts and numbers of shares between May 31, 20X6, and June 15, 20X6. We compared the amounts and numbers of shares listed under the caption "Amount Outstanding As of June 15, 20X6," adjusted for the issuance of the debentures to be offered by means of the registration statement and for the proposed use of a portion of the proceeds thereof to prepay portions of certain notes, as described under "Use of Proceeds," with the amounts and numbers of shares shown under the caption, "As Adjusted," and found such amounts and numbers of shares to be in agreement. (However, we make no comments regarding the reasonableness of the "Use of Proceeds," or whether such use will actually take place.) We compared the description of the securities and the information (except certain information in Note 2, referred to in 7) included in the notes to the table with the corresponding descriptions and information in the company's consolidated financial statements, including the notes thereto included in the registration statement, and found such descriptions and information to be in agreement.
b	We compared the amounts of military sales, commercial sales, and total sales shown in the registration statement with the balances in

---

13 *In some cases it may be considered desirable to combine in one paragraph the substance of paragraphs 7 and 9. This may be done by expanding the identification of items in paragraph 9 to provide the identification information contained in paragraph 7. In such cases, the introductory sentences in paragraphs 7 and 9 and the text of paragraph 8 might be combined as follows: "For purposes of this letter, we have also read the following information and have performed the additional procedures stated below with respect to such information. Our audit of the consolidated financial statements . . ."*

14 *In some cases the company or the underwriter may request that the independent accountants report on "selected financial data" as described in Section 552, "Reporting on Condensed Financial Statements and Selected Financial Data." When the accountants report on this data and the report is included in the registration statement, separate comments should not be included in the comfort letter.*

the appropriate accounts in the company's accounting records for the respective fiscal years and for the unaudited interim periods and found them to be in agreement. We proved the arithmetic accuracy of the percentages of such amounts of military sales and commercial sales to total sales for the respective fiscal years and for the unaudited interim periods. We compared such computed percentages with the corresponding percentages appearing in the registration statement and found them to be in agreement.

c We compared the dollar amounts of compensation (salary, bonus, and other compensation) for each individual listed in the table Annual Compensation, with the corresponding amounts shown by the individual employee earnings records for the year 20X5 and found them to be in agreement. We compared the dollar amount of aggregate executive officers' cash compensation on page twenty-two with the corresponding amount shown in an analysis prepared by the company and found the amounts to be in agreement. We traced every item over $10,000 on the analysis to the individual employee records for 20X5. We compared the dollar amounts shown under the heading of "Long-Term Compensation" on page twenty-four for each listed individual and the aggregate amounts for executive officers with corresponding amounts shown in an analysis prepared by the company and found such amounts to be in agreement.

We compared the executive compensation information with the requirements of item 402 of Regulation S-K. We also inquired of certain officials of the company who have responsibility for financial and accounting matters whether the executive compensation information conforms in all material respects with the disclosure requirements of item 402 of Regulation S-K. Nothing came to our attention as a result of the foregoing procedures that caused us to believe that this information does not conform in all material respects with the disclosure requirements of item 402 Regulation S-K.

d We compared the amounts of net sales, income from continuing operations, income from continuing operations per common share, and cash dividends declared per common share for the years ended December 31, 20X5, 20X4, and 20X3, with the respective amounts in the consolidated financial statements on pages 27 and 28 and the amounts for the years ended December 31, 20X2, and 20X1, with the respective amounts in the consolidated financial statements included in the company's annual reports to stockholders for 20X2 and 20X1 and found them to be in agreement.

We compared the amounts of total assets, long-term obligations, and redeemable preferred stock at December 31, 20X5 and 20X4, with the respective amounts in the consolidated financial statements on pages 27 and 28 and the amounts at December 31, 20X3, 20X2, and 20X1, with the corresponding amounts in the consolidated financial statements included in the company's annual reports to stockholders for 20X3, 20X2, and 20X1 and found them to be in agreement.

We compared the information under the heading, "Selected Financial Data" with the requirements of item 301 of Regulation S-K. We also inquired of certain officials of the company who have responsibility for financial and accounting matters whether this information conforms in all material respects with the disclosure requirements of item 301 of Regulation S-K. Nothing came to our attention as a result of the foregoing procedures that caused us to believe that this information does not conform in all material respects with the disclosure requirements of item 301 of Regulation S-K.

10. It should be understood that we make no representations regarding questions of legal interpretation or regarding the sufficiency for your purposes of the procedures enumerated in the preceding paragraph; also such procedures would not necessarily reveal any material misstatement of the amounts or percentages listed above. Further, we have addressed ourselves solely to the forego-

ing data as set forth in the registration statement and make no representations regarding the adequacy of disclosure or regarding whether any material facts have been omitted.

11. This letter is solely for the information of the addressees and to assist the underwriters in conducting and documenting their investigation of the affairs of the company in connection with the offering of the securities covered by the registration statement, and it is not to be used, circulated, quoted, or otherwise referred to within or without the underwriting group for any other purpose, including but not limited to the registration, purchase, or sale of securities, nor is it to be filed with or referred to in whole or in part in the registration statement or any other document, except that reference may be made to it in the underwriting agreement or in any list of closing documents pertaining to the offering of the securities covered by the registration statement.

ILLUSTRATION 7. COMMENTS ON TABLES, STATISTICS, AND OTHER FINANCIAL INFORMATION—SUMMARIZED DESCRIPTION OF PROCEDURES AND FINDINGS REGARDING TABLES, STATISTICS, AND OTHER FINANCIAL INFORMATION

Illustration 7 illustrates, in paragraph 9a, a method of summarizing the description of procedures and findings regarding tables, statistics, and other financial information in order to avoid repetition in the comfort letter. The summarization of the descriptions is permitted. Each of the comments is in response to a specific request. The paragraphs in Illustration 7 are intended to follow paragraph 6 in Illustration 1.[15]

7. For purposes of this letter, we have also read the following, set forth in the registration statement on the indicated pages.

Item	Page	Description
a	4	**Capitalization.** The amounts under the captions, "Amount Outstanding As of June 15, 20X6," and, "As Adjusted." The related notes, except the following in Note 2: " See 'Transactions With Interested Persons.' From the proceeds of this offering the company intends to prepay $900,000 on these notes, pro rata. See 'Use of Proceeds.'"
b	13	**History and Business—Sales and Marketing.** The table following the first paragraph.
c	22	**Executive Compensation—20X5 Compensation.**
d	33	**Selected Financial Data.**[16]

8. Our audit of the consolidated financial statements for the periods referred to in the introductory paragraph of this letter comprised audit tests and procedures deemed necessary for the purpose of expressing an opinion on such financial statements taken as a whole. For none of the periods referred to therein, or any other period, did we perform audit tests for the purpose of expressing an opinion on individual balances of accounts or summaries of selected transactions such as those enumerated above, and, accordingly, we express no opinion thereon.

9. However, for purposes of this letter and with respect to the items enumerated in 7 above

   a Except for item 7a, we have (1) compared the dollar amounts either with the amounts in the audited consolidated financial statements described in the introductory paragraph of this letter or, for prior years, included in the company's annual report to stockholders for the years 20X1, 20X2, and 20X3, or with amounts in the unaudited consolidated financial statements described in paragraph 3 to the extent such amounts are included in or can be derived from such statements and found them to be in agreement; (2) compared the amounts of military sales, commercial sales, and total sales and the dollar amounts of compensation for each listed individual with amounts in the company's accounting records and found them to be in agreement; (3) compared other dollar amounts with amounts shown in analyses prepared by the company and found them to be in agreement; and (4) proved the arithmetic accuracy of the percentages based on the data in the above-mentioned financial statements, accounting records, and analyses.

   We compared the information in items 7c and 7d with the disclosure requirements of Regulation S-K. We also inquired of certain officials of the company who have responsi-

---

15 *Other methods of summarizing the descriptions may also be appropriately used. For example, the letter may present a matrix listing the financial information and common procedures employed and indicating the procedures applied to specific items.*

16 *See footnote 10.*

bility for financial and accounting matters whether this information conforms in all material respects with the disclosure requirements of Regulation S-K. Nothing came to our attention as a result of the foregoing procedures that caused us to believe that this information does not conform in all material respects with the disclosure requirements of items 402 and 301, respectively, of Regulation S-K.

b With respect to item 7a, we compared the amounts and numbers of shares listed under the caption "Amount Outstanding As of June 15, 20X6," with the balances in the appropriate accounts in the company's general ledger at May 31, 20X6 (the latest date for which postings had been made), and found them to be in agreement. We were informed by officials of the company who have responsibility for financial and accounting matters that there had been no changes in such amounts and numbers of shares between May 31, 20X6, and June 15, 20X6. We compared the amounts and numbers listed under the caption "Amount Outstanding As of June 15, 20X6," adjusted for the issuance of the debentures to be offered by means of the registration statement and for the proposed use of a portion of the proceeds thereof to prepay portions of certain notes, as described under "Use of Proceeds," with the amounts and numbers of shares shown under the caption, "As Adjusted," and found such amounts and numbers of shares to be in agreement. (However, we make no comments regarding the reasonableness of "Use of Proceeds," or whether such use will actually take place.) We compared the description of the securities and the information (except certain information in Note 2, referred to in 7) included in the notes to the table with the corresponding descriptions and information in the company's consolidated financial statements, including the notes thereto, included in the registration statement and found such descriptions and information to be in agreement.

10. It should be understood that we make no representation regarding questions of legal interpretation or regarding the sufficiency for your purposes of the procedures enumerated in the preceding paragraph; also, such procedures would not necessarily reveal any material misstatement of the amounts or percentages listed above. Further, we have addressed ourselves solely to the foregoing data as set forth in the registration statement and make no representations regarding the adequacy of disclosure or regarding whether any material facts have been omitted.

11. This letter is solely for the information of the addressees and to assist the underwriters in conducting and documenting their investigation of the affairs of the company in connection with the offering of the securities covered by the registration statement, and it is not to be used, circulated, quoted, or otherwise referred to within or without the underwriting group for any other purpose, including but not limited to the registration, purchase, or sale of securities, nor is it to be filed with or referred to in whole or in part in the registration statement or any other document, except that reference may be made to it in the underwriting agreement or in any list of closing documents pertaining to the offering of the securities covered by the registration statement.

Illustration 8. Comments on Tables, Statistics, and Other Financial Information: Descriptions of Procedures and Findings Regarding Tables, Statistics, and Other Financial Information—Attached Registration Statement (or Selected Pages) Identifies with Designated Symbols Items to Which Procedures Were Applied

This illustration illustrates an alternate format which could facilitate reporting when the accountant is requested to perform procedures on numerous statistics included in a registration statement. Each of the comments is in response to a specific request. The paragraph in Illustration 8 is intended to follow paragraph 6 in Illustration 1.

7. For purposes of this letter, we have also read the items identified by you on the attached copy of the registration statement (prospectus), and have performed the following procedures, which were applied as indicated with respect to the symbols explained below.

 Compared the amount with the XYZ (Predecessor Company) financial statements for the period indicated and found them to be in agreement.

 Compared the amount with the XYZ (Predecessor Company) financial statements for the period indicated contained in the registration statement and found them to be in agreement.

 Compared the amount with ABC Company's financial statements for the period indicated contained in the registration statement and found them to be in agreement.

 Compared with a schedule or report prepared by the Company and found them to be in agreement.

The letter would also contain paragraphs 8, 10, and 11 of the letter in Illustration 6. [*The following is an extract from a registration statement that illustrates how an accountant can document procedures performed on numerous statistics included in the registration statement.*]

The following summary is qualified in its entirety by the financial statements and detailed information appearing elsewhere in this Prospectus.

The Company

ABC Company (the Company) designs, constructs, sells, and finances single-family homes for the entry-level and move-up homebuyer. The Company and its predecessor have built and delivered more single-family homes in the metropolitan area than any other homebuilder for each of the last five years. The Company delivered 1,000 ✓ homes in the year ending December 31, 20X5, and at December 31, 20X5, had 500 homes [17] under contract with an aggregate sales price of approximately $45,000,000. The Company's wholly owned mortgage banking subsidiary, which commenced operations in March 20X5, currently originates a substantial portion of the mortgages for homes sold by the Company.

The Company typically does not engage in land development without related home-building operations and limits speculative building. The Company purchases only that land which it is prepared to begin developing immediately for home production. A substantial portion of the Company's homes are under contract for sale before construction commences.

The DEF area has been among the top five markets in the country in housing starts for each of the last five years, with more than 90,000 single-family starts during that period. During the same period, the DEF metropolitan area has experienced increases in population, personal income, and employment at rates above the national average. The Company is a major competitive factor in three of the seven market areas, and is expanding significantly in a fourth area.

The Offering

Common Stock Offered by the Company................	750,000 Ⓦ shares of Common Stock—$.01 par value (the Common Stock)*
Common Stock to Be Outstanding	3,250,000 Ⓦ shares*
Use of Proceeds	To repay indebtedness incurred for the acquisition of the Company.
Proposed NASDAQ Symbol	ABC

**Assumes no exercise of the Underwriters' overallotment option. See Underwriting.*

Summary Financial Information
(*In thousands, except per share data*)

	XYZ (Predecessor Company) Year Ended December 31,				*ABC Company Year Ended December 31,*
Income Statement Data	*20X1*	*20X2*	*20X3*	*20X4*	*20X5*
Revenue from home sales	$106,603⊘	$88,977⊘	$140,110✗	$115,837✗	$131,032✓
Gross profit from sales	15,980⊘	21,138⊘	23,774✗	17,099✗	22,407✓
Income from home building net of tax	490⊘	3,473⊘	7,029✗	1,000✗	3,425✓
Earnings per share	--	--	--	--	$1.37✓

Illustration 9. Alternate Wording When Accountants' Report on Audited Financial Statements Contains an Explanatory Paragraph

Illustration 9 is applicable when the accountants' report on the audited financial statements included in the registration statement contains an explanatory paragraph regarding a matter that would also affect the unaudited condensed interim financial statements included in the registration statement. The introductory paragraph of Illustration 1 would be revised as follows:

Our reports with respect thereto (which contain an explanatory paragraph that describes a lawsuit to which the Company is a defendant, discussed in note 8 to the consolidated financial statements) are also included in the registration statement.

The matter described in the explanatory paragraph should also be evaluated to determine whether it also requires mention in the comments on the unaudited condensed consolidated interim financial information (paragraph 5b of Illustration 1). If it is concluded that mention of such a matter in the

[17] *See paragraph .55 of SAS 72.*

comments on unaudited condensed financial statements is appropriate, a sentence should be added at the end of paragraph 5b in Illustration 1.

> Reference should be made to the introductory paragraph of this letter which states that our audit report covering the consolidated financial statements as of and for the year ended December 31, 20X5, includes an explanatory paragraph that describes a lawsuit to which the company is a defendant, discussed in note 8 to the consolidated financial statements.

ILLUSTRATION 10. ALTERNATE WORDING WHEN MORE THAN ONE ACCOUNTANT IS INVOLVED

Illustration 10 applies when more than one accountant is involved in the audit of the financial statements of a business and the principal accountants have obtained a copy of the comfort letter of other accountants. Illustration 10 consists of an addition to paragraph 4c, a substitution for the applicable part of paragraph 5, and an addition to paragraph 6 of Illustration 1.

4c. We have read the letter dated _____ of [*the other accountants*] with regard to [*the related company*].

5. Nothing came to our attention as a result of the foregoing procedures (which, so far as [*the related company*] is concerned, consisted solely of reading the letter referred to in 4c) however, that caused us to believe that . . .

6. On the basis of these inquiries and our reading of the minutes and the letter dated _____ of [*the other accountants*] with regard to [*the related company*], as described in 4, nothing came to our attention that caused us to believe that there was any such change, increase, or decrease, except in all instances for changes, increases, or decreases that the registration statement discloses have occurred or may occur.

ILLUSTRATION 11. ALTERNATE WORDING WHEN THE SEC HAS AGREED TO A DEPARTURE FROM ITS PUBLISHED ACCOUNTING REQUIREMENTS

Illustration 11 is applicable when (1) there is a departure from the applicable accounting requirements of the Act and the related rules and regulations adopted by the SEC and (2) representatives of the SEC have agreed to the departure. Paragraph 2 of Illustration 1 would be revised to read as follows:

2. In our opinion [*include the phrase "except as disclosed in the registration statement," if applicable*], the consolidated financial statements and financial statement schedules audited by us and included (incorporated by reference) in the registration statement comply as to form in all material respects with the applicable accounting requirements of the Act and the related rules and regulations adopted by the SEC; however, as agreed to by representatives of the SEC, separate financial statements and financial statement schedules of ABC Company (an equity investee) as required by Rule 3-09 of Regulation S-X have been omitted.

ILLUSTRATION 12. ALTERNATE WORDING WHEN RECENT EARNINGS DATA ARE PRESENTED IN CAPSULE FORM

Illustration 12 is applicable when (1) the statement of income in the registration statement is supplemented by later information regarding sales and earnings (capsule financial information), (2) the accountants are asked to comment on that information, and (3) the accountants have conducted a review in accordance with Section 722 of the financial statements from which the capsule financial information is derived. The same facts exist as in Illustration 1, except for the following:

1. Sales, net income (no extraordinary items), and earnings per share for the six-month periods ended June 30, 20X6 and 20X5 (both unaudited), are included in capsule form more limited than that specified by APB Opinion 28 [AC Section 173.146].
2. No financial statements later than those for June 20X6 are available.
3. The letter is dated July 25, 20X6, and the cutoff date is July 20, 20X6.

Paragraphs 4, 5, and 6 of Illustration 1 should be revised to read as follows:

4. For purposes of this letter we have read the 20X6 minutes of the meetings of the stockholders, the board of directors, and [*include other appropriate committees, if any*] of the company and its subsidiaries as set forth in the minute books at July 20, 20X6, officials of the company having ad-

vised us that the minutes of all such meetings[18] through the date were set forth therein; we have carried out other procedures to July 20, 20X6, as follows (our work did not extend to the period from July 21, 20X6 to July 25, 20X6, inclusive):

a. With respect to the three-month periods ended March 31, 20X6 and 20X5, we have

   (1) Performed the procedures specified by the American Institute of Certified Public Accountants for a review of interim financial information as described in SAS 71,[19] *Interim Financial Information*, on the unaudited condensed consolidated balance sheet as of March 31, 20X6, and unaudited condensed consolidated statements of income, retained earnings (stockholders' equity), and cash flows for the three-month periods ended March 31, 20X6 and 20X5, included in the registration statement.

   (2) Inquired of certain officials of the company who have responsibility for financial and accounting matters whether the unaudited condensed consolidated financial statements referred to in (1) comply as to form in all material respects with the applicable accounting requirements of the Act and the related rules and regulations adopted by the SEC.

b. With respect to the six-month periods ended June 30, 20X6 and 20X5, we have

   (1) Read the unaudited amounts for sales, net income, and earnings per share for the six-month periods ended June 30, 20X6 and 20X5, as set forth in paragraph [*identify location*].

   (2) Performed the procedures specified by the American Institute of Certified Public Accountants for a review of financial information as described in SAS 71,[19] *Interim Financial Information,* on the unaudited condensed consolidated balance sheet as of June 30, 20X6, and the unaudited condensed consolidated statements of income, retained earnings (stockholders' equity), and cash flows for the six-month periods ended June 30, 20X6 and 20X5, from which the unaudited amounts referred to in b(1) are derived.

   (3) Inquired of certain officials of the company who have responsibility for financial and accounting matters whether the unaudited amounts referred to in (1) are stated on a basis substantially consistent with that of the corresponding amounts in the audited consolidated statements of income.

The foregoing procedures do not constitute an audit conducted in accordance with generally accepted auditing standards. Also, they would not necessarily reveal matters of significance with respect to the comments in the following paragraph. Accordingly, we make no representations regarding the sufficiency of the foregoing procedures for your purposes.

5. Nothing came to our attention as a result of the foregoing procedures, however, that caused us to believe that

   a. (1) Any material modification should be made to the unaudited condensed consolidated financial statements described in 4a(1), included in the registration statement, for them to be in conformity with generally accepted accounting principles.

      (2) The unaudited condensed consolidated financial statements described in 4a(1) do not comply as to form in all material respects with the applicable accounting requirements of the Act and the related rules and regulations adopted by the SEC.

   b. (1) The unaudited amounts for sales, net income, and earnings per share for the six-month periods ended June 30, 20X6 and 20X5, referred to in 4b(1) do not agree with the amounts set forth in the unaudited consolidated financial statements for those same periods.

      (2) The unaudited amounts referred to in b(1) were not determined on a basis substantially consistent with that of the corresponding amounts in the audited consolidated statements of income.

   c. At June 30, 20X6, there was any change in the capital stock, increase in long-term debt, or decrease in consolidated net current assets or stockholders' equity of the consolidated companies as compared with amounts shown in the March 31, 20X6 unaudited condensed consolidated balance sheet included in the registration statement, except in all instances for changes, increases, or decreases that the registration statement discloses have occurred or may occur.

---

[18] *See footnote 3.*

[19] *See footnote 1.*

6. Company officials have advised us that no consolidated financial statements as of any date for any period subsequent to June 30, 20X6, are available; accordingly, the procedures carried out by us with respect to changes in financial statement items after June 30, 20X6, have been, of necessity, even more limited than those with respect to the periods referred to in 4. We have inquired of certain officials of the company who have responsibility for financial and accounting matters regarding whether (1) at July 20, 20X6, there was any change in the capital stock, increase in long-term debt, or any decreases on consolidated net current assets or stockholders' equity of the consolidated companies as compared with amounts shown on the March 31, 20X6 unaudited condensed consolidated balance sheet included in the registration statement; or (2) for the period from July 1, 20X6, to July 20, 20X6, there were any decreases, as compared with the corresponding period in the preceding year, in consolidated net sales or in the total or per share amounts before extraordinary items or of net income. On the basis of these inquiries and our reading of the minutes as described in 4., nothing came to our attention that caused us to believe that there was any such change, increase, or decrease, except in all instances for changes, increases, or decreases that the registration statement discloses have occurred or may occur.

Illustration 13. Alternate Wording When Accountants Are Aware of a Decrease in a Specified Financial Statement Item

Illustration 13 covers a situation in which accountants are aware of a decrease in a financial statement item on which they are requested to comment. The same facts exist as in Illustration 1, except for the decrease covered in the following change in paragraph 5b.

b. (1) At May 31, 20X6, there was any change in the capital stock, increase in long-term debt or any decrease in consolidated stockholders' equity of the consolidated companies as compared with amounts shown in the March 31, 20X6 unaudited condensed consolidated balance sheet included in the registration statement, or

(2) For the period from April 1, 20X6, to May 31, 20X6, there were any decreases, as compared with the corresponding period in the preceding year, in consolidated net sales or the total or per share amounts of income before extraordinary items or of net income, except in all instances for changes, increases, or decreases that the registration statement discloses have occurred or may occur and except that the unaudited consolidated balance sheet as of May 31, 20X6, which we were furnished by the company, showed a decrease from March 31, 20X6, in consolidated net current assets as follows (in thousands of dollars):

	Current assets	*Current liabilities*	*Net current assets*
March 31, 20X6	$4,251	$1,356	$2,895
May 31, 20X6	3,986	1,732	2,254

6. As mentioned in 4b, company officials have advised us that no consolidated financial statements as of any date or for any period subsequent to May 31, 20X6, are available; accordingly, the procedures carried out by us with respect to changes in financial statement items after May 31, 20X6, have been, of necessity, even more limited than those with respect to the periods referred to in 4. We have inquired of certain officials of the company who have responsibility for financial and accounting matters regarding whether (1) there was any change at June 23, 20X6, in the capital stock, increases in long-term debt, or any decreases in consolidated net current assets or stockholders' equity of the consolidated companies as compared with amounts shown on the March 31, 20X6 unaudited condensed consolidated balance sheet included in the registration statement; or (2) for the period from April 1, 20X6, to June 23, 20X6, there were any decreases, as compared with the corresponding period in the preceding year, in consolidated net sales or in the total or per share amounts of income before extraordinary items of net income. On the basis of these inquiries and our reading of the minutes as described in 4, nothing came to our attention that caused us to believe that there was any such change, increase, or decrease, except in all instances of changes, increases, or decreases that the registration statement discloses have occurred or may occur and except as described in the following sentence. We have been informed by officials of the company that there continues to be a decrease in net current assets that is estimated to be approximately the same amount as set forth in 5b [*or whatever other disclosure fits the circumstances*].

Illustration 14. Alternate Wording of the Letter for Companies That Are Permitted to Present Interim Earnings Data for a Twelve-Month Period

Certain types of companies are permitted to include earnings data for a twelve-month period to the date of the latest balance sheet furnished in lieu of earnings data for both the interim period between the end of the latest fiscal year and the date of the latest balance sheet and the corresponding period of the preceding fiscal year. The following would be substituted for the applicable part of paragraph 3 of Illustration 1.

3. . . .was to enable us to express our opinion on the financial statements as of December 31, 20X5, and for the year then ended, but not on the financial statements for any period included in part within that year. Therefore, we are unable to and do not express an opinion on the unaudited condensed consolidated balance sheet as of March 31, 20X6, and the related unaudited condensed consolidated statements of income, retained earnings (stockholders' equity), and cash flows for the twelve months then ended included in the registration statement. . .

Illustration 15. Alternate Wording When the Procedures That the Underwriter Has Requested the Accountant to Perform on Interim Financial Information Are Less Than a SAS 71[20] Review

The illustration assumes that the underwriter has asked the accountants to perform specified procedures on the interim financial information and report thereon in the comfort letter. The letter is dated June 28, 20X6; procedures were performed through June 23, 20X6, the cutoff date. Since a SAS 71[20] (Section 722) review was not performed on the interim financial information as of March 31, 20X6, and for the quarter then ended, the accountants are limited to reporting procedures performed and findings obtained on the interim financial information. In addition to the information presented below, the letter would also contain paragraph 7 of the typical comfort letter in Illustration 1.

June 28, 20X6

[*Addressee*]

Dear Sirs:

We have audited the consolidated balance sheets of The Basic Company, Inc. (the company) and subsidiaries as of December 31, 20X5 and 20X4, and the consolidated statements of income, retained earnings (stockholders' equity), and cash flows for each of the three years in the period ended December 31, 20X5, and the related financial statements schedules all included in the registration statement (No. 33-00000) on Form S-1 filed by the company under the Securities Act of 1933 (the Act); our reports with respect thereto are included in that registration statement. The registration statement as amended on June 28, 20X6, is herein referred to as the registration statement.

Also, we have compiled the forecasted balance sheet and consolidated statements of income, retained earnings (stockholders' equity), and cash flows as of December 31, 20X6, and for the year then ending, attached to the registration statement, as indicated in our report dated May 15, 20X6, which is attached.

In connection with the registration statement

1. We are independent certified public accountants with respect to the company within the meaning of the Act and the applicable rules and regulations thereunder adopted by the SEC.
2. In our opinion [*include the phrase "except as disclosed in the registration statement," if applicable*], the consolidated financial statements and financial statement schedules audited by us and included in the registration statement comply as to form in all material respects with the applicable accounting requirements of the Act and the related rules and regulations adopted by the SEC.
3. We have not audited any financial statements of the company as of any date or for any period subsequent to December 31, 20X5; although we have conducted an audit for the year ended December 31, 20X5, the purpose (and therefore the scope) of the audit was to enable us to express our opinion on the consolidated financial statements as of December 31, 20X5, and for the year then ended, but not on the financial statements for any interim period within that year. Therefore, we are unable to and do not express any opinion on the unaudited condensed consolidated balance sheet as of March 31, 20X6, and the unaudited condensed consolidated statements of income, retained earnings (stockholders' equity), and cash flows for the three-month periods ended

[20] *See footnote 1.*

March 31, 20X6 and 20X5, included in the registration statement, or on the financial position, results of operations, or cash flows, as of any date or for any period subsequent to December 31, 20X5.

4. For purposes of this letter we have read the 20X6 minutes of meetings of the stockholders, the board of directors, and [*include other appropriate committees, if any*] of the company as set forth in the minute books at June 23, 20X6, officials of the company having advised us that the minutes of all such meetings[21] through that date were set forth herein; we have carried out other procedures to June 23, 20X6, as follows (our work did not extend to the period from June 24, 20X6, to June 28, 20X6, inclusive):

   a. With respect to the three-month periods ended March 31, 20X6 and 20X5, we have

      (1) Read the unaudited condensed consolidated balance sheet as of March 31, 20X6, and unaudited condensed consolidated statements of income, retained earnings (stockholders' equity), and cash flows for the three-month periods ended March 31, 20X6 and 20X5, included in the registration statement, and agreed the amounts contained therein with the company's accounting records as of March 31, 20X6 and 20X5, and for the three-month periods then ended.

      (2) Inquired of certain officials of the company who have responsibility for financial and accounting matters whether the unaudited condensed consolidated financial statements referred to in a(1): (a) are in conformity with generally accepted accounting principles[22] applied on a basis substantially consistent with that of the audited consolidated financial statements included in the registration statement, and (b) comply as to form in all material respects with the applicable accounting requirements of the Act and the related rules and regulations adopted by the SEC. Those officials stated that the unaudited condensed consolidated financial statements (a) are in conformity with generally accepted accounting principles applied on a basis substantially consistent with that of the audited financial statements, and (b) comply as to form in all material respects with the applicable accounting requirements of the Act and the related rules and regulations adopted by the SEC.

   b. With respect to the period from April 1, 20X6, to May 31, 20X6, we have

      (1) Read the unaudited consolidated financial statements of the company[23] for April and May of both 20X5 and 20X6 furnished us by the company, and agreed the amounts contained therein to the company's accounting records. Officials of the company have advised us that no such financial statements as of any date or for any period subsequent to May 31, 20X6, were available.

      (2) Inquired of certain officials of the company who have responsibility for financial and accounting matters whether (a) the unaudited financial statements referred to in b(1) are stated on a basis substantially consistent with that of the audited consolidated financial statements included in the registration statement, (b) at May 31, 20X6, there was any change in the capital stock, increase in long-term debt or any decrease in consolidated net current assets or stockholders' equity of the consolidated companies as compared with amounts shown in the March 31, 20X6 unaudited condensed consolidated balance sheet included in the registration statement, and (c) for the period from April 1, 20X6, to May 31, 20X6, there were any decreases, as compared with the corresponding period in the preceding year, in consolidated net sales or in the total or per share amounts of income before extraordinary items or of net income.

      Those officials stated that (a) the unaudited consolidated financial statements referred to in 4b(1) are stated on a basis substantially consistent with that of the audited consolidated financial statements included in the registration statement, (2) at May 31, 20X6, there was no change in the capital stock, no increase in long-term debt, and no decrease in net current assets or stockholders' equity of the consolidated companies as compared with amounts shown in the March 31, 20X6 unaudited condensed consolidated balance sheet included in the registration statements, and (3) there were no decreases for the period from April 1, 20X6, to May 31, 20X6, as compared with the corresponding period in the preceding year, in consolidated net sales or in the total or per share amounts of income before extraordinary items or of net income.

---

[21] *See footnote 3.*
[22] *See footnote 5.*
[23] *See footnote 4.*

c. As mentioned in 4b(1), company officials have advised us that no financial statements as of any date or for any period subsequent to May 31, 20X6, are available; accordingly, the procedures carried out by us with respect to changes in financial statement items after May 31, 20X6, have, of necessity, been even more limited than those with respect to the periods referred to in 4a and 4b. We have inquired of certain officials of the company who have responsibility for financial and accounting matters whether (1) at June 23, 20X6, there was any change in the capital stock, increase in long-term debt or any decreases in consolidated net current assets or stockholders' equity of the consolidated companies as compared with amounts shown on the March 31, 20X6 unaudited condensed consolidated balance sheet included in the registration statement or (2) for the period from April 1, 20X6, to June 23, 20X6, there were any decreases, as compared with the corresponding period in the preceding year, in consolidated net sales or in the total or per share amounts of income before extraordinary items or of net income. Those officials stated that (1) at June 23, 20X6, there was no change in the capital stock, no increase in long-term debt and no decreases in consolidated net current assets or stockholders' equity of the consolidated companies as compared with amounts shown on the March 31, 20X6 unaudited condensed consolidated balance sheet, and (2) for the period from April 1, 20X6, to June 23, 20X6, there were no decreases as compared with the corresponding period in the preceding year, in consolidated net sales or in the total or per share amounts of income before extraordinary items or of net income.

The foregoing procedures do not constitute an audit conducted in accordance with generally accepted auditing standards. We make no representations regarding the sufficiency of the foregoing procedures for your purposes. Had we performed additional procedures or had we conducted an audit or a review, other matters might have come to our attention that would have been reported to you.

5. At your request we also performed the following procedures:

a. Read the unaudited pro forma condensed consolidated balance sheet as of March 31, 20X6, and the unaudited pro forma condensed consolidated statements of income for the year ended December 31, 20X5, and the three-month period ended March 31, 20X6, included in the registration statement.

b. Inquired of certain officials of the company and of XYZ Company (the company being acquired) who have responsibility for financial and accounting matters as to whether all significant assumptions regarding the business combination had been reflected in the pro forma adjustments and whether the unaudited pro forma condensed consolidated financial statements referred to in a. comply as to form in all material respects with the applicable accounting requirements of Rule 11-02 of Regulation S-X.

Those officials referred to above stated, in response to our inquiries, that all significant assumptions regarding the business combination had been reflected in the pro forma adjustments and that the unaudited pro forma condensed consolidated financial statements referred to in a. comply as to form in all material respects with the applicable accounting requirements of Rule 11-02 of Regulation S-X.

c. Compared the historical financial information for the company included on page 20 in the registration statement with historical financial information for the company on page 12 and found them to be in agreement.

We also compared the financial information included on page 20 of the registration statement with the historical information for XYZ Company on page 13 and found them to be in agreement.

d. Proved the arithmetic accuracy of the application of the pro forma adjustments to the historical amounts in the unaudited pro forma condensed consolidated financial statements.

The foregoing procedures are substantially less in scope than an examination, the objective of which is the expression of an opinion on management's assumptions, the pro forma adjustments, and the application of those adjustments to historical financial information. Accordingly, we do not express such an opinion. We make no representation about the sufficiency of the foregoing procedures for your purposes. Had we performed additional procedures or had we made an examination of the pro forma financial information, other matters might have come to our attention that would have been reported to you.

6. At your request, we performed the following procedures with respect to the forecasted consolidated balance sheet and consolidated statements of income and cash flows as of December 31, 20X6, and for the year then ending. With respect to forecasted rental income, we compared the

occupancy statistics about expected demand for rental of the housing units to statistics for existing comparable properties and found them to be the same.

Because the procedures described above do not constitute an examination of prospective financial statements in accordance with standards established by the American Institute of Certified Public Accountants, we do not express an opinion on whether the prospective financial statements are presented in conformity with AICPA presentation guidelines or on whether the underlying assumptions provide a reasonable basis for the presentation. Furthermore there will usually be differences between the forecasted and actual results, because events and circumstances frequently do not occur as expected, and those differences may be material. We make no representations about the sufficiency of such procedures for your purposes. Had we performed additional procedures or had we made an examination of the forecast in accordance with standards established by the AICPA, matters might have come to our attention that would have been reported to you.

ILLUSTRATION 16. A TYPICAL COMFORT LETTER IN A NON-1933 ACT OFFERING, INCLUDING THE REQUIRED UNDERWRITER REPRESENTATIONS

Illustration 16 is applicable when a comfort letter is issued in a non-1933 Act offering. The underwriter has given the accountants a letter including the representations regarding their due diligence review process, and the comfort letter refers to those representations. In addition, the illustration assumes that the accountants were unable, or were not requested, to perform a SAS 71[24] (Section 722) review of a subsequent interim period and therefore no negative assurance has been given.

November 30, 20X5

[Addressee]

Dear Sirs:

We have audited the balance sheets of Example City, Any State Utility System, as of June 30, 20X5 and 20X4, and the statements of revenues, expenses, and changes in retained earnings and cash flows for the years then ended, included in the Official Statement for $30,000,000 of Example City, Any State Utility System Revenue Bonds due November 30, 20X5. Our report with respect thereto is included in the Official Statement. This Official Statement, dated November 30, 20X5, is herein referred to as the Official Statement.

This letter is being furnished in reliance upon your representation to us that

1. You are knowledgeable with respect to the due diligence review process that would be performed if this placement of securities were being registered pursuant to the Securities Act of 1933 (the Act).
2. In connection with the offering of revenue bonds, the review process you have performed is substantially consistent with the due diligence review process that you would have performed if this placement of securities were being registered pursuant to the Act.

In connection with the Official Statement

1. We are independent certified public accountants with respect to Example City, Any State and its Utility System under Rule 101 of the AICPA's *Code of Professional Conduct*, and its interpretations and ruling.
2. We have not audited any financial statements of Example City, Any State Utility System as of any date or for any period subsequent to June 30, 20X5; although we have conducted an audit for the year ended June 30, 20X5, the purpose (and therefore the scope) of the audit was to enable us to express our opinion on the financial statements as of June 30, 20X5, and for the year then ended, but not on the financial statements for any interim period within that year. Therefore, we are unable to and do not express any opinion on the financial position, results of operations, or cash flows as of any date or for any period subsequent to June 30, 20X5, for the Example City, Any State Utility System.
3. For purposes of this letter we have read the 20X5 minutes of the meetings of the City Council of Example City, Any State, as set forth in the minutes books as of November 25, 20X5, the City Clerk of Example City having advised us that the minutes of all such meetings through that date were set forth therein.

---

[24] *See footnote 1.*

4. With respect to the period subsequent to June 30, 20X5, we have carried out other procedures to November 25, 20X5, as follows (our work did not extend to the period from November 26, 20X5, to November 30, 20X5, inclusive):
   a. We have required of, and received assurance from, city officials who have responsibility for financial and accounting matters, that no financial statements as of any date or for any period subsequent to June 30, 20X5, are available.
   b. We have inquired of those officials regarding whether (a) at November 25, 20X5, there was any increase in long-term debt or any decrease in net current assets of Example City, Any State Utility System as compared with amounts shown on the June 30, 20X5 balance sheet, included in the Official Statement, or (b) for the period from July 1, 20X5, to November 25, 20X5, there were any decreases, as compared with the corresponding period in the preceding year, in total operating revenues, income from operations or net income. Those officials stated that (1) at November 25, 20X5, there was no increase in long-term debt and no decrease in net current assets of the Example City, Any State Utility System as compared with amounts shown in the June 30, 20X5 balance sheet; and (2) there were no decreases for the period from July 1, 20X5, to November 25, 20X5, as compared with the corresponding period in the preceding year, in total operating revenues, income from operations, or net income, except in all instances for changes, increases, or decreases that the Official Statement discloses have occurred or may occur.
5. For accounting data pertaining to the years 20X3 through 20X5, inclusive, shown on page 11 of the Official Statement, we have (1) for data shown in the audited financial statements, compared such data with the audited financial statements of the Example City, Any State Utility System for 20X3 through 20X5 and found them to be in agreement; and (2) for data not directly shown in the audited financial statements, compared such data with the general ledger and accounting records of the Utility System from which such information was derived, and found them to be in agreement.
6. The procedures enumerated in the preceding paragraph do not constitute an audit conducted in accordance with generally accepted auditing standards. Accordingly, we make no representations regarding the sufficiency of the foregoing procedures for your purposes.
7. This letter is solely for the information of the addressees and to assist the underwriters in conducting and documenting their investigation of the affairs of the Example City, Any State Utility System in connection with the offering of securities covered by the Official Statement, and it is not to be used, circulated, quoted, or otherwise referred to for any purpose, including but not limited to the purchase or sale of securities, nor is it to be filed with or referred to in whole or in part in the Official Statement or any other document, except that reference may be made to it in the Purchase Contract or in any list of closing documents pertaining to the offering of securities covered by the Official Statement.

ILLUSTRATION 17. LETTER TO A REQUESTING PARTY THAT HAS NOT PROVIDED THE NORMALLY REQUIRED LETTER[25]

Illustration 17 assumes that the procedures were performed at the request of a placement agent on information included in an offering circular in connection with a private placement of unsecured notes with two insurance companies. The letter is dated June 30, 20X6; procedures were performed through June 25, 20X6, the cutoff date.

June 30, 20X6

[*Addressee*]

Dear Sirs:

We have audited the consolidated balance sheets of XYZ Company, Inc. (the company) and subsidiaries as of December 31, 20X5 and 20X4, and the consolidated statements of income, retained earnings (stockholders' equity), and cash flows for each of the three years in the period ended December 31, 20X5, included in the offering circular for $40,000,000 of notes due June 30, 20X6. Our report with respect thereto is included in the offering circular. The offering circular dated June 30, 20X6, is herein referred to as the offering circular.

We are independent certified public accountants with respect to the company under Rule 101 of the AICPA's Code of Professional Conduct, and its interpretations and rulings.

---

[25] *This illustration is effective for letters issued after April 30, 1996.*

We have not audited any financial statements of the company as of any date or for any period subsequent to December 31, 20X5; although we have conducted an audit for the year ended December 31, 20X5, the purpose (and, therefore, the scope) of the audit was to enable us to express our opinion on the consolidated financial statements as of December 31, 20X5, and for the year then ended, but not on the financial statements for any interim period within that year. Therefore, we are unable to and do not express any opinion on the unaudited condensed consolidated balance sheet as of March 31, 20X6, and the unaudited condensed consolidated statements of income, retained earnings (stockholders' equity), and cash flows for the three-month periods ended March 31, 20X6 and 20X5, included in the offering circular, or on the financial position, results of operations, or cash flows as of any date or for any period subsequent to December 31, 20X5.

1. At your request, we have read the 20X6 minutes of meetings of the stockholders, the board of directors, and [*include other appropriate committees, if any*] of the company as set forth in the minutes books at June 25, 20X6, officials of the company having advised us that the minutes of all such meetings through that date were set forth therein; we have carried out other procedures to June 25, 20X6 (our work did not extend to the period from June 26, 20X6, to June 30, 20X6, inclusive) as follows:

   a. With respect to the three-month periods ended March 31, 20X6 and 20X5, we have

      (1) Read the unaudited condensed consolidated balance sheet as of March 31, 20X6, and the unaudited condensed consolidated statements of income, retained earnings (stockholders' equity), and cash flows of the company for the three-month periods ended March 31, 20X6 and 20X5, included in the offering circular, and agreed the amounts contained therein with the company's accounting records as of March 31, 20X6 and 20X5, and for the three-month periods then ended.

      (2) Inquired of certain officials of the company who have responsibility for financial and accounting matters whether the unaudited condensed consolidated financial statements referred to in a(1) are in conformity with generally accepted accounting principles applied on a basis substantially consistent with that of the audited consolidated financial statements included in the offering circular. Those officials stated that the unaudited condensed consolidated financial statements are in conformity with generally accepted accounting principles applied on a basis substantially consistent with that of the audited consolidated financial statements.

   b. With respect to the period from April 1, 20X6, to May 31, 20X6, we have

      (1) Read the unaudited condensed consolidated financial statements of the company for April and May of both 20X5 and 20X6, furnished us by the company, and agreed the amounts therein with the company's accounting records. Officials of the company have advised us that no financial statements as of any date or for any period subsequent to May 31, 20X6, were available.

      (2) Inquired of certain officials of the company who have responsibility for financial and accounting matters whether (a) the unaudited condensed consolidated financial statements referred to in b(1) are stated on a basis substantially consistent with that of the audited consolidated financial statements included in the offering circular, (b) at May 31, 20X6, there was any change in the capital stock, increase in long-term debt, or any decrease in consolidated net current assets or stockholders' equity of the consolidated companies as compared with amounts shown in the March 31, 20X6, unaudited condensed balance sheet included in the offering circular, or (c) for the period from April 1, 20X6, to May 31, 20X6, there were any decreases, as compared with the corresponding period in the preceding year, in consolidated net sales or in the total or per share amounts of income before extraordinary items or of net income.

      Those officials stated that (a) the unaudited condensed consolidated financial statements referred to in b(2) are stated on a basis substantially consistent with that of the audited consolidated financial statements included in the offering circular, (b) at May 31, 20X6, there was no change in the capital stock, no increase in long-term debt, and no decrease in consolidated net current assets or stockholders' equity of the consolidated companies as compared with amounts shown in the March 31, 20X6 unaudited condensed balance sheet included in the offering circular, and (c) there were no decreases for the period from April 1, 20X6, to May 31, 20X6, as compared with the corresponding period in the preceding year, in consolidated net sales or in the total or per share amounts of income before extraordinary items or of net income.

c. As mentioned in 1b, company officials have advised us that no financial statements as of any date or for any period subsequent to May 31, 20X6, are available; accordingly, the procedures carried out by us with respect to changes in financial statement items after May 31, 20X6, have, of necessity, been even more limited than those with respect to the periods referred to in 1a and 1b. We have inquired of certain officials of the company who have responsibility for financial and accounting matters whether

(1) At June 25, 20X6, there was any change in the capital stock, increase in long-term debt, or any decreases in consolidated net current assets or stockholders' equity of the consolidated companies as compared with amounts shown on the March 31, 20X6 unaudited condensed consolidated balance sheet included in the offering circular or

(2) For the period from April 1, 20X6, to June 26, 20X6, there were any decreases, as compared with the corresponding period in the preceding year, in consolidated net sales or in the total or per share amounts of income before extraordinary items or of net income.

Those officials referred to above stated that (1) at June 25, 20X6, there was no change in the capital stock, no increase in long-term debt, and no decreases in consolidated net current assets or stockholders' equity of the consolidated companies as compared with amounts shown on the March 31, 20X6 unaudited condensed consolidated balance sheet, and (2) there were no decreases for the period from April 1, 20X6, to June 25, 20X6, as compared with the corresponding period in the preceding year, in consolidated net sales or in the total or per share amounts of income before extraordinary items or of net income.

2. At your request we have read the following items in the offering circular on the indicated pages.

Item	Page	Description
a	13	**History and Business—Sales and Marketing.** The table following the first paragraph.
b	22	**Executive Compensation—20X5 Compensation.**
c	33	**Selected Financial Data.**

3. Our audits of the consolidated financial statements for the periods referred to in the introductory paragraph of this letter comprised audit tests and procedures deemed necessary for the purpose of expressing an opinion on such financial statements taken as a whole. For none of the periods referred to therein, nor for any other period, did we perform audit tests for the purpose of expressing an opinion on individual balances of accounts or summaries of selected transactions such as those enumerated above, and accordingly, we express no opinion thereon.

4. However, for purposes of this letter we have performed the following additional procedures, which were applied as indicated with respect to the items enumerated above.

Item in 2	Procedures and findings
a	We compared the amounts of military sales, commercial sales, and total sales shown in the registration statement with the balances in the appropriate accounts in the company's accounting records for the respective fiscal years and for the unaudited interim periods and found them to be in agreement. We proved the arithmetic accuracy of the percentages of such amounts of military sales and commercial sales to total sales for the respective fiscal years and for the unaudited interim periods. We compared such computed percentages with the corresponding percentages appearing in the registration statement and found them to be in agreement.
b	We compared the dollar amounts of compensation (salary, bonus, and other compensation) for each individual listed in the table "Annual Compensation," with the corresponding amounts shown by the individual employee earnings records for the year 20X5 and found them to be in agreement. We compared the dollar amounts shown under the heading of "Long-Term Compensation" on page 24 for each listed individual and the aggregate amounts for executive officers with corresponding amounts shown in an analysis prepared by the company and found such amounts to be in agreement.
c	We compared the amounts of net sales, income from continuing operations, income from continuing operations per common share, and cash dividends declared per common share for the years ended

December 31, 20X5, 20X4, and 20X3, with the respective amounts in the consolidated financial statements on pages 27 and 28 and the amounts for the years ended December 31, 20X2 and 20X1, with the respective amounts in the consolidated financial statements included in the company's annual reports to stockholders for 20X2 and 20X1 and found them to be in agreement.

We compared the amounts of total assets, long-term obligations, and redeemable preferred stock at December 31, 20X5 and 20X4, with the respective amounts in the consolidated financial statements on pages 27 and 28 and the amounts at December 31, 20X3, 20X2, and 20X1, with the corresponding amounts in the consolidated financial statements included in the company's annual reports to stockholders for 20X3, 20X2, and 20X1 and found them to be in agreement.

5. It should be understood that we have no responsibility for establishing (and did not establish) the scope and nature of the procedures enumerated in paragraphs 1 through 4 above; rather, the procedures enumerated therein are those the requesting party asked us to perform. Accordingly, we make no representations regarding questions of legal interpretation or regarding the sufficiency for your purposes of the procedures enumerated in the preceding paragraphs; also, such procedures would not necessarily reveal any material misstatement of the amounts or percentages listed above as set forth in the offering circular. Further, we have addressed ourselves solely to the foregoing data, and make no representations regarding the adequacy of disclosures or whether any material facts have been omitted. This letter relates only to the financial statement items specified above and does not extend to any financial statement of the company taken as a whole.
6. The foregoing procedures do not constitute an audit conducted in accordance with generally accepted auditing standards. Had we performed additional procedures or had we conducted an audit or a review of the company's March 31, April 30, or May 31, 20X6 and 20X5 condensed consolidated financial statements in accordance with standards established by the American Institute of Certified Public Accountants, other matters might have come to our attention that would have been reported to you.
7. These procedures should not be taken to supplant any additional inquiries or procedures that you would undertake in your consideration of the proposed offering.
8. This letter is solely for your information and to assist you in your inquiries in connection with the offering of the securities covered by the offering circular, and it is not to be used, circulated, quoted, or otherwise referred to for any other purpose, including but not limited to the registration, purchase, or sale of securities, nor is it to be filed with or referred to in whole or in part in the offering document or any other document, except that reference may be made to it in any list of closing documents pertaining to the offering of the securities covered by the offering document.
9. We have no responsibility to update this letter for events and circumstances occurring after June 25, 20X6.

Illustration 18. Comfort Letter That Includes Reference to Examination of Annual MD&A and Review of Interim MD&A[26]

Illustration 18 assumes the following circumstances. The prospectus (part I of the registration statement) includes audited consolidated balance sheets as of December 31, 20X5 and 20X4, and audited consolidated statements of income, retained earnings (stockholders' equity), and cash flows for each of the three years in the period ended December 31, 20X5. Part I also includes an unaudited condensed consolidated balance sheet as of March 31, 20X6, and unaudited condensed consolidated statements of income, retained earnings (stockholders' equity), and cash flows for the three-month periods ended March 31, 20X6 and 20X5. Part II of the registration statement includes audited consolidated financial statement schedules for the three years ended December 31, 20X5. The accountants have examined the company's management's discussion and analysis (MD&A) for the year ended December 31, 20X5, in accordance with Statement on Standards for Attestation Engagements (SSAE) 8; the accountants have also performed reviews of the company's unaudited condensed consolidated financial statements, referred to above, in accordance with SAS 71,[27] and the company's MD&A for the three-

[26] *This example is effective for letters issued after June 30, 1998.*

[27] *See footnote 1.*

month period ended March 31, 20X6, in accordance with SSAE 8. The accountant's reports on the examination and review of MD&A have been previously issued, but not distributed publicly; none of these reports is included in the registration statement. The cutoff date is June 23, 20X6, and the letter is dated June 28, 20X6. The effective date is June 28, 20X6.

Each of the comments in the letter is in response to a requirement of the underwriting agreement. For purposes of Illustration 18, the income statement items of the current interim period are to be compared with those of the corresponding period of the preceding year.

June 28, 20X6

[*Addressee*]

Dear Sirs:

We have audited the consolidated balance sheets of The Basic Company, Inc. (the company) and subsidiaries as of December 31, 20X5 and 20X4, and the consolidated statements of income, retained earnings (stockholders' equity), and cash flows for each of the three years in the period ended December 31, 20X5, and the related financial statement schedules, all included in the registration statement (No. 33-00000) on Form S-1 filed by the company under the Securities Act of 1933 (the Act); our reports with respect thereto are also included in that registration statement. The registration statement, as amended on June 28, 20X6, is herein referred to as the registration statement. Also, we have examined the company's Management's Discussion and Analysis for the year ended December 31, 20X5, included in the registration statement, as indicated in our report dated March 28, 20X6; our report with respect thereto is attached. We have also reviewed the unaudited condensed consolidated financial statements as of March 31, 20X6 and 20X5, and for the three-month periods then ended, included in the registration statement, as indicated in our report dated May 15, 20X6, and have also reviewed the company's Management's Discussion and Analysis for the three-month period ended March 31, 20X6, included in the registration statement, as indicated in our report dated May 15, 20X6; our reports with respect thereto are attached.

In connection with the registration statement

1. We are independent certified public accountants with respect to the company within the meaning of the Act and the applicable rules and regulations thereunder adopted by the SEC.
2. In our opinion [*include the phrase "except as disclosed in the registration statement," if applicable*] the consolidated financial statements and financial statement schedules audited by us and included in the registration statement comply as to form in all material respects with the applicable accounting requirements of the Act and the related rules and regulations adopted by the SEC.
3. We have not audited any financial statements of the company as of any date or for any period subsequent to December 31, 20X5; although we have conducted an audit for the year ended December 31, 20X5, the purpose (and therefore the scope) of the audit was to enable us to express our opinion on the consolidated financial statements as of December 31, 20X5, and for the year then ended, but not on the financial statements for any interim period within that year. Therefore, we are unable to and do not express any opinion on the unaudited condensed consolidated balance sheet as of March 31, 20X6, and the unaudited condensed consolidated statements of income, retained earnings (stockholders' equity), and cash flows for the three-month periods ended March 31, 20X6 and 20X5, included in the registration statement, or on the financial position, results of operations, or cash flows as of any date or for any period subsequent to December 31, 20X5.
4. We have not examined any management's discussion and analysis of the company as of or for any period subsequent to December 31, 20X5; although we have made an examination of the company's Management's Discussion and Analysis for the year ended December 31, 20X5, included in the company's registration statement, the purpose (and therefore the scope) of the examination was to enable us to express our opinion on such Management's Discussion and Analysis, but not on the management's discussion and analysis for any interim period within that year. Therefore, we are unable to and do not express any opinion on the Management's Discussion and Analysis for three-month period ended March 31, 20X6, included in the registration statement, or for any period subsequent to March 31, 20X6.
5. For purposes of this letter we have read the 20X6 minutes of meetings of the stockholders, the board of directors, and [*include other appropriate committees, if any*] of the company and its subsidiaries as set forth in the minutes books at June 23, 20X6, officials of the company having advised us that the minutes of all such meetings through that date were set forth therein; we have carried out other procedures from June 23, 20X6, as follows (our work did not extend to the period from June 24, 20X6, to June 28, 20X6, inclusive):

a. With respect to the three-month periods ended March 31, 20X6 and 20X5, we have inquired of certain officials of the company who have responsibility for financial and accounting matters whether the unaudited condensed consolidated balance sheet as of March 31, 20X6, and the unaudited condensed consolidated statements of income, retained earnings (stockholders' equity), and cash flows for the three-month periods ended March 31, 20X6 and 20X5, included in the registration statement, comply as to form in all material respects with the applicable accounting requirements of the Act and the related rules and regulations adopted by the SEC.

b. With respect to the period from April 1, 20X6, to May 31, 20X6, we have

(1) Read the unaudited consolidated financial statements of the company and subsidiaries for April and May of both 20X5 and 20X6 furnished to us by the company, officials of the company having advised us that no such financial statements as of any date or for any period subsequent to May 31, 20X6, were available.

(2) Inquired of certain officials of the company who have responsibility for financial and accounting matters whether the unaudited consolidated financial statements referred to in b(1) are stated on a basis substantially consistent with that of the audited consolidated financial statements included in the registration statement.

The foregoing procedures do not constitute an audit of financial statements conducted in accordance with generally accepted auditing standards. Also, they would not necessarily reveal matters of significance with respect to the comments in the following paragraph. Accordingly, we make no representations regarding the sufficiency of the foregoing procedures for your purposes.

6. Nothing came to our attention as a result of the foregoing procedures, however, that caused us to believe that

a. The unaudited condensed consolidated financial statements described in 5a do not comply as to form in all material respects with the applicable accounting requirements of the Act and the related rules and regulations adopted by the SEC.

b. (1) At May 31, 20X6, there was any change in the capital stock, increase in long-term debt, or decrease in consolidated net current assets or stockholders' equity of the consolidated companies as compared with amounts shown in the March 31, 20X6 unaudited condensed consolidated balance sheet included in the registration statement, or

(2) For the period from April 1, 20X6, to May 31, 20X6, there were any decreases, as compared with the corresponding period in the preceding year, in consolidated net sales or in the total or per share amounts of income before extraordinary items or of net income, except in all instances of changes, increases, or decreases that the registration statement discloses have occurred or may occur.

7. As mentioned in 5b, company officials have advised us that no consolidated financial statements as of any date or for any period subsequent to May 31, 20X6, are available; accordingly, the procedures carried out by us with respect to changes in financial statement items after May 31, 20X6, have, of necessity, been even more limited than those with respect to the periods referred to in 5. We have inquired of certain officials of the company who have responsibility for financial and accounting matters whether (1) at June 23, 20X6, there was any change in the capital stock, increase in long-term debt, or any decreases in consolidated net current assets or stockholders' equity of the consolidated companies as compared with amounts shown on the March 31, 20X6, unaudited condensed consolidated balance sheet included in the registration statement or (2) for the period from April 1, 20X6, to June 23, 20X6, there were any decreases, as compared with the corresponding period in the preceding year, in consolidated net sales or in the total or per share amounts of income before extraordinary items or of net income. On the basis of these inquiries and our reading of the minutes as described in 5., nothing came to our attention that caused us to believe that there was any such change, increase, or decrease, except in all instances for changes, increases, or decreases that the registration statement discloses have occurred or may occur.

8. This letter is solely for the information of the addressees and to assist the underwriters in conducting and documenting their investigation of the affairs of the company in connection with the offering of the securities covered by the registration statement, and it is not to be used, circulated, quoted, or otherwise referred to within or without the underwriting group for any purpose, including but not limited to the registration, purchase, or sale of securities, nor is it to be filed with or referred to in whole or in part in the registration statement or any other document, except that reference may be made to it in the underwriting agreement or in any list of closing documents pertaining to the offering of the securities covered by the registration statement.

711 FILINGS UNDER FEDERAL SECURITIES STATUTES

EFFECTIVE DATE AND APPLICABILITY

Original Pronouncement	SAS 37, April 1981.
Effective Date	When issued, April 1981.
Applicability	Reports of independent accountants included in registration statements filed with the SEC under the Securities Act of 1933.

DEFINITIONS OF TERMS

Registration statement. A statement required to be filed with the SEC by a company before its securities may be offered for sale to the public. Its primary purpose is to provide prospective investors with financial and other information concerning the company and the securities being offered for sale. Registration of an initial public offering of securities is governed by the Securities Act of 1933 and related regulations.

Prospectus. The major component of the registration statement. It also is distributed to prospective purchasers of the securities that will be offered for sale. It contains financial and other information of the issuer.

Shelf registration statement. A registration statement in which the issuer registers the amount of securities it reasonably expects to offer and sell within the next two years. Ordinarily, the issuer does not have to prepare and file a new prospectus and registration statement for each sale. A shelf registration statement can be updated after its original effective date by

- Filing a posteffective amendment.
- Incorporation by reference of subsequently filed material.
- Addition of a supplemental prospectus (sometimes referred to as a "sticker").

Effective date. The date after which securities registered with the SEC may be offered for sale to the public. Ordinarily it is the date that the SEC completes its review of the registration statement.

OBJECTIVES OF SECTION

Section 11 of the Securities Act of 1933 imposes civil liability for material misstatements or omissions in registration statements on "every accountant...who has, with his consent, been named as having prepared or certified any part of the registration statement." Section 11 provides that the accountant will not incur this liability, however, if he or she sustains the burden of proof that as to the part of the registration statement purporting to be made on his or her authority as an expert, the accountant had, "after **reasonable investiga-**

tion, **reasonable ground** to believe and did believe, **at the time such part of the statement became effective,** that the statements therein were true." The courts have interpreted this statement to mean that **as of the effective date** of the registration statement the accountant must have **reasonable ground** for believing that statements expertized by him or her were, in fact, true. For example, if the effective date of a registration statement is May 10, 20X1, the auditor must have **reasonable ground** on that date for believing that the December 31, 20X0 financial statements were true and that there were no material omissions.

To sustain the burden of proof under Section 11 of the Securities Act of 1933 that he or she has made a **reasonable investigation,** the auditor must apply certain additional procedures. This section describes procedures the accounting profession believes the auditor should follow to fulfill his or her responsibility as an expert under the 1933 act. The procedures relate to

- The independent accountant's review report on interim financial information.
- Subsequent events.
- Reports of predecessor auditors.

FUNDAMENTAL REQUIREMENTS

ACCOUNTANT'S RESPONSIBILITY

In a filing under the Securities Act of 1933, the prospectus frequently contains a statement that certain information is included in reliance on the reports of certain named experts. The accountant should read the section containing that statement and all other sections of the prospectus to make certain that the issuer of the securities is not attributing to the accountant greater responsibility than he or she intended. There should be no implication that the financial statements have been prepared by the accountant or that they are not the direct representations of management.

ACCOUNTANT'S REPORT: REVIEW OF INTERIM FINANCIAL INFORMATION

In Accounting Series Release (ASR) 274, the SEC ruled that an accountant's report on a review of unaudited interim financial information is not considered part of the registration statement prepared or certified by an accountant or a report prepared or certified by an accountant within the meaning of Section 11 of the Securities Act of 1933. The SEC requires a statement to this effect whenever the accountant's review report is presented or incorporated by reference in a registration statement. The accountant should read the registration statement to ensure that such a statement has been made.

SUBSEQUENT EVENTS PROCEDURES

Predecessor Auditor

An auditor who has not audited the financial statements for the most recent fiscal year, but whose reports on audits of prior years' financial statements are included in the registration statement, has a responsibility for material subsequent events from the date of the prior year financial statements through to the effective date. The predecessor auditor should

1. Read relevant parts of the prospectus and the registration statement.
2. Obtain a representation letter from the successor auditor regarding whether his or her audit revealed any matters that might materially affect the financial statements reported on by the predecessor or would require disclosure in the notes.

3. Make inquiries and perform other procedures to satisfy himself or herself about the appropriateness of adjustments or disclosures affecting the financial statements covered by the reports (see Section 508).

NOTE: In addition to the three procedures above, the authors believe that the procedures in Section 508 on "Reissuance of Predecessor Auditor's Report" should be followed. Thus, the predecessor auditor should obtain a letter of representation from the management of the former client.

Current Auditor

The auditor should extend his or her procedures for subsequent events from the date of the audit report up to the effective date, or as close as possible to the effective date. Those procedures include the following:

1. Arrange with the client to be kept informed of the progress of the registration proceedings.
2. Read the entire prospectus and other relevant parts of the registration statement.
3. Inquire of and obtain written representations from officers and other executives responsible for financial and accounting matters about whether any events have occurred, other than those reflected or disclosed in the registration statement, that materially affect the audited financial statements in the registration statement or that should be disclosed to keep the financial statements from being misleading.

In addition to the preceding procedures, the auditor should have applied the subsequent events procedures described in Section 560 up to the report date. They are as follows:

1. Compare latest interim financial statements to the statements being audited.
2. Ask officers and other executives responsible for financial and accounting matters whether
    a. Interim statements are prepared on same basis as annual statements.
    b. During the subsequent period there were any
        (1) Unusual adjustments.
        (2) Significant changes in
            (a) Capital stock.
            (b) Long-term debt.
            (c) Working capital.
            (d) Status of items accounted for on the basis of tentative or inconclusive data.
            (e) Existence of substantial contingent liabilities or commitments.
3. Read minutes of meetings of stockholders, directors, and relevant committees. Inquire about matters dealt with at meetings for which minutes are not available.
4. Inquire of client's legal counsel concerning litigation, claims, and assessments (see Section 337).
5. Obtain written representations from management (see Section 333) concerning subsequent events.
6. Make additional inquiries or apply other procedures to the extent necessary to resolve issues raised in applying the foregoing procedures.

    NOTE: Normally, an auditor obtains supplementary representation letters from the client and the client's lawyer that update the original letters from the report date to the effective date.

Response to Subsequent Events and Subsequently Discovered Facts: Audited Financial Statements

1. If, after the date of the report on audited financial statements, the auditor discovers subsequent events that require adjustment of or disclosure in the financial statements, he or she should follow the guidance in Section 560.
2. If, after the date of the report on audited financial statements, the auditor becomes aware that facts may have existed at the date of the report that might have affected the report had he or she then been aware of them, he or she should follow the guidance in Section 561.
3. In situations described in 1. and 2., if the financial statements are adjusted or the required additional disclosure is made, the auditor should follow the guidance in Section 530 on dating the report.
4. In situations described in 1. and 2., if the client refuses to adjust the financial statements or make the required additional disclosure, the auditor should apply the procedures described in Section 561. The auditor also should consider consulting with his or her lawyer about withholding consent to the use of the report on the audited financial statements in the registration statement.

Response to Subsequent Events and Subsequently Discovered Facts: Unaudited Financial Statements or Unaudited Interim Financial Information

If the accountant concludes that unaudited financial statements or unaudited interim financial information presented or incorporated by reference in a registration statement are not in conformity with GAAP, he or she should insist that the statements or information be revised.

If the client refuses to make the revisions

1. If he or she has reported on a review of the interim financial information and the subsequently discovered facts would have affected the report had they been known to him or her at the date of the report, the accountant should refer to Section 561.
2. If he or she has not reported on a review of the unaudited financial statements or interim financial information, the accountant should modify the report on the audited financial statements to describe the GAAP departure in the unaudited financial statements or interim financial information.
3. In situations described in 1. or 2., the accountant should consider consulting with his or her lawyer about withholding consent to the use of the report on the audited financial statements in the registration statement.

NOTE: This is sometimes called the reach-out theory of auditor responsibility. Even though the auditor is not explicitly reporting on the unaudited data, if he or she is aware of a GAAP departure in unaudited statements, the report should be modified to add a separate paragraph disclosing the departure. The opinion on the audited financial statements would remain unqualified. Naturally, the auditor's objective is to persuade the client to correct the departure. Should the client fail to do so, the auditor has no alternative but to add a paragraph to the audit report that describes the departure.

INTERPRETATIONS

Subsequent Events Procedures for Shelf Registration Statements Updated After the Original Effective Date (May 1983)

This interpretation states that the accountant should perform the subsequent events procedures described in Section 711 (for predecessor auditor or current auditor, as appropriate) when

1. A posteffective amendment is filed in accordance with the provisions of Item 512(a) of Regulation S-K.
2. A filing under the Securities and Exchange Act of 1934 that includes or amends audited financial statements is incorporated by reference into the shelf registration statement.

Posteffective Amendment

A posteffective amendment is considered to be a new registration statement. Therefore, whenever a posteffective amendment is filed, the accountant should perform the subsequent events procedures to a date as close as possible to the new effective date.

Incorporation by Reference

Each filing of a registrant's annual report (Form 10-K) and each filing of an employee benefit plan annual report (Form 11-K) that is incorporated by reference into a shelf registration statement is considered to be a new registration statement. Therefore, whenever a Form 10-K or Form 11-K is incorporated by reference into a shelf registration statement, the accountant should perform the subsequent events procedures to a date as close as possible to the date of the filing of the Form 10-K or Form 11-K. In these circumstances, the accountant should date his or her consent as of the date of completion of the subsequent events procedures.

Whenever other filings under the Securities and Exchange Act of 1934 (Form 10-Q, Form 8-K, etc.) include or amend audited financial statements and the filings are incorporated into a registration statement, the accountant who audited those statements must give a currently dated consent. Also, the accountant should perform subsequent events procedures to a date as close as possible to the date of incorporation.

Update by Sticker

When a shelf registration is updated by a supplemental prospectus (or sticker) the effective date is considered unchanged. Thus, the accountant has no responsibility to update performance of subsequent event procedures.

Consenting to Be Named as an Expert in an Offering Document in Connection with Securities Offerings other than Those Registered under the Securities Act of 1933 (Issued June 1992; Amended March 1995)

The auditor should not consent to be named, or referred to, as an expert in an offering document in connection with securities offerings other than those registered under the Securities Act of 1933. The term **expert** is typically undefined, other than in connection with the 1933 Act and therefore the auditor's responsibility is not defined. The auditor's resultant responsibility would also be undefined.

If the term **expert** is defined under applicable state law, or in other instances in which the term and responsibilities are explicit, the accountant might agree to be named as an expert in an offering document.

Consenting to the Use of an Audit Report in an Offering Document in Securities Offerings other than One Registered under the Securities Act of 1933 (June 1992)

The auditor may consent to the use of an audit report in an offering document other than one registered under the 1933 Act by use of the following language:

> We agree to inclusion in this offering circular of our report dated [XX] on our audit of the financial statements of [name of entity].

TECHNIQUES FOR APPLICATION

General

SEC work is complex and highly specialized. The accountant who performs this work should be familiar with the following accounting-related pronouncements of the SEC:

1. Regulation S-X.
2. Regulation S-K.
3. Financial Reporting Releases (FRR).
4. Staff Accounting Bulletins (SAB).

References

If he or she performs SEC work, the accountant might wish to use one or more of the following or similar references:

1. Commerce Clearing House, *Federal Securities Law Reporter* (Chicago). (This is a CCH loose-leaf updated publication.)
2. Commerce Clearing House, *SEC Accounting Rules* (Chicago). (This is a CCH loose-leaf updated publication.)
3. Commerce Clearing House, *Accountants SEC Practice Manual* (Chicago). (This is a CCH loose-leaf updated publication.)
4. Warren, Gorham and Lamont/Research Institute of America Group, *SEC Compliance: Financial Reporting and Forms* (Boston, MA). (This is a WGL/RIA Group loose-leaf updated publication.)
5. John Wiley & Sons, Inc., *The Coopers & Lybrand SEC Manual,* 7th edition (New York, NY).

ILLUSTRATION

The wording of the following illustration would be considered a satisfactory description of the status of the accountant's review report that was included in a Form 10-Q filing that was later presented or incorporated by reference in a registration statement. The accountant should make certain that this wording from SAS 37 (AU 711), or similar wording, appears in the prospectus.

ILLUSTRATION 1. REVIEW REPORT INCLUDED IN FORM 10-Q

Independent Public Accountants

The consolidated balance sheets as of December 31, 20X2 and 20X1, and the consolidated statements of income, retained earnings, and cash flows for each of the three years in the period ended December 31, 20X2, incorporated by reference in this prospectus, have been included herein in reliance on the report of Guy & Co., independent public accountants, given on the authority of that firm as experts in auditing and accounting.

With respect to the unaudited interim financial information for the periods ended March 31, 20X3 and 20X2, incorporated by reference in this prospectus, the independent public accountants have reported that they have applied limited procedures in accordance with professional standards for a review of such information. However, their separate report included in the company's quarterly report on Form 10-Q for the quarter ended March 31, 20X3, and incorporated by reference herein, states that they did not audit and they do not express an opinion on that interim financial information. Accordingly, the degree of reliance on their report on such information should be restricted in light of the limited nature of the review procedures applied. The accountants are not subject to the liability provisions of Section 11 of the Securities Act of 1933 for their report on the unaudited interim financial information because that report is not a "report" or a "part" of the registration statement prepared or certified by the accountants within the meaning of Sections 7 and 11 of the Act.

722 INTERIM FINANCIAL INFORMATION[1, 2]

EFFECTIVE DATE AND APPLICABILITY

Original Pronouncement SAS 100, November 2002.

Effective Date Interim periods within fiscal years beginning after December 15, 2002, with earlier application permitted.

Applicability

1. Interim financial information of
   a. SEC registrants.
   b. Subsidiaries, corporate joint ventures, or investees of SEC registrants, when that review is performed in the context of the review of the interim financial information of the SEC registrant.
   c. Non-SEC registrants that make a filing with a regulatory agency in preparation for a public offering or listing, if the latest annual financial statements have been or are being audited.
2. Reviews of the entity's fourth quarter interim financial information that are required, even when a quarterly report on Form 10-Q is not filed, because certain selected quarterly financial data are required to be presented under item 302(a) of Regulation S-K.

---

1 *The Auditing Standards Board has issued two Exposure Drafts of proposed SASs which would impact this section. The first is* ***Amendment to Statement on Auditing Standards No. 100, Interim Financial Information****. The proposed SAS would amend SAS 100 to require that the accountant conducting a review ask management about significant changes in the design or operation of internal control affecting annual or interim information that have occurred since the last audit or review. It would also require that the accountant consider whether such significant changes may introduce significant control deficiencies.*

The second Exposure Draft that would affect this section is ***Sarbanes-Oxley Omnibus SAS,*** *which is designed to address certain provisions of the Sarbanes-Oxley Act of 2002. This proposed amendment would add a requirement that the accountant retain review documentation for a period of seven years after the annual audit for the period under review is concluded, and states that interim reviews should be subject to a reviewing partner's inspection.*

The Public Company Accounting Oversight Board (PCAOB) has replaced the ASB as the standards-setting authority for public company audits. Therefore, the ASB's Exposure Drafts will not be issued as final standards by the AICPA. The documents will, however, be considered by the PCAOB in developing a standard or amendments to an existing standard. Please check for updates to this section on the John Wiley & Sons, Inc. website at www.wiley.com/gaas.

2 *SAS 71 remains in effect for interim periods within fiscal years beginning before or on December 15, 2002. The guidance in SAS 71 can be found in Section 722A.*

3. A review required when an accountant performs an initial audit of an entity that includes selected quarterly data and the accountant has not previously reviewed one or more of the quarters in the year. (The accountant should perform a review of those quarters to report on the audited financial statements containing such interim financial information.)

   NOTE: SAS 100 does not require that an accountant issue a written report on a review. However, the SEC requires a review report to be filed with interim financial information if the entity states in a filing that interim financial information has been reviewed by an independent public accountant.

   NOTE: Statements on Standards for Accounting and Review Services (SSARSs) apply to reviews of interim financial information not covered by this statement.

DEFINITIONS OF TERMS

Interim financial information or statement. Financial information or statements for less than a full year or for a twelve-month period ending on a date other than the entity's fiscal year-end.

Likely misstatement. The accountant's best estimate of the total misstatement in the account balances or classes of transactions on which he or she has performed review procedures.

Specified regulatory agencies. For purposes of this section, specified regulatory agencies are the SEC and the following agencies with which an entity files periodic reports pursuant to the Securities Exchange Act of 1934: Office of the Comptroller of the Currency, Federal Deposit Insurance Corporation, Federal Reserve System, and Office of Thrift Supervision.

OBJECTIVES OF SECTION

The objective of a review of interim financial information is to provide the accountant with a basis for communicating whether he or she is aware of any material modifications that should be made to the information for it to conform with generally accepted accounting principles. Review procedures consist primarily of inquiries, analytical procedures, and reading of certain documents and reports. A review is premised on the accountant's base of knowledge about the company's accounting and financial reporting practices and other aspects of its internal control. It is expected that this base of understanding will have been acquired by the accountant who audited the entity's financial statements for one or more annual periods. An accountant who has not audited annual financial statements can review interim financial information **if** he or she can acquire equivalent knowledge and understanding.

The service of review of interim information of a public entity is a product of the natural tension between government regulation and professional standard setting. Using its regulatory powers over financial reporting by public companies, the SEC pushed the AICPA's auditing standard-setting group to develop a level of service for interim data somewhere in between an audit and the minimal responsibility for association with unaudited statements. Initially, when first considered in 1975, the idea of providing negative, or limited, assurance based on the limited scope of a review was very controversial.

In December 1999, the Auditing Standards Board (ASB), as a result of a recommendation made by the 1999 Blue Ribbon Committee on Improving the Effectiveness of Corporate Audit Committees, amended SAS 71 (the predecessor SAS to SAS 100) by issuing SAS 90, *Audit Committee Communications*, to require that auditors of SEC clients determine that SAS 61 (see Section 380) matters identified in a review engagement be brought to the attention of the audit committee by management or the auditor. At the same time, the SEC required that auditors of all public companies perform timely interim reviews.

Finally, in November 2002, the Auditing Standards Board issued SAS 100, *Interim Financial Information*, which supersedes SAS 71. The Auditing Standards Board decided to issue this new standard to provide additional guidance on performing interim reviews, incorporate the requirements of the SEC for timely filings of interim financial information, and incorporate recommendations from the Public Oversight Board's Panel on Audit Effectiveness. The SAS also includes recommendations from the AICPA's Professional Issues Task Force that were included in PITF 2000-4, "Quarterly Review Procedures for Public Companies."

FUNDAMENTAL REQUIREMENTS: REVIEW PROCEDURES

STANDARDS

The three general standards of GAAS apply to reviews. SAS 100 provides guidance on application of the fieldwork and reporting standards to reviews.

SEC REQUIREMENTS

Under Rule 10-01(d) of Regulation S-X for Form 10-Q and Item 301(b) of Regulation S-B for Form 10-QSB, a registrant is required to engage an independent accountant to review the registrant's interim financial information before filing its quarterly Form 10-Q or Form 10-QSB. An accountant's review report must be filed with the interim financial information if the entity states that the interim financial information has been reviewed by an independent public accountant.

UNDERSTANDING WITH CLIENT

A clear understanding should be established with the client regarding the services to be performed in an engagement to review interim financial information. The accountant should document the understanding, preferably in writing, with the client. If an understanding has not been established with the client, the accountant should not accept or perform the engagement.

The understanding is specifically required to include

1. Objectives of the engagement.
2. Responsibilities of management.
3. Responsibilities of the accountant.
4. Limitations of the engagement.

NOTE: The best way to establish this understanding is to use an engagement letter (see ***Techniques for Application****).*

KNOWLEDGE OF THE ENTITY'S BUSINESS AND INTERNAL CONTROL

The accountant should have knowledge of the entity's business and internal controls that is sufficient to

- Identify types of potential material misstatements and the likelihood of such misstatements occurring.
- Determine the inquiries and analytical procedures to be performed. (The accountant should also use this knowledge to identify particular events, transactions, or assertions to determine where to direct inquiries or apply analytical procedures.)

Planning the Review

When planning the review, the accountant should perform procedures to update his or her knowledge of the entity's business and its internal control. This knowledge should be sufficient to aid in determining the inquiries to be made and the analytical procedures to be performed, and identify relevant events, transactions, or assertions to subject to inquiries or analytical procedures. The accountant should read

- Prior year's audit documentation. (The accountant should also consider whether results of audit procedures performed impact the current year's financial statements.)
- Documentation for prior interim period reviews of the current year.
- Documentation of prior year's corresponding quarterly and year-to-date interim period reviews.

  NOTE: The accountant should specifically evaluate (1) corrected material misstatements; (2) issues identified in a summary of uncorrected misstatements (see Section 312); (3) identified risks of material misstatement due to fraud, including the risk of management override of controls; and (4) significant continuing financial accounting and reporting matters (e.g., weaknesses in internal control).

- The most recent annual and comparable prior interim period financial information.

The accountant should ask management about

- Changes in business activities of the entity.
- The nature and extent of significant changes in internal control, including changes in policies, procedures, or personnel, occurring after the prior annual audit or review of interim financial information.

The accountant should also consider the results of any audit procedures performed with respect to the current year's financial statements.

Initial Review of Interim Information

In an initial review of interim information, the accountant should perform procedures to enable him or her to obtain the understanding of the business and internal controls necessary to address the objectives of the review. In addition, the accountant should make inquiries of the predecessor accountant and, if permitted by the predecessor, review the predecessor's documentation for

- The preceding annual audit, and
- Any prior interim periods in the current year reviewed by the predecessor.

  NOTE: The accountant may also want to review the predecessor's documentation for reviews of prior year's interim periods.

  The accountant should specifically evaluate the nature of any (1) corrected material misstatements, (2) issues identified in any summary of uncorrected misstatements, (3) identified risks of material misstatement due to fraud, including the risk of management override of controls, (4) significant continuing financial accounting and reporting matters (e.g., weaknesses in internal control).

The inquiries and procedures performed in the initial review and the conclusions reached are solely the responsibility of the successor accountant. The successor accountant should not make reference in his or her report to the predecessor's work as the basis for the successor's report. If the predecessor does not respond to inquiries or make documentation available for review, the accountant should perform alternative procedures to obtain the required knowledge.

If the accountant has not audited the most recent annual financial statements, the accountant should obtain sufficient knowledge of the entity's internal control as it relates to preparing interim financial information. Such knowledge includes relevant aspects of the control environment, the entity's risk assessment process, control activities, information and communication, and monitoring. (See Section 319.) The accountant should be aware that internal control over the preparation of interim information may differ from that over annual financial information because different accounting principles may be permitted for interim financial information by APB Opinion 28, *Interim Financial Reporting*.

REQUIRED REVIEW PROCEDURES

The following procedures should be tailored to the engagement based on the accountant's knowledge of the entity's business and internal control.

Analytical Procedures

The accountant should perform the following analytical procedures to identify and provide a basis for asking about the relationships and individual items that appear to be unusual and that may indicate a material misstatement in the interim financial information.

The accountant should compare

- Quarterly interim financial information with comparable information for the immediately preceding interim period and the prior year's corresponding quarterly and year-to-date interim financial information. The accountant should factor in his or her knowledge of changes in the business or transactions.
- Recorded amounts, or ratios developed from such amounts, to the account's expectations.
- Disaggregated revenue data, such as comparing the current interim period's revenue reported by month and by operating segment with that of comparable prior periods.

The accountant should also consider plausible relationships among financial and relevant nonfinancial information. The accountant may want to consider information developed by the entity such as a director's information package.

Illustration 9 provides examples of analytical procedures.

The accountant should keep in mind that, although expectations from analytical procedures in a review are normally less precise than those of an audit, and the accountant is not required to corroborate management's responses with other evidence, the accountant should consider whether such responses are reasonable and consistent with other information from the review.

Inquiries and Other Procedures

The accountant should make the following inquiries of financial and accounting management:

- Has the interim financial information been prepared in conformity with GAAP consistently applied?
- Are there any unusual or complex situations potentially affecting interim financial information? (See Illustration 10.)
- Have any significant transactions occurred or been recorded in the last several days of the interim period?

- Were uncorrected misstatements identified during the previous audit and interim review subsequently recorded? If so, when, and what were the final amounts of the adjustments?
- Were any issues identified while performing review procedures?
- Are there any subsequent events that could have a material effect on interim financial information?
- Does management know about any actual or suspected fraud involving management, employees who have significant roles in internal controls, or anyone else in a position to commit fraud that would materially affect the financial statements?
- Does management know about any actual or suspected fraud alleged by anyone including employees, former employees, analysts, regulators, or short sellers?
- Are there any significant journal entries and other adjustments?
- Are there any communications from regulatory agencies?
- Are there any significant deficiencies, including material weaknesses, in internal control?

The accountant should also read the following:

- Available minutes of meetings of stockholders, directors, and appropriate committees. The accountant should ask about issues discussed at meetings for which minutes are not available in order to identify issues that might affect interim financial information.
- The interim financial information to consider whether it conforms with GAAP, based on the results of review procedures and other information that comes to the accountant's attention.
- Other accompanying information contained in reports (1) to holders of securities or beneficial interests, or (2) filed with regulatory authorities under the Securities Exchange Act of 1934 (such as Form 10-Q or 10-QSB), to consider whether the information or the manner of presentation is materially inconsistent with the interim financial information.

  NOTE: The accountant should follow the guidance in Section 550, "Other Information in Documents Containing Audited Financial Statements," if the accountant concludes that there is a material inconsistency or a material misstatement of fact.

The accountant should also perform the following procedures:

- Obtain reports from other accountants engaged to perform a review of the interim financial information of significant components of the reporting entity, its subsidiaries, or its other investees. If reports haven not been issued, make inquiries of those accountants.

  NOTE: The accountant may also find the guidance in Section 543, "Part of the Audit Performed by Other Independent Auditors" helpful.

- Obtain evidence that the interim financial information agrees or reconciles with the accounting records. The accountant should consider asking management about the reliability of the records to which the interim information is compared or reconciled.

Inquiries Concerning Litigation, Claims, and Assessments

In a review, the accountant is ordinarily not required to send an inquiry letter to the entity's lawyer about litigation, claims, or assessments. However, it would be appropriate for the accountant to ask legal counsel about any specific matters that come to the accountant's attention that lead him or her to question whether there is a GAAP departure related to litigation, claims, or assessments.

Inquiries Concerning Going Concern Issues

Although a review is not designed to identify conditions or events indicating substantial doubt about the entity's ability to continue as a going concern, such conditions may already exist, or the accountant may become aware of them while performing the review. In either case, the auditor should ask management about its plans for dealing with the adverse effects of conditions and events, and consider whether these matters are adequately disclosed in the interim financial information.

Extension of Interim Review Procedures

During a review, an accountant may become aware of information that leads him or her to believe that the interim financial information may not be in conformity with GAAP in all material respects. In this case, the accountant should make additional inquiries or perform other appropriate procedures to provide a basis for communicating whether he or she is aware of any material modifications that should be made to the interim information.

NOTE: For example, if an accountant questions whether a significant sales transaction is recorded in conformity with GAAP, the accountant may perform procedures to resolve the question such as discussing the terms of the transaction with senior accounting and marketing personnel and/or reading the sales contract.

Timing of Review Procedures and Coordination with the Audit

Many review procedures can be performed before or at the same time that the entity is preparing interim financial information. Early performance of certain review procedures allows for early identification and consideration of significant accounting matters. Also, since the accountant performing the review is usually engaged to perform the year-end audit, the accountant may perform certain auditing procedures, such as reading the minutes of board of directors' meetings, concurrently with the interim review.

Management Respresentation Letter

The accountant should obtain written representations from management for all interim financial information presented and for all periods covered by the review. According to AU 722.24, specific representations should cover the following:

Financial Statements

1. Management's acknowledgment of its responsibility for the fair presentation of the interim financial information in conformity with GAAP.
2. Management's belief that the interim financial information has been prepared and presented in conformity with GAAP applicable to interim financial information.

Internal Control

3. Disclosure of all significant deficiencies, including material weaknesses, in the design or operation of internal controls which could adversely affect the issuer's ability to record, process, summarize, and report financial data.
4. Acknowledgment of management's responsibility for the design and implementation of programs and controls to prevent and detect fraud.
5. Knowledge of fraud or suspected fraud affecting the entity involving (a) management, (b) employees who have significant roles in internal control, or (c) others where fraud could have a material effect on the financial statements.
6. Knowledge of any allegations of fraud or suspected fraud affecting the entity received in communications from employees, former employees, analysts, regulators, short sellers, or others.

Completeness of Information

7. Availability of all financial records and related data.
8. Completeness and availability of all minutes of meetings of stockholders, directors, and committees of directors.
9. Communications with regulatory agencies concerning noncompliance with or deficiencies in financial reporting practices.
10. Absence of unrecorded transactions.

Recognition, Measurement, and Disclosure

11. Management's belief that the effects of any unrecorded financial statement misstatements aggregated by the accountant during the current review engagement and pertaining to the interim period(s) in the current year are immaterial, both individually and in the aggregate, to the interim financial information taken as a whole. (A summary of such items should be included in or attached to the letter.)
12. Plans or intentions that may materially affect the carrying value or classification of assets or liabilities.
13. Information concerning related-party transactions and amounts receivable from or payable to related parties.
14. Guarantees, whether written or oral, under which the entity is contingently liable.
15. Significant estimates and material concentrations known to management that are required to be disclosed in accordance with the AICPA's Statement of Position 94-6, *Disclosure of Certain Significant Risks and Uncertainties.*
16. Violations or possible violations of laws or regulations whose effects should be considered for disclosure in the interim financial information or as a basis for recording a loss contingency.
17. Unasserted claims or assessments that are probable of assertion and must be disclosed in accordance with Financial Accounting Standards Board (FASB) Statement of Financial Accounting Standards 5, *Accounting for Contingencies.*
18. Other liabilities or gain or loss contingencies that are required to be accrued or disclosed by FASB Statement 5.
19. Satisfactory title to all owned assets, liens or encumbrances on such assets, and assets pledged as collateral.
20. Compliance with aspects of contractual agreements that may affect the interim financial information.

Subsequent Events

21. Information concerning subsequent events.

The representation letter should be tailored to include additional representations specific to the entity's business or industry. See *Illustrations* for examples of representation letters.

Evaluating the Results of Interim Review Procedures

During a review, the accountant may become aware of likely misstatements and should accumulate such misstatements for further evaluation. The account should evaluate misstatements individually and in the aggregate to determine whether a material modification to the interim financial statements is necessary for it to conform to GAAP. The accountant should use professional judgment in evaluating the materiality of uncorrected likely misstatements. When evaluating the materiality of uncorrected misstatements, the accountant should consider

- The nature, cause, and amount of misstatements.
- When the misstatement occurred (prior year or interim periods of the current year).
- Materiality judgments made in the prior or current year annual audit.
- The potential effect of the misstatements on future interim or annual periods.

When evaluating whether uncorrected likely misstatements, individually or in the aggregate, are material, the accountant should also consider

- Whether it is appropriate to offset a misstatement of an estimated item with a misstatement of an item that can be precisely measured.
- That accumulating immaterial misstatements in the balance sheet may contribute to material misstatements in the future.

A review is incomplete and a review report cannot be issued if the accountant is not able to

- Perform procedures necessary for a review engagement.
- Obtain required written representations from management.

In this case, the accountant should communicate that information, following the guidance in *Fundamental Requirements: Communication with Management and Audit Committees.*

DOCUMENTATION

The accountant should prepare documentation for the review engagement. The form and content of such documentation should be designed to meet the particular engagement's circumstances. The accountant should use professional judgment when evaluating the quantity, type, and content of the documentation. However, such documentation should

1. Include any significant findings or issues, such as indications that the interim financial information is materially misstated.
2. Include any actions taken to address these findings.
3. Include the basis for final conclusions reached.
4. Enable engagement team members with supervision and review responsibilities to understand the nature, timing, extent, and results of the review procedures performed.
5. Identify the engagement team members who performed and reviewed the work.
6. Identify the evidence obtained to support the conclusion that the interim financial information reviewed agreed or reconciled with accounting records.

FUNDAMENTAL REQUIREMENTS: COMMUNICATION WITH AUDIT COMMITTEES

REQUIRED SAS 61 COMMUNICATIONS

The accountant should determine whether any of the matters described in SAS 61, *Communication with Audit Committees* (see Section 380), as they relate to interim financial information, have been identified (for example, the process used by management for particularly sensitive accounting estimates or changes in significant accounting policies affecting the interim financial information.) If so, the accountant should communicate such matters to the audit committee or be satisfied, through discussions with the audit committee, that management has communicated these matters to the committee. Such communications with the committee, or at least its chairman and a representative of financial management, should be made prior to the filing of 10-Q or 10-QSB or as soon as practicable under the circumstances.

Since the objective of a review is significantly different from that of an audit, any discussion about the quality of an entity's accounting principles for interim financial information would generally be limited to the impact of significant events, transactions, and changes in accounting estimates considered by the accountant when conducting the review. Interim review procedures do not provide assurance that the accountant will become aware of all matters affecting the accountant's judgment that would be identified as a result of an audit.

REPORTABLE CONDITIONS

If the accountant becomes aware of matters relating to internal control over financial reporting that might be of interest to the audit committee, he or she should communicate those matters to the audit committee (see SAS 60, *Communication of Internal Control Related Matters Noted in an Audit* [Section 325]).

FUNDAMENTAL REQUIREMENTS: COMMUNICATION WITH MANAGEMENT AND AUDIT COMMITTEES

COMMUNICATIONS TO MANAGEMENT

The accountant should communicate with management as soon as practicable, if he or she believes that material modification should be made to the interim financial information for it to conform with GAAP, or that the entity filed Form 10-Q or Form 10-QSB before the review was complete.

LACK OF APPROPRIATE MANAGEMENT RESPONSE

The accountant should inform the audit committee, or others with equivalent authority and responsibility, of these matters as soon as practicable, if management does not respond appropriately to his or her communication within a reasonable period of time.

ORAL COMMUNICATION

The accountant should document the communication with the audit committee if that communication is oral.

LACK OF APPROPRIATE AUDIT COMMITTEE RESPONSE

The accountant should decide whether to resign from the engagement related to interim financial information and whether to remain as the auditor of the entity's financial statements, if the audit committee does not respond appropriately to his or her communication within a reasonable period of time. The accountant may wish to consult with his or her attorney when making these decisions.

FRAUD OR ILLEGAL ACTS

If the accountant becomes aware of fraud, the accountant should communicate this to management. If the fraud involves senior management, or if it materially misstates the financial statements, then the accountant should communicate directly with the audit committees. (See Section 316.)

If the accountant becomes aware of a possible illegal act, and the effect is not inconsequential, the accountant should assure himself or herself that the audit committee is informed.

FUNDAMENTAL REQUIREMENTS: ACCOUNTANT'S REPORT

Description of Interim Financial Information

Each page of the interim financial information should be marked as "unaudited."

Date of Report and Addressee

The report should be dated as of the date of completion of the review procedures.

NOTE: SAS 100 does not provide guidance on addressing the report. As discussed in Section 508, under the Sarbanes-Oxley Act, the audit committee is responsible for appointment and oversight of the external auditor. Therefore, the authors recommend that interim review reports, as well as year-end audit reports, be addressed to the audit committee. The authors believe that it is acceptable to also address the report to the stockholders and boards of directors.

Form of Accountant's Review Report

According to AU 722.37, the accountant's report accompanying interim financial information that he or she has reviewed should consist of the following:

1. A title that includes the word **independent**.
2. Statements that
   a. The interim financial information identified in the financial statements was reviewed.
   b. The financial information is the responsibility of the entity's management.
   c. The review of interim financial information was conducted in accordance with standards established by the AICPA.
3. A description of the procedures for a review of interim financial information.
4. Statements that
   a. A review of interim financial information is substantially less in scope than an audit conducted in accordance with generally accepted auditing standards, the objective of which is an expression of opinion regarding the financial statements taken as a whole, and accordingly, no such opinion is expressed.
   b. Whether the accountant is aware of any material modifications that should be made to the accompanying financial information so that it conforms with generally accepted accounting principles. (This should include an identification of the country of origin of the accounting principles used.)
5. The manual or printed signature of the accountant's firm.
6. The date of the review report.

Reference to Report of Another Accountant

When he or she reports on the review of interim financial information, the accountant may use and make reference to the review reports of other accountants (see *Illustrations*).

Going Concern or Lack of Consistency

The accountant is not required to modify the review report if there is substantial doubt about an entity's ability to continue as a going concern or a lack of consistency in the application of GAAP as long as these matters are adequately disclosed in the interim financial information. If a change in accounting principle is not in conformity with GAAP, however, the accountant should modify the review report.

NOTE: A change in accounting principle might not be in conformity with GAAP due to lack of justification of preferability by management, improper accounting treatment of the effect of the change, or inadequate disclosure.

When there is substantial doubt about an entity's ability to continue as a going concern, the accountant should apply the following guidance:

1. If a going concern paragraph was included in the prior year's audit report, conditions giving rise to the paragraph continue to exist, and such conditions are adequately disclosed in the interim financial statements, the accountant does not need to modify the report. The accountant may add an explanatory paragraph emphasizing the matter, as shown in Illustration 6a.
2. If a going concern paragraph was **not** included in the prior year's audit report, but there are indications of an inability to continue as a going concern at the interim reporting date, the accountant does not need to modify the report as long as these conditions are adequately and appropriately disclosed. The accountant may add an explanatory paragraph, as shown in Illustration 6b.

DEPARTURE FROM GAAP

A departure from GAAP that has a material effect on the interim financial information requires the accountant to modify the review report. The modified report should describe the nature of the departure and, if practicable, should state the effects of the departure on the interim financial information (see *Illustrations*).

INADEQUATE DISCLOSURE

Disclosure requirements for interim financial information are described in APB Opinion 28. If information necessary for adequate disclosure is not included in the interim financial information, the accountant should modify the report and, if practicable, include the necessary information (see *Illustrations*).

CLIENT REPRESENTATION ABOUT ACCOUNTANT'S REVIEW

If a client states in documents filed with a regulatory agency or issued to stockholders or third parties that the accountant has reviewed the interim financial information included in the document, the accountant should advise the entity that his or her report must also be included.

NOTE: SEC regulations require the accountant's report to accompany the interim financial information if the company makes a representation that the accountant performed a review of the information.

If the client does not agree to include the report the accountant should

- Request that neither his or her name nor reference to him or her be associated with the interim financial information.
- If the client does not comply, notify the client that the accountant does not consent either to the use of his or her name or the reference.
- Recommend that the client consult with legal counsel about applicable laws and regulations, if appropriate.
- Consider other appropriate actions.

NOTE: In these circumstances, it is prudent for the accountant to consult with his or her lawyer.

If the accountant cannot complete his or her review and the client has represented that the accountant has reviewed interim financial information in a document filed with a regulatory agency or issued to stockholders or third parties, the accountant cannot issue the report and must notify the appropriate level of management as soon as practicable.

NOTE: If management does not respond on a timely basis, the accountant should follow the steps listed under ***Fundamental Requirements: Communication with Management and Audit Committees****.*

FUNDAMENTAL REQUIREMENTS: INTERIM FINANCIAL INFORMATION ACCOMPANYING AUDITED FINANCIAL STATEMENTS

PRESENTATION OF INTERIM FINANCIAL INFORMATION

Interim financial information ordinarily is presented as supplementary information outside the audited financial statements. Each page of the interim financial information should be clearly marked "unaudited." If this information is presented in a note to the audited financial statements, it should be clearly marked "unaudited."

THE AUDITOR'S REPORT

Because interim financial information is not audited and is not required to be presented by GAAP, the auditor need not modify the audit report for the review of interim financial information accompanying audited financial statements. However, the auditor should modify his or her report in the following circumstances:

a. The interim financial information in a note to the financial statements is not marked as unaudited, in which case the auditor should disclaim an opinion on the interim financial information.
b. The interim financial information does not conform to GAAP. The audit report does not need to be modified if the separate review report is presented with the information and addresses this issue.
c. The selected quarterly financial data required by Item 302(a) of SEC Regulation S-K is omitted or has not been reviewed. The auditor's report on the audited financial statements should be expanded in these circumstances (see *Illustrations*).

INTERPRETATIONS

There are no interpretations for this section.

PROFESSIONAL ISSUES TASK FORCE PRACTICE ALERTS

00-4 QUARTERLY REVIEW PROCEDURES FOR PUBLIC COMPANIES

This Practice Alert provides auditors with information to help them improve the efficiency and effectiveness of quarterly reviews. SAS 100 includes recommendations from this Practice Alert, and therefore a summary is not included here. However, accountants wishing to review the information in the Practice Alert can find it on the AICPA website at www.aicpa.org/members/div/secps/lit/practice.htm

TECHNIQUES FOR APPLICATION

The following aspects of conducting a review of interim financial information are discussed below:

1. Engagement letter.
2. Analytical procedures.
3. Extent of procedures.

4. Subsequent discovery of facts existing at the date of report.
5. Other information.
6. Successor auditors.
7. Additional guidance.

ENGAGEMENT LETTER

It is prudent for the accountant to confirm the nature and scope of his or her engagement in a letter to the client. The engagement letter includes the following matters:

1. The objective of the review is to provide the accountant with a basis for communicating whether he or she is aware of any material modifications that should be made to the interim financial information for it to conform with accounting principles generally accepted in the United States of America.
2. Management is responsible for
   a. The interim financial information.
   b. Effective financial control over reporting.
   c. Compliance with laws and regulations.
   d. Providing all financial records and related information to the accountant.
   e. Providing a written representation letter to the accountant at the end of the engagement.
   f. Adjusting the interim information to correct material misstatements.
   g. Affirming in the management representation letter that any uncorrected misstatements are immaterial, both individually and in the aggregate to the interim financial statements as a whole.
3. The accountant is responsible for conducting the review in accordance with AICPA standards. A review of interim financial information
   a. Consists principally of performing analytical procedures and making inquiries of persons responsible for financial and accounting matters. It is substantially less in scope than an audit conducted in accordance with generally accepted auditing standards, the objective of which is the expression of an opinion regarding the financial statements taken as a whole. Accordingly, the accountant will not express an opinion on the interim financial information.
   b. Includes obtaining sufficient knowledge of the entity's business and its internal controls to (1) identify the types of potential material misstatements and the likelihood of their occurrence, and (2) select the inquiries and analytical procedures that will provide the basis for communicating whether the accountant is aware of any material modifications that should be made to the interim financial information for it to conform with GAAP.
   c. Is not designed to provide assurance on internal control or identify reportable conditions. However, the accountant is responsible for communicating any reportable conditions that come to his or her attention to the audit committee or equivalent body.

ANALYTICAL PROCEDURES

In applying analytical procedures, it is prudent for the accountant to develop a permanent file similar to the one illustrated in Section 329, "Analytical Procedures." The file contains the following:

1. Comparative financial information.

a. Current quarter and preceding quarters.
b. Current quarter and year-to-date and the same periods of preceding years.
c. Current quarter and year-to-date and budgets for similar periods.

2. Analysis of relationships. Computation of relevant ratios (gross profit, net income, current, etc.) and comparison of these ratios with similar ratios of preceding years.
3. Sources of information for analytical procedures.

a. Financial information for comparable prior periods giving consideration to known changes.
b. Anticipated results; for example, budgets or forecasts including extrapolations from interim or annual data.
c. Relationships among elements of financial information within the period.
d. Information regarding the industry in which the client operates; for example, gross margin data.
e. Relationships of financial information with relevant nonfinancial information; for example, the relationship of sales to interest rates in the housing industry.

NOTE: In applying analytical procedures, it is prudent for the accountant to follow the guidance of Section 329, "Analytical Procedures."

4. Comparisons of disaggregated revenue data and other required procedures.

EXTENT OF PROCEDURES

The extent of procedures is influenced by significant changes in the client's accounting practices or in the nature or volume of its business activities. Examples of these changes are provided in Illustration 10.

NOTE: Interim financial information requires more estimates than annual financial statements. The accountant, therefore, might wish to refer to the guidance of Section 342, "Auditing Accounting Estimates."

SUBSEQUENT DISCOVERY OF FACTS EXISTING AT THE DATE OF REPORT

If, subsequent to the date of the report, the accountant becomes aware of facts that existed at the date of the report that might have affected the report had he or she been aware of those facts, he or she is well-advised to refer to Section 561, "Subsequent Discovery of Facts Existing at the Date of the Auditor's Report," for guidance.

OTHER INFORMATION

If interim financial information and the accountant's review report on such information appears in a document containing other information, the accountant might wish to refer to the guidance in Section 550. For example, the SEC requires Form 10-Q to include a management's discussion and analysis (MD&A) in addition to quarterly financial statements. The accountant might wish to read the MD&A and consider whether it is consistent with the accountant's knowledge obtained in reviewing the quarterly data.

SUCCESSOR AUDITORS

Successor auditors must complete inquiries of the predecessor auditor as required under AU Section 315, "Communications between Predecessor and Successor Auditors," before accepting an engagement to perform an initial review of interim information.

ADDITONAL GUIDANCE

When performing reviews, the accountant may find that audit guidance for relevant sections is useful. Specifically, the accountant may wish to consider

- Section 319, "Consideration of Internal Control in a Financial Statement Audit," when evaluating internal control. The accountant may find that internal control over interim financial information may vary from that over annual financial statements because of differences permitted by APB Opinion 28, *Interim Financial Reporting*.
- Section 329, "Analytical Procedures," when performing analytical procedures. The accountant should keep in mind that expectations developed during a review of interim information would ordinarily be less precise than those developed in an audit. In addition, the accountant is not required to corroborate management's answers with other evidence when performing a review, but should instead consider whether the response is reasonable and consistent with the results of other review procedures and the accountant's knowledge of the entity's business and its internal control.
- Section 380, "Communication with Audit Committees," when making communications to the audit committee.

ILLUSTRATIONS

The following illustrations are presented:

1. Accountant's standard review report.
2. Accountant's standard review report on comparative interim financial information.
3. Accountant's review report referring to the review report of another accountant.
4. Accountant's review report, departure from generally accepted accounting principles.
5. Accountant's review report, inadequate disclosure.
6. Additional going concern paragraph when
   a. A going concern paragraph was included in the prior year's audit report and the conditions continue to exist.
   b. A going concern paragraph was **not** included in the prior year's audit report and conditions exist that cause substantial doubt.
7. Additional paragraph for auditor's report on audited financial statements when
   a. Selected quarterly financial data required by Item 302(a) of SEC Regulation S-K are omitted.
   b. Selected quarterly financial data required by Item 302(a) of SEC Regulation S-K have not been reviewed.
8. Management representation letters for a review of interim financial information.
   a. Short form
   b. Long form
9. Analytical procedures to consider performing when conducting a review.
10. Unusual or complex situations to consider in a review.

Illustrations 1-10 are reproduced or adapted from Section 722.

ILLUSTRATION 1. ACCOUNTANT'S STANDARD REVIEW REPORT

Independent Accountant's Report

We have reviewed the accompanying [*describe the statements or information reviewed*] of DMG Company and consolidated subsidiaries as of September 30, 20X1, and for the three-month and nine-month periods then ended. These interim financial statements [*information*] are [*is*] the responsibility of the company's management.

We conducted our review in accordance with standards established by the American Institute of Certified Public Accountants. A review of interim financial information consists principally of applying analytical procedures to financial data and making inquiries of persons responsible for financial and accounting matters. It is substantially less in scope than an audit conducted in accordance with generally accepted auditing standards, the objective of which is the expression of an opinion regarding the financial statements taken as a whole. Accordingly, we do not express such an opinion.

Based on our review, we are not aware of any material modifications that should be made to the accompanying financial statements [*information*] for them (it) to be in conformity with accounting principles generally accepted in the United States of America.

[*Signature*]

[*Date*]

ILLUSTRATION 2. ACCOUNTANT'S STANDARD REVIEW REPORT ON COMPARATIVE INTERIM FINANCIAL INFORMATION[3] (CONDENSED INFORMATION INCLUDED)

Independent Accountant's Report

We have reviewed the condensed consolidated balance sheet of DMG Company and subsidiaries as of March 31, 20X1, and the related condensed consolidated statements of income and cash flows for the three-month periods ended March 31, 20X1 and 20X0. These financial statements are the responsibility of the company's management.

We conducted our review in accordance with standards established by the American Institute of Certified Public Accountants. A review of interim financial information consists principally of applying analytical procedures and making inquiries of persons responsible for financial and accounting matters. It is substantially less in scope than an audit conducted in accordance with generally accepted auditing standards, the objective of which is the expression of an opinion regarding the financial statements taken as a whole. Accordingly, we do not express such an opinion.

Based on our reviews, we are not aware of any material modifications that should be made to the condensed financial statements referred to above for them to be in conformity with accounting principles generally accepted in the Untied States of America.

We have previously audited, in accordance with auditing standards generally accepted in the United States of America, the consolidated balance sheet of DMG Company and subsidiaries as of December 31, 20X0, and the related consolidated statements of income, retained earnings, and cash flows for the year then ended (not presented herein); and in our report dated February 15, 20X1, we expressed an unqualified opinion on those consolidated financial statements. In our opinion, the information set forth in the accompanying condensed consolidated balance sheet as of December 31, 20X0, is fairly stated, in all material respects, in relation to the consolidated balance sheet from which it has been derived.[4]

[*Signature*]

[*Date*]

---

[3] *Regulation S-X specifies that the following financial information should be provided on filings on Form 10-Q:*

a. An interim balance sheet as of the end of the most recent fiscal quarter and a balance sheet as of the end of the preceding fiscal year that may be condensed to the same extent as the interim balance sheet.

b. Interim condensed statements of income for the most recent fiscal quarter, for the period between the end of the preceding fiscal year and the end of the most recent fiscal quarter, and for the corresponding periods of the preceding fiscal year.

c. Interim condensed cash flow statements for the period between the end of the preceding fiscal year and the end of the most recent fiscal quarter and for the corresponding period for the preceding fiscal year.

[4] *If the auditor's report in the prior year was other than qualified, made reference to other auditors, or included a paragraph describing a going concern issue or inconsistency in the application of GAAP, the last paragraph of this report should be modified.*

Illustration 3. Accountant's Review Report Referring to the Review Report of Another Accountant

Independent Accountant's Report

We have reviewed the accompanying [*describe the statements or information reviewed*] of DMG Company and consolidated subsidiaries as of September 30, 20X1, and for the three-month and nine-month periods then ended. These interim financial statements [*information*] are [*is*] the responsibility of the company's management.

We were furnished with the report of other accountants on their review of the interim financial information of Basic Subsidiary, whose total assets as of September 30, 20X1, and whose revenues for the three-month and nine-month periods then ended, constituted 10%, 12%, and 15%, respectively, of the related consolidated totals.

We conducted our review in accordance with standards established by the American Institute of Certified Public Accountants. A review of interim financial information consists principally of applying analytical procedures to financial data and making inquiries of persons responsible for financial and accounting matters. It is substantially less in scope than an audit conducted in accordance with generally accepted auditing standards, the objective of which is the expression of an opinion regarding the financial statements taken as a whole. Accordingly, we do not express such an opinion.

Based on our review and the report of other accountants, we are not aware of any material modifications that should be made to the accompanying financial statements [*information*] for them [*it*] to be in conformity with accounting principles generally accepted in the United States of America.

[*Signature*]

[*Date*]

Illustration 4. Accountant's Review Report, Departure from Generally Accepted Accounting Principles

[*Standard first and second paragraphs*]

Based on information furnished to us by management, we believe that the company has excluded from property and debt in the accompanying balance sheet certain lease obligations that should be capitalized to conform with accounting principles generally accepted in the United States of America. This information indicates that if these lease obligations were capitalized at September 30, 20X1, property would be increased by $_____, long-term debt by $_____, and net income and earnings per share would be increased [*decreased*] by $_____, $_____, $_____, and $_____, respectively, for the _____ and _____ periods then ended.

Based on our review, with the exception of the matter(s) described in the preceding paragraph(s), we are not aware of any material modifications that should be made to the accompanying financial statements [*information*] for them [*it*] to be in conformity with accounting principles generally accepted in the United States of America.

Illustration 5. Accountant's Review Report, Inadequate Disclosure

[*Standard first and second paragraphs*]

Management has informed us that the company is presently contesting deficiencies in federal income taxes proposed by the Internal Revenue Service for the years 20X1 through 20X2 in the aggregate amount of approximately $25,500, and that the extent of the company's liability, if any, and the effect on the accompanying statements [*information*] are [*is*] not determinable at this time. The statements [*information*] fail(s) to disclose these matters, which we believe are required to be disclosed in conformity with accounting principles generally accepted in the United States of America.

Based on our review, with the exception of the matter(s) described in the preceding paragraph(s), we are not aware of any material modifications that should be made to the accompanying financial statements [*information*] for them [*it*] to be in conformity with accounting principles generally accepted in the United States of America.

Illustration 6A. Additional Going Concern Paragraph When a Going Concern Paragraph Was Included in Prior Year's Audit Report and the Conditions Continue to Exist

Note 4 of the Company's audited financial statements as of December 31, 20X1, and for the year then ended discloses that the Company was unable to renew its line of credit or obtain alternative financing at December 31, 20X1. Our auditor's report on those financial statements includes an explanatory paragraph referring to the matters in Note 4 of those financial statements and indicating that these matters raised substantial doubt about the Company's ability to continue as a going concern. As indicated in Note 3 of the Company's unaudited interim financial statements as of March 31, 20X2, and for the three months then ended, the Company was still unable to renew its line of credit or obtain alternative financing as of March 31, 20X2. The accompanying interim financial information does not include any adjustments that might result from the outcomes of this uncertainty.

Illustration 6B. Additional Going Concern Paragraph When a Going Concern Paragraph Was Not Included in Prior Year's Audit Report and the Conditions Continue to Exist

As indicated in Note 3, certain conditions indicate that the Company may be unable to continue as a going concern. The accompanying interim financial information does not include any adjustments that might result from the outcome of this uncertainty.

Illustration 7A. Additional Paragraph for Auditor's Report on Audited Financial Statements When Selected Quarterly Financial Data Required by Item 302(a) of SEC Regulation S-K Are Omitted

The company has not presented the selected quarterly financial data, specified by Item 302(a) of Regulation S-K, that the Securities and Exchange Commission requires as supplementary information to the basic financial statements.

Illustration 7B. Additional Paragraph for Auditor's Report on Audited Financial Statements When Selected Quarterly Financial Data Required by Item 302(a) of SEC Regulation S-K Have Not Been Reviewed

The selected quarterly financial data on page xx contain information that we did not audit, and, accordingly, we do not express an opinion on that data. We attempted but were unable to review the quarterly data in accordance with standards established by the American Institute of Certified Public Accountants because we believe that the company's internal control for the preparation of interim financial information does not provide an adequate basis to enable us to complete such a review.

Illustration 8A. Management Representation Letter for a Review of Interim Financial Information (Short Form)

NOTE: This representation letter is used with the representation letter for the prior year audit. Management confirms the audit representations as they apply to the interim financial information, and makes any needed additional representations for the interim financial information.

[*Date*]

To [*Independent Accountant*]

We are providing this letter in connection with your review of the [*identification of interim financial information (statements)*] of [*name of entity*] as of [*dates*] and for the [*periods*] for the purpose of determining whether any material modifications should be made to the [*consolidated*] interim financial information (statements) for it (them) to conform with accounting principles generally accepted in the Untied States of America. We confirm that we are responsible for the fair presentation of the [*consolidated*] interim financial information (statements) in conformity with generally accepted accounting principles.

Certain representations in this letter are described as being limited to matters that are material. Items are considered material, regardless of size, if they involve an omission or misstatement of accounting information that, in light of surrounding circumstances, makes it probable that the judgment of a reasonable person relying on the information would be changed or influenced by the omission or misstatement.

We confirm, to the best of our knowledge and belief, [*as of (date of accountant's report or the completion of the review)*], the following representations made to you during your review.

1. The interim financial information (statements) referred to above has (have) been prepared and presented in conformity with generally accepted accounting principles applicable to interim financial information.
2. We have made available to you
   a. All financial records and related data.
   b. All minutes of the meetings of stockholders, directors, and committees of directors, or summaries of actions of recent meetings for which minutes have not yet been prepared. All significant board and committee actions are included in the summaries.
3. We believe that the effects of any uncorrected financial statement misstatements aggregated by you during the current review engagement and pertaining to the interim period(s) in the current year, as summarized in the accompanying schedule, are immaterial, both individually and in the aggregate, to the interim financial information (statements) taken as a whole.[5]
4. There are no significant deficiencies, including material weaknesses, in the design or operation of internal controls which could adversely affect the company's ability to record, process, summarize, and report interim financial data.
5. We acknowledge our responsibility for the design and implementations of programs and controls to prevent and detect fraud.
6. We have no knowledge of any fraud or suspected fraud affecting the company involving
   a. Management;
   b. Employees who have significant roles in internal control; or
   c. Others where the fraud could have a material effect on the interim financial information.
7. We have no knowledge of any allegations of fraud or suspected fraud affecting the company in communications from employees, former employees, analysts, regulators, short sellers, or others.
8. We have reviewed our representation letter to you dated [*date of representation letter relating to most recent audit*] with respect to the audited financial statements for the year ended [*prior year-end date*]. We believe that representations A, B, and C, within that representation letter do not apply to the interim financial information (statements) referred to above. We now confirm those representations 1 through X, as they apply to the interim financial information (statements) referred to above, and incorporate them herein, with the following changes:

   [*Indicate any changes*]
9. [*Add any representations related to new accounting or auditing standards that are being implemented for the first time.*]

To the best of our knowledge and belief, no events have occurred subsequent to the balance sheet date and through the date of this letter that would require adjustment to or disclosure in the aforementioned interim financial information (statements).

____

[*Name of Chief Executive Officer and Title*]

____

[*Name of Chief Financial Officer and Title*]

____

[*Name of Chief Accounting Officer and Title*]

[5] *If a summary of uncorrected misstatements is unnecessary because no uncorrected misstatements were identified, this representation should be eliminated.*

ILLUSTRATION 8B. MANAGEMENT REPRESENTATION LETTER FOR A REVIEW OF INTERIM FINANCIAL INFORMATION (LONG FORM)

NOTE: This representation letter is similar in detail to the management representation letter used for the audit of the financial statements of the prior year and thus need not refer to the written management representations received in the most recent audit.

[*Date*]

To [*Independent Accountant*]

We are providing this letter in connection with your review of the [*identification of interim financial information (statements)*] of [*name of entity*] as of [*dates*] and for the [*periods*] for the purpose of determining whether any material modifications should be made to the [*consolidated*] interim financial information (statements) for it (them) to conform with accounting principles generally accepted in the Untied States of America. We confirm that we are responsible for the fair presentation of the [*consolidated*] interim financial information (statements) in conformity with generally accepted accounting principles.

Certain representations in this letter are described as being limited to matters that are material. Items are considered material, regardless of size, if they involve an omission or misstatement of accounting information that, in light of surrounding circumstances, makes it probable that the judgment of a reasonable person relying on the information would be changed or influenced by the omission or misstatement.

We confirm, to the best of our knowledge and belief, [*as of (date of accountant's report or the completion of the review)*], the following representations made to you during your review.

1. The interim financial information (statements) referred to above has (have) been prepared and presented in conformity with generally accepted accounting principles applicable to interim financial information (statements).
2. We have made available to you
    a. All financial records and related data.
    b. All minutes of the meetings of stockholders, directors, and committees of directors, or summaries of actions of recent meetings for which minutes have not yet been prepared. All significant board and committee actions are included in the summaries.
3. There have been no communications from regulatory agencies concerning noncompliance with or deficiencies in financial reporting practices.
4. There are no material transactions that have not been properly recorded in the accounting records underlying the interim financial information.
5. We believe that the effects of any uncorrected financial statement misstatements aggregated by you during the current review engagement and pertaining to the interim period(s) in the current year, as summarized in the accompanying schedule, are immaterial, both individually and in the aggregate, to the interim financial information (statements) taken as a whole.[6]
6. There are no significant deficiencies, including material weaknesses, in the design or operation of internal controls which could adversely affect the company's ability to record, process, summarize, and report interim financial data.
7. We acknowledge our responsibility for the design and implementation of programs and controls to prevent and detect fraud.
8. We have no knowledge of any fraud or suspected fraud affecting the company involving
    a. Management;
    b. Employees who have significant roles in internal control; or
    c. Others where the fraud could have a material effect on the interim financial information.
9. We have no knowledge of any allegations of fraud or suspected fraud affecting the company in communications from employees, former employees, analysts, regulators, short sellers, or others.
10. The company has no plans or intentions that may materially affect the carrying value or classification of assets and liabilities.

---

[6] *If a summary of uncorrected misstatements is unnecessary because no uncorrected misstatements were identified, this representation should be eliminated.*

11. The following have been properly recorded or disclosed in the interim financial information (statements):
    a. Related-party transactions, including sales, purchases, loans, transfers, leasing arrangements, and guarantees, and amounts receivable from or payable to related parties.
    b. Guarantees, whether written or oral, under which the company is contingently liable.
    c. Significant estimates and material concentrations known to management that are required to be disclosed in accordance with the AICPA's Statement of Position 94-6, *Disclosure of Certain Significant Risks and Uncertainties.* [*Significant estimates are estimates at the balance sheet date that could change materially within the next year. Concentrations refer to volumes of business, revenues, available sources of supply, or markets or geographic areas for which events could occur that would significantly disrupt normal finances within the next year.*]
12. There are no
    a. Violations or possible violations of laws or regulations whose effects should be considered for disclosure in the interim financial information (statements) or as a basis for recording a loss contingency.
    b. Unasserted claims or assessments that are probable of assertion and must be disclosed in accordance with Financial Account Standards Board (FASB) Statement No. 5, *Accounting for Contingencies.*
    c. Other liabilities or gain or loss contingencies that are required to be accrued or disclosed by FASB Statement No. 5.
13. The company has satisfactory title to all owned assets, and there are no liens or encumbrances on such assets; nor has any asset been pledged as collateral.
14. The company has complied with all aspects of contractual agreements that would have a material effect on the financial statements in the event of noncompliance.
15. [*Add additional representations that are unique to the entity's business or industry. See Section 333.*]
16. [*Add any representations related to new accounting or auditing standards that are being implemented for the first time.*]

To the best of our knowledge and belief, no events have occurred subsequent to the balance sheet date and through the date of this letter that would require adjustment to or disclosure in the aforementioned interim financial information (statements).

____

[*Name of Chief Executive Officer and Title*]

____

[*Name of Chief Financial Officer and Title*]

____

[*Name of Chief Accounting Officer and Title*]

ILLUSTRATION 9. ANALYTICAL PROCEDURES TO CONSIDER PERFORMING WHEN CONDUCTING A REVIEW

Examples of analytical procedures an accountant may consider performing in a review of interim financial information include (reproduced with permission from SAS 100)

- Comparing current interim financial information with anticipated results, such as budgets or forecasts (for example, comparing tax balances and the relationship between the provision for income taxes and pretax income in the current interim financial information with corresponding information in (1) budgets, using expected rates, and (2) financial information for prior periods).[7]

[7] *The accountant should exercise caution when comparing and evaluating current interim financial information with budgets, forecasts, or other anticipated results because of the inherent lack of precision in estimating the future and susceptibility of such information to manipulation and misstatement by management to reflect desired interim results.*

- Comparing current interim financial information with relevant nonfinancial information.
- Comparing ratios and indicators for the current interim period with expectations based on prior periods, for example, performing gross profit analysis by product line and operating segment using elements of the current interim financial information and comparing the results with corresponding information for prior periods. Examples of key ratios and indicators are the current ratio, receivable turnover or days' sales outstanding, inventory turnover, depreciation to average fixed assets, debt to equity, gross profit percentage, net income percentage, and plant operating rates.
- Comparing ratios and indicators for the current interim period with those of entities in the same industry.
- Comparing relationships among elements in the current interim financial information with corresponding relationships in the interim financial information of prior periods, for example, expense by type as a percentage of sales, assets by type as a percentage of total assets, and percentage of change in sales to percentage of change in receivables.
- Comparing disaggregated data. The following are examples of how data may be disaggregated.

  —By period, for example, financial statement items disaggregated into quarterly, monthly, or weekly amounts.
  —By product line or operating segment.
  —By location, for example, subsidiary, division, or branch.

Analytical procedures may include such statistical techniques as trend analysis or regression analysis and may be performed manually or with the use of computer-assisted techniques.

ILLUSTRATION 10. UNUSUAL OR COMPLEX SITUATIONS TO CONSIDER IN A REVIEW OF INTERIM FINANCIAL INFORMATION

The following are examples, reproduced with permission from SAS 100, of situations about which the accountant would ordinarily inquire of management:

- Business combinations
- New or complex revenue recognition methods
- Impairment of assets
- Disposal of a segment of a business
- Use of derivative instruments and hedging activities
- Sales and transfers that may call into question the classification of investments in securities, including management's intent and ability with respect to the remaining securities classified as held to maturity.
- Computation of earnings per share in a complex capital structure
- Adoption of new stock compensation plans or changes to existing plans
- Restructuring charges taken in the current and prior quarters
- Significant, unusual, or infrequently occurring transactions
- Changes in litigation or contingencies
- Changes in major contracts with customers or suppliers
- Application of new accounting principles
- Changes in accounting principles or the methods of applying them
- Trends and developments affecting accounting estimates,[8] such as allowances for bad debts and excess or obsolete inventories, provisions for warranties and employee benefits, and realization of unearned income and deferred charges.
- Compliance with debt covenants
- Changes in related parties or significant new related-party transactions
- Material off-balance-sheet transactions, special-purpose entities, and other equity investments.
- Unique terms for debt or capital stock that could affect classification.

---

[8] *The accountant may wish to refer to the guidance in AU 342.*

722A INTERIM FINANCIAL INFORMATION[1]

EFFECTIVE DATE AND APPLICABILITY

Original Pronouncement

SAS 71, May 1992; and SAS 90, December 1999.

Effective Date

Interim periods within fiscal years beginning after September 15, 1992. (Reports issued or reissued after September 15, 1992, should conform with the reporting guidance in this section.) Revised to reflect SAS 90, effective for reviews of interim financial information for interim periods ending on or after March 15, 2000.

Applicability

1. Interim financial information.
   a. Engagements to review interim financial information or statements of a public entity that are presented alone, either in the form of financial statements or in a summarized form, that purports to conform with the provisions of Accounting Principles Board (APB) Opinion 28 (Financial Accounting Standards Board, *Current Text*, vol. 1, AC sec. I73).
   b. Interim financial information that accompanies, or is included in a note to, audited financial statements of a public entity.
   c. Interim financial information that is included in a note to the audited financial statements of a nonpublic entity.
2. Reporting by the auditor when certain selected quarterly financial data required to be presented with audited annual financial statements by item 302 (a) of Regulation S-K are not presented or are presented but have not been reviewed.
3. Communications to management and, in certain situations, audit committees, about departures from GAAP when
   (a) The accountant's report accompanies the entity's most recent audited financial statements filed with a specified regulatory

---

[1] *SAS 71 remains in effect for interim periods within fiscal years beginning on or before December 15, 2002. SAS 71 will be superseded by SAS 100,* ***Interim Financial Information,*** *which is effective for interim periods within fiscal years beginning after December 15, 2002, with earlier application permitted. Guidance on SAS 100 can be found in Section 722.*

agency (see *Definitions of Terms*), or the accountant has been engaged to audit the entity's annual financial statements for the current period, as stated in a document filed by the entity with a specified regulatory agency, and

(b) The accountant is engaged to either

   (1) Assist the entity in preparing its interim financial information or
   (2) Perform specified procedures (see *Fundamental Requirements: Review Procedures*) on the interim financial information.

NOTE: An accountant who reviews interim financial information of a public entity is not obligated to issue a written report on the information. Even if the accountant reports on interim information, the public entity is not obligated to publish the report in its release of quarterly information.

This section does not apply to comparative presentations of audited and unaudited financial data as discussed in Section 504.

NOTE: Statements on Standards for Accounting and Review Services (SSARSs) apply to reviews of interim financial information of nonpublic companies and reviews of financial statements of public entities that do not have an annual audit.

DEFINITIONS OF TERMS

Interim financial information or statement. Financial information or statements for less than a full year or for a twelve-month period ending on a date other than the entity's fiscal year-end.

Public entity. A public entity is any entity

1. Whose securities trade in a public market either on a domestic or foreign stock exchange or in the over-the-counter market, including securities quoted only locally or regionally.
2. That makes a filing with a regulatory agency in preparation for the sale of any class of its securities in a public market.
3. That is a subsidiary, corporate joint venture, or other entity controlled by an entity covered by 1. or 2. above.

Specified regulatory agencies. For purposes of this section, specified regulatory agencies are the SEC and the following agencies with which an entity files periodic reports pursuant to the Securities Exchange Act of 1934: Office of the Comptroller of the Currency, Federal Deposit Insurance Corporation, Federal Reserve System, and Office of Thrift Supervision.

OBJECTIVES OF SECTION

The objective of a review of interim financial information is to provide the accountant with a basis for reporting whether material modifications should be made to the information for it to conform with generally accepted accounting principles. Review procedures consist primarily of inquiries, analytical procedures, and reading of certain documents and reports.

A review is premised on the accountant's base of knowledge about the company's accounting and financial reporting practices and other aspects of its internal control. It is expected that this base of understanding will have been acquired by the accountant who audited the entity's financial statements for one or more annual periods. An accountant who has not audited annual financial statements can review interim financial information **if** he or she can acquire equivalent knowledge and understanding.

The service of review of interim information of a public entity is a product of the natural tension between government regulation and professional standard setting. Using its regulatory powers over financial reporting by public companies, the SEC pushed the AICPA's auditing standard-setting group to develop a level of service for interim data somewhere in between an audit and the minimal responsibility for association with unaudited statements. Initially, when first considered in 1975, the idea of providing negative, or limited, assurance based on the limited scope of a review was very controversial.

In June 1991, again as a result of pressure from the SEC, new responsibilities for interim information were created. These responsibilities are described in *Fundamental Requirements: Communication with Audit Committees*. The responsibilities exist when the accountant is involved with the interim information even though the accountant has **not** been engaged to review and report on interim information.

Finally, in December 1999, the Auditing Standards Board (ASB), as a result of a recommendation made by the 1999 Blue Ribbon Committee on Improving the Effectiveness of Corporate Audit Committees, amended SAS 71 by issuing SAS 90, *Audit Committee Communications*, to require that auditors of SEC clients determine that SAS 61 (see Section 380) matters identified in a review engagement be brought to the attention of the audit committee by management or the auditor. At the same time, the SEC required that auditors of all public companies perform timely interim reviews. However, there is no obligation for the audit committee to review the interim financial information.

FUNDAMENTAL REQUIREMENTS: REVIEW PROCEDURES

UNDERSTANDING WITH CLIENT

A clear understanding should be established with the client regarding the nature of the procedures to be performed on the interim financial information.

*NOTE: The best way to establish this understanding is to use an engagement letter (see **Techniques for Application** and **Illustrations**).*

INQUIRIES ABOUT CONTROLS AND FINANCIAL REPORTING

Inquiries about Internal Control

Inquire about

1. The internal control, including the control environment, risk assessment, control activities, information and communication, and monitoring for both annual and interim financial information.
2. Any significant changes in internal control since the most recent financial statement audit or review of financial information.

NOTE: The objective of these inquiries is to evaluate whether differences in the controls over interim financial reporting create an increased potential for material misstatements in interim information.

Inquiries of Those Responsible for Financial and Accounting Matters

Make inquiries concerning

1. Whether the interim financial information was prepared in conformity with GAAP consistently applied.
2. Changes in the entity's business activities or accounting practices.
3. Events subsequent to the date of the interim financial information that would have a material effect on that information.
4. Questions that arose from applying the other procedures in the review.

NOTE: The accountant should consider the consistency of responses to inquiries in light of the results of other inquiries and the application of analytical procedures.

Analytical Procedures

1. Make comparisons of
   a. The current interim financial information with the same information for the immediately preceding interim period and for corresponding previous periods.
   b. Recorded amounts, or ratios developed from recorded amounts, to expectations developed by the accountant. (See *Techniques for Application* for sources of information for developing expectations.)
2. Evaluate the interim financial information by considering plausible relationships among both financial and, where relevant, nonfinancial data.
3. Consider the types of matters that, in the preceding year or quarters, have required accounting adjustments.

Reading Minutes and Interim Information

Minutes

Identify actions that may affect interim financial information by

1. Stockholders.
2. Board of directors.
3. Committees of the board of directors.

Interim Financial Information

Consider whether the information conforms with GAAP.

Other Reports

Obtain reports from other accountants who have been engaged to review interim financial information of significant components, subsidiaries, or other investees of the entity.

Management Representation Letter

Obtain written representations from management about

1. Its responsibility for the financial information.
2. Completeness of minutes.
3. Subsequent events.
4. Other relevant matters (see Section 333; see also *Illustrations*).

Timing of Procedures

Interim financial information ordinarily is issued more promptly than annual financial information. To ensure this promptness, some review procedures may be performed before the end of the interim period being reported on. This permits the review to be completed at an early date and allows sufficient time for consideration of significant accounting matters affecting the interim financial information.

Extent of Procedures

The extent to which review procedures are applied depends on the following:

1. The accountant's knowledge of changes in accounting practices.
2. The accountant's knowledge of changes in the nature or volume of business activity.

NOTE: If changes come to the accountant's attention, he or she should inquire about the manner in which the changes and their effects are to be reported in the interim financial information. (For examples of changes, see ***Techniques for Application****.)*

3. Litigation, claims, and assessments. An inquiry of the entity's lawyer is appropriate if
   a. Information comes to the accountant's attention that leads him or her to question whether the interim financial information departs from generally accepted accounting principles concerning litigation, claims, and assessments, and
   b. The accountant believes the company's lawyer may have information about that matter.
4. Questions raised in performing review procedures. The accountant should make additional inquiries or employ other appropriate procedures if he or she becomes aware of information that leads him or her to question whether the interim financial information conforms with generally accepted accounting principles.
5. Results of procedures applied in an audit. The accountant may modify the review procedures to take into consideration the results of the audit of the client's financial statements.

NOTE: When the general accounting records are kept at corporate headquarters as well as at other locations, the accountant should apply review procedures at both corporate headquarters and selected other locations.

New Pronouncements

In performing a review of interim financial information, the accountant should consider the applicability of

1. New pronouncements on financial accounting standards to the client's interim financial information.
2. Existing pronouncements to new types of transactions or events.

Questions Raised during the Review

Information that leads the accountant to question whether the interim financial information conforms with GAAP should be followed up with additional inquiries of other appropriate procedures.

Internal Control

1. The accountant should have sufficient knowledge of internal control over financial reporting as it relates to the preparation of both annual and interim financial information to
   a. Identify types of potential material misstatements in the interim financial information and consider the likelihood of their occurrence.
   b. Select the appropriate inquiries and analytical procedures.
2. The accountant should perform procedures to obtain knowledge of the client's internal control if he or she does not have sufficient knowledge of the internal control (for example, the accountant has not audited the most recent annual financial statements).
3. The accountant should consider whether he or she can complete the review when the internal control appears to contain deficiencies so significant that it is impracticable for the accountant to effectively apply his or her knowledge to the interim financial information.
4. If, as a result of the audit, the accountant becomes aware of specific strengths or deficiencies in the client's internal control, he or she should modify the review procedures accordingly.

FUNDAMENTAL REQUIREMENTS: COMMUNICATION WITH AUDIT COMMITTEES

Required SAS 61 Communications

The accountant should consider whether any of the matters described in SAS 61, *Communication with Audit Committees* (see Section 380), as they relate to interim financial information, have been identified (for example, the process used by management for particularly sensitive accounting estimates or changes in significant accounting policies affecting the interim financial information.) If so, the accountant should communicate such matters to the audit committee or be satisfied, through discussions with the audit committee, that management has communicated these matters to the committee. Such communications with the committee, or at least its chairman and a representative of financial management, should be made prior to the filing of 10-Q or as soon as practicable under the circumstances.

Since the objective of a review is significantly different from that of an audit, any discussion about the quality of an entity's accounting principle for interim financial information would generally be limited to the impact of significant events, transactions, and changes in accounting estimates. Interim review procedures do not provide assurance that the auditor will become aware of all matters affecting the accountant's judgment that would be identified as a result of an audit.

Reportable Conditions

If the accountant becomes aware of matters relating to internal control over financial reporting that might be of interest to the audit committee, he or she should communicate those matters to the audit committee (see SAS 60, *Communication of Internal Control Related Matters Noted in an Audit* [Section 325]).

FUNDAMENTAL REQUIREMENTS: COMMUNICATION WITH MANAGEMENT AND AUDIT COMMITTEES WHEN ENGAGED TO ASSIST IN PREPARING OR TO PERFORM SPECIFIC PROCEDURES OR TO REVIEW INTERIM FINANCIAL INFORMATION

APPLICABILITY

These requirements apply when the accountant has audited a public entity's most recent annual financial statements or been engaged to audit the current period's annual financial statements and also been engaged to assist in preparing its interim financial information or to apply any inquiry or analytical procedures to the information.

NOTE: The accountant need not have been engaged to review the interim financial information. In fact, any involvement with the interim information beyond a mere reading of it will trigger these responsibilities.

DEPARTURE FROM GAAP

The accountant should communicate with management as soon as practicable, if he or she believes that the interim financial information filed or to be filed with a specified regulatory agency is probably materially misstated because of a departure from GAAP.

LACK OF APPROPRIATE MANAGEMENT RESPONSE

The accountant should inform the audit committee, or others with equivalent authority and responsibility, of the departure from GAAP as soon as practicable, if management does not respond appropriately to his or her communication within a reasonable period of time.

ORAL COMMUNICATION

The accountant should document the communication with the audit committee if that communication is oral.

LACK OF APPROPRIATE AUDIT COMMITTEE RESPONSE

The accountant should decide whether to resign from the engagement related to interim financial information and whether to remain as the auditor of the entity's financial statements, if the audit committee does not respond appropriately to his or her communication within a reasonable period of time. The accountant may wish to consult with his or her attorney when making these decisions.

FUNDAMENTAL REQUIREMENTS: ACCOUNTANT'S REPORT

DESCRIPTION OF INTERIM FINANCIAL INFORMATION

Each page of the interim financial information should be marked as "unaudited."

USE OF ACCOUNTANT'S NAME AND REPORT

If he or she has made a review of interim financial information, the accountant may permit the use of his or her name and the inclusion of the report in a document containing the interim financial information.

NOTE: The accountant is free to permit inclusion of the report, but is not required to insist on inclusion unless the accountant is named in the document containing the interim financial information of a public entity.

SCOPE LIMITATION

If a scope limitation prevents the accountant from completing the review, he or she should not permit the use of his or her name in a document containing interim financial information.

DATE OF REPORT AND ADDRESSEE

The report should be dated as of the date of completion of the review, and it may be addressed to the company, its board of directors, or its stockholders.

FORM OF ACCOUNTANT'S REVIEW REPORT

According to AU 722.29, the accountant's report accompanying interim financial information that he or she has reviewed should consist of the following:

1. A title that includes the word **independent**.
2. Identification of the interim financial information reviewed.
3. A statement that the financial information is the responsibility of the entity's management.
4. A statement that the review of interim financial information was conducted in accordance with standards established by the AICPA.
5. A description of the procedures for a review of interim financial information.
6. A statement that a review of interim financial information is substantially less in scope than an audit conducted in accordance with generally accepted auditing standards, the objective of which is an expression of opinion regarding the financial statements taken as a whole, and accordingly, no such opinion is expressed.
7. A statement about whether the accountant is aware of any material modifications that should be made to the accompanying financial information so that it conforms with generally accepted accounting principles.
8. The manual or printed signature of the accountant's firm.
9. The date of the review report.

REFERENCE TO REPORT OF ANOTHER ACCOUNTANT

When he or she reports on the review of interim financial information, the accountant may use and make reference to the review reports of other accountants (see *Illustrations*).

UNCERTAINTY OR LACK OF CONSISTENCY

The existence of an uncertainty, including substantial doubt about an entity's ability to continue as a going concern, or a lack of consistency in the application of GAAP does not require the accountant to modify the review report if these matters are disclosed in the interim financial information. If a change in accounting principle is not in conformity with GAAP, however, the accountant should modify the review report.

NOTE: A change in accounting principle might not be in conformity with GAAP due to lack of justification of preferability by management, improper accounting treatment of the effect of the change, or inadequate disclosure.

DEPARTURE FROM GAAP

A departure from GAAP that has a material effect on the interim financial information requires the accountant to modify the review report. The modified report should describe the nature of the departure and, if practicable, should state the effects of the departure on the interim financial information (see *Illustrations*).

Inadequate Disclosure

Disclosure requirements for interim financial information are described in APB Opinion 28. If information necessary for adequate disclosure is not included in the interim financial information, the accountant should modify the report and, if practicable, include the necessary information (see *Illustrations*).

Client Representation about Accountant's Review

If a client states in documents issued to stockholders or third parties that contain interim financial information or in SEC Form 10-Q that the accountant has reviewed the interim financial information, the accountant should request that the report be included.

NOTE: SEC regulations require the accountant's report to accompany the interim financial information if the company makes a representation that the accountant performed a review of the information.

If the client does not agree to include the report, or if the accountant has not completed the review, the accountant should request that neither his or her name nor reference to him or her be associated with the interim financial information. If the client does not comply with this request, the accountant should notify the client that the accountant does not consent either to the use of his or her name or to the reference. Also, the accountant should consider other appropriate actions.

NOTE: In these circumstances, it is prudent for the accountant to consult with his or her lawyer.

FUNDAMENTAL REQUIREMENTS: INTERIM FINANCIAL INFORMATION ACCOMPANYING AUDITED FINANCIAL STATEMENTS

Application of Review Procedures

Certain companies are required by Item 302(a) of SEC Regulation S-K to include selected quarterly financial data in their annual reports or other documents filed with the SEC that contain audited financial statements. If he or she has audited the financial statements of annual periods for which the selected quarterly financial data are required to be presented, the accountant should apply the review procedures described earlier (see *Fundamental Requirements: Review Procedures*).

If a company voluntarily includes in documents containing audited financial statements the selected quarterly financial data specified in Item 302(a) of SEC Regulation S-K, the accountant should apply the review procedures described earlier (see *Fundamental Requirements: Review Procedures*). It is not necessary to apply these procedures, however, if the company indicates that the data have not been reviewed or if the auditor expands the report on the audited financial statements to state that the data have not been reviewed.

NOTE: The accountant may perform the review procedures quarterly before the issuance of the data (called a timely review) or at the time of the audit of the annual financial statements (called a retrospective review).

Presentation of Interim Financial Information

Interim financial information ordinarily is presented as supplementary information outside the audited financial statements. Each page of the interim financial information should be clearly marked "unaudited." If this information is presented in a note to the audited financial statements, it should be clearly marked "unaudited."

The Auditor's Report

Because interim financial information is not audited and is not required to be presented by GAAP, the auditor need not report on the review of interim financial information accompanying audited financial statements.

Modification of Auditor's Report

If the selected quarterly financial data required by Item 302(a) of SEC Regulation S-K are omitted or have not been reviewed, the auditor's report on the audited financial statements should be expanded (see *Illustrations*).

The auditor's report also should be expanded in the following circumstances:

1. Interim financial information included in a note to the financial statements is not marked "unaudited."
2. Item 302(a) information that has not been reviewed is voluntarily presented by a public entity in a client-prepared document containing audited financial statements, and the information is not appropriately marked as not reviewed.
3. Interim financial information in 1. or 2. above does not appear to be presented in conformity with GAAP.
4. Interim financial information includes an indication that a review was made but fails to state the limitations of a review.

NOTE: For items 3. and 4., the auditor need not expand the report on the audited financial statements if the separate review report, which refers to those circumstances, is presented with the interim financial information.

INTERPRETATIONS

There are no interpretations for this section.

PROFESSIONAL ISSUES TASK FORCE PRACTICE ALERTS

00-4 Quarterly Review Procedures for Public Companies

This Practice Alert provides auditors with information to help them improve the efficiency and effectiveness of quarterly reviews The alert points out that a Form 10-Q or 10-QSB that is filed prior to the completion of the auditor's review is not considered to be timely filed or a complete document filing. A company that files its quarterly report without the auditor having performed a review of the interim financial information is considered to be in violation of securities laws.

SAS No. 71 identifies certain procedures discussed under *Fundamental Requirements: Review Procedures* for conducting a review of interim financial information. The Professional Issues Task Force identified certain other procedures that should be considered in performing quarterly reviews. The goal of these procedures is to assist in the timely identification of material accounting issues, and minimize the likelihood of quarterly restatements. The procedures listed in the Practice Alert include

- Reading the Form 10-Q or 10-QSB, including management's discussion and analysis, to determine if such information is consistent with the interim financial statements.
- Reviewing and understanding current and prior period restructuring charges and extraordinary items, as well as details of significant transactions taking place in the last days of the quarter.
- Reviewing revenue recognition methods and whether they comply with GAAP. Consider having management confirm that there are no side agreements.

- Reviewing nonstandard journal entries and significant account fluctuations, especially items such as business combinations, disposal of a segment of a business, litigation, changes in major contracts with customers or suppliers, changes in accounting principles, trends affecting accounting estimates, or other extraordinary, unusual, or infrequently occurring transactions.

  NOTE: The Panel on Audit Effectiveness points out that "nonstandard entries" is a term that is not precisely defined, although it is commonly used among accountants and auditors. Such entries sometimes are referred to as "top-side entries," "post-closing entries," "manual adjustments," "management entries," or "unusual adjustments." In general, they are financial statement changes or entries made in books and records (including computer records) of an entity that usually are initiated by management-level personnel and are not routine or associated with the normal processing of transactions. Auditors should be aware that

  - *When information technology is used to maintain the general ledger and prepare financial statements, such nonstandard entries may exist only in electronic form and may be more difficult to identify through physical inspection of printed documents.*
  - *Financial statement misstatements are often perpetrated by using nonstandard entries to record fictitious transactions or other events and circumstances, particularly near the end of the reporting period.*

- Reviewing and recalculating the company's earnings per share.
- Tracing and agreeing financial statement amounts to the general ledger or other appropriate records to avoid classification or other errors.
- Considering fraud risk factors, and asking management about the risk of fraud in the company and whether they know of any frauds committed.
- Performing analytical review procedures, such as those discussed in *Techniques for Application.*
- Inquiring about compliance with debt covenants.
- Following up on material contingencies from prior audits and reviews.

The alert also makes the following points:

- Neither the SEC nor the AICPA's SEC Practice Section requires a concurring partner review for a review of interim financial information, although certain judgmental matters may warrant consultation with the concurring review partner.
- If a review is properly planned and executed, it can assist and strengthen the annual audit. Certain procedures performed at quarter-end may help streamline the year-end audit. A review does not preclude the use of audit procedures.
- Auditors are reminded that APB No. 28, *Interim Financial Reporting*, requires disclosure of significant fourth quarter items and adjustments in a note to the annual financial statements.
- Auditors are reminded of the responsibility to communicate matters required by SAS 90, *Audit Committee Communications.*
- When the auditor becomes aware of a probable misstatement due to a GAAP departure, the auditor should discuss the matter with management as soon as possible. If management fails to appropriately respond, the auditor should notify the audit committee orally or in writing. If the audit committee fails to appropriately respond in a reasonable period of time, the auditor should consider whether to resign. The auditor should also consider consulting with his or her attorney to determine whether there is a responsibility to report fraud under Section 10A of the 1934 Act.
- Many review procedures can be performed prior to or simultaneously with the preparation of the quarterly financial statements.

- Some companies will want to issue their earnings release prior to the completion of the review, in which case the auditor should attempt to perform as much of the review as possible prior to the release. The auditor should not be publicly associated with the release.

TECHNIQUES FOR APPLICATION

The following aspects of conducting a review of interim financial information are discussed below:

1. Engagement letter.
2. Documentation
3. Analytical procedures.
4. Extent of procedures.
5. Subsequent discovery of facts existing at the date of report.
6. Other information.
7. Timely vs. retrospective review.

ENGAGEMENT LETTER

It is prudent for the accountant to confirm the nature and scope of his or her engagement in a letter to the client. The engagement letter includes

1. A general description of procedures.
2. An explanation that the procedures are substantially less in scope than an audit made in accordance with generally accepted auditing standards.
3. An explanation that the financial information is the responsibility of the entity's management.
4. A description of the form of report (see *Illustrations*).

DOCUMENTATION

The accountant should document when he or she conducts a review of interim financial information. The documentation ordinarily includes

1. The management representation letter (see *Illustrations*).
2. Documentation listing responses to inquiries and results of analytical procedures.
3. A review checklist (see *Illustrations*).

ANALYTICAL PROCEDURES

In applying analytical procedures, it is prudent for the accountant to develop a permanent file similar to the one illustrated in Section 329, "Analytical Procedures." The file contains the following:

1. Comparative financial information.
    a. Current quarter and preceding quarters.
    b. Current quarter and year-to-date and the same periods of preceding years.
    c. Current quarter and year-to-date and budgets for similar periods.
2. Analysis of relationships. Computation of relevant ratios (gross profit, net income, current, etc.) and comparison of these ratios with similar ratios of preceding years.
3. Sources of information for analytical procedures.
    a. Financial information for comparable prior periods giving consideration to known changes.

b. Anticipated results; for example, budgets or forecasts including extrapolations from interim or annual data.
c. Relationships among elements of financial information within the period.
d. Information regarding the industry in which the client operates; for example, gross margin data.
e. Relationships of financial information with relevant nonfinancial information; for example, the relationship of sales to interest rates in the housing industry.

NOTE: In applying analytical procedures, it is prudent for the accountant to follow the guidance of Section 329, "Analytical Procedures."

EXTENT OF PROCEDURES

The extent of procedures is influenced by significant changes in the client's accounting practices or in the nature or volume of its business activities. Examples of those changes are the following:

1. Business combinations.
2. Disposal of a segment of the business.
3. Extraordinary, unusual, or infrequently occurring transactions.
4. Significant changes in related parties or related-party transactions.
5. Initiation of litigation or the development of other contingencies.
6. Changes in accounting principle or the methods of applying them.
7. Trends in sales or costs that could affect accounting estimates relating to the valuations of receivables and inventories, realization of deferred charges, provisions for warranties and employee benefits, and unearned income.

   NOTE: Interim financial information requires more estimates than annual financial statements. The accountant, therefore, might wish to refer to the guidance of Section 342, "Auditing Accounting Estimates."

SUBSEQUENT DISCOVERY OF FACTS EXISTING AT THE DATE OF REPORT

If, subsequent to the date of the report, the accountant becomes aware of facts that existed at the date of the report that might have affected the report had he or she been aware of those facts, he or she is well-advised to refer to Section 561, "Subsequent Discovery of Facts Existing at the Date of the Auditor's Report," for guidance.

OTHER INFORMATION

If interim financial information and the accountant's review report on it appears in a document containing other information, the accountant might wish to refer to the guidance in Section 550. For example, the SEC requires Form 10-Q to include a management's discussion and analysis (MD&A) in addition to quarterly financial statements. The accountant might wish to read the MD&A and consider whether it is consistent with the accountant's knowledge obtained in reviewing the quarterly data.

TIMELY VS. RETROSPECTIVE REVIEW

When review procedures are performed quarterly before release of the financial data, that is called a **timely review**. When the quarterly data is reviewed as part of the audit of the annual financial statements, that is called a **retrospective review**. These terms are commonly used in practice, but not in the SAS. Because a timely review is more costly, the decision of whether to have one is made by the client. Even when the accountant is specifically engaged to do a timely review, the client decides whether a written report is needed and whether it should be published.

ILLUSTRATIONS

The following illustrations are presented:

1. Accountant's standard review report.
2. Accountant's review report referring to the review report of another accountant.
3. Accountant's review report, departure from generally accepted accounting principles.
4. Accountant's review report, inadequate disclosure.
5. Additional paragraph for auditor's report on audited financial statements when
   a. Selected quarterly financial data required by Item 302(a) of SEC Regulation S-K are omitted.
   b. Selected quarterly financial data required by Item 302(a) of SEC Regulation S-K have not been reviewed.
6. An engagement letter for a review of interim financial information.
7. A management representation letter for a review of interim financial information.
8. A checklist for the review of interim financial information.

Illustrations 1-6 illustrate the first five preceding items which are adapted from Section 722.

ILLUSTRATION 1. ACCOUNTANT'S STANDARD REVIEW REPORT

We have reviewed the accompanying [*describe the statements or information reviewed*] of Widget Company and consolidated subsidiaries as of September 30, 20X1, and for the three-month and nine-month periods then ended. These financial statements [*information*] are [*is*] the responsibility of the company's management.

We conducted our review in accordance with standards established by the American Institute of Certified Public Accountants. A review of interim financial information consists principally of applying analytical procedures to financial data and making inquiries of persons responsible for financial and accounting matters. It is substantially less in scope than an audit conducted in accordance with generally accepted auditing standards, the objective of which is the expression of an opinion regarding the financial statements taken as a whole. Accordingly, we do not express such an opinion.

Based on our review, we are not aware of any material modifications that should be made to the accompanying financial statements [*information*] for them (it) to be in conformity with generally accepted accounting principles.

[*Signature*]

[*Date*]

ILLUSTRATION 2. ACCOUNTANT'S REVIEW REPORT REFERRING TO THE REVIEW REPORT OF ANOTHER ACCOUNTANT

We have reviewed the accompanying [*describe the statements or information reviewed*] of Widget Company and consolidated subsidiaries as of September 30, 20X1, and for the three-month and nine-month periods then ended. These financial statements [*information*] are [*is*] the responsibility of the company's management.

We were furnished with the report of other accountants on their review of the interim financial information of Basic Subsidiary, whose total assets as of September 30, 20X1, and whose revenues for the three-month and nine-month periods then ended, constituted 15%, 20%, and 22%, respectively, of the related consolidated totals.

We conducted our review in accordance with standards established by the American Institute of Certified Public Accountants. A review of interim financial information consists principally of applying analytical procedures to financial data and making inquiries of persons responsible for financial and accounting matters. It is substantially less in scope than an audit conducted in accordance with generally accepted auditing standards, the objective of which is the expression of an opinion regarding the financial statements taken as a whole. Accordingly, we do not express such an opinion.

Based on our review and the report of other accountants, we are not aware of any material modifications that should be made to the accompanying financial statements [*information*] for them [*it*] to be in conformity with generally accepted accounting principles.

[*Signature*]

[*Date*]

ILLUSTRATION 3. ACCOUNTANT'S REVIEW REPORT, DEPARTURE FROM GENERALLY ACCEPTED ACCOUNTING PRINCIPLES

[*Standard first and second paragraphs*]

Based on information furnished us by management, we believe that the company has excluded from property and debt in the accompanying balance sheet certain lease obligations that should be capitalized to conform with generally accepted accounting principles. This information indicates that if these lease obligations were capitalized at September 30, 20X1, property would be increased by $_____, long-term debt by $_____, and net income and earnings per share would be increased [*decreased*] by $_____, $_____, $_____, and $_____, respectively, for the _____ and _____ periods then ended.

Based on our review, with the exception of the matter(s) described in the preceding paragraph(s), we are not aware of any material modifications that should be made to the accompanying financial statements [*information*] for them [*it*] to be in conformity with generally accepted accounting principles.

ILLUSTRATION 4. ACCOUNTANT'S REVIEW REPORT, INADEQUATE DISCLOSURE

[*Standard first and second paragraphs*]

Management has informed us that the company is presently contesting deficiencies in federal income taxes proposed by the Internal Revenue Service for the years 20X1 through 20X2 in the aggregate amount of approximately $25,500, and that the extent of the company's liability, if any, and the effect on the accompanying statements [*information*] are [*is*] not determinable at this time. The statements [*information*] fail(s) to disclose these matters, which we believe are required to be disclosed in conformity with generally accepted accounting principles.

Based on our review, with the exception of the matter(s) described in the preceding paragraph(s), we are not aware of any material modifications that should be made to the accompanying financial statements [*information*] for them [*it*] to be in conformity with generally accepted accounting principles.

ILLUSTRATION 5A. ADDITIONAL PARAGRAPH FOR AUDITOR'S REPORT ON AUDITED FINANCIAL STATEMENTS WHEN SELECTED QUARTERLY FINANCIAL DATA REQUIRED BY ITEM 302(A) OF SEC REGULATION S-K ARE OMITTED

The company has not presented the selected quarterly financial data, specified by Item 302(a) of Regulation S-K, that the Securities and Exchange Commission requires as supplementary information to the basic financial statements.

ILLUSTRATION 5B. ADDITIONAL PARAGRAPH FOR AUDITOR'S REPORT ON AUDITED FINANCIAL STATEMENTS WHEN SELECTED QUARTERLY FINANCIAL DATA REQUIRED BY ITEM 302(A) OF SEC REGULATION S-K HAVE NOT BEEN REVIEWED

The selected quarterly financial data on page xx contain information that we did not audit, and, accordingly, we do not express an opinion on that data. We attempted but were unable to review the quarterly data in accordance with standards established by the American Institute of Certified Public Accountants because we believe that the company's internal control over financial reporting for the preparation of interim financial information does not provide an adequate basis to complete such a review.

ILLUSTRATION 6. ENGAGEMENT LETTER FOR A REVIEW OF INTERIM FINANCIAL INFORMATION

Chief executive officer
Name of company
Address
City, State

Dear __________:

This letter confirms your engagement of our firm to perform a timely review of [name of company] interim financial information for each of the quarters in the year ending __________, 20X1, and the resulting data prepared for submission to shareholders and to the Securities and Exchange Commission on Form 10-Q.

The review will be performed in accordance with standards established by the American Institute of Certified Public Accountants. Accordingly, our review procedures will consist principally of obtaining an understanding, by inquiries, of internal control over financial reporting used in the preparation of interim financial information, applying analytical procedures to pertinent financial information, reading minutes, and making inquiries of certain officials of the Company who have responsibility for financial and accounting matters. Also, we will obtain copies of reports on reviews from other accountants who have been engaged to make a review of the interim financial information of significant segments of the Company, including subsidiaries and other investee companies.

It should be understood that these review procedures do not constitute an audit made in accordance with generally accepted auditing standards, and therefore we cannot express any opinion as to the fairness of presentation in conformity with generally accepted accounting principles of the Company's interim financial information. Furthermore, because the procedures to be performed are limited, they would not necessarily reveal all significant matters concerning the interim financial information, including errors, fraud, or deficiencies in internal control. However, we will report to you such matters of significance that come to our attention.

Our fee for these services will be based on our standard hourly rates plus reimbursement for out-of-pocket costs, if any.

If this letter correctly expresses your understanding, please sign the duplicate copy and return it to us.

Very truly yours,

Name of firm

APPROVED:

By: ___________
Title: ___________
Date: ___________

ILLUSTRATION 7. MANAGEMENT REPRESENTATION LETTER FOR A REVIEW OF INTERIM FINANCIAL INFORMATION

Client letterhead

Date of accountant's review report

Name of CPA firm
Address
City, State

In connection with your review of the unaudited interim financial information of [*name of client*] for the quarter ended September 30, 20X2, to be included in the quarterly report to shareholders and in the Form 10-Q filing with the Securities and Exchange Commission, we represent that, to the best of our knowledge and belief, the aforementioned interim financial information is presented fairly in conformity with generally accepted accounting principles applied on a basis consistent with that of the interim financial information for the quarter ended September 30, 20X1, and on a basis substantially consistent with the audited financial statements as of and for the year ended December 31, 20X1. Further, we represent that in preparing the interim financial information, we have, to the best of our knowledge and belief, complied with the applicable provisions of Accounting Principles Board (APB) Opinion 28 and applicable Financial Accounting Standards Board (FASB) statements and interpretations.

We confirm, to the best of our knowledge and belief, [*as of (date of auditor's report),*] the following representations made to you during your audit(s).[2]

1. The financial statements referred to above are fairly presented in conformity with accounting principles generally accepted in the United States of America.
2. We have made available to you all
   a. Financial records and related data.
   b. Minutes of the meetings of stockholders, directors, and committees of directors, or summaries of actions of recent meetings for which minutes have not yet been prepared.
3. There have been no communications from regulatory agencies concerning noncompliance with or deficiencies in financial reporting practices.
4. There have been no material transactions that have not been properly recorded in the accounting records underlying the financial statements.
5. There has been no
   a. Fraud involving management or employees who have significant roles in internal control.
   b. Fraud involving others that could have a material effect on the financial statements.
6. The company has no plans or intentions that may materially affect the carrying value or classification of assets and liabilities.
7. The following have been properly recorded or disclosed in the financial statements:
   a. Related-party transactions, including sales, purchases, loans, transfers, leasing arrangements, and guarantees, and amounts receivable from or payable to related parties.
   b. Guarantees, whether written or oral, under which the company is contingently liable.
   c. Significant estimates and material concentrations known to management that are required to be disclosed in accordance with the AICPA's Statement of Position 94-6, *Disclosure of Certain Significant Risks and Uncertainties.* [*Significant estimates are estimates at the balance sheet date that could change materially within the next year. Concentrations refer to volumes of business, revenues, available sources of supply, or markets or geographic areas for which events could occur that would significantly disrupt normal finances within the next year.*]
8. There are no
   a. Violations or possible violations of laws or regulations whose effects should be considered for disclosure in the financial statements or as a basis for recording a loss contingency.
   b. Unasserted claims or assessments that our lawyer has advised us are probable of assertion and must be disclosed in accordance with Financial Accounting Standards Board (FASB) Statement 5, *Accounting for Contingencies.*
   c. Other liabilities or gain or loss contingencies that are required to be accrued or disclosed by FASB Statement 5.
9. The company has satisfactory title to all owned assets, and there are no liens or encumbrances on such assets nor has any asset been pledged as collateral.
10. The company has complied with all aspects of contractual agreements that would have a material effect on the financial statements in the event of noncompliance.

Consider adding representations that cover the unique aspects of interim financial information such as

> Annual inventory is determined by a physical count. Inventory at the end of each quarter is estimated using the gross profit method. In establishing the gross profit ratio for use in this estimation, we have considered the results of the most recent annual physical inventory and any significant changes in operations that would be expected to influence the gross profit ratio.

[*Add additional representations that are unique to the entity's business or industry.*]

---

[2] *When proposed adjustments have not been booked by the client, practitioners may wish to add a representation to this letter stating "We believe that the uncorrected financial statement misstatements summarized in the accompanying schedule are immaterial, both individually and in the aggregate."*

To the best of our knowledge and belief, no events have occurred subsequent to the balance sheet date and through the date of this letter that would require adjustment to or disclosure in the aforementioned financial statements.

____

[Name of Chief Executive Officer and Title]

____

[Name of Chief Financial Officer and Title]

ILLUSTRATION 8. REVIEW OF INTERIM FINANCIAL INFORMATION CHECKLIST

Client ______________________ Quarter ended ______________

Approved by ______________________ Date ______________

Instructions

This checklist should be used for all engagements to make a timely review of interim financial information. It should be completed no later than the last day of the review.

If a procedure is not applicable, N/A should be inserted in the working paper reference column with the reason for its inapplicability.

Procedures	*Performed by*	*Date*	*Working paper reference*
General			
1. Obtain engagement letter or prepare engagement memorandum.			
2. Inquire of financial vice president or controller about internal control over financial reporting relevant to gathering data for the preparation of interim financial information.			
3. Inquire about whether there were any major changes in internal control since the last interim review and consider whether these changes have affected our review procedures or the quality of the interim information (list changes in the working papers).			
4. Document the understanding of internal control or update existing documentation.			
5. Inquire about the following:			
a. Whether the interim financial information has been prepared in conformity with GAAP consistently applied.			
b. Changes in accounting policies or reporting practices, including the effect of new financial accounting standards.			
c. Changes in the nature of the company's business activities, including mergers, acquisitions, sales of segments, or discontinuance of operations.			
d. Status of revenue agents' reviews, if any are in progress.			
e. Amendments to pension or profit-sharing plans.			
f. Existence of related parties and related-party transactions.			
g. Errors or fraud discovered by management.			
h. Errors in estimation discovered in prior financial statements or prior interim financial information.			
i. Status of, or change in, commitments and contingencies, including new leases or similar significant commitments, resolution of prior litigation, and new litigation.			
j. Significant changes in major contracts with customers or suppliers.			
k. New debt agreements.			

Procedures	*Performed by*	*Date*	*Working paper reference*
l. The method of determining inventories, including quantities, prices, and provisions for estimated losses.			
m. Events subsequent to the date of the interim financial information that would have a material effect on the information.			
6. Read minutes of meetings of			
a. Stockholders.			
b. Board of directors.			
c. Committees of board of directors.			
7. Read interim financial information to determine if it appears on its face and based on our knowledge to conform to GAAP.			
8. Read filings with SEC and other regulatory agencies.			
9. Obtain representation letter dated as of the date of completion of our review.			
10. Inquire of company's counsel about the status of any litigation and asserted or unasserted claims.			
Analytical Procedures and Inquiry			
1. Obtain interim financial information and make the following comparisons:			
a. Current quarter to immediately preceding quarter.			
b. Current quarter to same quarter in preceding year.			
c. Current year-to-date to preceding year-to-date.			
Consider whether additional comparisons, such as month-to-month comparisons, would be appropriate in the circumstances.			
2. Obtain or prepare the following data and selected ratios on a comparative basis:			
a. Current ratio.			
b. Quick ratio.			
c. Receivable turnover.			
d. Inventory turnover.			
e. Depreciation to average fixed assets.			
f. Debt to equity ratio.			
g. Receivable allowances (discounts, bad debts, etc.) as a percentage of accounts receivable.			
h. Gross profit percentage.			
i. Net income percentage.			
3. For the comparisons made in 1. and 2., above, obtain reasons for significant variances from prior periods.			
4. Accounts receivable			
a. Obtain current aged schedule and compare with preceding quarter's schedule.			
b. Read schedule and consider whether there are amounts due from related parties. Make inquiries about significant amounts.			
c. Inquire about procedures for sales cutoff at end of quarter.			
d. Inquire about disputed items and significant write-offs during the period.			
e. Inquire about procedures for estimation allowances, such as bad debts, discounts, and other adjustments.			

Procedures	Performed by	Date	Working paper reference
5. Inventory			
a. Inquire about method of determining inventory.			
b. If the method used in a. is different from the method used the preceding quarter, obtain explanation for change and determine the effects of the change on the inventory amount.			
c. Inquire about whether inventory is valued at the lower of cost or market.			
d. Inquire about method of determining cost (FIFO, LIFO, etc.).			
e. Inquire about procedures for purchases cutoff at end of quarter.			
f. Inquire about whether the inventory was observed, and if so, inquire about adjustments required because of differences between the perpetual records and the physical observations.			
g. Inquire about provisions for obsolescence and spoilage.			
h. Inquire about overhead rates used in the inventory computation, and if different from the preceding quarter, obtain explanations of significant differences.			
i. Compare inventory classifications (raw materials, work in process, finished goods) with those of the preceding quarter and obtain explanations of significant differences.			
6. Property, plant, and equipment			
a. Inquire about additions and disposals and compare additions with capital budgets and authorizations.			
b. Inquire about changes in methods of depreciation and amortization.			
c. Obtain schedule of repairs and maintenance and inquire about significant amounts.			
d. Inquire about new leases and the method of accounting for them.			
7. Other assets			
a. Inquire about significant changes from the preceding quarter in items such as			
(1) Cash.			
(2) Marketable securities.			
(3) Prepayments.			
(4) Long-term investments.			
(5) Goodwill and other intangibles.			
(6) Other significant assets.			
8. Long-term debt			
a. Inquire about compliance with covenants.			
b. Review classification of current portion.			
c. Inquire about significant changes from preceding quarter.			
d. Calculate expected overall interest expense and compare with amount charged to expense. Inquire about significant differences.			
9. Income taxes			
a. Obtain reconciliation between effective tax rate and statutory tax rate.			

Procedures	*Performed by*	*Date*	*Working paper reference*
b. Review assumptions used in calculating taxes and determine that they are in conformity with the requirements of APB Opinion 28 and applicable FASB statements and interpretations.			
c. Inquire about significant differences between the current quarter and the preceding quarter.			
10. Other liabilities			
a. Inquire about significant changes in similar accounts from the preceding quarter.			
11. Stockholders' equity			
a. Inquire about changes other than those caused by recognition of net income and declaration of dividends.			
b. Compare amount charged for dividends with amount declared by board of directors and inquire about any differences.			
Other Procedures			
1. Inquire about			
a. Changes in key management personnel.			
b. Changes in legal counsel.			
c. Major interruption of operations due to strike, or casualty such as a fire, etc.			
2. Compare interim financial information with information in client's audit documentation and schedules. If interim information from multiple locations is consolidated at a higher level, inquire about top level adjustments made in this process.			
3. Obtain review reports from other accountants, if any.			
4. Evaluate whether the interim financial information has been materially misstated.			
5. If the interim financial information is materially misstated, or is "probably" materially misstated, discuss the matter with management and consider the need to communicate to the audit committee any implied deficiencies in internal control.			
6. If management does not respond appropriately, inform the audit committee or its equivalent. If the audit committee does not respond appropriately, with the advice of legal counsel, consider whether to resign the engagement and take further action (e.g., consider whether there is a material illegal act that requires communicating with the SEC).			

801 COMPLIANCE AUDITING CONSIDERATIONS IN AUDITS OF GOVERNMENTAL ENTITIES AND RECIPIENTS OF GOVERNMENTAL FINANCIAL ASSISTANCE

EFFECTIVE DATE AND APPLICABILITY

Original Pronouncements	SAS 74, February 1995.
Effective Date	Audits of financial statements and of compliance with laws and regulations for fiscal periods ending after December 31, 1994, unless subsequently amended.
Applicability	Engagements to audit the financial statements of a governmental entity under GAAS and to test and report on compliance with laws and regulations under Government Auditing Standards (the Yellow Book)[1] or in certain other circumstances involving governmental financial assistance such as a single or organization-wide audit or a program specific audit under certain federal or state audit regulations.

DEFINITIONS OF TERMS

Government auditing standards. The publication, *Government Auditing Standards,* was issued by the Comptroller General of the United States. It is often referred to as "the Yellow Book" or as GAGAS (generally accepted government auditing standards).[1] It prescribes fieldwork and reporting standards for financial audits beyond those required by GAAS as well as requirements of other types of audits that are not part of an audit of financial statements.

Compliance audit procedures. Tests of compliance with laws and regulations. The tests are intended to determine whether there have been events of noncompliance that may have a material effect on the financial statements or to provide a basis of reporting on the entity's compliance with such laws and regulations. (Tests of compliance with laws and

---

[1] *In June 2003, the GAO issued revisions to its* ***Government Auditing Standards.*** *This revision supercedes the 1994 revision, including Amendments 1 through 3. The new standards will be effective for financial audits and attestation engagements of periods ending on or after January 1, 2004, and for performance audits beginning on or after January 1, 2004, although the standards may be applied earlier. Practitioners can view the revisions on the GAO's website at www.gao.gov.*

regulations are **substantive tests** usually accomplished by examining supporting documentation.) This section is concerned with laws and regulations concerning **governmental financial assistance**. Engagements related to laws and regulations or internal control over compliance with specified requirements concerning laws, regulations, or rules not involving governmental financial assistance are covered by Chapter 6 of SSAE 10, *Compliance Attestation* (Section 2601).

Government entity. States, counties, townships, cities, towns, other municipalities, school districts, authorities, etc.

Recipients of governmental financial assistance. Not-for-profit organizations and business enterprises that receive financial assistance from some level of government. Federal, state, and local governmental units provide financial assistance to nongovernmental units in the form of cash and other assets, loans, loan guarantees, interest rate, or other subsidies. Examples of governmental agencies that provide such assistance include the Department of Education, National Endowment for the Arts, Department of Health and Human Services, and the Department of Housing and Urban Development at the federal level and similar agencies at the state and local level.

Single audit. An audit of an entity's financial statements and of compliance with regulations relating to governmental financial assistance. (Generally, a single audit is a GAAS and GAGAS audit plus additional requirements as described in the Office of Management and Budget [OMB] circulars and releases. The additional requirements relate to testing and reporting on compliance requirements and internal control related to compliance requirements. Single audits are also called organization-wide audits.)

General requirements. Compliance requirements that involve national policy and apply to all or most federal financial assistance programs.

Specific requirements. Compliance requirements that apply to a particular federal program and generally arise from statutory requirements and regulations.

Major program. A major federal financial assistance program is defined by a federal regulation or law or by the federal grantor agency's audit guide.

OBJECTIVES OF SECTION

There is a tendency to associate compliance audit procedures with audits of governmental units. However, tests of compliance with laws and regulations may also be a significant factor in the audit of not-for-profit organizations and certain business enterprises.

This section is applicable to audits of the financial statements of governmental units and of certain not-for-profit organizations and business enterprises. By accepting governmental financial assistance, both governmental and nongovernmental entities may be subject to laws and regulations that may have a direct and material effect on the determination of amounts in their financial statements.

Examples of not-for-profit organizations that often receive governmental financial assistance include

1. Community-based action agencies, such as crisis intervention centers and shelters for the homeless.
2. Day care centers.
3. Libraries.
4. Museums and other cultural centers.
5. Colleges and universities.
6. Hospitals and other health care providers.

Examples of business enterprises that receive governmental assistance include some for-profit organizations that provide services similar to not-for-profit organizations and such organizations as private vocational schools and housing projects and programs.

The auditor's responsibility for consideration of laws and regulations and how they affect the audit is described in SAS 54 (Section 317), for audits performed in accordance with GAAS. SAS 54, *Illegal Acts by Clients*, states that illegal acts with a direct and material effect on the financial statements are to be treated the same as misstatements caused by fraud and that the auditor is responsible for applying audit procedures to provide reasonable assurance of detecting them. This section on compliance auditing explains these responsibilities in greater detail for audits of governmental entities and of nongovernmental entities that receive financial assistance from a governmental agency.

FUNDAMENTAL REQUIREMENTS

GAAS Audit—Effects of Laws on Financial Statements

According to AU 801.06-.07 the auditor should design the audit to provide reasonable assurance that the financial statements are free of material misstatements resulting from violations of laws and regulations that have a direct and material effect on the determination of financial statement amounts.

- The auditor should obtain an understanding of the possible effects on financial statements of laws and regulations that are generally recognized by auditors to have a direct and material effect on determination of financial statement amounts.
- The auditor should assess whether management has identified laws and regulations that have a direct and material effect on determination of financial statement amounts and obtain an understanding of the effect on financial statements.

Government Auditing Standards (GAGAS)

If the audit is of the financial statements of a government organization or a contractor, not-for-profit organization, or other nongovernment organization required by law, regulation, agreement, contract, or policy to have an audit in accordance with *Government Auditing Standards*, the auditor should follow those requirements for financial audits. GAGAS prescribe fieldwork and reporting standards beyond those required by GAAS.

Federal Audit Requirements—Planning

In planning the audit of a recipient of federal financial assistance, the auditor should determine and consider the specific federal audit requirements applicable to the engagement, including the issuance of additional reports. Generally, the auditor is required to determine whether the recipient has complied with the general and specific requirements of federal programs as identified in guidelines issued by the Office of Management and Budget (OMB) or in grantor agency audit guides.

NOTE: Generally, the audit is to be conducted in accordance with GAAS and ***Government Auditing Standards*** *and requires additional testing and reporting on consideration of internal control established to ensure compliance with laws and regulations applicable to federal financial assistance and administration of programs in accordance with applicable laws and regulations.*

Federal Audit Requirements—Evaluating Results of Compliance Audit Procedures

According to AU 801.17 in evaluating whether an entity has complied with laws and regulations that, if not complied with, could have a material effect on each major federal financial assistance program, the auditor should consider the effect of identified instances of noncompliance on each major program. The auditor should consider

1. The frequency of noncompliance identified.
2. The adequacy of a primary recipient's system for monitoring subrecipients.
3. Whether any instances of noncompliance identified resulted in questioned costs and whether such costs are material to the program.

In evaluating the effect of questioned costs on the compliance opinion, the auditor should project known questioned costs to estimate likely questioned costs.

In reporting instances of noncompliance, the auditor should follow the provisions of *Government Auditing Standards*. Regardless of the effect on the opinion on compliance, the auditor should report any instances of noncompliance found and any resulting questioned costs.

The auditor should also consider whether identified instances of noncompliance affect his or her opinion.

COMMUNICATIONS REGARDING APPLICABLE AUDIT REQUIREMENTS

If the auditor becomes aware that an entity is subject to an audit requirement (in addition to GAAS) that is not encompassed in the terms of the engagement, the auditor should communicate to management and the audit committee, or to bodies with equivalent authority and responsibility, that an audit in accordance with GAAS may not satisfy legal, regulatory, or contractual requirements.

The communication may be oral or written, but if oral, should be documented.

If management does not arrange for an audit that meets the applicable requirements, the auditor should follow the guidance in Section 317 for the auditor's response to detected illegal acts.

NOTE: By law, regulation, or contractual agreement, the entity may be required to have an audit performed in accordance with

1. *Government Auditing Standards.*
2. *OMB Circular A-133,* ***Audits of States, Local Governments, and Nonprofit Organizations****.*
3. *Other state or local laws or federal program-specific audits.*

INTERPRETATIONS

There are no interpretations for this section.

TECHNIQUES FOR APPLICATION

PROCEDURES TO OBTAIN AN UNDERSTANDING OF THE LAWS AND REGULATIONS AND ASSESS AUDIT RISK

A possible approach to obtaining an understanding of specific laws and regulations concerning federal financial assistance includes the following steps:

1. The auditor requests management to identify the amount of financial assistance received, the government source of that assistance, and the requirements that govern that financial assistance that, if not complied with, could have a material effect on the financial statements.
2. The auditor assesses the materiality of the financial assistance in relation to the financial statements taken as a whole, and assesses the risk that noncompliance with requirements governing financial assistance could occur and have a material effect

on the financial statements. A significant factor in the risk assessment is the auditor's understanding of the internal control.

3. The auditor corroborates management's identification of requirements and obtains an understanding of those requirements. If applicable, the auditor refers to any relevant government agency circulars or releases. The auditor might also discuss compliance requirements with the entity's chief financial official and legal counsel, and review any directly related agreements, such as grant or loan documents. Program administrators of the entities that provided the grants may also provide information about requirements.
   - For federal programs, the auditor might also inquire of the inspector general of the federal agency providing assistance.
   - For state and local programs, the auditor might also inquire of the audit function of the agency that provided assistance, or inquire of the state auditor or other state audit oversight organization, or review information about compliance requirements made available by state societies of CPAs.
   - For a governmental entity, the minutes of meetings of the legislative body may indicate enactment of relevant laws and regulations.
4. The auditor designs the audit to include specific audit procedures to provide reasonable assurance of detecting material misstatements resulting from violations of the requirements determined to have a direct and material effect on determination of financial statement amounts.
5. The auditor requests management to make written representations on their responsibility for compliance governing the assistance received, their disclosure to the auditor of the sources and amounts of assistance, and the adequacy of identification of requirements governing assistance.

PROCEDURES TO TEST COMPLIANCE WITH LAWS AND REGULATIONS

The laws and regulations that may require testing for compliance in the audit of a governmental unit or of a not-for-profit organization or a business enterprise that receives governmental financial assistance include

1. Laws or regulations that specify the types of goods or services allowed or not allowed, that is, the types that the entity may purchase with the financial assistance.
2. Laws or regulations that specify eligibility requirements, that is, the characteristics of individuals or groups to whom entities may give financial assistance or to whom they may provide services.
3. Laws or regulations that specify matching, level of effort, or earmarking requirements. These laws establish requirements for amounts that the entity should contribute from their own resources towards projects paid for with financial assistance.

Allowability and eligibility are often tested as part of tests of transactions. For example, the auditor might select a sample of cash disbursements charged to governmental assisted programs and consider the allowability of costs charged, or the auditor might select a sample from recipient records and test for eligibility.

Allowability of costs may include specific requirements of the program or more general requirements for federal programs specified in circulars issued by OMB.

In addition to tests of the eligibility of individual recipients (such as legal aid, health care, student loans, etc.) the auditor may need to test whether the entity is an eligible provider of the service.

AUDIT PROCEDURES FOR A SINGLE AUDIT

The auditor should plan and perform audit procedures to test compliance with the general requirements for federal financial assistance programs and the specific requirements of those programs under which financial assistance is received. The auditor should also test compliance with the requirements relating to federal financial reports and claims for advances and reimbursements (i.e., test whether such reports contain information that is supported by the books and records from which the basic financial statements were prepared).

Matching, level of effort, and earmarking requirements (i.e., whether such limitations were met and amounts used for matching were determined in accordance with OMB circulars) should also be subjected to audit procedures.

As part of testing expenditures, the auditor should consider whether evidence obtained from the audit procedures performed in evaluating the validity, completeness, or valuation of expenditures charged to governmental assistance programs selected for financial audit purposes indicates noncompliance with applicable specific requirements related to

Allowability of the cost as set forth in OMB circulars or, if applicable, state or local equivalent requirements.

Eligibility of the recipient of the expenditure to receive aid under the program. (Generally, this would involve some form of social welfare program.)

In addition, the auditor should select and test a representative number of expenditures charged to each major program.

REPRESENTATIVE NUMBER

OMB circulars may state that for single audits the auditor should determine whether the recipient has complied with laws and regulations that may have a material effect on each major federal program and test a "representative number" of charges from each major program.

What is a "representative number"? The term is not explicitly defined in OMB circulars or in AICPA standards. However, it is reasonable to interpret the requirement as an audit sample selected using one of the representative selection methods described in SAS 39 on audit sampling (see Section 350) with an adequate sample size in light of factors that may affect the auditor's judgment, such as the following:

- The amount of expenditures for the program.
- The newness of the program or changes in its conditions.
- Prior experience with the program, particularly as revealed in prior audits.
- The extent to which the program is carried out through subrecipients.
- The extent to which the program contracts for goods or services.
- The level to which the program is already subject to program reviews or other forms of independent oversight.
- The adequacy of the controls for ensuring compliance.
- The expectation of adherence or lack of adherence to the applicable laws and regulations.
- The potential impact of adverse findings.

GENERAL REQUIREMENTS

In performing a single audit, should the auditor always perform tests of all the general requirements? The auditor tests only the general requirements that apply to the programs for which the client receives assistance. For example, the Davis-Bacon Act requires that laborers working on federal financial construction contracts be paid a wage established by the US

Secretary of Labor. If the client's major programs do not involve construction, no testing of compliance with the Davis-Bacon Act is required. However, some general requirements, such as a drug-free environment and the need not to discriminate based on sex or race are matters of national policy, and such general requirements are always tested.

NOT-FOR-PROFIT ORGANIZATIONS

Does this section apply to the audits of all not-for-profit organizations? No. It applies only to those organizations that receive direct financial assistance from federal, state, or local governments, or that receive governmental assistance passed through from a level of government. For example, a city receives a grant from a federal program. The city provides funds to a not-for-profit corporation as a part of the efforts of the program. This section applies to the audits of both the city and the not-for-profit corporation. The audit of a not-for-profit corporation supported entirely from private contributions would generally not be subject to the requirements of this section.

NO REPORTABLE CONDITIONS REPORT

SAS 60 (Section 325) prohibits the auditor from issuing a report stating that no reportable conditions were noted during the audit. However, audits in accordance with Government Auditing Standards require the issuance of a report on internal control. What should the report say if no reportable conditions were noted? The report should specifically identify the categories of internal control policies and procedures considered and provide assurance that no material weaknesses were identified. The expression of assurance on the absence of material weaknesses combined with no reference to reportable conditions is implicit assurance on the absence of reportable conditions.

901 PUBLIC WAREHOUSES: CONTROLS AND AUDITING PROCEDURES FOR GOODS HELD

EFFECTIVE DATE AND APPLICABILITY

Original Pronouncements	SAP 37, September 1966 (codified in SAS 1, November 1972); SAS 43, August 1982.
Effective Date	When issued, September 1966.
Applicability	Internal control of 1. A warehouseman for goods in his or her custody. 2. An owner of goods in the custody of a warehouseman. Auditing procedures to be applied by 1. An auditor of a warehouseman for goods in the custody of the warehouseman. 2. An auditor of an owner of goods in the custody of a warehouseman.

DEFINITIONS OF TERMS

Warehouse. A facility operated by a warehouseman whose business is maintaining effective custody of goods for others.

Terminal warehouse. A warehouse that ordinarily furnishes storage only; however, it may provide other services, such as packaging and billing.

Field warehouse. A warehouse that is established as part of a financing arrangement. It might be established on the premises of either

1. The owner of the goods, or
2. A customer of the owner of the goods.

A field warehouse is established so that the warehouseman may take and maintain custody of the goods. The warehouseman does the following:

1. Leases space on the premises of the owner or the customer of the owner.
2. Ordinarily temporarily employs personnel at the warehouse who are employees of the owner or the customer of the owner.
3. Issues warehouse receipts to be used as collateral for a loan or other form of credit.

Refrigerated warehouse. A warehouse constructed and equipped to meet controlled-temperature and special-handling requirements. Ordinarily it stores perishable products and food.

Commodity warehouse. A warehouse that stores certain bulk commodities, such as agricultural products and chemicals. Ordinarily this type of warehouse stores only one commodity.

General merchandise warehouse. A warehouse that stores merchandise not requiring special storage facilities, such as furniture, other household goods, and personal effects.

Warehouse receipt. A document that represents goods stored in warehouse.

Negotiable warehouse receipt. A warehouse receipt that must be surrendered to the warehouseman before the release of the goods.

Nonnegotiable warehouse receipt. A warehouse receipt that need not be surrendered in order for goods to be released by the warehouseman. Goods may be released upon valid instructions to the warehouseman.

OBJECTIVES OF SECTION

In the early 1960s the Allied Crude Vegetable Oil Company case, or, as it is sometimes called, the DeAngelis fraud, shocked accountants and caused the AICPA Committee on Auditing Procedure (forerunner to the Auditing Standards Board) to reexamine the existing position that a confirmation from the warehouseman provided sufficient evidence on inventory held in a public warehouse. After all, the warehouseman is not a disinterested party and cannot necessarily be relied on to disclose shortcomings in his or her own performance.

The main change made by the committee was to indicate that if inventory was a significant portion of current assets or total assets, confirmation from the warehouseman is not sufficient. More reliable evidence is necessary. The auditor may use judgment, however, in deciding how extensive his or her procedures need to be. One or more of several procedures, in addition to confirmation, might be appropriate depending on the circumstances.

FUNDAMENTAL REQUIREMENTS: CONTROLS FOR WAREHOUSEMAN

AU 901.15 provides guidance on suggested controls for a warehouse. It emphasizes the segregation of duties in the performance of operating functions of the warehouse. Controls are classified as follows:

1. Receiving goods.
2. Storing goods.
3. Delivering goods.
4. Warehouse receipts.
5. Insurance.
6. Additional controls for field warehouses.

RECEIVING GOODS

1. Receipts should be issued for all goods admitted.
2. Receiving clerks should prepare reports for all goods received.
3. Quantities on receiving reports should be compared with quantities shown on bills of lading or other documents received from outside sources by an employee independent of receiving, storing, and delivering.
4. Goods received should be inspected, counted, weighed, measured, or graded. Machinery (or computers) used for these purposes should be periodically checked for accuracy.

Storing Goods

1. When possible, goods should be stored so that each lot is segregated and identified with its warehouse receipt. (This may not be possible with fungible goods.)
2. Warehouse records should show the location of goods represented by each warehouse receipt.
3. Access to the storage area should be limited to employees whose duties require it.
4. Custody of keys to the storage area should be controlled.
5. Periodic statements to customers should identify the goods held and request that discrepancies be reported to a named employee who is not connected with receiving, storing, or delivering.
6. Stored goods should be physically counted or tested periodically and quantities agreed to the records by an employee who is not connected with the storage function.
7. For perishable goods, a regular schedule for inspection of condition should be established.
8. Protective devices—burglar alarms, fire alarms, sprinkler systems, and temperature and humidity controls—should be inspected regularly.

Delivering Goods

1. Instructions should be issued that goods may be released only on proper authorization. In the case of negotiable receipts, this includes surrender of the receipt.
2. Goods should be released only on written instructions from an authorized employee who does not have access to the goods.
3. Counts of goods to be released made by stock clerks should be independently checked by shipping clerks or others, and the two counts should be compared before the goods are released.

Warehouse Receipts

1. Prenumbered warehouse receipts should be used.
2. Procedures should be established for accounting for all receipts used and for cancellation of negotiable receipts when goods have been delivered.
3. Unused receipts should be safeguarded, and their custody should be assigned to a responsible employee who is not authorized to prepare or sign receipts.
4. Receipts should be furnished only to authorized persons and in a quantity limited to the number required for current use.
5. The signer of receipts should ascertain that the receipts are supported by receiving records.
6. Receipts should be prepared and completed in a manner designed to prevent alteration.
7. Authorized signers of receipts should be a limited number of responsible employees.

Insurance

1. Insurance coverage should be reviewed periodically.

Additional Controls for Field Warehouses

1. Only nonnegotiable warehouse receipts should be issued from field locations.

2. Receipt forms should be furnished to field locations by the central office in quantities limited to current requirements.
3. According to AU 901.18, other internal control procedures suggested for the central office are
   a. Consideration of the business reputation and financial standing of the depositor.
   b. Preparation of field warehouse contract in accordance with requirements of depositor and lender.
   c. Determination that leased warehouse premises meet the physical requirements for segregation and effective custody of goods.
   d. Satisfaction about legal matters pertaining to the lease of the warehouse premises.
   e. Investigation and bonding of employees at field locations.
   f. Providing employees at field locations with written instructions.
   g. Maintenance of inventory records showing quantity and stated value, where applicable, of goods represented by each outstanding warehouse receipt.
   h. Examination of field warehouse, including inspection of the facilities, observation as to compliance with prescribed procedures, physical counts or tests of goods in custody and reconciliation of quantities to records at both the central office and the field locations, accounting for all receipts furnished to the field locations, and confirmation of outstanding warehouse receipts with registered holders.

FUNDAMENTAL REQUIREMENTS: WAREHOUSEMAN'S AUDITOR

INTERNAL CONTROL POLICIES AND PROCEDURES

Obtain an understanding of controls relating to the accountability for, and the custody of, all goods placed in the warehouse and perform tests of controls to evaluate their effectiveness.

ACCOUNTABILITY

According to AU 901.19, the independent auditor of the warehouseman should perform the following procedures.

Goods Placed in Custody

Test the warehouseman's records to evaluate accountability for all goods placed in his or her custody.

Outstanding Warehouse Receipts

Test the warehouseman's accountability under recorded outstanding warehouse receipts. Procedures relating to accountability might include, on a test basis, the following:

1. Comparison of documentary evidence of goods received and delivered with warehouse receipts records.
2. Accounting for issued and unissued warehouse receipts by number.
3. Comparison of records of goods stored with billings for storage.

In some circumstances, the auditor may consider it necessary to confirm with the printer of the warehouse receipts the serial numbers supplied.

Observation

Observe physical counts of goods in custody and reconcile test counts with records of goods stored. In the case of a field warehouse where goods are stored at many scattered locations, the auditor may observe physical counts at certain selected locations.

Confirmation

Confirm accountability by direct communication with holders of warehouse receipts. Confirmation of negotiable receipts with holders may not be practicable because the holder's identity usually is not known to the warehouseman. Confirmation with the depositor to whom the outstanding receipt was originally issued, however, is evidence of accountability for certain designated goods. In some circumstances, it may be desirable to request confirmations from former depositors who are not currently holders of record.

Other Procedures Considered Necessary

The auditor might review

1. Bonding arrangements.
2. Financial statements of, and credit reports on, some depositors.
3. Insurance coverage.
4. Adequacy of reserves for losses for damage claims.

FUNDAMENTAL REQUIREMENTS: OWNER OF GOODS

Investigation of Warehouseman before Placing Goods in His or Her Custody

According to AU 901.26, the auditor should

1. Consider the business reputation and financial standing of the warehouseman.
2. Inspect facilities.
3. Review warehouseman's financial statements and the related auditor's reports.
4. Make inquiries about
   a. The warehouseman's controls and whether he or she holds goods for his or her own account.
   b. The type and adequacy of the warehouseman's insurance.
   c. Government or other licensing and bonding requirements and the nature, extent, and results of any inspection by government or other agencies.

Evaluation of Warehouseman's Performance

According to AU 901.27, the auditor should

1. Review and update information developed from investigation described earlier.
2. Perform physical counts of goods at the warehouse, if practicable and reasonable.
3. Reconcile quantities shown on statements from warehouseman with owner's records.

Other Procedures

1. Review the owner's insurance, if any, on goods at warehouse.

FUNDAMENTAL REQUIREMENTS: OWNER'S AUDITOR

Section 331.14 describes the procedures the owner's auditor should consider applying if inventories are held in a public warehouse. The auditor should obtain direct confirmation, in writing, from the warehouseman. If inventories at a warehouse are a significant proportion of current assets or total assets, the auditor should apply one or more of the following procedures:

1. Assess control risk related to the client's procedures for investigating the warehouseman and evaluating his or her performance.
2. Observe physical counts of goods at warehouse, if practicable.
3. If warehouse receipts have been pledged as collateral, confirm with lenders details of pledged receipts (see Section 330).
4. Do one of the following:
    a. Obtain auditor's report on the warehouse's controls relevant to custody of goods and pledging of receipts (see Section 324).
    b. Apply procedures at the warehouse to gain reasonable assurance that information received from the warehouse is reliable.

INTERPRETATIONS

There are no interpretations for this section.

2101 ATTEST ENGAGEMENTS[1]

EFFECTIVE DATE AND APPLICABILITY

Original Pronouncements

Statement on Standards for Attestation Engagements (SSAE) 10, *Attestation Standards: Revision and Recodification,* January 2001, as amended by SSAE 11, January 2002, and SSAE 12, September 2002.

Effective Date

Effective when the subject matter or assertion is as of, or for a period ending on or after, June 1, 2001. Revised to reflect SSAE 11, which is effective for attest engagements when the subject matter or assertion is as of, or for a period ending on or after December 15, 2002, with early application permitted, and SSAE 12, effective upon issuance.

Applicability

Attest engagements, as defined below, performed by a certified public accountant in the practice of public accounting (practitioner). See Section 2301 for additional guidance on applicability when engaged to provide an attest service on a financial forecast or projection.

NOTE: Practitioners performing agreed-upon procedures must follow the general, fieldwork, and reporting standards for attest engagements described in the section, but should refer to Section 2201 for specific guidance on performing such engagements. When a practitioner accepts an attest engagement for a government body or agency and agrees to follow specified government standards, guides, procedures, statutes, rules, and regulations, the practitioner must follow those governmental requirements as well as the applicable attestation standards.

DEFINITIONS OF TERMS

Attest engagement. An engagement in which a practitioner is engaged to issue or does issue an examination, a review, or an agreed-upon procedures report on subject matter, or an assertion about the subject matter, that is the responsibility of another party.

NOTE: Professional services that are not covered by this section include the following:

1. *Services performed under SASs.*
2. *Services performed under SSARSs.*
3. *Services performed under the Statement on Standards for Consulting Services (SSCS) including litigation services.*

---

[1] *In AICPA publications this section is codified as AT 101.*

4. *Engagements to advocate a client's position, such as representing the client when dealing with the Internal Revenue Service.*
5. *Engagements to prepare tax returns or provide tax advice.*

Assertion. A declaration, or set of related declarations, about whether the subject matter is based on, or in conformity with, the selected criteria.

NOTE: A conclusion on the reliability of a written assertion may refer to that assertion or to the subject matter to which the assertion relates. However, if there are one or more material deviations from the criteria, the practitioner should modify the report and should ordinarily express his or her conclusion directly on the subject matter, not on management's assertion.

Responsible party. The person or persons (either as individuals or representatives of the entity) responsible for the subject matter. If no such party exists due to the nature of the subject matter, then a party who has a reasonable basis for making a written assertion about the subject matter may provide such an assertion.

Subject matter. Examples of the subject matter of an attest engagement include

- Historical or prospective performance or condition, such as prospective financial information, performance measurements, and backlog data.
- Physical characteristics, such as a narrative description or square footage of facilities.
- Historical events, such as the price of a market basket or goods on a certain date.
- Analyses, such as breakeven analyses.
- Systems and processes, such as internal control.
- Behavior, such as corporate governance or compliance with laws and regulations.

Criteria. The standards or benchmarks used to measure and present the subject matter and against which the practitioner evaluates the subject matter.

Attestation risk. The risk that the practitioner may unknowingly fail to appropriately modify his or her attest report on an assertion that is materially misstated. It consists of the risk (inherent and control risk) that the assertion contains errors that could be material and the risk (detection risk) that the practitioner will not detect such errors.

OBJECTIVES OF SECTION

At one time attest services provided by CPAs were limited to expressing a positive opinion on historical financial statements on the basis of an audit made in accordance with generally accepted auditing standards (GAAS). However, CPAs are increasingly requested to provide assurance on representations other than historical financial statements and in forms other than the positive opinion. The main objective of adopting the attestation standards was to provide guidance and establish a broad framework for the variety of attest services demanded of CPAs.

There are eleven attestation standards and two levels of attest assurance that can be reported for general distribution, as follows:

1. Positive assurance in reports that express conclusions on the basis of an **examination**.
2. Moderate assurance in reports that express conclusions on the basis of a **review**.

The guidance on attest services also provides for reports based on agreed-upon procedures or agreed-upon criteria as long as the use of the report is limited to the parties who agreed upon the procedures or criteria.

In January 1999, the Auditing Standards Board issued Statement on Standards for Attestation Engagements 9, *Amendments to SSAE Nos. 1, 2, and 3.* SSAE 9

- Provided the option of reporting directly on the subject matter of the assertion, while still permitting practitioners to report on management's assertion. (The practitioner would continue to be required to obtain management's assertion as a condition of engagement performance.)

- Eliminated the requirement for a separate presentation of management's assertion in certain cases where the assertion is included in the introductory paragraph of the practitioner's report. (This limited approach to direct reporting was modified by SSAE 10.)
- Conformed the reporting guidance to include reporting elements similar to those required in auditor reports on historical financial statements as contained in SAS 58, *Reports on Audited Financial Statements* (see Section 508).
- Provided guidance on the relationship between SSAEs and the Statements on Quality Control Standards.

In January 2001, the Auditing Standards Board issued SSAE 10, *Attestation Standards: Revision and Recodification*. SSAE 10 superseded SSAEs 1 through 9 and renumbered the AT sections in the AICPA's *Codification*. The primary driver behind the issuance of SSAE 10 was not the need for substantive changes, but the need to make the guidance among attest services more consistent. The revisions to this section included

- Changing the title of this section to *Attest Engagements*.
- Changing the definition of an attest engagement.
- Clarifying that the attestation standards may be applied to a broad range of subject matter.
- Clarifying the relationship between the responsible party, the client (if different from the responsible party), and the practitioner.
- Clarifying that the essential elements of criteria referred to in the third general standard are that the criteria must be suitable, available to users, and the subject matter must be capable of reasonably consistent measurement.
- Providing guidance on restricting the use of the report when a practitioner performs and reports on engagements when written assertion cannot be obtained.
- Permitting true direct reporting on the subject matter. There is no requirement to make reference to an assertion in the practitioner's report. The practitioner would also be permitted to report on the written assertion.
- Expanding guidance on the circumstances in which the use of attest reports should be restricted to specified parties is provided.

Additional changes made by SSAE 10 are described in Sections 2201 to 2701.

In January 2002, the Auditing Standards Board issued SSAE 11, *Attest Documentation*. SSAE 11 incorporates in the attestation standards the concepts and terminology in SAS 96, *Audit Documentation*. (See Section 339.) In September 2002, SSAE 12, *Amendment to Statement on Standards for Attestation Engagements No. 10,* ***Attestation Standards: Revision and Recodification,*** was issued. SSAE 12 clarifies that although an effective quality control system will assist in complying with attestation standards, deficiencies in or noncompliance with the quality control system does, not by itself, indicate that an engagement was not performed according to the appropriate standards.

FUNDAMENTAL REQUIREMENTS

A practitioner who is engaged to issue or does issue an examination, a review, or an agreed-upon procedures report on subject matter, or an assertion about the subject matter that is the responsibility of another party should do so in accordance with the eleven attestation standards described below.

Any professional engagement which results in an expression of assurance must be performed under the applicable AICPA standards. Reports issued in connection with other professional standards should be clearly distinguished from attest reports.

An identified responsible party is a prerequisite for an attest engagement. A practitioner may accept an examination, a review, or an agreed-upon procedures engagement on subject matter or a related assertion if one of the following is met:

- The client is responsible for the subject matter. If, due to the nature of the subject matter, a responsible party does not otherwise exist, then the client must have a reasonable basis for providing a written assertion about the subject matter.
- If the client is not responsible for the subject matter, then he or she must be able to provide the practitioner, or have a responsible third party provide the practitioner, with evidence of the third party's responsibility for the subject matter.

NOTE: The practitioner should not take on the role of the responsible party in an attest engagement.

The practitioner should obtain written acknowledgement or other evidence (e.g., reference to legislation, a regulation, or a contract) of the responsible party's responsibility for the subject matter.

The eleven attestation standards are a natural extension of, **but do not supersede,** the ten generally accepted auditing standards. Further, they do not supersede existing standards in Statements on Auditing Standards (SASs) and Statements on Standards for Accounting and Review Services (SSARSs). The practitioner who is engaged to perform an engagement subject to these existing standards should follow such standards and not look to the eleven attestation standards or the discussion of them in Section 2101 (AT 101) for guidance.

ATTESTATION STANDARDS

The 11 standards are classified as follows:

General: 1 through 5.
Fieldwork: 6 and 7.
Reporting: 8 through 11.

1. **First general standard.** The engagement shall be performed by a practitioner having adequate technical training and proficiency in the attest function. (AT 101.19)
2. **Second general standard.** The engagement shall be performed by a practitioner having adequate knowledge of the subject matter. (AT 101.21)
3. **Third general standard.** The practitioner shall perform the engagement only if he or she has reason to believe that the subject matter is capable of evaluation against reasonable criteria that are suitable and available to users. (AT 101.23)
    a. *Suitable* criteria must be
        (1) *Objective* – Free from bias.
        (2) *Measurable* – Permit reasonably consistent measurements (qualitative or quantitative) of subject matter. The practitioner should consider whether the criteria are sufficiently precise to permit people having competence in and using the same measurement criterion to be able to obtain materially similar measurements.
        (3) *Complete* – Relevant factors that would alter a conclusion about the subject matter are not omitted.
        (4) *Relevant* – Be relevant to the subject matter.

    Criteria issued by a body designated by Council under the AICPA's *Code of Professional Conduct*, or issued by regulatory agencies and other bodies composed of experts that follow due-process procedures, are considered suitable. Other criteria that lack authoritative support should be evaluated according to the characteristics described above. Regardless of who establishes the criteria, the responsible party or client is responsible for selecting the criteria. The client is responsible for determining whether the criteria are appropriate for its purpose.

b. The criteria must be *available* to users in one or more of the following ways:
   (1) Publicly.
   (2) Through inclusion in a clear manner in the presentation of the subject matter or the assertion, or in the practitioner's report.
   (3) By being well understood by most users, although not formally available.

If the criteria are only available to specified parties, such as the terms of a contract or criteria issued by an industry association and available only to those in the industry, the practitioner's report should be restricted to parties that have access to the criteria.

4. **Fourth general standard.** In all matters relating to the engagement, an independence in mental attitude shall be maintained by the practitioner. (AT 101.35)
5. **Fifth general standard.** Due professional care shall be exercised in the planning and performance of the engagement. (AT 101.39)
6. **First standard of fieldwork.** The work shall be adequately planned and assistants, if any, shall be properly supervised. (AT 101.42) Factors to be considered in planning an attest engagement include the following (AT 101.45):
   a. The criteria to be used.
   b. Preliminary judgments about attestation risk and materiality.
   c. Nature of the subject matter or the items within the assertion that are likely to require revision or adjustment.
   d. Conditions that may require extension or modification of attest procedures.
   e. Nature of report (see reporting standards) to be issued.
7. **Second standard of fieldwork.** Sufficient evidence shall be obtained to provide a reasonable basis for the conclusion that is expressed in the report. (AT 101.51)

   NOTE: The standard also covers engagements designed solely to meet the needs of specified users who have participated in establishing the nature and scope of the engagement (agreed-upon procedures or agreed-upon criteria).

   In establishing an appropriate combination of procedures to accumulate evidence and appropriately restrict attestation risk, the practitioner should consider the following:

   a. Evidence obtained from sources outside an entity, such as through confirmation, provides greater assurance of an assertion's reliability than evidence secured solely from within the entity.
   b. Information obtained from the attester's direct personal knowledge, such as through physical examination, observation, computation, operating tests, or inspection, is more persuasive than information obtained indirectly.
   c. The more effective the controls over the subject matter, the more assurance they provide about the subject matter or the assertion.

   In an attest engagement designed to provide a high level of assurance (an examination), the practitioner should select from **all** available procedures any combination that can limit attestation risk to an appropriately low level.

In an attest engagement designed to provide a moderate level of assurance (a review), the practitioner's procedures are ordinarily limited to inquiries and analytical procedures and do not include search and verification procedures, such as confirmation and physical examination.

NOTE: In an attest engagement designed solely to meet the needs of specified parties who have participated in establishing the nature and scope of the engagement, the practitioner is required to perform only those procedures that have been designed or agreed to by the parties.

If the practitioner cannot obtain a written assertion from the responsible party, the practitioner should consider the effects on his or her ability to obtain sufficient evidence to form a conclusion about the subject matter. If the practitioner's client is the responsible party, the practitioner should ordinarily conclude that a scope limitation exists. If the practitioner's client is not the responsible party, the practitioner may be able to conclude that he or she has sufficient evidence to form a conclusion about the subject matter.

8. **First standard of reporting.** The report shall identify the subject matter or the assertion being reported on and state the character of the engagement. (AT 101.63) The statement of the character of the attest engagement includes

   a. A description of the nature and scope of the work performed, and
   b. A reference to the professional standards governing the engagement (see *Illustrations*).

   NOTE: When the assertion does not accompany the practitioner's report, the first paragraph of the report should also contain a statement of the assertion. This requirement would be met by using a "hot link" within the practitioner's report to management's assertion.

9. **Second standard of reporting.** The report shall state the practitioner's conclusion about the subject matter or the assertion in relation to the criteria against which the subject matter was evaluated. However, if conditions exist that, individually or in combination, result in one or more material deviations from the criteria, the practitioner should modify the report and should ordinarily express his or her conclusion directly on the subject matter, not on the assertion. (AT 101.66)

10. **Third standard of reporting.** The report shall state all of the practitioner's significant reservations about the engagement, the subject matter, and, if applicable, the assertion related thereto. (AT 101.71)

    Reservations about the engagement include unresolved problems that the practitioner had in complying with the attestation, other interpretative standards, or specified agreed-upon procedures.

    Reservations about the engagement also include scope limitations. Scope restrictions may require the practitioner

    a. To qualify the assurance provided,
    b. To disclaim any assurance, or
    c. To withdraw from the examination or review engagement.

    Ordinarily, if the scope limit is pervasive or imposed by the client, a disclaimer of opinion or withdrawal is appropriate.

    In a review engagement, the review is incomplete and the practitioner should withdraw from the engagement when

    - The practitioner is unable to perform the necessary inquiry and analytical procedures.
    - The client is the responsible party and does not provide a written assertion.

Reservations about the subject matter or assertion refers to questions about whether the subject matter or assertion is fairly stated, in all material respects, based on established or stated criteria, including adequacy of disclosure. They can result in either qualified or adverse opinions.

Reservations also include questions about measurement, form, arrangement, content or underlying judgments and assumptions applicable to the subject matter or the assertion. Reservations may require modification of the practitioner's report.

11. **Fourth standard of reporting.** The report shall state that the use of the report is restricted to specified parties under the following circumstances (AT 101.78):

- When the criteria used to evaluate the subject matter are determined by the practitioner to be appropriate only for a limited number of parties who either participated in their establishment or can be presumed to have an adequate understanding of the criteria.
- When the criteria used to evaluate the subject matter are available only to specified parties.
- When reporting on subject matter and a written assertion has not been provided by the responsible party.
- When the report is on an attest engagement to apply agreed-upon procedures to the subject matter.

A number of circumstances may affect the need to restrict a report, including

- The purpose of the report.
- The criteria used in preparation of the subject matter.
- The extent to which the procedures performed are known or understood.
- The potential for the report to be misunderstood when taken out of context.

Although a practitioner should consider informing the client that restricted-use reports are not intended for distribution to nonspecified parties, regardless of whether they are included in a document containing a separate general-use report, a practitioner is not responsible for controlling a client's distribution of restricted-use reports.

Restricted-use reports should contain

a. A statement indicating that the report is intended solely for the information and use of the specified parties.
b. An identification of the specified parties to whom use is restricted.
c. A statement that the report is not intended to be and should not be used by anyone other than these specified parties.

NOTE: A practitioner may restrict the use of any report.

If a practitioner issues a single combined report covering both subject matter or presentations that require restrictions and those that do not require restrictions, the use of a single combined report should be restricted to the specified parties.

If a separate restricted-use report is included in a document that contains a general-use report, this does not affect the intended use of either report (i.e., the restricted-use report remains restricted and the general-use report continues to be for general use).

Examination Reports

In an attest engagement designed to achieve a high level of assurance (an examination), the practitioner's conclusion should be expressed in the form of an opinion (see *Illustrations: Examination Reports*).

According to AT 101.84, when expressing an opinion, the practitioner should clearly state whether (1) the subject matter is based on (or in conformity with) the criteria, in all material respects, or (2) the assertion is presented (or fairly stated), in all material respects, based on the criteria. However, reports expressing an opinion may be qualified or modified for some aspect of the subject matter, the assertion, or the engagement. Reports also may emphasize certain matters relating to the engagement.

The form of the practitioner's report depends on whether the practitioner's opinion is on the subject matter or assertion. According to AT 101.85, the practitioner's examination report on subject matter should include the following:

- A title that includes the word **independent**.
- An identification of the subject matter and the responsible party.
- Statements that
  - The subject matter is the responsibility of the responsible party.
  - The practitioner's responsibility is to express an opinion on the subject matter based on his or her examination.
  - The examination was conducted in accordance with attestation standards established by the AICPA, and accordingly, included procedures that the practitioner considered necessary in the circumstances.
  - The practitioner believes the examination provides a reasonable basis for his or her opinion.
- The practitioner's opinion on whether the subject matter is based on (or in conformity with) the criteria in all material respects.
- A statement restricting the use of the report to specified parties when the criteria used to evaluate the subject matter are determined to be appropriate only for a limited number of parties who understand the criteria, or when such criteria are available only to the specified parties. The report should also be restricted when a written assertion has not been provided by the responsible party, and a statement to that effect should be included in the introductory paragraph.
- The manual or printed signature of the practitioner's firm.
- The date of the examination report.

Under AT 101.86 the practitioner's examination report on an assertion should include the following:

- A title that includes the word **independent**.
- An identification of the assertion and the responsible party. (When the assertion does not accompany the practitioner's report, the first paragraph of the report should also contain a statement of the assertion.)
- Statements that
  - The assertion is the responsibility of the responsible party.
  - The practitioner's responsibility is to express an opinion on the assertion based on his or her examination.
  - The examination was conducted in accordance with attestation standards established by the American Institute of Certified Public Accountants, and accordingly, included procedures that the practitioner considered necessary in the circumstances.

  - The practitioner believes the examination provides a reasonable basis for his or her opinion.
- The practitioner's opinion on whether the assertion is presented (or fairly stated), in all material respects, based on the criteria.
- A statement restricting the use of the report to specified parties when the criteria used to evaluate the subject matter are appropriate only for a limited number of parties who understand the criteria, or when such criteria are available only to the specified parties.
- The manual or printed signature of the practitioner's firm.
- The date of the examination report.

The practitioner is not precluded from examining an assertion but opining directly on the subject matter.

Review Reports

In an attest engagement designed to achieve only a moderate level of assurance (a review), the practitioner's conclusion should be expressed in the form of negative assurance (see *Illustrations: Review Reports*). According to AT 101.88 the practitioner's conclusion should state whether any information came to the practitioner's attention that indicated (1) subject matter is not based on (or in conformity with) the criteria or (2) the assertion is not presented in all material respects based on established or stated criteria.

According to AT 101.89 the practitioner's review report on subject matter should include

- A title that includes the word **independent**.
- An identification of the subject matter and the responsible party.
- Statements that
  - The subject matter is the responsibility of the responsible party.
  - The review was conducted in accordance with attestation standards established by the AICPA.
  - A review is substantially less in scope than an examination, the objective of which is an expression of opinion on the subject matter, and accordingly, no such opinion is expressed.
- A statement about whether the practitioner is aware of any material modifications that should be made to the subject matter in order for it to be based on (or in conformity with), in all material respects, the criteria, other than those modifications, if any, indicated in his or her report.
- A statement restricting the use of the report to specified parties when the criteria used to evaluate the subject matter are appropriate only for a limited number of parties who understand the criteria, or when such criteria are available only to the specified parties. The report should also be restricted when a written assertion has not been provided by the responsible party, and a statement to that effect should be included in the introductory paragraph.
- The manual or printed signature of the practitioner's firm.
- The date of the examination report.

Under AT 101.90 the practitioner's review report on an assertion should include the following:

- A title that includes the word **independent**.

- An identification of the assertion and the responsible party. (When the assertion does not accompany the practitioner's report, the first paragraph of the report should also contain a statement of the assertion.)
- Statements that
  - The assertion is the responsibility of the responsible party.
  - The review was conducted in accordance with attestation standards established by the American Institute of Certified Public Accountants.
  - A review is substantially less in scope than an examination, the objective of which is an expression of opinion on the assertion, and accordingly, no such opinion is expressed.
- A statement about whether the practitioner is aware of any material modifications that should be made to the assertion in order for it to be presented (or fairly stated), in all material respects, based on (or in conformity with) the criteria, other than those modifications, if any, indicated in his or her report.
- A statement restricting the use of the report to specified parties when the criteria used to evaluate the subject matter are appropriate only for a limited number of parties who understand the criteria, or when such criteria are available only to the specified parties.
- The manual or printed signature of the practitioner's firm.
- The date of the review report.

RELATIONSHIP TO QUALITY CONTROL STANDARDS

Attestation and quality control standards are related, since attestation standards relate to the conduct of individual attest engagements and quality control standards relate to the firm's whole attest practice. The quality control policies and procedures that a firm adopts may affect both the conduct of individual attest engagements and the conduct of a firm's attest practice as a whole. Therefore, SSAE 10 requires firms to adopt a system of quality control in the conduct of their attest practice. However, deficiencies in or noncompliance with the quality control system does not, by itself, indicate that an engagement was not performed according to the appropriate standards.

ATTEST DOCUMENTATION

The practitioner should prepare and maintain documentation of the attest engagement. The form and content of the attest documentation will depend on the particular engagement's circumstances. The quantity, type, and content of attest documentation are matters of the practitioner's professional judgment.

Attest documentation is the principal record of the procedures applied, information obtained, and conclusions or findings reached by the practitioner. It serves to provide the primary support for the practitioner's report and assist in the conduct and supervision of the engagement. It should be sufficient to

- Allow members of the engagement team with supervisory and review responsibilities to understand the nature, timing, extent, and results of attest procedures performed, and the information obtained, and
- Indicate which engagement team members performed and reviewed the work.

Attest documentation, which may be in paper or electronic form, includes work programs, analyses, memoranda, letters of confirmation and representation, abstracts or copies of the entity's documents, and schedules or commentaries prepared or obtained by the practitioner.

The practitioner owns the attest documentation, and some states recognize this right of ownership in their statutes. However, the practitioner has an ethical, and sometimes legal, obligation to maintain the confidentiality of the client or responsible party. The practitioner should adopt reasonable procedures to maintain the confidentiality of information contained in the attest documentation, and to prevent unauthorized access to that documentation. The practitioner should also retain the attest documentation for a period sufficient to meet the needs of his or her practice, and to satisfy any pertinent legal or regulatory requirements for records retention. (The practitioner should be able to access electronic documentation throughout the retention period.)

Sometimes attest documentation may serve as a source of reference for the client, but such documentation should not be considered as part of, or a substitute for, the client's accounting records.

When performing an examination of prospective financial statements, attest documentation ordinarily should indicate that the practitioner considered the process by which the entity develops its prospective financial statements in determining the scope of the engagement.

NOTE: Although the requirement to maintain attest documentation is stated in SSAE 10, changes have been made by SSAE 11, which reflect the concepts and terms used in SAS 96. SSAE 11 is effective for attest engagements when the subject matter or assertion is as of or for a period ending on or after December 15, 2002, with earlier application permitted.

ESTABLISHING AN UNDERSTANDING WITH THE CLIENT

According to AT 101.46, the practitioner should establish an understanding with the client on the services to be performed for each engagement that includes

1. The objectives of the engagement.
2. Management's responsibilities.
3. Practitioner's responsibilities.
4. Limitations of the engagement.

The understanding should be documented, preferably through a written communication with the client. If the practitioner believes that an understanding has not been established, he or she should not accept the engagement.

REPRESENTATION LETTER

In an examination or review engagement, a practitioner should consider obtaining a representation letter from the responsible party. According to AU 101.60, examples of representations that may by included are

- A statement acknowledging responsibility for the subject matter and the assertion (if applicable).
- A statement acknowledging responsibility for selecting the criteria (if applicable).
- A statement acknowledging responsibility for determining that such criteria are appropriate for its purposes, where the responsible party is the client.
- The assertion about the subject matter based on the selected criteria.
- A statement that all known matters contradicting the assertion and any communication from regulatory agencies affecting the subject matter or the assertion have been disclosed to the practitioner.
- Availability of all records relevant to the subject matter.
- A statement that any known events subsequent to the period (or point in time) of the subject matter being reported on that would have a material effect on the subject matter (or assertion, if applicable) have been disclosed to the practitioner.

If the client is not the responsible party, the practitioner should consider obtaining a representation letter from the client. According to AU 101.61, examples of representations included in the letter are

- A statement that any known material subsequent events have been disclosed.
- A statement acknowledging the client's responsibility for selecting the criteria, if applicable.
- A statement acknowledging the client's responsibility for determining that such criteria are appropriate.

If the responsible party or client refuses to furnish necessary written representations in an examination engagement, the practitioner should consider the impact on the ability to issue a conclusion about the subject matter. If the representation is necessary to obtain sufficient evidence to issue a report, the responsible party or client's refusal may cause the practitioner to disclaim an opinion or withdraw. However, in other circumstances, a qualified opinion may be appropriate. The practitioner should also consider whether the refusal affects his or her ability to rely on other representations.

If the engagement is a review and a scope limitation exists, the practitioner should withdraw from the engagement.

NOTE: Written representations are part of the evidential matter that the practitioner obtains.

OTHER INFORMATION IN A CLIENT-PREPARED DOCUMENT CONTAINING THE PRACTITIONER'S ATTEST REPORT

A practitioner's report may appear in

- Annual reports to holders of securities or beneficial interests.
- Annual reports of organizations for charitable or philanthropic purposes.
- Annual reports filed with regulatory authorities under the Securities Exchange Act of 1934.
- Other documents to which the practitioner, at the client's request, devotes attention.

In this case, the auditor should

1. Read the other information.

   NOTE: This is the knowledgeable study of information by an auditor who has an understanding of the client's business, organization, and operating characteristics, as well as its financial characteristics.

2. Consider whether the other information is materially inconsistent with information in the audited financial statements. This consideration includes the manner of presentation of both the other information and comparable information in the financial statements.
3. If there is a material inconsistency

   a. Determine whether the financial statements, the report, or both require revision.

      NOTE: This means the auditor should decide if the difference is caused by a misstatement in the financial statements.

   b. Request that the client revise the other information if it, rather than the financial statements, is misstated.
   c. If the other information is not revised, consider other actions such as

      (1) Revising the report to include an explanatory paragraph describing the material inconsistency.

    (2) Withholding the use of the report in the document.
    (3) Withdrawing from the engagement.

4. If the auditor's reading makes him or her aware of a material misstatement of fact, he or she should

    a. Discuss the matter with the client.
    b. Consider that

        (1) He or she may not have the expertise to assess the validity of the statement.
        (2) There may be no standards by which to assess its presentation.
        (3) There may be valid differences of judgment or opinion.

        NOTE: This means that concluding there is a material misstatement is a lot more subjective than concluding there is a material inconsistency.

    c. Request that the client seek the advice of legal counsel on the matter.
    d. If the auditor concludes after discussion with the client that there is, in fact, a material misstatement of fact, he or she should consider steps such as

        (1) Notifying the client in writing of his or her views.
        (2) Consulting his or her own legal counsel on what other action is appropriate.

SUBSEQUENT EVENTS

Subsequent events are events or transactions that occur after the point in time or period of time of the subject matter being tested but not before the date of the practitioner's report that have a material effect on the subject matter and therefore require adjustment or disclosure in the financial statements.

According to AT 101.96-.97, the two types of events that a practitioner must consider include

1. Events that provide additional evidence about conditions that existed at the point in time or during the period of time of the subject matter being tested. The practitioner should use this information in considering whether the subject matter is presented in conformity with the criteria and may affect the presentation of the subject matter, the assertion, or the practitioner's report.
2. Events that provide evidence about conditions that arose after the point in time or period of time of the subject matter being tested that need to be disclosed to keep the subject matter from being misleading. This type of subsequent event will not normally affect the practitioner's report if the information is disclosed.

The practitioner is not responsible for to detecting subsequent events. However, the practitioner should ask the responsible party if they are aware of any subsequent events through the date of the practitioner's report that would have a material effect on the subject matter or assertion. If a representation letter is obtained, the letter should include a representation concerning subsequent events.

If the practitioner subsequently becomes aware of conditions that existed at the date of the practitioner's report that might have affected the report had the practitioner been aware of them, the practitioner should consider the guidance in Section 561.

COMPARISON OF ATTESTATION STANDARDS WITH GENERALLY ACCEPTED AUDITING STANDARDS

Below is a table that compares attestation standards with generally accepted auditing standards.

Attestation standards	Generally accepted auditing standards
General Standards	
1. The engagement shall be performed by a practitioner having adequate technical training and proficiency in the attest function.	1. The audit is to be performed by a person or persons having adequate technical training and proficiency as an auditor.
2. The engagement shall be performed by a practitioner having adequate knowledge of the subject matter.	
3. The practitioner shall perform the engagement only if he or she has reason to believe that the subject matter is capable of evaluation against criteria that are suitable and available to users.	
4. In all matters relating to the engagement, an independence in mental attitude shall be maintained by the practitioner.	2. In all matters relating to the assignment, an independence in mental attitude is to be maintained by the auditor or auditors.
5. Due professional care shall be exercised in the planning and performance of the engagement.	3. Due professional care is to be exercised in the performance of the audit and the preparation of the report.
Standards of Fieldwork	
1. The work shall be adequately planned and assistants, if any, shall be properly supervised.	1. The work is to be adequately planned and assistants, if any, are to be properly supervised.
	2. A sufficient understanding of internal control is to be obtained to plan the audit and to determine the nature, timing, and extent of tests to be performed.
2. Sufficient evidence shall be obtained to provide a reasonable basis for the conclusion that is expressed in the report.	3. Sufficient competent evidential matter is to be obtained through inspection, observation, inquiries, and confirmations to afford a reasonable basis for an opinion regarding the financial statements under audit.
Standards of Reporting	
1. The report shall identify the subject matter or the assertion being reported on and state the character of the engagement.	
2. The report shall state the practitioner's conclusion about the subject matter or the assertion in relation to the criteria against which the subject matter was evaluated.	1. The report shall state whether the financial statements are presented in accordance with generally accepted accounting principles.
	2. The report shall identify those circumstances in which such principles have not been consistently observed in the current period in relation to the preceding period.
	3. Informative disclosures in the financial statements are to be regarded as reasonably adequate unless otherwise stated in the report.

<u>*Attestation standards*</u>

3. The report shall state all of the practitioner's significant reservations about the engagement, the subject matter, and if applicable, the assertion related thereto.
4. The report shall state that the use of the report is restricted to specified parties under the following circumstances:
   - When the criteria used to evaluate the subject matter are determined by the practitioner to be appropriate only for a limited number of parties who either participated in their establishment or can be presumed to have an adequate understanding of the criteria.
   - When the criteria used to evaluate the subject matter are available only to specified parties.
   - When reporting on subject matter and a written assertion has not been provided by the responsible party.
   - When the report is on an attest engagement to apply agreed-upon procedures to the subject matter.

<u>*Generally accepted auditing standards*</u>

4. The report shall either contain an expression of opinion regarding the financial statements taken as a whole, or an assertion to the effect that an opinion cannot be expressed. When an overall opinion cannot be expressed, the reasons therefore should be stated. In all cases where an auditor's name is associated with financial statements, the report should contain a clear-cut indication of the character of the auditor's work, if any, and the degree of responsibility he or she is taking.

INTERPRETATIONS

DEFENSE INDUSTRY QUESTIONNAIRE ON BUSINESS ETHICS AND CONDUCT (ISSUED AUGUST 1987; AMENDED FEBRUARY 1989; MODIFIED MAY 1989)

This interpretation provides detailed guidance to a practitioner engaged to examine or review a defense contractor's responses to a questionnaire related to principles of business ethics and conduct adopted by certain companies in the defense industry.

RESPONDING TO REQUESTS FOR REPORTS ON MATTERS RELATING TO SOLVENCY (ISSUED MAY 1988; AMENDED FEBRUARY 1993; REVISED JANUARY 2001)

An accountant should not provide any form of assurance, through examination, review, or agreed-upon procedures, that an entity

1. Is not insolvent at the time debt is incurred or would not be rendered insolvent thereby.
2. Does not have unreasonably small capital.
3. Has the ability to pay its debts as they mature.

An accountant may provide a client with various professional services that might be useful to a client in connection with a financing, but the scope of services and form of report have to conform to the requirements of the relevant professional standards.

If an accountant reports on the results of applying agreed-upon procedures, in addition to the normal requirements, the report should make clear that no representations are provided on questions of legal interpretation and no assurance is provided concerning the borrower's solvency, adequacy of capital, or ability to pay its debts.

Applicability of Attestation Standards to Litigation Services (July 1990; Revised January 2001)

Attestation standards do not apply to litigation services unless the practitioner has been specifically engaged to express a written conclusion about the reliability of a written assertion that is the responsibility of another party and that conclusion and assertion are for the use of others who, under the rules of the proceedings, do not have an opportunity to analyze and challenge such work. The attestation standards would apply if the practitioner is specifically requested by a litigant to issue an attestation services report.

A practitioner is not prohibited from providing expert testimony on matters relating to solvency. The prohibition on providing written reports related to solvency does not apply in a legal forum in which the legal definition and interpretation of matters relating to solvency can be analyzed and challenged by the opposing party.

Providing Access to, or Photocopies of, Working Papers to a Regulator (May 1996; Revised January 2001; Revised January 2002)

A regulator's request for access to or photocopies of working papers in an attestation engagement should be treated in the same manner as a request related to audit working papers (see Section 339).

ILLUSTRATIONS: EXAMINATION REPORTS

These illustrations are adapted from SSAE 10.

Illustration 1. Standard Examination Report on Subject Matter for General Use

This report pertains to subject matter for which suitable criteria exist and are available to all users through inclusion in a clear manner in the presentation of the subject matter. A written assertion has been obtained from the responsible party.

Independent Accountant's Report

We have examined the [*identify the subject matter—e.g., the accompanying schedule of investment returns of Widget Company for the year ended December 31, 20X1*]. Widget Company's management is responsible for the schedule of investment returns. Our responsibility is to express an opinion on this statement based on our examination.

Our examination was conducted in accordance with attestation standards established by the American Institute of Certified Public Accountants and, accordingly, included examining on a test basis, evidence supporting [*identify the subject matter—e.g., Widget Company's schedule of investment returns*] and performing such other procedures as we considered necessary in the circumstances. We believe that our examination provides a reasonable basis for our opinion.

[*Additional paragraph(s) may be added to emphasize certain matters relating to the attest engagement or the subject matter.*]

In our opinion, the schedule referred to above presents, in all material respects, [*identify the subject matter—e.g., the investment returns of Widget Company for the year ended December 31, 20X1*] based on [*identify criteria—e.g., the [XXX] criteria set forth in Note 1*].

Guy and Carmichael
February 15, 20X2

Illustration 2. Standard Examination Report on an Assertion for General Use

This report pertains to subject matter for which suitable criteria exist and are available to all users through inclusion in a clear manner in the presentation of the subject matter. A written assertion has been obtained from the responsible party.

Independent Accountant's Report

We have examined management's assertion that [*identify the assertion—e.g., the accompanying schedule of investment returns of Widget Company for the year ended December 31, 20X1, is presented in accordance with [XXX] criteria set forth in Note 1*]. Widget Company's management is responsible for the assertion. Our responsibility is to express an opinion on the assertion based on our examination.

Our examination was conducted in accordance with attestation standards established by the American Institute of Certified Public Accountants and, accordingly, included examining, on a test basis, evidence supporting management's assertions and performing such other procedures as we considered necessary in the circumstances. We believe that our examination provides a reasonable basis for our opinion.

[*Additional paragraph(s) may be added to emphasize certain matters relating to the attest engagement or the assertion.*]

In our opinion, management's assertion referred to above is fairly stated, in all material respects, based on [*identify established or stated criteria—e.g., the [XXX] criteria set forth in Note 1*].

Guy and Carmichael
February 15, 20X2

Illustration 3. Examination Report for General Use

The introductory paragraph states the practitioner has examined management's assertion, but the practitioner opines directly on the subject matter. The report pertains to subject matter for which suitable criteria exist and are available to all users through inclusion in a clear manner in the presentation of the subject matter. A written assertion has been obtained from the responsible party.

Independent Accountant's Report

We have examined management's assertion that [*identify the assertion—e.g., the accompanying schedule of investment returns of Widget Company for the year ended December 31, 20X1, is presented in accordance with the [XXX] criteria set forth in Note 1*]. Widget Company's management is responsible for the assertion. Our responsibility is to express an opinion on this statement based on our examination.

Our examination was conducted in accordance with attestation standards established by the American Institute of Certified Public Accountants and, accordingly, included examining on a test basis, evidence supporting [*identify the subject matter—e.g., Widget Company's schedule of investment returns*] and performing such other procedures as we considered necessary in the circumstances. We believe that our examination provides a reasonable basis for our opinion.

[*Additional paragraph(s) may be added to emphasize certain matters relating to the attest engagement or the assertion.*]

In our opinion, the schedule referred to above presents, in all material respects, [*identify the subject matter—e.g., the investment returns of Widget Company for the year ended December 31, 20X1*] based on [*identify criteria—e.g., the [XXX] criteria set forth in Note 1*].

Guy and Carmichael
February 15, 20X2

Illustration 4. Examination Report on Subject Matter; Use of Report Restricted

In this example, use of the report is restricted because although suitable criteria exist, the criteria are available only to specified parties. A written assertion has been obtained from the responsible party.

Independent Accountant's Report

We have examined the accompanying schedule of investment returns of Widget Company for the year ended December 31, 20X1. Widget Company's management is responsible for the schedule of investment returns. Our responsibility is to express an opinion on this statement based on our examination.

Our examination was conducted in accordance with attestation standards established by the American Institute of Certified Public Accountants and, accordingly, included examining on a test basis, evidence supporting [*identify the subject matter—e.g., Widget Company's schedule of investment returns*] and performing such other procedures as we considered necessary in the circumstances. We believe that our examination provides a reasonable basis for our opinion.

[Additional paragraph(s) may be added to emphasize certain matters relating to the attest engagement or the assertion.]

In our opinion, the schedule referred to above presents, in all material respects, [*identify the subject matter—e.g., the investment returns of Widget Company for the year ended December 31, 20X1*] based on the [XXX] criteria referred to in the investment management agreement between Widget Company and Basic Investment Managers, Ltd., dated November 15, 20X2.

This report is intended solely for the information and use of Widget Company and [*identify other specified parties—e.g., Basic Investment Managers, Ltd.*] and is not intended to be and should not be used by anyone other than these specified parties.

Guy and Carmichael
February 15, 20X2

Illustration 5. Examination Report: Qualified Opinion

In this example, the opinion is qualified because conditions exist that, individually or in combination, result in one or more material misstatements or deviations from the criteria. The report is for general use and pertains to subject matter for which suitable criteria exist and are available to all users through inclusion in a clear manner in the presentation of the subject matter. A written assertion has been obtained from the responsible party.

Independent Accountant's Report

We have examined the accompanying schedule of investment returns of Widget Company for the year ended December 31, 20X1. Widget Company's management is responsible for the schedule of investment returns. Our responsibility is to express an opinion based on our examination.

Our examination was conducted in accordance with attestation standards established by the American Institute of Certified Public Accountants and, accordingly, included examining, on a test basis, evidence supporting [*identify the subject matter—e.g., Widget Company's schedule of investment returns*] and performing such other procedures as we considered necessary in the circumstances. We believe that our examination provides a reasonable basis for our opinion.

Our examination disclosed the following [*describe condition(s) that, individually or in the aggregate, resulted in a material misstatement or deviation from the criteria].*

In our opinion, except for the material misstatement (or deviation from the criteria) described in the preceding paragraph, the schedule referred to above presents, in all material respects, [*identify the subject matter—e.g., the investment returns of Widget Company for the year ended December 31, 20X1*] based on [*identify criteria—e.g., the [XXX] criteria set forth in Note 1*].

Guy and Carmichael
February 15, 20X2

Illustration 6. Examination Report: Disclaimer of Opinion

This example illustrates a disclaimer of opinion because of a scope restriction. The report pertains to subject matter for which suitable criteria exist and are available to all users through inclusion in a clear manner in the presentation of the subject matter.

Independent Accountant's Report

We were engaged to examine the accompanying schedule of investment returns of Widget Company for the year ended December 31, 20X1. Widget Company's management is responsible for the schedule of investment returns.

[Scope paragraph should be omitted.]

[Include paragraph to describe scope restrictions.]

Because of the restriction on the scope of our examination discussed in the preceding paragraph, the scope of our work was not sufficient to enable us to express, and we do not express, an opinion on whether the schedule referred to above presents, in all material respects, [*identify the subject matter—e.g., the investment returns of Widget Company for the year ended December 31, 20X1*] based on [*identify criteria—e.g., the [XXX] criteria set forth in Note 1*].

Guy and Carmichael
February 15, 20X2

ILLUSTRATION 7. EXAMINATION REPORT: SUBJECT MATTER IS THE RESPONSIBILITY OF A PARTY OTHER THAN THE CLIENT

In this example, the report is restricted as to use, since a written assertion has not been provided by the responsible party. The subject matter pertains to criteria that are suitable and are available to the client.

Independent Accountant's Report

To the Board of Directors

Basic Company

We have examined the [*identify the subject matter—e.g., the accompanying schedule of investment returns of Widget Company for the year ended December 31, 20X1*]. Widget Company's management is responsible for the schedule of investment returns. Widget management did not provide us a written assertion about their schedule of investment returns for the year ended December 31, 20X1. Our responsibility is to express an opinion based on our examination.

Our examination was conducted in accordance with attestation standards established by the American Institute of Certified Public Accountants and, accordingly, included examining on a test basis, evidence supporting [*identify the subject matter—e.g., Widget Company's schedule of investment returns*] and performing such other procedures as we considered necessary in the circumstances. We believe that our examination provides a reasonable basis for our opinion.

[*Additional paragraph(s) may be added to emphasize certain matters relating to the attest engagement or the subject matter.*]

In our opinion, the schedule referred to above presents, in all material respects, [*identify the subject matter—e.g., the investment returns of Widget Company for the year ended December 31, 20X1*] based on [*identify criteria—e.g., the [XXX] criteria set forth in Note 1*].

This report is intended solely for the information and use of the management and the board of directors of Basic Company and is not intended to be and should not be used by anyone other than these specified parties.

Guy and Carmichael
February 15, 20X2

ILLUSTRATIONS: REVIEW REPORTS

These illustrations are adapted from SSAE 10.

ILLUSTRATION 1. STANDARD REVIEW REPORT ON SUBJECT MATTER FOR GENERAL USE

This report pertains to subject matter for which suitable criteria exist and are available to all users through inclusion in a clear manner in the presentation of the subject matter. A written assertion has been obtained from the responsible party.

Independent Accountant's Report

We have reviewed the [*identify the subject matter—e.g., the accompanying schedule of investment returns of Widget Company for the year ended December 31, 20X1*]. Widget Company's management is responsible for the schedule of investment returns.

Our review was conducted in accordance with attestation standards established by the American Institute of Certified Public Accountants. A review is substantially less in scope than an examination, the objective of which is the expression of an opinion on [*identify the subject matter—e.g., Widget Company's schedule of investment returns*]. Accordingly, we do not express such an opinion.

[*Additional paragraph(s) may be added to emphasize certain matters relating to the attest engagement or the subject matter.*]

Based on our review, nothing came to our attention that caused us to believe that the [*identify the subject matter—e.g., schedule of investment returns of Widget Company for the year ended December 31, 20X1*] is not presented, in all material respects, in conformity with [*identify criteria—e.g., the [XXX] criteria set forth in Note 1*].

Guy and Carmichael
February 15, 20X2

Illustration 2. Review Report: Subject Matter Is the Responsibility of a Party other than the Client

This review report is restricted as to use since a written assertion has not been provided by the responsible party. The subject matter pertains to criteria that are suitable and are available to the client.

Independent Accountant's Report

To the Board of Directors

Basic Company

We have reviewed [*identify the subject matter—e.g., the accompanying schedule of investment returns of Widget Company for the year ended December 31, 20X1*]. Widget Company's management is responsible for the schedule of investment returns. Widget Company's management did not provide us a written assertion about their schedule of investment returns for the year ended December 31, 20X1.

Our review was conducted in accordance with attestation standards established by the American Institute of Certified Public Accountants. A review is substantially less in scope than an examination, the objective of which is the expression of an opinion on [*identify the subject matter—e.g., Widget Company's schedule of investment returns*]. Accordingly, we do not express such an opinion.

[*Additional paragraph(s) may be added to emphasize certain matters relating to the attest engagement or the subject matter.*]

Based on our review, nothing came to our attention that caused us to believe that [*identify the subject matter—e.g., schedule of investment returns of Widget Company for the year ended December 31, 20X1*] is not presented, in all material respects, in conformity with [*identify criteria—e.g., the [XXX] criteria set forth in Note 1*].

This report is intended solely for the information and use of the management and the board of directors of Basic Company and is not intended to be and should not be used by anyone other than these specified parties.

Guy and Carmichael
February 15, 20X2

Illustration 3. Review Report on an Assertion

Although suitable criteria exist for the subject matter, the report is restricted since the criteria are available only to specified parties. A written assertion has been obtained from the responsible party.

Independent Accountant's Report

We have reviewed management's assertion that [*identify the assertion—e.g., the accompanying schedule of investment returns of Widget Company for the year ended December 31, 20X1 is presented in accordance with the [XXX] criteria referred to in Note 1*]. Widget Company's management is responsible for the assertion.

Our review was conducted in accordance with attestation standards established by the American Institute of Certified Public Accountants. A review is substantially less in scope than an examination, the objective of which is the expression of an opinion on management's opinion. Accordingly, we do not express such an opinion.

[*Additional paragraph(s) may be added to emphasize certain matters relating to the attest engagement or the assertion.*]

Based on our review, nothing came to our attention that caused us to believe that management's assertion referred to above is not fairly stated, in all material respects, based on [*identify criteria—e.g., the [XXX] criteria referred to in the investment management agreement between Widget Company and Basic Investment Managers, Ltd., dated November 15, 20X2*].

This report is intended solely for the information and use of Widget Company and [*identify other specified parties—e.g., Basic Investment Managers, Ltd.*] and is not intended to be and should not be used by anyone other than these specified parties.

Guy and Carmichael
February 15, 20X2

2201 AGREED-UPON PROCEDURES ENGAGEMENTS[1, 2]

EFFECTIVE DATE AND APPLICABILITY

Original Pronouncement

SSAE 10, *Attestation Standards: Revision and Recodification,* January 2001, as amended by SSAE 11, January 2002.

Effective Date

This Statement is effective when the subject matter or assertion is as of, or for a period ending on or after June 1, 2001. Revised to reflect SSAE 11, which is effective for attest engagements when the subject matter or assertion is as of, or for a period ending on or after, December 15, 2002, with earlier application permitted.

Applicability

All agreed-upon procedures engagements, except the following:

1. Situations in which an accountant reports on specified compliance requirements based solely on an audit (see SAS 62, *Special Reports*, Section 623).
2. Engagements for which the objective is to report in accordance with SAS 74, *Compliance Auditing Considerations in Audits of Governmental Entities and Recipients of Governmental Financial Assistance* (Section 801).
3. Circumstances covered by SAS 70, *Reports on the Processing of Transactions by Service Organizations* (Section 324) when the service

---

[1] *In AICPA publications this section is codified as AT 201.*

[2] *The Auditing Standards Board has issued Statement of Position (SOP) 01-3,* ***Performing Agreed-upon Procedures Engagements That Address Internal Control over Derivative Transactions as Required by the New York State Insurance Law****, which is effective upon issuance. (See August 2001, Journal of Accountancy, pages 97-103.) The SOP provides guidance to practitioners on performing an agreed-upon procedures engagement that enables insurance companies to meet the requirements of the New York Derivative Law (the Law) that amends Article 14 of the New York Insurance Law. The Law requires insurers who enter into derivative transactions to file with the State of New York Insurance Department (Department) a statement describing an independent CPA's assessment of the insurance company's internal control over derivative transactions. This assessment is considered part of the evaluation of internal control prescribed by section 307(b) of the New York State Insurance Law. An assessment is required regardless of whether the derivative transactions are material to the insurer's financial statements.*

auditor is requested to apply substantive procedures to user transactions or assets at the service organization and he or she makes specific reference in the service auditor's report to having carried out designated procedures.

4. Engagements covered by SAS 72, *Letters for Underwriters and Certain Other Requesting Parties*, (Section 634).

When performing agreed-upon procedures on prospective information or compliance matters, the practitioner should refer to Section 2301, "Forecasts and Projections," and Section 2601, "Compliance Attestation."

DEFINITIONS OF TERMS

Agreed-upon procedures engagement. An agreed-upon procedures engagement is one in which a practitioner is engaged by a client to issue a report of findings based on specific procedures performed on subject matter. The client engages the practitioner to assist specified parties in evaluating subject matter or an assertion. The specified parties assume responsibility for the sufficiency of the agreed-upon procedures. In this type of engagement, the practitioner does not perform an examination or review and does not provide an opinion or negative assurance about the assertion. The practitioner's report is in the form of procedures and findings.

Assertion. An assertion is any declaration or set of declarations about whether the subject matter is based on, or in conformity with, the criteria selected.

OBJECTIVES OF SECTION

This section presents attestation standards and provides guidance to a practitioner concerning performance and reporting in all agreed-upon engagements, except those noted above in "Effective Date" and "Applicability." It was issued because of the diversity in practice in performing and reporting on agreed-upon procedures engagements.

In January 2001, the Auditing Standards Board issued SSAE 10, *Attestation Standards: Revision and Recodification*. SSAE 10 superseded SSAEs 1 through 9 and renumbered the AT sections in the AICPA's *Codification*. The revisions to this section include

- Eliminating the requirement for the practitioner to obtain a written assertion in an agreed-upon procedures engagement.
- Providing guidance on engagements to apply agreed-upon procedures to specified elements, accounts, or items of a financial statement previously covered by SAS 75, *Engagements to Apply Agreed-Upon Procedures to Specified Elements, Accounts, or Items of a Financial Statement.* (SAS 75 was withdrawn as part of SAS 93, *Omnibus Statement on Auditing Standards—2000*).

In January 2002, SSAE 11 amended this section to delete the guidance on working papers. Documentation requirements for attest engagements are now covered in Section 2101, "Attest Engagements."

FUNDAMENTAL REQUIREMENTS

STANDARDS

The general, fieldwork, and reporting standards for attestation engagements (see Section 2101) should be followed by the practitioner in performing and reporting on agreed-upon procedures engagements as interpreted in this section.

SUBJECT MATTER

In an agreed-upon procedures engagement, the agreed-upon procedures are applied to the specific subject matter using the selected criteria. The subject matter may take many different forms and be at a point in time or covering a period of time. However, the subject matter and the criteria must meet the conditions in the third general standard (see Section 2101). The criteria may be stated with the enumerated procedures or referred to in the practitioner's report.

ASSERTION

A written assertion is generally not required in an agreed-upon procedures engagement unless specifically required by another attest standard (see Section 2601). If, however, the practitioner asks that the responsible party provide an assertion, the assertion may be presented in writing in a representation letter or another written communication from the responsible party (such as a statement, narrative description, or schedule appropriately identifying what is being presented and the point in time or period of time covered). The responsible party's refusal to furnish a written assertion constitutes a limitation on the performance of the engagement that requires the practitioner to withdraw from the engagement.

ACCEPTANCE OF ENGAGEMENT

The practitioner may perform an agreed-upon procedures attestation engagement if

1. He or she establishes an understanding with the client about the services to be performed.
2. He or she has adequate knowledge of the subject matter to which the agreed-upon procedures are to be applied.
3. He or she is independent (ordinarily engagement team independence, not firmwide independence).
4. One of the following conditions is met:
   a. The client is responsible for the subject matter, or has a reasonable basis for providing a written assertion about the subject matter when a responsible party does not exist due to the nature of the subject matter.
   b. The client is not responsible for the subject matter but is able to provide the practitioner, or have a third party who is responsible for the subject matter provide the practitioner, with evidence of the third party's responsibility for the subject matter.
5. He or she and the specified parties agree upon the nature, timing, and extent of procedures performed or to be performed. Furthermore, the procedures agreed to should not be overly subjective and possibly open to varying interpretations. The practitioner should not report on the engagement if the specified users do not agree to the procedures.
6. The specified parties take responsibility for the sufficiency of the agreed-upon procedures for their purposes.
7. The specific subject matter to which the procedures are to be applied is subject to reasonably consistent measurement.
8. Criteria to be used in the determination of findings are agreed upon between the practitioner and the specified parties.
9. The procedures to be applied to the specific subject matter are expected to result in reasonably consistent findings using the criteria.

10. Evidence related to the specific subject matter to which the procedures are applied is expected to exist to provide a reasonable basis for expressing the findings in the practitioner's report.
11. If applicable, the practitioner and the specified parties agree to any materiality limits for reporting purposes.
12. The report is restricted to the specified parties.
13. For agreed-upon procedures engagements on prospective financial information, a summary of significant assumptions is included in the prospective financial statements (see Section 2301).

INVOLVEMENT OF A SPECIALIST

The practitioner and the specified parties should explicitly agree to the involvement of a specialist, if any, in assisting the practitioner in performing an agreed-upon procedures engagement. The practitioner should not agree to merely read the specialist's report solely to describe or repeat the specialist's findings in his or her report. The latter does not constitute assistance to the practitioner.

INVOLVEMENT OF INTERNAL AUDITORS OR OTHERS

Except as referred to above, "Involvement of a Specialist," the practitioner must perform the agreed-upon procedures included in his or her report. Internal auditors or others may prepare schedules and accumulate data or provide other information for the practitioner, but cannot perform agreed-upon procedures reported on by the practitioner.

ELEMENTS OF PRACTITIONER'S REPORT

According to AT 201.38, the practitioner's report on agreed-upon procedures should be in the form of procedures and findings. The report should contain the following elements:

1. A title that includes the word **independent**.
2. Identification of the specified parties.
3. Identification of the subject matter (or the written assertion related thereto) and the character of the engagement.
4. Identification of the responsible party.
5. A statement that the subject matter is the responsibility of the responsible party.
6. A statement that the procedures performed were those agreed to by the specified parties identified in the report.
7. A statement that the agreed-upon procedures engagement was conducted in accordance with attestation standards established by the American Institute of Certified Public Accountants.
8. A statement that the sufficiency of the procedures is solely the responsibility of the specified parties and a disclaimer of responsibility for the sufficiency of those procedures.
9. A list of procedures performed (or reference thereto) and all related findings. Negative assurance should not be given, and vague or ambiguous language in reporting findings should be avoided.
10. If applicable, a description of any agreed-upon materiality limits.
11. A statement that the practitioner was not engaged to, and did not, conduct an examination of the subject matter, the objective of which would be the expression of an opinion, a disclaimer of opinion on the assertion, and a statement that if the

practitioner had performed additional procedures, other matters might have come to his or her attention that would have been reported.

12. A statement of restrictions on the use of the report because it is intended to be used solely by the specified parties.
13. For an agreed-upon procedures engagement on prospective financial information, all items included in Section 2301.
14. If applicable, a description of the nature of the assistance provided by a specialist.
15. If applicable, and the practitioner does not withdraw from the engagement, describe any restrictions (not agreed to) or reservations on the performance of the procedures.
16. The manual or printed signature of the practitioner's firm.
17. The date of the report.

Other requirements are as follows:

1. If desired, explanatory language about matters such as disclosure of stipulated facts, assumptions, or interpretations; description of the conditions of records, controls, or data; explanation that the practitioner has no responsibilities to update the report; and explanation of sampling risk.
2. If applicable, and the practitioner does not withdraw from the engagement or change the engagement to another form of engagement, disclose in his or her report the inability to obtain representations from the responsible party. (see "Representation Letter").
3. If, in connection with the application of agreed-upon procedures, matters come to the practitioner's attention by other means that significantly contradict the subject matter (or written assertions) include this matter in the report.

Dating of Report

The practitioner's report should be dated as of the date of completion of the agreed-upon procedures.

Adding Specified Parties

The practitioner may be asked to consider adding another party as a specified party (a nonparticipant party) after the completion of the agreed-upon procedures engagement. If the practitioner agrees to add the nonparticipant party as a specified party, he or she should obtain affirmative acknowledgment from that party, normally in writing, agreeing to the procedures performed and agreeing to take responsibility for the sufficiency of those procedures.

If a nonparticipant party is added after the practitioner has issued his or her report, the practitioner may reissue the report or provide written acknowledgment that a party has been added. If the report is reissued, the report date should not be changed. If written acknowledgment is provided, the acknowledgment ordinarily should state that no procedures have been performed subsequent to the date of the report.

Restrictions on the Performance of Procedures

The practitioner should attempt to have specified parties agree to any modification of the agreed-upon procedures when circumstances impose restrictions on the performance of those procedures. If an agreement cannot be obtained (for example, when the agreed-upon procedures are published by a regulatory agency that will not modify those procedures), the practitioner should either describe any restrictions in his or her report or withdraw from the engagement.

Representation Letter

Practitioners may find that a representation letter is useful in obtaining representations from the responsible party. Generally, a representation letter is not required for this type of engagement. However, a representation letter is required in an agreed-upon procedures engagement related to compliance with specified requirements (see Section 2601). If the practitioner decides to request a representation letter from the responsible party and that party refuses to furnish one, the practitioner should do one of the following:

1. Disclose in the accountant's report the inability to obtain representations from the responsible party.
2. Withdraw from the engagement (required for an agreed-upon procedures engagement related to compliance with specified requirements).
3. Change the engagement to another form of engagement.

Knowledge of Outside Matters

If matters come to the practitioner's attention by other means outside the agreed-upon procedures that significantly contradict the assertion referred to in the report, the practitioner should include the matter in the report.

Change from Another Engagement (Attest or Nonattest) to an Agreed-upon Procedures Engagement

According to AT 201.42, before agreeing to change another type of engagement to an agreed-upon procedures engagement, the practitioner should consider the

1. Possibility that certain procedures performed as part of the other engagement are not appropriate to include in an agreed-upon procedures engagement.
2. Reason given for the request, especially any scope restrictions or restrictions on matters to be reported related to the other engagement.
3. Additional effort required to complete the other engagement.
4. Reason for changing from a general-use to a restricted-use report.
5. Propriety of accepting a change in engagement if agreed-upon procedures are substantially complete (or effort to complete the procedures is relatively insignificant).

INTERPRETATIONS

There are no interpretations for this section.

TECHNIQUES FOR APPLICATION

Meaning of Independence

Independence requirements for an agreed-upon procedures engagement are less stringent than the independence requirements for other attest and audit engagements (refer to the Code of Professional Conduct, Interpretation 101.11, *Modified Application of Rule 101 for Certain Engagements to Issue Restricted-use Reports under the SSAEs* [Revised].

Engagement Letter

The practitioner should establish a clear understanding regarding the terms of engagement, preferably in an engagement letter. Engagement letters should be addressed to the client, and, in some circumstances, to all specified parties. According to AT 201.10, the practitioner should consider including the following matters in the engagement letter:

1. Nature of the engagement.
2. Identification of the subject matter (or the assertion related thereto), the responsible party, and the criteria to be used.
3. Identification of specified parties.
4. Specified parties' acknowledgment of their responsibility for the sufficiency of the procedures.
5. Responsibilities of the practitioner.
6. Reference to attestation standards established by the AICPA.
7. Agreement on procedures by enumerating, or referring to, the procedures.
8. Disclaimers expected to be included in the practitioner's report.
9. Use restrictions.
10. Assistance to be provided to the practitioner.
11. Involvement of a specialist, if applicable.
12. Agreed-upon materiality limits, if applicable.

Communication with Specified Parties

Ordinarily, the practitioner should communicate directly with, and obtain affirmative acknowledgment from, each of the specified parties. This may be accomplished by

1. Meeting with the specified parties.
2. Distributing a draft of the anticipated report to the specified parties and obtaining their agreement.
3. Distributing a copy of the engagement letter to the specified parties and obtaining their agreement.

If the practitioner is unable to communicate directly with all of the specified parties, he or she should consider applying one or more of the following procedures:

1. Compare the procedures to be applied to written requirements of the specified parties.
2. Discuss the procedures to be applied with appropriate representatives of the specified parties.
3. Review relevant contracts with, or correspondence from, the specified parties.

Procedures to Be Performed

The procedures that the practitioner and the specified parties agree upon may be as limited or as extensive as the specified parties desire. Mere reading of an assertion or specified information, however, does not constitute a procedure sufficient to permit a practitioner to report on the results of applying agreed-upon procedures.

According to AT 201.17, examples of appropriate procedures include the following:

1. Execution of a sampling application after agreeing on relevant parameters.
2. Inspection of specified documents.
3. Confirmation of information with third parties.
4. Comparison of documents, schedules, or analyses with specified attributes.
5. Performance of specific procedures on work performed by others, including the work of internal auditors.
6. Work of mathematical computations.

Examples of inappropriate procedures include evaluating the competency or objectivity of another party or interpreting documents outside the scope of the practitioner's professional expertise.

REPRESENTATION LETTER

Although, as a general rule, a representation letter is not required, it is advisable to obtain one. According to AT 201.38, examples of matters that might appear in a representation letter include

1. A statement acknowledging responsibility for the subject matter or the assertion.
2. A statement acknowledging responsibility for selecting the criteria and for determining that the criteria are appropriate.
3. The assertion about the subject matter based on the criteria selected.
4. A statement that all known matters contradicting the subject matter or the assertion and any communication from regulatory agencies affecting the subject matter or the assertion have been disclosed to the practitioner.
5. Availability of all records relevant to the subject matter and the agreed-upon procedures.
6. Other matters the practitioner deems appropriate.

REPORT ON AGREED-UPON PROCEDURES IN A DOCUMENT CONTAINING FINANCIAL STATEMENTS

When the practitioner consents to the inclusion of his or her report on agreed-upon procedures in a document containing the entity's financial statements, he or she is associated with those financial statements. For a public entity, the practitioner should include his or her audit report (see Section 508), review report (see Section 722), or unaudited disclaimer (see Section 504) in such document. For a private entity, the practitioner should include his or her audit report (see Section 508), review report (see Section 3100), or compilation report (see Section 3100) in such document. If the practitioner has not audited, reviewed, or compiled the private entity financial statements, the document should state that the practitioner has not audited, reviewed, or compiled the financial statements and assumes no responsibility for them. All combined reports (agreed-upon procedure and other reports) should be restricted to specified parties (see Section 2101).

ILLUSTRATIONS

ILLUSTRATION 1. ACCOUNTANT'S STANDARD REPORT ON AN AGREED-UPON PROCEDURES ENGAGEMENT (FROM SSAE 10)

Independent Accountant's Report on Applying Agreed-upon Procedures

To the Audit Committees and Managements of Widget Inc. and Basic Fund:

We have performed the procedures enumerated below, which were agreed to by the audit committees and managements of Widget Inc., and Basic Fund, solely to assist you in evaluating the accompanying Statement of Investment Performance Statistics of Basic Fund (prepared in accordance with the criteria specified therein) for the year ended December 31, 20X1. Basic Fund's management is responsible for the statement of investment performance statistics. This agreed-upon procedures engagement was conducted in accordance with attestation standards established by the American Institute of Certified Public Accountants. The sufficiency of these procedures is solely the responsibility of the parties specified in the report. Consequently, we make no representation regarding the sufficiency of the procedures described below either for the purpose for which this report has been requested or for any other purpose.

The procedures and associated findings are as follows:

[*Include paragraphs to enumerate procedures and findings.*]

We were not engaged to, and did not conduct an examination, the objective of which would be the expression of an opinion on the accompanying Statement of Investment Performance Statistics of

Basic Fund. Accordingly, we do not express such an opinion. Had we performed additional procedures, other matters might have come to our attention that would have been reported to you.

This report is intended solely for the information and use of the audit committees and managements of Widget Inc. and Basic Fund, and is not intended to be and should not be used by anyone other than these specified parties.

[*Signature*]

[*Date*]

NOTE: The following are additional illustrations of reporting on applying agreed-upon procedures to elements, accounts, or items of a financial statement.

ILLUSTRATION 2. REPORT IN CONNECTION WITH A PROPOSED ACQUISITION

Independent Accountant's Report on Applying Agreed-upon Procedures

To the Board of Directors and Management of Widget Company:

We have performed the procedures enumerated below, which were agreed to by the Board of Directors and management of Widget Company, solely to assist you in connection with the proposed acquisition of Generic Company as of December 31, 20X1. Generic Company is responsible for its cash and accounts receivable records. This agreed-upon procedures engagement was conducted in accordance with attestation standards established by the American Institute of Certified Public Accountants. The sufficiency of these procedures is solely the responsibility of the parties specified in this report. Consequently, we make no representation regarding the sufficiency of the procedures described below either for the purpose for which this report has been requested or for any other purpose.

The procedures and the associated findings are as follows:

Cash

1. We obtained confirmation of the cash on deposit from the following banks, and we agreed the confirmed balance to the amount shown on the bank reconciliations maintained by Generic Company. We mathematically checked the bank reconciliations and compared the resultant cash balance per book to the respective general ledger account balances.

Bank	*General ledger account balances as of December 31, 20X1*
XY Bank	$ 2,500
AB Bank	4,200
Town Trust Company regular account	67,341
Town Trust Company payroll account	11,240
	$ 85,281

We found no exceptions as a result of the procedures.

Accounts Receivable

2. We added the individual customer account balances shown in an aged trial balance of accounts receivable (identified as Exhibit A) and compared the resultant total with the balance in the general ledger account.

   We found no difference.

3. We compared the individual customer account balances shown in the aged trial balance of accounts receivable (Exhibit A) as of December 31, 20X1 to the balances shown in the accounts receivable subsidiary ledger.

   We found no exceptions as a result of the comparisons.

4. We traced the aging (according to invoice dates) for fifty customer account balances shown in Exhibit A to the details of outstanding invoices in the accounts receivable subsidiary ledger. The balances selected for tracing were determined by starting at the eighth item and selecting every fifteenth item thereafter.

   We found no exceptions in the aging of the amounts of the fifty customer account balances selected. The sample size traced was 9.8% of the aggregate amount of the customer account balances.

5. We mailed confirmations directly to the customers representing the 150 largest customer account balances selected from the accounts receivable trial balance, and we received responses as indicated below. We also traced the items constituting the outstanding cus-

tomer account balance to invoices and supporting shipping documents for customers from which there was no reply. As agreed, any individual differences in a customer account balance of less than $300 were to be considered minor, and no further procedures were performed.

Of the 150 customer balances confirmed, we received responses from 140 customers; 10 customers did not reply. No exceptions were identified in 120 of the confirmations received. The differences disclosed in the remaining twenty confirmation replies were either minor in amount (as defined above) or were reconciled to the customer account balance without proposed adjustment thereto. A summary of the confirmation results according to the respective aging categories is as follows:

	Accounts receivable December 31, 20X1		
Aging categories	*Customer account balances*	*Confirmations requested*	*Confirmations received*
Current	$225,000	$ 115,000	$ 90,000
Past due:			
Less than one month	52,000	27,000	20,000
One to three months	36,000	20,000	9,000
Over three months	24,000	24,000	7,000
	$337,000	$186,000	$126,000

We were not engaged to and did not conduct an audit, the objective of which would be the expression of an opinion on cash and accounts receivable. Accordingly, we do not express such an opinion. Had we performed additional procedures, other matters might have come to our attention that would have been reported to you.

This report is intended solely for the information and use of the board of directors and management of Widget Company and is not intended to be and should not be used by anyone other than these specified parties.

[*Signature*]

[*Date*]

ILLUSTRATION 3. REPORT IN CONNECTION WITH CLAIMS OF CREDITORS

Independent Accountant's Report on Applying Agreed-upon Procedures

To the Trustees of Widget Company:

We have performed the procedures described below, which were agreed to by the Trustees of Widget Company with respect to the claims of creditors, solely to assist you in determining the validity of claims of Widget Company as of May 31, 20X1 as set forth in the accompanying Schedule A. Widget Company is responsible for maintaining records of claims submitted by creditors of Widget Company. This agreed-upon procedures engagement was conducted in accordance with attestation standards established by the American Institute of Certified Public Accountants. The sufficiency of these procedures is solely the responsibility of the party specified in this report. Consequently, we make no representation regarding the sufficiency of the procedures described below either for the purpose for which this report has been requested or for any other purpose.

The procedures and associated findings are as follows:

1. Compare the total of the trial balance of accounts payable at May 31, 20X1 prepared by Widget Company, to the balance in the related general ledger account.

   The total of the accounts payable trial balance agreed with the balance in the related general ledger account.

2. Compare the amounts for claims received from creditors (as shown in claim documents provided by Widget Company) to the respective amounts shown in the trial balance of accounts payable. Using the data included in the claims documents and in Widget Company's accounts payable detail records, reconcile any differences found to the accounts payable trial balance.

   All differences noted are presented in column 3 of Schedule A. Except for those amounts shown in column 4 of Schedule A, all such differences were reconciled.

3. Obtain the documentation submitted by creditors in support of the amounts claimed and compare it to the following documentation in Widget Company's files: invoices, receiving reports, and other evidence of receipt of goods or services.

   No exceptions were found as a result of these comparisons.

We were not engaged to and did not conduct an audit, the objective of which would be the expression of an opinion on the claims of creditors set forth in the accompanying Schedule A. Accordingly, we do not express such an opinion. Had we performed additional procedures, other matters might have come to our attention that would have been reported to you.

This report is intended solely for the information and use of the Trustees of Widget Company and is not intended to be and should not be used by anyone other than this specified party.

[*Signature*]

[*Date*]

2301 FINANCIAL FORECASTS AND PROJECTIONS[1]

EFFECTIVE DATE AND APPLICABILITY

Original Pronouncement	SSAE 10, *Attestation Standards: Revision and Recodification*, January 2001, as amended by SSAE 11, January 2002.
Effective Date	This Statement is effective when the date of the practitioner's report is on or after June 1, 2001. Revised to reflect SSAE 11, which is effective for attest engagements when the subject matter or assertion is as of, or for a period ending on or after, December 15, 2002, with earlier application permitted.
Applicability	The Statement applies to engagements in which a practitioner either (1) submits, to his or her clients or others, prospective financial statements that he or she has assembled or assisted in assembling or (2) reports on prospective financial statements, and also believes under (1) or (2) that those financial statements are, or reasonably might be, expected to be used by a third party. (See below.)

APPLICABILITY

The practitioner should report when the practitioner **submits** to the client or others prospective financial statements the practitioner has assembled or assisted in assembling and also believes the prospective financial statements might by used by a third party.

This section also provides standards for a practitioner engaged to examine, compile, or apply agreed-upon procedures to partial presentations. (See *Definitions of Terms.*)

There are also several circumstances in which the pronouncement does not apply, as explained in the following paragraphs.

The Statement does not apply to a financial analysis of a potential project where the practitioner obtains the information, makes the assumptions, and assembles the presentation. This type of analysis is not for general use; **however,** if the responsible party (see below) reviews and adopts the assumptions and presentation, or bases its assumption and presentation on the analysis, the Statement does apply.

The Statement does not apply to engagements involving prospective financial statements used solely in connection with litigation services if the practitioner's work is subject to analysis and challenge by all parties. This exception does not apply if

---

[1] *In AICPA publications, this section is codified as AT 301.*

1. The practitioner is specifically engaged to issue or does issue an examination, a compilation, or an agreed-upon procedures report on prospective financial statements.
2. The prospective financial statements are for use by third parties who, under the rules of the proceedings, do not have the opportunity for analysis and challenge by each party.

The Statement also does not apply to services involving the following:

1. Prospective financial statements restricted to internal use.
2. Current year budgets presented with interim period historical financial statements.

DEFINITIONS OF TERMS

For purposes of this section, the following definitions apply

Prospective financial statement. Financial forecasts or financial projections (see below) **including** summaries of significant assumptions and accounting policies. Prospective financial statements may cover a period that has **partially** expired. The following are **not** prospective financial statements:

1. Statements for periods that have completely expired.
2. Pro forma financial statements (see Section 2401).
3. Partial presentations.

Partial presentation. A presentation of prospective financial information that excludes one or more of the items required for prospective financial statements (see *Fundamental Requirements: General*). Partial presentations are not ordinarily appropriate for general use and should be restricted for use by specified parties who will be negotiating directly with the responsible party.

Financial forecast. Prospective financial statements that present to the best of the responsible party's (see below) knowledge and belief, an entity's (see below) expected financial position, results of operations, and cash flows. It is based on the responsible party's assumptions about conditions it expects to exist and the course of action it expects to take. A financial forecast may be expressed in specific monetary amounts as a single point estimate of forecasted results or as a range.

Financial projection. Prospective financial statements that present, to the best of the responsible party's knowledge and belief, **given one or more hypothetical assumptions** (see below), an entity's expected financial position, results of operations, and cash flows. Ordinarily, it is prepared to answer the question, "What would happen if . . .?" A financial projection may contain a range.

Entity. Any unit, **existing or to be formed,** for which financial statements could be prepared in accordance with generally accepted accounting principles or another comprehensive basis of accounting. It may be an individual, partnership, corporation, trust, estate, association, or governmental unit.

Hypothetical assumption. An assumption used in a financial projection to present a condition or a course of action that may not occur, but is consistent with the purpose of the projection.

Responsible party. Person or persons responsible for the assumptions underlying prospective financial statements. Ordinarily, the responsible party is management; however, it can be outsiders, such as a party considering acquiring the entity.

Assembly. Manual or computer processing of mathematical or other clerical functions related to the presentation of prospective financial statements.

Key factors. Significant matters on which an entity's future results are expected to depend. Key factors encompass matters that affect items such as sales, production, service, and financing activities. They are the foundation for prospective financial statements and are the bases for assumptions.

General use of prospective financial statements. Use of prospective financial statements by persons with whom the responsible party is not negotiating directly (e.g., prospective financial statements in an offering statement for an entity's debt or equity securities). Recipients of general-use prospective financial statements are unable to ask the responsible party directly about the presentation. **Only a financial forecast is appropriate for general use.**

Limited use of prospective financial statements. Use of prospective financial statements by the responsible party alone or by the responsible party and **third parties with whom the responsible party is negotiating directly** (e.g., prospective financial statements used in loan negotiations, submission to a regulatory agency, or solely within the entity). **Financial forecasts and financial projections are appropriate for limited use.**

Compilation of prospective financial statements. A professional service that involves

1. Assembling prospective financial statements.
2. Performing required procedures (see below), including reading the prospective financial statements and the accompanying summary of significant assumptions and accounting policies, and considering whether they appear to be presented in conformity with AICPA presentation guidelines (see AICPA *Guide for Prospective Financial Information*) and are not obviously inappropriate.
3. Issuing a compilation report.

A compilation does not provide assurance that the practitioner will become aware of significant matters that might be disclosed by more extensive procedures such as those performed in an examination of prospective financial statements.

Examination of prospective financial statements. A professional service that involves

1. Evaluating the preparation of the prospective financial statements.
2. Evaluating the support underlying the assumptions.
3. Evaluating the presentation of the financial statements for conformity with AICPA presentation guidelines (see AICPA *Guide for Prospective Financial Information*).
4. Issuing an examination report.

An examination provides the practitioner with a basis for reporting on whether, in his or her opinion, the prospective financial statements are presented in conformity with AICPA guidelines and the assumptions provide a reasonable basis for the responsible party's forecast or projection given the hypothetical assumptions.

OBJECTIVES OF SECTION

For many years, practitioners have been requested to provide and have provided services relating to forecasts and projections. There was, however, little in the authoritative literature to guide the practitioner in these types of engagements for some time. In 1980, the AICPA issued a guide on reviews of financial forecasts, but many areas of practice were not covered by that guide. There was a need for more comprehensive guidance. This Statement provides that guidance.

The Statement does the following:

1. Defines a financial forecast and a financial projection, and related terms.

2. Established procedures and reporting standards for prospective financial statements that require the following services:
   a. Compilation.
   b. Examination.
   c. Application of agreed-upon procedures.

The service that was previously called a "review" was renamed an "examination" because that is the highest level of service available. Now there is no review service.

In January 2001, the Auditing Standards Board issued SSAE 10, *Attestation Standards: Revision and Recodification*. SSAE 10 superseded SSAEs 1 through 9 and renumbered the AT sections in the AICPA's codification. The revisions to this section include

- Changing elements of the standard reports to conform to those elsewhere in the attestation standards.
- Making the section applicable to partial presentations of prospective financial information.
- Changing references to statements of changes in financial position to statement of cash flows.

Additional guidance for practitioners' services relating to prospective financial statements is found in the AICPA *Guide for Prospective Financial Information*.

In January 2002, SSAE 11 amended this section to delete the guidance on working papers. Documentation requirements for attest engagements are now covered in Section 2101, "Attest Engagements."

FUNDAMENTAL REQUIREMENTS: GENERAL

A practitioner should perform one of the services described in this Statement—compilation, examination, or application of agreed-upon procedures—whenever he or she does the following:

1. Submits to the client or others prospective financial statements that he or she has assembled, or assisted in assembling, that are, or reasonably might be, expected to be used by others.
2. Reports on prospective financial statements that are, or reasonably might be, expected to be used by others.

A practitioner may **not** compile, examine, or apply agreed-upon procedures to prospective financial statements that omit the summary of significant assumptions.

A practitioner should **not** compile, examine, or apply agreed-upon procedures to a financial projection that excludes either an identification of hypothetical assumptions or a description of the limitations on the usefulness of the presentation.

A practitioner may **not** consent to the use of his or her name in conjunction with a financial projection if the projection is to be used by persons not negotiating directly (general use) with the responsible party **unless** the projection is used to supplement a forecast.

Prospective financial statements preferably should be in the format of the historical financial statements. According to AT 301, Appendix A, paragraph 1, at a minimum, however, the following must be presented:

1. Sales or gross revenues.
2. Gross profit or cost of sales.
3. Unusual or infrequently occurring items.
4. Provision for income taxes.
5. Discontinued operations or extraordinary items.

6. Income from continuing operations.
7. Net income.
8. Basic and diluted earnings per share, if applicable.
9. Significant changes in financial position (for examples, see AICPA *Guide for Prospective Financial Information*).
10. Summary of significant assumptions.
11. Summary of significant accounting policies.
12. A description of what the responsible party intends the prospective financial statements to present.
13. A statement that the assumptions are based on the responsible party's judgment at the time the prospective information was prepared.
14. A caveat that the prospective results may not be achieved.

A presentation that omits any of the items 1. through 9. is a partial presentation, which would not ordinarily be appropriate for general use. If an omitted applicable minimum item is derivable from the information presented, the presentation would not be deemed to be a partial presentation. A presentation that contains items 1. through 9. but omits 10. through 14. is **not** a partial presentation and is subject to the provisions of this section applicable to complete presentations.[2]

PARTIAL PRESENTATIONS

A practitioner who is engaged to or does compile, examine, or apply agreed-upon procedures to a partial presentation should follow the guidance in this section for complete presentations and make modifications necessary to reflect the nature of the presentation.

Procedures on a partial presentation may be affected by the nature of the information presented. When engaged to compile or examine a partial presentation, the practitioner should consider whether key factors affecting elements, accounts, or items that are interrelated with those in the partial presentation he or she has been engaged to examine or compile have been evaluated, including key factors that may not necessarily be obvious to the partial presentation. (An example of this might be productive capacity relative to a sales forecast.) The practitioner should also consider whether all significant assumptions have been disclosed. The scope of the examination or compilation of some partial presentations may need to be similar to that for the examination or compilation of a presentation of prospective financial statements.

Because partial presentations are generally appropriate only for limited use, reports on partial presentations of both forecasted and projected information should describe any limitations on the usefulness of the presentation.

NOTE: Chapter 23 of the AICPA ***Guide for Prospective Financial Information*** *explains how to apply the guidance for complete prospective financial statements to partial presentations.*

FUNDAMENTAL REQUIREMENTS: COMPILATION OF PROSPECTIVE FINANCIAL STATEMENTS

STANDARDS

The following standards apply to the compilation of prospective financial statements and the practitioner's report on these statements:

---

[2] *Complete presentation guidelines for entities that choose to issue prospective financial statements are included in the AICPA Audit and Accounting Guide,* ***Guide for Prospective Financial Information****. The* ***Guide*** *also presents presentation guidelines for partial presentations.*

1. The person or persons performing the compilation should have adequate technical training and proficiency to compile prospective financial statements.
2. The practitioner should exercise due professional care in performing the compilation and preparing the report.
3. The work should be adequately planned, and assistants, should be properly supervised.
4. The practitioner should perform the applicable compilation procedures.
5. The practitioner's report should conform to the guidance described below.

NOTE: Applicable compilation procedures should be performed (see Appendix B).

PRACTITIONER'S REPORT

According to AT 301.18, the standard report on the compilation of prospective financial statements should include the following:

1. An identification of the prospective financial statements.
2. A statement that the practitioner has compiled the prospective financial statements in accordance with attestation standards established by the American Institute of Certified Public Accountants (AICPA).
3. A statement that a compilation is limited in scope and does not enable the practitioner to express an opinion or any other form of assurance on the prospective financial statements or the assumptions.
4. A warning that the prospective results may not be achieved.
5. A statement that the practitioner assumes no responsibility to update the report for events and circumstances occurring after the date of the report.
6. The manual or printed signature of the practitioner's firm.
7. The date of the compilation report.

Other requirements are as follows:

1. The date of the practitioner's report is the date of completion of the practitioner's compilation procedures.
2. If prospective financial statements contain a range, the practitioner's report should include a separate paragraph related to the circumstances.
3. For the compilation of a projection, the practitioner's report should include a statement describing the special purpose for which the projection was prepared, as well as a separate paragraph that restricts the use of the report to the specified parties.
4. A practitioner who is not independent may issue a compilation report. The last paragraph of the report is as follows:

   We are not independent with respect to XYZ Company.

5. If prospective financial statements contain presentation deficiencies or omit disclosures other than those relating to significant assumptions, the practitioner's report should disclose the deficiency or omission.
6. If prospective financial statements are presented on a comprehensive basis of accounting other than generally accepted accounting principles and this is not disclosed, the practitioner's report should disclose the basis of presentation.

Examples of compilation reports on prospective financial statements are presented in Illustrations 1-3.

FUNDAMENTAL REQUIREMENTS: EXAMINATION OF PROSPECTIVE FINANCIAL STATEMENTS

STANDARDS

The practitioner should follow the general, fieldwork, and reporting standards for attestation engagements described in Section 2101.

NOTE: Standards concerning technical training and proficiency and planning the examination engagement, as well as applicable examination procedures, are described in Appendix C.

ACCOUNTANT'S REPORT

The standard report on the examination of prospective financial statements should include the following:

1. A title that includes the word **independent**.
2. An introductory paragraph with statements that
    a. Identify the prospective financial statements.
    b. Identify the responsible party.
    c. The prospective financial statements are the responsibility of the responsible party.
    d. The practitioner's responsibility is to express an opinion on the prospective financial statements based on his or her examination.
3. A scope paragraph with statements that
    a. The examination was made in accordance with attestation standards established by the AICPA, and accordingly, included such procedures as the practitioner considered necessary in the circumstances.
    b. The practitioner believes that the examination provides a reasonable basis for his or her opinion.
4. An opinion paragraph that presents
    a. The practitioner's opinion that the prospective financial statements are presented in conformity with AICPA presentation guidelines (see AICPA *Guide for Prospective Financial Statements*) and that the underlying assumptions provide a reasonable basis for the forecast. If a projection is presented, the practitioner's opinion should be that the underlying assumptions provide a reasonable basis for the projection given the hypothetical assumptions.
    b. A warning that the prospective results may not be achieved.
    c. A statement that the practitioner assumes no responsibility to update the report for events and circumstances occurring after the date of the report.
5. The manual or printed signature of the practitioner's firm.
6. The date of the examination or report.

Other requirements are as follows:

1. The date of the practitioner's report is the date of completion of the practitioner's examination procedures.
2. If prospective financial statements contain a range, the practitioner's report should include a separate paragraph that describes the responsible party's election to present a range and the assumptions involved.

3. For the examination of a projection, the practitioner's report should include a statement describing the special purpose for which the projection was prepared and a separate paragraph that restricts the report to the specified parties.

MODIFICATIONS OF PRACTITIONER'S OPINION

The practitioner should modify his or her opinion in the following circumstances.

1. If prospective financial statements depart from AICPA presentation guidelines, issue a qualified opinion or an adverse opinion.
2. If prospective financial statements fail to disclose significant assumptions, issue an adverse opinion.
3. If one or more of the significant assumptions do not provide a reasonable basis for the forecast, issue an adverse opinion.
4. If one or more of the significant assumptions do not provide a reasonable basis for the projection, given the hypothetical assumptions, issue an adverse opinion.
5. If there is a scope limitation, disclaim an opinion and describe the limitation.
6. If there is a departure from generally accepted accounting principles (e.g., failure to capitalize a capital lease), issue an adverse opinion.

Examples of modified reports on prospective financial statements are presented in *Illustrations*.

Qualified Opinion

A practitioner's report with a qualified opinion should include a separate explanatory paragraph that states all substantive reasons for the qualification and describes the departure from AICPA presentation guidelines. The opinion should include the words "except" or "exception" and should refer to the separate explanatory paragraph.

NOTE: A qualified opinion cannot be issued for a measurement (GAAP) departure, unreasonable or omitted assumption, or scope limitation.

Adverse Opinion

A practitioner's report with an adverse opinion should include a separate explanatory paragraph that states all substantive reasons for the adverse opinion. The opinion should state that the presentation is not in conformity with AICPA presentation guidelines and should refer to the separate explanatory paragraph.

If the assumptions do not provide a reasonable basis for the financial statements, the opinion paragraph should make that statement.

If a significant assumption is not disclosed, the practitioner should describe the assumption in the report.

Disclaimer of Opinion

A practitioner's report with a disclaimer of opinion should include a separate explanatory paragraph that states how the examination did not comply with appropriate standards. The disclaimer of opinion paragraph should state that the scope of the examination was not sufficient to enable the practitioner to express an opinion on the prospective financial statements. The disclaimer of opinion should include a direct reference to the separate explanatory paragraph.

If there is a scope limitation and also material departures from presentation guidelines, the practitioner should describe the departures in the report.

MODIFICATION OF STANDARD EXAMINATION REPORT

There are circumstances under which the practitioner should modify the report without modifying the opinion included in the report. The circumstances and the modifications are explained in this section.

Emphasis of a Matter

The practitioner may present explanatory information or other informative material regarding the prospective financial statements in a separate paragraph of the report.

Part of Examination Made by Another Accountant

If more than one practitioner is involved in the examination, the guidance provided in Section 543 is generally applicable.

Comparative Historical Financial Information

Prospective financial statements may be included in a document that also contains audited, reviewed, or compiled historical financial statements and the practitioner's report on those financial statements. In addition, the historical financial statements in the document may also be summarized and presented comparatively with the prospective financial statements. In these circumstances, the concluding sentence of the last paragraph of the practitioner's report on the examination of the prospective financial statements is as follows:

> The historical financial statements for the year ended December 31, 20X1, (from which the historical data are derived) and our report thereon are set forth on pages xx-xx of this document.

Examination Is Part of Larger Engagement

If the practitioner's examination of prospective financial statements is part of a larger engagement (for example, a financial feasibility study or business acquisition study), the practitioner may expand the report on the examination of the prospective financial statements to describe the entire engagement.

Examples of reports on the examination of prospective financial statements are presented in *Illustrations*.

FUNDAMENTAL REQUIREMENTS: APPLYING AGREED-UPON PROCEDURES TO PROSPECTIVE FINANCIAL STATEMENTS (See also Section 2201)

GENERAL

According to AT 301.52, a practitioner may accept an engagement to apply agreed-upon procedures to prospective financial statements under the following conditions:

1. The practitioner is independent.
2. The specified parties and the practitioner agree upon the procedures to be performed by the practitioner, and the specified parties take responsibility for the sufficiency of the procedures to be performed.
3. Use of the report is restricted to the specified parties involved.
4. The prospective financial statements include a summary of significant assumptions.
5. The prospective financial statements to which the procedures are to be applied are subject to reasonably consistent evaluation against criteria that are suitable and available to the specified parties.

6. Criteria to be used in the determination of findings are agreed upon between the practitioner and the specified parties.
7. The procedures to be applied to the prospective financial statements are expected to result in reasonably consistent findings using the criteria.
8. Evidential matter is expected to exist to provide a reasonable basis for expressing the findings in the practitioner's report.
9. Where applicable, the practitioner and the specified parties agree on any materiality limits for reporting purposes.

The practitioner ordinarily should meet with the specified parties to discuss procedures to be followed. If the practitioner is not able to discuss the procedures directly with all specified parties who will receive the report, he or she should apply one of the following or similar procedures:

1. Discuss the procedures to be applied with appropriate representatives of the specified parties.
2. Review relevant correspondence from the specified parties.
3. Compare the procedures to written requirements of the specified parties.
4. Distribute a draft of the report or a copy of the client's engagement letter to the specified parties and obtain their agreement.

While the agreed-upon procedures generally may be as extensive or limited as the parties specify, mere reading of the prospective financial statements is not a procedure sufficient to permit a practitioner to report on the results of applying agreed-upon procedures to those statements.

PRACTITIONER'S REPORT

The practitioner's report on the results of applying agreed-upon procedures should include the elements as indicated in the example report presented in Illustration 11.

FUNDAMENTAL REQUIREMENTS: OTHER

PRACTITIONER-SUBMITTED DOCUMENT

If a practitioner-submitted document contains the practitioner's compilation, review, or audit report on historical financial statements and prospective financial statements, the practitioner should compile, examine, or apply agreed-upon procedures to the prospective financial statements and report accordingly. However, the practitioner does not have to compile, examine, or apply agreed-upon procedures to the prospective financial statements if (1) they are labeled "budget," (2) the budget is only for the current fiscal year, and (3) the budget is presented with current year interim financial statements. In these circumstances, the practitioner should report on the budget and indicate that he or she did not compile or examine it and disclaim an opinion or any other form of assurance.

The budgeted information may omit the summaries of significant assumptions and accounting polices required by the AICPA presentation guidelines provided the omission is not undertaken with the intention of misleading a user of the budgeted information and is disclosed in the practitioner's report (see Illustration 12).

CLIENT-PREPARED DOCUMENT

According to AT 301.60, if a client-prepared document contains the practitioner's compilation, review, or audit report on historical financial statements and prospective financial statements, the practitioner should not consent to the use of his or her name in the document unless one of the following conditions exist:

1. The practitioner has compiled, examined, or applied agreed-upon procedures to the prospective financial statements and the practitioner's report accompanies them.
2. The prospective financial statements are accompanied by an indication by the responsible party or the practitioner that the practitioner has not compiled, examined, or applied agreed-upon procedures to the prospective financial statements and that the practitioner assumes no responsibility for them.
3. Another practitioner has compiled, examined, or applied agreed-upon procedures to the prospective financial statements and that practitioner's report is included in the document.

If the practitioner audited historical financial statements that accompany prospective financial statements that he or she did not compile, examine, or apply agreed-upon procedures to, he or she should refer to SAS 8, *Other Information in Documents Containing Audited Financial Statements* (Section 550), and determine if that pronouncement applies.

According to AT 301.61, if a client-prepared document contains the practitioner's report on prospective financial statements and historical financial statements, the practitioner should not consent to the use of his or her name in the document unless one of the following conditions exist:

1. The practitioner has compiled, reviewed, or audited the historical financial statements and the practitioner's report accompanies them.
2. The historical financial statements are accompanied by an indication by the responsible party or the practitioner that the practitioner has not compiled, reviewed, or audited the historical financial statements and that the practitioner assumes no responsibility for them.
3. Another practitioner has compiled, reviewed, or audited the historical financial statements and that practitioner's report is included in the document.

Inconsistent Information

An entity may publish documents that contain information other than historical financial statements in addition to the compiled or examined prospective financial statements and the practitioner's report thereon. In these circumstances, the practitioner should read the other information and consider whether there are inconsistencies with the information appearing in the prospective financial statements.

If the practitioner examined prospective financial statements included in a document containing inconsistent information, the practitioner should consider whether the prospective financial statements, the practitioner's report, or both require revision. Depending on the conclusion reached, the practitioner should consider other actions, such as issuing an adverse opinion, disclaiming an opinion because of a scope limitation, withholding use of the practitioner's report in the document, or withdrawing from the engagement.

If the practitioner compiled the prospective financial statements included in the document containing inconsistent information, the practitioner should try to obtain additional or revised information. If the additional or revised information is not received, the practitioner should withhold use of the compilation report or withdraw from the compilation engagement.

Material Misstatement of Fact

If, in the document containing the compiled or examined prospective financial statements, the practitioner becomes aware of information he or she believes is a material misstatement of fact, he or she should discuss the matter with the responsible party. If the practitioner concludes that there is a valid basis for concern, he or she should suggest that the responsible party consult with a party whose advice might be useful, such as the entity's attorney.

If, after discussing the possible material misstatement of fact, the practitioner concludes that a material misstatement of fact exists, he or she should consider notifying the responsible party in writing and consulting his or her attorney.

INTERPRETATIONS

There are no interpretations for this section. The AICPA has issued the *Guide for Prospective Financial Information,* which provides comprehensive guidance for engagements related to prospective financial statements. The *Guide* was recently updated to reflect the changes made by SSAEs 10 and 11.

ILLUSTRATIONS

The illustrations on the following pages are adapted from SSAE 10.

NOTE: These report forms are appropriate whether the presentation is based on GAAP or an OCBOA. If the responsible party is other than management, the references to management in these reports should be changed to refer to the party who assumes responsibility for the assumptions.

ILLUSTRATION 1. STANDARD REPORT: COMPILATION OF FORECAST (DOES NOT CONTAIN A RANGE)

> We have compiled the accompanying forecasted balance sheet, statements of income, retained earnings, and cash flows of Widget Company as of December 31, 20X1, and for the year then ending, in accordance with attestation standards established by the American Institute of Certified Public Accountants.[3]
>
> A compilation is limited to presenting in the form of a forecast information that is the representation of management and does not include evaluation of the support for the assumptions underlying the forecast. We have not examined the forecast, and, accordingly, do not express an opinion or any other form of assurance on the accompanying statements or assumptions. Furthermore, there will usually be differences between the forecasted and actual results, because events and circumstances frequently do not occur as expected, and those differences may be material. We have no responsibility to update this report for events and circumstances occurring after the date of this report.
>
> Guy and Carmichael
> February 15, 20X2

ILLUSTRATION 2. STANDARD REPORT: COMPILATION OF PROJECTION (DOES NOT CONTAIN A RANGE)

> We have compiled the accompanying projected balance sheet, statements of income, retained earnings, and cash flows for Widget Company as of December 31, 20X1, and for the year then ending, in accordance with attestation standards established by the American Institute of Certified Public Accountants.[4] The accompanying projection and this report were prepared for [*state special purpose, for example, "the Anytown National Bank for the purpose of negotiating a loan to expand Widget Company's plant,"*].

---

[3] *When the presentation is summarized as discussed in* **Fundamental Requirements—General,** *this sentence might read, "We have compiled the accompanying summarized forecast of Widget Company as of December 31, 20X1, and for the year then ended in accordance with attestation standards established by the American Institute of Certified Public Accountants."*

[4] *When the presentation is summarized as discussed in* **Fundamental Requirements—General,** *this sentence might read, "We have compiled the accompanying summarized projection of Widget Company as of December 31, 20X1, and for the year then ended in accordance with attestation standards established by the American Institute of Certified Public Accountants."*

A compilation is limited to presenting in the form of a projection information that is the representation of management and does not include evaluation of the support for the assumptions underlying the projection. We have not examined the projection and, accordingly, do not express an opinion or any other form of assurance on the accompanying statements or assumptions. Furthermore, even if [*describe hypothetical assumption, for example, "the loan is granted and the plant is expanded,"*] there will usually be differences between the projected and actual results, because events and circumstances frequently do not occur as expected, and those differences may be material. We have no responsibility to update this report for events and circumstances occurring after the date of this report.

The accompanying projection and this report are intended solely for the information and use of Widget Company and Anytown National Bank and are not intended to be and should not be used by anyone other than these specified parties.

Guy and Carmichael
February 15, 20X2

Illustration 3. Standard Compilation Report: Separate Paragraph—Prospective Financial Statements Contain a Range

As described in the summary of significant assumptions, management of Widget Company has elected to portray forecasted [*describe financial statement element or elements for which the expected results of one or more assumptions fall within a range, and identify the assumptions expected to fall within a range, for example, "revenue at the amounts of $X,XXX and $Y,YYY, which is predicated upon occupancy rates of XX percent and YY percent of available apartments,"*] rather than as a single point estimate. Accordingly, the accompanying forecast presents forecasted financial position, results of operations, and cash flows [*describe one or more assumptions expected to fall within range, for example, "at such occupancy rates."*] However, there is no assurance that the actual results will fall within the range of [*describe one or more assumptions expected to fall within a range, for example, "occupancy rates"*] presented.

Guy and Carmichael
February 15, 20X2

Illustration 4. Standard Report: Examination of Forecast

Independent Accountant's Report

We have examined the accompanying forecasted balance sheet, statements of income, retained earnings, and cash flows of Widget Company as of December 31, 20X1, and for the year then ending.[5] [*Client*]'s management is responsible for the forecast. Our responsibility is to express an opinion on the forecast based on our examination.

Our examination was conducted in accordance with attestation standards established by the American Institute of Certified Public Accountants and, accordingly, included such procedures as we considered necessary to evaluate both the assumptions used by management and the preparation and presentation of the forecast. We believe that our examination provides a reasonable basis for our opinion.

In our opinion, the accompanying forecast is presented in conformity with guidelines for presentation of a forecast established by the American Institute of Certified Public Accountants, and the underlying assumptions provide a reasonable basis for management's forecast. However, there will usually be differences between the forecasted and actual results, because events and circumstances frequently do not occur as expected, and those differences may be material. We have no responsibility to update this report for events and circumstances occurring after the date of this report.

Guy and Carmichael
February 15, 20X2

---

[5] *When the presentation is summarized as discussed in* ***Fundamental Requirements—General****, this sentence might read, "We have examined the accompanying summarized forecast of Widget Company as of December 31, 20X1, and for the year then ending."*

Illustration 5. Standard Report: Examination of Projection

Independent Accountant's Report

We have examined the accompanying projected balance sheet, statements of income, retained earnings, and cash flows of Widget Company as of December 31, 20X1, and for the year then ending.[6] [*Client*]'s management is responsible for the projection, which was prepared for [state special purpose]. Our responsibility is to express an opinion on the projection based on our examination.

Our examination was conducted in accordance with attestation standards for an examination of a projection established by the American Institute of Certified Public Accountants and, accordingly, included such procedures as we considered necessary to evaluate both the assumptions used by management and the preparation and presentation of the projection. We believe that our examination provides a reasonable basis for our opinion.

In our opinion, the accompanying projection is presented in conformity with guidelines for presentation of a projection established by the American Institute of Certified Public Accountants, and the underlying assumptions provide a reasonable basis for management's projection [*describe the hypothetical assumption, for example, "assuming the granting of the requested loan for the purpose of expanding Widget Company's plant as described in the summary of significant assumptions."*] However, even if [*describe hypothetical assumption, for example, "the loan is granted and the plant is expanded,"*] there will usually be differences between the projected and actual results, because events and circumstances frequently do not occur as expected, and those differences may be material. We have no responsibility to update this report for events and circumstances occurring after the date of this report.

The accompanying projection and this report are intended solely for the information and use of [*identify specified parties*] and are not intended to be and should not be used by anyone other than these specified parties.

Guy and Carmichael
February 15, 20X2

Illustration 6. Standard Examination Report: Separate Paragraph —Prospective Financial Statements (Forecast) Contain a Range

As described in the summary of significant assumptions, management of Widget Company has elected to portray forecasted [*describe financial statement element or elements for which the expected results of one or more assumptions fall within a range, and identify assumptions expected to fall within a range, for example, "revenue at the amounts of $X,XXX and $Y,YYY, which is predicated upon occupancy rates of XX percent and YY percent of available apartments,"*] rather than as a single point estimate. Accordingly, the accompanying forecast presents forecasted financial position, results of operations and cash flows [*describe one or more assumptions expected to fall within a range, for example, "at such occupancy rates."*] However, there is no assurance that the actual results will fall within the range of [*describe one or more assumptions expected to fall within a range, for example, "occupancy rates"*] presented.

Guy and Carmichael
February 15, 20X2

Illustration 7. Examination Report: Qualified Opinion on Forecast

Independent Accountant's Report

We have examined the accompanying forecasted balance sheet, statements of income, retained earnings, and cash flows of Widget Company as of December 31, 20X1, and for the year then ending. Widget Company's management is responsible for the forecast. Our responsibility is to express an opinion on the forecast based on our examination.

Our examination was conducted in accordance with attestation standards established by the American Institute of Certified Public Accountants and, accordingly, included such procedures as we considered necessary to evaluate both the assumptions used by management and the preparation and presentation of the forecast. We believe that our examination provides a reasonable basis for our opinion.

---

[6] *When the presentation is summarized as discussed in* ***Fundamental Requirements—General,*** *this sentence might read, "We have examined the accompanying summarized projection of Widget Company as of December 31, 20X1, and for the year then ending."*

The forecast does not disclose reasons for the significant variation in the relationship between income tax expense and pretax accounting income as required by generally accepted accounting principles.

In our opinion, except for the omission of the disclosure of the reasons for the significant variation in the relationship between income tax expense and pretax accounting income as discussed in the preceding paragraph, the accompanying forecast is presented in conformity with guidelines for presentation of a forecast established by the American Institute of Certified Public Accountants and the underlying assumptions provide a reasonable basis for management's forecast. However, there will usually be differences between the forecasted and actual results, because events and circumstances frequently do not occur as expected, and those differences may be material. We have no responsibility to update this report for events and circumstances occurring after the date of this report.

Guy and Carmichael
February 15, 20X2

Illustration 8. Examination Report: Adverse Opinion on Forecast

Independent Accountant's Report

We have examined the accompanying forecasted balance sheet, statements of income, retained earnings, and cash flows of Widget Company as of December 31, 20X1, and for the year then ending. Widget Company's management is responsible for the forecast. Our responsibility is to express an opinion on the forecast based on our examination.

Our examination was conducted in accordance with attestation standards for an examination of a financial forecast established by the American Institute of Certified Public Accountants and, accordingly, included such procedures as we considered necessary to evaluate both the assumptions used by management and the preparation and presentation of the forecast. We believe that our examination provides a reasonable basis for our opinion.

As discussed under the caption "Sales" in the summary of significant forecast assumptions, the forecasted sales include, among other things, revenue from the Company's federal defense contracts continuing at the current level. The Company's present federal defense contracts will expire in March 20X2. No new contracts have been signed and no negotiations are under way for new federal defense contracts. Furthermore, the federal government has entered into contracts with another company to supply the items being manufactured under the Company's present contracts.

In our opinion, the accompanying forecast is not presented in conformity with guidelines for presentation of a financial forecast established by the American Institute of Certified Public Accountants because management's assumptions, as discussed in the preceding paragraph, do not provide a reasonable basis for management's forecast. We have no responsibility to update this report for events or circumstances occurring after the date of this report.

Guy and Carmichael
February 15, 20X2

Illustration 9. Examination Report: Disclaimer of Opinion on Forecast

Independent Accountant's Report

We were engaged to examine the accompanying forecasted balance sheet, statements of income, retained earnings, and cash flows of Widget Company as of December 31, 20X1, and for the year then ending. Widget Company's management is responsible for the forecast.

As discussed under the caption "Income From Investee" in the summary of significant forecast assumptions, the forecast includes income from an equity investee constituting 23% of forecasted net income, which is management's estimate of the Company's share of the investee's income to be accrued for 20X1. The investee has not prepared a forecast for the year ending December 31, 20X1, and we were therefore unable to obtain suitable support for this assumption.

Because, as described in the preceding paragraph, we are unable to evaluate management's assumption regarding income from an equity investee and other assumptions that depend thereon, the scope of our work was not sufficient to express, and we do not express, an opinion with respect to the presentation of or the assumptions underlying the accompanying forecast. We have no responsibility to update this report for events and circumstances occurring after the date of this report.

Guy and Carmichael
February 15, 20X2

ILLUSTRATION 10. EXPANSION OF PRACTITIONER'S REPORT ON OR FOR A FINANCIAL FEASIBILITY STUDY[7]

Independent Accountant's Report

The Board of Directors
Example Hospital
Example, Texas

We have prepared a financial feasibility study of Example Hospital's plans to expand and renovate its facilities. The study was undertaken to evaluate the ability of Example Hospital (the Hospital) to meet the Hospital's operating expenses, working capital needs, and other financial requirements, including the debt service requirements associated with the proposed $25,000,000 [*legal title of bonds*] issue, at an assumed average annual interest rate of 10.0% during the five years ending December 31, 20X5.

The proposed capital improvements program (the Program) consists of a new two-level addition, which is to provide 50 additional medical-surgical beds, increasing the complement to 275 beds. In addition, various administrative support service areas in the present facilities are to be remodeled. The Hospital administration anticipates that construction is to begin June 30, 20X1, and to be completed by December 31, 20X2.

The estimated total cost of the Program is approximately $30,000,000. It is assumed that the $25,000,000 of revenue bonds that the Example Hospital Finance Authority proposes to issue would be the primary source of funds for the Program. The responsibility for payment of debt service on the bonds is solely that of the Hospital. Other necessary funds to finance the Program are assumed to be provided from the Hospital's funds, from a local fund drive, and from interest earned on funds held by the bond trustee during the construction period.

Our procedures included analysis of

- Program history, objectives, timing, and financing.
- The future demand for the Hospital's services including consideration of
  - Economic and demographic characteristics of the Hospital's defined service area.
  - Locations, capacities, and competitive information pertaining to other existing and planned area hospitals.
  - Physician support for the Hospital and its programs.
  - Historical utilization levels.
- Planning agency applications and approvals.
- Construction and equipment costs, debt service requirements, and estimated financing costs.
- Staffing patterns and other operating considerations.
- Third-party reimbursement policy and history.
- Revenue/expense/volume relationships.

We also participated in gathering other information, assisted management in identifying and formulating its assumptions, and assembled the accompanying financial forecast based on those assumptions.

The accompanying financial forecast for the annual periods ending December 31, 20X1 through 20X5, is based on assumptions that were provided by or reviewed with and approved by management. The financial forecast includes

- Balance sheets.
- Statements of operations.
- Statements of cash flows.
- Statements of changes in net assets.

We have examined the financial forecast. Example Hospital's management is responsible for the forecast. Our responsibility is to express an opinion on the forecast based on our examination.

---

[7] *This form of report is also applicable to other entities such as hotels or stadiums. Although the illustrated report format and language should not be departed from in any significant way, the language used should be tailored to fit the circumstances that are unique to a particular engagement (e.g., the description of the proposed capital improvement program; the proposed financing of the program; the specific procedures applied by the practitioner; and any explanatory comments included in emphasis-of-matter paragraphs).*

Our examination was conducted in accordance with attestation standards established by the American Institute of Certified Public Accountants and, accordingly, included such procedures as we considered necessary to evaluate both the assumptions used by management and the preparation and presentation of the forecast. We believe that our examination provides a reasonable basis for our opinion.

Legislation and regulations at all levels of government have affected and may continue to affect revenues and expenses of hospitals. The financial forecast is based on legislation and regulations currently in effect. If future legislation or regulations related to hospital operations are enacted, such legislation or regulation could have a material effect on future operations.

The interest rate, principal payments, Program costs, and other financing assumptions are described in the section entitled "Summary of Significant Forecast Assumptions and Rationale." If actual interest rates, principal payments, and funding requirements are different from those assumed, the amount of the bond issue and debt service requirements would need to be adjusted accordingly from those indicated in the forecast. If such interest rates, principal payments, and funding requirements are lower than those assumed, such adjustments would not adversely affect the forecast.

Our conclusions are presented below.

- In our opinion, the accompanying financial forecast is presented in conformity with guidelines for presentation of a financial forecast established by the American Institute of Certified Public Accountants.
- In our opinion, the underlying assumptions provide a reasonable basis for management's forecast. However, there will usually be differences between the forecasted and actual results, because events and circumstances frequently do not occur as expected, and those differences may be material.
- The accompanying financial forecast indicates that sufficient funds could be generated to meet the Hospital's operating expenses, working capital needs, and other financial requirements, including the debt service requirements associated with the proposed $25,000,000 bond issue, during the forecast periods. However, the achievement of any financial forecast is dependent on future events, the occurrence of which cannot be assured.

We have no responsibility to update this report for events and circumstances occurring after the date of this report.

Guy and Carmichael
February 15, 20X2

Illustration 11. Practitioner's Report: Applying Agreed-upon Procedures to a Forecast

Independent Practitioner's Report on Applying Agreed-upon Procedures

Board of Directors—Widget Corporation

Board of Directors—Basic Company

At your request, we have performed certain agreed-upon procedures, as enumerated below, with respect to the forecasted balance sheet and the related forecasted statements of income, retained earnings, and cash flows of Generic Company, a subsidiary of Basic Company, as of December 31, 20X1, and for the year then ending. These procedures, which were agreed to by the Boards of Directors of Widget Corporation and Basic Company, were performed solely to assist you in evaluating the forecast in connection with the proposed sale of Generic Company to Widget Corporation. [*Client*]'s management is responsible for the forecast.

This agreed-upon procedures engagement was conducted in accordance with attestation standards established by the American Institute of Certified Public Accountants. The sufficiency of these procedures is solely the responsibility of the specified parties. Consequently, we make no representation regarding the sufficiency of the procedures described below either for the purpose for which this report has been requested or for any other purpose.

[*Include paragraphs to enumerate procedures and findings*]

We were not engaged to, and did not, conduct an examination, the objective of which would be the expression of an opinion on the accompanying prospective financial statements. Accordingly, we do not express an opinion on whether the prospective financial statements are presented in conformity with AICPA presentation guidelines or on whether the underlying assumptions provide a reasonable basis for the presentation. Had we performed additional procedures, other matters might have come to our attention that would have been reported to you. Furthermore, there will usually be differences between the forecasted and actual results, because events and circumstances frequently do not occur as expected, and those differences may be material. We have no responsibility to update this report for events and circumstances occurring after the date of this report.

This report is intended solely for the information and use of the Boards of Directors of Basic Company and Widget Corporation and is not intended to be and should not be used by anyone other than these specified parties.

Guy and Carmichael
February 15, 20X2

Illustration 12. Standard Paragraphs Added to Practitioner's Report in a Practitioner-Submitted Document: Budgeted Financial Statements—Summaries of Significant Assumptions and Accounting Policies Omitted

The accompanying budgeted balance sheet, statements of income, retained earnings, and cash flows of Widget Company as of December 31, 20X1, and for the six months then ending, have not been compiled or examined by us, and, accordingly, we do not express an opinion or any other form of assurance on them.

Management has elected to omit the summaries of significant assumptions and accounting policies required under established guidelines for presentation of prospective financial statements. If the omitted summaries were included in the budgeted information, they might influence the user's conclusion about the company's budgeted information. Accordingly, this budgeted information is not designed for those who are not informed about such matters.

APPENDICES

The following appendices are reproduced with permission from SSAE 10. Appendix B is concerned with compilation of prospective financial statements, and Appendix C is concerned with examination of prospective financial statements. The appendices deal with the following:

1. Training and proficiency of the practitioners.
2. Planning the engagement.
3. Procedures to be applied.

Appendix A from the Statement is included in *Fundamental Requirements—General* (list of fourteen minimum presentation requirements).

APPENDIX B: TRAINING AND PROFICIENCY, PLANNING AND PROCEDURES APPLICABLE TO COMPILATIONS

Training and proficiency

1. The practitioner should be familiar with the guidelines for the preparation and presentation of prospective financial statements. The guidelines are contained in the AICPA *Guide for Prospective Financial Information.*
2. The practitioner should possess or obtain a level of knowledge of the industry and the accounting principles and practices of the industry in which the entity operates or will operate, that will enable him to compile prospective financial statements that are in appropriate form for an entity operating in that industry.

Planning the compilation engagement

3. To compile the prospective financial statements of an existing entity, the practitioner should obtain a general knowledge of the nature of the entity's business transactions and the key factors upon which its future financial results appear to depend. He or she should also obtain an understanding of the accounting principles and practices of the entity to determine if they are comparable to those used within the industry in which the entity operates.
4. To compile the prospective financial statements of a proposed entity, the practitioner should obtain knowledge of the proposed operations and the key factors upon which its future results appear to depend and that have affected the performance of entities in the same industry.

Compilation procedures

5. In performing a compilation of prospective financial statements the practitioner should, where applicable
   a. Establish an understanding with the client, preferably in writing, regarding the services to be performed. The understanding should include the objectives of the engagement, the client's responsibilities, the practitioner's responsibilities, and the limitations of the engagement. The practitioner should document the understanding, preferably through a written communication with the client. If the practitioner believes an understanding with the client has not been established, he or she should decline to accept or perform the engagement.
   b. Inquire about the accounting principles used in the preparation of the prospective financial statements.
      (1) For existing entities, compare the accounting principles used to those used in preparation of previous historical financial statements and inquire whether such principles are the same as those expected to be used in the historical financial statements covering the prospective period.
      (2) For entities to be formed or entities formed that have not commenced operations, compare specialized industry accounting principles used, if any, to those typically used in the industry. Inquire about whether the accounting principles used for the prospective financial statements are those that are expected to be used when, or if, the entity commences operations.
   c. Ask how the responsible party identifies the key factors and develops its assumptions.

d. List, or obtain a list of, the responsible party's significant assumptions providing the basis for the prospective financial statements and consider whether there are any obvious omissions in light of the key factors upon which the prospective results of the entity appear to depend.
e. Consider whether there appear to be any obvious internal inconsistencies in the assumptions.
f. Perform, or test the mathematical accuracy of, the computations that translate the assumptions into prospective financial statements.
g. Read the prospective financial statements, including the summary of significant assumptions, and consider whether

    (1) The statements, including the disclosures of assumptions and accounting policies, appear to be not presented in conformity with the AICPA presentations guidelines for prospective financial statements.[8]
    (2) The statements, including the summary of significant assumptions, appear to be not obviously inappropriate in relation to the practitioner's knowledge of the entity and its industry and, for a

    Financial forecast, the expected conditions and course of action in the prospective period.
    Financial projection, the purpose of the presentation.

h. If a significant part of the prospective period has expired, inquire about the results of operations or significant portions of the operations (such as sales volume), and significant changes in financial position, and consider their effect in relation to the prospective financial statements. If historical financial statements have been prepared for the expired portion of the period, the practitioner should read such statements and consider those results in relation to the prospective financial statements.
i. Confirm his or her understanding of the statements (including assumptions) by obtaining written representations from the responsible party. Because the amounts reflected in the statements are not supported by historical books and records but rather by assumptions, the practitioner should obtain representations in which the responsible party indicates its responsibility for the assumptions. The representations should be signed by the responsible party at the highest level of authority who the practitioner believes is responsible for and knowledgeable, directly or through others, about matters covered by the representations.

    (1) For a **financial forecast,** the representations should include the responsible party's assertion that the financial forecast presents, to the best of the responsible party's knowledge and belief, the expected financial position, results of operations, and cash flows for the forecast period and that the forecast reflects the responsible party's judgment, based on present circumstances, of the expected conditions and its expected course of action. The representations should also include a statement that the forecast is presented in conformity with guidelines for presentation of a forecast established by the American Institute of Certified Public Accountants. The representations should also include a statement that the assumptions on which the forecast is based are reasonable. If the forecast contains a range, the representation should also include a statement that, to the best of the responsible party's knowledge and belief, the item or items subject to the assumption are expected to actually fall within the range and that the range was not selected in a biased or misleading manner.
    (2) For a **financial projection,** the representations should include the responsible party's assertion that the financial projection presents, to the best of the responsible party's knowledge and belief, the expected financial position, results of operations, and cash flows for the projection period given the hypothetical assumptions, and

---

[8] *Presentation guidelines for entities that issue prospective financial statements are set forth and illustrated in the AICPA* ***Guide for Prospective Financial Information.***

that the projection reflects its judgment based on present circumstances, of expected conditions and its expected course of action given the occurrence of the hypothetical events. The representations should also

(a) Identify the hypothetical assumptions and describe the limitations on the usefulness of the presentation.
(b) State that the assumptions are appropriate.
(c) Indicate if the hypothetical assumptions are improbable.
(d) If the projection contains a range, include a statement that, to the best of the responsible party's knowledge and belief, given the hypothetical assumptions, the item or items subject to the assumption are expected to actually fall within the range and that the range was not selected in a biased or misleading manner.

The representations should also include a statement that the projection is presented in conformity with guidelines for presentation of a projection established by the American Institute of Certified Public Accountants.

j. Consider, after applying the above procedures, whether he has received representations or other information that appears to be obviously inappropriate, incomplete, or otherwise misleading and, if so, attempt to obtain additional or revised information. If he does not receive such information, the practitioner should ordinarily withdraw from the compilation engagement.[9] (Note that the omission of disclosures, other than those relating to significant assumptions, would not require the practitioner to withdraw; see *Fundamental Requirements.*)

APPENDIX C: TRAINING AND PROFICIENCY, PLANNING AND PROCEDURES APPLICABLE TO EXAMINATIONS

Training and proficiency

1. The practitioner should be familiar with the guidelines for the preparation and presentation of prospective financial statements. The guidelines are contained in the AICPA *Guide for Prospective Financial Information.*
2. The practitioner should posses or obtain a level of knowledge of the industry and the accounting principles and practices of the industry in which the entity operates or will operate, that will enable him to examine prospective financial statements that are in appropriate form for an entity operating in that industry.

Planning an examination engagement

3. Planning the examination engagement involves developing an overall strategy for the expected scope and conduct of the engagement. To develop such a strategy, the practitioner needs to have sufficient knowledge to enable him to adequately understand the events, transactions, and practices that, in his judgment, may have a significant effect on the prospective financial statements.
4. Factors to be considered by the practitioners in planning the examination include

   a. The accounting principles to be used and the type of presentation.
   b. The anticipated level of attestation risk[10] related to the prospective financial statements.

---

[9] *The accountant need not withdraw from the engagement if the effect of such information on the prospective financial statements does not appear to be material.*

[10] ***Attestation risk*** *is the risk that the practitioner may unknowingly fail to appropriately modify his examination report on prospective financial statements that are materially misstated, that is, that are not presented in conformity with AICPA presentation guidelines or have assumptions that do not provide a reasonable basis for management's forecast, or management's projection given the hypothetical assumptions. It consists of (1) the risk (consisting of inherent risk and control risk) that the prospective financial statements contain errors that could be material and (2) the risk (detection risk) that the accountant will not detect such errors.*

c. Preliminary judgments about materiality levels.
d. Items within the prospective financial statements that are likely to require revision or adjustment.
e. Conditions that may require extension or modification of the practitioner's examination procedures.
f. Knowledge of the entity's business and its industry.
g. The responsible party's experience in preparing prospective financial statements.
h. The length of the period covered by the prospective financial statements.
i. The process by which the responsible party develops its prospective financial statements.

5. The practitioner should obtain knowledge of the entity's business, accounting principles, and the key factors upon which its future financial results appear to depend. The practitioner should focus on such areas as

   a. The availability and cost of resources needed to operate. Principal items usually include raw materials, labor, short-term and long-term financing, and plant and equipment.
   b. The nature and condition of markets in which the entity sells its goods or services, including final consumer markets if the entity sells to intermediate markets.
   c. Factors specific to the industry, including competitive conditions, sensitivity to economic conditions, accounting policies, specific regulatory requirements, and technology.
   d. Patterns of past performance for the entity or comparable entities, including trends in revenue and costs, turnover of assets, uses and capacities of physical facilities, and management policies.

Examination procedures

6. The practitioner should establish an understanding with the responsible party regarding the services to be performed. The understanding should include the objectives of the engagement, the responsible party's responsibilities, the practitioner's responsibilities, and the limitations of the engagement. The practitioner should document the understanding, preferably through a written communication with the responsible party. If the practitioner believes an understanding with the responsible party has not been established, he or she should decline to accept or perform the engagement. If the responsible party is different than the client, the practitioner should establish the understanding with both the client and the responsible party, and the understanding also should include the client's responsibilities.
7. The practitioner's objective in an examination of prospective financial statements is to accumulate sufficient evidence to limit attestation risk to a level that is, in his or her professional judgment, appropriate for the level of assurance that may be imparted by his or her examination report. In a report on an examination of prospective financial statements, he or she provides assurance only about whether the prospective financial statements are presented in conformity with AICPA presentation guidelines and whether the assumptions provide a reasonable basis for management's forecast, or a reasonable basis for management's projection given the hypothetical assumptions. He or she does not provide assurance about the achievability of the prospective results because events and circumstances frequently do not occur as expected and achievement of the prospective results is dependent on the actions, plans, and assumptions of the responsible party.
8. In the examination of prospective financial statements, the practitioner should select from all available procedures—that is, procedures that assess inherent and control risk and restrict detection risk—any combination that can limit attestation risk to such an appropriate level. The extent to which examination procedures will be performed should be based on the practitioner's consideration of

   a. The nature and materiality of the information to the prospective financial statements taken as a whole.
   b. The likelihood of misstatements.
   c. Knowledge obtained during current and previous engagements.
   d. The responsible party's competence with respect to prospective financial statements.

e. The extent to which the prospective financial statements are affected by the responsible party's judgment (i.e., its judgment in selecting the assumptions used to prepare the prospective financial statements).

f. The adequacy of the responsible party's underlying data.

9. The practitioner should perform those procedures he considers necessary in the circumstances to report on whether the assumptions provide a reasonable basis for the

a. **Financial forecast.** The practitioner can form an opinion that the assumptions provide a reasonable basis for the forecast if the responsible party represents that the presentation reflects, to the best of its knowledge and belief, its estimate of expected financial position, results of operations, and cash flows for the prospective period[11] and the practitioner concludes, based on his examination

(1) That the responsible party has explicitly identified all factors expected to materially affect the operations of the entity during the prospective period and has developed appropriate assumptions with respect to such factors.[12]

(2) That the assumptions are suitably supported.

b. **Financial projection given the hypothetical assumptions.** The practitioner can form an opinion that the assumptions provide a reasonable basis for the financial projection, given the hypothetical assumptions, if the responsible party represents that the presentation reflects, to the best of its knowledge and belief, expected financial position, results of operations, and cash flows for the prospective period, given the hypothetical assumptions,[13] and the practitioner concludes, based on his examination

(1) That the responsible party has explicitly identified all factors that would materially affect the operations of the entity during the prospective period if the hypothetical assumptions were to materialize and has developed appropriate assumptions with respect to such factors.

(2) That the other assumptions are suitably supported given the hypothetical assumptions. However, as the number and significance of the hypothetical assumptions increase, the practitioner may not be able to satisfy himself about the presentation as a whole by obtaining support for the remaining assumptions.

10. The practitioner should evaluate the support for the assumptions.

a. **Financial forecast.** The practitioner can conclude that assumptions are suitably supported if the preponderance of information supports each significant assumption.

b. **Financial projection.** In evaluating support for assumptions other than hypothetical assumptions, the practitioner can conclude that they are suitably supported if the preponderance of information supports each significant assumption given the hypothetical assumptions. The practitioner need not obtain support for the hypothetical assumptions, although he should consider whether they are consistent with the purpose of the presentation.

11. In evaluating the support for assumptions, the practitioner should consider

---

[11] *If the forecast contains a range, the representation should also include a statement that, to the best of the responsible party's knowledge and belief, the item or items subject to the assumption are expected to actually fall within the range and that the range was not selected in a biased or misleading manner.*

[12] *An attempt to list all assumptions is inherently not feasible. Frequently, basic assumptions that have enormous potential impact are considered to be implicit, such as conditions of peace and absence of natural disasters.*

[13] *If the projection contains a range, the representation should also include a statement that, to the best of the responsible party's knowledge and belief, given the hypothetical assumptions, the item or items subject to the assumption are expected to actually fall within the range and that range was not selected in a biased or misleading manner.*

a. Whether sufficient pertinent sources of information about the assumptions have been considered. Examples of external sources the practitioner might consider are government publications, industry publications, economic forecasts, existing or proposed legislation, and reports of changing technology. Examples of internal sources are budgets, labor agreements, patents, royalty agreements and records, sales backlog records, debt agreements, and actions of the board of directors involving entity plans.
b. Whether the assumptions are consistent with the sources from which they are derived.
c. Whether the assumptions are consistent with each other.
d. Whether the historical financial information and other data used in developing the assumptions are sufficiently reliable for that purpose. Reliability can be assessed by inquiry and analytical or other procedures, some of which may have been completed in past examinations or reviews of the historical financial statements. If historical financial statements have been prepared for an expired part of the prospective period, the practitioner should consider the historical data in relation to the prospective results for the same period, where applicable. If the prospective financial statements incorporate such historical financial results and that period is significant to the presentation, the practitioner should make a review of the historical information in conformity with the applicable standards for review.[14]
e. Whether the historical financial information and other data used in developing the assumptions are comparable over the periods specified or whether the effects of any lack of comparability were considered in developing the assumptions.
f. Whether the logical arguments, or theory, considered with the data supporting the assumptions are reasonable.

12. In evaluating the preparation and presentation of the prospective financial statements, the practitioner should perform procedures that will provide reasonable assurance that the

a. Presentation reflects the identified assumptions.
b. Computations made to translate the assumptions into prospective amounts are mathematically accurate.
c. Assumptions are internally consistent.
d. Accounting principles used in the

(1) **Financial forecast** are consistent with the accounting principles expected to be used in the historical financial statements covering the prospective period and those used in the most recent historical financial statements, if any.
(2) **Financial projection** are consistent with the accounting principles expected to be used in the prospective period and those used in the most recent historical financial statements, if any, or that they are consistent with the purpose of the presentation.[15]

e. Presentation of the prospective financial statements follows the AICPA guidelines applicable for such statements.[16]
f. Assumptions have been adequately disclosed based on AICPA presentation guidelines for prospective financial statements.

13. The practitioner should consider whether the prospective financial statements, including related disclosures, should be revised because of

a. Mathematical errors.
b. Unreasonable or internally inconsistent assumptions.

---

[14] *If the entity is a public company, the accountant should perform the procedures in Section 722, "Interim Financial Information." If the entity is nonpublic, the accountant should perform the procedures in SSARS 1,* ***Compilation and Review of Financial Statements*** *(Section 3100).*

[15] *The accounting principles used in a financial projection need not be those expected to be used in the historical financial statements for the prospective period if use of different principles is consistent with the purpose of the presentation.*

[16] *Presentation guidelines for entities that issue prospective financial statements are set forth and illustrated in the AICPA* ***Guide for Prospective Financial Information***.

c. Inappropriate or incomplete presentation.
d. Inadequate disclosure.

14. The practitioner should obtain written representations from the responsible party acknowledging its responsibility for both the presentation and the underlying assumptions. The representations should be signed by the responsible party at the highest level of authority who the practitioner believes is responsible for and knowledgeable, directly or through others in the organization, about the matters covered by the representations. Appendix B, paragraph 5i, describes the specific representations to be obtained for a financial forecast and a financial projection. See "Disclaimer of Opinion" under *Fundamental Requirements: Examination of Prospective Financial Statements* for guidance on the form of report to be rendered if the practitioner is not able to obtain the required representations.

2401 REPORTING ON PRO FORMA FINANCIAL INFORMATION[1]

EFFECTIVE DATE AND APPLICABILITY

Original Pronouncement	SSAE 10, *Attestation Standards: Revision and Recodification*, January 2001.
Effective Date	Effective when the presentation of pro forma financial information is as of, or for a period ending, on or after June 1, 2001.
Applicability	Reports on an examination or a review of pro forma financial information. When pro forma information is provided outside the financial statements and the accountant is not engaged to report on it, the guidance in Section 550, "Other Information in Documents Containing Audited Financial Statements," applies.

DEFINITIONS OF TERMS

Pro forma financial information. Shows "what the significant effects on historical financial information **might have been** had a **consummated or proposed** transaction (or event) occurred at an earlier date." (Emphasis added.)

OBJECTIVES OF SECTION

A high rate of mergers and acquisitions in the late 1980s increased the need for guidance on pro forma financial information. The Auditing Standards Board started a project that resulted in an Exposure Draft of an SAS on reporting on pro forma information that the SEC requires public companies to file under Article 11 of Regulation S-X. That Exposure Draft was dropped without ever being issued as an SAS.

The Auditing Standards Board issued a Statement on Standards for Attestation Engagements, *Reporting on Pro Forma Financial Information* (the Statement) in September 1988. Unlike the previous Exposure Draft, the attestation statement applies to the accountant's involvement with all presentations of pro forma financial information, not just to information required by Article 11.

The statement explains the application of the general guidance for attestation engagements to engagements to report on pro forma information. The permitted levels of service that the accountant can provide related to pro forma information are a **review** or an **examination**.

---

[1] *This section is codified in AICPA publications as AT 401. If procedures are applied to pro forma information in connection with a comfort letter see SAS 76 (Section 634).*

The statement does not apply to the GAAP requirements in historical financial statements related to disclosure of a transaction consummated after the balance sheet date to achieve a more meaningful presentation, such as presentation of earnings per share revised for a subsequent stock split.

USE OF PRO FORMA INFORMATION

Pro forma information might be used to show the effects of a business combination, change in capitalization, disposition of a significant portion of a business, a change in form or status of a business (for example, from a division to a separate entity), or a proposed sale of securities and application of the proceeds.

In January 2001, the Auditing Standards Board issued SSAE 10, *Attestation Standards: Revision and Recodification.* SSAE 10 superseded SSAEs 1 through 9 and renumbered the AT sections in the AICPA's Codification. The revisions to this section include

- Conforming the required reporting elements and reporting examples to other attest reports.
- Including required reporting elements for a report on reviews of pro forma financial information.

FUNDAMENTAL REQUIREMENTS

CONDITIONS FOR REPORTING AND THE ACCOUNTANT'S OBJECTIVES

A practitioner may **examine** or **review** pro forma financial information if all three of the following conditions are achieved:

1. The document including the pro formas also includes complete historical financial statements (or incorporates them by reference) of the entity for the most recent year. If pro formas are for an interim period, historical interim information for that period is also presented (or incorporated by reference). If the circumstances are a business combination, the document includes historical data for significant constituent parts of the combined entity.
2. The historical financial statements on which the pro forma information is based have been audited or reviewed by a practitioner.

   NOTE: The level of assurance on the pro formas should be no greater than the level on the related historical statements. For a nonpublic entity, the review may be performed under Section 3100.

3. The practitioner reporting on the pro forma information should have an appropriate level of knowledge of the entity's accounting and financial reporting practices.

   NOTE: Generally this knowledge will be the result of having audited or reviewed the historical statements. If the practitioner was not the auditor or reviewer of the historical statements, the practitioner "should consider whether, under the particular circumstances, he or she can acquire sufficient knowledge."

ENGAGEMENT OBJECTIVES

Examination

The objective of a practitioner's **examination** of pro forma information is to provide reasonable assurance that

1. Management's assumptions provide a reasonable basis for presenting the significant effects of the underlying transaction or event.

2. Pro forma adjustments give appropriate effect to the assumptions.
3. The pro forma column (historical information modified by adjustments) reflects the proper application of the adjustments.

Review

The objective of a practitioner's **review** of pro forma information is to provide negative assurance on the three aspects of the pro forma information listed in the preceding paragraph.

NOTE: "Negative assurance" indicates that no information came to the practitioner's attention that would cause him or her not to believe the three statements.

*The objectives of an examination or review do not focus on the final pro forma column alone. The assurance is **not** that the pro forma column conforms with established criteria. The practitioner's objectives relate to the three **separate** aspects of a pro forma presentation:*

- *Assumptions (reasonable)*
- *Adjustments (give effect to assumptions)*
- *Final column (application of adjustments is proper)*

PROCEDURES

The procedures for an examination or review are

1. Obtain an understanding of the underlying transaction or event.
2. Obtain a level of knowledge of each significant constituent part of the combined entity in a business combination.
3. Discuss with management their assumptions about the effects of the transaction or event.
4. Evaluate whether pro forma adjustments are included for all significant effects of the transaction or event.
5. Obtain sufficient evidence in support of such adjustments.

NOTE: In considering the level of attestation risk the practitioner is willing to accept in a pro forma information engagement, the level of assurance on the underlying historical financial statements is a key factor. Accordingly, the procedures the practitioner should apply to the assumptions and pro forma adjustments are substantially the same for either an examination or a review engagement. The evidence needed is a matter of judgment and may vary with the level of service involved.

6. Evaluate whether management's assumptions are presented in a sufficiently clear and comprehensive manner, and are consistent with each other and with the data used to develop them.
7. Determine whether computations of pro forma adjustments are mathematically correct and that the pro forma column reflects proper application of the adjustments.
8. Obtain management's written representations on
   a. Their responsibility for the assumptions.
   b. Assertion that the assumptions provide a reasonable basis for presenting all of the significant effects directly attributable to the transaction or event.
   c. Assertion that the related pro forma adjustments give appropriate effect to the assumptions.
   d. Assertion that the pro forma column reflects the proper application of adjustments.
   e. Their belief that significant effects of the transaction or event are appropriately disclosed.

9. Read the pro forma financial information and evaluate the appropriateness of the descriptions of
   a. The underlying transaction or event
   b. The pro forma adjustments, and
   c. The significant assumptions and significant uncertainties about those assumptions.

   Also, evaluate whether the source of the historical information base is appropriately identified.

FORM OF REPORT ON PRO FORMA FINANCIAL INFORMATION

According to AT 401.12, a practitioner's examination report on pro forma financial information should include

1. A title that includes the word **independent**.
2. An identification of the pro forma financial information.
3. A reference to the financial statements from which the historical financial information is derived and a statement as to whether such financial statements were audited. (The report on pro forma financial information should refer to any modification in the practitioner's report on the historical financial information.)
4. An identification of the responsible party and a statement that the responsible party is responsible for the pro forma financial information.
5. Statements that
   a. The practitioner's responsibility is to express an opinion on the pro forma financial information based on his or her examination.
   b. The examination of the pro forma financial information was conducted in accordance with attestation standards established by the American Institute of Certified Public Accountants and, accordingly, included such procedures as the practitioner considered necessary in the circumstances.
   c. The practitioner believes that the examination provides a reasonable basis for his or her opinion.
6. A separate paragraph explaining the objective of pro forma financial information and its limitations.
7. The practitioner's opinion as to whether management's assumptions provide a reasonable basis for presenting the significant effects directly attributable to the transaction (or event), whether the related pro forma adjustments give appropriate effect to those assumptions, and whether the pro forma column reflects the proper application of those adjustments to the historical financial statements.
8. The manual or printed signature of the practitioner's firm.
9. The date of the examination report.

According to AT 401.13, a practitioner's review report on pro forma financial information should include the following:

1. A title that includes the word **independent**.
2. An identification of the pro forma financial information.
3. A reference to the financial statements from which the historical financial information is derived and a statement as to whether such financial statements were audited or reviewed. (The report on pro forma financial information should refer to any modification in the practitioner's report on the historical financial information.)

4. An identification of the responsible party and a statement that the responsible party is responsible for the pro forma financial information.
5. A statement that the review of the pro forma financial information was conducted in accordance with attestation standards established by the American Institute of Certified Public Accountants.
6. A statement that a review is substantially less in scope than an examination, the objective of which is the expression of an opinion on the pro forma financial information and, accordingly, the practitioner does not express such an opinion.
7. A separate paragraph explaining the objective of pro forma financial information and its limitations.
8. The practitioner's conclusion as to whether any information came to the practitioner's attention to cause him or her to believe that management's assumptions do not provide a reasonable basis for presenting the significant effects directly attributable to the transaction (or event), or that the related pro forma adjustments do not give appropriate effect to those assumptions, or that the pro forma column does not reflect the proper application of those adjustments to the historical financial statements.
9. The manual or printed signature of the firm.
10. The date of the review report.

The practitioner's report on the pro forma financial information

- Should be dated as of the completion of the appropriate procedures.
- May be added to the practitioner's report on historical financial information or may appear separately.

If the reports are combined and the date of completion of procedures on the pro forma financial information is after the completion of fieldwork for the audit or review of the historical financial information, the combined report should be dual-dated, as shown in the following:

> February 15, 20X2, except for the paragraphs regarding pro forma financial information as to which the date is March 20, 20X2.

See *Illustrations* for example reports on examinations (Illustration 1) and reviews (Illustration 2) of pro forma information.

NOTE: A practitioner's report may combine a review of some pro forma information and an examination of other pro forma information (for example, an examination of annual pro formas with a review of quarterly pro forma information). An example of such a report is presented in Illustration 3.

Report Modifications

A practitioner should modify the report (qualify, adverse, or disclaim) or withdraw from the engagement for (1) restrictions on the scope of the engagement, or (2) reservations about the propriety of the assumptions or the conformity of the presentation with those assumptions, including inadequate disclosure of significant matters. Examples of modified reports appear as Illustrations 4 through 7.

NOTE: Uncertainty about whether the transaction/event will be consummated does not require a report modification.

INTERPRETATIONS

There are no interpretations for this section.

TECHNIQUES FOR APPLICATION

PRESENTATION OF PRO FORMA FINANCIAL INFORMATION

Pro forma financial information

1. Should be labeled to distinguish it from historical financial information.
2. Should describe the transaction or event that is presented as pro forma, the source of the historical information on which it is based, significant assumptions underlying the information, and any significant uncertainties.
3. Should indicate that it should be read in conjunction with the related historical information.
4. Should indicate that it is not necessarily indicative of results that would have been obtained if the transaction had taken place earlier.

NOTE: For presentation of pro forma information for a public company, the practitioner should also refer to Article 11 of Regulation S-X.

NONAUDIT AND NONREVIEW CLIENTS

Can a practitioner who has not audited or reviewed the historical base financial statements have a sufficient level of knowledge of the entity's accounting and financial reporting practices to accept a pro forma review or examination engagement? The knowledge would have to be obtained to permit the practitioner to report on the pro forma information. A practitioner may be able to obtain this knowledge in some cases. For example, if the 20X1 pro forma information were based on historical financial statements audited by someone else, but the practitioner has audited the historical financial statements for 20X2, and as part of that audit, reviewed the workpapers of the predecessor auditors, the practitioner should have obtained an appropriate level of knowledge.

MOST RECENT YEAR HISTORICAL FINANCIAL STATEMENTS

There is a requirement that the historical financial statements for the most recent year be included in the document containing the pro forma financial information. If the historical financial statements for the most recent year are not yet available, can the practitioner accept the engagement to report on the pro formas? Yes. The Statement indicates that the historical financial statements for the preceding year should be included if financial statements for the most recent year are not available.

COMPILED HISTORICAL FINANCIAL STATEMENTS

An entity with audited financial statements acquires a small closely held business for which the practitioner has compiled the financial statements. Is it permissible for the practitioner to accept an engagement to report on pro forma financial information? No, not if the operating results of the closely held business are material to the combined entity. The historical base should be audited or reviewed. Compilation is not enough, but the practitioner can accept the engagement if he or she is able to perform a retroactive review or audit.

QUALIFIED REPORT ON HISTORICAL FINANCIAL STATEMENTS

The practitioner's report on pro forma financial information refers to the financial statements from which the historical financial information was derived, and states whether the financial statements were audited or reviewed. If the report on the historical financial statements was a qualified opinion or was otherwise modified, a reference to the modification should be included in the report on pro forma information.

ILLUSTRATIONS

The following are examples of reports on pro forma financial information (adapted from SSAE 10).

ILLUSTRATION 1. REPORT ON EXAMINATION OF PRO FORMA FINANCIAL INFORMATION

Independent Accountant's Report

We have examined the pro forma adjustments reflecting the transaction [*or event*] described in Note 1 and the application of those adjustments to the historical amounts in [*the assembly of*] the accompanying pro forma condensed balance sheet of Widget Company as of December 31, 20X1, and the pro forma condensed statement of income for the year then ended. The historical condensed financial statements are derived from the historical financial statements of Widget Company, which were audited by us, and of Basic Company, which were audited by other accountants, appearing elsewhere herein [*or incorporated by reference*]. Such pro forma adjustments are based upon management's assumptions described in Note 2. Widget Company's management is responsible for the pro forma financial information. Our responsibility is to express an opinion on the pro forma financial information based on our examination.

Our examination was conducted in accordance with attestation standards established by the American Institute of Certified Public Accountants and, accordingly, included such procedures as we considered necessary in the circumstances. We believe that our examination provides a reasonable basis for our opinion.

The objective of this pro forma financial information is to show what the significant effects on the historical financial information might have been had the transaction [*or event*] occurred at an earlier date. However, the pro forma condensed financial statements are not necessarily indicative of the results of operations or related effects on financial position that would have been attained had the above-mentioned transaction [*or event*] actually occurred earlier.

[*Additional paragraph(s) may be added to emphasize certain matters relating to the attest engagement or the subject matter.*]

In our opinion, management's assumptions provide a reasonable basis for presenting the significant effects directly attributable to the above-mentioned transaction [*or event*] described in Note 1, the related pro forma adjustments give appropriate effect to those assumptions, and the pro forma column reflects the proper application of those adjustments to the historical financial statement amounts in the pro forma condensed balance sheet as of December 31, 20X1, and the pro forma condensed statement of income for the year then ended.

Guy and Carmichael
February 15, 20X2

ILLUSTRATION 2. REPORT ON REVIEW OF PRO FORMA FINANCIAL INFORMATION

Independent Accountant's Report

We have reviewed the pro forma adjustments reflecting the transaction [*or event*] described in Note 1 and the application of those adjustments to the historical amounts in [*the assembly of*] the accompanying pro forma condensed balance sheet of Widget Company as of March 31, 20X2, and the pro forma condensed statement of income for the three months then ended. These historical condensed financial statements are derived from the historical unaudited financial statements of Widget Company, which were reviewed by us, and of Basic Company, which were reviewed by other accountants, appearing elsewhere herein [*or incorporated by reference*]. Such pro forma adjustments are based on management's assumptions as described in Note 2. Widget Company's management is responsible for the pro forma financial information.

Our review was conducted in accordance with attestation standards established by the American Institute of Certified Public Accountants. A review is substantially less in scope than an examination, the objective of which is the expression of an opinion on management's assumptions, the pro forma adjustments, and the application of those adjustments to historical financial information. Accordingly, we do not express such an opinion.

The objective of this pro forma financial information is to show what the significant effects on the historical financial information might have been had the transaction [*or event*] occurred at an earlier date. However, the pro forma condensed financial statements are not necessarily indicative of the results of operations or related effects on financial position that would have been attained had the above-mentioned transaction [*or event*] actually occurred earlier.

[*Additional paragraph(s) may be added to emphasize certain matters relating to the attest engagement or the subject matter.*]

Based on our review, nothing came to our attention that caused us to believe that management's assumptions do not provide a reasonable basis for presenting the significant effects directly attributable to the above-mentioned transaction [*or event*] described in Note 1, that the related pro forma adjustments do not give appropriate effect to those assumptions, or that the pro forma column does not reflect the proper application of those adjustments to the historical financial statement amounts in the pro forma condensed balance sheet as of March 31, 20X2, and the pro forma condensed statement of income for the three months then ended.

Guy and Carmichael
February 15, 20X2

ILLUSTRATION 3. REPORT ON EXAMINATION OF PRO FORMA FINANCIAL INFORMATION AT YEAR-END WITH A REVIEW OF PRO FORMA FINANCIAL INFORMATION FOR A SUBSEQUENT INTERIM DATE

Independent Accountant's Report

We have examined the pro forma adjustments reflecting the transaction [*or event*] described in Note 1 and the application of those adjustments to the historical amounts in [*the assembly of*] the accompanying pro forma condensed balance sheet of Widget Company as of December 31, 20X1, and the pro forma condensed statement of income for the year then ended. The historical condensed financial statements are derived from the historical financial statements of Widget Company, which were audited by us, and of Basic Company, which were audited by other accountants, appearing elsewhere herein [*or incorporated by reference*]. Such pro forma adjustments are based upon management's assumptions described in Note 2. Widget Company's management is responsible for the pro forma financial information. Our responsibility is to express an opinion on the pro forma financial information based on our examination.

Our examination was conducted in accordance with attestation standards established by the American Institute of Certified Public Accountants and, accordingly, included such procedures as we considered necessary in the circumstances. We believe that our examination provides a reasonable basis for our opinion.

In addition, we have reviewed the related pro forma adjustments and the application of those adjustments to the historical amounts in [*the assembly of*] the accompanying pro forma condensed balance sheet of Widget Company as of March 31, 20X2, and the pro forma condensed statement of income for the three months then ended. The historical condensed financial statements are derived from the historical financial statements of Widget Company, which were reviewed by us, and Basic Company, which were reviewed by other accountants, appearing elsewhere herein [*or incorporated by reference*]. Such pro forma adjustments are based upon management's assumptions as described in Note 2. Our review was conducted in accordance with attestation standards established by the American Institute of Certified Public Accountants. A review is substantially less in scope than an examination, the objective of which is the expression of an opinion on management's assumptions, the pro forma adjustments, and the application of those adjustments to historical financial information. Accordingly, we do not express such an opinion on the pro forma adjustments or the application of such adjustments to the pro forma condensed balance sheet as of March 31, 20X2, and the pro forma condensed statement of income for the three months then ended.

The objective of this pro forma financial information is to show what the significant effects on the historical information might have been had the transaction [*or event*] occurred at an earlier date. However, the pro forma condensed financial statements are not necessarily indicative of the results of operations or related effects on financial position that would have been attained had the above-mentioned transaction [*or event*] actually occurred earlier.

[*Additional paragraph(s) may be added to emphasize certain matters relating to the attest engagement or the subject matter.*]

In our opinion, management's assumptions provide a reasonable basis for presenting the significant effects directly attributable to the above-mentioned transaction [*or event*] described in Note 1, the related pro forma adjustments give appropriate effect to those assumptions, and the pro forma column reflects the proper application of those adjustments to the historical financial statement amounts in the pro forma condensed balance sheet as of December 31, 20X1, and the pro forma condensed statement of income for the year then ended.

Based on our review, nothing came to our attention that caused us to believe that management's assumptions do not provide a reasonable basis for representing the significant effects directly attributable to the above-mentioned transaction [*or event*] described in Note 1, that the related pro forma adjustments do not give appropriate effect to those assumptions, or that the pro forma column does not reflect the proper application of those adjustments to the historical financial statement amounts in the pro forma condensed balance sheet as of March 31, 20X2, and the pro forma condensed statement of income for the three months then ended.

Guy and Carmichael
February 15, 20X2

Illustration 4. Report on Examination of Pro Forma Financial Information—Scope Limitation Qualification

Independent Accountant's Report

We have examined the pro forma adjustments reflecting the transaction [*or event*] described in Note 1 and the application of those adjustments to the historical amounts in [*the assembly of*] the accompanying pro forma condensed balance sheet of Widget Company as of December 31, 20X1, and the pro forma condensed statement of income for the year then ended. The historical condensed financial statements are derived from the historical financial statements of Widget Company, which were audited by us, and of Basic Company, which were audited by other accountants, appearing elsewhere herein [*or incorporated by reference*]. Such pro forma adjustments are based upon management's assumptions described in Note 2. Widget Company's management is responsible for the pro forma financial information. Our responsibility is to express an opinion on the pro forma financial information based on our examination.

Except as described below, our examination was conducted in accordance with attestation standards established by the American Institute of Certified Public Accountants and, accordingly, included such procedures as we considered necessary in the circumstances. We believe that our examination provides a reasonable basis for our opinion.

We are unable to perform the examination procedures we considered necessary with respect to assumptions relating to the proposed loan described as Adjustment E in Note 2.

The objective of this pro forma financial information is to show what the significant effects on the historical financial information might have been had the transaction [*or event*] occurred at an earlier date. However, the pro forma condensed financial statements are not necessarily indicative of the results of operations or related effects on financial position that would have been attained had the above-mentioned transaction [*or event*] actually occurred earlier.

In our opinion, except for the effects of such changes, if any, as might have been determined to be necessary had we been able to satisfy ourselves as to the assumptions relating to the proposed loan, management's assumptions provide a reasonable basis for presenting the significant effects directly attributable to the above-mentioned transaction [*or event*] described in Note 1, the related pro forma adjustments give appropriate effect to those assumptions, and the pro forma column reflects the proper application of those adjustments to the historical financial statement amounts in the pro forma condensed balance sheet as of December 31, 20X1, and the pro forma condensed statement of income for the year then ended.

Guy and Carmichael
February 15, 20X2

Illustration 5. Report on Examination of Pro Forma Financial Information—Qualification—Propriety of Assumptions

Independent Accountant's Report

We have examined the pro forma adjustments reflecting the transaction [*or event*] described in Note 1 and the application of those adjustments to the historical amounts in [*the assembly of*] the accompanying pro forma condensed balance sheet of Widget Company as of December 31, 20X1, and the pro forma condensed statement of income for the year then ended. The historical condensed financial statements are derived from the historical financial statements of Widget Company, which were audited by us, and of Basic Company, which were audited by other accountants, appearing elsewhere herein [*or incorporated by reference*]. Such pro forma adjustments are based upon management's assumptions described in Note 2. Widget Company's management is responsible for the pro forma financial information. Our responsibility is to express an opinion on the pro forma financial information based on our examination.

Our examination was conducted in accordance with attestation standards established by the American Institute of Certified Public Accountants and, accordingly, included such procedures as we considered necessary in the circumstances. We believe that our examination provides a reasonable basis for our opinion.

The objective of this pro forma financial information is to show what the significant effects on the historical financial information might have been had the transaction [*or event*] occurred at an earlier date. However, the pro forma condensed financial statements are not necessarily indicative of the results of operations or related effects on financial position that would have been attained had the above-mentioned transaction [*or event*] actually occurred earlier.

As discussed in Note 2 to the pro forma financial statements, the pro forma adjustments reflect management's assumption that X Division of the acquired company will be sold. The net assets of this division are reflected at their historical carrying amount; generally accepted accounting principles require these net assets to be recorded at estimated net realizable value.

In our opinion, except for inappropriate valuation of net assets of X Division, management's assumptions described in Note 2 provide a reasonable basis for presenting the significant effects directly attributable to the above-mentioned transaction [*or event*] described in Note 1, the related pro forma adjustments give appropriate effect to those assumptions, and the pro forma column reflects the proper application of those adjustments to the historical financial statement amounts in the pro forma condensed balance sheet as of December 31, 20X1, and the pro forma condensed statement of income for the year then ended.

Guy and Carmichael
February 15, 20X2

ILLUSTRATION 6. DISCLAIMER OF OPINION ON PRO FORMA FINANCIAL INFORMATION—SCOPE LIMITATION

Independent Accountant's Report

We were engaged to examine the pro forma adjustments reflecting the transaction [*or event*] described in Note 1 and the application of those adjustments to the historical amounts in [*the assembly of*] the accompanying pro forma condensed balance sheet of Widget Company as of December 31, 20X1, and the pro forma condensed statement of income for the year then ended. The historical condensed financial statements are derived from the historical financial statements of Widget Company, which were audited by us, and of Basic Company, which were audited by other accountants, appearing elsewhere herein [*or incorporated by reference*]. Such pro forma adjustments are based upon management's assumptions described in Note 2. Widget Company's management is responsible for the pro forma financial information.

As discussed in Note 2 to the pro forma financial statements, the pro forma adjustments reflect management's assumptions that the elimination of duplicate facilities would have resulted in a 30% reduction in operating costs. Management could not supply us with sufficient evidence to support this assertion.

The objective of this pro forma financial information is to show what the significant effects on the historical financial information might have been had the transaction [*or event*] occurred at an earlier date. However, the pro forma condensed financial statements are not necessarily indicative of the results of operations or related effects on financial position that would have been attained had the above-mentioned transaction [*or event*] actually occurred earlier.

Since we were unable to evaluate management's assumptions regarding the reduction in operating costs and other assumptions related thereto, the scope of our work was not sufficient to express and, therefore, we do not express an opinion on the pro forma adjustments, management's underlying assumptions regarding those adjustments, and the application of those adjustments to the historical financial statement amounts in the pro forma condensed financial statement amounts in the pro forma condensed balance sheet as of December 31, 20X1, and the pro forma condensed statement of income for the year then ended.

Guy and Carmichael
February 15, 20X2

2501 REPORTING ON AN ENTITY'S INTERNAL CONTROL OVER FINANCIAL REPORTING[1, 2]

EFFECTIVE DATE AND APPLICABILITY

Original Pronouncements	SSAE 10, *Attestation Standards: Revision and Recodifications,* January 2001.
Effective Date	Effective when the subject matter or assertion is as of, or for a period ending on or after, June 1, 2001.
Applicability	Applicable when an independent accountant is engaged to issue or does issue an examination report on the effectiveness of an entity's internal control over financial reporting as of a point in time. *NOTE: A practitioner may also be engaged to examine the effectiveness of an entity's internal control over financial reporting for a period of time (instead of a point in time). In that case, the guidance in this section should be appropriately modified.*

---

1 *In AICPA publications this section is codified as AT 501.*

2 *Auditors of publicly held companies should be aware that Section 404 of the Sarbanes-Oxley Act of 2002 requires that all public company annual reports on Form 10-K include a report containing a statement of management's responsibility to establish and maintain adequate internal controls over financial reporting, and an assessment, as of the end of the issuer's fiscal year, of the effectiveness of those internal controls. The company's auditors must attest to and report on management's assessment of the effectiveness of internal control over financial reporting. (The Act states that these attestations cannot be separate engagements.) The SEC has issued its final rule on Section 404 (see "Management's Reports on Internal Control over Financial Reporting and Certification of Disclosure in Exchange Act Periodic Reports," Release No. 33-8238, at www.sec.gov, governing this requirement.*

The SEC's implementing rule on Section 404 notes that the existing SSAE 10 chapter on internal control has been adopted in the PCAOB's interim standards. However, the PCAOB is expected to issue an Exposure Draft and a final standard to replace the guidance on internal control over financial reporting in SSAE 10 before the requirement for a management report and related auditor attestation becomes effective in 2004. The ASB, among other things, has submitted a proposed replacement to the chapter in SSAE 10 on internal control over financial reporting and a proposed new auditing standard, ***Auditing an Entity's Internal Control over Financial Reporting in Conjunction with the Financial Statement Audit*** *to the PCAOB for its consideration in developing a new standard(s) on internal control over financial reporting. Please check for updates to this section on the John Wiley & Sons, Inc., website at www.wiley.com/gaas.*

Review engagements are prohibited, but agreed-upon procedures engagements are not.

This statement does not change the auditor's responsibility for considering or communicating internal control related matters in an audit. See SAS 60 (Section 325).

For reports on the processing of transactions at service organizations, SAS 70 (Section 324) continues to apply.

DEFINITIONS OF TERMS

Reportable conditions. Matters coming to an auditor's attention that represent significant deficiencies in the design or operation of internal control that could adversely affect the entity's ability to record, process, summarize, and report financial data consistent with the assertions of management in the financial statements.

Material weakness. A reportable condition in which the design or operation of one or more of the internal control components does not reduce to a relatively low level the risk that errors or fraud in amounts that would be material in relation to the financial statements may occur and not be detected within a timely period by employees in the normal course of performing their assigned functions.

Responsible party. As used in this section, management personnel who accept responsibility for the effectiveness of an entity's internal control.

OBJECTIVES OF SECTION

The history of public reporting on internal control has been long and controversial. In the mid-1940s there was a debate about whether an auditor had a duty to modify the audit report to disclose serious deficiencies in accounting control. In the late 1960s, several large banks included accountants' reports on internal control in their annual reports. These reports were brief and stated, in effect, that the accountants had reviewed controls and believed that the control systems were effective.

There was disagreement about the desirability of this type of reporting. Some accountants believed that reports on internal control served no useful purpose unless the recipients were in a position to do something about internal control effectiveness.

In late 1971, SAP 49 was issued to put an effective halt to the small but growing practice of public reporting on internal control. It required two caveat paragraphs on the limitations of accounting control, and the only form of assurance permitted was negative assurance on the absence of material weaknesses. Critics of the accounting profession, most notably officials of the SEC, publicly derided the report as a triumph of technical precision over meaningful reporting and common sense.

There were no significant developments in the area until the illegal payments scandal broke in the mid-1970s. One outcome of the scandal was passage of the Foreign Corrupt Practices Act of 1977. The act adopted the accounting profession's definition of internal accounting control and required that all public companies have a system of internal accounting control sufficient to meet the objectives stated in the definition.

The SEC began what appeared to be a concerted drive to require independent accountants to report publicly on the internal accounting systems of public companies. Despite the momentum of the illegal payments scandal, the drive faltered because of unanticipated strong opposition from public companies and lack of support from large CPA firms. Ultimately, the SEC backtracked and withdrew its proposals. In response to the Foreign Corrupt Practices

Act and related SEC proposals, however, the accounting profession had started several initiatives, and many of them had been virtually completed before the SEC's withdrawal.

In late 1977, even before passage of the act was achieved, SAS 20 had been issued. It imposed a responsibility on the auditor to communicate material weaknesses in accounting control to management. A footnote to the SAS pledged that the subject of public reporting on accounting control was being given continued study.

In the mid-1980s, SAS 30 was issued. It provided a vehicle for an accountant to issue a positive opinion on accounting control. The unmodified opinion stated

> *In our opinion, the system of internal accounting control of XYZ Company and subsidiaries in effect at [date], taken as a whole, was sufficient to meet the objectives stated above insofar as those objectives pertain to the prevention or detection of errors or irregularities in amounts that would be material in relation to the consolidated financial statements.*

However, this report was largely of academic interest only. Without the pressure of an SEC requirement, there was little incentive even for public companies to engage an independent accountant to express an opinion on an internal accounting control system. Small and privately owned companies never had any great interest in such reports. The report was a service that was all dressed up but had no place to go.

In the wake of the savings and loan crisis in the late 1980s, there was considerable regulatory and legislative activity to help reduce fraudulent financial reporting. A National Commission on Fraudulent Financial Reporting, known as the Treadway Commission, was created, formed of representatives of the Financial Executives Institute, the AICPA, Institute of Management Accountants, Institute of Internal Auditors, and the American Accounting Association. The Commission's report, issued in 1987, included as one of its recommendations the requirement for a management report on internal control. Legislators and regulators agreed. The Federal Deposit Insurance Corporation Improvement Act of 1991 affecting financial institutions was passed, and the SEC issued another rule proposal, *Report of Management's Responsibilities*, proposing a requirement for public companies to provide such a management report publicly. However, a common definition of "internal control" was needed to make such management reporting consistent. A group called "The Committee of Sponsoring Organizations of the Treadway Commission (COSO)" developed a common definition to provide a standard for reporting. Their report, *Internal Control—Integrated Framework*, was issued in September 1992.

Statement on Standards for Attestation Engagements 2 was issued by the AICPA in May 1993. This Statement substantially changed the approach to reporting on control by requiring that management issue its report and the accountant provide an opinion on management's assertion. This parallels the audit process in which management issues the financial statements and the auditor provides an opinion on the statements. The report continued to include caveat paragraphs about the inherent limitation of internal control similar to those required by SAP 49 and SAS 30.

SSAE 6 was issued in December 1995 to make the guidance compatible with the COSO definitions and criteria for internal control. Theoretically, management may use any reasonable criteria for effective internal control established by a recognized body. However, COSO is the only recognized body specifically identified in the SSAEs.

SSAE 9 was issued by the AICPA in January 1999. This SSAE enabled the practitioner to report directly on a specified subject matter, such as internal control, rather than management's assertion. The practitioner continued to be required to obtain management's assertion in order to perform the engagement. SSAE 9 also eliminated the requirement for a separate presentation of management's assertion in certain cases where the assertion is included in the introductory paragraph of the practitioner's report.

In January 2001, the Auditing Standards Board issued SSAE 10, *Attestation Standards: Revision and Recodification.* SSAE 10 superseded SSAEs 1 through 9 and renumbered the AT sections in the AICPA's Codification. The revisions to this section include clarifying that

- The responsible party's refusal to provide a written assertion as part of an examination engagement should cause the practitioner to withdraw from the engagement. (An exception exists if an examination of internal control is required by law or regulation. In this case, the practitioner should disclaim an opinion unless he or she obtains evidential matter that warrants expressing an adverse opinion.)
- The responsible party's refusal to furnish the required representations constitutes a limitation on the scope of the engagement.
- If, in a multiple-party arrangement, the practitioner's client is not the responsible party, the practitioner has no responsibility to communicate reportable conditions to the responsible party. (However, the practitioner is not precluded from making that communication.)

FUNDAMENTAL REQUIREMENTS

The statement (1) establishes conditions that should be met for a practitioner to examine the effectiveness of an entity's internal control over financial reporting and (2) establishes the engagement performance and reporting requirements for four types of such engagements. These types are engagements to examine

1. The effectiveness of an entity's internal control.
2. The design and operating effectiveness of a segment of an entity's internal control.
3. Only the suitability of design of an entity's internal control when no assertion is made about the operating effectiveness.
4. The design and operating effectiveness of an entity's internal control based on criteria established by a regulatory agency.

STANDARDS

An engagement conducted in accordance with this section should comply with the general, fieldwork, and reporting standards in Section 2101.

REQUIRED CONDITIONS FOR ENGAGEMENT ACCEPTANCE

According to AU 501.04, the following conditions should be present for the practitioner to accept the engagement to examine the effectiveness of an entity's internal control. These are

1. Management accepts responsibility for the effectiveness of the entity's internal control.
2. The responsible party evaluates the effectiveness of the entity's internal control using suitable criteria.
3. Sufficient evidential matter exists or could be developed to support the responsible party's evaluation.

The practitioner should obtain a written assertion about the effectiveness of the entity's internal control from the responsible party. The written assertion may be provided in a representation letter to the practitioner or in a separate report accompanying the practitioner's report.

Regardless of whether the client is the responsible party, the responsible party's refusal to provide as assertion requires that the practitioner withdraw from an examination engagement. Withdrawal is **not** required if the engagement is required by law or regulation. In that case, the practitioner should disclaim an opinion on internal control unless an adverse opinion is warranted. If the practitioner expresses an adverse opinion and the responsible party does not provide an assertion, the practitioner's report should be restricted.

The responsible party's written assertion may take various forms but should be specific enough that individuals having competence in and using the same or similar measurement and disclosure criteria ordinarily would be able to arrive at similar conclusions.

Management Representations and Responsibilities

The statement requires the practitioner to obtain in writing certain specific representations from the responsible party. If the responsible party refuses to furnish all of the required written representations, a scope limitation exists which ordinarily is sufficient to require that the practitioner disclaim an opinion or withdraw from the engagement. However, depending on the nature of the representations not obtained or the circumstances of the refusal, the practitioner may decide that a qualified opinion is appropriate. According to AT 501.44, the required representations are

1. Acknowledgment of the responsible party's responsibility for establishing and maintaining internal control.
2. A statement that the responsible party has performed an evaluation of the effectiveness of the entity's internal control, specifying the control criteria used.
3. A statement of the responsible party's assertion about the effectiveness of the entity's internal control based on the control criteria as of a specified date.
4. A statement that the responsible party has disclosed to the practitioner all significant deficiencies in the design or operation of internal control which could adversely affect the entity's ability to record, process, summarize, and report financial data consistent with the assertions of management in the financial statements and has identified those that it believes to be material weaknesses in internal control.
5. A description of any material fraud and any other fraud that, although not material, involves management or other employees who have a significant role in the entity's internal control.
6. A statement whether there were, subsequent to the date being reported on, any changes in internal control or other factors that might significantly affect internal control, including any corrective actions taken by the responsible party with regard to significant deficiencies and material weaknesses.

A sample management representation letter is included in Illustration 11. Section 333 provides guidance on the date as of which management should sign such a representation letter and which members of management should sign it.

Criteria

Criteria issued by bodies composed of experts that follow a formal process of developing and exposing drafts of pronouncements to the public before issuance are generally reasonable criteria. Such bodies include the AICPA, some regulatory agencies, and the Committee of Sponsoring Organizations of the Treadway Commission (COSO).

Criteria established by groups that do not follow due process or "do not as clearly represent the public interest" should be evaluated by the practitioner to determine that the criteria are reasonable for general-use reporting. If such criteria are used, the criteria should be available to users as discussed in Section 2101.

Criteria suitable only for limited distribution. In some cases, criteria may be suitable only for reports that are limited to the parties, generally a regulatory agency, who developed the criteria. For example, a regulatory agency may include specific criteria in its audit guide that are suitable to its specific needs. When such criteria are used, the practitioner's report should be modified to limit its use to the regulatory agency. If the criteria has been subject to due process procedures and the criteria are available to users, the practitioner may use the report in Illustration 1 or 2.

Evidential Matter

To be able to express an opinion, the practitioner performs procedures to gather sufficient competent evidential matter.

1. In considering the effectiveness of the design of a specific control, the practitioner evaluates whether the policy or procedure is suitably designed to prevent or detect material misstatements in specific financial statement assertions.
2. In considering operating effectiveness of a control, the practitioner evaluates whether the control was applied consistently, whether the control is effectively achieving its purpose, and considers who applied it.

Tests performed by the responsible party. The responsible party may have performed tests and may provide their results to the practitioner. The practitioner may consider such results, but it is the practitioner's responsibility to obtain sufficient evidence to support the opinion. The practitioner's tests may corroborate the results of the responsible party's tests. In considering whether the evidence obtained is sufficient, the practitioner should recognize that evidence obtained directly by the practitioner is more persuasive than that obtained indirectly, such as from the responsible party.

Time period covered. The time period to be covered by tests of controls is a matter of judgment. The practitioner should perform tests of controls over a period of time that is adequate to determine whether, as of the date selected, the controls necessary for achieving the objectives of the control criteria are operating effectively.

NOTE: In considering the time period to be covered by the tests of controls, the practitioner recognizes that some controls operate continuously while others (e.g., controls over physical inventory counts) operate only at certain times.

Changes in controls. Management may change controls to make them more effective or efficient. If the change occurs before the date as of which management's assertion about internal control over financial reporting is made, and they have been in effect for a sufficient period to be able to assess them, the practitioner should consider the design and operating effectiveness of the new controls and not be concerned with superseded controls.

If the change is a subsequent event (after the date as of which the internal control over financial reporting is being examined but before the date of the practitioner's report), the treatment is analogous to a subsequent event in an audit. The practitioner considers

1. Does the subsequent event significantly affect the effectiveness of the entity's internal control as of the date specified in the assertion?
2. Does management adequately describe the subsequent event and its effects in the assertion?

Subsequent events. If the practitioner becomes aware of subsequent events that he or she believes significantly affect the effectiveness of the entity's internal control as of the date specified in the assertion, the practitioner should report directly on the effectiveness of the entity's internal control and issue a qualified or adverse opinion. The practitioner should disclaim an opinion if he or she cannot determine the effect of the subsequent event on the effectiveness of the entity's internal control.

The practitioner may become aware of subsequent events related to conditions that did not exist at the date specified in the assertion but arose after that date. Occasionally, the impact of this kind of subsequent event is so significant that the practitioner may want to add an explanatory paragraph to his or her report that either describes the event and its effects or directs the reader's attention to the event and its effects.

Guidance on conditions that existed at the date of the practitioner's report but were discovered only after the date of the report is also analogous to the audit guidance in Section 561. The practitioner needs to determine

1. Is the new information reliable?
2. Did the conditions/facts exist at the date of the report?
3. Would the practitioner have changed the report if the conditions/facts were known at that time?
4. Is anyone likely to be relying on the practitioner's report on the effectiveness of the entity's internal control?

Documentation

The controls and control objectives that they were designed to achieve should be documented to serve as a basis for the responsible party's assertion, and to support the practitioner's report. The responsible party generally prepares the documentation of controls, but the practitioner, at the responsible party's request, may assist in preparing or gathering documentation. No particular form of documentation (narratives, policy manuals, flowcharts, etc.) is specifically required.

Reporting Requirements

The practitioner may examine and report on

- An entity's effectiveness of internal control over financial reporting
- The responsible party's written assertion.

The practitioner's examination report on the effectiveness of an entity's internal control over financial reporting should include the following:

1. A title that includes the word **independent**.
2. An introductory paragraph with statements that
   a. Identify the subject matter (internal control over financial reporting) and the responsible party.
   b. The responsible party (management) is responsible for maintaining effective internal control over financial reporting.
   c. The practitioner's responsibility is to express an opinion on the effectiveness of an entity's internal control based on his or her examination.
3. A scope paragraph with statements that
   a. The examination was conducted in accordance with attestation standards established by the American Institute of Certified Public Accountants and, accordingly, included obtaining an understanding of internal control over financial reporting, testing and evaluating the design and operating effectiveness of internal control, and performing other such procedures as the practitioner considered necessary in the circumstances.
   b. The practitioner believes the examination provides a reasonable basis for his or her opinion.

4. An inherent limitations paragraph that states that, because of inherent limitations of any internal control, misstatements due to errors or fraud may occur and not be detected. (In addition, the paragraph should state that projections of any evaluation of internal control over financial reporting to future periods are subject to the risk that internal control may become inadequate because of changes in conditions, or that the degree of compliance with the policies or procedures may deteriorate.)
5. An opinion paragraph that presents the practitioner's opinion on whether the entity has maintained, in all material respects, effective internal control over financial reporting as of the specified date, based on the control criteria.
6. A statement restricting the use of the report to the specified parties when the criteria used to evaluate internal control over financial reporting are
   a. Determined by the practitioner to be appropriate only for a limited number of parties who either participated in their establishment or can be presumed to have an adequate understanding of the criteria.
   b. Available only to specified parties.
7. The manual or printed signature of the practitioner's firm.
8. The date of the examination report.

The practitioner's examination report on a written assertion about the effectiveness of an entity's internal control over financial reporting should include the following:

1. A title that includes the word **independent**.
2. An introductory paragraph with statements that
   a. Identify the written assertion about the effectiveness of the entity's internal control over financial reporting as of a specified date and the responsible party (when the written assertion does not accompany the practitioner's report, the first paragraph of the report should also contain a statement of the assertion).
   b. The assertion is the responsibility of the responsible party.
   c. The practitioner's responsibility is to express an opinion on the written assertion based on his or her examination.
3. A scope paragraph with statements that
   a. The examination was conducted in accordance with attestation standards established by the American Institute of Certified Public Accountants and, accordingly, included obtaining an understanding of internal control over financial reporting, testing and evaluating the design and operating effectiveness of internal control, and performing such other procedures as the practitioner considered necessary in the circumstances.
   b. The practitioner believes the examination provides a reasonable basis for his or her opinion.
4. An inherent limitations paragraph that states that, because of inherent limitations of any internal control, misstatements due to error or fraud may occur and not be detected (In addition, the paragraph should state that projections of any evaluation of internal control over financial reporting to future periods are subject to the risk that internal control may become inadequate because of changes in conditions, or that the degree of compliance with the policies or procedures may deteriorate.)
5. An opinion paragraph that presents the practitioner's opinion on whether the assertion about the effectiveness of the entity's internal control over financial reporting as of the specified date is fairly stated, in all material respects, based on the control criteria.

6. A statement restricting the use of the report to specified parties when the criteria used to evaluate the effectiveness of internal control over financial reporting are
   a. Determined by the practitioner to be appropriate only for a limited number of parties who either participated in their establishment or can be presumed to have an adequate understanding of the criteria.
   b Available only to specified parties.
7. The manual or printed signature of the practitioner's firm.
8. The date of the examination report.

NOTE: If a practitioner is requested by one party to examine the effectiveness of another entity's internal control, he or she may want to restrict the report to the party making the request. Section 2101 provides guidance on restricting the use of an attest report.

Material weakness. During the course of the engagement, the practitioner may become aware of reportable conditions, some of which may be material weaknesses. The practitioner has a responsibility to communicate reportable conditions to the audit committee and to identify those reportable conditions that are material weaknesses. Such communication should be in writing.

NOTE: The practitioner should not issue a written report representing that no reportable conditions were noted because of the potential for misinterpretation of the limited degree of assurance.

If, in a multiple-party arrangement, the client is not the responsible party, the practitioner has no responsibility to communicate reportable conditions to the responsible party.

The practitioner should also modify his or her report

1. If a reportable condition is of such magnitude that it is a material weakness, or
2. If the combined effect of several reportable conditions that would not individually be material weaknesses results in a material weakness existing.

To most effectively communicate with the reader of the modified report, the practitioner should express his or her opinion directly on the effectiveness of internal control, not on the assertion (see Illustration 3).

If a written assertion accompanying the practitioner's report contains a statement that the responsible party believes that the cost of correcting the weakness would be greater than benefits of the new controls, the practitioner should disclaim an opinion on the responsible party's cost-benefit statement. If the practitioner believes the cost-benefit statement is a material misstatement of fact, he or she should consider the guidance in Section 2101.

Other report modifications. Other reasons that the practitioner may decide to modify the report include

1. Scope limitation.
2. Reference to the report of another practitioner.
3. Significant subsequent event.
4. Reporting on only a segment of internal control.
5. Reporting on only the suitability of the design (and not the operating effectiveness).
6. Criteria are not suitable for general use.

Examples of several of these reports are included in *Illustrations*.

Other Information in Client-Prepared Documents

Other information may be contained in the document that contains the practitioner's attest report on internal control (or an assertion related thereto). When the information is contained in annual reports to owners, annual reports of not-for-profit entities distributed to the public, or annual reports filed with SEC, or other documents to which the practitioner devotes attention at the client's request, then the practitioner should

- Read such information not covered by the practitioner's report, and
- Consider whether it or its manner of presentation is materially inconsistent with the practitioner's report or whether it contains a material misstatement of fact.

See Section 2101 for additional guidance.

Agreed-upon Procedures Engagements

Agreed-upon procedure engagements are permitted by the standards. The guidance in Section 2201 applies.

INTERPRETATIONS

Pre-Award Surveys (Issued February 1997; Revised January 2001)

A practitioner may not issue a report on a pre-award assertion (survey) by management about the effectiveness (suitability) of the design of an entity's internal control based solely on consideration of internal control in an audit of financial statements. A pre-award survey is often part of the process in applying for a government grant or contract.

To issue a report on the design effectiveness of an entity's internal control or a portion thereof for a pre-award survey, the practitioner should perform an examination of or apply agreed-upon procedures to management's written assertion. An examination report is described in "Reporting on an Entity's Internal Control over Financial Reporting" (AT 501 in AICPA publications and Section 2501 herein). For an engagement to apply agreed-upon procedures to a written assertion about the design effectiveness of the entity's internal control over compliance with specified requirements, the practitioner should also follow the provisions of "Compliance Attestation" (AT 601 in AICPA publications and Section 2601 herein) and "Agreed-upon Procedures Engagements" (AT 201 in AICPA publications and Section 2201 herein).

If the practitioner is requested to sign a form prescribed by a government agency in connection with a pre-award survey, the practitioner should refuse to sign unless he or she has performed an attestation engagement (either an examination or an agreed-upon procedures engagement). Also, the practitioner should consider whether the prescribed form wording conforms to professional standards and modify the wording as necessary or attach a separate report.

The practitioner should refuse to provide any report on an entity's ability to establish suitably designed internal control. Neither an audit nor an attestation engagement provides a basis for such a report because an assertion about **ability** is not capable of reasonably consistent estimation or measurement.

TECHNIQUES FOR APPLICATION

Planning the Engagement

According to AT 501.18, in planning the engagement, the practitioner should consider factors such as the following:

1. Matters affecting the industry in which the entity operates, such as financial reporting practices, economic conditions, laws and regulations, and technological changes.
2. Knowledge of the entity's internal control obtained during other professional engagements.
3. Matters relating to the entity's business, including its organization, operating characteristics, capital structure, and distribution methods.
4. The extent of recent changes, if any, in the entity, its operations, or its internal control.

5. Management's method of evaluating the effectiveness of the entity's internal control based upon control criteria.
6. Preliminary judgments about materiality levels, inherent risk, and other factors relating to the determination of material weaknesses.
7. The type and extent of evidential matter pertaining to the effectiveness of the entity's internal control.
8. The nature of specific controls designed to achieve the objectives of the control criteria, and their significance.
9. Preliminary judgments about the effectiveness of the internal control.

Obtaining an Understanding of Internal Control

The practitioner obtains an understanding through a combination of the following techniques:

1. Inquiry of personnel (staff level through supervisory).
2. Inspection of documentation.
3. Observation of activities and operations.

The statement indicates that documentation of internal control "is generally prepared by the responsible party." However, the first year that an entity issues a report on internal control, the responsible party often finds such documentation to be lacking, outdated, or organized in a manner that makes comparison to the control objectives difficult. Such documentation is a requirement to support both the assertion and the practitioner's report. In estimating the time required and fees for an engagement to report on the assertion, the practitioner should carefully consider the quality of the existing documentation. If it is poor, the practitioner may wish to offer his or her services in a separate consulting engagement to prepare or organize such documentation.

Evaluating the Design

Guidance on techniques for evaluating the entity's internal control in Section 319 is generally helpful in engagements to report on internal control.

Testing and Evaluating the Operating Effectiveness

Techniques for performing tests of controls are also presented in Section 319.

Evaluating Whether a Material Weakness Exists

When the practitioner identifies a reportable condition, he or she evaluates whether it is of such magnitude that it is a material weakness. When evaluating the magnitude of a reportable condition, the practitioner should consider

1. The amount or range of misstatement that might occur in the account balance or class of transactions because of the reportable condition.
2. The risk of the misstatement within the range in 1. above.

In addition, the practitioner needs to consider the combined effect of reportable conditions that individually may not be material weaknesses. The joint effect may be a material weakness. According to AT 501.39, the practitioner should assess

1. The range or distribution of the amount of misstatement caused by error or fraud that may result during the same accounting period from two or more individual reportable conditions.
2. The joint risk or probability that such a combination of errors or fraud would be material.

ILLUSTRATIONS

The following illustrations are adapted from SSAE 10.

Illustration 1. Practitioner's Opinion Directly on the Effectiveness of an Entity's Internal Control

Independent Accountant's Report

We have examined the effectiveness of Widget Company's internal control over financial reporting as of December 31, 20X1, based on criteria established in *Internal Control—Integrated Framework* issued by the Committee of Sponsoring Organizations of the Treadway Commission (COSO). Widget Company's management is responsible for maintaining effective internal control over financial reporting. Our responsibility is to express an opinion on the effectiveness of internal control based on our examination.

Our examination was conducted in accordance with attestation standards established by the American Institute of Certified Public Accountants and, accordingly, included obtaining an understanding of the internal control over financial reporting, testing, evaluating the design and operating effectiveness of internal control, and performing such other procedures as we considered necessary in the circumstances. We believe that our examination provides a reasonable basis for our opinion.

Because of inherent limitations in any internal control, misstatements due to error or fraud may occur and not be detected. Also, projections of any evaluation of internal control over financial reporting to future periods are subject to the risk that internal control may become inadequate because of changes in conditions, or that the degree of compliance with the policies or procedures may deteriorate.

In our opinion, Widget Company maintained in all material respects, effective internal control over financial reporting as of December 31, 20X1, based on criteria established in *Internal Control—Integrated Framework* issued by the Committee of Sponsoring Organizations of the Treadway Commission (COSO).

Guy and Carmichael
February 15, 20X2

Illustration 2. Practitioner's Opinion on Management's Assertion

Independent Accountant's Report

We have examined management's assertion, included in the accompanying [*title of management report*], that Widget Company maintained effective internal control over financial reporting as of December 31, 20X1, based on criteria established in *Internal Control—Integrated Framework* issued by the Committee of Sponsoring Organizations of the Treadway Commission (COSO).[3] Widget Company's management is responsible for maintaining effective internal control over financial reporting. Our responsibility is to express an opinion on management's assertion based on our examination.

[*Standard scope and inherent limitations paragraphs*]

In our opinion, management's assertion that Widget Company maintained effective internal control over financial reporting as of December 31, 20X1, is fairly stated, in all material respects, based on criteria established in *Internal Control—Integrated Framework* issued by the Committee of Sponsoring Organizations of the Treadway Commission (COSO).

Guy and Carmichael
February 15, 20X2

---

[3] *The practitioner should identify the responsible party's report examined by referring to the title used by the responsible party in its report. Further, he or she should use the same description of the entity's internal control as the responsible party uses in its report, including the types of controls (that is, controls over the preparation of annual financial statements, interim financial statements, or both) on which the responsible party is reporting. If the presentation of the assertion does not accompany the practitioner's report, the phrase "included in the accompanying [title of the responsible party's report]" would be omitted.*

ILLUSTRATION 3. MATERIAL WEAKNESS IN INTERNAL CONTROL—QUALIFIED OPINION

Independent Accountant's Report

We have examined the effectiveness of Widget Company's internal control over financial reporting as of December 31, 20X1, based on criteria established in *Internal Control—Integrated Framework* issued by the Committee of Sponsoring Organizations of the Treadway Commission (COSO). Widget Company's management is responsible for maintaining effective internal control over financial reporting. Our responsibility is to express an opinion on the effectiveness of internal control based on our examination.

[*Standard scope and inherent limitations paragraphs*]

[*Include sentence(s) describing the material weakness and its effect on the achievement of the objectives of the control criteria.*] We believe such condition represents a material weakness. A material weakness is a condition that precludes the entity's internal control from providing reasonable assurance that material misstatements in the financial statements will be prevented or detected on a timely basis.[4]

In our opinion, except for the effect of the material weakness described in the preceding paragraph on the achievement of the objectives of the control criteria, Widget Company has maintained, in all material respects, effective internal control over financial reporting as of December 31, 20X1, based on criteria established in *Internal Control—Integrated Framework* issued by the Committee of Sponsoring Organizations of the Treadway Commission (COSO).

Guy and Carmichael
February 15, 20X2

ILLUSTRATION 4. MATERIAL WEAKNESS IN INTERNAL CONTROL—ADVERSE OPINION

Independent Accountant's Report

We have examined the effectiveness of Widget Company's internal control over financial reporting as of December 31, 20X1, based on criteria established in *Internal Control—Integrated Framework* issued by the Committee of Sponsoring Organizations of the Treadway Commission (COSO). Widget Company's management is responsible for maintaining effective internal control over financial reporting. Our responsibility is to express an opinion on the effectiveness of internal control based on our examination.

[*Standard scope and inherent limitations paragraphs*]

[*Include sentence(s) describing the material weakness and its effect on the achievement of the objectives of the control criteria.*] We believe such condition represents a material weakness. A material weakness is a condition that precludes the entity's internal control from providing reasonable assurance that material misstatements in the financial statements will be prevented or detected on a timely basis.[5]

In our opinion, because of the effect of the material weakness described above on the achievement of the objectives of the control criteria, Widget Company has not maintained effective internal control over financial reporting as of December 31, 20X1, based on criteria established in *Internal Control—Integrated Framework* issued by the Committee of Sponsoring Organizations of the Treadway Commission (COSO).

Guy and Carmichael
February 15, 20X2

ILLUSTRATION 5. SCOPE LIMITATION—QUALIFIED OPINION

Independent Accountant's Report

[*Standard introductory paragraph*]

Except as described below, our examination was conducted in accordance with attestation standards established by the American Institute of Certified Public Accountants and, accordingly, in-

---

4 *This description of a material weakness differs from the definition of material weakness in Section 325. Although a practitioner should consider the definition contained in Section 325 when determining whether a material weakness exists, the description above should be used to describe a material weakness in the practitioner's report.*

5 *See footnote 4.*

cluded obtaining an understanding of the internal control over financial reporting, testing, evaluating the design and operating effectiveness of the internal control, and performing such other procedures as we considered necessary in the circumstances. We believe that our examination provides a reasonable basis for our opinion.

Prior to December 20, 20X1, Widget Company had an inadequate system for recording cash receipts, which could have prevented the Company from recording cash receipts on accounts receivable completely and properly. Therefore, cash received could have been diverted for unauthorized use, lost, or otherwise not properly recorded to accounts receivable. We believe this condition was a material weakness in the design or operation of the internal control of Widget Company in effect at [*date*]. A material weakness is a condition that precludes the entity's internal control from providing reasonable assurance that material misstatements in the financial statements will be prevented or detected on a timely basis. Although the Company implemented a new cash receipts system on December 20, 20X1, the system has not been in operation for a sufficient period of time to enable us to obtain sufficient evidence about its operating effectiveness.

[*Standard inherent limitations paragraph*]

In our opinion, except for the effect of matters we may have discovered had we been able to examine evidence about the effectiveness of the new cash receipts system, Widget Company maintained, in all material respects, effective internal control over financial reporting as of December 31, 20X1, based on criteria established in *Internal Control—Integrated Framework* issued by the Committee of Sponsoring Organizations of the Treadway Commission (COSO).

Guy and Carmichael
February 15, 20X2

ILLUSTRATION 6. SCOPE LIMITATION—DISCLAIMER OF OPINION

Independent Accountant's Report

We were engaged to examine the effectiveness of Widget Company's internal control over financial reporting as of December 31, 20X1, based on criteria established in *Internal Control—Integrated Framework* issued by the Committee of Sponsoring Organizations of the Treadway Commission (COSO). Widget Company's management is responsible for maintaining effective internal control over financial reporting.

[*Scope paragraph should be omitted*]

[*Explanatory paragraph to describe scope restrictions*]

Since management [*describe scope restrictions*] and we were unable to apply other procedures to satisfy ourselves as to the entity's internal control over financial reporting, the scope of our work was not sufficient to enable us to express, and we do not express, an opinion on the effectiveness of the entity's internal control over financial reporting.

Guy and Carmichael
February 15, 20X2

ILLUSTRATION 7. OPINION BASED IN PART ON THE REPORT OF ANOTHER PRACTITIONER

Independent Accountant's Report

We have examined the effectiveness of Widget Company's internal control over financial reporting as of December 31, 20X1, based on criteria established in *Internal Control—Integrated Framework* issued by the Committee of Sponsoring Organizations of the Treadway Commission (COSO). Widget Company's management is responsible for maintaining effective internal control over financial reporting. Our responsibility is to express an opinion on the effectiveness of internal control based on our examination. We did not examine the effectiveness of internal control over financial reporting of Basic Company, a wholly owned subsidiary, whose financial statements reflect total assets and revenues constituting 20% and 30%, respectively, of the related consolidated financial statement amounts as of and for the year ended December 31, 20X1. The effectiveness of Basic Company's internal control over financial reporting was examined by other accountants whose report has been furnished to us, and our opinion, insofar as it relates to the effectiveness of Basic Company's internal control over financial reporting, is based solely on the report of the other accountants.

Our examination was conducted in accordance with attestation standards established by the American Institute of Certified Public Accountants and, accordingly, included obtaining an understanding of the internal control over financial reporting, testing, and evaluating the design and operating effectiveness of the internal control, and performing such other procedures as we considered necessary in the circumstances. We believe that our examination and the report of the other accountants provide a reasonable basis for our opinion.

[*Standard inherent limitations paragraph*]

In our opinion, based on our examination and the report of the other accountants, Widget Company maintained, in all material respects, effective internal control over financial reporting as of December 31, 20X1, based on criteria established in *Internal Control—Integrated Framework* issued by the Committee of Sponsoring Organizations of the Treadway Commission (COSO).

Guy and Carmichael
February 15, 20X2

ILLUSTRATION 8. REPORTING ON A SEGMENT OF THE ENTITY'S INTERNAL CONTROL

Independent Accountant's Report

We have examined the effectiveness of Widget Company's internal control over financial reporting for its retail division as of December 31, 20X1, based on criteria established in *Internal Control—Integrated Framework* issued by the Committee of Sponsoring Organizations of the Treadway Commission (COSO). Widget Company's management is responsible for maintaining effective internal control over financial reporting. Our responsibility is to express an opinion on the effectiveness of internal control based on our examination.

[*Standard scope and inherent limitations paragraph*]

In our opinion, Widget Company's retail division maintained, in all material respects, effective internal control over financial reporting as of December 31, 20X1, based on criteria established in *Internal Control—Integrated Framework* issued by the Committee of Sponsoring Organizations of the Treadway Commission (COSO).

Guy and Carmichael
February 15, 20X2

ILLUSTRATION 9. REPORTING ON THE SUITABILITY OF DESIGN

Independent Accountant's Report

We have examined the suitability of Widget Company's design of internal control over financial reporting to prevent or detect material misstatements in the financial statements on a timely basis as of December 31, 20X1, based on criteria established in *Internal Control—Integrated Framework* issued by the Committee of Sponsoring Organizations of the Treadway Commission (COSO). Widget Company's management is responsible for the suitable design of internal control over financial reporting. Our responsibility is to express an opinion on the design of internal control based on our examination.

Our examination was conducted in accordance with attestation standards established by the American Institute of Certified Public Accountants and, accordingly, included obtaining an understanding of the internal control over financial reporting, evaluating the design of internal control, and performing such other procedures as we considered necessary in the circumstances. We believe that our examination provides a reasonable basis for our opinion.

[*Standard inherent limitations paragraph*]

In our opinion, Widget Company's internal control over financial reporting is suitably designed, in all material respects, to prevent or detect material misstatements in the financial statements on a timely basis as of December 31, 20X1, based on criteria established in *Internal Control—Integrated Framework* issued by the Committee of Sponsoring Organizations of the Treadway Commission (COSO).

Guy and Carmichael
February 15, 20X2

ILLUSTRATION 10. CRITERIA SPECIFIED BY A REGULATORY AGENCY

Independent Accountant's Report

We have examined the adequacy of Widget Company's internal control over financial reporting as of December 31, 20X1, based on [*identify criteria, e.g., the criteria established by* __________ *Agency, as set forth in its audit guide dated* __________]. Widget Company's management is responsible for maintaining adequate internal control over financial reporting. Our responsibility is to express an opinion on whether the internal control is adequate to meet such criteria based on our examination.

[*Standard scope and inherent limitations paragraph*]

We understand that the agency considers the controls over financial reporting that meet the criteria referred to in the first paragraph of this report adequate for its purpose. In our opinion, based on this understanding and on our examination, Widget Company's internal control over financial reporting is adequate, in all material respects, based on the criteria established by [__________ *Agency*].

This report is solely intended for the information and use of the board of directors and management of Widget Company and [__________ *Agency*] and is not intended to be and should not be used by anyone other than these specified parties.

Guy and Carmichael
February 15, 20X2

ILLUSTRATION 11. MANAGEMENT REPRESENTATIONS

[*Client letterhead*]

[*Date of practitioner's report*]

[*Practitioner's name*]

[*Address*]
[*City, State*]

Dear__________:

In connection with your examination of the effectiveness of Widget Company's internal control over financial reporting as of December 31, 20X1, based on criteria established in *Internal Control—Integrated Framework* issued by the Committee of Sponsoring Organizations of the Treadway Commission (COSO), as of December 31, 20X1, we confirm, to the best of our knowledge and belief, the following representations made to you during your examination.

1. We are responsible for establishing and maintaining internal control over financial reporting.
2. We have performed an evaluation of the effectiveness of Widget Company's internal control over financial reporting using the criteria established in *Internal Control—Integrated Framework* issued by the Committee of Sponsoring Organizations of the Treadway Commission (COSO).
3. Based on our evaluation, we assert that Widget Company maintained effective internal control over financial reporting as of December 31, 20X1, based on the above specified control criteria.
4. We have disclosed to you all significant deficiencies in the design or operation of internal control that could adversely affect Widget Company's ability to record, process, summarize, and report financial data consistent with our assertions in the financial statements.
5. There are no material weaknesses in internal control. [*We have identified all deficiencies in internal control we believe to be material weaknesses.*]
6. There has been no [*We have disclosed to you all*]
    a. Fraud involving management or employees who have significant roles in internal control.
    b. Fraud involving other employees that could have a material effect on the financial statements.
7. Subsequent to the date being reported on, there have been no [*we have disclosed to you all*] significant changes to internal control and no other factors have arisen that might significantly affect internal control. [*We have disclosed to you the corrective actions taken by us with regard to significant deficiencies and material weaknesses.*]

Very truly yours,

____
Chief Executive Officer

____
Chief Financial Officer

2601 COMPLIANCE ATTESTATION[1]

EFFECTIVE DATE AND APPLICABILITY

Original Pronouncements

SSAE 10, *Attestation Standards: Revision and Recodification,* January 2001.

Effective Date

Effective when the subject matter or assertion is as of, or for a period ending, June 1, 2001.

Applicability

Applicable to agreed-upon procedures related to either of the following:

1. Compliance with requirements of specified laws, regulations, rules, contracts, or grants (specified requirements).
2. The effectiveness of internal control over compliance with specified requirements.
3. Or both 1. and 2.

Also applicable to engagements to examine the entity's compliance with specified requirements or a written assertion thereon.

The Statement does not apply to the following:

1. Situations in which an auditor reports on specified compliance requirements based solely on an audit of financial statements (see Section 623, "Special Reports").
2. Engagements for which the objective is to report in accordance with *Government Auditing Standards*, or the Single Audit Act, or Office of Management and Budget (OMB) circulars and releases (see Section 801).
3. Program-specific audits as addressed in Section 801 performed in accordance with federal audit guides issued prior to the effective date of this SSAE.
4. Engagements covered by Section 634, "Letters for Underwriters and Certain Other Requesting Parties" (comfort letters).
5. The report that encompasses the internal control over compliance for a broker or dealer in securities as required by Rule

[1] *In AICPA publications this section is codified as AT 601.*

17a-5 of the Securities Exchange Act of 1934.

6. Audits performed in accordance with generally accepted auditing standards.

NOTE: An accountant is discouraged from accepting an engagement to examine the effectiveness of internal control over compliance or an assertion thereon because reasonable criteria for evaluation are typically not available. If such an engagement is accepted, the appropriate guidance is in AT 101 in AICPA publications (Section 2101 herein). Additionally, AT 601 (Section 2601 herein) may be helpful, but it is intended for reporting on internal control over financial reporting, not over compliance.

DEFINITIONS OF TERMS

Attestation risk.[2] The risk that the practitioner may unknowingly fail to modify appropriately his or her opinion. It is composed of inherent risk, control risk, and detection risk.

Inherent risk.[2] The risk that material noncompliance with specified requirements could occur, assuming there are no related controls.

Control risk.[2] The risk that material noncompliance that could occur will not be prevented or detected on a timely basis by the entity's internal control.

Detection risk.[2] The risk that the practitioner's procedures will lead him or her to conclude that material noncompliance does not exist when, in fact, such noncompliance does exist.

Internal control over compliance. The process by which management obtains reasonable assurance of compliance with specified requirements.

Specified requirements. A term that is used to refer to an entity's compliance with requirements of specified laws, regulations, rules, contracts, or grants.

OBJECTIVES OF SECTION

This SSAE provides guidance for engagements related to either (1) compliance with requirements of specified laws, regulations, rules, contracts, or grants (specified requirements) or (2) the effectiveness of internal control over compliance with specified requirements.

A practitioner may be engaged to perform agreed-upon procedures to assist users in evaluating management's written assertion about an entity's compliance with specified requirements, the effectiveness of internal control over compliance, or both. A practitioner also may be engaged to examine compliance with specified requirements or a written assertion thereon. For example, some electronic funds transfer associations or networks require their members who process transactions to complete a compliance exam.

In January 2001, the Auditing Standards Board issued SSAE 10, *Attestation Standards: Revision and Recodification.* SSAE 10 superseded SSAEs 1 through 9 and renumbered the AT sections in the AICPA's Codification. The revisions to this section include clarifying that

- The responsible party's refusal to furnish the required representations constitutes a limitation on the scope of the engagement.

---

[2] *Terms that are related to risk in an examination engagement.*

- The responsible party's refusal to provide a written assertion as part of an examination engagement should cause the practitioner to withdraw from the engagement. (An exception exists if an examination of an entity's compliance with specified requirements is required by law or regulation. In this case, the practitioner should disclaim an opinion on compliance unless he or she obtains evidential matter that warrants expressing an adverse opinion.)
- If the engagement is to perform agreed-upon procedures and
  - The client is the responsible party, that party's refusal to provide an assertion requires that the practitioner withdraw from the engagement.
  - The client is not the responsible party, the practitioner is not required to withdraw, but should consider the effects of the refusal on the engagement and report.

FUNDAMENTAL REQUIREMENTS: GENERAL (APPLICABLE TO BOTH AGREED-UPON PROCEDURES AND EXAMINATION ENGAGEMENTS)

General

An engagement conducted in accordance with this section should comply with the general, fieldwork, and reporting standards in Section 2101.

Criteria

The practitioner cannot accept an agreed-upon procedures or an examination engagement unless reasonable criteria have been established by a recognized body or are stated in or attached to the practitioner's report.

Prohibited Engagements

A practitioner should not accept an engagement to perform a review (see Section 2101) about compliance with specified requirements or about the effectiveness of internal control over compliance or assertions thereon.

Using the Work of a Specialist

The practitioner should follow the guidance of Section 336, "Using the Work of a Specialist," if he or she decides that a specialist is necessary for an engagement covered by this section.

Management's Representations

According to AT 601.68, for both an agreed-upon procedures engagement and an examination engagement, the practitioner should obtain the responsible party's written representations that

1. Acknowledge the responsible party's responsibility for complying with the specified requirements.
2. Acknowledge the responsible party's responsibility for establishing and maintaining effective internal control over compliance.
3. State that the responsible party has performed an evaluation of (1) the entity's compliance with specified requirements, or (2) the entity's internal controls for ensuring compliance and detecting noncompliance with requirements, as applicable.

4. State the responsible party's assertion about the entity's compliance with the specified requirements or about the effectiveness of the internal control over compliance, as applicable, based on the stated or established criteria.
5. State that the responsible party has disclosed to the practitioner all known noncompliance.
6. State that the responsible party has made available all documentation related to compliance with specified requirements.
7. State the responsible party's interpretation of any compliance requirements that have varying interpretations.
8. State that the responsible party has disclosed any communications from regulatory agencies, internal auditors, and other practitioners concerning possible noncompliance with the specified requirements, including communications received between the end of the period addressed in the written assertion and the date of the practitioner's report.
9. State that the responsible party has disclosed any known noncompliance occurring subsequent to the period for which, or date as of which, the responsible party selects to make its assertion.

Section 333, "Management Representations," provides guidance on the dating and signatories of the representation letter.

The responsible party's refusal to furnish the required representations constitutes a limitation on the scope of the engagement. In an examination engagement, the practitioner ordinarily should disclaim an opinion or withdraw. However, based on the nature of the representations or circumstances, a qualified opinion may be appropriate.

In an agreed-upon procedures engagement in which the practitioner's client is the responsible party, the responsible party's refusal to provide written assertions is a scope limitation sufficient to cause the practitioner to withdraw. When the practitioner's client is not the responsible party, the practitioner

- Is not required to withdraw, but should consider the effects of the responsible party's refusal on his or her report, as well as the ability to rely on other representations of the responsible party.
- May also want to obtain written representations from the client (e.g., knowledge of any noncompliance).

Other Information in a Client-Prepared Document

The practitioner's report on either compliance with specified requirements or the effectiveness of internal control over compliance or written assertions thereon may be included in a client-prepared document that includes other information. In those circumstances, the practitioner should read the other information and follow the procedures discussed in Section 2101.

FUNDAMENTAL REQUIREMENTS: AGREED-UPON PROCEDURES ENGAGEMENT

Conditions for Acceptance

According to AT 601.09, a practitioner may accept an agreed-upon procedures engagement related to an entity's compliance with specified requirements or the effectiveness of internal control over compliance, if the following conditions are met:

1. The responsible party accepts responsibility for the entity's compliance with specified requirements and the effectiveness of the entity's internal control over compliance.
2. The responsible party evaluates the entity's compliance with specified requirements or the effectiveness of the entity's internal control over compliance.

In addition, the conditions that apply to acceptance of all agreed-upon procedures engagements have to be met (see Section 2201).

NOTE: A written management representation letter is required in agreed-upon procedure engagements relating to compliance matters.

The practitioner should obtain a written assertion about compliance with specified requirements or internal control over compliance from the responsible party. The written assertion may be provided in the representation letter or in a separate report accompanying the practitioner's report. If the client is the responsible party, that party's refusal to provide an assertion requires that the practitioner withdraw from the engagement. Withdrawal is **not** required if the engagement is required by law or regulation. If the client is not the responsible party, the practitioner is not required to withdraw but should consider the effects of the refusal on the engagement and report.

UNDERSTANDING WITH SPECIFIED PARTIES

The specified parties should participate in establishing the procedures to be performed and take responsibility for the adequacy of those procedures. The practitioner should determine whether the specified parties understand the procedures to be performed by discussing the nature of management's assertion and the procedures with the specified parties (see *Techniques for Application*).

UNDERSTANDING THE SPECIFIED COMPLIANCE REQUIREMENTS

The practitioner should obtain an understanding of the specified compliance requirements stated in management's assertion. To obtain this understanding, the practitioner should consider the following:

1. Laws, regulations, rules, contracts, and grants relevant to the specified compliance requirements.
2. Knowledge about the specified compliance requirements obtained from the following:
   a. Prior engagements and regulatory reports.
   b. Discussions with appropriate individuals within the entity.
   c. Discussions with appropriate individuals outside the entity, such as regulators or specialists.

SCOPE RESTRICTIONS

The practitioner should attempt to obtain agreement from the specified parties for modification of the agreed-upon procedures if circumstances impose restrictions on the scope of those procedures. If an agreement for modification cannot be obtained, the practitioner should describe the restrictions in the attestation report or withdraw from the engagement.

SUBSEQUENT EVENTS

If the practitioner becomes aware of noncompliance related to management's assertion that occurs after the period addressed by that assertion but before the date of the report, he or she should consider including that information in the report. According to AT 601.24, the practitioner has no obligation to perform procedures to detect noncompliance in the subsequent period.

Practitioner's Report

The practitioner's report on agreed-upon procedures on an entity's compliance with specified requirements or about the effectiveness of an entity's internal control over compliance should be in the form of procedures and findings. The report should be dated as of the date of completion of the agreed-upon procedures. According to AT 601.24, the practitioner's report should contain the following elements:

1. A title that includes the word independent.
2. Identification of the specified parties.
3. Identification of the subject matter of the engagement (or management's assertion thereon), including the period or point in time addressed,[3] and a reference to the character of the engagement.
4. An identification of the responsible party.
5. A statement that the subject matter is the responsibility of responsible party.
6. A statement that the procedures, which were agreed to by the specified parties identified in the report, were performed to assist the specified parties in evaluating the entity's compliance with the specified requirements or the effectiveness of its internal control over compliance.
7. A statement that the agreed-upon procedures engagement was conducted in accordance with attestation standards established by the American Institute of Certified Public Accountants.
8. A statement that the sufficiency of the procedures is solely the responsibility of the specified parties and a disclaimer of responsibility for the sufficiency of those procedures.
9. A list of the procedures performed (or reference thereto) and related findings. The practitioner should not provide negative assurance.
10. Where applicable, a description of any agreed-upon materiality limits.
11. A statement that the practitioner was not engaged to and did not conduct an examination of the entity's compliance with specified requirements or about the effectiveness of an entity's internal control over compliance, a disclaimer of opinion thereon, and a statement that if the practitioner had performed additional procedures, other matters might have come to his or her attention that would have been reported.
12. A statement restricting the use of the report to the specified parties. (However, if the report is a matter of public record, the practitioner should include the following sentence: "However, this report is a matter of public record and its distribution is not limited.")
13. Where applicable, reservations or restrictions concerning procedures or findings.
14. Where applicable, a description of the nature of the assistance provided by the specialist.
15. The manual or printed signature of the practitioner's firm.
16. The date of the report.

---

[3] *Generally, management's assertion about compliance with specified requirements will address a* ***period*** *of time, whereas an assertion about internal control over compliance will address a* ***point*** *in time.*

FUNDAMENTAL REQUIREMENTS: EXAMINATION ENGAGEMENT

CONDITIONS FOR ENGAGEMENT PERFORMANCE

According to AT 601.10, a practitioner may accept an examination engagement related to an entity's compliance with specified requirements if the following conditions are met:

1. The responsible party accepts responsibility for the entity's compliance with specified requirements and the effectiveness of the entity's internal control over compliance.
2. The responsible party evaluates the entity's compliance with specified requirements.
3. Sufficient evidential matter exists or could be developed to support the responsible party's evaluation.

A practitioner may examine the effectiveness of the entity's internal control over compliance or an assertion thereon only if he or she has reason to believe that the subject matter is capable of reasonably consistent evaluation against criteria that are suitable and available to users. If such criteria exist for internal control over compliance, the practitioner should perform the engagement in accordance with Section 2101. Section 2501 may also be helpful on such an engagement.

The practitioner should obtain a written assertion about compliance with specified requirements or internal control over compliance from the responsible party. The written assertion may be provided in a representation letter to the practitioner or in a separate report accompanying the practitioner's report. The responsible party's written assertion may take various forms but should be specific enough that users having competence in and using the same or similar measurement and disclosure criteria ordinarily would be able to arrive at materially similar conclusions.

The responsible party's refusal to provide a written assertion as part of an examination engagement should cause the practitioner to withdraw from the engagement, regardless of whether the client is the responsible party. An exception exists if an examination of an entity's compliance with specified requirements is required by law or regulation. In this case, the practitioner should disclaim an opinion on compliance unless he or she obtains evidential matter that warrants expressing an adverse opinion. If the practitioner expresses an adverse opinion and the responsible party does not provide an assertion, the practitioner's report should be restricted.

EXTENT OF EVIDENCE

To express an opinion on an entity's compliance (or assertion related thereto), the practitioner should accumulate sufficient evidence about the entity's compliance with specified requirements and limit attestation risk to an appropriately low level.

ASSESSMENT OF INHERENT RISK

The practitioner should consider factors affecting inherent risk similar to the factors an auditor would consider when planning an audit of financial statements (see Section 316). According to AT 601.33, in addition, the practitioner should consider the following factors:

1. The complexity of the specified compliance requirements.
2. The length of time the entity has been subject to the specified compliance requirements.
3. Prior experience with the entity's compliance.
4. Potential impact of noncompliance.

Assessment of Control Risk

The practitioner should assess control risk. To assess control risk for compliance with specified requirements and to plan the engagement, the practitioner should obtain an understanding of those parts of the internal control related to compliance.

Engagement Procedures

According to AT 601.39, in an examination of the entity's compliance with specified requirements, the practitioner should do the following:

1. Obtain an understanding of the specified compliance requirements.
2. Plan the engagement.
3. Consider relevant portions of the entity's internal control over compliance.
4. Obtain sufficient evidence including testing compliance with specified requirements.
5. Consider subsequent events.
6. Form an opinion about whether the entity complied, in all material respects, with specified requirements (or whether the responsible party's assertion about such compliance is fairly stated in all material respects) based on the specified criteria.

Subsequent Events

The practitioner should consider information about subsequent events that comes to his or her attention between the end of the period addressed by the practitioner's report and prior to the issuance of the report.

The practitioner has no responsibility to detect noncompliance after the period being reported on but before the date of the report. However, if the practitioner becomes aware of this type of noncompliance and its nature and significance may make management's assertion misleading, the practitioner should include in the report an explanatory paragraph describing the nature of the noncompliance.

Practitioner's Report

According to AT 601.55, the practitioner's report on an examination, which is ordinarily addressed to the entity, should include the following:

1. A title that includes the word **independent**.
2. An identification of the specified compliance requirements, including the period covered, and of the responsible party.[4]
3. A statement that compliance with the specified requirements is the responsibility of the entity's management.
4. A statement that the practitioner's responsibility is to express an opinion on the entity's compliance with those requirements based on his or her examination.
5. A statement that the examination was conducted in accordance with attestation standards established by the American Institute of Certified Public Accountants and, accordingly, included examining, on a test basis, evidence about the entity's compliance with those requirements and performing such other procedures as the practitioner considered necessary in the circumstances.

---

[4] *A practitioner also may be engaged to report an entity's compliance with specified requirements as of a point in time. In this case, the reports in* ***Illustrations*** *should be adapted as appropriate.*

6. A statement that the practitioner believes the examination provides a reasonable basis for his or her opinion.
7. A statement that the examination does not provide a legal determination on the entity's compliance.
8. The practitioner's opinion on whether the entity complied, in all material respects, with specified requirements based on the specified criteria.
9. A statement restricting the use of the report to the specified parties when the criteria used to evaluate compliance
   a. Are determined by the practitioner to be appropriate only for a limited number of parties who either participated in establishing the criteria or who can be assumed to have an adequate understanding of the criteria.
   b. Are available only to specified parties.
10. The manual or printed signature of the practitioner's firm.
11. The date of the examination report.

The practitioner's report should be dated as of the date of completion of the examination procedures.

REPORT MODIFICATIONS

The practitioner should modify the standard report whenever any one of the following conditions exist:

1. There is material noncompliance with specified requirements (qualified or adverse opinion).
2. The scope of the engagement is restricted (qualified or disclaimer of opinion).
3. The practitioner refers to the report of another practitioner as the basis, in part, for the report (see Illustration 9 in Section 2501).

INTERPRETATIONS

There are no interpretations for this section.

TECHNIQUES FOR APPLICATION

PLANNING THE ENGAGEMENT—GENERAL

For either an agreed-upon procedures engagement or an examination, the practitioner should properly plan the engagement. In planning the engagement, the practitioner should consider doing the following:

1. Discuss the purpose of the engagement with management.
2. Read or obtain an understanding of relevant laws and documents.
3. Obtain an engagement letter.
4. Design a program of procedures to be applied.

AGREED-UPON PROCEDURES ENGAGEMENT

In this type of engagement, the practitioner should try to meet with the specified parties or a representative of the specified parties to establish the procedures. If a meeting is not possible, the practitioner should do one of the following:

1. Compare the procedures to be applied to written requirements of the specified parties.
2. Review relevant contracts with or correspondence from the specified parties.

3. Distribute a draft of the anticipated report or a copy of a proposed engagement letter to the specified parties with a request for their comments.
4. Discuss the procedures to be applied with appropriate representatives of the specified parties involved.

The manner in which the procedures are established should be documented in the practitioner's workpapers.

At the conclusion of this type of engagement, the practitioner should obtain a management representation letter. If the management refuses, the practitioner should withdraw from the engagement.

PLANNING THE EXAMINATION ENGAGEMENT

The practitioner should consider the following when planning the engagement:

1. For an entity with multiple components, determine if it is necessary to examine all components for compliance. In making this determination, consider
   a. The degree to which the specified compliance requirements apply at the component level.
   b. Judgments about materiality.
   c. The degree of centralization of records.
   d. The effectiveness of the control environment, particularly management's direct control over the exercise of authority delegated to others and its ability to supervise activities at various locations effectively.
   e. The nature and extent of operations conducted at the various components.
   f. The similarity of controls over compliance for different components.
2. The need to use the work of a specialist (see Section 336).
3. The existence of an internal audit function and the extent to which internal auditors are involved in monitoring compliance with specified requirements (see Section 322).
4. Obtain an understanding of the parts of the internal control related to compliance with the specified requirements. This understanding may be obtained by
   a. Inquiries.
   b. Inspection of documents.
   c. Observation of activities.
5. Identify types of potential noncompliance.
6. Assess control risk. If the practitioner wishes to assess control risk below the maximum, he or she should perform tests of controls.

EXAMINATION PROCEDURES

The nature of procedures and the sufficiency of evidence are matters of practitioner judgment. Procedures to be considered include the following:

1. For engagements involving regulatory requirements
   a. Review communication between regulatory agencies and the entity.
   b. Review examination reports of the regulatory agencies.
   c. If appropriate, make inquiries of regulatory agencies including inquiries about examinations in progress.
   d. Make inquiries of entity's outside and inside counsel responsible for such matters.

2. Identify subsequent events for the period from the reporting period to the date of the report that would provide evidence about compliance during the period under examination. Information concerning subsequent events would be obtained from the following sources:
   a. Relevant internal auditors' reports issued during the subsequent period.
   b. Other practitioners' reports identifying noncompliance, issued during the subsequent period.
   c. Regulatory agencies' reports on the entity's noncompliance, issued during the subsequent period.
   d. Information about the entity's noncompliance, obtained through other professional engagements for that entity.
3. If the specified requirements relate to financial statement matters, compare the relevant parts of these statements with the specified requirements.
4. Obtain a management representation letter. If management refuses, the practitioner should consider issuing a qualified opinion or a disclaimer of opinion.

MATERIALITY

Materiality in an examination of compliance differs from materiality in an audit. In an examination, the practitioner should consider the

1. Nature of the compliance requirements, which may or may not be quantifiable in monetary terms
2. Nature and frequency of noncompliance, including sampling risks
3. Qualitative considerations, including user needs and expectations

ILLUSTRATIONS

The following illustrations are adapted from SSAE 10.

ILLUSTRATION 1. AGREED-UPON PROCEDURES REPORT IN WHICH THE PROCEDURES AND FINDINGS CONCERNING COMPLIANCE WITH SPECIFIED REQUIREMENTS ARE ENUMERATED[5]

Independent Accountant's Report on Applying Agreed upon Procedures

We have performed the procedures enumerated below, which were agreed to by [*list specified parties*], solely to assist the specified parties in evaluating Widget Company's compliance with [*list specified requirements*] during the [*period*] ended [*date*]. Management is responsible for Widget Company's compliance with those requirements. This agreed-upon procedures engagement was performed in accordance with attestation standards established by the American Institute of Certified Public Accountants. The sufficiency of these procedures is solely the responsibility of the parties specified in this report. Consequently, we make no representation regarding the sufficiency of the procedures described below either for the purpose for which this report has been requested or for any other purpose.

[*Include paragraphs to enumerate procedures and findings.*]

We were not engaged to, and did not, perform an examination, the objective of which would be the expression of an opinion on compliance. Accordingly, we do not express such an opinion. Had we performed additional procedures, other matters might have come to our attention that would have been reported to you.

This report is intended solely for the information and use of [*list or refer to specified parties*] and is not intended to be and should not be used by anyone other than these specified parties.

---

[5] *In some agreed-upon procedures engagements, the practitioner may issue one report on a combined management assertion about compliance with specified requirements and the effectiveness of internal control over compliance. The practitioner's combined report should address both specified requirements and internal control over compliance.*

Illustration 2. Agreed-upon Procedures Report in Which the Procedures and Findings Concerning the Effectiveness of Internal Control over Compliance Are Enumerated[6]

Independent Accountant's Report on Applying Agreed-upon Procedures

We have performed the procedures enumerated below, which were agreed to by [*list specified parties of report*], solely to assist the specified parties in evaluating the effectiveness of Widget Company's internal control over compliance with [*list specified requirements*] as of [*date*]. Management is responsible for Widget Company's internal control over compliance with those requirements. This agreed-upon procedures engagement was performed in accordance with attestation standards established by the American Institute of Certified Public Accountants. The sufficiency of these procedures is solely the responsibility of the parties specified in the report. Consequently, we make no representation regarding the sufficiency of the procedures described below either for the purpose for which this report has been requested or for any other purpose.

[*Include paragraphs to enumerate procedures and findings.*]

We were not engaged to, and did not, perform an examination, the objective of which would be the expression of an opinion on the effectiveness of internal control over compliance. Accordingly, we do not express such an opinion. Had we performed additional procedures, other matters might have come to our attention that would have been reported to you.

This report is intended solely for the information and use of [*list or refer to specified parties*] and is not intended to be and should not be used by anyone other than these specified parties.

Illustration 3. Examination Report Expressing an Opinion on Compliance with Specified Requirements

Independent Accountant's Report

We have examined Widget Company's compliance with [*list specified compliance requirements*] during the [*period*] ended [*date*]. Management is responsible for Widget Company's compliance with those requirements. Our responsibility is to express an opinion on Widget Company's compliance based on our examination.

Our examination was conducted in accordance with attestation standards established by the American Institute of Certified Public Accountants and, accordingly, included examining, on a test basis, evidence about Widget Company's compliance with those requirements and performing such other procedures as we considered necessary in the circumstances. We believe that our examination provides a reasonable basis for our opinion. Our examination does not provide a legal determination on Widget Company's compliance with specified requirements.

In our opinion, Widget Company complied in all material respects with the aforementioned requirements for the year ended December 31, 20X1.

Illustration 4. Examination Report When Expressing an Opinion on Management's Assertion about Compliance with Specified Requirements

Independent Accountant's Report

We have examined management's assertion, included in the accompanying [*title of management report*], that Widget Company complied with [*list specified compliance requirements*] during the [*period*] ended [*date*]. Management is responsible for Widget Company's compliance with those requirements. Our responsibility is to express an opinion on management's assertion about Widget Company's compliance based on our examination.

[*Standard scope paragraph*]

In our opinion, management's assertion that Widget Company complied with the aforementioned requirements during the [*period*] ended [*date*] is fairly stated, in all material respects.

---

6 *In some agreed-upon procedures engagements, the practitioner may issue one report on a combined management assertion about compliance with specified requirements and the effectiveness of internal control over compliance. The practitioner's combined report should address both specified requirements and internal control over compliance.*

ILLUSTRATION 5. MODIFIED REPORT WHEN PRACTITIONER HAS IDENTIFIED MATERIAL NONCOMPLIANCE AND MANAGEMENT HAS APPROPRIATELY MODIFIED ITS ASSERTION

Independent Accountant's Report

We have examined Widget Company's compliance with [*list specified compliance requirements*] for the [*period*] ended [*date*]. Management is responsible for compliance with those requirements. Our responsibility is to express an opinion on Widget Company's compliance based on our examination.

[*Standard scope paragraph*]

Our examination disclosed the following material noncompliance with [*type of compliance requirement*] applicable to Widget Company during the [*period*] ended [*date*]. [*Describe noncompliance.*]

In our opinion, except for the material noncompliance described in the third paragraph, Widget Company complied, in all material respects, with the aforementioned requirements for the [*period*] ended [*date*].

ILLUSTRATION 6. ADVERSE REPORT WHEN PRACTITIONER HAS IDENTIFIED MATERIAL NONCOMPLIANCE AND MANAGEMENT HAS APPROPRIATELY MODIFIED ITS ASSERTION

Independent Accountant's Report

We have examined Widget Company's compliance with [*list of specified compliance requirements*] for the [*period*] ended [*date*]. Management is responsible for compliance with these requirements. Our responsibility is to express an opinion on Widget Company's compliance based on our examination.

[*Standard scope paragraph*]

Our examination disclosed the following material noncompliance with [*type of compliance requirement*] applicable to Widget Company during the [*period*] ended [*date*]. [*Describe noncompliance*].

In our opinion, because of the effect of the noncompliance described in the third paragraph, Widget Company has not complied with the aforementioned requirements for the [*period*] ended [*date*].

2701 MANAGEMENT'S DISCUSSION AND ANALYSIS (MD&A)[1]—A SUMMARY[2, 3]

EFFECTIVE DATE AND APPLICABILITY

Original Pronouncement	SSAE 10, *Attestation Standards: Revision and Recodification,* January 2001.
Effective Date	Effective when management's discussion and analysis is for a period ending on or after June 1, 2001.
Applicability	When a practitioner is engaged by a public entity that prepares MD&A in accordance with the rules and regulations adopted by the SEC (or a non-public entity following the same requirements) to either perform an examination or review of MD&A. A practitioner engaged to perform agreed-upon procedures on MD&A should follow the guidance in Section 2201.

DEFINITION OF TERM

MD&A. Management's Discussion and Analysis of Financial Condition and Results of Operations adopted by the SEC and found in Item 303 of Regulation S-K, as interpreted by Financial Reporting Release (FRR) 36.

OBJECTIVES OF SECTION

The SEC adopted requirements for MD&A in 1974 to have management provide a narrative explanation of the financial statements. The idea was to allow the user to see the com-

---

[1] *In AICPA publications this section is codified as AT 701.*

[2] *The SSAE on examination or review of MD&A is essentially a detailed manual on how to perform examinations and reviews, and only the highlights are summarized here. A practitioner seeking to provide these services should refer to SSAE 10 and the SEC's rules and regulations on MD&A. Only the considerations for a public entity are covered here. The considerations for a nonpublic entity are very similar because only the SEC has, at this point, issued rules and regulations that provide guidance on the presentation of MD&A.*

[3] *Practitioners should be aware that, on April 15, 2002, the SEC issued "Commission Statement about Management's Discussion and Analysis of Financial Condition and Results of Operations." The release sets forth certain views of the SEC regarding disclosures that should be considered by registrants. Disclosure matters covered in the release are liquidity and capital resources, including off-balance-sheet arrangements; certain trading activities that include nonexchange traded contracts accounted for at fair value; and the effects of transactions with related and certain other parties. The release can be found on the SEC's website at www.sec.gov.*

pany's financial position and operating results through management's eyes. The SEC has periodically changed the requirements and the most recent comprehensive explanation of the requirements is in FRR 36.

Two levels of service are possible—an examination or a review. A review report is restricted as to use and is not intended to be filed with the SEC. An examination report is intended for general use, but at this stage, whether there will be a significant demand for this service is unknown. The SEC does not require a practitioner's report on MD&A—the narrative presentation is management's responsibility and not a part of the audited financial statements.

The practitioner's objective in an examination of MD&A is to express an opinion on the presentation taken as a whole by reporting whether

1. The presentation includes, in all material respects, the required elements of the rules and regulations adopted by the SEC.
2. The historical financial amounts included in the presentation have been accurately derived, in all material respects, from the entity's financial statements.
3. The underlying information, determinations, estimates and assumptions of the entity provide a reasonable basis for the disclosures contained in the presentation.

The objective of a review of MD&A is to provide negative assurance on the three items listed above.

NOTE: "Negative assurance" indicates that no information came to the accountant's attention that would cause him or her not to believe the three statements.

An examination of MD&A would generally be expected to relate to the MD&A for annual periods, but a review might relate to the MD&A for annual or interim periods or some combination.

In an examination, the practitioner seeks to obtain reasonable assurance by accumulating sufficient evidence in support of the disclosures and assumptions, thereby limiting attestation risk to an appropriately low level. A review consists principally of applying analytical procedures and making inquiries and does not provide assurance that a practitioner would become aware of all significant matters that would be disclosed in an examination.

In January 2001, the Auditing Standards Board issued SSAE 10, *Attestation Standards: Revision and Recodification*. SSAE 10 superseded SSAEs 1 through 9 and renumbered the AT sections in the AICPA's Codification. SSAE 10 made only minor changes to this section, including modifying the reports in this section to conform to changes made by SAS 93, *Omnibus Statement on Auditing Standards—2000*.

FUNDAMENTAL REQUIREMENTS: EXAMINATION

ACCEPTANCE

To accept an engagement to examine MD&A, the practitioner should audit the financial statements for at least the latest period to which the MD&A presentation relates and the financial statements for the other periods covered by the MD&A presentation should have been audited by the practitioner or a predecessor auditor.

PERFORMANCE

According to AT 701.41, the practitioner should do the following:

1. Obtain an understanding of the rules and regulations adopted by the SEC for MD&A and management's method of preparing MD&A.

2. Plan the engagement by developing an overall strategy considering factors such as matters affecting the entity's industry and similar knowledge obtained during the audit of financial statements.
3. Consider relevant portions of internal control applicable to the preparation of MD&A.
4. Obtain sufficient evidence, including testing completeness, by comparing the content of the MD&A to the information obtained in the audit of financial statements and considering whether the explanations in the MD&A are consistent with this information.
5. Consider the effect of events subsequent to the balance sheet date by extending subsequent events review procedures in the audit to the MD&A information.
6. Obtain written representations from management concerning its responsibility for MD&A, completeness of minutes, events subsequent to the balance sheet date, and other matters the practitioner considers relevant to the MD&A presentation.
7. Form an opinion about whether the MD&A presentation meets the objectives for an opinion on such a presentation.

REPORTING

The financial statements for the periods covered by the MD&A presentation and the related auditors' report should accompany the presentation or be incorporated by reference to information filed with a regulatory agency.

The report should include the elements as found in the example in Illustration 1.

FUNDAMENTAL REQUIREMENTS: REVIEW

ACCEPTANCE

A practitioner may accept an engagement to review an MD&A presentation for an annual period under the same circumstances as an examination.

In order to accept an engagement to review the MD&A presentation for an interim period the practitioner should

1. Either
    a. Review and report on the historical financial statements for the related comparative interim periods, or
    b. Audit the interim financial statements, and
2. The MD&A presentation for the most recent fiscal year has been or will be examined by either the practitioner or a predecessor auditor.

PERFORMANCE

According to AT 701.76, the practitioner should do the following:

1. Obtain an understanding of the rules and regulations adopted by the SEC for MD&A and management's method of preparing MD&A.
2. Plan the engagement considering factors such as matters affecting the industry, the types of information management reports to external analysts, and matters identified during the audit or review of historical financial statements.
3. Consider relevant portions of the entity's internal control applicable to the MD&A.
4. Apply analytical procedures and make inquiries of management and others.
5. Consider the effects of events subsequent to the balance sheet date.
6. Obtain written representations from management.

7. Form a conclusion as to whether any information came to the practitioner's attention that would cause him or her to believe the objectives related to the MD&A presentation were not achieved.

REPORTING

The financial statements for the periods covered by the MD&A presentation and the related auditors' or accountants' reports should accompany the presentation or be incorporated by reference to information filed with a regulatory agency.

The report should include the elements as found in the examples in Illustrations 2 and 3.

INTERPRETATIONS

There are no interpretations for this section.

ILLUSTRATIONS

The following reports are adapted from SSAE 10:

1. An illustration of the wording of a standard examination report.
2. A standard review report on an annual MD&A presentation.
3. A standard review report on an MD&A presentation for an interim period.

ILLUSTRATION 1. STANDARD EXAMINATION REPORT

Independent Accountant's Report

We have examined Widget Company's Management's Discussion and Analysis taken as a whole, included [*incorporated by reference*] in the Company's [*insert description of registration statement or document*]. Management is responsible for the preparation of the Company's Management's Discussion and Analysis pursuant to the rules and regulations adopted by the Securities and Exchange Commission. Our responsibility is to express an opinion on the presentation based on our examination. We have audited, in accordance with auditing standards generally accepted in the United States of America, the financial statements of Widget Company as of December 31, 20X2 and 20X1, and for each of the years in the three-year period ended December 31, 20X2, and in our report dated Month XX, 20X3, we expressed an unqualified opinion on those financial statements.[4]

Our examination of Management's Discussion and Analysis was conducted in accordance with attestation standards established by the American Institute of Certified Public Accountants and, accordingly, included examining, on a test basis, evidence supporting the historical amounts

---

[4] *If prior financial statements were audited by other auditors, this sentence would be replaced by the following:*

> *We have audited, in accordance with auditing standards generally accepted in the United States of America, the financial statements of Widget Company as of and for the year ended December 31, 20X2, and in our report dated Month XX, 20X3, we expressed an unqualified opinion on those financial statements. The financial statements of Widget Company as of December 31, 20X1, and for each of the years in the two-year period then ended were audited by other auditors, whose report dated Month XX, 20X2, expressed an unqualified opinion on those financial statements.*

If the practitioner's opinion on the financial statements is based on the report of other auditors, this sentence would be replaced by the following:

> *We have audited, in accordance with auditing standards generally accepted in the United States of America, the financial statements of Widget Company as of December 31, 20X2 and 20X1, and for each of the years in the three-year period ended December 31, 20X2, and in our report dated Month XX, 20X3, we expressed an unqualified opinion on those financial statements based on our audits and the report of other auditors.*

and disclosures in the presentation. An examination also includes assessing the significant determinations made by management as to the relevancy of information to be included and the estimates and assumptions that affect reported information. We believe that our examination provides a reasonable basis for our opinion.

The preparation of Management's Discussion and Analysis requires management to interpret the criteria, make determinations as to the relevancy of information to be included, and make estimates and assumptions that affect reported information. Management's Discussion and Analysis includes information regarding the estimated future impact of transactions and events that have occurred or are expected to occur, expected sources of liquidity and capital resources, operating trends, commitments, and uncertainties. Actual results in the future may differ materially from management's present assessment of this information because events and circumstances frequently do not occur as expected.[5]

In our opinion, the Company's presentation of Management's Discussion and Analysis includes, in all material respects, the required elements of the rules and regulations adopted by the Securities and Exchange Commission; the historical financial amounts included therein have been accurately derived, in all material respects, from the Company's financial statements; and the underlying information, determinations, estimates, and assumptions of the Company provide a reasonable basis for the disclosures contained therein.

Illustration 2. Standard Review Report on an Annual MD&A Presentation

Independent Accountant's Report

We have reviewed Widget Company's Management's Discussion and Analysis taken as a whole, included [*incorporated by reference*] in the Company's [*insert description of registration statement or document*]. Management is responsible for the preparation of the Company's Management's Discussion and Analysis pursuant to the rules and regulations adopted by the Securities and Exchange Commission. We have audited, in accordance with auditing standards generally accepted in the United States of America, the financial statements of Widget Company as of December 31, 20X2 and 20X1, and for each of the years in the three-year period ended December 31, 20X2, and in our report dated Month XX, 20X3, we expressed an unqualified opinion on those financial statements.

We conducted our review of Management's Discussion and Analysis in accordance with attestation standards established by the American Institute of Certified Public Accountants. A review of Management's Discussion and Analysis consists principally of applying analytical procedures and making inquiries of persons responsible for financial, accounting, and operational matters. It is substantially less in scope than an examination, the objective of which is the expression of an opinion on the presentation. Accordingly, we do not express such an opinion.

The preparation of Management's Discussion and Analysis requires management to interpret the criteria, make determinations as to the relevancy of information to be included, and make estimates and assumptions that affect reported information. Management's Discussion and Analysis includes information regarding the estimated future impact of transactions and events that have occurred or are expected to occur, expected sources of liquidity and capital resources, operating trends, commitments, and uncertainties. Actual results in the future may differ materially from management's present assessment of this information because events and circumstances frequently do not occur as expected.[6]

---

[5] *The following sentence should be added to the beginning of the explanatory paragraph if the entity is a nonpublic entity:*

> *Although Widget Company is not subject to the rules and regulations of the Securities and Exchange Commission, the accompanying Management's Discussion and Analysis is intended to be a presentation in accordance with the rules and regulations adopted by the Securities and Exchange Commission.*

[6] *The following sentence should be added to the beginning of the explanatory paragraph if the entity is a nonpublic entity:*

> *Although Widget Company is not subject to the rules and regulations of the Securities and Exchange Commission, the accompanying Management's Discussion and Analysis is intended to be a presentation in accordance with the rules and regulations adopted by the Securities and Exchange Commission.*

Based on our review, nothing came to our attention that caused us to believe that the Company's presentation of Management's Discussion and Analysis does not include, in all material respects, the required elements of the rules and regulations adopted by the Securities and Exchange Commission; that the historical financial amounts included therein have not been accurately derived, in all material respects, from the Company's financial statements; or that the underlying information, determinations, estimates, and assumptions of the Company do not provide a reasonable basis for the disclosures contained therein.

This report is intended solely for the information and use of [*list or refer to the specified parties*] and is not intended to be, and should not be, used by anyone other than the specified parties.

ILLUSTRATION 3. STANDARD REVIEW REPORT ON AN INTERIM MD&A PRESENTATION

Independent Accountant's Report

We have reviewed Widget Company's Management's Discussion and Analysis taken as a whole, included in the Company's [*insert description of registration statement or document*]. Management is responsible for the preparation of the Company's Management's Discussion and Analysis pursuant to the rules and regulations adopted by the Securities and Exchange Commission. We have reviewed, in accordance with standards established by the American Institute of Certified Public Accountants, the interim financial information of Widget Company as of June 30, 20X3 and 20X2, and for the three-month and six-month periods then ended and have issued our report thereon dated July XX, 20X3.

We conducted our review of Management's Discussion and Analysis in accordance with attestation standards established by the American Institute of Certified Public Accountants. A review of Management's Discussion and Analysis consists principally of applying analytical procedures and making inquiries of persons responsible for financial, accounting, and operational matters. It is substantially less in scope than an examination, the objective of which is the expression of an opinion on the presentation. Accordingly, we do not express such an opinion.

The preparation of Management's Discussion and Analysis requires management to interpret the criteria, make determinations as to the relevancy of information to be included, and make estimates and assumptions that affect reported information. Management's Discussion and Analysis includes information regarding the estimated future impact of transactions and events that have occurred or are expected to occur, expected sources of liquidity and capital resources, operating trends, commitments, and uncertainties. Actual results in the future may differ materially from management's present assessment of this information because events and circumstances frequently do not occur as expected.[7]

Based on our review, nothing came to our attention that caused us to believe that the Company's presentation of Management's Discussion and Analysis does not include, in all material respects, the required elements of the rules and regulations adopted by the Securities and Exchange Commission; that the historical financial amounts included therein have not been accurately derived, in all material respects, from the Company's financial statements; or that the underlying information, determinations, estimates, and assumptions of the Company do not provide a reasonable basis for the disclosures contained therein.

This report is intended solely for the information and use of [*list or refer to the specified parties*] and is not intended to be, and should not be, used by anyone other than the specified parties.

---

[7] *The following sentence should be added to the beginning of the explanatory paragraph if the entity is a nonpublic entity:*

> *Although Widget Company is not subject to the rules and regulations of the Securities and Exchange Commission, the accompanying Management's Discussion and Analysis is intended to be a presentation in accordance with the rules and regulations adopted by the Securities and Exchange Commission.*

3100 COMPILATION AND REVIEW OF FINANCIAL STATEMENTS [1,2]

EFFECTIVE DATE AND APPLICABILITY

Original Pronouncement	SSARS 1, December 1978; as amended by SSARS 8, October 2000, and SSARS 9, November 2002.
Effective Date	For financial statements issued after December 1978. Revised to reflect SSARS 8, which is effective for financial statements submitted after December 31, 2000. Revised to reflect SSARS 9, which is effective upon issuance, except for the amendments to the required review representation letter, which is effective for review reports dated January 1, 2003, or after.
Applicability	Whenever the accountant submits financial statements of a nonpublic entity to a client or others, he or she should compile or review those financial statements in accordance with the requirements of this section. (See the interpretation on litigation services in this section and Sections 3300 and 3600 for the only exceptions.) The accountant is also required to issue a report whenever he or she completes a compilation (unless the compilation engagement is for management-use-only financial statements) or a review of the financial statements of a nonpublic entity. The section does not apply to accounting services such as

---

[1] *In 2000, the ASB issued SAS 93,* ***Omnibus Statement of Auditing Standards—2000,*** *which amended SAS 58 to modify the basic elements of the auditor's standard report to include a reference to the country of origin of (a) the accounting principles used to prepare the financial statements and (b) the auditing standards followed in performing the audit. Questions have been raised as to whether the country of origin language described by SAS 93 should be incorporated in a compilation or review report. Although ARSC believes that nothing in SSARS 1 would preclude CPAs from including such language in the standard compilation or review report if they so choose, they concluded that there is no pressing need to make a change to the report language at this time.*

[2] *Practitioners involved with compilation or review engagements of common interest realty associations (CIRAs) should be aware of Statement of Position (SOP) 93-5,* ***Reporting on Required Supplementary Information Accompanying Compiled or Reviewed Financial Statements of Common Interest Realty Associations****. The AICPA's Audit and Accounting Guide,* ***Common Interest Realty Associations,*** *requires that CIRAs disclose certain information outside the basic financial statements. This SOP provides performing and reporting guidance when required supplementary information accompanies the basic financial statements for compilation or review engagements of CIRAs.*

1. Preparing a working trial balance.
2. Assisting in adjusting the books.
3. Consulting on accounting, tax, or similar matters.
4. Preparing tax returns (of any kind).
5. Providing manual or electronic bookkeeping services.
6. Processing financial data for clients of other accountants.

NOTE: If a public entity does not have its annual financial statements audited, the accountant may review the entity's annual or interim financial statements in accordance with this section.

DEFINITIONS OF TERMS

Accounting and Review Services Committee (ARSC). A committee of the AICPA that is charged with developing pronouncements on the procedures and standards of reporting on unaudited financial statements or other unaudited financial information of nonpublic entities.

Nonpublic entity. Any entity other than one (1) whose securities trade in a public market (i.e., a domestic or foreign stock exchange or over-the-counter market, including securities quoted only locally or regionally, (2) that makes a filing with a regulatory agency to sell any of its securities publicly, or (3) a subsidiary, corporate joint venture, or other entity controlled by an entity in (1) or (2).

Financial statements. A presentation of financial data, including notes thereto, derived from accounting records and intended to present an entity's economic resources or obligations at a point in time, or changes therein for a period of time, in accordance with GAAP or OCBOA, excluding financial forecasts and projections (see Section 2301) and financial presentations in tax returns. Financial statements may also be presented for management use only. Management-use-only financial statements may be prepared on GAAP, OCBOA, or a combination of GAAP or OCBOA, including other bases of accounting (e.g., current value).

Submission of financial statements. Presenting to a client or others financial statements that the accountant has prepared.

Entity. Includes financial statements of a corporation, a consolidated group of corporations, a combined group of affiliated entities, a not-for-profit organization, a governmental unit, an estate or trust, a partnership, a proprietorship, a segment of any of these, or an individual.

Compilation. Presenting financial statements that are the representation of management or owners without expressing any assurance on those statements. (There are two types of compilations: (1) traditional compilations and (2) management-use-only engagements.)

Review. Applying inquiry and analytical procedures to financial statements to provide a basis for expressing limited assurance that there are no material modifications that should be made to those statements for them to be in conformity with GAAP or OCBOA.

OBJECTIVES OF SECTION

In 1977, the AICPA formed the Accounting and Review Services Committee to develop pronouncements on the procedures and standards for reporting on unaudited financial statements and other unaudited information of nonpublic entities. Practice for unaudited financial statements of nonpublic entities prior to SSARS 1 was diverse. Some CPAs did substantial work on the client's financial statements; others did minimal work. Both practices resulted in the same unaudited disclaimer report. SSARS 1 codified these two practices and referred to the first as a review and the latter as a compilation. SSARS 1 provides standards for compilations and reviews of a nonpublic entity's financial statements. After years of debate, SSARS 8 was issued in October 2000 (codified as amended SSARS 1) to (1) clarify the applicability of SSARS (i.e., the meaning of submission of financial statements) and (2) create a new type of compilation engagement for management-use-only financial statements of nonpublic entities.

SSARS 9 was issued in November 2002 and includes numerous revisions to Section 3100, such as adding footnotes stating (1) that the statement of retained earnings is not a required statement and, if not presented as a separate statement, reference in the compilation and review report is not needed and (2) if the statement of comprehensive income is presented, reference should be made in the appropriate paragraphs of the report. SSARS 9 also requires a signature on a compilation or review report, provides additional guidance on management representation letters for review engagements, explicitly allows a separate report on supplementary information for compilations, and explicitly states that the Statements on Quality Control Standards apply to compilation and review engagements. Finally, SSARS 9 provides example wording, analogous to wording provided in Section 504 when an accountant is associated with financial statements of a public company but has not audited or reviewed them, but modified for situations appropriate for compilations and reviews of nonpublic entities.

FUNDAMENTAL REQUIREMENTS

General Guidance

Reporting Obligation

When the accountant performs more than one service such as a compilation and an audit, he or she should issue the highest level report (i.e., an audit report).

The accountant should not consent to the use of his or her name in a written communication containing financial statements of a nonpublic entity unless

1. He or she compiles or reviews the financial statements and reports on them.
2. The financial statements are accompanied by a statement that the accountant has not compiled or reviewed the financial statements and he or she assumes no responsibility for them. According to AR 100.03, that statement may be worded as follows:

> The accompanying balance sheet of Widget Company as of December 31, 20X1, the related statements of income, and cash flows for the year then ended were not audited, reviewed, or compiled by us and, accordingly, we do not express an opinion or any other form of assurance on them.

If the accountant becomes aware that his or her name has been used improperly, he or she should advise the client and consider what other actions are needed, including consulting with an attorney.

Submitting Financial Statements

Whenever the accountant submits financial statements of a nonpublic entity to clients or others, he or she has to at least compile (traditional or management-use-only compilation) those financial statements.

Submitting financial statements is defined as

1. Preparing (manually or via the computer) financial statements.
2. Presenting such financial statements to clients or others.

Understanding with the Client

According to AR 100.05, the accountant should establish an understanding, preferably in writing, regarding the services to be performed. (Example engagement letters for a traditional compilation and a review, taken from SSARS 1, are included in Illustration TC-1 and Illustration R-1.) However, if the compilation engagement is for a management-use-only financial statement, an engagement letter is required. (An example engagement letter for a management-use-only compilation is included in Illustration MUO-1.)

When the Accountant Is Not Independent

The accountant cannot perform a review if he or she is not independent. Furthermore, if not independent, the accountant should issue a compilation report that discloses the lack of independence. The reason for the lack of independence should not be included. The compilation report should be modified by adding the following as the last paragraph: "I am (we are) not independent with respect to XYZ Company."

NOTE: If the accountant is engaged to prepare and issue a management-use-only financial statement, the lack of independence should be disclosed in the required engagement letter (a compilation report is ordinarily not issued).

TRADITIONAL COMPILATIONS

Performance Requirements

Before completing a traditional compilation engagement, the accountant should possess a level of knowledge of the accounting principles and practices of the client's industry that will enable him or her to compile appropriate financial statements. The accountant should also possess

1. A general understanding of the entity's business transactions.
2. The form of its accounting records.
3. The stated qualifications of its accounting personnel.
4. The accounting basis of its financial statements.
5. The form and content of the financial statements.

If the accountant becomes aware of information that is incorrect, incomplete, or otherwise unsatisfactory, he or she should obtain additional or revised information. If the client refuses to provide that information, the accountant should withdraw from the engagement.

The accountant should read the compiled financial statements to see if they appear to be appropriate in form and free from obvious material misstatement or omission.

Subsequent to the date of the compilation report, the accountant may become aware of facts that existed at the compilation report date that suggest certain information was incorrect, incomplete, or otherwise unsatisfactory. In such circumstances, the accountant should refer to Section 561 of the SAS and should consider consulting an attorney. (Illustration TC-2 presents a checklist for a traditional compilation engagement.)

Reporting Requirements

According to AR 100.11, the compiled financial statements should be accompanied by a compilation report (see Illustration TC-3 for the standard compilation report) stating that

1. A compilation was performed in accordance with SSARS issued by the AICPA.
2. A compilation is limited to presenting financial information that is the representation of management.
3. The financial statements have not been audited or reviewed, and no opinion or assurance has been expressed on them.

The report should be signed and dated the date of the completion of the compilation. Each page of the financial statements should include a reference such as "See Accountant's Compilation Report."

If the accountant becomes aware of material measurement or disclosure departures from GAAP or OCBOA (except for compiled financial statements that omitted substantially all disclosures) and the client does not revise the financial statements, the accountant should disclose the departure in a separate paragraph of the report. The effects of the departure should also be disclosed if such effects have been determined by the client or are known by the accountant. An example of a compilation report with a measurement departure is presented in Illustration TC-4.

If the accountant believes that the modification of the standard compilation report is not adequate to call attention to the financial statement deficiencies, he or she should withdraw from the engagement and may wish to consult with an attorney.

When the basic financial statements are accompanied by supplementary information and the accountant has compiled that information, the compilation report should cover the supplementary information or a separate report should be issued on that information. If a separate report is presented, the report should state that the other data accompanying the financial statements are presented only for supplemental analysis purposes and that the information has been compiled from information that is the representation of management, without audit or review, and the accountant does not express an opinion or any other form of assurance on such data.

Reporting on Financial Statements That Omit All or Substantially All Disclosures

An accountant may compile financial statements that omit all or substantially all disclosures required by GAAP or OCBOA provided that

1. The omission (of notes) is clearly indicated in the compilation report.
2. It is not, to his or her knowledge, done to mislead users.
3. When only a few notes are presented, the notes that are presented should be labeled "Selected Information—Substantially All Disclosures Required by Generally Accepted Accounting Principles Are Not Included."

(The paragraph that should be added to the compilation report to indicate that all or substantially all disclosures are omitted is illustrated in the compilation engagement letter presented in Illustration TC-1.)

MANAGEMENT-USE-ONLY COMPILATIONS

Definition of Management-Use-Only Financial Statements

To qualify as management-use-only financial statements, the financial statements must meet the following conditions:

1. Be compiled by the accountant (i.e., prepared by the accountant and presented to management).
2. Be restricted in use (and distribution) to certain members of management who are deemed to be knowledgeable of the entity and the context of its financial statements.

Illustration MUO-2 presents a checklist for a management-use-only compilation.

Performance and Communication Requirements

The performance requirements that apply to a traditional compilation (see steps 1-4 in Illustration TC-2) also apply to a management-use-only compilation (see steps 4-7 in Illustration MUO-2). However, the reporting requirements of a traditional compilation (see steps 5-13 of TC-2) do not apply to a management-use-only compilation. Instead, the management-use-only compilation requirements obligate the accountant to use an engagement letter and mark each page of the financial statements with an appropriate restriction on use (see steps 1-3 and step 9 in Illustration MUO-2). In a management-use-only compilation, the accountant ordinarily does not issue a compilation report—the required engagement letter takes the place of the compilation report.

Essential Conditions Necessary for a Management-Use-Only Compilation

An accountant can compile financial statements of a nonpublic entity for management-use-only, if and only if, those financial statements are reasonably expected to be used only by knowledgeable members of management. To qualify as knowledgeable, members of management must understand the nature of the procedures applied and the basis of accounting and assumptions used in preparing the financial statement.

Unless information comes to the accountant's attention indicating otherwise, the accountant may rely on the client's representation that members of management have the necessary knowledge to understand the financial statements.

NOTE: Management includes members of the board of directors, the chief executive officer, chief operating officer, vice presidents in charge of principal business functions (such as sales, administration, or finance), and others who perform similar policy-making functions.

SSARS 1 uses the term "third party" to refer to all users of the compiled financial statements that are

1. *Not members of management, or*
2. *Members of management who are not knowledgeable about the financial statements.*

If the accountant anticipates that the compiled financial statements for management-use-only are to be used by anyone in group 1. or 2. above, a traditional compilation (with a compilation report) should be performed.

Management-Use-Only Financial Statements Distributed to Inappropriate Parties

If the accountant becomes aware that the compiled management-use-only financial statements have been distributed to inappropriate parties, the accountant should

1. Discuss the situation with the client.
2. Request that the client have the financial statements returned to them.
3. If the client does not comply with 2. above within a reasonable period of time, notify known third parties (inappropriate parties) that the financial statements are not intended for their use.

NOTE: Before performing step 3. above, the accountant should consider consulting with his or her attorney.

The Required Engagement Letter for Performing a Management-Use-Only Compilation

A written engagement letter (preferably signed by management) should be used. The engagement letter, among other things, should contain an acknowledgment

1. That management has knowledge about the nature of the procedures applied and the basis of the accounting and assumptions used in the preparation of the financial statements.
2. Of management's representation and agreement that the financial statements will not be used by third parties (inappropriate parties as discussed above).

3. That material departures from established GAAP or OCBOA may exist and the effects of those departures may not be known departures may be disclosed.
4. That the accountant is not independent, if applicable.

These and other required statements or comments are presented in Illustration MUO-1.

NOTE: The example engagement letter in Illustration MUO-1 also contains an optional paragraph that the authors believe is important to reduce and control the malpractice risk relating to management-use-only financial statements. That risk stems from two sources: (1) knowledgeable management's misunderstanding and misuse of the financial statements, and (2) use by an inappropriate party. The paragraph reads as follows:

> *...you agree not to take or assist in any action seeking to hold us liable for damages due to any deficiency in the financial statements we prepare and you agree to hold us harmless from any liability and related legal costs arising from any third-party [or other inappropriate party distribution to or] use of the financial statements in contravention of the terms of this agreement.*

Acceptable Bases of Accounting in a Management-Use-Only Compilation

The management-use-only financial statements may be generally based on GAAP, OCBOA, or they may be a mixture of GAAP, cash-basis, income-tax basis, or other bases (e.g., estimated current value). The accountant should design the financial statements based on the needs of management.

Required Legend on Each Page of the Financial Statements

The accountant should place a legend on each page of the management-use-only financial statements. The legend should restrict the financial statements to management's use only. Acceptable wording for a legend may be:

- Restricted for Management's Use Only
- Solely for the Information and Use by the Management of XYX Company and Not Intended to Be and Should Not Be Used by Any Other Party

NOTE: SSARS does not specify the exact wording of a legend; therefore, the wording is flexible. Because of the possibility of the financial statements being inadvertently distributed to inappropriate parties, the two illustrative legends above may be made even stronger by adding a sentence such as: "These restricted-use financial statements contain material departures from established bases of accounting and the effects of those departures on the financial statements is not disclosed."

An appropriate legend may be affixed to the financial statements by computer software, a rubber stamp, manual notation, or any other method. The legend and the engagement letter may also identify the specific members of management (by name) that are intended users.

REVIEWS

Performance Requirements

Before completing the review engagement, the accountant should possess a level of knowledge of the accounting principles and practices of the industry. The accountant should also obtain an understanding of the client's business that will enable him or her, through the performance of inquiry and analytical procedures to express limited assurance that there are no material modifications that should be made to the financial statements for them to be in conformity with GAAP or OCBOA.

To understand the client's business, the accountant should have a

1. General understanding of the client's organization (operating characteristics and nature of assets, liabilities, revenues, and expenses).
2. General knowledge of its production, distribution, compensation methods, types of products and services, operating locations, and material related-party transactions.

According to AR 100.28, the accountant's inquiry and analytical procedures should ordinarily include (see Illustration R-6 for illustrative inquiries taken from SSARS 1)

1. Inquiries about accounting principles and practices and how they are applied.
2. Inquiries about the accounting system.
3. Analytical procedures to identify unusual relationships and items.
4. Inquiries about actions taken at meetings of stockholders, board of directors, and its committees that may affect financial statements.
5. Inquiries of persons having responsibility for the financial statements about
   a. Whether the statements have been prepared in conformity with GAAP or OCBOA.
   b. Changes in the client's business or accounting principles or practices.
   c. Questions that have arisen from applying other inquiries and analytical procedures.
   d. Material subsequent events.

The accountant should also read the financial statements and obtain reports from other accountants, if any, who have audited or reviewed significant components of the reporting entity.

NOTE: A review does not require obtaining an understanding of internal control or assessing control risk, testing accounting records, or obtaining corroborating evidence.

If the accountant becomes aware of information that appears to be incorrect, incomplete, or otherwise unsatisfactory, he or she should perform additional procedures to resolve the matter.

The accountant should describe in his or her working papers

1. Inquiries covered and analytical procedures performed.
2. Unusual matters and how they were resolved.

The accountant should also obtain a representation letter (see Illustration R 7). The representation letter should normally be signed by the chief executive and chief financial officer. The representation letter should cover all periods reported on. In addition, according to AR 100.29, the specific representations included in the letter should be tailored to the circumstances of the engagement, but should include specific representations on

1. Management's acknowledgement of its responsibility for the fair presentation of the financial statements in accordance with GAAP.
2. Management's belief that the financial statements are fairly presented in accordance with GAAP.
3. Management's full and truthful response to all inquiries.
4. Completeness of information.
5. Information covering subsequent events.

The representation letter should be dated no earlier than the date of the review report.

Subsequent to the date of the review report, the accountant may become aware of facts that existed at the review report date that suggest certain information was incorrect, incomplete, or otherwise unsatisfactory. In such circumstances, the accountant should refer to Section 561 of the SASs and should consider consulting an attorney.

Reporting Requirements

According to AR 100.34, the reviewed financial statements should be accompanied by a review report (see Illustration R-4 for the standard report) stating that

1. A review was performed in accordance with the SSARS issued by the AICPA.

2. Information included in the financial statements is the representation of management.
3. A review consists of inquiries and analytical procedures.
4. A review is substantially less than an audit, the objective of which is the expression of an opinion, and no opinion is expressed.
5. The accountant is not aware of any material modifications that should be made to the financial statements in order for them to be in conformity with GAAP or OCBOA.

The report should be signed and dated the date of completion of the review. Each page of the financial statements should include a reference such as "See Accountant's Review Report."

If the accountant becomes aware of material measurement or disclosure departures from GAAP or OCBOA and the client does not revise the financial statements, the accountant should disclose the departure in a separate paragraph of the report. The effects of the departure should also be disclosed if such effects have been determined by the client or are known by the accountant. An example of a review report with a measurement departure is presented in Illustration R-5.

If the accountant believes that the modification of the standard review report is not adequate to call attention to the financial statement deficiencies, he or she should withdraw from the engagement and may wish to consult with an attorney.

When the basic financial statements are accompanied by supplementary information, the accountant should either indicate in the review report or in a separate report that

1. The additional information is presented only for supplementary analysis and it has been subjected to the inquiry and analytical procedures applied in the review of the financial statements, and the accountant did not become aware of any material modifications that are needed, or
2. The additional information is presented only for supplementary analysis and it has not been subjected to the inquiry and analytical procedures applied in the review of the financial statements, but was compiled without audit or review and no opinion or assurance is expressed.

CHANGE IN ENGAGEMENT FROM AUDIT TO REVIEW OR COMPILATION (OR FROM REVIEW TO COMPILATION)

According to AR 100.47, before an accountant agrees to change an engagement from an audit to a review/compilation or a review to a compilation, he or she should consider

1. Reasons given for the client's request, particularly the implications of a restriction on the scope of work whether imposed by the client or caused by circumstance.
2. Additional effort required to complete the engagement.
3. Additional costs to complete the engagement.

NOTE: A change in circumstances that affects the client's need for an audit or review or a misunderstanding concerning the nature of an audit, review, or compilation is ordinarily a reasonable basis for requesting a change.

If the engagement was an audit and the accountant was prohibited by the client from corresponding with the client's legal counsel, the accountant ordinarily should not issue a review or compilation report.

If the engagement was an audit or a review and the client would not sign a representation letter, the accountant ordinarily should not issue a compilation report.

If the audit or review procedures are substantially complete or the cost to complete such procedures is relatively insignificant, the accountant should consider the propriety of accepting the change.

Illustration R-3 presents a "Checklist for Change in Engagement from Audit to Review or Review to Compilation."

INTERPRETATIONS

OMISSION OF DISCLOSURES IN REVIEWED FINANCIAL STATEMENTS (DECEMBER 1979; NOVEMBER 2002)

This interpretation precludes the accountant from accepting an engagement to review financial statements that omit substantially all the disclosures required by GAAP. This interpretation gives guidance on the reporting implications if an accountant who has undertaken to review financial statements subsequently finds that the client declines to include substantially all required disclosures.

FINANCIAL STATEMENTS INCLUDED IN SEC FILINGS (DECEMBER 1979; REVISED OCTOBER 2000)

This interpretation basically concludes that a SSARS compilation or review report should not be filed with the SEC.

REPORTING ON THE HIGHEST LEVEL OF SERVICE (DECEMBER 1979; REVISED OCTOBER 2000)

This interpretation requires that if an accountant provides more than one level of service on the same financial statements, the financial statements should be accompanied by the accountant's report that is appropriate for the highest level of service provided. This interpretation does not preclude the accountant from using procedures that go beyond those required for the level of assurance expressed. Nor does this interpretation require that the accountant "step up" the level of his or her report if the accountant uses procedures that go beyond those required for the level of assurance expressed. (In other words, deciding to perform some types of procedures such as confirmation of receivables or payables does not convert the engagement to an audit. Similarly, performing some analytical procedures does not convert the engagement from a compilation to a review.)

DISCOVERY OF INFORMATION AFTER THE DATE OF THE ACCOUNTANT'S REPORT (NOVEMBER 1980; REVISED NOVEMBER 2002)

The interpretation emphasizes the need for professional judgment in determining an appropriate course of action when information becomes available after the date of the accountant's report and that information causes the accountant to believe that the compiled or reviewed financial statements may be incorrect, incomplete, or otherwise unsatisfactory. This interpretation instructs the accountant to consider the reliability of the information and the existence of persons known to be relying on or likely to rely on the financial statements when making a decision about an appropriate course of action.

PLANNING AND SUPERVISION (ISSUED AUGUST 1981; REVISED NOVEMBER 2002)

The interpretation clarifies that Section 311, "Planning and Supervision," does not apply to compilation or review engagements. However, this interpretation suggests that the accountant may wish to consider SAS 22 (AU 311) and other references when planning and supervising a compilation or review engagement.

WITHDRAWAL FROM COMPILATION OR REVIEW ENGAGEMENT (ISSUED AUGUST 1981; REVISED NOVEMBER 2002)

The interpretation identifies circumstances in which it is appropriate for an accountant to withdraw from an engagement. Circumstances suggested include those in which the nature, extent, and probable effect of GAAP departures or departures from an OCBOA might cause the accountant to question whether the departures are a result of the preparer's intention to mislead those who might reasonably be expected to use the financial statements. The accountant would also withdraw from a compilation or review engagement if the financial statements are not revised after the accountant requests that revisions be made, and the client refuses to accept the modified standard report that the accountant believes is appropriate.

REPORTING WHEN THERE ARE SIGNIFICANT DEPARTURES FROM GENERALLY ACCEPTED ACCOUNTING PRINCIPLES (ISSUED AUGUST 1981; REVISED NOVEMBER 2002)

The interpretation indicates that a statement in a compilation or review report that the financial statements are not in conformity with GAAP or an "other comprehensive basis of accounting" would be tantamount to expressing an adverse opinion on the financial statements taken as a whole; therefore, an accountant is precluded from making such a statement. Such an opinion can be expressed only in the context of an audit engagement. This interpretation does not preclude the accountant from emphasizing the limitation of the financial statements in a separate paragraph of the report. This separate paragraph is not, however, a substitute for disclosure of the specific GAAP or OCBOA departures or the effects of the departures. Also, the accountant should withdraw from the engagement when the accountant believes modification of the standard report is not adequate to indicate deficiencies in the financial statements taken as a whole. The authors believe that generally it is advisable to withdraw when there are significant GAAP or OCBOA departures.

REPORTS ON SPECIFIED ELEMENTS, ACCOUNTS, OR ITEMS OF A FINANCIAL STATEMENT (NOVEMBER 1981; REVISED JANUARY 2001; REVISED NOVEMBER 2002)

The interpretation clarifies that the SSARS 1 reporting requirements for a review do not apply to presentations of specified elements, accounts, or items of financial statements because these presentations do not meet the definition of a financial statement. SSAE provide guidance on reporting on (1) the results of applying agreed-upon procedures to specified elements, accounts, or items of a financial statement, and (2) such presentations when the accountant is engaged to express moderate assurance in a review report.

REPORTING WHEN MANAGEMENT HAS ELECTED TO OMIT SUBSTANTIALLY ALL DISCLOSURES (ISSUED MAY 1982)

The interpretation allows the accountant to modify the language in the sample report in paragraph 18 of SSARS 1 from "Management has elected to omit substantially all disclosures." However, this interpretation stresses that the language used should clearly indicate that the omission of substantially all disclosures is the entity's decision, not the accountant's. The interpretation encourages the use of the language in the sample report in paragraph 18 of SSARS 1.

Reporting on Tax Returns (Issued November 1982)

SSARS do not apply to tax returns. The interpretation exempts the accountant from compiling the financial information contained in a tax return, although the accountant may accept an engagement to compile or review such a presentation.

Reporting on Uncertainties (Issued December 1982; Revised November 2002)

The interpretation directs the accountant to paragraphs 10 and 11 of SAS 59, *The Auditor's Consideration of an Entity's Ability to Continue as a Going Concern* (see Section 341), for guidance in evaluating the disclosure of uncertainties. This interpretation does not require the accountant to modify his or her report if uncertainties are appropriately disclosed in the financial statements; nor does the interpretation require modification of a compilation report on financial statements that omit substantially all disclosures required by GAAP, provided the report clearly indicates the omission and the client's decision to omit the disclosures was not, to the accountant's knowledge, undertaken with the intention of misleading users of the statements. The interpretation suggests, but does not require, language that may be used if an accountant wishes to draw attention to an uncertainty in an emphasis paragraph of a compilation or review report.

Reporting on a Comprehensive Basis of Accounting other than Generally Accepted Accounting Principles (Issued December 1982; Revised November 1992; Revised October 2000)

The interpretation illustrates how the standard compilation and review reports should be modified if financial statements are prepared on another comprehensive basis of accounting. Notes to the financial statements should state the basis of presentation and describe how that basis differs from GAAP. If notes present this information, the standard compilation and review reports should be used appropriately modified to identify the financial statement title (e.g., Balance Sheet—Income Tax Basis).

When an accountant compiles OCBOA financial statements that omit substantially all disclosures, either a note to those statements should disclose the basis of accounting or the face of the financial statements should be marked with a description of the basis of accounting. If that disclosure is not made, the following sentence should be added to the first paragraph of the accountant's report:

> The financial statements have been prepared on the accounting basis used by the Entity for federal income tax purposes, which is a comprehensive basis of accounting other than generally accepted accounting principles.

Additional Procedures (March 1983; Revised October 2000; Revised November 2002)

The interpretation permits the accountant to perform additional procedures in a compilation or review engagement without requiring the accountant to change the engagement level.

Differentiating a Financial Statement Presentation from a Trial Balance (September 1990; Revised October 2000)

The interpretation identifies the attributes of a financial statement and those of a trial balance. It assists an accountant in determining whether a financial statement presentation is a financial statement, requiring compliance with the provisions of SSARS 1, or a trial balance that does not require compliance with the provisions of SSARS 1.

SUBMITTING DRAFT FINANCIAL STATEMENTS (SEPTEMBER 1990; REVISED OCTOBER 2000)

Except in cases when the financial statements are not expected to be used by a third party (management-use-only financial statements), the interpretation prohibits an accountant from submitting draft financial statements without intending to submit those financial statements in final form accompanied by an appropriate compilation or review report. This interpretation requires that draft financial statements be so marked and suggests that an accountant document the reasons why he or she intended to submit, but never submitted final financial statements, should that situation occur.

SPECIAL-PURPOSE FINANCIAL PRESENTATIONS TO COMPLY WITH CONTRACTUAL AGREEMENTS OR REGULATORY PROVISIONS (SEPTEMBER 1990)

The interpretation permits an accountant, if asked to report on special-purpose financial statements prepared to comply with a contractual agreement or regulatory provision that specifies a special basis of presentation, to issue a compilation or review report on those financial statements in accordance with SSARS 1. The interpretation describes how to report on presentations based on contractual agreements or regulatory provisions that require a financial presentation that (1) does not constitute a complete presentation of the entity's assets, liabilities, revenues, or expenses but is otherwise prepared in conformity with GAAP or OCBOA or (2) uses a prescribed basis of accounting that does not result in a presentation in conformity with GAAP or OCBOA.

REPORTING WHEN FINANCIAL STATEMENTS CONTAIN A DEPARTURE FROM PROMULGATED ACCOUNTING PRINCIPLES THAT PREVENTS THE FINANCIAL STATEMENTS FROM BEING MISLEADING (FEBRUARY 1991; REVISED OCTOBER 2000; REVISED NOVEMBER 2002)

The interpretation addresses Rule 203, *Accounting Principles* of the AICPA *Code of Professional Conduct,* which prohibits a member from expressing an opinion that financial statements are presented in conformity with GAAP if the member is aware that the statements contain a departure from an authoritative pronouncement (such as a FASB Statement or Interpretation). If the statements contain a departure from an authoritative pronouncement, and the member can demonstrate that due to unusual circumstances compliance with the pronouncement would render the financial statements misleading, the member can comply with Rule 203 by describing in the report the departure; its approximate effects, if practicable; and the reasons why compliance with an authoritative pronouncement would result in misleading statements.

The interpretation indicates that if the circumstances contemplated by Rule 203 exist in a review engagement, the accountant's review opinion should be unmodified, but the accountant's review report should be modified to contain a separate paragraph, including the information required by Rule 203. The interpretation clarifies that Rule 203 does not apply to compilation engagements. If the circumstances contemplated by Rule 203 exist in a compilation engagement, an accountant should follow the guidance in paragraphs 40 through 42 of SSARS for reporting on a compilation of financial statements with a GAAP departure. (The interpretation does not state the rationale for not permitting departure from authoritative pronouncements in compiled financial statements in the circumstances contemplated in Rule 203. However, in a compilation engagement, an accountant is much less likely to be able to conclude that application of an authoritative pronouncement would be misleading.)

NOTE: The authors believe the situation described in this interpretation would almost never occur in practice.

Applicability of Statements on Standards for Accounting and Review Services to Litigation Services (May 1991; Revised October 2000)

SSARS do not apply to financial statements submitted in litigation services that involve pending or potential proceedings before a court, regulatory body, or governmental authority (or the agent of any of these) such as a grand jury or an arbitrator (mediator) when the

- Accountant is an expert witness or a "trier of fact" (or an agent for one).
- Accountant's work is subject to detailed analysis and challenge by each party to the dispute.
- Accountant is engaged by the attorney and protected by the attorney's work product privilege.

Applicability of SSARS No. 1 When Performing Controllership or Other Management Services (July 2002)

An accountant who is

- In the practice of public accounting
- Providing an entity with controllership or other management services that involve the submission of financial statements, and
- **Not** a stockholder, partner, director, officer, or employee of the entity

must follow the performance and reporting requirements of SSARS 1, including any requirement to disclose the lack of independence. (If the financial statements are for management's use only, the accountant should follow the guidance as presented in Fundamental Requirements.) A public accountant who provides such controllership services but is also a stockholder, partner, director, officer, or employee of the entity may either comply with SSARS 1's requirements or communicate the accountant's relationship to the entity, preferably in writing. An example of such a communication is as follows:

> The accompanying balance sheet of Company X as of December 31, 20XX, and the related statements of income and cash flows for the year then ended have been prepared by [*name of accountant*], CPA. I have prepared such financial statements in my capacity [*describe capacity, for example, as a director*] of Company X.

If an accountant is not engaged in the practice of public accounting, the issuance of a report under SSARS would be inappropriate. However, the accountant may communicate the accountant's relationship to the entity, using a communication similar to the above example.

Accountants may also wish to refer to Ruling 10, "Submission of Financial Statements by a Member in Public Practice," in the AICPA's *Code of Professional Conduct* for additional guidance.

Use of "Selected Information—Substantially All Disclosures Required by Generally Accepted Accounting Principles Are Not Included" (December 2002)

When more than a few required disclosures are included in the financial statements, the notes that are presented should not be labeled as "Selected Information—Substantially All Disclosures Required by Generally Accepted Accounting Principles Are Not Included." Instead, the omitted notes should be treated as GAAP departures.

APPLICABILITY OF STATEMENTS ON STANDARDS FOR ACCOUNTING AND REVIEW SERVICES WHEN AN ACCOUNTANT ENGAGED TO PERFORM A BUSINESS VALUATION DERIVES INFORMATION FROM AN ENTITY'S TAX RETURN (APRIL 2003)

This interpretation states that SSARS do not apply when an accountant derives financial information from a tax return for use in a report on a business valuation engagement. (Deriving such information is not considered "submission of financial statements" under SSARS 1.) However, the interpretation does note that the accountant, in the business valuation report, should refer to the source of the information and note that the accountant assumes no responsibility for it. The interpretations states that the following wording may be used:

> In preparing our business valuation report, we have relied upon historical financial information provided to us by management and derived from [*refer to the appropriate source of the information, such as tax return, audit report issued by another auditor, and so on*]. This financial information has not been audited, reviewed, or compiled by us and accordingly we do not express an opinion or any form of assurance on this financial information.

However, if the accountant does submit financial statements as part of the business valuation engagement, the accountant should comply with SSARS.

TECHNIQUES FOR APPLICATION

WHEN SSARS 1 APPLIES

One of the most complex practice decisions involving SSARS 1 concerns when the accountant is governed by it versus when he or she is not. SSARS 8 was issued in part to clarify the applicability of SSARS 1. SSARS 8 redefined "submission" (see *Definitions of Terms*). The question hinges on what constitutes "submission of financial statements." The following services are excluded from SSARS 1.

- Reading client-prepared financial statements.
- Typing or reproducing client-prepared financial statements as a client accommodation.
- Proposing correcting journal entries or disclosures to financial statements (orally or in writing) that materially change client-prepared financial statements.
- Preparing standard monthly journal entries such as depreciation.
- Providing a client with a standard financial statement format without dollar amounts.
- Advising a client about software that will generate financial statements.
- Providing the client with the use of computer hardware or software that the client will use to generate financial statements.

Given the difficulty that has historically surrounded the applicability of SSARS 1, especially when computer processing is involved, the following scenarios will assist accountants in making that decision.

Scenarios on the Applicability of SSARS 1

Scenarios numbers 1 and 5 are the only ones governed by SSARS 1. The others are not deemed to be compilations.

1. The CPA prepares financial statements for a client and attaches them to a tax return. The financial statement information correlates with the information requested on the tax return. The CPA gives the returns and the statements to the client, who submits them to the taxing authority.

2. A client gives client-prepared financial statements to a CPA. The CPA posts adjustments to the client's financial statements in a worksheet format (either manually or using a computer) to reflect the tax closing and carries the adjusted balances forward. The CPA gives the client the trial balance worksheet so the client can enter the adjustments into his or her client's accounting system to reflect the tax closing.
3. On a separate sheet of paper, the CPA prepares adjustments to client-prepared financial statements and gives the adjustments to the client. The client posts the adjustments to the financial statements and sends the adjusted financial statements to the CPA for his or her consideration.
4. The CPA enters adjustments to the client's financial statement database using the client's computer, prints the adjusted financial statements, and takes the financial statements with him or her. The client has the ability to access the adjusted financial statements by viewing them on the computer monitor or printing them.
5. The CPA is engaged to compile the client's financial statements. The CPA prepares the financial statements and shows them to the client for his or her review. The client or CPA notes a problem in the statements, and the CPA adjusts the statements and shows a revised draft of the statements to the client. Several additional versions of the financial statements are prepared for the client's review.
6. The CPA meets with the client's bookkeeper to discuss client-prepared financial statements. The CPA notes a problem in the statements and communicates the required adjusting entries to the bookkeeper. The bookkeeper enters the adjusting entries into the computer, prints the revised financial statements, and shows them to the CPA. The CPA reads the financial statements and informs the bookkeeper that no further adjustments are required. The bookkeeper gives the CPA and the client a copy of the financial statements, which the CPA discusses with the client.
7. The client sends the CPA a computer disk that contains client-prepared financial statements. The CPA adjusts the client's accounting data on the disk, which results in revised financial statements. The CPA returns the disk to the client.

Engagement Letters for Traditional Compilations and Reviews

SSARS 1 requires that an understanding be reached with the client, but does not require an engagement letter. However, the authors strongly recommend that one be used. The required understanding, in writing or otherwise, should include (see the illustrative engagement letters in Illustrations TC-1 and R-1).

1. A description of the nature and limitations of the engagement.
2. A description of the report.
3. An indication that the engagement cannot be relied on to disclose errors, fraud, or illegal acts.
4. An indication that the accountant will communicate matters identified in 3. above, unless they are clearly inconsequential.

Although SSARS 1 specifies that the communication responsibility in 4. above be included in the understanding, the accountant may wish to consult with an attorney to limit the degree of responsibility assumed by using more cautionary language. For example, the accountant may wish to indicate the communication is not a separate undertaking and may not be made when the engagement is terminated before report issuance.

Engagement Letters for Management-Use-Only Compilations: Required Contents

The engagement letter should contain statements or comments

1. About the nature and limitation of services to be performed.
2. Definition of a compilation.
3. That the financial statements are not audited or reviewed.
4. That no opinion or assurance is provided.
5. That management has knowledge of the procedures applied and basis of accounting used.
6. An acknowledgement from management that the financial statements will be used only by knowledgeable members of management.
7. That the engagement cannot be relied upon to disclose errors, fraud, or illegal acts.

And, when applicable

8. That the financial statements may contain (or do contain) material departures from GAAP or OCBOA and the effect of those departures is not disclosed.
9. That substantially all disclosures (i.e., footnotes) are omitted.
10. That the accountant is not independent.
11. A reference to supplemental information that is presented, if any.

And the following statements or comments should strongly be considered

12. That the client will not hold the accountant liable for any damages due to deficiencies in the financial statements.
13. That the client will hold the accountant harmless from any liability and related legal costs arising from any third-party use of the financial statements.

Required Level of Industry Knowledge

SSARS 1 does not preclude an accountant from accepting an engagement in an industry where the accountant has no previous experience. However, before completing the compilation or review engagement, the requisite level of knowledge should be obtained. Such knowledge may be acquired by consulting AICPA guides, industry publications, financial statements of other entities in the industry, textbooks and periodicals, and knowledgeable individuals.

Reporting on a Single Financial Statement

SSARS 1 permits the accountant to report on one financial statement, such as a balance sheet.

Incomplete Review Engagement

When the accountant is not able to apply the inquiry and analytical procedures he or she deems appropriate, the review is incomplete and a review report should not be issued. As discussed in the change of engagements checklist in Illustration R-3, the accountant may not be able to issue a compilation report in this situation.

Identity of the Basis of Accounting and Titles of Financial Statements for Management-Use-Only Financial Statements

The basis of accounting will not ordinarily be identified and is not necessary since the financial statements are restricted to members of management who are knowledgeable about them. Traditional GAAP financial statement titles may be used such as "balance sheet" and "income statement." Any reasonable title that management understands is acceptable since the financial statements are not designed for general use.

AN ALTERNATIVE TO MANAGEMENT-USE-ONLY COMPILATIONS

CPAs frequently prepare monthly financial statements for a significant number of clients. To reduce the costs of preparing the financial statement and to meet the client's needs, one alternative that the accountant should consider is management-use-only financial statements for those monthly financial statements. Another alternative, especially for those firms who decide not to prepare management-use-only financial statements, is to consider a cash or modified cash basis financial statement with disclosures omitted. This alternative is appealing because the resulting financial statements are general use and do not have to be restricted to management use.

An accountant who is engaged to prepare a traditional cash basis compilation has to follow the SSARS performance and reporting standards. But, one of the significant efficiencies is that other than the (1) client's name/address, (2) titles of the financial statements, and (3) the dates of the financial statements and report date, the compilation report does not change from month to month or from client to client. The following example report presents the standard format for the monthly compilation report. The illustrative compilation report derives its efficiency, in part, from the fact that it does not need to be modified because of departures from the cash or modified cash basis of accounting. Such departures are extremely rare.

> We have compiled the accompanying statement of assets, liabilities, and equity—cash basis of XYZ Company, Inc. as of January 31, 20X1, and the related statement of revenues, expenses, and retained earnings—cash basis for the one month then ended, in accordance with *Statements on Standards for Accounting and Review Services* issued by the American Institute of Certified Public Accountants. The financials statements have been prepared on the cash basis (or modified cash basis) of accounting, which is a comprehensive basis of accounting other than generally accepted accounting principles.
>
> A compilation is limited to presenting in the form of financial statements information that is the representation of management. We have not audited or reviewed the accompanying financial statements and, accordingly, do not express an opinion or any other form of assurance on them.
>
> Management has elected to omit substantially all of the disclosures ordinarily included in financial statements prepared on the cash basis of accounting. If the omitted disclosures were included in the financial statements, they might influence the user's conclusions about the Company's assets, liabilities, equity, revenues and expenses. Accordingly, these financial statements are not designed for those who are not informed about such matters.

NOTE: The above report assumes that the financial statements do not define the basis of accounting.

ILLUSTRATIONS: TRADITIONAL COMPILATION ENGAGEMENT

The following items are presented:

TC-1. Traditional Compilation Engagement Letter.
TC-2. Checklist for a Traditional Compilation Engagement.
TC-3. Standard Compilation Report.
TC-4. Compilation Report with GAAP Measurement Departure.

ILLUSTRATION TC-1. TRADITIONAL COMPILATION ENGAGEMENT LETTER (ADAPTED FROM SSARS 1)

[*Appropriate Salutation*]

This letter is to confirm our understanding of the terms and objectives of our engagement and the nature and limitations of the services we will provide.

We will perform the following services:

1. We will compile, from information you provide, the annual and interim balance sheets and related statements of income, retained earnings, and cash flows of Widget Company for the year 20X1. We will not audit or review such financial statements. Our report on the annual financial statements of Widget Company is presently expected to read as follows:

> I [*we*] have compiled the accompanying balance sheet of Widget Company as of December 31, 20X1, and the related statements of income, retained earnings, and cash flows for the year then ended, in accordance with Statement on Standards for Accounting and Review Services issued by the American Institute of Certified Public Accountants.
>
> A compilation is limited to presenting in the form of financial statements information that is the representation of management. We have not audited or reviewed the accompanying financial statements and, accordingly, do not express an opinion or any other form of assurance on them.

Our report on your interim financial statements, which statements will omit substantially all disclosures, will include an additional paragraph that will read as follows:

> Management has elected to omit substantially all of the disclosures required by generally accepted accounting principles. If the omitted disclosures were included in the financial statements, they might influence the user's conclusions about the company's financial position, results of operations, and cash flows. Accordingly, these financial statements are not designed for those who are not informed about such matters.

If, for any reason, we are unable to complete the compilation of your financial statements, we will not issue a report on such statements as a result of this engagement.

2. We will also...[*description of other services*].

Our engagement cannot be relied upon to disclose errors, fraud, or illegal acts that may exist. However, we will inform the appropriate level of management of any material errors that come to our attention and any fraud or illegal acts that come to our attention, unless they are clearly inconsequential. (An accountant may wish to add this sentence: "…or unless our engagement is terminated before it is completed and our report issued.")

Our fees for these services....

We shall be pleased to discuss this letter with you at any time.

If the foregoing is in accordance with your understanding, please sign the copy of this letter in the space provided and return it to us.

Sincerely yours,

____

[*Signature of accountant*]

Accepted and agreed to:
Widget Company

____

President

____

Date

ILLUSTRATION TC-2. CHECKLIST FOR A TRADITIONAL COMPILATION ENGAGEMENT

Step No.	*Action/Decision*
1.	Obtain an understanding with the client, preferably in writing, about the engagement. (For a new client, determine if communication with the predecessor accountant is desirable.)
2.	Acquire the necessary knowledge of the client industry's accounting principles and practices.
3.	Acquire a general understanding of the nature of the client's business transactions, the form of the accounting records, the stated qualifications of the accounting personnel, the accounting basis used, and the form and content of the financial statements. (It is not necessary to make inquiries or perform other procedures; however, if the accountant becomes aware that information supplied by the entity is incorrect, incomplete, or unsatisfactory, the accountant should obtain additional or revised information.)
4.	Read the financial statements and determine if they are appropriate in form and free from obvious material error.

Step No.	*Action/Decision*
5.	Consider whether all disclosures required by GAAP are provided. If they are not, go to step 6. If they are, go to step 7.
6.	If the client has engaged the accountant to prepare financial statements that omit all or substantially all of the disclosures required by GAAP, indicate this in a separate paragraph in the report. If most, but not all, disclosures are omitted, notes to the financial statements should be labeled "Selected Information—Substantially All Disclosures Required by Generally Accepted Accounting Principles Are Not Included."
7.	Consider whether the financial statements contain departures from GAAP. If they do, go to step 8. If they do not, go to step 9.
8.	Request the client to revise the financial statements. Failing that, consider modifying the report by adding a separate paragraph that describes the departure. If the effect of the departure has been determined by management or is known by the accountant, disclose the dollar effects in the report. (The report need not be modified for uncertainties, going concern matters, or inconsistencies if they are properly disclosed—see step 5.) Withdraw from the engagement if the departures are designed to mislead financial statement users.
9.	Determine whether the firm is independent. If the firm is not, go to step 10. If the firm is, go to step 11.
10.	If the firm is not independent, add a separate paragraph to the report stating "We are not independent with respect to XYZ Company."
11.	Mark each page of the financial statements, including notes to the financial statements, "See Accountant's Compilation Report."
12.	Sign and date (manual, stamped, electronic, or typed signature) the report using the date the compilation was completed.
13.	Issue the financial statements and related compilation report.

NOTE: This checklist is designed for a GAAP basis compilation. If the accounting basis is an OCBOA, questions should be added to address (1) disclosure of the basis of accounting and (2) appropriate titles for the financial statements. See the interpretation on "Reporting on a Comprehensive Basis of Accounting other than GAAP" in this section.

ILLUSTRATION TC-3. STANDARD COMPILATION REPORT (ADAPTED FROM SSARS 1)

We have compiled the accompanying balance sheet of Widget Company as of December 31, 20X1, and the related statements of income, retained earnings, and cash flows for the year then ended, in accordance with Statements on Standards for Accounting and Review Services issued by the American Institute of Certified Public Accountants.

A compilation is limited to presenting in the form of financial statements information that is the representation of management [*owners*]. We have not audited or reviewed the accompanying financial statements and, accordingly, do not express an opinion or any other form of assurance on them.

[*Signature*]

[*Date*]

NOTE: The statement of retained earnings is not a required statement and changes therein (along with other changes in capital) may be presented as part of another basic financial statement (or in notes). In that case, the reference to retained earnings is not needed. If the statement of comprehensive income is included, the reference to that statement should be included.

ILLUSTRATION TC-4. COMPILATION REPORT WITH GAAP MEASUREMENT DEPARTURE (ADAPTED FROM SSARS 1)

We have compiled the accompanying balance sheet of Widget Company as of December 31, 20X1, and the related statements of income, retained earnings, and cash flows for the year then ended, in accordance with Statements on Standards for Accounting and Review Services issued by the American Institute of Certified Public Accountants.

A compilation is limited to presenting in the form of financial statements information that is the representation of management [*owners*]. We have not audited or reviewed the accompanying financial statements and, accordingly, do not express an opinion or any other form of assurance on them. However, we did become aware of a departure from generally accepted accounting principles that is described in the following paragraph.

As disclosed in Note X to the financial statements, generally accepted accounting principles require that land be stated at cost. Management has informed us that the company has stated its land at appraised value and that, if generally accepted accounting principles had been followed, the land account and stockholders' equity would have been decreased by $500,000.

[*Signature*]

[*Date*]

ILLUSTRATIONS: MANAGEMENT-USE-ONLY COMPILATION ENGAGEMENT

The following items are presented:

MUO-1. Required Engagement Letter.

MUO-2. Checklist for Compilation of Management-Use-Only Financial Statements.

ILLUSTRATION MUO-1. REQUIRED ENGAGEMENT LETTER (ADAPTED FROM SSARS 1)

[*Appropriate Salutation*]

This letter is to confirm our understanding of the terms and objectives of our engagement and the nature and limitations of the services we will provide.

We will perform the following services:

1. We will compile, from information you provide, the monthly financial statements of Widget Company for the year 20X1. A compilation is limited to presenting in the form of financial statements information that is the representation of management. We will not audit or review the financial statements and, accordingly, will not express an opinion or any other form of assurance on them. The financial statements will not be accompanied by a report.

Based upon our discussions with you, these statements are for management's use only and are not intended for third-party use.

Material departures from generally accepted accounting principles (GAAP) or other comprehensive bases of accounting (OCBOA) may exist and the effects of those departures, if any, on the financial statements may not be disclosed. In addition, substantially all disclosures required by GAAP or OCBOA may be omitted. Notwithstanding these limitations, you represent that you have knowledge about the nature of the procedures applied and the basis of accounting and assumptions used in the preparation of the financial statements that allows you to place the financial information in the proper context. Further, you represent and agree that the use of the financial statements will be limited to members of management with similar knowledge.

The financial statements are intended solely for the information and use of [*include list of specified members of management*] and are not intended to be and should not be used by any other party. [*optional*]

2. We will also [*discussion of other services—optional*]

Our engagement cannot be relied upon to disclose errors, fraud, or illegal acts that may exist. However, we will inform the appropriate level of management of any material errors that come to our attention and any fraud or illegal acts that come to our attention, unless clearly inconsequential.

We are not independent with respect to Widget Company. [*if applicable*]

The other data accompanying the financial statements are presented only for supplementary analysis purposes and will be compiled from information that is the representation of management, without audit or review, and we do not express an opinion or any other form of assurance on such data. [*if applicable*]

In view of the limitations described above, you agree not to take or assist in any action seeking to hold us liable for damages due to any deficiency in the financial statements we prepare and you agree to hold us harmless from any liability and related legal costs arising from any third-party use of the financial statements in contravention of the terms of this agreement. [*optional*]

Our fees for these services....

Should you require financial statements for third-party use, we would be pleased to discuss with you the requested level of service. Such engagement would be considered separate and not deemed to be part of the services described in this engagement letter.

If the foregoing is in accordance with your understanding, please sign the copy of this letter in the space provided and return it to us.

Sincerely yours,

____

[*Signature of accountant*]

Accepted and agreed to:
Widget Company

____
President

____
Date

ILLUSTRATION MUO-2. CHECKLIST FOR COMPILATION OF MANAGEMENT-USE-ONLY FINANCIAL STATEMENTS

Step No.	*Action/Decision*
1.	Prepare an engagement letter for the services to be performed and note the limitations on the use/distribution of the financial statements. (For a new client, determine if communication with the predecessor accountant is desirable.)
2.	Determine whether the CPA firm is independent. If the firm is not, disclose the lack of independence in the engagement letter.
3.	Obtain management's signature on the engagement letter to establish the client's agreement with the terms of engagement. *NOTE: SSARS indicates that this step is preferable, not required.*
4.	Acquire the necessary knowledge of the client's industry's accounting principles and practices.
5.	Acquire a general understanding of the nature of the client's business transactions, the form of the accounting records, and the stated qualifications of the accounting personnel.
6.	Obtain an understanding (based on management's stated needs) of the accounting basis used and the form and content of the management-use-only financial statements.[3]
7.	Draft and read the financial statements to determine if they are based on management's design and free from material error.
8.	If the management-use-only financial statements appear to be incorrect, incomplete, or unsatisfactory, given management's stated needs, obtain additional or revised information.
9.	Mark each page of the financial statements with an appropriate restriction on use such as: "Solely for the information and use by management [exact names of individuals may be used] of XYZ Company and not intended to be and should not be used by any other party." (SSARS does not require that the legend be place on supplemental information, if any.)
10.	Issue the restricted-use financial statements to management. (Do not attach a compilation report to the financial statements.)
11.	If after issuance, the accountant becomes aware that the management-use-only financial statements have been distributed to inappropriate parties, discuss the situation with the client and see that the client has the financial statements returned. (If the client does not comply with the request, in consultation with an attorney, notify known inappropriate parties that the financial statements are not intended for their use.)

ILLUSTRATIONS: REVIEW ENGAGEMENT

The following items are presented:

R-1. Review Engagement Letter.
R-2. Checklist for a Review Engagement.
R-3. Checklist for Change in Engagement from Audit/Review to Review/Compilation.
R-4. Standard Review Report.
R-5. Review Report with GAAP Measurement Departure.
R-6. Illustrative Inquiries for a Review.
R-7. Illustrative Representation Letter.

---

[3] *Management-use-only financial statements are designed according to management's explicit needs, not necessarily according to GAAP or OCBOA.*

ILLUSTRATION R-1. REVIEW ENGAGEMENT LETTER (ADAPTED FROM SSARS 1)

[*Appropriate Salutation*]

This letter is to confirm our understanding of the terms and objectives of our engagement and the nature and limitations of the services we will provide.

We will perform the following services:

1. We will review the balance sheet of Widget Company as of December 31, 20X1, and the related statements of income, retained earnings, and cash flows for the year then ended, in accordance with Statements on Standards for Accounting and Review Services issued by the American Institute of Certified Public Accountants. Our review will consist primarily of inquiries of company personnel and analytical procedures applied to financial data, and we will require a representation letter from management. A review does not contemplate obtaining an understanding of internal control or assessing control risk, tests of accounting records and responses to inquiries by obtaining corroborating evidential matter, and certain other procedures ordinarily performed during an audit. Thus, a review does not provide assurance that we will become aware of all significant matters that would be disclosed in an audit. Our engagement cannot be relied upon to disclose errors, fraud, or illegal acts that may exist. However, we will inform the appropriate level of management of any material errors that come to our attention and any fraud or illegal acts that come to our attention, unless they are clearly inconsequential. (An accountant may wish to add to this sentence: "…or unless our engagement is terminated before it is completed and our report issued.") We will not perform an audit of such financial statements, the objective of which is the expression of an opinion regarding the financial statements taken as a whole, and, accordingly, we will not express such an opinion on them.

Our report on the financial statements is presently expected to read as follows:

> We have reviewed the accompanying balance sheet of Widget Company as of December 31, 20X1, and the related statements of income, retained earnings, and cash flows for the year then ended, in accordance with Statements on Standards for Accounting and Review Services issued by the American Institute of Certified Public Accountants. All information included in these financial statements is the representation of the management of Widget Company.
>
> A review consists principally of inquiries of company personnel and analytical procedures applied to financial data. It is substantially less in scope than an audit in accordance with generally accepted auditing standards, the objective of which is the expression of an opinion regarding the financial statements taken as a whole. Accordingly, we do not express such an opinion.
>
> Based on our review, we are not aware of any material modifications that should be made to the accompanying financial statements in order for them to be in conformity with generally accepted accounting principles.

If, for any reason, we are unable, to complete our review of your financial statements, we will not issue a report on such statements as a result of this engagement.

2. We will also...[*description of other services*].

Our fees for these services....

We shall be pleased to discuss this letter with you at any time.

If the foregoing is in accordance with your understanding, please sign the copy of this letter in the space provided and return it to us.

Sincerely yours,

____

[*Signature of accountant*]

Accepted and agreed to:
Widget Company

____

President

____

Date

Illustration R-2. Checklist for a Review Engagement

Step No.	Action/Decision
1.	Obtain an understanding with the client, preferably in writing, regarding the engagement. (For a new client, determine if communication with the predecessor accountant is desirable.)
2.	Determine whether the firm is independent. If the firm is, go to step 3. If the firm is not, do not issue a review report. (However, it may be possible to issue a compilation report—see Illustration TC-2 "Checklist for a Compilation Engagement.")
3.	Acquire the necessary knowledge of the client industry's accounting principles and practices.
4.	Acquire an understanding of the client's business, including (1) a general understanding of the entity's organization, (2) its operating characteristics, and (3) the nature of its assets, liabilities, revenues, and expenses.
5.	Apply appropriate inquiry and analytical procedures to obtain a reasonable basis for expressing limited assurance that no material modifications should be made to the financial statements.
6.	Read the financial statements to determine whether, based on the information presented, they appear to conform to GAAP. Obtain reports of other accountants for subsidiaries, investees, etc., if any. Indicate division of responsibility if reference is made to other accountants.
7.	Perform additional procedures if information appears to be incorrect, incomplete, or otherwise unsatisfactory.
8.	Describe in the working papers matters covered in steps 5. and 7. Also, describe unusual matters that were considered and how they were resolved.
9.	Determine whether the inquiry and analytical procedures considered necessary to achieve limited assurance are incomplete or restricted in any way. If they are, go to step 10. If they are not, go to step 11.
10.	Consider whether a compilation report should be issued rather than a review report. (A review that is incomplete or restricted is not an adequate basis for issuing a review report.)
11.	Consider whether the financial statements contain departures from GAAP, including disclosure departures. If they do, go to step 12. If they do not, got to step 13.
12.	Request that the client revise the financial statements. Failing that, consider modifying the review report by adding a separate paragraph or paragraphs. If the effect of the departure has been determined by management or is known by the accountant, disclose the dollar effects in the report. (However, the report need not be modified for uncertainties, going concern matters, or inconsistencies if they are properly disclosed.) Withdraw from the engagement if the departures are designed to mislead financial statement users.
13.	Obtain a representation letter from the client.
14.	Mark each page of the financial statements, including notes to the financial statements, "See Accountant's Review Report."
15.	Sign and date (manual, stamped, electronic, or typed signature) the report using the date the inquiry and analytical procedures were completed.
16.	Issue the financial statements and the related review report.

Illustration R-3. Checklist for Change in Engagement from Audit/ Review to Review/Compilation

Step No.	Action/Decision
1.	Consider (a) the reason given for the client's request, (b) the additional effort required to complete the engagement, and (c) the estimated additional cost to complete the engagement.
2.	Determine whether the request for the change is caused by (a) a change in circumstances affecting the need for an audit or review, (b) a misunderstanding as to the nature of alternative services, or (c) restrictions caused by the client or by circumstances on the scope of the engagement. If (a) or (b)—which provide a reasonable basis for requesting a change—go to step 3. If (c), go to step 4.
3.	Consider issuing an appropriate compilation or review report. Make no mention in the report of the original engagement, the procedures performed, or the scope limitations. Go to step 5.
4.	Evaluate the possibility that the information affected by the scope restriction may be incorrect, incomplete, or otherwise unsatisfactory. If the client prohibited you from corresponding with the company's legal counsel or refused to sign a client representation letter, do not issue a review or compilation report.
5.	If the audit or review is substantially complete or the cost to complete is insignificant, consider the propriety of accepting a changed engagement.
6.	If an engagement letter has been obtained, revise the understanding with the client regarding the nature of the services to be rendered.

ILLUSTRATION R-4. STANDARD REVIEW REPORT (ADAPTED FROM SSARS 1)

We have reviewed the accompanying balance sheet of Widget Company as of December 31, 20X1, and the related statements of income, retained earnings, and cash flows for the year then ended, in accordance with Statements on Standards for Accounting and Review Services issued by the American Institute of Certified Public Accountants. All information included in these financial statements is the representation of the management of Widget Company.

A review consists principally of inquiries of company personnel and analytical procedures applied to financial data. It is substantially less in scope than an audit in accordance with generally accepted auditing standards, the objective of which is the expression of an opinion regarding the financial statements taken as a whole. Accordingly, we do not express such an opinion.

Based on our review, we are not aware of any material modifications that should be made to the accompanying financial statements in order for them to be in conformity with generally accepted accounting principles.

[*Signature*]

[*Date*]

NOTE: The statement of retained earnings is not a required statement and changes therein (along with other changes in capital) may be presented as part of another basic financial statement (or in notes). In that case, the reference to retained earnings is not needed. If the statement of comprehensive income is included, the reference to that statement should be included.

ILLUSTRATION R-5. REVIEW REPORT WITH GAAP MEASUREMENT DEPARTURE (ADAPTED FROM SSARS 1)

We have reviewed the accompanying balance sheet of Widget Company as of December 31, 20X1, and the related statements of income, retained earnings, and cash flows for the year then ended, in accordance with Statements on Standards for Accounting and Review Services issued by the American Institute of Certified Public Accountants. All information included in these financial statements is the representation of the management of Widget Company.

A review consists principally of inquiries of company personnel and analytical procedures applied to financial data. It is substantially less in scope than an audit in accordance with generally accepted auditing standards, the objective of which is the expression of an opinion regarding the financial statements taken as a whole. Accordingly, we do not express such an opinion.

Based on our review, with the exception of the matter described in the following paragraph, we are not aware of any material modifications that should be made to the accompanying financial statements in order for them to be in conformity with generally accepted accounting principles.

As disclosed in Note X to the financial statements, generally accepted accounting principles require that inventory cost consist of material, labor, and overhead. Management has informed us that the inventory of finished goods and work-in-progress is stated in the accompanying financial statements at material and labor cost only, and that the effects of this departure from generally accepted accounting principles on financial position, results of operations, and cash flows have not been determined.

[*Signature*]

[*Date*]

ILLUSTRATION R-6. ILLUSTRATIVE INQUIRIES FOR A REVIEW (FROM APPENDIX B IN SSARS 1)

1. General
   a. What are the procedures for recording, classifying, and summarizing transactions (relates to each section discussed below)?
   b. Do the general ledger control accounts agree with subsidiary records (for example, receivables, inventories, investments, property and equipment, accounts payable, accrued expenses, noncurrent liabilities)?
   c. Have accounting principles been applied on a consistent basis?
2. Cash
   a. Have bank balances been reconciled with book balances?
   b. Have old or unusual reconciling items between bank balances and book balances been reviewed and adjustments made where necessary?
   c. Has a proper cutoff of cash transactions been made?

   d. Are there any restrictions on the availability of cash balances?
   e. Have cash funds been counted and reconciled with control accounts?

3. Receivables
   a. Has an adequate allowance been made for doubtful accounts?
   b. Have receivables considered uncollectible been written off?
   c. If appropriate, has interest been reflected?
   d. Has a proper cutoff of sales transactions been made?
   e. Are there any receivables from employees and related parties?
   f. Are any receivables pledged, discounted, or factored?
   g. Have receivables been properly classified between current and noncurrent?

4. Inventories
   a. Have inventories been physically counted? If not, how have inventories been determined?
   b. Have general ledger control accounts been adjusted to agree with physical inventories?
   c. If physical inventories are taken at a date other than the balance sheet date, what procedures were used to record changes in inventory between the date of the physical inventory and the balance sheet date?
   d. Were consignments in or out considered in taking physical inventories?
   e. What is the basis of valuation?
   f. Does inventory cost include material, labor, and overhead where applicable?
   g. Have write-downs for obsolescence or cost in excess of net realizable value been made?
   h. Have proper cutoffs of purchases, goods in transit, and returned goods been made?
   i. Are there any inventory encumbrances?

5. Prepaid expenses
   a. What is the nature of the amounts included in prepaid expenses?
   b. How are these amounts amortized?

6. Investments, including loans, mortgages, and intercorporate investments
   a. Have gains and losses on disposal been reflected?
   b. Has investment income been reflected?
   c. Has appropriate consideration been given to the classification of investments between current and noncurrent, and the difference between the cost and market value of investments?
   d. Have consolidation or equity accounting requirements been considered?
   e. What is the basis of valuation of marketable equity securities?
   f. Are investments unencumbered?

7. Property and equipment
   a. Have gains or losses on disposal of property or equipment been reflected?
   b. What are the criteria for capitalization of property and equipment? Have such criteria been applied during the fiscal period?
   c. Does the repairs and maintenance account only include items of an expense nature?
   d. Are property and equipment stated at cost?
   e. What are the depreciation methods and rates? Are they appropriate and consistent?
   f. Are there any unrecorded additions, retirements, abandonments, sales, or trade-ins?
   g. Does the entity have material lease agreements? Have they been properly reflected?
   h. Is any property or equipment mortgaged or otherwise encumbered?

8. Other assets
   a. What is the nature of the amounts included in other assets?
   b. Do these assets represent costs that will benefit future periods? What is the amortization policy? Is it appropriate?
   c. Have other assets been properly classified between current and noncurrent?
   d. Are any of these assets mortgaged or otherwise encumbered?

9. Accounts and notes payable and accrued liabilities
   a. Have all significant payables been reflected?
   b. Are all bank and other short-term liabilities properly classified?
   c. Have all significant accruals, such as payroll, interest, and provisions for pension and profit-sharing plans been reflected?
   d. Are there any collateralized liabilities?
   e. Are there any payables to employees and related parties?

10. Long-term liabilities
    a. What are the terms and other provisions of long-term liability agreements?
    b. Have liabilities been properly classified between current and noncurrent?
    c. Has interest expense been reflected?
    d. Has there been compliance with restrictive covenants of loan agreements?
    e. Are any long-term liabilities collateralized or subordinated?
11. Income and other taxes
    a. Has provision been made for current and prior-year federal income taxes payable?
    b. Have any assessments or reassessments been received? Are there tax examinations in process?
    c. Are there timing differences? If so, have deferred taxes been reflected?
    d. Has provision been made for state and local income, franchise, sales, and other taxes payable?
12. Other liabilities, contingencies, and commitments
    a. What is the nature of the amounts included in other liabilities?
    b. Have other liabilities been properly classified between current and noncurrent?
    c. Are there any contingent liabilities, such as discounted notes, drafts, endorsements, warranties, litigation, and unsettled asserted claims? Are there any unasserted potential claims?
    d. Are there any material contractual obligations for construction or purchase of real property and equipment and any commitments or options to purchase or sell entity securities?
13. Equity
    a. What is the nature of any changes in equity accounts?
    b. What classes of capital stock have been authorized?
    c. What is the par or stated value of the various classes of stock?
    d. Do amounts of outstanding shares of capital stock agree with subsidiary records?
    e. Have capital stock preferences, if any, been disclosed?
    f. Have stock options been granted?
    g. Has the entity made any acquisitions of its own capital stock?
    h. Are there any restrictions on retained earnings or other capital?
14. Revenue and expenses
    a. Are revenues from the sale of major products and services recognized in the appropriate period?
    b. Are purchases and expenses recognized in the appropriate period and properly classified?
    c. Do the financial statements include discontinued operations or items that might be considered extraordinary?
15. Other
    a. Are there any events that occurred after the end of the fiscal period that have a significant effect on the financial statements?
    b. Have actions taken at stockholder, board of directors, or comparable meetings that affect the financial statements been reflected?
    c. Have there been any material transactions between related parties?
    d. Are there any material uncertainties? Is there any change in the status of material uncertainties previously disclosed?

ILLUSTRATION R-7. ILLUSTRATIVE REPRESENTATION LETTER[4] (ADAPTED FROM SSARS 1, AS AMENDED BY SSARS 9)

(*Date [No earlier than the date of the Accountant's Report*])

(*To the Accountant*)

We are providing this letter in connection with your review of the (*identification of financial statements*) of (*name of entity*) as of (*dates*) and for the (*periods of review*) for the purpose of expressing limited assurance that there are no material modifications that should be made to the statements in order for them to be in conformity with generally accepted accounting principles. We con-

[4] *This representation letter is for illustrative purposes only. The accountant may decide, based on the circumstances of the review engagement or the industry in which the entity operates, that other matters should be specifically included in the letter or that some of the representation included in the illustrative letter are not necessary.*

firm that we are responsible for the fair presentation in the financial statements of financial position, results of operations, and cash flows in conformity with generally accepted accounting principles.

Certain representations in this letter are described as being limited to matters that are material. Items are considered material, regardless of size, if they involve an omission or misstatement of accounting information that, in light of surrounding circumstances, makes it probable that the judgment of a reasonable person relying on the information would be changed or influenced by the omission or misstatement.[5]

We confirm, to the best of our knowledge and belief, (*as of [a date no earlier than the date of review report]*), the following representations made to you during your review.

1. The financial statements referred to above are fairly presented in conformity with generally accepted accounting principles.
2. We have made available to you all
   a. Financial records and related data.
   b. Minutes of the meetings of stockholders, directors, and committees of directors, or summaries of actions of recent meetings for which minutes have not yet been prepared.
3. There are no material transactions that have not been properly recorded in the accounting records underlying the financial statements.
4. We have no plans or intentions that may materially affect the carrying amounts or classification of assets and liabilities.
5. There are no material losses (such as from obsolete inventory or purchase or sales commitments) that have not been properly accrued or disclosed in the financial statements.
6. There are no
   a. Violations or possible violations of laws or regulations, whose effects should be considered for disclosure in the financial statements or as a basis for recording a loss contingency.
   b. Unasserted claims or assessments that our lawyer has advised us are probable of assertion that must be disclosed in accordance with Financial Accounting Standards Board (FASB) Statement No. 5 [AC section C59], *Accounting for Contingencies.*[6]
   c. Other material liabilities or gain or loss contingencies that are required to be accrued or disclosed by FASB Statement No. 5.
7. The company has satisfactory title to all owned assets, and there are no liens or encumbrances on such assets, nor has any asset been pledged as collateral.
8. We have complied with all aspects of contractual agreements that would have a material effect on the financial statements in the event of noncompliance.
9. The following have been properly recorded or disclosed in the financial statements:
   a. Related party transactions, including sales, purchases, loans, transfers, leasing arrangements, and guarantees, and amounts receivable from or payable to related parties.
   b. Guarantees, whether written or oral, under which the company is contingently liable.
   c. Significant estimates and material concentrations known to management that are required to be disclosed in accordance with the AICPA's Statement of Position 94-6, *Disclosure of Certain Significant Risks and Uncertainties.* (Significant estimates are estimates at the balance sheet date that could change materially with the next year. Concentrations refer to volumes of business, revenues, available sources of

---

[5] *The qualitative discussion of materiality used in this letter is adapted from Financial Accounting Standards Board Statement of Financial Accounting Concepts 2,* ***Qualitative Characteristics of Accounting Information.***

[6] *If management has not consulted a lawyer regarding litigation, claims, and assessments, the representation might be worded as follows:*

> *We are not aware of any pending or threatened litigation, claims, or assessments or unasserted claims or assessments that are required to be accrued or disclosed in the financial statements in accordance with Financial Accounting Standards Board Statement No. 5 [AC section C59],* ***Accounting for Contingencies,*** *and we have not consulted a lawyer concerning litigation, claims, or assessments.*

supply, or markets or geographic areas for which events could occur that would significantly disrupt normal finances within the next year.)

(Add additional representations that are unique to the entity's business or industry. See below for additional illustrative representations.)

10. To the best of our knowledge and belief, no events have occurred subsequent to the balance-sheet date and through the date of this letter that would require adjustment to or disclosure in the aforementioned financial statements.
11. We have responded fully and truthfully to all inquiries made to us by you during your review.

____

(Name of Owner or Chief Executive Officer and Title)

____

(Name of Chief Financial Officer and Title, when applicable)

The following additional representations may be appropriate in certain situations. This list of additional representations is not intended to be all-inclusive. In drafting a representation letter, the effects of other applicable pronouncements should be considered.

- The financial statements disclose all of the matters of which we are aware that are relevant to the entity's ability to continue as a going concern, including significant conditions and events, and our plans.
- We have reviewed long-lived assets to be held and used for impairment in accordance with FASB Statement 144, *Accounting for the Impairment or Disposal of Long-Lived Assets,* whenever events or changes in circumstances have indicated that the carrying amount of those assets might not be recoverable and have appropriately recorded the adjustment.
- We have tested goodwill and indefinite-lived intangibles for impairment in accordance with FASB Statement 142, *Goodwill and Other Intangible Assets* and, when an asset has been impaired, we have appropriately recorded the adjustment to the carrying value of the impaired asset.
- Debt securities that have been classified as held-to-maturity have been so classified due to our intent to hold such securities to maturity and our ability to do so. All other debt securities have been classified as available-for sale or trading.
- We consider the decline in value of debt or equity securities classified as either available-for-sale or held-to-maturity to be temporary.
- Receivables reported in the financial statements represent valid claims against debtors for sales or other charges arising on or before the balance-sheet date and have been appropriately reduced to their estimated net realizable value.
- We believe that the carrying amounts of all material assets will be recoverable.
- All agreements to repurchase assets previously sold have been properly disclosed.
- We have made provisions for losses to be sustained in the fulfillment of, or from the inability to fulfill, sales commitments.

See Section 333 for other representations that may be appropriate from management relating to matters specific to the entity's business or industry.

If matters exist that should be disclosed to the accountant, they should be indicated by listing them following the representation. For example, if an event subsequent to the date of the balance sheet has been disclosed in the financial statements, the subsequent events paragraph could be modified as follows: "To the best of our knowledge and belief, except as discussed in Note X to the financial statements, no events have occurred…" Similarly, in appropriate circumstances, item 4 could be modified as follows: "The company has no plans or intentions that may materially affect the carrying value or classification of assets and liabilities, except for our plans to dispose of Segment A, as disclosed in Footnote X to the financial statements, which are discussed in the minutes of the December 7, 20X1, meeting of the board of directors."

3200 REPORTING ON COMPARATIVE FINANCIAL STATEMENTS[1]

EFFECTIVE DATE AND APPLICABILITY

Original Pronouncement

SSARS 2, October 1979.

Effective Date

Reports on comparative financial statements for periods ending on or after November 30, 1979.

Applicability

When comparative financial statements of a nonpublic entity are presented and the current period has been compiled and reported on or reviewed in conformity with GAAP or OCBOA.

NOTE: When current period financial statements of a nonpublic entity are audited and the prior period compiled or reviewed, the guidance in SASs applies.

The current status of the entity—public or nonpublic—governs whether SASs or SSARSs apply. If the entity was nonpublic but now public, SASs apply. If the entity was public but now nonpublic, SSARSs apply.

This section only applies to traditional compilations, not management-use-only compilations. The guidance in this section addresses reporting requirements, and a report ordinarily is not issued in a management-use-only compilation engagement.

DEFINITIONS OF TERMS

Comparative financial statements. Financial statements of two or more periods presented in columnar form.

Continuing accountant. An accountant who has been engaged to audit, review, or compile and report on the financial statements of the current period and one or more consecutive periods immediately prior to the current period.

Updated report. A report issued by a continuing accountant that takes into consideration information that he becomes aware of during his current engagement and that reex-

[1] *In 2000 the ASB issued SAS 93, **Omnibus Statement of Auditing Standards—2000,** which amends SAS 58 to modify the basic elements of the auditor's standard report to include a reference to the country of origin of (1) the accounting principles used to prepare the financial statements and (2) the auditing standards followed in performing the audit. Questions have been raised as to whether the country of origin language described by SAS 93 should be incorporated in a compilation or review report. Although ARSC believes that nothing in SSARS 1 would preclude CPAs from including such language in the standard compilation or review report if they so choose, they concluded that there is no pressing need to make a change to the report language at this time.*

presses his previous conclusions or, depending on the circumstances, expresses different conclusions on the financial statements of a prior period as of the date of his current report.

Reissued report. A report issued subsequent to the date of the original report that bears the same date as the original report. A reissued report may need to be revised for the effects of specific events; in these circumstances, the report should be dual-dated with the original date and a separate date that applies to the effects of such events.

OBJECTIVES OF SECTION

This section established standards for reporting on comparative financial statements of a nonpublic entity when financial statements of the current period have been compiled and reported on or reviewed. SSARS 2 was issued to provide coverage for reporting on comparative financial statements in situations when the SASs do not apply.

FUNDAMENTAL REQUIREMENTS

GENERAL

When comparative financial statements of a nonpublic entity are presented, the accountant should issue a report covering each period presented.

If the accountant becomes aware that financial statements of other periods that have not been audited, reviewed, or compiled are presented in comparative form in a document containing financial statements that he or she has reported on and the accountant's name or report is used, the accountant should advise the client that the use of his or her name or report is not appropriate. The accountant may also wish to consult with an attorney.

The accountant should not report on comparative statements when statements for one or more of the periods, but not all, omit all or substantially all disclosures.

NOTE: Financial statements in columnar form with disclosures are comparative; financial statements that omit all or substantially all disclosures are comparative; but financial statements with disclosures are not comparative to financial statements without disclosures.

CONTINUING ACCOUNTANT'S STANDARD REPORT

A continuing accountant who performs the same or higher level of service on the current period financial statements should update his or her report on the prior period financial statements.

A continuing accountant who performs a lower level of service (20X2 compiled, 20X1 reviewed) should either

1. Include a separate paragraph in the report describing the responsibility for the prior period financial statements.
2. Reissue the report on the prior period financial statements.

If option 1. above is selected, the description should include the original date of the report and should state that no review procedures were performed after that date.

If option 2. is selected, the report may be

1. A combined compilation and reissued review report. (The combined report should state that no review procedures were performed after the date of the review report.)
2. Presented separately.

Illustrations presents example reports on comparative financial statements for the continuing accountant when

1. Each period is compiled.

2. Each period is reviewed.
3. Current period is reviewed and prior period is compiled.

Continuing Accountant's Changed Reference to GAAP

The accountant should consider the effects on the prior period report of circumstances or events that came to his or her attention. When the accountant's report contains a changed reference to a GAAP departure, the report should include a separate paragraph indicating

1. Date of previous report.
2. Circumstances or events that caused the change.
3. If applicable, that the prior period financial statements have been changed.

Illustrations presents an example explanatory paragraph for a changed reference to GAAP.

Predecessor's Compilation or Review Report

A predecessor accountant is not required, but may reissue his or her report. If the predecessor's compilation or review report is not presented, the successor should either

1. Make reference to the predecessor's report.
2. Perform a compilation, review, or audit of the prior period financial statements and report thereon.

If "reference to the predecessor's report" option is selected, the successor's reference should include

1. A statement that the prior period financial statements were compiled or reviewed by another accountant (without identifying the predecessor by name).
2. The date of prior accountant's report.
3. A description of the disclaimer or limited assurance report.
4. A description or quotation of any report modification or emphasis paragraphs.

Illustrations contain examples of successor paragraphs when the predecessor reviewed or compiled the prior period financial statements.

According to AR 200.20, if the predecessor report is to be reissued, before reissuing the predecessor should consider

1. The current form and presentation of the prior period financial statements.
2. Subsequent events not previously known.
3. Changes in the financial statements that alter modifications to the report.

The predecessor should also perform the following procedures listed in AR 200.21:

1. Read the current period financial statements and the successor's report.
2. Compare the prior period financial statements with those previously issued, and with the current period.
3. Obtain a letter from the successor indicating whether he or she is aware of any matter that affects the prior period financial statements.

If the predecessor becomes aware of any matter that affects the prior period financial statements, he or she should

1. Make inquiries or perform analytical procedures similar to those that would have been applied to the information if it had been known at the report date.
2. Perform other procedures considered necessary such as discussing the matter with the successor or reviewing the successor's working papers.

When reissuing the report, the predecessor should use the date of the previous report. However, if the financial statements are revised, the report should be dual-dated. Also, if the financial statements are revised, the predecessor should obtain a written statement from the former client describing the new information and its effect on the prior period financial statements.

If the predecessor is unable to complete the reissue procedures described above, he or she should not reissue the report and may wish to consult with an attorney.

Changed Prior Period Financial Statements

Either the predecessor (as discussed above) or the successor should report on restated financial statements when the financial statements have been changed. If the successor reports on them, he or she should audit, review, or compile the financial statements and report accordingly. No references to the predecessor's report should be made in the successor's report.

Reporting When Prior Period Is Audited

The accountant should issue a compilation or review report on the current period financial statements and either

1. Reissue the audit report on the prior period or
2. Add a separate paragraph to the current period report that includes the following information:
    a. The financial statements of the prior period were audited.
    b. The date of the audit report.
    c. The type of opinion.
    d. Substantive reasons for other than unqualified opinion.
    e. No audit procedures were performed after b. above.

Illustrations presents an example paragraph for the above situation.

Reporting on Financial Statements That Previously Did Not Omit All or Substantially All Disclosures

The accountant may report on comparative financial statements that omit all or substantially all disclosures even if the prior period statements were originally compiled, reviewed, or audited (with disclosures) provided that his or her report includes an additional paragraph stating the nature of the previous service and the date of the previous report. *Illustrations* presents an example report. (See also *Interpretation* below.)

Change of Status—Public/Nonpublic Entity

A previously issued compilation or review report should not be reissued or referred to in the current report if the entity is currently a public entity.

INTERPRETATION

If the financial statements are compiled (disclosures omitted) from financial statements that previously did not omit disclosures, the accountant's reference to the previous reports should include a description or quotation of any report modification or emphasis matter.

TECHNIQUES FOR APPLICATION

CLIENT-PREPARED FINANCIAL STATEMENTS PRESENTED WITH COMPILED OR REVIEWED FINANCIAL STATEMENTS

Client-prepared financial statements of some periods that have not been audited, reviewed, or compiled should not be presented in columnar/comparative format. However, they may be presented on separate pages of a document (containing financial statements that the accountant has reported on) if they are accompanied by an indication by the client (1) that they have not been compiled, reviewed, or audited, and (2) that the accountant assumes no responsibility for them.

DECIDING REPORT OPTIONS UNDER SSARS 2

SSARS 2 is rather complex. The following summary decision aid helps simplify the report decision process in SSARS 2. The comparative statements are for years 20X1 and 20X2.

1. If 20X2 is audited, SASs apply.
2. If the entity's current status for 20X2 is a public company, SASs apply.
3. For continuing accountant
    a. If 20X2 level of service is equal to or higher than 20X1, update report.
    b. If 20X2 is lower level of service, either refer to or reissue prior report.
4. For successor accountant
    a. If predecessor does not reissue, refer to report of predecessor or perform audit, review, or compilation of 20X1.
    b. If financial statements are restated because of an error and predecessor doesn't report on restated financials, perform audit, review, or compilation of 20X2.

ILLUSTRATIONS

The following reports on comparative financial statements adapted from SSARS 2 are presented for continuing accountants:

1. Compiled each period.
2. Reviewed each period.
3. Current period reviewed and prior period compiled.
4. An explanatory paragraph for a changed reference to a GAAP departure.

The following reports are also presented:

5. An explanatory paragraph referencing the predecessor's report.
6. An explanatory paragraph when prior period is audited.
7. A report on financial statements that previously did not omit disclosures.

ILLUSTRATION 1. COMPILED EACH PERIOD—CONTINUING ACCOUNTANT

I (we) have compiled the accompanying balance sheets of Widget Company as of December 31, 20X2 and 20X1, and the related statements of income, retained earnings, and cash flows for the years then ended, in accordance with Statements on Standards for Accounting and Review Services issued by the American Institute of Certified Public Accountants.

A compilation is limited to presenting in the form of financial statements information that is the representation of management (owners). I (we) have not audited or reviewed the accompanying financial statements and, accordingly, do not express an opinion or any other form of assurance on them.

Guy and Carmichael
February 15, 20X3

ILLUSTRATION 2. REVIEWED EACH PERIOD—CONTINUING ACCOUNTANT

I (we) have reviewed the accompanying balance sheets of Widget Company as of December 31, 20X2 and 20X1, and the related statements of income, retained earnings, and cash flows for the years then ended, in accordance with Statements on Standards for Accounting and Review Services issued by the American Institute of Certified Public Accountants. All information included in these financial statements is the representation of the management (owners) of Widget Company.

A review consists principally of inquiries of company personnel and analytical procedures applied to financial data. It is substantially less in scope than an audit in accordance with generally accepted auditing standards; the objective of which is the expression of an opinion regarding the financial statements taken as a whole. Accordingly, I (we) do not express such an opinion.

Based on my (our) reviews, I am (we are) not aware of any material modifications that should be made to the accompanying financial statements in order for them to be in conformity with generally accepted accounting principles.

Guy and Carmichael
February 15, 20X3

ILLUSTRATION 3. CURRENT PERIOD REVIEWED AND PRIOR PERIOD COMPILED —CONTINUING ACCOUNTANT

I (we) have reviewed the accompanying balance sheet of Widget Company as of December 31, 20X2, and the related statements of income, retained earnings, and cash flows for the year then ended, in accordance with Statements on Standards for Accounting and Review Services issued by the American Institute of Certified Public Accountants. All information included in these financial statements is the representation of the management (owners) of Widget Company.

A review consists principally of inquiries of company personnel and analytical procedures applied to financial data. It is substantially less in scope than an audit in accordance with generally accepted auditing standards; the objective of which is the expression of an opinion regarding the financial statements taken as a whole. Accordingly, I (we) do not express such an opinion.

Based on my (our) review, I am (we are) not aware of any material modifications that should be made to the accompanying financial statements in order for them to be in conformity with generally accepted accounting principles.

The accompanying 20X1 financial statements of Widget Company were compiled by me (us). A compilation is limited to presenting in the form of financial statements information that is the representation of management (owners). I (we) have not audited or reviewed the 20X1 financial statements and, accordingly, do not express an opinion or any other form of assurance on them.

Guy and Carmichael
February 15, 20X3

ILLUSTRATION 4. EXPLANATORY PARAGRAPH FOR A CHANGED REFERENCE TO A GAAP DEPARTURE—CONTINUING ACCOUNTANT

In my (our) previous (compilation) (review) report dated March 1, 20X2, on the 20X1 financial statements, I (we) referred to a departure from generally accepted accounting principles because the company carried its land at appraised values. However, as disclosed in Note X, the company has restated its 20X1 financial statements to reflect its land at cost in accordance with generally accepted accounting principles.

ILLUSTRATION 5. EXPLANATORY PARAGRAPH REFERENCING THE PREDECESSOR'S REPORT

1. For a review

   The 20X1 financial statements of Widget Company were reviewed by other accountants whose report dated March 1, 20X2, stated that they were not aware of any material modifications that should be made to those statements in order for them to be in conformity with generally accepted accounting principles.

2. For a compilation

   The 20X1 financial statements of Widget Company were compiled by other accountants whose report dated February 1, 20X2, stated that they did not express an opinion on any other form of assurance on those statements.

ILLUSTRATION 6. EXPLANATORY PARAGRAPH WHEN PRIOR PERIOD IS AUDITED

The financial statements for the year ended December 31, 20X1, were audited by us (other accountants) and we (they) expressed an unqualified opinion on them in our (their) report dated March 1, 20X2, but we (they) have not performed any auditing procedures since that date.

ILLUSTRATION 7. REPORT ON FINANCIAL STATEMENTS THAT PREVIOUSLY DID NOT OMIT DISCLOSURES

I (we) have compiled the accompanying balance sheet of Widget Company as of December 31, 20X2 and 20X1, and the related statements of income, retained earnings, and cash flows for the years then ended, in accordance with Statements on Standards for Accounting and Review Services issued by the American Institute of Certified Public Accountants.

A compilation is limited to presenting in the form of financial statements information that is the representation of management (owners). I (we) have not audited or reviewed the accompanying financial statements and, accordingly, do not express an opinion or any other form of assurance on them.

Management has elected to omit all of the disclosures required by generally accepted accounting principles. If the omitted disclosures were included in the financial statements, they might influence the user's conclusions about the company's financial position, results of operations, and cash flows. Accordingly, these financial statements are not designed for those who are not informed about such matters.

The accompanying 20X1 financial statements were compiled by me (us) from financial statements that did not omit all of the disclosures required by generally accepted accounting principles and that I (we) previously reviewed as indicated in my (our) report dated March 1, 20X2.

Guy and Carmichael
February 15, 20X3

3300 COMPILATION REPORTS ON FINANCIAL STATEMENTS INCLUDED IN CERTAIN PRESCRIBED FORMS

EFFECTIVE DATE AND APPLICABILITY

Original Pronouncement	SSARS 3, December 1981.
Effective Date	Issue date.
Applicability	The section provides for an alternative form of standard compilation report on financial statements in prescribed forms that call for departures from GAAP (or OCBOA) by either (1) specifying a measurement principle not in conformity with GAAP, or (2) failing to request the disclosures required by GAAP. The section does not apply to tax returns or to forms designed or adopted by the client. Also, the section does not apply to review engagements or to management-use-only financial statements that are provided to clients without issuing a compilation report.

DEFINITION OF TERM

Prescribed form. Any standard preprinted form designed or adopted by the body to which it is to be submitted, for example, forms used by banks, credit agencies, industry trade associations, or governmental and regulatory agencies.

OBJECTIVES OF SECTION

There is a presumption that the information required by a prescribed form is sufficient to satisfy the body that designed or adopted the form; thus, there is no need to call attention to departures required by the form.

FUNDAMENTAL REQUIREMENTS

GENERAL

The standards for performing a compilation as described in SSARS 1 (Section 3100) also apply to SSARS 3 engagements.

An accountant may issue either a compilation report as described in SSARS 1 or the alternative SSARS 3 report (see *Illustration*).

Measurement and Disclosure Departures

The SSARS 3 report does not require GAAP measurement or disclosure departures required by the prescribed form or the instructions to the form to be identified.

Departures from GAAP that are not permitted by the form or its requirements should be described in the SSARS 3 compilation report in accordance with SSARS 1.

Preprinted Accountant's Report

The accountant should not sign a preprinted prescribed report that does not meet the requirements of SSARS 1 or SSARS 3. Instead, the accountant should attach an acceptable report.

INTERPRETATION

Omission of Disclosures in Financial Statements Included in Certain Prescribed Forms (May 1982)

An accountant who has reviewed financial statements of a nonpublic entity may issue a compilation report on financial statements for the same period in a prescribed form that calls for a departure from GAAP. When the difference between the previously reviewed financial statements and the financial statements included in the prescribed form is limited to the omission of disclosures not requested by the form, the accountant may wish to refer to the review report in the prescribed-form compilation report.

ILLUSTRATION

The standard compilation report for a prescribed form presented is adapted from SSARS 3.

Illustration 1. Compilation Report for a Prescribed Form

We have compiled the balance sheet of Widget Company as of December 31, 20X1, included in the accompanying prescribed form in accordance with Statements on Standards for Accounting and Review Services issued by the American Institute of Certified Public Accountants.

Our compilation was limited to presenting in the form prescribed by Third National Bank information that is the representation of management. We have not audited or reviewed the financial statement referred to above and, accordingly, we do not express an opinion or any other form of assurance on it.

This financial statement is presented in accordance with the requirements of Third National Bank, which differ from generally accepted accounting principles. Accordingly, this financial statement is not designed for those who are not informed about such differences.

[*Signature*]

[*Date*]

3400 COMMUNICATIONS BETWEEN PREDECESSOR AND SUCCESSOR ACCOUNTANTS

EFFECTIVE DATE AND APPLICABILITY

Original Pronouncement	SSARS 4, December 1981, as amended by SSARS 9, December 2002.
Effective Date	Issue date.
Applicability	Compilation and review engagements when a successor accountant decides (not mandatory) to communicate with the predecessor accountant about acceptance of an engagement. SSARS 4 obligates the successor accountant to request the client to communicate with the predecessor when the successor believes that the financial statements reported on by the predecessor are materially misstated.

DEFINITIONS OF TERMS

Successor accountant. An accountant who has been invited to propose on a new engagement and is considering accepting the engagement or who has accepted an engagement to compile or review financial statements.

Predecessor accountant. An accountant who has reported on the most recent financial statements or was engaged to do so but did not complete the engagement and has resigned, declined to stand for reappointment, or been terminated.

OBJECTIVES OF SECTION

SSARS 4 discusses the circumstances when communications between predecessor and successor accountants may be desirable and the types of inquiries a successor may decide to make. The section was initially based on SAS 7, *Communications between Predecessor and Successor Accountants* (superceded by SAS 84; see Section 315). However, unlike the auditor-to-auditor communications in SAS 84, communications are not required in a compilation or review engagement (with the exception noted when the financial statements are believed to be materially misleading).

FUNDAMENTAL REQUIREMENTS

GENERAL

According to AR 400.03, a successor accountant may decide to communicate with a predecessor accountant when

1. The information obtained about the prospective client is limited or requires special attention.
2. The change in accountants takes place substantially after the end of the accounting period for which financial statements are to be compiled or reviewed.
3. There have been frequent changes in accountants.

The successor accountant should (1) obtain the client's permission before communicating with the predecessor, and (2) ask the client to authorize the predecessor to respond fully to inquiries. The successor's inquiries may be either oral or written.

INQUIRIES ABOUT ENGAGEMENT ACCEPTANCE

Ordinarily, inquiries would include questions that might assist a successor in deciding whether to accept the engagement. Inquiries may cover

1. Management's integrity.
2. Disagreements about accounting principles or about the need to perform certain procedures.
3. Management's cooperation in providing information.
4. The predecessor's understanding of the reasons for the change in accountants.

The predecessor should respond promptly and completely to the inquiries noted above. If the predecessor limits his or her response because of unusual circumstances, such as litigation, that should be disclosed. The successor should evaluate the reasons and implications of a limited response in deciding whether to accept the engagement.

ACCESS TO WORKING PAPERS

A successor may also wish, after the client obtains authorization from the predecessor, to review the predecessor's working papers. The predecessor and successor should agree on those working papers that are available and those that may be copied. Valid business reasons (e.g., unpaid fees) may cause the predecessor not to allow access to working papers.

MATERIALLY MISLEADING FINANCIAL STATEMENTS

If during the engagement, the successor accountant becomes aware of information that causes him or her to believe that the financial statements reported on by the predecessor may need to be revised, the successor should ask the client to communicate the matter to the predecessor. If the client refuses to do so or if the predecessor's response is inadequate, the successor should evaluate the implications for the engagement and consider whether to resign. The accountant may also wish to consult with legal counsel.

INTERPRETATIONS

REPORTS ON THE APPLICATION OF ACCOUNTING PRINCIPLES (AUGUST 1987)

An accountant who has been asked to provide written or oral advice on the application of accounting principles to a client whose financial statements are compiled or reviewed by another accountant is obligated to follow SAS 50, *Reports on the Application of Accounting Principles* (see Section 625).

TECHNIQUES FOR APPLICATION

APPLICABILITY OF SAS 84

SAS 84 does not apply to engagements governed by SSARS 4. Furthermore, no standards apply to situations where the prior years' financial statements were compiled or reviewed and the current year is to be audited, or vice versa. Footnote 3 of SAS 84 indicates that a successor **auditor** may find the guidance in Section 315 useful in communicating with the predecessor **accountant** who compiled or reviewed the prior financial statements. Similarly, a successor **accountant** may find the guidance in SSARS 4 useful in communicating with a predecessor **auditor**.

FACILITATING ACCESS TO WORKING PAPERS OF THE PREDECESSOR ACCOUNTANT

Before permitting access to the working papers, the predecessor accountant may wish to obtain a consent letter and an acknowledgement letter from the successor accountant. An example consent letter and an acknowledgement letter is presented in *Illustrations*.

ILLUSTRATIONS

Following are illustrations of (1) a client consent and acknowledgement letter and (2) a successor accountant acknowledgement letter. The letters are not required by SSARS 4. The first letter is based on a similar letter that is illustrated in SAS 84, and the second letter is taken from SSARS 4, as amended by SSARS 9.

ILLUSTRATION 1. ILLUSTRATIVE CLIENT CONSENT LETTER

[*Date*]

Widget Company
[*Address*]

You have given your consent to allow [*name of successor CPA firm*] as successor accountants for Widget Company, access to our working paper documentation for our [*compilation or review*] of the December 31, 20X1 financial statements of Widget Company. You also have given your consent to respond fully to [*name of successor CPA firm*] inquiries. You understand and agree that the review of our working paper documentation is undertaken solely for the purpose of obtaining an understanding about Widget Company and certain information about our [*compilation or review*] to assist [*name of successor CPA firm*] in [*compiling or reviewing*] the December 31, 20X2 financial statements of Widget Company.

Please confirm your agreement with the foregoing by signing and dating a copy of this letter and returning it to us.

Attached is the form of the letter we will furnish [*name of successor CPA firm*] regarding the use of the working paper documentation.

Very truly yours,

[*Predecessor Accountant*]

By:____________________

Accepted:

Widget Company

By:____________________ Date:____________________

ILLUSTRATION 2. ILLUSTRATIVE SUCCESSOR ACCOUNTANT ACKNOWLEDGEMENT LETTER (ADAPTED FROM SSARS 4)

[*Date*]

[*Successor Accountant*]

[*Address*]

We have previously [*reviewed or compiled*], in accordance with Statements on Standards for Accounting and Review Services, the December 31,20X1 financial statements of Widget Company. In connection with your [*review or compilation*] of Widget's 20X2 financial statements, you have requested access to our working papers prepared in connection with that engagement. Widget has authorized our firm to allow you to review those working papers.

Our [*review or compilation*], and the working papers prepared in connection therewith, of Widget Company's financial statements were not planned or conducted in contemplation of your [*review or compilation*]. Therefore, items of possible interest to you may not have been specifically addressed. Our use of professional judgment for the purpose of this engagement means that matters may have existed that would have been assessed differently by you. We make no representation about the sufficiency or appropriateness of the information in our working papers for your purposes.

We understand that the purpose of your review is to obtain information about Widget Company and our 20X1 results to assist you in your 20X2 engagement of Widget Company. For that purpose only, we will provide you access to our working papers that relate to that objective.

Upon request, we will provide copies of those working papers that provide factual information about Widget Company. You agree to subject any such copies or information otherwise derived from our working papers to your normal policy for retention of working papers and protection of confidential client information. Furthermore, in the event of a third-party request for access to your working papers prepared in connection with your [*reviews or compilations*] of Widget Company, you agree to obtain our permission before voluntarily allowing any such access to our working papers or information otherwise derived from our working papers, and to obtain on our behalf any releases that you obtain from such third party. You agree to advise us promptly and provide us a copy of any subpoena, summons, or other court order for access to your working papers that include copies of our working papers or information otherwise derived therefrom.

Please confirm your agreement with the foregoing by signing and dating a copy of this letter and returning it to us.

Very truly yours,

[*Predecessor Accountant*]

By:_________________________

Accepted:

[*Successor Accountant*]

By:_________________________ Date:______________________

NOTE: According to AR 400.12, even with the client's consent, access to the predecessor accountant's working papers may still be limited. Experience has shown that the predecessor accountant may be willing to grant broader access if given additional assurance concerning the use of the working papers. Accordingly, the successor accountant might consider agreeing to the following limitations on the review of the predecessor accountant's working papers in order to obtain broader access:

- *The successor accountant will not comment, orally or in writing, to anyone as a result of the review about whether the predecessor accountant's engagement was performed in accordance with the Statements on Standards for Accounting and Review Services.*
- *The successor accountant will not provide expert testimony or litigation services or otherwise accept an engagement to comment on issues relating to the quality of the predecessor accountant's engagement.*

The paragraph below illustrates the above.

Because your review of our working papers is undertaken solely for the purpose described above and may not entail a review of all our working papers, you agree that (1) the information obtained from the review will not be used by you for any other purpose, (2) you will not comment, orally or in writing, to anyone as a result of that review about whether our engagement was performed in accordance with Statements on Standards for Accounting and Review Services, (3) you will not provide expert testimony or litigation services or otherwise accept an engagement to comment on issues relating to the quality of our engagement.

3600 REPORTING ON PERSONAL FINANCIAL STATEMENTS INCLUDED IN WRITTEN PERSONAL FINANCIAL PLANS[1]

EFFECTIVE DATE AND APPLICABILITY

Original Pronouncement	SSARS 6, September 1986.
Effective Date	September 30, 1986.
Applicability	An accountant may opt for an exemption from SSARS 1 for certain personal financial statements included in written personal financial plans. The section does not preclude an accountant from complying with SSARS 1. The section applies to personal financial statements whether the basis of accounting is GAAP or OCBOA.

DEFINITIONS OF TERMS

This section does not contain any definitions.

OBJECTIVES OF SECTION

Personal financial statements included in personal financial plans (1) frequently omit disclosures and (2) contain departures from GAAP (or OCBOA). If the purpose of those financial statements is solely to assist in developing the personal financial plan, SSARS 6 provides for an exemption from SSARS 1 and an alternative report that should be used if the exemption is followed.

FUNDAMENTAL REQUIREMENTS

EXEMPTION

According to AR 600.03 an accountant may submit a written personal financial plan containing unaudited personal financial statements to a client without following SSARS 1, if

1. The accountant establishes an understanding, preferably in writing, with the client that the personal financial statements will

---

[1] *The accountant has the option of preparing management-use-only financial statements when preparing personal financial statements. However, in most cases, the authors believe that accountants will find it more useful to follow the guidance in this section.*

   a. Be used solely to assist the client and his or her advisers to develop the client's personal goals and objectives.
   b. Not be used for credit or any other purposes other than those in a. above.
2. Nothing comes to the accountant's attention during the engagement indicating anything other than a. and b. above.

Alternative Report Required

An accountant electing the SSARS 6 exemption should issue a report. The report should indicate that the financial statements

1. Are designed solely to help develop the financial plan.
2. May be incomplete or contain other GAAP departures.
3. Should not be used to obtain credit or for any other purpose (exception for 1. above).
4. Have not been audited, reviewed, or compiled. Illustration 1 presents an appropriate report.

Marking on Each Page

Each page of the personal financial statements should refer to the accountant's report.

INTERPRETATIONS

Submitting a Personal Financial Plan to a Client's Advisers (May 1991)

The interpretation allows the accountant to submit a written personal financial plan, to be implemented by the client or his or her advisers, without complying with SSARS 1. Examples of implementation include an

1. Insurance broker to identify specific products.
2. Investment adviser to provide investment portfolio recommendations.
3. Attorney to draft a will or trust agreement.

ILLUSTRATION

The following is an illustrative report adapted from SSARS 6.

Illustration 1. Report on Personal Financial Statements Included in a Personal Financial Plan

The accompanying Statement of Financial Condition of X, as of December 31, 20X1, was prepared solely to help you develop your personal financial plan. Accordingly, it may be incomplete or contain other departures from generally accepted accounting principles and should not be used to obtain credit or for any purposes other than developing your financial plan. We have not audited, reviewed, or compiled the statement.

[*Signature*]

[*Date*]

APPENDIX A

CROSS-REFERENCES TO SASs, SSAEs, AND SSARSs

Statements on Auditing Standards

No.	*Date issued*	*Title*	*Guide section*
1	Nov. 1972	Codification of Auditing Standards and Procedures	
2	Oct. 1974	(Superseded by SAS 58.)	
3	Dec. 1974	(Superseded by SAS 48.)	
4	Dec. 1974	(Superseded by SAS 25.)	
5	July 1975	(Superseded by SAS 69.)	
6	July 1975	(Superseded by SAS 45.)	
7	Oct. 1975	(Superseded by SAS 84.)	
8	Dec. 1975	Other Information in Documents Containing Audited Financial Statements	550
9	Dec. 1975	(Superseded by SAS 65.)	
10	Dec. 1975	(Superseded by SAS 24.)	
11	Dec. 1975	(Superseded by SAS 73.)	
12	Jan. 1976	Inquiry of a Client's Lawyer Concerning Litigation, Claims, and Assessments	337
13	May 1976	(Superseded by SAS 24.)	
14	Dec. 1976	(Superseded by SAS 62.)	
15	Dec. 1976	(Superseded by SAS 58.)	
16	Jan. 1977	(Superseded by SAS 53.)	
17	Jan. 1977	(Superseded by SAS 54.)	
18	May 1977	(Withdrawn by Auditing Standards Board)	
19	June 1977	(Superseded by SAS 85.)	
20	Aug. 1977	(Superseded by SAS 60.)	
21	Dec. 1977	(Rescinded by Auditing Standards Board)	
22	Mar. 1978	Planning and Supervision	311
23	Oct. 1978	(Superseded by SAS 56.)	
24	Mar. 1979	(Superseded by SAS 36.)	
25	Nov. 1979	The Relationship of Generally Accepted Auditing Standards to Quality Control Standards	161
26	Nov. 1979	Association with Financial Statements	504
27	Dec. 1979	(Superseded by SAS 52.)	
28	June 1980	(Withdrawn by SAS 52.)	
29	July 1980	Reporting on Information Accompanying the Basic Financial Statements in Auditor-Submitted Documents	551
30	July 1980	(Superseded by SSAE 2.)	
31	Aug. 1980	Evidential Matter	326
32	Oct. 1980	Adequacy of Disclosure of Financial Statements	431
33	Oct. 1980	(Superseded by SAS 45.)	
34	Mar. 1981	(Superseded by SAS 59.)	
35	April 1981	(Superseded by SAS 75.)	
36	April 1981	(Superseded by SAS 71.)	
37	April 1981	Filings under Federal Securities Statutes	711
38	April 1981	(Superseded by SAS 49.)	
39	June 1981	Audit Sampling	350
40	Feb. 1982	(Superseded by SAS 52.)	
41	April 1982	(Superseded by SAS 96.)	

Statements on Auditing Standards (Continued)

No.	*Date issued*	*Title*	*Guide section*
42	Sept. 1982	Reporting on Condensed Financial Statements and Selected Financial Data	552
43	Aug. 1982	Omnibus Statement on Auditing Standards	331, 350, 420, 901
44	Dec. 1982	(Superseded by SAS 70.)	
45	Aug. 1983	Omnibus Statement on Auditing Standards—1983	313, 334
46	Sept. 1983	Consideration of Omitted Procedures after the Report Date	390
47	Dec. 1983	Audit Risk and Materiality in Conducting an Audit	312
48	July 1984	The Effects of Computer Processing on the Audit of Financial Statements	311, 326
49	Sept. 1984	(Superseded by SAS 72.)	
50	July 1986	Reports on the Application of Accounting Principles	625
51	July 1986	Reporting on Financial Statements Prepared for Use in Other Countries	534
52	April 1988	Omnibus Statement on Auditing Standards—1987	551, 558
53	April 1988	(Superseded by SAS 82.)	
54	April 1988	Illegal Acts by Clients	317
55	April 1988	Consideration of Internal Control in a Financial Statement Audit	319
56	April 1988	Analytical Procedures	329
57	April 1988	Auditing Accounting Estimates	342
58	April 1988	Reports on Audited Financial Statements	508
59	April 1988	The Auditor's Consideration of an Entity's Ability to Continue as a Going Concern	341
60	April 1988	Communication of Internal Control Related Matters Noted in an Audit	325
61	April 1988	Communication with Audit Committees	380
62	April 1989	Special Reports	623
63	April 1989	(Superseded by SAS 68.)	
64	Dec. 1990	Omnibus Statement on Auditing Standards—1990	341, 508, 543
65	April 1991	The Auditor's Consideration of the Internal Audit Function in an Audit of Financial Statements	322
66	June 1991	(Superseded by SAS 71.)	
67	Nov. 1991	The Confirmation Process	330
68	Dec. 1991	(Superseded by SAS 74.)	
69	Jan. 1992	The Meaning of *Present Fairly in Conformity with Generally Accepted Accounting Principles*	411
70	April 1992	Service Organizations	324
71	May 1992	Interim Financial Information (Superseded by SAS 100 for interim periods within fiscal years beginning after December 15, 2002.)	722A
72	Feb. 1993	Letters for Underwriters and Certain Other Requesting Parties	634
73	July 1994	Using the Work of a Specialist	336
74	Feb. 1995	Compliance Auditing Considerations in Audits of Governmental Entities and Recipients of Governmental Financial Assistance	801
75	Sept. 1995	(Withdrawn by SAS 93.)	
76	Sept. 1995	Amendments to Statement on Auditing Standards 72, *Letters for Underwriters and Certain Other Requesting Parties*	634, 2401

Statements on Auditing Standards (Continued)

No.	*Date issued*	*Title*	*Guide section*
77	Nov. 1995	Amendments to Statements on Auditing Standards 22, *Planning and Supervision;* 59, *The Auditor's Consideration of an Entity's Ability to Continue as a Going Concern;* and 62, *Special Reports*	311, 341, 544, 623
78	Dec. 1995	Consideration of Internal Control in a Financial Statement Audit: An Amendment to Statement on Auditing Standards 55	319
79	Dec. 1995	Amendment to Statement on Auditing Standards 58, *Reports on Audited Financial Statements*	508
80	Dec. 1996	Amendment to Statement on Auditing Standards 31, *Evidential Matter*	326
81	Dec. 1996	[Superseded by SAS 92]	
82	Feb. 1997	Consideration of Fraud in a Financial Statement Audit (Superseded by SAS 99 for audits of financial statements for periods beginning on or after December 15, 2002.)	316A
83	Oct. 1997	Establishing an Understanding with the Client	310
84	Oct. 1997	Communications between Predecessor and Successor Auditors	315
85	Nov. 1997	Management Representations	333
86	Mar. 1998	Amendment to Statement on Auditing Standards 72, *Letters for Underwriters and Certain Other Requesting Parties*	634
87	Sept. 1998	Restricting the Use of an Auditor's Report	532
88	Dec. 1999	Service Organizations and Reporting on Consistency	324, 420
89	Dec. 1999	Audit Adjustments	310, 333, 380
90	Dec. 1999	Audit Committee Communications	380, 722
91	Apr. 2000	Federal GAAP Hierarchy	411
92	Sept. 2000	Auditing Derivative Instruments, Hedging Activities, and Investments in Securities	332
93	Oct. 2000	Omnibus Statement on Auditing Standards—2000	315, 411, 508
94	May 2001	The Effect of Information Technology on the Auditor's Consideration of Internal Control in a Financial Statement Audit	319
95	Dec. 2001	Generally Accepted Auditing Standards	150
96	Jan. 2002	Audit Documentation	312, 329, 339, 341
97	June 2002	Amendment to Statement on Auditing Standards 50, *Reports on the Application of Accounting Principles*	625
98	Sept. 2002	Omnibus Statement on Auditing Standards—2002	150, 161, 312, 324, 508, 530, 550, 551, 558, 560, 561
99	Oct. 2002	Consideration of Fraud in a Financial Statement Audit	316
100	Nov. 2002	Interim Financial Information	722
101	Jan. 2003	Auditing Fair Value Measurements and Disclosures	328

Statements on Standards for Attestation Engagements

No.	*Date issued*	*Title*	*Guide section*
1	Oct. 1985	Superseded by SSAE 10	
1	Mar. 1986	Superseded by SSAE 10	
1	Sept. 1988	Superseded by SSAE 10	
1	Dec. 1987	Superseded by SSAE 10	
2	May 1993	Superseded by SSAE 10	
3	Dec. 1993	Superseded by SSAE 10	
4	Sept. 1995	Superseded by SSAE 10	
5	Nov. 1995	Superseded by SSAE 10	
6	Dec. 1995	Superseded by SSAE 10	
7	Oct. 1997	Superseded by SSAE 10	
8	Mar. 1998	Superseded by SSAE 10	
9	Jan. 1999	Superseded by SSAE 10	
10	Jan. 2001	Attestation Standards: Revision and Recodification	2101-2701
11	Jan. 2002	Attest Documentation	2101, 2201, 2301
12	Sept. 2002	Amendment to SSAE 10, *Attestation Standards: Revision and Recodification*	2101

Statements on Standards for Accounting and Review Services

1	Dec. 1978	Compilation and Review of Financial Statements	3100
2	Oct. 1979	Reporting on Comparative Financial Statements	3200
3	Dec. 1981	Compilation Reports on Financial Statements Included in Certain Prescribed Forms	3300
4	Dec. 1981	Communications between Predecessor and Successor Accountants	3400
5	July 1982	(Deleted by SSARS 7.)	
6	Sept. 1986	Reporting on Personal Financial Statements Included in Written Personal Financial Plans	3600
7	Nov. 1992	Omnibus Statement on Standards for Accounting and Review Services—1992	3100, 3200, 3300, 3400
8	Oct. 2000	Amendment to Statement on Standards for Accounting and Review Services No. 1, *Compilation and Review of Financial Statements*	3100
9	Nov. 2002	Omnibus Statement on Standards for Accounting and Review Services – 2002	3100, 3400

APPENDIX B

LIST OF AICPA AUDIT AND ACCOUNTING GUIDES AND AUDITING STATEMENTS OF POSITION[1]

Along with auditing Interpretations of SASs, which are integrated in the appropriate sections, the auditing guidance in the following AICPA Audit and Accounting Guides and auditing Statements of Positions are Tier 2 Interpretive Publications in the GAAS hierarchy established by SAS 95 (see Section 100-230). Interpretive publications are recommendations on how to apply the SASs in specific circumstances and for entities in specialized industries that are issued under the authority of the ASB. Auditors who do not follow the guidance in an applicable interpretive publication should be prepared to explain how they complied with the relevant SAS requirements addressed by such guidance.

AICPA *Audit and Accounting Guides* summarize the practices applicable to specific industries and describe relevant matters, conditions, and procedures unique to these industries. In addition, general audit and accounting guides listed below may be of interest to CPAs performing audit and attest engagements. The accounting guidance included in AICPA *Audit and Accounting Guides* is in the GAAP hierarchy as authoritative GAAP. Guides are available from the AICPA.

Analytical Procedures
Audit Sampling
Auditing Derivative Instruments, Hedging Activities, and Investments in Securities
Auditing Revenue in Certain Industries
Audits of Agricultural Producers and Agricultural Cooperatives
Audits of Airlines
Audits of Casinos
Audits of Colleges and Universities
Audits of Credit Unions
Audits of Employee Benefit Plans
Audits of Entities with Oil and Gas Producing Activities
Audits of Federal Government Contractors
Audits of Finance Companies (Including Independent and Captive Financing Activities of Other Companies)
Audits of Investment Companies
Audits of Property and Liability Insurance Companies
Audits of State and Local Governmental Units (Non-GASB 34 Edition)
Audits of State and Local Governments
Audits of Voluntary Health and Welfare Organizations
Banks and Savings Institutions
Brokers and Dealers in Securities
Common Interest Realty Associations
Consideration of Internal Control in a Financial Statement Audit
Construction Contractors
Guide for Prospective Financial Information
Guide for the Use of Real Estate Appraisal Information
Health Care Organizations

---

[1] *Accounting Statements of Position are not included in this listing.*

Life and Health Insurance Entities
Not-for-Profit Organizations
Personal Financial Statements Guide
Service Organizations: Applying SAS No. 70, as Amended

Statements of Position—Auditing and Attestation

Auditing and Attestation Statements of Position are issued to achieve one or more of several objectives: to revise, clarify, or supplement guidance in previously issued Audit and Accounting Guides; to describe and provide implementation guidance for specific types of audit and attestation engagements; or to provide guidance on specialized areas in audit and attestation engagements. The auditing and attestation guidance in a Statement of Position has the same authority as auditing and attestation guidance in an Audit and Accounting Guide.

Confirmation of Insurance Policies in Force
Auditing Property and Liability Reinsurance
Auditing Life Reinsurance
Reports on Audited Financial Statements of Investment Companies
Questions Concerning Accountants' Services on Prospective Financial Statements
Report on the Internal Control Structure in Audits of Investment Companies
Accountants' Services on Prospective Financial Statements for Internal Use Only and Partial Presentations
Report on the Internal Control Structure in Audits of Futures Commission Merchants
Questions and Answers on the Term Reasonably Objective Basis and Other Issues Affecting Prospective Financial Statements
Auditing Insurance Entities' Loss Reserves
Auditing Property/Casualty Insurance Entities' Statutory Financial Statements Applying Certain Requirements of the NAIC Annual Statement Instructions
Reporting on Required Supplementary Information Accompanying Compiled or Reviewed Financial Statements of Common Interest Realty Associations
The Auditor's Consideration of Regulatory Risk-Based Capital for Life Insurance Enterprises
Inquiries of State Insurance Regulators
Letters for State Insurance Regulators to Comply with the NAIC Model Audit Rule
Auditor's Reporting on Statutory Financial Statements of Insurance Enterprises
Audits of States, Local Governments, and Not-for-Profit Organizations Receiving Federal Awards
Reporting on Management's Assessment Pursuant to the Life Insurance Ethical Market Conduct Program of the Insurance Marketplace Standards Association
Guidance to Practitioners in Conducting and Reporting on an Agreed-upon Procedures Engagement to Assist Management in Evaluating the Effectiveness of Its Corporate Compliance Program
Auditing Health Care Third-Party Revenues and Related Receivables
Performing Agreed-upon Procedures Engagements That Address Internal Control over Derivative Transactions as Required by the New York State Insurance Law
Reporting Pursuant to the Association for Investment Management and Research Performance Presentation Standards
Performing Agreed-Upon Procedures Engagements That Address Annual Claims Prompt Payment Reports as Required by the New Jersey Administrative Code

To order the guides, call 888-777-7077 or go to www.aicpa.org

APPENDIX C

OTHER AUDITING PUBLICATIONS IN THE GAAS HIERARCHY

PART 1: LIST OF AICPA PRACTICE ALERTS

Practice Alerts are issued by the AICPA's SEC Practice Section Professional Issues Task Force (PITF). The PITF accumulates and considers practice issues that appear to present accounting and auditing concerns for practitioners. They do not represent an official position of the AICPA. Previously issued Practice Alerts can be obtained from the AICPA website

www.aicpa.org/members/div/secps/lit/practice.htm

and are as follows (as of July 31, 2003):

94-1: Dealing with Audit Differences (Section 312)
94-2: Auditing Inventory—Physical Observations (Section 331)
94-3: Acceptance and Continuance of Audit Clients (Section 315)
95-1: Revenue Recognition Issues (Superceded by Practice Alert 98-3)
95-2: Complex Derivatives (Deleted due to the issuance of FASBs 133 and 137)
95-3: Auditing Related Parties and Related-Party Transactions (Section 334)
96-1: The Private Securities Litigation Reform Act of 1995 (Not included)
97-1: Financial Statements on the Internet (Section 550)
97-2: Audit of Employee Benefit Plans (Not included)
97-3: Changes in Auditors and Related Topics (Section 315)
98-1: The Auditor's Use of Analytical Procedures (Section 329)
98-2: Professional Skepticism and Related Topics (Section 316)
98-3: Revenue Recognition Issues (Supercedes Practice Alert 95-1) (Section 316)
99-1: Guidance for Independence Discussions with Audit Committees (Section 380)
99-2: How the Use of a Service Organization Affects Internal Control Considerations (Section 324)
00-1: Accounting for Certain Equity Transactions (Not included)
00-2: Quality of Accounting Principles—Guidance for Discussions with Audit Committees (Section 380)
00-3: Auditing Construction Contracts
00-4: Quarterly Review Procedures for Public Companies (Section 722)
01-1: Common Peer Review Recommendations (Not included)
01-2: Audit Considerations in Times of Economic Uncertainty (Not included)
02-1: Communications with the Securities and Exchange Commission (Not included)
02-2: Use of Specialists (Section 336)
02-3: Reauditing Financial Statements (Not included)
03-1: Audit Confirmations (Section 330)
03-2: Journal Entries and Other Adjustments (Section 316)

PART 2: LIST OF AUDITING PRACTICE RELEASES, CURRENT AICPA RISK ALERTS, AICPA TECHNICAL PRACTICE AIDS, AND OTHER PUBLICATIONS

Auditing Practice Releases

Auditing Practice Releases (formerly titled *Auditing Procedures Studies*) provide practitioners with nonauthoritative practical assistance concerning auditing procedures. The releases available from the AICPA are listed below.

- The Information Technology Age: Evidential Matter in the Electronic Environment (1997)
- Audit Implications of EDI (1995)
- Confirmation of Accounts Receivable (1995)

Current AICPA Risk Alerts

- Audit Risk Alert—2001/2002: Current Risks, Accounting, Auditing, and Professional Developments
- Auto Dealerships
- Banks, Credit Union, and Other Lenders and Depository Institutions
- Common Interest Realty Associations
- Construction Contractors
- Compilation and Review Alert
- E-Business
- Employee Benefit Plans
- Health Care
- High Technology
- Insurance
- Investment Companies
- Not-for-Profit Organizations
- Real Estate
- Retail Enterprises
- Securities
- State and Local Governments

AICPA Technical Practice Aids, Accounting and Auditing Publications Technical Questions and Answers

- TIS Section 8000, *Audit Fieldwork*
- TIS Section 9000, *Auditor's Reports*

Other Publications

- *Assets Acquired in a Purchase Business Combination to Be Used in Research and Development Activities*
- *Auditing Estimates and Other Soft Accounting Information*, by Michael J. Ramos
- *Considering Fraud in a Financial Statement Audit: Practical Guidance in Applying SAS 82*, by Michael J. Ramos

A

Acceptance of clients and engagements, 9, 680, 696, 751
Accounting and Review Services Committee (ARSC), 713
Accounting changes
Adverse opinions, 389
Cash flow presentation, 369
Classification, 369
Comparability, 366
Consistency affected, 368, 386
Consistency not affected, 369
Correction of error, 369
Definition, 366
Effect on auditor's report, 367, 389, 402
Estimates, 369
Explanatory paragraph added, 367, 386
FIFO to LIFO, 370
Future change, 370
Qualified opinions, 386, 389
Reporting entity, 368
Special reports, 487
Subsequent years' reports, 386, 389
Substantially different, 369
Accounting principles, quality of, 345
Accounts payable
List of evidential matter, 168
Accounts receivable
Confirmation process, 193
Definition, 193
List of evidential matter, 163, 176
Accrued expenses
List of evidential matter, 168
Adverse opinions
Accounting changes, 389
Condensed financial statements, 454
Definition, 382
Description, 389, 649
Disagreements with management, 689
Explanatory paragraph, 385, 386
GAAP departures, 387, 388, 397, 401
Illegal acts by clients, 104
Illustrations
Condensed financial statements, 454
Forecast, 656
GAAP departures, 401
Inadequate disclosure, 402
Omission of statement, 402
Uncertainties, 388
Affiliated companies
Definition, 248
Related parties, 248
Agreed-upon procedures
Acceptance of engagement, 633, 696
Accountants' reports, 634, 651
Communication with specified parties, 637
Definitions, 632
Engagement letter, 636
Illustrative examples
Compliance reports, 703
Report in connection with proposed acquisition, 639
Standard accountant's report, 638
Independence, 636
Internal control, 684
Planning the engagement, 702
Procedures, 635, 637, 702
Prospective financial statements, 650, 658
Report on, 638, 698
Elements of, 696
Representation letter, 636, 638
Scope restrictions, 697
Subsequent events, 697
American Bar Association policy on audit inquiries, 273
Analytical procedures
Application of, 181
Audit procedures, 188
Auditor's use of, 178
Common-size financial statements, 186
Definition, 177
Documentation, 190
Fraud, 181
Illustrative case studies, 190
Industry comparisons, 182
National economic data comparisons, 183
Overall review, 178, 179, 188
Permanent files, 187
Planning, 178, 188
Precision of expectation, 190
Ratio analysis, 182, 183
Recommended audit procedures, 188
Regression analysis, 186
Reliability of data, 189
Review of interim financial information, 580, 587
Substantive tests, 178, 189
Trend analysis, 182, 185
Variance analysis, 182, 185
Annual reports
Internal control, 435
Types, 432
Assertions
Completeness, 153, 157, 160, 222
Definition, 153, 169
Existence, 153, 159
Presentation and disclosure, 154, 158, 160, 226
Rights and obligations, 153, 160
Valuation and allocation, 154, 160
Assessment
Audit procedures, 274
Client without a lawyer, 277, 280
Disclosure, 274
Inquiries of client's lawyer, 275
Unasserted, 272
Association with financial statements
Client-prepared communication, 378, 432
Definition, 374
Unaudited, 375
Attest documentation
Preparation, 620
Attest engagement
Agreed-upon procedures, 631, 695
Assertions, 612
Attestation risk, 612
Compliance attestation, 694
Definition, 611
Responsible party, 612
Subject matter, 612
Attest reports
Agreed-upon procedures, 638, 698
Examination, 626
Review, 629
Attestation standards
Comparison with GAAS, 624
Fieldwork standards, 615
General standards, 614
Relationship to quality control standards, 620
Reporting standards, 616
Audit committee
Audit adjustments, 339
Auditor's responsibilities under GAAS, 341
Communication with auditor, 339, 345, 562, 582
Illustration of written communication to, 350
Illustrative questionnaire, 347
Independence discussions with, 343
Reportable conditions, 146
Audit documentation
Application of accounting principles, 505
Auditor's letter to regulator, 293
Communications to client regarding access, 293, 294

Content, 288
Deficiencies, 292
Definition, 286
Documentation requirements on auditing standards, 294
Fieldwork standard, 288
Nonstatistical sampling, 325, 327
Ownership, 289
Preparation, 290
Quality, 292
Related accounts, 291
Requirement, 288
Standardization, 290

Audit engagement
Objective, 2
Planning, 13
Professional skepticism, 92
Quality control standards, 5
Timing of audit work, 14
Withdrawal by auditor, 91, 104, 438

Audit objectives, 154, 155, 170
Illustration, 159

Audit programs
Illustrative source list, 162
Inventory observation, 213

Audit risk
Audit sampling, 45
Consideration of, 43
Definition, 31, 317
Detection risk, 32, 36, 45
Errors or fraud, 64, 88
Incremental audit risk, 49
Inherent risk, 32, 36, 44
Management characteristics, 89, 99
Materiality, 32, 33, 38, 39, 89
Professional skeptcism, 75, 92
Relative risk, 44
Risk assessment questionnaire, 28

Audit sampling
Confidence limits, 332
Definition, 317
Documentation, 324, 327
Dual-purpose sample, 318
Misstatements, 320
Nonsampling, 321
Nonsampling risk, 317
Nonstatistical, 321
Population, 318, 325
Preliminary judgement of materiality, 40
Risk, 317, 330
Sample selection, 319, 322
Sampling risk, 317, 327
Size of sample, 320, 323, 325, 328, 330
Statistical, 328
Stratification, 319
Tests of controls, 323
Tolerable misstatement, 36, 318, 326
Tolerable rate, 318
Unexamined items, 318, 319

Auditor, independent
Appoinment, 14
Association with financial statements, 374
Lack of independence, 376
Relationship between appointment and planning, 14
Responsibilities, 2, 7, 254

Auditor's reports
Accounting changes, 389
Addressee, 384
Application of accounting principles, 500
Auditor-submitted document, 441, 446
Circumstances requiring modification, 395
Comparative financial statements, 377, 390
Components of standard report, 383
Condensed financial statements, 451, 453
Consistency, 367, 386
Date of report, 407
Departures from GAAP, 365, 431
Dual statements, 417, 418
Dual-dated, 407, 410
Emphasis of a matter, 258, 386
Explanatory language added, 382, 384
Fair presentation, 357
Financial statements prepared for use outside US, 414
GAAP departures, 376, 385, 387
Going concern, 306
Government entities, 600
Illegal acts by clients, 104
Illustrations
Accounting change, 402
Application of accounting principles, 504
Comparative financial statements, 398, 406
Compilation of forecast, 653
Compilation of projection, 653
Condensed financial statements, 454
Dual statements, 418
Examination of forecast, 654
Examination of projection, 655
Financial feasibility study, 657
GAAP departure, 400
Inadequate disclosure, 402
Internal control, 688
Liquidation basis of accounting, 405
Modified US style report, 418
Oil and gas producing activities, 459
Omission of statement, 402
One basic financial statement, 398
Other auditors, 399, 426, 690
Predecessor's report not presented, 404
Pro forma financial information, 672
Reports with differing opinions, 403
Restricted-use, 413
Review report, 569, 590
Rule 203 opinion, 401
Scope limitation, 400
Selected data, 455
Single year, 398, 405
Standard report, 398
Supplementary information, 461
Unaudited financial statements, 379
Inadequate disclosure, 372, 376, 388
Interim financial information, 548, 564, 583
Introductory paragraph, 383
Lack of independence, 376
Material weaknesses, 151
Modified US style report, 414, 416
Negative assurance, 378
Notes to financial statements, 387
OCBOA financial statements, 375
One financial statement, 387, 398
Opinion paragraph, 383
Other auditors, 385, 420, 422
Other information in documents, 432
Reference to specialists, 264
Regulated industries, 430
Related-party transactions, 257
Reportable conditions, 150
Reporting standards, 4, 358, 367, 372
Reports with differing opinions, 377
Restatement of prior period's financial statements, 392
Restricting use of, 411
Review of interim financial information, 583

Revisions, 438, 474
Scope limitations, 387, 396
Scope paragraph, 383
Signature, 384
Standard report, 381
Subsequent events, 407, 408, 466
Supplementary information reference, 459
Tax returns, 379
Title, 383
Unaudited financial statements, 375
Uncertainties, 387, 388
Unqualified opinion, 382
Updated report, 382
Work performed by other auditor, 420

B

Basis of accounting
Cash, 478, 492
Liquidation, 393, 405
Other comprehensive basis of accounting, 375, 478, 492
Regulatory, 478
Tax, 478, 492
Blank confirmation form, 193
Business combinations
Consistency, 368
Pooling of interests, 421
Business risk, 31

C

Cash
List of evidential matter, 162
Cash flows
Change in presentation, 369
Change in accounting principle, 368
Change in estimate, 369
Change in reporting entity, 368
Change of auditors
Communication between auditors, 54
Procedures, 394
Checklists
Compilations, 730
Management-use-only (MUO), 733
Evaluating work of internal auditors, 129
Going concern, 308
Inventory observation checklist, 214
Receivables confirmation, 203
Related-party, 258
Review of interim financial information, 594
Reviews, 735
Subsequent events, 468
Claims
Audit procedures, 274
Auditor discovery of, 280
Client without a lawyer, 277, 280
Disclosure, 274
Inquiries of client's lawyer, 275
Unasserted, 272
Clients
Auditor-submitted documents, 441, 456, 651
Client-prepared documents, 378, 441, 456, 651
Developing accounting estimates, 313
Disclosure and discovery of facts, 473
Litigation, claims, and assessments, 272
Other information in documents, 432
Preparation of audit documentation, 290
Refusal to revise information, 437, 439
Common-size financial statements, 186
Communication
Audit adjustments, 339
Auditor and audit committee, 330, 562, 582
Illustrations, 347, 350
Auditor's responsibilities under GAAS, 340
Engagement letters, 346
Errors or fraud, 91
Illegal acts by clients, 104
Independence discussions, 343
Internal control, 108
Predecessor auditor, 55, 750
Quality control policies, 7
Reportable conditions, 149
Successor auditor, 55, 750
Comparability
Accounting changes, 367
Definition, 366
Comparative financial statements
Auditor's reports, 390, 398
Change of opinion, 390
Continuing accountant, 390, 741
Continuing accountant's report, 742
Date of auditor's report, 390
Definition, 741
Financial statements restated, 392, 744
Illustrative auditor's report, 398, 745
Negative assurance, 378
Predecessor's report, 391, 743, 746
Reissued report, 742
Reports with differing opinions, 377, 403
Special reports, 487
Unaudited, 377
Updated report, 741
Competence
Definition, 154
General guides, 156
General standard, 3
Compilation of financial statements
Application of standards, 725
Change from audit, 720
Change from review, 720
Checklist, 730
Condensed financial statements, 449
Definition, 713
Engagement letter, 728
Entity, 713
Illustrations
Engagement letter, 729
Standard report, 731
Management-use-only (MUO), 728
Nonpublic entity, 713
Performance requirements, 715
Prospective financial statements, 646, 660
Reporting, 714, 715
Reports
Illustration, 731, 749
Prescribed form, 748
Compliance attestation
Acceptance of engagement, 696, 699
Control risk, 700
Definitions, 694
Inherent risk, 699
Management's representations, 695
Materiality, 703
Planning the engagement, 701
Procedures, 700, 704
Report, 698, 700
Examples of, 703
Modification of, 701
Scope restrictions, 697
Subsequent events, 697, 700
Compliance auditing
Definitions, 598
Descriptions of, 599
Government auditing standards, 598, 600
No reportable conditions report, 604
Procedures, 602
Recipients of governmental financial assistance, 599

Single audit, 599, 603
Understanding of laws and regulations, 601
Condensed financial statements
Adverse opinion, 454
Auditor's report, 451
Auditor-submitted document, 443, 450
Comparative presentation, 452
Compilation report, 451, 749
Definition, 449
Letters for underwriters, 509
Nonpublic entities, 451
Public entities, 450
Confirmations
Blank, 193
Checklist, 202
Control of, 196
Definitions, 193
Description, 194
Design of, 195
Evaluation of results, 196, 197
Illustrative checklist, 202
Illustrative confirmations, 204, 218
Inventories, 217
Negative, 193, 198, 205
Nonresponses, 196, 202
Positive, 193, 204
Preparation and mailing, 199
Prior to year-end, 198
Procedures, 198
Public warehouses, 609
Respondents, 195
Responses, 200
Selection of accounts, 193, 199
Subsequent payments, 205
Summarize results, 201
Timing, 198
Worksheet, 206
Consistency
Accounting requirements, 367
APB 28, 370
Auditor's standard report, 367, 381
Comparability, 366
Explanatory paragraph, 386
First year audits, 370
Lack of, 386
Other information, 433
Periods covered, 368
Reporting standard, 4, 367, 382
Consolidated financial statements
Auditor's report, 444, 448
Continuance of clients and engagements, 9
Contracts
Compliance reports, 483
Special-purpose financial presentations, 484
Control activities, 108, 112
Control environment, 108, 112
Control risk
Assessed level, 109
Assessment by auditor, 44, 112, 114, 117, 221
Audit sampling, 318
Definition, 32, 108
Documentation of, 116
Illustrative documentation, 119
Maximum level, 109
Reduction, 115
Substantive tests, 51, 52
Correction of error
Application of principle, 369
Not involving principle, 369
Corroborating information, 154
Tests to develop, 155

D

Data processing
Use of service organizations, 133
Date of auditor's report
Completion of fieldwork, 410
Definition, 407
Dual-dated report, 407, 410, 467
Reissued report, 407, 409
Subsequent events, 407, 408, 462, 466
Debt
List of evidential matter, 168
Restructure, 303
Defalcation, 63, 88
Deferred charges
List of evidential matter, 165
Departures from promulgated principles
Accounting changes, 368, 387
Adverse opinion, 389, 401
Justification for departure, 385, 400
Materiality, 397
Qualified opinion, 386, 400
Regulated companies, 430
Review of interim financial information, 565, 584, 589
Rule 203, 361, 365, 401
Special reports, 487
Derivatives, 219
Assertions
Completeness, 222
Examples of substantive procedures, 233
Control risk assessment, 230
Existence
Examples of substantive procedures, 233
Inherent risk assessment, 228
Management's ability and intent, 226
Occurrence
Examples of substantive procedures, 233
Presentation and disclosure, 226
Rights and obligations
Examples of substantive procedures, 234
Tests of valuation, 222
Collateral in evaluating fair value, 225
Control risk assessment, 221
Definition, 219
Designing audit procedures, 222
Effect of service organization on audit approach and procedures, 230
Fair value determined using a model, 224
Impairment losses, 225
Management representations, 227
Risk assessment in planning, 221
Sources of fair value information, 224
Special skill or knowledge, 227
Substantive procedures based on risk assessment, 222
Tests of valuation assertions, 222
Unrealized appreciation or depreciation in fair value, 225
Valuation based on cost, 223
Valuation based on fair value, 224
Valuation based on investee's financial results, 223
Detection risk, 32, 36, 45, 108
Disclaimer of opinion
Definition, 382
Description, 390, 649
GAAP departures, 390
Going concern assumption, 308
Illegal acts by clients, 104
Illustrations
Forecast, 656
Information accompanying financial statements, 446
Scope limitations, 400, 690
Supplementary information, 448
Inadequate disclosure, 376, 380
Lack of independence, 376
Negative assurance, 378
Pro forma financial information, 676
Reports of other auditors, 421
Scope limitations, 387, 390, 396, 400

Supplementary information, 443, 459
Timing of auditor appointment, 14
Unaudited financial statements, 375
Uncertainties, 387, 388, 488

Disclosure
Adverse opinion, 372, 389
Fair value of financial instruments, 312
Going concern assumption, 306
Inadequate, 372, 388, 402
Litigations, claims, and assessments, 273
Oil and gas producing activities, 459
Omission of statement, 388
Qualified opinion, 372, 386, 389
Related-party transactions, 250, 254, 257
Reporting standard, 4, 372
Segment information, 158
Subsequent discovery of facts, 474
Subsequent events, 408, 464
Supplementary information, 458

Discovery
Auditor disclosure, 474
Auditor's responsibilities, 472
Client disclosure, 472
Lawyer's advice, 472
Letters for underwriters, 518
Notification, 474
Omitted auditing procedures, 353
Refusal to disclose, 473
Reliability of information, 472
Resignation or discharge of auditor, 474
Sampling, 328
Subsequent discovery of facts, 471

Documentation
Assessed level of control risk, 115
Audit sampling, 324, 327
Fraud risk assessment, 91, 96
Internal control, 683
Reportable conditions, 148
Understanding of internal control, 114
Work performed by specialist, 268

Due professional care
General standard, 3, 6

E

Elements of financial statements
Applicability of GAAS, 481
Auditor's report, 482
Materiality, 481
Scope of audit, 481

Emphasis of matter, 386

Engagement letters
Agreed-upon procedures, 636
Client to specialists, 270
Illustrative engagement letter, 15, 270, 592, 729, 732, 733
Management-use-only (MUO), 732
Matters covered in, 15
Relation to representation letter, 240
Review engagement, 728
Review of interim financial information, 585, 592

Equity method
Long-term investments, 425

Errors or fraud
Analytical procedures, 181
Assessing risk, 89, 96
Audit tests results, 91
Communications, 81, 91, 97
Definitions, 63, 88
Disclosure to outside parties, 92
Documentation, 91, 96
Illustrative risk factors, 84, 99
Withdrawal by auditor, 91

Estimation
Accounting changes, 369
Accounting estimates, 316
Auditor's responsibilities, 311, 315
Definition, 310
Developing accounting estimates, 313
Effect of internal control, 314
Fair value disclosures, 312
Identification, 311, 314
Key factors, 310
Reasonableness, 34, 312, 315
Subsequent events, 315
Unreasonable, 315

Evidential matter
Audit objectives, 154, 155, 159
Audit programs, 162
Competence, 154, 156
Corroborating information, 154, 155
Definition, 154
Evaluation, 156
Fieldwork standard, 3
Illustrative source list for audit program, 162
Income tax accruals, 157
Interim financial statements, 157
Internal control, 682
Segment disclosures, 158
Substantive tests, 155, 170
Sufficiency, 154, 156
Underlying accounting data, 154, 155

Expense
List of evidential matter, 168

Explanatory language
Attorney-client privilege, 278
Auditor's report, 384
Circumstances requiring, 384
Definition, 382
GAAP departures, 385
Lack of consistency, 386
Scope limitations, 387
Supplementary information, 458
Uncertainties, 387, 388
Use of other auditor's work, 385

F

Fair presentation
Field warehouse, 605
Meaning in auditor's report, 358

Fair value
Assessing risk, 170, 174
Communication with audit committees, 173
Determining fair value, 170, 174
Engaging a specialist, 171
Evaluating conformity, 170
Evaluating the results of audit procedures, 173
Fair value disclosures, 172
General, 173
Management's responsibilities, 174
Testing, 171, 175
Written management representations, 173

Fieldwork standards
Attestation standards, 614, 624
Audit documentation, 290
Evidential matter, 3
Financial statements on foreign country's accounting principles, 414
Internal control, 3
Planning and supervision, 3

Financial statements
Accompanying information, 440, 445
Assertions, 153
Auditor's association, 374
Coexisting financial statements, 441, 444
Comparability, 366
Definition, 440, 477
Dual statements, 414, 417, 418

Effects of laws on regulations, 600
Fair presentation, 2, 358
Management's responsibilities, 3, 6
Management-use-only (MUO), 728
Material misstatements, 32, 43, 89, 91, 433, 438
Non-GAAP financial statements, 430
Other comprehensive basis of accounting, 375, 478, 486
Other information in documents, 433
Personal, 755
Regulated companies, 430
Related-party transactions, 249
Revisions required, 474
SEC filings, 377, 379
Subsequent events, 464
Used in foreign countries, 414

Fixed assets
List of evidential matter, 166

Foreign Corrupt Practices Act
Internal control, 105

Foreign country
Reporting on financial statements, 414

Fraud
Assessing identified risks, 69
Basic requirement, 65
Characteristics of, 78, 95
Communication, 81, 91, 97
Communication to audit committee, 74
Communication to management, 74
Communication to others, 74
Detection of, 102, 105
Documentation, 74, 91, 96
Engagement team discussion, 65
Evaluating analytical procedures, 81
Evaluating audit evidence, 72
Identifying fraud risks, 68
Management antifraud programs and controls, 83
Management's responsibilities, 78
Obtaining information to identify fraud risks, 66
Professional skepticism, 65
Responding to results of assessment, 69
Risk factors, 64, 79, 88, 95
Examples of, 84, 85, 99
Risk of material misstatement, 43, 79, 89, 95

G

General standards
Attestation standards, 614, 624
Due professional care, 3
Financial statements on foreign country's accounting principles, 415, 417
Independence, 3
Training and proficiency, 3

Generally accepted accounting principles
Definition, 357
Elements of financial statements, 482
Foreign country's accounting principles, 415, 417
Hierarchy–Nongovernmental entities, 359
Hierarchy–State and local governmental entities, 359
Regulated companies, 430
Reporting standards, 4, 358, 367, 372
Reports on application, 500

Generally accepted auditing standards
Audit of financial statements for use outside US, 414, 417
Comparison with attestation standards, 624
Due care, 3
Fieldwork standards, 3
General standards, 3
Generally accepted governmental auditing standards, 600
Independence, 5
Management representation letter, 6
Other comprehensive basis of accounting, 478
Quality control policies and procedures, 7
Quality control standards, 5
Reporting standards, 4, 358, 367, 372
Responsibilities of auditors, 2, 7
Training and proficiency, 5

Going concern
Audit procedures, 298, 300
Auditor's report, 306
Auditor's responsibilities, 298
Borrowing money, 303
Description, 297
Disclaimer of opinion, 307
Disclosure, 299, 306
Eliminating explanatory paragraph, 300
Financial statement effects, 306
Illustrative checklist, 308
Indications of problems, 301
Management forecasts, 305
Management's plans, 302

H

Hedging activities, 219

I

Illegal acts
Audit procedures, 103, 106
Auditor's report, 104
Auditor's responsibilities, 102, 105
Communication, 104
Definition, 102
Description, 102
Disclosure to outside parties, 105
Evaluation of, 104
Evidential matter, 103
Foreign Corrupt Practices Act, 105
Internal control, 105
Withdrawal by auditor, 104

Impairment
Investments, 225

Income tax accrual
Evidential matters, 157

Incremental audit risk
Assessment of, 50, 52
Definition, 49
Factors that increase, 50

Independence
Agreed-upon procedures, 636
General standard, 3
Lack of, 376
Letter for specialist, 271
Letters for underwriters, 513
Other auditors, 424
Quality control policies and procedures, 7, 9

Information
Annual report, 432
Audit procedures, 434
Auditor-submitted document, 441
Client-prepared document, 441
Consistency of other information, 433, 437
Internal control, 108, 113
Material misstatements, 433, 438

Information technology
Effect on internal control, 118
Need for skills, 111

Inherent risk, 32, 36, 44, 108, 699

Inquiries
Internal auditor's work, 125

Litigation, claims, and assessments, 272
Principal auditor, 422
Supplementary information, 458
Intangible assets
List of evidential matter, 167
Interim audit work
Attorney letter, 282
Evidential matter, 156
Observation of inventories, 14
Timing of auditor appointment, 14
Interim financial information
Accompanying audited financial statements, 566, 585
Additional guidance, 569
Addressee, 564
Analytical procedures, 567, 580, 587
Audit documentation, 562, 588
Checklist, 594
Client representation about accountant's review, 565
Communication to management, 563
Communication with audit committee, 562, 582
Coordination with the audit, 560
Date of report, 564
Defined, 555, 578
Discussion of, 555, 578
Engagement letter, 566, 588, 592
Evaluating results of review procedure, 561
Extension of interim review procedures, 560
Form of accountant's review report, 564
Fraud or illegal acts, 563
Going concern, 564
Going concern issues, 560
Inquiries
Financial reporting, 580
Internal control, 579
Inquiries concerning litigation, claims, and assessments, 559
Internal control, 582
Lack of appropriate audit committee response, 563
Lack of appropriate management response, 563
Lack of consistency, 564
Management representation letter, 560, 572, 574, 580, 592
Oral communication, 563
Other information, 568
Presentation of, 566
Procedures, 568, 581, 589
Report on, 564, 583
Reportable conditions, 563
Required review procedures, 558
SAS 61 communications, 562
Subsequent discovery of facts, 568, 589
Successor auditors, 568
Timing of, 560
Internal auditors
Agreed-upon procedures, 634
Auditor's understanding of function, 122, 125
Competence, 123, 127
Definition, 121
Directly assisting auditor, 124, 129
Effect on audit, 124, 127
Evaluating work, 123, 128
Functions, 121
Illustrative checklist
Evaluating work of, 129
Objectivity, 123, 127
Substantive tests, 125
Internal control
Accounting estimates, 314
Auditor's responsibilities, 109, 112
Components, 108
Control activities, 108, 112
Control environment, 108, 112
Definitions, 108
Detection risk, 108
Documentation, 114, 116
Fieldwork standard, 3, 110
Foreign Corrupt Practices Act, 105
Illustrative documentation, 119
Illustrative reports, 150
Information and communication, 108, 113
Inherent risk, 108
Interim financial information, 582
Internal auditors, 121
Limitations, 111
Management's responsibilities, 3
Material inconsistencies, 437
Material weaknesses, 146, 687
Monitoring, 108, 114
Placed in operation, 108
Public warehouses, 608
Reportable conditions, 146, 604
Responsibile party, 678
Risk assessment, 108, 112
Risk of material misstatement, 108
Service organizations, 132
Tests of controls, 108
Understanding, 109, 687
Inventories
Alternative procedures, 392
Audit program, 213
Beginning inventory not observed, 208
Confirmations, 208, 210, 217
Held by custodian, 210
Illustrative audit objectives, 159
List of evidential matter, 164
Observation by auditor, 207
Observation checklist, 214
Outside inventory-taking firm used, 214
Periodic inventory system, 210
Perpetual inventory, 208
Physical inventory, 207, 213
Public warehouses, 208, 210, 218, 605, 606
Scope limitations, 209
Timing of auditor appointment, 210
Investments
Assertions
Completeness
Examples of substantive procedures, 233
Control risk assessment, 228
Existence
Examples of substantive procedures, 233
Inherent risk assessment, 228
Management's ability and intent, 226
Occurrence
Examples of substantive procedures, 233
Presentation and disclosure, 226
Rights and obligations
Examples of substantive procedures, 234
Tests of valution, 222
Collateral in evaluating fair value, 225
Control risk assessment, 221
Cost method, 425
Designing audit procedures, 221
Effect of service organization on audit approach and procedures, 230
Equity method, 425
Fair value determined using a model, 225
Impairment losses, 225
Management representations, 227
Risk assessment in planning, 221
Sources of fair value information, 224
Special skills or knowledge, 227
Subsequent events, 223

Substantive procedures based on risk assessment, 222
Test of valuation assertions, 222
Types, 220
Unrealized appreciation or depreciation in fair value, 225
Valuation
Based on cost, 223
Based on investee's financial results, 223

L

Lawyers
Audit inquiry letter, 275, 283
Audit procedures other than inquiry of, 274
Client without a lawyer, 280
Date of response, 276, 280
Evaluation of response, 276, 280
Illustrative audit inquiry letter, 283
Internal vs. outside counsel, 282
Limited scope of response, 276
Policy on audit inquires, 273
Refusal to respond, 282
Resignation of client's lawyer, 282
Legislation
Errors or fraud, 64, 88
Expectation gap, 64, 88
Letters for underwriters
Accountants' reports, 511
Addressee, 511
Capsule information, 507, 515, 534
Comfort letters, 506
Compliance with SEC requirements, 513
Concluding paragraph, 518
Condensed financial statements, 514
Dates, 508, 511
Discovery of facts, 518
Financial forecasts, 515
Format and contents, 511
Illustrative reports
Capsule information, 534
Interim earning data, 537
Other financial information, 528
Pro forma financial information, 527
Reports of other accountants, 534
SEC filing, 525, 534
Typical, 522
Independence, 513
Introductory paragraph, 512
Negative assurance, 509, 512
Other financial information, 516, 528
Principal accountant, 510
Pro forma adjustments, 515, 527
Reports of other accountants, 534
Scope of procedures, 509
Shelf registration statement, 508, 510
Subsequent changes, 516
Unaudited financial statements, 514
Underwriter, 507
Liquidation
Auditor's report, 405
Uncertainties, 387
Litigation
Audit procedures, 274
Client represented by insurance company, 281
Client without a lawyer, 280
Disclosure, 274
Inquiries of client's lawyer, 275
Lawyer unaware of litigation, 281
Loss contingencies
Accounting considerations, 273
Definitions, 272
Disclosures, 273
Probable, 272
Reasonably possible, 272
Remote, 272
Uncertainties, 387, 388

M

Management
Accounting changes, 389
Accounting estimates, 311
Appointment of auditor, 14
Discussion and analysis, 706
Fundamental requirements for examination, 707
Fundamental requirements for reviews, 708
Illustrations
Annual MD&A presentation, 710
Interim MD&A presentation, 711
Standard examination report, 709
Going concern assumptions, 300
Illegal acts, 103
Internal control, 3, 435
Reportable conditions, 147
Reports on internal control, 11, 435
Responsibilities, 3, 6, 254, 681
Supplementary information, 458
Marketable securities
List of evidential matter, 153
Material weakness, 685
Materiality
Audit concept of, 33
Auditor's judgment, 40
Comparative financial statements, 377
Compliance attestation, 703
Definition, 32
Effect on audit, 31
Errors or fraud, 43, 89
Factor in planning audit, 35
Letters for underwriters, 508
Management representations, 239
Misstatements, 31, 433, 652
Preliminary judgment, 39
Segment information, 158
Tolerable misstatement, 36, 40
Monitoring, 108, 114

N

National Commission on Fraudulent Financial Reporting
Reporting on internal control, 679
Negative assurance
Comparative financial statements, 378
Letters for underwriters, 509
Negative confirmations, 193, 198
Example of, 205
Negotiable warehouse receipt, 606
Nonaudit and nonreview clients, 672
Nonnegotiable warehouse receipt, 606
Nonpublic enterprises
Comparative financial statements, 377
Condensed financial statements, 451
Segment information, 158
Selected data, 451
Unaudited financial statements, 375
Nonsampling, 321
Nonstatistical sampling
Audit documentation, 324, 327
Control risk, 44
Detection risk, 45
Deviation rate, 324
Inherent risk, 43
Population, 325

Preliminary judgement of materiality, 40
Risk of incorrect acceptance, 326
Sample selection, 322
Sampling risk, 324, 327
Size of sample, 323, 325
Substantive tests, 325
Tests of controls, 323
Tolerable misstatements, 36, 43, 326
Vs. statistical sampling, 321

Notes to financial statements
Disclosure, 372
Related-party transactions, 250, 257
Segment information, 158
Subsequent events, 462

O

Objective of audit
Audit programs, 162
Definition, 154
Development, 155
Evidential matter, 154
Examination, 668
Review, 669
Source list for audit program, 162
Working paper checklist, 162, 174

Objectivity
Assessment of, 123

Oil and gas producing activities
Auditor's report, 460
FASB requirements, 459
SEC requirements, 459

Omitted auditing procedures
Application of, 352
Definition, 351
Determining importance of, 353, 354
Professional disagreements, 352
Review of audit work, 354
Threatened litigation, 351

Organization charts, 126

Outstanding warehouse receipts, 608

Overall review, 188

P

Planning
Analytical procedures, 178
Appointment of auditor, 14
Assessement of audit risk, 32
Audit program, 18
Audit risk, 31
Continuing client, 26
Economic factors, 22
Errors or fraud, 43, 89
Evidential matter, 3
Extent of planning, 19
Fieldwork standard, 3
Firm requirements, 27
Industry factors, 23
Internal control, 3, 112
Knowledge of client's business, 20
Management discussions, 26
Materiality, 31
New client, 23
Procedures, 20
Professional skepticism, 90
Relationship to appointment of auditor, 14
Segment information, 158
Supervision, 21
Timing of audit work, 14
Use of computer processing, 20

Pooling of interests
Auditor's report, 427
Procedures, 421

Positive confirmations, 193
Examples of, 204
Practitioner's report, 634, 698

Predecessor auditor/accountant
Availability of audit documentation, 57
Availability of working papers, 751
Change of auditors, 56
Communication with successor, 56, 751
Definition, 55, 750
Illustrative communication, 60
Misstatements, 58
Reaudit, 57
Reissuance of report, 60, 391, 403
Representation letter from successor, 405
Response to successor, 56
Revisions of financial statements, 60
Subsequent discovery of facts, 58
Subsequent events, 548

Prepaid assets
List of evidential matter, 165

Principal auditor
Auditor's report, 426
Representation letter, 427
Responsibilities, 420

Pro forma financial information
Accountant's objectives, 668
Attest engagement, 668
Examination, 668
Illustrations, 673
Letters for underwriters, 515, 527
Procedures, 669
Purpose, 668
Review, 669
Unaudited information, 387

Processing of transactions by service organizations, 133

Professional skepticism, 75, 92, 96

Projections
Definition, 643
Hypothetical assumption, 643
Use of accountant's name, 645

Prospective financial statements
Agreed-upon procedures, 645, 650
Compilation of, 644, 646, 653
Definition, 643
Examinations, 644, 648, 654
General use of, 644
Key factors of, 644
Limited use, 644
Material misstatements, 652
Planning, 660
Responsible party, 643
Training and proficiency, 660
Use of, 644

Public warehouses
Accountability, 608
Commodity, 606
Confirmations, 609
Definition, 605
Field, 605, 607
General merchandise, 606
Goods, 606
Insurance, 607
Internal control policies and procedures, 606
Inventories, 208, 210, 218
Refrigerated, 605
Terminal, 605
Warehouse receipts, 606, 607

Publicly traded entities
Auditor's association with financial statements, 374
Comparative financial statements, 377
Condensed financial statements, 450
Definition, 374
Oil and gas producers, 459
Segment information, 158
Selected data, 451

Q

Qualified opinion
Accounting changes, 389
Accounting principles inappropriate, 388
Definition, 382
Description, 386
Estimates unreasonable, 388
Explanatory paragraph, 386
GAAP departures, 387, 400

Illegal acts by clients, 104
Illustrations
Accounting changes, 402
GAAP departures, 400
Inadequate disclosures, 402
Information accompanying financial statements, 447
Omission of statement, 402
Scope limitations, 400
Inadequate disclosure, 388, 402
Letters for underwriters, 512
Notes to financial statements, 387
Omission of statement, 388, 402
Reports of other auditors, 422
Scope limitations, 387, 399
Segment information, 158
Subsequent years' reports, 389
Timing of auditor appointment, 14
Uncertainties, 388
Quality control
Acceptance and continuance of clients and engagements, 9
Administration of quality control system, 10
Audit engagement standards, 3
Communicating policies and procedures, 8
Due care, 6
Elements, 8
Establishing policies and procedures, 7
Independence, 5, 9
Monitoring, 9
Performance, 9
Personnel, 8
Supervision, 3
Training and proficiency, 3, 5
Questionnaires
Audit risk assessment, 28, 96
Communications to audit committee, 347

R

Ratio analysis, 183
Reaudit, 57
Receivables
Aged schedule, 199
Alternative procedures, 194
Confirmation, 193
Reasons for not conforming, 197
Refrigerated warehouse, 605
Regression analysis, 186
Regulated industries
Basis of accounting, 430
GAAP departures, 431
Regulatory agencies
Compliance reports, 483
Reports on internal accounting controls, 678
Special-purpose financial presentations, 484
Reissued reports
Date of report, 391
Definition, 407
Explanatory paragraph, 391
Illustrative auditor's report, 403
Predecessor reports, 60, 391, 403
Procedures before reissuing, 391
Subsequent events, 468
Related parties
Audit procedures, 250
Communication between auditors, 252
Control, 249
Definitions, 248
Disclosure requirements, 249, 254, 258
Emphasis in auditor's report, 258
Family relationships, 249
Illustration of notes to financial statements, 258
Illustrative related-party checklist, 258
Management representation letter, 257
Owners, 249
Questionable transactions, 250
Reportable conditions
Agreed-upon criteria, 146, 148
Auditor's responsibilities, 147
Communication to audit committee, 146, 148
Content of report, 147
Definition, 146
Documentation, 148
Examples, 150
Governmental authorities, 149
Identification, 148
Illustrative reports, 150
Management, 147
Material weakness, 146, 148, 149, 151
Reporting obligation, 4
Reporting standards
Application of accounting principles, 503
Attestation standards, 614
Auditor's expression of opinion, 4
Consistency, 4, 368, 382
Disclosure, 4
Financial statements used in foreign countries
Dual statements, 417
Foreign report form, 417
Modified US style report, 416
US distribution, 417
Generally accepted accounting principles, 4, 357
Reports on comparative financial statements
Changed prior period financial statements, 744
Changed reference to GAAP, 743, 746
Illustrations, 745
Predecessor's report, 743, 746
Prior period audited, 744, 747
Standard report, 742, 745
Reports on compiled financial statements, 748
Reports on internal control
Communication of internal control related matters noted in an audit, 145, 150
Reporting on an entity's internal control over financial reporting, 677
Reporting requirements, 683
Reports on personal financial statements
Exemption, 756
Illustration, 756
Required, 755
Reports on pro forma financial information
Form, 670
Historical financial statements, 672
Illustrations
Disclaimer of opinion, 676
Examination, 673
Qualified opinions, 675
Review, 673
Scope limitation, 675
Modifications, 671
Reports on prospective financial statements
Adverse opinion, 649
Agreed-upon procedures, 650
Comparative historical information, 650
Compilation reports, 646, 715
Disclaimer of opinion, 649
Emphasis of a matter, 650
Examination reports, 648
Illustrations
Adverse opinion, 656
Agreed-upon procedures, 658
Budgeted financial statements, 659
Compilation, 654, 731
Disclaimer of opinion, 656
Examination, 654

Financial feasibility study, 657
Qualified opinion, 655
Review, 736
Modifications of accountant's opinion, 649
Part of larger engagement, 650
Qualified opinion, 649
Report of other accountant, 650
Review, 612, 713, 718
Reports, other auditors'
Auditing procedures, 420, 423
Auditor's responsibilities, 420
Coordination of activities, 425
Decision not to make reference, 420, 424
Decision to make reference, 420, 424
Disclaimer of opinion, 421
Explanatory language added to standard report, 384
Illustrative auditor's report, 399, 426
Inquiries, 422, 428
Long-term investments, 425
Pooling of interests, 421, 427
Principal auditor decision, 420, 423
Qualified opinion, 422
Representation letters, 427
Reputation, 424
Review of interim financial information, 564, 569, 584, 590
SEC requirements, 423
Reports, restrictive use
Adding new parties, 412
Combined, 412
Definition, 411
Example, 413
General-use, 411
Language, 411
Required restrictive reports, 412
Restricted parties, 412
Representation letters
Audit requirement, 6, 236
Dating of letters, 238, 240
Definition, 235
Evidential matter, 236
Examples of information included, 237, 243
Illegal acts by clients, 106
Illustrative letter, 241, 405, 427
Management's assurances, 237
Materiality, 238
Reliance on representations, 236
Reporting on internal control, 683, 691
Reports, other auditors', 426
Responsibility for financial statements, 6
Review of interim financial information, 572, 574, 581, 592
Scope limitations, 239
Signatures, 235, 238
Specialized industries, 238
Successor and predecessor auditors, 405
Updating, 239, 247
Responsible party, 643
Restatements
Financial statements reported on by predecessor auditor, 57, 391
Prior period financial statements, 391
Revenue
List of evidential matter, 168
Recognition issues, 75, 93
Review of financial statements
Application of standards, 725
Change from audit, 720
Checklist, 735
Definition, 713
Engagement letter, 727, 734
Entity, 713
Illustrations
Engagement letter, 734
GAAP departures, 736
Inquiries, 736
Management report, 11
Representation letter, 738
Standard report, 736
Nonpublic entity, 713
Performance requirements, 715
Reporting obligation, 714
Review of interim financial information
Accountant's report, 564, 571, 583, 590
Analytical procedures, 580, 587
Auditor's report, 566, 586
Communication with audit committee, 562, 582
Documentation, 562, 588
Engagement letter, 567, 588, 592
GAAP departures, 565, 583, 584
Illustrative checklist, 594
Inadequate disclosures, 565, 585
Inquiries, 579
Internal control, 581
Knowledge of entity's business and internal control, 556
Litigation, claims, and assessment, 282
Procedures, 568, 581, 589
Reports of other auditors, 564, 571, 584, 590
Representation letter, 572, 574, 580, 592
Review report
Analytical procedures to consider, 575
Comparative, 570
Departure from GAAP, 571
Inadequate disclosure, 571
Unusual or complex situations, 576
SEC requirements, 556
Standards, 556
Subsequent discovery of facts, 568, 589
Understanding with client, 556, 579
Use of accountant's name, 583
Review reports
Condensed financial statement, 453
GAAP departures, 565, 584
Inadequate disclosures, 565, 585
Interim financial information, 583
Use of other accountant's report, 583
Risk
Attestation, 612, 694
Audit, 31
Business, 31
Control, 32, 221, 694, 700
Detection, 32, 694
Incremental audit, 49, 50
Inherent, 32, 43, 694, 699
Relative, 44
Risk of material misstatement due to fraud, 43
Risk assessment, 108, 112

S

Scope of audit
Client-imposed restrictions, 397
Common restrictions, 396
Elements of financial statements, 482
First year audits, 370
Lawyer's responses to inquiries, 276, 280
Limitations
Disclaimer of opinion, 400
Inventories, 209, 392
Management's refusal to furnish written representations, 239
Pro forma financial information, 675
Qualified opinion, 386, 400
Segment information, 158

Uncertainties, 387, 388
Securities and Exchange Commission
Accountant's report, 548
Accountant's responsibilities, 548
Comparative financial statements, 377
Condensed financial statements, 450
Current auditor, 549
Effective date, 547
Engagement, 339
Federal securities statutes, 547
Letters for underwriters, 513
Level of authority, 362
Material misstatements, 547
Posteffective amendment, 551
Predecessor auditor, 548
Registration statements, 547
Review of interim financial information, 548
Selected financial data, 449
Shelf registration statement, 508, 510, 547, 551
Subsequent discovery of facts, 550
Subsequent events, 548
Unaudited financial statements, 375
Segment information, 158
Service oganizations, 136
Selected financial data
Auditor's report, 452
Auditor-submitted documents, 450
Client-prepared document, 451
Comparative presentation, 452
Compilation report, 451
Definition, 449
Form of report, 452
Nonpublic enterprises, 451
Publicly traded companies, 450
SEC regulations, 450
Service auditor, 132
Service organizations
Reports on the processing of transactions, 133
Special reports
Accounting changes, 487
Applicability, 476
Basis of accounting other than GAAP, 478
Comparative financial statements, 488
Compliance reports, 483
Components of report, 479
Consistency, 487
Disclosures, 480
Elements of financial statements, 481
Explanatory language required, 487
Explanatory paragraph, 482, 486, 487
GAAP departures, 486
Illustrations
Cash basis, 492
Compliance reports, 495
Current value, 490, 499
Internal Revenue Service Form 990, 498
Property and liability insurance companies, 497
Regulatory basis, 493
Tax basis, 492
Internal Revenue Service Form 990, 489, 498
Introductory paragraph, 482, 485
Opinion paragraph, 483, 486
Prescribed forms, 488
Property and liability insurance companies, 489, 497
Reports of other auditors, 488
Scope limitations, 480
Scope paragraph, 482, 486
Service organization, 141
Special-purpose financial presentation, 484
Title of financial statements, 480
Uncertainties, 488
Specialists
Auditing procedures, 263
Definition, 261
Engagement letter, 270
Evidential matter, 263
Examples of use of, 267
Professional qualifications, 263
Reference in auditor's report, 264
Relationship with client, 263, 268, 271
Using findings of, 263
Statistical sampling
Confidence levels, 332
Detection risk, 45, 330
Discovery sampling, 328
Equal probability sampling, 332
Fundamental requirements, 319
Inventories, 208
Misstatements, 329
Nonstatistical sampling vs., 321
Point estimate, 331, 333
Preliminary judgment of materiality, 40
Risk of incorrect acceptance, 317
Risk of incorrect rejection, 318
Sample selection, 328
Sampling risk, 317
Size of sample, 328, 330
Substantive tests of details, 330
Tolerable misstatements, 36, 40
Subsequent events
Accounting considerations, 463
Adjustment events, 462, 464
Adjustments to financial statements, 408
Auditing procedures, 463
Compliance attestation, 697
Cutoff point, 463
Date of auditor's report, 407, 462, 466
Definition, 407, 462
Disclosure necessary, 408, 463, 465
Dual dating of auditor's report, 467
Illustrative checklist, 468
Minutes of meetings, 466
Review, 408
SEC filings, 548
Shares outstanding, 465
Subsequent period, 462
Unaudited information, 550
Substantive tests
Alternative procedures, 49
Analytical procedures, 177, 179, 188
Assessing audit risk, 50
Assessing control risk, 52, 114
Completeness assertion, 157
Convenience-timed tests, 48
Cost effectiveness, 50
Examples of, 159
Financial statement assertions, 154
Incremental audit risk, 49
Interim vs. anual date, 48
Principal, 49
Selection, 155
Timing and extent, 48, 51
Successor auditor/accountant
Acceptance and continuance of audit clients, 58
Audit evidence, 57
Communication with predecessor, 56, 750
Definition, 55, 750
Illustrative communications, 61
Misstatements, 58
Reaudit, 57
Reference to predecessor, 57
Reissuance of predecessor's report, 60, 391
Representation letter from predecessor, 405
Revisions of financial statements, 60
Subsequent discovery of facts, 58
Working papers, 751
Supervision

Definition, 18
Disagreements among staff, 21
Extent, 21
Fieldwork standard, 3
Instructing assistants, 21
Quality control policies and procedures, 7
Reviewing work, 21
Supplementary information
Auditor's responsibilities, 458
Audits of, 457
Disclaimer of opinion, 443, 446
Illustrative auditor's reports, 461
Limited procedures, 458
Material departures, 459, 461
Oil and gas producing activities, 459
SEC requirements, 457, 459
Voluntary presentations, 456

T

Terminal warehouse, 605
Tests of controls
Attribute sampling, 323
Definition, 108
Nonstatistical sampling, 321
Use of internal auditors, 122
Time period covered, 682
Timeliness
Communication of reportable conditions, 149
Scheduling audit work, 14
Training and proficiency
General standard, 3
Quality control policies and procedures, 7
Treadway commission, 679
Trend analysis, 185

U

Unaudited financial statements
Accountant's association, 375
Compartive financial statements, 377
GAAP departures, 376
Illustrative report on GAAP financial statements, 379
Letters for underwriters, 514
Negative assurance, 378
SEC filings, 379
Subsequent events, 550
Unaudited information
Subsequent events, 408, 550
Uncertainties
Accounting estimates, 387
Accounting principles, 387
Auditor's report, 387, 388
Explanatory language in auditor's report, 387
Going concern, 488
Materiality, 388
Special reports, 487
Underlying accounting data, 154
Tests of, 155

V

Variance analysis, 185

W

Working papers
Analytical procedures, 189